NOTES:
  PAGE 97 - THIS IS NOT THE RUBY
30" GAGE CORTEZ MINING RAILROAD (MINE TO MILL, NO CO..
RAILS). NOTES ON PAGE 337.

RAILROADS OF NEVADA

VOLUME I

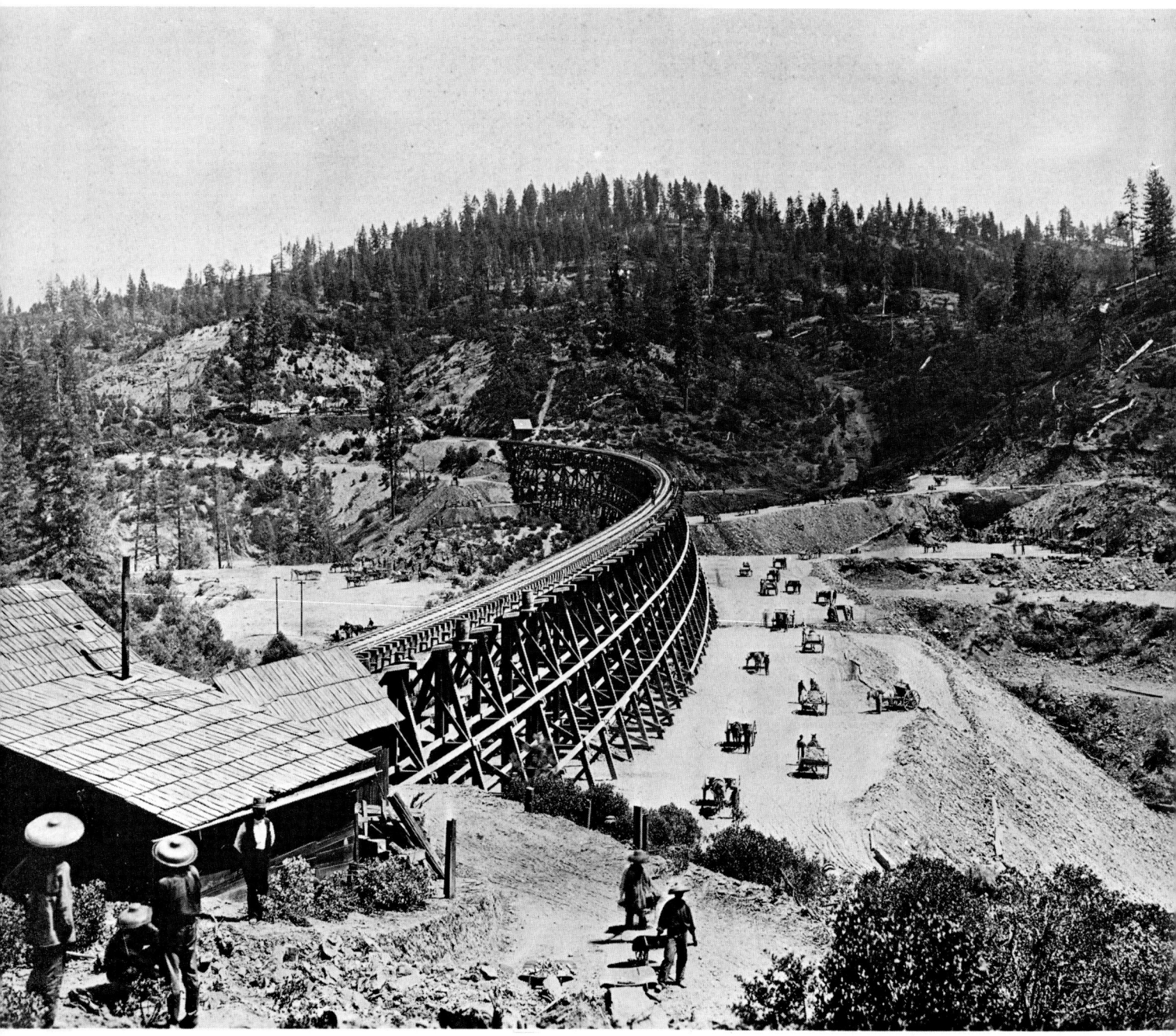

Undoubtedly one of the best, most typical and most famous of early railroad construction scenes is this superb view of the filling in of the Central Pacific's gigantic 1100-foot Secrettown Trestle in 1876. In the haste of initial construction, pioneer railroads spanned depressions in their paths with wooden trestles such as this one, then filled them in at leisure with solid earth embankments. In this striking scene a score or more of plodding Chinese may be seen, leading their small, horse-drawn, hand-filled dump carts and looking for all the world like human ants on a tremendous ant hill. The work was slow and laborious, consuming months in the process, but the finished embankment still carries SP main line trains today and may be seen from U. S. Highway 40 which parallels the railroad at this point. *(Southern Pacific Collection.)*

RAILROADS OF NEVADA AND EASTERN CALIFORNIA

Volume I,
The Northern Roads

DAVID F. MYRICK

University of Nevada Press
Reno Las Vegas London

Railroads of Nevada and Eastern California by David F. Myrick: Volume I was originally published by Howell-North Books of Berkeley, California, in 1962; it was reprinted by Howell-North Books of San Diego, California, in 1980; the University of Nevada Press edition reproduces the original except for changes to the front matter, which has been modified to reflect the new publisher, and the addition of a new preface by the author. Volume II was originally published by Howell-North Books of Berkeley, California, in 1963; the University of Nevada Press edition reproduces the original except for changes to the front matter, which has been modified to reflect the new publisher, and to the Roster of Locomotives at the back of the book, which was updated by the author. In both volumes, minor corrections to the text have been made throughout and newly designed dust jackets have been provided; the folding map included in Howell-North's original edition has been reduced in size and now appears as an endsheet in each volume.

The paper used in this book meets the requirements of American National Standard for Information Sciences—Permanence of Paper for Printed Library Materials, ANSI Z39.48-1984. The binding is sewn for strength and durability.

Library of Congress Cataloging-in-Publication Data

Myrick, David F.
  Railroads of Nevada and eastern California / David F. Myrick.
    p.   cm.
  Reprint, with revisions. Originally published: Berkeley, Calif. : Howell-North Books. 1962–1963.
  Includes index.
  Contents: v. 1. The northern roads — v. 2. The southern roads.
  ISBN 0-87417-195-4 (set : alk. paper) —
  ISBN 0-87417-193-8 (vol. 1 : alk. paper) —
  ISBN 0-87417-194-6 (vol. 2 : alk. paper)
  1. Railroads—Nevada—History. 2. Railroads—California—History. I. Title.
HE2771.N3M9 1992
385'.06'5793—dc20   92-21672
                                  CIP

BOOKS AND PAMPHLETS BY DAVID F. MYRICK

Railroads of Nevada and Eastern California
  Volume I, The Northern Roads (1962; reprinted 1992)
  Volume II, The Southern Roads (1963; reprinted 1992)
San Francisco's Telegraph Hill (1972)
Railroads of Arizona
  Volume I, The Southern Roads (1975)
  Volume II, Phoenix and the Central Roads (1980)
  Volume III, Clifton, Morenci and Metcalf, Rails and Copper Mines (1984)
Pioneer Arizona Railroads (1968)
Refinancing and Rebuilding the Central Pacific, 1899–1910 (1969)
Land Grants: Aids and Benefits to the Government and Railroads (1969)
New Mexico's Railroads; An Historical Survey (1970; revised and reprinted 1990)
Rails Around the Bohemian Grove (1973)
Potosí, An Empire of Silver (1980)
Montecito and Santa Barbara
  Volume I, From Farms to Estates (1988)
  Volume II, The Days of the Great Estates (1991)

University of Nevada Press, Reno, Nevada 89557 USA

Copyright © 1962 Howell-North Books
Copyright © 1990, 1992 David F. Myrick
All rights reserved

Jacket design by Ann Lowe

Printed in the United States of America
9 8 7 6 5 4 3 2

CONTENTS

PREFACE TO THE NEW EDITION ix

PREFACE xi

ACKNOWLEDGMENTS xiv

CHRONOLOGICAL LIST OF SELECTED EVENTS xvi

THE CENTRAL PACIFIC — PIONEER 1
    Original construction 1863-69 — Early operations — Southern Pacific ownership — The new Central Pacific (refinanced and reconstructed) — Shops moved from Wadsworth to Sparks — Lucin Cut-Off — Branches to Fallon and Metropolis — Fernley & Lassen Ry. to Susanville and Westwood — Improvements (1923-30).

EAGLE SALT WORKS RAILROAD COMPANY 51
    B. F. Leete — Eagle Salt Works — Railroad construction and abandonment.

THE NEVADA RAILROAD COMPANY 52
    Mining and life at Olinghouse — Railroad construction — Railroad Day celebration — Abandonment.

NEVADA SHORT LINE RAILWAY 57
    Joseph F. Nenzel — Oreana — Rochester — A. A. Codd — Railroad construction — Panama — "The Silver Belt Railroad" — Aerial tramway — Railroad abandonment.

GOLCONDA & ADELAIDE RAILROAD 63
    Golconda Hot Springs — Glasgow & Western Exploration Co. — Adelaide Star Mines, Ltd. — Railroad construction and abandonment.

NEVADA CENTRAL RAILWAY 66
    Discovery and development of Reese River Mining District and growth of Austin — Nevada Railway formed and route surveyed — Project taken over by Col. Bridges with bond financing provided by Anson Phelps Stokes and built to Clifton (Austin) as Nevada Central Railway — Nevada Northern Railway, Nevada Southern Railway and Southern Nevada Railway surveyed — Union Pacific buys stock, later defaults on bonds — Property reverts to Stokes — J. G. Phelps Stokes takes over — Tasker Oddie finds fraud in Austin — Later railroad operations and abandonment.

BATTLE MOUNTAIN & LEWIS RAILWAY 78
    Silver ore discovered in Lewis Canyon — Lewis booms — Labor trouble at Starr Grove Mine — Railroad constructed — Financial difficulties at mine and railroad — Operations suspended — Abandoned — Battle Mountain Mines & Development Co. railroad.

AUSTIN CITY RAILWAY 83
    Allen A. Curtis builds mule power railroad from Clifton to Austin — Later steam power substituted for mules (Mules' Relief) — Serious wreck — Railroad abandoned.

NEVADA MIDLAND RAILROAD COMPANY 84
    Under Simon Bamberger's unrealized plan, surveys were made for a railroad from Austin to Tonopah in connection with the proposed acquisition of the Nevada Central.

MID-PACIFIC RAILROAD 86
    Plan developed by Andrew Stevenson to merge six Nevada railroads with four connecting links to be built.

EUREKA & PALISADE RAILROAD 90
  Discovery of silver-lead ore at Eureka — Development of mining and smelting — Organization and construction of E&P — Ruby Hill Railroad built — Long period of dull times — Mark Requa assumes management of property — Reorganized as Eureka & Palisade Railway — Ruby Hill branch reconstructed — Railroad out of service two years following washouts of 1910 — Reorganized as Eureka-Nevada Railway, operated under lease by Nevada Transportation Co., J. E. Sexton, manager — Later operations and abandonment.

NEVADA NORTHERN RAILWAY 113
  Discovery of gold and naming of Ely — Discovery of copper and development of mines by Mark Requa — Surveys for railroad — Construction to Ely — Railroad Days at Ely — Ely City controversy — Tracks built to mines and smelter — Current operations of Nevada Northern and Kennecott Copper trains — Corporate name changes.

GIROUX CONSOLIDATED MINES COMPANY 134
  Development of copper claims near Ely — Building of narrow gauge railroad — Reorganization as Consolidated Coppermines Co. and widening of tracks — Sale of property to Kennecott Copper.

VIRGINIA & TRUCKEE RAILROAD 136
  Railroad needed to haul ore from Comstock mines to mills — Organization of Virginia, Carson & Truckee Railroad Co. — Virginia and Truckee Railroad Co. — Virginia & Truckee River Rail Road Co. — Virginia & Truckee Rail Road Co. — Organization and construction of Virginia & Truckee Railroad Co. — Busy operations followed by dull times — Later surge of traffic from Tonopah — Extension to Minden — Abandonment of Virginia City line — Abandonment of entire railroad.

GARDNERVILLE AND SOUTHERN RAILROAD 162
  Organization — Surveying and grading of short railroad from Minden to Gardnerville — Abandonment of entire project.

EUREKA MILL RAILROAD 163
  Construction of mill railroad along Carson River.

CARSON & COLORADO RAILROAD 166
  Mining districts south of Virginia City — Organization and building of first section from Mound House to Candelaria — Hawthorne town lot sale — Carson and Colorado Railroad Company, Second Division, formed to build from Filben to state line — Carson and Colorado Railroad Company, Third Division formed to build in California — Construction terminated at Keeler (Hawley) — Mining towns along the route — Inyo Development Co. and Natural Soda Products Co. operate short lines at Keeler — Rumored short lines at Luning and Kearsarge — Mining slump — All corporations consolidated as Carson & Colorado Railway — Cottonwood Branch built — C&C sold to Southern Pacific — Part of route standard gauged — Name changed to Nevada & California Railway — Hawthorne by-passed — Terminal established at Mina — Mojave-Owenyo standard gauge tracks built to aid in construction of Los Angeles aqueduct — Red Rock Railroad — Line change in Owens Valley and subsequent abandonment.

DAYTON, SUTRO & CARSON VALLEY RAILROAD 210
  Stamp mills at Dayton — Fred Birdsall builds horse-drawn railroad — Converted to steam power and extended as Lyon Mill and Mining Co. — Sold to J. M. Douglass and lengthened under name of DS&CVRR.

NEVADA COPPER BELT RAILROAD 214
  Copper mining in Yerington district — Construction of NCB — Mason Valley Mines Co. aerial tramway and smelter at Thompson — Bluestone Copper Co. standard gauge steam and narrow gauge electric railroad — Difficulties of operation — Abandonment.

RAWHIDE WESTERN RAILWAY 229
  Discovery of ore and boom at Rawhide — Railroad graded — Bad fire at Rawhide — Railroad project abandoned before tracks laid.

TONOPAH & GOLDFIELD RAILROAD 236
    Tonopah Railroad (236): Jim Butler and burro discover silver at Tonopah — Development of mines and town — Various proposals for railroad — Tonopah Railroad incorporated — Control passes to Tonopah Mining Co. — Narrow gauge railroad built — Railroad Days at Tonopah — Serious washouts — Conversion to standard gauge — Goldfield Railroad (256): Discovery of gold at Grandpa — Later at Goldfield and growth of town — Railroad built by Goldfield Syndicate — Railroad Days at Goldfield — T&G RR (258) formed as consolidation — Great prosperity in mines and cities — Operating problems — Competition from Las Vegas and Tonopah Railroad and Bullfrog Goldfield Railroad — Hard times — Recovery and resumption of dividends — Goldfield flood of 1913 and fire of 1923 — Connecting railroad to Gilbert proposed — Financial difficulties of the 1930's — Tonopah Mining Co. sells control to Dulien Steel Products — World War II booms traffic — Loss of postwar traffic and abandonment.

GOLDFIELD CONSOLIDATED MILLING & TRANSPORTATION CO. . . . 288
    Goldfield Consolidated Mines Co. (Nixon and Wingfield) builds short railroad to mill — Mill and railroad transferred to GCM&T Co. — Later operation of railroad by T&G RR.

SILVER PEAK RAILROAD COMPANY 292
    Short railroad graded and tramway built in 1860's to serve Drinkwater mine — Property acquired by John I. Blair — Later sold to Oliver and Flinn — Under name of Pittsburg Silver Peak Gold Mining Co., large mill built and subsidiary, Silver Peak Railroad, constructed — Electric mine railroad brought ores to aerial tramway — Townsite of Blair laid out — Water problems — Profitable mining operation ceased — Mill dismantled and railroad abandoned.

BODIE & BENTON RAILWAY 298
    Discovery of gold by William S. Bodey — Reputation of Bodie as rough and wicked town — Railroad needed to bring lumber to mines — Bodie Railway & Lumber Co. formed — Neighboring towns of Mammoth and Lundy — Construction problems: anti-Chinese feeling, labor difficulties — Completed and renamed The Bodie & Benton Railway & Commercial Co. and line partially graded to Benton — Diminished mining activity affected railroad — Later sold to become Mono Lake Railway & Lumber Co. and surveys made to connect with other railroads — Name changed to Mono Railway Co. — Later abandoned.

OWENS RIVER VALLEY ELECTRIC RAILWAY CO. 313
    Three lines proposed from Bishop — Line from Laws to Bishop graded — Locally known as "The Red Apple Route" — Project abandoned before rails laid.

WESTERN PACIFIC RAILROAD 316
    Construction of main line across Nevada — Acquisition of part of Nevada-California-Oregon (Reno Branch) — Line change (Arnold Loop) and construction of other branches — Proposed control by AT&SF or SP.

OREGON SHORT LINE (IDAHO CENTRAL) 333
    Surveys of Idaho Central Railroad — Inability to raise funds — Project taken over by OSL (Union Pacific) and railroad constructed — Celebration at Wells on completion.

OTHER NORTHERN NEVADA SHORT LINES 337
    Deep Creek Railroad (Wendover-Gold Hill, Utah) — Pacific Portland Cement Co. (Empire-Gerlach) — Nevada Massachusetts Co. (Mill City) — Cortez Mines (Tenabo).

NEVADA-CALIFORNIA-OREGON RAILWAY 341
    Western Nevada Railroad Co. incorporated to build south from Wadsworth — Abandoned in favor of The Nevada and Oregon Railroad to build north and south from Reno — Col. Moore begins construction northward from Reno — Company reorganized as Nevada and Oregon Railroad Co. and work moves ahead — Dissension — Scoville shot at directors' meeting — Railroad completed and placed in operation to Oneida — Financial difficulties — Interest unpaid — Bankruptcy follows and road acquired by Moran Bros. (bondholders) who operated it as Nevada & California Railroad and later as Nevada-California-Oregon Railway — Railway extended to Amedee, then Termo —

NEVADA-CALIFORNIA-OREGON RAILWAY (Continued)

Locally called "The Great Northern" — Tracks reach Madeline — Branch built to Reno Fair Grounds — Sierra Valleys Ry. acquired — Main line built north to Likely, Alturas and Lakeview, Oregon — Sale of tracks for WP Reno branch — Shops and offices moved to Alturas — Operating conditions on N-C-O — Abandonment threatened — Acquisition and standard gauging by SP — Construction of SP line from Alturas to Klamath Falls — Lumber railroads: Pickering at Hackamore, Big Lakes at Canby (Canby Railroad), Crane Creek at Willow Ranch.

SIERRA VALLEYS RAILWAY 384

Feather River gold discoveries of 1849 — Plumas-Eureka mine and short railroad — Proposed Sierra Iron & Quincy Railroad — Sierra Valley & Mohawk Railroad built by California Land & Timber Co. interests — Activity at Beckwith (Beckwourth) and Kerby — Financial problems of railroad — Eventually sold to Henry Bowen — Renamed as Sierra Valleys Ry. and pushed on to Clairville — Life at Clairville — Fires at Clairville and Vinton — Bowen financially undermined by serious accident — Road taken over by N-C-O Ry. — Name changed to Sierra & Mohawk Railway and later fully absorbed by N-C-O — Tracks reach Davies Mill — Line sold to WP and abandoned.

BOCA & LOYALTON RAILROAD 398

Early mill of Lewis brothers — Later joined by Capt. Roberts — Short track of Boca Mill & Ice Co. at Boca — Lewis and Roberts build B&L to replace steam wagons — Sawmills at Loyalton — Joint track with WP near Portola — Gulling's Grizzly Creek Ice Co. — B&L defaults on interest — Property acquired by WP — Most abandoned.

VERDI LUMBER COMPANY 410

Early lumbering activities — Life at Verdi (fires) — Construction of "Verdi Scenic Railway" to timber in Dog Valley — Then north to Long Valley Canyon — Later pushed westward to Lemon Canyon — Timber exhausted — Sawmill burns — Railroad abandoned.

LOGGING RAILROADS — LAKE TAHOE AND TRUCKEE RIVER BASIN . . 416

CARSON AND TAHOE LUMBER AND FLUMING CO.
(LAKE TAHOE NARROW GAUGE R.R.) 417

Sawmill at Glenbrook — Flume from Spooner's Summit to Carson City — Railroad built from Glenbrook to Spooner's Summit — Later dismantled.

M. C. GARDNER (CAMP RICHARDSON) 423

G. W. CHUBBUCK (LAKE VALLEY RAILROAD) (Bijou) 424

SIERRA NEVADA WOOD AND LUMBER COMPANY 425

Construction of great incline and flume — "Crystal Bay Railroad" built along lake shore — Operations — Dismantled and moved to Hobart Mills.

LAKE TAHOE RAILWAY AND TRANSPORTATION CO. 430

Construction of railroad from Truckee to Tahoe City — Branches to Ward Creek and Squaw Valley — Leased to SP — Track widened — Later abandoned.

OTHER EARLY LUMBER RAILROADS IN THE TRUCKEE AREA . . . 436

Truckee Lumber Co. — George Schaffer — Richardson Brothers — Pacific Lumber and Wood Co. (Clinton Narrow Gauge RR) — Miscellanea (Boca Mill Co., Nevada and California Lumber Co.).

SIERRA NEVADA WOOD AND LUMBER CO. 439

Construction of railroad from Truckee to Hobart Mills — Narrow gauge logging lines to the woods — Name changed to Hobart Estate Co. — Part operated as Hobart Southern.

CROWN WILLAMETTE PAPER COMPANY (Alder Creek) 442

FIBREBOARD PRODUCTS, INC. (Hobart Mills) 443

PREFACE TO THE NEW EDITION

Since these two volumes first appeared almost thirty years ago, much has happened in the nation's transportation scene. Nevada's railroads were affected by the many changes. The superhighways, now nearing the time for extensive rehabilitation, enabled the trucking industry to lure high-rated traffic from the railroads. The same highways made the extended use of private automobiles more compelling, and the faster airplanes pulled business travelers from the Pullman cars. Thirty years ago, Nevada had three Class I railroads and all had impressive dividend records. Today, there are only two large railroads and only one is paying dividends. Formerly unthinkable changes in ownership have taken place and the U.S. government has been operating main-line passenger service since the spring of 1971.

The steam locomotive was on the wane during the 1950s. Aside from special excursions, the Western Pacific's last steamer operated in 1953. Five years later, diesels were in complete command on the Union Pacific, the same year that steam power bowed out on the Southern Pacific (with the exception of its affiliated Nacozari Rail Road in Mexico, where steam operations terminated in 1959).

It was a sad day when the *California Zephyr,* a joint operation with the Rio Grande and Burlington between San Francisco and Chicago, vanished in March 1970. Though held high in public esteem, patronage had been declining and expenses were marching upward without a pause. Typical was the attitude of one businessman who said he always wanted to enjoy the *Zephyr* and the wonderful scenery of Feather River Canyon and the Rockies but never could spare the extra time required.

Southern Pacific's famed *City of San Francisco* was also operating under financial stress and by the end of 1970 had been reduced to a triweekly train. When the National Railroad Passenger Corporation (Amtrak) took over May 1, 1971, it scheduled the *San Francisco Zephyr* over SP lines from Ogden to Reno and Oakland. Until the *Desert Wind* was inaugurated in October 1979, Amtrak operated no passenger service over the former Salt Lake Route of the Union Pacific.

Back in 1960, Southern Pacific tried to acquire the Western Pacific in an effort to eliminate the expense of duplicating parallel operations. The Interstate Commerce Commission denied this move and the Western Pacific, a plucky little road, maintained its independence for almost another two decades.

The Rock Island and the Milwaukee roads once held important places in the Midwest; today both are only fading memories. Beginning in 1962, the Rock Island became a merger candidate contested by two pairs of railroads. After a long series of hearings before the Interstate Commerce Commission, the ICC examiner, as part of his proposed decision, recommended that the SP lines in Nevada be carved up and turned over to other lines. Ownership of SP's track from Ogden to Roseville and beyond would have been transferred to the Union Pacific together with the Fallon and Mina branches. The examiner called for the Santa Fe's acquisition of the entire Western Pacific and the purchase of the SP tracks from Klamath Falls to Flanigan. After long delays the final decision was rendered in December 1974, and then nobody liked it even though the examiner's radical proposals were excluded. The Rock Island's condition had deteriorated badly so that neither the UP nor SP wanted the system any longer. (Through an affiliate, SP acquired the short line from New Mexico to Kansas City and St. Louis in a separate transaction in 1980.)

The Union Pacific flexed its muscles in January 1980 and entered into a friendly agreement to acquire the Missouri Pacific Railroad; two weeks later it announced that a similar arrangement had been made with the Western Pacific. Ironically, in earlier times, the Western Pacific had been constructed as a solution for the problems that E. H. Harriman had created for George Gould. Harriman, boss of the UP and SP, had closed the Ogden gateway to the traffic of the Denver and Rio Grande, the western end of George Gould's contemplated transcontinental railroad system.

Just before Christmas of 1982, the Union Pacific took over both the Missouri Pacific and the Western Pacific. For a time, the Missouri Pacific name was retained, but the WP was swallowed by the UP to become its Fourth Division. Lost was the name and the orange and black color scheme of the WP diesel locomotives.

In 1969, the Southern Pacific Company became a holding company and the railroad was transferred to a subsidiary, the Southern Pacific Transportation Company. Santa Fe Industries, Inc., the holding company of the Santa Fe Railway, and the Southern Pacific Company were merged in 1983, but the ICC refused to allow a merger of the two rail systems. Accordingly, the Santa Fe Pacific Company sold the Southern Pacific Transportation Company to Rio Grande Industries, Inc., effective October 13, 1988, and it is now operated in conjunction with the Denver and Rio Grande Western Railroad.

Physically, the railroad plant in Nevada and elsewhere, along with a number of employees, has been reduced. The great shops of the SP at Sparks are a fitting topic of old-timers' recollections; today the underlying land is occupied by a major hotel and gasoline tank farms. Similarly, the SP facilities at Carlin are but a shadow of their former stature. The WP terminals at Winnemucca and Elko, along with the UP plants at Caliente, Utah, and Las Vegas, no longer provide employment for hundreds of workers. Section men, characteristically living in lonely houses by the railroad track or in outfit cars, are part of railroad folklore; in their place, track maintenance forces move about the system engaging in program work with state-of-the-art mechanical aids as budgeted.

Pioche, county seat of Lincoln County and for years an important mining community, saw its last UP train in 1983; fifteen years earlier, the same railroad gave up its link between Wells and Idaho. Freight trains no longer pass by Pyramid Lake, as SP now detours over the WP from Flanigan to Winnemucca. Similarly, in 1990, rails were removed from another portion of the historic Carson & Colorado Railroad—the road that its builder stated was 300 miles too long or built 300 years too soon—so that only 55 miles of the original line remain in operation.

The fortunes of the Nevada Northern Railway declined with the ending of Kennecott's copper operations near Ely. After the last freight train was operated to the SP connection at Cobre in 1983, the railroad became dormant. The main line was sold in 1987 to the Los Angeles Department of Water and Power to provide rail delivery of coal to a proposed power plant. The power plant has not yet been built, but in 1991 arrangements were under way for resumption of freight service over this line by contract with the California Southern Railroad Co. During the summer months, the trackage around Ely, McGill, and Keystone is utilized for popular passenger excursions as part of the Nevada Northern Railway Museum.

Still, Nevada has not been devoid of railroad construction. By the end of 1983, the UP (WP) and SP had finished relocating their lines around Elko, which eased downtown congestion. It should be noted that new or rebuilt railroads still manifest themselves in Nevada. For example, the Virginia & Truckee Railroad has been rebuilt in part and is very much alive as a summer tourist railroad. And in 1977 the WP completed a three-mile spur from its Reno branch to serve the Lear Reno Industrial Site.

The romance of the railroads has popular appeal as reflected by public attendance at railroad museums. Foremost in Nevada are the Nevada State Railroad Museum at Carson City and at Henderson (on the former UP line to Boulder City), and the Nevada Northern Railway Museum at Ely. In California, the State Railroad Museum at Sacramento, with its fine exhibits of old railroad equipment, including historic locomotives from Nevada short lines rescued by Gilbert Kniess and others many decades ago, are on display. At Rio Vista, some 25 miles southwest of Sacramento, the Western (formerly California) Railway Museum has a notable operating railroad system, as does the Orange Empire Museum at Perris, not far from San Bernardino in southern California.

The foregoing is but a glimpse of the events which have taken place in recent decades. Various proposed railroad and streetcar lines in Nevada and eastern California, as well as boats on the inland lakes, spectacular aerial tramways, lumber railroads, and previously unreported local railroad history will constitute a future third volume of *Railroads of Nevada and Eastern California*.

April 1992   DAVID F. MYRICK

PREFACE

You are standing on an old right-of-way in Nevada. It is early in the morning, the air is clear and brisk, and shadows flow from the sagebrush. Your eye follows the old railroad grade as it curves to the shoulder of the hill and stems down the plain before turning into a canyon. Is that the shrill of a locomotive whistle you hear? Are those echoing exhausts? "Look out for the train!"

How many years ago was it? Five? Ten? No, more likely it was 20, or 40 years ago, or more. But no matter; that is all in the past now. Those railroads, the lives of the men who built them, the few or the hordes who rode them into new mining camps in search of riches or returned with the long faces of disappointment—we may never see or meet them. We can only review the poignant record of their activities which has been left behind. And that we are about to do.

This book is an attempt to recreate the history, the people, the lives and the times surrounding each of the many different railroads built during the last century in Nevada and Eastern California. Each had some particular purpose, however minute—to service an industry, to serve a town, to develop a territory. There were times when the only purpose was to line the pockets of a promoter, or to bolster some inner personal pride where money alone could not entirely erase a feeling of recent impecuniosity.

Most of the material for these volumes has been obtained from old-time contemporary local newspapers, court records and government reports. Investigation of the more recent railroads has afforded an opportunity for personal interviews with many of the principals involved, developing an understanding and a flavor too frequently lacking on the printed page.

The story of some of the Nevada railroads has already been reasonably thoroughly recorded, that of the Virginia & Truckee is a prime example. To avoid repetition, the coverage of such lines herein will be confined largely to that additional information which has come to light together with enough of the basic facts necessary to make the story cohesive. It is to the other, more obscure railroads that the author has devoted his attention in an attempt to shed some light upon their obfuscations; and the stories of these lines, heretofore neglected, are given in greater detail. Indulgence is requested for the sometimes dry, though essential, references to the financial status of such lines; it is because no man will work without expecting compensation, and therefore no railroad could be built or continued in operation, if funds were not forthcoming to sustain its existence. Without adequate revenues, the demise of any business concern becomes certain; it is only a question of time.

Similarly, it is hoped that the sprinkling of dates and names will serve a dual purpose. Aside from being genuinely informative and of help in identifying and dating pictures, it would be most rewarding if their inclusion in this writing would help to stimulate further research and discovery of additional unknown facts, whether in the form of maps, photographs, documents or recollections. So much of this subject remains to be explored and chronicled, it would be most gratifying if in some small way this book might serve as a stimulus to that end.

Now a word about Nevada. Its history is colorful and varied, and this book is a supplement to general histories and is not intended as a replacement for available publications. Any chronological comparison of Nevada's development with that of the state of California should be made cautiously, keeping in mind that the first white explorers came to California some 250 years before they ventured into Nevada. The first permanent white settlement in California predated that in Nevada (in 1851) by at least 80 years.

Nevada and Eastern California were developed and populated mostly as a result of the development of the mining industry. In general there were two basic eras of consideration. The first (1859 to the early 1880's) began with the discovery of gold and later silver at Virginia City, but by 1894 production had shrunk to less than $2,000,000, a far cry from the $46,700,000 of 1877. Rich veins pinched out or were lost by faulting, and silver prices declined over a period of several decades.

Then, beginning with the twentieth century, the trend was reversed. Rich ore was found first at Tonopah, then followed by numerous other discoveries. Metal prices recovered. During the first decade of the century, riches from the earth created a whole new set of millionaires and thousands of less fortunate hopefuls.

Since mining was the principal industry of Nevada, it was only logical that railroad development paralleled the eras of mining prosperity. The majority of the railroads were constructed within two periods—from 1868 to 1883 and from 1903 to 1912. Later, highway improvements plus a general decline of mining, except in a few limited areas, brought about abandonments, the procession starting about the time of World War I.

Sitting in a comfortable chair and reading tales about the old mining camps, which over the years have emphasized the romance, excitement and riches of those times, an incomplete picture is fabricated. Pushed into the background are the difficulties and privations encountered by most of the people participating in the early-day life of those mining camps. Mere subsistence was a distinct mode of discomfort; the heat in the summer could be abnormally extreme while the cold in the winter would be equally vexatious, particularly when aided by strong winds. At such times, miners' tents offered little protection.

It is to be remembered that man needed companionship and conviviality then as now, particularly after a series of discouraging days of seeking elusive riches. The only relief was the tent saloon, usually the first tent erected, where men could take the curse off their plight. Crowding into the tent at night, drinking—perhaps too much in an effort to warm up or forget the bad day, or to encourage a better spirit for the morrow—could easily create an outburst of verbal or physical expression. A quick gun at the hip, brought into play because of some initially minor irritation, frequently resulted in shootings in "self defense." A moderate number of such incidents were of normal commonplace, as they were to be associated with the lower element; a larger quantity gave the camp a "reputation," and made all such events of newsworthy comment.

Perhaps the following letter from Henry Cutting, one of the first storekeepers in Tonopah, written to the *Reno Evening Gazette* on February 3, 1901, will lend some impression of the vicissitudes of early-day camp life, although it should be borne in mind that the embryonic Tonopah of that time had little of the lawlessness usually associated with incipient mining camps.

"There are two frame buildings which have been thrown together and are tight enough to screen the icy winds of winter but not keep them out. One of them is the Tonopah store, 12 x 14 feet, the other the necessary adjunct of every mining camp, the saloon, which is 12 x 16 feet. Into these the whole male population—about sixty men—crowd every evening and stormy days, for a tent is pretty cold quarters when one is out of bed. The one redeeming feature of Tonopah, besides the richness of the ore, is the boarding house. Of course you folks in Reno who can go over to the Riverside and get one of those dinners that Harry Gosse sets up, might scorn a dinner of tough beef and canned goods served in a tent with a box for a seat. You who sit around a comfortable house cannot imagine what a luxury this is in Tonopah, but had you been here as I was before the boarding house started you would have no depreciatory remarks to make. . . ."

For ease of comprehension and facility of reference, the railroads of Nevada have been divided into two groups—Volume I encompasses the northern trunk lines and the connecting roads which normally fed traffic to them; Volume II encompasses the southern trunk lines and connecting roads which normally routed traffic to the south. Isolated railroads have been assigned to either of these groups on a geographical basis. Most ultra-short lines, and those for which but little information has been found, have been combined into a single chapter in each of the major groups. As an aid to chronological orientation, the list of selected events will assist in placing the various major railroad incidents mentioned in the text in proper perspective.

While this is not a guide book per se, a number of identifying landmarks and mileages have been included in maps and text as purposeful aids to those on field trips. Local details are highlighted for the same reason, as well as for the benefit of current residents of the areas involved. To one familiar with the country, the yet uncovered former railroad grades can be spotted from the air. Regular transcontinental flights pass over Tonopah, Coaldale and Mount Montgomery Pass, while other flights follow the routes of the T&G, the BG and the LV&T to Las Vegas.

In any book about railroads, the number and variety of corporate names and spellings can become onerously multiplied and complex. In these pages every attempt has been made to give the correct spelling of the full road name at the time of its introduction; thereafter abbreviations are frequently used (particularly in the use of "&" for "and") or merely the initials representing the corporate name. The advantage will become apparent where several road names appear in series, an unfortunately unavoidable circumstance in any work of this nature.

Lest a descendant fail to find his worthy ancestor mentioned or identified by name in the course of events as related in this book, it should be understood that such omission in no way is intended to belittle or ignore that worthy ancestor's accomplishments—space limitations have forced the omission of many important names and events. However, the writer would welcome correspondence of import concerning any portion of this work—pictures, maps or text—which will help to clarify or expand our knowledge of the railroads of Nevada. Such letters should be addressed to him in care of the publisher.

DAVID F. MYRICK

San Francisco, California
1962

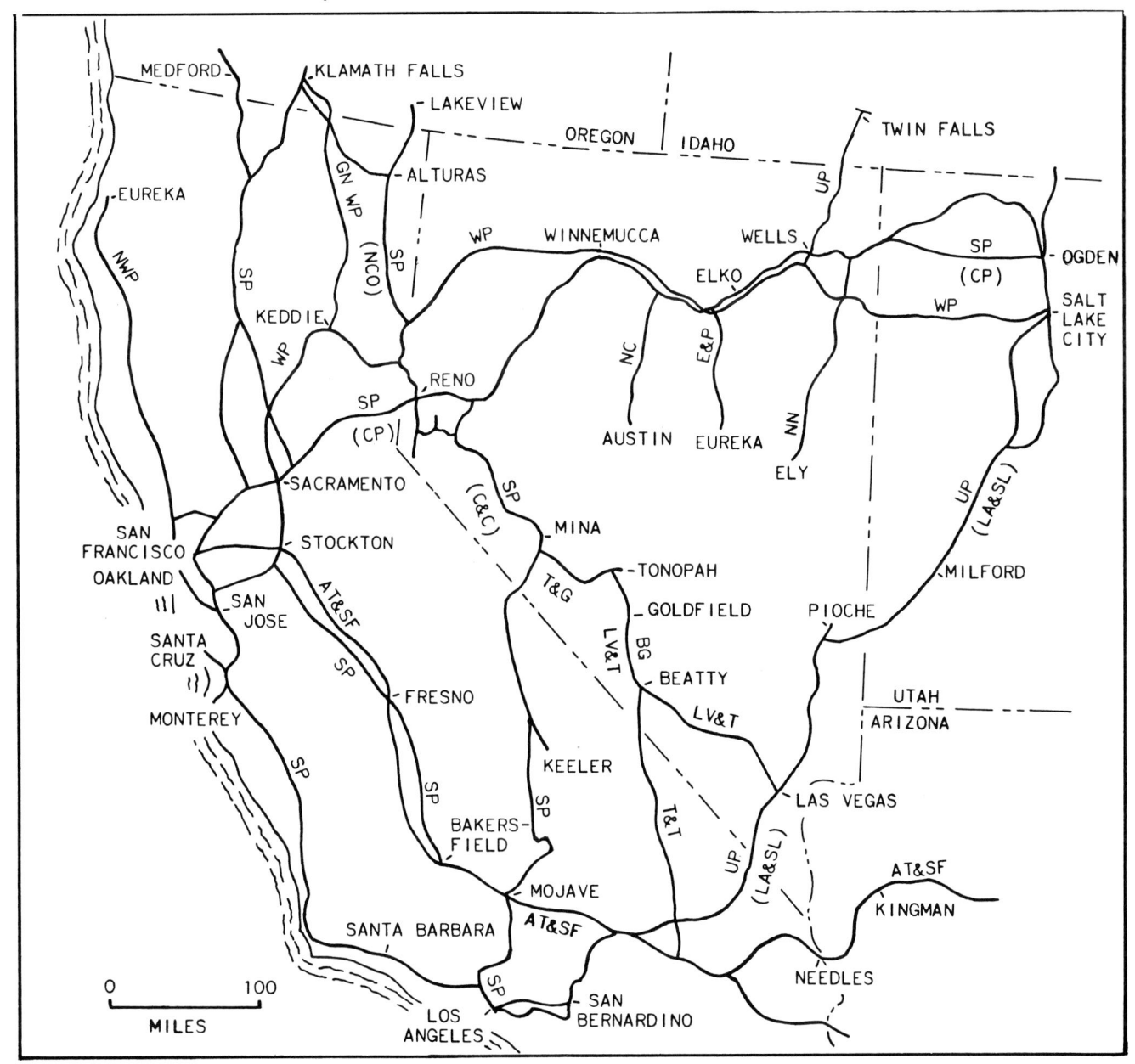

ACKNOWLEDGMENTS

Entering the Nevada scene when most of the fabled railroads are only memories of the past, one is dependent on gracious people with fine memories and a generous spirit. Fortunately a good number still exist—many were among the earliest residents of the twentieth century boom camps—although their number is being thinned as time takes its toll. Other people, although not a part of the active scene, have made substantial contributions to this volume in the form of suggestions or pictures from their collections. To all who aided me in this effort, I express my thanks, whether they acted as individuals or representatives of corporations, historical societies, libraries or government agencies. Among those who have contributed in a general manner to the development of this first volume are the following:

Walter Averett, the late Don Ashbaugh, Mrs. Clara Beatty, Mrs. Myrtle Myles, Mrs. Andy Welliver, Miss Delle Boyd, Dr. Effie Mona Mack, Donald and Nancy Bowers, Lucius Beebe, F. L. Green, E. W. Darrah, Dr. Russell Elliott, Louis D. Gordon, Grahame Hardy, John Koontz, Mrs. Emily P. Wood and Mrs. Byrd Sawyer, all residents of Nevada.

In California, I have been assisted many times by Brian Thompson, Gilbert Kneiss, Hugh Tolford, W. A. Pennington, Doug Richter, Stanley Borden, Robert Hancocks, W. C. Hendrick, Henry Carlisle, Guy L. Dunscomb and Jack Gibson.

For assistance with the Olinghouse story, I thank Mr. and Mrs. George F. Dallimore, also Ernie Mack and Mrs. Lucille Liebling. George F. White and John G. Huntington provided information concerning the Nevada Short Line, while James C. Martin's legal research yielded facts about the Eagle Salt Works. Material for the Nevada Central and Nevada Midland was supplied by the late J. G. Phelps Stokes, who, with Andrew Stevenson, Jr., also made available certain files, data and drafts of contracts of the proposed Mid Pacific Railroad. Burt Acree added knowledge for the Nevada Central and Austin City Railroad chapters, while Linn Ball, John Ball, Donald B. McGuire, Louis E. Lemaire, Adrian Ramsdell and his sister, Mrs. Eads, passed on their recollections of the Lewis area and the B&ML RR. Mr. Belton O. Bryan, American Consul General at Glasgow, Scotland, obtained helpful background information about the Golconda and Adelaide RR.

I was aided in the E&P chapter by Ed Delaney, Victor Goodwin and Stanley Borden. One fine source of information was Lawrence K. Requa, who helped with the story of Ely and the Nevada Northern Ry. Others contributing to this chapter were F. Sommer Schmidt, John D. East, Adolph Judell, H. M. Peterson and Walter Armstrong. John Eaby and A. J. O'Connor sent useful data on Giroux trackage and locomotives.

New stories about the V&T are not easy to obtain, however, Ted Wurm and Gordon Sampson came forward with previously unrecorded tales. At Dayton, Chester Barton, W. H. Scott and Ray Walmsley were kind enough to fill in the railroad and mill situation in that area. W. R. Curry and Jim Knapp offered fresh data relating to the C&C, while E. W. Billeb did the same thing for Bodie. A number of people helped to round out the Tonopah and Goldfield chapter—Oro Parker, Henry Carlisle, Mrs. R. T. Morris, L. Dulien, Hon. G. W. Malone, Col. Thomas W. Miller, Eugene Rebarb, Herb Witt, Alfred E. Perlman and three who have passed on in the last two years—Walter Rowson, Clarence M. Oddie and Mark Bradshaw. Orlando McCraney has my thanks for his personal recollections of the construction of the Silver Peak RR. W. A. Swann furnished a fine map of the GCM RR and other data. James C. Martin, Clark J. Guild and Anson S. Blake (now deceased) filled in details concerning the Nevada Copper Belt.

Although the last through line constructed in Nevada, the OSL line from Twin Falls to Wells was an elusive subject. The search was solved thanks to John A. Elliott, Allan Krieg and Robert W. Edwards. Assisting with the Western Pacific were Eric Thomsen, Louis Stein, Jr., and Vic Goodwin.

As the former president of the N-C-O, letters from Charles Moran were always helpful and visits with him in New York most delightful. Other N-C-O material was furnished by the late S. H. McCartney, formerly vice president and general manager, and Miss Maud Miller, the former secretary. Additional information and stories came from T. A. Smith, C. R. Chapman, Sam Boney, Ira Moore, Mrs. A. V. Small, Mrs. Fisk and Mrs. MacDonald of Madeline, J. H. Mahan (formerly traffic manager of the N-C-O), Mrs. Patricia Fee Olmsted and the late Henry Kober of Ft. Bidwell, Alfred Coffman, Jr., Mr. Galleppi and Mr. Brubeck, both ranchers in Honey Lake Valley, Dr. E. F. Auble, Joe Leonard, Mrs. Beth Parliman and Mrs. A. C. Riesenman of Wendel. Thanks to E. K. Bramblett, I obtained a photostat copy of an early trial involving the N-C-O. Especially helpful were H. E. Gasaway, former roadmaster of the N-C-O and Mrs. Ora Dimick, long-time Alturas resident.

Assistance on the stories of the lumber roads came from various kind, well-informed people. Mrs. Vinton Bowen White was particularly helpful, recalling many events in her father's struggle to hang on to his equity in the Sierra Valleys Railway. The late R. F. Ramelli and the late Steve A. Pezzola supplied additional information as did the City Bank Farmers Trust Co. of New York. Victor Goodwin, E. E. Jackman and Arthur Revert gave me many details respecting the Verdi Lumber Co. F. F. Thomas, Jr., Peter Morrison, W. A. Lawrence, Oscar Lindsay, Charles Oliver, Norman J. Hearn, O. C. Majors, and Paul E. Shively filled the reservoir of information concerning the railroads around Hobart Mills, while Hal Wright, J. S. Rees, Vern Lingren, Clyde D. Spradling and the late J. S. Conklin supplied data about the Clover Valley Lumber Co. and the Boca & Loyalton Railroad.

For illustrations, selections were made from 2,000 pictures. Individual credit is given each picture (except those few where the source is not known or those taken by the author) but the following unusually fine collections deserve special mention and again I express my appreciation to all concerned, particularly to the Nevada Historical Society, Donald Duke of the *Pacific Railway Journal,* Guy Dunscomb, Dr. Stanley Palmer, Grahame Hardy, Ted Wurm, Louis Stein, Jr., Chester Barton, Mrs. Hugh Brown, Sewell Thomas, Clarence Oddie, William A. Pennington, H. E. Gasaway, Mrs. Vinton Bowen White, Southern Pacific, Western Pacific and the U. S. Geological Survey.

Compiling and drawing the maps presented another challenge but, thanks to Miss Carolyn Henderson, Mrs. Jean Molleskog, Stanley Borden and Robert Adams (whose skill resulted in many fine maps) the task was made much lighter.

Editorial assistance was contributed by Brian Thompson, E. P. Humphrey, Jr., and Stanley Borden. I would particularly like to express my sincere thanks to Robert Adams for his patience and notable contribution in this respect.

Many other people—some whose names I shall never know as they were part of a government organization, a fine library or an historical society—made contributions either in facts or stories. From the following libraries and offices, I was able to make use of almost eighty different newspapers. To the staffs of these libraries and commissions, I offer my thanks for their help and interest. Among them are: the Nevada Historical Society, the University of Nevada and the Nevada State Library, Bancroft Library at Berkeley, the University of California at Los Angeles, the library of the California Division of Mines and the library of the California Historical Society in San Francisco as well as the Stanford University Library. Away from the area, I found material of great value in the New York City Public Library, the National Archives, Library of Congress, U. S. Supreme Court Law Library, the Library of the Association of American Railroads, as well as the Santa Barbara Public Library, the Plumas County Library and the Inyo County Free Library.

Historical societies in Oregon, Nebraska and New York kindly answered questions concerning individuals. Much useful information came from the transcripts of testimony of hearings before the Public Service Commission of Nevada (Miss Austin was particularly helpful), and the California Public Utilities Commission. The Oregon Public Utilities Commissioner supplied answers to my questions as did the Interstate Commerce Commission, who not only supplied maps but copies of reports. My special thanks to them. Material respecting incorporations was furnished by the Secretaries of State in Nevada, California, Oregon, Utah, Idaho, Arizona and even Maine.

One of the most rewarding aspects of the entire project was the confidence displayed by old friends and the interest of new friends acquired along the many paths of research. Last but not least, I should like to acknowledge with pleasure the sparkling presence of pretty companions who joined me in the field trips in the search for ghost towns and old lines of railroads.

DAVID F. MYRICK

Telegraph Hill, San Francisco
October 1962

CHRONOLOGICAL LIST OF SELECTED EVENTS

Railroad Construction	Other Nevada, California or National Events	Railroad Abandonments
1853 Pacific R.R. surveys	1851 First Settlement – Mormon Station 1859 Rush to Comstock 1860 Nevada Population 6,857	
1861 Central Pacific R.R. incorporated. 1863 Central Pacific construction begun 1867 Railroad at Silver Peak graded First locomotive in Nevada (December 13) 1868 CP opened to Reno 1869 V&T ground broken February 18 CP completed – gold spike V&T operating Gold Hill to Carson City December 21	1861 Territory of Nevada started 1862 Austin – Gold and silver discovered 1864 Nevada became a state Eureka – Lead-silver discoveries 1868 Austin and Belmont – peak production 1869 Comstock – end first bonanza 1870 Hamilton – peak production Nevada population 42,491	
1872 V&T completed Reno to Virginia City (August 24) Eureka Mill R.R. built 1873 Pioche & Bullionville R.R. constructed 1875 Eureka & Palisade completed Lake Tahoe R.R. (Glenbrook) completed 1880 Nevada Central R.R. completed Carson & Colorado R.R. – work begun Nevada & Oregon R.R. – ground broken	1871-73 Pioche booming 1871-85 Eureka – good production 1873 Comstock – Big bonanza discovered 1875 Virginia City and Eureka – Big fires 1877 Nevada mineral production – $46 million 1879 Reno – bad fire 1880 Silver price $1.29 oz. Nevada population 62,266	
1881 C&C opened to Hawthorne (April 7) Bodie & Benton and Battle Mountain & Lewis opened. 1882 C&C opened to Candelaria (March 1) Nevada & Oregon operating to Evans (October 2) SP Mojave-Needles construction begun 1883 C&C opened to Keeler (August 1) SP-A&P connected at Needles (August 9) 1884 AT&SF bought SP line from Mojave to Needles 1885 Battle Mountain & Lewis R.R. revived 1890 UP graded Milford-Pioche Nevada & California R.R. reached Amedee	1881 Comstock – Big bonanza over Calico, Calif. – silver discovered 1881-83 Candelaria booming 1882 Sutro Tunnel completed 1883-84 Calico booming – borate discovered 1884 Nevada mineral production – $7 million 1890 Severe winter, blockades, etc. Eureka production shut down Nevada population 47,335	1890 Battle Mountain & Lewis R.R. dismantled (approx.)
1891 Pioche Pacific R.R. built 1893 Nevada Southern R.R. built UP in receivership 1898 Randsburg R.R. completed Borate & Daggett R.R. opened 1899 Golconda & Adelaide opened Utah & Pacific construction reached Uvada 1900 Lake Tahoe Ry. & Transp. Co. R.R. opened to Truckee SP purchased C&C N-C-O opened to Termo	1891 Candelaria – long strike started 1893 National depression set in 1894 Nevada mineral production – $2 million 1896 Silver price down to 53¢ oz. 1898 Klondike, Alaska, gold rush War with Spain Austin mines closed (fraud) 1900 Tonopah discovered (May 17) Nevada population 42,335	1896 Dayton, Sutro & Carson Valley R.R. abandoned (approx.)
1901 Clark-Harriman war UP bought control of SP 1902 Calif. Eastern R.R. reached Ivanpah Quartette R.R. built at Searchlight 1903 Ludlow & Southern R.R. completed 1904 Tonopah R.R. built Nevada Transit (Reno) opened 1905 Salt Lake Route (SP, LA&SL) opened C&C widened to standard gauge T&G reached Goldfield	1901 Tonopah mines operated under leases 1904 Goldfield boom started 1905 Rhyolite boomed Las Vegas town lot auction Nevada mineral production – $6 million	1904 SP's Wadsworth Shops moved to Sparks

Railroad Construction	Other Nevada, California or National Events	Railroad Abandonments
1906 Nevada Northern R.R. completed to Ely Silver Peak R.R. opened Las Vegas & Tonopah R.R. completed to Rhyolite 1907 Nevada R.R. to Olinghouse opened AT&SF built Barnwell to Searchlight LV&T completed to Goldfield Tonopah & Tidewater R.R. opened to Beatty Bullfrog Goldfield R.R. opened to Beatty 1908 Rawhide Western R.R. graded 1909 Western Pacific R.R. opened 1910 Nevada Copper Belt R.R. completed to Yerington SP built Mojave to Owenyo	1906 Greenwater boomed Silver price – 68¢ oz. 1907 Heavy storms in March Labor troubles in Goldfield Panic – banks closed 1908 Carson irrigation project opened Rawhide boomed – promotion Rawhide fire (September 4) 1909 Rawhide flood (August 31) 1910 Gambling made illegal (October 1) Nevada mineral production – $31 million Nevada population 81,875	1906 Eureka Mill R.R. abandoned 1908 Rawhide Western R.R. given up 1909 Nevada R.R. to Olinghouse abandoned
1911 Owens River Valley Electric Ry. graded Yellow Pine Ry. opened 1912 NCB completed to Ludwig Salt Lake Route Moapa branch opened N-C-O completed to Lakeview, Oregon 1913 Nevada Short Line opened 1914 SP (Fernley & Lassen Ry.) completed to Westwood Trona Ry. completed Death Valley R.R. completed LV&T-BG consolidation 1915 Nevada Short Line extended to Upper Rochester 1918 Western Pacific entered Reno	1913 Los Angeles Aqueduct completed Goldfield flood (September 13) 1914 Borax production started at (New) Ryan Metal prices decline 1914-18 World War I 1916-18 Metal prices soar Goodsprings boomed 1918 Silver price $1.00 ounce Nevada mineral production – $49 million 1919 Excitement at Divide 1920 Nevada population 77,407	1912 Owens River Valley Electric Ry. given up 1914 Colconda & Adelaide R.R. dismantled 1916 Eagle Salt Works abandoned 1917 Bodie & Benton abandoned 1918 Silver Peak R.R. abandoned LV&T abandoned Boca & Loyalton R.R. abandoned 1920 Reno trolleys abandoned in part Nevada Short Line abandoned
1925 SP bought N-C-O 1926 UP built Idaho-Wells branch 1927-28 N-C-O standard-gauged 1929 SP opened new Fernley to Klamath Falls line	1923 First Goldfield fire 1924 Second Goldfield fire 1927 Nevada mineral production – $24 million Naval Ammunition Depot established at Hawthorne Borax production shifted to Boron, California Death Valley opened to tourists 1930 Nevada population 91,058	1924 AT&SF Searchlight branch abandoned 1927 Reno-Sparks trolley abandoned Verdi Lumber R.R. abandoned 1928 Bullfrog-Goldfield abandoned 1930 Arden Plaster R.R. abandoned
1931 UP built Boulder City Branch 1932 Mid-Pacific R.R. proposed 1936 "City" Streamliners started in operation 1940 UP acquired Prince Consolidated Mines R.R.	1930-35 Economic Depression 1931 Gambling legalized in Nevada 6-week divorce law in Nevada 1931-35 Hoover Dam (Boulder) constructed 1932 Nevada mineral production – $4 million Silver price 28¢ ounce 1935 Nevada mineral production – $16 million Silver price 52¢ ounce 1940 Nevada mineral production – $44 million Nevada population 110,247	1931 Death Valley R.R. abandoned 1934 SP's Mound House branch abandoned 1935 Ludlow & Southern rails removed 1937 Nevada Central abandoned 1938 Eureka-Nevada R.R. abandoned SP (C&C) narrow-gauge line Mina to Benton abandoned 1939 V&T old main Carson City to Virginia City abandoned 1940 T&T abandoned (Rails up 1942)
	1942 Air Force Base established at Tonopah 1950 Nevada mineral production – $48 million	1946 T&G abandoned 1947 NCB abandoned 1950 V&T final abandonment
	1957 Zinc, lead, tungsten mines closed 1960 Nevada mineral production – $80 million Nevada population 285,278	1960 SP (C&C) narrow-gauge line Laws to Keeler abandoned

CHRONOLOGICAL LIST OF SELECTED EVENTS

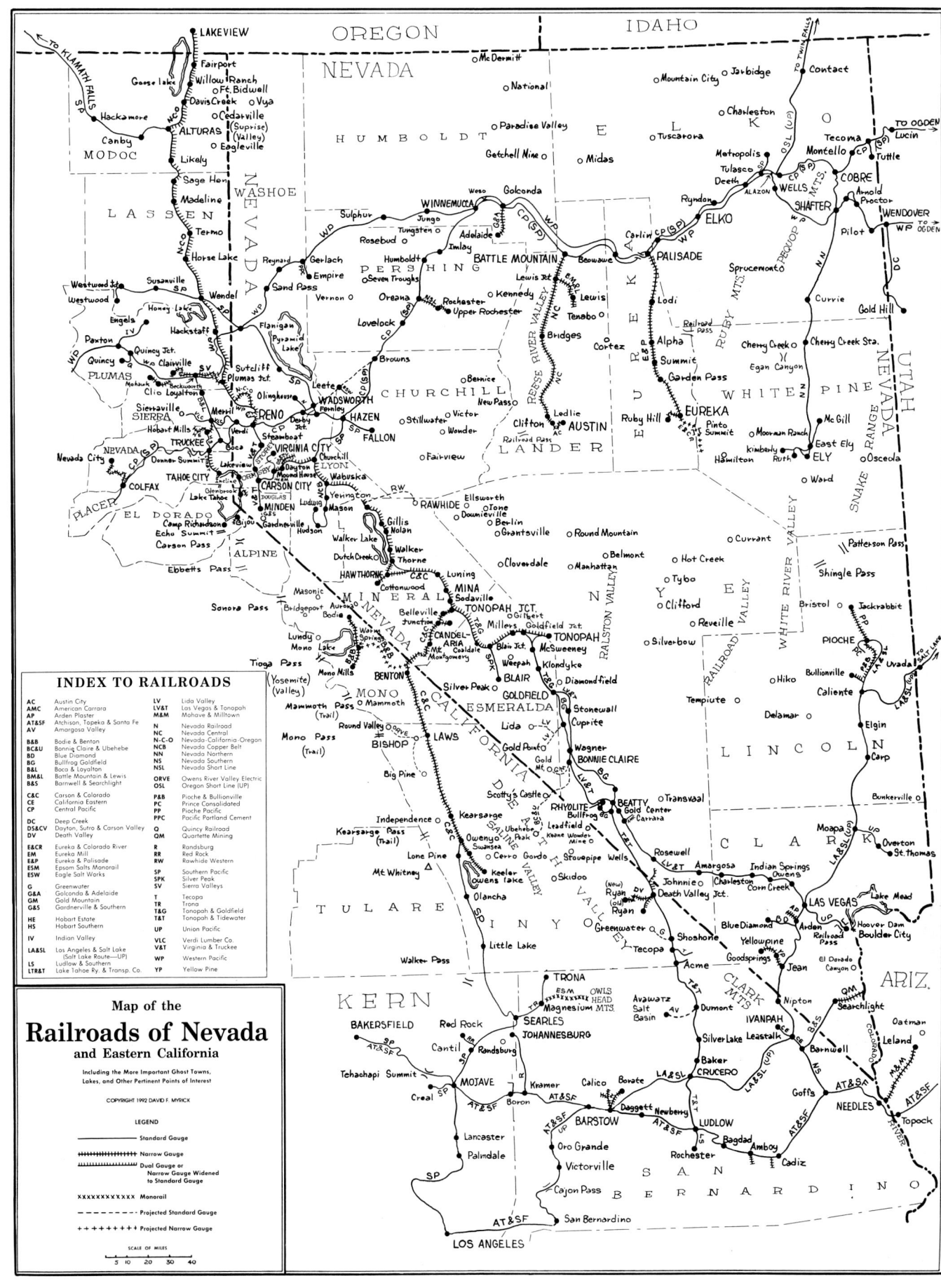

THE CENTRAL PACIFIC... PIONEER

Excepting the occasional sporadic forays engaged in by the Hudson Bay Company's trappers plus some Spanish explorations in the southern part of the state, it may be said that the territory comprising the state of Nevada was never viewed by white men until the year 1826, nearly three centuries following the first exploration of California. During the ensuing two decades such famous explorers as Jedediah Smith, Walker, Fremont and Kit Carson traversed the territory, as did various emigrant parties on their way across the country to California. The first of this latter group was the Bartelson-Bidwell party of 1841.

In 1849 a great wave of gold seekers emigrated westward, and a trading post was established in the Carson Valley called Mormon Station, which became the first permanent settlement in that area, then known as Western Utah. Subsequently in 1856 a town was surveyed, and the name was changed to Genoa. Later, in 1864, the territory became the state of Nevada. The only thought given to the area traversed by these nineteenth century travellers was respectful consideration for its many hazards and an idle wish that some means be found to minimize them. The Pacific Coast was their goal, and it remained the big objective until 1859, when a great backwash arose and swept eastward in the reverse direction, up and over the Sierras, returning to the very brim of Carson Valley where those fortunes were sought on the Comstock Lode which had escaped them in California.

The first proposals for a railroad across this country, initiated as early as the 1830's, envisioned just such a better means of travel by which to gain access to the state of California as the gold seekers desired. Asa Whitney brought the matter to the attention of Congress as early as 1845-47, but it was not until 1853 that the Pacific Railroad Surveys were authorized. Another three years and 13 volumes later, the five major, practical routes for such a railroad had not only been delineated, but even the flora and fauna were circumspectly depicted at the cost of hundreds of additional pages. Still another section outlined the various Indian dialects together with their English equivalents. It was indeed a masterful, albeit expensive, compilation.

Naturally, there were strong supporters for each of the routes under consideration. However, with the advent of the Civil War in 1861 stressing the need to bind California to the Union cause, the southern route was dropped from consideration, and the central route was chosen. On July 1, 1862, President Lincoln affixed his signature to that famous document, the Pacific Railroad Act, and the first transcontinental railroad was officially born.

The full story of the race between the Union Pacific and Central Pacific railroads in the construction of this first monumental enterprise is entertaining, enlightening and highly spiced with the flavor of rugged, primitive living conditions of the times. It is an oft-told tale, far beyond the compass of the boundaries of any one state, and ample works of reference are extant to satisfy the desires of the interested. The remarks contained herein will largely be confined to those applicable to that area of territory comprising the eastern slopes of the Sierra Nevada mountains in eastern California, all of the state of Nevada, and appropriate portions of the western part of the state of Utah.

Construction

Theodore Dehone Judah, the engineer and surveyor, was the man who sparked the Central Pacific Rail Road into existence and subsequently into prominence. Wherever agitation for a transcontinental railroad was expressed, whether in the halls of Congress or along the California coast, there was Judah, propounding the basic facts based upon scientific studies and sound engineering principles. It was Judah who succeeded in enlisting the financial support of Huntington, Hopkins, Crocker and Stanford — the "Big Four" of western railroading; it was Judah who succeeded, on June 28, 1861, in incorporating the Central Pacific Rail Road Company of California (the first of four separate corporations to use the Central Pacific name); it was Judah who obtained formal acceptance of the contract between the government and the Central Pacific as witnessed by proper signatories on No-

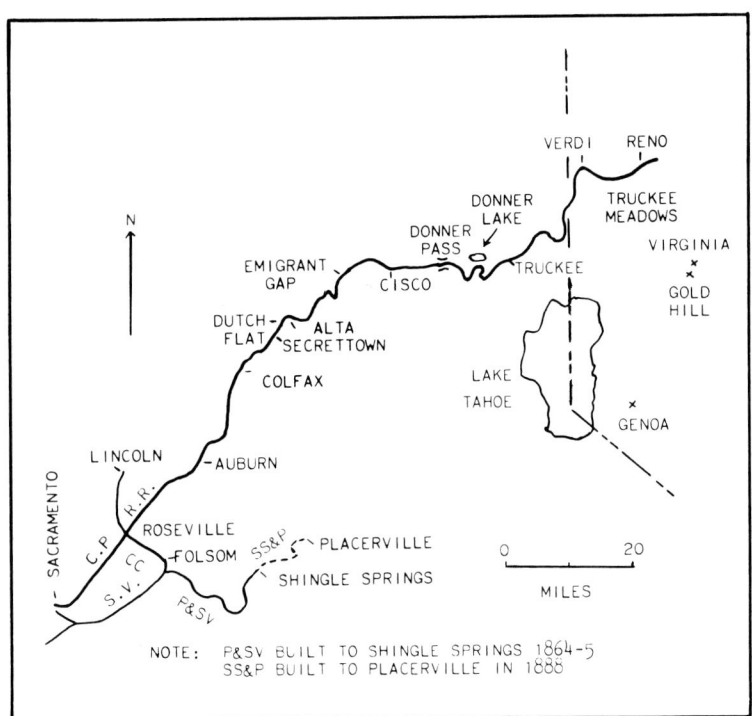

NOTE: P&SV BUILT TO SHINGLE SPRINGS 1864-5
SS&P BUILT TO PLACERVILLE IN 1888

vember 1, 1862; and it was Judah who set sail for New York in October 1863, contracted Panama fever at the Isthmus, and died a few days later on November 2 at a mere 38 years of age. A monument erected to his memory stands today on the lawn in front of the station building of the Southern Pacific Railroad in the city of Sacramento, capital of the state of California.

Construction of the Central Pacific started at Sacramento with the breaking of ground on January 8, 1863. The first 138 miles up and over the Sierra Mountains, through the 7,042-foot Donner Pass and on to the California-Nevada border were not completed for nearly five long years. It was an eventful Friday, the thirteenth (of December 1867), when the first locomotive nosed its way across the state line into Nevada at Camp 24. The reasons for the delay were obvious.

Initial rail deliveries at Sacramento were not made on time, with the result that track laying eastward from the city did not commence until October of 1863. By then, compounded delays had begun to take their toll with the result that the first, easiest, 18-mile section to a place called Junction (now Roseville) was not opened until April 26, 1864. At this point the Central Pacific crossed the older California Central Railroad out of Folsom, and business began to be attracted. In the month of May, some 8,906 passengers paid a total of $4,291.25 to ride the new line, but freight revenues held to a disquieting $160.50.

During the next 36 miles of line, the effects of the foothills of the Sierras began to be noticed.

Even though balmy, summer weather favored the project, it was September 1864 before service was instituted up the 2,255-foot climb to Colfax where the continuing grade increased to 2.42% for the climb to and beyond Dutch Flat (an additional 13 miles and approximately 1,000 feet higher).

1864 faded into 1865 as a heavy winter set in with snow storms and gales. That year travel eastward to Virginia City was possible only on runners, and for a time the Pioneer Stage Company withdrew its stages from the road between Colfax and Dutch Flat. Snowballing, a leading winter sport in Dutch Flat, got out of hand. All top hats were fair game, as were Chinamen; but the local magistrate took a dim view after one man had been arrested for snowballing a Chinaman, and he gave the active party a fine of $60. Unable to pay, the arrested man was sent to the county jail for 30 days.

In spite of the bad weather, work was being pushed as was necessary. On the eastern end, the Union Pacific was picking up speed, and their track was beginning to move westward at an alarming rate up the broad, flat valley of the Platte River. To the contrary, progress on the Central Pacific was slow, for deep cuts in the granite hills were required with increasing profusion. Each operation required the drilling of several holes 18 or 20 feet long and the insertion of a keg or two of black powder. When several of these charges were touched off in rapid succession the local reporters insisted that the concussion was unsurpassed even by the bombardment of Fort Sumter. Sometimes carelessness caused the blasting to be premature. Near Gold Run, seven men were blown up following a somewhat similar explosion in downtown San Francisco the day previous.

By May, 1866, Central Pacific cars were operating into Secrettown, and Charles Crocker, superintendent of construction, was feeling rather confident when, on June 2, he penned the following note to Phillip Lynch of the *Gold Hill* (Nevada) *News:* "The work goes bravely on. We are working between 9,000 and 10,000 men and 1,000 horses; and will employ more if they offer. The material we have encountered has proved much easier than we had expected to find; and in the Fall of 1867 I will meet you at Truckee Meadows and will pass you through to Sacramento by rail in seven hours." Crocker was overly optimistic. Only 60-odd miles of line had been completed, and there were over 50 miles yet to go. Heavy weather delayed completion of the line to Truckee Meadows, and when operations did commence two years later, a full eight and one-half hours were required to make the trip to Sacramento.

At the end of June people could "hear, distinctly, the 'iron horse' snorting" as work trains approached Dutch Flat (altitude 3,390 feet). Most of the town took advantage of the special Fourth of July excursion and paid $3.00 a head to ride to Sacramento. The return portion of the trip was interrupted with a delay due to a lumber fire along the railroad, and the passengers were most unhappy nid-nodding in the cars until nearly five o'clock the next morning. However, ten days later nearly 1,000 people from Sacramento crowded aboard an excursion train to the new station of Alta (two miles farther and 209 feet higher), while a special train for the benefit of stockholders was later operated. The public was beginning to acquire a taste for the steamcars.

A typesetter on the *Dutch Flat Enquirer* could not resist inserting this "local item" about his editor, E. B. Boust, who went down to Sacramento and then mislaid his ticket for the return trip. The editor "was as usual 'out of funds' to buy another. The conductor listened to, but heeded not, the pretty tale of the suspicious looking cove, and offered him the alternative of assisting the Engineer to 'wood' on the trip or go ashore. Boust 'wooded' extensively."

To accomplish as much work as possible before winter storms set in, a night grading shift was instituted. Such good progress was made (the night shift typically claimed they accomplished more than the day shift) that rail laying on the 21-mile section from Alta through Emigrant Gap to Cisco was begun in September. As the graders needed to keep ahead of the track layers, the cry went out for more labor. Chinese, probably ex-miners from Angels Camp, Vallecito and other places in Calaveras County, were recruited and assembled in Stockton before going up the hill to work on the CP. (It is interesting to note that, from 1847 to October, 1860, some 48,070 Chinese came to California to work in the mines, and it was not until 1862 that serious resentment toward the "Celestials" began to develop.)

In spite of these additions to the forces, the track layers overtook the graders just above Polley's, a scant five miles below Cisco, and Mr. Swift, the foreman, ranged all the way to Sacramento in his search for additional manpower. The success of his enterprise is indicated in that on Thanksgiving Day, November 29, 1866, the first through cars were run to Cisco (92 miles from Sacramento) at an elevation of 5933 feet. The race against winter had been won by the railroad.

But the success was short-lived. Two weeks later the heaviest snowstorm in years set in, while down in San Francisco the heaviest December rainfall in history was recorded. Trains stopped running as fills washed out and cuts caved in. For a few days no trains reached Alta, and for the next three months the new line to Cisco was out of service completely. Near the summit, a gang of Chinese graders was caught in a snowslide and five died before they could be rescued. On the Friday night before Christmas the snow fell so heavily that a whole camp of Chinese laborers was buried and had to be dug out. In other instances, camps were carried away in avalanches, the men buried and not found until the snow melted the next summer.

Nature continued to torment the construction forces all winter. Each week there was a new snowstorm, some leaving as much as 72 inches of additional, fresh snow. Newspapers favoring other trans-Sierra routes which, it was hoped, would pass through their local cities, were full of abusive comments about the Dutch Flat route and the railroad's eternal battle with the elements. The *Red Bluff Independent* called the project a fizzle and doubted it could ever be finished.

At the beginning of this trouble, late in 1866, Crocker moved his operations over the summit and down the east slope to the Truckee River canyon where more moderate weather prevailed. As he said later, "The men were driven out of the mountains by storms . . . the snow would fill up just as fast as they could dig it out, so I moved them down on the Truckee River. We hauled locomotives (and when I say 'we' I mean myself) and we hauled iron and cars." In this way three locomotives, 40 cars and material for 40 miles of track were hauled from Cisco to Donner Lake. Work commenced westward on the section of track from Corburn's Station (soon renamed Truckee) toward the Summit. By tunneling under the snow, excavation of the 1,650 foot tunnel at Donner Summit (elevation 7,017 feet) was continued all during the winter on a three shift basis.

The railroad line from Alta to Cisco was finally freed from snow on March 19, 1867. By April it was snowed in again. The stage agent at Cisco telegraphed Bill Crandell, the agent at Virginia City, Nevada, the discouraging news: "Snowplow only got half mile below Cisco at noon today. Plow

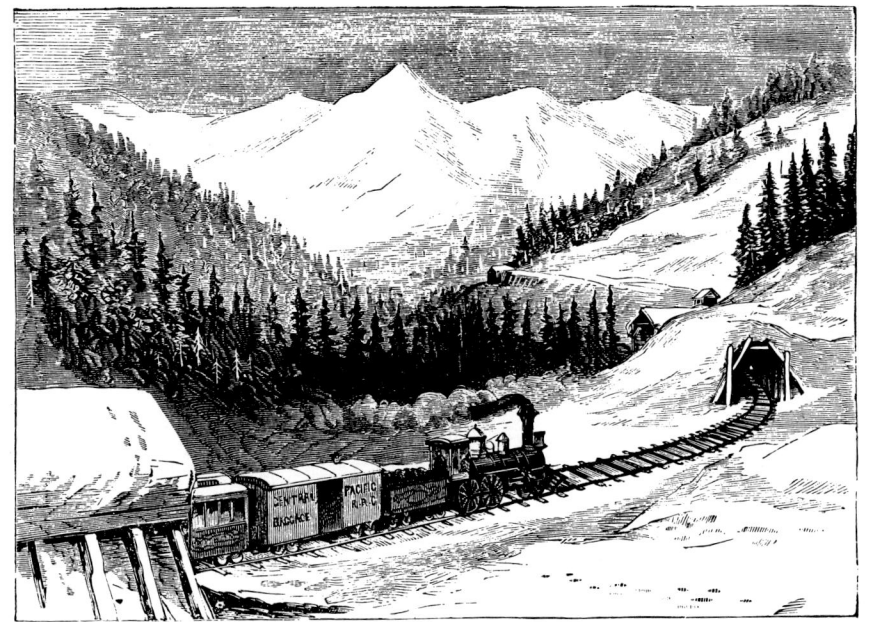

THE SUMMIT OF THE SIERRA NEVADA MOUNTAINS.
Drawn by NAHL BROS., San Francisco.   Engraved by G. W. SHOURDS.

From time immemorial, winter snows have plagued the crossing of the Sierra Nevada. The Central Pacific's route over Donner Summit was no exception. An artist depicts *(left)* the early designs of snowsheds along the western approach to the summit, a type of construction which became the prelude to 40 miles of such man-made, smoke-filled, timber tunnels to keep the right-of-way open at the most strategic places. SP's eastbound cab-in-front locomotive No. 4164 *(below)* trails the load of tonnage which it has successfully negotiated over the serpentine summit crossing. *(Top: Bancroft Library; Bottom: Southern Pacific.)*

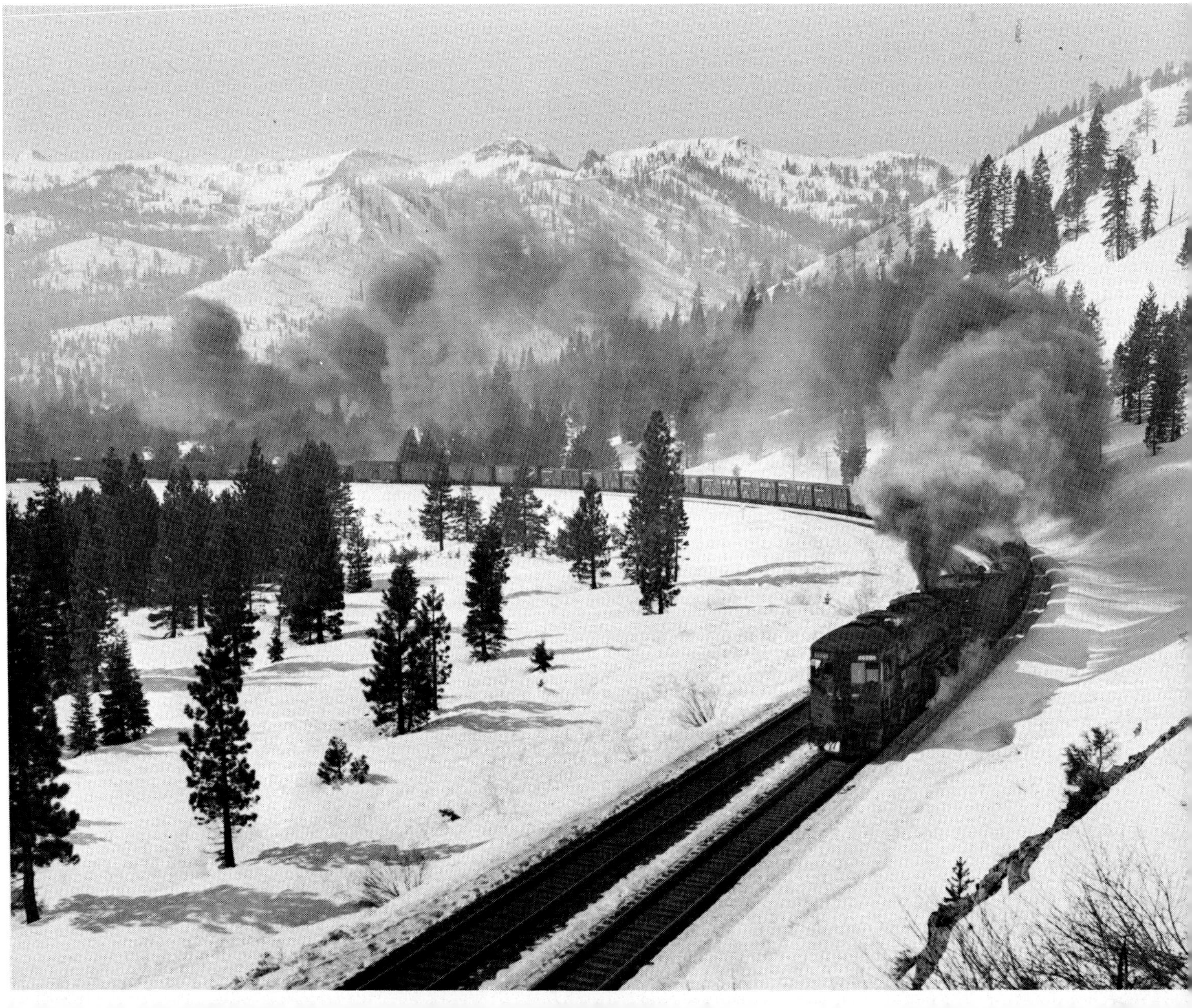

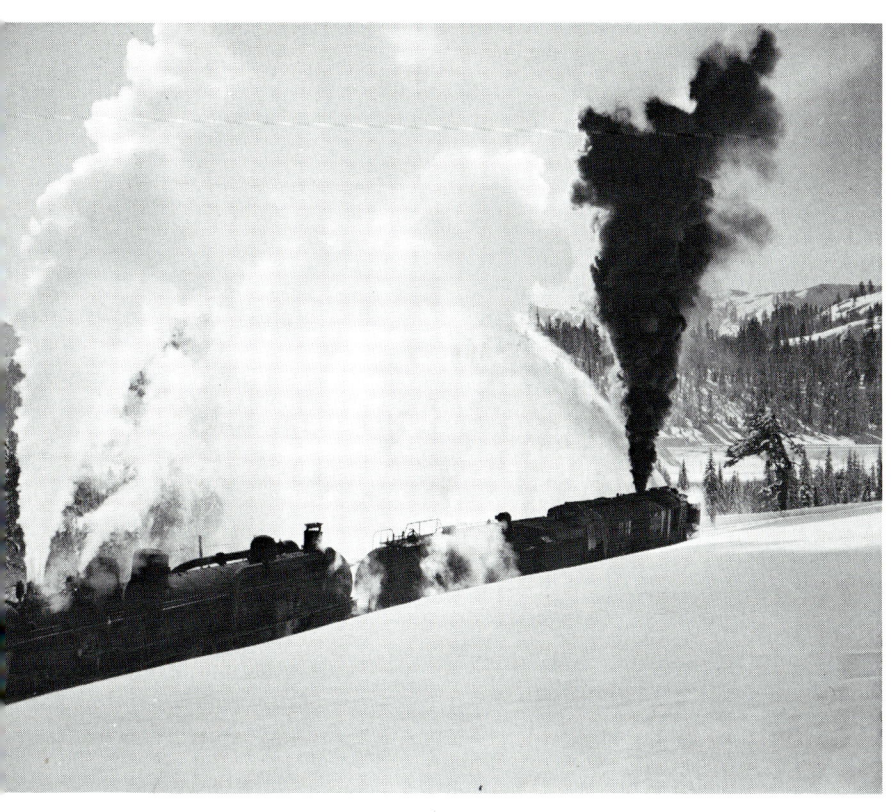

Modern rotary snowplows have enabled the railroad effectively to reduce the costly miles of snowsheds to but six miles of short, sporadic lengths. A rotary plow *(left)* may be seen at work on the west slope of Donner Summit, while *(below)* in the wake of a vanishing snowstorm, a critical length of modern snowshed still protects the treacherous eastern approach to the same crossing. *(Two Photos: Southern Pacific.)*

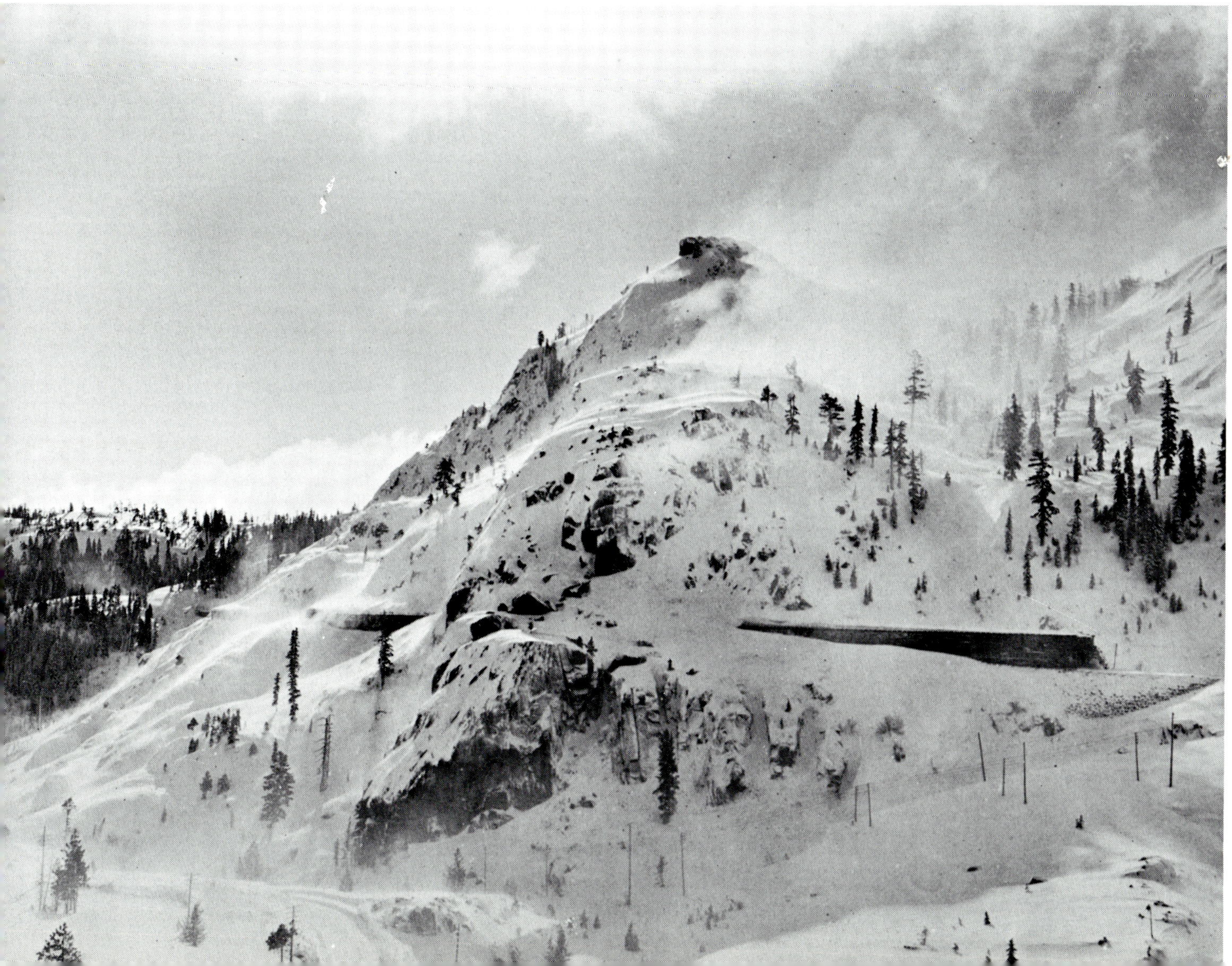

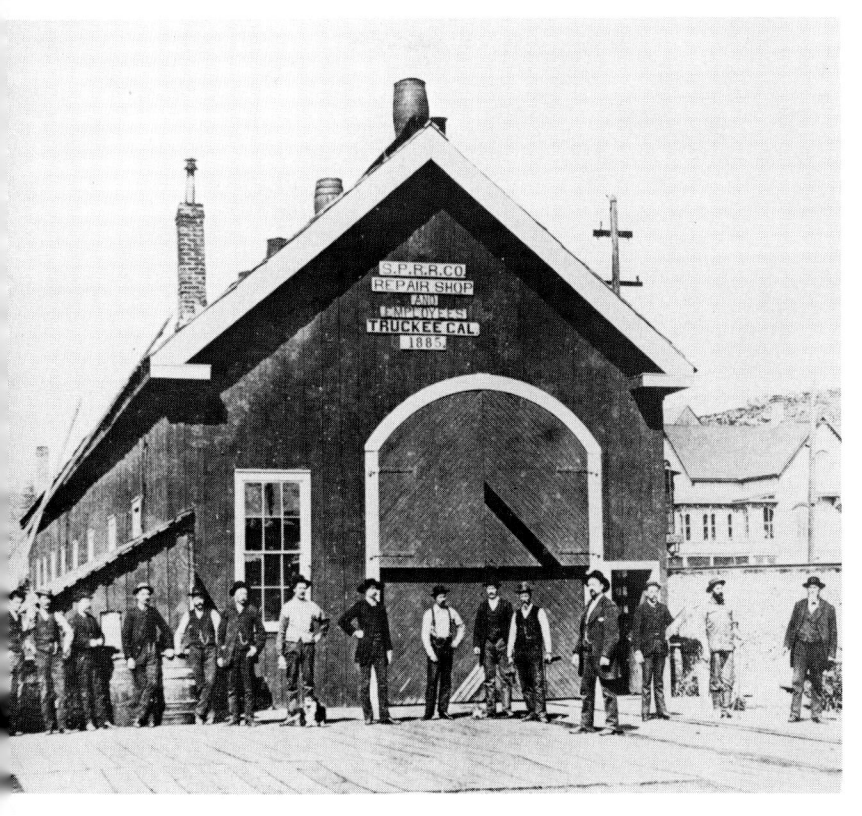

Situated at the foot of the steep climb up the east slope of Donner Summit, Truckee, California, rapidly became an essential helper station and repair center. Although the Repair Shop *(left)* was built by the Central Pacific and continued (at the time of the photo) to carry its complement of strategic water barrels along the peak of the roof in case of fire, the "S.P.R.R.CO." designation of ownership on the front postdates this group-shopmen picture into the early part of the present century. (*Southern Pacific Collection.*)

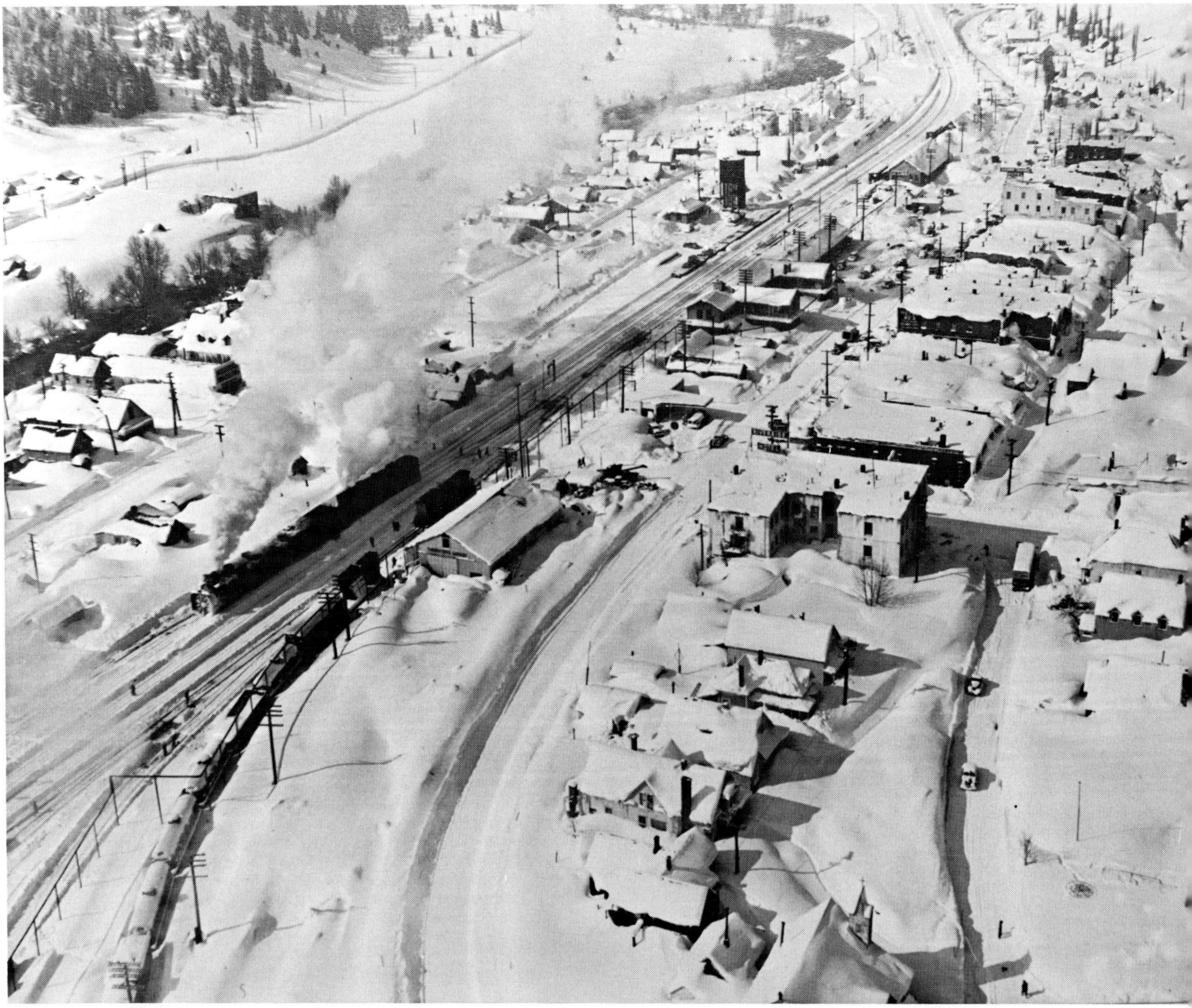

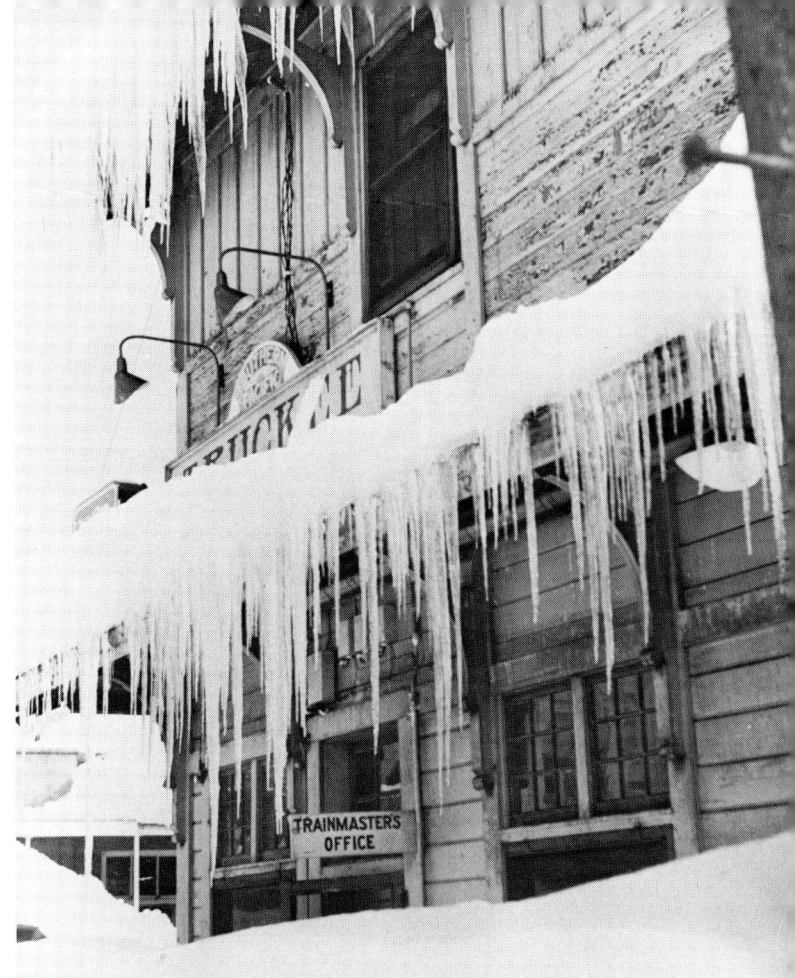

That winters in Truckee were, and still are, picturesquely severe is amply demonstrated in this group of photos. Peeling paint on the station side walls *(right)* is indicative of the depression year of 1932. Two decades later in January 1952, a rotary plow and cab-forward pusher *(left, below)* paused for this striking winter portrait of a railroad center minus such early necessities as the famous Truckee covered roundhouse *(below, right)* built by the Central Pacific in wood-burning days to protect the turntable and pit from mid-winter snows. *(Bottom, Left: Sacramento Bee Photo; This Page: Southern Pacific Collection.)*

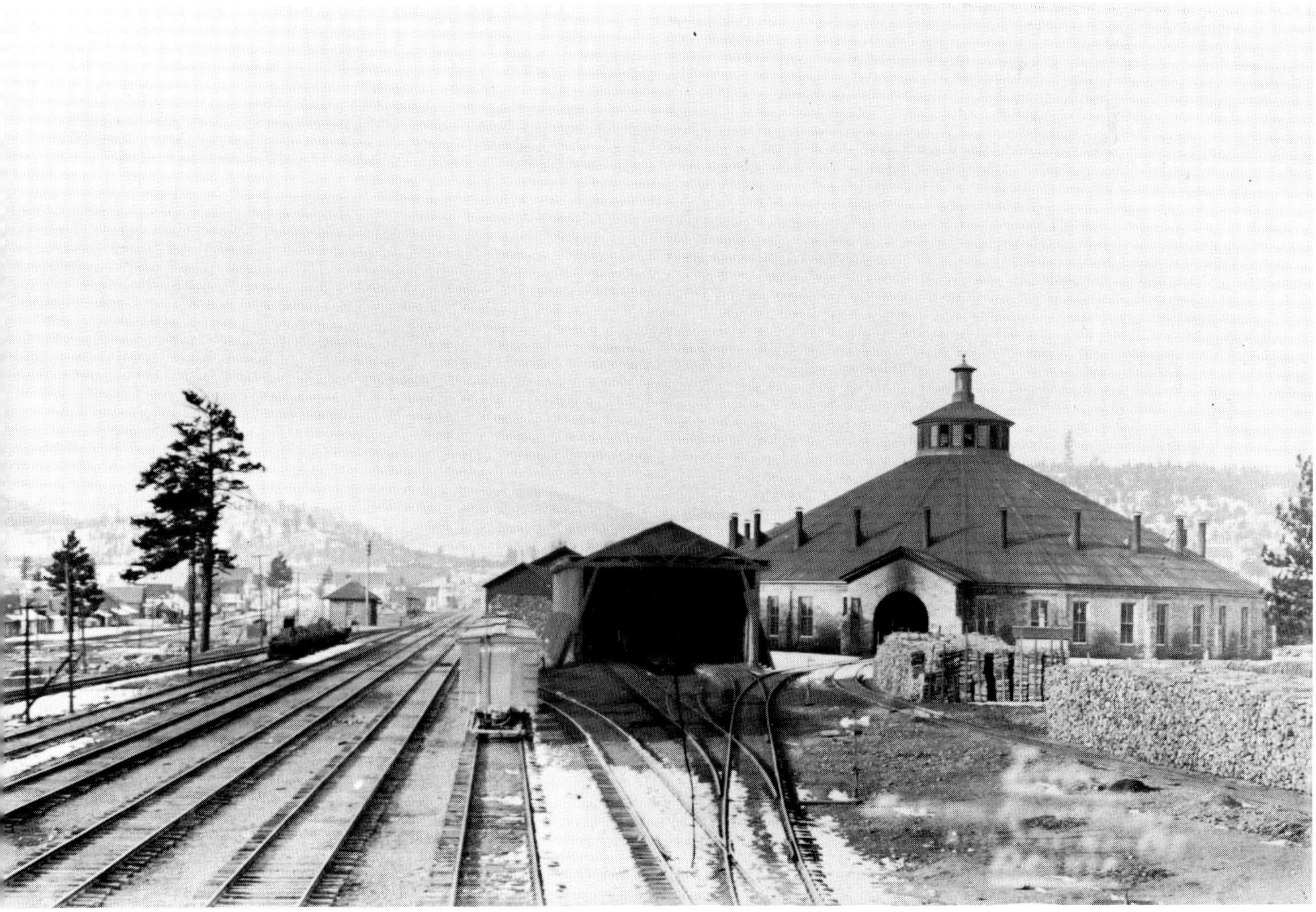

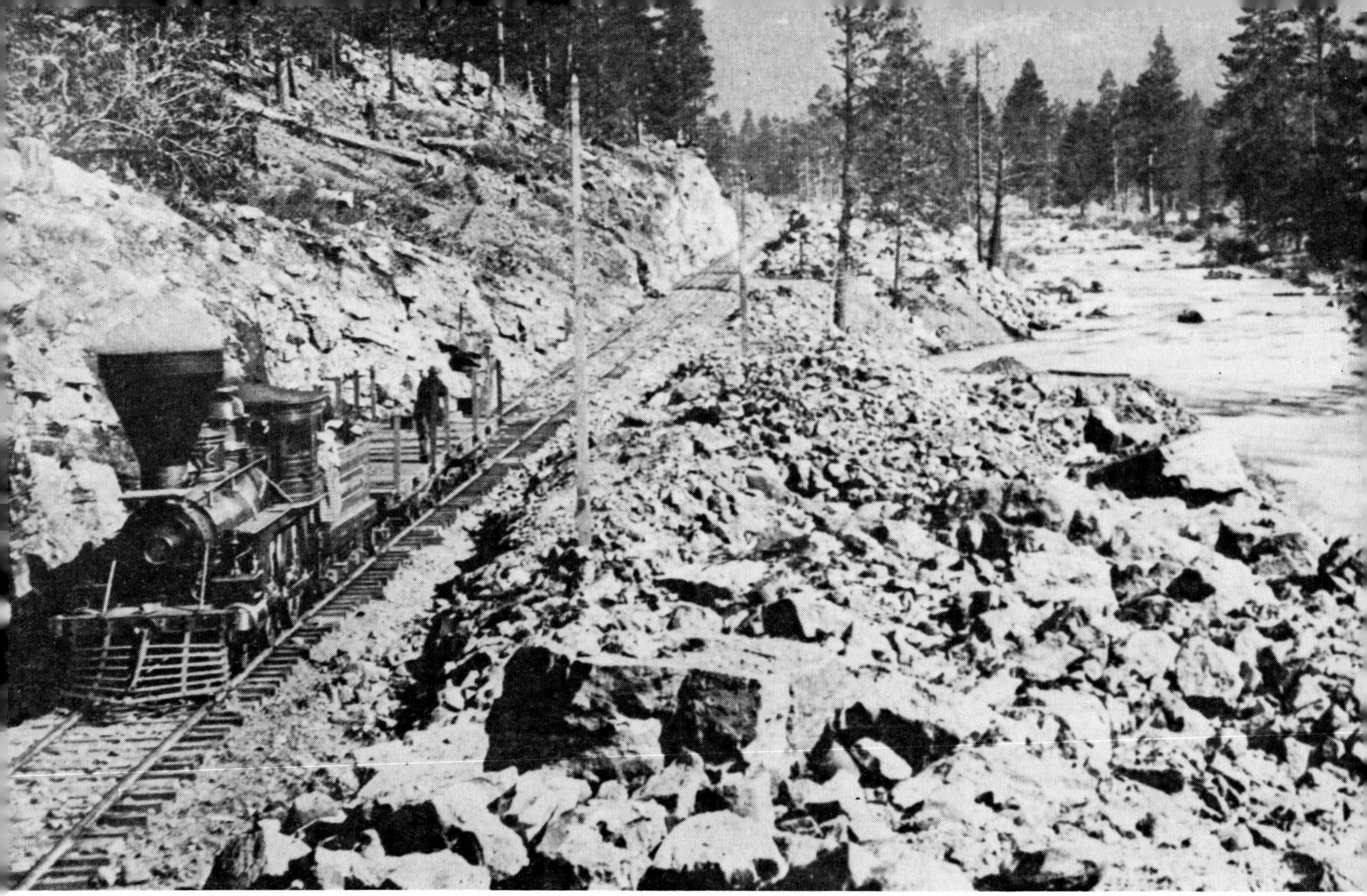

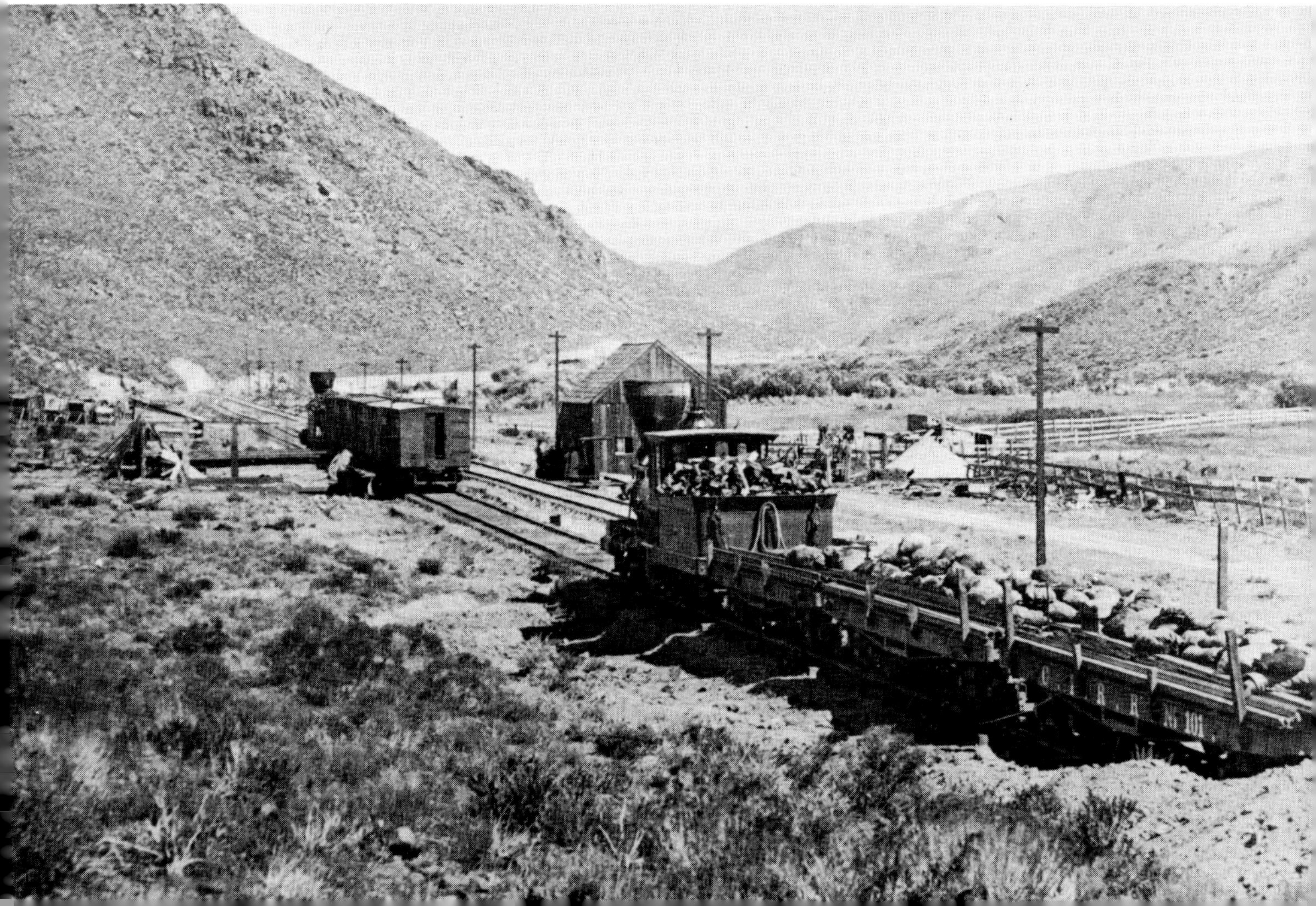

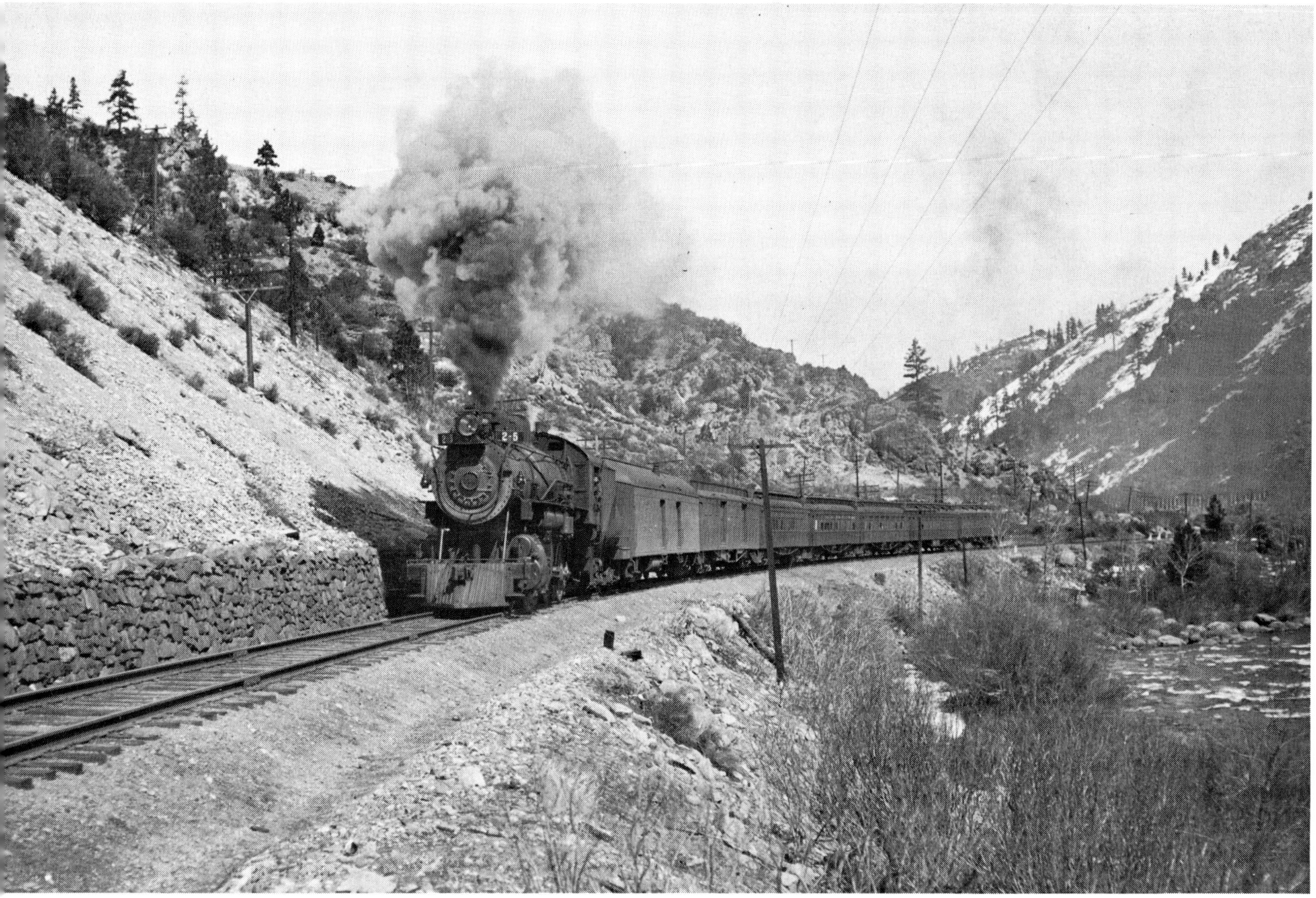

In 1867 Crocker dragged engines, cars and rails over the Donner Summit on sledges so that work on the Central Pacific, stalled for a year by construction of the lengthy summit tunnel, could proceed eastward along the banks of the Truckee River in the valley below. One of the earliest pictures of this construction *(top, left)* shows a work train gingerly threading its way along the uneven rails, while the presence of the lady in the cab is suggestive of most informal and unofficial sanction. Sidings in this mountain fastness *(left, below)* were infrequent and heavily trafficked. East of Reno near the Mary Wall Ranch two construction trains, the nearer loaded with rails and sacks of spikes and rail joiners, pause briefly for clearance of a main line train. Bridges of the period were largely of standard wooden construction knit together with wooden nails (trepins), as witness this one of Birge Arch Truss design *(right, below)* which graced the first crossing of the Truckee River at Eagle Gap, California. *(Three Photos: Southern Pacific Collection.)*

In startling contrast is the portrait in a later era *(top, right)* of the Second Section of Train No. 5, the *Western Express*, galloping along behind SP 10-wheeler No. 2313 in a similar section of the same canyon supported by a manicured roadbed on which rails rest on individual tie plates securely anchored to each individual tie. *(Photo: Stanley Palmer.)*

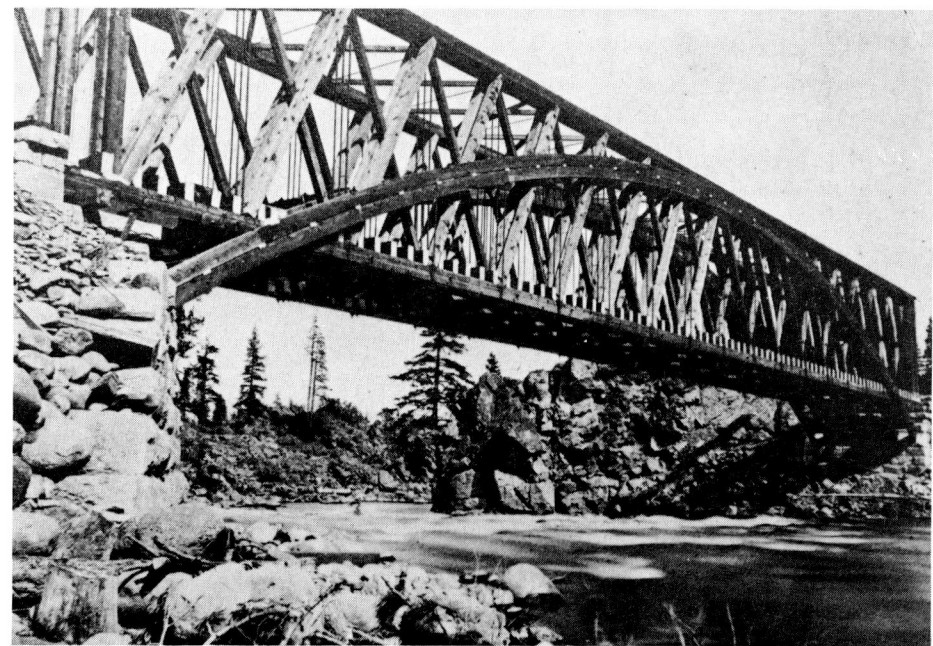

—9—

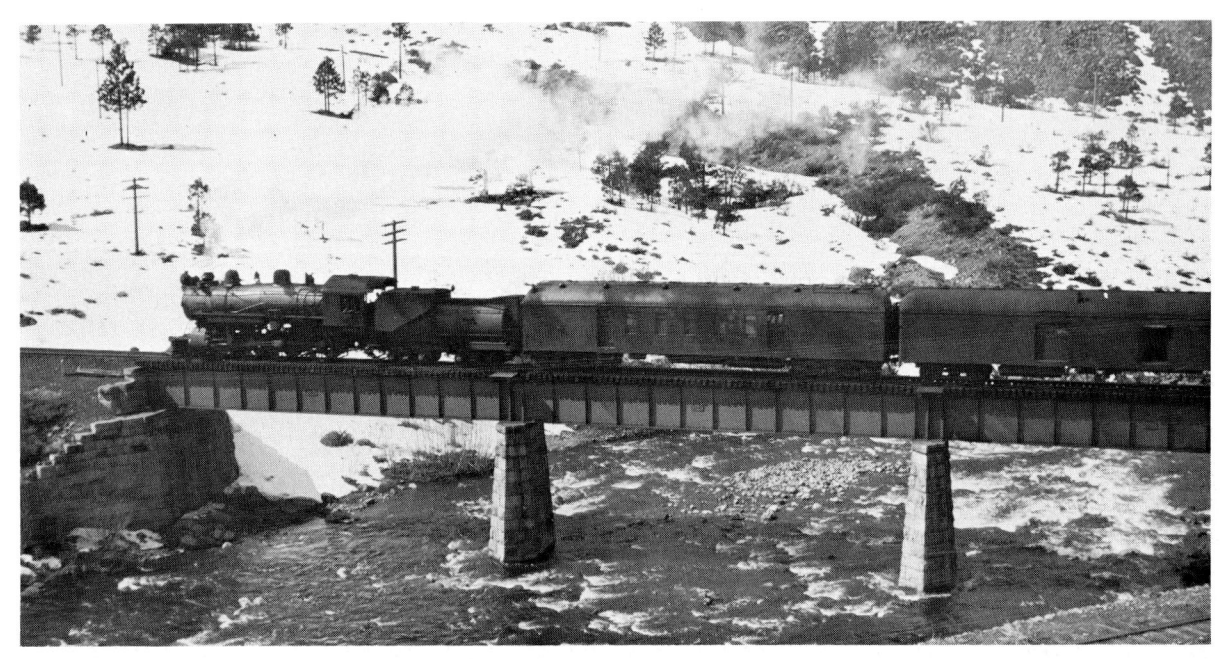

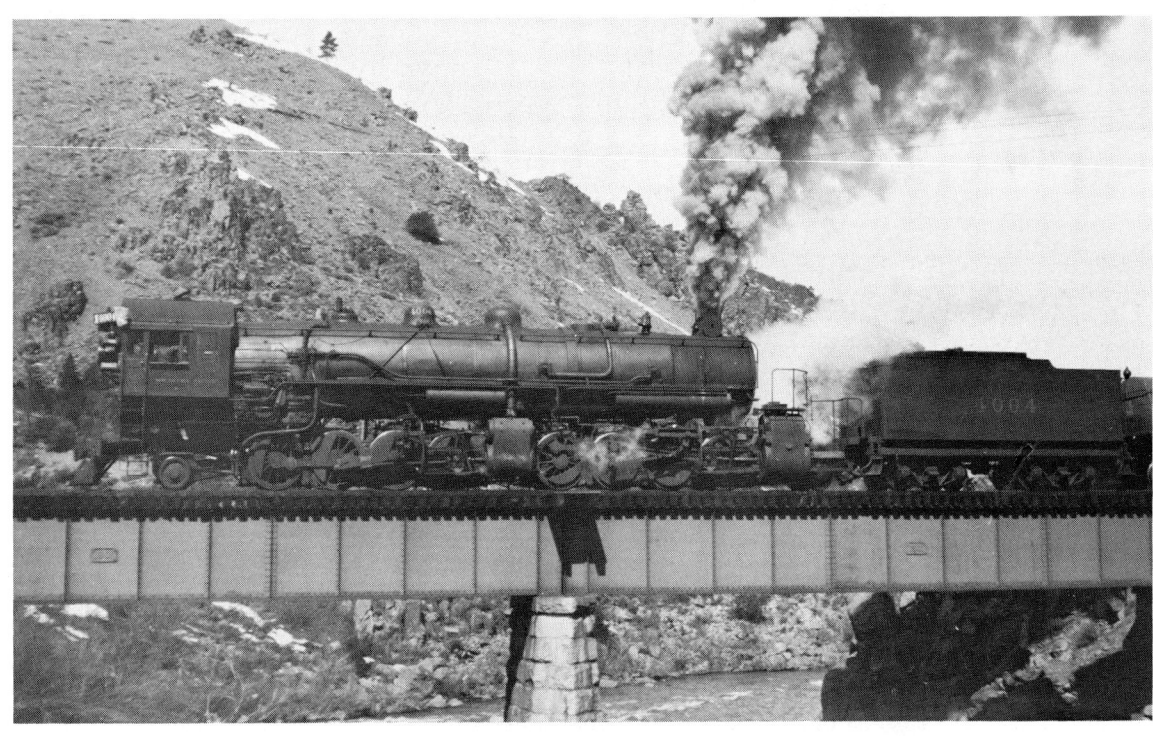

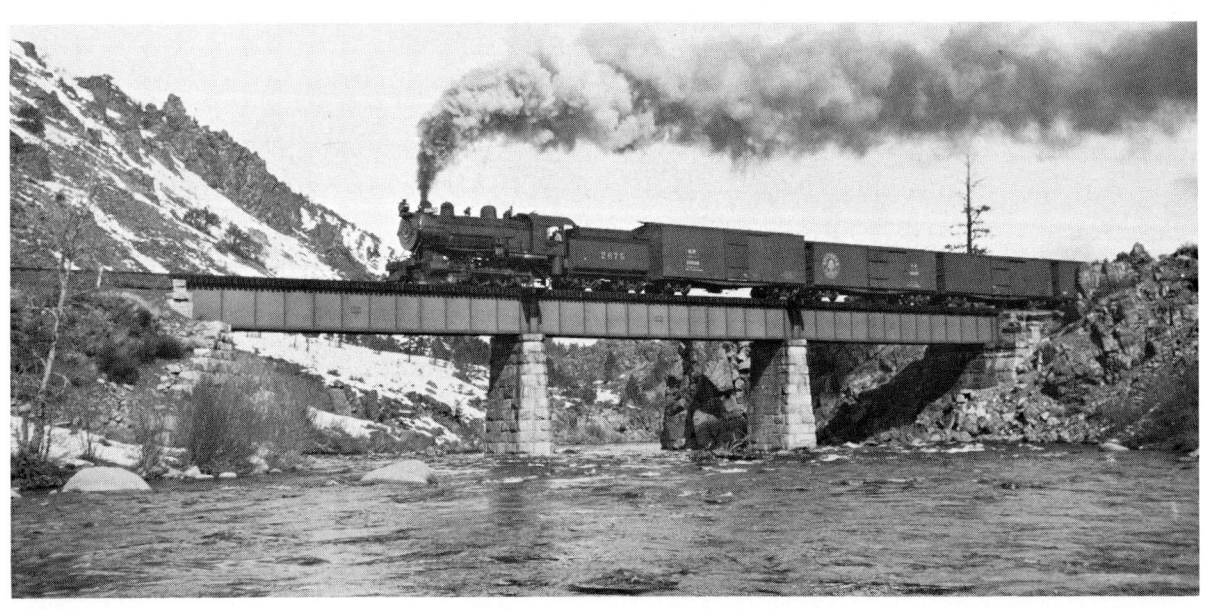

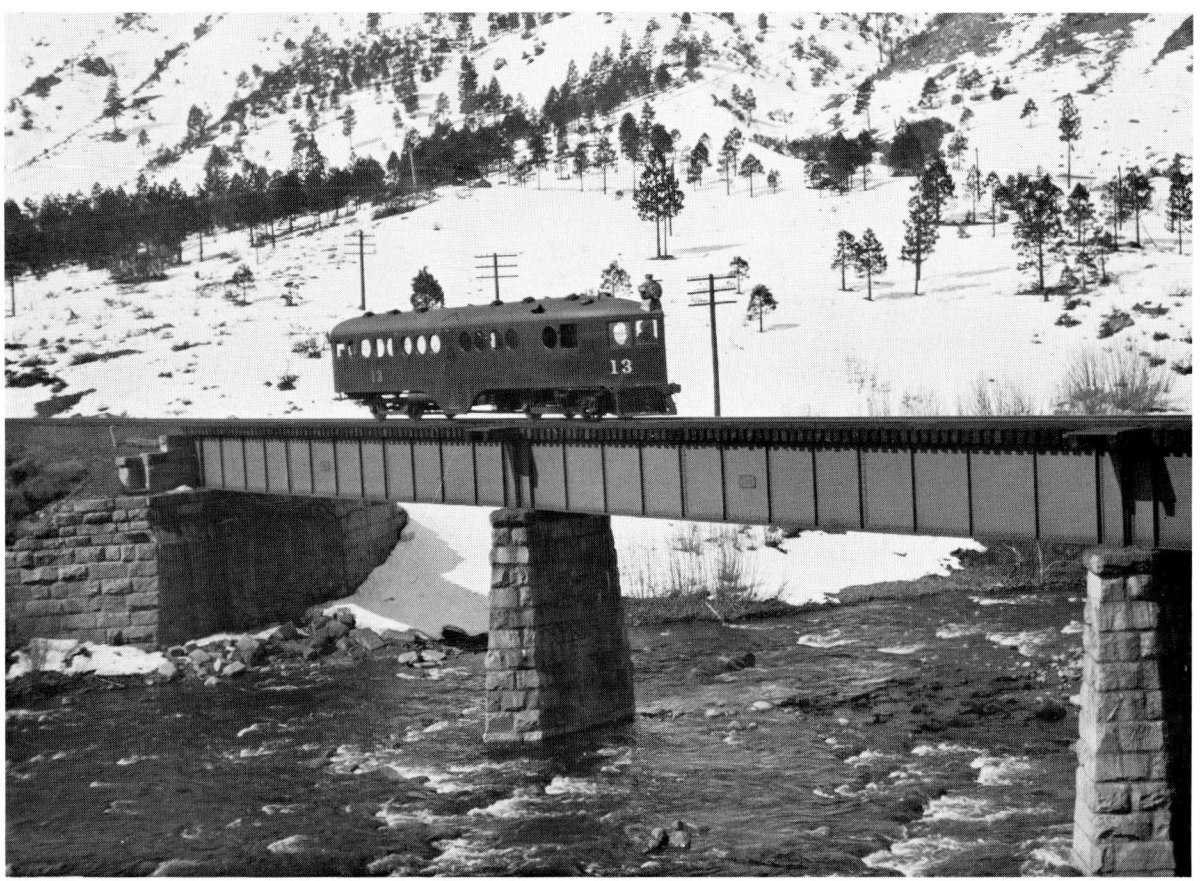

Train watching in the Truckee River Canyon in 1911 was interesting and spectacular. West of Verdi, Nevada, near Fleish, the railroad crossed from the east to the west bank of the river on a bridge consisting of three 70-foot, deck girder spans originally installed in 1902. In this sequence we see *(top, left)* an eastbound passenger train headed by a 2300-series 10-wheeler equipped with a special Vanderbilt tender incorporating a car-diaphragm buffer at the rear; next *(center)* a freight train headed by cab-forward articulated No. 4004, one of the first group of such locomotives to be delivered to the SP in 1909; and *(bottom)* a light freight extra, powered by (2-8-0) Consolidation No. 2675. On this page *(top)* McKeen Motor Car No. 13 may be seen headed west on its scheduled Reno-Truckee run, although during warmer weather many uncarded stops may be made en route at likely fishing places to pick up or let off sporting anglers. Not so sporting was the wreck *(bottom)* which occurred at an earlier date in 1905 as a result of a broken axle. *(All Photos: Stanley Palmer.)*

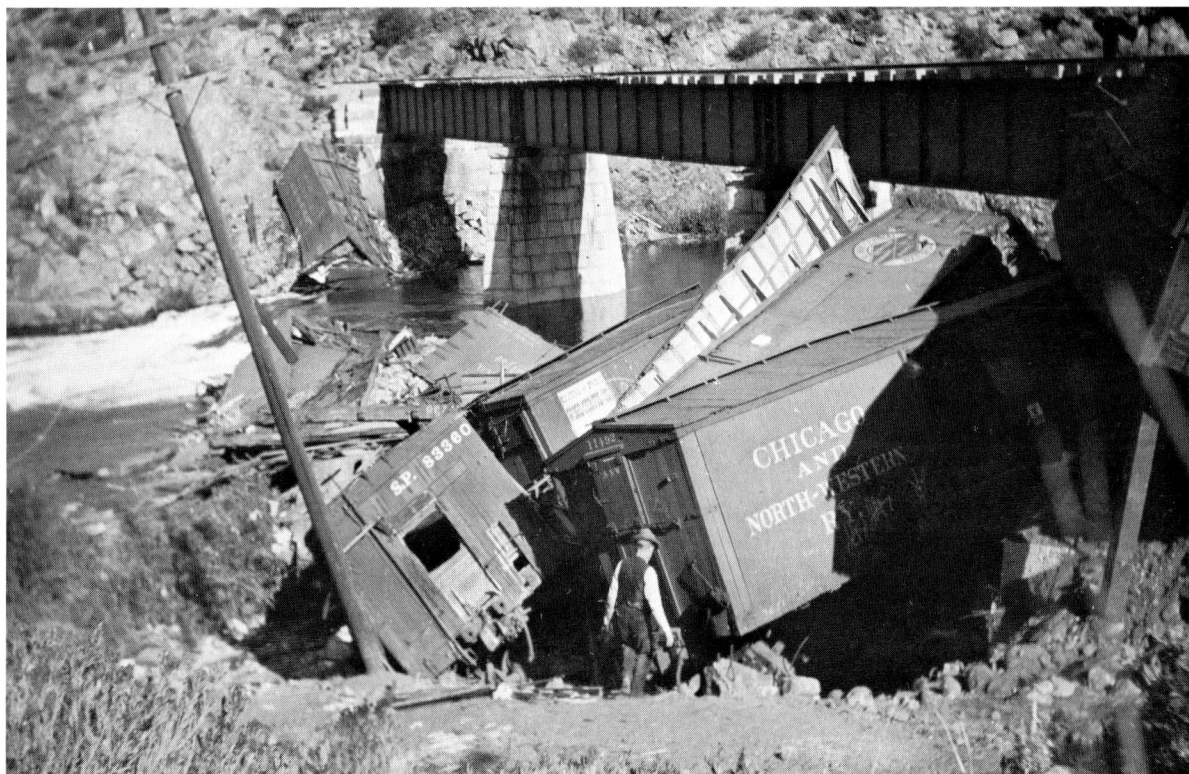

now broke; don't know when passengers will get down." Passengers suffered a further blow on April 23rd when Pollard's Hotel at the west end of Donner Lake burned. It had been the principal stopping point between Cisco and Virginia City.

Spring, in 1867, finally did arrive, and with the advent of better weather the men returned to the pass from their work below. The introduction of nitroglycerin in lieu of black powder helped move the grading along in the upper Sierras. Back in New York, however, Huntington was having a hard time selling Central Pacific bonds — only a million dollars' worth could be sold after the most strenuous efforts.

Work continued along the Truckee River at a less ambitious pace. Then the docile Chinamen surprised everyone by being not so docile and going out on strike for ten days to demand a $40 a month wage and a ten hour work day. The strike was settled on the old basis—$30 for a month of twelve hour days with the men supplying their own board. However, their pay later was increased to $35 for a 26-day month.

By the time the bulk of the forces were sent back to the mountains in July, 25 miles of roadbed along the Truckee River had been completed to a point just two and one-half miles from the California-Nevada line. In September the "Dutch Flat Company," as the *Gold Hill News* called the Central Pacific, was operating a construction train over a few miles of track near Truckee.

Blasting continued on the upper part of the railroad at all hours of the day and night. On August 30, 1867, the great summit tunnel was holed through, while two more months were required to clear it for ties and tracks. East of the tunnel, the route lay along the south side of Donner Lake. Its cost for 2.6 miles of construction was $692,000. A shorter route along the north side of Donner Lake would have cost $968,000 to construct.

By the time winter had set in again, much of the roadbed was ready from the summit to Donner Lake Valley, but in view of the painful experience of the previous winter, the decision was made to wait for spring thaws before testing the cutting and filling. Consequently, 4,000 men were brought down from the summit to the Truckee River to help push the line into Nevada (138 miles from Sacramento), an achievement of record on December 13, 1867, as previously noted.

The reasons for the concentration of construction activity upon the line over the Sierra Nevada mountains in California were manifold. Primarily, a more dependable construction supply route to the interior was the most immediate objective, for which Congress had given its authorization in 1862 with the formation of the Central Pacific Rail Road Company of California to construct a railroad across that state. Subsequently these powers were amplified by the Pacific Railroad Act of 1864, which permitted the Central Pacific to penetrate into the state of Nevada for a distance of 150 miles. Two years later (in 1866) these powers were further augmented by authorization to proceed with construction eastward until the CP rails met with those of the Union Pacific. It was the logistics of the situation, coupled with the financial problems, that confined virtually all efforts to the California segment.

This is not to imply that Huntington and his associates were oblivious to the imminence of such extension. One of the early acts of the Territorial Legislature of Nevada was to grant the CP a non-exclusive franchise to build along the Truckee River to the Big Bend (near Wadsworth) and on to the eastern boundary of the state. Final approval came on November 25, 1861, in spite of considerable opposition from the interests of operators of toll roads, stages and freight lines. During this period some 3,000 teams were employed in handling material destined for the Comstock over the rough wagon roads of El Dorado County. Freight charges on shipments from Sacramento to Virginia City were $120 per ton. In 1862 the total bill amounted to a then staggering $5,000,000. This was the Central Pacific's most immediate market.

Another railroad, the San Francisco & Washoe Railroad Company, also had its eye on the same pot of gold. Surveyed in 1862, the line was to be an extension of the Sacramento Valley and the Placerville & Sacramento Valley railroads, would have run from Placerville around the southern end of Lake Tahoe to Virginia City, with further plans to venture on to Austin. It would have reached many towns the Central Pacific by-passed and would have superseded that ambitious undertaking of the Big Four. Although incorporation was finally accomplished in 1864, by that time the Central Pacific had gained the upper hand, and the SF&W was never constructed.

Thus by the spring of 1868 the Central Pacific was completely in the saddle and pressing its advantages. The Secretary of the Interior had approved the route, selected as a result of the 1866 surveys, across the state of Nevada from the Big Bend in the Truckee River (Wadsworth) to and along the Humboldt River to (Humboldt) Wells. Although the important mining towns of Austin and Eureka were by-passed, there was a greater compensation in the avoidance of seven mountain ranges which would have had to be crossed on the alternate route. Since the Humboldt Canyon, which the present line was to follow, had three particularly difficult places to grade, advance forces were dispatched to these areas.

Snow blockades again tied up traffic to some extent that spring and delayed movement of materials to the front. Supplies, to be used in pushing the line eastward through Nevada, were brought over the Sierras on sleds. In the reverse direction, passengers from Virginia City took the stage to the railhead near Verdi, the train to Truckee, another stage to the summit of the mountains where the final train to Sacramento was met.

A terrific storm in January 1868 culminated in a flood at Stone & Gates Crossing, just east of Reno. This made it necessary for the railroad to deviate from its survey to circumvent the flooded area, and tracks were laid along what is now Prater Way in Sparks before returning to the planned route at the entrance to Lower Truckee Canyon.

As the rails moved forward, the stages retrogressed. By April 30 interchange was being effected at J. M. Hunter's place; on May 5 it was Lake's Crossing.

Myron C. Lake acquired the property bearing his name from a Mr. Fuller who had established a roadside inn on the south bank of a ford of the Truckee River. Later a bridge was built to expedite travel to the Comstock area, and when floods carried it away in the winter of 1862, Myron Lake came into possession and rebuilt the bridge in 1863. With the bridge title also came title to the lands on either bank of the river, and when the Central Pacific rails approached the area, Lake arranged with the railroad to construct a town on the north bank which would serve as the vital transfer point for freight destined to Virginia City and the Washoe area. Some 80 acres of land were turned over to Charlie Crocker with the understanding that the Central Pacific would erect a station on the railroad and deed back alternate lots to Lake. First called "The End of Track" when the rails reached there on May 4; briefly considered as Argenta, a name coined by Judge E. B. Crocker, Charlie's brother, as indicative of the importance of silver to the area; it was finally named Reno in honor of Jesse Lee Reno, a West Point general killed in the battle of South Mountain in 1862.

"Reno, Virginia Station, on the Pacific Railroad" came into prominence the early part of May 1868. A grand auction for the sale of town lots was held on Saturday, May 9. Well planned preliminary advertising and promotion attracted people from all over the surrounding countryside the day before the auction. That night, there being no town as such, comfortable spots in the sagebrush were at a premium, and exorbitant amounts were freely offered for so much as a single blanket. Food was scarce, though fortunately whiskey was plentiful with which to ward off the chill of the night air. The next morning, D. A. Haskell, a former state senator, transferred his oratorical talents to the auctioneer's platform in front of the audience of 1,500 people and brought success to the enterprise. The first lot to be sold, on the east corner of Commercial Row and Virginia Street, brought a resounding $600. Others brought equally good prices, with a few being sold for an astounding $1,000 each.

Phillip Lynch, the editor of the *Gold Hill News*, went down to Reno to take in the auction and met his old friend, Mark Hopkins, who invited him aboard for a special train ride to Verdi. Lynch properly reported it as the smoothest and most comfortable road he had ever been over, then promptly disqualified himself as a competent judge by adding that he had not ridden on a railroad for five years.

A week later, as the rails were approaching the entrance to the Lower Truckee Canyon, another crisis arose. High waters had flooded the roads, and a supply of heavy bridge timbers was urgently needed by the contractors at Wadsworth, 30 miles downstream to the east. Arthur Brown, then superintendent of bridges and buildings (subsequently an architect of note with a famous son), was being hard pressed by the Big Four to do the impossible and get the timbers on their way when a man named Dan O'Conner sauntered up and offered to put the timbers in Wadsworth in three days for a mere $30 a thousand feet. It was a stiff price to pay, but an agreement was signed. O'Conner posted a $4,000 performance bond. When Collis P. Huntington asked, "How do you propose to get these big timbers to Wadsworth in three days, a distance of nearly 30 miles over impossible roads?" the answer came quickly and clearly, "Why float 'em down the

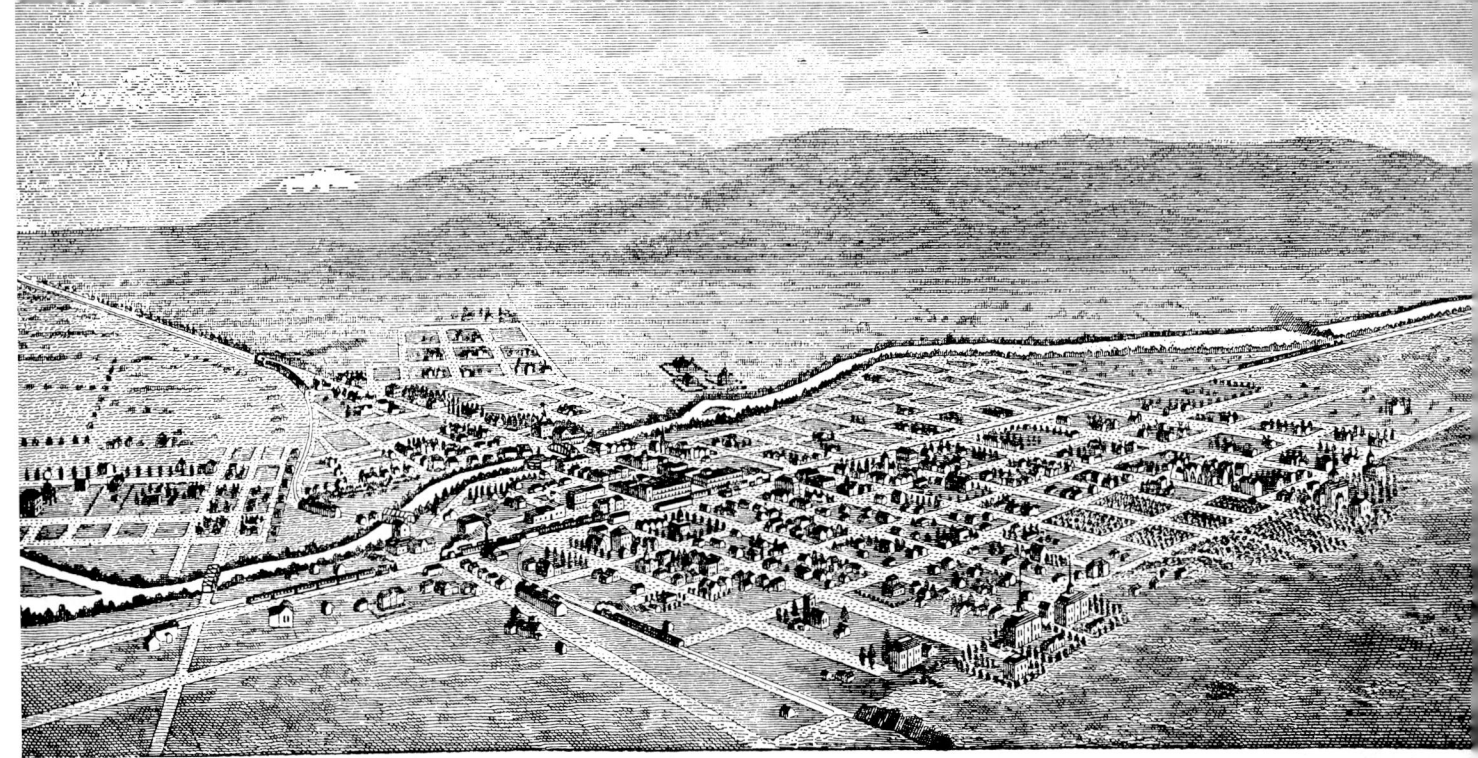

This early view of Reno *(above)* looking south was first published in 1890 and demonstrates how well Central Pacific engineers originally platted the town in April 1868. The first CP passenger train reached Reno on June 19, 1868; the Virginia & Truckee connection to Carson City to the south was opened August 24, 1872; and the Nevada-California-Oregon Ry. started extending its belabored narrow-gauge rails northward late in 1880. In the right foreground the buildings of the University of Nevada may be clearly identified, but the Central Pacific station, center, was a replacement of the original, spacious Depot Hotel *(below)* which served as the focal point of town life until it was destroyed in the great fire of March 1879. *(Bottom Photo: Southern Pacific Collection.)*

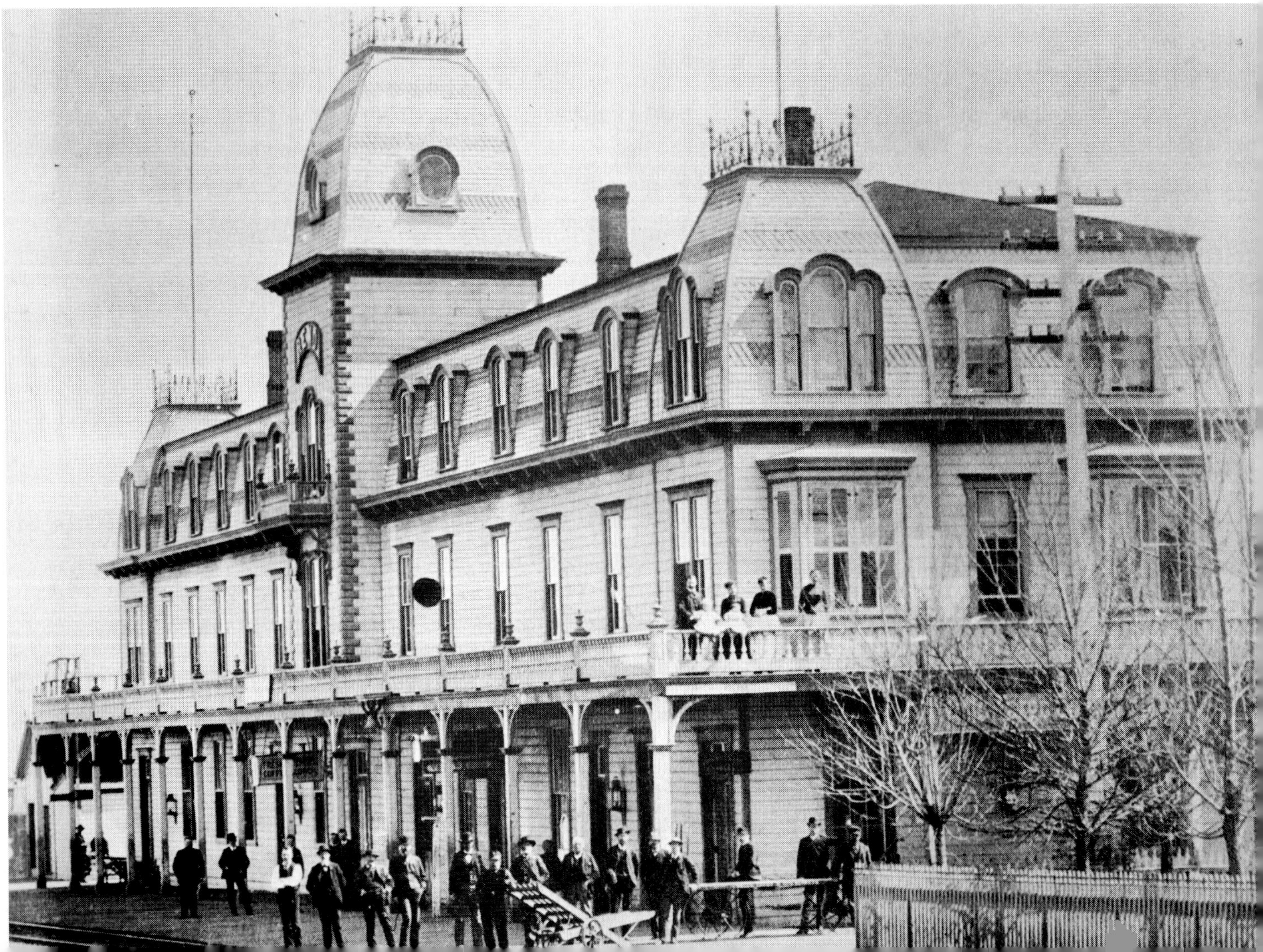

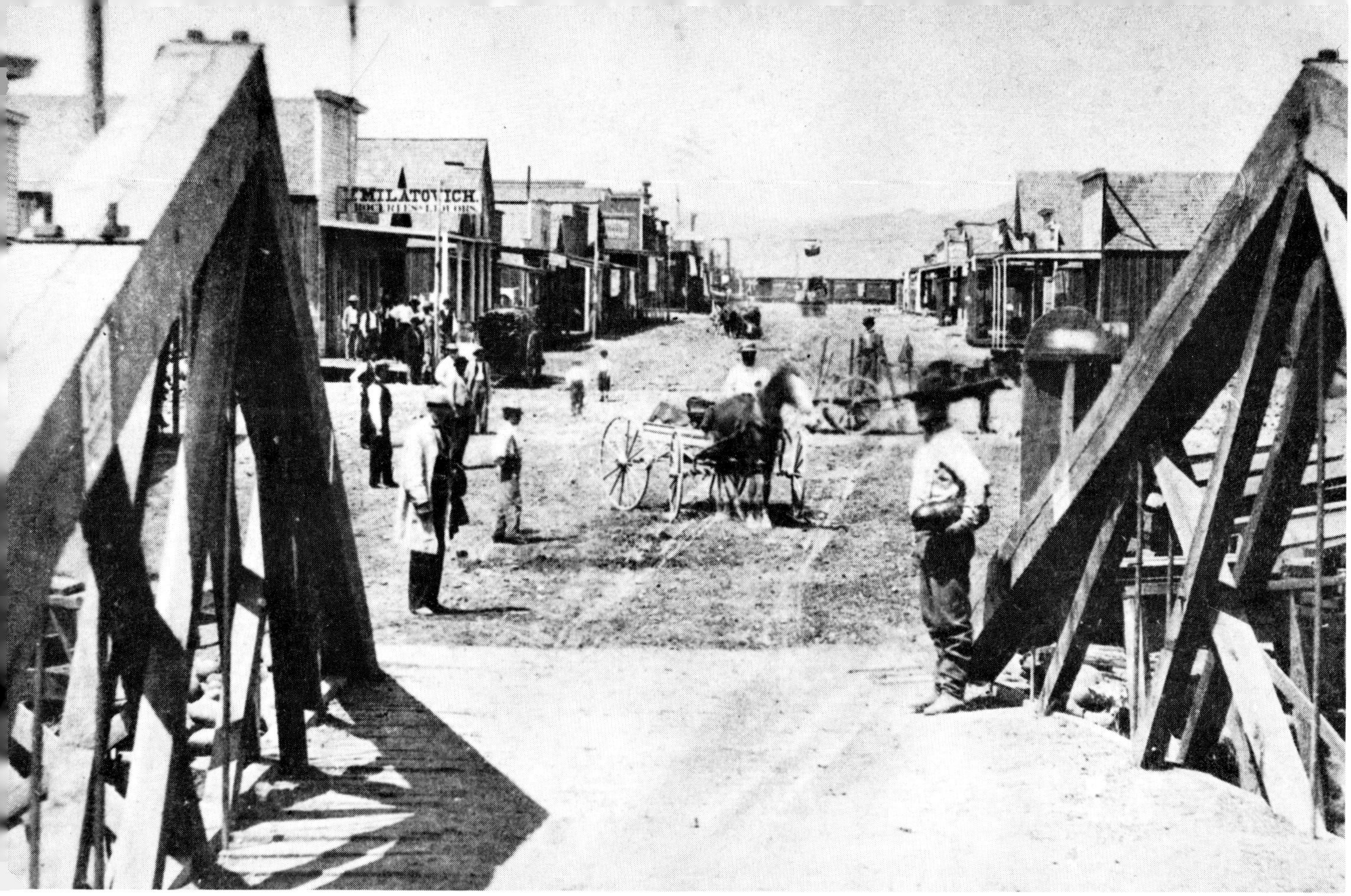

The dirt street and wooden sidewalks characterizing Virginia Street in the 1870's were probably impressive sights to visitors approaching Reno from the south over the Truckee River bridge. More impressive than the cars of the Central Pacific at the end of the street *(above)* or the freight depot *(below)* was the efficacy of the sign painter's art as demonstrated for V. Milatovich's Groceries and Liquors as well as the Pioneer Hall & Brewery just up the street. Modern viewers will find it difficult to recognize in these simple beginnings the spectacular gaming establishments which line these same blocks today. *(Both Photos: Southern Pacific Collection.)*

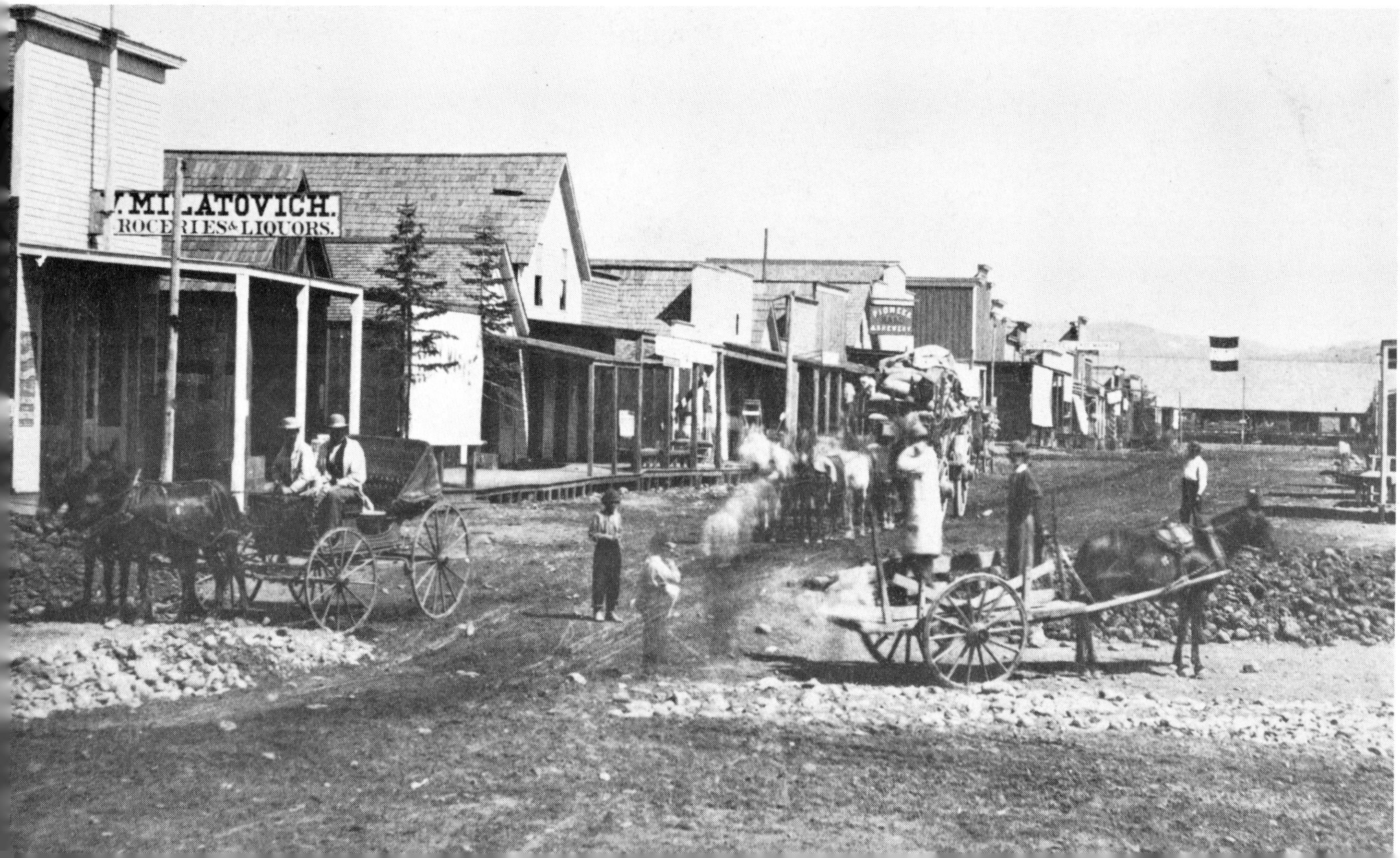

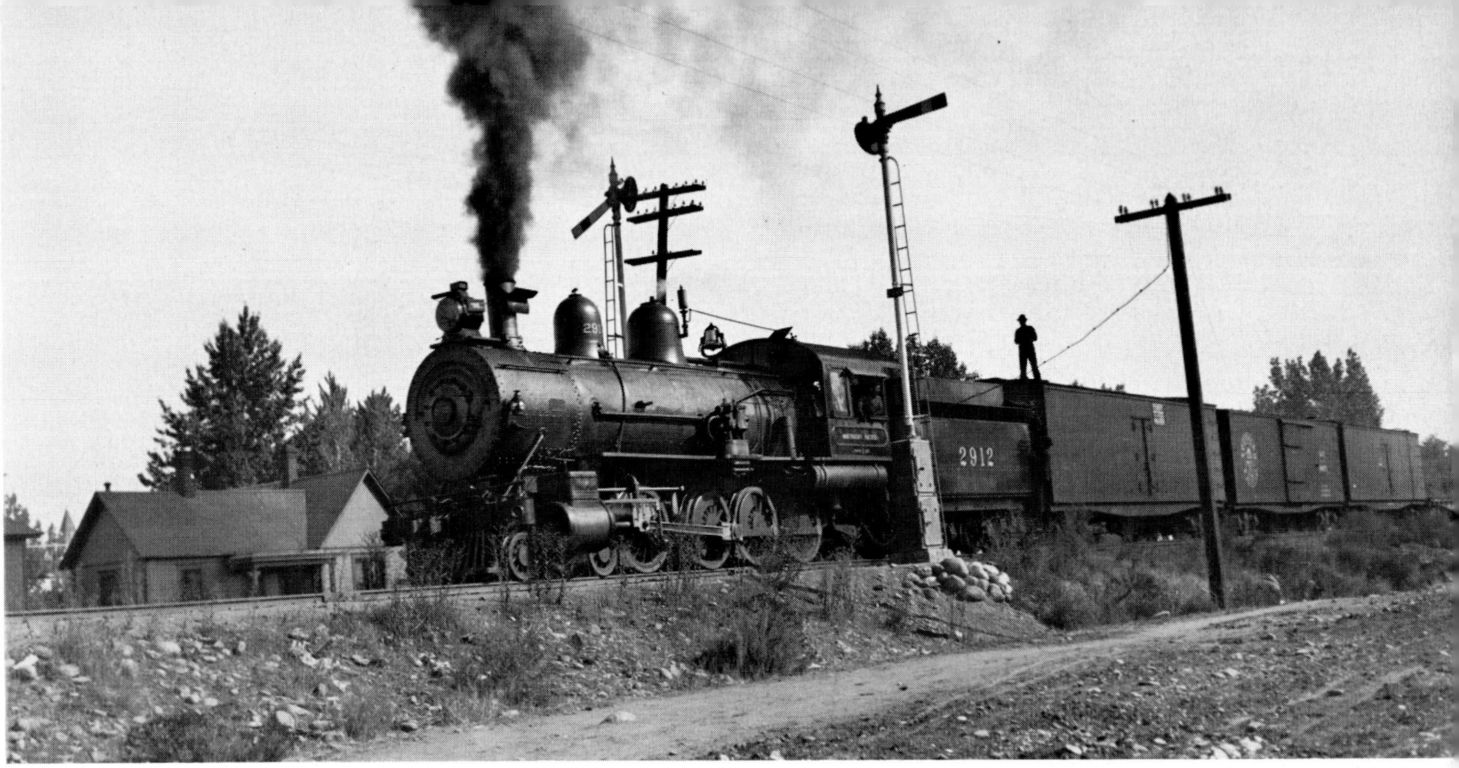

At Reno in 1909 (*above*) Mastodon (or 12-wheeler) No. 2912 starts its heavy train under the watchful gaze of the head brakeman atop the box car. The lower quadrant semaphore blade on the far side is just rising to horizontal (red) position as the locomotive enters the block, while the blade on the near side will drop with the passing of the caboose. In town (*below*) the Pacific Limited has stopped at the station near the heart of the city. Vintage autos at the crossing and the presence of display billboards for liquors date this scene in the post-prohibition 1930's, while visible on the arch over Virginia Street is the slogan generally credited to Oscar Morgan, for many years the fiery little editor of the *Reno Evening Gazette*. (*Top: Stanley Palmer; Bottom: Southern Pacific.*)

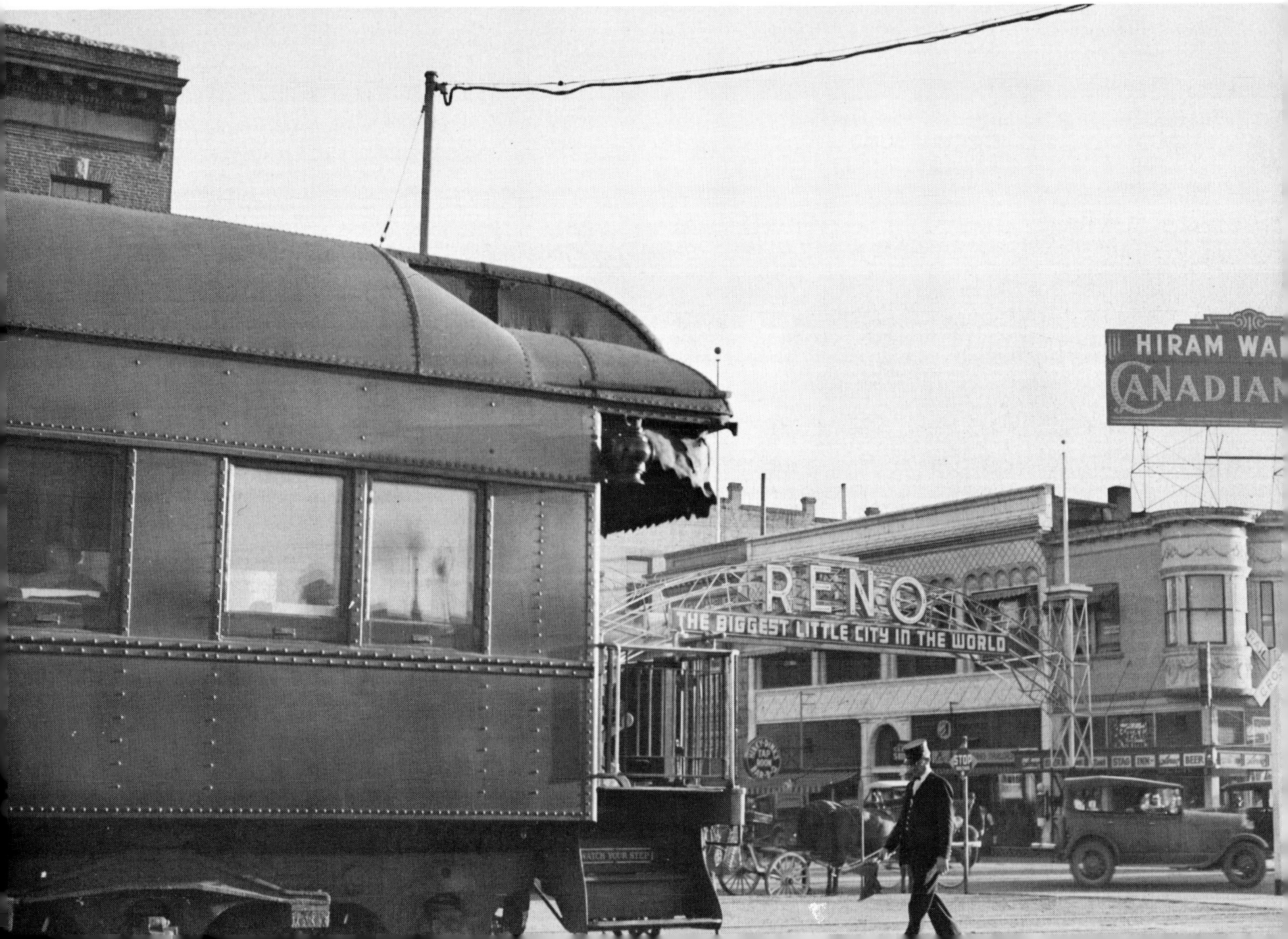

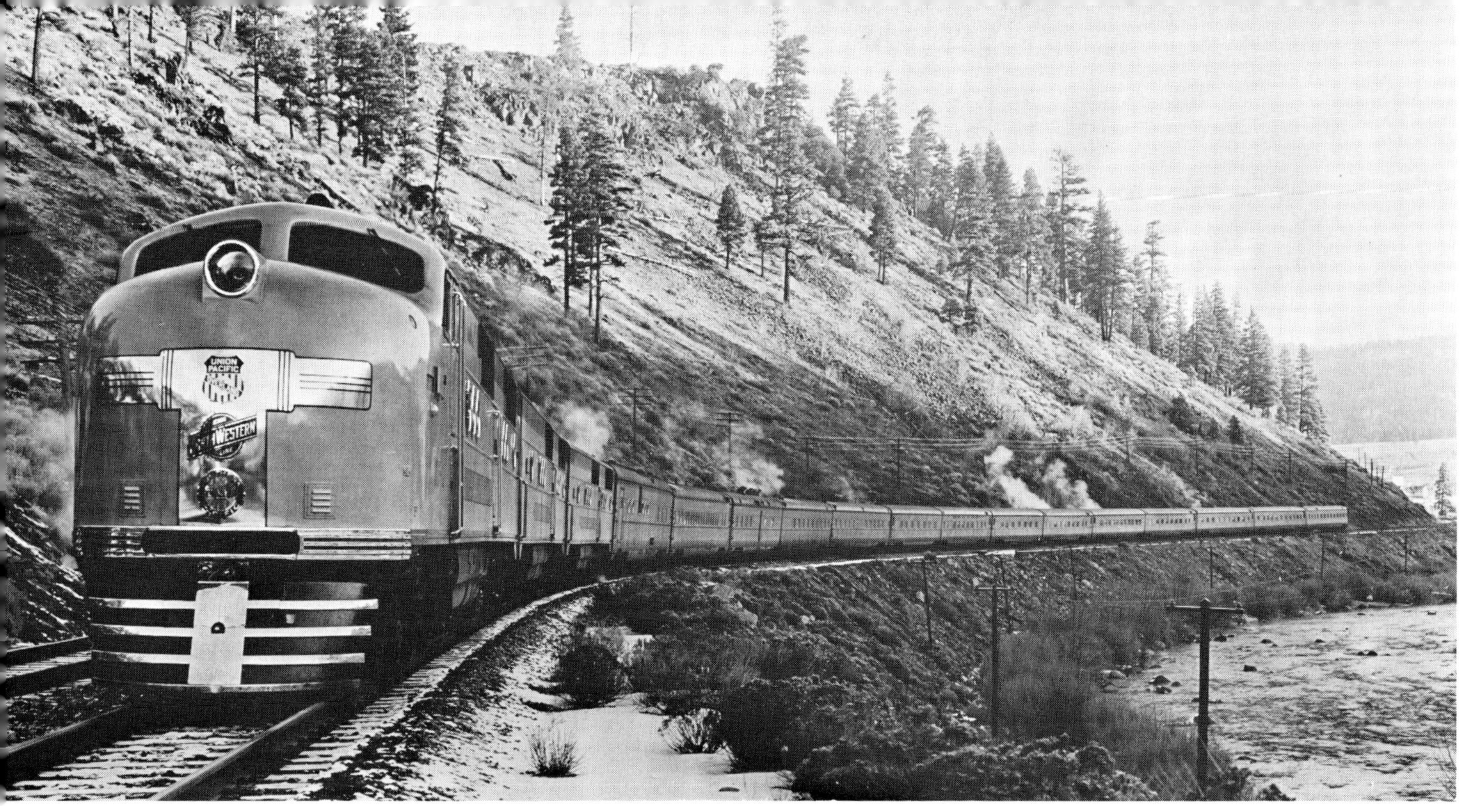

In the 1940's the Truckee River Canyon was playing host to the burbling Diesels of such low rumbling trains as the City of San Francisco *(above)* bearing the triple nose insignia of its joint owners—the Union Pacific, the Chicago & Northwestern and the Southern Pacific. The practice of pooled ownership of locomotives was limited to those for this one train and was discontinued in 1948. Freight trains of that era were still hauled by the versatile cab-in-front articulateds, typified by Extra 4185 *(below)*. Left hand operations predominated over this section of railroad due to peculiar grade conditions resulting from the addition of the second track in 1913. *(Upper: Louis Stein, Jr. Collection; Lower: Southern Pacific.)*

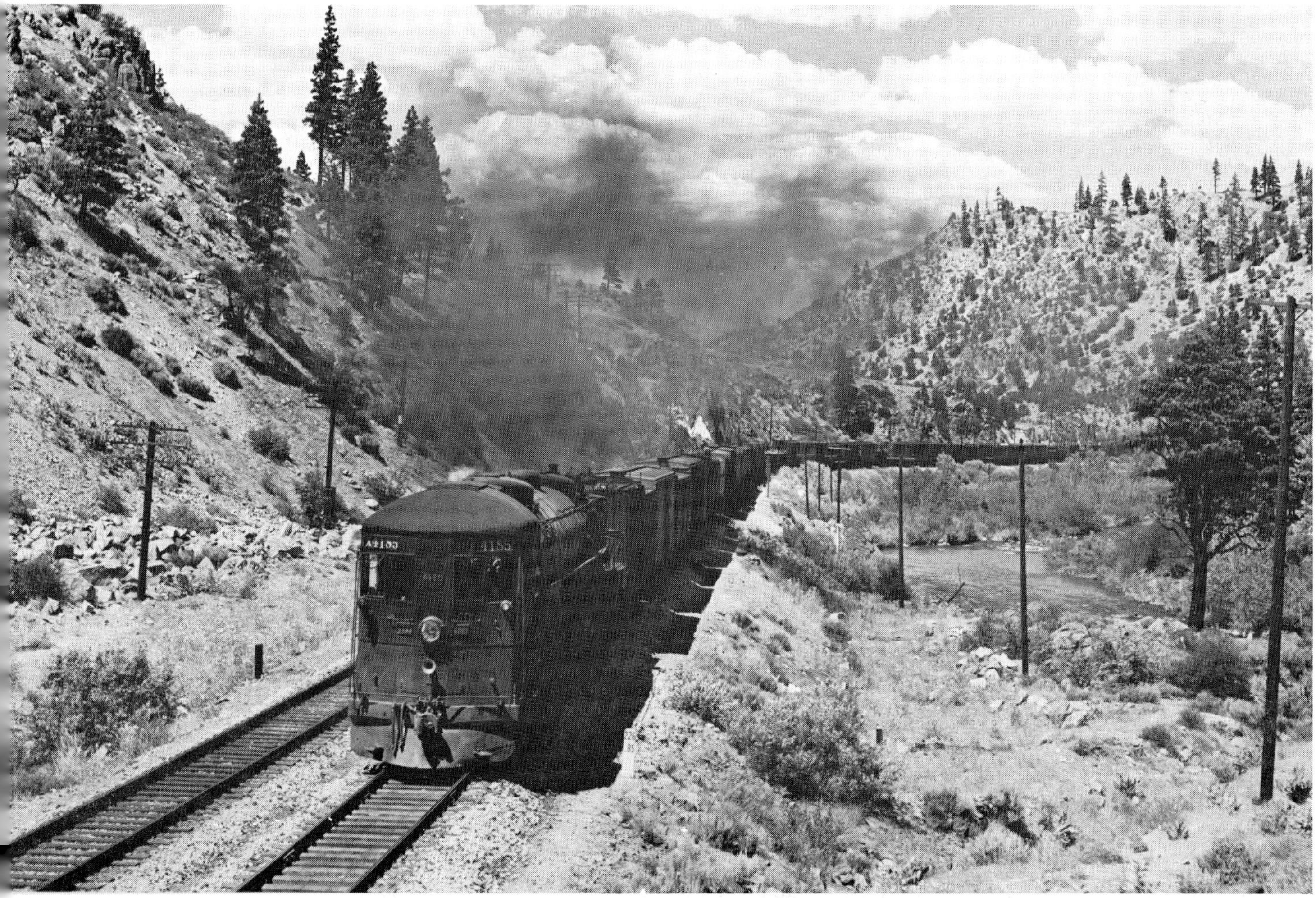

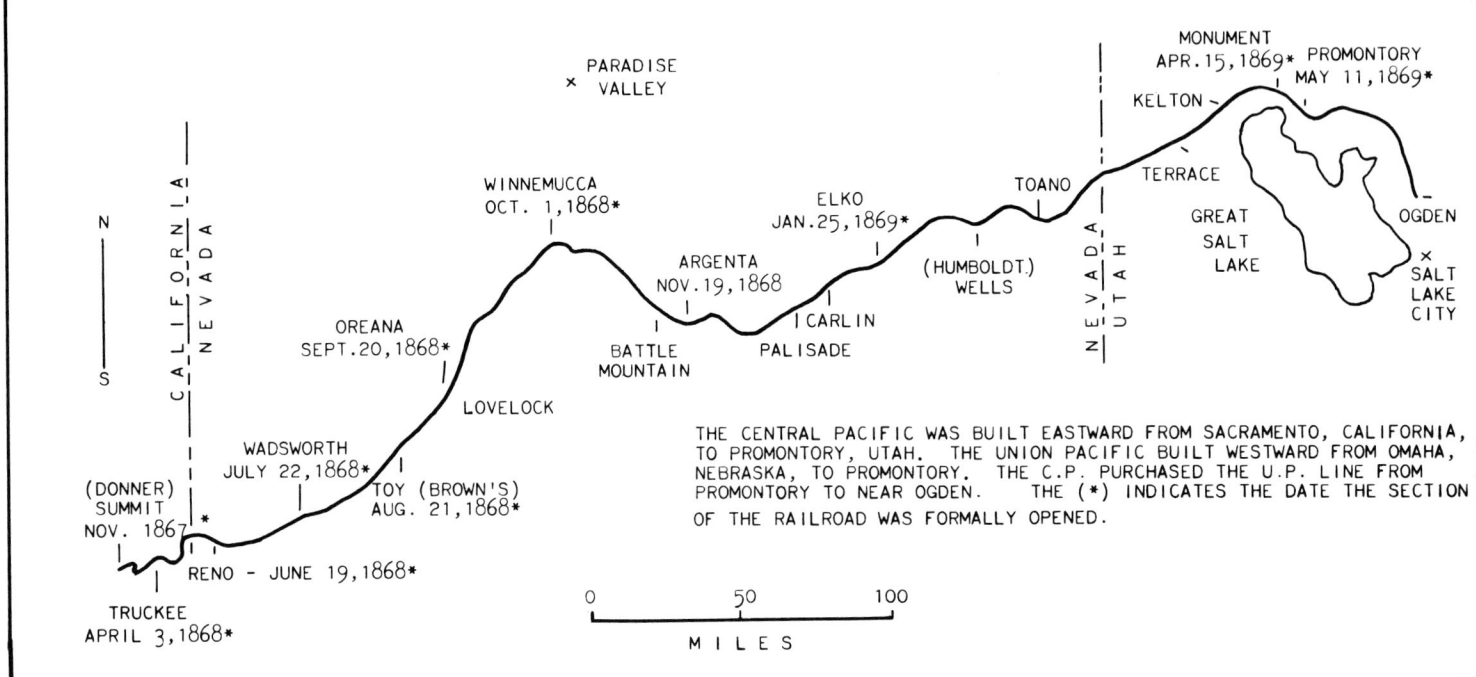

river, of course." The logic was simple; not so the tirade released by Brown when he heard the news. Dan wasted no time. Lashing the poles into four rafts, he sent them downstream that very day. Except for a small delay caused by an eddy in the stream at Clark's, no problems were encountered and the rafts cast anchor at Wadsworth by sundown.

The final gap on the east slope of the Sierras near Truckee, California, was officially closed on June 18, 1868, when the rails were joined just west of the town. Effective July 6 a passenger train left Sacramento each morning except Sunday at 6:30, arrived at Reno at 4:00 P.M. and proceeded on to the new terminal at Wadsworth, arriving at 5:42 P.M. Returning, a train left Wadsworth at 1:47 A.M., Reno at 3:30 A.M. and arrived at Sacramento at 1:00 P.M. Along with these "convenient" schedules came the announcement that "second class cars accompany Freight Trains, on which passengers are carried at reduced rates."

Thus, to construct a railroad to Reno and Wadsworth, the latter 188 miles from Sacramento, had taken five and one-half years of getting materials, bringing them around the Horn, fighting storms, blasting granite, and a lot of just plain, hard cussed work. The next 501 miles of track to Promontory, Utah, were to be laid in a brief nine months and twenty days. This meant keeping the graders some 200 miles ahead of the track forces. Instead of cold weather and snow, there was to be heat and the eternal problem of drinking water. Hauls of 40 miles were a normal occurrence, while at one point it was necessary to haul water 84 miles to rail head.

Winnemucca, 136 miles northeastward from Wadsworth, had the CP very much in mind during the summer of 1868. In anticipation of its arrival, the town boasted a Railroad Livery Stable, a Railroad Saloon and a Railroad Stage Line operated by one Hill Beachey. The latter met all trains at the advancing end of track, brought the people to Winnemucca and then headed north to Paradise Valley, Owyhee and Boise, Idaho. The boys in the mining district of Owyhee must have been delighted to welcome the stage the time it arrived with a load of "gurdies."

Track layers, working two eight-hour shifts, were advancing at the rate of three miles a day as long as material was available. At least 21 sawmills around Truckee were cutting ties and lumber for the big push. A temporary shortage of rails forced suspension of work at Lovelock, midway between Wadsworth and Winnemucca, during the early part of August.

Indians, generally, were not a problem to the CP forces. True, some wily, lazy ones were involved in specious blackmail with the Chinese graders for food, but it was "Chief" Huntington's personal pow-wow with an old Piute chief that set up harmonious relations. The great white chief told his Indian brother that they must take care of the railway and the railway would take care of them. In like manner, Crocker arranged a treaty with the Shoshones. Passes were given to the Indian chiefs to allow them to ride in the coaches, while the rest of the tribes were given to understand they could ride on freight trains without question. This became a favorite pastime and, when the custom was carried over to other railroads, men such as Gest of the Nevada-California-Oregon Railway never could fathom the basis of what appeared to be a God-given right. The Indians were friendly to the CP and more than once warned of washouts.

Rails were going down faster and faster as the organization improved. A mile was laid in three hours; then four miles went down in one day; and on August 19, with the contest with the Union Pacific growing hotter and hotter, eight miles were spiked from sun-up to sun-down.

At 10:00 A.M. on September 16, 1868, on the very outskirts of Winnemucca, the tracklayers used up the last of the inventory of rails on hand. Just then a train arrived with a new supply, and before noon the "Champion" became celebrated as the first locomotive to enter Winnemucca.

Some of the delays were caused by a shortage of locomotives. Each 100 miles of new track required a fresh complement of power. It also meant 400 tons of rail — a good shipload — several thousand ties, innumerable bridge timbers, new water tanks, and countless additional items. To Winnemucca reporters, Crocker explained that all the iron and engines needed to connect with the UP were either afloat or in port. Still, at times, only sufficient rail would trickle through the supply lines to keep the track workers busy for three or four hours on any one day.

Winnemucca became a bustling community, and its citizens began to be alarmed by the looseness of certain things around town. "Many are not accustomed to the musical click of the six shooter at all hours of the night," it was reported; "on the other hand, a majority are chagrined because there is not enough killing for the amount of flourishing." Demands for a calaboose and more policemen (only one private night watchman being available) were echoed.

In October, an outburst in Twelve Mile Canyon (eastward near Palisade) occurred when a teamster, on lighting his pipe, dropped a spark among some powder kegs. Four men went up with the powder and were instantly stricken from all future payrolls, while others were injured.

Judge Crocker finally got his wish when, a few miles west of Palisade, a new station was named Argenta. The first trains to this location arrived on November 5.

With some foresight, the Union Pacific was busy too. Although their construction was still some 200 miles east of Ogden, Utah, their surveyors were well out along the Humboldt River in Nevada with the planned intent of working backward from Wells, Nevada, to Ogden, Utah, a mere additional 219 miles. On October 16, Durant of the UP had telegraphed a California agent to send 3,000 Chinamen to Wells. Some work was actually done by the UP at Wells, but it constituted lost motion when a later agreement fixed the meeting point between the two lines at Promontory, Utah.

By the end of the year Central Pacific surveyors were laying out town lots in both Carlin and Elko, Nevada. A few weeks later when the first stage reached the area from booming Hamilton, a silver town some 120 miles to the south, Elko was already boasting three stores, a lodging house, a restaurant and, of course, the inevitable gambling saloon.

Regular trains reached Elko on January 28, 1869; by April 13 the end of track was at Indian Springs, near Kelton, Utah; and by the end of the month the job was almost finished. A demonstration of highly organized track-laying skill was made on April 28, said to be the result of a $10,000 wager between Crocker of the CP and Durant of the UP. Crocker won the bet when the track layers put down ten miles of track in one day, a feat never since equalled. On May 1 the last CP ties and rail were placed in position, following which a week of waiting ensued while the UP finished some rock cutting on its portion of the line.

Officially the rails met at Promontory, Utah. The last spike celebration was to have been held on Saturday, May 8, but due to some confusion and delay on the part of the Union Pacific, the ceremony was postponed until May 10. At that, the Central Pacific was nearly responsible for a further delay, as the special train carrying Governor Stanford and his party to the celebration hit a fallen tree just west of Reno. The signal "Done" was received by telegraph in Washington, D.C., at 2:47 P.M. on Monday, May 10, 1869, and the job was finished.

In Nevada, the event was celebrated in various ways. Firemen from Virginia City and Gold Hill were accorded free passage (if in uniform) to Sacramento for a Saturday celebration. On the Com-

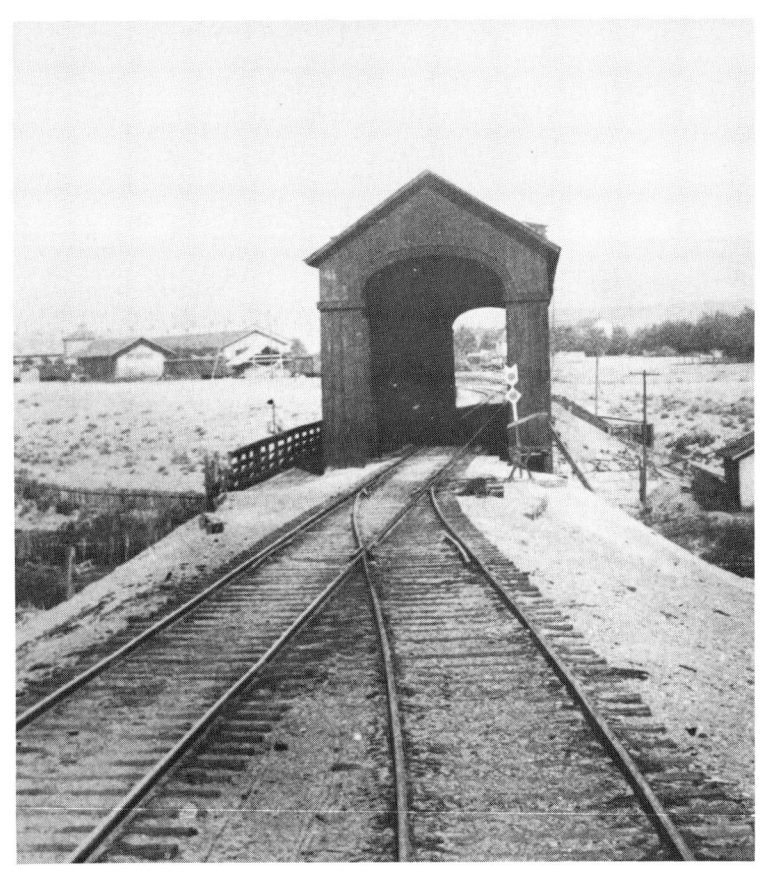

Surely the first and probably the only covered bridge in Nevada was this structure *(top)*, photographed in 1884, which carried the Central Pacific's tracks over the Truckee River to the original, large Wadsworth shops and roundhouse visible in background on the east bank. For 36 years (1868-1904), throughout the era of wood-burners, link-and-pin couplings and wooden brake beams, the Wadsworth shops *(below)* were symbolic of the main terminal and division point, while company stores and dwellings encroached on the area in direct proportion to the size of the operating and maintenance crews stationed there. *(Top: Nevada Historical Society; Bottom: Southern Pacific Collection.)*

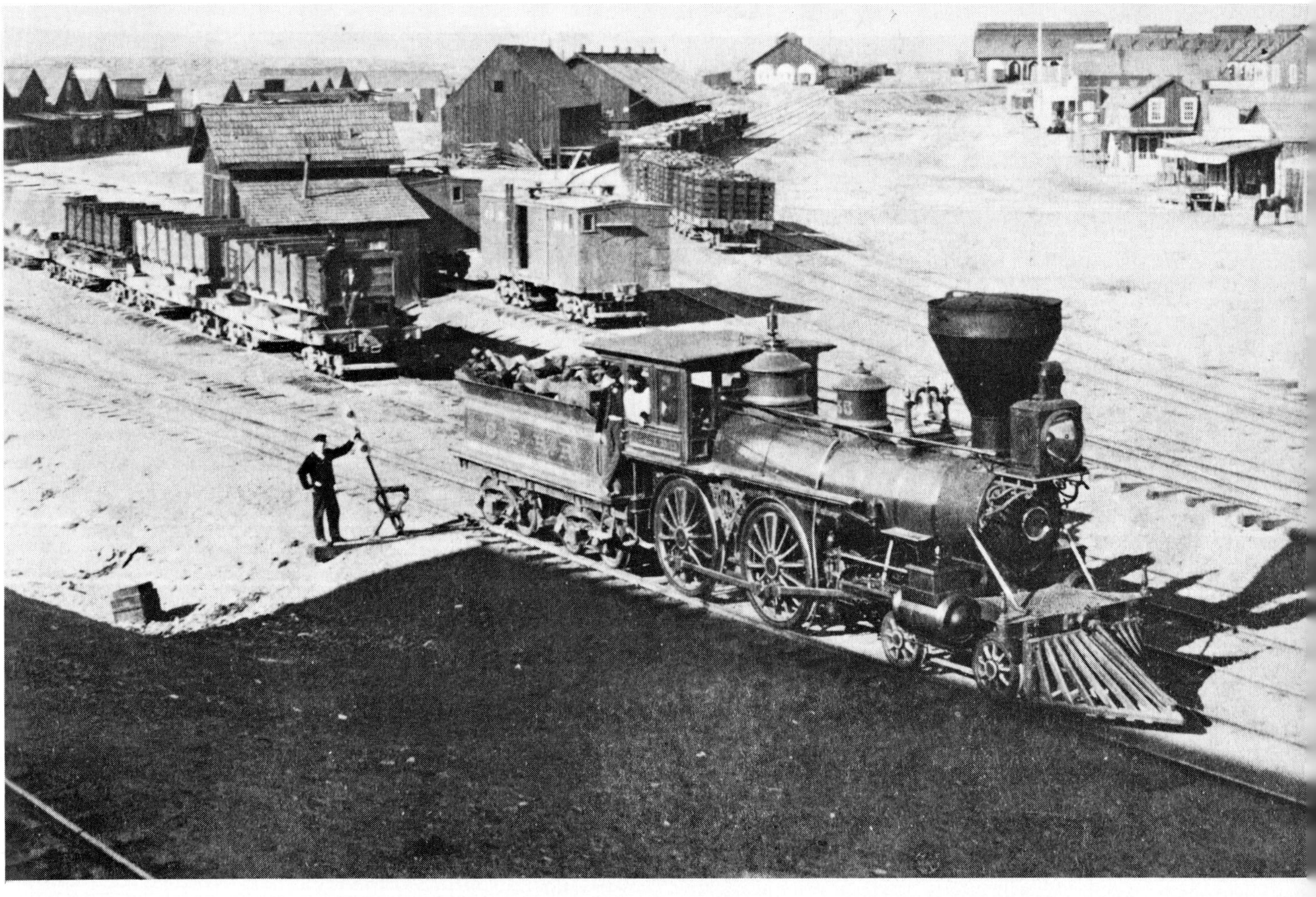

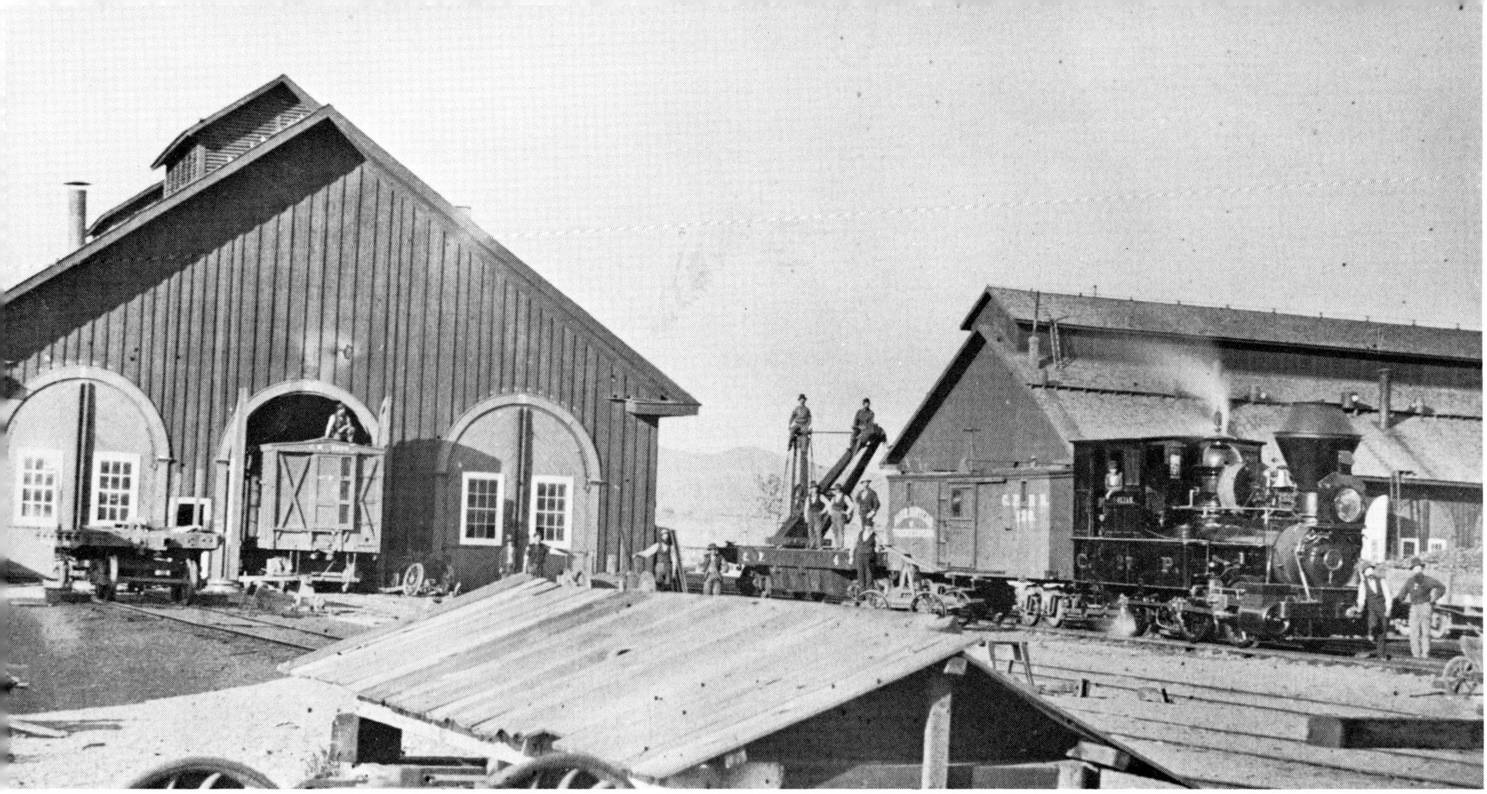

In the close-up of the Wadsworth shop buildings *(above)*, the absence of the customary water barrels along the roof peaks is offset by the presence of CP's 0-6-0-T No. 27, GOLIATH, a six-wheel, saddle-tank switcher replete with water pump and fire-hose reel atop the boiler. Wadsworth station *(below)* was impressive and commodious to accommodate division operating offices on the second floor. Patronage was substantial, as witness these early arrivals for train time and the freight stacked near the baggage room door. *(Both Photos: Southern Pacific Collection.)*

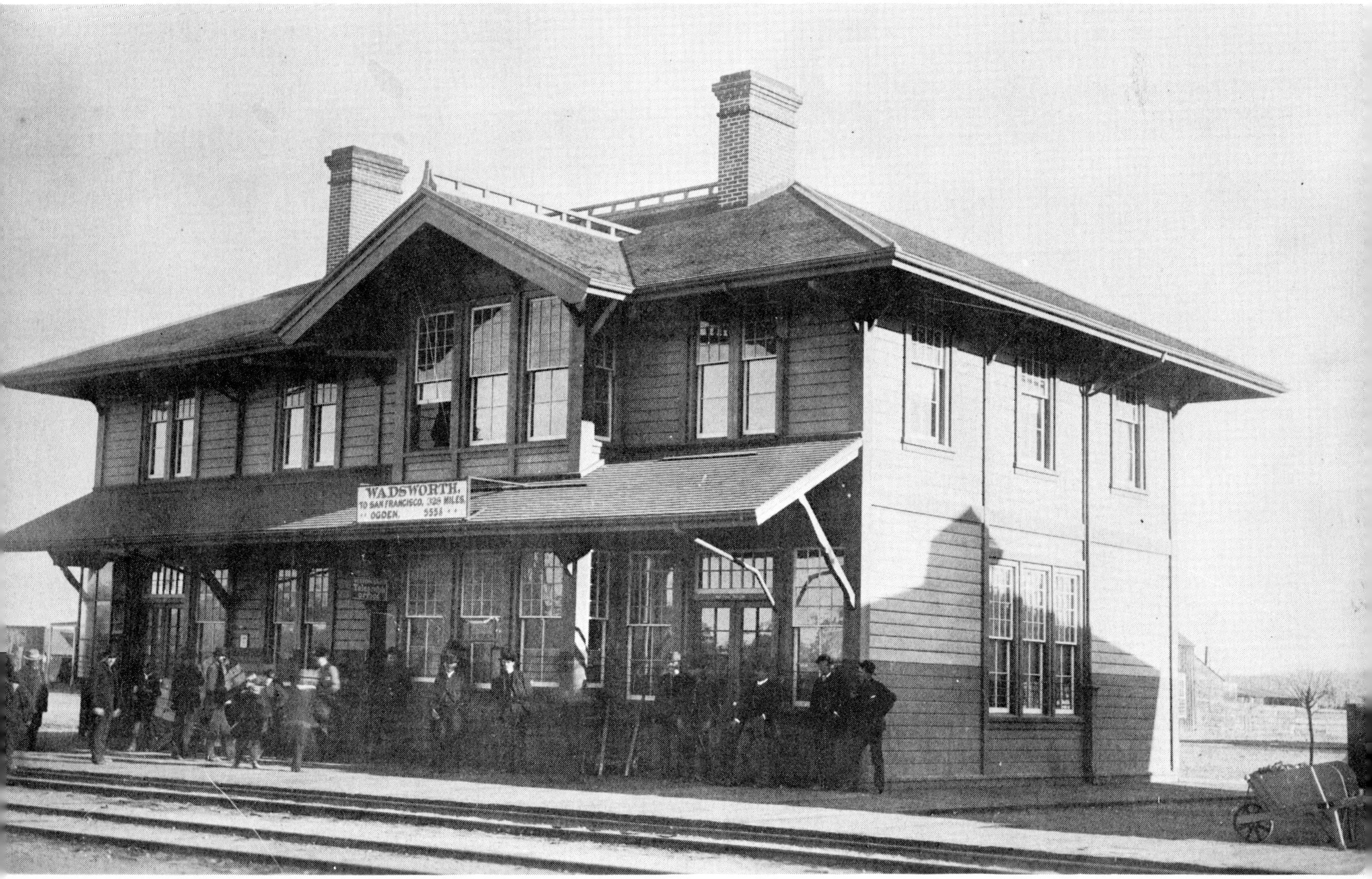

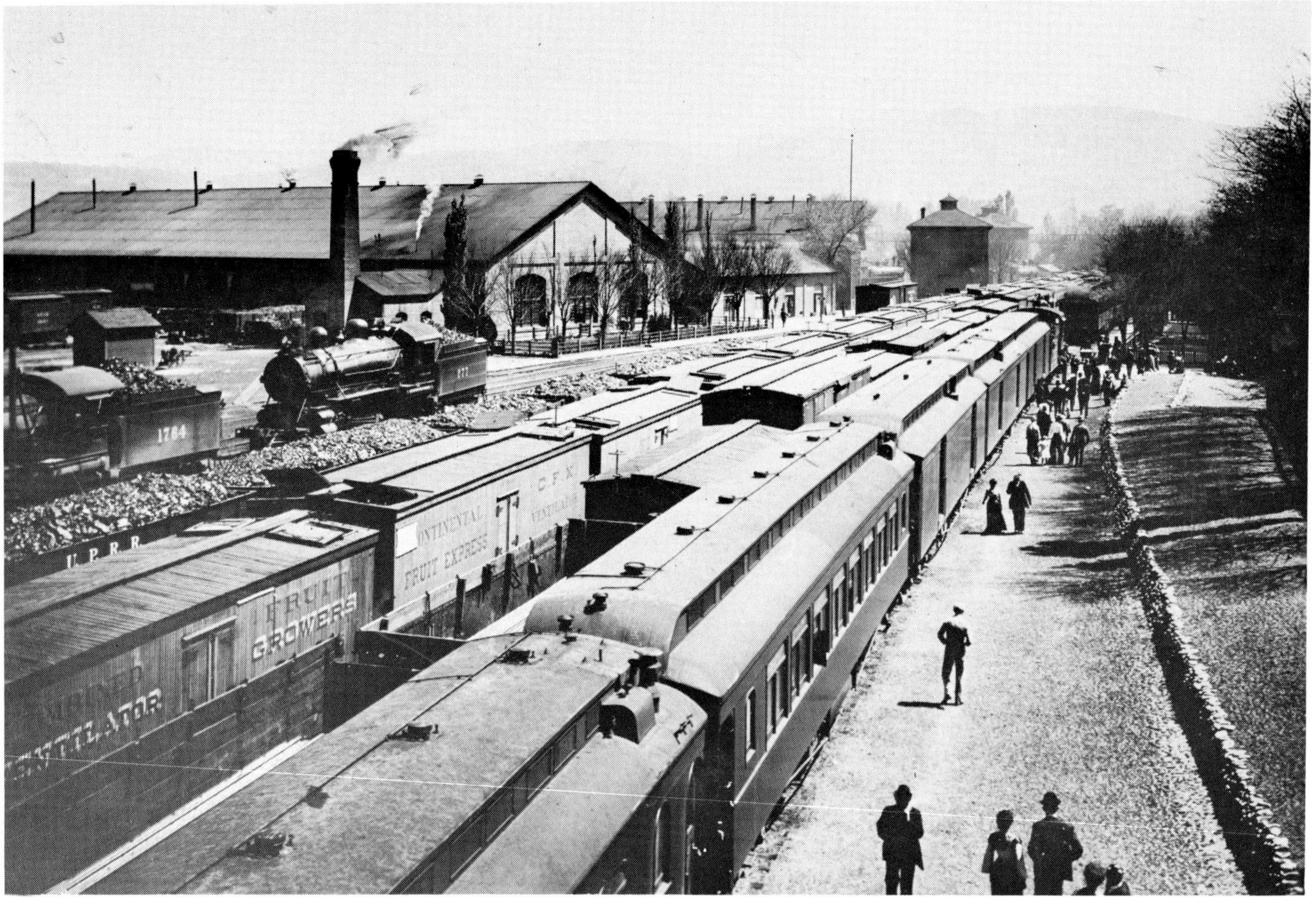

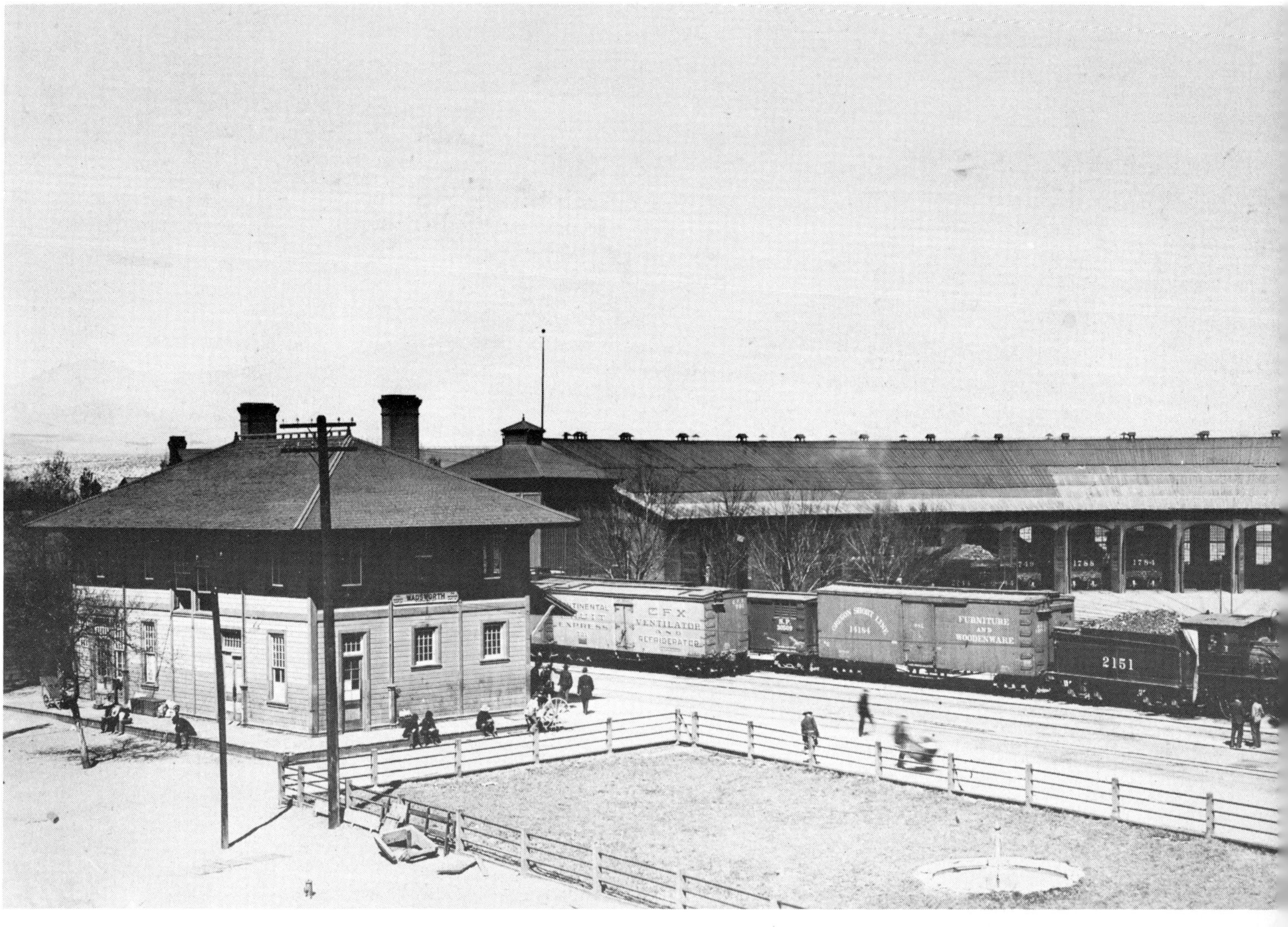

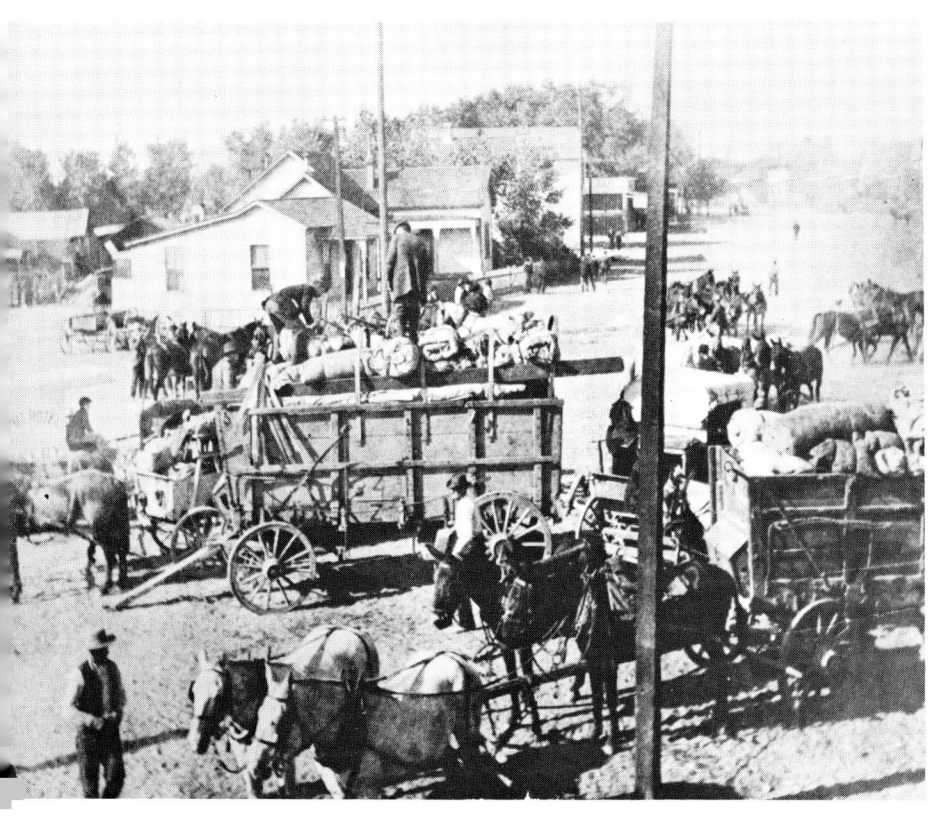

By the turn of the century Wadsworth had become cosmopolitan. In these photos, ca. 1901–1904, taken just before a series of major line changes outmoded and bypassed the Wadsworth location, passenger trains were lining up end-to-end along the station platform *(top, left)*; main line tracks were choked with freight trains. The division headquarters *(left, bottom)* was considered sufficiently substantial to warrant its being moved to Sparks in 1904, where the building remains in use to this day. A constant parade of locomotive power *(bottom, right)* kept the Wadsworth roundhouse eternally busy around the clock. When Wadsworth terminal was closed in 1904, "moving day" to Sparks *(immediate left)* became a lengthy experience extending over several months, as witness these horse-powered "vans" ready to roll with their loads of furnishings. *(All Photos: Southern Pacific Collection.)*

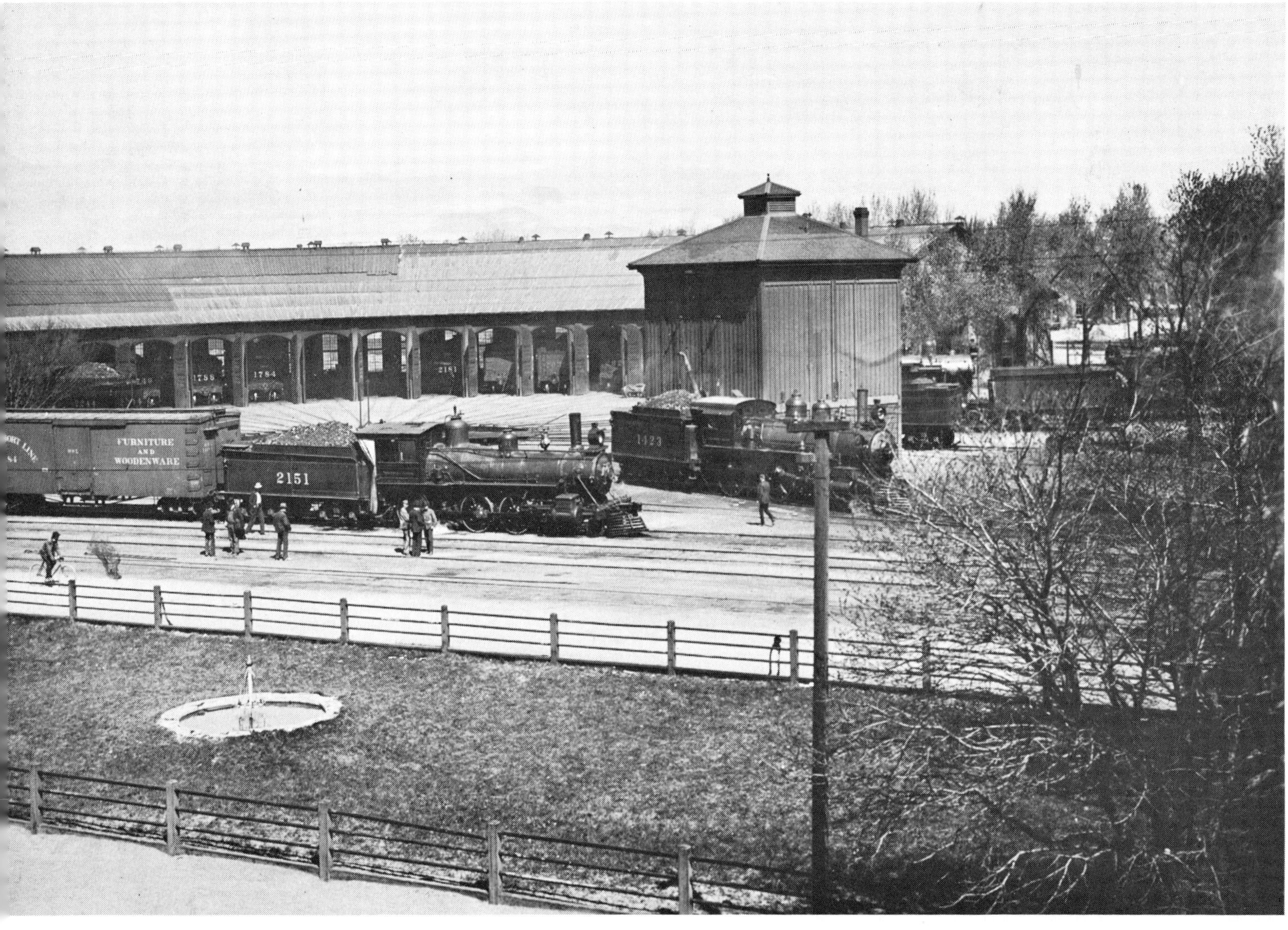

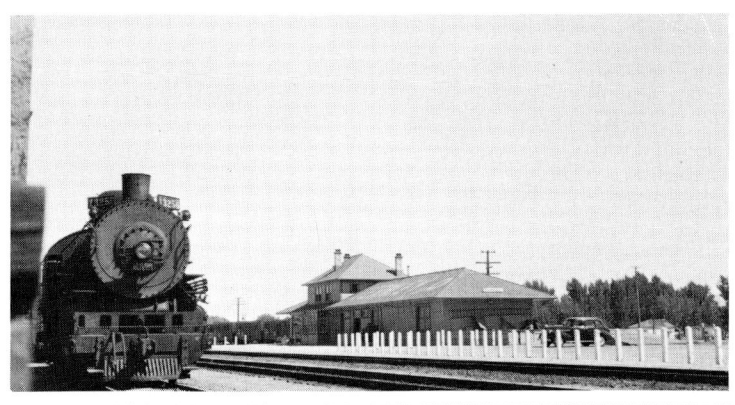

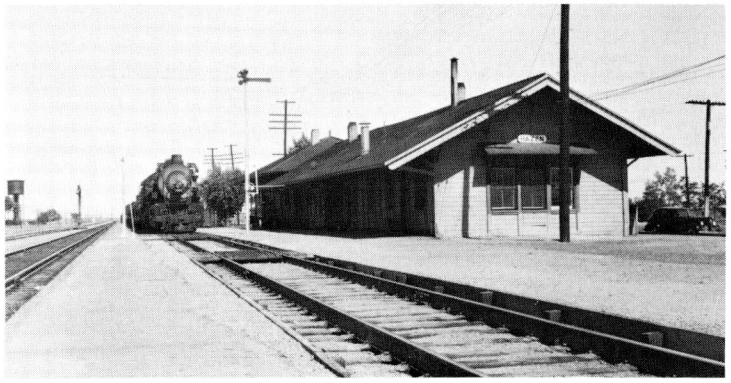

East of Wadsworth lie several important junction points. In these 1946 views we see in quick succession Fernley *(top, left)*, connection for the CP's Fernley & Lassen Railway to Susanville (1912-14); Hazen station *(next below)* and Hazen roundhouse *(third below)* comprised the junction facilities for the Hazen Cut-Off to Churchill (1905) and the 15-mile Fallon branch (1906). The roundhouse nestled within a wye, the south leg of which (at right in photo) furnished the lead to the two branches.

Northeast from Hazen toward Winnemucca, the division point of Imlay was prominent for a time. In the two 1912 views *(below)* the one *(left)* illustrates the power house, machine shop and roundhouse *(left to right)* while Consolidation (2-8-0) No. 2826 in foreground relieves her boiler pressure as she awaits assignment. The panorama *(right)* looks south past the 12-stall roundhouse to the employees' Club House. The little shed in the middle foreground contains fire hoses in the event of emergency. *(Top Three Photos: Ted Wurm; Bottom Photos: Stanley Palmer.)*

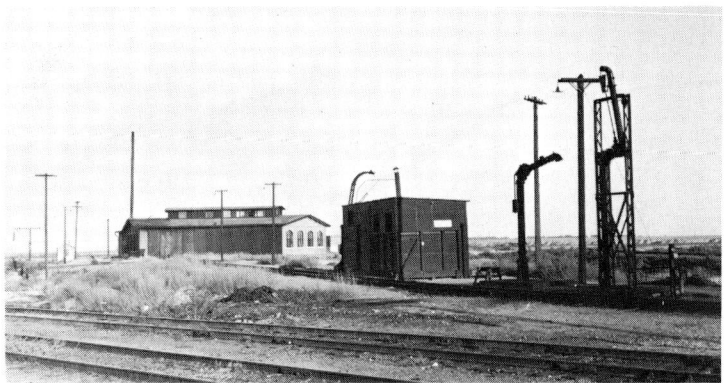

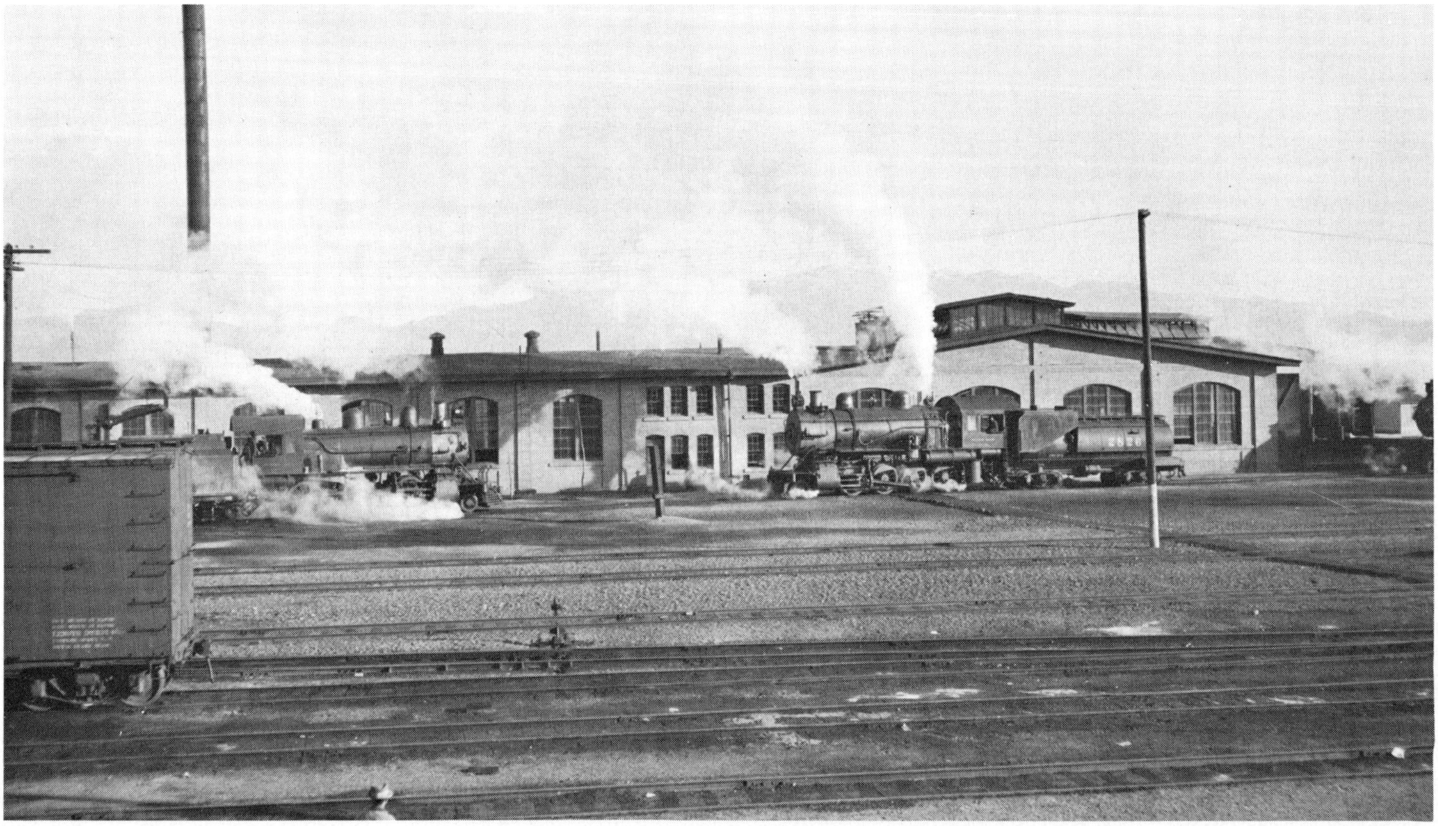

stock, Fort Homestead's famous cannon, the "General Grant," was fired, and that night rockets filled the skies. Down at Dayton, on the Carson River, as soon as the telegrapher announced "Done," all hands made a mad rush to the National Hotel to drink a toast to the railroad and to Charlie Crocker. Virginia City had a special interest in the Last Spike event for, in addition to the gold spike from California, a silver spike had come from Nevada fashioned by Robert Lodge at Dowling's Blacksmith Shop at Taylor and B Streets in Virginia City. Over 100 people had taken the sledge and cast a blow to help form the notable memento.

Stanford said later: "We were exceedingly relieved and we 'jollified' a little. We thought we had succeeded in accomplishing a great work . . ." They had indeed, and all four eventually became very rich men subjected to much criticism and abuse before they passed on.

Early Operations

Operations over the next 30 years were not spectacular. True there were wrecks, snow blockades, fires, personality problems and dividends (1873-77, 1880-84 and 1888-93, inclusive). No branches were built in Nevada, even though a line from Winnemucca to Eastern Washington with a branch to Wood River (Ketchum), Idaho, was shown in heavy red ink on an 1883 map.

Some of the operating problems were unusual. In May, 1879, No. 6, the emigrant train, tried to start up after making a scheduled stop at Clark's, 20 miles east of Reno, but was unable to do so until brooms were procured and crickets swept from the rails.

The following February the Eureka *Leader* carried the following story concerning certain personalities: "Conductor Hopkins on the Humboldt Division says that a fly, alighting on one of the glasses of the engineer's spectacles, caused the engineer to think it was a cow on the track and turned on the air brakes to avoid disaster." On the other hand: "The engineer retorts that one night the conductor saw what he thought was the headlight of an approaching locomotive. He kept his own train waiting for a while and then, somewhat confusedly, started her. 'He is the safest man I ever ran with,' said the engineer. 'Venus is millions of miles away and he waited twelve minutes on a side track to allow her to pass.'"

One of the most famous of all train robberies, but not the first, took place at Verdi, Nevada, on November 5, 1870. Much careful watching spotted an anticipated shipment of gold out of San Francisco. The robbers sent a confederate to the city with instructions to send a coded telegram when the shipment was actually made. The rest was easy. The train was stopped; the engine and express car were detached and run down the track a few miles; the car was broken into and the Wells Fargo safe conveniently opened. The program worked to perfection except that the men subsequently were caught and most served long terms in the penitentiary. The most remarkable thing about this robbery was that the same train on the same day was the

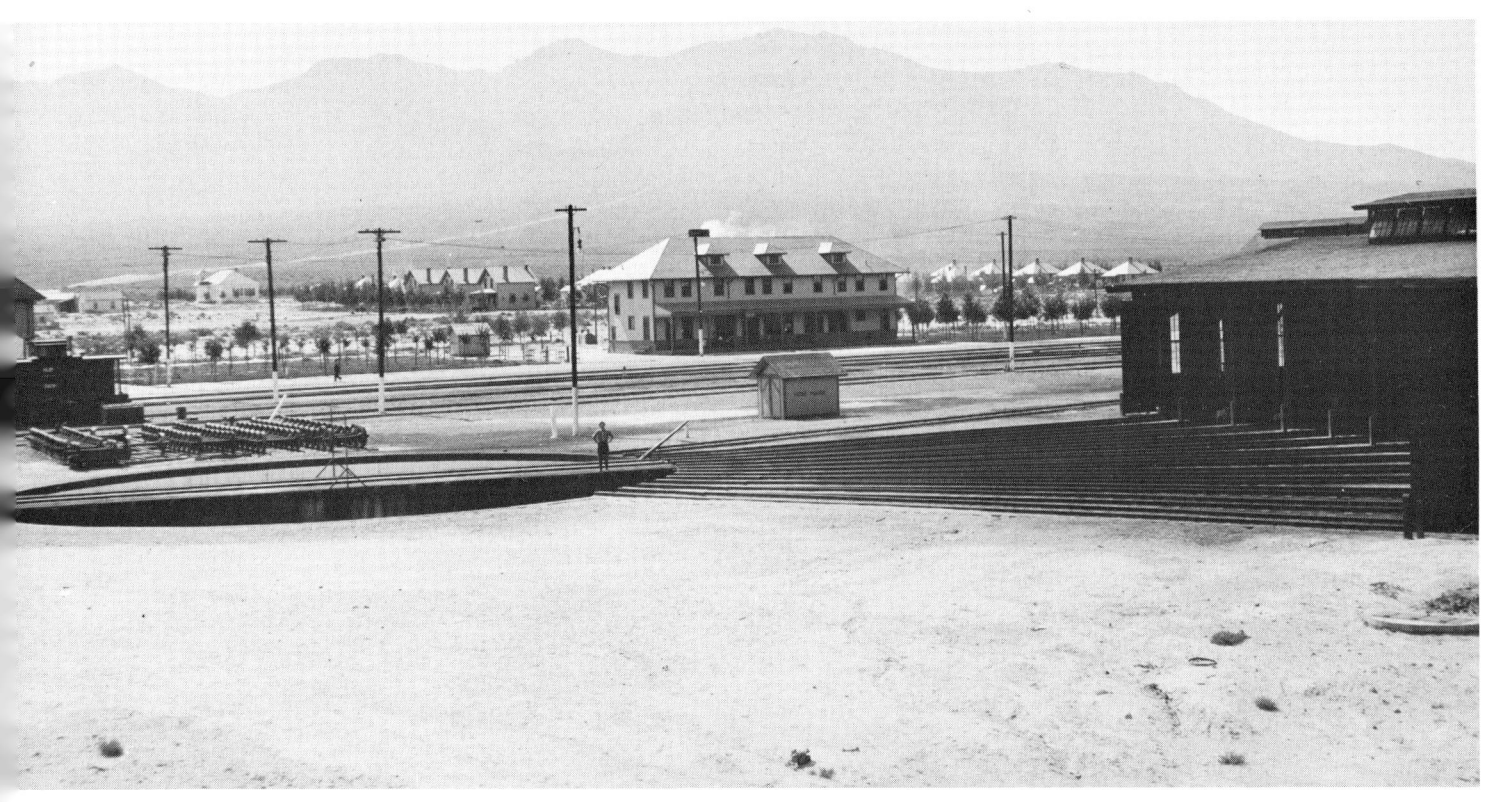

victim of another set of robbers some 400 miles farther east in the Pequop Mountains near Wells. The exact spot is in dispute — some say Independence; others say Pequop, 11 miles beyond — but there is no doubt that the methods used by this second set of robbers were identical to those of the first group. Oddly enough, there was still $300 in the safe following the first robbery plus a sizeable quantity of registered mail.

Robbers attacked the express car of a train near Montello late on the Sunday night of January 21, 1883. The brave messenger shot it out with the bandits, and they departed, to vent their spite by harassment of nearby ranchers. Wells Fargo presented the live hero, A. G. Ross, with a $1,000 check plus a gold watch for his good deed.

The robbery a mile east of Humboldt (House) was more successful. The time was 2:00 A.M.; the date, July 14, 1898. Train No. 1 was eastbound. Two masked men suddenly appeared from over the tender and commanded the engineer to halt his train. The crew were then marched down to the express car, told to identify themselves to the express man and have him open the door. A few shots were fired into the ground to emphasize the point, whereupon the messenger promptly turned out the lights. The robbers then placed a small stick of dynamite under the door and touched it off with the remark, "I guess that will fetch him." It did. With the door partly open, the messenger had no other recourse except to turn on the lights and come out like a good fellow. Along with the engine crew, he was marched to the head of the train, while a large blast of dynamite blew up the safe as well as blowing out the sides of the car and raising the roof. While one of the bandits scooped up the valuables, the three members of the crew were told to join hands and walk ahead. Some distance from the train they were instructed to stop; the robbers shook hands, bid them "Adios" and calmly disappeared in the darkness.

During the 1870's the original iron rail was replaced by steel, while new roundhouses were erected at Truckee, Wadsworth, Winnemucca and Carlin. Wood was used to fire the locomotives for years, but in 1880 coal burning locomotives made their advent in Nevada and were used as far west as Truckee. Division repair shops were maintained at Rocklin and Truckee in California, at Wadsworth, Winnemucca, Carlin and Toano in Nevada, and at Terrace and Ogden in Utah, the average division being approximately 200 miles in length.

The traffic elements were interesting. Tea was an important commodity, amounting to 18 million pounds of revenue freight or approximately ten per cent of the 1877 total. Sometimes 60 cars of tea and other Chinese goods would pass Battle Mountain in a two day period. Considering the small volume of traffic (only two regularly scheduled freight trains each way daily) and the modest train lengths of the period, this was rather an impressive statistic. Wool was another important cargo, while in 1876 over a million pounds of seal skins were carried.

Westbound, through passengers from Ogden numbered 34,040 in 1872, while those eastbound only totaled 21,645. By 1883 the volume had increased to 73,700 and 40,107, respectively, the westbound traffic still predominating. 1875 was a particularly heavy year for passenger travel. But passengers could not always be counted as statistics, as was the case of one San Francisco-bound voyager. He was in a great hurry, but still had time for a few rounds with the boys before boarding the "Lightning Express" at Reno. By train time he could not tell a clothes line from a picket fence, but he boarded what he thought to be the "Lightning" and ensconced himself in a seat. Shortly he was dreaming away at the rate of 30 m.p.h. About 4:00 A.M. he awoke, somewhat sobered, to find the train was making an unusually long stop. Turning to ask a neighbor the reason, he found he was the only one on the coach. Stepping outside he discovered he was still in Reno. He had boarded one of the coaches used temporarily as a depot following the big fire which had just consumed the regular station.

Other passengers were waylaid in Reno for a different reason, and were distinctly not pleased as the days went by. It happened during the terrific storms of January, 1890, when so much of Nevada's livestock perished and the Central Pacific was completely snowbound. The blockade over the Sierras lasted a full 14 days, but after nine days of waiting the 600 stranded passengers held an indignation meeting in Reno. They even published their own paper, appropriately called *The Snowbound*, to air their woes. A single issue did the job, for the trains moved a few days later. But in February the trains again were tied up for three days. One passenger train was reported to have had 18 engines on the head end plus a push plow. Even with all this power, it stalled near Emigrant Gap. Rotary snowplows were developed shortly thereafter and generally were able to keep the line clear, although as

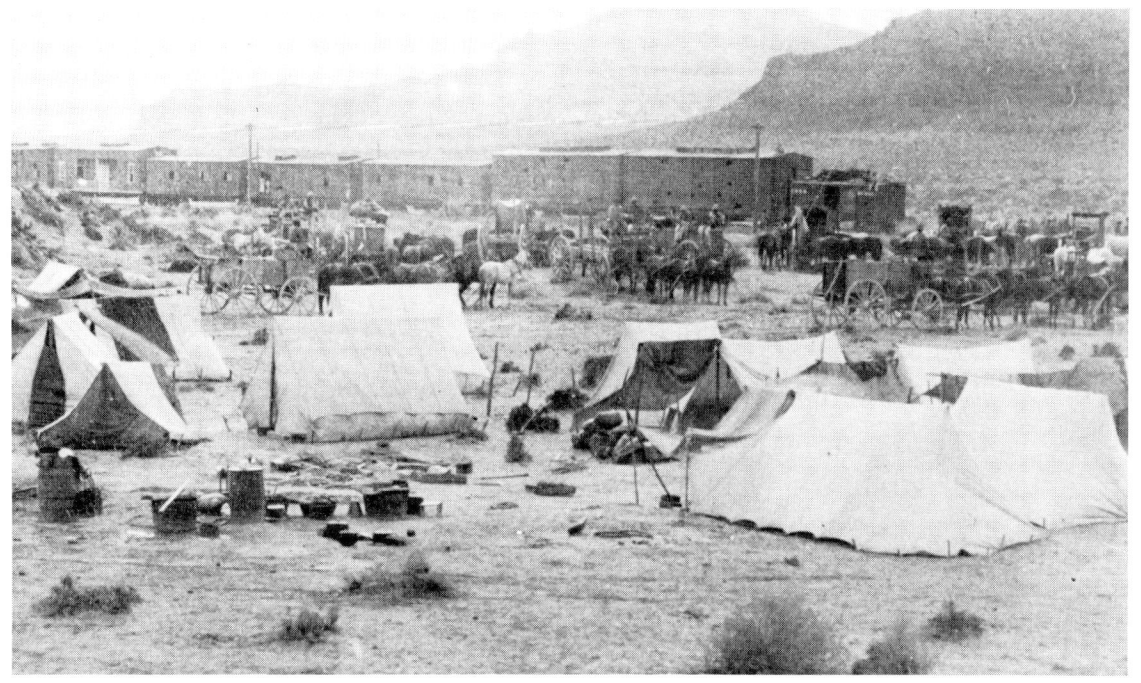

Primitive times in the Winnemucca area are amply portrayed by these two scenes. In the summer of 1868 the end of track lay near Humboldt Lake (top). The temporary tents and crude camping equipment typical of "front" towns lie plainly in the foreground, while the bunk and work cars of the construction men line the siding at rear. Rails were then heading for Winnemucca (below) whose Winnemucca Hotel (left, rear) served as terminus for stage lines to Paradise Valley and the Owyhee Mining District of Idaho. (Southern Pacific Collection.)

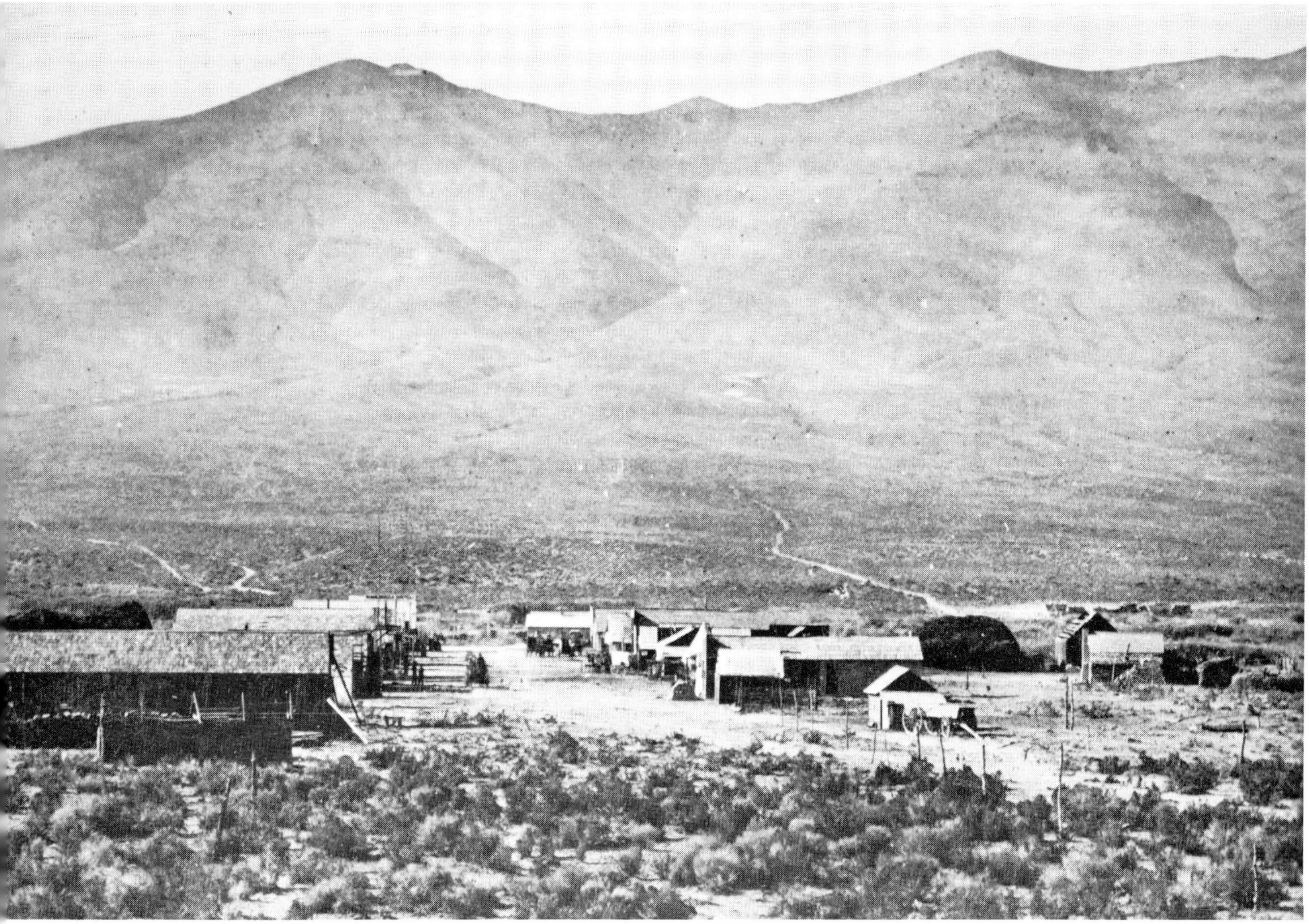

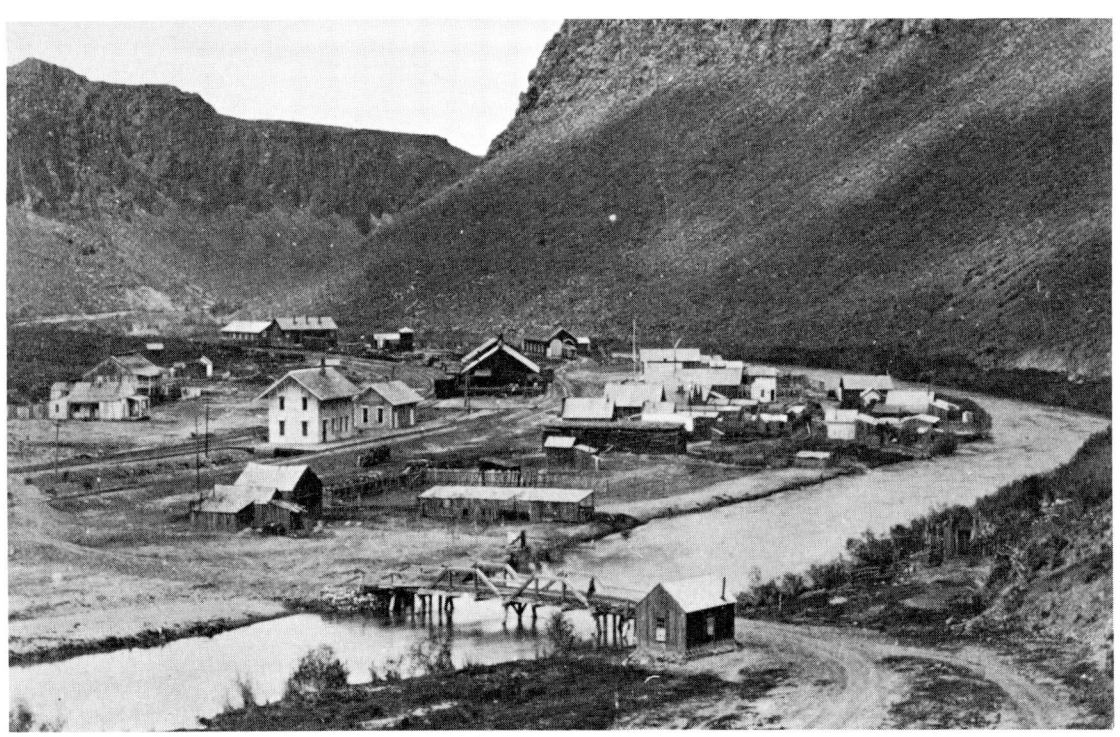

Palisade, Nevada, in the Humboldt River Canyon, was strictly a railroad town in the 1880's when the photo *(top)* was taken. Tracks of the transcontinental Central Pacific lay toward the north, while on the near side lay those of the 3-foot gauge Eureka & Palisade Railroad which terminated at this junction. Between the two may be seen the CP's two-story station, just beyond, the freight interchange buildings, and to the right behind those the E&P's car shed and shop with a passenger car in front. In the far distance (over the roof of the CP station) lie the roundhouse and shops of the E&P. Circumscribing this pastoral scene on the right is the Humboldt River, through the canyon of which *(below)* the CP's Pacific Limited of a later era threads its way behind Mountain-type (4-8-2) locomotive No. 4350, built by the Sacramento Shops in 1926. *(Both Photos: Southern Pacific.)*

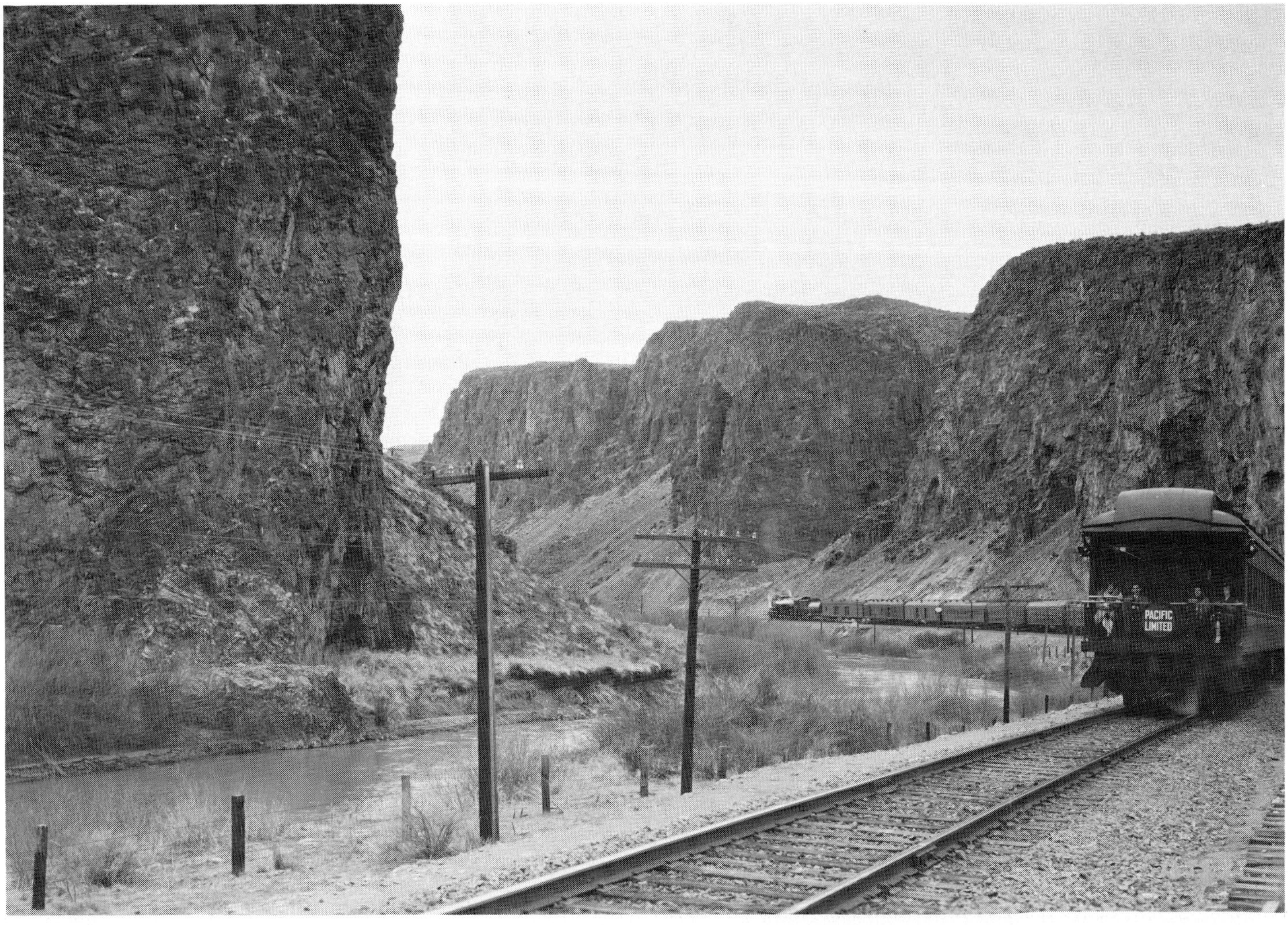

recently as January 1952 a modern diesel train was snowed in at approximately the same location.

Although the Big Four had sold most of their stock in the Central Pacific by 1883, they were able to continue to control the company through its lease to the Southern Pacific Company, a corporation newly-formed the following year. From 1887 to 1893 the Central Pacific enjoyed a guaranteed annual net income of $1,360,000 under the terms of the SP's lease, but when the contract was amended in the early part of 1894, the SP had become tired of making up the difference between actual and guaranteed income, and the guaranty was eliminated. As a solace to the stockholders (many of whom resided in Europe), it was pointed out that all of the principal "Pacific" railroad companies (except the CP and the SP) were in the hands of receivers.

Following the death of Leland Stanford in June 1893, Isaac Requa (of Comstock mining fame) became president of the Central Pacific. The future looked dark indeed, for the Government bonds together with 30 years of accumulated interest were maturing from January 16, 1895 to January 1, 1899. Improvements to the railroad had been deferred as the CP had little money of its own; in fact, the railroad had operated at small losses during the years 1895 and 1896. Receivership appeared to be the most promising solution to the problem for, with poor credit and a heavy debt, the possibilities of refunding were slim. But Huntington, that master of money, working in collaboration with Speyer & Company, put together an agreement whereby the stockholders of the CP traded their shares for stock and bonds of the SP Company. The old bonds were then refunded and the debt to the U. S. Government which, with interest, totaled $58,812,715, was paid off serially in full, the last payment being made on February 1, 1909. A new company, the Central Pacific Railway, fully owned by the Southern Pacific Co., began business on August 1, 1899.

The New Central Pacific

Now that the Southern Pacific owned the stock of the Central Pacific, it could properly pour money into the property. Things began to happen.

In the fall of 1899 surveyors were scattered all across Nevada, running lines and checking for possible cut-offs and improvements which would result in operating economies. A new passenger train, the Overland Limited, brought the number of daily trains over the Ogden Route to three. "The Great Salt Lake Cut-Off has become a certainty," general manager J. A. Fillmore declared in December 1899; engineers were already at work on it.

First mention of this line across the lake had appeared in the *Ogden Standard* some years before. It was around 1889 that a Lt. Von Gorp, an engineer who had worked on the Trans-Siberian Railway, had come to the United States in the interests

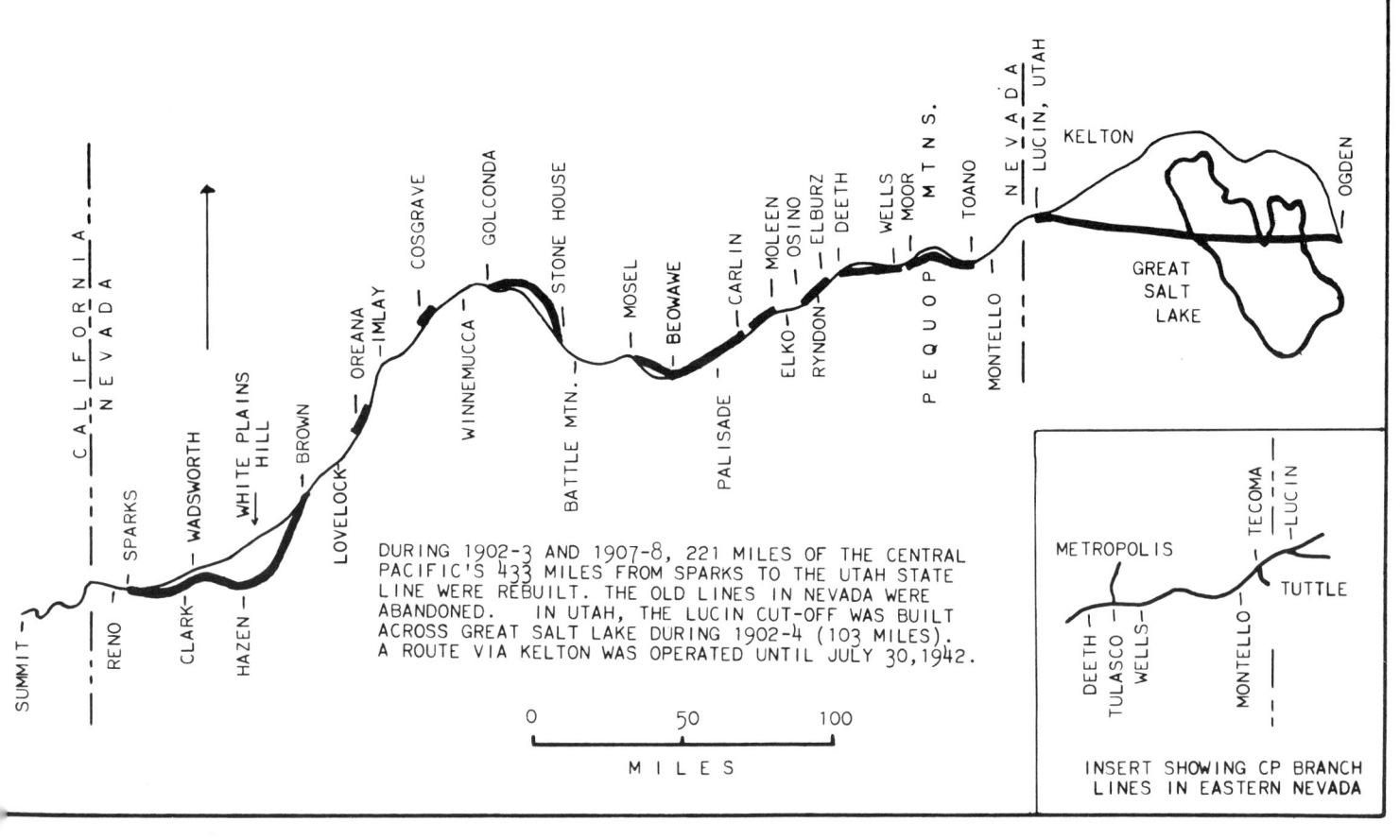

DURING 1902-3 AND 1907-8, 221 MILES OF THE CENTRAL PACIFIC'S 433 MILES FROM SPARKS TO THE UTAH STATE LINE WERE REBUILT. THE OLD LINES IN NEVADA WERE ABANDONED. IN UTAH, THE LUCIN CUT-OFF WAS BUILT ACROSS GREAT SALT LAKE DURING 1902-4 (103 MILES). A ROUTE VIA KELTON WAS OPERATED UNTIL JULY 30, 1942.

INSERT SHOWING CP BRANCH LINES IN EASTERN NEVADA

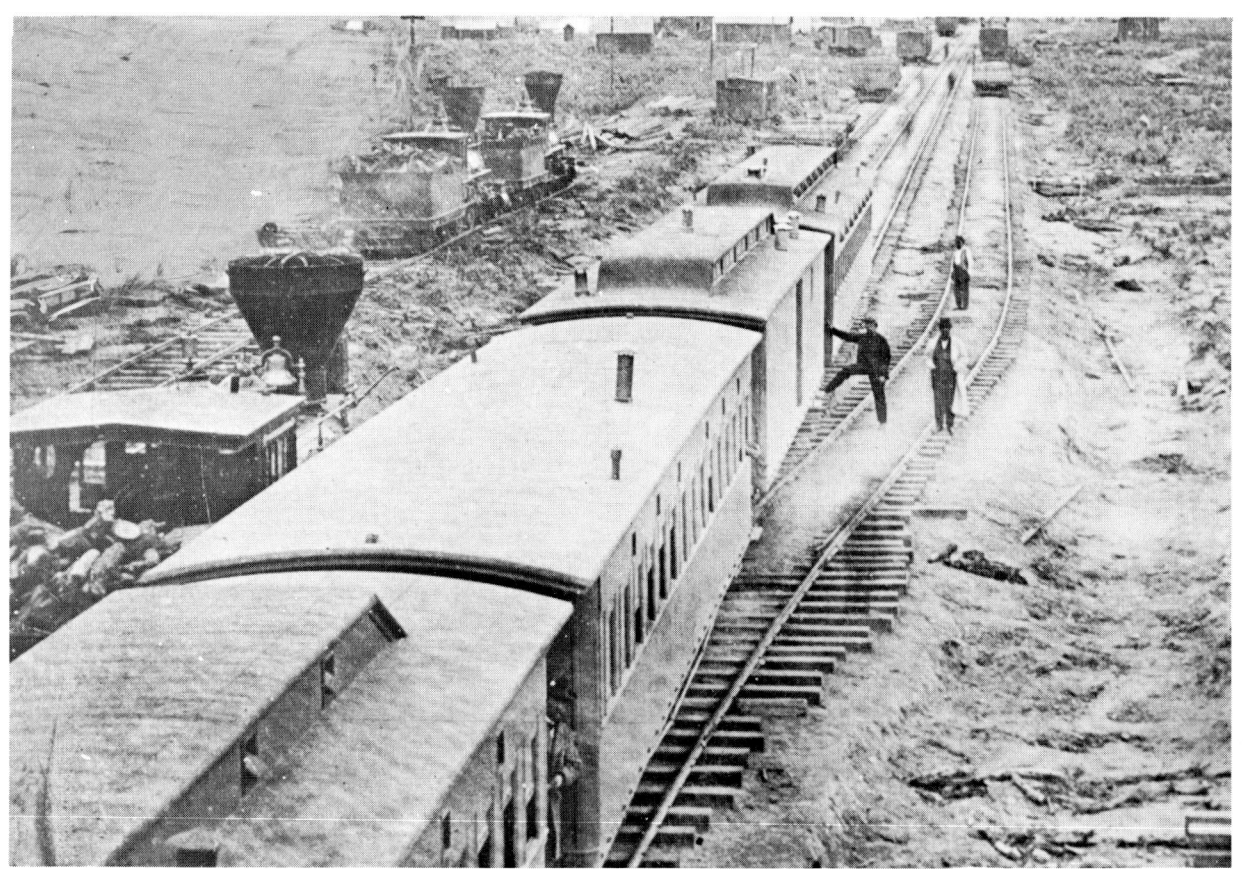

East of Palisade, where the Humboldt River valley broadens into an oasis, the Central Pacific established a division point called Carlin. In these two fine 1869 views taken during a routine train service stop we see, looking west from the roof of the water tower *(top)*, the last four cars of the train of earliest coaches. Interposition of the baggage car before the rear coach would indicate the last car was reserved for the exclusive use of the crew, while some passengers were obliged to ride with less ventilation in the older coach (third from rear) without benefit of clerestory. At right lie the ready tracks of the engine terminal, and behind the freight yards of the terminus. Looking east *(below)* nine wood-burning locomotives may be spotted around the shops and enginehouse, while *(below, right)* is a superb portrait of one of the locomotives of the period in front of the Carlin roundhouse on a wintry day in the early 1870's. The decorative valve chests on the cylinders as well as the round smokebox front proudly announce that SP No. 25, the INDUSTRY, was built by the J. A. Norris Locomotive Works of Lancaster, Pa., in 1864 under builder's identification No. 14. *(Three Photos: Southern Pacific Collection.)*

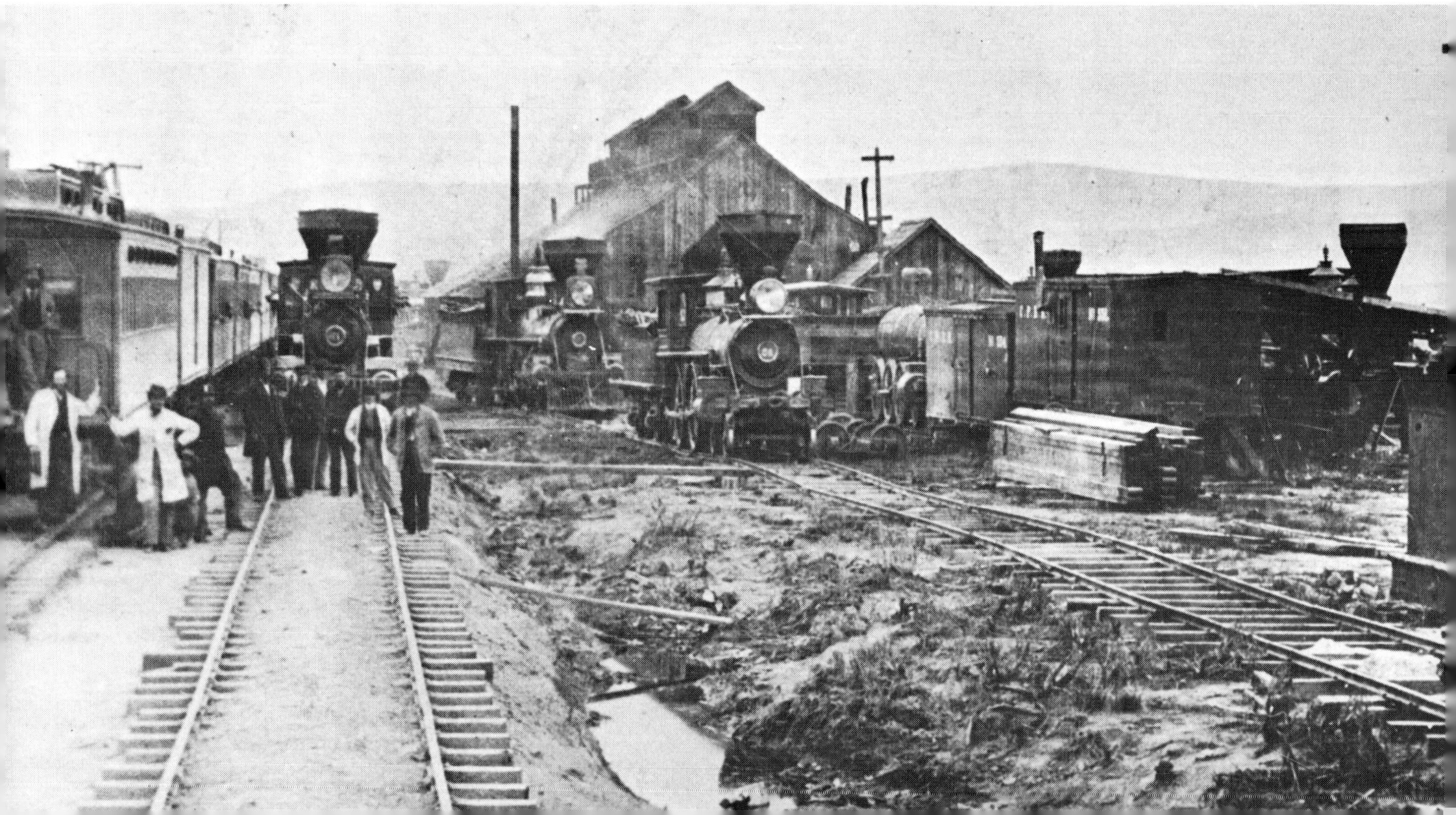

of Dutch investors. Some New York promoters had shown him plans for a railroad from Ogden to San Francisco via Lucin, Fort McDermitt and Beckwourth Pass, in which a crossing of the lake had been contemplated. In his preliminary survey, Von Gorp had found the crossing to be feasible, but the project died a-borning in 1890 with the failure of Baring Bros., the London banking house, a calamity which placed all American railway projects under a cloud.

However, the article from the *Standard* had been widely circulated and studied by many. Huntington felt that the project was feasible and that no problems would be encountered. In his view, the low water level of the Great Salt Lake would continue indefinitely as the streams feeding the lake were being tapped regularly for irrigation purposes. In anticipation of construction, four steam shovels were brought to Ogden, ready to begin work on the Lucin Cut-Off.

Of the many line improvements, the first to be undertaken was in the vicinity of Reno. The level of the roadbed from Laughton, five miles to the west, was raised and a right-of-way through various ranches to the east was acquired to circumvent the big detour made in the original alignment due to the flood conditions of 1868. According to Robert L. Fulton, long the station agent at Reno, the whole Central Pacific from Reno to Ogden was to be rebuilt to eliminate helper districts except for that portion over the Pequop Mountains.

At this time, also, the Central Pacific purchased its first (isolated) feeder line in Nevada. In March 1900 it secured the Carson & Colorado Railroad running from a connection with the Virginia & Truckee Railroad at Mound House, Nevada, for 300 miles southward to Keeler on Owens Lake in southeastern California.

This, then, was the situation when Harriman set his eye on a second route to the Pacific Coast for his Union Pacific. Harriman had tried to buy the Central Pacific from the Southern Pacific, but the latter would not sell. So he did the next best thing and bought control of the Southern Pacific. In August 1900 Huntington of the SP died, and in February 1901 the large block of SP stock held by his estate passed into Union Pacific hands.

Harriman did not concur with Huntington in his views that the water level of the Great Salt Lake would remain a constant, and plans for the Lucin Cut-Off were shelved. Work did go ahead on some 15 other line changes during the period from 1901 to 1903. The longest was from East Reno (Sparks) eastward to Brown's via Hazen, 84 miles. Although the new line was five miles longer, it avoided the long 1½% Hot Springs grade. At Oreana there was

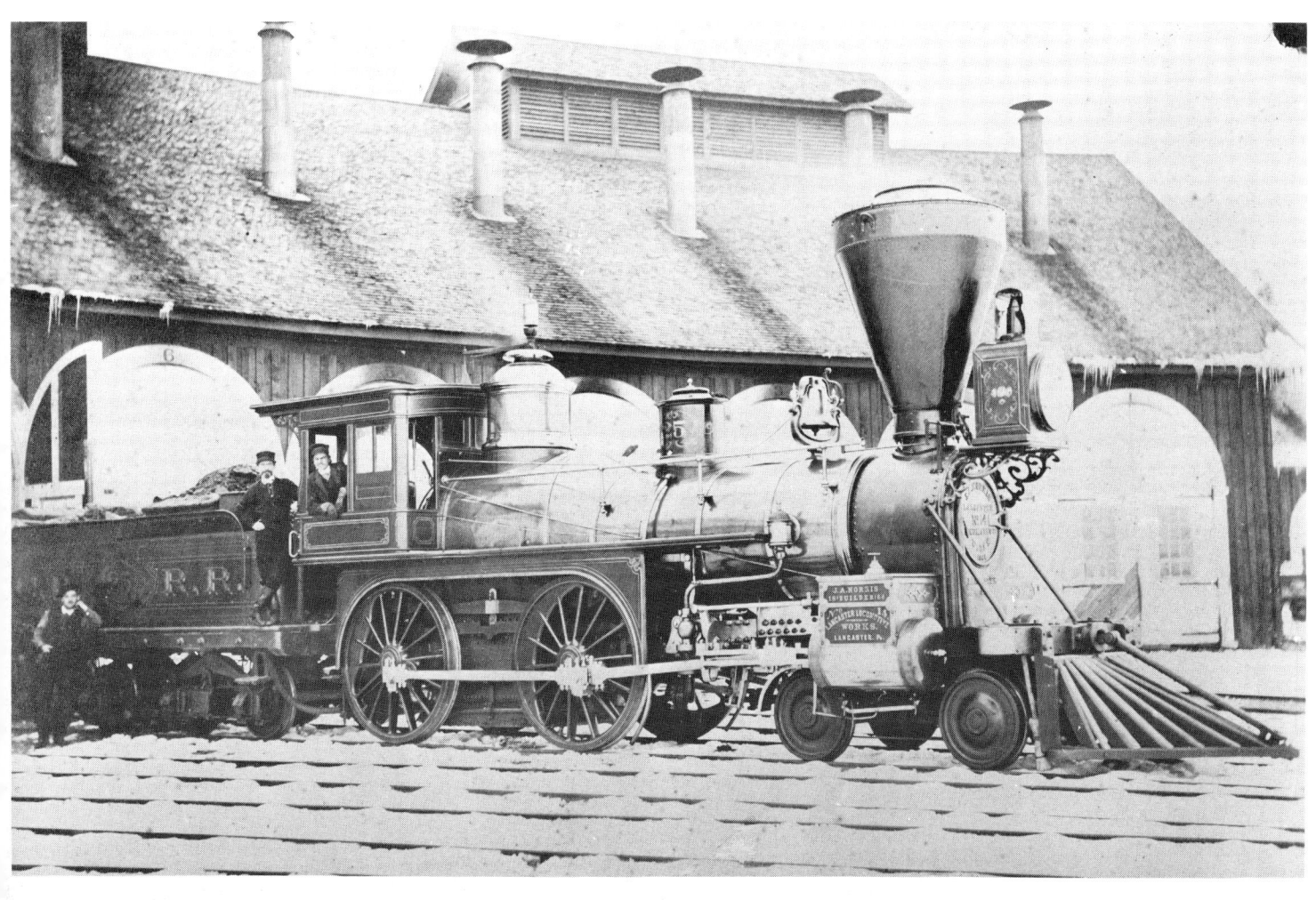

a 10-mile change, a 25-mile change from Golconda to Stone House, a 15-mile revision from Mosel to Beowawe, followed by another 15-mile change from there to Palisade. A new line, 27 miles long, was built from Moor to Toano. Near Elko four tunnels were bored, the longest being at Ryndon, 3,918 feet in length. In the entire stretch from Brown's to Lucin, only 8.4 route miles were saved, but curves were reduced from 10° to 4° or less. Except for the climb over the Pequops, and in two other places, the grade was reduced to a mere .4%. A proposed change around Battle Mountain was never made, and it was not until 1909 that the 16-mile Deeth-Wells change was completed.

The years 1901 to 1903 also encompassed the beginnings of Nevada's second great mining era. Although Tonopah attracted the greatest interest (its fame spread throughout the world), the people in Reno were primarily excited over Olinghouse, near Wadsworth, and a mine just northeast of Reno being developed by an ex-piano tuner named George Wedekind. Although discovered in 1896, it was not until 1901 that his Star Mine began to be exploited and work begun in earnest. It was news of the Star Mine that commanded the biggest space in the *Reno Gazette*, and Sunday prospecting north of town became so popular that the supply of rigs at local liveries were frequently exhausted by prospective mining millionaires.

Wadsworth became a very lively town in 1902, thanks to unwelcome guests. Virtually every train brought in its complement of hoboes — including some mighty rough characters — who were looking for work on the various railroad cut-offs. Quickly tiring of manual labor, they drifted back to Wadsworth. Street fights became common occurrences, although the combatants were usually too full of liquor to do serious harm. Many landed in jail. As some 2,000 men were working on the Hazen line alone, the Wadsworth jail was normally taxed to capacity, and the overflow had to be taken to Reno.

In the vicinity of Palisade, in order to keep the men on the job, the Southern Pacific issued orders that no liquor was to be sold along the right-of-way. Still further east in the Pequop Mountains, one man nearly starved the workers at the grading camp of Fenelon in September 1902 when he attempted to dynamite the commissary. He wasn't mad at the whole camp; he merely wanted to kill the man in charge of the commissary.

In February 1902 Kilpatrick Brothers & Collins, a concern which held many of the construction contracts, was working the 14-mile section eastward from Clark to Wadsworth. The original line had been kept on the north bank of the river, but as the new route was to be constructed as straight as possible, nine heavy bridges were being erected to compensate for the bends of the river. Hundreds

---

Elko, Nevada, was largely a tent city when the Central Pacific reached that locality in January 1869. Crowds gathered to welcome the arrival of one of the first scheduled trains *(left, below)*. While the curious timidly inspected the head end with its fire-breathing locomotive and observed the incompleted trackwork in the foreground, a line-up of stage coaches (at left) waited to cross the tracks and load *(right, below)* at the rear of the station to carry passengers into the hinterlands. *(Both Photos: Southern Pacific Collection.)*

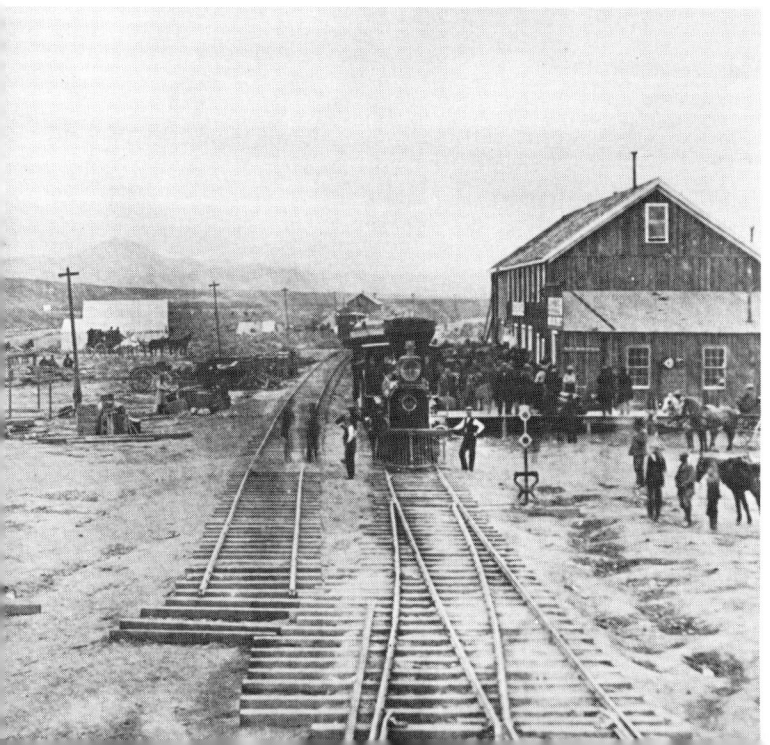

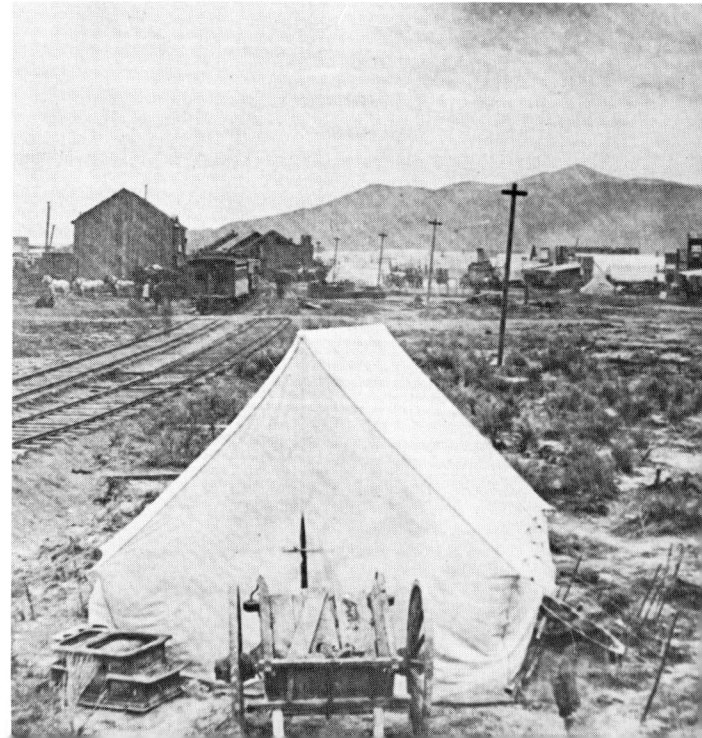

of tents were stretched along the water to accommodate the large crew of men required, while some 500 horses and a half-dozen narrow-gauge locomotives were brought in for the job. In April 1902 one little train dashed into a gully when a trestle gave way, resulting in serious injuries to a man.

To provide lighting for the night shift, the contractors erected a generating plant at Clark. An emergency hospital was also established with two doctors in attendance. One report on life in the camp noted that "bathing facilities have been provided, and every employee is made to keep himself clean and a discharge is awaiting the man who neglects to do this . . . A superintendent of the dining departments is also instructed to see that the men come to their meals in a tidy way and the man who so forgets himself as to use profane language is summarily discharged." Kilpatrick would make gentlemen out of these hoboes, or else . . .

Early in 1902 the people of Reno learned that the shops and facilities located at Wadsworth were to be moved to the Mary Wall ranch in the Truckee Meadows, three miles east of Reno. William Hood, chief engineer of the Southern Pacific, made the formal announcement on April 30. A mass meeting was held in Wadsworth, and a representative was sent to call on J. Kruttschnitt, then vice-president and general manager of the Southern Pacific and years later to become its head. The information was startling. Each employee would be entitled to purchase a lot at the new location at a nominal cost (actually $1.00), and houses and belongings would be moved free of charge by the railroad.

The new locality existed for quite some time without any official designation. At first it was called East Reno; sometimes New Reno. In August 1903 it became Harriman, but subsequently, following a visit by that dignitary later in the year, it was discovered that he would prefer that a different designation be chosen. Accordingly it was again renamed, this time in honor of John Sparks, rancher, mine owner and then governor of the state of Nevada. At one time there was some talk of establishing a union station at Sparks for the joint usage of the Southern Pacific (Central Pacific), the Virginia & Truckee and the N-C-O. These plans did not materialize.

Because a large portion of the ground was swampy, it was necessary to bring in 18 inches of fill before any construction could take place. In June 1903 some 44 cars began moving rock and gravel from a point known as Poor's ranch, two

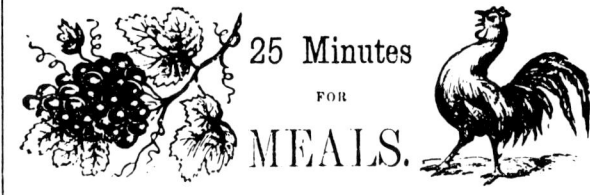

Nevada's preference for hard coin (as against the unstable dollar of the period) is amply evidenced in the Cosmopolitan Hotel's 1870 advertising in the *Railroad Gazetteer* for the 25-minute meal stop of all trains at Elko, Nevada. (*Southern Pacific Collection.*)

miles west of Reno. For approximately six months a constant movement of 360 cars a day (two shifts) kept the mainline humming. At East Reno, 350 men were occupied in spreading the fill. By fall, the foundation for the roundhouse had been laid, and the walls were taking form with bricks brought from Pleasanton, California. The building's large, 40-stall capacity dictated that it be built in a complete circle. Installation of approximately 15 of the 30 miles of yard tracks was also accomplished by this time.

Commencing in February 1904, transfer of the shop equipment was started. Then, during the latter

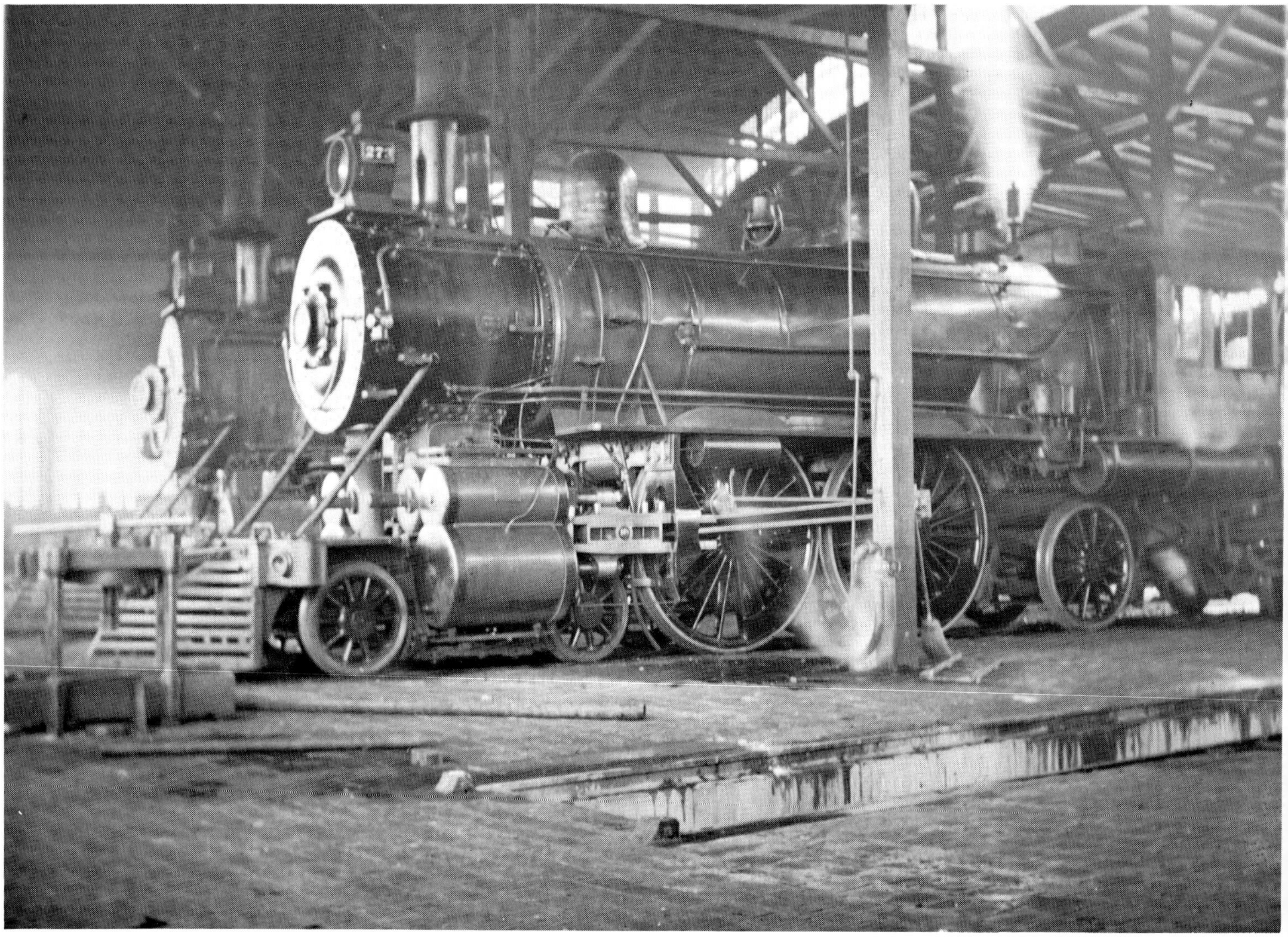

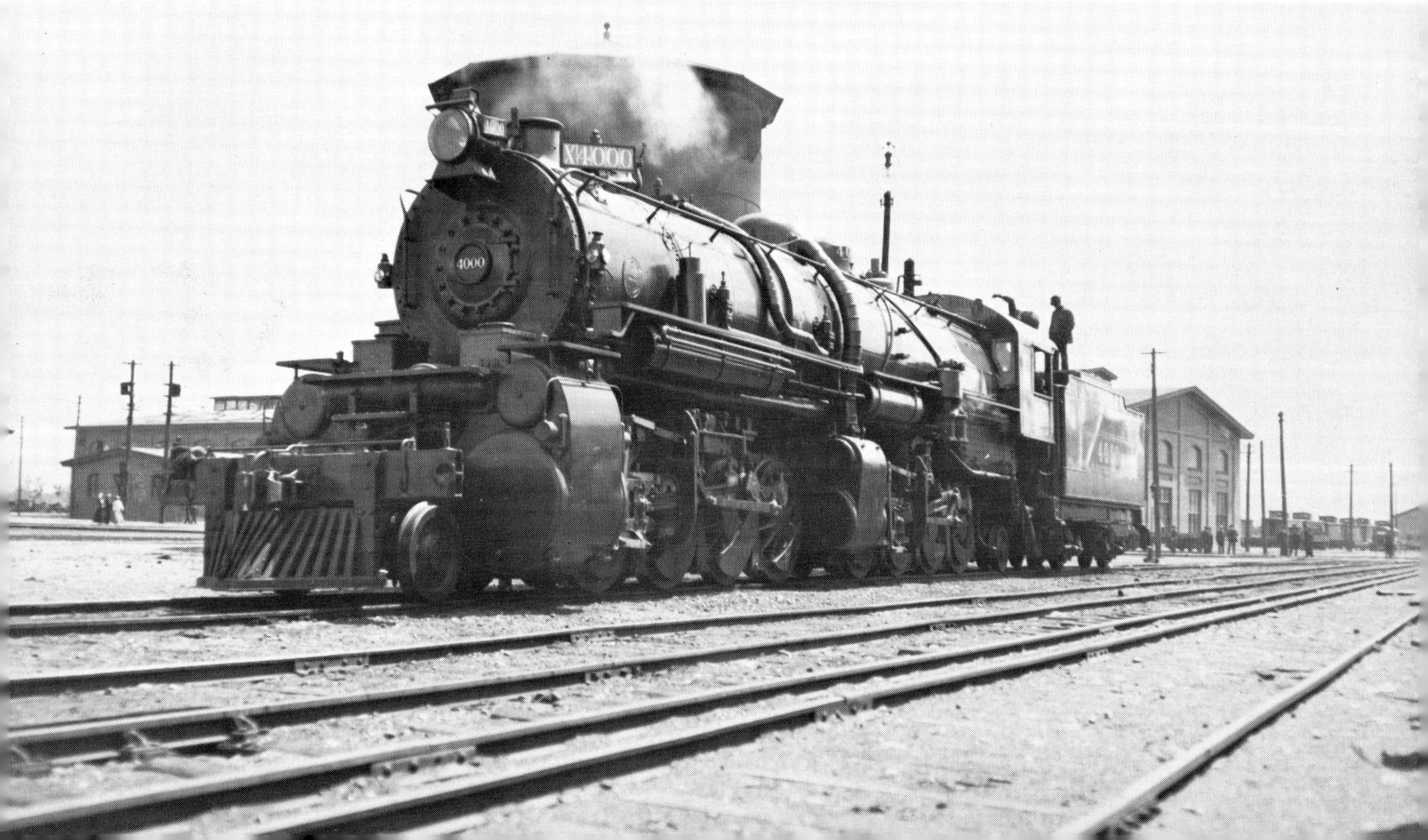

Sparks new (1904) roundhouse and shop facilities were to play host to a wide variety of motive power including such high stepping, compound Atlantics as No. 273 *(left, above)* and lumbering, compound articulated 2-8-8-2 No. 4000 *(left, below)* which paused on its way to Sacramento delivery. The 4000 and its sister 4001 were the first two compound Mallet articulated locomotives to be delivered to the Southern Pacific, and the smoke and gas of their passing through the snowsheds and tunnels of the Sierra Nevada caused the SP to wire Baldwin to change the balance of its order to cab-forward oil burners. The 4000 and 4001 were then relegated to service on the tunnelless hill out of Colton in southern California, ultimately to be converted to cab-in-fronts in 1928. To manage the Sparks works in 1905, 16 shop foremen *(top, right)* were required. An idea of the extent of the facilities may be gleaned from the view *(center, right)* of the erecting shop floor with the heavy machine shop immediately beyond. The circular roundhouse under construction *(below)* completely surrounded the turntable, entrance to which was confined to specific tracks passing through the building's walls. *(Right, Top and Bottom: Southern Pacific; All Others: Stanley Palmer.)*

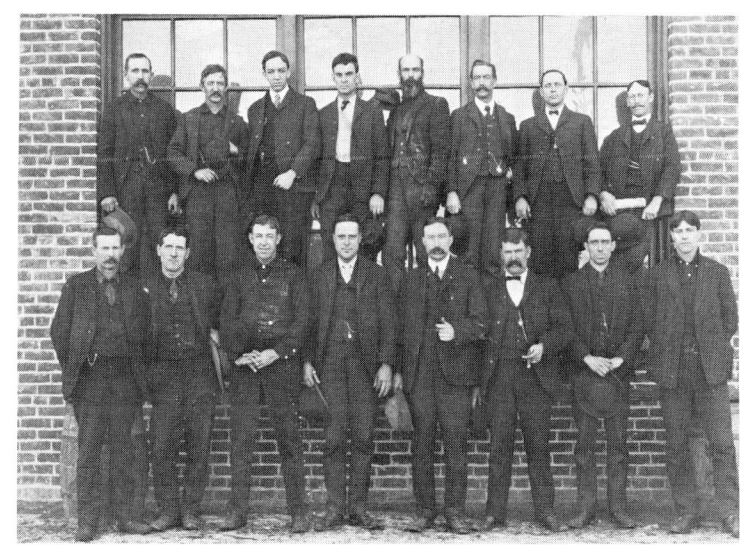

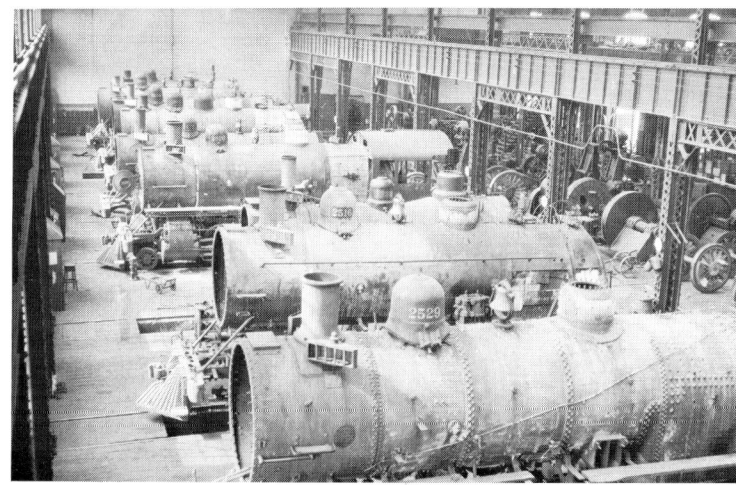

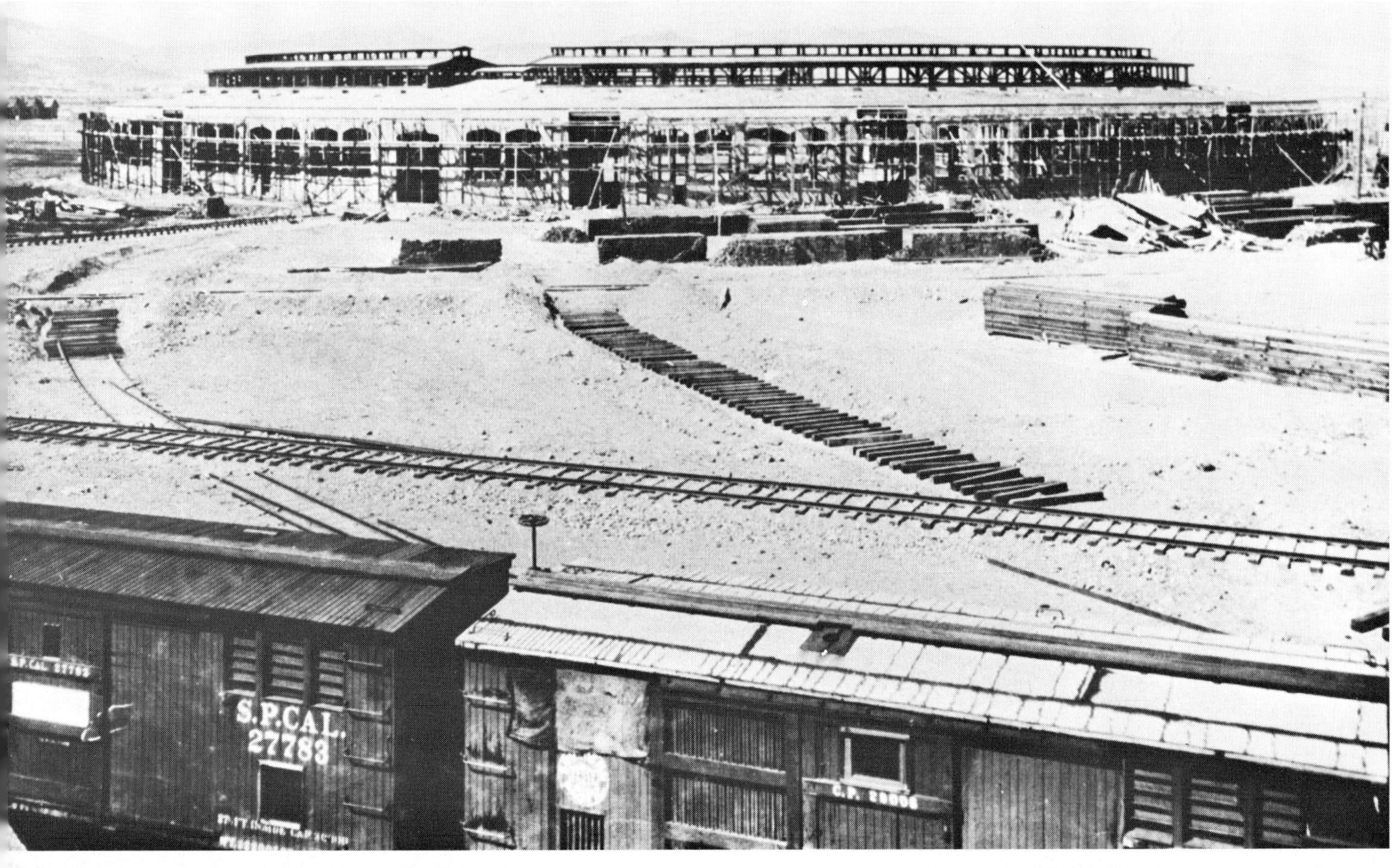

part of June, transplantation of the workers' families and their belongings to the new site was begun.

In Sparks, the first store was established in October 1903. The following month work was instituted on a new hotel. A few months later 1,000 shade trees were planted. When a trainload of oranges became the first to operate over the new main line to the south of Wadsworth, the official beginning of that town's decline was noted on the record, and Sparks began to assume its planned importance. When Wadsworth's depot was dismantled and reassembled at its new location, just prior to the moving of the division headquarters on June 19, 1904, Sparks became a real town. Additional prestige accrued when Harriman, as part of his program for a closely knit organization, elected to have the Oregon Short Line (the northwest arm of the Union Pacific) operate the CP lines east from Sparks from April 1, 1904 to the year 1912.

The roundhouse at Wadsworth was torn down in December 1904, bringing back many memories to W. B. Sheldon, who supervised its demolition. It was he who had been in charge of its construction 21 years before, and he well recalled the day the flagpole had been placed atop its peak. The names of the contributors to the Engineers and Mechanics Library had been carefully scribed on a piece of paper and sealed in the little brass ball at the top of the staff. By now some had departed; others had passed beyond; perusal of the names would be interesting. So before dynamiting the brick walls, the pole was carefully cut down, and the men rushed to read the names of their old friends. On opening the ball, nothing was found except a little disappointing dust; the climate had disintegrated the paper.

Harriman had some second thoughts about the Great Salt Lake Cut-Off, and in 1902 decided to go ahead with the project. A gun fire salute at sunrise on March 17 signalled the start of work on the project, while general pandemonium ensued in Ogden as the permanency of the project seemed assured. The new 103-mile line, extending from Ogden across the lake to Lucin (Umbria Junction) would shorten the old main line by 43 miles and avoid a number of steep grades. Of the 27½ miles across the lake, four would be on fill, eleven on permanent trestlework, while twelve would be built on temporary trestles for replacement by an embankment at a later date.

The big problem was not one of the depth of the lake, but in finding a stable bottom under the mud deposited through the centuries. Enormous quantities of fill were poured into the embankment, only to have it sink and disappear overnight. At least three times the trestles gave way under trains, but

---

With five cars of head-end revenue and seven cars for the accommodation of passengers, the Pacific Limited pauses at Sparks for a routine service stop. Cab-forward No. 4204 was the last of an order for 28 Class AC-8 locomotives of 4-8-8-2 wheel arrangement built by Baldwin in 1939. (*Nevada State Highway Dept. Photo.*)

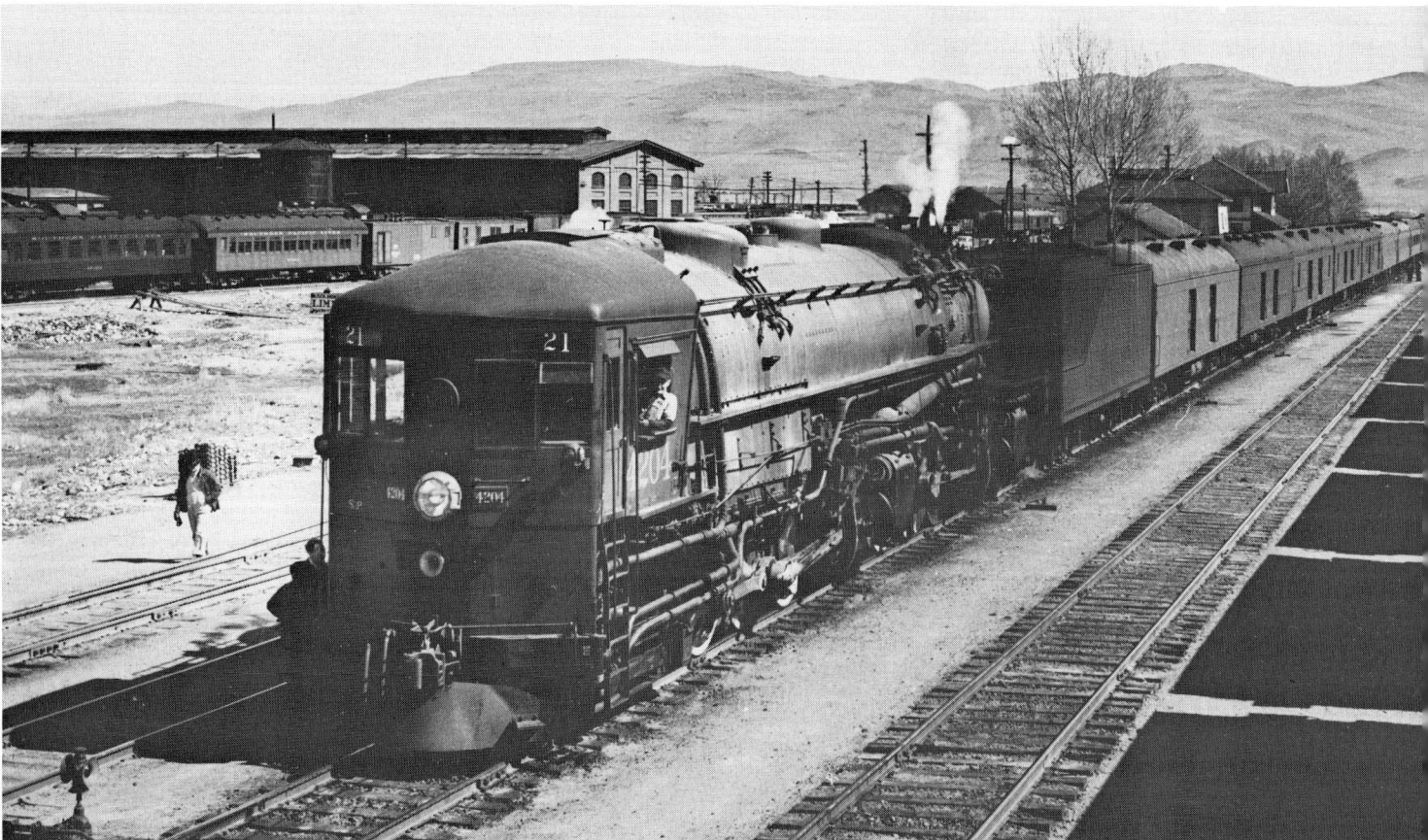

the men and cars were fished out satisfactorily. Chided about the rumored abandonment of the whole idea after these events, Harriman bristled and said, "We are going ahead with the cut-off, and successfully too. This talk of engineers being up [against it], as it were, and unable to find bottom in the Lake is all bosh."

And the project did move ahead, though not as fast as "The Little Giant" anticipated. By July 1903 the south nose of Promontory Point had been blasted away, and the east end was finished. Four hundred Greek laborers were discharged; they were among the lucky ones as events unfolded. On July 22, in spite of a five-mile gap, the governors of Utah and New York made a "first crossing" utilizing a boat to bridge the gap between the ends. Three months later the last pile was pounded; on November 13 the rails were physically joined; and on November 26, 1903, the official "last spike" celebration was held. A work train crossed the entire distance three days later.

An air brake failure was blamed for the head-on crash between two trains at Jackson, 13 miles east of Lucin, Utah, on February 14, 1904. The force of the collision exploded a carload of dynamite which went up with a blast that shook Terrace, 15 miles away, with the force of an earthquake. The two locomotives were thrown incredible distances; the station building was blown to splinters; and the ground was torn up for a distance of 1,000 feet to a depth of 30 feet. Seeing a great white cloud arise, a telegrapher immediately wired Ogden for a relief train without waiting to ascertain the casualties. The death toll came to 29, most of them the unfortunate Greek laborers who were living in outfit cars on a siding.

The Lucin Cut-Off was opened for freight service service March 8, 1904; passenger trains continued using the old main line via Kelton until September 18. A new advertising slogan was born: "Go to Sea by Rail," but sometimes the water became a bit rough. During the heavy storms of March, 1907, high seas short circuited the block signals. In some quarters there was a fear that the trestle might be washed out. On Saturday, August 17, 1907, Train No. 5 was caught on the Cut-Off during a raging storm. The roadbed was under water for over a mile (in some places two feet deep) so the engi-

---

The setting is the same Sparks enginehouse and terminal as that of the 4204 (*page opposite*); the locomotive numbers are but two digits apart; and both engines are of cab-forward design; but there the similarity ends. Locomotive 4206 (*below*) is of the original Class MM-2, 2-6-6-2, cab-forward, compound articulated design, one of a series of 12 (Nos. 4200-4211) which were built by Baldwin in 1911. Subsequently these locomotives were rebuilt to Class AM-2, 4-6-6-2, cab-forward, simple articulateds and renumbered in the 3900 series (Nos. 3900-3911). Note the early cylindrical tender design which was later superseded by rectangular tenders of greater capacity. (*Stanley Palmer Photo.*)

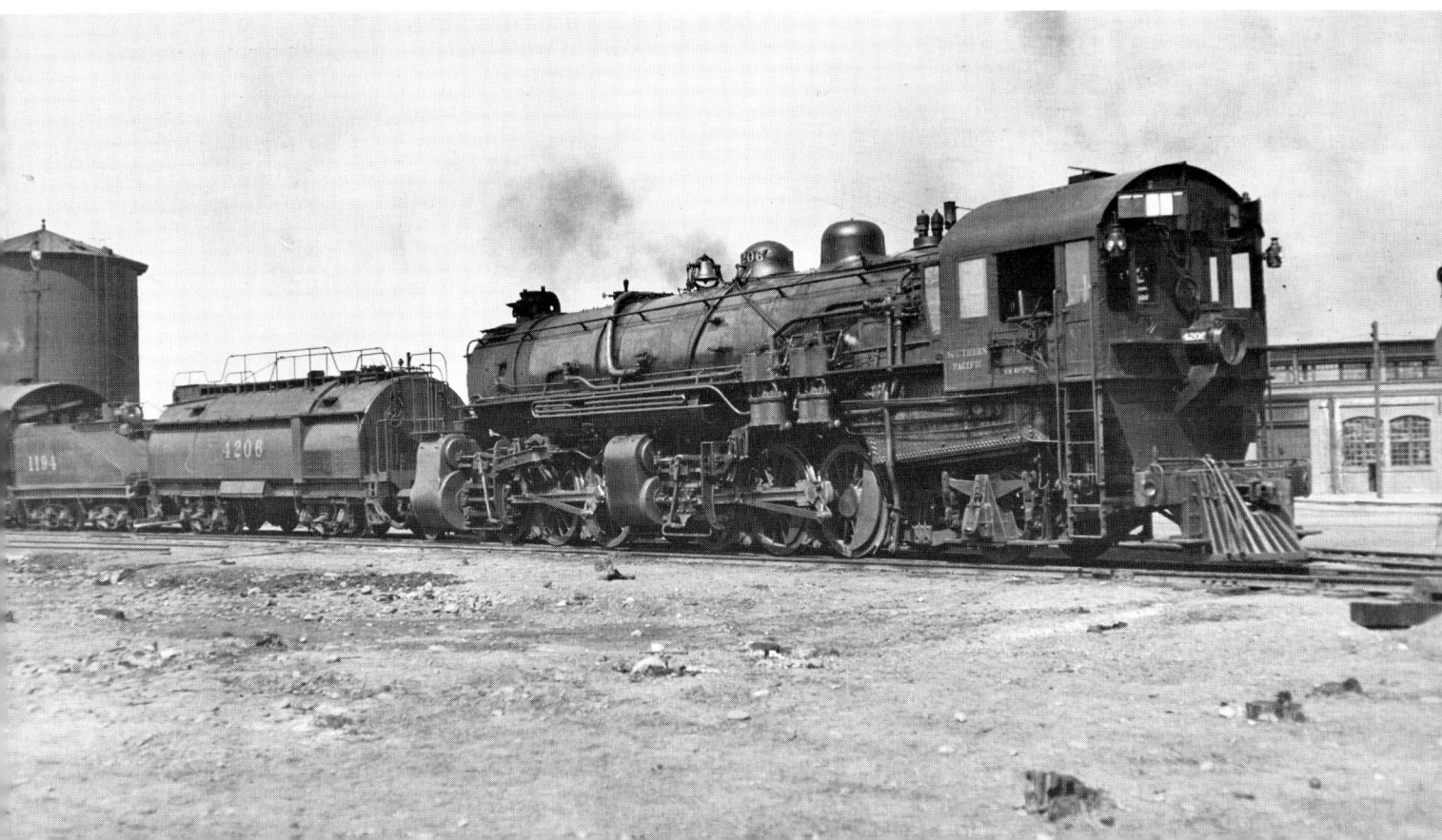

neer decided to back out. The rear brakeman certainly earned his wages for that day as he walked back in water up to his knees to flag possible approaching trains. Passengers became excited as water splashed against the windows of the cars. Women had white faces. Some passengers, particularly the foreign element in the smoker, turned panicky and tried to get out. Three women in the last Pullman fainted. Finally arriving at a safe station, many passengers went forward to thank the engineer and shake his hand. The delay lasted 36 hours.

In 1903 the Truckee-Carson irrigation project was well under way. The first Federal project of its kind in the country, it extended from a point near Wadsworth (on the Truckee River) 31 miles to the Carson Sink, northeast of Fallon. Warren & Co. had the contract for the first 18 miles and Stone Bros., contractors, the balance.

With all of the men brought into the country to work on the realignment of the railroad plus those required for the canal construction, many thugs came along in the crowd. One gang was arrested in 1903 after robbing freight cars, passenger trains and even hoboes themselves, but other thugs followed in their footsteps. One railway passenger suffered the indignity of having his pants removed from his berth while the train was on a siding at Ryndon (near Elko). The only solution to his problem was to remain in bed until another pair could be found for him at Ogden.

If the canal workers were not blowing their funds at Wadsworth, then Derby and Hazen were ready to relieve them of their pay checks. The Derby dives became infamous; after a good night on the town, bodies might be found in the Truckee River the next morning. Along with those of Camp 6 and Hazen, some 50 saloons could be tallied for relief for the weary canal men. At Hazen, things became so rough a vigilante committee was under consideration.

A notorious Derby thug, "Red" Wood, became the first occupant of the new graveyard at Hazen. He had run the Monte Carlo saloon at Derby, but when his partner perished under suspicious circumstances, "Red" was asked to leave town. He tried Fallon, but only lasted a short while before shifting over to Hazen in February, 1905. Unable to restrain his old habits, he soon became involved in a hold-up of two men outside the railroad station. A few shots from the alert station agent stopped Wood, and he was caught and locked up in jail.

No special attention was considered necessary, but in the wee hours of the following morning some callers arrived at the jail and, finding the door barred, broke it down. At daylight Mr. Wood was discovered swinging from a convenient telephone pole. Nobody knew who was in the mob; nobody really cared; for the job was done. Legislation was finally passed limiting saloons in the vicinity of construction jobs. Subsequently a fire leveled most of Hazen, rather obviating the problem for that municipality.

Across Nevada, railroad changes and improvements continued unabated. The shortening of the line, following completion of the Lucin Cut-Off, resulted in a rearrangement of engine districts. Terrace, Utah, and Toano, Nevada, vanished. Banvard blossomed for a time as an engine terminal, but it was soon replaced by neighboring Montello. New roundhouses, in addition to the one at Sparks, were built at Imlay and Carlin, and they became engine terminals.

In 1905 Hazen assumed a more exalted status when it became the northern terminus of that portion of the former Carson & Colorado Railroad newly laid to standard gauge from Tonopah Jct. north to Churchill and Mound House (on the V&T). A 28-mile connection from Hazen south to old Fort Churchill was completed on September 1, 1905, and forced interchange with the V&T at Mound House and at Reno became a thing of the past.

In addition, a 15-mile branch was built eastward from Hazen to Fallon. First talked about in 1905, actual construction did not commence until May 1906. By the end of June, four miles of rail and eight miles of grading were completed. Then time dragged by. An inability to obtain rail was blamed on the aftermath of the San Francisco earthquake and fire with its reconstruction problems. In October the men left the job for a brief period when their pay checks were late. Fallon talked of a "last spike" celebration for Thanksgiving Day, but waiting for the last spike caused constant postponements of festivities, first to December 4, then to some time in the spring when better weather would prevail. The first train sneaked in quietly after noon on January 10, 1907, and the celebration was forgotten.

Three months later the SP was reported to have finished its survey for an extension of the line from Fallon to Wonder via Stillwater and Hercules. A bit of switch shanty gossip included a report that the necessary rail for the 42 miles of track was on its way from the East. No delivery was ever made, nor any construction recorded.

There were other projected routes in this same area. One was surveyed from Wabuska (on the C&C) southward to Yerington (one report contended trains would be running in 90 days), thence onward to Masonic, Aurora and Bodie, eventually to extend to a connection with the SP's Owens Valley line. A later projection (about 1912) envisioned a cut-off from Fallon northeasterly to Battle Mountain. As with so many surveys, a tightening of credit, a downward forecast in business, a poor report from a geologist, or even an executive whim would block actual construction.

Over in eastern Nevada, two short branches were actually constructed. The first ran southward from the old town of Tecoma to the copper mines at Tuttle, then being revived following the increase in copper prices which prevailed during the first half of 1907. The 3.88-mile branch was opened September 6, 1907, and connected with the four-mile tramway of the Buel Copper Mining Co. which brought ore from its mine. The short line

Humboldt House at Humboldt Station (west of Imlay), was a most important meal stop for hungry passengers and water stop for trains in the arid desert country. Appetites were whetted (it was hoped) by this amusing advertisement *(right)* which was published in the perennial traveler's guide of the period, the *Railroad Gazetteer;* while *(below)* with train in photographer's selected position, is a rare 1871 portrait of the famous establishment. Nothing remains today of the former Humboldt Station. *(Top: Southern Pacific Collection; Bottom: Louis L. Stein, Jr. Collection.)*

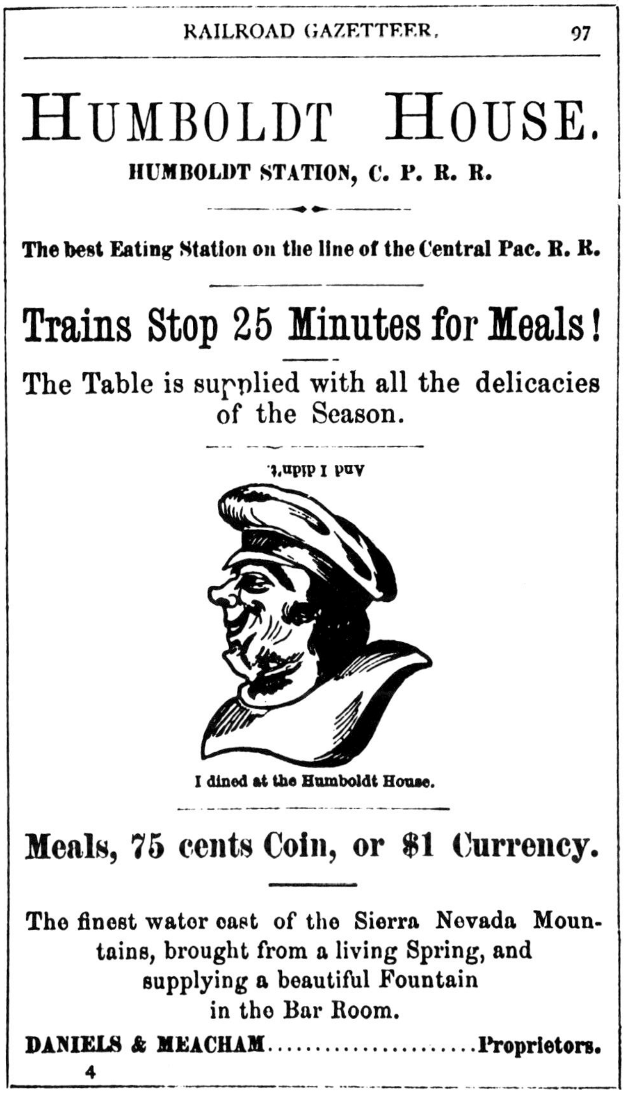

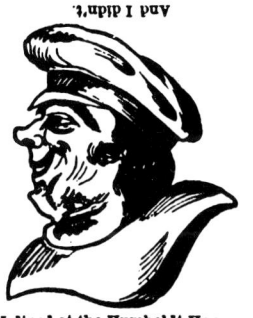

RAILROAD GAZETTEER. 97

HUMBOLDT HOUSE.

HUMBOLDT STATION, C. P. R. R.

The best Eating Station on the line of the Central Pac. R. R.

Trains Stop 25 Minutes for Meals!

The Table is supplied with all the delicacies of the Season.

I dined at the Humboldt House.

Meals, 75 cents Coin, or $1 Currency.

The finest water east of the Sierra Nevada Mountains, brought from a living Spring, and supplying a beautiful Fountain in the Bar Room.

DANIELS & MEACHAM......................Proprietors.

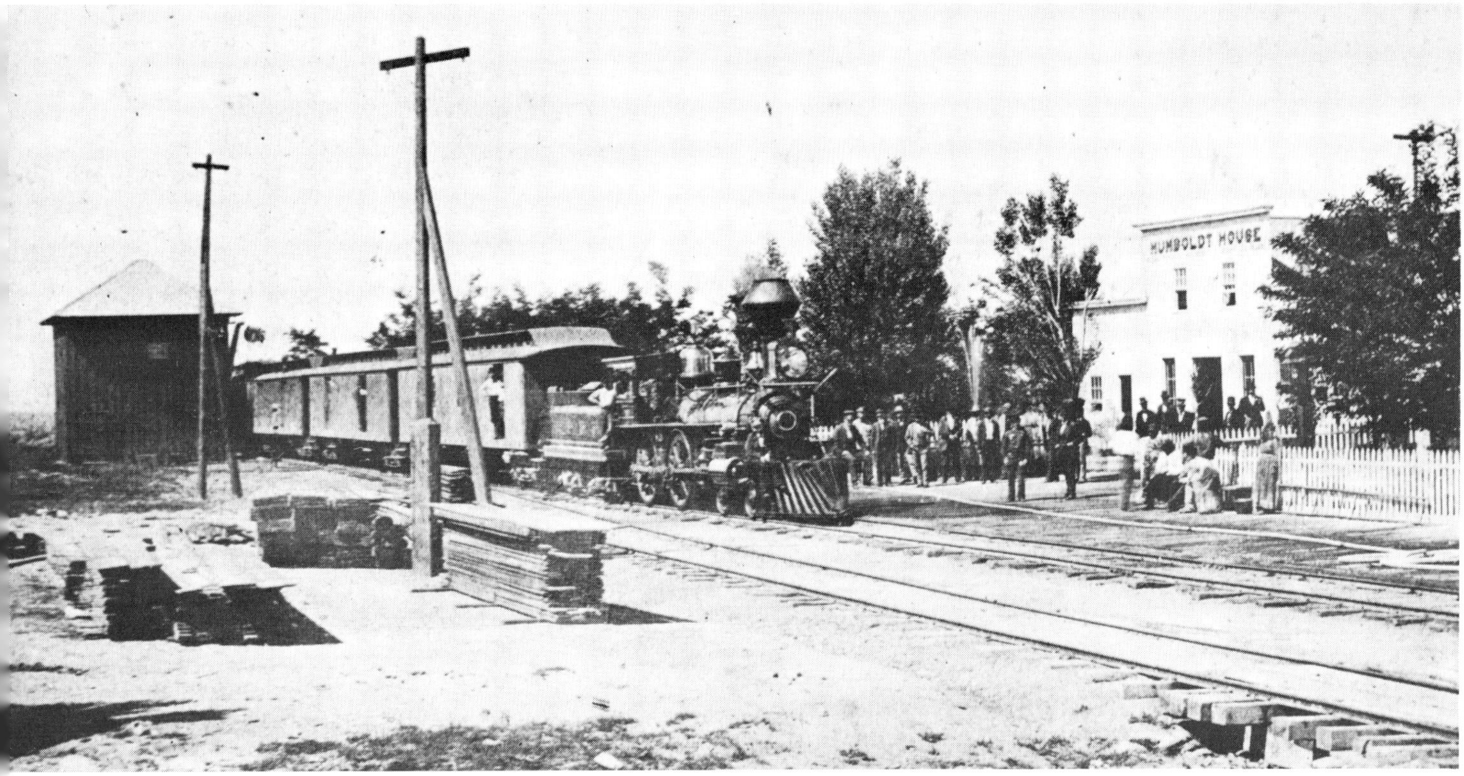

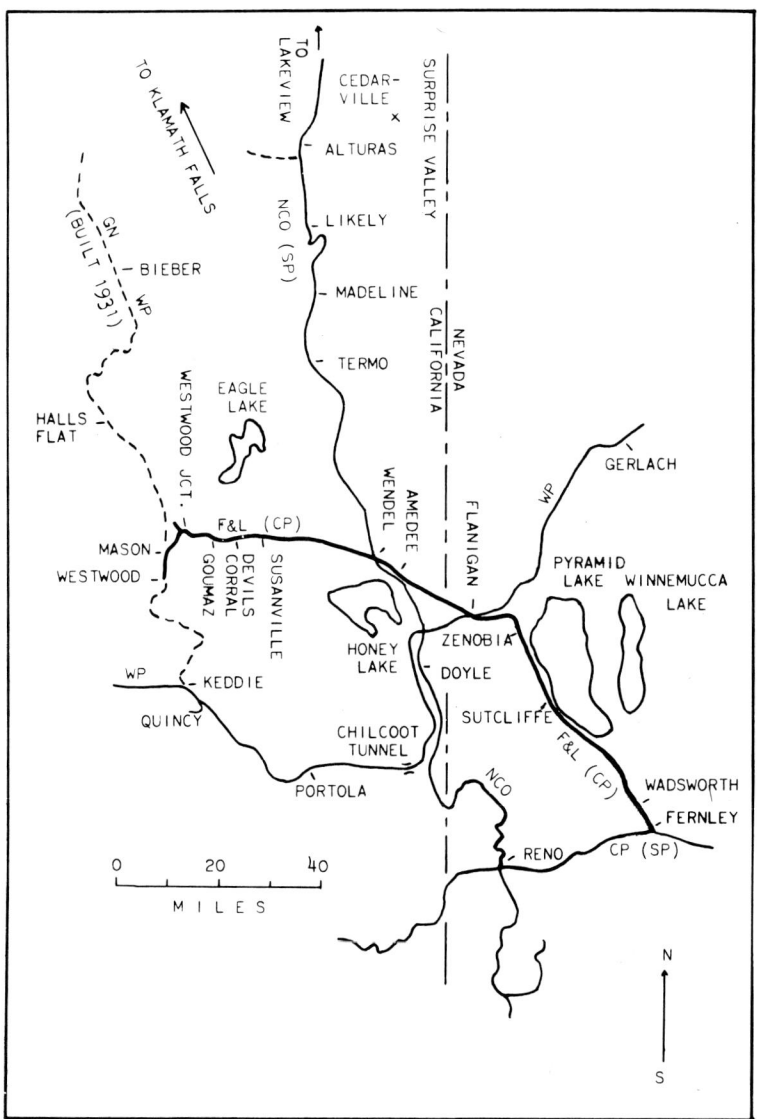

lasted for 33 years, finally being abandoned on May 1, 1940.

The second branch did not fare as well. Metropolis, to the north and slightly west of Wells, was to be made the center of a great irrigation project, and in May 1910 the Pacific Reclamation Company embarked on a colonization and reclamation program involving some 25,000 acres of desert. The Southern Pacific built a 7.89-mile line from Tulasco north to the budding Metropolis at a cost of $117,780. Work began July 10, and the job was finished December 8, 1911. The Reclamation Company planned to store and use water from three creeks in the area, but a 1912 lawsuit limited the water appropriation to but one creek. As a result, only 4,000 acres could be brought under irrigation, and subsequent droughts forced the 500 settlers eventually to wander elsewhere in search of a livelihood. The original daily mixed train on the branch gave way to a tri-weekly freight in September 1913, and this in turn was reduced to a weekly freight in January 1916. Trains were run intermittently when the I.C.C. authorized abandonment in August 1922, but the line was kept in operation for another three years before it was dismantled in August 1925.

For a number of years SP and UP surveyors had been planning a network of lines along the Pacific Coast in central and eastern Oregon, with extensions to be made southward into California and Nevada. One route was to begin at Klamath Falls, Oregon, head south past Halls Flat, California, to what was then called Walker Mill Jct. (now Westwood Jct.), then proceed eastward past Susanville to the west side of Pyramid Lake in Nevada, and thence southward again to join the main line of the Central Pacific at Fernley, 30 miles east of Reno.

But the SP and the UP were not the only railroads interested in this area. The Nevada-California-Oregon Railway had been pushing its narrow-gauge tracks northward from Reno into Oregon and was talking of going on north to the Columbia River. Gould was expected to run an important branch of his Western Pacific northward into the same area. Actually, in May 1912, WP engineers commenced surveying a route from the vicinity of Gerlach, Nevada, northwesterly to Cedarville, California, to tap the Surprise Valley farming area. A truck line was already in operation between these two points, with rates of 70¢ per cwt. from Gerlach northward and 35¢ per cwt. for traffic destined in the reverse direction to the railroad connection.

The big threat, however, was James J. Hill and his Great Northern Railway. Through a subsidiary, the Oregon Trunk Railway, a line had been built to Bend, Oregon, 152 miles south of the Columbia River, late in 1911. Harriman had passed away two years before, but the Union Pacific was not without strong-willed men ready to contest this encroachment. Following a physical encounter in the narrow confines of the Deschutes River Canyon (south of the Columbia) involving a matter of parallel lines, the situation was held in check by an arrangement for joint operation of part of the trackage. In spite of this Hill was still subjected to careful scrutiny, and when his son, Louis, who succeeded to the presidency of the GN, was reported to have acquired substantial Madeline Plains (Lassen County) acreage from J. Noble Jones, a local promoter, early in 1912, support was given to the expectation that the GN was ready to move southward. This it ultimately did, via Klamath Falls and Bieber to join the Western Pacific in 1931.

When T. B. Walker acquired large tracts of timber in Lassen County, west of Susanville, he prepared to move his Red River Lumber Company from cut-over lands in Minnesota to the new location which was to be called Westwood. The SP stood to pick up their entire business by following the route of its original survey, and this it proceeded to do through organization of the Fernley & Lassen Railway to construct the necessary line of road. While contracts for the construction of the southerly portion of the line from Fernley to Susanville and Westwood were being awarded, a singular event in the last few hours of May 28, 1912, must have caused some uneasiness in the minds of SP officials. For that was the day the Western Pacific's Chilcoot Tunnel caught fire, and Susanville's *Lassen Advocate,* with almost a smug attitude, blatantly pointed out that this could have been avoided had the WP built its line from Keddie to the Nevada boundary via Susanville rather than tunneling under Beckwourth Pass. For many months the WP used a temporary shoo-fly track over the summit of the range as repairs could not be made due to the accumulated heat and gases. With the long blockade, it appeared for a time that the WP might see things clearly and build a line via Susanville, which would have divided the lumber traffic of the Red River Lumber Company, but the WP failed to move.

In June 1912 work began on the SP line on a grand scale with thousands of men and horses stretched over the 106 miles between Fernley and Susanville. The Utah Construction Company was the principal contractor. Along the shores of Pyramid Lake in Nevada where considerable rock cutting was necessary, 15 grading camps were established. Another hundred men were put to work at the foot of Weatherlow Street on the southern edge of Susanville, California, where a long, wide cut had to be made to allow room for a passenger station and several side tracks.

Some tracklaying began almost immediately; in August about 25 miles were completed and construction trains were operating from Fernley as far as Dead Ox Canyon, a few miles north of Wadsworth. At the western end, the Red River Lumber Co. was building a modest sawmill on Robbers Creek where a small celebration attended the cutting of the first tree on September 10. In 1912-13 the Lumber Company removed a great amount of machinery from its old plant at Akeley, Minnesota, for transfer to the new site. Some of the supplies were trucked in from the WP at Keddie, while others were hauled in wagons by Caterpillar tractors from Doyle through Susanville. The sawmill, although at first considered to be temporary, actually became the nucleus of the Westwood plant, and sawing commenced in February 1913.

Not everything could be expected to run smoothly, and it did not. Two Italian workmen signaled the construction train one day to stop to take them into Wadsworth, but the engineer, pulling his train up a heavy grade, was disinclined to halt and went on. The two men shook their fists as he went on by and planned a little surprise for him on his return trip by placing two angle bars on the track. Fortunately for the crew and the 25 men aboard the returning train, the locomotive pilot knocked the bars off the track and no damage was done except to the liberty of the two workmen who were given a forced rest in jail. Assigned to separate cells, each protested his own innocence, naming the other as the responsible party.

At the end of February 1913, the tracks had crossed those of the Western Pacific at a place that became known as Flanigan and were approaching Amedee. Encouraged by the progress, the Lassen Development League started making plans for a gala Railroad Day which never materialized. By April 25 the tracks had been extended across the slough at the Winchester place (where yards were later established), about a mile east of Susanville, and arrived at the big cut on the southern edge of town a day later. The SP agent was busy soliciting business, and the first freight arrived on May 7, 1913. Shipments included a large order for the Hallowell Hardware Co. Passengers were handled on the trains, although service was irregular for several months. Many people appeared to prefer the new auto stage line to Doyle where they could connect with the WP for San Francisco.

Work was rushed on the remaining 29 miles to Westwood in an effort to have the line in service by the end of the year before the winter storms set in. T. B. Walker, described as having the appearance of a country preacher, was spending considerable time in the SP engineering offices "expediting" the work. The first 14 miles along the Susan River Canyon to Hog Flat required difficult construction. After Hog Flat, the railroad continued to climb to the summit at Westwood Jct. (el. 5,520 feet), then turned south around Pegleg Mountain to Westwood, eleven miles away. Two tunnels, a change in

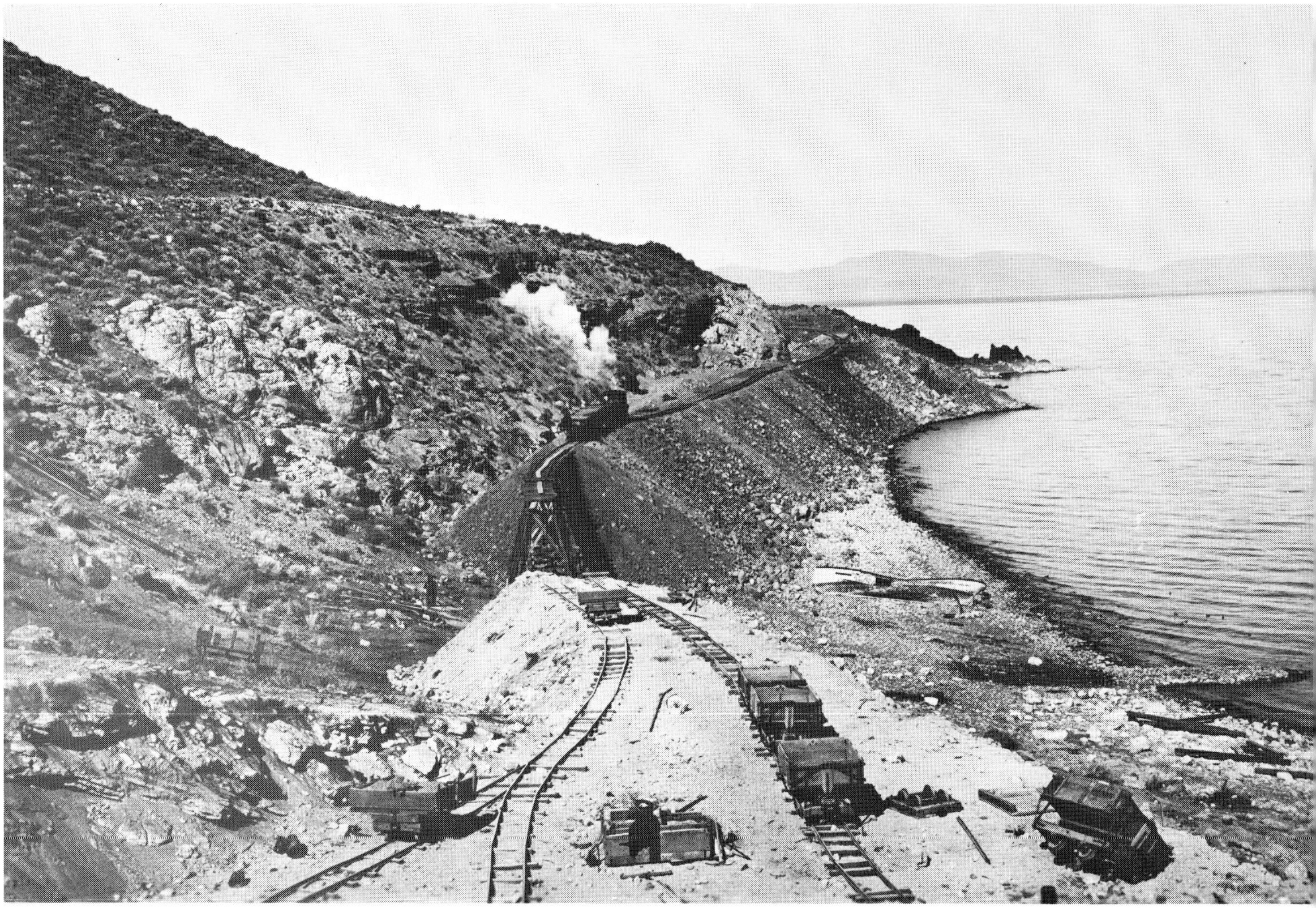

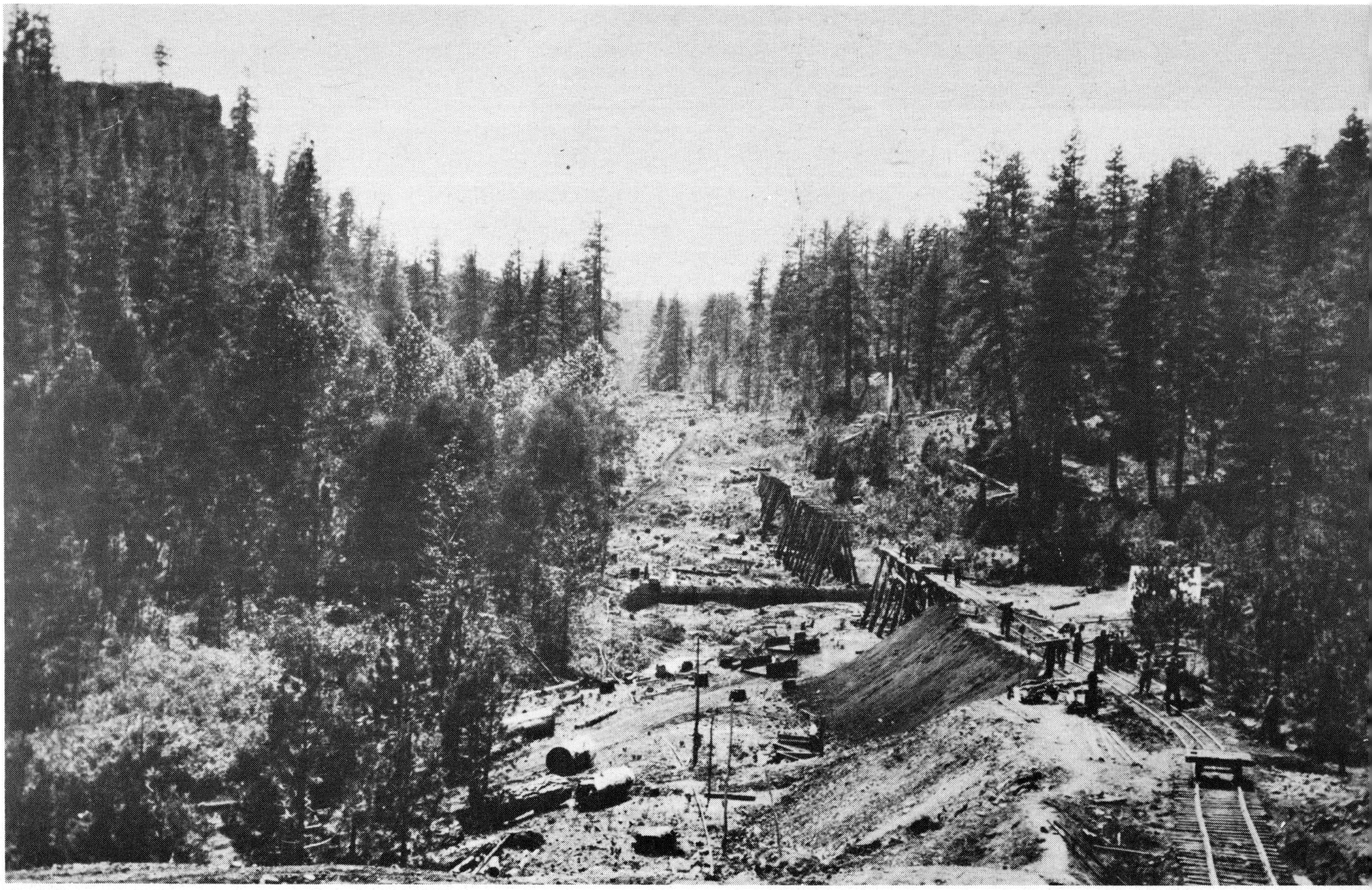

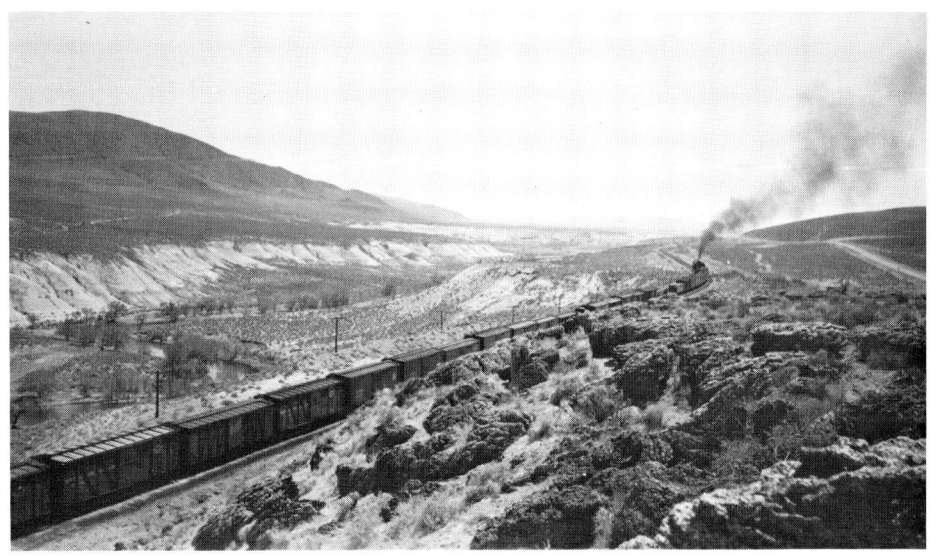

Construction of the Fernley & Lassen Railway to Susanville and Westwood was a difficult, two-year project undertaken in 1912-14. Along the shores of Pyramid Lake *(left, above)* heavy cuts and fills were required, earth moving being conducted in trainloads of tiny dump cars by dinky locomotives over roller coaster narrow-gauge tracks. Beyond Susanville near the west end of Goumaz Siding *(left, below)*, heavy timbering was also required. The uncompleted light trestlework was erected to support the work trains as they brought fill to cover the four-foot drainage arch in the bottom of the defile. In spectacular scenic style, the railroad climbed high along the bank of the Truckee River *(right, above)* or wound its way past such interesting rock formations as this tufa *(below)* near Pyramid Lake. *(Top Right: W. A. Pennington Photo; All Others: Southern Pacific.)*

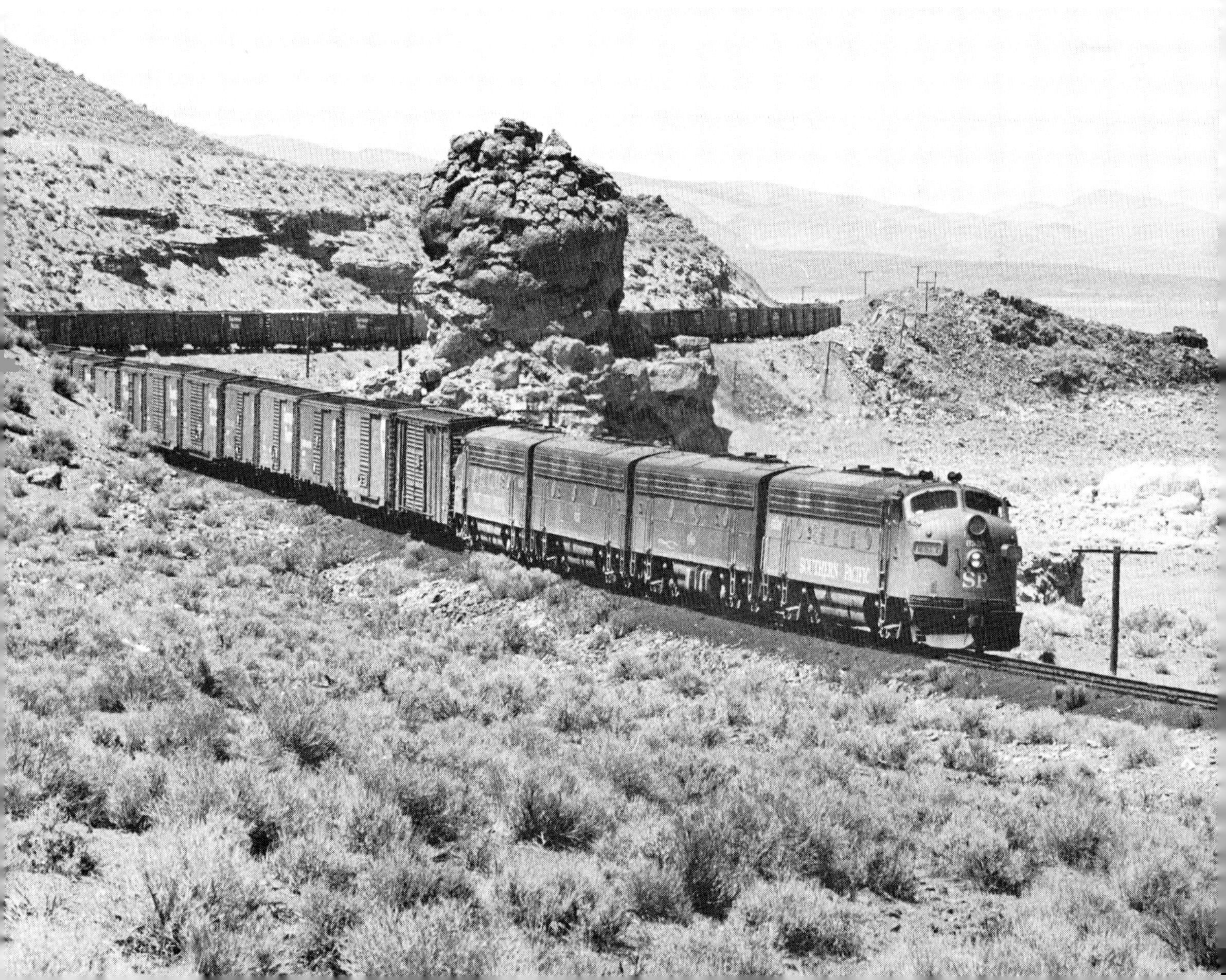

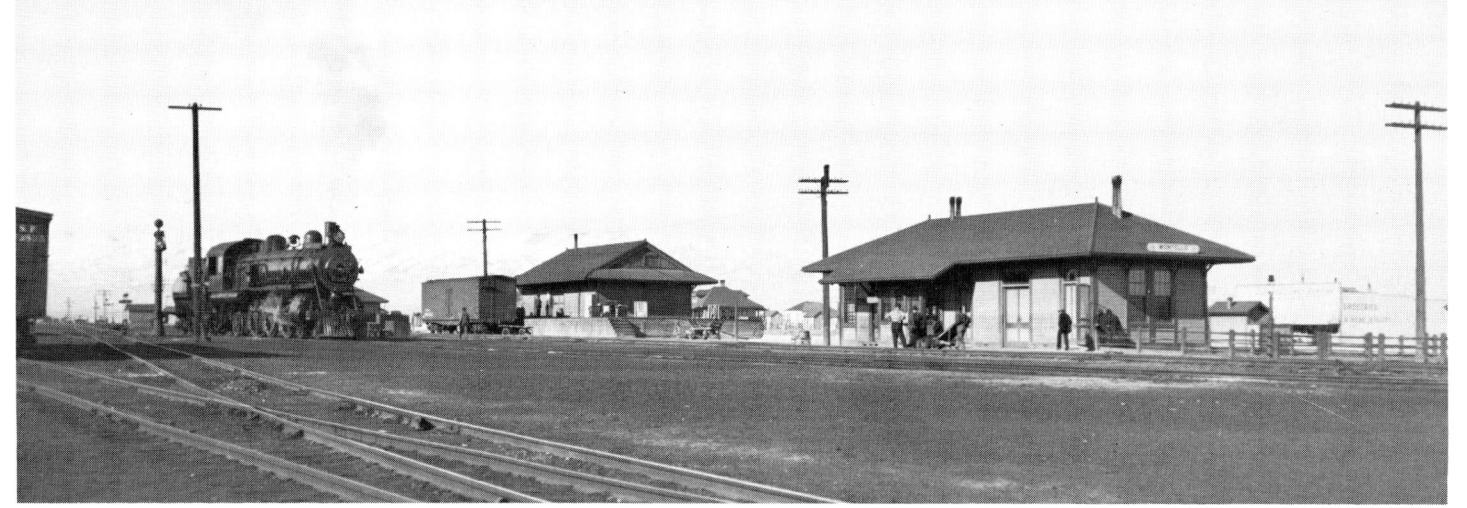

Montello was the easternmost division point in the state of Nevada and the last major terminal before crossing the Great Salt Lake to Ogden, Utah. The 1912-vintage pictures on this page graphically illustrate the station facilities on the main line *(above)*, the huge water tank and large coal bunker in left background *(middle)*, and the seven-stall enginehouse of rectangular rather than circular design *(bottom)*. The strange-looking engine at left was SP No. 2527, a 1907 Baldwin-built Consolidation (2-8-0) which was undergoing a series of steam input tests. The wooden housing on the pilot beam protected the engineers as they watched special gauges under varying operating conditions. *(Three Photos: Stanley Palmer.)*

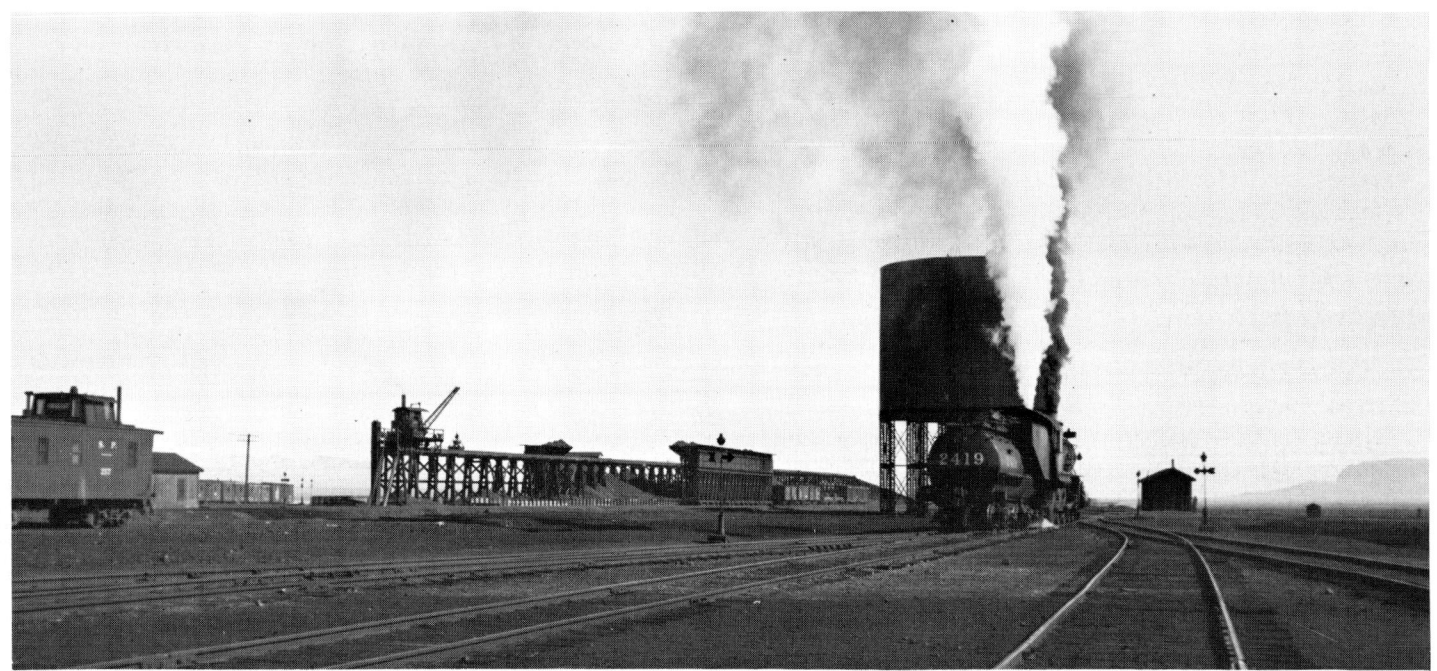

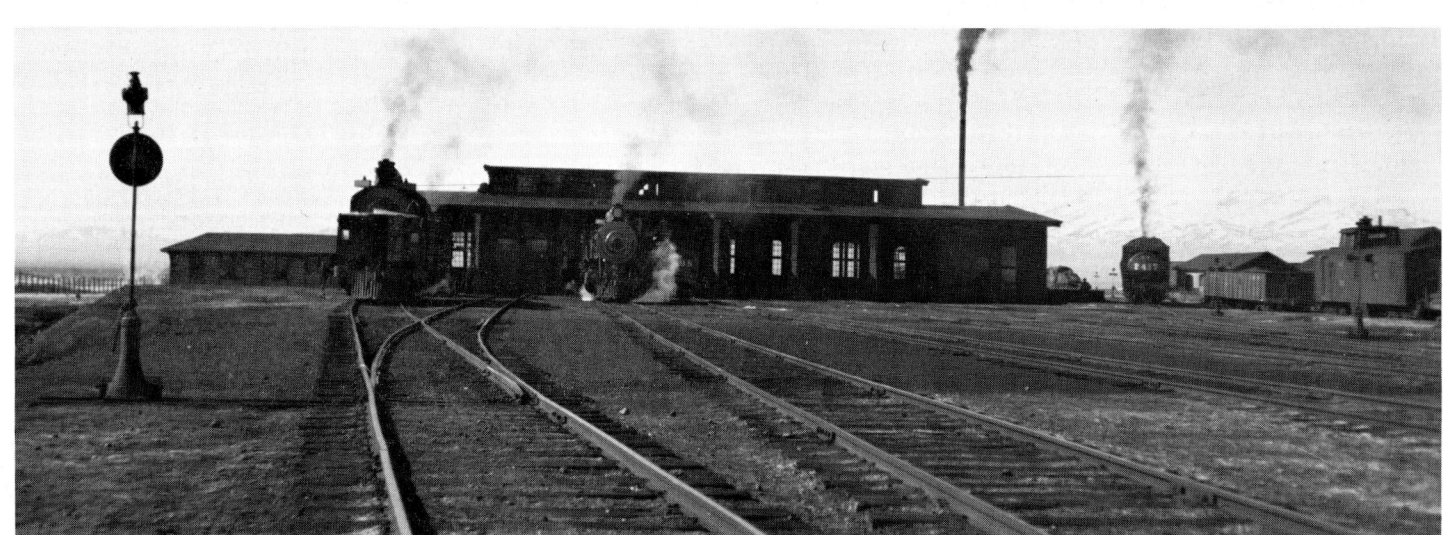

the river channel, and a 2.2 per cent grade were necessary between Susanville and the summit.

Construction crews passed through Susanville regularly to work in the canyon. Dinky construction engines were moved up on their own temporary tracks, two track sections at a time. Steam shovels were moved the same way. One pair of shovels became involved in a race with a $500 bet at stake. A thousand men were working on the seven miles between Susanville and Devil's Corral, while still others were working beyond. Heavy blasting was necessary. One blast, set off to remove a rocky ledge near a tunnel, not only moved the ledge but the entire construction camp as well. No reports of injuries were made, and the demolished camp was quickly restored.

William Sproule, president of the Southern Pacific, inspected the line at the end of August, along with a number of SP officials. An informal luncheon with the local people was held in Susanville which was disappointing to reporters, for the SP men said little, preferring to listen to the words of the natives.

September 1913 was an unfortunate month. One engineer was killed when his dinky tipped over, and a tunnel cave-in claimed the life of another man. By early October the grade was substantially completed, and track laying to Devil's Corral began. At the other end of the line, the new track from Fernley to Susanville was being ballasted in anticipation of regular passenger train service.

The first excursion on the new railroad was held in October, when a hundred Susanville people traveled east for a day's outing at Pyramid Lake. Tri-weekly Pullman service from Susanville to San Francisco was inaugurated the same month. Later, daily service to Westwood was established, following completion of the line, and for many years a standard sleeper left Oakland Pier in the Tonopah Express bound for Westwood. The depression of the 1930's forced curtailment of this service, including that of the Tonopah sleeper as well.

By Christmas, trains were operating to Devil's Corral, but frozen ground and snow — two feet in Susanville and four feet in Westwood — seriously hampered further work. More bad storms came in January 1914. Then there was an unseasonal rain. Slides trapped two construction engines. One engineer saw the whole hillside — trees and all — moving toward the track. He stopped, reversed his locomotive, and although the slide still hit the engine it only removed the pilot. However, another slide came down behind the equipment, effectively landlocking the little locomotive and its crew.

In spite of the storms, the rails reached Westwood during the latter part of February 1914. The first wreck occurred in March at Zenoiba, Nevada, when heavy rains soaked the new roadbed, making it unstable. The victim was a cattle train, and nearly a hundred head of cattle escaped to roam the sage brush. A dozen cowboys were recruited to round up the strays. Ballasting, grading and other finishing touches were applied to the line during the summer of 1914, and on October 1 official recognition was accorded its completion.

Four lumber companies built railroads into the woods from points along the Fernley & Lassen in succeeding years. The Red River Lumber Co. was the major operator with some 50 miles of railroad, of which a portion was electrified.

During all these years of construction and improvement (1901-1914), the Union Pacific continued its attempts to strengthen its financial control over the Southern Pacific. Additional purchases of stock were added to the original Huntington block until UP ownership represented 46% of the total shares outstanding. In 1908 legal proceedings were instituted under the Sherman Anti-Trust Act to separate the UP and the SP. The efforts culminated in the U. S. Supreme Court decision of December 2, 1912, wherein the UP was directed to divest itself of its holdings of SP stock.

Still the UP did not give up fighting. In February 1914 another anti-trust suit was instituted, this time to split the CP from the balance of the SP System. The events of the next nine years would fill many pages of interesting legal history. Ultimately the Supreme Court ordered the separation, but the I.C.C. found that SP control of the CP was in the public interest, and the case was closed in August 1923.

During this latter period of litigation (1914-23), extensions and other major improvements were sharply curtailed. Double tracking, which had been started following San Francisco's earthquake and fire of 1906 with its ensuing serious congestion, was halted with only 197 miles completed. Plans for a 28,000-foot tunnel under the Sierras (discussed as early as 1874) together with a program for electrification of the line were completely discarded. A subsidiary company, formed to acquire the water rights for hydro-electric power generation, was discarded. Such improvements as were made after 1923 reflected considerably higher prices and interest rates than those prevailing in 1914, and were more modest in concept.

An additional 37 miles of double track were completed in the latter part of 1923 which, together with the paired track agreement (1924) with the Western Pacific for the lines along the Humboldt River in Nevada, brought the mileage of double track operated to a total of 500 miles. A second 10,230-foot tunnel under Donner Summit (one of the longest railroad tunnels in the U.S.), completed in 1925, added to the second track mileage, and by 1930 the SP's tally showed 570 miles of dual trackage.

June 14, 1936, was the date of the operation of the first streamliner over this route. It was also the first on the entire Southern Pacific System. Diesel powered, the "City of San Francisco" began operations with a single 11-car train, making five "sailings" a month on a 39¾-hour schedule from San Francisco to Chicago (passengers using the ferry to cross the bay from San Francisco to Oakland Pier). A modified streamliner, the "Forty-Niner," started alternate service the following July. Lightweight equipment, later obtained in sufficient quantities, permitted daily operation of these trains.

Although the fame of the "City" has spread far and wide, perhaps the one thing for which the SP is most famous in the eyes of the early twentieth century traveler is the cab-in-front steam locomotive. Following the arrival of the first heavy duty locomotives of the 4000 series (2-6-6-2's) in 1909, the enginemen were so bothered by smoke and gas in the long tunnels and snowsheds, the motive power department adopted an idea from the North Pacific Coast Railroad and placed the cabs on the front of the oil burning locomotives. After that initial experience, most of the articulated locomotives built for the SP had their cabs in front.

Tremendous tonnages developed over the "Overland Route," initially constructed as the Central Pacific nearly a century ago. Lumber from Oregon, copper and iron from Nevada, fresh fruits and vegetables from the San Joaquin and Salinas Valleys in California, and auto parts from Detroit, Michigan, are some of the thousands of different items carried over its rails. During 1943-46 and in 1959-60, Centralized Traffic Control was installed over those remaining portions of the line still single track in order to increase its capacity. Thousands of people have been carried every year. Soldiers, statesmen, politicians, theatrical personalities, miners, immigrants to the West—all have handed over their little pasteboard tickets to conductors to be punched and turned in to SP auditors. Each ticket holder, driven by ambition, despair, greed, or other emotion, brought with him another contribution to the total which now forms the character of the West.

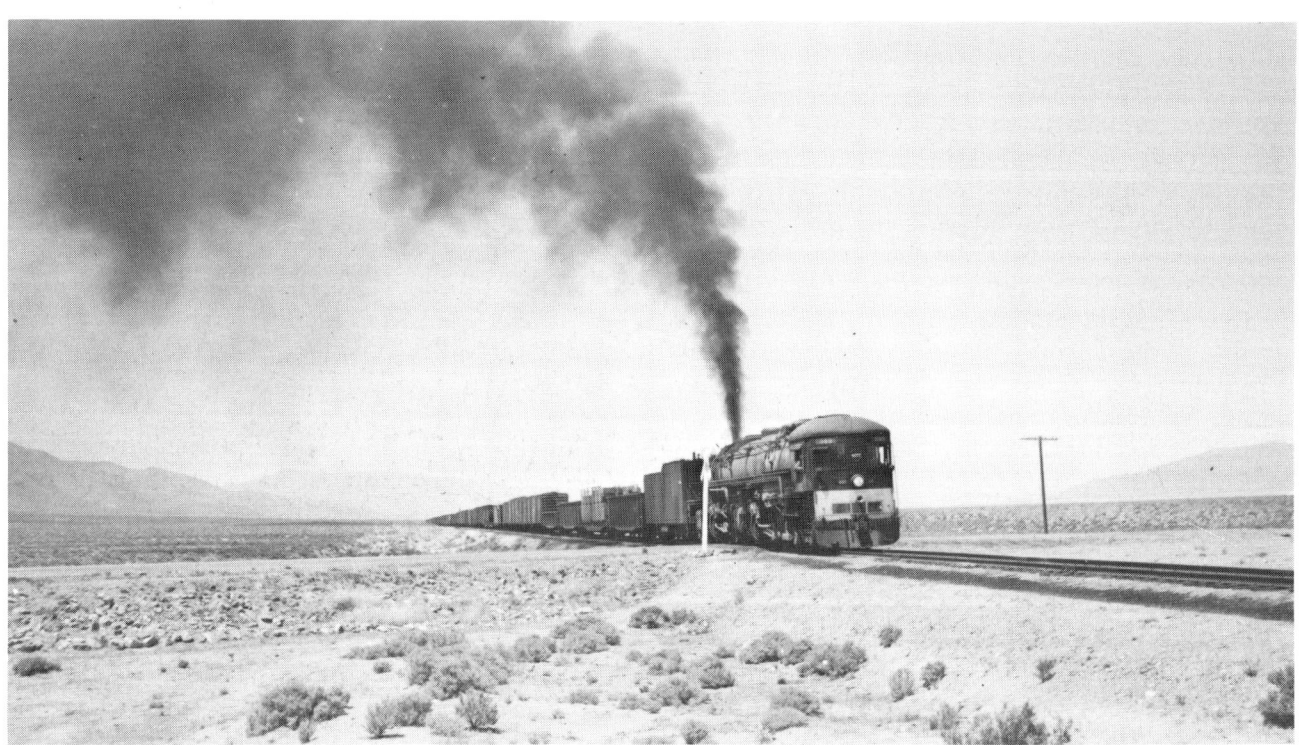

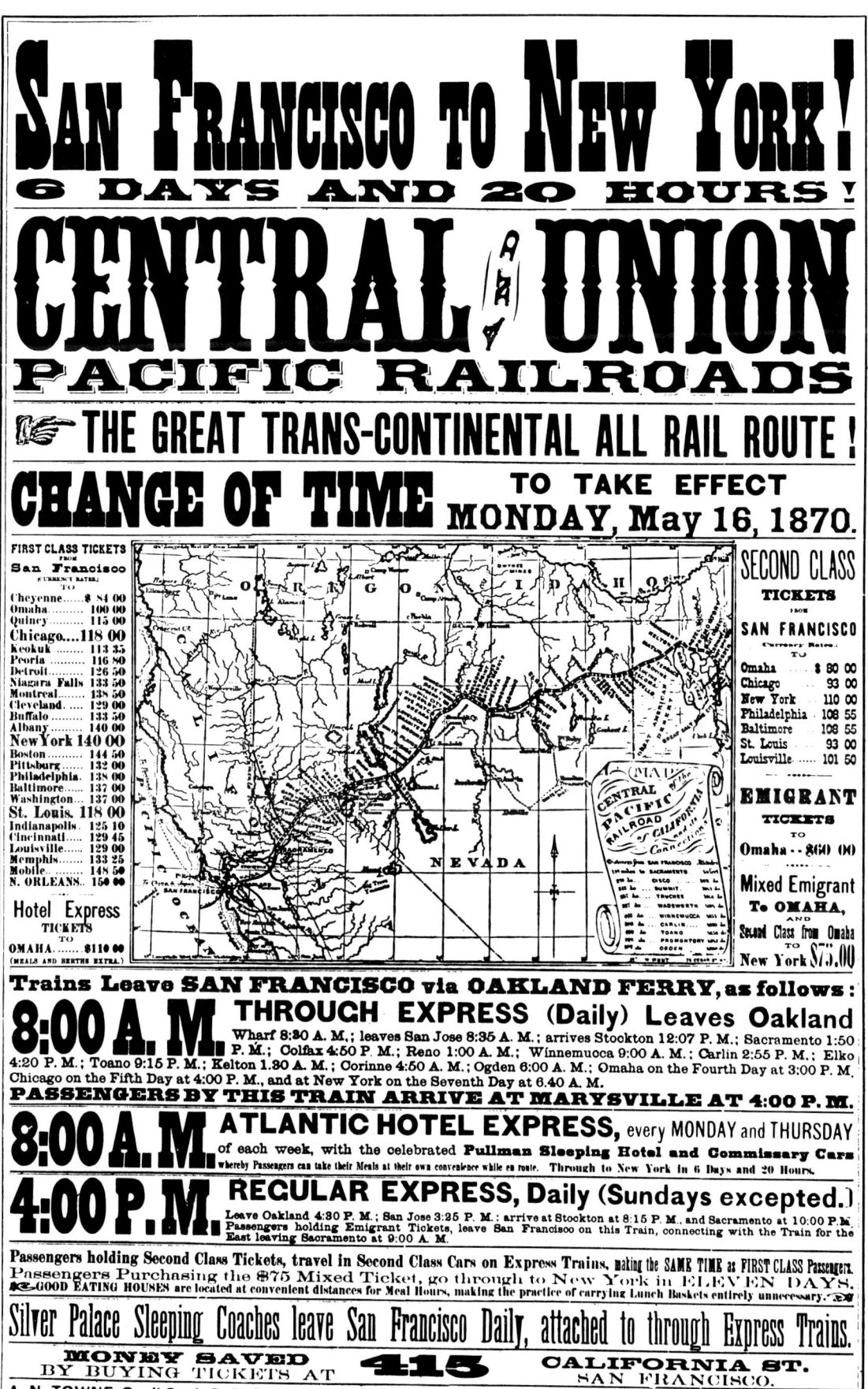

This poster, published a year after the Central Pacific was completed, shows some interesting fares for the "6 days and 20 hours" trip from San Francisco to New York. (*Society of California Pioneers.*)

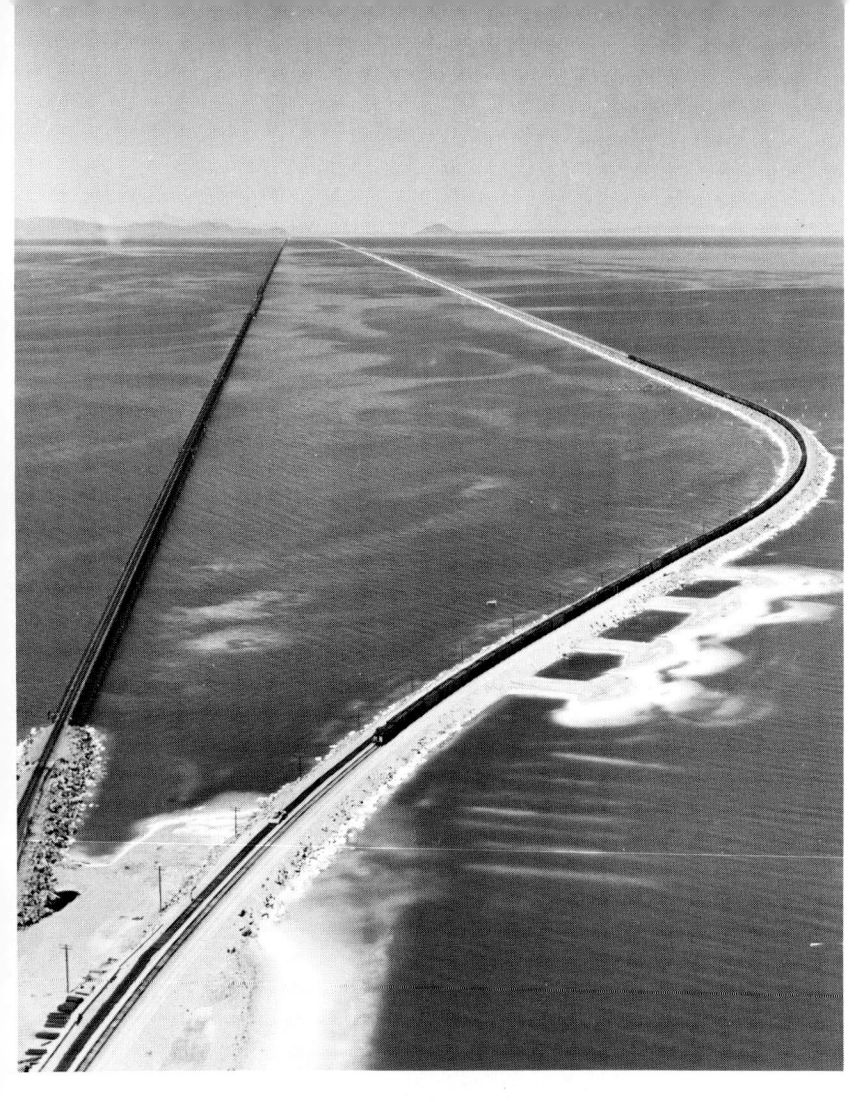

As far as eye can see *(left)* the Lucin Cut-Off stretches in an unbroken straight line across the 27½ miles of water of the Great Salt Lake in Utah. When the older wooden trestle (at left in photo) required extensive retimbering it was deemed better to build a new, 13-mile section of solid rock-based fill. Completed in July 1959, it has been used by trains such as the freight in the photo and resulted in faster schedules due to elimination of slow orders.

Construction of the original trestle and fill in 1903 was a work of great magnitude for its day. Temporary trestles were built on the lake bottom *(below)*, and trainloads of gravel in dump cars were backed cautiously out over the water before dumping the fill.

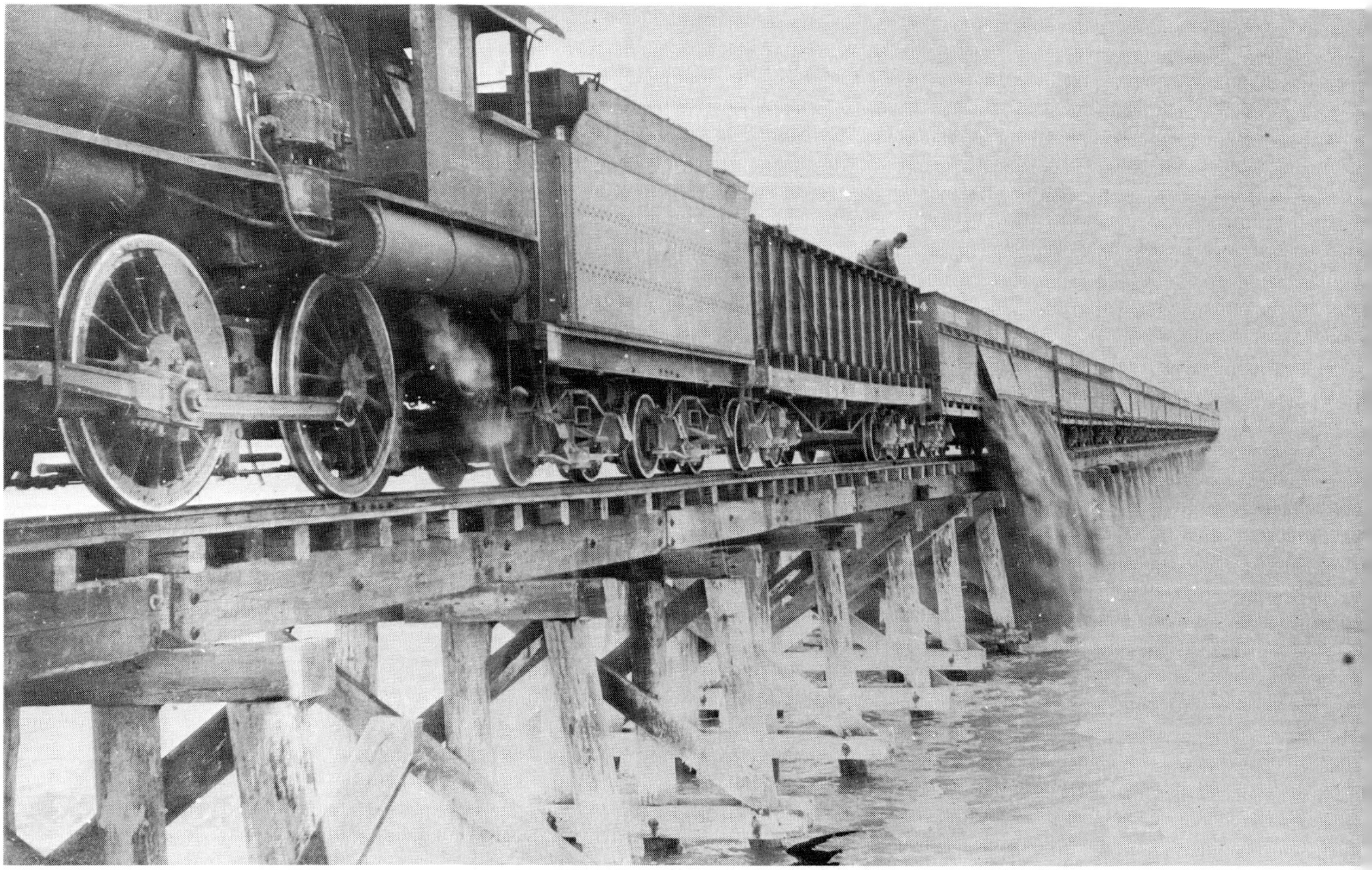

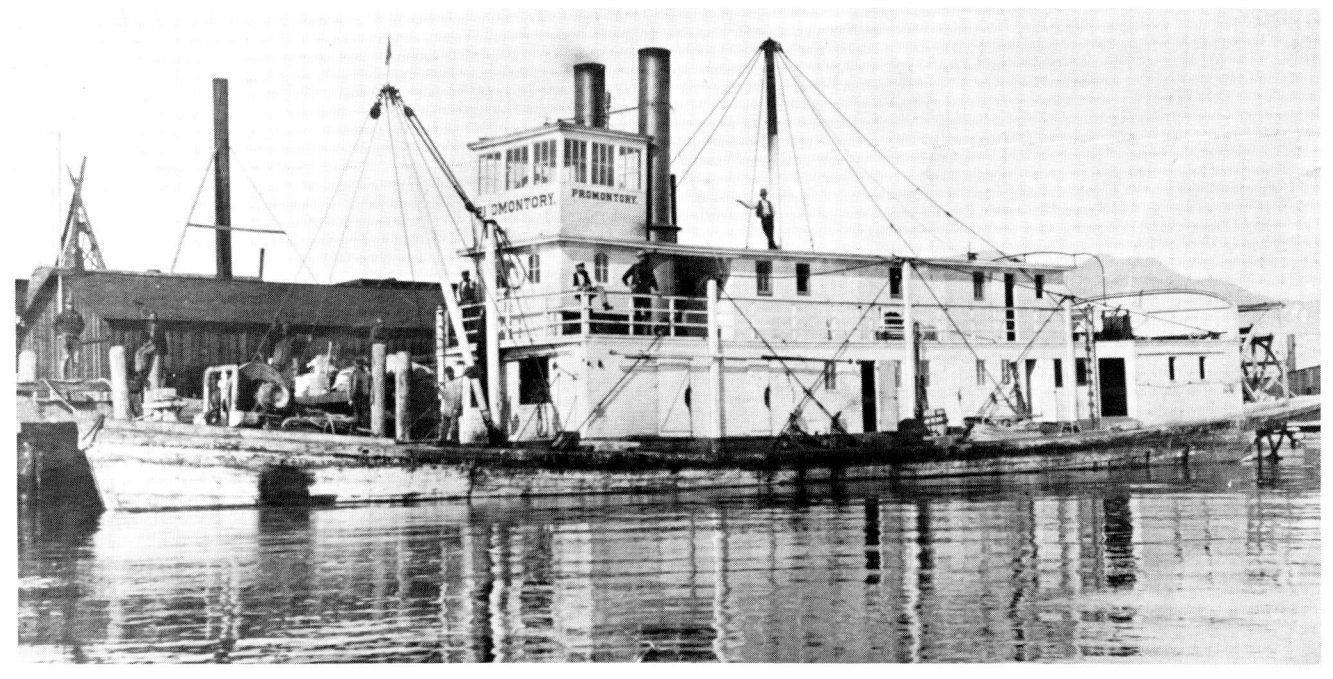

As work progressed farther over the lake, the *Promontory* (top), a double-stacked stern-wheeler was utilized to help carry supplies to the end-of-track. After the last pile was pounded, the rails were joined on November 13, 1903. On November 26, the official "last spike" celebration was held. *(All Photos: Southern Pacific.)*

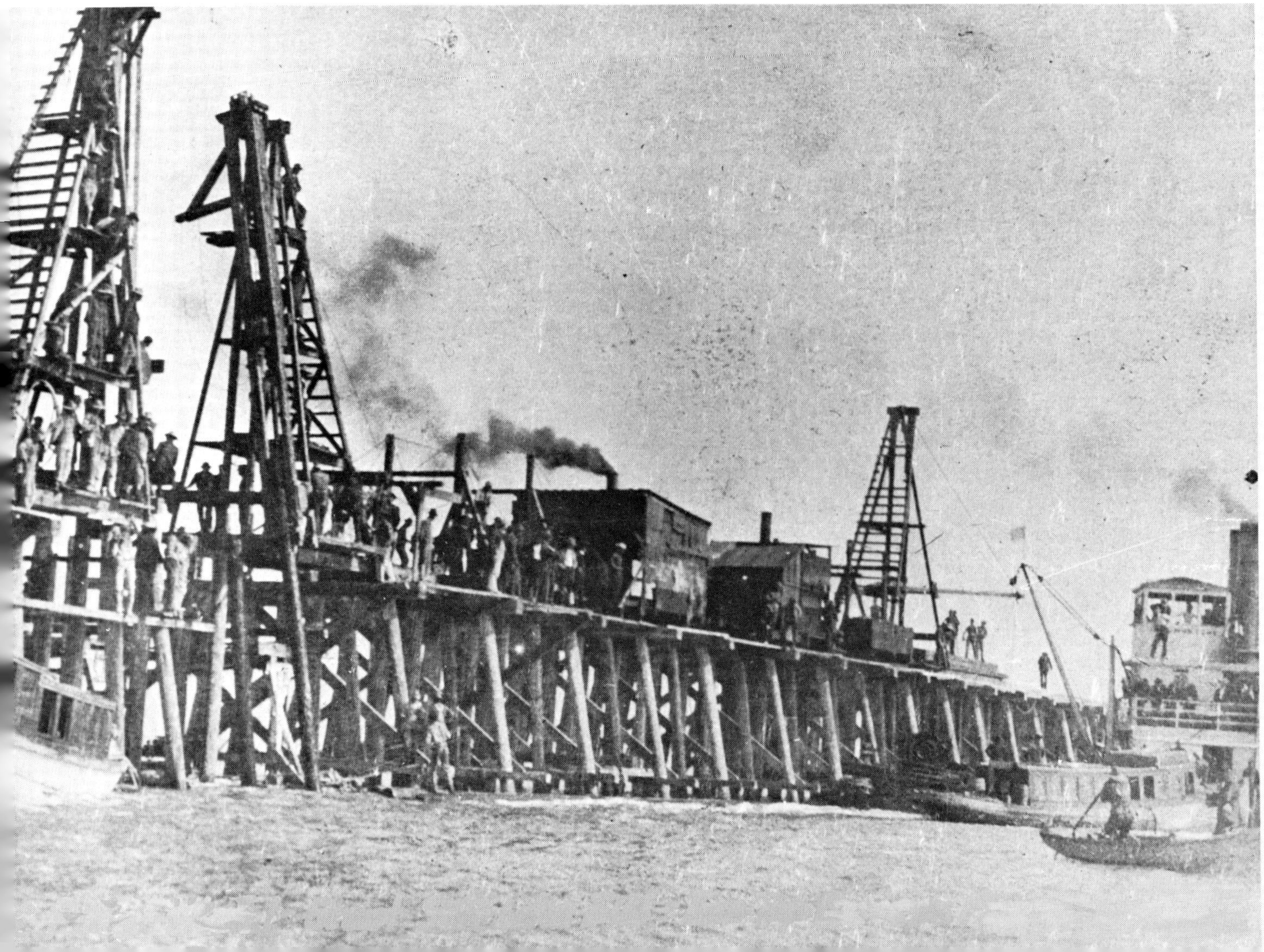

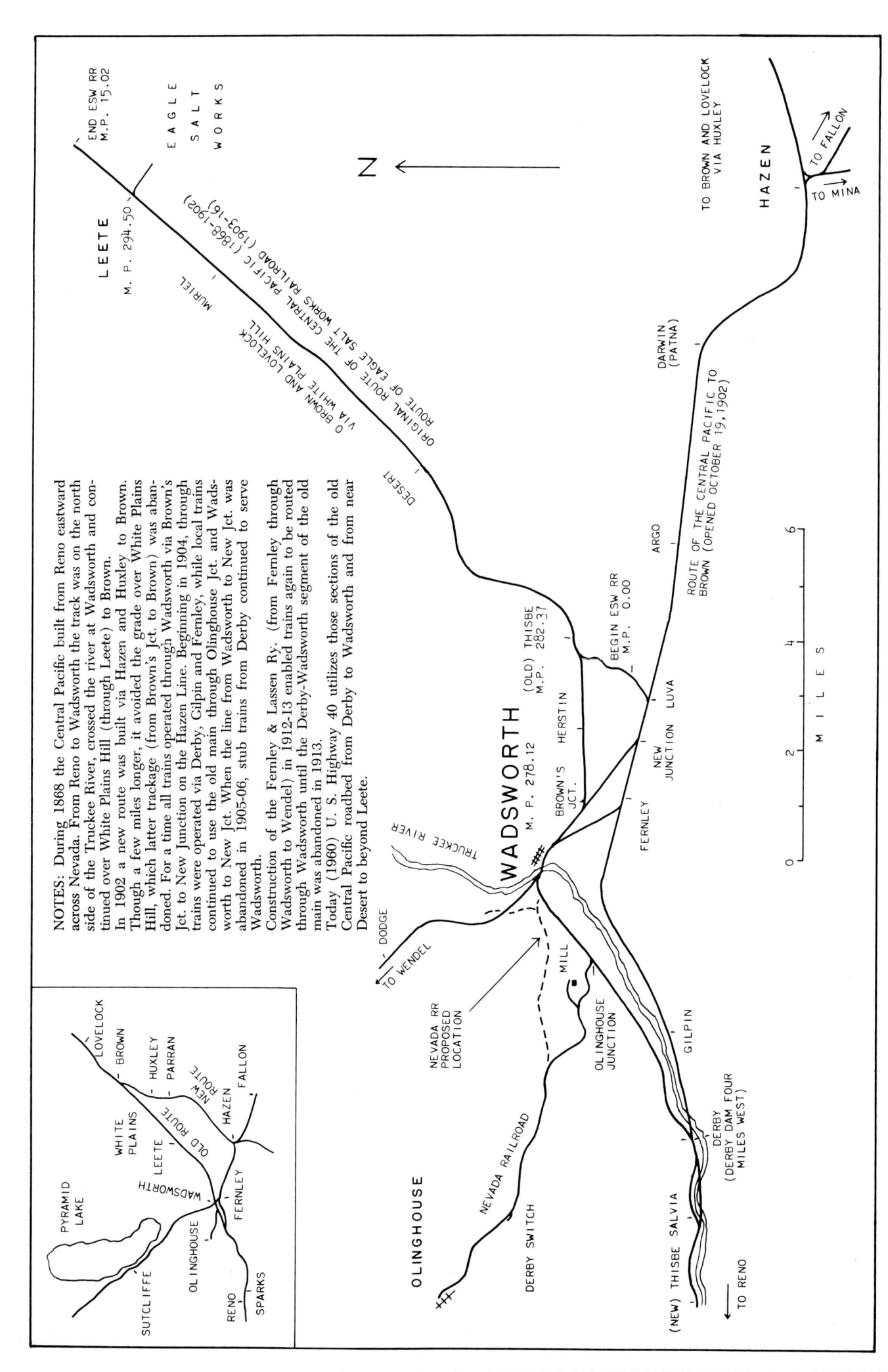

Eagle Salt Works Railroad Company

Conveniently located 15 miles east of Wadsworth, and only a short distance from the original main line of the Central Pacific Railroad up the Hot Springs grade, lay some salt beds, ignored and unnoticed. It took a man named B. F. Leete to recognize their possibilities and exploit their usefulness.

Leete had been engaged in railroad surveying in his home state of New York before coming west to join Theodore Judah on the preliminary surveys for the Central Pacific. Other engineering activities followed until, about the year 1869, he stumbled onto the hot springs and figured their potential in the light of the need for salt in the reduction of Comstock ores. Under the name of the Eagle Salt Works, Leete commenced operations in 1871 and supplied some 3,000 tons of salt to the silver mills that year at a considerable savings over the cost from previous sources.

Production was a simple process. Water from the springs, containing a 30% salt solution, was led to flow into a series of open air vats covering some seven acres of ground. In the desert sun, the water evaporated, leaving pure salt crystals which were gathered and shipped. During the extreme hot weather cycles, an acre of vats could produce approximately 10 tons of salt in one day.

With time the process was improved and production increased. The greatest period of activity occurred during the years 1879-1884 when some 334,000 tons were shipped and a moderate amount of table salt was also distributed. In the ensuing years production slackened until, in 1901-1903, when the CP relocated its main line from Wadsworth to Brown's via Hazen, Leete's Salt Works was left with the prospect of being without a railroad connection.

In January 1903 the Central Pacific removed the rails from its old main line. However, during the previous August, Leete had negotiated an agreement whereby every other tie would be left in place so that a light railway could be constructed. In February 1903 he organized the Eagle Salt Works Railroad Company to build a standard gauge railroad from Luva on the main line of the CP to (old) Thisbee on the former CP alignment, thence along the old main line right-of-way to the former Leete station, then onward a short distance to the Eagle Salt Works. A small steam locomotive (the "Three Spot," as it was familiarly called) was thoroughly overhauled in the CP shops and sent out near the end of March to assist in construction of the line.

The 14.5-mile railroad ultimately was completed in June 1903 and was hailed as a boon to the old Nezelda silver mine, six miles to the northwest of Leete, which was staging a revival at the time. History records that production from the Nezelda mine was disappointing, and despite the new railroad, even the salt operation had become quite inactive. The first shipment from the works was not made until three years later in March 1906. Over the next four years, daily shipments never exceeded two carloads (many times none), and up to September 1910 when the last car rolled over the line under Leete management, the cumulative total only amounted to a meager 171 cars.

In financing the construction of his railroad in 1903, Leete had borrowed $23,535 from the Southern Pacific, using as collateral the stock of the railroad plus that of his Eagle Salt Works Company which he had incorporated in 1896. The agreement of July 1, 1903, stipulated that annual payments of $4,000 were to be made, but Leete could never meet those requirements. Foreclosure action was finally filed in 1910, and the SP acquired the little road together with the salt works itself. No reports of operations (if any) during the next two years have been found, but those for the years ended June 30, 1913 and 1914 show an investment in the road of slightly over $30,000 while the revenues (all freight) were $602 and $1,509, respectively, with net losses after expenses of $4,877 and $2,430, respectively. Indicated total tonnage carried was a mere 583 tons and 1,032 tons, consisting of salt, a few cars of coal and a little hay.

The coal-fired steam locomotive (there is also a report of a small gasoline engine) hauled one car at a time and apparently operated approximately 70 days out of each year. Following a long period of inactivity, the railroad was finally abandoned in March 1916, and the rails were taken up the next month. Evaporation (of salt) had created a business; evaporation (of traffic) had brought it to a close.

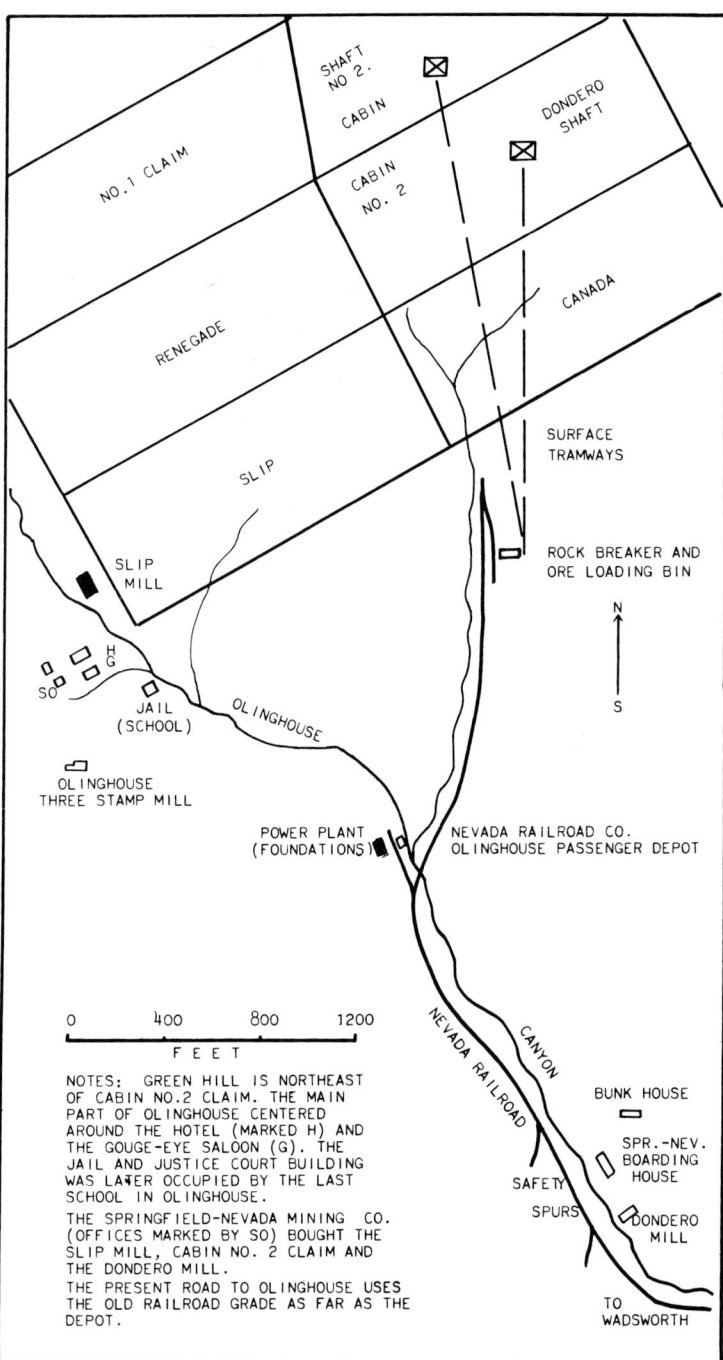

The Nevada Railroad Company

"Woman Wins Foreclosure Suit on Husband's Railroad Company." So screamed a headline in a 1908 edition of the *Goldfield Review*. Women were scarce in Nevada, and any news item involving the female sex always made interesting reading. Inevitably, other papers would pick up the story.

The situation was the direct result of a small railroad bringing disappointment to its investors when the mines, the chief source of revenue carloadings, failed. The big story, completely overlooked, lay in the swiftness with which it all happened — so fast that most people scarcely remember the line. Operated slightly more than a year, the Nevada Railroad survives with only a brief mention in Poor's Manual, plus a small scar on some maps.

Elias Olinghouse had been a teamster between Denver and Salt Lake City before the arrival of the Union Pacific Railroad disrupted his business. The desecration resulted in a shift farther west into Nevada where another teamster line from Wadsworth southeast to Belmont, near Tonopah, was established. When the inexorable advancement of age dictated that Olinghouse search for a less strenuous occupation, he finally settled down quietly in a canyon northeast of Wadsworth to raise sheep. Although not a miner, he witnessed the activities of strangers in the canyon as various placer deposits began to be worked, and his interest in mining commenced to grow, culminating in the purchase of several claims from a man named McClane and the erection, in 1903, of a small mill to process ores. Needing assistance as the operation grew, he called on his nephew, Henry I. Olinghouse, to join in management of the enterprise.

Two men, Brooks McClane and F. Plane, originally located the source of the placer deposits on Green Hill in the year 1897. As the word spread, interest developed in the area, and people began to pour in. Some men pedalled their way on bicycles from Reno, 30 miles to the west; others came from Wadsworth, 8 miles to the east. Many mining claims were recorded, and a two-stamp mill was brought to the new settlement, on the left fork of the canyon creek, originally named McClanesburg, or Ora Post Office, and subsequently retitled Olinghouse. Old W. Cattawalder "Bill" Williams was ever ready to claim fatherhood of the new town, for he was the one to locate Cabin No. 2, one of the main producers of the area, even though a later sale was made to a man named Dondero and a Reno restaurant keeper named Frankovitch. The pair of them, in turn, sold it to the Springfield-Nevada Mining Co.

Enthusiasm ran rampant. With partial ownership of a good claim, one man confided to friends that he fully expected to be a millionaire before the end of 1897. A 25-pound rock yielded $800 in gold,

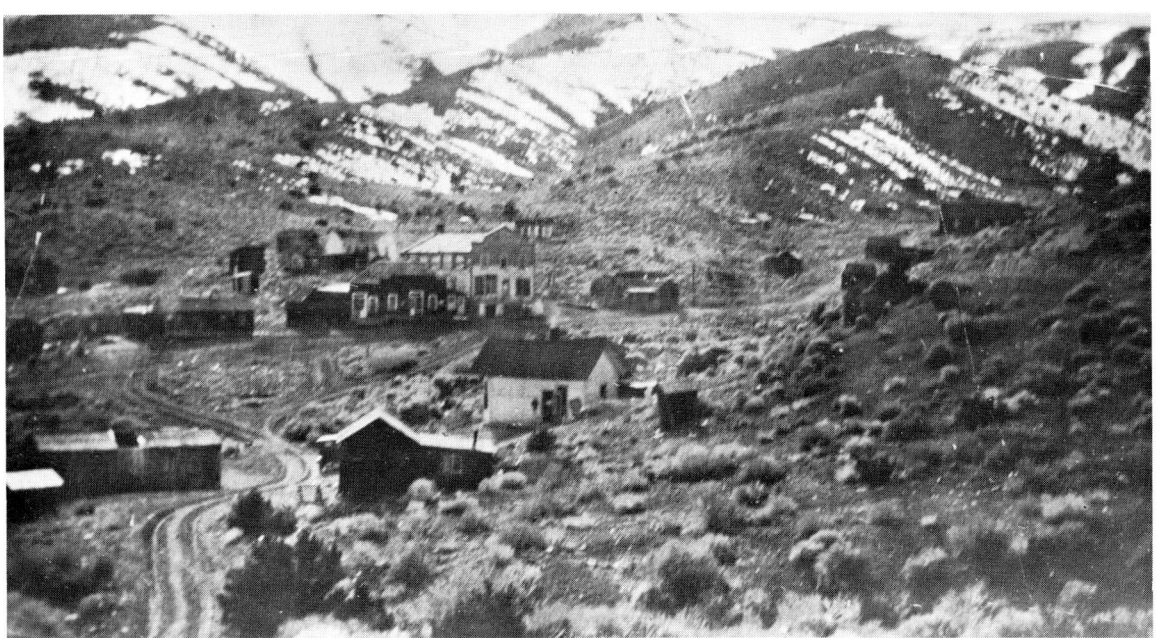

In 1904 two years before the arrival of the railroad, Olinghouse was a scattered collection of business establishments and small homes. The two-story building in the center of the photo is Crosby and McCoy's hotel; immediately to its left is Dan Cozzen's pioneer saloon, The Gouge Eye, which also housed the assay office; the low building still farther left was Grutt's General Store. In the foreground at left is the Springfield-Olinghouse barn; across the road is Odett's house where Mrs. Dondero lived; and behind that is the O'Farrell house which was the location of the first Post Office (building burned in 1958). (*George Dallimore.*)

resulting in expressed opinions that the new camp was the most flattering prospect since the days of the Comstock. The ensuing talk was so prevalent that H. H. Beck, a realistic business man, said, "My impression of the camp is that the day of talk, horning and panning, assaying and general slobber has passed. So far there has been too much location and too little development." Some shipments were made the month following this outburst, but the production never even began to approach that of the Comstock, with which it had been compared. Output for 1903 was $39,130, a fraction of that of the previous year, nearly half of it coming from Cabin No. 2.

One man alone contributed in large part to the decline of production. Dondero became involved in a murder charge. His trial was held in Reno. As a large number of witnesses were involved, considerable time and money was spent in going the 30 miles to court, and but little productive work was done in the mines. Dondero was subsequently released; not so the ore.

The new owners of Cabin No. 2 became interested in the plans of Henry Esden of the Wadsworth Electric Light & Power Co. to bring electricity into the camp and to build a tramway from the mines to the Truckee River where a mill would be erected. Also at that time (May 1903), plans were developed for a railroad which, it was felt, could haul ore from the mines to the mill for seven cents a ton. Proof of the contention never materialized.

Two years later, with the mining companies commencing to pay dividends, the town was definitely prosperous. One long main street wound along the bed of the canyon. The Home Restaurant, operated by Mrs. T. L. Bowers, dispensed food to the hungry, while the thirsty found solace at Frank Wheeler's Union Saloon or Dan Cozzens' pioneer saloon, The Gouge Eye. Other establishments included an assay office, Smith Brothers' eating house and the power company. Passengers for Wadsworth rode one of John Hamilton's stages at a 75 cents fare.

New strikes continued to stimulate interest in the area. J. Aaron "Buck" Ingalls finally struck pay dirt following four years of hard work and 3,500 assays. Prichitt & Dahl's claim in neighboring Secret Canyon to the east was the next to attract attention. Governor Sparks was the fortunate owner of the Ora when a new and "marvelous strike" was made. Reports filled the Reno papers with increasing regularity. One mine sample assayed $88,000 a ton. The jubilation of the Reno stockholders was short-lived, however, when it was discovered that the amount of this ore was extremely limited, as so often happened.

Meanwhile, the prosperity of near-by Wadsworth was seriously declining at this time. The Central Pacific's shops and division headquarters had been moved from town to Sparks, near Reno, and the only economic salvation for the inhabitants lay in the neighboring mining district or in the Truckee-Carson irrigation project. Consequently, when a promoter arrived on the scene in February, 1906, and told a mass meeting of the townsfolk that his Green Hill Mining Company had taken over certain of the mines at Olinghouse and proposed to build a mill at Wadsworth together with a connecting railroad between the two, the people were overjoyed and extremely happy to pledge the required labor, valued at $2,000, to aid in its construction.

William L. Stevenson, the promoter, lost no time in getting the project under way. Moneyed Reno people organized the railroad under the corporate name, Nevada Railroad Company. Among the chief backers were Judge C. E. Mack and Richard Kirman, a Reno banker, later mayor and still later the governor of Nevada. Two sisters joined the group: Ann M. Warren, a U. S. Commissioner, and Mrs. Litti R. Mudd, a school teacher. Civil engineer Edward L. Haft came up from Los Angeles to run the survey for the railroad, while ample power for the mill (and possibly for the railroad) was assured when the stockholders of the power company voted to sell out to the new group.

Then came a set-back. Ground for the mill had been broken, and the machinery, on order from the Joshua Hendy Iron Works, was almost ready for shipment. But on the morning of April 18, 1906, San Francisco suffered its great earthquake, and in the resulting conflagration and destruction, all was lost. A complete new set of equipment was ordered from Denver, but several months were to go by before delivery could be accomplished.

In early June the Summit Construction Company began work on the railroad with an initial force of 50 men and 85 horses. Grading was completed by the middle of August, and the delivery of rails was expected momentarily. The third week of September 1906 found a leased 4-4-0 locomotive plying its way over two miles of completed track while rail laying was being pushed forward. Superintendent Will Kearney had trains operating from Wadsworth to the mouth of Olinghouse Canyon on November 26, and the site of the passenger depot was finally determined. A 9% grade from this point up the right fork of the canyon to the ore bins dictated the use of the first Shay geared locomotives in Nevada.

Excitement prevailed in the early part of 1907. The new 50-stamp mill near Wadsworth was ready to handle the freshly mined ore of the Nevada Consolidated Mining and Milling Company (successor to the Green Hill Mining Company). Two laborers of the railroad became involved in a cutting affray. One was sent to the hospital; the other to jail. But February 4 was the big day for Olinghouse when, for the first time, "the iron horse rumbled and snorted right into the heart of town." The inhabitants were delighted; their future was "assured."

Two Shays were used to haul the two daily mixed trains between the Junction (with the SP) and Olinghouse depot. Shortly after leaving the Junction, the train would be halted while the locomotive switched the ore cars about the mill. The passengers would wait in discomfort, the only provision for their accommodation being a box car with crude, hard seats along either side.

A private car, the *Sunland*, was also used which belonged to Kirman's bank. Initially it had been the *Stanford*, built by the Central Pacific in its Sacramento shops in 1882. The 60-foot length brought disappointment to Stevenson, however, as the curves at the upper end of the line near Olinghouse proved to be too tight to allow the car to be brought into town. On the main lines of other railroads it served its purpose admirably by helping Stevenson to impress the investing public and disengage hesitant investors from their money.

Life continued to boom in the canyon. Ore poured down from the mines to the chutes; and the railroad hauled it in cars down the hill to the mill, always stopping at the depot near the mouth of the canyon for those passengers who presented themselves for transportation. A Railroad Day appeared to be in order, so the Olinghouse Improvement Association selected May 28, 1907 for the big day. J. M. Thomas, also a promoter in Stevenson's camp, arranged for a special train from Reno to Olinghouse. For $1.25 a ticket, the purchaser was entitled to a round trip from Reno with the option to return that evening or stay for the dance and return the following day. Interest was further heightened by a well-timed announcement that the first bar of bullion turned out at the mill was worth $4,000. Talk was also circulated of the prospects of doubling the size of the mill. Editorials in the Reno newspapers urged people to attend the celebration.

Although falling on a Tuesday, Railroad Day was undoubtedly the biggest event in the history of Olinghouse. Certainly the population, temporary or permanent, never again approached the number of people in attendance for the festivities. A four-car special train left Reno that morning with 230 people aboard. At Sparks another 23 passengers entrained. A stop was made at Olinghouse Junction to switch the train from the SP tracks to those of the Nevada Railroad, and another was made at the NCM&M's custom mill so visitors could see the heavy investment and the work which had been accomplished. Then the train proceeded to Olinghouse and the mines.

Other people joined the throng, arriving on foot, on horseback, by carriage and bicycle. Governor and Mrs. Sparks were on hand to greet the visitors in spite of the fact that the Governor had arrived the day before and worked the entire night getting the feast ready and preparing the meat. When the barbecue was finally ready, over 800 people sat down at the rough tables for the festivities.

Speech making followed the feast—first Governor Sparks, who was soundly acclaimed for his efforts and for his culinary achievements, and then Stevenson who said, "My friends, I wish to thank you all for your assistance in what has been done here. If I could have as hearty cooperation in every undertaking as I have had from the people of Olinghouse and vicinity in this enterprise, the task of delivering ice in hell would be a little one." Stevenson, the man with the push for the project, enigmatically was described as a quiet man with tremendous energy, but according to one recollection, it was his tall, gaunt secretary, Maude "Kit" Carson, who ran much of the show.

For entertainment, horse racing and a wrestling match were provided. Some people visited the mines; others roamed up and down the mile-long main street, stopping for liquid or solid refreshment at the Olinghouse Restaurant operated by George Dallimore and T. O. Carmen. The Riverside Park Band from Reno under the direction of Professor Cushman, provided the music and remained after the concerts to play for the dance that evening. According to the recollection of a former band member many years later, it was quite an evening, as he drank so much he fell off the bandstand. The professor must have conducted his music under extreme difficulties that night.

Not all of the excursionists were happy with the event. Oscar R. Morgan wrote a long lament in the *Reno Evening Gazette* severely criticizing the train service which required four hours each way for the 40 mile ride with stops at every telegraph pole to pick up the men, women and children who wanted to join the fun. The rival morning paper, the *Nevada State Journal*, treated the matter more kindly, attributing the delays to the steepness of the mountain railroad and the fact that, "The Southern Pacific locomotive tugged and puffed ahead of the four coaches to about half way up the mountain, where with a final snort and three wheezy, asthmatic toots, it acknowledged defeat. Then the hill climbing Shay engine with three flat cars came to the relief of the visitors . . ."

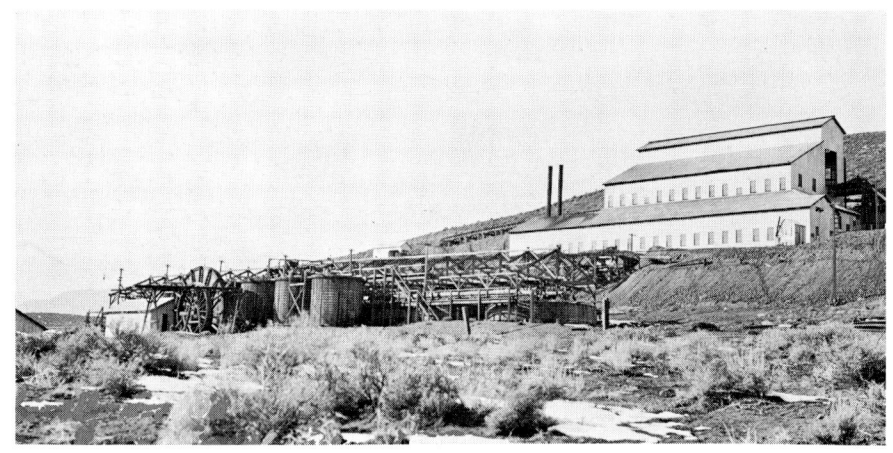

This 50-stamp mill near Wadsworth was completed by W. L. Stevenson in the early part of 1907 to process ores from the mines in Olinghouse. Tracks of the Nevada Railroad can be seen on the hillside (to left of the smokestacks) leading to the ore bins above, and again in the lower right corner leading to the lower level. (Nevada Historical Society.)

A description of the camp in the same issue placed the Nevada Consolidated mine on the tall hill at the extreme right (north) side of the canyon. Up and down the hill, little two-ton gravity cars traveled 1,700 feet in 46 seconds under the direction of one man. A total of 250 tons of ore was dumped daily into the loading bins over the freight cars of the Nevada Railroad. From here, the standard gauge cars would start their descent to the mill.

The Nevada Consolidated custom mill, near Wadsworth, was so busy with its own ores it was unable to do any outside work. For several months, general appearances continued bright. Some 84 men were working underground for the mill owners providing ore for a mill that was considered very efficient. It could handle ore assaying $2.50 a ton at a profit, as the cost of mining, milling and transportation for a ton of ore was a mere $1.80. With current assays at $40 a ton, the money should have been pouring in.

But something was wrong—the mill was not yielding the anticipated gold bars. Stevenson, with $22,000 in outstanding checks and unable to raise additional funds, became alarmed. For assistance he called on Eugene Grutt (one of the famous brothers at Rawhide), who took some samples for assaying in the dark of night. The resultant truth was a shock—the ore assayed less than $1.00 per ton.

On receipt of this news, Stevenson immediately closed down the operation and, by selling a block of his personal holdings of C&NW Railway stock, paid off some of the outstanding bills. In retrospect, it was said that Stevenson was a spendthrift, that he was influenced by his thinking that he could always raise money. Considered comments were that too much money was spent on top of the ground and too little under the surface.

Ore production continued in a small way for many months, but the custom mill of the Nevada Consolidated became idle. There was some talk of using the mill to work ores from the Goldfield Consolidated mines, but that company decided against it. The railroad was operated regularly until November 1, 1907 and then occasionally until the end of the year when operations ceased altogether. By that time the Panic of 1907 had set in, and there was little hope of revival.

Mary J. Mack, the wife of the Reno judge, held a one-year mortgage on the Nevada Railroad in the amount of $20,409 with interest at the rate of 1% per month—probably one of the highest interest rates for a railroad mortgage anywhere in the country at that time. When the railroad defaulted its interest payments, Mrs. Mack filed foreclosure action, and the sheriff sold the railroad and equipment (2 locomotives, 7 ore cars, 10 miles of main track plus 2 miles of sidings) in front of the Washoe County Courthouse on December 12, 1908. As Mrs. Mack was the only bidder, she acquired her husband's railroad for $23,647 (face amount of the mortgage plus court costs and interest).

It was then that the newspapers picked up the story. Judge Mack, whose law firm acted for Mrs. Mack, said, "It was simply a case where the company did not pay the interest when it was due, thus placing the note in prejudice and making it become due. The insurance companies declared under such conditions they would not continue insurance protection on the properties unless a receiver was appointed at once and there remained nothing else to do but to foreclose on the note. The holder was forced to act."

In September 1909 a crew of thirty men tore up the rails. Approximately eight miles of track were sold to the Nevada Copper Belt Railroad, then under construction, while the balance went to a P. E. O'Brien of San Francisco. By 1911 there was not a single tie or rail to point out the location of the former railroad, although a sharp eye can still trace most of the old grade. The ore mill was torn down, and the machinery was sold piece by piece whenever a purchaser could be found. Its foundations remain as a stark reminder of another unfortunate mining gamble and can be seen on the hillside along the highway between Reno and Wadsworth.

The private car, *Sunland,* was expediently sold back to the Southern Pacific in February 1911 by Mr. Kirman. Taken to Sacramento, it was refurbished and renamed *Tucson.* Ironically, two months after its release from the shops, it was destroyed by fire.

People have continued to inhabit the town of Olinghouse since the days of the railroad. The number of houses is constantly diminishing; on a windy day in September 1958 fire consumed three houses. The area is full of peace and quiet, and a few people engage in minor mining activities. Over the years the trees have grown in size, and today they are the most prominent feature of this historic Nevada ghost town.

Nevada Short Line Railway

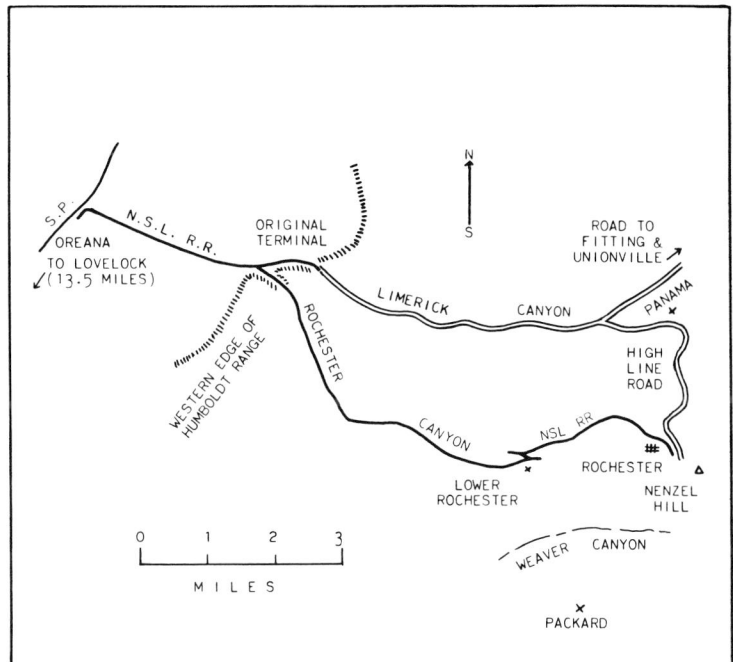

Short in life, short in miles, and the very last of the independent railroads built in Nevada, the narrow (3-foot) gauge Nevada Short Line Railway was unique. Initially constructed in 1913, then twice extended — once in 1914 and again in 1915 — the line never exceeded a multifarious 12 measured miles of linear length, yet it climbed an average grade of 6% in the last 8 miles and incorporated a switchback in its 2,100 feet of vertical ascent. Its mélange of motive power was a master mechanic's nightmare and entirely inadequate for the traffic, the conditions, or the innumerable breakdowns which occurred with unmitigating frequency. In short, the situation was hopeless — almost from the very beginning.

The genesis of activity in the Rochester Canyon dates back to the early 1860's when a silver mining district was established by migrant New Yorkers. The canyon started at the peak of the Humboldt Mountain Range and stretched 6 miles westward to the floor of the Humboldt River Valley, where four more miles of arid, desert country separated it from the town of Oreana on the east bank of the Humboldt River. One of the first lead smelters in the west had been erected in Oreana in 1867 to reduce the ores of the Montezuma Mine in the near-by Arabia District on the west slopes of the valley. (Although references have appeared in print regarding a railroad west from Oreana to this vicinity, no such railroad was ever constructed.)

For 40 years production in Rochester Canyon was most insignificant. The real spark of life was struck by Joseph F. Nenzel when he staked his claim and located his monuments on what became Nenzel Hill on June 25, 1912. Rising above (Upper) Rochester at the summit of the Humboldt Range, the hill still bears his name today, for his fame was skyrocketed over the area and was soon compared with that of Jim Butler, the discoverer of Tonopah.

Inevitably a rush of miners to the area ensued, and that first winter 2,200 men were spread among the three separate camps which stretched for 2½ miles up Rochester Canyon. Of these "700 were the undesirable, the unworthy and unsuccessful." Frequent shootings marked the opening of new saloons, as well as their closing. Of the 24 establishments which were operating early in the first year of the camps, 19 were casualties before the year's end.

But wealth attracts good men as well as bad, and Rochester was the subject of considerable publicity. George Wingfield of Goldfield invested in several claims for a short while, then sold out to Nenzel. Another ex-Goldfielder, who also stopped to try his luck at Rawhide along the way, was Arthur Ashton Codd. Taking over the No. 2 lease of the Rochester Mines Co. in December 1912, he modestly changed its name to the Codd Lease and formed the Rochester Hills Mining Company to operate it, naming himself as president.

With the increased mining activity on top of the range, the problem of transporting ores from these mines to the river became increasingly acute. Limerick Canyon, immediately to the north and parallel to Rochester Canyon, was selected for the site of the tortuous route known as the "high line" wagon road. Branching off the old road near Nenzel Hill, it crossed the saddle into Limerick Canyon to a place called Panama, then wound down the hill to rejoin the old road on the flats of the Humboldt River Valley. The settlement of Panama does not show on many maps of the region for it was comprised of from 30 to 60 people who lived there only briefly the early part of the year 1913. The briefness of their habitation is indicated by the tactful comment of a returning visitor later that year that "the majority of the Panamanians seemed to be away on vacation."

The intense activity in the Rochester area was having its effect in the valley below. So much

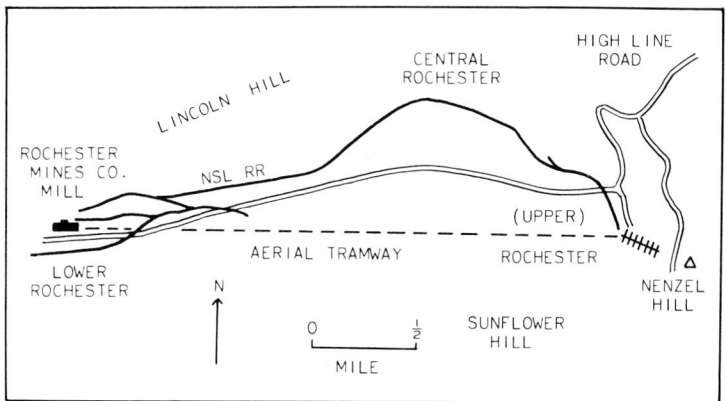

material was being delivered by the SP at Oreana for Rochester and the mines that the railroad decided to change the name of the station to Nixon to avoid possible penmanship or other confusion with Oceana, California. However, postal authorities refused to sanction the new name of Nixon as that would be confused with a post office of the same name at Pyramid Lake, about 70 miles to the south and west. Undaunted, the railroad next tried to use the name of Nenzel for a time, but confusion again arose between that station name and the post office name of Oreana for the same location. The railroad finally capitulated and reverted to the original title.

The terrific increase in volume of traffic, coupled with the marginal nature of Codd Lease production (it was described as a good producer but never a money maker), induced Codd to announce in May 1913 that he would build a narrow-gauge railroad from Oreana eastward four miles across the sandy flats of the valley to ore bins at the mouth of Limerick Canyon. This would serve both the "high line" wagon road and the mining camps in the bed of Rochester Canyon at the canyon mouth. His Nevada Short Line Railway was ambitiously started as a sole proprietorship, though subsequently it was found expedient to file articles of incorporation.

The grading contract was awarded to a Mr. Maguire of Rochester before the end of the month, and some used equipment from the SP's Fernley-Lassen line construction job through Susanville was purchased from the Utah Construction Co. Grading was completed in a matter of weeks with 35 men on the job, and the final track work was finished on July 31 with the exception of one solitary spike. This was a special, silver spike which Codd was reputedly having fashioned by a San Francisco jeweler so that, following the celebration, it could be gainfully employed as a paper weight. Just what transpired has been lost in the annals of history, as no further mention has been found of the celebration, the silver spike, or the memento conversation piece on the desk of one Arthur Ashton Codd.

A gasoline locomotive, purchased in San Francisco, was used to haul the first ore trains on August 9, 1913, following a few days of trial runs. Before the end of the month the main crankshaft broke, and service was not restored until a steam locomotive was procured from Hobart Mills, California, just north of Truckee. At the time of delivery Codd's engineer was absent due to the illness of his mother and Codd, with a reputation for being well dressed, was obliged to don overalls and take over operations.

The "Silver Belt Railroad," as it was familiarly called, could never be said to have been born with a silver spoon in its mouth. Vicissitudes were a commonplace. Aside from the initial broken crankshaft and subsequent disruption of service, the following month a windstorm leveled the engine house at Nenzel (Oreana). Motive power breakdowns were a constant source of difficulty. Yet still the little road operated. Increasing ore tonnage kept the line busy both day and night until finally an extension was planned up the canyon to Lower Rochester.

The principal stimulation for this latest move lay in the very nature of the "high line" wagon road and its inability to handle the heavy volume of traffic. It was variously described as having a smooth grade but an inadequate number of turnouts, spaced "so far apart that the mahout (sic) is compelled to refer to his field glasses in order to make out passing points, for the ore wagons . . . are constantly making their way down." An extension of the railroad into Rochester Canyon would provide direct service to the lower mines and reduce the length of haul for those mines on the hill in (Upper) Rochester.

In April 1914 incorporation of the railroad became an accomplished fact, with Codd holding the stock. The extension necessitated removal of the last mile of existing roadbed to the ore bins at the foot of Limerick Canyon and a rebuilding in the direction of the mouth of Rochester Canyon. Continuation then proceeded for six additional miles up steep 5% grades to Lower Rochester. William Simkins ran the survey coincident with the pushing of the grade over the first two miles under the supervision of H. G. Dunbar, a relatively easy section to construct. To compensate for the increased capacity of the extended line, an additional locomotive was purchased from the former Golconda & Adelaide Railroad through the intermediary of a scrap dealer, and was routed to the Central Pacific shops at Sparks for repairs before being pressed into service.

Completion of the extension was commemorated at Christmas 1914 with the presentation to Codd of a Hamilton gold watch on behalf of his employees. Codd gave the town a present on January 15, 1915, when he initiated passenger service into Lower Rochester with two round trips daily. Such bountiful service must have taxed the road's facilities to the utmost as the roster of equipment of the time showed one steam locomotive, two box cars, a number of flat cars, a passenger car, and "Mike." "Mike" was an aberration — the frame and motor of a 60 H.P. Winton auto ensconced on two light railroad trucks and completely blanketed with a homemade cab of crude design. The "thing" was called a locomotive.

Joseph F. Nenzel was not apathetic to these goings-on. With transportation being supplied right to the foot of his doorstep, a new and improved mill could be built in Lower Rochester which would benefit everyone, he reasoned. Currently ore shipped to distant smelters needed to assay 35 ounces to the ton to be profitable, whereas a modern mill right on the site in Lower Rochester would enable the processing of ores with as little as 8 ounces of silver to the ton. Mines in (Upper) Rochester then would have but a short haul downgrade to reach the new facilities. In conjunction with his surface tramway from the top of Nenzel Hill to the bins in (Upper) Rochester which was already installed and operating, his haulage costs would be reduced to an absolute minimum.

In September 1914 work on the new 100-ton custom mill of the Rochester Mines Co. was begun. But Nenzel did not stay to see the fruition of his plans. Two months later he resigned as president of the Rochester Mines Co. and left for Cactus, 27 miles east of Goldfield, where he purchased and operated the rich Fairday claims. L. A. Friedman, a successful mining man from Seven Troughs, succeeded to the presidency and the job of completing the new works. This was accomplished by the early part of 1915, and on February 4, in the Lower Rochester Hotel, a dance was held to celebrate jointly the completion of the custom mill and the completion of the railroad. Such a large crowd was attracted to the celebration, it defeated its own purpose — dancing on the crowded floor was impossible. However, as long as the liquid refreshments held out, the miners proved capable of improvising their own entertainment.

The new mill proved beneficial in every way anticipated, but the after-effects on the (over-)extended railway were drastic. Gone were the long hauls of bulky crude ore to Oreana. In their stead were substituted fewer and lighter shipments of refined ore which brought decreased revenues to the till to compensate for the overextension of finances to construct the line. Only one salvation remained, and that was to garner the hauling of the crude ore from the mines in (Upper) Rochester down the hill to the custom mill.

In April 1915 contracts were let to build the third and final extension of the line. Two miles long, the rails left the upper leg of the custom mill siding (forming a switchback) and wound up the side of the canyon on a nearly impossible grade. The saving grace in the whole project was that loads could be lowered down the hill while only empties need be pushed up the grade.

Work was temporarily suspended when a controversy arose over right-of-way matters through the East (Upper) Rochester Townsite, and it was only after satisfying a $2,500 bond that work could be resumed. Then the Shay locomotive, which was nursing two cars of rails and ties up the grade, ran away. It didn't go far before landing in a ditch surrounded by the scattered remnants of its train. The locomotive was so badly damaged it had to be sent to the SP shops in Sparks for major repairs.

On August 23, 1915, the last rails were spiked in place, but the accomplishment was nearly overlooked in the confusion attending the aftermath of a bakery fire in Lower Rochester which swept through two business blocks and ruined the Brunswick Hotel, not to mention the economy of the region. Although the rails had now reached (Upper) Rochester, Codd faced personal financial adversity of stupendous proportions and was forced to sell his Codd Lease to the Rochester Mines Co.

On September 9, 1915, the first train made a trial run to test the newly installed air brakes. Three days later Codd rode the first ore train down the hill to the mill at Lower Rochester. That fall business boomed on the road as trains of ore drifted down to the mill on a regular basis, the Shay lifting the empties back again for refilling.

The real disaster for the railroad was the fire that destroyed the shops in Nenzel (Oreana) on November 30. Started by a gasoline explosion which

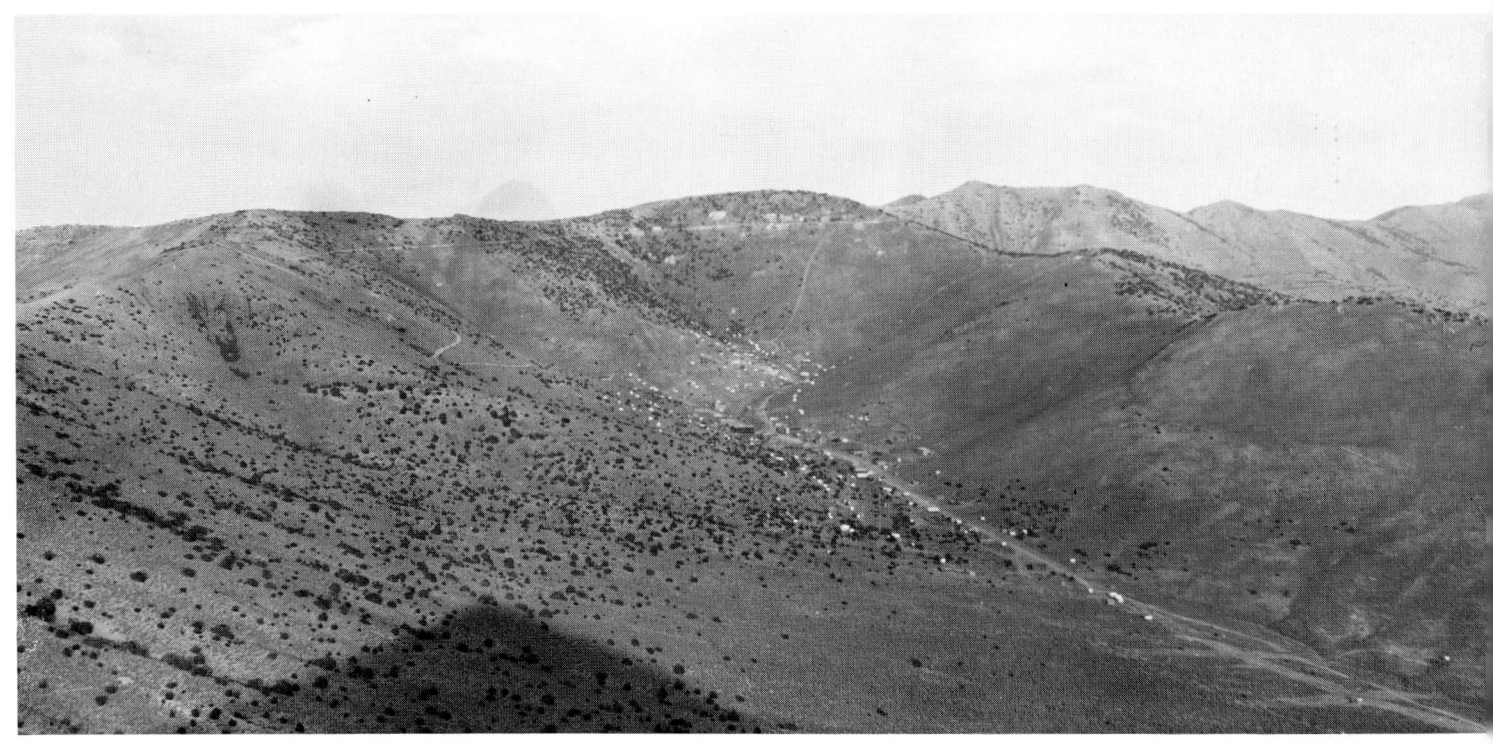

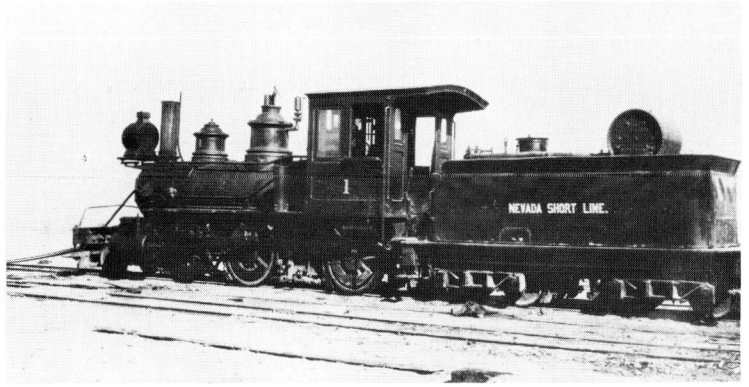

Rochester Canyon stretched for six miles from the peak of Nenzel Hill (center background) to the Humboldt River Valley. The town of (lower) Rochester in the center of the valley became the site of the Rochester Mines Co. mill, second terminus of the NSL. On the slopes of the hills above Upper Rochester may be seen faint traces of the steep grade of the High Line Road.

Nevada Short Line No. 1 was this ex-Golconda & Adelaide locomotive, delivered in 1914.

Heavy equipment delivered at Upper Rochester was laboriously hauled into position by block and tackle on an improvised wooden skidway. *(Top: U. S. Geological Survey; Center: Ted Wurm Collection; Bottom: George White Collection.)*

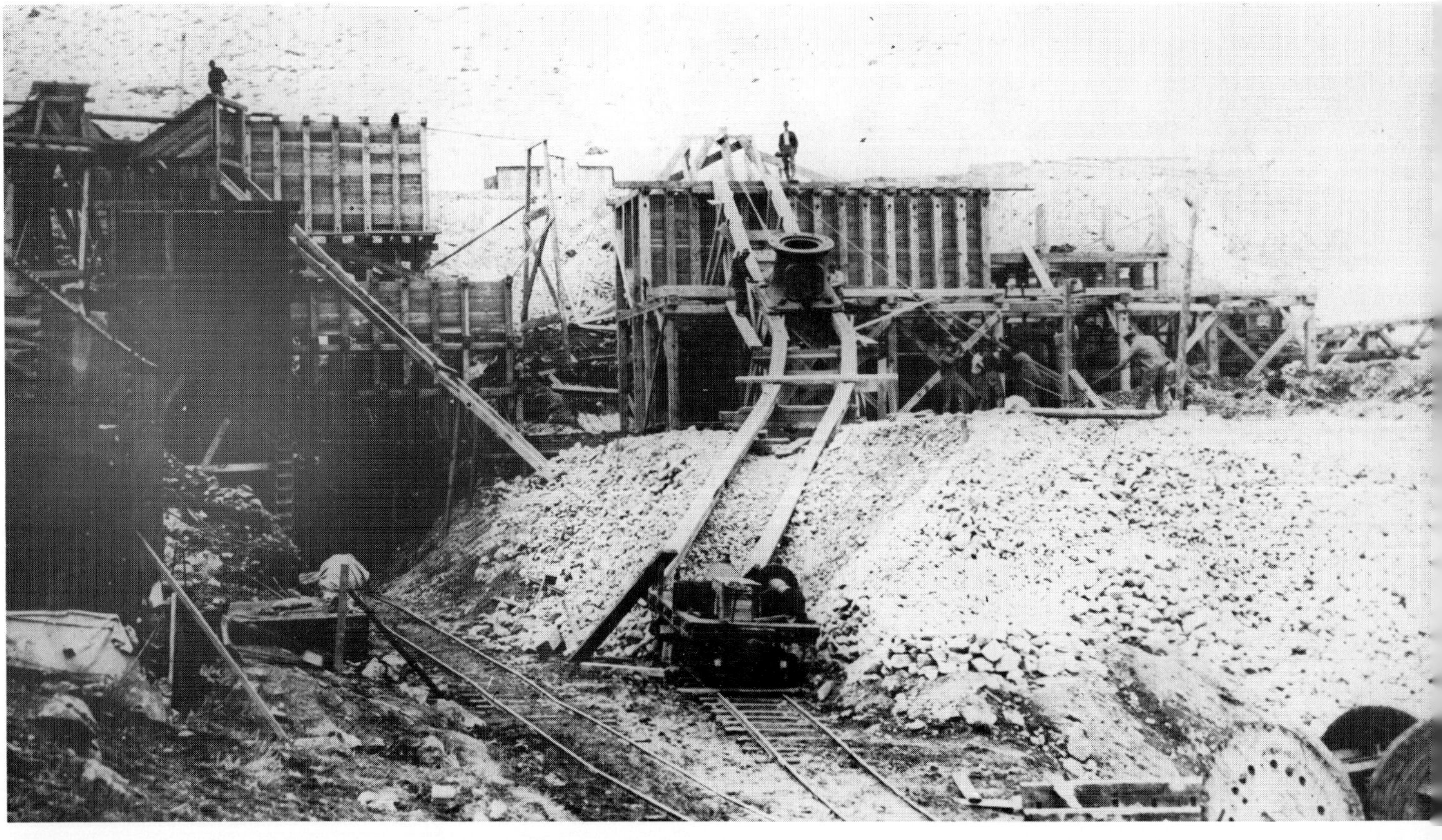

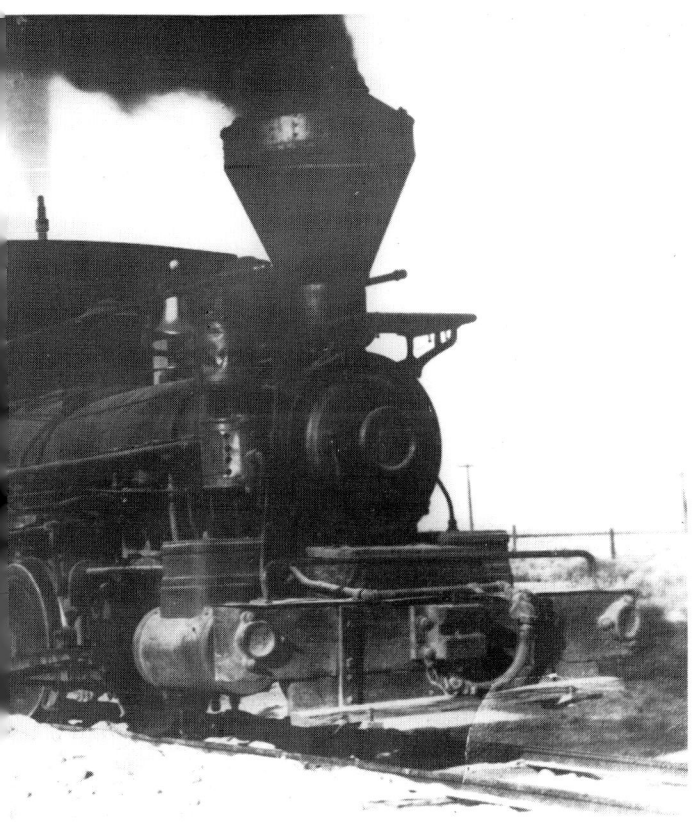
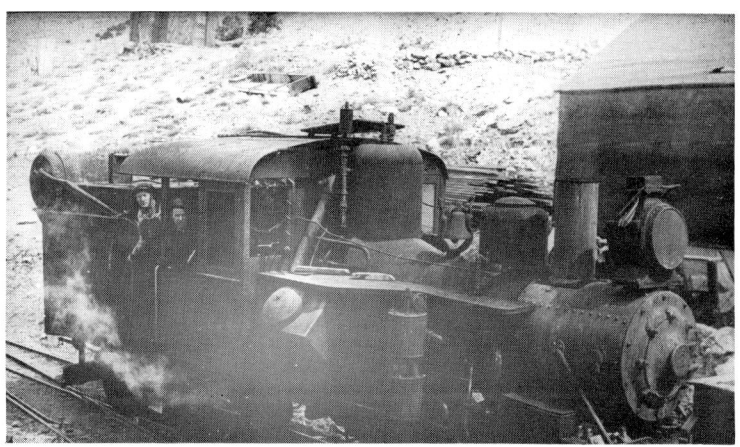

The Nevada Short Line's "Preferred Investment," so glamorously advertised in the *Western Miner* of July 1915, was backed by such unglamorous items of motive power as the second-hand, four-wheel, construction dinky, the tired Heisler "Francis," from Borax Smith's Borate & Dagget Railroad at Calico, and the still plodding No. 1. The mill in the background was the new (1915) innovation of the Rochester Mines Co. *(Two Top Photos: George White Collection.)*

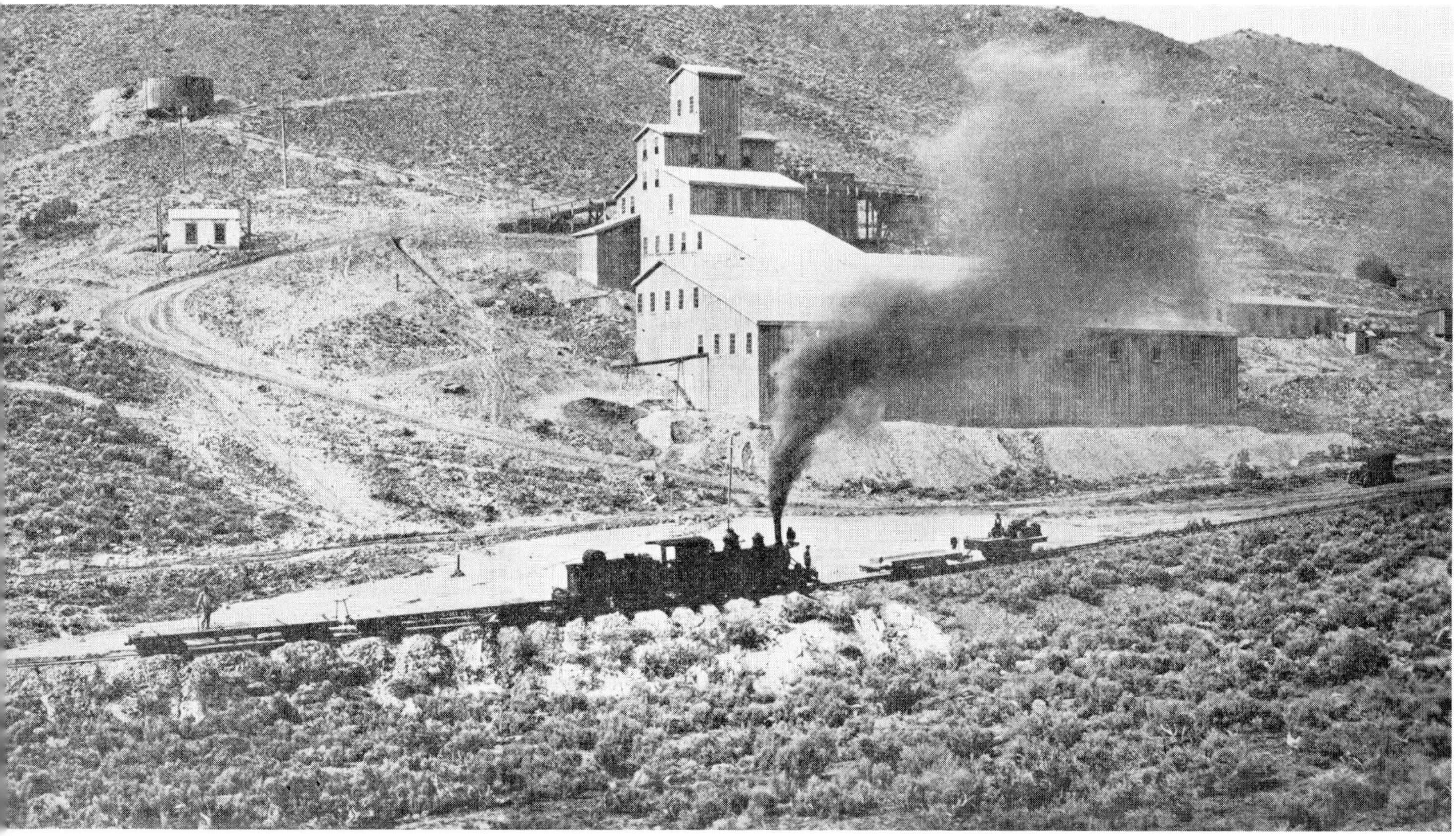

Nevada Short Line Railway Co.
Preferred Stock Offering
12 to 15 Per Cent Interest Assured

5000 shares of treasury stock of the **NEVADA SHORT LINE RAILWAY COMPANY** are offered for sale for the purpose of securing funds to reduce the bond issue. Par value of shares is $10.00 each, but 5000 shares are now offered at $5.00 each as

A Preferred Investment

The company has constructed and has in operation 12 miles of railroad connecting the rich Rochester Mining District with the main line of the Southern Pacific Railway at Oreana, Nevada. It has assets worth $178,000, including the railway, four locomotives, passenger and flat cars, and 22 ore cars. All of the cars are being equipped with air brakes and automatic couplers.

The company has a gross income of $4,500 per month under contracts for hauling ores, mail and express, making a total assured income of $54,000 per year. Its operating expenses are only $1500 per month, which leaves an earning capacity that will easily pay 12 to 15 per cent interest per annum on the issue of Preferred Treasury Stock which is now offered and which is the first offering of this kind ever made by the company.

For Further Particulars, Address A. A. CODD, President

Nevada Short Line Railway Co.
Reno, Nevada

singed the night watchman, it destroyed two of the locomotives yet spared the ingenious "Mike," the least powerful unit in the motive power stud. The situation was unendurable for Codd, and receivership followed. Frank Manson, was named receiver, while C. W. Poole, was appointed manager of the railroad.

For weeks no ore moved to the mill at Lower Rochester. The former mule teams had long been dispersed. Of necessity, the mill was closed. The popularity of the railroad declined. It was admitted that the road "was absolutely inadequate to handle the tonnage necessary to keep the mill going."

The new management did obtain another Shay from the Mammoth Copper Co. and even succeeded in bringing its crew from Kennett, California, to operate it. Tried out during the most severe snow storm in the history of Rochester, the performance was pronounced beautiful, and it was reported: "On December 16 the new locomotive came and wreathed the ore bins with a halo of new smoke. The inhabitants cheered, for the steady progress of the newcomer indicated that the days of ore failures were past. The next day 100 tons went down and the following day, 220 tons went to the mill." The long period of idleness at last was over.

Late in 1915 the surface tramway, which had carried a million dollars in ore from the top of Nenzel Hill to the ore bins in (Upper) Rochester, was abandoned. The new Friedman tunnel, extending 1,600 feet into the base of Nenzel Hill, had been completed and ore mined in the upper levels was dropped to bins in the tunnel where ore cars carried it to the portal for conveyance to the mill. Following 1915, ore production increased several times due to the greater mill capacity as well as the higher market price of silver.

Even under new management, the railroad continued to encounter difficulties. Five feet of snow halted trains for a week in January, 1916. Income proved insufficient to meet the installments on the bonds as they became due, and the Washoe County Bank asked the District Court in Reno to foreclose. A contractor was also seeking his money. In court Frank Manson, the receiver, told Judge Moran that the little line could not operate profitably in heavy winter snow but should be able to make money during good weather. The principal source of business was the two-mile movement of ore from the mines on the hill to the mill in Lower Rochester.

Disaster struck again a few months later. The motor car jumped the rails near the mouth of Rochester Canyon. Five passengers escaped with minor abrasions, but motorman Robert Enslow suffered head injuries.

Motive power failures further delayed the railroad's operations. During 1916 a 24-ton Porter locomotive was in use while a Heisler was acquired from the Pacific Coast Borax Co. Three ore cars were purchased. At the end of the year the equipment list presented a meager, diversified picture: three flat cars, two bottom cars, three ore cars, one freight motor, one passenger motor, and two steam locomotives.

The climax came toward the end of September 1916 when L. A. Friedman announced plans for a 12,017-foot aerial tram line from the ore bins at the mouth of Friedman tunnel to the mill at Lower Rochester. Handling ore by railroad cost 50 cents a ton; by tramway it would be a mere 6 to 9 cents a ton. Annual savings would tally at least $24,000.

The contract for the tram (approximate cost $35,000) was given to the Leschen Wire Rope Co., and in November timbers started arriving from the Red River Lumber Company's plant at Westwood, California. The tramway towers went up; the cables were strung; the ore buckets were attached; and after a test run, ore began moving by air in April 1917. No longer was the mill dependent upon the whims of a balky steam locomotive. In celebration, a dance was held in Lower Rochester.

This was the end of heavy tonnage for the railroad, although some ore continued to move by rail from other mines in the area. The railroad was put up for sale for delinquent taxes in the summer of 1917, but no buyer could be found for the line. Even the county did not want it at the bargain arrearage price of $120.23, as Treasurer Hoenstine did not wish to be an unsalaried railroad manager. So the railroad was stricken from the tax rolls.

Service became more erratic than ever due to locomotive failures, lack of traffic, and snow. Early in 1918 the new receiver, H. J. Humphries, tried to instill some life through the purchase of four freight cars and an auto passenger track car from the NCO Railway. Additionally, it was awarded the U. S. Mail contract on July 1, 1918. A major flood in June 1918 badly damaged the town of Rochester and virtually destroyed the railroad. The line was doomed and service soon ceased entirely. Scrap dealers moved in and tore up the rails in 1920, distributing some equipment to other railroads in the territory including the Eureka-Nevada.

Rochester continued to produce, quite prolifically too. In fact, over one-half of the camp's production was made in the eight years following the railroad's demise. A few of the old buildings remain today; some tramway towers still stand; the scars of the Nenzel Hill tramway are still visible; and the old railroad grade can still be spotted, particularly on the hillsides. Between Upper and Lower Rochester the railroad had had its ups and downs, but by and large its progress was downhill most of the way.

Golconda & Adelaide Railroad

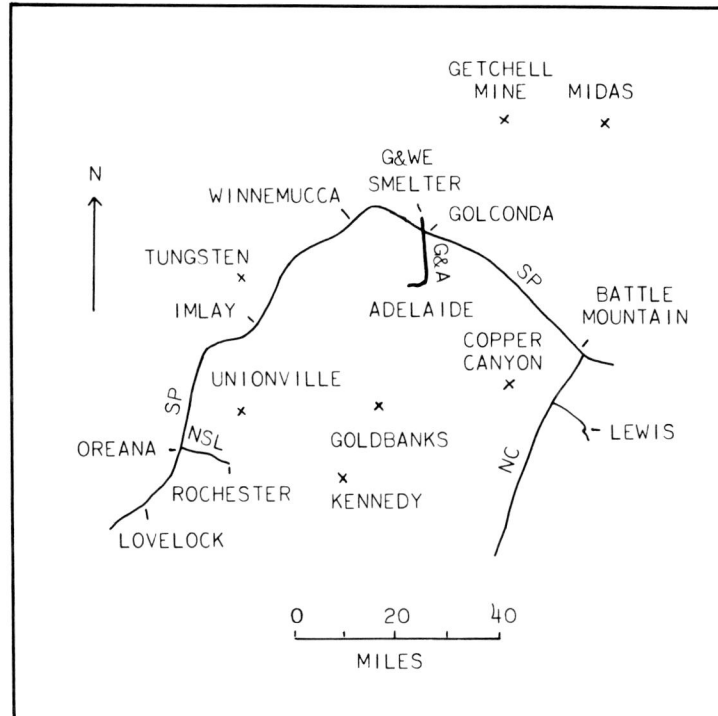

Golconda!

The very name implies fabulous wealth found in romantic settings. The original Golconda was an ancient city in India, renowned for its fine diamonds and royal fortresses and mausoleums. Perhaps the Nevada town was named by its founders in the hope that great riches would flow from the earth. If such were the case, they were doomed to disappointment.

The Golconda Hot Springs were located 16 miles east of Winnemucca on the Humboldt River. In 1866 the settlement around the springs became unofficial headquarters for all activity in the near-by Gold Run Mining District. The principal mine in the area for many years had been the Adelaide, adjoining the old settlement of Cumberland to the south. By the time the Central Pacific rails had been laid to Golconda Hot Springs in October 1868, mining was on the decline and the Springs had come to be considered something of a health resort. In fact, for several decades following the year 1870, only desultory mining was carried on, highlighted by the brief Adelaide mine and furnace development during 1888-89.

In 1896 a group of Scotsmen, including members of the famous (thread manufacturing) Coats family, became interested in the possibilities of profitable mining in Nevada, and on October 28 they organized the Glasgow & Western Exploration Company, Ltd., with Joseph Farren, a Salt Lake City mining man, as their agent. Taking an option on the old Adelaide Copper Mine, Farren put 25 men to work exploring its possibilities. The results looked so promising, it was estimated the Adelaide might outrival the now famous Anaconda. The option was quickly exercised; plans were made for a smelter; and a subsidiary company was formed in April 1897, called the Adelaide Star Mines, Ltd., to acquire this mine plus that of the Star and Grey Eagle Mines at Cherry Creek in eastern Nevada. Another addition to their properties, the old mines at Copper Canyon near Battle Mountain, was made a year later.

Golconda began to boom. A townsite was laid out, and the few original houses surrounding the hot springs were rapidly augmented as people began to arrive in town. Teamsters started hauling timbers to the mine at Adelaide which was rapidly being reconditioned, but most activity centered about the new smelter to be erected on the east side of town. In May 1897 a quarry was blasted open to provide the stone for the foundations; men came from Montana to construct the building and install the equipment which would duplicate that of the smelter in Anaconda; and L. Dutertre, owner and recent developer of the Hot Springs, constructed a dam across the Humboldt River three miles to the east and brought water to the site through the old Humboldt Canal. By November the smelter was ready for a trial run.

The year 1898 was one of feverish activity and suspenseful anticipation for the residents of Golconda. Town life centered around the six hotels and the Reinhart Brothers' store which optimistically advertised: "No concern in the country can sell you goods cheaper or as cheap as we can" — quite an extensive claim for a small town store.

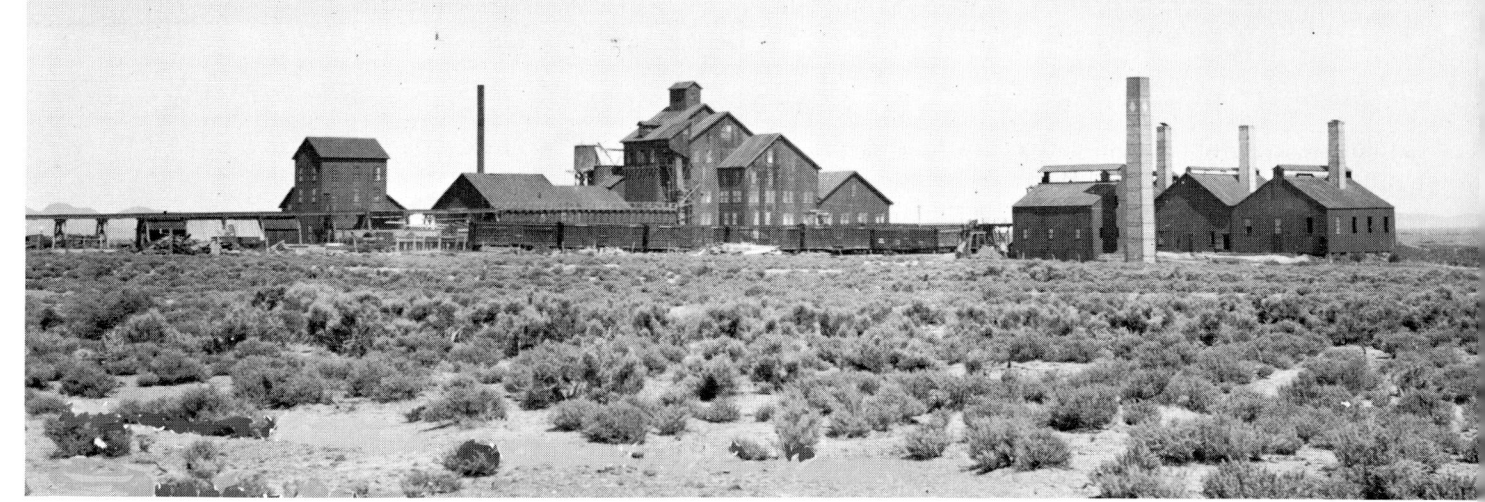

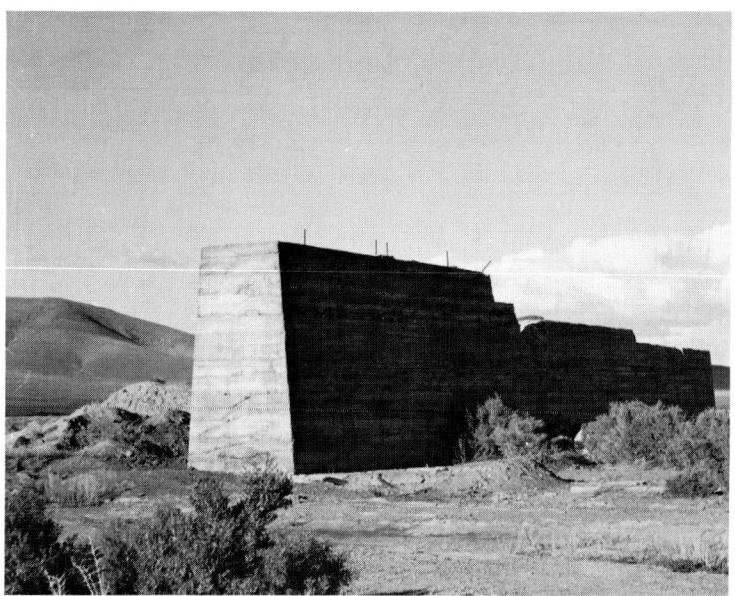

The massive concentrating plant and smelter of the Glasgow & Western Exploration Company at Golconda, Nevada.

Only these concrete foundations remain today as a sporting ground for jack rabbits. All traces of the narrow gauge Golconda & Adelaide Railroad have vanished, as have Golconda's six hotels and most of its 500 population.

In 1915 a grove of trees and a few buildings still marked the site of the Golconda Hot Springs, but the vigorous mining which gave the area its impetus had already dissipated in the desert air a full five years earlier. *(Top: Nevada Historical Society; Bottom: Southern Pacific.)*

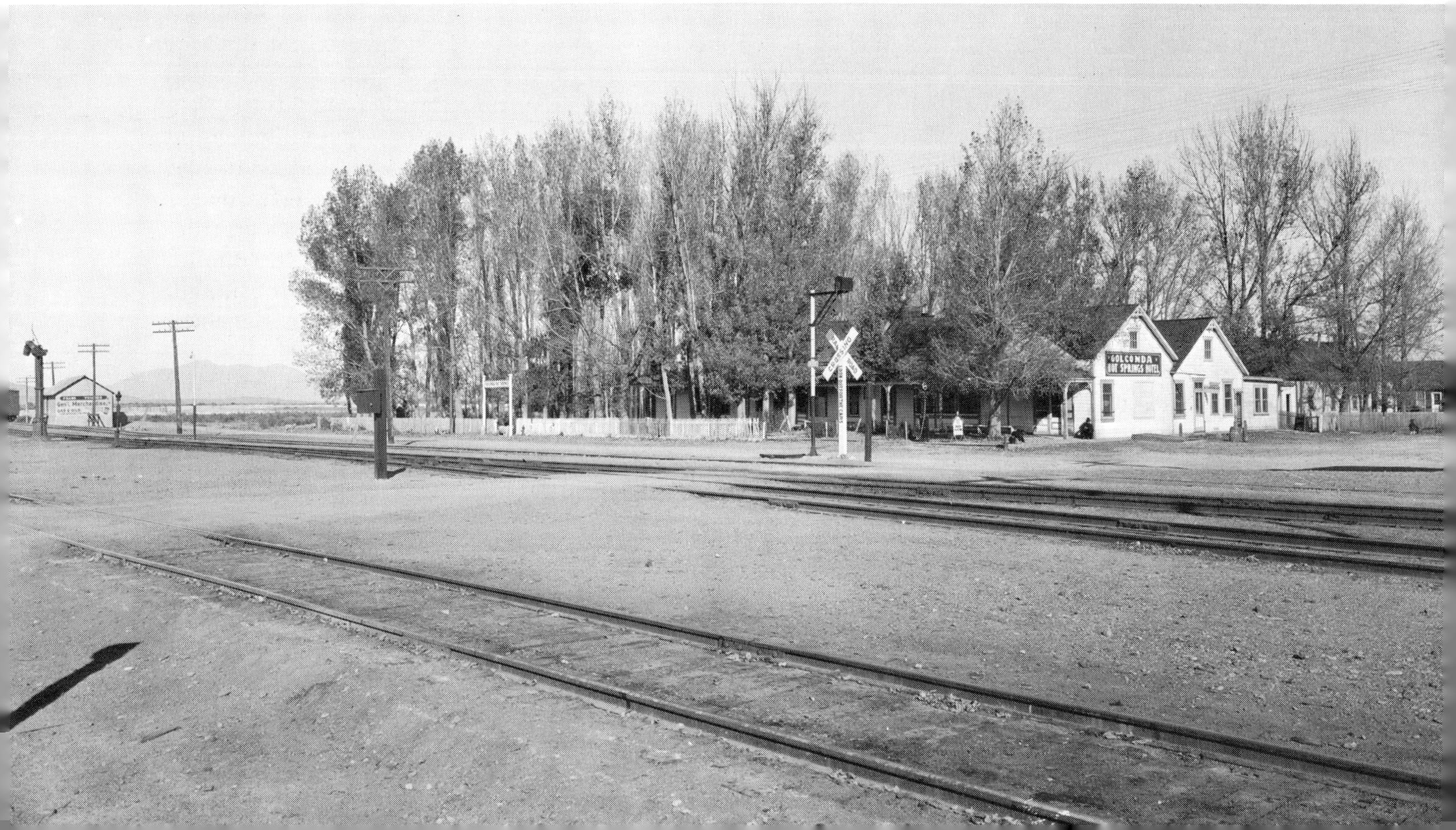

Employment at the smelter totaled 70 men, while another 50 men were busily engaged at the Adelaide mine. Otto Stahlman, general manager of G&WE Co.'s operations, announced plans to enlarge the smelter. Economic benefits for Golconda were also anticipated from activities at George Lovelock's iron mines which, although some distance away, were employing 60 men and planning a railroad north to a connection with the Central Pacific. Extensive developments of sulphur deposits and an expanded farm irrigation program were also in the offing. There was even talk of building a railroad to the mining town of Tuscarora, 80 miles to the northeast. Why, in another two years the smelter alone would be employing 900 men, and Golconda eventually would become the largest city in Nevada with a population of 10,000!

Initially, it was the suggestion of a Reno man that instigated town talk and cracker barrel speculation over the possibilities of an electric railroad from Golconda to the Adelaide mines. Possibly it was the ensuing discussions which prompted the Glasgow & Western Exploration Company to decide to build a narrow (3-foot) gauge railroad over the 11¾ miles between Golconda and Adelaide. Whatever the stimulation, the Golconda & Adelaide Railroad (as it was normally titled, although occasional references have used the cognomen, Glasgow & Western Railroad) had a very quiet birth without benefit of formal title or incorporation. The surveys were completed in the early part of September 1898, and orders for the necessary rails and 33,000 ties were placed. The grading was swiftly accomplished — work was started on October 10 and completed before the end of the month. Then the enterprise stalled on dead center. The rails were on hand, and a locomotive had been acquired; but without ties, nothing further could be done.

It was early December before the shipment was received. Again, no time was lost in proceeding. By December 15th ties and rails were in place over the first four miles, and Charles Smith, an ex-SP engineer, was operating the locomotive in supply train service. The smelter, which had been shut down during construction of the railroad, was reactivated; and ore shipments commenced even before the advancing railhead had reached the mines. Some thought was entertained of electrifying the line, but for reasons unknown this was never accomplished. The final rails were spiked in place the early part of January 1899, and shipments rapidly rose to 90 tons and subsequently to 250 tons of ore daily. Although unrealized, Golconda had now reached the height of its boom, boasted a population of 500 people, and supported a weekly newspaper.

Unfortunately, the ore proved to be difficult to reduce, and in June 1900 the mine and the mill were closed down, which forced suspension of the railroad service as well. During December 1904 there was some talk of extending the line 50 miles farther south to Kennedy, a mining town which had been active in 1894, but renewed interest in the area failed to last and the project died a-borning. Another much shorter extension was surveyed from the coal trestle at Adelaide to the mines of the Humboldt Smelting & Reduction Co. around 1904. Although only a few miles long, a switchback was included in the plans.

More years passed, and the smelter was redesigned and rebuilt. Once again the railroad was reactivated (1907-1910) to haul ore for the modernized milling process. This, too, failed to live up to expectations, so the mill was again closed. The railroad lay idle for several years, subsequently being sold to the Sugarman Iron & Metal Company. In 1914 the Sugarman interests, in turn, sold the rails and equipment to the Nevada Short Line Railroad at Rochester, Nevada.

According to information available in Glasgow, Scotland, the Glasgow & Western Exploration Company's operations were never a financial success. The company was voluntarily liquidated in March 1913, and an agent was sent over to close out its affairs in the United States. The basic contention was that the Coats' name was used too liberally, and that the company did not consider itself responsible for the actions of the former management, which it considered wasteful. Arrangements were made to settle the general obligations on the basis of 45% plus $15,000 for the delinquent payroll.

Golconda today still has a few of the old buildings. There is still a tunnel entrance to the mine at Adelaide together with the obvious mine dumps. However, all the machinery and hoists of G&WE Co. and of its purchaser in 1916, the Yerington Mountain Mining Company, have been removed. Of the Golconda & Adelaide there is little trace. The Nevada desert has reclaimed its own.

NEVADA CENTRAL RAILWAY

A former Pony Express rider, William H. Talcott, started the famous Austin mining boom. The year was 1862, a mere three years subsequent to the dramatic Comstock mining discoveries, and the whole eastern part of Nevada was largely unexplored territory. At that time Talcott was working at the Jacobsville station of the Overland stage route, and on one of his spring rides into the hills in May of that year, he discovered silver ore on a hillside to the east.

As a result of his discovery, the Reese River Mining District came into being, and the town of Austin was spawned as its nucleus. Austin grew in size, stature and popularity, for it was men from Austin who located and founded many of the famous camps in the central Nevada region including Eureka, Hamilton, Belmont and others. Speculation in Reese River mining stocks became rampant; the name of Austin was on everyone's lips; and by 1872 the embryo town had grown to become the second largest city in Nevada.

A great deal of the usual, early mining litigation was avoided in Austin and the Reese River District because the Manhattan Silver Mining Co., over a period of six years ending in 1871, managed to consolidate the majority of the mining claims in the area. The company became an influential factor in the development of the District, and M. J. Farrell, its secretary, was elevated to the rank of state senator from Lander County. Austin in general, and the Manhattan mines in particular, greatly needed a railroad to provide transportation over the 93 miles northward to Battle Mountain on the Central Pacific Railroad. In 1874 Farrell set out to stimulate interest in such a project. True, there had been several previous ambitious proposals, but none had attained the remotest maturity. Austin needed a railroad — and right now.

In February 1875 the Nevada legislature authorized Lander County to grant $200,000 of its bonds as a subsidy to encourage the railroad, but to add stimulus to the encouragement, they set a time limit of five years for accomplishment of the objective. Farrell immediately went to work on the proposition, but his efforts to interest others in a railroad proved fruitless until finally one of his letters caught the eye of Col. Lyman Bridges, a Chicago engineer. Bridges came west, looked the proposition over, and liked it.

The Nevada Railway was formally organized at a meeting held in San Francisco's Baldwin Hotel on March 25, 1878. It would connect Austin with Battle Mountain (on the Central Pacific) and would be of narrow (3-foot) gauge, a type of construction which Farrell had previously studied and liked due to the economies involved. Economy was a major factor, for money was difficult to find. The Nevada Bank turned a deaf ear to the railroad's pleas. Another bank, owned by Allen Curtis, one of the railroad's directors, was reluctant to advance money other than "for discount commercial paper having a short time to run. There was nothing in the Nevada Railway's proposal for the Bank to entertain." In desperation the directors hired an agent at 2½% commission to locate $200,000 of financing at an interest not to exceed 12%. The agent found nothing, and his contract was cancelled after three months.

In spite of these discouragements, Lyman Bridges started his survey that spring. The course of the railroad was not a difficult one, for it followed the valley of the Reese River for almost the entire distance. By July 1878 the route was completely staked, but there was still no money and no railroad. And time, on the County bond subsidy, was beginning to run out.

A year went by. Then Anson Phelps Stokes became interested. Stokes was a grandson of the founder as well as a partner in Phelps Dodge, and it was his intention to develop Nevada silver properties in much the same manner as his company was developing Arizona copper. Already an investor in the Manhattan Silver Mining Co., he was anxious that Austin have outside rail connections and was willing to arrange for the bond financing.

Consequently, late in August 1879 a new company was formed utilizing virtually the same executive talent, but with a change of name to Nevada

Central Railway (no connection with the 1872 railroad of the same name between Pioche and Bullionville). The transfer of the surveys and franchises was accomplished at the Capital Hotel in Battle Mountain on September 15, 1879. Starting at 5:00 A.M., the Nevada Central Railway directors met to authorize the purchase of the assets of the Nevada Railway for $8,938.58. Then, one hour later, the directors of the latter company met and authorized the sale of their assets for the same amount. The early morning start was most appropriate, for little time was left in which to complete the railroad. February 9, 1880, was the expiration date set for the county bond subsidy and less than five months of primarily winter weather was rather short shrift for the construction of some 93 miles of railroad, narrow gauge or not.

To complicate the situation, no sooner had work been started than the graders decided to go on strike. Even though a settlement was quickly reached, there was still an annoying supply problem. The only near-by source of rail was the Pacific Rolling Mills in San Francisco, and they were solidly booked with orders. Fortunately, the narrow gauge Monterey & Salinas Valley Railroad in central California had just been taken over by the SP and was being converted to standard gauge with heavier rail. The Nevada Central hastily acquired the old rail together with that line's two locomotives. As a further measure, the directors authorized the contractor to buy an additional supply of unused rail which had originally been rolled for the Stockton & Ione Railroad in California. Additional purchases included two turntables from the SP for installation at Austin and at Station No. 2295 and a wye to be installed in the mouth of Big Creek near Jacobsville.

On October 21, 1879, the first 10 miles of line had been completed. Another 10 miles were finished 10 days later. The next 10 miles took 18 days to spike in place, thus bringing the calendar up to November 19. Including Thanksgiving, Christmas and New Years, 82 days were left in which to finish the remaining 63 miles — and winter was at hand.

Matters became desperate in December; only four additional miles of track were laid. Then General Ledlie took over, and the work moved ahead more expeditiously. The greatest problem to be faced was a continuing shortage of rail. Obtaining and keeping the engine crews was another, so Ledlie suggested their pay be increased. The arrival of another locomotive helped the situation tremendously; and by doubling the number of engine crews, utilization of equipment was vastly improved. By January 2, 1880, completed trackage had been increased to 40 miles of line, and 20 succeeding miles were laid during the month at the rate of a mile per day. Still faster progress was reported during the last few weeks of the month as rails and ties were thrown across the frozen ground with but scanty attempts at ballasting.

The critical day—February 9, 1880—arrived with inescapable finality. Unless claimed, the Lander County bond subsidy would cease to exist at mid-

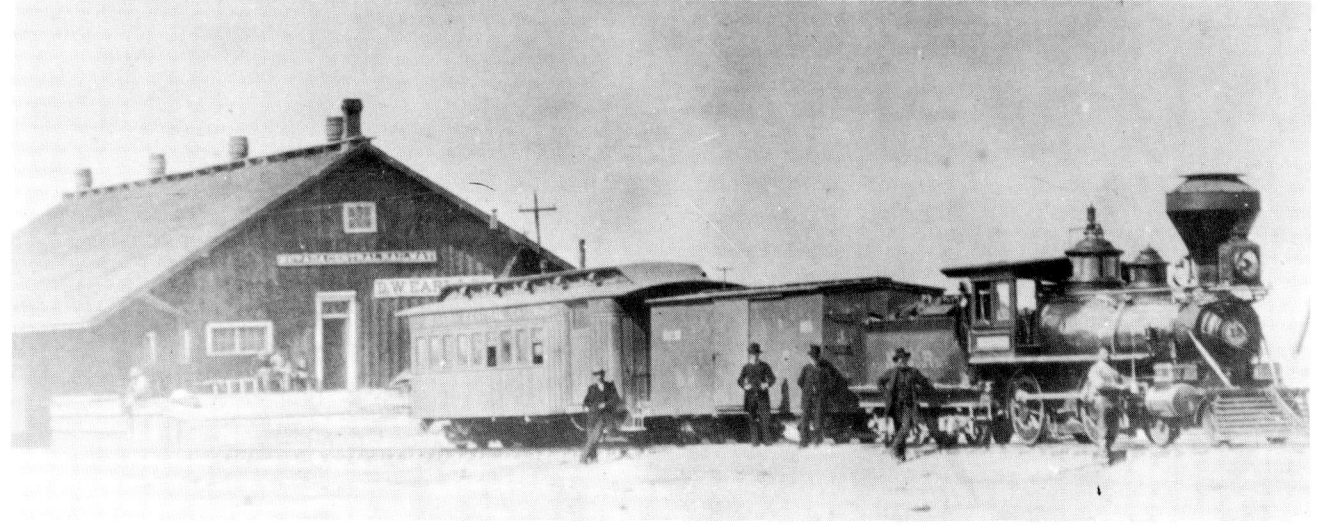

Still wearing Number Plate 12 of its former owner, the North Pacific Coast Railroad, Nevada Central No. 5 stands at Battle Mountain in 1886 with its abbreviated mixed train, awaiting the highball. (*T. L. Williamson Collection.*)

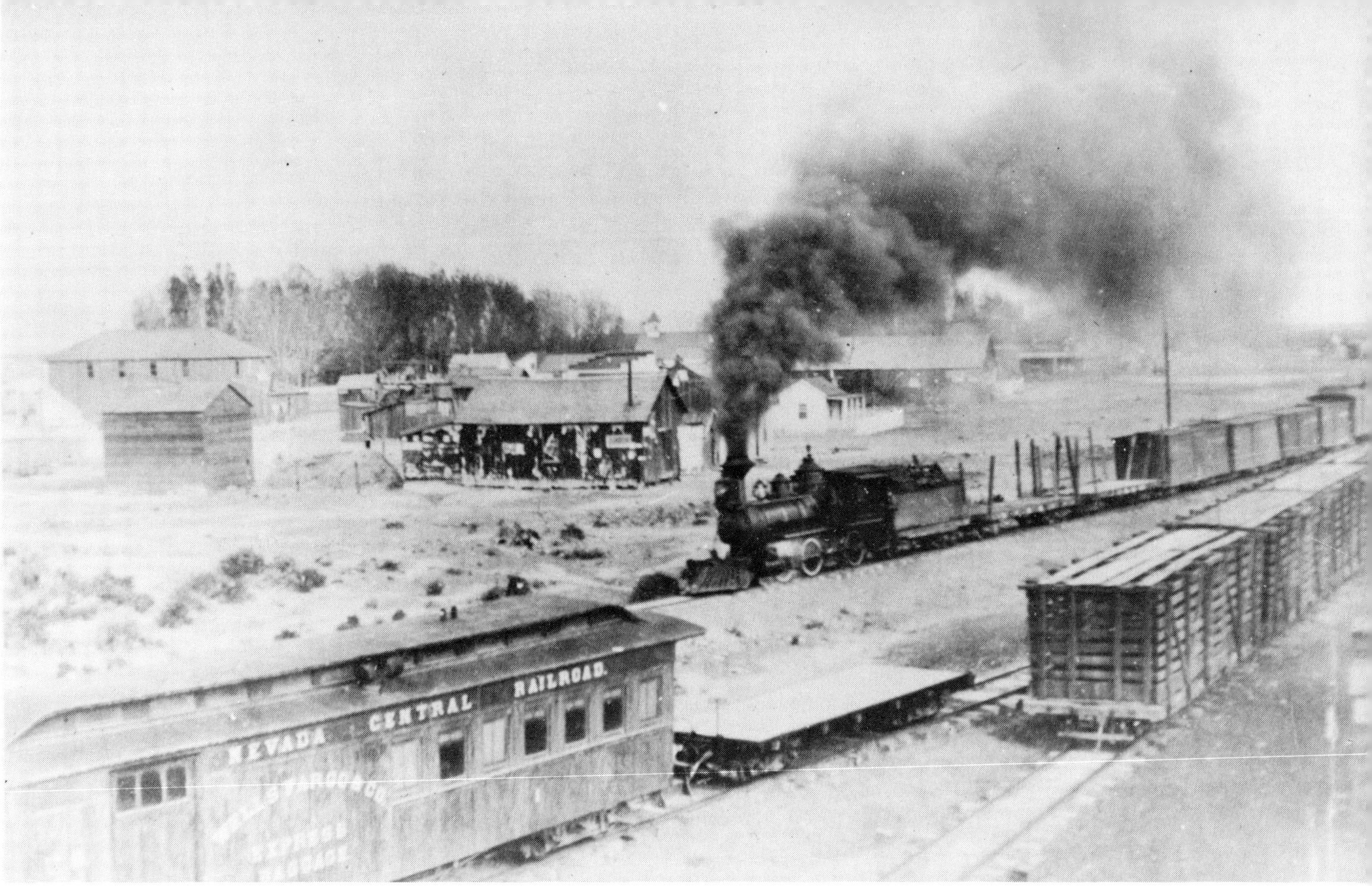

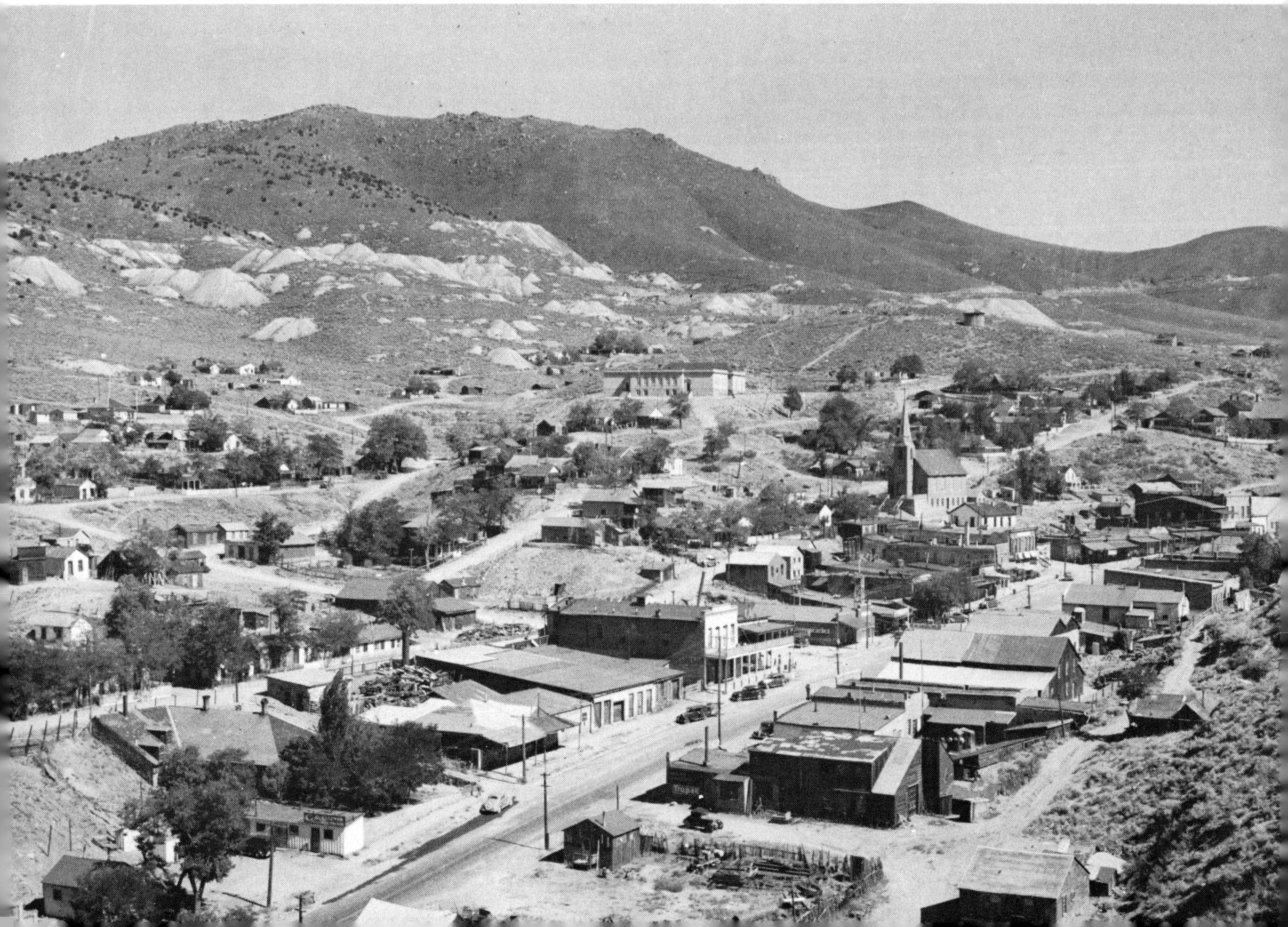

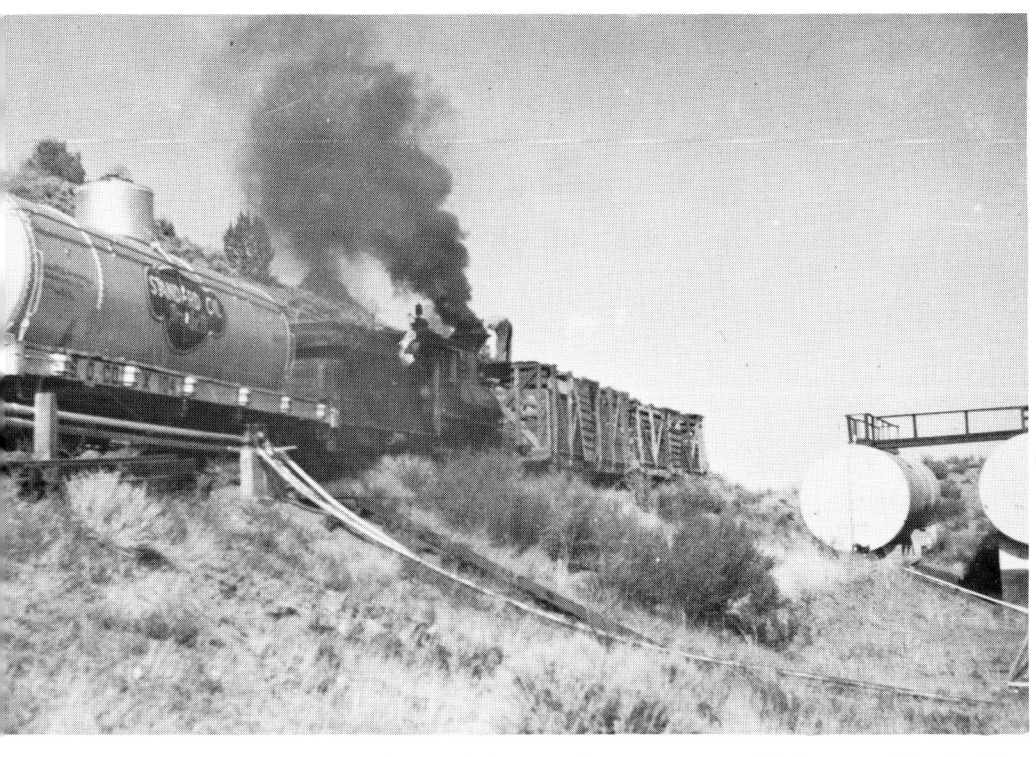

These tanks and storage building still extant 2011 summer

Rare in the extreme are action photos of the Nevada Central such as this *(top, page opposite)* 1884 portrait of a mixed train leaving Battle Mountain, or the switching operation at a bulk oil plant *(above)* involving an ornate tank car hand-fashioned from a standard flat car body. At Battle Mountain *(below)* American (4-4-0) No. 5, built by Baldwin in 1876, stands ready in early morning sunlight for departure on its 87-mile journey to Clifton, NC terminus for the city of Austin shown *(below, left)* in a 1930's view. The building (center), with the balcony over the sidewalk, is the famed International Hotel, destroyed by fire about 1950 and subsequently rebuilt along different lines. The former Austin City Railway ran easterly (to right) up the main street to the mines and reduction works at the upper end of town. U. S. Highway 50 climbs the hill in the background. *(Top Left: Williamson Collection; Bottom Right: Southern Pacific; Others: U. S. Geological Survey.)*

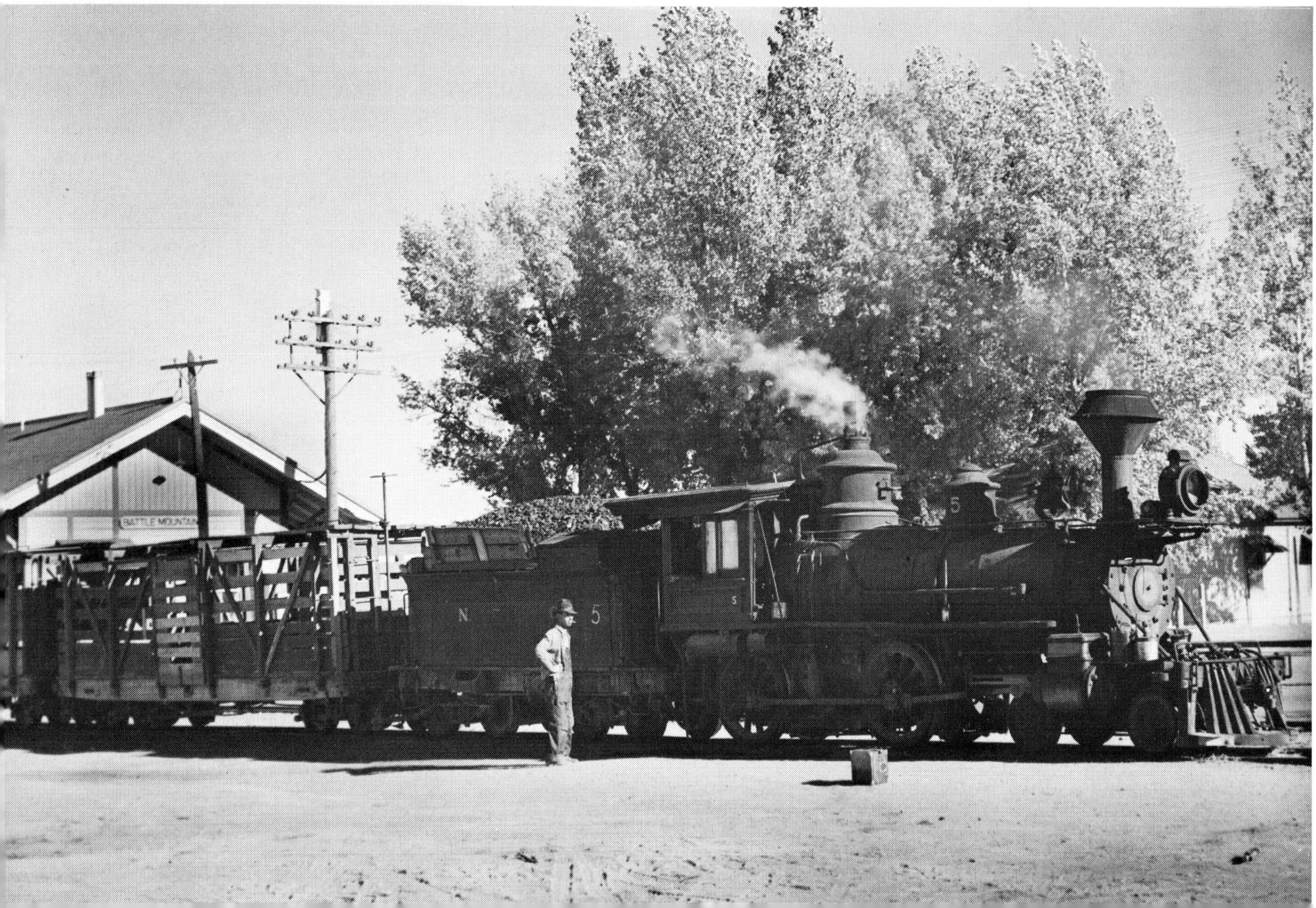

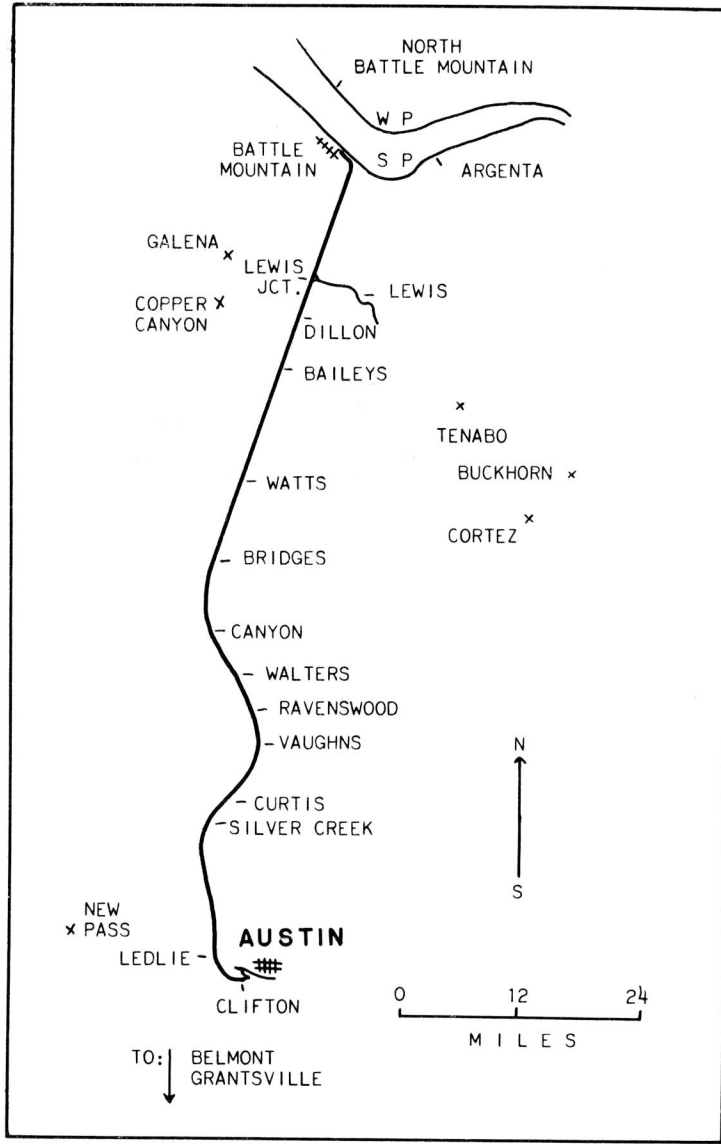

night; yet to claim it the railroad must accomplish the impossible and finish its line to the City of Austin. The story, oft repeated, is that Austin City officials recognized the railroad's plight and, in empathic resolve, enlarged the city limits to bring them closer to the advancing railhead. But repetition, per se, does not establish the veracity of a statement; and it is an established fact that Bert Acree, long the Lander County recorder, has searched for years in vain for the formal papers. Interesting, then, is the basis of authorization for issuance of the bonds which the Nevada Central collected when, at 10 minutes before midnight, track was completed by torchlight to stake 4811, 900 feet inside the expanded city limits.

The celebration was explosive. Melville Curtis sent up rockets; at 1:00 A.M. two engines appeared at end of track, and the accompanying blast of their whistles blended with the din from all the mill whistles which were tied down for one full hour. "Main Street, at 2:00 A.M., presented an appearance of metropolitan proportions, so numerous were the people," reported the *Reese River Reveille* in an account of the event in its extra edition which was soon exhausted. So great was the demand, the story had to be reprinted two days later.

Luck was with the construction forces — a bad storm broke the very next day causing widespread damage which had to be repaired. Too, much of the hastily laid track near Austin needed reworking to put it in shape for regular operation of trains. Although the contractor commenced operating the road on a regular schedule on February 24, the official "Open for business day" was set for March 1. Track was extended a short distance to Clifton at the bottom of the hill where connecting stages accommodated passengers the rest of the way up the hill to Austin. The railroad as completed was 93¾ miles long, although later (1888) it was commonly referred to as being 93 miles; passenger fare for the one-way trip was $9.00.

The overall running time from Austin to Battle Mountain required eight hours; travel in the reverse direction required an additional 20 minutes. Instructions from the superintendent established passenger fares at 10 cents a mile and freight rates at 1 cent per hundred pounds for each mile of haulage. All trains were required to reduce speed to five miles per hour when passing switches. With meal stops established at Hallsville for outbound trains to Battle Mountain and at Bridges for the return trip, it is not surprising that the average speed for the 93 mile trip was only 11 miles per hour.

With the advent of spring weather, the frozen ground heaved, then thawed, and the roadbed had to be thoroughly reworked. A force of 200 men was assigned to the job. By June 10 sufficient stabilization had been achieved to enable the schedule to be trimmed by one full hour. Freight business was not overburdening, averaging approximately 10 carloads per day. Picnic trains were inaugurated in June, the first operating to Walters (60 miles from Battle Mountain) where the day's events were highlighted by a baseball game in which the Austin nine subdued the Battle Mountain team by the extreme margin of one run. At the second, big holiday picnic on July Fourth the tables were somewhat reversed — Battle Mountain was leading the Austinites with a score of 38 to 26 when the game was called at dusk. Early, unexpected fireworks developed on the way to the picnic, when two railroad officials elected to ride the locomotive pilot for the trip. En route, the engineer thought he smelled something burning and sent the fireman ahead to investigate. Sure enough, while the two men on the pilot had been talking about fireworks, unaware that sparks had set fire to the clothes of one of the men. The train was stopped; the blaze extinguished; but the victim was reported to have "walked kind of sideways" for a considerable time afterward.

In the autumn of 1880 the daily mixed train was abolished. In its stead a full-fledged passenger train was inaugurated on a 5½-hour schedule, while a tri-weekly freight handled the carload and less-than-carload freight routines. The railroad appeared to be coming of age, in spite of the fact that the census that year counted 1,679 people in Austin, 216 in Lewis and 522 in Battle Mountain. Obviously, additional business would have to be developed.

The idea was not new. Immediately following the railroad's dramatic entrance into Austin in February, Nevada Central men had organized two new projects to expand their horizons. The "Nevada Northern Railway, First Division" was to start from the Battle Mountain terminus and build northward 120 miles to the Idaho state line with the objective of continuing on to the Columbia River. The contra-companion project, the "Nevada Southern Railway, First Division," was to start from a point near Austin and build southward to Cloverdale, passing within a few miles of Grantsville, and encompassing the hopeful objective of continuing on to Columbus, Silver Peak and even the Southern Pacific RR far to the south. At this particular moment the Carson & Colorado Railroad was still just a gleam in the eyes of its founder, Darius Mills, while the Nevada Central was successfully soliciting business with special rates and other inducements from such mining camps as Ione, Grantsville, Belmont and even Gold Mountain, then an active metropolis of 50 shacks and 6 saloons some 150 miles to the southwest.

In March 1880 a group of surveyors under Col. Bridges went to work on the Nevada Northern route, while another group under Bridges' assistant, J. R. Hudson, set out from Austin on the projected Nevada Southern. Even the Central Pacific joined in the act and surveyed its own route northward from Battle Mountain into the Snake River country in Idaho. Bridges was the first to return with his report, after traversing over 300 miles of territory. He had made arrangements to meet with Henry Villard (of OR&N and later Northern Pacific fame) at Baker City in eastern Oregon, and it was anticipated that Villard's line would run along the Columbia River, thence over the Blue Mountains in southeastern Washington, and on down to a connection with the Nevada Northern.

On the home front, the newspapers were having a heyday making all manner of allegations and counter-allegations. The *Battle Mountain Messenger*, ever the more optimistic, quoted the *Reese River Reveille* as saying: "We would advise the press not to get excited over the reported new rail-

Trains could not exceed 20 miles per hour when Employees' Timetable No. 11 went into effect on November 12, 1899. Service was light (one train each way per day), but so was traffic, for the Austin Mining Co. had suspended operations the year previous. (*J. G. Phelps Stokes Papers in Nevada Historical Society.*)

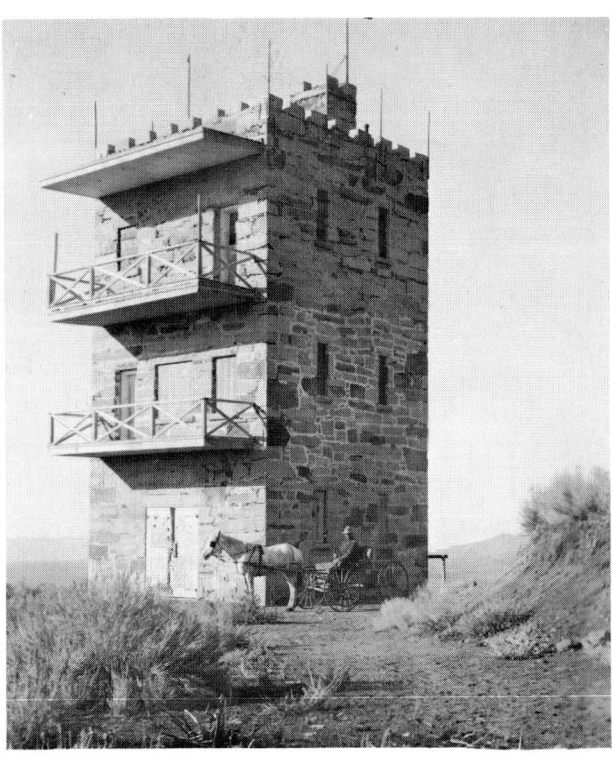

When J. G. Phelps Stokes went to Nevada to look after his father's interests, this famous Stokes Tower was erected for his residence (shown here in 1907). *(Sewell Thomas Photo.)*

roads, one to run north from Battle Mountain and the other from Austin southwest. There is nothing in it. Two sheets of legal cap paper have been spoiled. That and nothing more." Then the *Messenger* commented caustically: "We would advise the *Reveille* to keep within the bounds of truth and not to go libeling new enterprises before it knows anything about them. For some reason or other, it was hostile to the Nevada Central and now it commences on the new roads before they get fairly started. Papers like the *Reveille* are the kind that are needed in a young state like Nevada. They help build the country so fast, the only trouble is they build the wrong way . . ." Actually, the harsh words of the *Reveille* bore the closest resemblance to the truth. When the *Territorial Enterprise*, after hearing that some New Yorkers had gone over the proposed Nevada Southern route, reported that the contracts had been let, the *Reveille* justifiably enjoined it for building the railroad "a little too fast." As a matter of fact, both the Nevada Northern and the Nevada Southern projects lapsed into quiescence during the summer of 1880.

In the fall there was a reshuffling of officers and directors, and a whole new organization came into being called the Southern Nevada Railway. Formal organization took place in November at which time it was announced that steel rails had already been ordered and that work would commence the following spring. The route would start from a junction with the Nevada Central at Ledlie, cross the Reese River Valley above Rooker's Ranch, then turn northwesterly through a pass in the mountains to Edwards Creek, thence down the west side of the range in a southerly direction to a point opposite Grantsville. (Undoubtedly Railroad Pass on U. S. Highway 50 received its name from this survey.)

But events in the 1880's were moving rapidly. By the spring of 1881 the Carson & Colorado Railroad had completed its line all the way from Mound House to Hawthorne, and traffic from Belmont, Grantsville, Ione and neighboring camps began to flow to the newer and shorter route. Business on the Nevada Central between Austin and Battle Mountain fell to half its former volume. Revenues proportionally reflected this decrease in traffic, and with the Grantsville boom subsiding, plans for the Southern Nevada Railway were shelved indefinitely. Even the newly organized, connecting Austin City Railway (May 1881) and the Battle Mountain & Lewis Railway (July 1881) failed to render a modicum of surcease to the eternal problem.

On the other hand, the Union Pacific was aggressively inclined. In 1881 it had plans for an extension to California and had already incorporated the Salt Lake & Western Railway to build across central Nevada somewhere in the vicinity of Belmont. By building an extension north to Austin and gobbling up the Nevada Central, the UP could virtually control the potential traffic of the entire area. In June 1881 the Nevada Central was purchased; Bridges congratulated the UP on its foresight and pocketed a $55,000 profit on the sale of his stock. That year the system map in the UP stockholders' report showed the new line together with a proposed extension from Austin to Silver Peak.

But the UP's rosy dreams were short-lived and failed of materialization. In the next few years the situation degenerated, and in June 1884 Charles Francis Adams was brought into the UP organization to straighten matters out. As Adams later commented, one of the first things he did when he became president was to throw the Nevada Central overboard together with the UP investment of some $450,000 in its stock and income bonds. There were no regrets. Even before Adams took office, almost a mile of Nevada Central track had been washed out, and this plus the general languishing spirit in Austin probably convinced him that the NC had no future. "Mining railroads are a species of railroad gambling," he declared and then went on to explain that things were fine when the mines were active, but if they were not, you merely had a railroad on your hands. Consequently, after having advanced $115,094 to the little road so it could pay the interest on the first mortgage bonds, the UP directors decided to let the October 1884 coupons go unpaid. Following this default, the Nevada Central was thrown into receivership the next year and sold at bankruptcy to the bondholders, which placed it right back in the hands of the original owners — Anson Phelps Stokes et al. A new company, the Nevada Central *Railroad*, took over the property on November 1, 1888, with Stokes firmly in control.

Other Austin enterprises suffered vicissitudes. The old Manhattan silver mines went through several reorganizations and were finally closed in 1890. To acquire the properties, Stokes organized the Austin Mining Company in 1891 and under that banner drove the Austin-Manhattan drainage and haulage tunnel almost 6,000 feet under Lander Hill for exploration purposes. The job was performed over a period of approximately 10 years, the tunnel portal being located in Pony Canyon near the railroad terminal at Clifton where a 40-stamp mill was erected.

In 1897 another star appeared on the horizon. J. G. Phelps Stokes, fresh out of Yale's Sheffield Scientific School and with a medical degree from Columbia University, arrived in Nevada to take charge of his father's interests. In anticipation of the event, his father erected the famous Stokes Tower, just west of Austin, to provide him with a Nevada residence.

Additional troubles developed in 1898. Tasker Oddie, a young attorney employed in the Stokes' (Woodbridge Co.) New York real estate business, was sent west to look over the family interests in Austin, Ione and Downieville. He returned to New York with the seemingly incredible contention that one of the trusted managers of the business had embezzled an estimated $300,000 from the Austin Mining Co. At first the story was not accepted; the manager disclaimed the charge as ridiculous. Subsequent investigation, however, proved that Oddie was correct. Operations were suspended; miners were laid off; and for the first time in a third of a century, not a single steam whistle was heard in Austin.

In the early 1900's the Nevada Central was variously eyed by others as an integral part of railroad schemes promulging. The Nevada Midland selected it in 1902 as the base for a line to Tonopah, then just beginning to blossom into bonanza. (For a time the Nevada Central itself entertained ideas of a route to Tonopah in 1905 and even went so far as to have surveys made.) Then, around 1910, the SP considered the road in conjunction with its proposed inland route from Los Angeles via the Owens Valley to Basalt, Battle Mountain and Ogden. Even George Gould was said to have purchased the line for the Western Pacific. Probably the last and most advertent project was the inopportune Mid Pacific enterprise of the 1930's.

In spite of all this attention, the affairs of the Nevada Central were decidedly importunate. Mining activity at Austin diminished around 1904 and virtually ceased after 1911. Traffic patterns shifted, and the majority of the road's business originated in new and different areas. The Nevada Company's mines at Berlin (another Stokes property) supplied a full one-third of the freight traffic in 1903. From 1907 to 1909 a substantial proportion of the road's business was derived from Manhattan and Round Mountain.

Then, on February 13, 1910, calamity struck. Water pouring from the foothills near Bailey's damaged five miles of track. Even before the two weeks' repair job was completed, the Reese River went on a rampage and the entire line, including the Battle Mountain yards, sustained untold damage. Traffic was suspended, the motor car and work train were stranded before repairs were effected by crews of Italian and Greek laborers. Regular service was not instituted again until May 30.

Unusual and singular was the year 1911. Livestock movements provided a greater volume of business than mining, and revenues reached the astounding figure of $84,614, highest in the company's history with the exception of the year 1881. The following year the mines closed down, and the livestock and wool businesses were virtually the sole sustenance of the railroad. Not until 1916 did mining come back into the picture, and then it was the copper mines at New Pass and Dillon that supplied over one-half of the traffic.

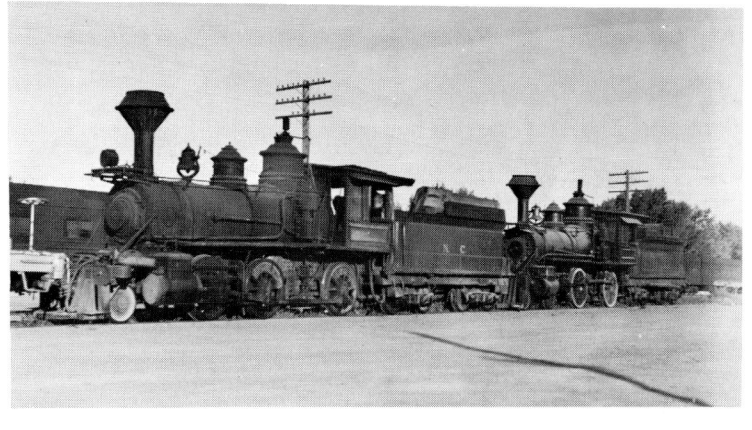
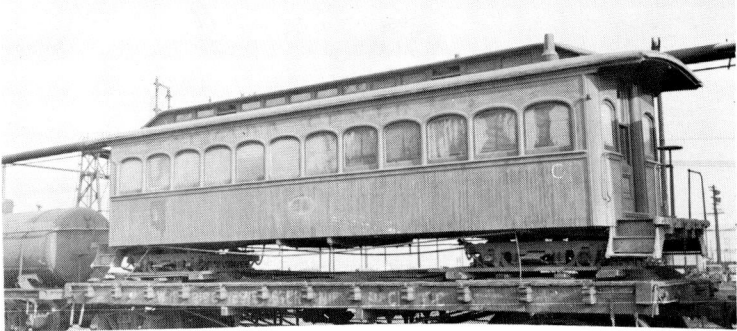
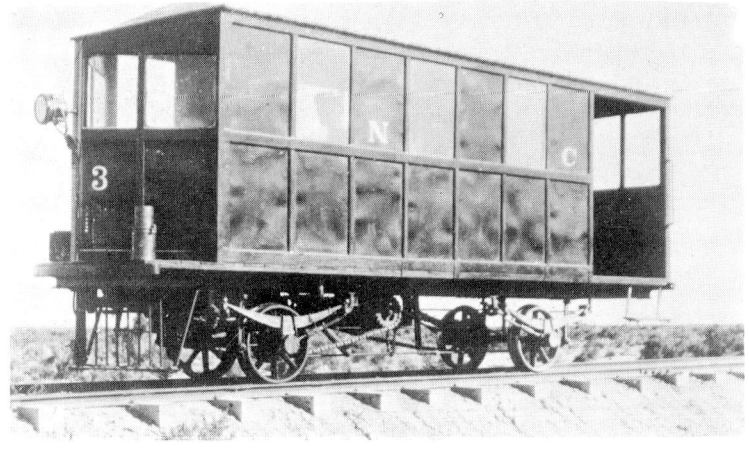

A lifespan of railroading is encompassed in this vignette of Nevada Central locomotives and equipment. The early days are represented by the two portraits *(right, top and center)* of locomotive No. 2 with passenger train and No. 1 with mixed train, respectively, both at Battle Mountain. On this page *(top)* are locomotives Nos. 2 and 5 at the end of their NC service in 1938; *(next below)* the *Silver State*, once the luxurious parlor car from the NC's Battle Mountain shops; and *(third below)* Nevada Central Motor No. 3, a home-crafted product of dubious distinction featuring automobile leaf springs and a chain drive to the front axle. In 1939 *(below, left and right)* Nevada Central's Nos. 6 and 5 were reincarnated as Union Pacific No. 119 and Central Pacific JUPITER, respectively, for the Treasure Island pageant, "Wedding of the Rails" at the San Francisco Exposition. *(Left, Top and Third: Albert C. Phelps; Left, Second, and Right, First and Second: Ted Wurm Collection; Bottom Left and Right: Guy Dunscomb.)*

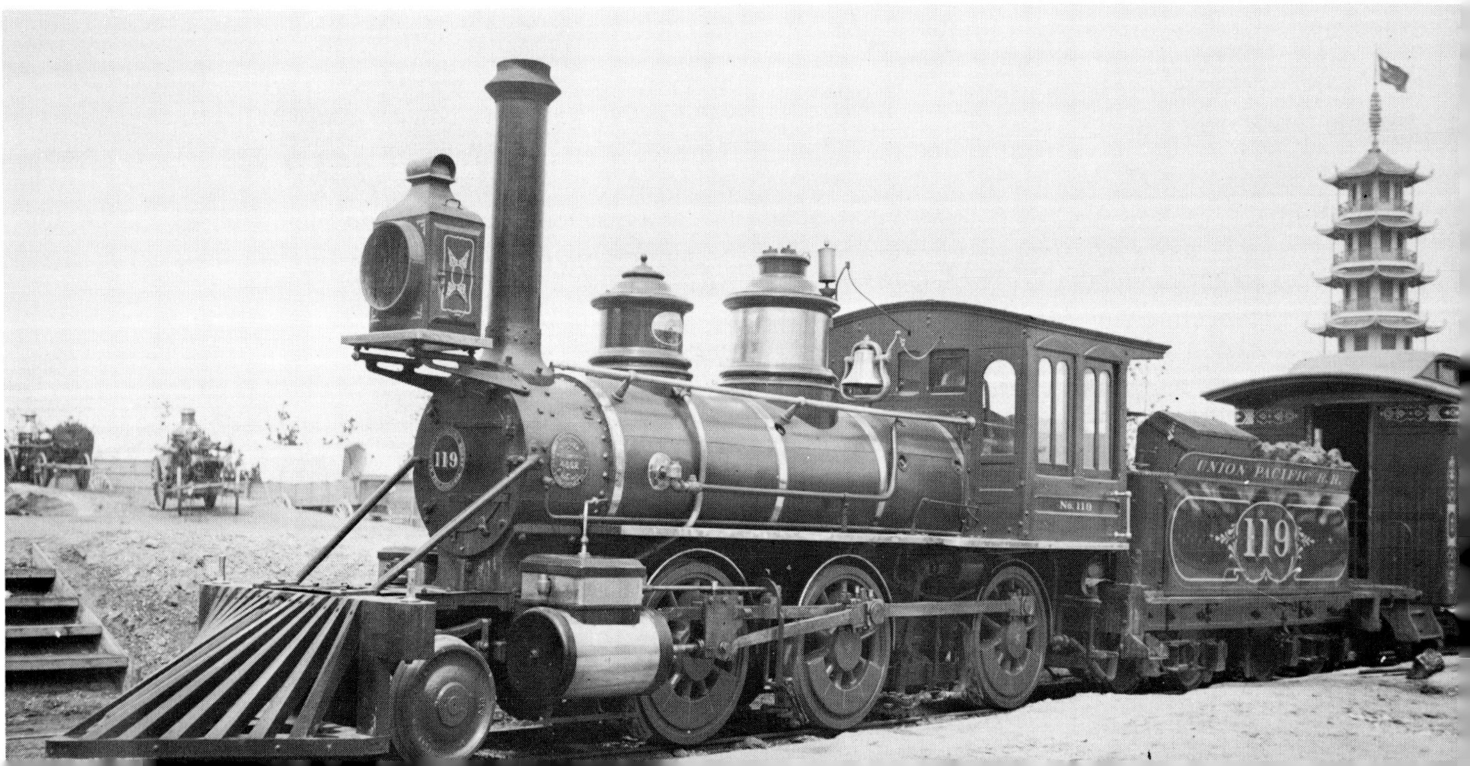

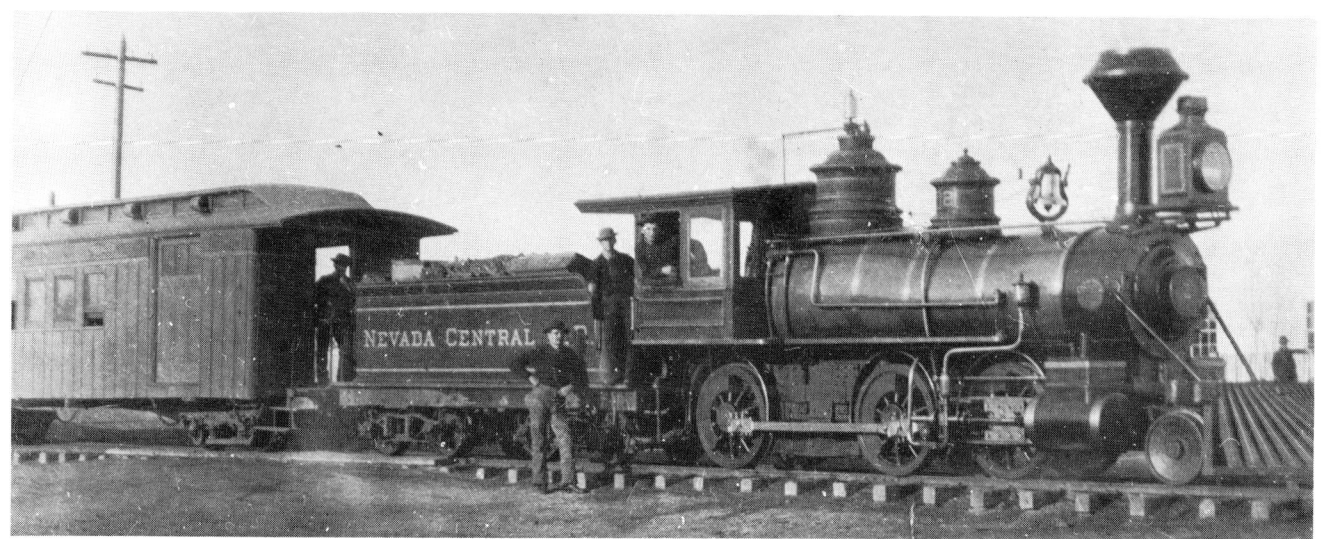

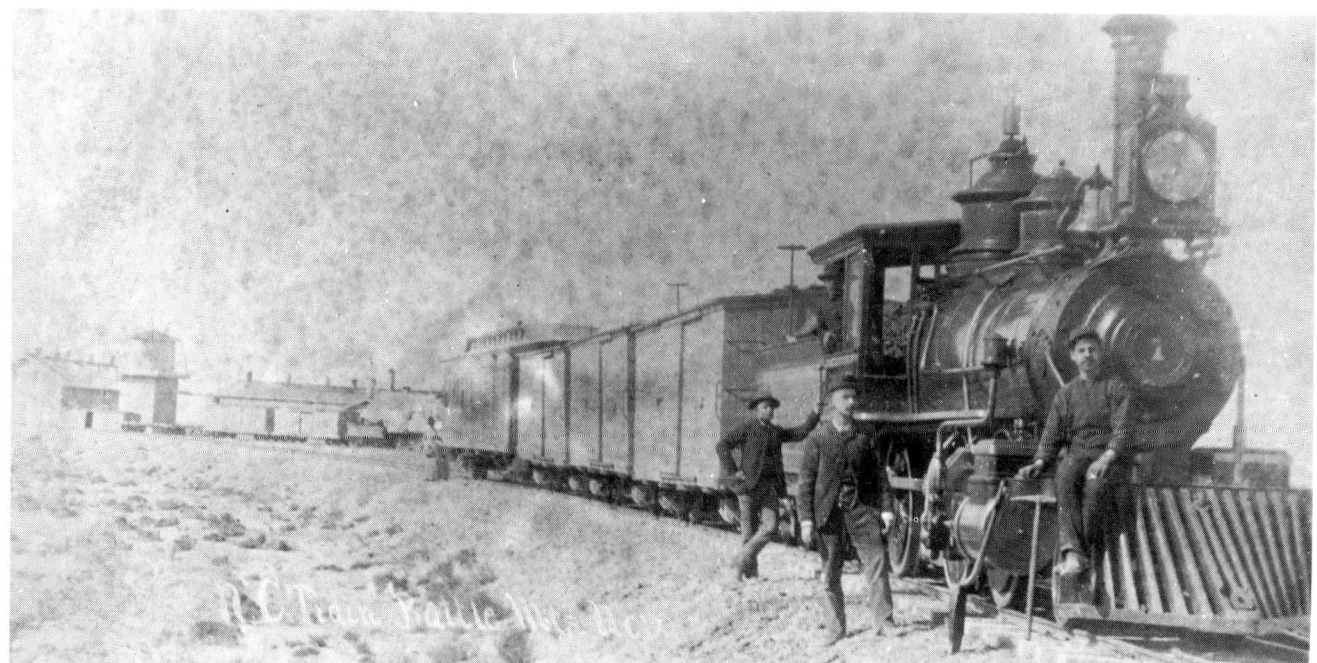

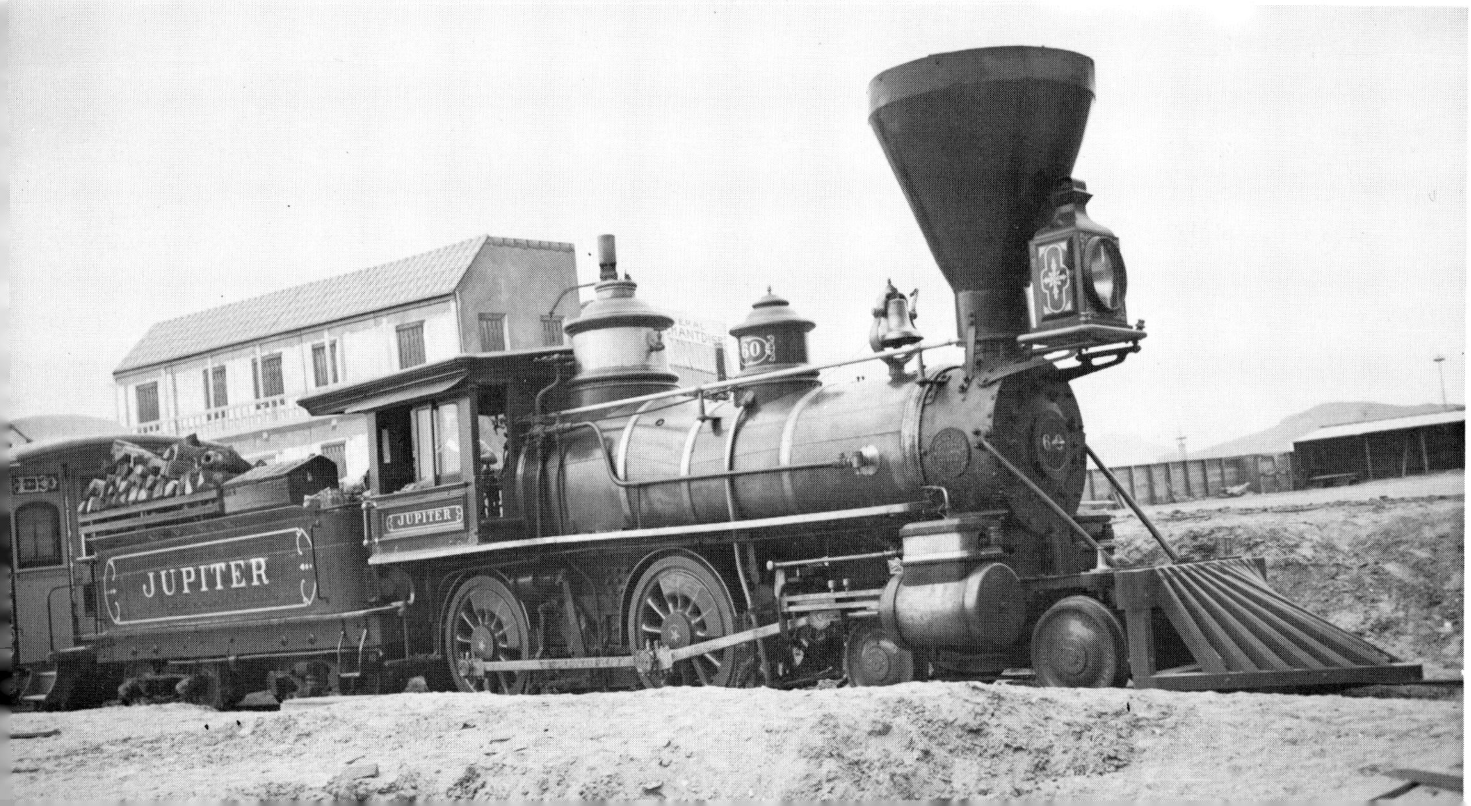

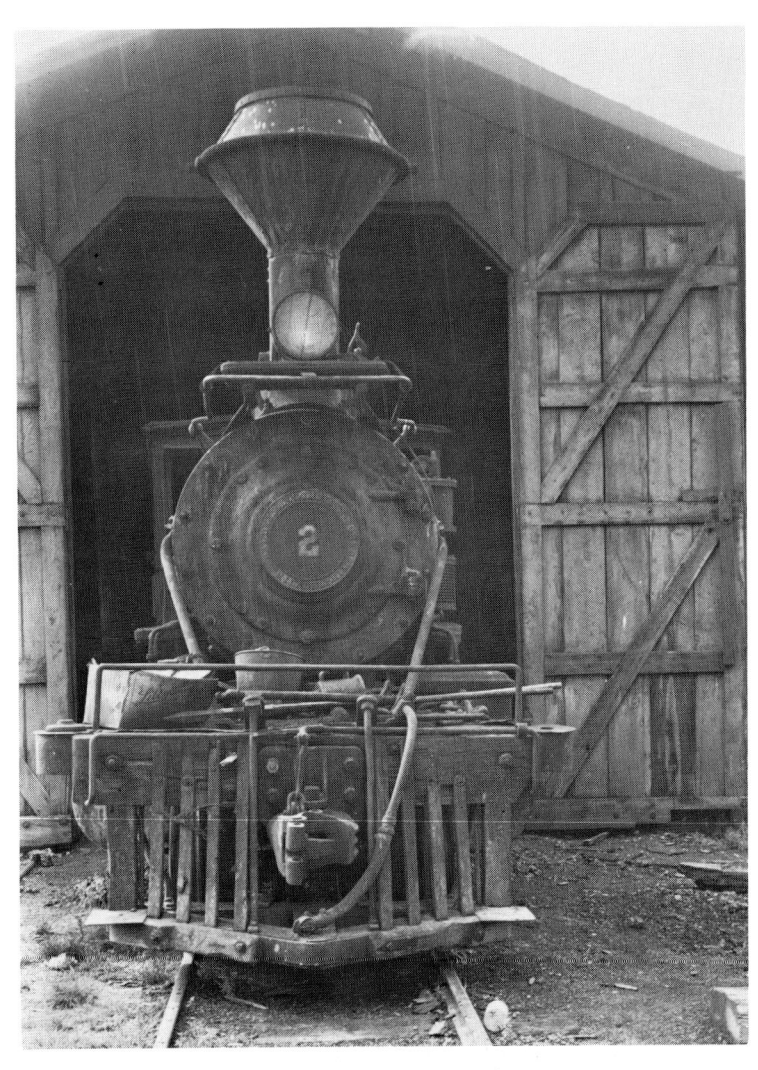

Officially the Nevada Central was abandoned on January 31, 1938, although much of the equipment remained on the Battle Mountain premises throughout the summer. On July 4, 1938, the profile of Mogul (2-6-0) No. 2 presented this drab appearance with its sickly, cracked electric headlight and the assorted tools of many derailments haphazardly stacked aboard its pilot beam.

In September the equipment was hauled away. No. 6 (loaded in gondola at left) and Combine No. 1 (at right) went to the Pacific Coast Chapter of the Railway & Locomotive Historical Society for preservation; engine No. 1 (right) was scrapped in San Francisco. (*Upper: Guy L. Dunscomb; Lower: Albert C. Phelps.*)

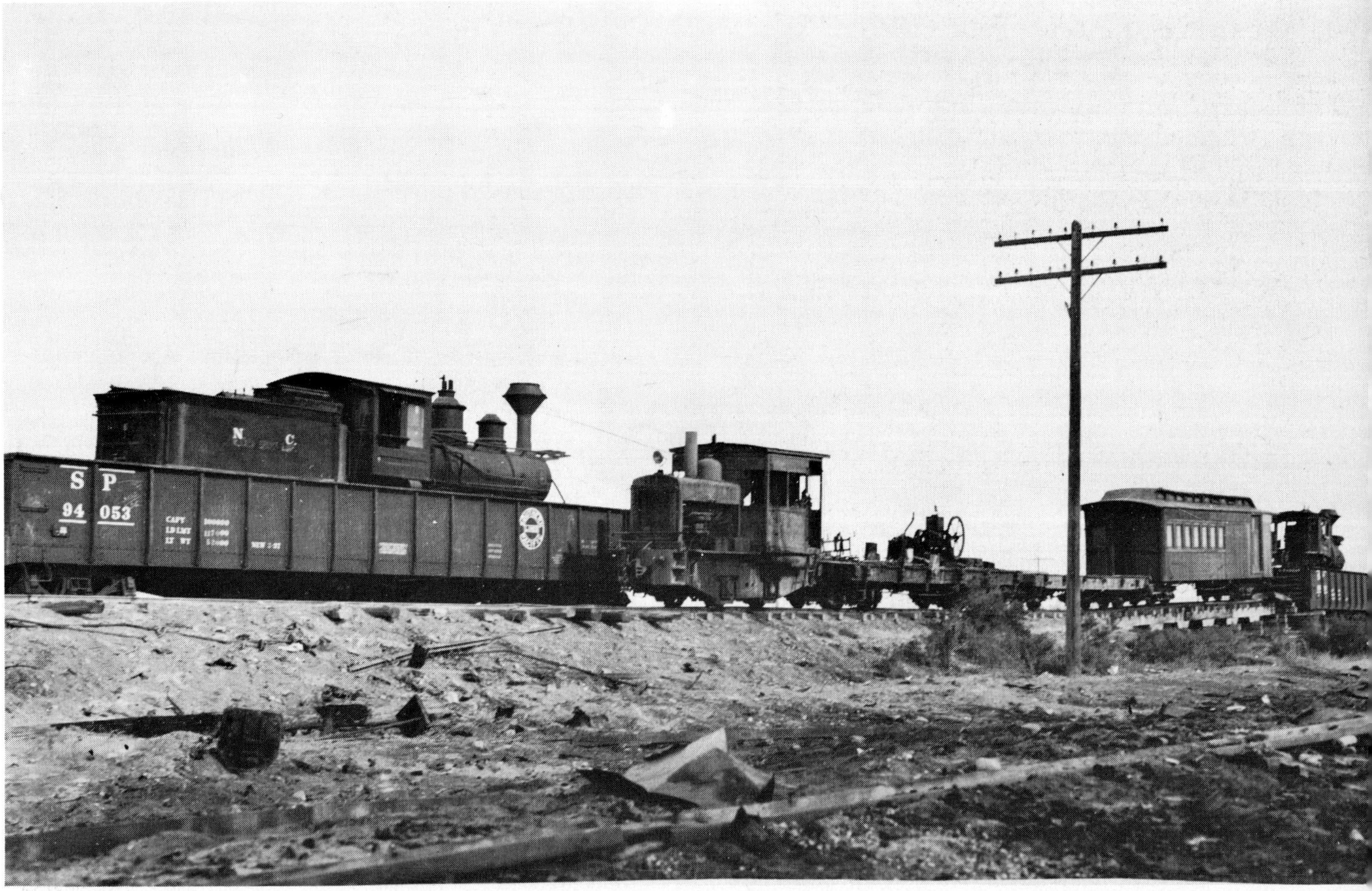

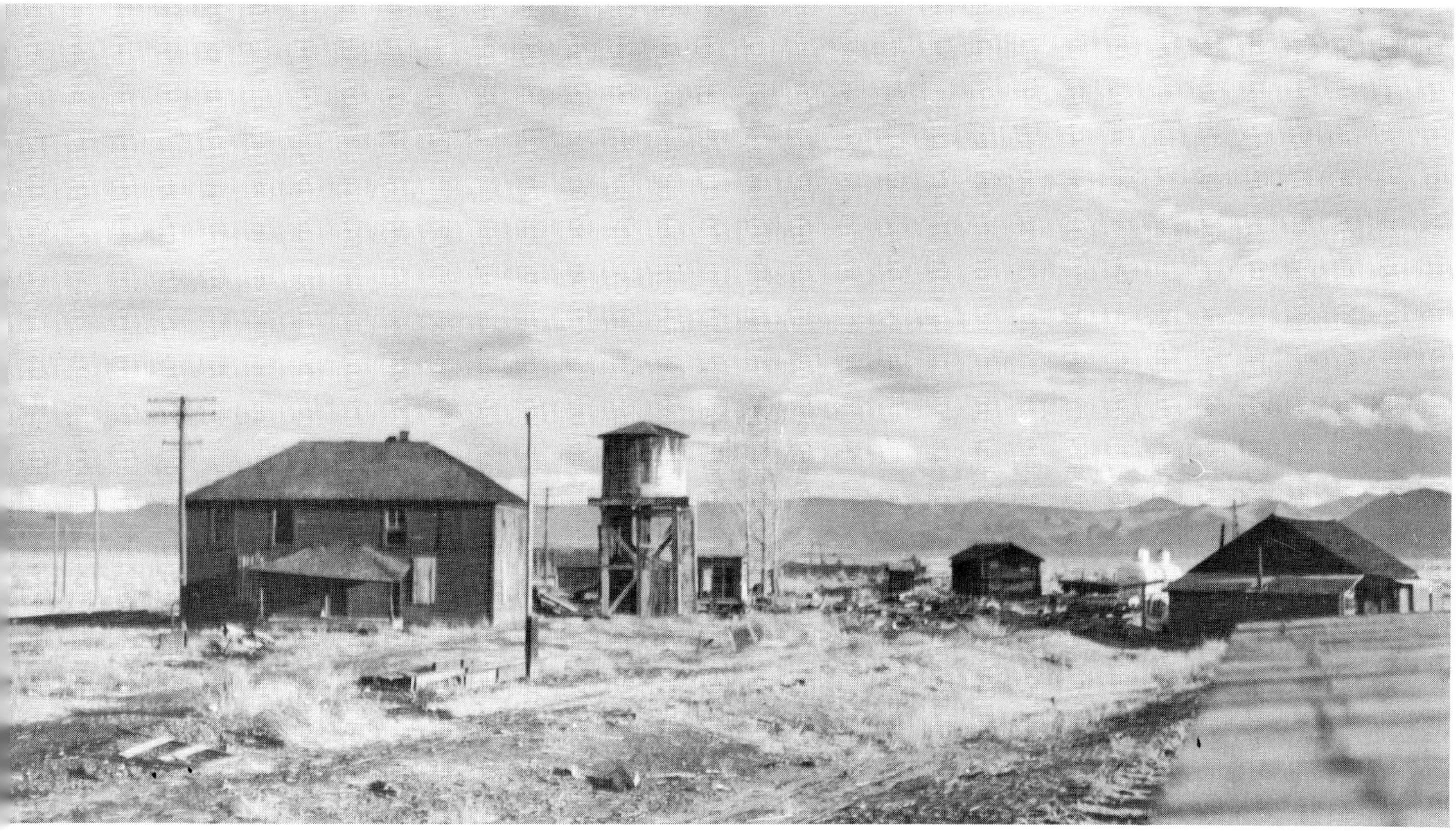

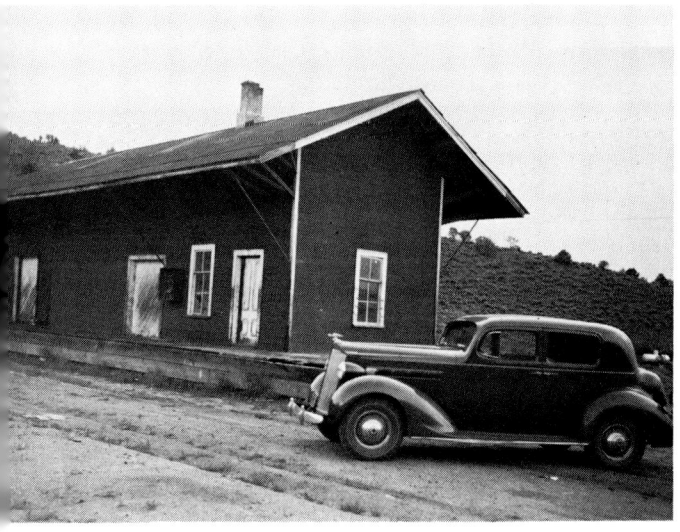

When the scrap dealers, Hyman-Michaels, had finished their job on the Nevada Central in 1938, there was little left at Battle Mountain *(above)* or at (Clifton) Austin *(center)* by which to recognize the once proud narrow gauge as typified by the view *(below)* of the Battle Mountain shops and terminal facilities in the more glorious year of 1887. *(Top and Bottom: Tom L. Williamson; Center: Ted Wurm Photo.)*

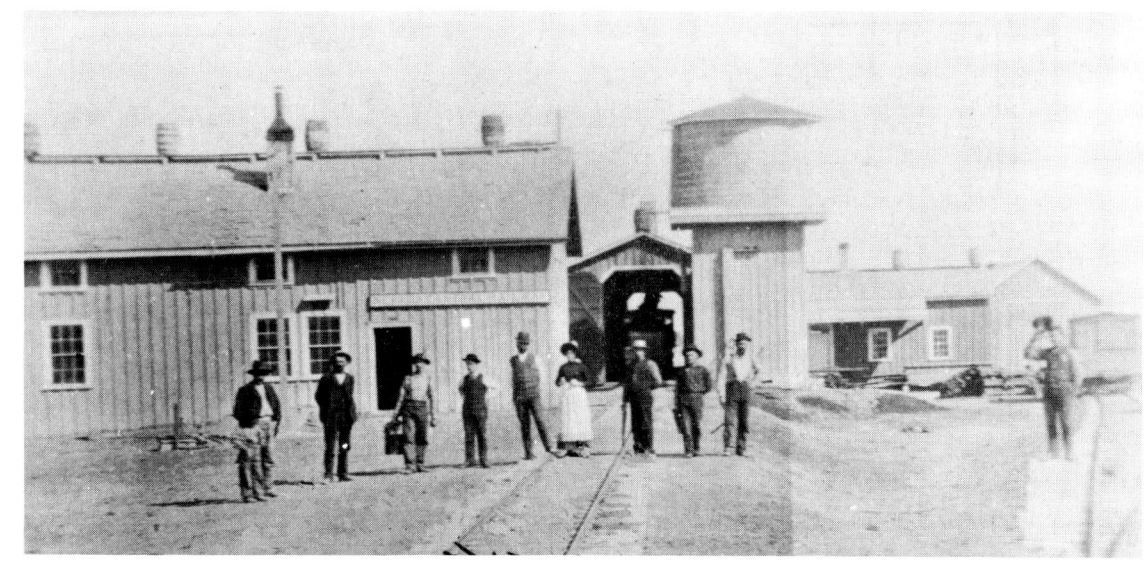

Generally speaking, the 1920's were rather dull years for the little road. There were the usual washouts and small fires, augmented by one conflagration of note when the engine house at Austin was consumed by flames on June 26, 1925. Succeeding years saw the rise of motor bus competition, so on April 27, 1927, the Nevada Central commenced to operate its own line of stages. At the end of the year they were turned over to an affiliated company, Nevada Central Motor Lines, more colloquially known as Hiskey Stages. J. M. Hiskey (from whom the name was derived) was a very active man in the area, holding five distinct titles on the railroad alone — secretary, treasurer, general manager, superintendent and auditor. It would appear that the internal accounting control in the financial affairs of the railroad left something to be desired with the combination of the second and last positions being vested in one individual.

In the late 1920's, gross income averaged around $25,000 annually, which was about half that of the NC's neighboring railroad to the east, the Eureka-Nevada. Moreover, there were no visible signs of improvement. To the contrary, in 1932 snow tied up the railroad completely for a period of 60 days; two of its locomotives had been out of service for some time; the other two needed repairs; and the motor cars, due to the loss of traction on the icy rails, could not operate effectively in the heavy snow. The following winter was not much better. Hiskey attempted to anticipate snow conditions, but still the railroad became snowbound while attempting to rescue a band of sheep. "The road could easily be kept open by continuous daily movement of steam trains," Hiskey reported to J. G. Phelps Stokes, "but the cost, in the absence of revenue business to be moved thereon, is prohibitive."

A review of the road's financial history showed that it had had 32 years of profitable operations and 25 years of losses. It had never paid a dividend. Its only debt, after the 1888 reorganization, was an issue of $750,000 5% income bonds. In no year was the interest paid in full on these bonds, and none at all was paid following 1917. There was nothing in the picture even remotely encouraging; so with the corporate charter about to expire, the road was abandoned on January 31, 1938.

What physical properties of rails and accessories remained were sold to Hyman-Michaels, scrap dealers, for $22,500. Fortunately, through the timely intervention of Gilbert Kneiss, many of the pieces of equipment (including the famed "Silver State" coach) have been preserved and will be placed on display in a transportation museum in the San Francisco Bay area.

Battle Mountain & Lewis Railway

Battle Mountain was the center of considerable activity in the 1880's. Social affairs centered around Huntsman's popular Capital Hotel where passengers from the Central Pacific's Palace Cars detrained for culinary respite. More plebeian activities surrounded the freight transfer station attending the junction of the standard gauge Central Pacific Railway and its narrow gauge counterpart, the Nevada Central. The town also served as the major supply center for an active mining region. Too, it had possibilities for becoming a major railroad crossroad if plans for the projected Nevada Northern and Nevada Southern Railroads were brought to fruition. Completion of these two lines would make the Nevada Central part and parcel of a major north-south routing.

South and somewhat west of Battle Mountain were other mining camps — Galena, Copper Basin and Copper Canyon — variously active from time to time for many years. Daily stages ran to Galena, operated by the same Alex Robertson who served as agent for Clugage & Parker's stages running northeasterly to Tuscarora. Ore from Copper Canyon was teamed to Battle Mountain to be loaded onto cars of the Central Pacific as the first step in the chain of circumstance that would see it conveyed all the way to Liverpool, England.

South and somewhat east of Battle Mountain were Crum (Krum) Canyon and Lewis Canyon. In the first named defile, a railroad was proposed but never built; in the latter, one did succeed of accomplishment, however short-lived. For it was in Lewis Canyon, as early as 1867, that Johnathan Green and E. J. George reportedly made the original locations of silver ore and developed the earliest mines. To attend their production, the Eagle and Starr Grove mills were constructed, and in 1877 a town called Lewis was laid out in the narrow confines of the canyon with but one (appropriately named) Main Street. When activities increased, Lewis enlarged in the only directions possible — to the north and south—and acquired a new name in the expanded hierarchy, Middletown. That area to the north (down the canyon) became Lowertown, while up the canyon to the south Uppertown was established.

On February 9, 1880, shortly after the Nevada Central Railway had completed its line to Austin, considerable excitement was experienced in the town of Lewis when ore assaying $3,000 to the ton was discovered in the Morgan mine in Lewis Canyon. By June 1880 other finds had been made, and regular shipments of gold bars were being made weekly from the Starr Grove and Betty O'Neal mines. In one three-week period a total of 21 bars were sent out. In November 1880, eastern interests incorporated the Starr Grove Silver Mining Co. to acquire the mine and 15-stamp mill of the same name. Then in January 1880 plans were announced for the formation of the Battle Mountain & Lewis Railway to be constructed from the Nevada Central Railway at Galena, 10.5 miles south of Battle Mountain (later Lewis Junction), easterly to Lewis Canyon and thence southerly up the canyon to the mines. The total distance amounted to approximately 12 miles. Backing the enterprise to an unknown extent were the eastern owners of the Starr & Grove mining properties.

Grading commenced on January 28, 1881. During February carloads of rails and ties were delivered on location. The job was short; but little grading was required for the first section of the line which followed a straight path across a flat valley and made but one turn approaching Lewis Canyon; and the job was finished to Lewis Station (Lowertown) on April 25, 1881. A ball was held that night to commemorate the event.

Even as the road was being constructed, there was difficulty on the labor scene. In February the Starr Grove management cut the miners' wages; the miners left their jobs; the mine was closed. An attempt at a reopening resulted in a clash of men, and three shootings (one fatal) resulted. Still later, in March of that year, 57 men petitioned the union to be allowed to work, but the 21 union members said "No." A telegram was dispatched to the Miners' Union at Austin, creating considerable excitement there. The Austinites held a meeting and decided the entire membership should go to Lewis, so 250 men armed themselves with guns, rifles and shotguns and chartered a train of box cars to Lewis. The train conductor was made to understand the necessity for a speedy trip, and the engine was

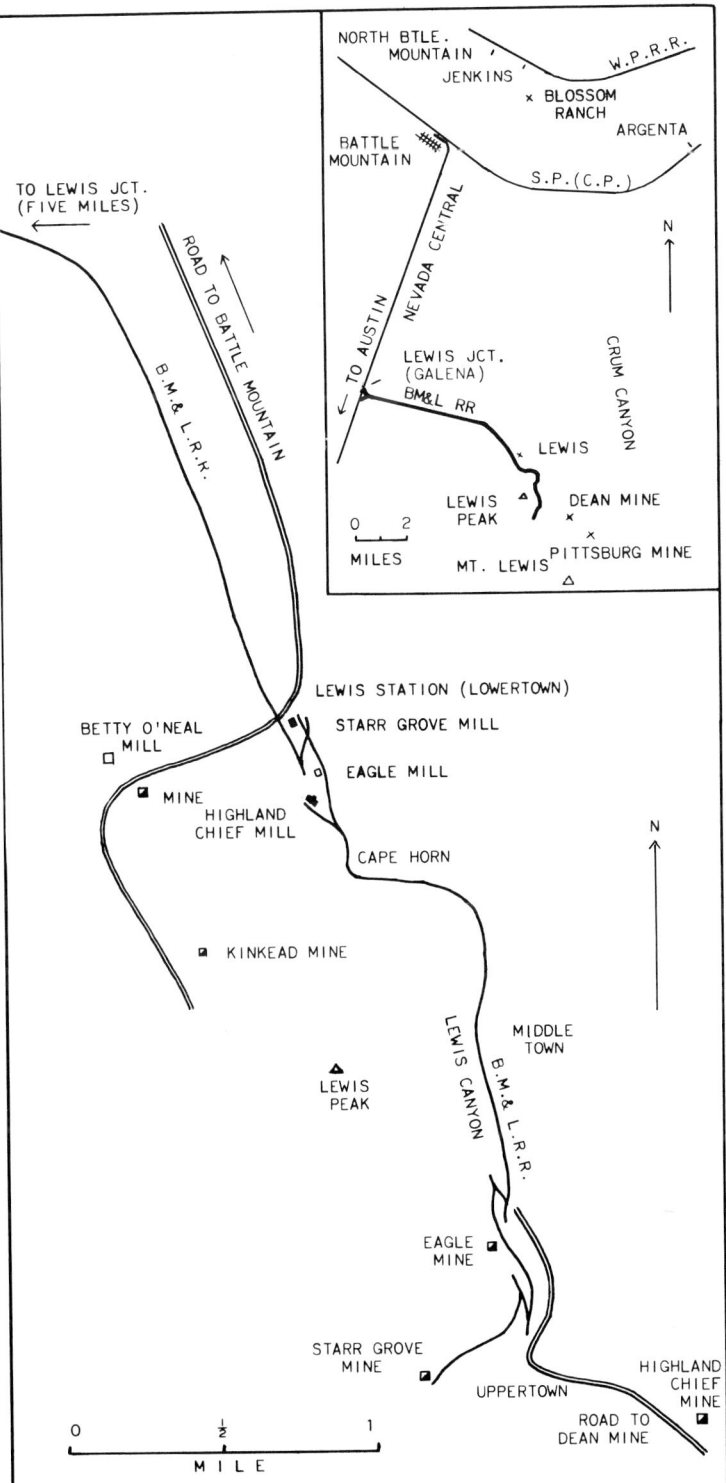

turned loose. However, before the special arrived at its destination, Bothwell had ordered the demands of the miners be met, and the men had returned to their jobs. Only one trouble-maker developed, and he was encouraged to leave town within 12 hours. The Austin miners, on their return home, were met with the Lander Brass Band and formed a victory parade up Austin's Main Street.

Service over the line was instituted on July 30, 1881, with a rented Nevada Central locomotive for motive power. Then on August 12 the BM&L received its own, personal engine, the "John D. Hall." Named for the president of the road and built by Prescott, Scott & Co. of San Francisco, at a cost of $7,500, the locomotive proved to be too light for the steep grades in the canyon (it only weighed 17 tons), and an exchange was subsequently effected for a larger, heavier engine. Meanwhile, however, the "John D. Hall" proudly headed the first excursion over the line to "The Switch" (the *Reveille's* name for Battle Mountain) where an evening dance and celebration was an occasion to remember.

With the railroad arrived, the town of Lewis became a roaring, booming camp claiming a population of 700 people. Of these some 300 were employed in the mines or mills. Starr Grove employed 50 men, as did the Highland Chief and the Betty O'Neal. Lou Pugh was proprietor of the famous Lewis Hotel where the "professor" and his bird show entertained twice weekly. A full deck of "hurdies" were brought over from Eureka and installed in the Arcade Hall. While the "hurdies" were available every night, the Rev. James was obliged to confine his efforts to visits on every third Sunday — a distinctly unfair advantage. To contain those led astray between visits, a jail was erected to accommodate the too-wayward guests. Bill Baugh, the manager, was ready to attend to the wants of all and sundry and assured evil doers that they would find first class accommodations and a very pressing invitation to stay with him.

Meanwhile, graders continued working up the narrow canyon on construction of the last 2½ miles of road to the mines. In October 1881 a reporter made a trip over the line and returned with rather glowing accounts of the activity he found. At Lewis Station (Lowertown) he noted a lumber yard, the 15-stamp Eagle Mill, and a new 40-stamp mill being erected by the Highland Chief Mining Co. Middletown was quite a metropolis with a first-class boarding house, a meat market, a saloon and a commodious Miners' Union Hall. Uppertown was developing rapidly as men were taken on at the Starr Grove Mine. One boarding house was already in operation, and more houses were under construction. As for the railroad proper, the majority of the line was completed except for the final section, and that was almost completely graded except for the last half-mile. One line change was being provided at Lowertown to obtain an easier grade, although the rails were not yet rolled, and the framing of two bridges still in progress. Then he went on: "The present management is first class and the roadbed is in good condition and engine No. 5 (a rented NC engine) pulled its burden up the 400-foot grade (7½%) without difficulty . . . It had been thought it would be difficult to operate an engine on the track in time of frosty and bad weather, but the skillful managers are preparing for the emergency. Sand boxes are being prepared that will, it is believed, answer all purposes for avoiding difficulty. They will be so placed that the track can be sanded at pleasure by the conductor's own hand, by the use of an attachment with the boxes that will open or close them at will . . . In order to make a passable grade up the canyon, there have been two or three, what are termed 'switchbacks,' formed, which is a cute and wise invention".

At the fork in Lewis Canyon near the end of the line, considerable blasting was required. Foreman T. Rice was pushing this work in November 1881 while bridge crews were setting the trestles in place. Additionally, the new engine house at Lewis Station (Lowertown) was a decided improvement. Decidedly not an improvement was the big fire which started in the early morning hours of December 5 in Dr. Sponogle's drug store and furnished the newly organized *Lewis Herald* with its first big headline. A stiff breeze boosted the flames along through two saloons, two barber shops and a meat market before a volunteer fire brigade could bring the situation under control. In spite of the conflagration, the Starr Grove mine managed to forward a shipment of $20,000 in bullion later the same day; but even this stirring news failed to stimulate the populace, for enthusiasm in Lewis was generally on the wane. When Tom Warren resigned his job as conductor to go to California, his letter of reference was published in the paper for all to see. Still the year 1881 ended in progressive fashion, for two carloads of rails and ties were being distributed along the mine branch in Uppertown.

On March 2, the Highland Chief mill was finally started following many delays in obtaining machinery. To celebrate the occasion, Lou Pugh's Lewis Hotel contributed a box of cigars, some champagne, and "something a little harder." The excitement was short-lived, however, for late in the same month the town was shocked to learn that its favorite railroad had been attached for debts amounting to $6,467, thus forcing suspension of operations. As

RAILROAD TIME TABLES.
BATTLE MOUNTAIN
—AND—
LEWIS
RAILWAY
TIME CARD.

O^N AND AFTER

SATURDAY, JULY 30TH, 1881,

TRAINS WILL LEAVE BATTLE MOUNTAIN for LEWIS, daily, at **4:55** o'clock P. M., arriving at Lewis at **6:15** P. M.

RETURNING WILL LEAVE LEWIS AT **8:45** o'clock A. M., arriving at Battle Mountain at **10:30** A. M.

Connects at Lewis Junction with Trains to and from Austin as follows:

LEAVES LEWIS FOR LEWIS JUNCTION at **4:45** o'clock P. M., connecting with train for Austin at **5:34** P. M.

LEAVES LEWIS JUNCTION FOR LEWIS on arrival of train from Austin at **9:53** A. M., arriving at Lewis at **10:40** A. M.

JNO. D. HALL, PRESIDENT.
L. B. BALL, SUPERINTENDENT.

General Office—Lewis, Nev.
jy30-tf

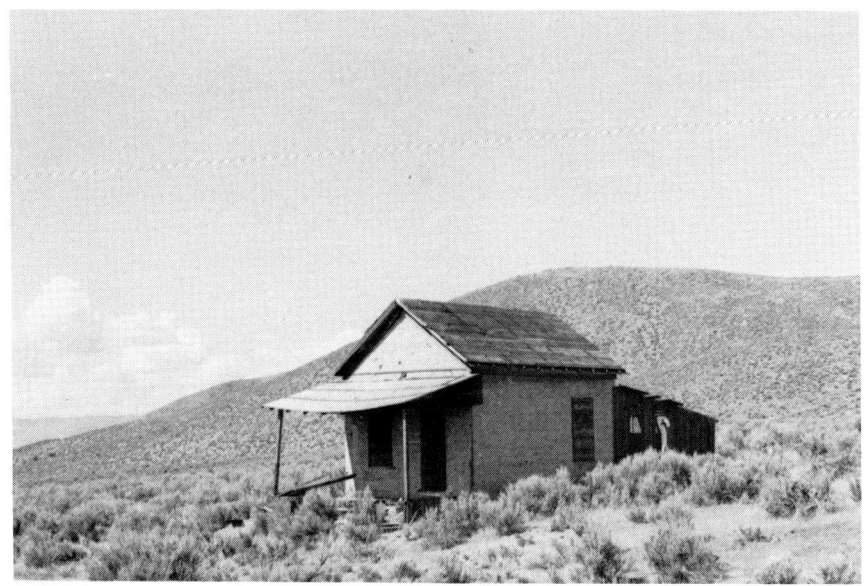

Although the Battle Mountain & Lewis Railway was completed on April 25, 1881, regular passenger service over the line was not inaugurated until the official announcement appeared in the *Battle Mountain Messenger*. The railroad's approach to Lewis (Lowertown) was easily made across a flat plain, but its extension in 1881 lay up the difficult Lewis Canyon *(below)*. The cut-away in the hill at left foreground was the site of the Starr Grove Mill; the Eagle Mill stood close to the creek; while the Highland Chief Mill was located on the hillside to the right. In 1958, when these pictures were taken, one of the few remaining buildings was the Lewis jail which had weathered appreciably. *(Top Left: Bancroft Library.)*

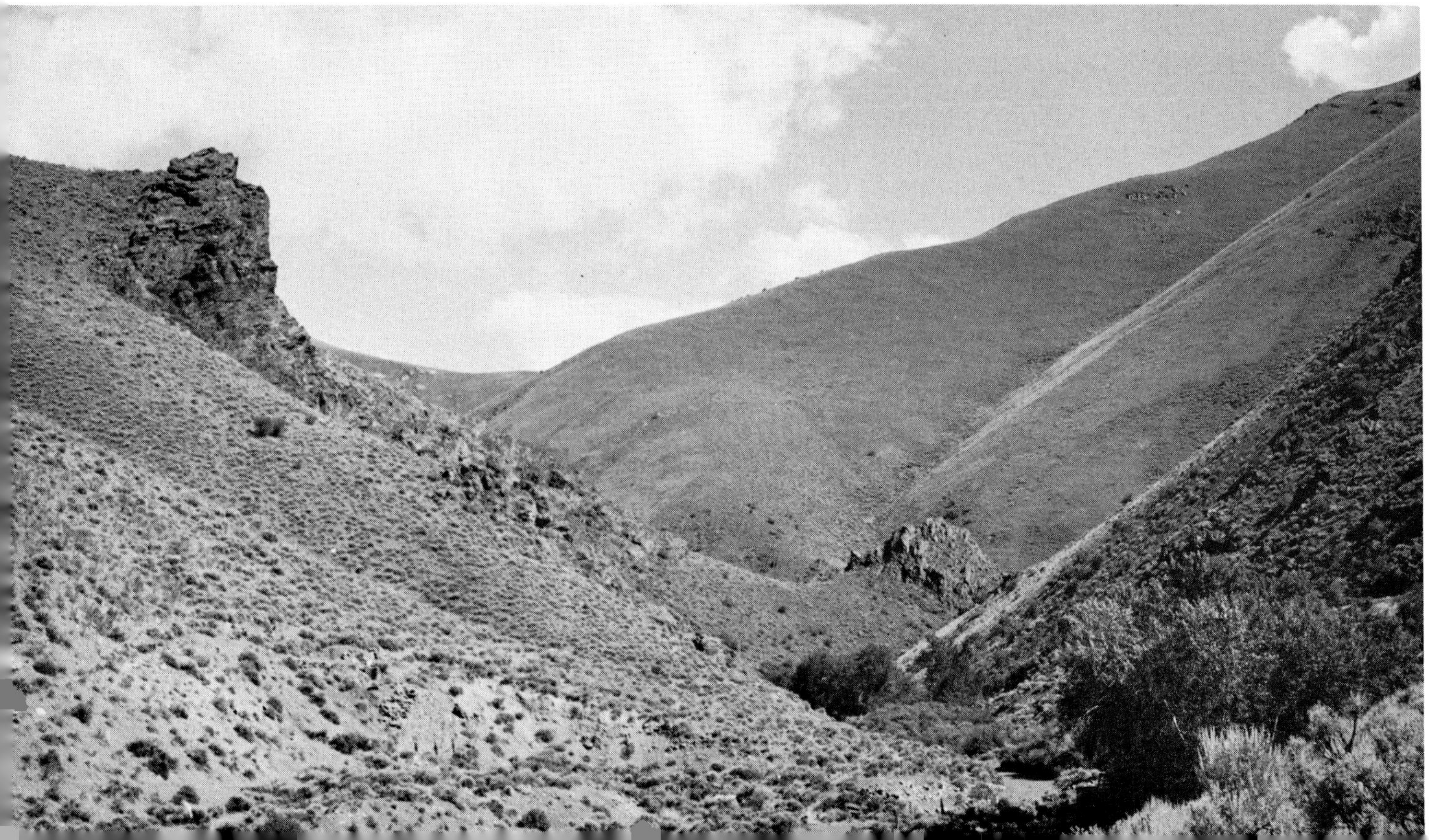

a temporary measure, a light wagon met Nevada Central trains at Lewis Junction and transferred passengers, mail and express from there into town.

The Nevada Central instigated the situation, which was purely a matter of a little money. There were unpaid interline freight charges from February 1 to March 17, 1882, of $4,898; there was another little matter of $552 of back rent on a locomotive; and it seemed the BM&L had also overlooked some $1,017 worth of coal which was not included in the locomotive rental. Even more surprising were two attachments levied against the Starr Grove properties amounting to a mere $519. Superintendent Bothwell of the Starr Grove hastily decided it was time to get to New York "to adjust matters."

During the days of waiting following Bothwell's departure, there was bold talk that the BM&L would take up its connecting track at Lewis Junction and build its own line north to Battle Mountain. Had ample funds been available, backed by productive ores, this might have happened. However, the situation was generally revealed when the Starr Grove property was sold at a sheriff's sale in April, 1882, and H. D. Gates of Lewis purchased the BM&L roadbed for $4,401 in May.

A spring freshet perpetrated considerable damage to the railroad in Lewis Canyon, but Gates soon had repair forces at work. Some stimulation was provided when a party of eastern investors arrived on a special train, and work was encouraged on the still uncompleted southern end of the line. But depression was under way at Lewis, and in June there was an epidemic of people leaving town in the still hours of the night "forgetting to settle sundry little accounts and not even leaving their future address or bidding their creditors goodbye." The Eagle mill closed down, and further work on the railroad was suspended. Linn Bradbury Ball, the one and only superintendent in the history of the BM&L (and famous for the two peculiar accoutrements to his trade—a black cat on his shoulder and a prominent gun in his belt), finally gave up and returned to his home in New Berlin, New York.

By the end of June 1882 all work of any nature on the railroad had ceased, and officially the line was considered to be closed. "Unofficially" the people in Middletown continued to operate between there and Lowertown through the medium of two light hand cars which were capable of making the trip down the hill in a scant six minutes.

Another set-back of economic significance to the area occurred on October 31, 1882, when a terrific explosion demolished the hoisting works and other mine buildings of the Betty O'Neal, approximately half a mile west of Lewis. L. W. Getchell had just gone to the bottom of the 260-foot shaft with another man on an inspection trip when the boiler blew up, killing one man and lodging a sizeable section of tubing half way down the shaft. Two months were required to rebuild the hoisting works, necessitating occasional trainloads of parts and supplies which the Nevada Central obligingly hauled over the BM&L rails. Normally, however, teams carted the more moderate quantities of supplies and ores between Lewis and Battle Mountain. A serious fire finally brought about the closing of the works in April 1883. To add insult to injury, four bars of bullion which were in the assay office immediately prior to the conflagration were never found in the ruins, and 800 pounds of mercury in flasks vanished into limbo.

During the days from February to July 1883, BM&L rails once again resounded to the rhythmic pound of midget drivers and the rumble of narrow gauge cars. Special trains were operated over the line by the Nevada Central to facilitate removal of parts of the dismantled Starr Grove mill. These were hauled from Lewis to the Junction and thence via NC rails to Ledlie where teams took over for the 60-mile haul west to the new mining excitement at Bernice.

Then Lewis subsided into quiescence. People continued to live there for the next two years, but mining activity was virtually at a standstill. Early in 1885 there was a small flurry of activity, and miners drifted back to the mines like ants to an ant hill. In March of that year the old BM&L track was reworked sufficiently to place it in operating condition, and the Nevada Central eased its trains over the line at such sporadic times as the traffic warranted. Bothwell and Morgan were happy to help revive the railroad with inbound traffic, but the impetuous miners stultified the whole revival program by once again going on strike. Activity ended; traffic ceased; and the Battle Mountain & Lewis was sold by the County Treasurer for taxes. The County bid on the property successfully (unfortunately), but without any business to sustain it, the railroad was superfluous and finally was permanently abandoned. The rails and ties subsequently were pulled up about 1890.

In 1916 the Battle Mountain Mines & Development Co. attempted activity in the area and built a short line in Lewis Canyon, but it operated for only a few years. Subsequently in 1920, Noble Getchell, son of L. W. Getchell, purchased the Betty O'Neal and in 1922-23 constructed a 200-ton flotation mill. In the succeeding six years over $2,000,000 was produced before the property was assigned to leasers in 1929. The ruins of this mill are still extant, while only a few crumbling foundations remain to mark the tri-sectional municipality of Lewis.

Austin City Railway

"This is a short but remarkable piece of road, running from Ledlie, [should be Clifton] the terminus of the Nevada Central Railroad, to the town of Austin and the Manhattan Company mines. The grades on this road are very heavy, being in places as high as 400 feet to the mile [7½%], and a few curves being as sharp as 40 degrees. It climbs the abrupt slope of the mountainside by means of a succession of Y's. With a very powerful engine only two, and sometimes but one, loaded car can be hauled at a time." Thus was the 2.80-mile, narrow (3-foot) gauge Austin City Railway described in the 1883-84 Report of the Surveyor General of Nevada.

The story began in March of the year 1880. The Nevada Central had just reached Clifton, at the foot of the hill to Austin, the month before; and stages and teamsters were enjoying spectacular rates for the short, steep haul between the two points. Allen A. Curtis, with the sagacity of a banker (which he was) and the shrewdness of a business man (he was also superintendent of the Manhattan Silver mill, a Phelps Stokes operation), had already analyzed the situation and applied to the Common Council of Austin for a right of way from the terminus of the Nevada Central to any point in the city. This the Council granted.

Work began May 31, 1880, following a route from Clifton up the hill, along Main Street to the Manhattan Mill in Upper Austin. Grading progressed smoothly; rails and ties were purchased from the Nevada Central; and by early August the line was completed to the International Hotel. Two months later the mule-power railroad was in operation, 11 mules being required to pull one loaded car to the mill. Early operations on the steep grades apparently were successful; one report noted that a long string of box and flat cars rattled down Main Street one evening with a number of Indians and Whites taking advantage of a free ride to Clifton.

Although originally it was considered impossible to operate a railroad with such steep grades with anything other than mule power, the matter was reconsidered and finally a locomotive was ordered from the Baldwin Works. The uncertainty of the operation and the novelty of the steam dummy type locomotive, completely hidden within its tremendous paneled and many-windowed cab, generated intense interest and curiosity. When the "Mules Relief" was first unloaded and tested on arrival in Battle Mountain, every move was carefully watched. Following a short trial trip, it had to be returned to the Nevada Central shops for minor adjustments.

The next day, May 31, 1881, the engine arrived in Clifton at the foot of the Austin grade. "Nearly every man, woman and child who had nothing else to do, went down to look at it." Clifton became a lively place for the moment as the populace gazed, poked and stared at the locomotive that looked like a passenger coach. Curtis took some friends for a trial run over a few miles of track north of Clifton while some unknown person, perhaps miffed because he was not invited to join the group, set two cars loose by Keystone's Stables and some damage resulted.

Actual operation was eagerly awaited. No other town in Nevada had a full fledged steam railroad on its main street, and as the local editor declared, "This will give us rail connection with Boston, city of culchaw." June 17, 1881, was the day finally set for the initial trip, and at eight o'clock in the morning sightseers were lining the grade waiting for the momentous event.

As the editor subsequently reported: "A little before eleven, the whistle tooted and a few minutes later the 'Mules Relief' was passing up the street with her bell ringing and whistle blowing, the sidewalks the while being thronged with people. Allen A. Curtis rode in the front of the engine seemingly as proud as a boy with his first long pants. Shortly before reaching the mill the big whistle there, as well as those at the mines, sounded a welcome to the iron horse, whose Cyclopean eye is in his forehead, whose lips are steel, whose wood is fire and whose breath is steam. For a time there was quite an excitement."

The next day the locomotive was pressed into service on the main line of the Nevada Central to haul the second section of a picnic train; then on June 22 the first working trip on the home line was accomplished, a car of lumber being taken up the hill at an estimated speed of at least five miles per hour. The ability of the mechanical substitute for mules was no longer in doubt. A freight depot was established just east of the courthouse and an engine house (still standing) was erected at the east end of town.

A year later on August 19, 1882, tragedy struck. Because the daylight hours were being utilized to effect track repairs, all freight hauling was performed at night. Although the engine's steam brake had become defective, leaving only the emergency hand brake still operable, engineer Andy Wright still thought he could accomplish the night's operations in spite of Curtis' admonitions against it. Everything went well until the next to the last trip when, just before 6:00 A.M. and while passing the *Reveille* office, even the hand brake refused to work. The engine rapidly gained momentum, whirled around a bad curve at the Citizen's mill, then hit the sharp reverse curvature opposite Horton's powder house. Frank Duffy, the fireman, was thrown out while Andy Wright continued to struggle with the controls. When Duffy regained his senses, he found the locomotive lying on its side some 20 or 30 yards below him on the edge of a cliff. The woodwork had been shattered; steam was blowing off; and no one was in sight. Andy Wright, the former CP engineer from Rocklin, California, had been crushed beneath the wreckage.

It took 16 mules to haul the wreck to the Manhattan Mill's shops and a month to recondition the locomotive and make it ready for test runs. In the reshopping process, the cab lost its clerestory roof and the length was abbreviated to enclose only the rear half of the boiler from the steam dome on back. Frank Duffy courageously returned to his old job of firing the mechanical monster while J. F. F. Hale of Ruby Hill became the new engineer.

Operation of the line continued regularly until the mines began to slow down and traffic dwindled. Around 1889 service was discontinued; the line was abandoned; and the track was removed. The "Mules Relief" had fulfilled its destiny.

Nevada Midland Railroad Company

Simon Bamberger is best known for his association with the one-time electric railroad in Utah which bore his name. But little known about Bamberger is his erstwhile effort at railroading in the state of Nevada.

Even as he was pushing completion of the Salt Lake & Ogden Railway (subsequently known as the Bamberger Electric), Simon Bamberger was also actively promoting a projected line called the Nevada Midland Railroad. Its articles of incorporation called for the acquisition and reconstruction of the Nevada Central Railroad from Battle Mountain to Austin, and the construction of an extending line of railroad from Austin via Tonopah to the California state line, possibly connecting with the Salt Lake Route then under construction far to the south. Useful indeed were the old 1880 surveys of the Nevada Southern from Austin Junction (Ledlie) as far as Cloverdale, but from that point to Tonopah (the immediate objective) new surveys were required.

Early in 1902 contracts were drawn to accomplish the primary objective of reaching the booming area of Tonopah, then without a railroad. Work was to commence on March 1, the line as far as Tonopah to be finished not later than October 1 of the same year.

As part of the Bamberger plan, virtually all of the stock and bonds of the (operating) Nevada Central Railroad were placed under option to the (projected) Nevada Midland, and were to be exchanged on the basis of two Nevada Central shares or bonds for each new Nevada Midland share or bond. Under this arrangement (had it materialized) the Nevada Central group would have held about 20% of the stock and 40% of the bonds of the new company. To perform the physical labors, the Nevada Construction Company was organized with the expressed, anticipated remuneration of $10,000 par value of Midland stock plus $10,000 of Midland bonds for each mile of completed road.

Before completing the arrangements, engineer E. A. Vail of the Nevada Midland and general manager Pearson of the Nevada Central went over

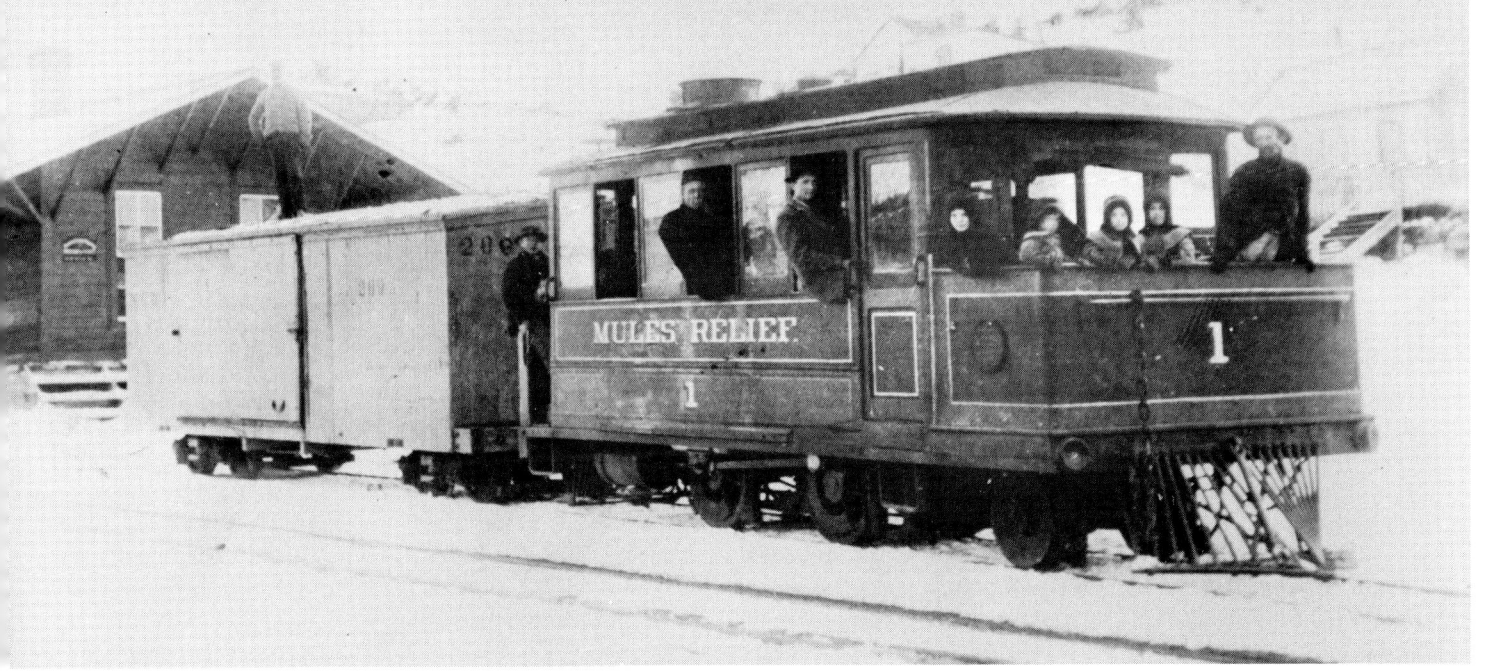

The "Mules' Relief," 0-4-2 steam dummy No. 1 of the Austin City Railway, was that road's only locomotive. In the early 1880's view at Clifton, a group of voyagers are ready to brave the wintry air for an early run.

Scorched paint on the side of the box-cab indicates that firebox heat from the severe 7½% grades and 40° curves of the 2.8-mile line had taken its toll before this later-day photo was made.

The absence of the ornate, full-length cabin dates this picture on the steep grade into Austin as having been taken some time after August 19, 1882, when, following an ill-advised attempt to operate the engine on the steep grades using only the hand brake, the engineer lost control and was crushed beneath his wrecked locomotive. *(Center: Silleman Collection; Others: Ken Kidder Collection.)*

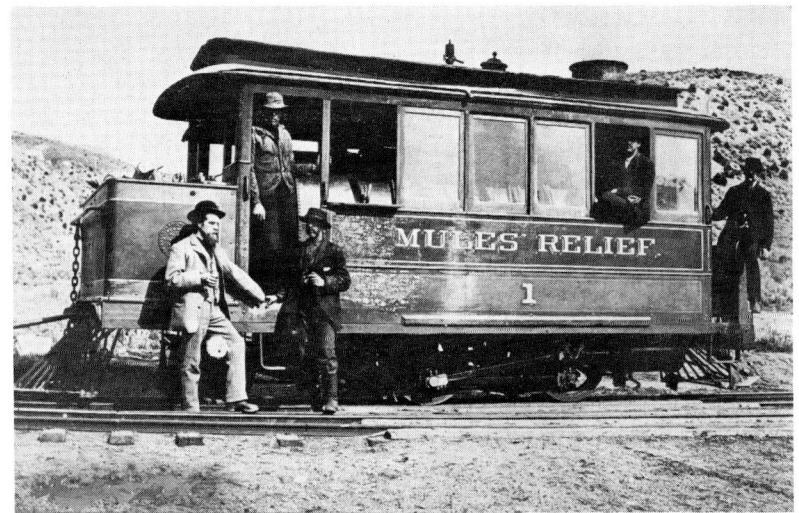

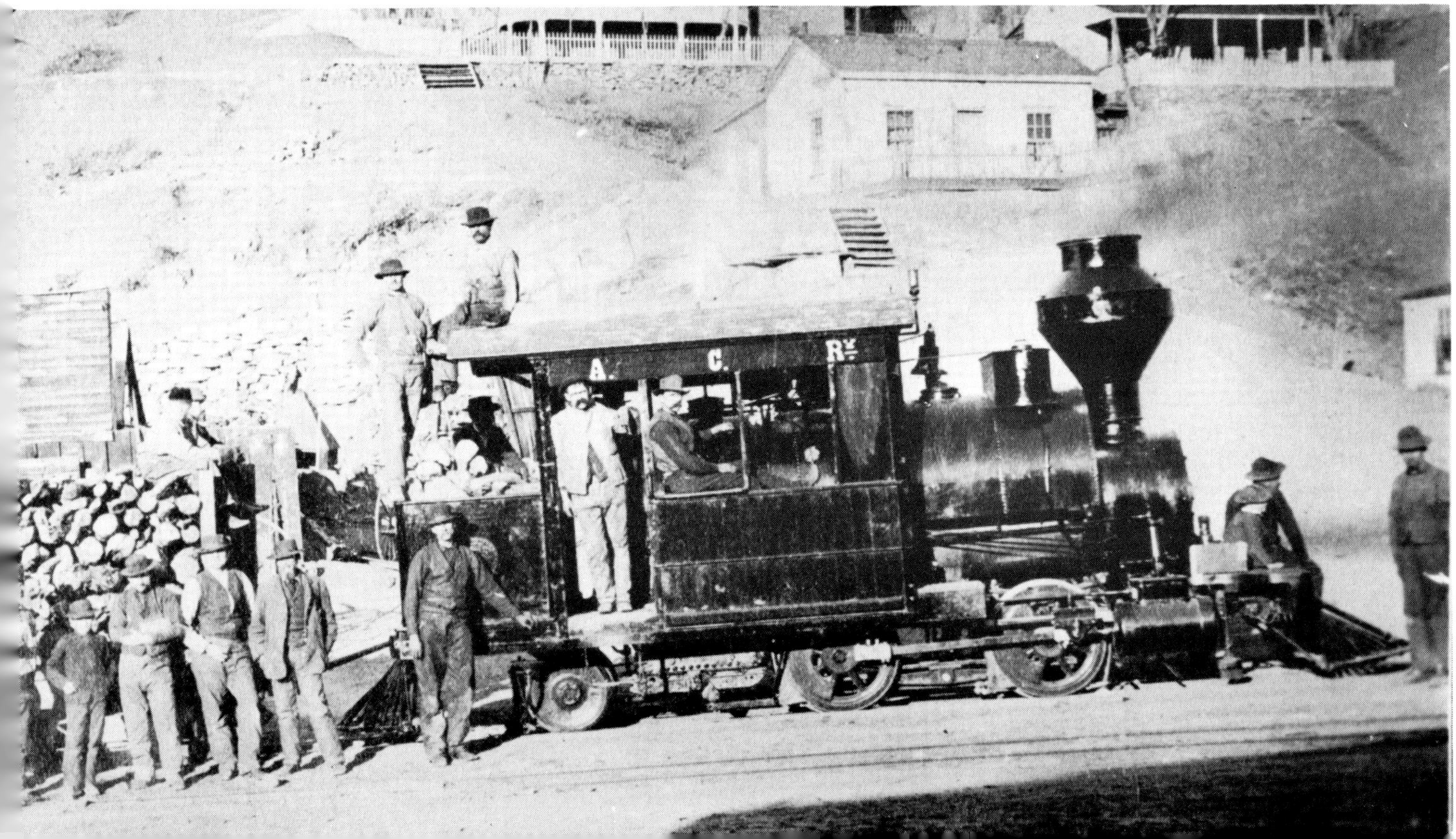

the proposed route in the early part of March 1902. Vail then left to organize his crew of surveyors, while John Everill spent some time in Austin making arrangements for grading teams. However, severe snow storms that month delayed the work for several weeks; then the project stalled on dead center.

There were several contributing factors which prevented the project from being brought to fruition. Bad weather delayed commencement of the work in accordance with the terms of the contract; there was a difficulty and inability to secure adequate, second-hand, 40-pound rail; but the greatest difficulty of all was in reconciling the mental reservations and uncertainty of realistic assessment of the future possibilities of booming Tonopah. This complete diversity of opinion was expressed in a letter from the railroad's agent which read in part: "Mr. Oddie was here this week. He called upon me, and he is as wild about his properties around Tonopah as ever, and I fear that he will not come to his senses until it is too late . . ."

Using his intuition and his best judgment based upon the facts at hand, Bamberger allowed the project to become permanently dormant. But Oddie was right; Bamberger was wrong; for Tonopah boomed with a suddenness, intensity and duration undreamed of by its founders. In the words of Shakespeare:

We must take the current when it serves,
Or lose our ventures.

Mid-Pacific Railroad

The year was 1929. Although the country was booming with inflation, non-ferrous metal prices had sunk to the lowest levels in their history. Nevada mining was in a doldrum from which it appeared it might not recover. The state's short-line railroads were in a likewise drastic predicament, being almost totally dependent upon the mining activities. Some of the weaker lines had already disappeared from corporate records and tax listings, leaving only their physical scars on the landscape to mark their passing; and of those remaining, the majority were destined to follow the same pathway to oblivion within the next decade.

Onto this stage stepped Andrew Stevenson, a man of previous railroad experience including a turn on each of the C&EI and Wabash railroads. With imagination and foresight, he evolved a plan to weld together six of Nevada's short lines into one big system 1,000 miles long. The route would form a gigantic "Y" in shape, with Reno and North Battle Mountain at the northern extremities of the arms, Millers (near Tonopah) at the vertex, and Barstow, California, at the tip of the tail. Four existing roads (V&T, T&G, NC and T&T) would be interconnected through the construction of four new lines (Nevada Central Extension RR, Los Angeles & Nevada RR, Nevada Southern RR, and the Santa Fe Connecting RR) plus the addition of trackage rights over portions of two other major systems (the SP and the AT&SF). In addition, two other supporting railroads would be absorbed (NCB and EN), neither of which directly connected with owned lines of the system. Individually, the roads were on the brink of disaster; put together at depressed valuations, they might be welded into a system of real value and importance.

Late in 1929 Stevenson met with a group of men to form the Nevada Manhattan Corporation for the purpose of exploring and developing the plan just outlined. The ensuing 2½-year study was amazingly thorough, including a physical examination of the existing lines, detailed analyses of traffic, financial and operating problems, and a study of necessary rehabilitation work. Projected connecting roads were surveyed and mapped most carefully. Then the possibilities of the hypothetical merged system were analyzed and explored, and the whole compiled into a proposed Consolidation and Merger Agreement between the Nevada Manhattan Corporation and the various railroads involved. The 400-page report was then presented to the board in August of 1932.

As a result of these studies, a financing plan was derived. Each line would cause its securities to be exchanged for those of the Mid-Pacific and additionally they would make a cash subscription for $100,000 of the common stock of the Mid-Pacific to cover part of the cost of the remaining field work plus the necessary legal expenses. The Nevada Manhattan Corporation would also receive stock in the new company as reimbursement for moneys spent on surveys and reports as well as for part of the cost of the construction of the connecting lines. Mid-Pacific bonds, to be sold to the public, would supply most of the money for the construction of these various connections.

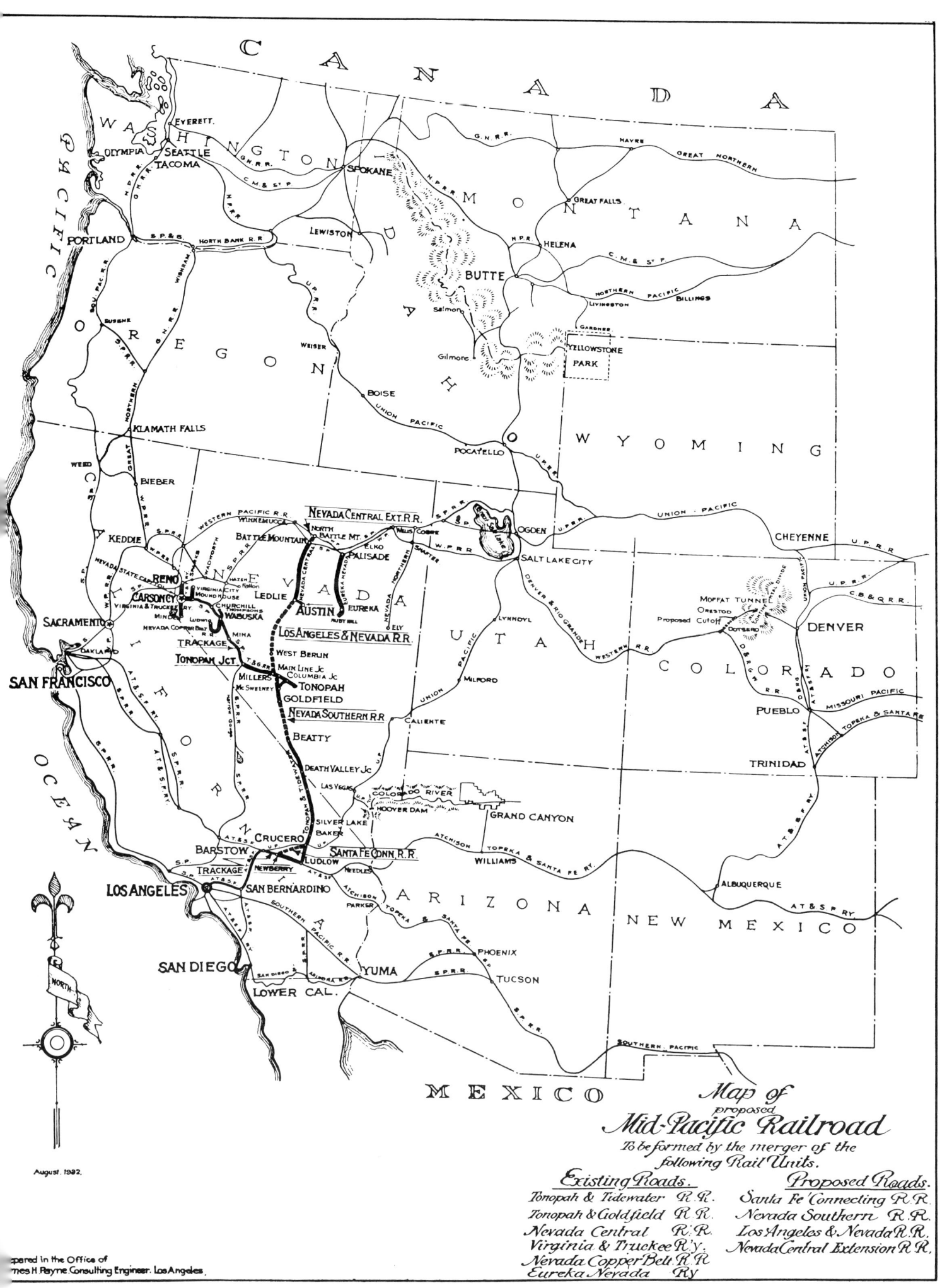

MID-PACIFIC RAILROAD
PLAN OF CONSOLIDATION AND CONSTRUCTION
MODIFICATIONS TO BE MADE

	ROAD	
LEFT ARM OF Y	Virginia & Truckee Railroad Company *(Existing)*	Acquire entire road and rehabilitate main line from Reno to Mound House, 41 miles. Plan to build a grade along the Carson River from Merrimac (5.6 miles east of Carson City) to Dayton on the SP Mound House branch. New grade would be .6% vs. 2.4% on V&T between Merrimac and Mound House and 2.5% on the SP between Dayton and Mound House. Minor grade reductions would also be made between Reno and Carson City.
	Southern Pacific Company *(Existing)*	Trackage rights to be acquired from Mound House to Tonopah Junction, Nevada, 137 miles.
	Tonopah & Goldfield Railroad Company *(Existing)*	Acquire and rehabilitate main line, including replacement of light rail between Tonopah and Goldfield with 90-lb., second-hand rail, plus rebuilding of abandoned cut-off between McSweeney Junction and Main Line Junction.
RIGHT ARM OF Y	Nevada Central Extension Railroad Company *(New road)*	Construct seven-mile connection between Battle Mountain (northern terminus of the Nevada Central) and the Western Pacific at North Battle Mountain, including several embankments 10 to 20 feet high plus the only bridge on the entire line (small trestles and wooden culverts would suffice elsewhere).
	Nevada Central Railroad Company *(Existing)*	Acquire and convert to standard gauge entire line, replacing light rail with 90-lb., second-hand rail. Establish complete, secondary system shop at Battle Mountain, Nevada.
	Los Angeles & Nevada Railroad Company *(New road)*	Construct 111-mile line from Ledlie on Nevada Central to Millers on the T&G, route passing through Ione Valley, crossing Ione Mountains at Railroad Pass, thence down Reese River Valley. Original plans provided for 7,392-foot tunnel at summit of pass (later discarded), and maximum grade of .8%.
STEM OF Y	Nevada Southern Railroad Company *(New road)*	Construct 79 miles from Goldfield to Beatty, Nevada. New grading 20 miles from Goldfield to three miles north of Ralston; old LV&T grade there to Wagner, 15 miles; new grading across desert Wagner to Ancram, 26 miles; old BG grade Ancram to Beatty, 18 miles.
	Tonopah & Tidewater Railroad Company *(Existing)*	Acquire and rehabilitate entire main line of 169 miles from Beatty to Ludlow, including relaying of main line with 90-lb., second-hand rail.
	Santa Fe Connecting Railroad Company *(New road, subsequently dropped)*	Construct low grade line from Crucero on the T&T to Newberry (Springs) on the Santa Fe, 36 miles. Line would parallel LA&SL for 15 miles from Crucero through Afton Canyon (trackage right possibilities), would avoid two 1.5% grades on T&T, and would be 25 miles shorter.
	Atchison, Topeka & Santa Fe Railway Company *(Existing)*	Trackage rights to be acquired from Newberry (Springs) to Barstow, California, 21 miles.
ADDITIONAL LINES	Nevada Copper Belt Railroad Company *(Existing)*	Minor additions for anticipated heavier motive power.
	Eureka Nevada Railway Company *(Existing)*	Minor additions and betterments. Install standard gauge ties, but leave line narrow gauge for present.

NOTE: The cost of rehabilitating the six existing lines was estimated to be $4,678,000, and the cost of building and equipping the four new lines was $5,980,000—a total cost of $10,658,000. A subsequent estimate by a Los Angeles construction firm (limiting the work to the minimum amount necessary to complete a through standard gauge line) was made at $5,123,000. This did not include $1,039,000 for the Santa Fe Connecting Railroad, and estimate for the cost of equipment and supplies of approximately $2,670,000, nor $275,000 for estimated engineering work.

Andrew Stevenson was a hard worker, and he might have accomplished his far-reaching merger if the nation, and the railroads involved in particular, had not been suffering economically. In 1931 the gross revenues of the six roads being combined totaled $585,000. Total net operating income of the same roads was a red figure of $104,000. After interest charges the loss for the same roads totaled $315,000. It was hoped that by connecting these roads, new traffic patterns could be established over the system, essentially a bridge line. But bridge traffic would largely have been dependent upon the effects of solicitation plus the willingness of the Santa Fe and the Western Pacific to share a division of the through rate with the Mid-Pacific, all of which would not be necessary by the direct interchange at Stockton, California. Had one of the northern transcontinental lines become interested in reaching southern California and been willing to lend a helping hand, the picture might have been improved. None came forward, however, even though the plan was described as bringing the Great Northern into Los Angeles. To make matters even more discouraging, local traffic prospects were very dim. A complete system certainly would have more appeal, and if built up properly could be sold far more readily than six little disconnected, unhappy rails.

Early in 1932 the project was strengthened when Robert W. Campbell joined the group. Campbell was an attorney with law offices in Chicago and Los Angeles; but perhaps even more important, he was Judge Gary's son-in-law. It was Campbell who drew up the many documents necessary for the merger. Shortly after they were distributed to the interested parties outlining the basis of exchange of the securities, Great Britain went off the gold standard and, with ownership of the Tonopah & Tidewater vested with Borax Consolidated, Ltd., of London, it was necessary to revalue the securities accordingly. Then, before the new agreements could be signed, the United States went off the gold standard.

The load proved to be too much for Stevenson, and he passed away in December of 1933 following a few weeks of illness. Campbell and his associate, John McHenry, attempted to carry on. Times were a bit better now, and there were some signs of encouragement. True, Ogden Mills of the V&T had some reservations as to the form of the merger, but it was expected that this would present no serious problem. W. L. Haehnlen, a receiver for the T&G was very enthusiastic about the project (even though short of cash), as it would put his road on the map and would be highly beneficial to the short lines of Nevada. In April 1934 he took the matter up with the famed Van Sweringen brothers. While they indicated some interest, the scheme was not sufficiently attractive to produce the necessary financial support.

Then other parties became involved. Senator Tasker Oddie took a hand in the project, but he too was unsuccessful in obtaining financial aid. John McHenry tried, through the offices of T. M. Schumacher, to interest Arthur Curtis James in the line as a southern California feeder for his Western Pacific but received a negative response.

Time was passing, and the date was now June 1934. The increasing number of railroad receiverships created a discouraging picture for any new railroad enterprise. Further work became futile, and the Mid-Pacific project quietly vanished as it had come. It was never really in the public eye, for it never reached a stage that called for any public announcement. However, a Carson City newspaper did reveal the general plan in 1934.

Unfortunately very little is known of this embryo major railroad system. The information gleaned here was made possible only by a fortunate examination of some private correspondence. Nothing further has been elicited.

Had the plans of the Mid-Pacific Railroad developed as contemplated, this North Battle Mountain station on the Western Pacific Railroad would have been one of the two northern termini (Reno, the other) of a railroad extending all the way south to Barstow, California. (Guy L. Dunscomb; Mid-Pacific Map: Andrew Stevenson, Jr.)

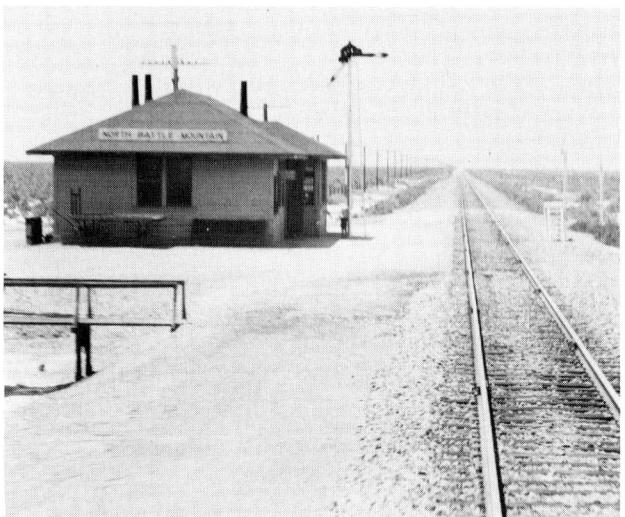

EUREKA & PALISADE RAILROAD

Illustrious, dramatic corroboration of the venerable adage, "Necessity is the mother of invention," will attend any archival research into the history of Eureka, Nevada. Silver-lead ore was first discovered in New York Canyon in 1864, immediately to the south of the present location of the town of Eureka, and during the ensuing years additional discoveries were made. Primal stumbling block to adequate development of the finds was the abortive effort to smelt the ore, which was of a consistency and composition not previously encountered. Five probationary years slipped by before an opportune effort was rewarded with the requisite success to enable establishment of an industry and a city.

Miners had drifted into Hamilton in the big rush of its reported bonanza in 1869 and had departed almost as swiftly in the wake of its saturated complement of manpower. Solace was sought in the shadow of Eureka's Prospect Mountain, and many claims were established on Ruby, McCoy, Adams and Cariboo Hills. Of them all, Ruby Hill was the most promising, and in 1870 a group of the claims were gathered together under the aegis of the Eureka Consolidated Mining Co., a legal entity created in far away San Francisco, for which extensive furnaces were erected at the north end of Eureka, virtually filling the narrow valley. A second group of claims, in juxtaposition to the mines of the Eureka Consolidated, were likewise banded together this time under the banner of the Richmond Consolidated Mining Co., an 1871 organization of even more distant London, England. Another elaborate set of furnaces were then established oppositely at the southern end of town. Thus Eureka lay bilaterally and malodorously between the two largest smoke-belching monsters, victim of the slightest breeze which could blow in either of two directions with baleful effect upon the citizens. The title, "Pittsburgh of the west" was approbriously earned, for Eureka entertained a total of some 16 volatile smelting entities, each contributing its proportionate share to the atmospheric pollution.

Inevitably a battle of the giants occurred. From the very beginning there was considerable friction between the Richmond and the Eureka Consolidated, and the physical proximity of the mines only served to aggravate the situation. The first major apex suit, carried all the way to the U. S. Supreme Court, evolved from the Richmond's zealous but angular pursuit of ore veins down the Tip Top shoot to Pott's Chamber, located in the ground of which the Eureka Consolidated claimed ownership. The ultimate Supreme Court decision in 1881 upheld the Eureka Consolidated as the lawful possessor of the property and sustained their claim to $2,000,000 of damages. It had been a long and bitter battle.

With the advent of important works and volume production, transportation became a major problem. To solve it, two stage operators (Gilmer and Salisbury), the Hamilton hotel man (J. P. Withington), and others banded together to form the Eureka & Palisade Railroad. Organization was accomplished in November 1873, and shortly thereafter work was started from Palisade on the Central Pacific over 84 miles of narrow (3-foot) gauge roadbed. In July 1874 new talent entered the picture as Isaac Requa, D. O. Mills, William Sharon, Thomas Bell and Edgar Mills took over the job of completing the line. These were substantial important men, representing the Bank of California, the V&T, and various other mining activities in Virginia City and the Comstock; they were unimpressed with the single engine which was all that was necessary to handle the entire rolling stock of the line (2 box cars and 11 flats); but they were interested in the fact that the road was operating as far as Lodi, where a hotel was under construction for the convenience of travelers. The next section to Alpha, slightly beyond mid-point of the line, was completed before the close of the year 1874; then activity ceased until June 1875.

That summer the renewed efforts were sincere and the work concentrated. Graders rushed the 14 miles of roadbed up the Sulphur Spring Mountains on maximum grades of 4% and pushed them on over the top at Garden Pass. Rails followed, and behind them came the trains. Operations to Summit, seven miles north of Garden Pass, started in September while the graders put the finishing touches to the last 25 miles to the depot in Eureka. Superintendent Everts fixed the Eureka station site through the timely purchase of Colonel Ray's toll house, though not so timely was the comment that it would have been nicer if the terminus had been closer to town. General jollification greeted the arrival of the first locomotive on Friday, October 22, 1875. The great day had arrived; the town was gaily decorated with all available flags and bunting; people "hurrahed, speechified, drank lager and other things." It was the "other things" which were to remain longest in their subconscious recollections of the big event.

Aside from the transcontinental implications of the Eureka & Palisade connections, railroading was no novelty in Eureka, Nevada. Back in May 1875, when the E&P was so abruptly terminated at Alpha some 40 route miles distant, Eureka had witnessed a "first spike" ceremony for its own Eureka & Ruby Hill Narrow Gauge Railroad. With facetious naivete it might best be described as a "3 by 3" — three miles long and three feet wide. Construction extended from the Eureka Consolidated mines atop Ruby Hill, down a tortuous descent which circumnavigated Cariboo Hill, to the company's furnaces in the valley at the north end of Eureka. Curious crowds gathered to witness the arrival of the new Baldwin saddle-tank locomotive with six wheels the same size; it was the first locomotive in Eureka. Initial operations involved the plebeian aspects of construction; then came the more exalted task of transporting ore. Daily, trainloads of 10 six-ton loaded ore cars were gently lowered down the hill to the ravenous furnaces of the Eureka Consolidated, while a compensating number of return trips escorted the empties back up to the mines. The residents fancied this new and faster mode of transport to such an extent that their impromptu incursions aboard the cars, accompanied by numerous near-calamitous avoidances under the rumbling wheels, quickly determined the management on providing a small coach of 20- to 25-passenger capacity for attachment to each train. Expediency dictated verbal reference to the line as the Ruby Hill Railroad, an appellation which remained to become a pseudonym following the purchase of the property by the E&P in 1875 and subsequent extension to serve the competing mines and furnaces of the Richmond Consolidated.

Eureka's population was explosive, rising from a few precursory souls to an agglomeration in excess of 9,000 people during the ten years of operations

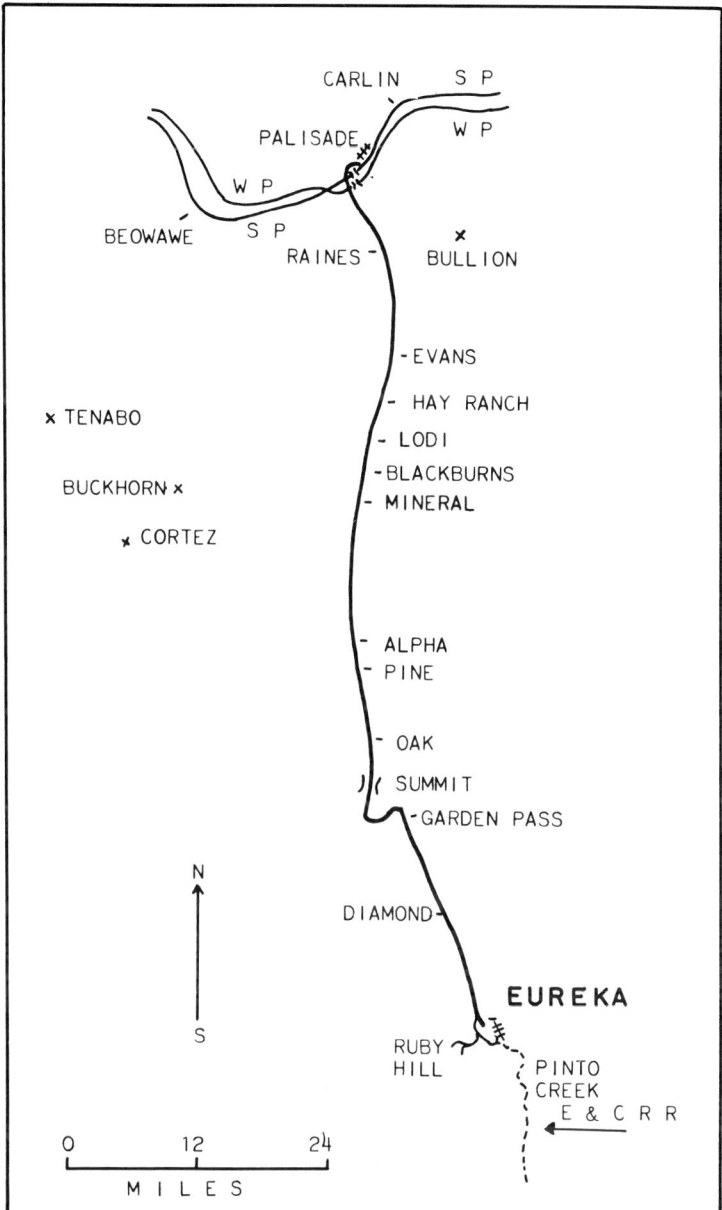

to 1878. Production in that latter year, as indicated by Wells Fargo bullion shipments, amounted to a substantial $7,000,000. The price of such success was measured in terms of hardship and adversity— a smallpox epidemic, two fires, two floods and the inevitable labor difficulties, most famous of which was the charcoal burners' war. People in general were friendly. One of the Centennial Guards' annual outings and picnics in 1881 provided participants with a ride over the freight-only Ruby Hill Railroad, wherein such benevolence was created in one individual, a sympathetic shooting occurred following arrival back in town. Frequently the "good neighbor" policy backfired, as witness the time that large quantities of water encountered in the Eureka Consolidated mines inadvertently spilled over into

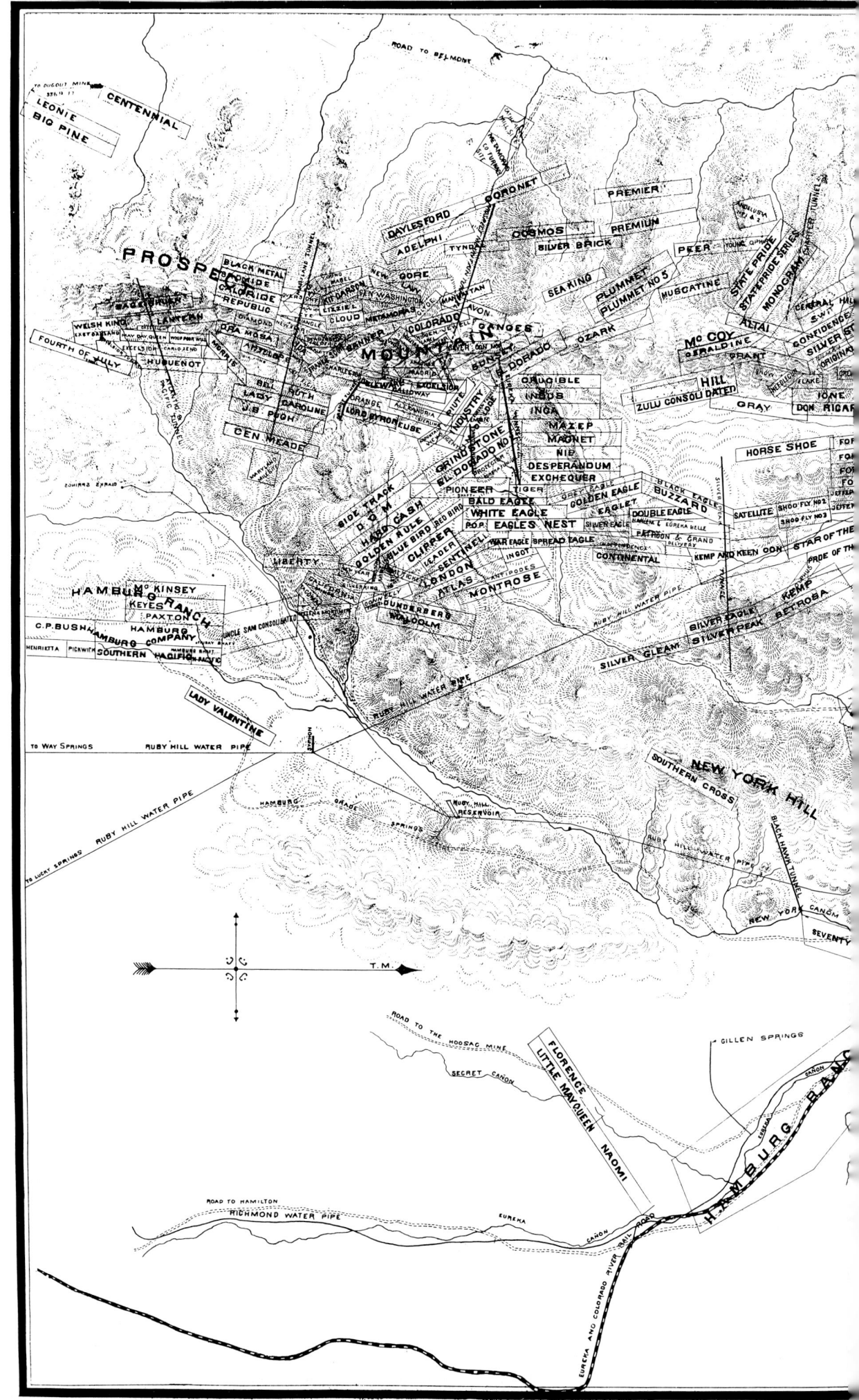

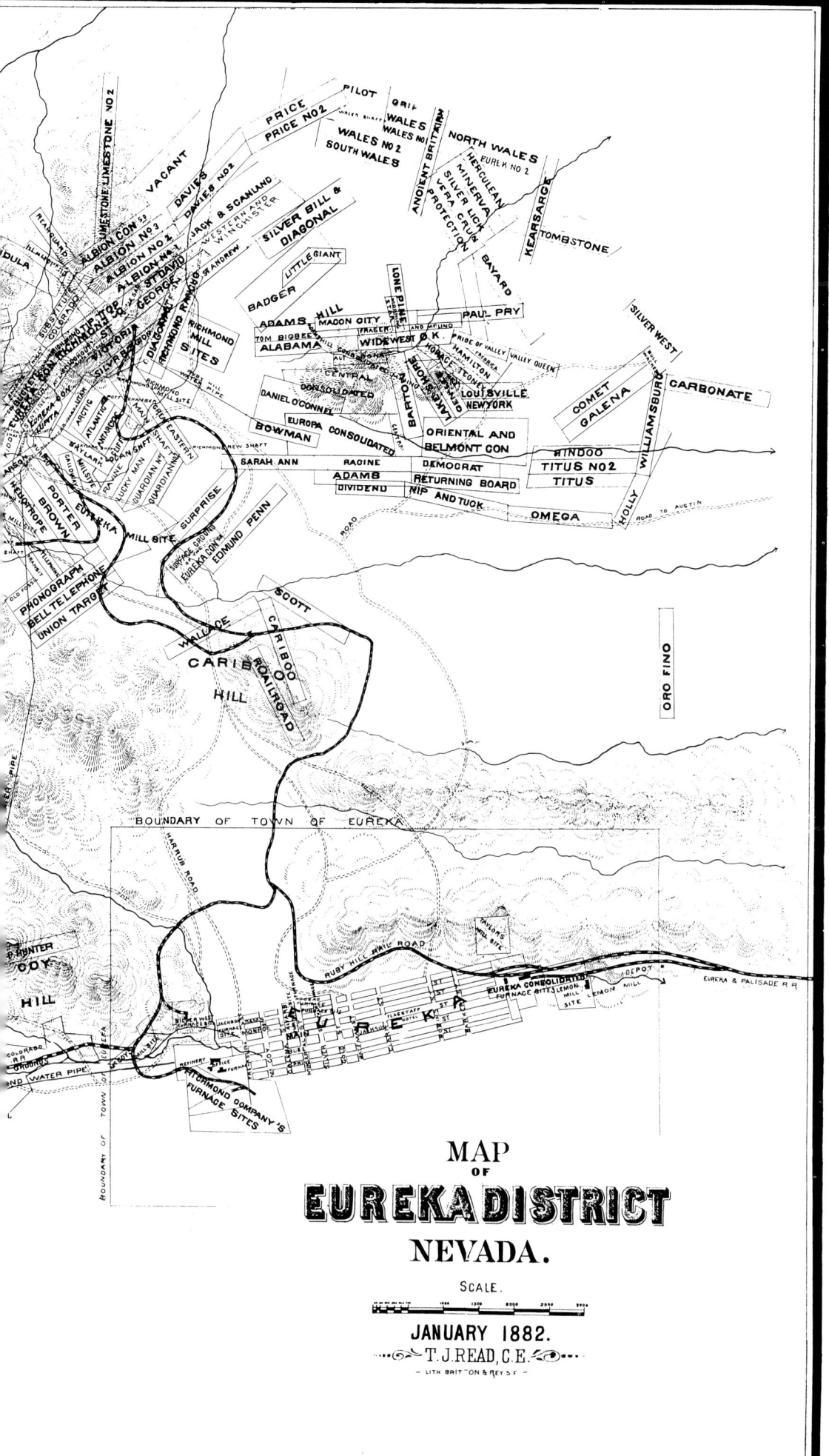

MAP OF EUREKA DISTRICT NEVADA.

Scale.

JANUARY 1882.

T. J. READ, C.E.

— LITH BRITTON & REY S.F —

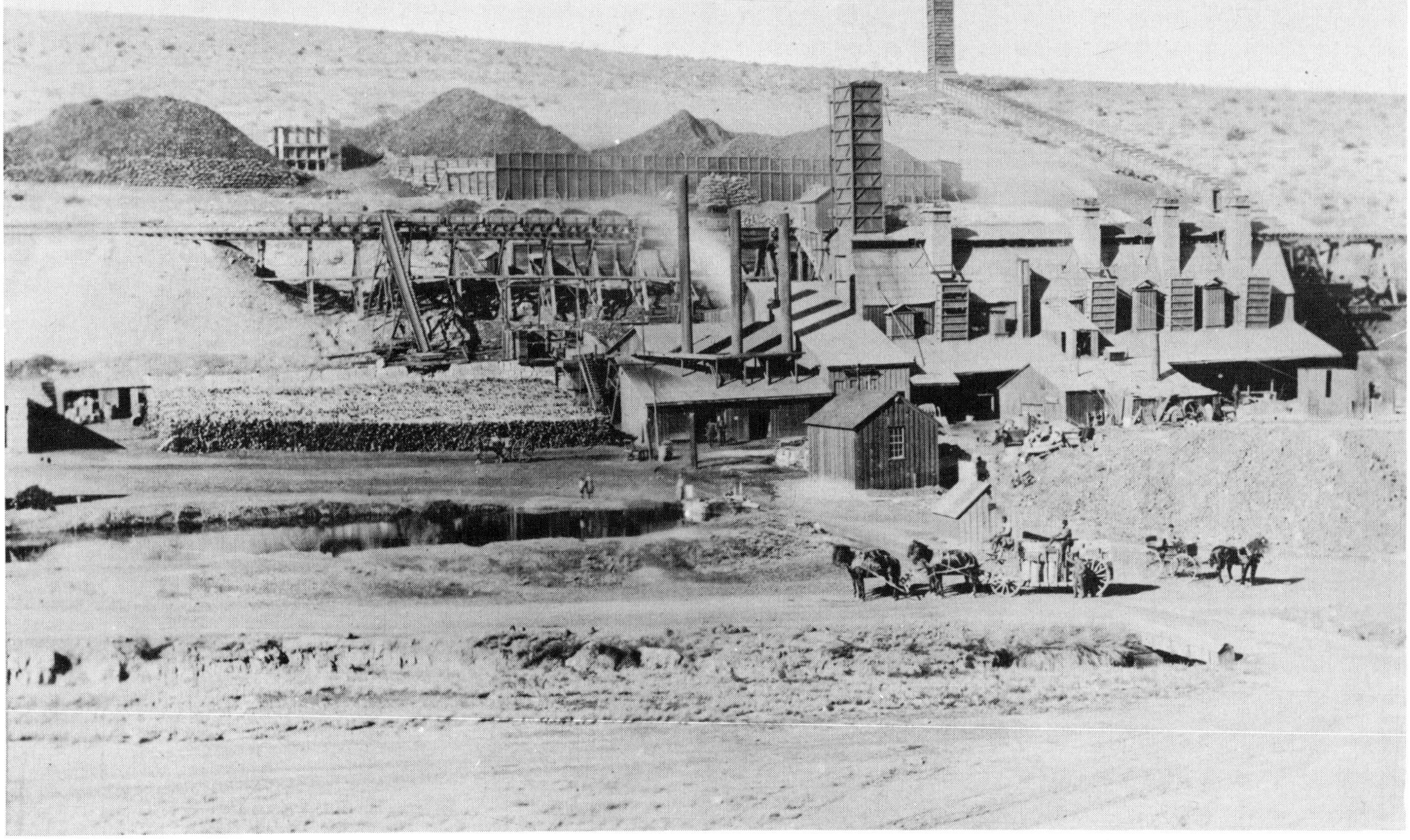

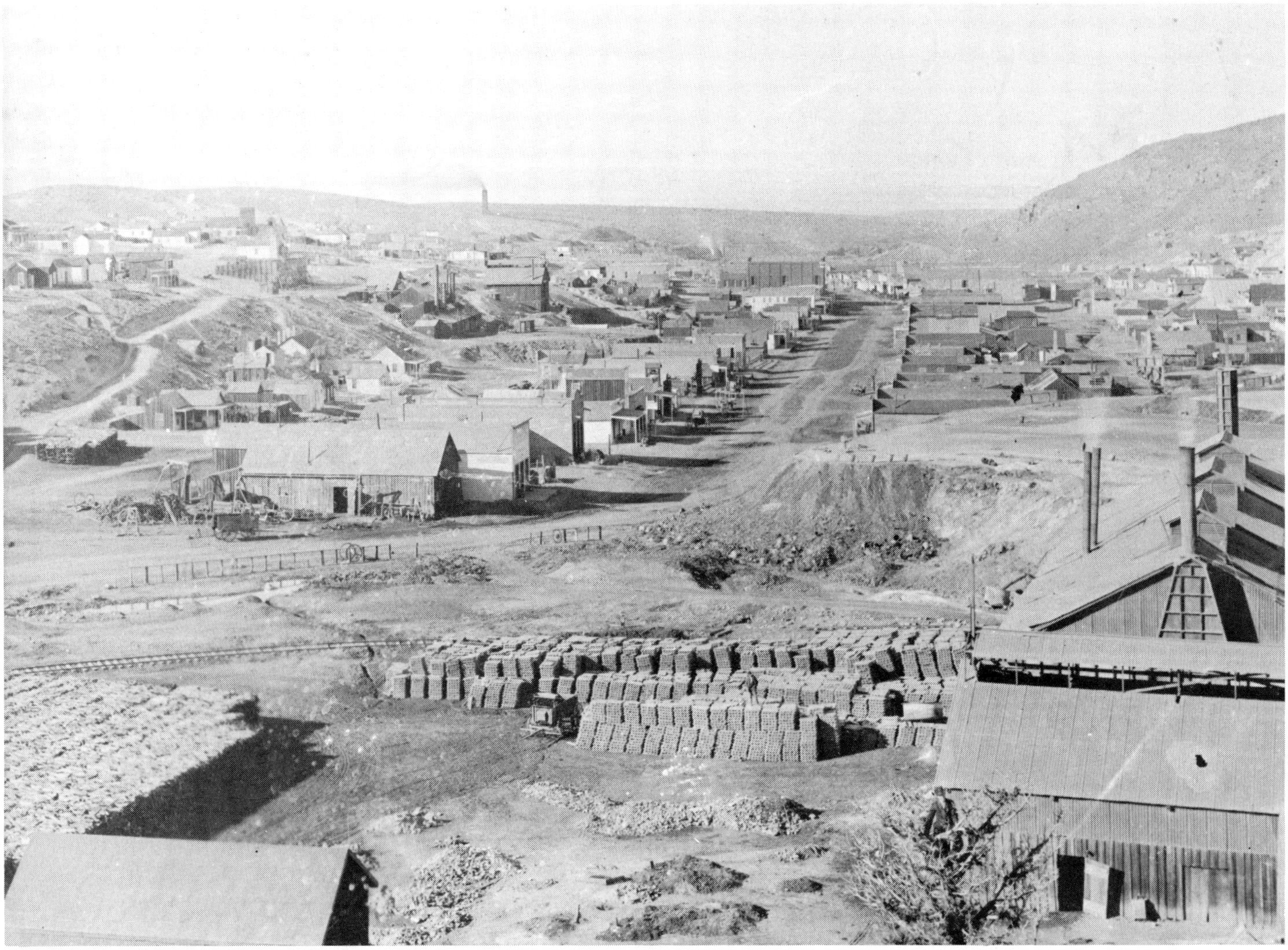

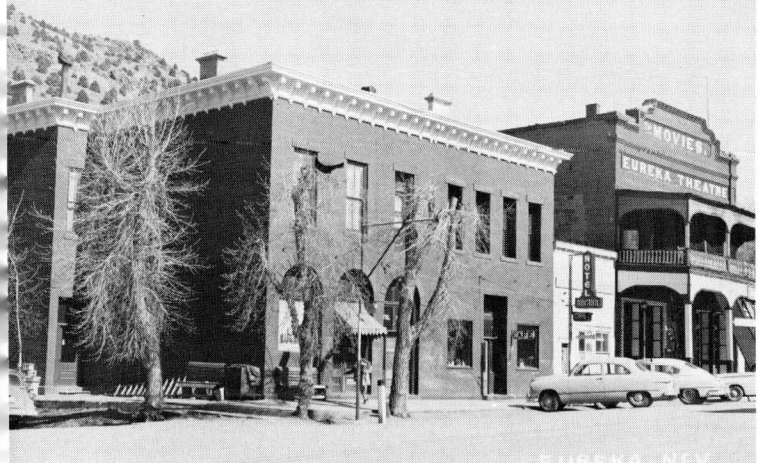

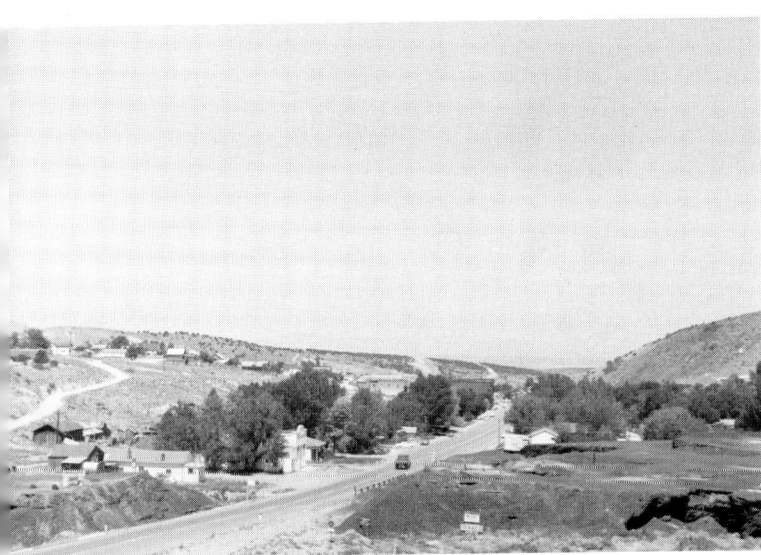

The Ruby Hill Railroad operated in the form of a gigantic "X". From the Eureka Con. mines on the south leg on Ruby Hill, ores were brought to the Eureka Consolidated furnaces *(top, page opposite)* on the north side of Eureka, from which the Eureka & Palisade Railroad hauled the refined ores to the Central Pacific connection at Palisade. In this view, loaded ore jimmies of the Ruby Hill Railroad stand ready to feed the hungry furnaces, while the smoke and fumes of the smelter are hopefully carried to the top of the hill through the elongated stack in an effort to diminish air pollution in the treeless town below. The Richmond Company's furnaces *(below, far left)*, located at the south side of Eureka, were fed by mines on the north leg of the Ruby Hill Railroad. Tracks of the Ruby Hill Railroad are plainly visible in the foreground, while the town of Eureka sprawled in a northerly direction toward the Eureka Con. furnaces, the stack of which can be plainly seen against the sky line in the left background. In the later-day views on this page may be seen the Eureka Hotel and theater *(top)*, a view north from the approximate site of the Richmond Works *(center)*, and a view south from the dumps of the former Eureka Consolidated Works *(below)*. The Eureka & Colorado Railroad was graded for 10 miles over the pass in the background before the project was abandoned. *(Far Left, Top and Bottom: Lambatucci Collection.)*

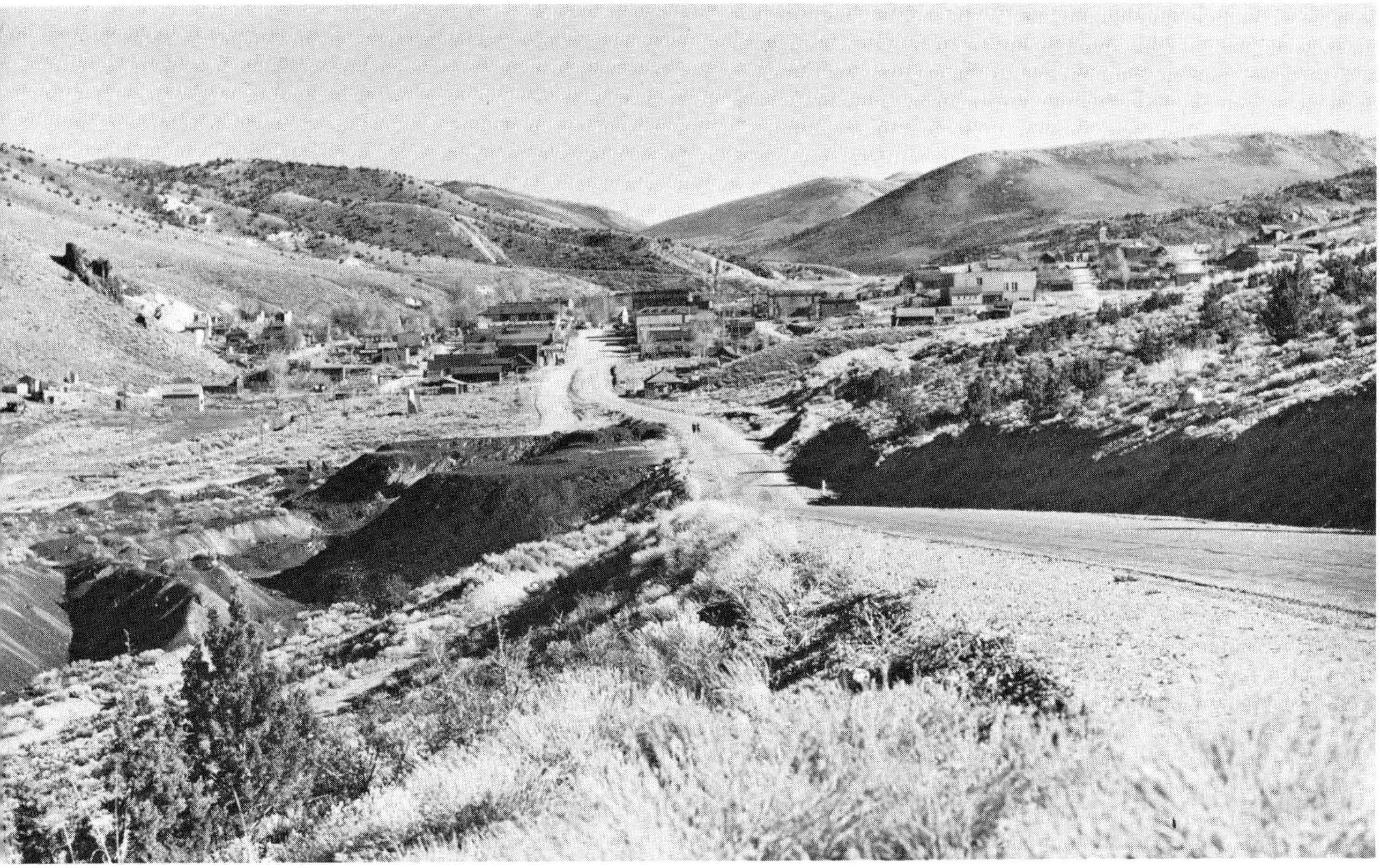

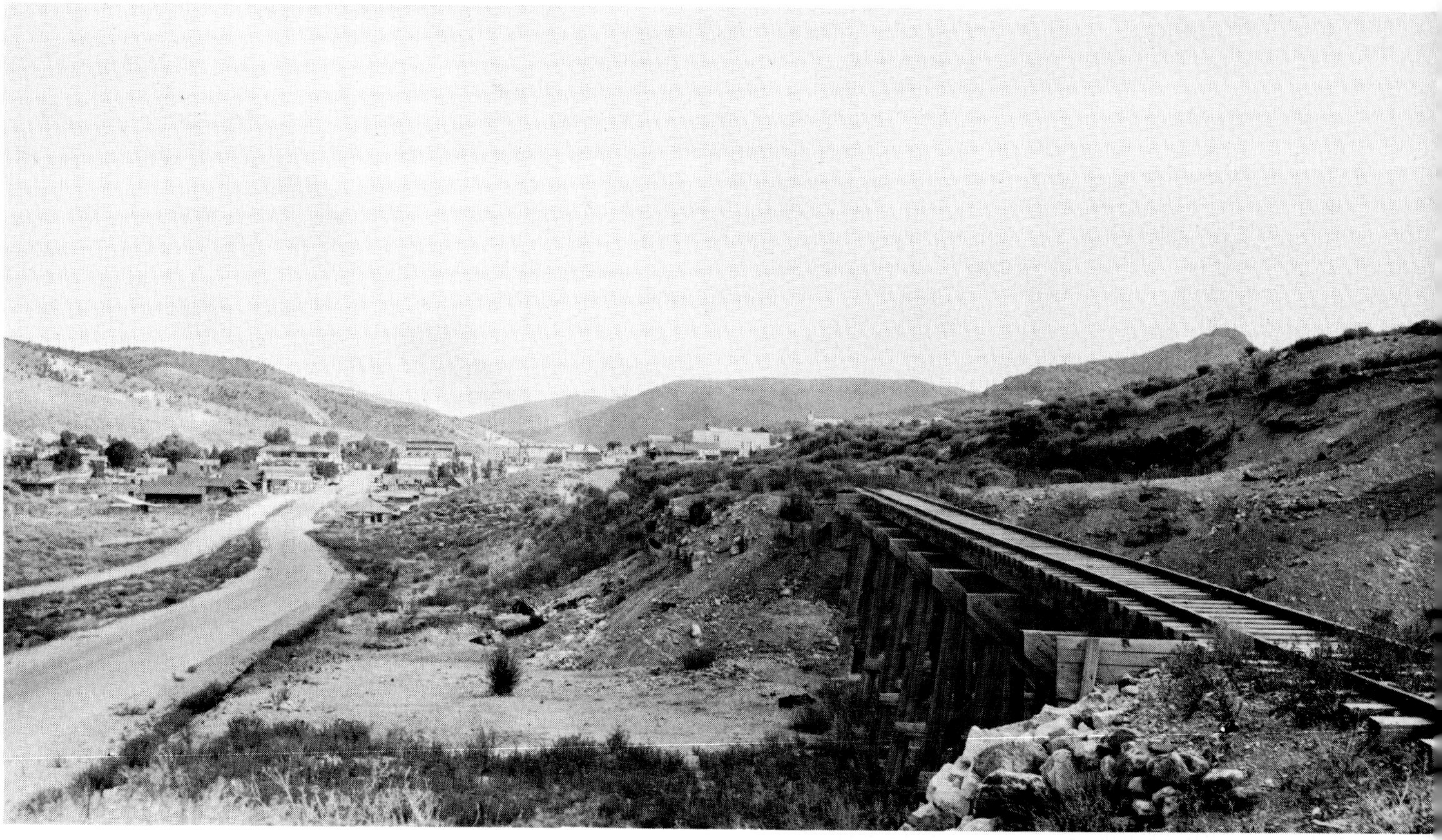

The Eureka & Palisade was abandoned two short months after this July 1938 photo *(above)* was taken looking south toward Eureka from the approximate location of the Eureka Con. furnaces and the Lemon Mill.

The Ruby Hill Railroad had disappeared, but its former presence is clearly indicated *(below)* just over the top of the E&P gondolas in this earlier view near the same site. *(Top: Ted Wurm Photo; Bottom: Louis Stein, Jr. Collection.)*

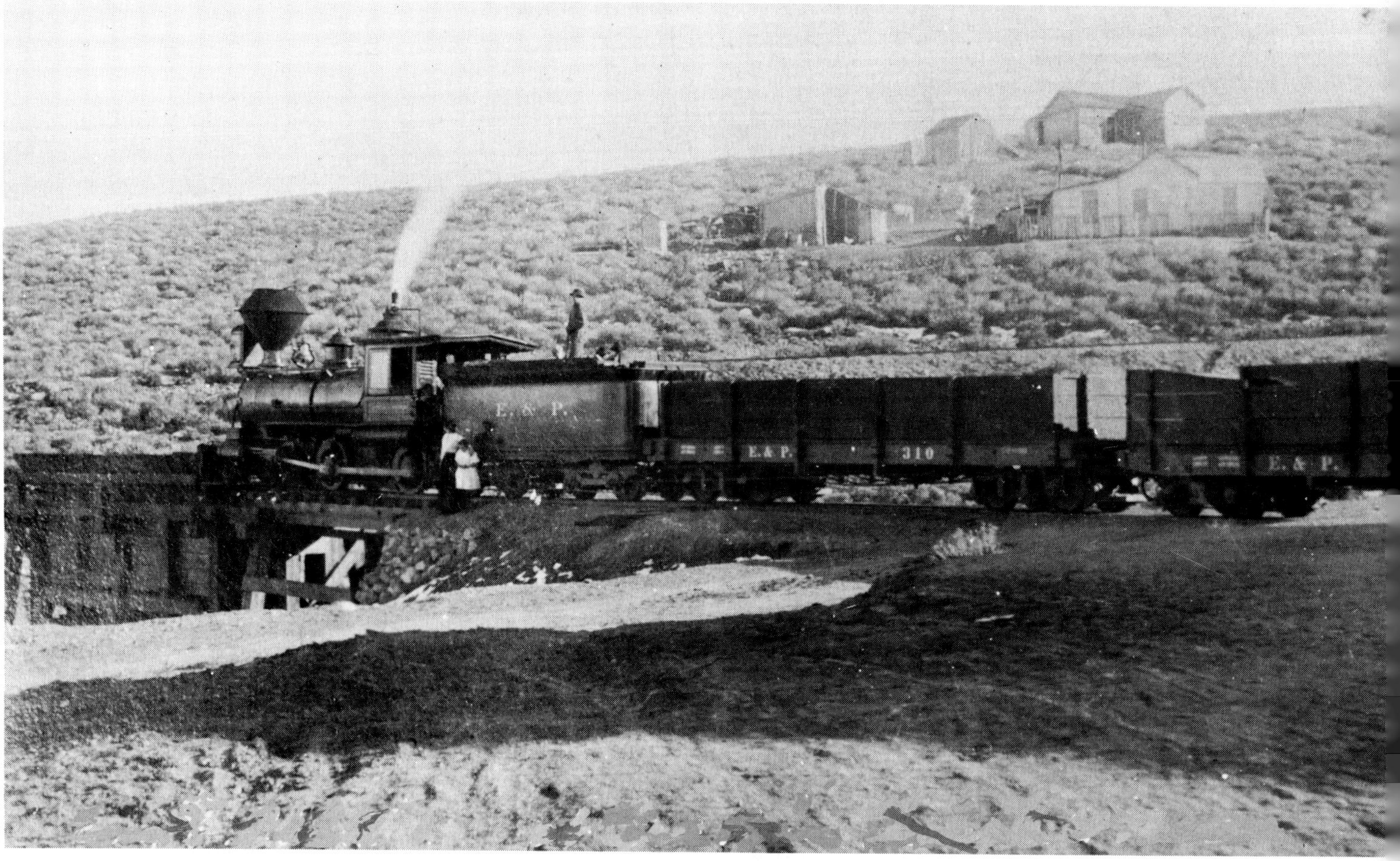

Cortez Mining R.R. Mine to Mill, no connections

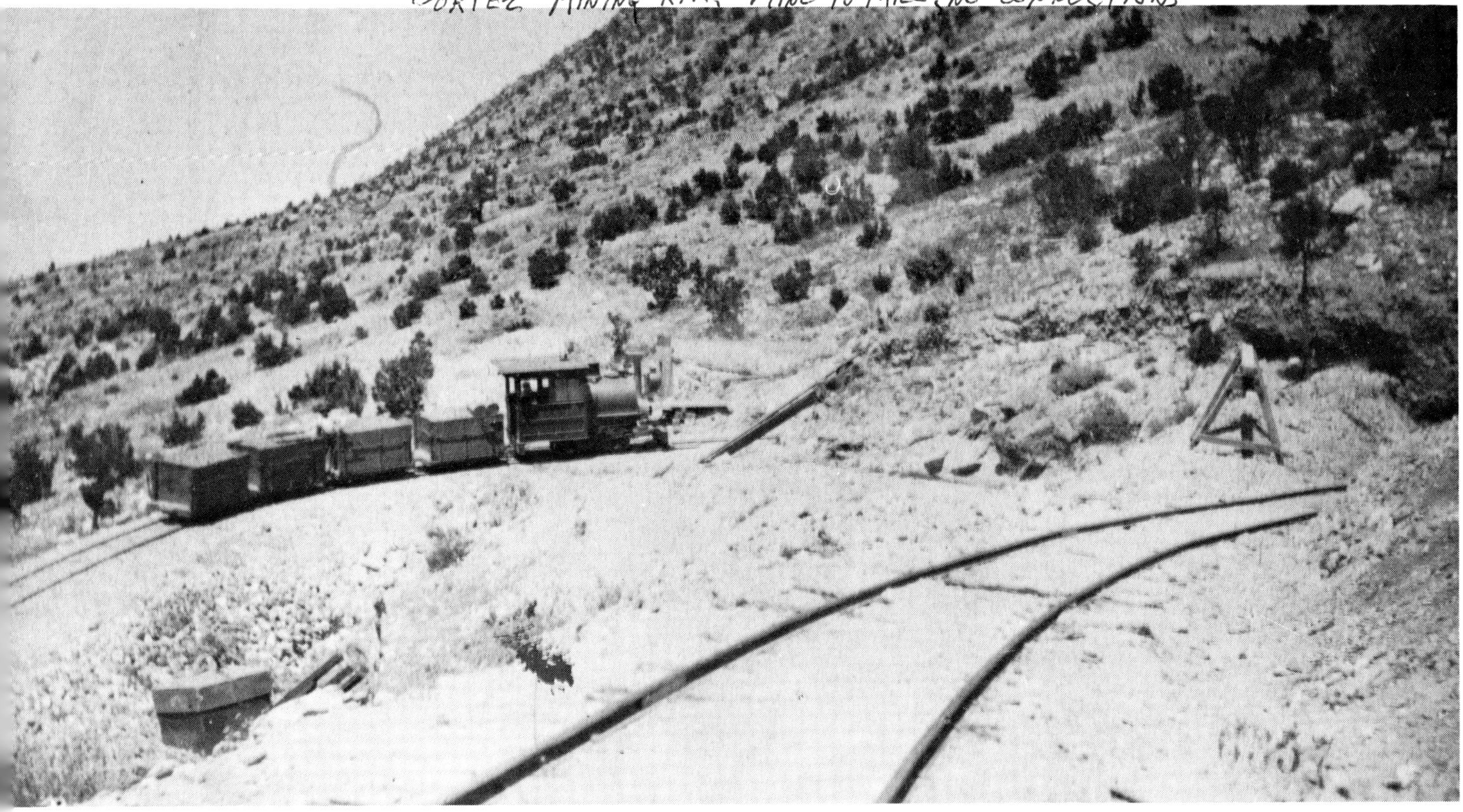

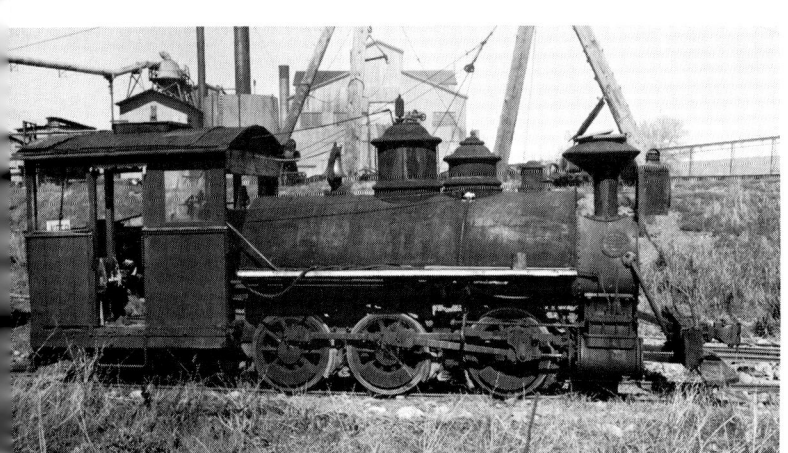

Climbing Ruby Hill was an ordeal for the fireman on the road's dinky locomotives, but descending the same steep grade with only the locomotive brakes to hold four loaded ore cars in check could be equally distressing to the engineer.

The RH's first locomotive in 1876 "with six wheels the same size" undoubtedly was similar to this 1890 product of Baldwin which formerly ran on the Ruby Hill but is here seen at Oroville, California, in the service of the Swayne Lumber Co.

Before construction of the railroad, people came to Ruby Hill—and stayed—as witness this pre-1875 view of the town's facilities. *(Top: Nevada Historical Society; Center: Ted Wurm Collection; Bottom: Louis L. Stein, Jr. Collection.)*

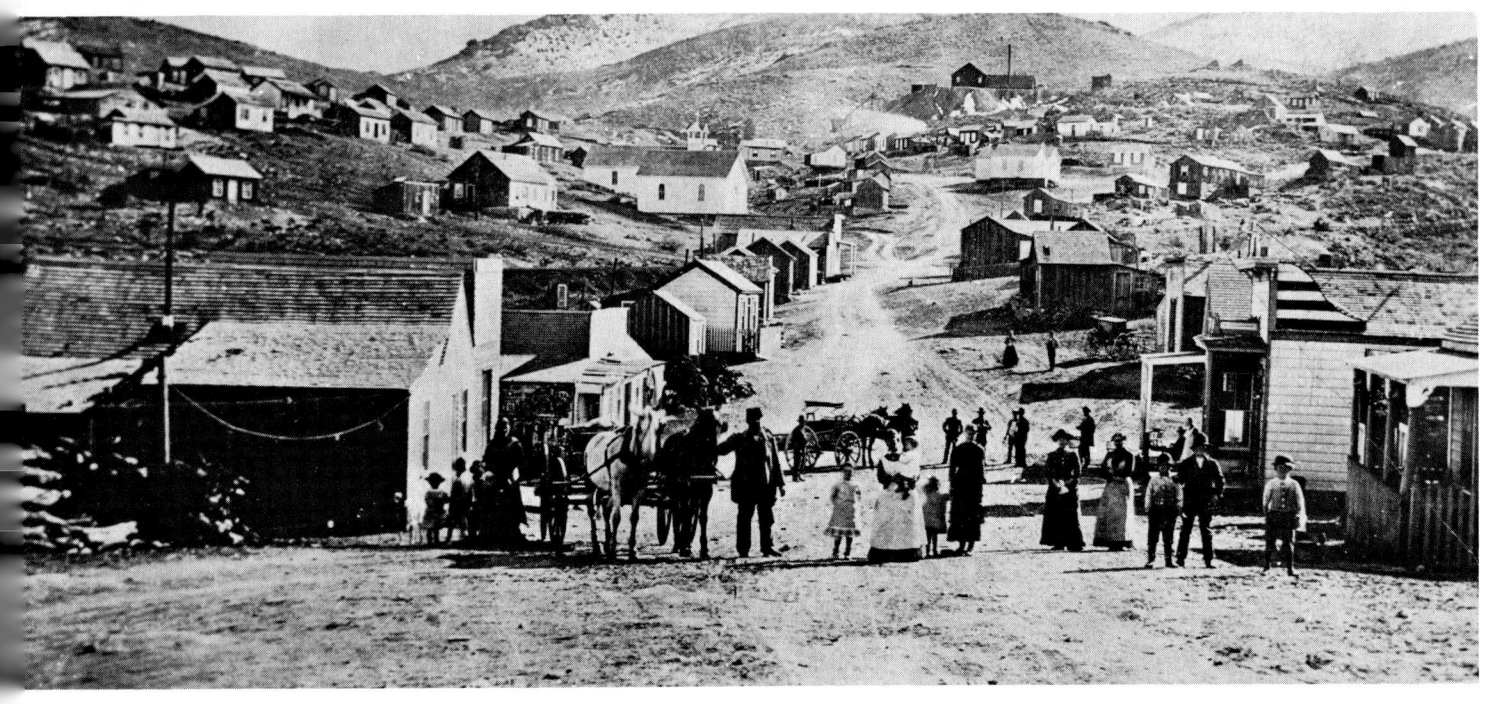

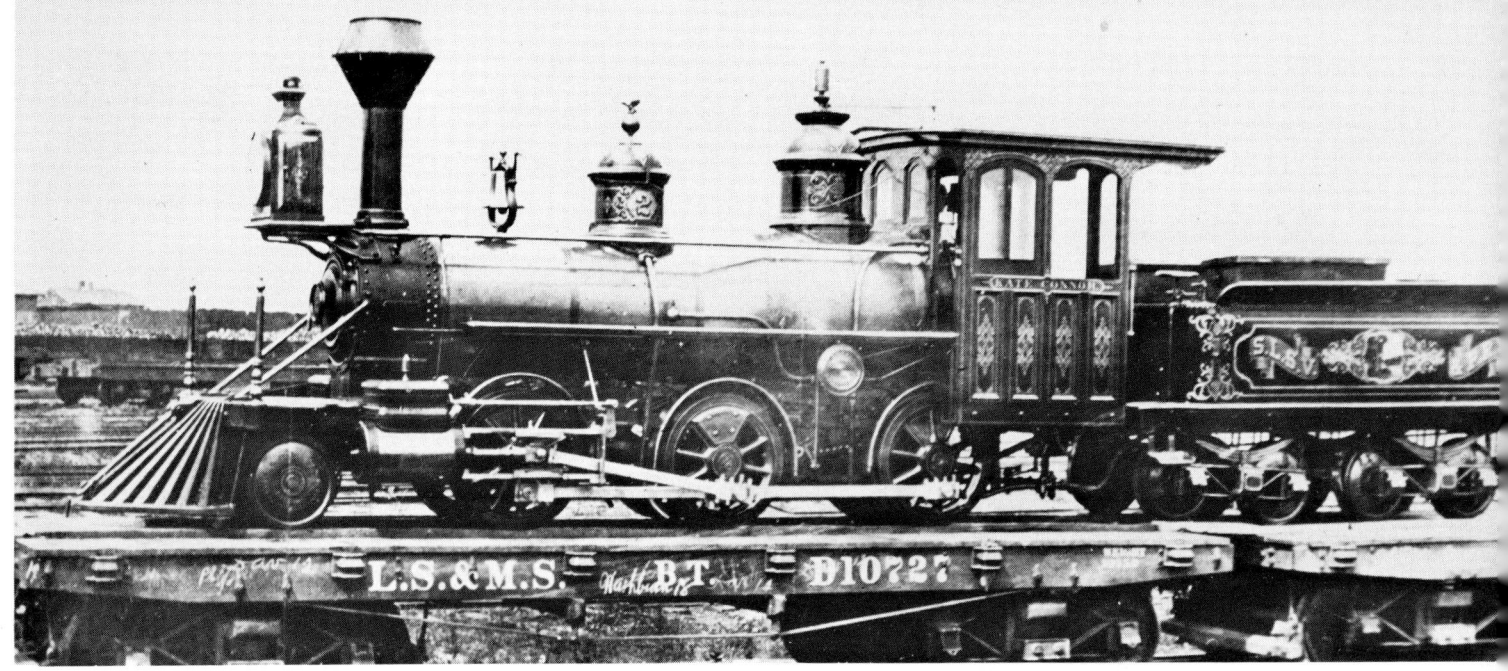

The E&P's first locomotive was an ornate Brooks Mogul (2-6-0) originally built in the early 1870's for General Connor's Salt Lake, Sevier Valley & Pioche Railroad and appropriately named the KATE CONNOR in honor of the General's daughter. When the SL,SV&P failed to materialize, the engine was diverted to the E&P and became its No. 1, EUREKA. Shown here *(above)* on delivery, it is interesting to note the scrollwork on the domes, the inlaid cab, the elaborate insignia on the tender and the supporting eliptical springs over arch bar trucks of the period. Other E&P motive power was not so glamorous. In the view *(right)* of No. 5, the posed crew obscures the fact that the PALISADE has paused for the more plebeian task of clearing a plugged flue, as evidenced by the open smokebox door. In the last year of operations, No. 10 posed with what might be the entire personnel of the Eureka Nevada in front of the Palisade terminus. *(Top and Center: Louis L. Stein, Jr. Collection; Bottom: Albert C. Phelps.)*

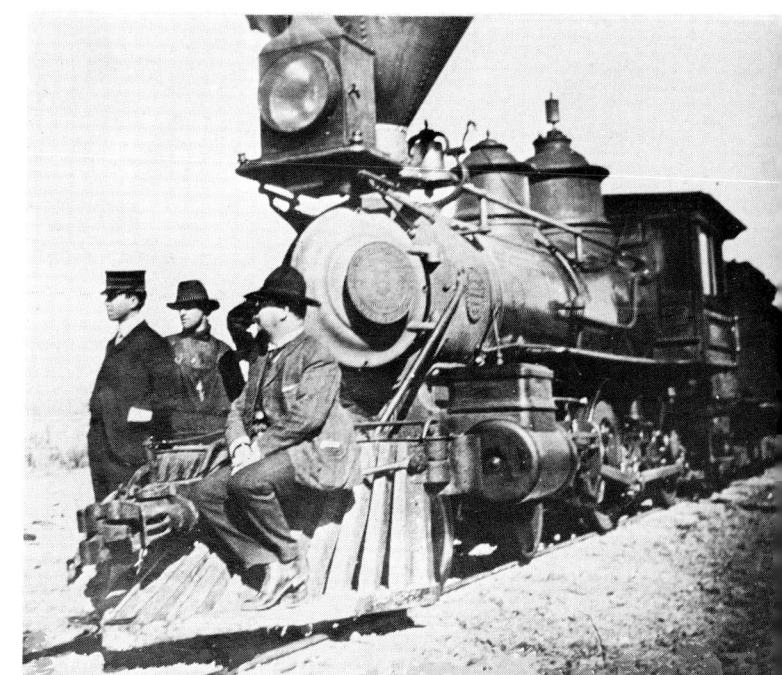

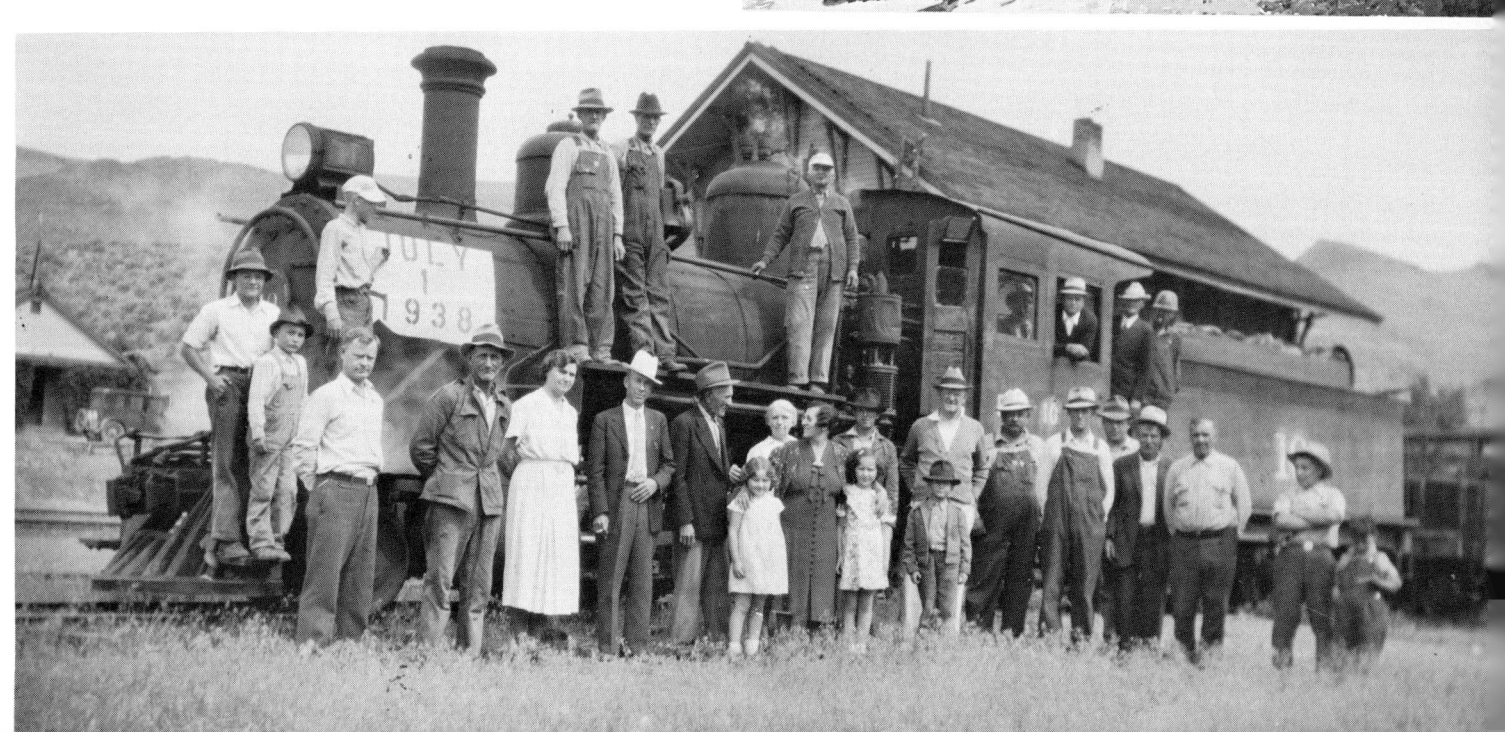

FREIGHTERS.

EUREKA AND PALISADE RAIL ROAD.

NOTICE TO SHIPPERS.

GREAT REDUCTION
—IN—
RATES OF FREIGHT!

SHORTEST AND QUICKEST ROUTE TO PIOCHE,

VIA EUREKA AND PALISADE R. R. AND FAST FREIGHT TEAMS.

Rates payable in United States gold coin or its equivalent.

All Consignments of Goods Forwarded with Promptness and Dispatch. **No Forwarding or Commission Charges.**

Mark Goods Care "E. & P. R. R."

All Liquors and Liquids will be transported only at the owner's risk of leakage.

On and after **May 1st and until November 1st, 1876**, Rates on all First-Class Freight from Palisade to Pioche will be **Three (3) Cents per Pound**, including transfer at Palisade and Eureka.

W. E. GRIFFIN,
a13-tf   Agent.

EUREKA AND PALISADE RAILROAD

TIME TABLE, NO. 16,

To take effect at 1 o'clock A. M., Sunday, July 1, 1883.

For the Government of Employes only.

BOUND NORTH.				STATIONS.		BOUND SOUTH.		
No. 5. FREIGHT.	No. 3. WAY FREIGHT.	No. 1. MAIL and EXP	Distance from Eureka. MILES.		Distance from Palisade. MILES.	No. 2. MAIL and EXP	No. 4. WAY FREIGHT.	No. 6 FREIGHT
3.25 p m	4.40 p m	90		Ar † PALISADE. Lv	0	5.35 p m	6.00 a m	
2.30	4.15	80¾		BULLION.	9¼	6.00	7.00	
2.15	4.05	77¾		EVANS.	12¼	6.10	7.20	
1.55	3.55	75		WILLARDS.	15	6.20	7.35	
1.35	3.45	71		HAY RANCH.	19	6.30	8.05	
12.50	3.20	61½		BOX SPRINGS.	28½	6.55	9.00	
12.30	3.10	56½		BLACKBURNS.	33½	7.05	9.25	
12.10 p m	3.00	52½		MINERAL.	37½	7.15	9.50	
11.45	2.45	47		DEEP WELLS.	43	7.30	10.15	
10.55	2.25	40		ALPHA.	50	7.50	10.55	
10.30	2.20	38		PINE.	52	7.55	10.10	
10.15	2.15	35½		CEDAR.	54½	8.05	11.25	
9.55	2.05	32		OAK.	58	8.15	11.45	
9.25	1.50	27		SUMMIT.	63	8.30	12.40 p m	
7.45	**1.30**	21		GARDEN PASS.	69	8.50	**1.30**	
7.00	1.05	12		DIAMOND.	78	9.15	2.25	
6.00 a m	12.35 p m	0		Lv † EUREKA. Ar	90	9.50	3.30	

† Telegraph Stations.

Trains will not run to exceed eight (8) miles per hour in passing over switches.

Trains Nos. 1 and 2 will only stop at Hay Ranch and Alpha, except when flagged, or to let off Passengers.

B. GILMAN, Gen'l Supt

Immediately upon completion in 1875, the E&P began reaching out to the surrounding mining camps for additional business. This 1876 advertisement in the *Pioche Weekly Record* offered a low 3¢-per-pound rate on first-class freight including transfer at both Palisade (to E&P cars) and Eureka (to E&P wagons for the nearly 200-mile southerly haul). Liquors appeared to be a particularly perishable commodity. (*Nevada Historical Society.*)

Eureka, Nevada, reached the peak of its production during the years 1880-82. Employees' Timetable No. 16 of July 1, 1883, reflects the early effects of the fall-off through elimination of trains 5 and 6. Presumably both the Way Freight and the Mail & Express catered to passengers desiring transportation. (*Louis L. Stein, Jr. Collection.*)

---

those of the adjoining Richmond Consolidated, resulting in considerable extra litigation.

The Eureka & Palisade Railroad prospered, returning to its owners a handsome profit in the initial year of operations and continuing in the ensuing years to add bounty upon bounty. In 1880 the reported return on investment in the E&P was in excess of 15%, and that of the Ruby Hill Railroad a magnificent 53%. Through the medium of connecting teamster service, freight lines were established throughout the surrounding area, extending as far south as Pioche. So lucrative was the traffic, a connecting Eureka & Colorado River Railroad (see Projected Railroads) was platted from the Richmond Furnace leg of the Ruby Hill Railroad southward over Pinto Summit. Ten miles of grading were accomplished before all work ceased, leaving vestigial lines on some cartographer's efforts of the 1882 period.

When the bonanza ore bodies became exhausted in 1885, mining properties generally were turned over to leasers. Such beneficence did not pertain to the smelters, then employing 170 men in the refinement of local ores as well as those from Hamilton to the east and from as far as Reveille to the south. Dividends from the Richmond, previously and magnanimously declared payable in English shillings, ultimately ceased.

With the decline in prosperity, service on the Eureka & Palisade Railroad also shrank. Daily passenger trains gave way to tri-weekly mixed service in 1888. Some small Eureka mines, instead of patronizing local smelters, shipped their ores to Salt Lake City on the contention they could net $3.00 to $12.00 more per ton in spite of the added shipping costs. In 1890 the Richmond smelter closed down, and to cap the climax the Eureka followed suit in 1891. Subsequently both works were reduced to scrap iron. Then in 1893 the Ruby Hill Railroad was abandoned, the same year in which the first of many annual deficits was incurred by the Eureka & Palisade.

The principal E&P stockholders were rapidly losing interest in their railroad. The primary institutions it was built to serve were gone; there was little left to furnish traffic for a one-purpose line. In desperation they turned the project over to Mark Requa, son of Isaac Requa, in 1897. Realizing the solution for badly needed traffic was not to be found in Eureka, Mark Requa actively pursued a policy of reaching out for business beyond the rail head. His constant solicitation of business managed to change the routing of various Ely-bound freight from the Wells-Steptoe Valley route to that via the E&P to Eureka and thence by teams over the intervening 40 miles to the east. Additional business was secured from Hamilton which was having a mild revival from activities at the Rocco Homestake mine. When Charlie Lane reopened the old Chainman mine near Ely, the E&P was the beneficiary of another few months of prosperity. Further surcease was enjoyed when Giroux started his operations at Pilot Knob near Ely in 1901.

Various extension schemes were considered and dropped. Tonopah looked inviting in the first blush of its bonanza, and a projection to the new camp was eagerly considered. D. O. Mills found little appeal in the project considering the outlay of money required, and his was still the large, tight hand on the company's purse strings. Shortly afterward, Mark Requa became interested in various copper mining properties near Ely and had surveys made for an extension of the E&P eastward to the promising new bonanza. Although the 75 route miles would mean far less construction mileage than a new road directly connecting Ely with the Central Pacific, there was a little matter of crossing four mountain ranges with the attendant operating problems. The difficulties were too great; a different route north from Ely up the Steptoe Valley to Wells was chosen; and a new Nevada Northern Railway was built as a separate enterprise in 1905-06.

Receivership came to the E&P on June 13, 1900 following default on its bond interest, and the property was sold in bankruptcy. Although Nevada's Governor Sadler and his associates bid $250,000 for the line (the initial cost had been in excess of $1,500,000), Mark Requa, I. W. Hellman and J. H. Moulton succeeded in wresting it away from them for $300,000 as trustees for the bondholders. On July 10, 1901, a new, debt-free Utah company, was formed called Eureka & Palisade *Railway,* and the properties were transferred on February 1, 1902.

The reorganization was timely; other upheavals were in the process. The old Richmond Consolidated and Eureka Consolidated mining properties passed into the hands of the U. S. Smelting, Refining & Mining Co. through a separate subsidiary called the Richmond-Eureka Mining Co. By 1905 Eureka was booming again as in days gone by, and once again Ruby Hill needed transportation. With some $70,000 advanced by the Richmond-Eureka the E&P rebuilt the Ruby Hill branch, altering the alignment wherever expedient in the light of more modern methods and equipment. Grading started in October 1905, and the resultant road was only four miles long as compared with the seven miles of line comprising the original Ruby Hill Narrow Gauge Railroad. Ore shipments from the mines commenced in 1906, loading being accomplished directly into the narrow-gauge cars of the E&P which were then marshalled into trains, dropped down the hill, and hauled the entire length of the line to Palisade. At the latter point erection of a large ore transfer trestle facilitated reloading into the standard-gauge cars of the Southern Pacific for the balance of the journey to the U.S.S.R.&M. smelter near Salt Lake City. By 1909 this phase of the railroad's business amounted to 200 tons daily, comprised 90% of the tonnage handled, and accounted for 75% of the road's revenues. Thus for a few years the E&P enjoyed a moderate volume of long-haul business and, being free of interest requirements, managed to pay a few small dividends to its shareholders.

The respite was short-lived. On March 1, 1910, tragedy struck again; the E&P was badly washed out; 11 miles of track were destroyed; operations ground to an abrupt halt.

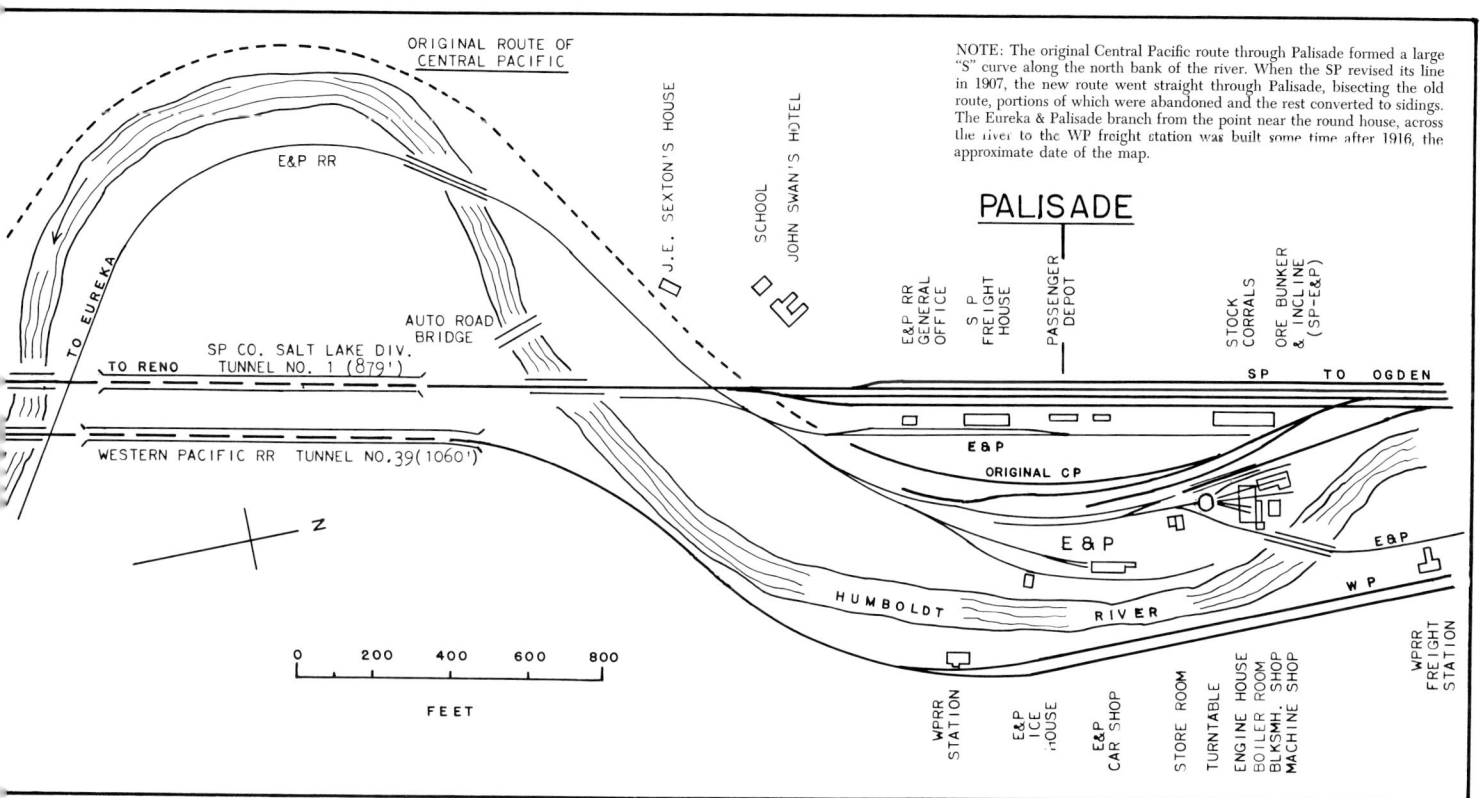

NOTE: The original Central Pacific route through Palisade formed a large "S" curve along the north bank of the river. When the SP revised its line in 1907, the new route went straight through Palisade, bisecting the old route, portions of which were abandoned and the rest converted to sidings. The Eureka & Palisade branch from the point near the round house, across the river to the WP freight station was built some time after 1916, the approximate date of the map.

The situation began innocently enough with normal heavy spring rains the latter part of February. However, instead of diminishing in intensity, they increased; and the railroad began operating under greater and greater difficulties. The southbound train out of Palisade became delayed by a washout at "The Chimneys," just south of Alpha, with the result that its scheduled Friday afternoon arrival in Eureka was postponed until Saturday noon, February 26. Before the train could be turned around for its northbound run back to Palisade, word was received that the temporary track repairs which had been effected were washed out again. There was nothing to do but wait, though no one dreamed the wait would last for two full years.

E&P locomotive No. 10 suffered a similar fate. A washout near Garden Pass three weeks earlier had sent the engine slithering into the mud. Track repairs had been rushed, but before the locomotive could be extricated from its predicament and placed back on the rails, the floods came. It, too, was not disturbed for two long years.

At the northern end of the line at Palisade, matters were definitely in no better shape. The southbound train (corresponding to the one stranded at Eureka) managed to leave town bravely enough, but it was forced to turn back at Blackburn. By the time the crew reached Palisade once again, they were congratulating themselves on their good fortune at being able to return at all. The double-header work train sent out to repair the break in the line at "The Chimneys" managed to struggle as far as Mineral Station, where it became marooned. The crew and work gangs bravely and hopefully waited for a few days; then they gave up. There was only one thing to do — walk home. The entire train, including locomotives Nos. 5 and 6, was abandoned, not to move for two years.

Instead of being the climax, these incidents were to be but the prelude to the main event. On March 1, 1910, the real floods came—extensive wet-mantle floods (complete saturation of the soil mantle) — and Pine Valley, the entire E&P route, and much of the rest of central Nevada were hard hit. Swirling waters brought all railroad operations in the area to a standstill. Pine Creek's channel, previously 100 yards wide, was expanded tenfold in places, washing out 11 miles of E&P tracks. A gigantic lake was formed in Pine Creek's valley extending southward from Palisade for 30 miles. (A subsequent, similar flood of smaller dimensions occurred in 1952, though the height and extent of the waters was nowhere near as great.)

That portion of the E&P roadbed that was not completely washed away became so seriously deteriorated by the standing flood waters it was useless. The E&P's roundhouse and shop buildings in Palisade were inundated to a depth of five feet. Tracks of both the SP and the WP were swept away, and the tunnels of both roads just west of

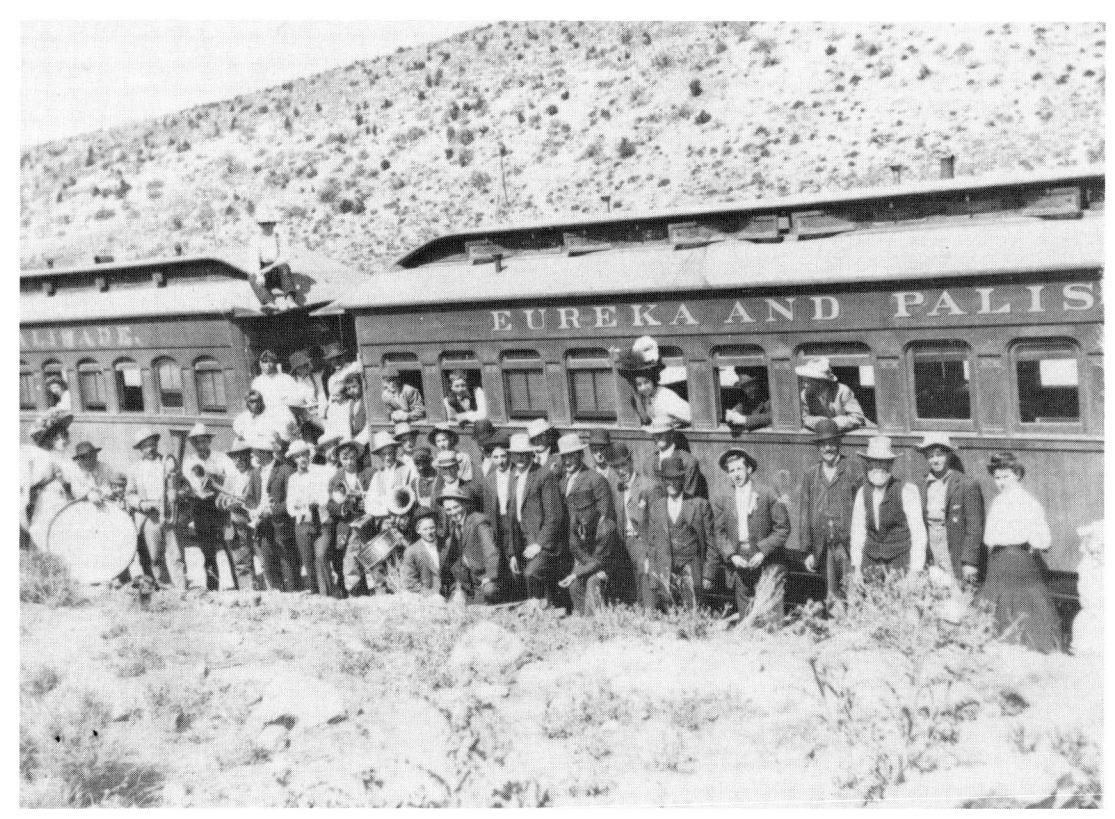

Around the turn of the century, the crew of men employed at the E&P shops in Palisade was sufficiently large to enable a band to be organized, the members of which received free transportation on picnics, such as this one at Eureka.

In the earlier portrait at Palisade two vested dignitaries posed with the crew of No. 5, the PALISADE, built by Baldwin in 1876. Note the fendered pony truck, the crosshead pump for supplying water to the boiler, and the single sand pipe from the dome to supply the forward drivers only. (*Top: Williamson Collection; Bottom: Louis L. Stein, Jr. Collection.*)

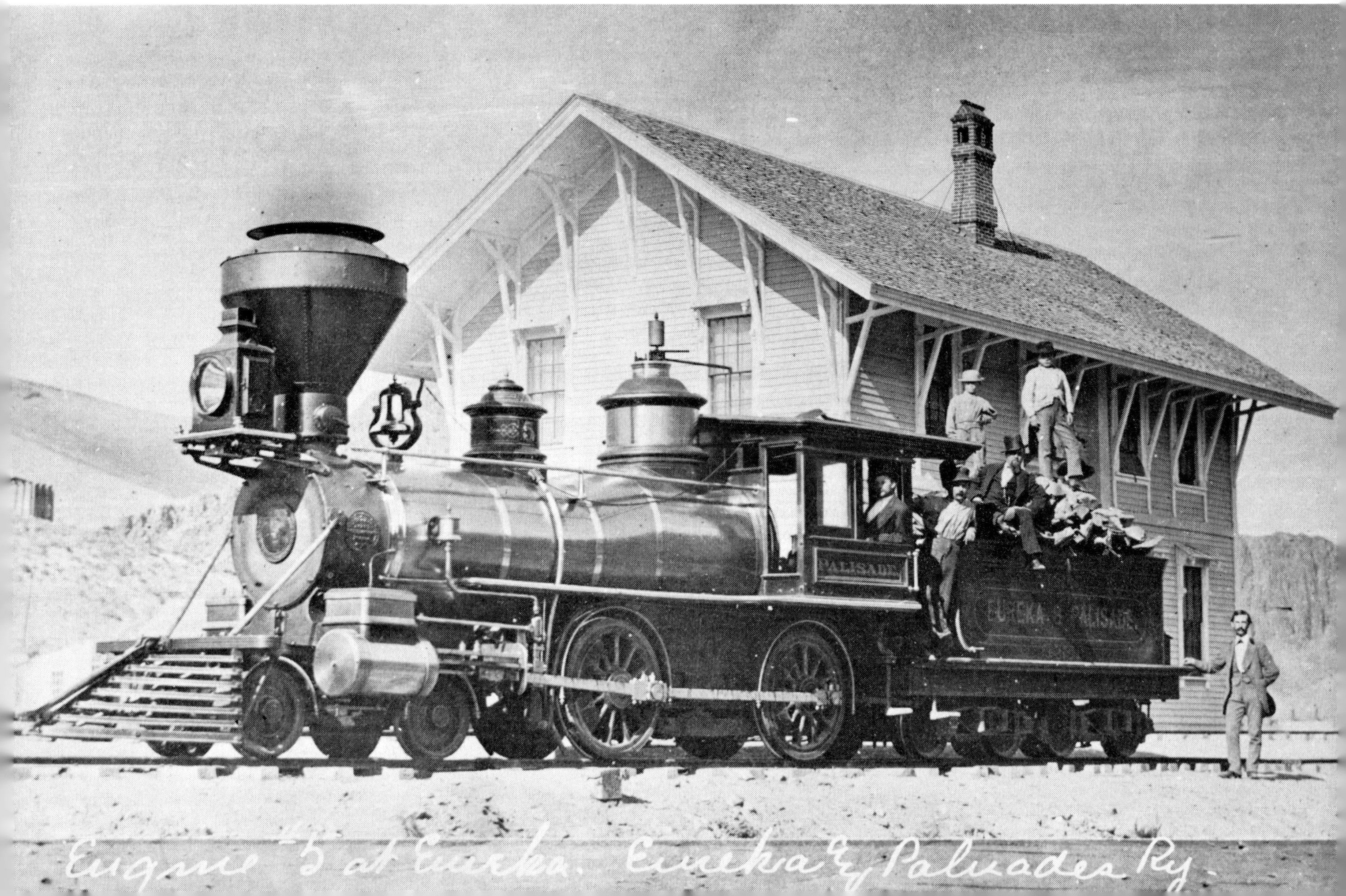

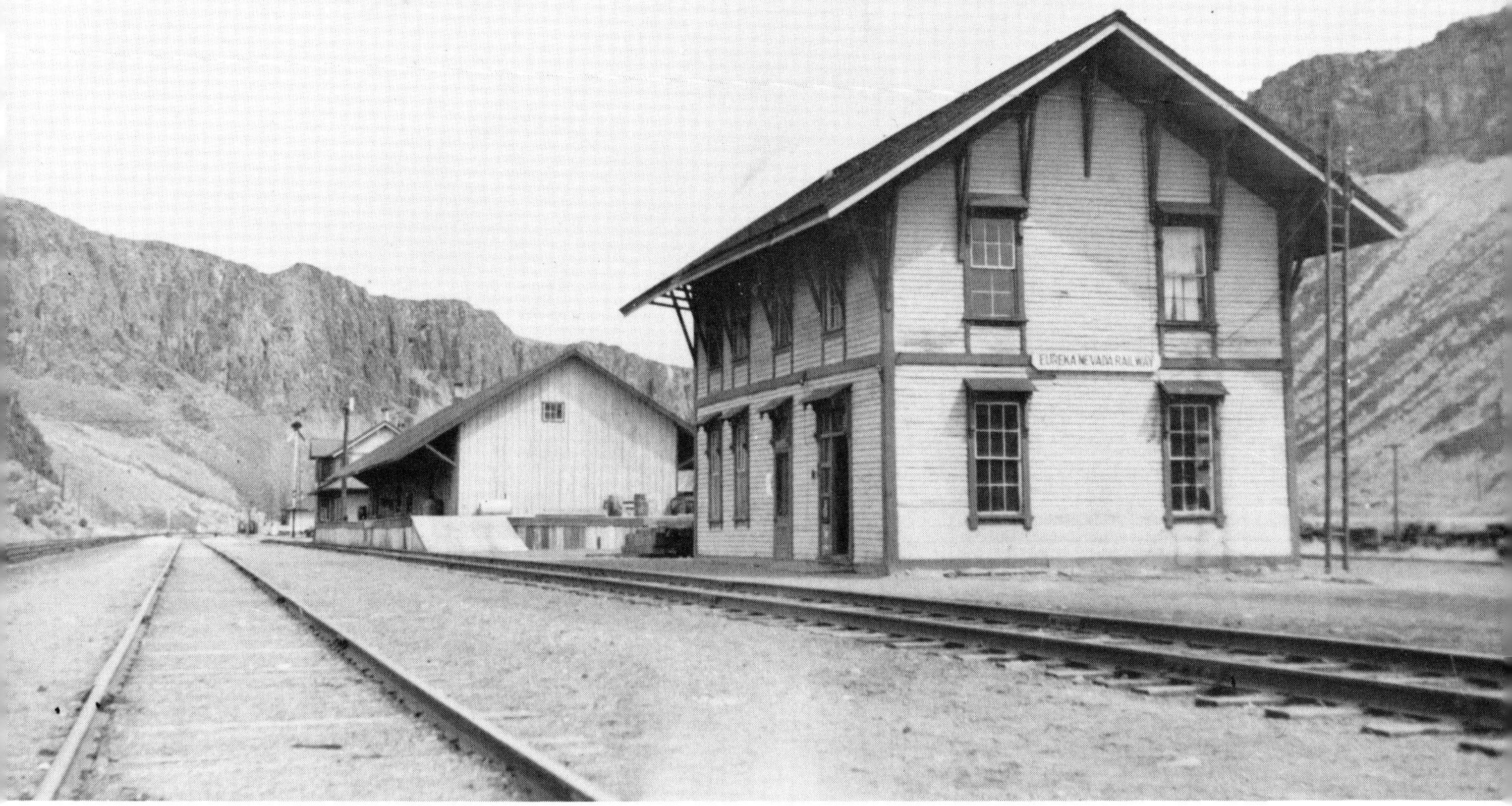

For two years following the floods of 1910 the Eureka & Palisade was immobilized; when it was finally reactivated, the name had been changed to Eureka Nevada Railway. *Above* is the Eureka Nevada general office building at Palisade in 1938, the final year of utility before abandonment.

The E&P roundhouse shops and crew in the more affluent year of 1909 when 200 tons of ore arrived each day to be pushed up the incline of the transfer trestle (at left in photo) for reloading into standard gauge cars of the Southern Pacific. *(Both: Williamson Collection.)*

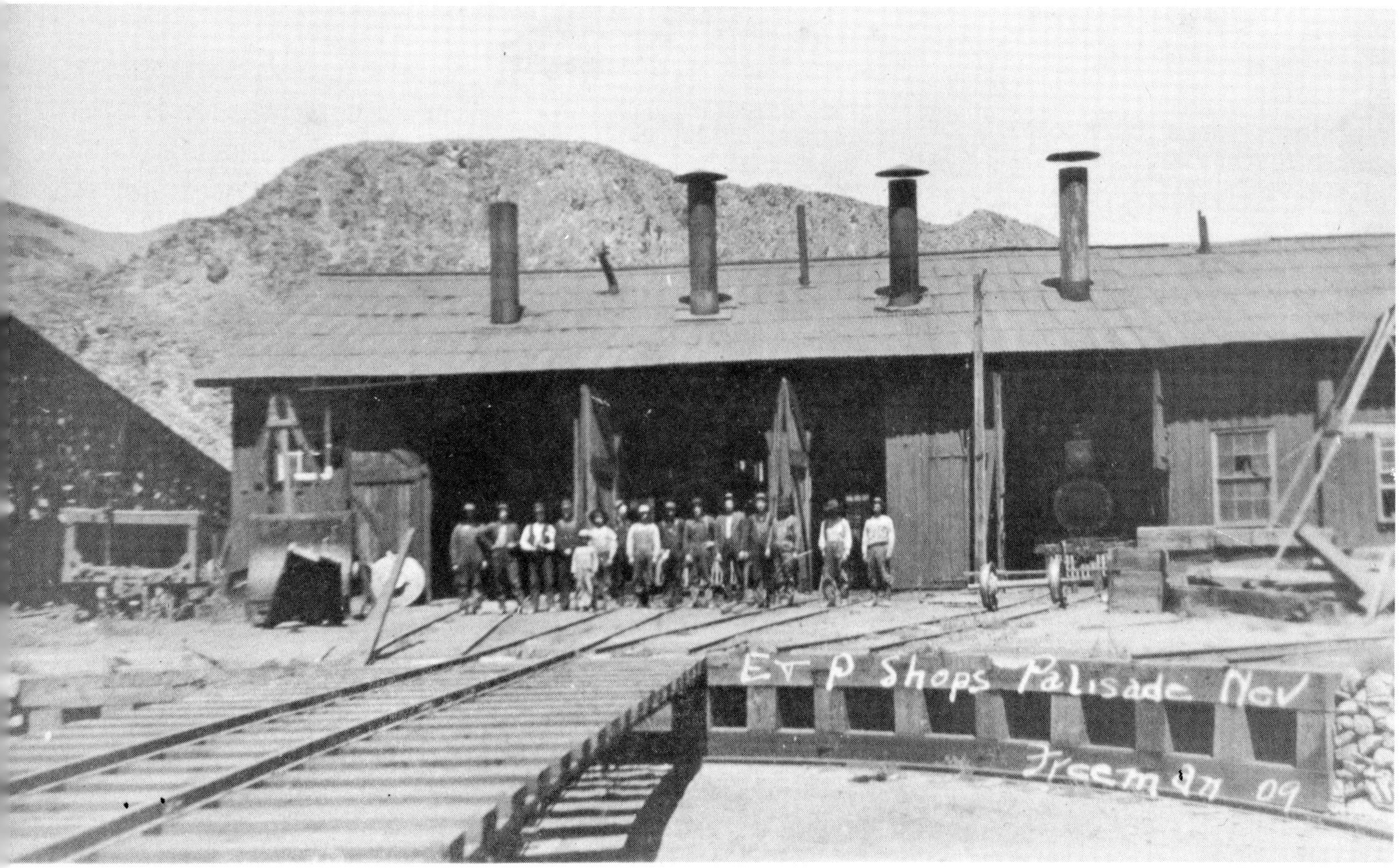

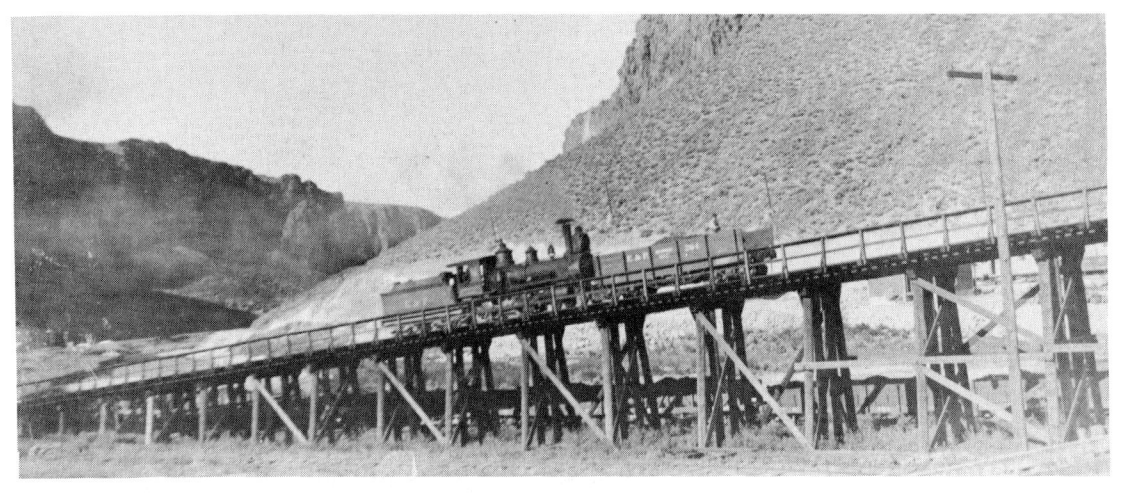

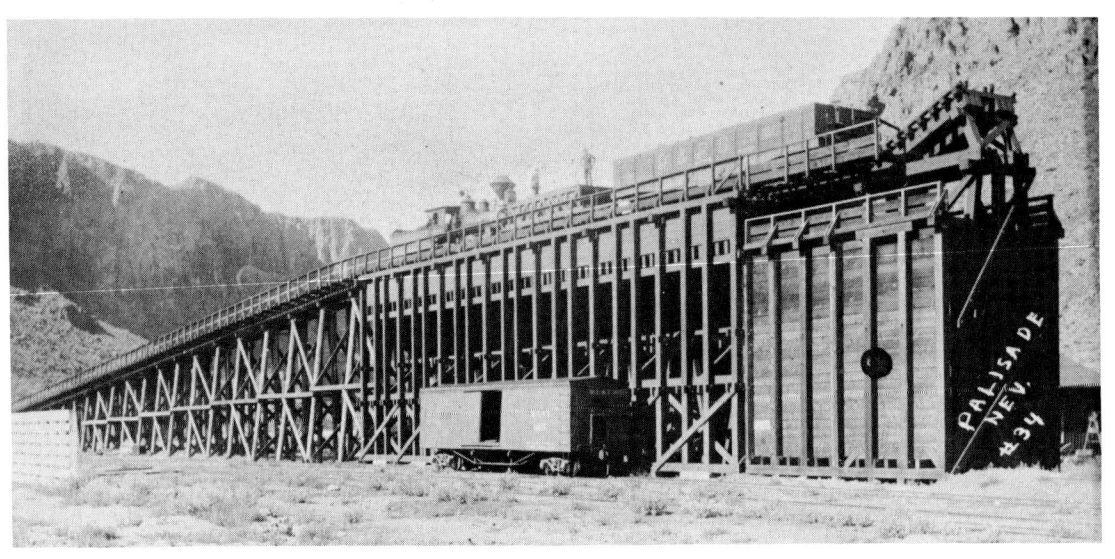

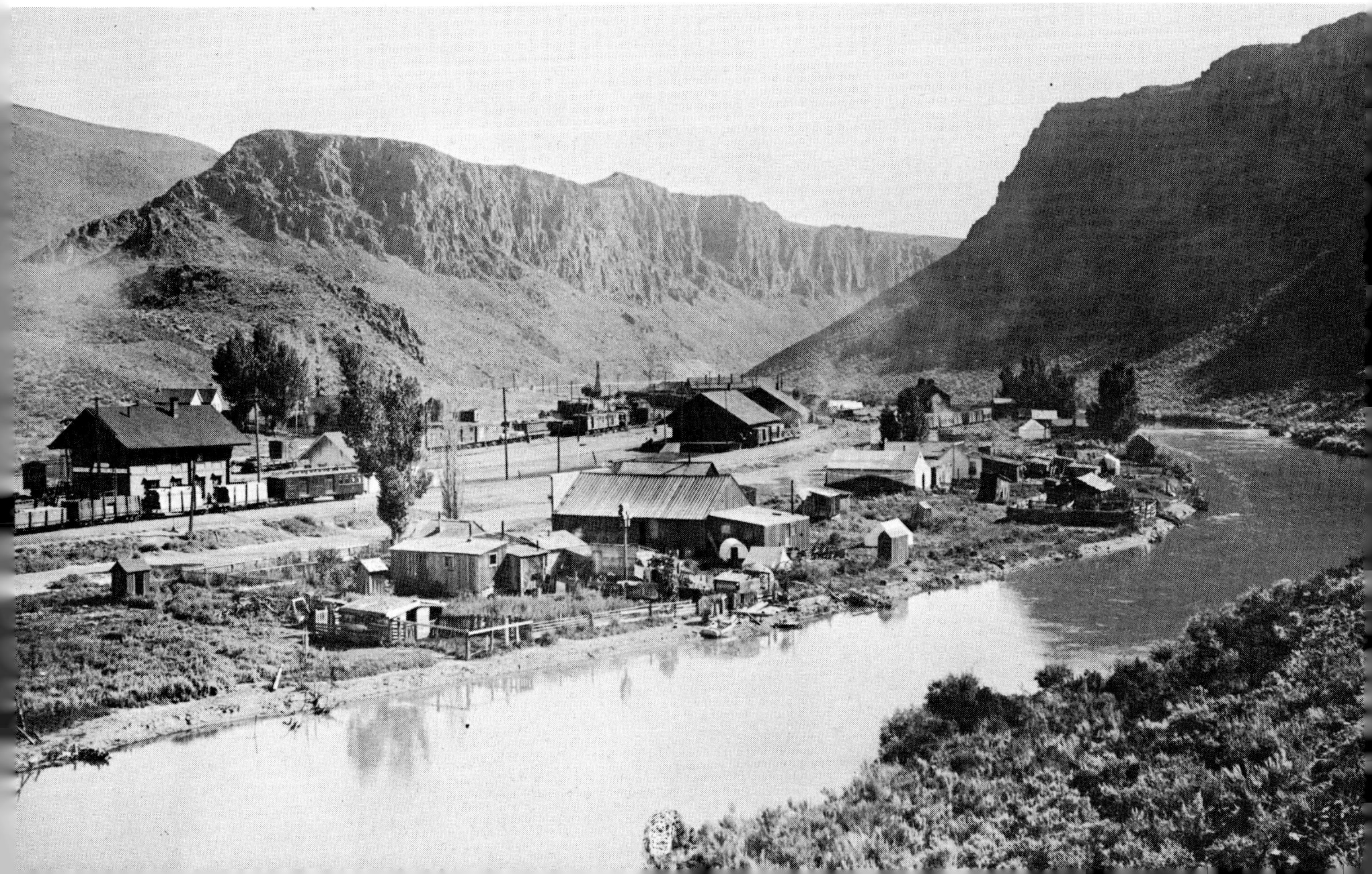

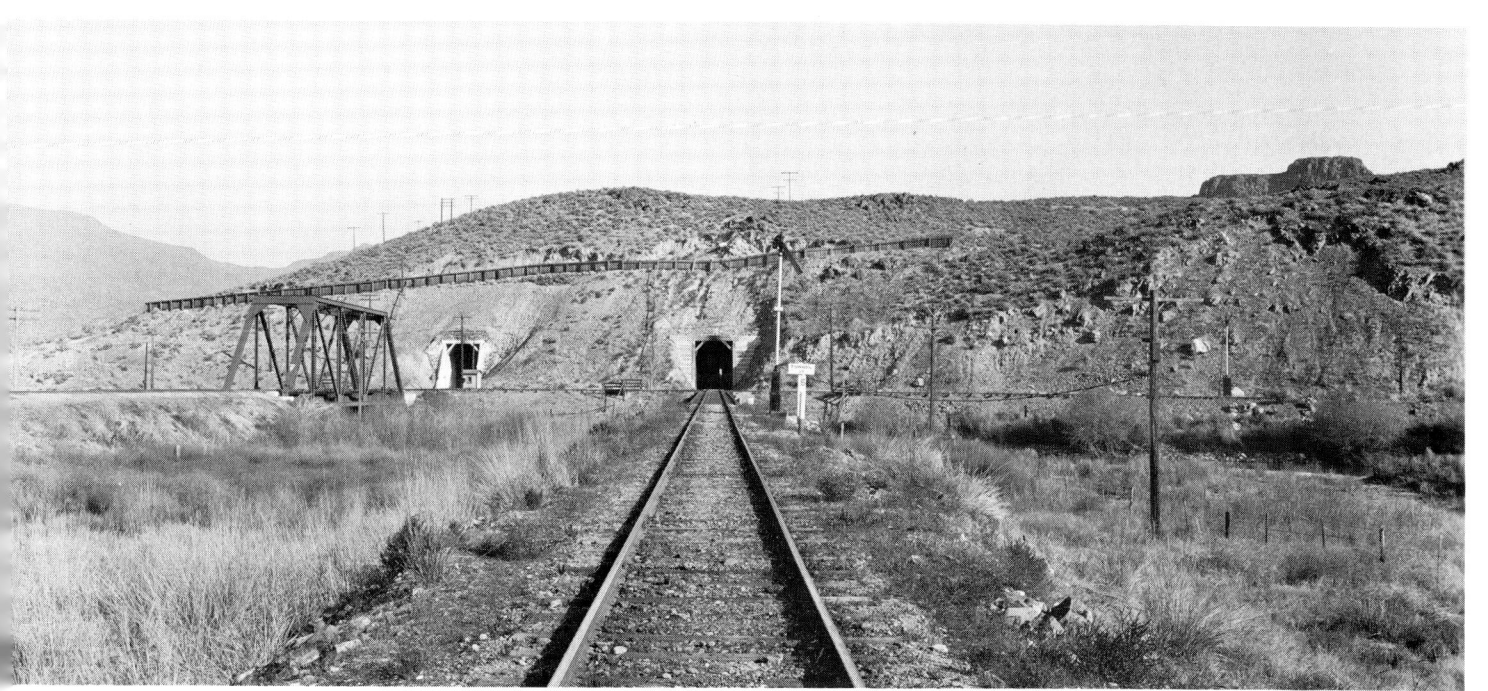

From 1905-09 Eureka boomed and the E&P prospered. Daily trainloads of ore were brought to Palisade and pushed up the incline *(top, left)* to the ore transfer bins *(center, left)*. In the latter view an ex-D&RG narrow gauge car can be seen. About the turn of the century, Palisade *(left, below)* was active. The abundance of the E&P mixed train whose rear portion shows in front of the station at left, and the presence of a derrick boom to left of center behind the freight station and E&P shops, suggests that business is increasing and that erection of the ore trestle is about to begin.

When the Western Pacific built through the Humboldt River Valley in 1907-08, its main line *(above)* paralleled that of the SP on the western approach to Palisade. Both lines bridged the Humboldt River, crossed the tracks of the E&P along the base of the bluff, then tunneled the ridge. On the far side the WP swung along the south bank of the river, while the SP again crossed the river and the tracks of the E&P to enter the town. In 1910 operations of all three railroads ground to an abrupt halt when floods hit the area. The town of Palisade *(below)* was so thoroughly inundated that workers from the E&P shops were unable to celebrate their enforced vacation at J. W. Ebert's Winchester Saloon and Restaurant where "Jessie Moore Whiskey in Bond" was the order of the day. The new Western Pacific grade and tracks may be seen at the base of the bluff in the background. *(Bottom Left, Upper Right: Southern Pacific; Lower Right: Milo Taber Collection.)*

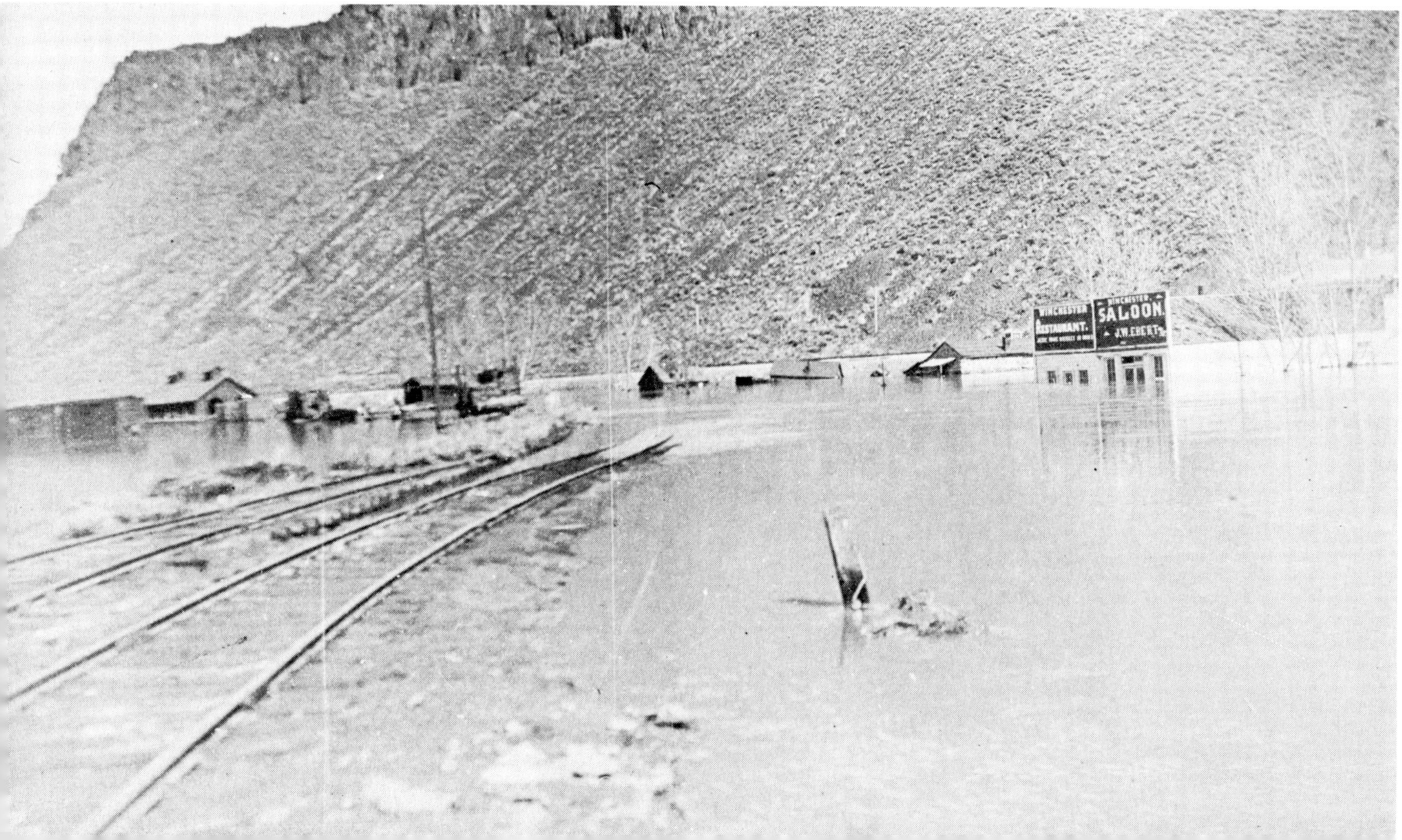

town were flooded. But for the strategic placement of the SP's railroad bridge at Palisade, that town's jail, eight houses and a store might have disappeared under the surging waters.

Floods can be devastating in the manner and unexpectedness of their occurrence, but frequently even more oppressive than the damage wrought is the aftermath of mud, silt and filth left in their wake. Two men were sent by Mark Requa to ascertain the extent of damage to E&P property; their report was most discouraging. A complete survey of the stricken area required a two-day trip in a horse and buggy and ended in a reported estimate of $150,000 to repair and rehabilitate the property. The sum was a staggering one to the little railroad, but a decision had to be made.

In a letter published in the *Eureka Sentinel* on April 2, 1910, Requa announced the sad news: the narrow gauge was suspending operations. As a faint ray of hope in an otherwise forlorn situation, Requa's letter went on to state that the railroad had been offered to the Richmond-Eureka interests, the principal shipper, without cost other than the obligation to repair the line and assume their own mortgage. As an added incentive, they could operate the reconditioned railroad until they had been reimbursed for the repair costs following which, if they wished, an interest in the company could still be maintained. When the Richmond-Eureka failed so much as to acknowledge the proffer, Requa arrived at the obvious conclusion that they were not interested.

With the suspension of railroad service, the economic activity of Pine Valley and Eureka lost the momentum it had gained over the previous four years of operations. The mining company, unable to ship its ores to the smelter, suspended operations with a resultant layoff of personnel. The cash flow in the area, already dwindled to a trickle, shrank even further with another community setback — the failure of the Eureka County Bank. Temporary (but limited) transportation was immediately provided following the flood by a twice-weekly, horse drawn stage which was superseded as quickly as possible by P. A. Pollock's light freight and passenger service with a Pope-Toledo automobile. The effect of the improved service was almost negligible — the region was dead on its feet.

Since the railroad and the mining company apparently were unable to arrive at any point of agreement, and since neither could operate successfully without the other, rumors of alternate solutions to the problem began to circulate. The one posing the greatest threat to the area involved a complete removal of the mining company's activities eastward to Ward, Nevada, to the south of Ely. There the Nevada United Mines Co. (a company not affiliated with the U.S.S.R.&M. Co.) held deposits of similar fluxing ores, and reportedly a survey had already been made for a 14-mile railroad north from Ward to Ely where a connection with the Nevada Northern Railway would provide access to the Salt Lake City smelter without any change of gauge or reloading of cars. Although the average grade of such a line of railway reputedly was only 1%, it was admitted that a one-mile stretch of 3% pitch would be required.

Most heartening to Eureka was the reported proposal involving a revival of the old Eastern Nevada Railroad project, originally instigated by some Elko people. The initial project (actively promoted during the period from 1871 to 1873), contemplated a line from Elko (on the SP) southward to Hamilton, approximately 45 miles southeast of Eureka. Although very little grading had been done at that time, the current (1910) plan involved rejuvenation of those portions of the old grade which could be used as part of the new route to Eureka. The excited flurry of interest was brief; talk then subsided; and the scheme joined its predecessor in oblivion. Another alternative was the suggested construction of a line east and south to Hamilton and to a connection with a then projected railroad between Ely and Goldfield.

During this period of mental and emotional turmoil Mark Requa and his E&P remained quiescent; but not so the Richmond-Eureka Mining Company. Obtaining a judgment for the money loaned to the railroad to rebuild the Ruby Hill branch, the mining company forced the railroad into receivership. Foreclosure proceedings commenced on October 29, 1910, and one month later, under a decree from the U. S. District Court, the property was sold at auction on November 29, 1910. George W. Heintz, general manager of the mining company (and acting in its behalf), then bought the railroad with a bid of $77,298.41, topping that of the National Bank of D. O. Mills & Co.

Under the law there was a six-month waiting period before any property sold in bankruptcy could be redeemed. Heintz and the mining company were most anxious to start rebuilding the railroad they had purchased, but according to one report the E&P shareholders refused to waive the right of redemption regardless of the mining company's efforts at persuasion. Finally on May 8, 1911, as the waiting period was drawing to a close, the E&P board of directors took positive action. Finding themselves still without funds and with little prospect of ever acquiring any, they officially refused to redeem the property. Whereupon George Whittell, a major stockholder of the railroad, acting independently in a surprise move, purchased the property from Heintz for $86,345.

Work on restoration of the line was immediately begun, but the task was long and arduous. The fall of 1911 in Pine Valley turned brutal. A cold wave settled in; the thermometer dropped to readings of -20 degrees on some days. Many of the laborers left the job, while those who remained faced hard and frozen ground. That winter a Fallon newspaper featured a story that some 1,000 people in Eureka faced famine due to the snow and the inability of the railroad to operate. For those who stuck it out, spring did finally come, and ultimately the railroad work was completed. On May 6, 1912, the first train steamed into Eureka following a period of over two years of waiting, and great was the celebration.

George Whittell was not entirely unprepared, although he had some last minute changes to make as operations commenced. On the same day (May 6) he formed the Nevada Transportation Company under California laws; the next day (May 7) he incorporated the Eureka-Nevada Railway Company in Utah to acquire ownership of the former Eureka & Palisade property and assets; then the following day (May 8, 1912) the Eureka-Nevada was leased to and become operated by the Nevada Transportation Co. Any potential legal liability was thus effectively spread.

Passengers were happy to have their little train returned, although the tri-weekly, 8-hour service may not have compared very favorably with the daily-except-Sunday, 5-hour schedules which prevailed during the early part of the first decade. Certain it is the principal shipper, the Richmond-Eureka Mining Company, was considerably less than pleased with the new freight rates which went into effect with restored operations, and they backed their displeasure with lengthy legal maneuverings before the Railroad Commission of Nevada. The railroad took the stand that it had spent large sums in repairing the line and that the increase in rate from $1.35 a ton to $2.60 a ton for hauling ores was completely justified. The mining company contended that the ores were not rich enough to support the increased tariff plus the smelting charges and indicated that in their opinion even the old rates were too high. The upshot of the matter was a stalemate in which the mines remained closed for many more years. Even when shipments were made during the 1920-23 period, only that ore from the old dumps containing a high arsenic content was moved.

For the next nine years the railroad remained leased to the Nevada Transportation Co. excluding, of course, the Ruby Hill line which had precipitated the foreclosure. John E. Sexton was placed in charge of operations, and he became one of the most colorful men in Nevada railroad history. He was outspoken and a law unto himself, yet he knew when to comply with authority so as to keep out of jail. His unorthodox methods inevitably brought results, while one bout with the federal government in Washington nearly caused an international incident and was only smoothed over when Sexton obtained the money the government owed him as manager of that impeccable railroad, the Eureka-Nevada.

One of Sexton's first acts was to remove a mile of track from the Ruby Hill branch for use in the main line of the E-N. Some upward rate adjustments were under negotiation with the (reluctant) mining company, and Sexton felt that the deed might help spur a little action for the E-N. It did. The Nevada Railroad Commission firmly suggested that no further dismantling be perpetrated, to which Sexton and Whittell agreed, but the Commission declined to issue an order that the branch be restored to its original condition. Years later the branch line track was rehabilitated and made operative, but its use was short-lived.

Washouts seemed to be the rule for the reconstructed E-N, each one tying up the road for several weeks at a time. Activity in Bullion, to the southeast of Palisade, stimulated surveys in 1914 for a 14-mile branch to that area from Raines Crossing. Work was to start as soon as the ground was free from frost, but an intervening storm perpetrated so much damage to the main line, nothing further was said or done about the branch. (Storm damage in the early part of 1917 and 1921 tied up the railroad for periods of several weeks; a train was wrecked in a washout in the later period.)

During 1917 Sexton entered into one of his infrequent bouts with the Post Office Department. To force the issue, service was abandoned for

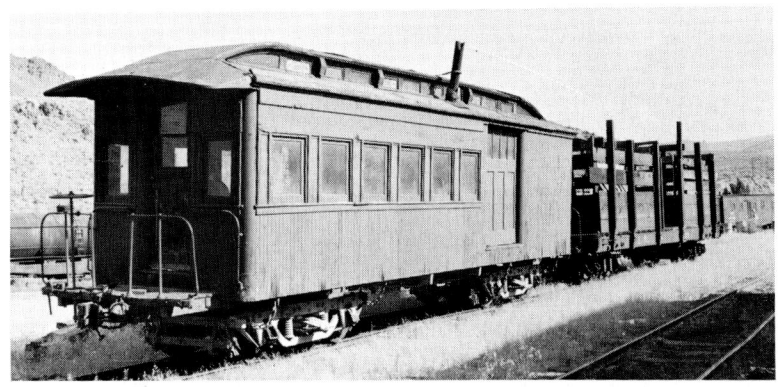

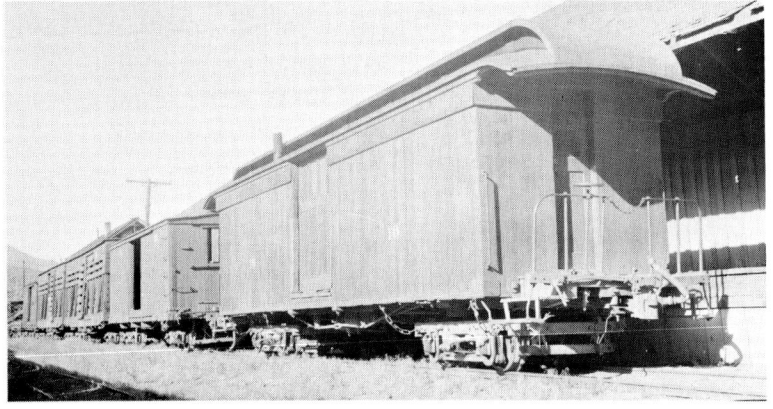

Latter-day equipment of the Eureka Nevada Railway was largely unnamed and unnumbered due to the bleaching action of the bright Nevada sunlight and the deferral of all except the most urgent maintenance and repairs. In these 1938 photos we see Combine No. 20 *(top)*, Baggage Car No. 10 *(next below)* which also saw service as a caboose in the final years of operations, and Combine No. 3 *(third below)*, the rounded windows of which denote the touch of expert car craftsmen. Mogul (2-6-0) No. 7 bears little resemblance to the E&P's first No. 7, an American (4-4-0) built by Baldwin in 1883. *(Top Three Photos: Ted Wurm; Bottom: Louis L. Stein, Jr. Collection.)*

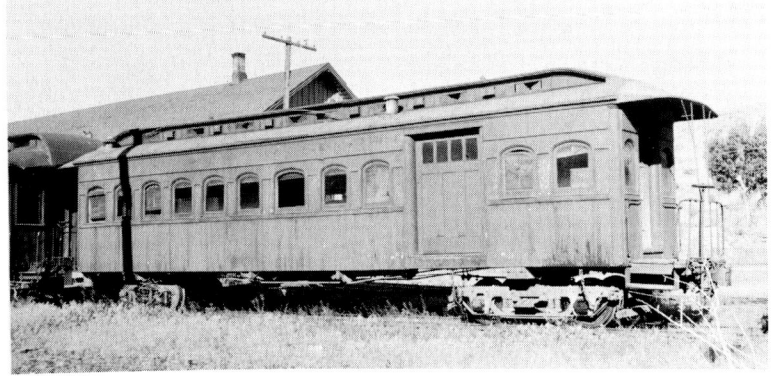

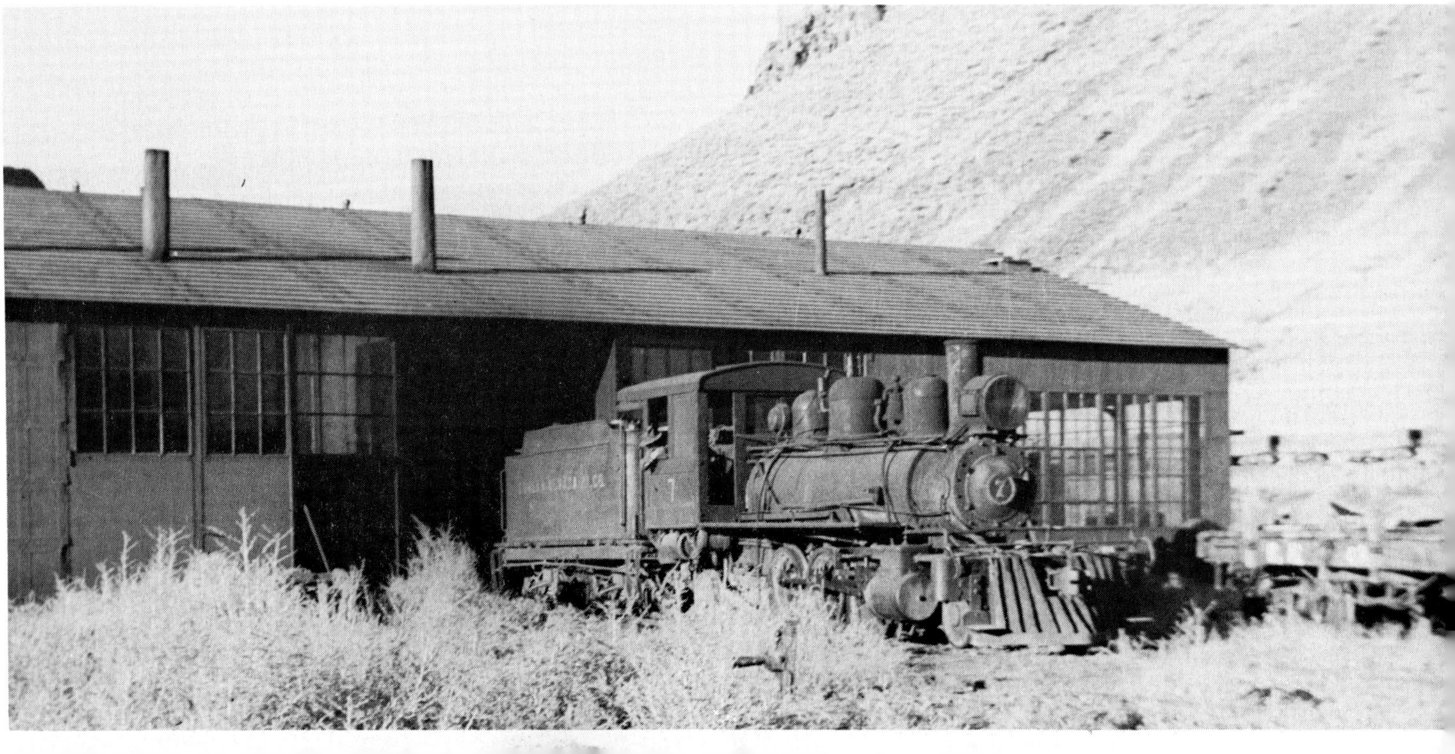

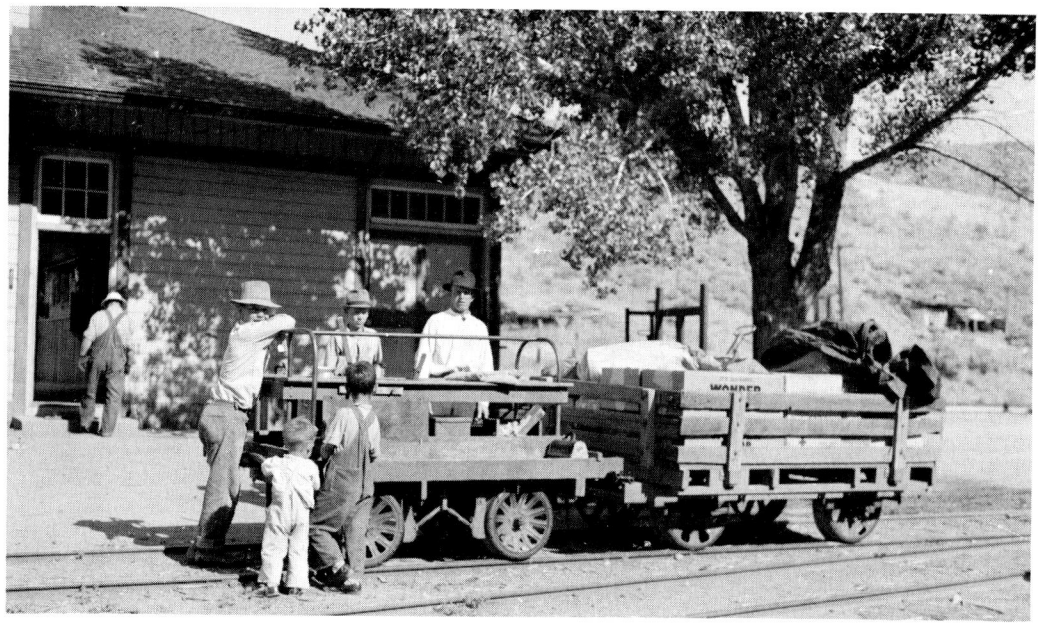

The gas motor car and trailer loaded with mail and express, constituted "the train" on July 11, 1938, when the regular motor stalled on the line. No. 23 (right center) normally performed the day's chores, being loaded (left center) at the Palisade freight house, switched, and allowed to set bravely forth (bottom) across the Southern Pacific diamond at the magnificent speed of five miles per hour. Westward around the bluff, the car will turn south up the Pine Creek Valley into the hinterlands toward Eureka. (Top: Al Phelps Photo; All Others: Ted Wurm.)

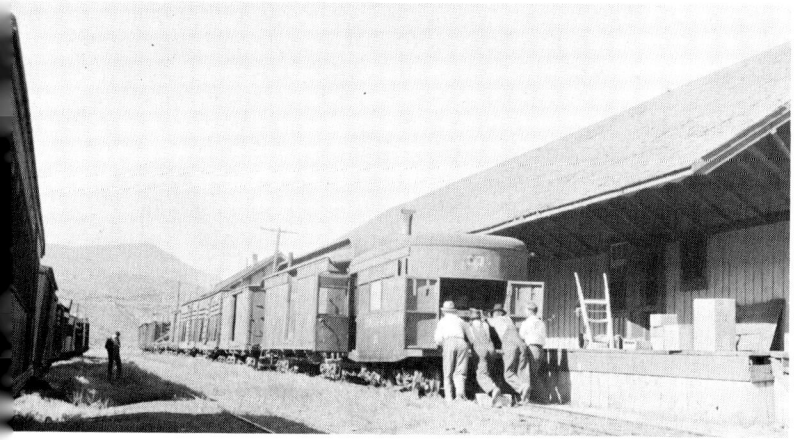
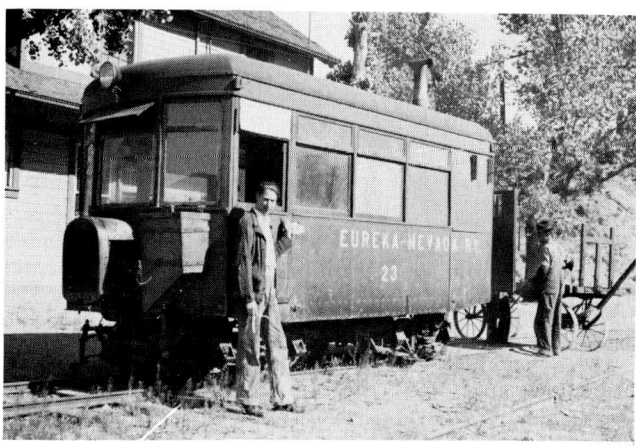
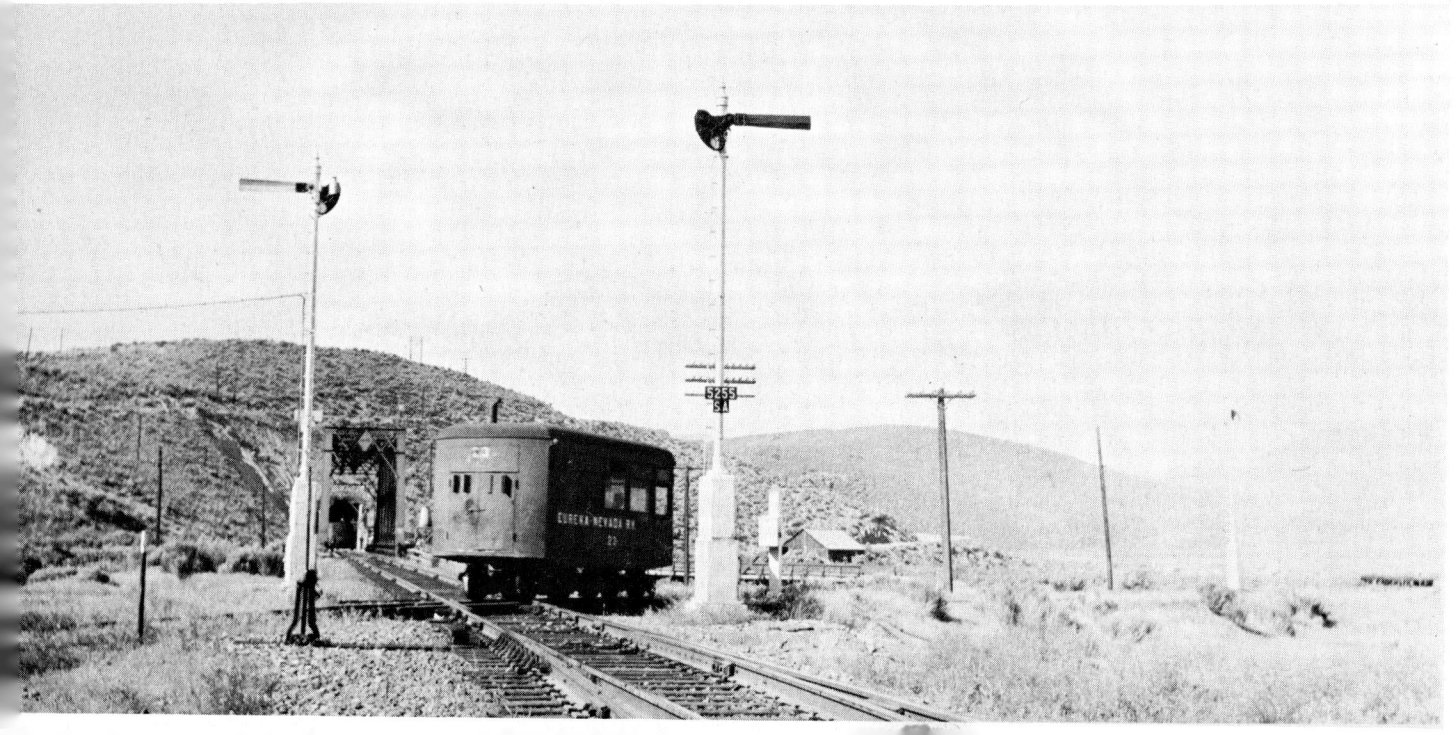

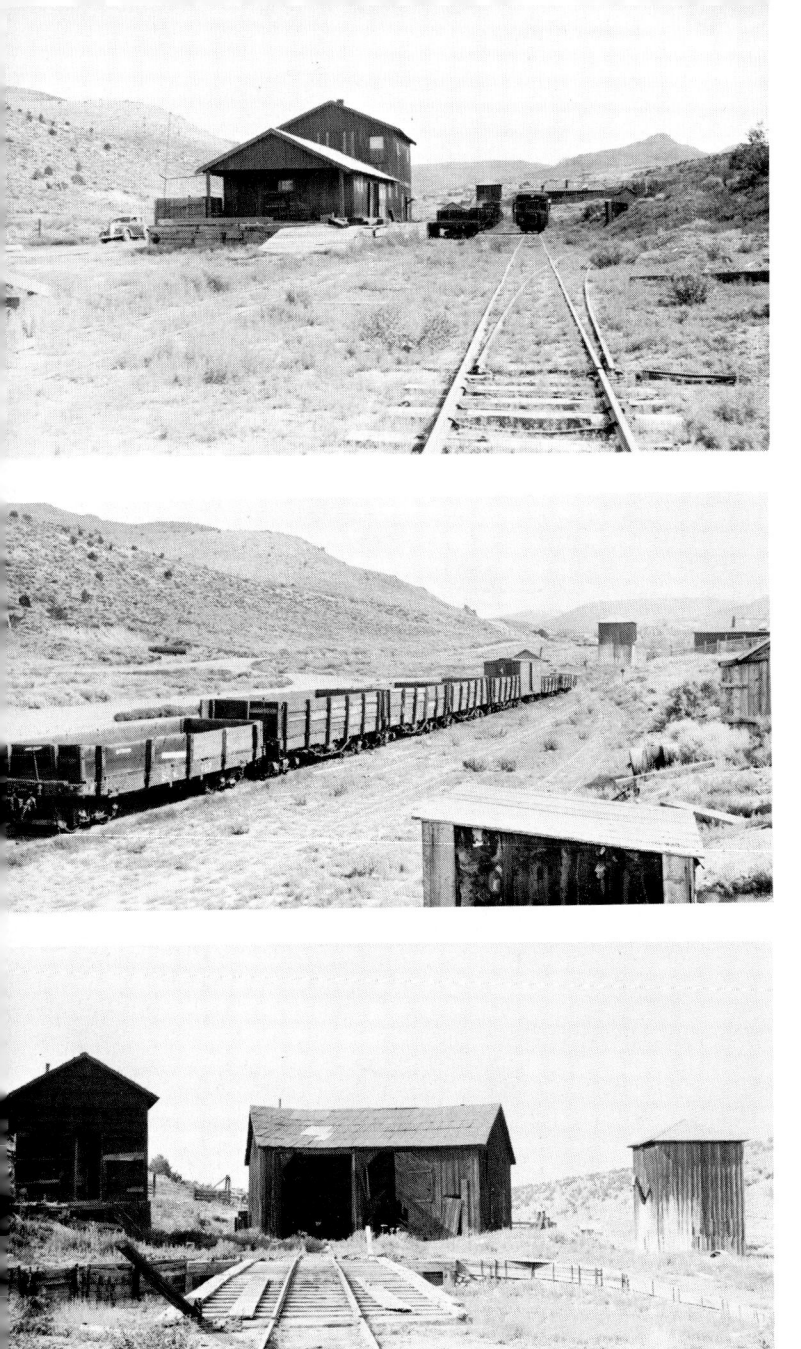
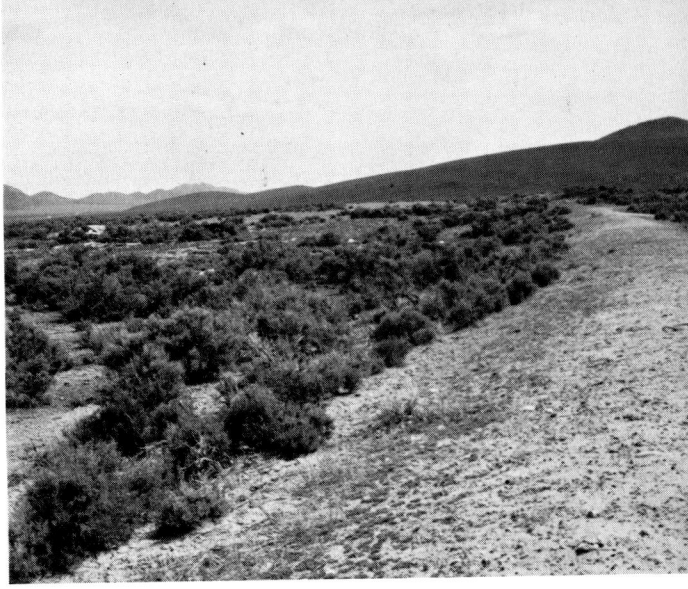

Just before abandonment in 1938, Eureka presented a forlorn appearance. The view *(top, left)* looks south toward the town which lies behind the hill to the left. Motor Car No. 23 holds the main behind the stub switch in the foreground which controls access to the yard tracks. Behind the motor may be seen the roundhouse (right) and the water tank (left), shown in more detail in the closer look *(next below)*, while the lead to the turntable and enginehouse approached from the opposite direction *(third, below)*. The Eureka Nevada acquired the former Uintah Railway Consolidation (2-8-0) No. 12 shown at Palisade, and operated the engine without benefit of repainting or relettering. When the EN was abandoned in September 1938, removal of the ties and rails left but vestigial traces of roadbed on the Nevada desert as seen *(above, right)* 22 years later at Alpha, 50 miles from Palisade. *(Three Photos Top Left: Ted Wurm; Bottom: Louis L. Stein, Jr. Collection; Top Right: Stanley Pahor.)*

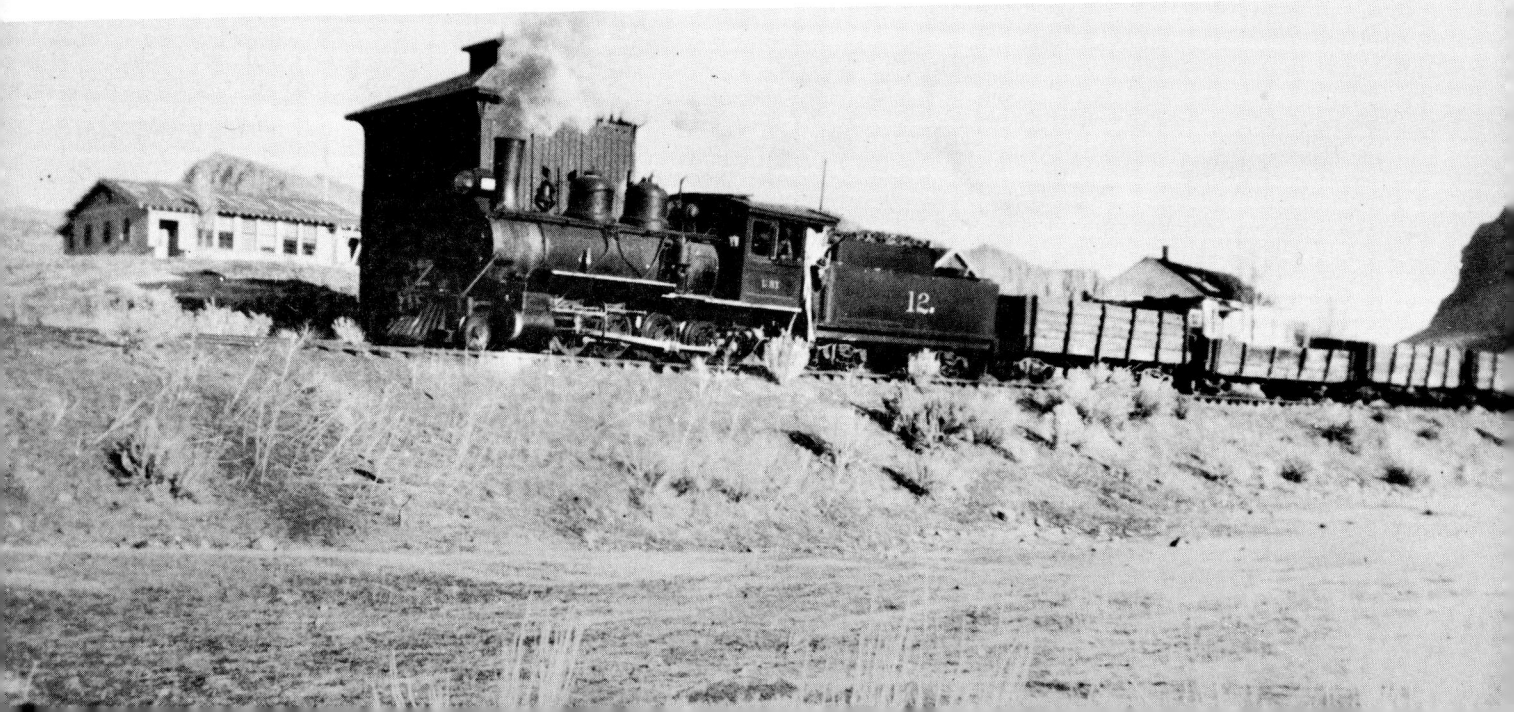

a period of several weeks. The plan backfired, however, when the Nevada Railroad Commission threatened to seek a court appointed receiver if service was not restored. Reluctantly Sexton complied with a once-weekly train.

Late in 1921 the Eureka County Chamber of Commerce picked up the dudgeons and filed a complaint with the Nevada Railroad Commission concerning the service. Sexton could hardly have been less interested. When a public hearing was planned, he uttered the quotable comment that he thought he had received some sort of a communication from the Commission but had not answered it, did not intend to answer it, and that he did not think he would appear at the meeting. Commissioner Shaughnessy arrived in Eureka to find the railroad suffering from one of its chronic washouts and Mr. Sexton in San Francisco instructing his auditor to lay off the entire force. When Shaughnessy failed to get a commitment from Sexton for restoration of the service, the Commission ordered that a specific number of track workers be hired and the railroad restored.

With all its vicissitudes, the Eureka-Nevada had been operated for over 15 years with about half the annual revenues realized in the years prior to 1910. By his positive (though somewhat unorthodox) methods, Sexton had been able to record a profit in each year of some lead production, and small dividends had been declared in all but two of the years between 1915 and 1927. After 1927 better highways and declining revenues resulted in deficits with the single exception of the year 1934, when a small boom netted the road a profit of $5,112. When John Sexton died, his brother took over operations, but the volume of business and the unusual drive were not present. With the slow haste of degeneration, the road finally was abandoned September 21, 1938.

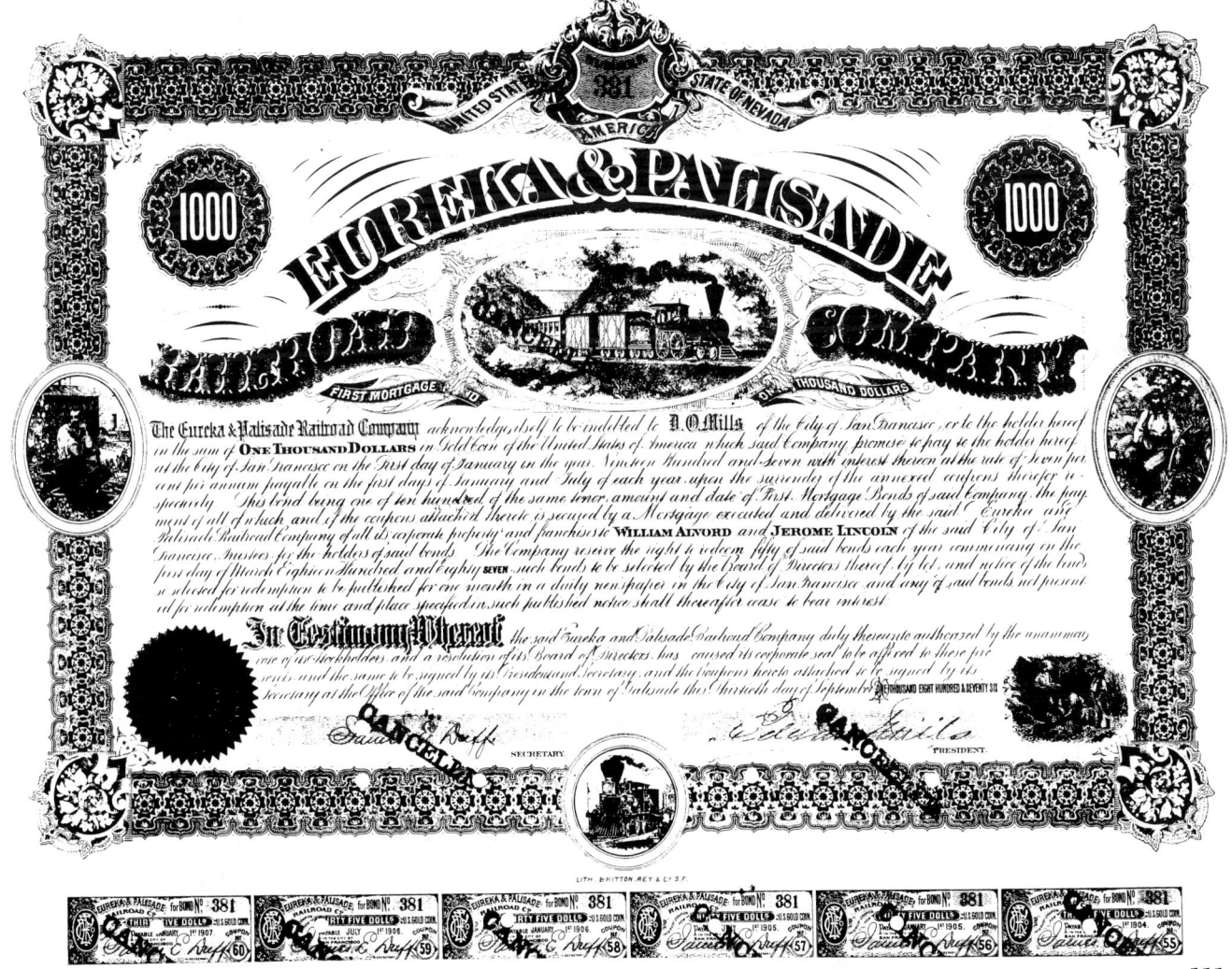

EUREKA & PALISADE RAILROAD

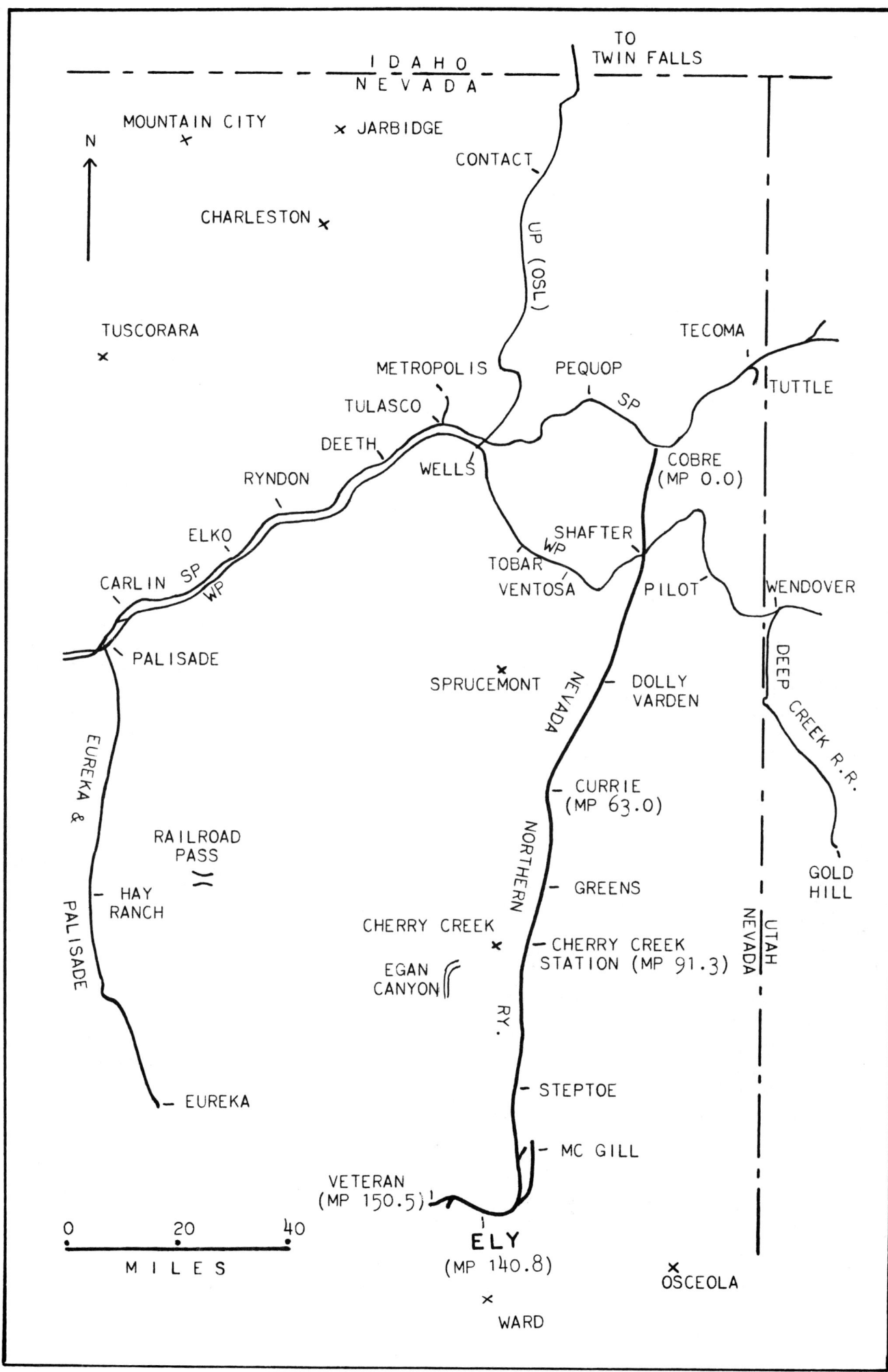

NEVADA NORTHERN RAILWAY

Ely, Nevada, switched horses in midstream. It rose to prominence as the "Johnny-come-lately" of Nevada mining camps, and continues today to be one of the outstandingly active mining areas in the state.

Gold was the initial motivating influence in the Ely area, and Thomas Robinson instigated the activity with discoveries in the canyon now bearing his name. Mining commenced in 1867, scant years following the silver-lead discoveries near Eureka, 75 miles to the west, and with its activity Mineral City (later the site of Lane City) blossomed and faded twice in the succeeding few years. Finally Frederick Thomas of Oakland, California, named the camp "Ely" in 1878 in honor of Smith Ely, a Vermont smelter operator and president of Selby Copper Mining & Smelting Co. In combination with J. W. Long and Thomas Selby, he erected a 10-stamp mill and put up a few houses where the Chainman mill was later located, in what is now a park on Mill Street in Ely. Annual production, if the term may be loosely applied, was extremely modest.

It was copper, not gold, that finally gave Ely its impetus; and it was Eureka, not Ely, that sponsored the uplift. In 1897 Mark Requa had assumed active management of the failing Eureka & Palisade Railroad, and, coupled with his diagnosis of insufficient traffic, was his recommended curative — reach out beyond the railhead and look for more business. As part of the program, Requa placed a mine scout named J. B. Stevens on the lookout for mining properties, and it was from Stevens that word came of extensive porphyry copper ore deposits in Copper Flat, just west of Ely. In 1902 Requa visited the area and was sufficiently impressed to purchase two properties, the Star Pointer and the Ruth, for $150,000.

Requa combined these properties in January 1903 and organized the White Pine Copper Company to take over and analyze the ore bodies. But little was known or understood about mining and refining such scattered crystals of metal in their granular base, the process having just been profitably demonstrated in Utah by D. C. Jackling using ore containing as little as 3% copper. For 18 months, experts checked and rechecked the possibilities for exploitation of the mine field. F. Somner Schmidt, then just out of college, recalls that the engineers were moderately embarrassed to discuss the proposed reduction plant because of its large capacity of 1,000 tons per day. Little did they realize that such production would be quadrupled and then more than doubled and redoubled again. Ultimately the plant's daily capacity reached 20,000 tons of 1% copper-bearing ore at the concentrator, which reduced it to 20-25% copper before going to the smelter for conversion into 99% blister copper. In turn, the blister copper was then trundled, via Nevada Northern, to SP connections for transportation to purification refineries farther east.

The magnitude of the over-all operations obviously necessitated the facilities of a railroad, and Requa immediately thought in terms of his existing Eureka & Palisade. Only 75 miles of new construction would be required to connect Eureka with Ely, while nearly double that amount would be necessary to bring Ely in direct contact with the normal channels of commerce along the Southern Pacific at Wells or some other convenient point. It was a matter of serious import, and with customary thoroughness Requa instituted surveys over both routes. The results were not difficult of analysis. Narrow gauge railroads as major entities were no longer in vogue. The expense of rehabilitating the E&P main line to standard gauge dimensions plus new construction eastward over four mountain ranges with their prospective attendant operating problems more than outweighed the advantages of the direct northward route down the Steptoe Valley with its easy grades.

A. C. Cleveland (an Ely cattle rancher, twice an unsuccessful gubernatorial candidate, and an organizer of several proposed railroad lines) had long advocated the route. His son-in-law, William McGill (owner of the famous McGill ranch on the east side of the valley with its valuable Duck Creek water right), and W. B. Graham (Ely's pioneer storekeeper) concurred in the thought. Men were sent out over the length and breadth of Steptoe

Valley to scour for sources of additional tonnage for the railroad as justification for its financing and construction. The private undertaking of development of a copper mine plus 140 miles of new railroad was one of stupendous proportions for which tremendous vision was required coupled with meticulous planning and constant surveying and checking. It was the close attention to these factors which led to the successful completion and operation of the project in the years to follow.

William Hood, the SP's chief engineer, was responsible for obtaining the talent to lay out the line. Adolph Judell, 27 years old, had just finished working on an SP project north of Chico, California, when Hood directed him to eastern Nevada in October 1904. With the Steptoe Valley the obvious choice as an avenue for the railroad, the problem became one of deciding which of the many possible routes through it should be selected.

Judell's reconnaisance survey from Wells to Ely was made very rapidly; on some days as many as seven miles were traversed. His selection of a grade down the flat part of the valley was seriously questioned by some who felt that a higher location along the hillsides would be preferable. Hood stood by Judell's location, judging that flood waters from the canyons along the hillsides would have great velocity on entering the valley, but that their force would be dissipated on reaching the flat, wide, central area where any damage would be minimized.

E. E. Carpenter, another SP engineer, was selected to run the final line. In reviewing Judell's work, he determined to keep to the east of the Pequop Mountains, feeling that the proposed tonnage would justify a new station on the SP near Omar in deference to a connection with the main line at Wells. At a conference of the mining engineers, various names were propounded for the new location, but it was Oscar Hershey, just returned from a trip to Mexico and still speaking Spanish words, who suggested Cobre (the Spanish word for copper). In later years Requa was wont to remark that the Wells newspaper never could print enough nice stories about him and his railroad as long as the terminal was planned for Wells, but once Cobre was announced as a more practical site, his popularity vanished overnight.

With the increasing activity and expanding plans, additional new money was needed in the organization. It arrived in the form of a combination, in November 1904, of Requa's White Pine Copper Co. and other mining properties into a new Nevada Consolidated Copper Company. President of the new organization was W. Hinckle Smith, a Philadelphia capitalist and also a member of the famous Bullfrog Syndicate, backers of the Bullfrog Goldfield Railroad. Mark Requa became the acting head of operations with the title of vice-president and general manager, in which capacity he continued to push construction of the railroad.

That winter blizzards arrived, borne on howling winds, to be followed by temperatures down to -22 degrees. The young engineers from the east found the cold unbearable. Living in tents became most unattractive, particularly when the tent stakes, driven in the frozen ground, would pop out unexpectedly to allow the cold canvas to collapse in the sleepers' faces. Apparently, however, the physical privations did not affect the quality of the engineers' accomplishments. When Judge Curtis Lindley (Requa's attorney) took the location maps back to Washington for approval, the remark was made that never before had such accuracy and delineation been seen.

Since certain traffic concessions were needed for Harriman's SP connection, Requa paid a visit to that magnate in his New York offices. As Requa later reminisced, he found a busy little man high up in an office building at 120 Broadway. The time was two o'clock; an untouched lunch waited on a side table; a stack of assorted papers on the desk were being given individual, scrupulous attention. Acknowledgement of the intrusion was curtly to the point: "Well, Mr. Requa, what can I do for you? I want you to talk quickly; I have no time to waste, not even enough time to eat my lunch." As the story of the Nevada Northern situation was developed, Harriman listened suspiciously, for every short line railroad could be a potential front for part of a well-organized scheme of a competitor. Once convinced that Requa would build no further than the mines at Ely, he assented and much to Requa's relief made no proposal that the Southern Pacific construct the line.

At the southern terminus of Ely there were other problems. A right-of-way was needed westward through the town in order to reach Robinson Canyon and the mine fields. Surprisingly, the county commissioners were amenable and in May 1905 granted a franchise to construct the railroad through Aultman Street, the main business street of Ely. Some townspeople, on the other hand, entertained a variety of controvertible misgivings. There were those who feared the advent of the railroad would sever Ely's pleasant isolation; others feared that tramps and undesirables would swamp the town; while a Steptoe rancher named Green, in granting a right-of-way through his lands, insisted on a clause in his contract that the whistle would be blown each time a train went by. He had waited so long for a railroad, the melodious notes would be welcome assurance of its actuality.

On June 1, 1905, the Nevada Northern Railway was formally incorporated. The surveyors completed their work in August, and the Utah Construction Co. was awarded the contract for building the line. Construction forces were moved over to Cobre following completion of work on the SP's Hazen Cut-Off, and grading commenced at Cobre on September 11, 1905, under the direction of Supt. W. H. Wattis. Rails were ordered from the Colorado Fuel & Iron Company in Pueblo, Colorado; bids were sought for 4,500 telegraph poles (30 to the mile); and orders were placed for various and sundry miscellaneous items requisite for the construction of a railroad. It was anticipated the line would reach Ely before the end of the year.

Grading moved ahead very rapidly at first, 20 miles of it being completed in the first four weeks. Then it grew colder, and difficulties were encountered in obtaining workmen. Most arrived in cotton work clothes, shivered their way through the first day of labor, then concluded they had all the money they needed and fled. But the worst was yet to come. In November the heaviest snow in years covered the ground, blocking stage traffic and presaging one of the worst winters in Nevada history. Of scant comfort were thoughts of the ultra hot days of summer when men would chase the jack rabbits away in order to have a few moments in the shade of a telegraph pole.

Quite understandably the Utah Construction Co. planned to have rail laying follow closely on the heels of the completed grade. When the railroad was unable to furnish rail due to adverse weather hampering production at the Colorado mill, the construction company threatened to quit the job. Judell managed to persuade them to stay, backing up his arguments with subsequent delivery of a moderate supply of ties and rail, plus 3 locomotives and 30 freight cars. In November and December some 15 miles of track were laid in spite of the weather conditions. However, as soon as their contracts were completed, six grading outfits of 25 teams each departed for warmer climate in southern Nevada where work on the LV&T looked far more promising. They refused to take any further contracts working with deeply frozen ground, and from December to March the work came to a virtual standstill.

Requa's Nevada Consolidated Copper Company owned the Nevada Northern Railway and guaranteed its bonds. In March 1906 the Guggenheim interests purchased sufficient stock to obtain working control of the NCCCo, and with it came control of the railroad. S. W. Eccles became the new president of both organizations. Immediately the announcement was made that the smelter would be doubled in size, causing the *White Pine News* to headline an article: "Great Ely, Greater Ely, Greatest Ely." The ensuing typography went on to claim that there were some 22 million tons of ore in the mines carrying copper worth $174 million. Apparently the *News* was inclined to be a bit pessimistic in its purportedly optimistic forecasts of production, as actual figures for the Eureka-Liberty pit alone reveal that from 1907 to 1955 over 138 million tons of ore were extracted.

March also signified the approximate end of winter, and the Nevada Northern commenced handling freight over the 30 miles of tracks south from Cobre which had been constructed between the winter's storms. In May an embargo was declared on commercial freight for a brief period as the entire railroad facilities were needed to expedite construction. Then on May 22, 1906, the first passenger train was operated, a "special" for the conveyance of Mark Requa and friends over the 63 miles of completed line to Currie's Ranch. The novelty of the occasion was such that reportedly even the coyotes ventured forth in the daylight to see the newly painted cars. Auto transportation was provided over the remaining 77 miles to Ely, and on the return trip, a late spring blizzard deposited two feet of snow on the desert roads. Though somewhat delayed, the party managed to reach the train wherein the warm comforts of railroad travel were amply demonstrated and appreciated.

Regular tri-weekly passenger service to Currie was instituted on June 2, 1906. The train left Cobre at 8:30 A.M. and averaged a pert 31 miles an hour to accomplish its destined 11:30 A.M. arrival at Currie. The return trip took equally as long, leaving Currie at 1:30 P.M. and arriving at Cobre at 4:30 P.M.

Work on the last 77 miles of line from Currie to Ely was rushed. President Eccles wanted to get the railroad operating as quickly as possible, and Requa obliged. Grading was skimped, it being decided to wait until after the line was in operation to bring the roadbed up to standard. (Later in 1910, the grade was further improved with a new alignment from a point near Hiline to East Ely.) Workers' tents were scattered along the right-of-way over the 28-mile span from Currie to Cherry Creek and even beyond. By July 4 the tracks reached Cherry Creek Station, and on the 16th a special Railroad Day celebration was held in the town, four miles to the west of the railroad. Champagne corks were pulled, and the townspeople entertained an impressive number of distinguished guests. In the speeches that followed, Requa foretold of future large scale mining developments, while Senator W. C. Gallagher paid praiseworthy compliment, stating that the people had frequently but vacuously been promised a railroad, but now Requa had actually constructed one.

On July 20, 1906, the first regularly scheduled train arrived at Cherry Creek Station. Rails were only 40 miles from Ely, while grading was completed except for the last 20 miles from Campbell's ranch at Steptoe. For Ely, an old era was about to bow out and a new one begin — an exciting prospect, for the old way of life left much to be desired.

A returning traveler described those early conditions in July 1906, mere months before they were superseded. The old route to town started at Palisade on the Southern Pacific where transfer was made for the 80-mile trip over the Eureka & Palisade —five hours of rail travel for $8.00 in fare. The next 75 miles from Eureka to Ely required a 24-hour stage ride over rough, dusty roads and four mountain ranges, for which privilege a $10.00 fare was extracted. Although the stage operated six times a week during the summer, a two- or a three-day delay might be encountered as the travel was heavy. Many passengers found it more desirable to delay another day en route by stopping at the Six Mile House near Hamilton, or a little farther on at the Moorman Ranch where Mrs. Moorman's superb cooking and clean beds were considered an essential luxury. Even following ultimate arrival at Ely, the passengers' problems were not alleviated. Into a town with insufficient accommodations were crowded 1,000 men, many of whom had no place to go. The more fortunate paid 50 cents for a cot in a tent; the less fortunate utilized saloon tables and chairs as makeshift couches or hollowed out hip space in the hard floor of the desert. Personal effects and baggage might take more than a month to catch up with the traveler. Following one of the worst winters in years which had left the roads in deplorable condition, the E&P had sold its big freight teams and suspended service. Supplies had been delayed so long, the town was on the verge of a famine. One team had taken three weeks for the round trip between the two centers. As one reporter commented: "The Ely of today is yet in the making, the rawest of mining camps, just awakened to its enormous possibilities after a lethargy of thirty years."

In August 1906 a controversy arose over the railroad's franchise on Aultman Street in Ely. W. N. McGill contended that a double track railroad through the main business street of the city was an untenable situation and that "unless a change were made to Garden Street, it would drive every business out of Ely." Vociferous objections were raised by the many people who had built homes on Garden (now Clark) Street during the intervening 15 months since the granting of the franchise; property values would be depreciated; it was an invasion of their privacy. Obviously the business element carried the greater weight; the objections were overruled and the route of the Nevada Northern was altered accordingly.

Ely's "Railroad Days" were celebrated on Saturday and Sunday, September 29 and 30, 1906. The Nevada Northern barely kept the appointment, being obliged to work right up to the last day to bring the rails into town. One special train came from Salt Lake City; another came from Ogden; while special cars from Reno brought Governor Sparks, Senator Newlands and other dignitaries. The last spike, appropriately fashioned of copper from the Ruth mine, was driven in place by Mark Requa on Saturday afternoon at a selected site just west of the court house. Cheers from the crowd gave audible approval of his splendid efforts. Miniature copper spikes were presented to the heads of the various committees participating in the event as mementos of the occasion. For the situation was unique — not only had a railroad been completed, but its actual cost had been decidedly less than estimated.

The celebration was contagiously enthusiastic, the merriment becoming more amplified as the day progressed. McGill handled all arrangements for feeding the more than 4,000 people attending, trenches were dug in the court house grounds wherein fires were ignited for the cooking of barbecued beef and beans. Although the event reportedly took place "under skies that drooped tenderly with azure tints of autumn . . ." the *White Pine News* failed to report the Steptoe Valley zephyr which blew down the tent where food was being prepared and sent paper plates soaring madly about in the skies. Liquidity advanced as the day progressed, and couples were in rare form by the time the two dances got under way on Saturday night in the new and still incomplete Northern Hotel. Unofficial and unrecorded highlight of the evening occurred when Kerosene Kate, the town's leading prostitute, found herself wedged in a toilet and was rescued only after her cries attracted four strong men who pulled her out. All in all, the event was best remembered by those concerned as Ely's one big drunk.

The following day was notorious for a number of awakenings. Adolph Judell had left the railroad with the driving of the last spike, ostensibly to enjoy a little leisure and delve into a private mining venture. Those of the populace who were capable, paid visits to the mines; those who could not, remained behind and listened to local urchins peddling yesterday's programs at half price or attempting to dispose of 5,000 special postcards which had been completely overlooked on the day preceding. Virtually anticlimactic was the inauguration of train service on Monday, October 1, 1906, from a temporary depot erected immediately in back of the *News* office at the corner of Murry and Garden Streets. Ultimately the site was abandoned for a more practical one near the edge of town.

Even before the railroad was completed it had faced a series of problems. Original plans had contemplated the construction of the mill on the west side of Steptoe Valley immediately to the north of Ely, utilizing water from Murry Creek for the milling operations. To this end the Georgetown Ranch had been acquired as a site for the mill tailings dump, and Judell had laid out the railroad yard on the site in June of 1906, acting with a free hand and using the best of engineering principles. Then Judge Lindley, an authority on water law, told Requa that Murry Creek water would not be available as the courts had held that domestic use (for Ely residents) would have superior rights. Subsequently the railroad made plans to locate the mill on the McGill Ranch on the east side of Steptoe Valley which held the water rights to the bountiful Duck Creek; the Georgetown property then became useless; the majority of the 2,000 acre site was sold to the Ely Townsite Co. in December 1906. In spite of this, a fine two-story depot and office was erected at a cost of $23,000 at the townsite which was now called Ely City, the Townsite Company absorbing approximately two-thirds of the cost of the building.

To furnish supplies for construction of the new McGill smelter, a three-mile line was projected from McGill Junction to McGill. Work started during the summer of 1906 before the main line had reached the area, and the project was completed and opened on October 1, 1906, immediately following the "Railroad Days" celebration. A few weeks later a dinky locomotive coupled to an improvised caboose provided daily service between McGill and Ely.

In spite of the harmony outwardly expressed during the big Railroad Days celebration, beneath the surface a bitter controversy was being waged between the citizens of Ely and those of the more newly created Ely City to the east. With the arrival of the Nevada Northern and the location of its yards and freight depot at the latter site, people had begun buying lots in Ely City where prices were lower than the inflated values of property in the older location. Ely was not only inconvenienced by the necessity of teaming all freight deliveries from Ely City, but more important, it was in fear that the new townsite would usurp the very name of Ely. Whereupon the Ely Commercial Club, composed of good and substantial citizens, filed suit to prevent the transference of the name of Ely to that other location of Ely City. Subsequently the action was further strengthened when the City Council of Ely actively joined the fracas.

In an effort to appease the situation, certain attorneys and real estate men sought a court order directing the Nevada Northern to build and maintain a freight depot in Ely, adding additional emphasis to their intent by making the matter one of the first service complaints before the new state Railroad Commission of Nevada. The railroad attempted to alleviate the situation for a time by unloading freight on Garden Street in Ely without benefit of a formal freight depot. However, protests from residents adjoining the area over the resultant congregations of drunken hoboes attracted by the operation caused cessation of the service. The situation was aggravated further when one A. J. Fesler filed a suit for $11,000 damages to his Garden Street property from the smoke and noise of passing trains, although it was later reported

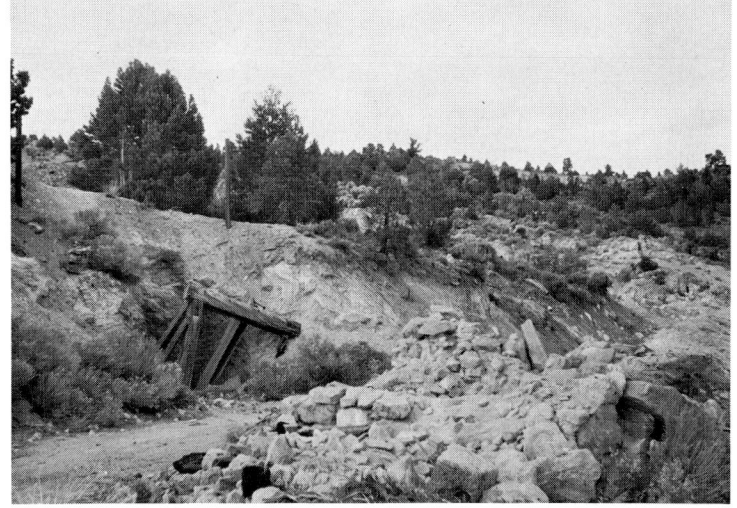

Decaying timbers in 1958 *(top, left)* mark the site of the Ruth Shaft, original copper mine which started the Ely boom. To right is the site of the house in which Mark Requa and his family spent the first lonely winter while the mine was being proved. Its success presaged the building of the Nevada Northern Railway whose first train to Ely was headed by SP 10-wheeler No. 2173.

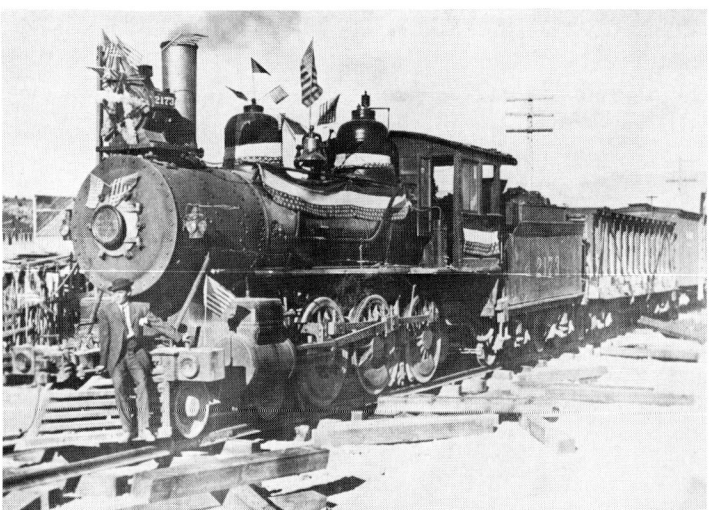

Ely's official Railroad Days were celebrated on September 29-30, 1906. Tents offered lodging to the visitors while the welcoming committee prepared to start on the day's activities.

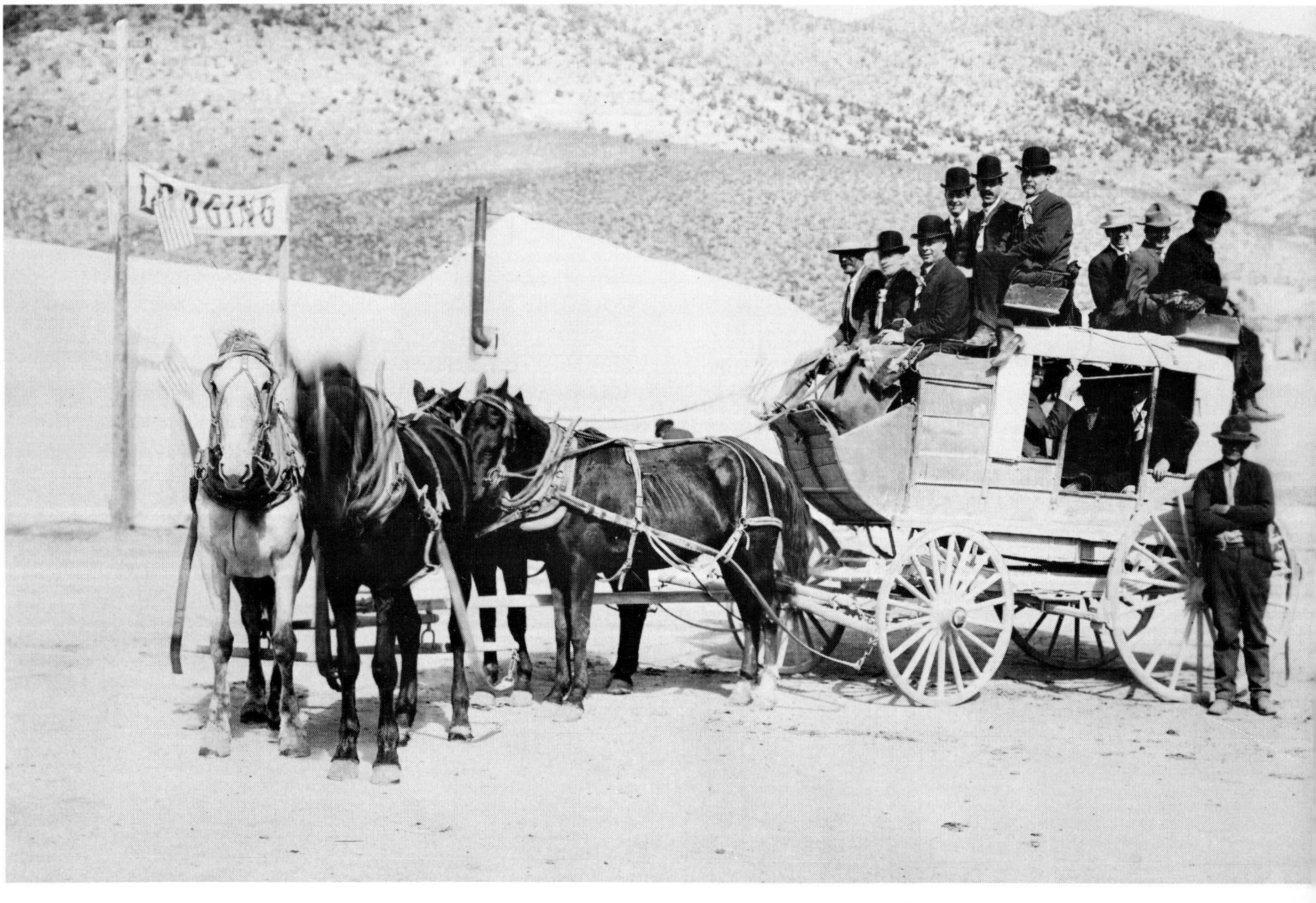

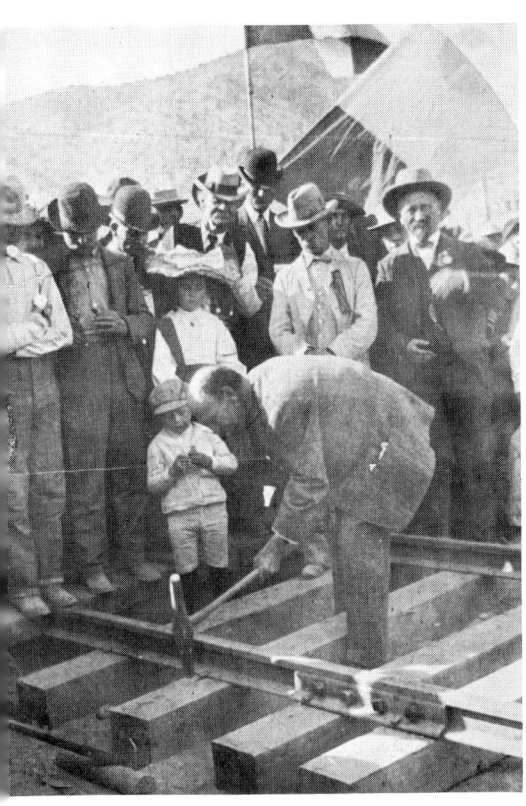
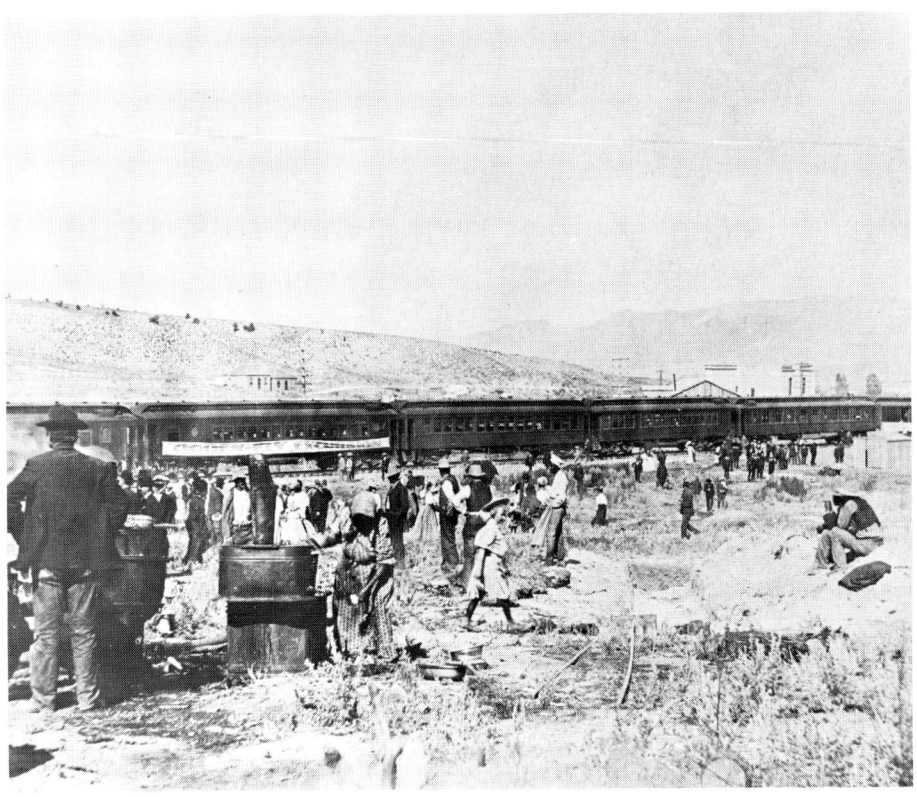

Citizens prepared the barbecue, digging the pit in full view of the train of coaches comprising the "Ogden-Ely Excursion" in background. Mark Requa drove the last spike, significantly fashioned of copper and subsequently preserved by Mrs. Amy Requa Russell who later donated it to the University of Nevada. Action-packed climax to the event (below) was provided by this flag- and flower-decked Nevada Northern 10-wheeler backing its string of coaches over the sacred site. (Center Left, Top Far Right: Nevada Northern Railway Collection; Top Near Right: L. K. Requa Collection; Bottom Left and Right: Mrs. Amy Requa Russell.)

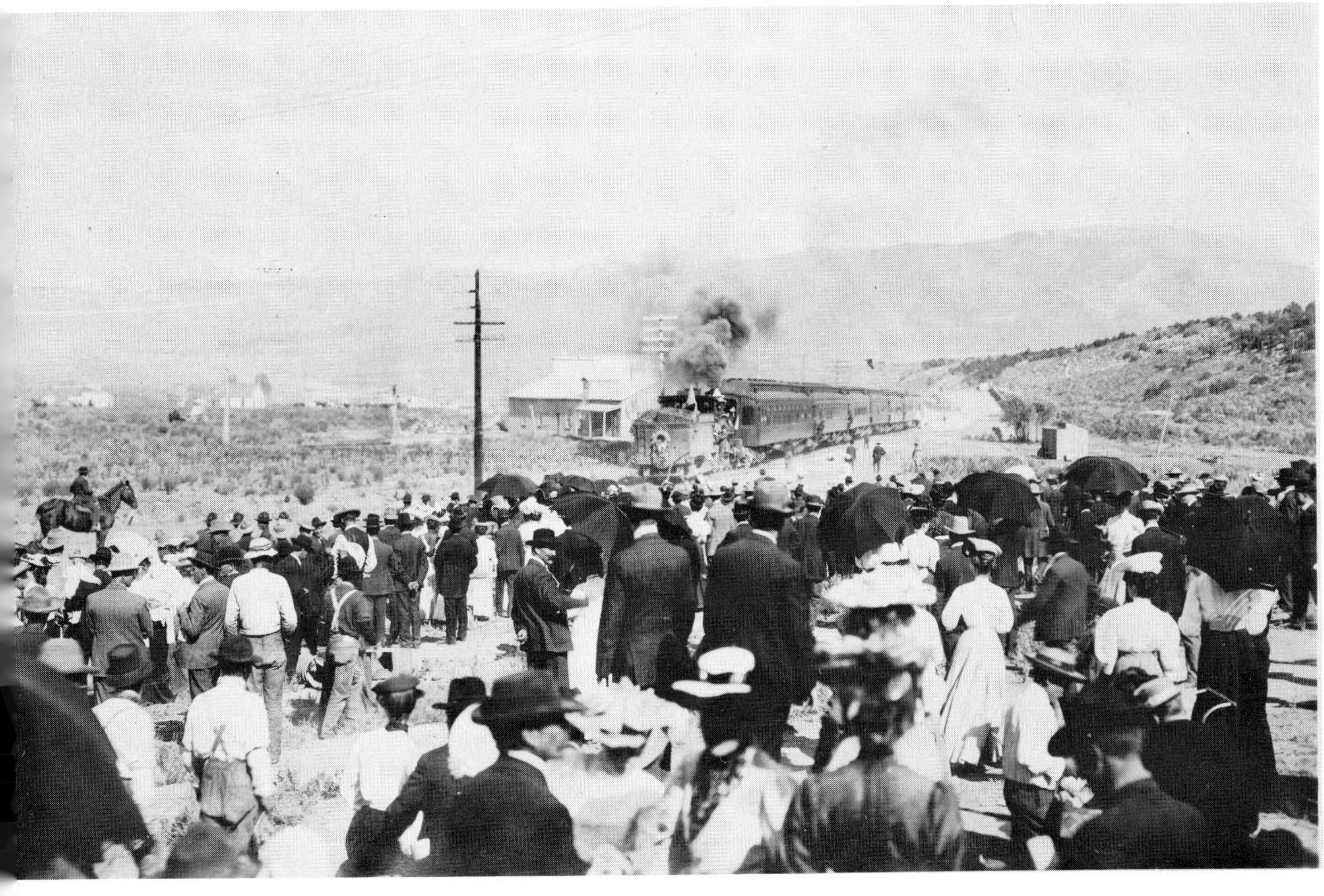

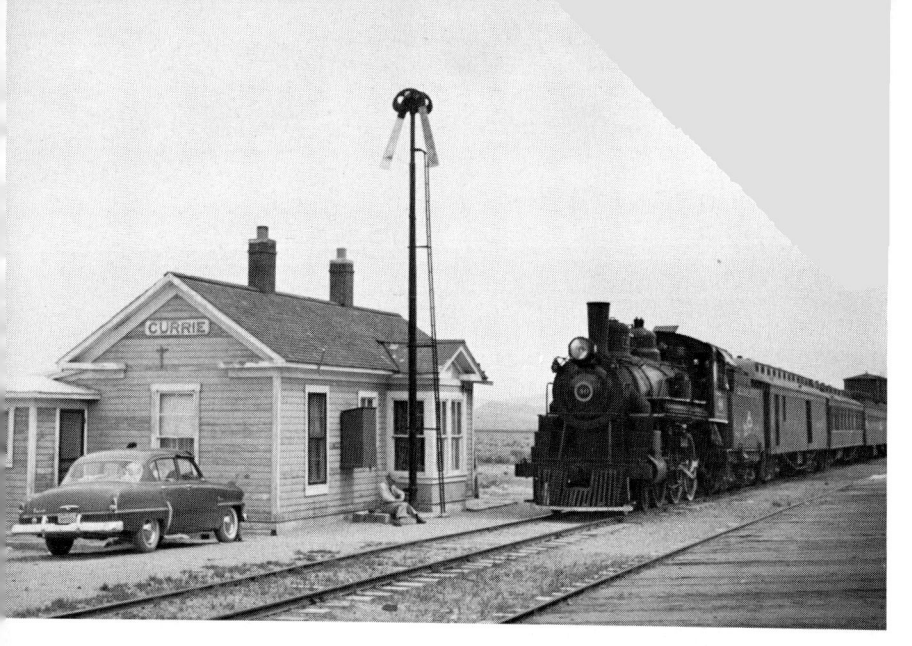

Nevada Northern 10-wheeler No. 40 is a favorite for railfan excursions and has posed at a number of historic spots along the line. In these 1958 views the engine is seen at Currie, approximate half-way point on the main line (63 miles from Cobre and 77 miles from Ely) first reached by the railroad on June 2, 1906. Cherry Creek was the gateway for a number of proposed lines projected westward through Egan Canyon in the hills beyond. Copper Flat *(top, right)* is the site of the strategic NN yards and point of confluence for the various branches in the Kimberly-Ruth mining area. Most critical construction problem on the NN was the curved tunnel just west of Ely from the eastern portal of which No. 40 is just emerging. *(Bottom Photos, Left and Right: Pacific Railway Journal.)*

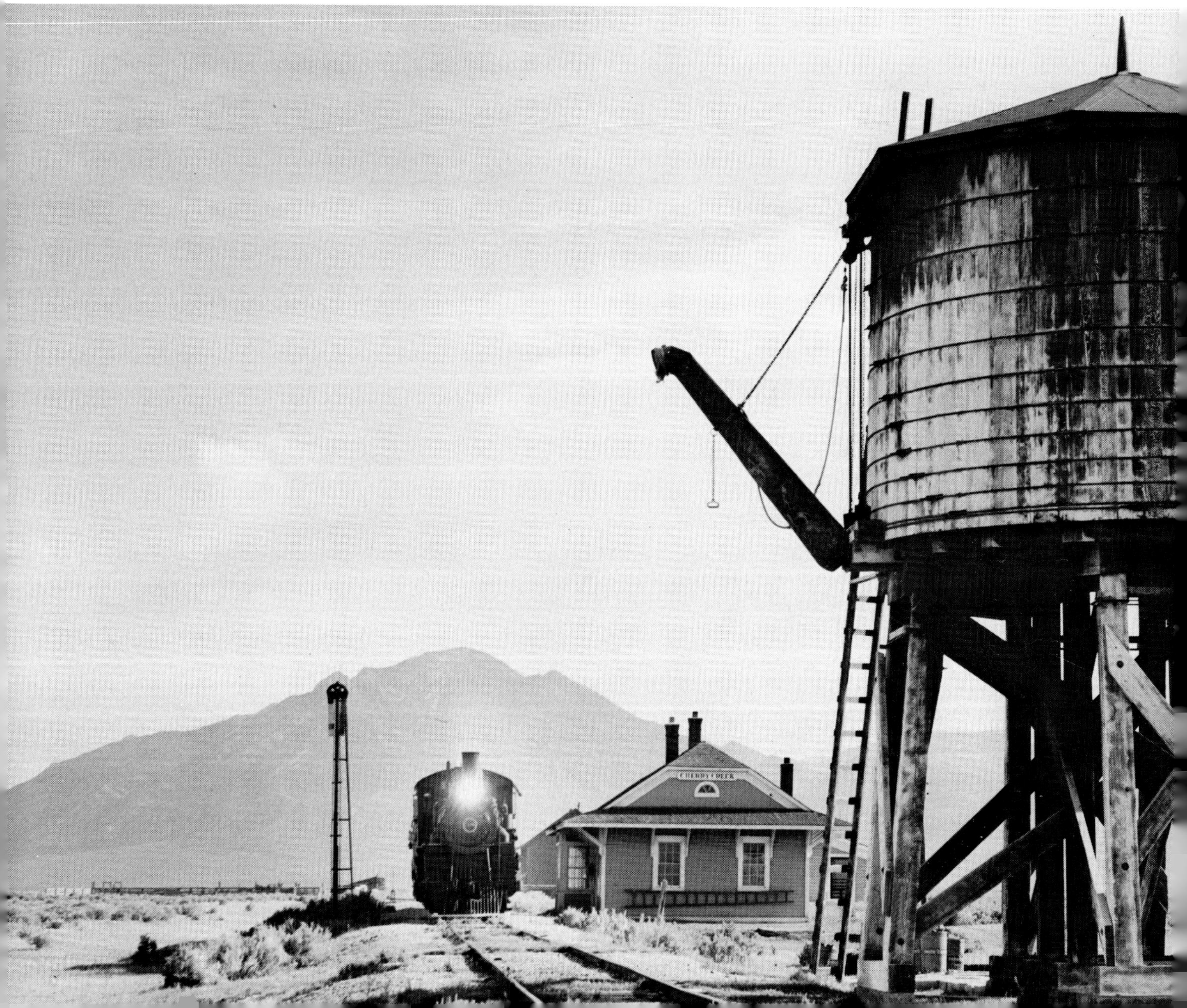

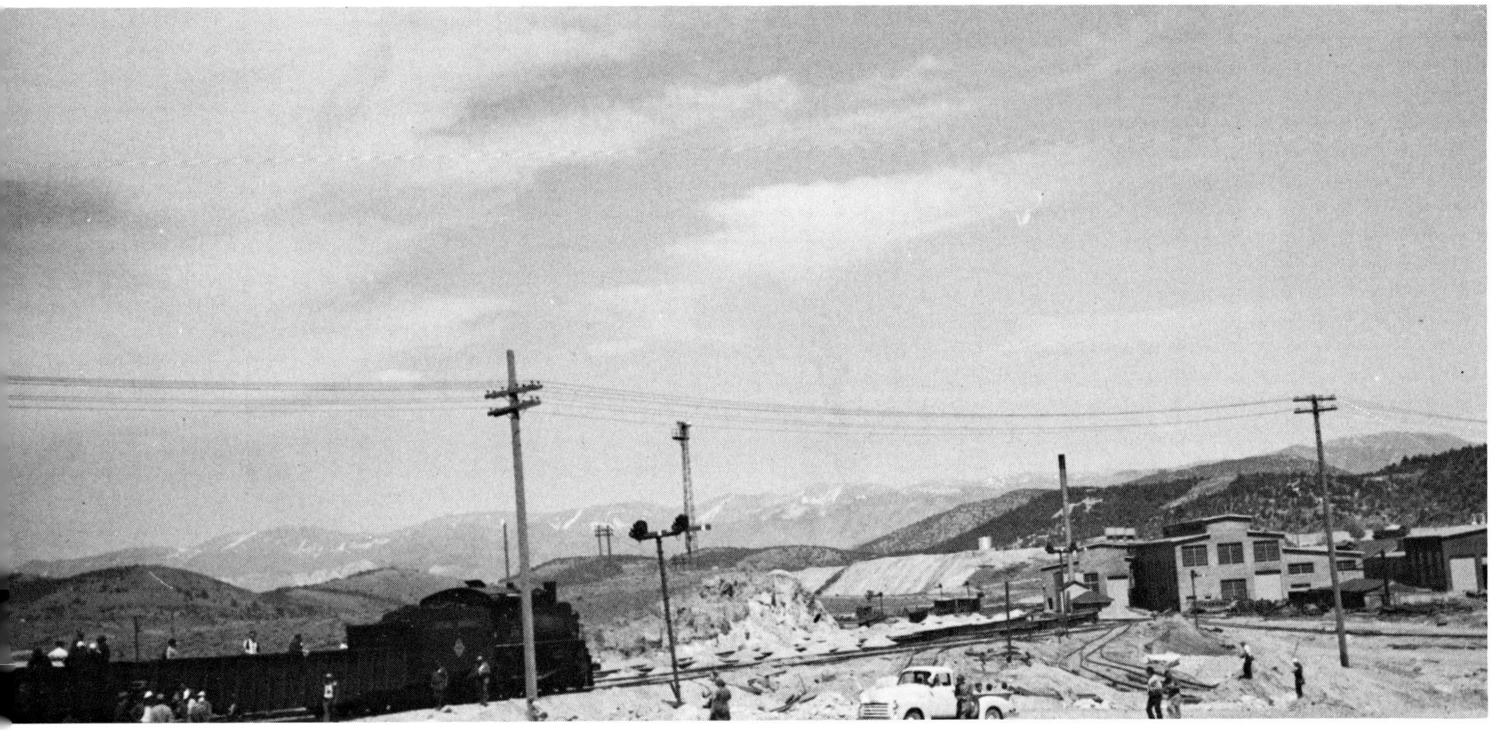

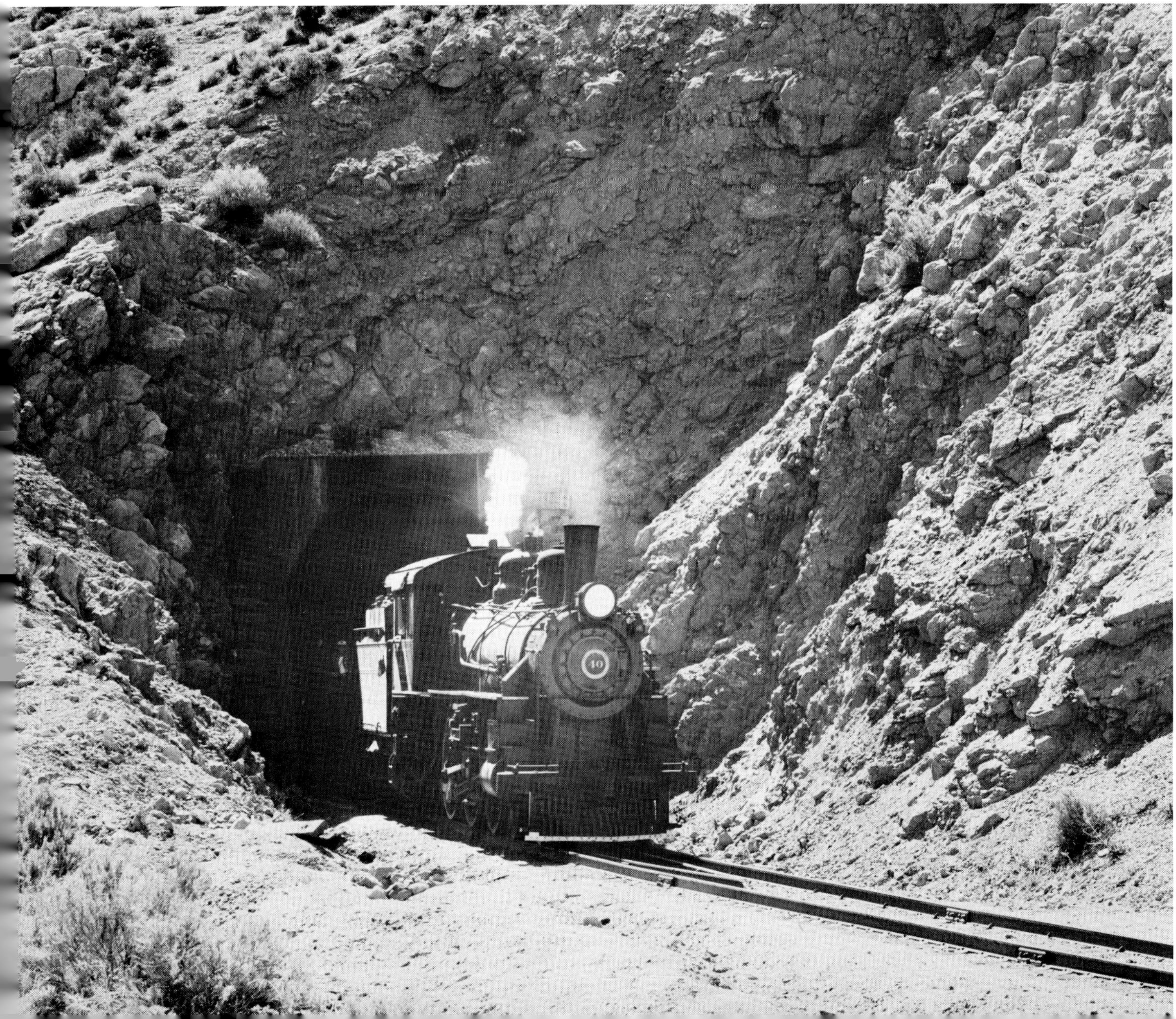

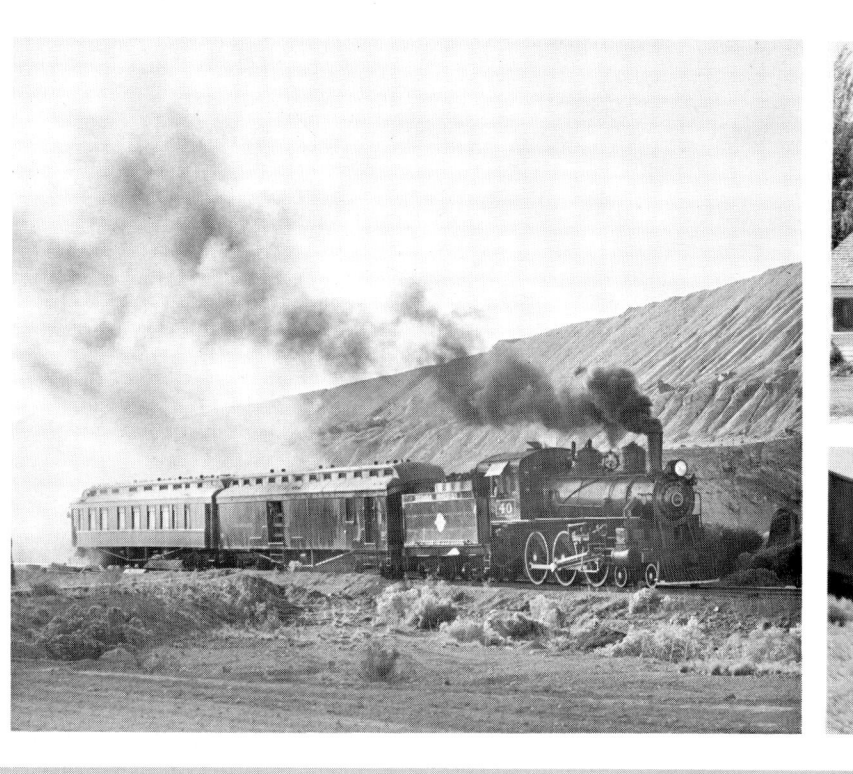
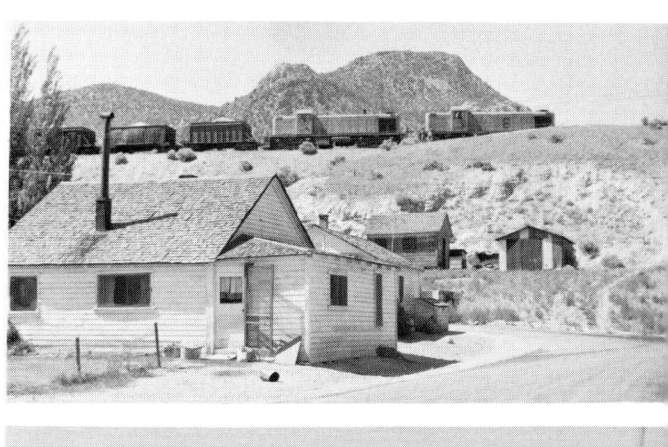
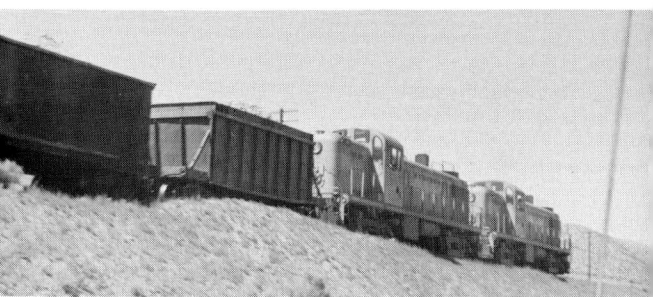

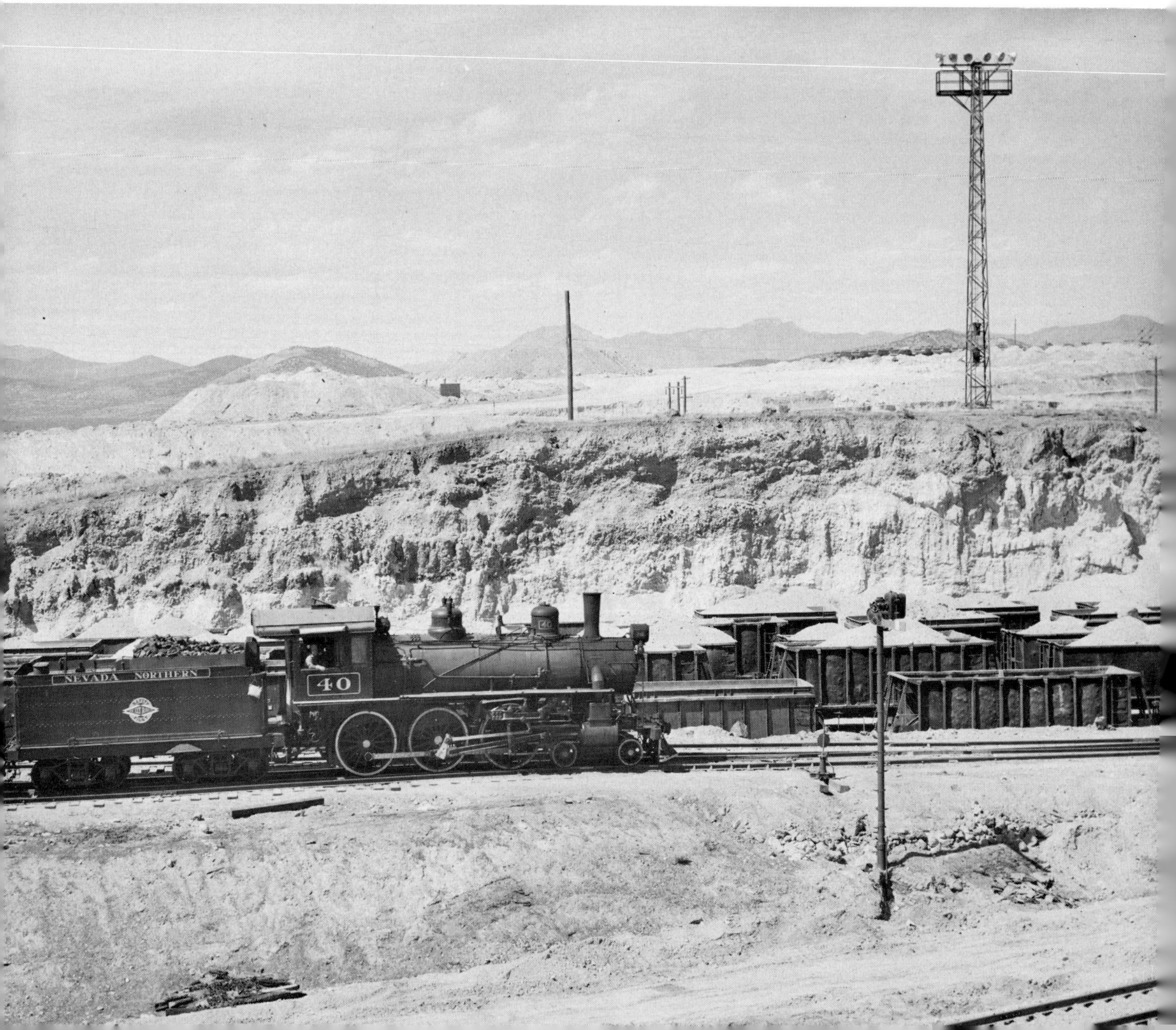

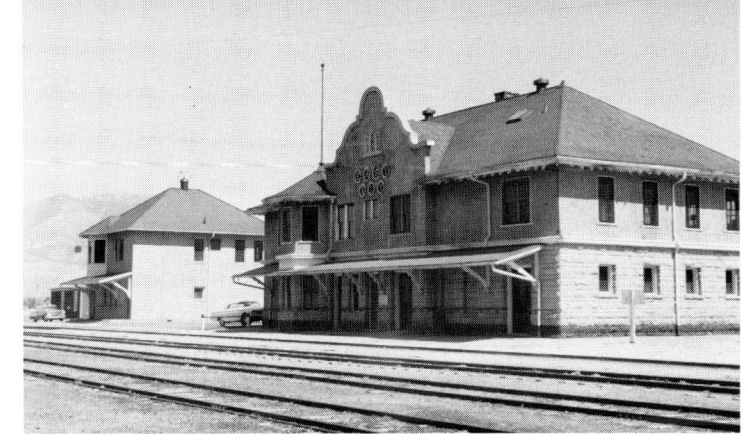

Copper Flat, near the southwestern tip of the Nevada Northern, is characterized by huge mine dumps, such as form the background for No. 40 and train *(top, far left)*, and railroad yards for the switching of loads and empties *(left, below)*. Round-the-clock operations are facilitated at night by illumination from floodlight towers, one of which stands on the bank above the ore cars. The East Ely station building *(top, right)* also houses the general office of the Nevada Northern Ry. The original line of the railroad continued through Ely along Garden Street and behind "Tex" Rickard's Northern Hotel *(right, center)*. Kennecott Copper ore trains use the three-mile by-pass along the hills to the north *(near left, top and center)*. Although regular passenger service has long been discontinued on the Nevada Northern, occasional passenger trains still pull into East Ely, as witness this special movement *(below)* in October 1959. *(Far Left, Top and Bottom, and Right, Below: Pacific Railway Journal.)*

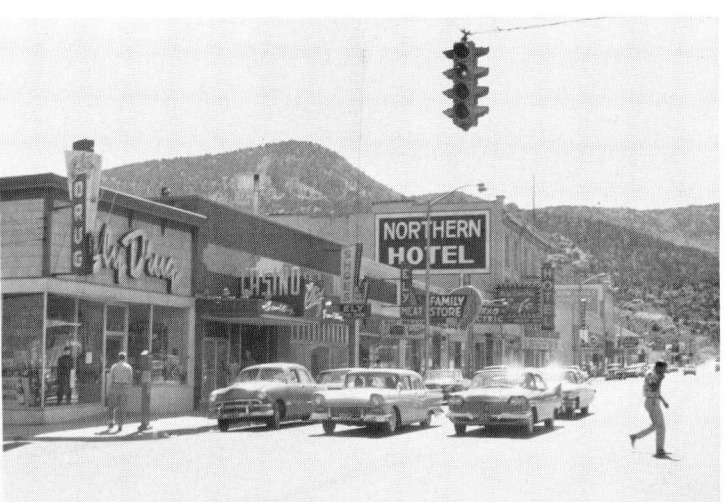

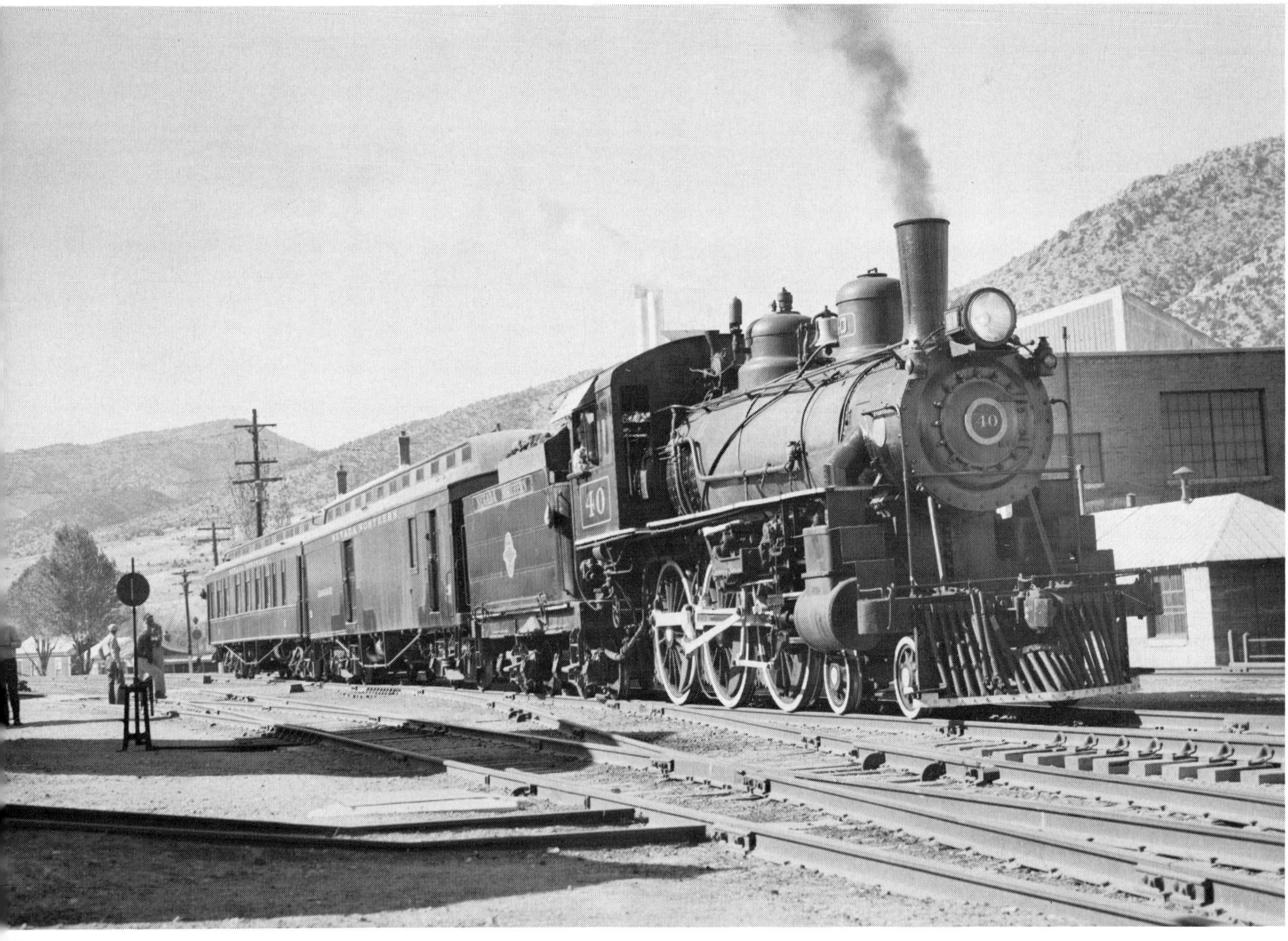

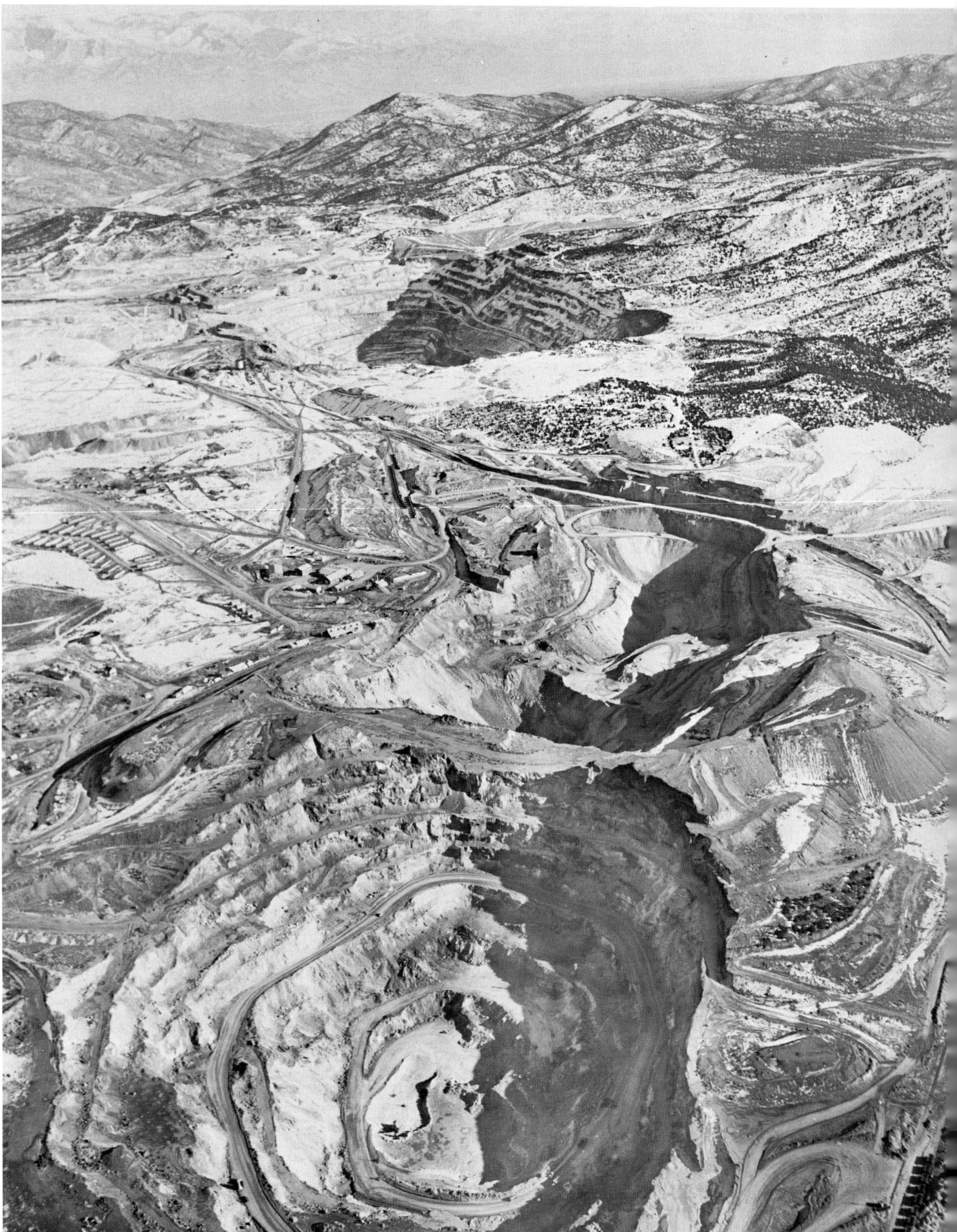

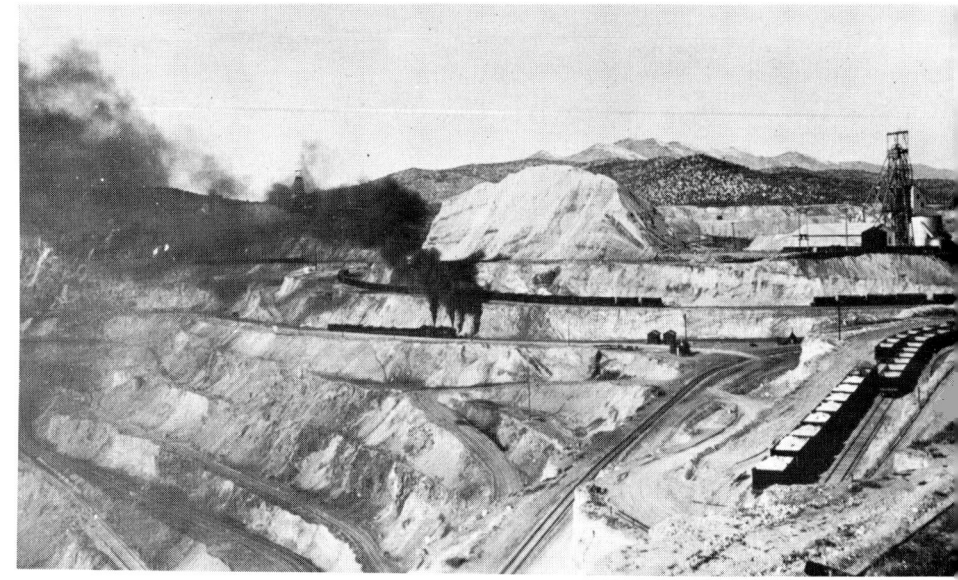

In the mid-morning sunlight of a wintry day *(left)* the three great mine pits of the Ely copper district stand stretched in half-shadowed relief across a six-mile area. In the middle background, with its southern half in deep shadow, is the mile-long Liberty Pit, largest of the three and the only one previously worked by railroad. (At the time of this photo, all three pits utilized truck and road transportation; the Liberty was the only active pit; the other two were on a stand-by basis.) On the far north lip of the Liberty are visible the yards and terminal of the Nevada Northern at Copper Flat. The path of the railroad westward toward the camera may be easily traced, whence it circles south, to the right of the Tripp Pit (center) and the Veteran Pit (foreground). To the left of the Tripp Pit are the buildings comprising the town of Kimberly, while just beyond (where the ore cars stand on sidings) lies Riepetown.

In the more animated days of steam railroad operation, two locomotives *(right)* appear to be working as four to lift eight loaded ore cars up the steep shelf of the pit bank as the morning sun multiplies their sooty exhaust. A full stable of iron horses was necessary to maintain schedules on an around-the-clock basis, for the many miles of tracks appear deceptively few against the massive walls of the big pit whose steep banks dwarf the combined workings of two of the largest steam shovels of the period. *(Left: Kennecott Copper Corp.; Right, Top and Center: Paul Russell Photos, Guy Dunscomb Collection; Bottom: U. S. Geological Survey.)*

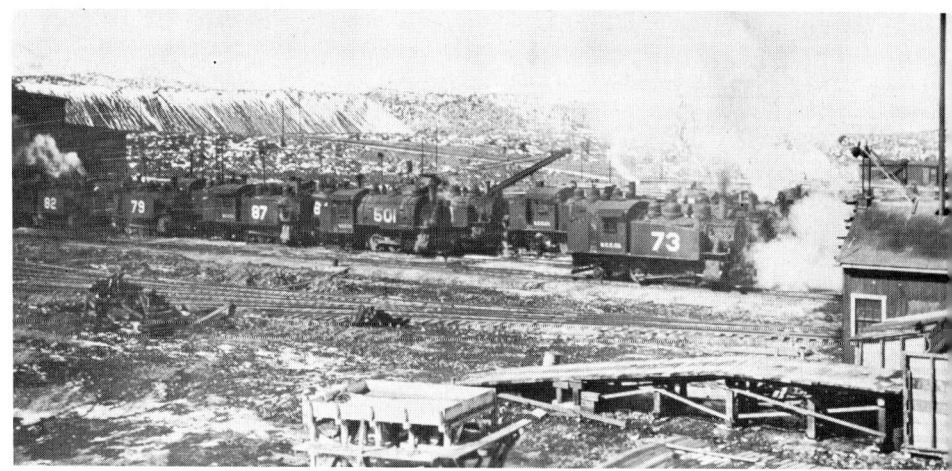

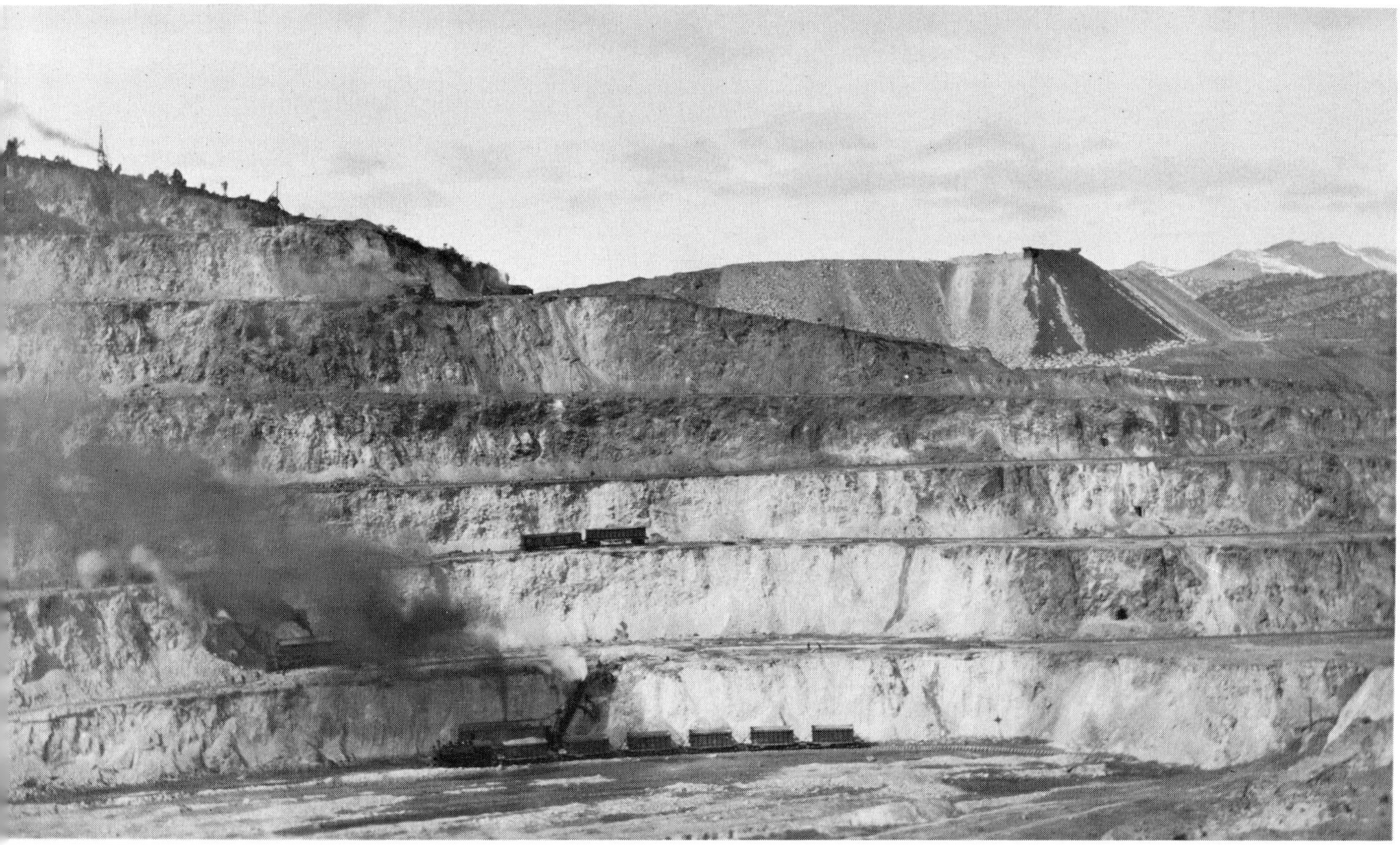

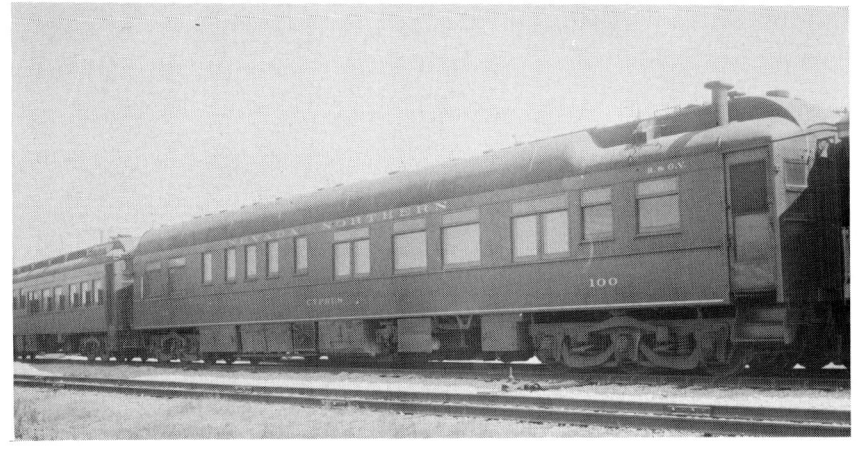

Nevada Northern car No. 100, the *Cyprus*, was formerly the private car of copper mogul D. C. Jackling. The initials "R&GV" near the ends of the letterboard designate the Ray & Gila Valley Railroad, a line in southern Arizona belonging to the Ray Consolidated Copper Company which merged with the NCCCo as part of the Kennecott Copper Corp. family.

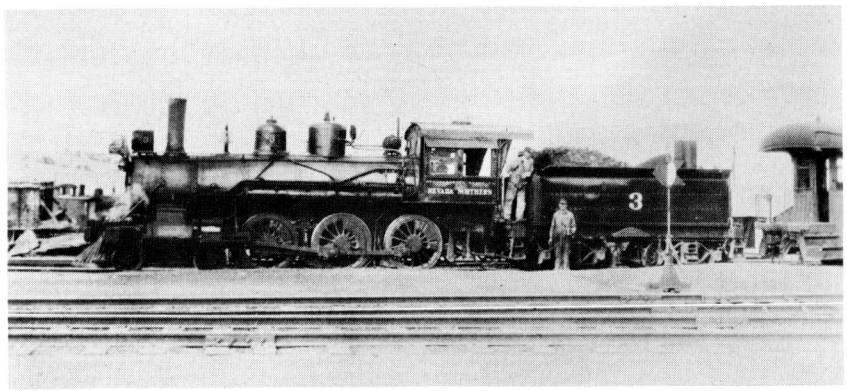

In June 1933 the Nevada Northern's school trains were usually headed by No. 3, a broad-wheelbased 10-wheeler from the Southern Pacific. Consolidation (2-8-0) No. 94 carried the initials of the Kennecott Copper Corp. when this portrait was taken in July 1946, while another variation of the same basic wheel arrangement may be seen in Nevada Northern No. 81 as photographed by builder Baldwin before delivery. *(Top: G. L. Dunscomb; Second: Ted Wurm; Third: B. H. Ward Photo, Dunscomb Collection; Bottom: H. L. Broadbelt Collection.)*

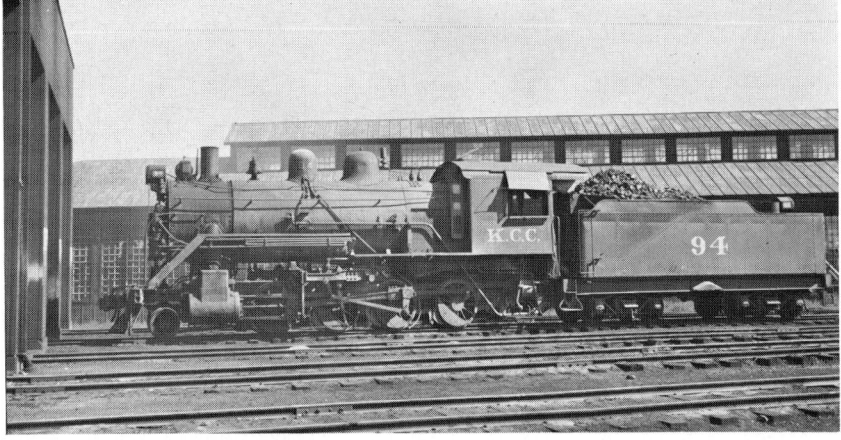

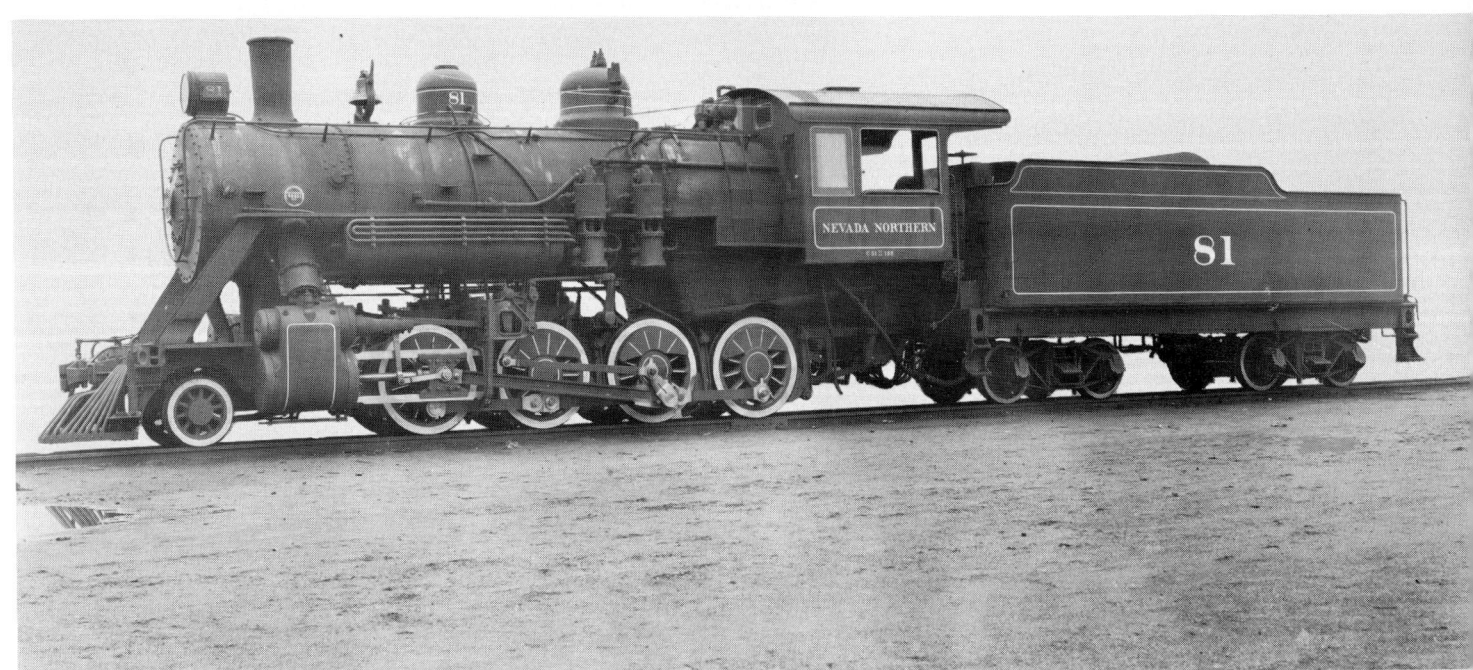

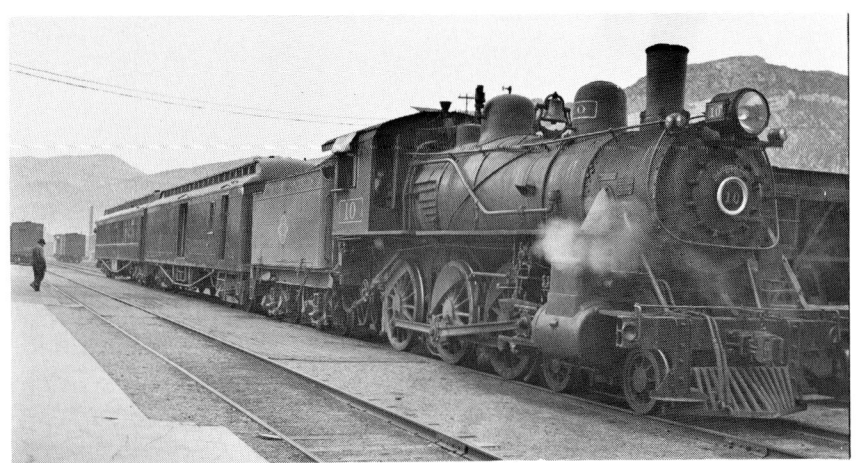

Typical of NN passenger trains of the 1930 era is the consist of 10-wheeler No. 10, a baggage-express-R.P.O. car and a solitary coach. Ore trains of the period were hauled by (2-8-0) Consolidations such as the No. 93 of the Nevada Consolidated Copper Co. which later became part of the Kennecott Copper Corp. as now exhibited in Ely with No. 81 on a parallel track. Contrast these letterings with that of No. 94 on the page opposite. When Nevada Northern No. 40 was first built by Baldwin in 1910 it differed but little from the locomotive of today with the exception of the location of the generator, the absence of a back-up sander line behind the second driver, ornate hand rails on the tender, and a transposition of the road name and locomotive number between tender and cab. This builder's photo shows the engine before delivery. *(Top: Doug Richter Photo, Guy L. Dunscomb Collection; Second: Ted Wurm Photo; Bottom: H. L. Broadbelt Collection.)*

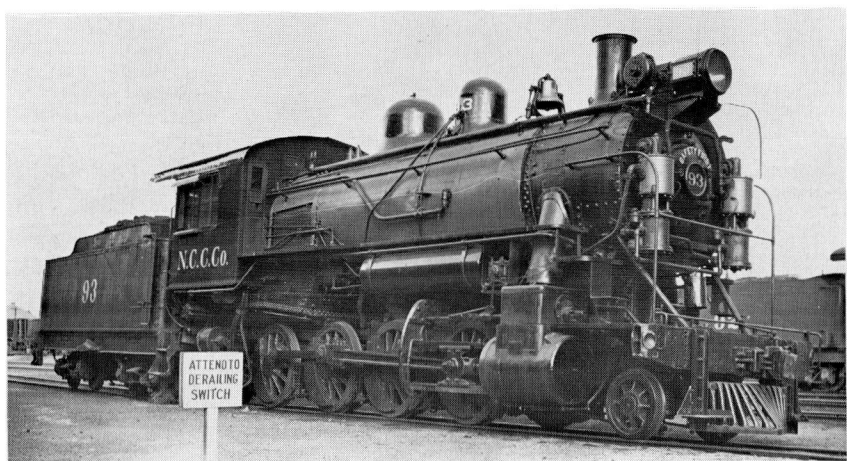

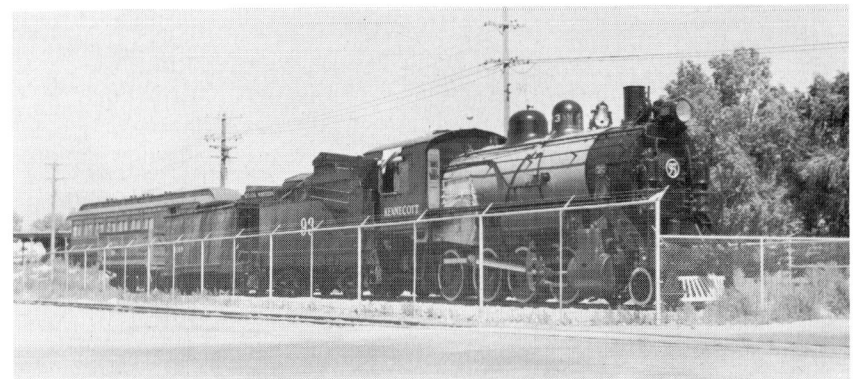

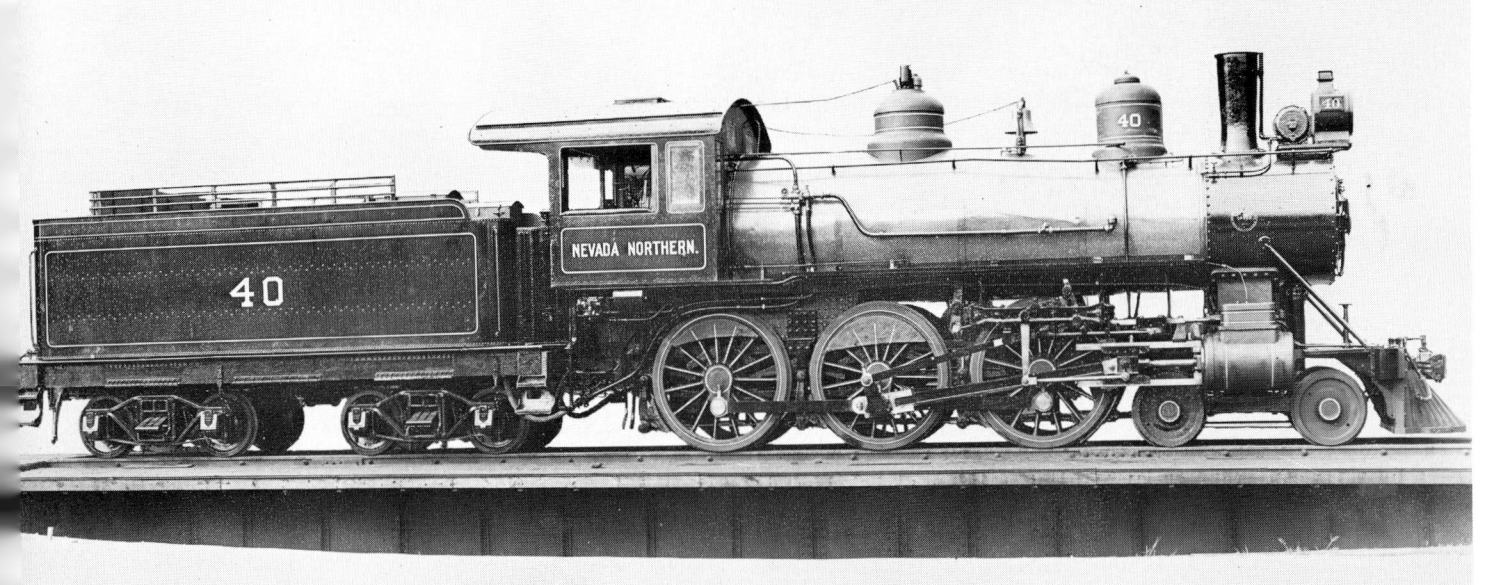

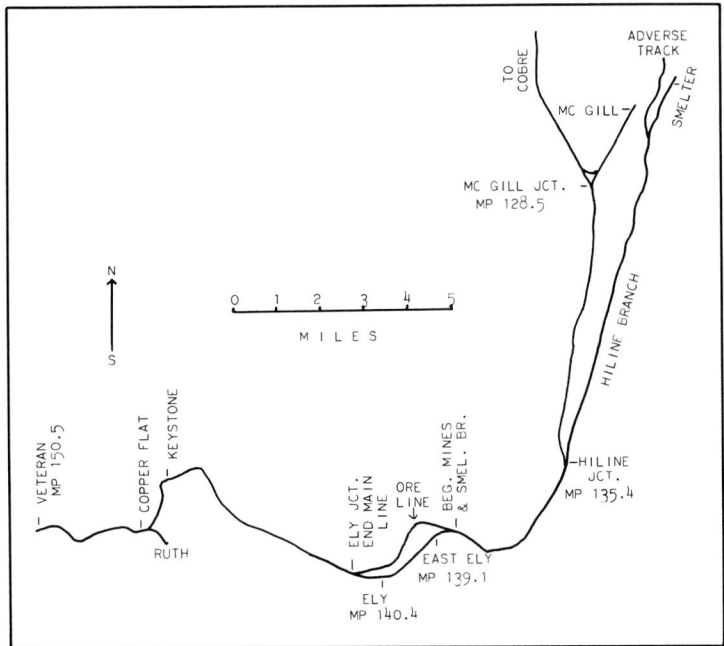

that he had purchased the property for a mere $6,400 *after* the tracks had been laid. Other suits were anticipated; one was filed in Lane City; Mr. Fesler even attempted a second suit for a more moderate $2,000. Ironically for the Nevada Northern, the first train to leave Ely was operated on Railroad Day when, in an errand of mercy, a special train removed a sick man to a hospital in Salt Lake City. The patient's name: A. J. Fesler.

President Eccles was approached concerning the freight depot situation, but he refused to commit himself pending the outcome of the suit. "We are powerless to do anything as a result of this action until this matter is settled," he commented. "If we were to go ahead now and construct a freight depot in Ely, how do you know some one would not ask to have that destroyed as they have our Garden Street line?"

The Railroad Commission listened to the evidence, although much of the testimony was based on hearsay. In March 1907 it ordered the railroad to build a freight depot in Ely, which order was challenged in the U. S. Circuit Court. The Commission filed an answer, but by this time interest was lagging in Ely. The Commercial Club had become insolvent the previous December (1906), and the attorneys had dropped out of the case. Ely City was eventually changed to East Ely in 1908, and the hassel was over.

With the advent of regular railroad service following the Railroad Days celebration, the building boom in Ely continued. "Tex" Rickard's Northern Hotel was opened on January 8, 1907 and was acclaimed by resident and tourist alike for its many fine features. Miners also found solace at its gambling tables where the proceeds of many a claim sale passed into the hands of the croupiers.

Passenger business was good on the railroad. The coaches were jammed with people on every trip, as many as 150 people being accommodated at a time. When overflow crowds failed to find room aboard the cars, freight conductors graciously consented to share the hospitality of their cabooses with a corresponding reduction in tariff to half-fare to compensate for the slowness and lack of conveniences. At the end of each day all cash proceeds were thrown up to the ceiling in the usual manner, any remaining affixed to the roof in defiance of gravity being turned in to the company. The trial test of a tourist Pullman brought complaints. The toilet was locked at inconvenient times, and the service was generally unsatisfactory. A standard Pullman was requested, and when the *Dana* ultimately was placed in service on April 8, 1907, it brought 25 people to Ely where a crowd of 200 were gathered to witness its arrival.

Mark Requa resigned from the railroad on December 1, 1906. He had helped the road over the majority of its hurdles, was well known as a fine person, unusually scrupulous and most careful with money. These were all factors to stand him in good stead when he subsequently formed his own mining engineering firm.

The bad weather of the previous winter was repeated the year the railroad was built. In a blinding January 1907 snowstorm a train on the McGill branch was pushing two flat cars when the dinky suddenly appeared in the swirling flakes. The resulting collision critically injured the engineer and killed H. E. Price, the assistant master mechanic.

Following completion of the grade into Ely and before the last spike was driven in eventful ceremony, the graders had moved on into Robinson Canyon to work on the 10-mile extension to the copper mines. The line was difficult, and it was expensive. Just west of Ely a 311-foot tunnel was required, while four miles farther west another 206-foot (Keystone) tunnel was necessary. (The latter ultimately was daylighted in 1944.) It is said that the 10-mile extension cost as much to build as the entire 140 mile line from Cobre to Ely.

Initially a grading camp was established at Copper Flat in March 1907, and the grade from Ely was roughed out most of the distance. The graders made progress, but with the adverse winter weather a succession of engineers made poor show-

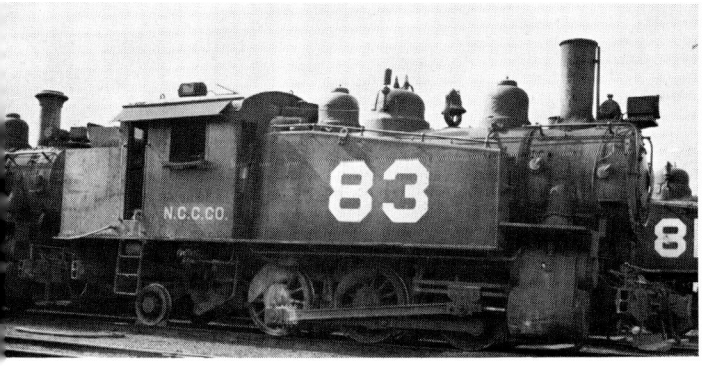

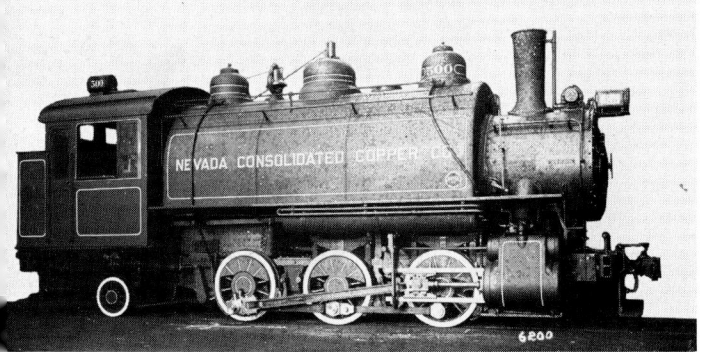

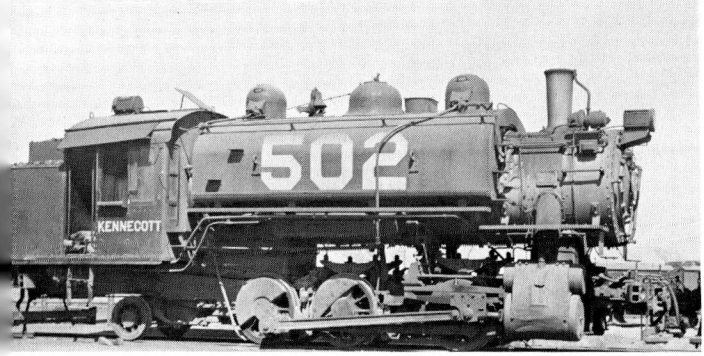

Due to the combination of switching and heavy line-haul duties, most pit locomotives were of the 0-6-2-T saddle-tank variety, which permitted the weight of larger coal bunkers to be hung on the extended frames. Here we see Nos. 83, 500 and 502 in varying stages of ownership and lettering. Contrast these with 0-6-0-T switcher No. 337 *(below)* as viewed in the clear cut print of a Baldwin Locomotive Works negative before that engine's delivery to the dusty ore region. *(Top: Ken Kidder Collection; Third: G. M. Best Photo; Other Two: H. L. Broadbelt Collection.)*

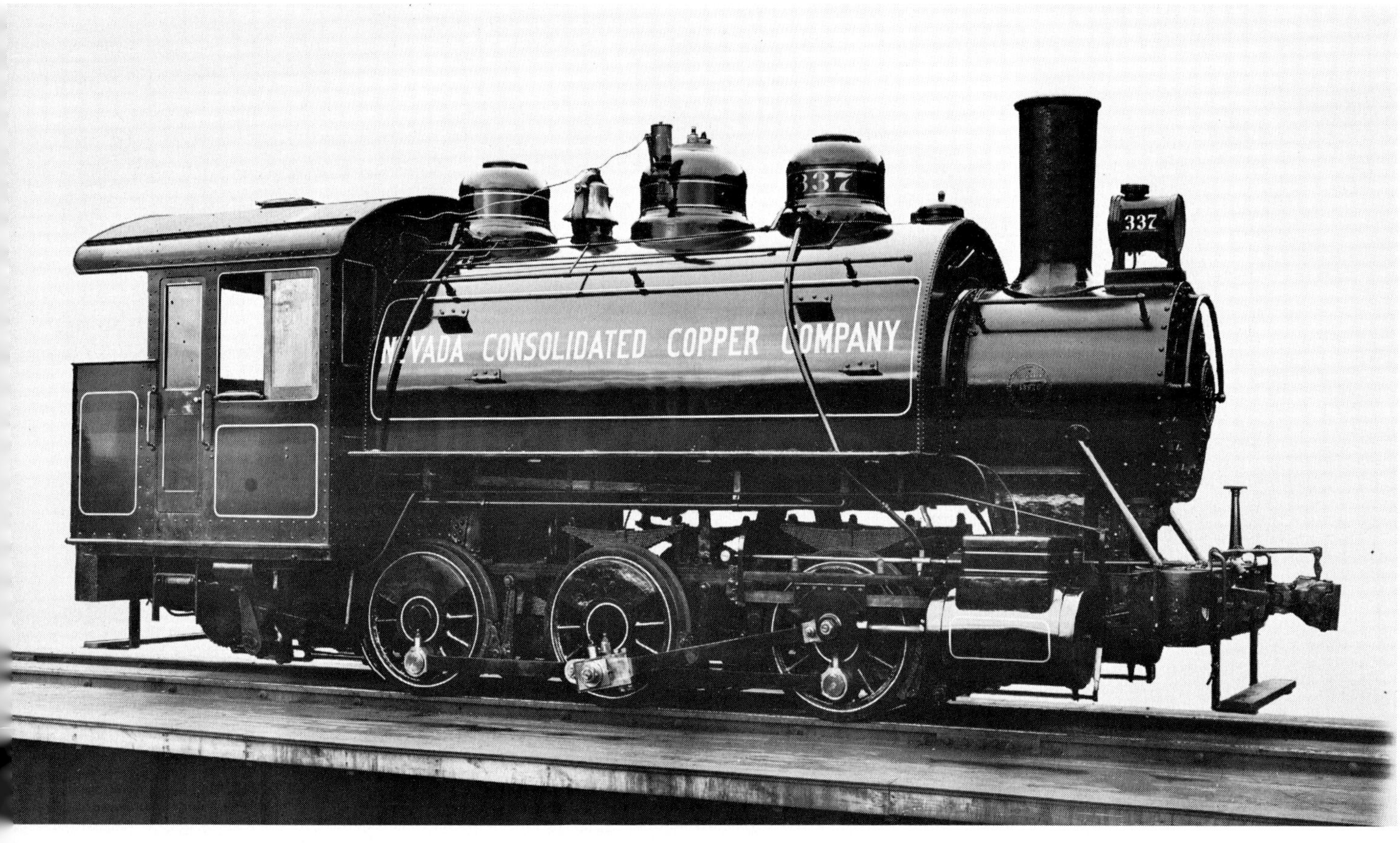

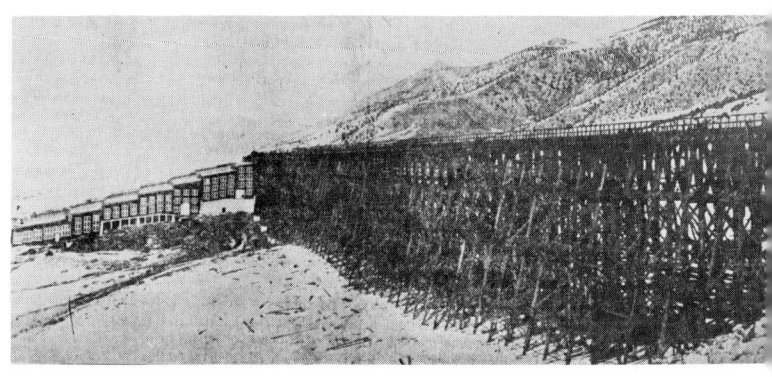

When the nine-mile "Hiline" was first built in April 1907 from a point near East Ely to the concentrator at McGill, this 1,720-foot, double-tracked trestle provided the only major obstacle to construction. Five months in the making, its 109 feet of maximum depth instigated the contention that it was the highest double-track trestle in the world at that time. The McGill station on the main line was distant from, and at a considerably lower altitude than the concentrator, part of whose buildings may be seen in background. Today, a solitary electric locomotive (probably the only one in Nevada) switches cars for the concentrator over approximately one mile of electrified trackage. *(Top: White Pine News Photo; Center: Ted Wurm; Bottom: Pacific Railway Journal.)*

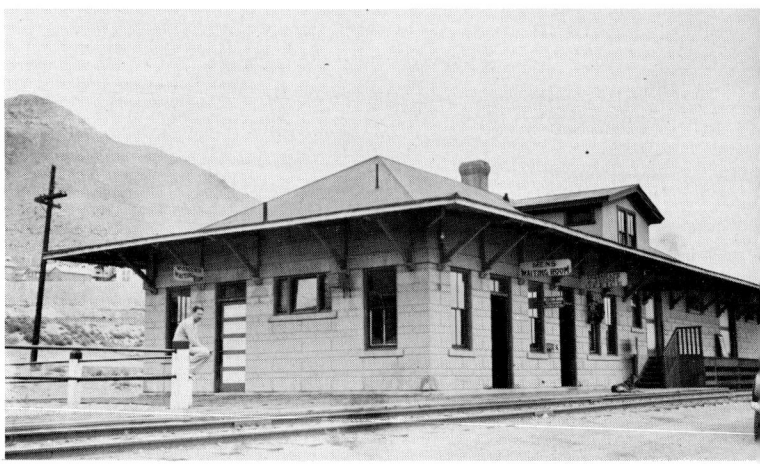

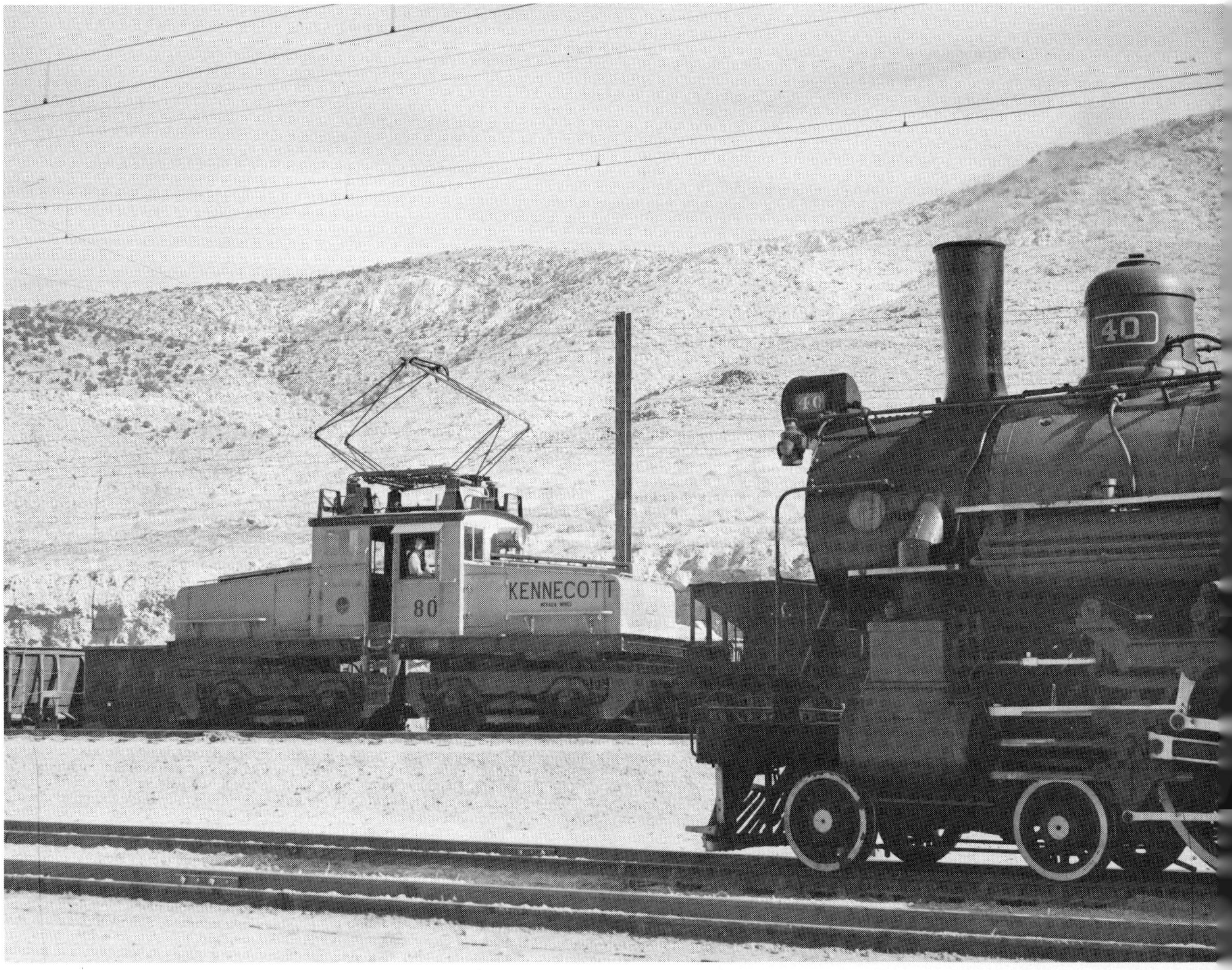

ings. President Eccles was disgusted. Adolph Judell, the road's original engineer, was enjoying his leisure in a little office in Ely, doing some reading and economically preparing his own food. Friends kept him informed of developments on the railroad, to which his ears were attuned. On April 30, 1907, the word came; Eccles wanted to see him in the *Oceanic,* his private car. The meeting was blunt and to the point. Eccles explained that he had had a succession of five engineers and that each one ordered sufficient supplies for a complete railroad. "You started the line and you should finish it," he said. Then he asked Judell what his salary should be. "Twice the old rate," replied Judell. And that is what it was.

When the lower tunnel was finished and lined with timber, the tracks were extended to Lane City, operations commencing in July 1907. A Railroad Day Celebration was held on August 11 with John Verzan as master of ceremonies, a veteran who had first walked into the area some 30 years previous. An improvised race track provided the main event of the occasion, although it is doubtful whether the spectators or the wind and dust had the greater sport.

The rails reached Keystone on July 19, 1907, and were completed across the trestle to the Star Pointer Shaft on August 16. Farther on near Ruth a mining company's boarding house obstructed the right of way. Since it could not be moved, the simplest arrangement was to blast it away. Complaints of employees to the New York office were useless; the deed was done and then corrected with a new boarding house. The incident was reminiscent of a previous situation when the railroad laid its tracks through a barn in Ely City, then moved the barn before the trains began to roll.

Other occasions were less premeditated; the I. W. W. took particular delight in annoying the railroad. Unannounced loaded gravel cars too frequently appeared from nowhere, rolling down the tracks. One crew of men working in the lower tunnel observed such a phenomenon traveling toward them at a high rate of speed, but before any action could be taken a pile of dirt near the tunnel mouth retarded the momentum sufficiently so that no one was hurt.

To prepare the Eureka Pit, near Copper Flat, for copper mining operations, considerable overburden had to be removed. Late in September 1907 a short line was built to the Pit as well as one to the dumping ground, and two dinkies pulling ore cars were assigned to help clear the ground. To speed ballasting a night shift was instituted, and first trains were operated to the Eureka Pit in the middle of November.

Work on the final 2½-mile extension of the line to Kimberly and Veteran was started in August 1907. Difficult rock work was encountered in the grading operations, and in an effort to beat the winter the Corey Bros. contractors doubled their force. Track laying started in November, but bad weather set in to slow the progress, and one particularly large cut delayed the initial operation until January 9, 1908.

At the east end of the Ely system one additional line was needed to bring ore into the upper part of the concentrator at McGill. In April 1907 work was started on the nine-mile "Hiline" which branched from the main line northeast of East Ely at a point designated as Hiline (Jct.). No particular problems were involved in its construction with the exception of a 1,720-foot trestle just before reaching the concentrator. Five months were required to fashion the double track structure, 109 feet above the ground at its greatest height, and it was contended that this was the highest double track trestle in the world at that time. When the mill burned in 1922, the trestle also caught fire and was replaced by a fill. The Hiline was completed on March 15, 1908, and three months later an additional spur was found necessary. Leaving the Hiline at a point approximately a mile distant from the concentrator, the "adverse line" (as it was officially termed) dropped downgrade to the smelter so that ore not requiring concentration could be fed directly to the furnaces. The line is presently used to bring supplies and lime rock to the smelter.

The Ore Line, consisting of the main line from the mines (including the extension trackage to Veteran) through Robinson Canyon to Ely and on to Hiline and the concentrator at McGill was to constitute the Mines and Smelter branch of the Nevada Northern. While construction was still in progress, a report was circulated that estimated traffic would require an ore train every 30 minutes passing through Ely. People immediately complained, so President Eccles instructed that an alternate ore line be constructed around the city at the foot of the hills to the north. A steam shovel was brought over from the smelter, and on June 4, 1907, work began on the three-mile by-pass which tallied just 1,000 extra linear feet over the length of the original route through the city. A 40-foot cut at Ninth Street entailed considerable blasting, which was re-echoed with vocal repercussions when some rocks went through the roof of a house and another fragment hit a drunk. Subsequently a second steam shovel was conscripted, and a night shift was instituted to push the work along. By December the job was done at a cost of $110,000, although ballasting of the track was deferred until spring.

A large crowd was on hand to witness the start of operations at the concentrator on April 12, 1908. The first train came down from Copper Flat the following day with ten carloads of ore, and shipments from the mines at Veteran were inaugurated the first of May. These events were the culmination of years of constructive effort and marked the beginning of a long period of successful large-scale, low-grade copper mining operations.

Passenger service to McGill was inaugurated on February 9, 1908, while in the other direction, service to Veteran commenced on Saturday, May 9, 1908. A large group of miners came down from Veteran for a gala night in Ely on that first trip. Later in the year the service was further improved when, in addition to the daily train to Cobre, four trains were scheduled to McGill, three to Veteran, and ten shuttled back and forth over the 1.2 miles between Ely and East Ely. The little road was full of traffic.

Substantial reductions in freight rates were made voluntarily by the Nevada Northern, while even more were made under pressure from the Railroad Commission. Passenger fares followed a similar pattern. Before the advent of the railroad, the Wells-Ely stage fare was $12.50; the initial railroad fare for the 140-mile trip from Cobre to Ely was $10.00; in 1908 the Railroad Commission ordered this cut to $8.00; four years later a further cut was ordered to $6.30, probably the lowest rate per mile of any short line in Nevada.

No sooner had the Nevada Northern started operating successfully than other proposals for railroads to the area were voiced. A direct line from Salt Lake City to Ely was the theme of one group of promoters. The Salt Lake Route also appeared to be a possible candidate with talk of extending their line from Tintic, Utah, to Ely.

The Nevada Northern itself was not without ambitions, contemplating new branches to Vulcan and to Cherry Creek. The latter had been a very active camp with a claimed population of 6,000 in the 1870's, and although the mining activity had shrunk considerably since that time, there were still hopes that a railroad would bring about a strong revival of interest and development. Although the town was only four miles west of the railroad, the ground was swampy and difficult. After particularly heavy rains, P. H. Cannon is reported to have appeared before the county commissioners to seek a franchise for a ferry service between "Requa's Island" (Cherry Creek station), then completely surrounded by water, and the mainland. In actuality, surveys for the branch line were made. The matter was under consideration for a period of a year, but the line was never constructed.

Augmenting the regular passenger service of the Nevada Northern were the famous school trains which furnished shuttle commuter facilities to McGill children attending Ely High School. The students are best remembered for their attentive endeavors at slashing the seats and pulling the signal cord. So deep was the impression created by their persistence, when the Nevada Northern celebrated its 50th anniversary in 1956, it operated trains all day long between Ely and East Ely and all children were permitted to ride free of charge. The event was reminiscent of a similar occasion in 1908 when Richard Riepe, an old resident of Ely, hired a train to take all of the Ely children for a free ride to McGill.

As the years went by, improved highways presaged the diminishing number of railroad passengers, and various trains were gradually discontinued. As late as 1939, it was still a pleasant sight to observe the Nevada Northern passenger train standing at the Cobre station, the locomotive's brass sparkling in the afternoon sun, waiting for passengers from the San Francisco-Overland Limited destined for Ely. Unfortunately, an insufficient number of people made the transfer, and the Cobre-Ely train was discontinued after July 31, 1941.

Ever since full scale operations commenced in 1908, most of the tonnage handled over the railroad has been copper ore bound from the Eureka-Liberty Pit at Copper Flat to the concentrator at McGill. In earlier days steam shovels loaded the ore directly into gondolas which were then assembled into trains for the winding, 11-mile climb up and around the sides of the pit, then over the edge to the assembly yard at Copper Flat. At this point heavier power replaced the pit locomotives, and road crews took over the train operations for the balance of the journey to the McGill concentrator.

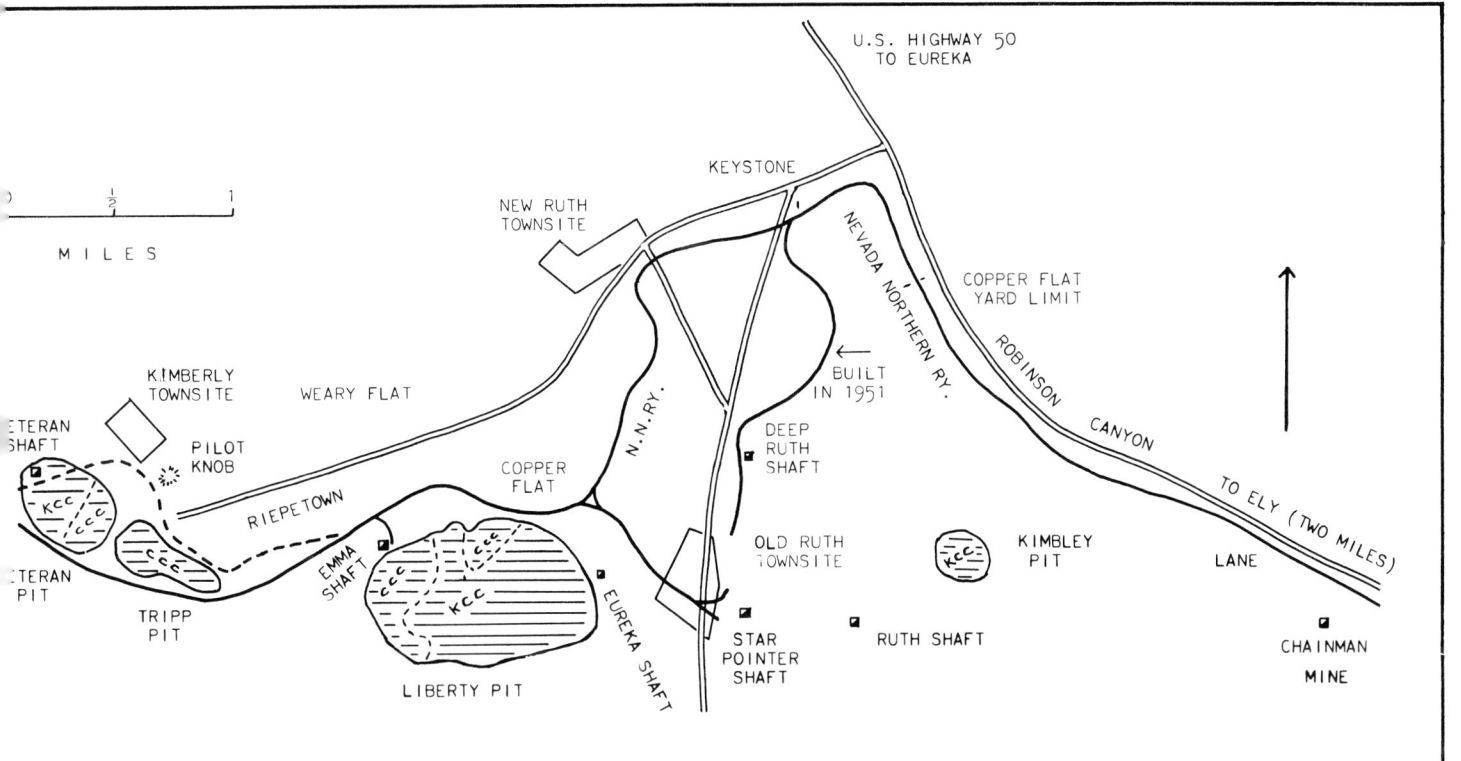

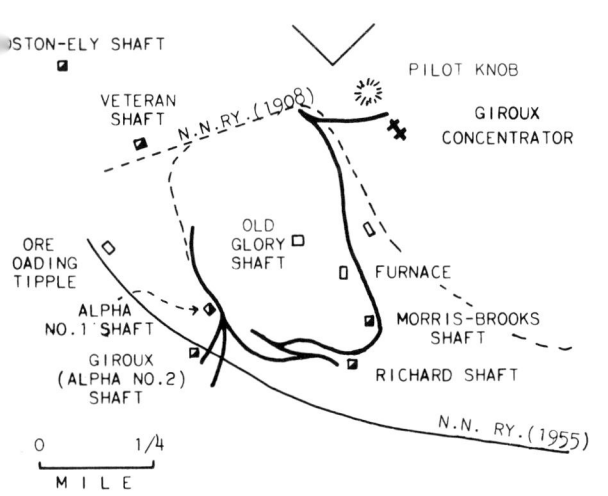

THE LIBERTY PIT (A COMBINATION OF THE EUREKA AND LIBERTY PITS) WAS PARTLY OWNED BY THE KENNECOTT COPPER CO. (NEV. CON.) AND BY CONSOLIDATED COPPERMINES (GIROUX). IN THIS PIT, 14 MILES OF RAILROAD WERE OPERATED WHEN ABANDONED IN 1958. THE TRIPP PIT (FORMERLY CON. COPPER) IS A COMBINATION OF THE MORRIS AND BROOKS PITS.
PRODUCTION BEGAN AT THE KIMBLEY PIT IN 1952 AND AT THE VETERAN PIT (FORMERLY JOINTLY OWNED) IN 1953. USING A BLOCK CAVING SYSTEM, ORE WILL BE MINED AT THE NEW DEEP RUTH SHAFT. THIS NECESSITATED RELOCATING THE TOWN OF RUTH.

NOTES CONCERNING THE GIROUX CONSOLIDATED MINES RAILROAD (INSERT):

THE DASHED LINE INDICATES THE NEVADA NORTHERN RY. TRACK BUILT TO VETERAN IN JANUARY 1908. A SPUR FROM VETERAN TO ALPHA SHAFT WAS BUILT IN 1938 AND WAS ABANDONED IN 1950. THE N.N. RY. TRACK TO VETERAN WAS ABANDONED IN 1953 AND THE SOLID THIN LINE IS THE NEW N.N. TRACK COMPLETED TO THE ORE LOADING TIPPLE AT THE VETERAN PIT IN 1955.
THE HEAVY LINE INDICATES GIROUX TRACKAGE. IN 1907, A NARROW GAUGE TRACK WAS BUILT FROM THE CONCENTRATOR TO THE ALPHA NO.1 SHAFT. IN 1912, THE PORTION OF THIS TRACK FROM THE CONCENTRATOR TO THE CROSSING OF THE N.N. RY. (1/4TH MILE) WAS ABANDONED WHILE THE REMAINING TRACK TO THE ALPHA SHAFT WAS WIDENED. THIS TRACK WAS ABANDONED IN 1938.

On April 1, 1958, the procedure was altered. Pit trains were discontinued, and trucks and a skip hoist were instituted to lift the ore and deliver it to the waiting gondolas in the Copper Flat yards.

Starting in 1920, the Nevada Consolidated Copper Co. operated over the Nevada Northern with its own locomotives and crews from Copper Flat all the way to the concentrator at McGill, a practice which continued after the shift from steam to diesel power and greater locomotive utilization and change of name to Kennecott in 1943. Today, Kennecott Copper diesel units in pairs escort trainloads of 40 to 50 gondolas, each loaded with 80 tons of ore, to the yard near the McGill concentrator. Here a solitary electric locomotive switches the cars to the concentrator over approximately a mile of electrified trackage. Eight trains a day constitute normal operations for the line, thus feeding the McGill plant with some 300 to 350 carloads. To handle this traffic, Kennecott maintains a fleet of over 600 ore cars, distinctive with their metal serial numbers welded to the car sides in lieu of being painted in the customary manner.

In spite of the concentrator's voracious appetite (some 20,000 tons of ore daily), it disgorges a comparatively minuscule three carloads a day of blister copper which moves out on the three-mile line from McGill via McGill Junction. Three trains a week are sufficient to transport the tonnage to Cobre for forwarding to the refinery, as well as to pick up the return loads of inbound freight consisting of approximately 50 carloads of coal, 7 carloads of coke, and miscellaneous loads of machinery, lumber, gasoline and diesel fuel, weekly.

Various are the insigne of equipment which have traversed the lines of the Nevada Northern. The early Nevada Consolidated Copper Co. (NCCCo.) joined hands with the Cumberland-Ely Co. at the instigation of the Guggenheim interests, and each owned a half-interest in the Nevada Northern. At the McGill smelter, the early steam locomotives bore the name of Steptoe Valley Mining & Smelting Co., another affiliated company. In 1909-10, the NCCCo purchased the C-ECo, and in turn itself became a subsidiary of the Utah Copper Co. The Kennecott Copper Corporation entered the picture in 1915 through an exchange of stock with the Guggenheim Exploration Co., acquiring full control of Utah Copper in 1923 and absorbing its assets in 1936. During this period, the Ray Consolidated Copper Company in 1926, including its subsidiary, the Ray & Gila Valley Railroad, both located in southern Arizona was merged with NCCCo. With acquisition of the assets of NCCCo in 1932, Kennecott formed the Nevada Consolidated Copper *Corporation* to manage its properties in Nevada, Arizona and New Mexico, ultimately dissolving the entity on December 31, 1942, to group the properties at Ely, McGill and Copper Flat under the cognomen of the Nevada Mines Division of the Kennecott Copper Corporation. Studies of pictures of early Nevada Northern rolling stock will reveal a reflection of this corporate progression.

The Nevada Northern has been a successful railroad. It has been able to report good earnings, has paid fine dividends, and is the last short line operating in Nevada. It is a favorite among railfans, because they are cordially received by crew members and operating officers alike, and it has the indubitable distinction of maintaining one of the last operating steam locomotives in Nevada.

Giroux Consolidated Mines Company

West of Ely and adjoining the mines of the Nevada Consolidated Copper Company were the properties of the Giroux Consolidated Mines Co., a less extensive, less prosperous, less publicized operation which ultimately was to contribute to Ely's welfare, regardless. A measure of its potentialities can be gleaned from a comparison of the total value of Giroux production (to the year 1940) of substantially over $50,000,000 with that of Nevada Consolidated's production during the same period of $316,000,000. Regardless of size, Giroux Consolidated Mines Co. was unique — it operated both a narrow gauge and a standard gauge railroad during its corporate existence.

Joseph L. Giroux, the founder, had had a major role in the development of Senator William Clark's United Verde Copper Company in Arizona and was looking for new fields to conquer. First attracted to the Ely District in 1900, he joined with J. A. Snedaker and others in May 1901 in the acquisition of 33 claims in the Pilot Knob area. Two years later Giroux Consolidated Mines Co. emerged as owner and operator of the Alpha, Taylor, Old Glory and Pilot Knob claims and as owner of the Kimberly townsite.

For six years the property remained virtually undeveloped while Requa acquired his claims and proceeded with the organization and construction of the Nevada Northern Railway. With the latter project assured, active development of the Giroux properties commenced in 1907. A narrow gauge railroad was projected from the Alpha mine shaft to a concentrator and small smelter at Kimberly. As the Nevada Northern was still extending its line to Copper Flat and Veteran, the Giroux equipment was arduously teamed up Robinson Canyon's muddy way from Ely. One ore crusher left the Ely freight depot in January 1907 and was still en route in May when rails began arriving for the narrow gauge. By July a portion of the track had been completed, just in time to test the newly arrived Porter-built locomotive "Alpha." In October the basic job was done, the locomotive and a handful of ore cars conveying sufficient material for an experimental run of the new concentrator. Ultimately the railroad was extended to a total of approximately three miles of line.

Then a series of disasters began. In December 1907 the Alpha shaft gave way, trapping three men 1,000 feet underground. Rescue was accomplished only after 46 days of effort; salvage of the shaft was impossible, its future use being confined to that of an air shaft.

Less than a year later, in the fall of 1908, control of the company changed hands, and Cole-Ryan interests acquired a majority of the stock. The small smelter (never used) caught fire, reportedly from the sparks of a passing locomotive. Work continued, however, and some production was recorded up to August 1911, when a fire in the main shaft took several lives and the mines became flooded. Drainage was accomplished the next year, only to have the men go on strike in October and the mines become flooded again.

In 1912 the railroad tracks were rearranged and widened to standard gauge, and two new locomotives were purchased to service the mines. Two years later, in 1914, the Giroux name disappeared when the company became a subsidiary of the Consolidated Coppermines Company. Active production at last became a reality, but the activity was of short duration. In 1920 the low price of copper following World War I forced a closing of the mines. In 1922 the Consolidated Coppermines *Corporation* was formed to purchase the property of the old company which was sold at foreclosure. This proved to be the end for the railroad as well. When operations commenced again the following year, all the Consolidated Copper ores were handled by the Nevada Consolidated for treatment at their McGill smelter, some being mined under contract by Nevada Consolidated out of Consolidated Copper mines.

In 1958, the Kennecott Copper Co. (successor to Nevada Consolidated) purchased all of Consolidated Copper's properties in Nevada for $8,400,000, thereby bringing virtually all of the Kimberly-Ruth operating mines under one ownership. A year later the name of Consolidated Copper disappeared when the Cerro de Pasco Copper Corporation (now the Cerro Corporation) purchased it.

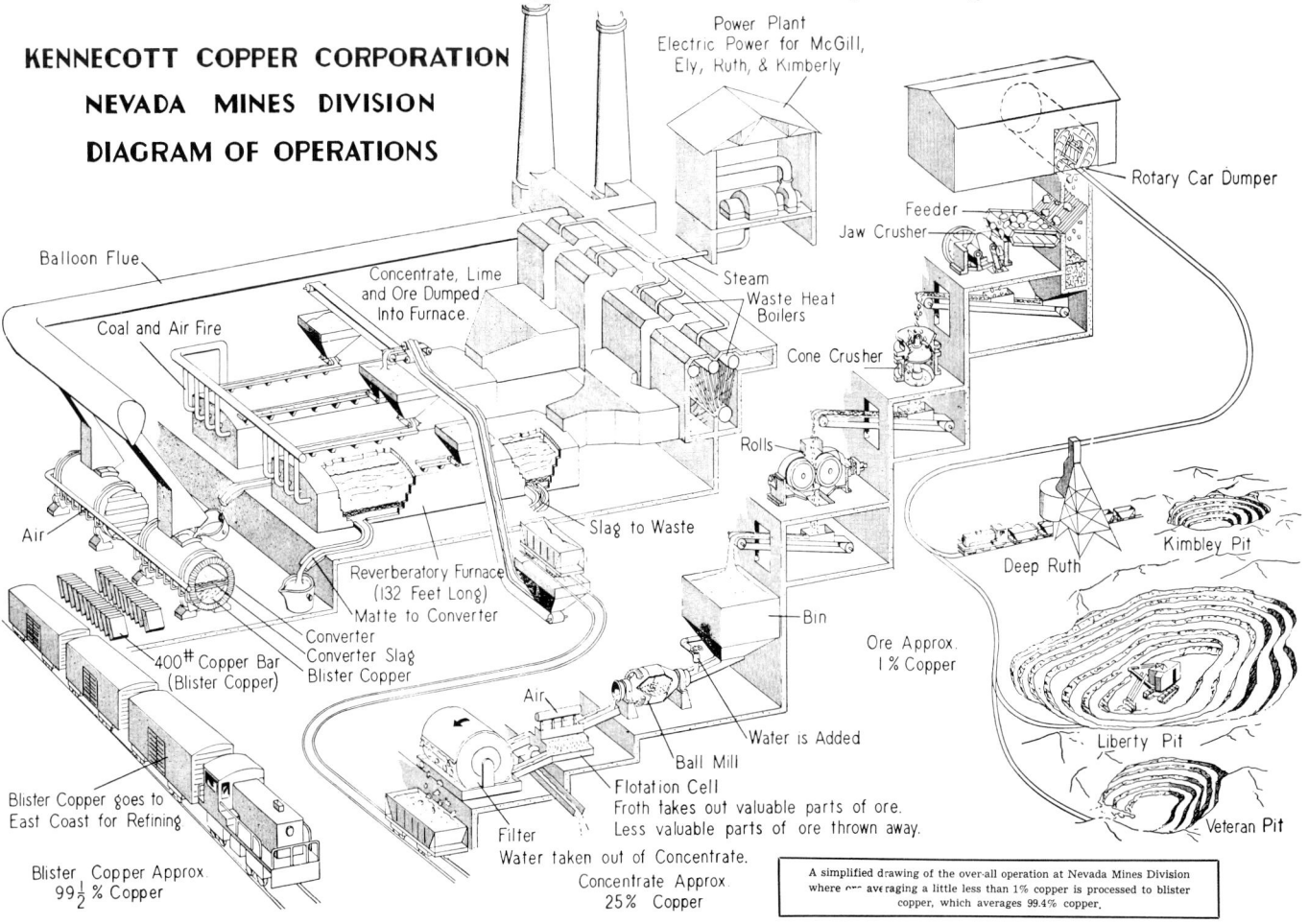

A simplified drawing of the over-all operation at Nevada Mines Division where ore averaging a little less than 1% copper is processed to blister copper, which averages 99.4% copper.

VIRGINIA & TRUCKEE RAILROAD

The "Queen of the Nevada Mining Camps," Virginia City, began life in 1859 following the discovery of gold along the Comstock. Extraction of gold and silver to the value of $310,000,000 over the next 20 years boomed it into a lusty, prosperous metropolis. Production of such stupendous enormity aroused the curiosity of many of the notables of the land and induced them to travel from the ends of the continent for a personal survey of the scene of such enterprise. Then the boom was over; the price of silver began to fall; the lesser mines played out. Yet during the next 70 declining years, the Comstock was to produce still another $76,000,000 of metallic treasure, a feat of sufficient magnitude to accord it recognition among the all-time greats.

Many fortunes were made (and sometimes lost and re-made) by owners of mines along the Comstock. An even greater number of people amassed wealth, however temporarily it may have been held, from non-mining and related activities. Treating ore, dealing in lumber and wood for the mines and mills, speculating in mining stocks, or even the operation of one of the ubiquitous saloons and gambling houses which populated the area could be a fruitful and lucrative experience. Attorneys handling litigation over mining claims waxed rich whether their clients won or lost their cases; but the miners usually had the last laugh for several fortunes, accumulated from preserving justice, disappeared into the ground.

Banking was often a profitable venture, one outstanding example being the Bank of California. Formed in 1864 by experienced bankers, it was headed by Darius Ogden Mills who was assisted by a financial genius, one William C. Ralston. Soon after opening its doors in San Francisco, the Bank of California started a branch in Virginia City with William Sharon in charge. Lower interest rates attracted Comstock mine and mill owners to its offices and subsequently, when these same owners encountered financial difficulties, their properties came into the hands of the Bank which in turn passed them on to the Union Mill & Mining Company whose shareholders comprised the same individuals identified with the Bank.

Since the earliest days, mine operators had been faced with discouragingly stiff teamster charges for hauling ore from the mines in Virginia City to the mills along the Carson River as well as for the equally important return traffic of wood and timber from the Tahoe region with which to fire the furnaces and erect the square-set timbers so essential to mining operations. As Mills, Ralston, Sharon, et al. drifted into mining and milling as a result of their banking activity, they too became faced with the same frustrating Gordian knot. But, like Alexander the Great, they resolved to cut the rope. In this instance, such action constituted the organization, construction and operation of a railroad.

The job was not easy; many groups made false starts before any project was brought to fruition. The first thought was to construct a road from Virginia City to the boundary line of California by way of the Eagle and Washoe Valleys and thence along the Truckee River. A branch from the main line would serve Carson City. This initial project was chartered November 29, 1861, as the Virginia, Carson & Truckee Railroad Co. A year of inactivity passed, during which two more railroads were proposed, one deeming Carson City, capital of Nevada, of sufficient importance to warrant main line routing. On December 20, 1862, a new charter was granted to other proponents of the same general scheme under the new name of the Virginia and Truckee Railroad Co. with a time limitation of three years for completion. Before the time limit had expired, new interests were propounding another railroad project resulting in the incorporation on September 1, 1865, of the Virginia & Truckee River Rail Road Co. When this effort, like the ones preceding, failed to produce a railroad, Sharon stepped into the picture. On May 8, 1867, he incorporated the Virginia & Truckee Rail Road Co. to build from Gold Hill northerly through Virginia City and along Lousetown Creek to a point on the Truckee River ten miles east of the future site of Reno, then known as Lake's Crossing. In September the route was surveyed, but a howl went up from the settlers in Eagle and Washoe Valleys who were being by-passed and left out of the picture. Sharon was amicable wherever money was concerned, and when the people of Ormsby and Storey Counties petitioned the legislature to authorize their counties to donate a total of $500,000 in county bonds, he agreed to move the route of the railroad westward so as to reach the Central Pacific through Carson City. A new and final Virginia & Truckee Railroad Co. resulted on March 5, 1868, and under this name the road was built.

Sharon was a busy man and had little time for conversation. With the preliminaries out of the way, it was time for action. His now famous three-sentence interview with Isaac James, a leading mining surveyor, was: "Can you run a railroad from Virginia City to the Carson River?" "Yes!" was the reply. "Do it then, at once!" was the order. And so it was done.

The greatest and most immediate problem faced by the V&T was one of elevation: traffic from the mines at Virginia City was forced to drop 1,575 feet to reach the mills along the Carson River. James managed to hold the maximum descending grade to 2.2%, but to do so he wrapped the railroad around the hills with a curvature equivalent to 17 complete circles in the 13½ route miles between those points.

Ground was broken on February 18, 1869, two miles below Gold Hill on American Flat. There was not much of a celebration; there was no time for such frivolity. A gang of forty men started work immediately while the officials who witnessed the commencement fought off the winter's cold snap with a few cups of whisky to toast the success of the enterprise.

Experienced miners were hired to build the three major tunnels (there was a total of seven tunnels on the line including the two in Virginia City). Two to five months were required to hole them through. The Fort Homestead Tunnel was opened with a terrific blast at five o'clock in the morning, thus waking up the entire town of Gold Hill. The two foremen, working from opposite ends, celebrated the event by reaching through the opening and shaking hands. A little later in the day, when the opening was enlarged, each man crawled through. Alf Doten, the famed editor of the *Gold Hill News*, and his dog Kyzer went through that afternoon and reported that the men seemed happy as several kegs of beer were observed going in their direction.

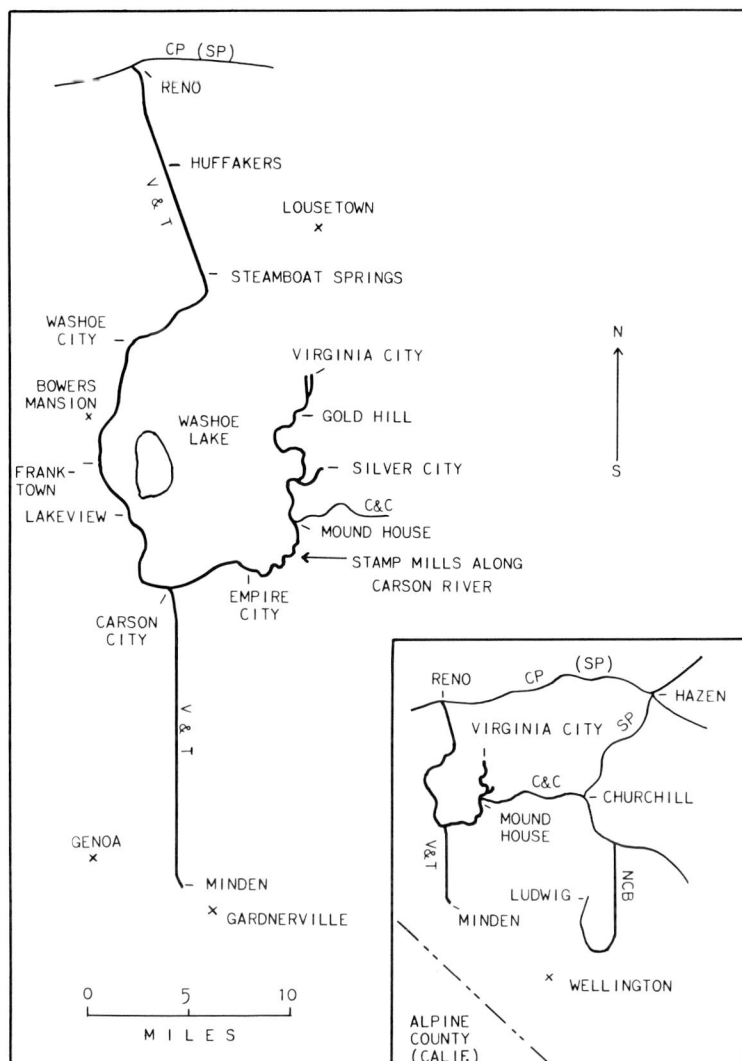

Some 38 grading camps were established along the line to house the workers. The majority were Chinese for whom the Virginia City miners held a particular aversion, and trouble began to brew until a few firm words from the sheriff quieted them down. Crown Point Ravine was crossed with a rather formidable trestle 85 feet high and 500 feet long. Its perilousness was emphasized when one workman (an ex-sailor) fell to his death while reaching for a rope. Later, another man working below the trestle at the Kentuck mine narrowly escaped the obituary columns when a heavy beam crashed near him.

Teams hauled the first locomotive into Carson City on August 6 and on September 28, 1869, just three hours after V&T superintendent H. M. Yerington drove the first spike, the locomotive was operating over rails rolled in England and shipped 'round the Horn. Memento of the occasion was the spike itself. Presented by W. C. Bousfield, Esq., well-known Virginia City assayer, it was made of

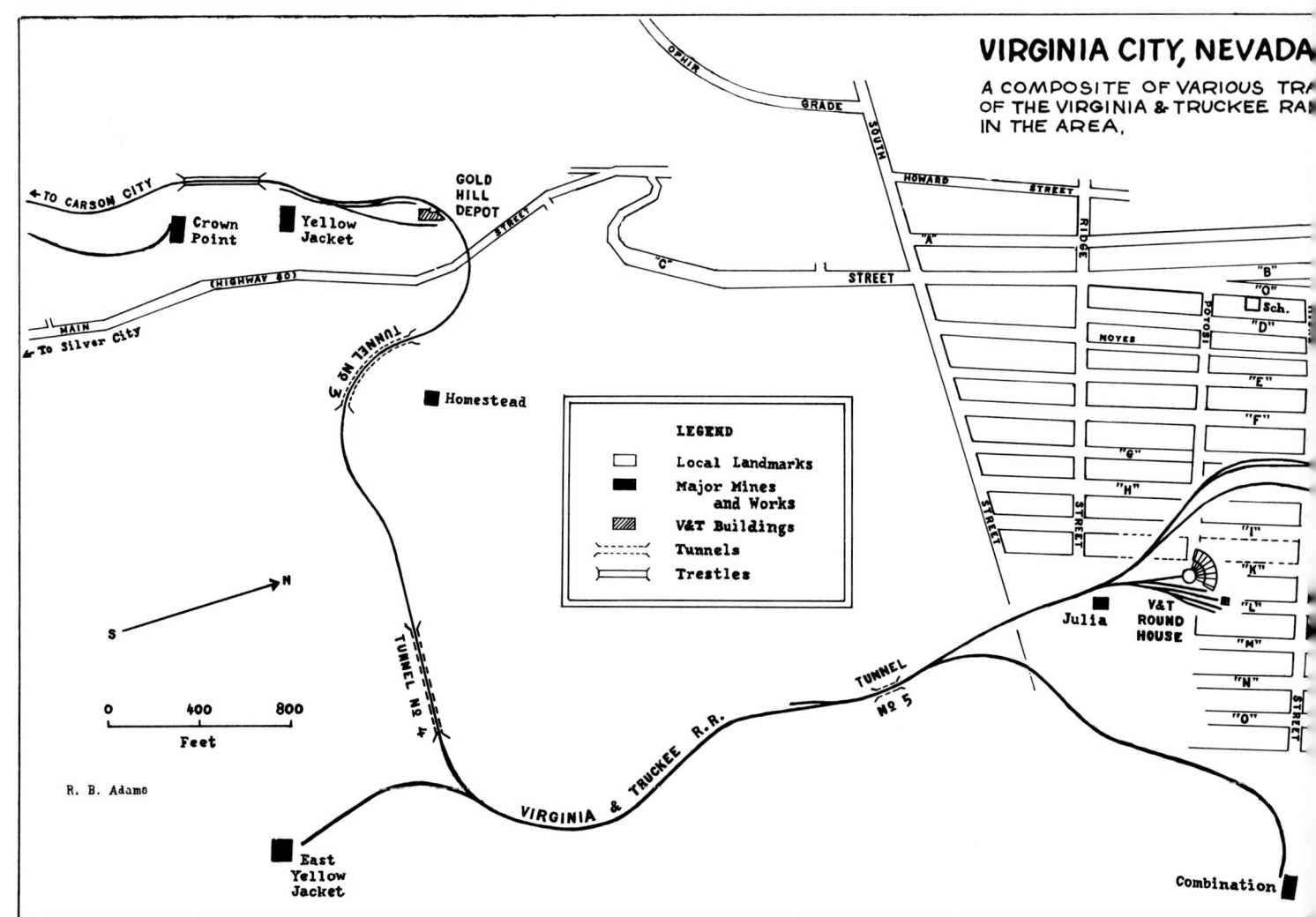

pure silver and contained a simple inscription on its shaft of the name of the road and the date.

Tracklaying started rapidly out of Carson City but halted almost as abruptly when miners chased the Chinese graders off the job. Work was not resumed until October 8, following an address delivered to the miners by Sharon assuring them that no Chinese would be used in the mines and none on the railroad north of the American Mine Hoisting Works.

On September 30, 1869, the Crown Point trestle was completed and crews were putting the finishing touches to a coat of fireproof, dark brown paint. Early the following month an assessment of $3.00 was levied on V&T stock subscriptions, and the Gold Hill News reported: "Virginia & Truckee rails are now laid from the foot of the Sierras to the greater part of the way to Empire. Superintendent Yerington is expected to have the rails laid all the way up to the timber last evening."

As a prelude to regular service, free rides on construction trains were prohibited the latter part of October. Men and boys had been crowding the tenders of the locomotives and climbing aboard the platform cars to the extent that the management became fearful for the lives and well being of these freeloaders.

When the first regular train appeared on the Crown Point Trestle on November 12, there was a grand celebration with a wide selection of spirits ranging from lager to champagne. On December 21, 1869, just a year following the terse Sharon-James interview, scheduled trains were operating from Carson City as far as Gold Hill whence, for an additional 25 cents, one of Hampton's omnibuses would gladly convey any rider the rest of the way to Virginia City. V&T advertisements in the Gold Hill News announced that the train would leave Carson City at 8:00 A.M. for Gold Hill and returning would leave Gold Hill "at or about 4 P.M." Obviously the V&T trains would be run on time, even if the timetable required some stretching.

January 29, 1870, the line was opened in its entirety. The News reported that, "About 10½ A.M. the locomotive, with regular passenger train

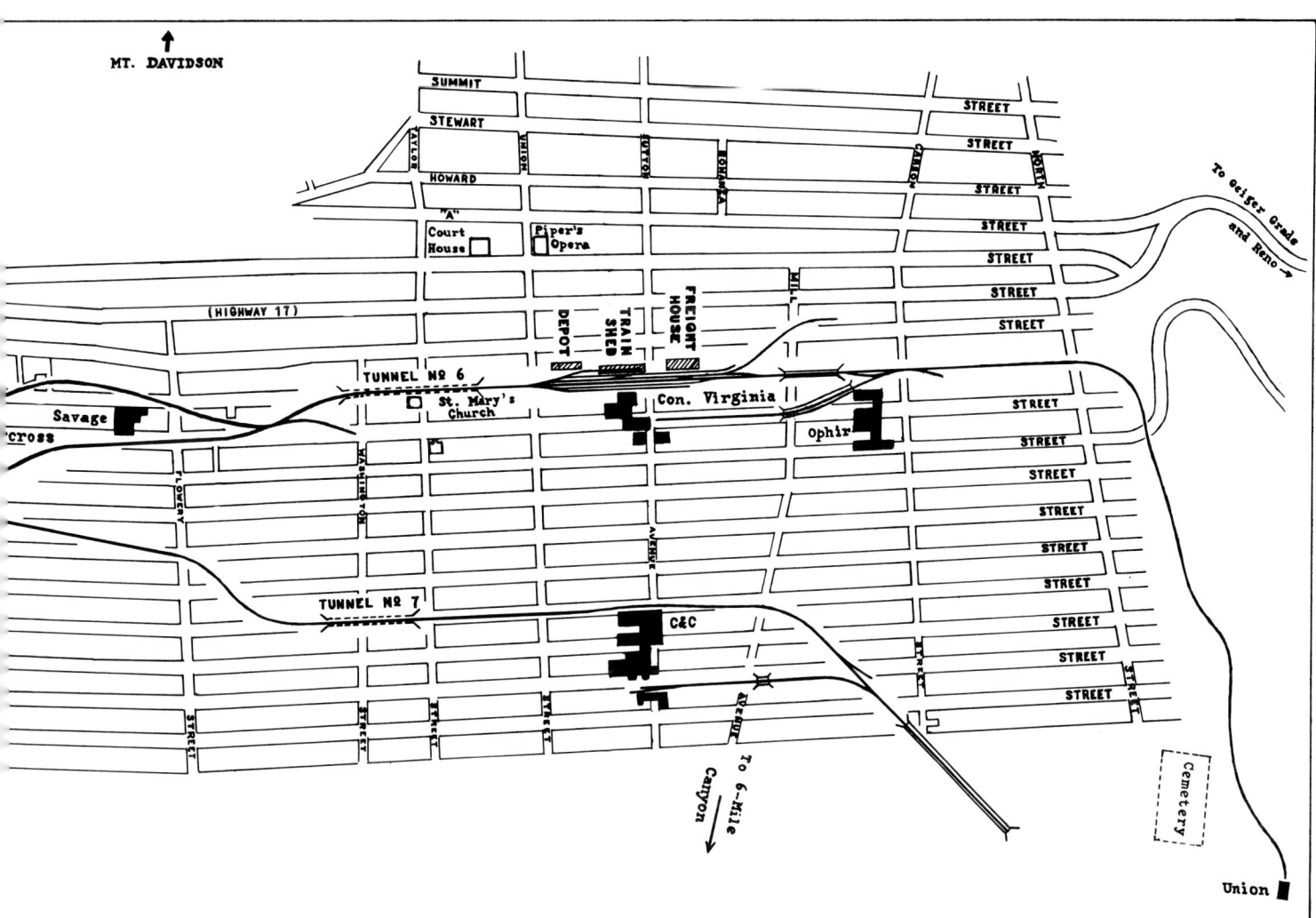

Following Page:

The superb panorama on the following two pages was taken by Virginia City photographer J. H. Crockwell, who climbed just a little bit farther up Mount Davidson than usual to give us this very detailed view looking easterly down into the streets of Virginia City about 1880. In the center right foreground, with the sun reflecting from its roof, is St. Mary's Church (still standing today), perched almost directly above the V&T's Tunnel No. 6 on E Street. Far down behind it are the white dumps of the giant C&C works, and immediately to the right and behind those (in the property enclosed by trees) is the Virginia City Hospital. The valley behind the hospital is Six Mile Canyon, winding down past Sugar Loaf Mountain (top, right) to the Carson River valley just north of Sutro.

Visible in the open space (front left from St. Mary's) can be seen the wooden northern portal of the V&T's Tunnel No. 6, while farther left along the line of the railroad is the large works of the Con. Virginia mine, whose four stacks stand like sentinels against the white of the dump behind. Across the tracks and directly in front of the Con. Virginia is the V&T's long train shed; to its right the roof of the passenger station; to its left the freight house. Still farther left are the two trestles of the V&T over Mill Avenue — the upper serving the main line, the lower the siding to the Con. Virginia. Behind the trestles are the works of the Ophir mine, while far behind those (upper left) lie the Union hoist works, also served by continuation of the upper line of the V&T.

The cemetery occupies the knoll (center left) against which abuts the V&T's large trestle carrying the dead-end tail track of the low-line switchback servicing the C&C ore loading bins. The lower leg branches off at the forward end of the trestle, while the lead to the V&T's main line climbs (toward camera) to pass by the rear of the C&C hoisting works, thence southward through Tunnel No. 7 under Washington Street, the exposed timber portal of which on the southern end may be seen immediately to the right rear of the large mine dump in the lower right hand corner of the photo.

Landmarks in town are the International Hotel (the large square building behind the V&T passenger depot, now burned and gone), Piper's Opera House (the long rectangular building behind it, toward camera), and the Court House (large square building to right).

Note that the presentation of the map of Virginia City (above) is diametric to the photographic view; the former facing westerly, the latter easterly.

VIRGINIA & TRUCKEE RAILROAD

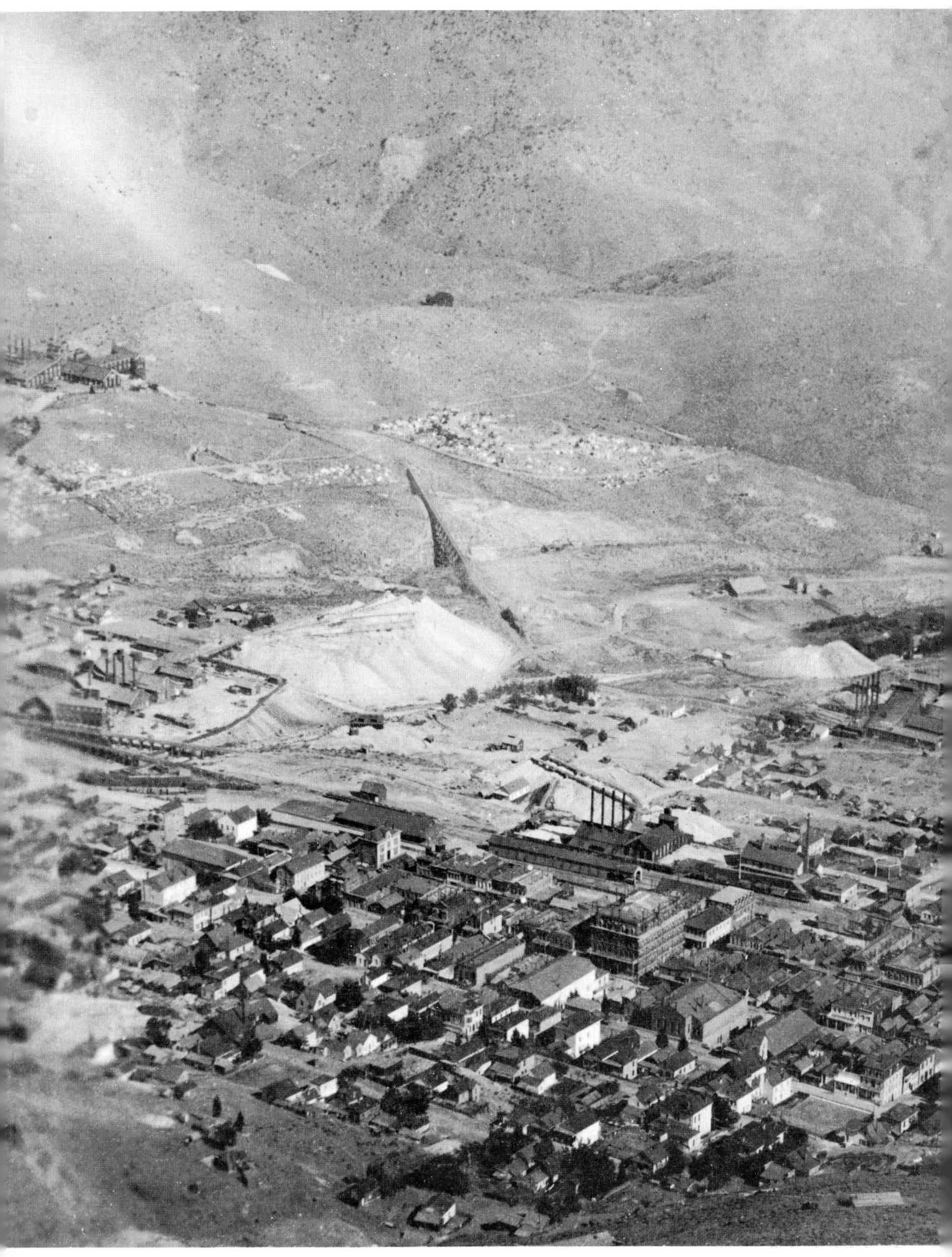

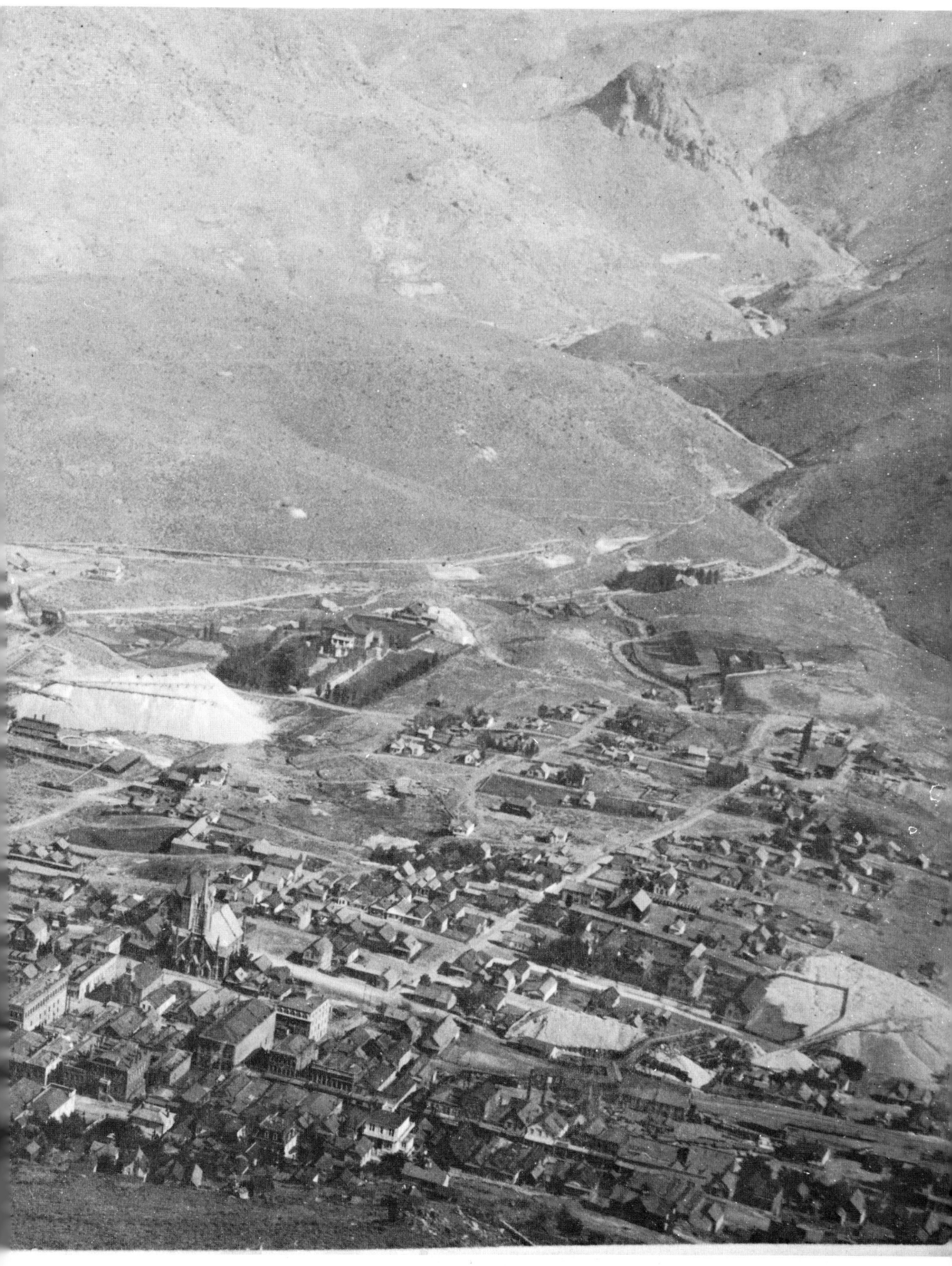

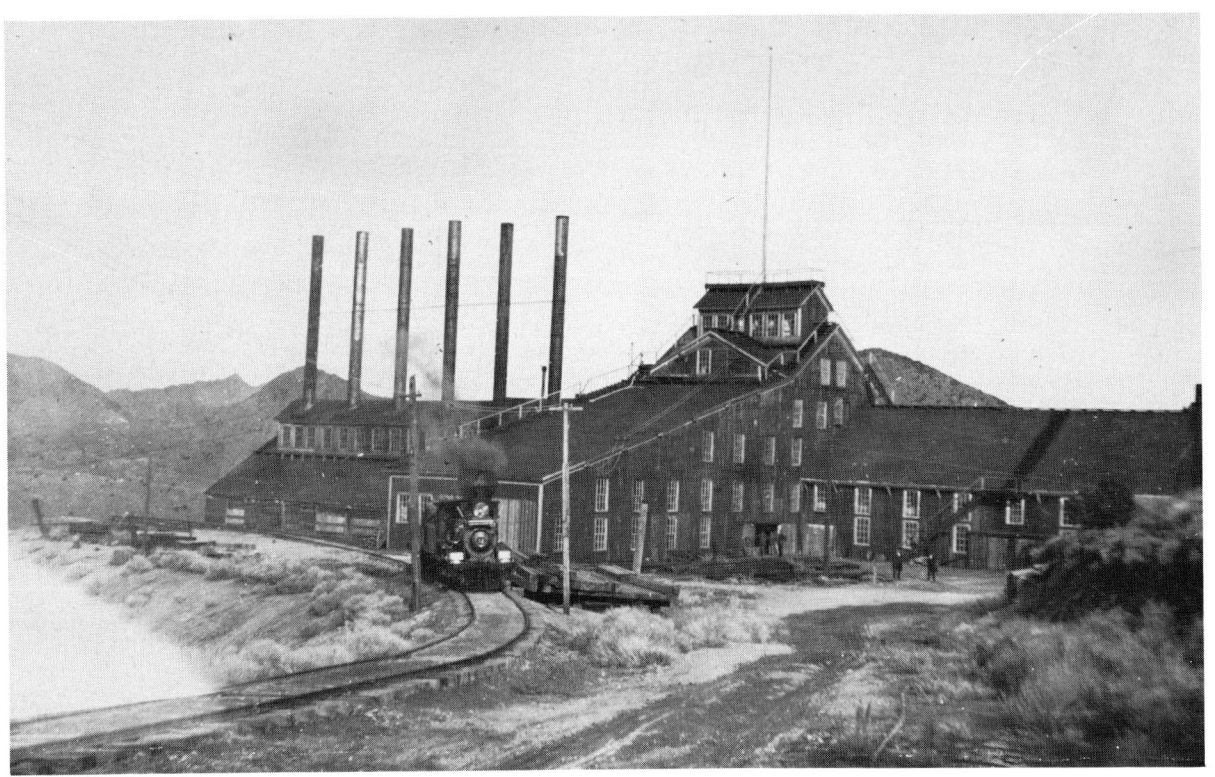

An extension of the V&T's main line from Virginia City station served the Union hoisting works, northeast of town. In the view (*above*), V&T No. 11 is paying a routine call. (*Chester Barton Collection.*)

Two engines with a push plow were attempting to clear the low-line one wintry day when the lead engine left the rails behind the C&C works (*below*). The little shoo-fly in the tracks to clear the end of the hoisting works is clearly evident, as is the low-line's Tunnel No. 7 under Washington Street to the rear just beyond the jutting end of the building. (*Chester Barton Collection.*)

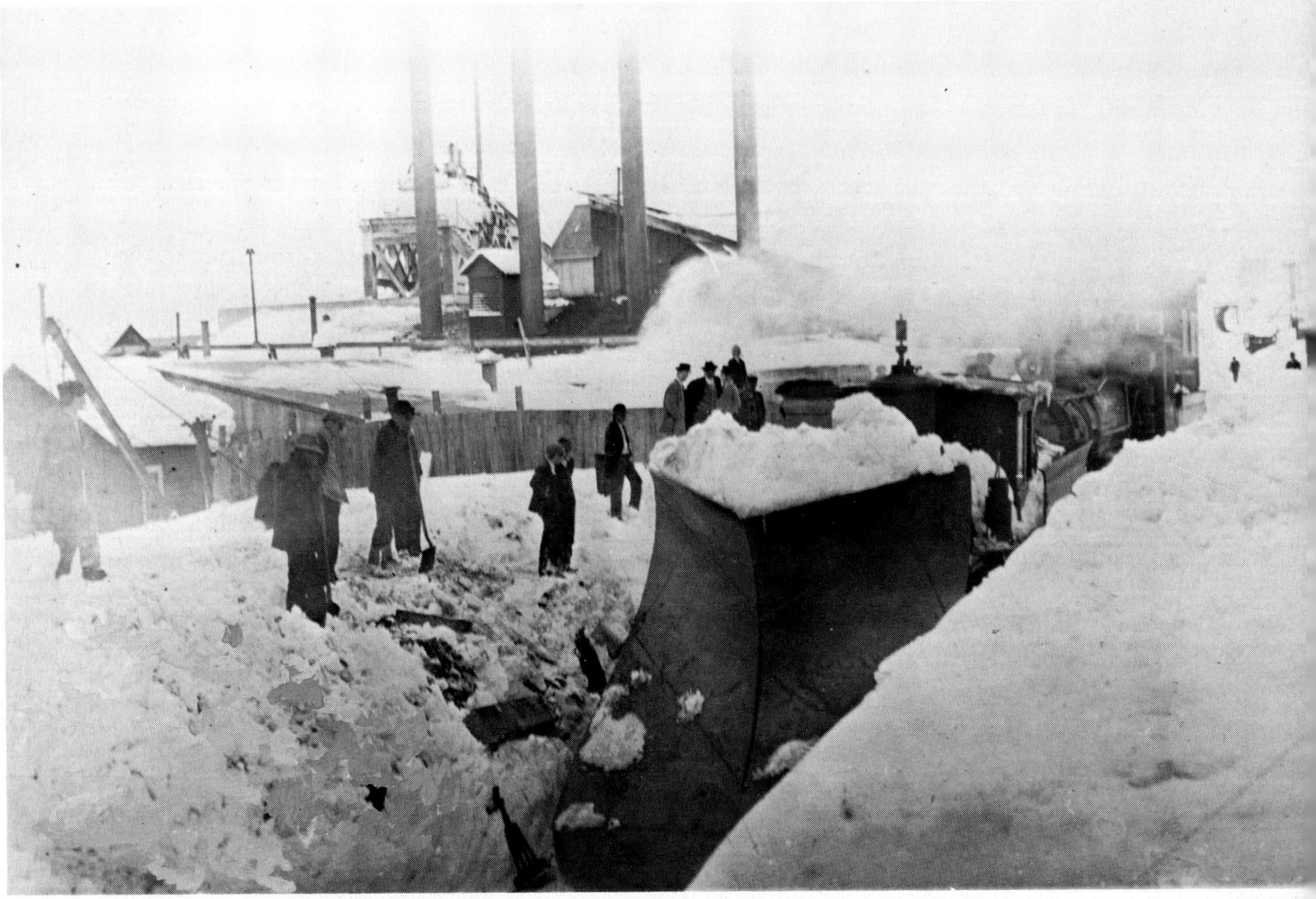

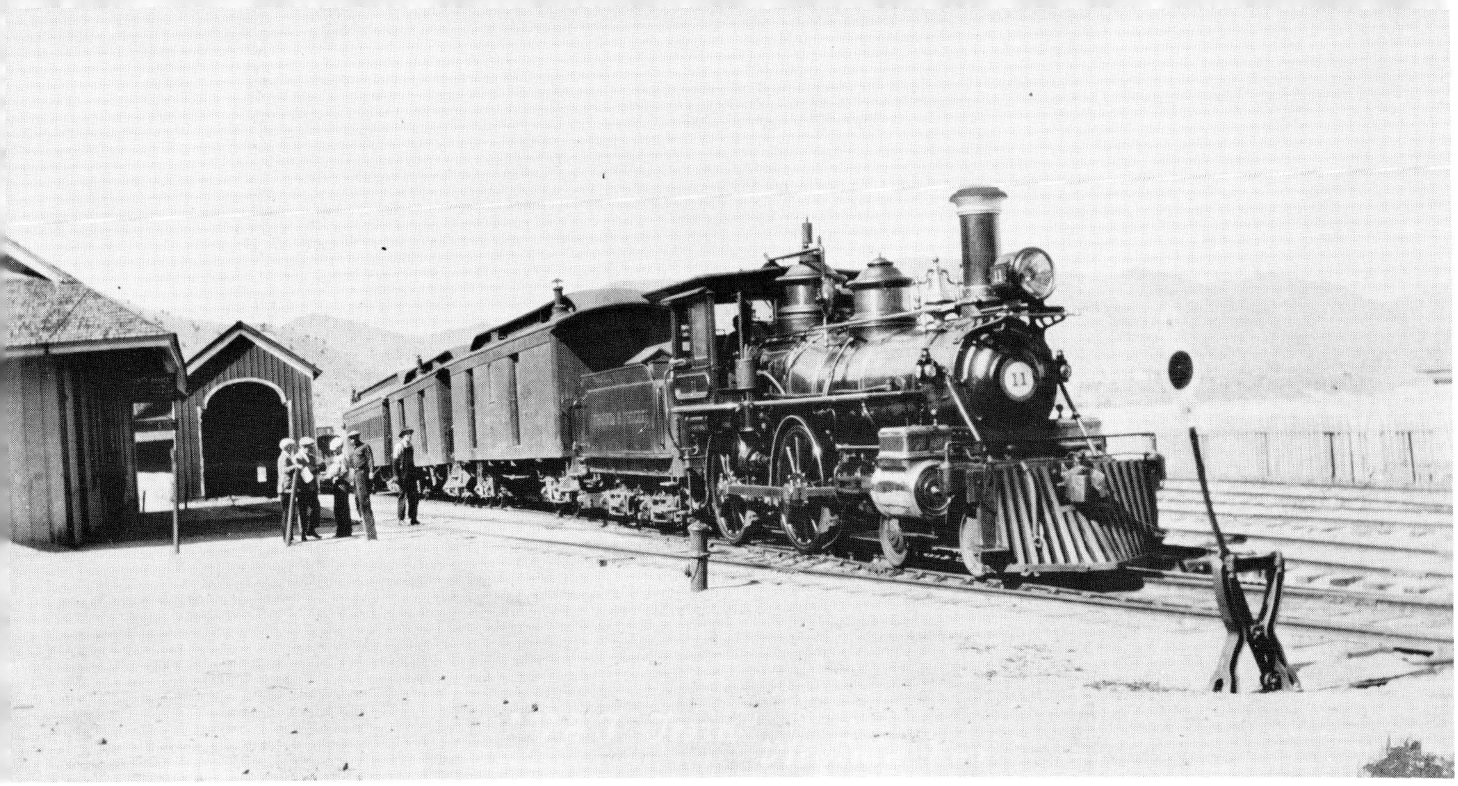

In classic pose, V&T No. 11 stands at the Virginia City passenger depot tailing its consist of two cars for head-end revenue and a solitary coach for passengers. Although the stub switch in the foreground is set for the train to roll, departure time is still some minutes away as attested by the listless group of passengers at trackside. An idea of the tremendous length of the train shed (between the train and the station) may be gleaned from the size of the northern portal as seen through the open doors at this end of the building.

In the northerly view *(below)* taken from the right-of-way of the spur to the Combination shaft, we see the V&T roundhouse situated almost equidistant from the Fourth Ward School at the foot of Mount Davidson on the left and St. Mary's Church on the right, whose spire is plainly visible against the barren slope of the hill in the background. The trestle carries the mine cars of the Chollar Potosi works over the V&T main to the dump at right. Behind the roundhouse, four stacks mark the Hale & Norcross works, while farther to the right (over the platform in the middle of the dump) the three stacks of the Savage works are faintly visible. The igloo-like huts in the right foreground are Piute Indian hogans, fashioned from scrap pipe and miscellaneous cast-offs and covered with flattened tin cans and other debris of an advancing mechanical age. *(Top: Southern Pacific Collection; Bottom: Grahame Hardy Collection.)*

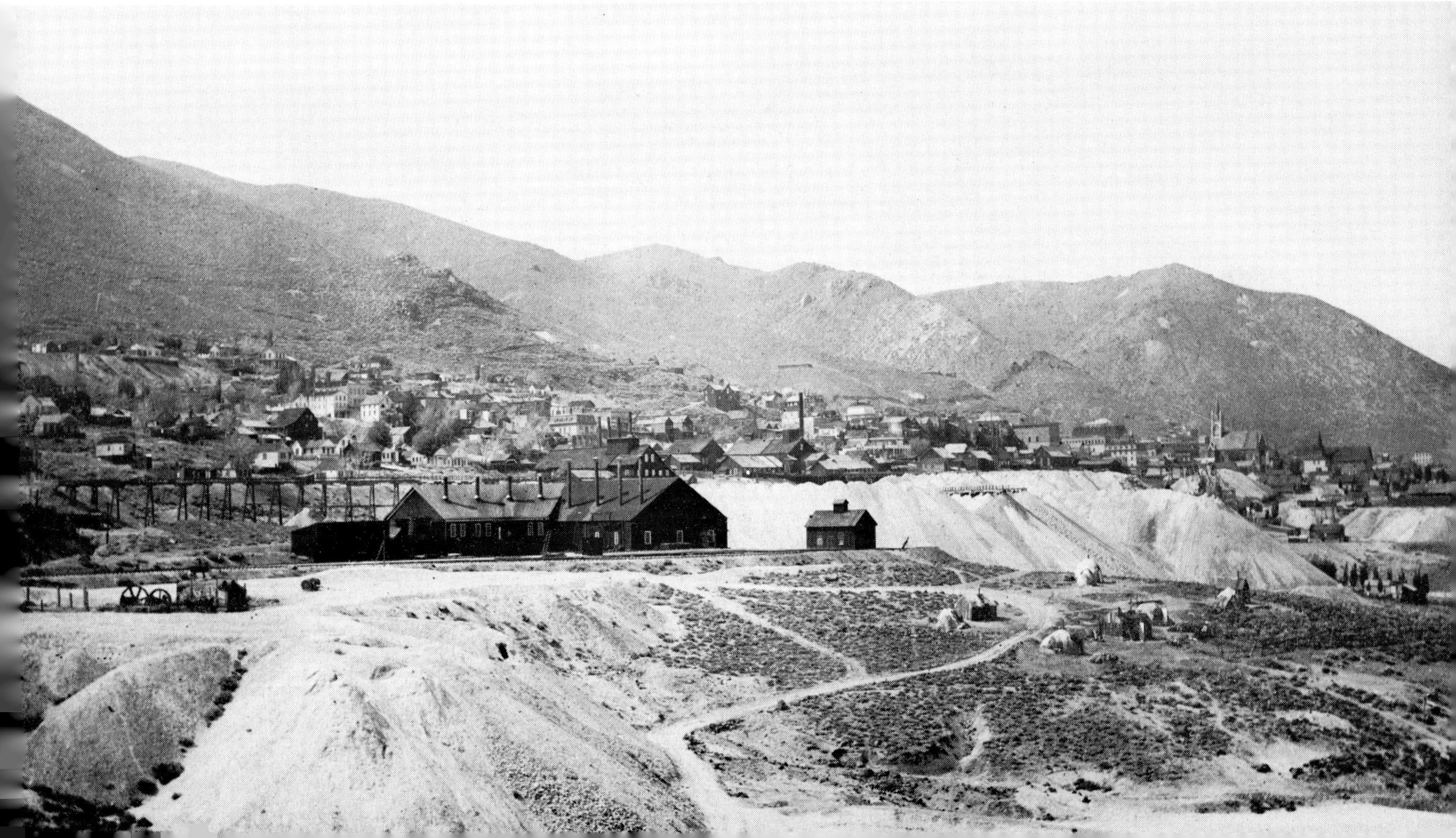

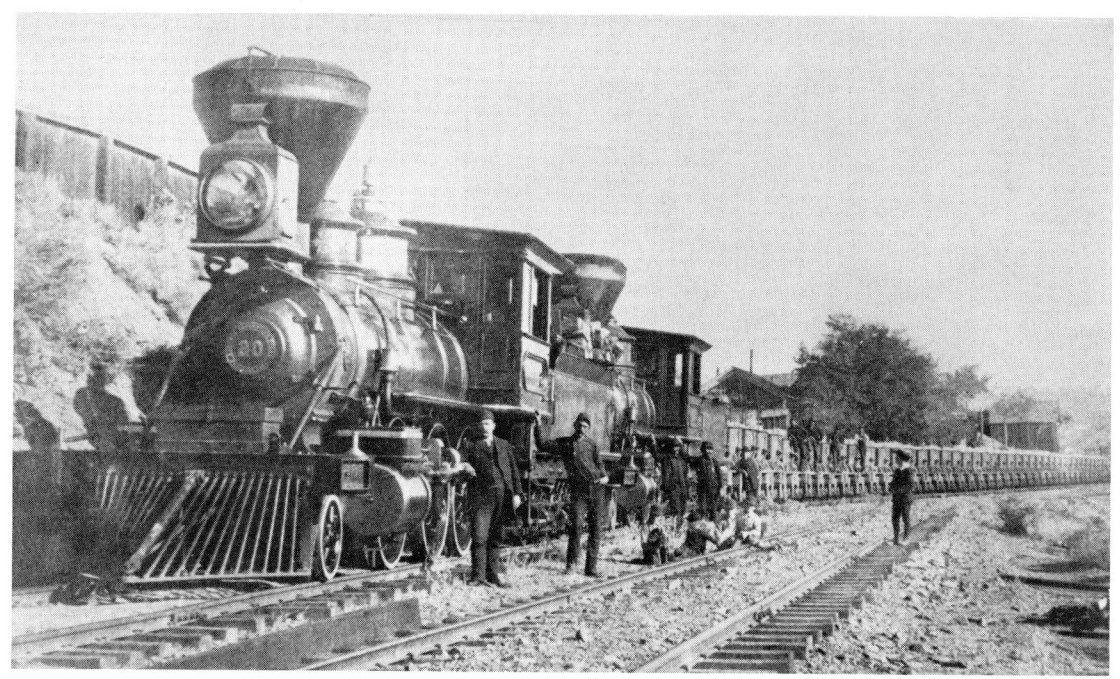

Although the V&T's early ore jimmies were small, light 4-wheeled bottom dump cars on a rigid frame, their individual weight when loaded was considerable in proportion to their size. Fortunately the loaded trains were eased downgrade over the 13½ miles to the mills along the Carson River, 1,575 feet lower, and only empty cars were hauled on the return uphill. Still, hand brakes prevailed, and in order to safeguard control of the cars on the steep grades, all mainline trains were normally double-headed. The freight *(above)* awaits clearance in Virginia City with approximately 30 loads for the hill. Four brakemen lounge on the sides of the cars while the two engineers, two firemen and the conductor strike casual poses for the benefit of the five admiring boys in the foreground.

The train with the single engine *(below)* is doing switching work on the Virginia City low-line. The locomotive VIRGINIA has just backed a cut of loaded ore cars from the C&C's bins out onto the huge trestle comprising the tail track of the switchback and stands ready to haul them up the grade through Tunnel No. 7 to a junction with the main line near the roundhouse. *(Upper: Grahame Hardy Collection; Lower: Southern Pacific Collection.)*

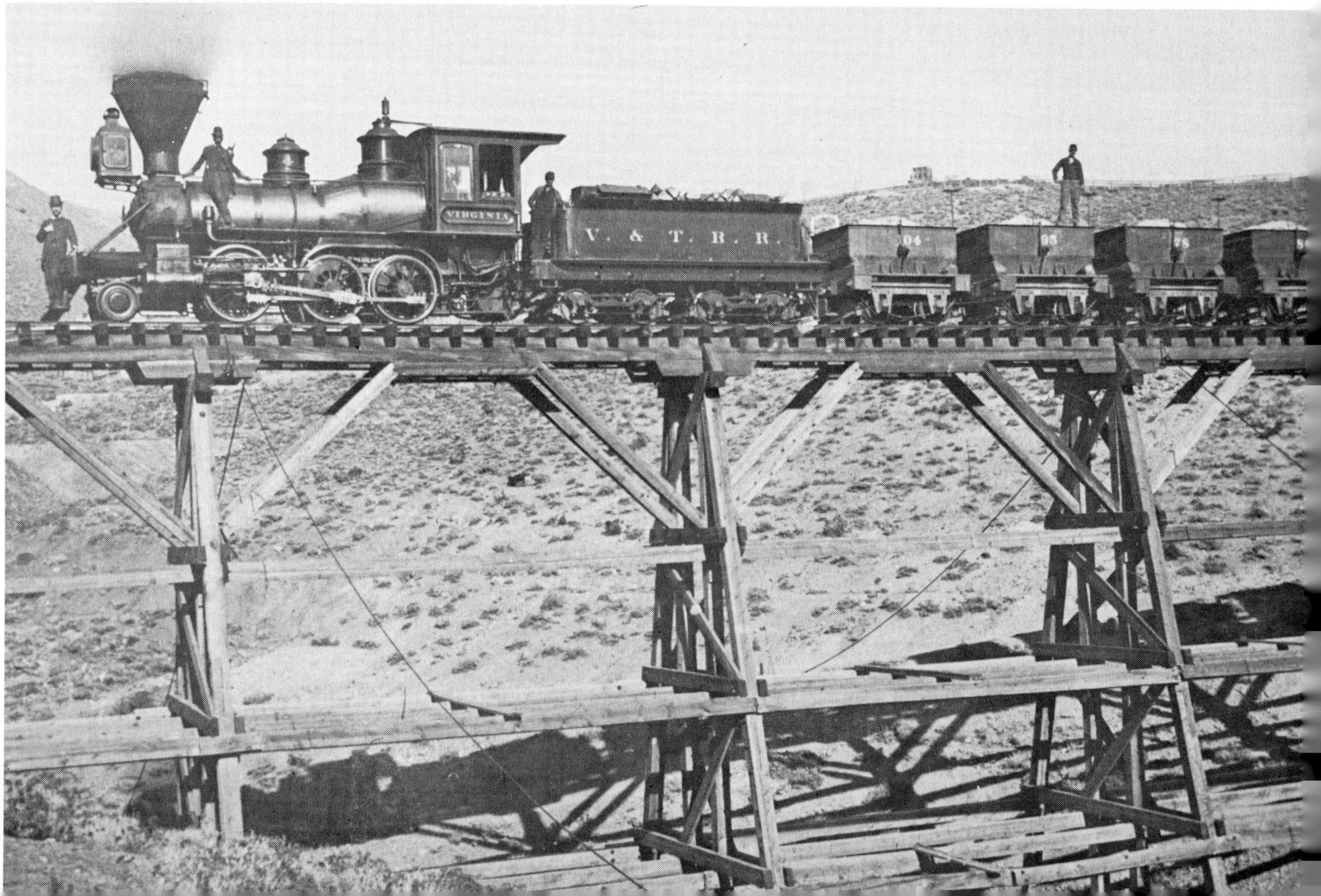

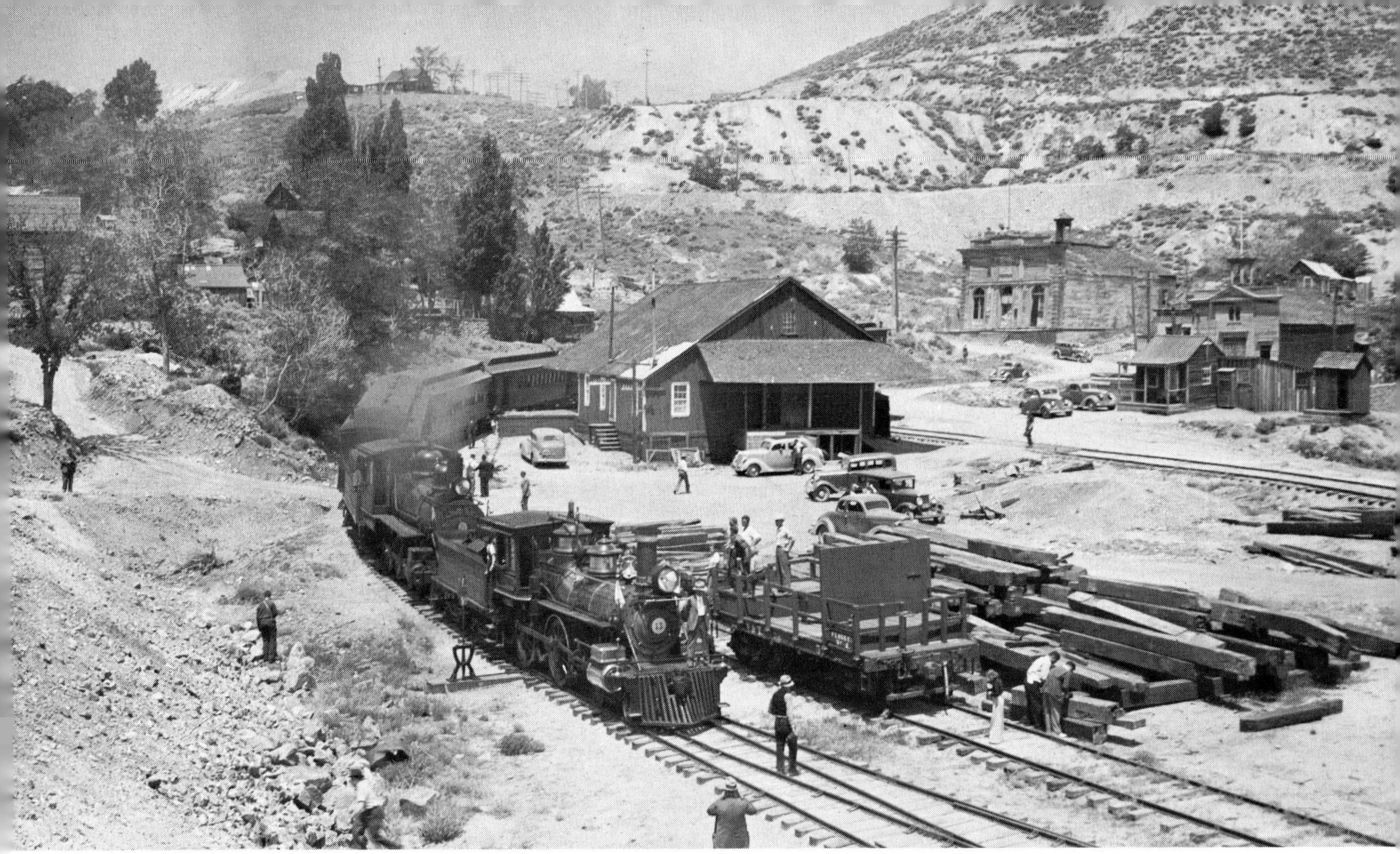

In the summer of 1938, a year before the Virginia City line was abandoned, this special passenger movement *(above)*, double-headed with American (4-4-0) No. 11 on the point, spiraled out of the curving Homestead Tunnel from Virginia City and pulled to a stop on the sharp reverse curvature at Gold Hill station. Flanger No. 2 sits idly by on the siding, harbinger of wintry storms to come which, in earlier years, frequently necessitated triple-heading with a pusher plow *(below)* for even the shortest trains. The train, in this memento of a by-gone era, is heading in the opposite direction, having just traversed the Crown Point Trestle and is currently whistling its approach to the Gold Hill station stop. *(Upper: Guy L. Dunscomb Photo; Bottom: Chester Barton Collection.)*

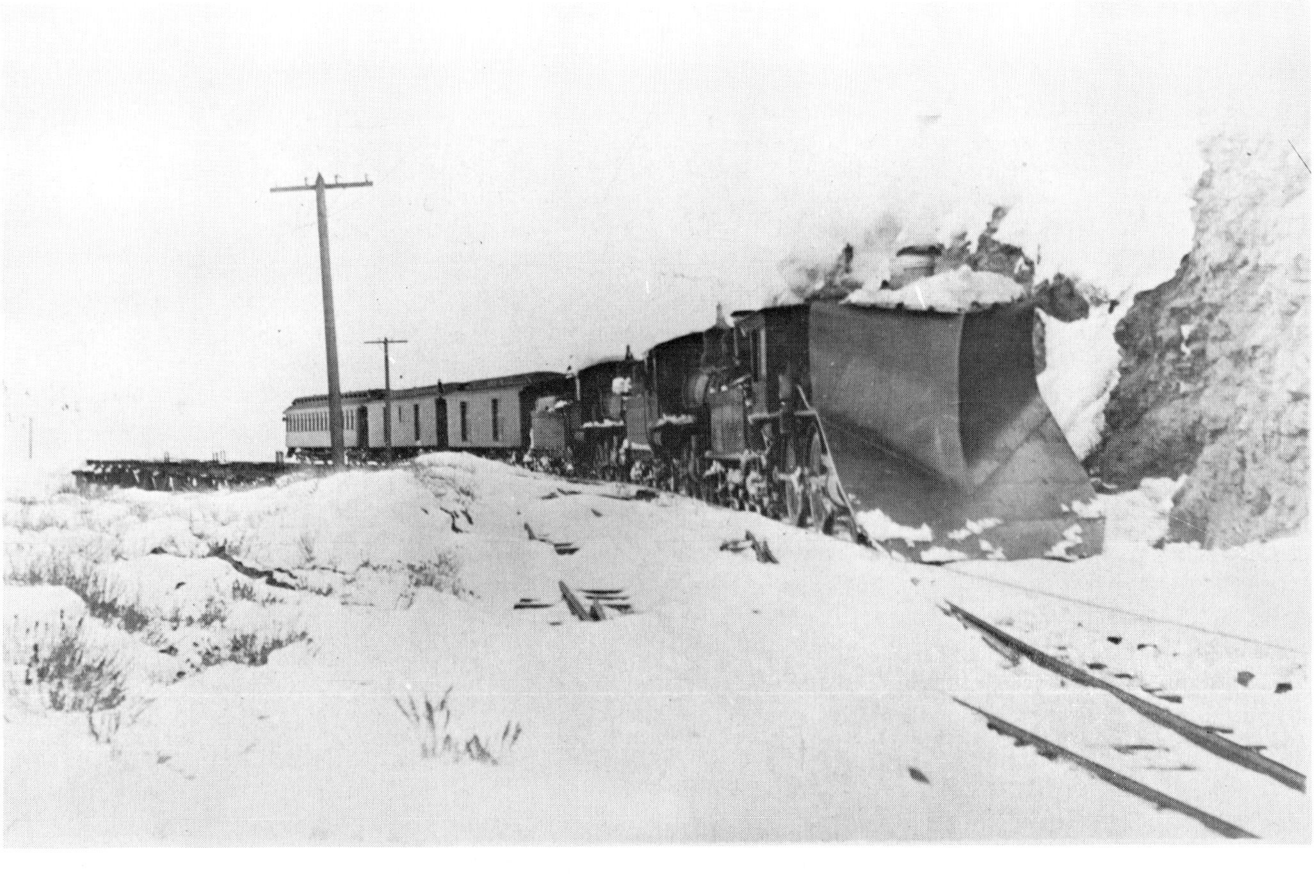

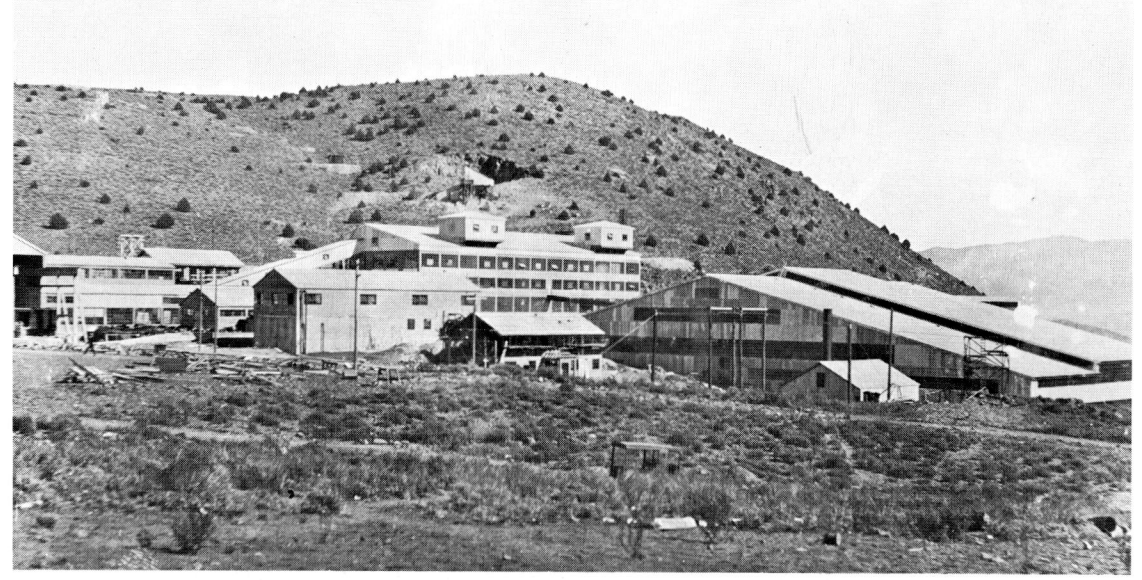

American Flat (probably in the 1880's) presented an impressive panorama. American City had been platted for location across the slopes of the valley through the center of the photo below the line of railroad. The tall stack in the near-center foreground marks the buildings and dumps of the Rock Island Mill, the siding for which leads directly (toward camera) to a connection with the V&T main line at The Scales station (right foreground). From Gold Hill (far right background) a double header freight is just visible as it rounds the shoulder of the hill ready to drop down the 2% (and greater) grade along the foot of the mountains. The deep railroad cut (left) is doubly protected by 6-foot snow fences, one above and one below the track, indicative of the varying winds and drifting snow anticipated in the winter months ahead. Below the railroad embankment is the cluster of buildings comprising part of the Jones Ranch, and just this side near the railroad crossing stands the old toll house and gate post. The railroad continues to circle the valley to right on a descending grade until it has made a gigantic "C," then dives through Tunnel No. 2, the "American Flat Tunnel," and comes out high on the cliff above American Ravine. The floor of the valley slopes downward to the right to the narrow neck of the canyon, just above the mouth of which, in the early 1920's, the last major mill in the area was erected. This was the United Comstock Merger Mine mill *(above)* which, although necessitating construction of the V&T's last major spur 1.6 miles in length on a continuous circular steep grade, failed to reach the anticipated volume of production and was shortly closed. *(Bottom: Grahame Hardy Collection.)*

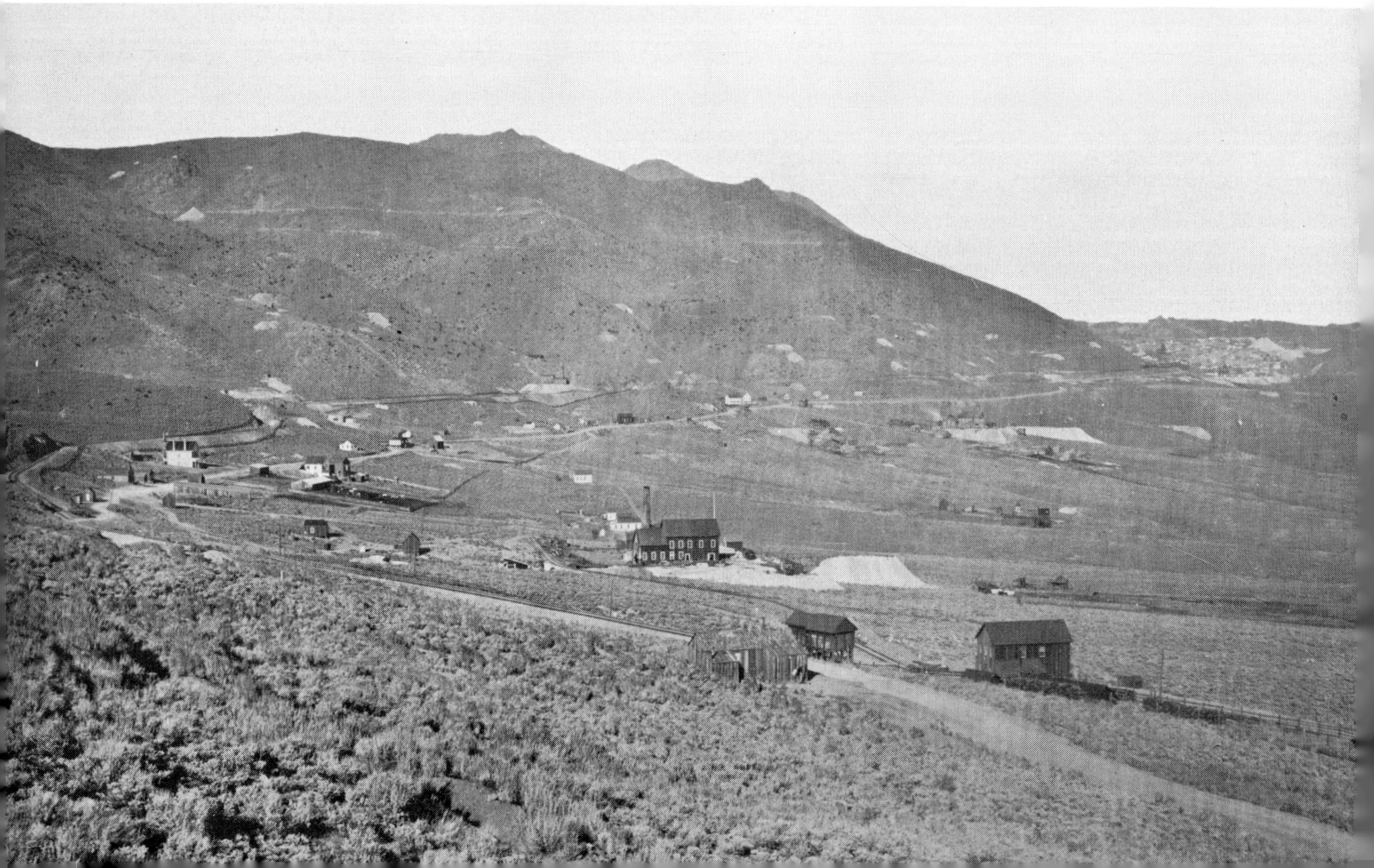

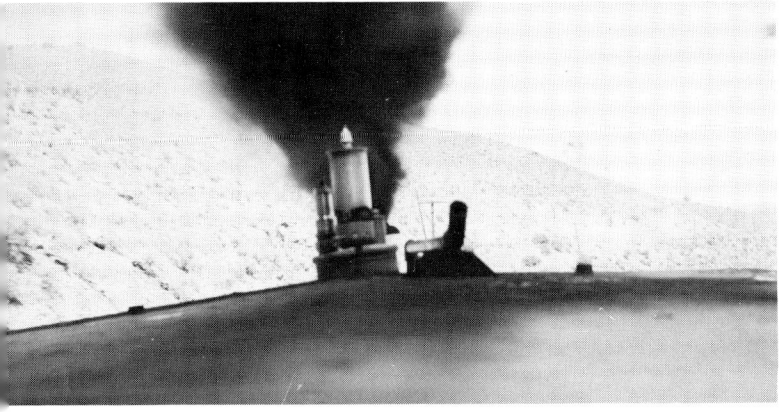

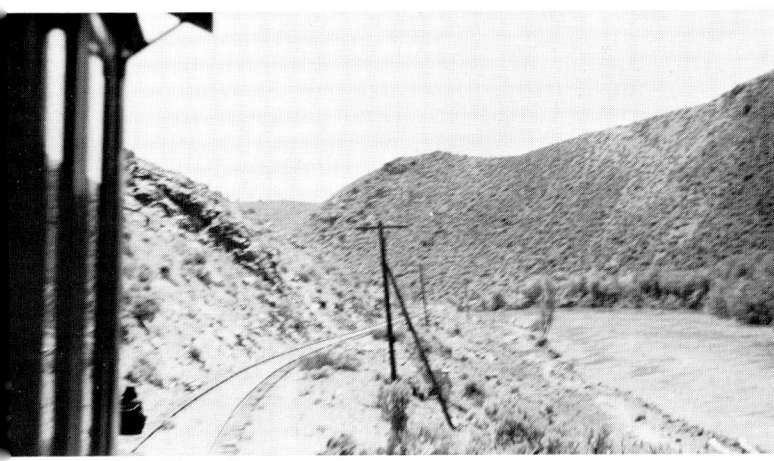

As quaintly photogenic in 1938 as it was in 1888, the V&T was beloved by railfans who made periodic visits to ride the colorful cars behind antique locomotives. Although converted to oil burners, the engines still maintained their original slide valve mechanisms and chuffed magnificently as they climbed the grade to Virginia City *(above)*. In the remote world of the Carson River valley *(center)*, or near Merrimac at a point colloquially called "double crossing" (both extremes of which are visible in the view *below*), the V&T reigned supreme. Cap-stacked American (4-4-0) No. 11 had been with the road since built by Baldwin in 1872; companion 10-wheeler (4-6-0) No. 27 was a product of the same works but of a later 1913 vintage. *(Three Photos: Ted Wurm.)*

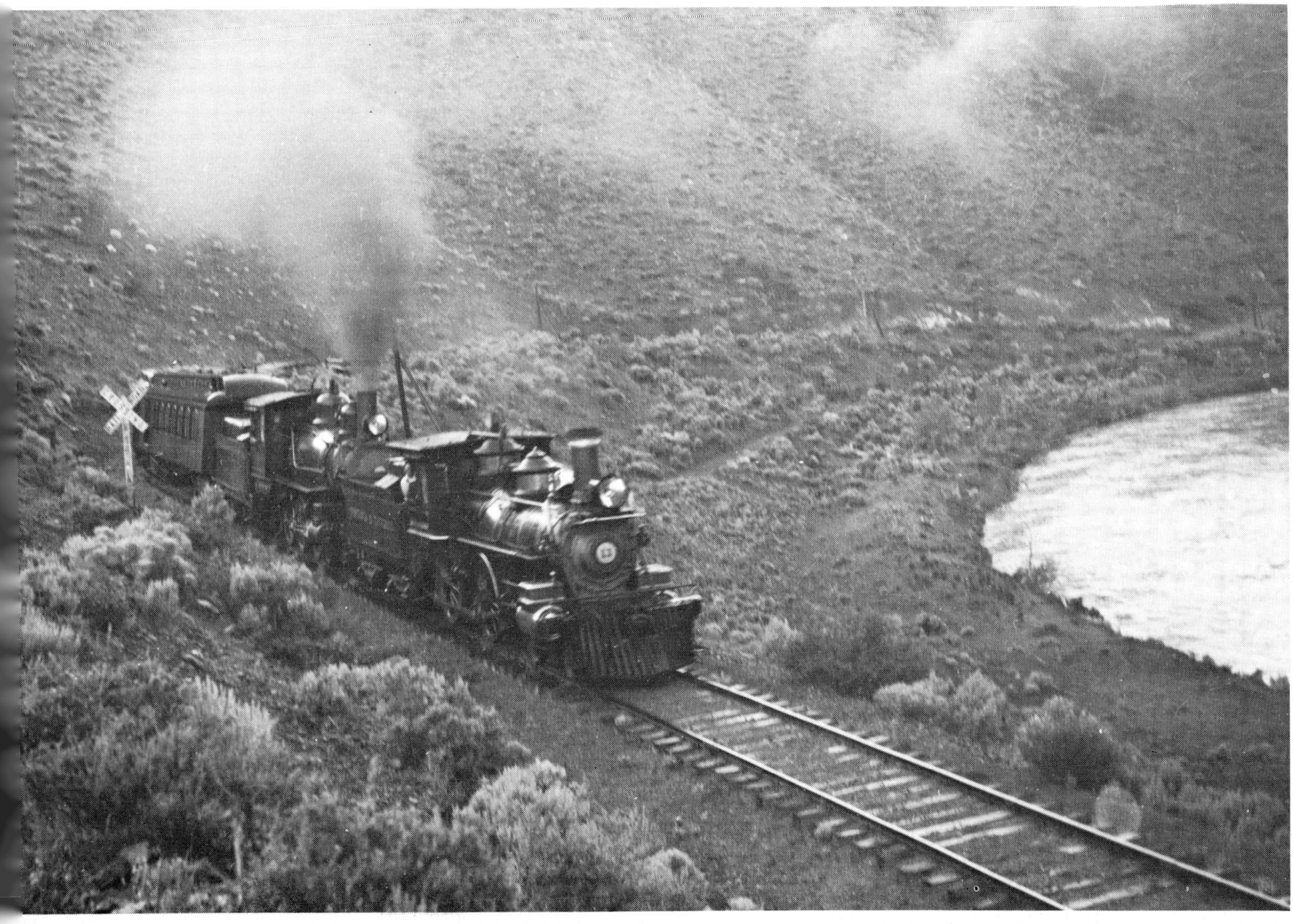

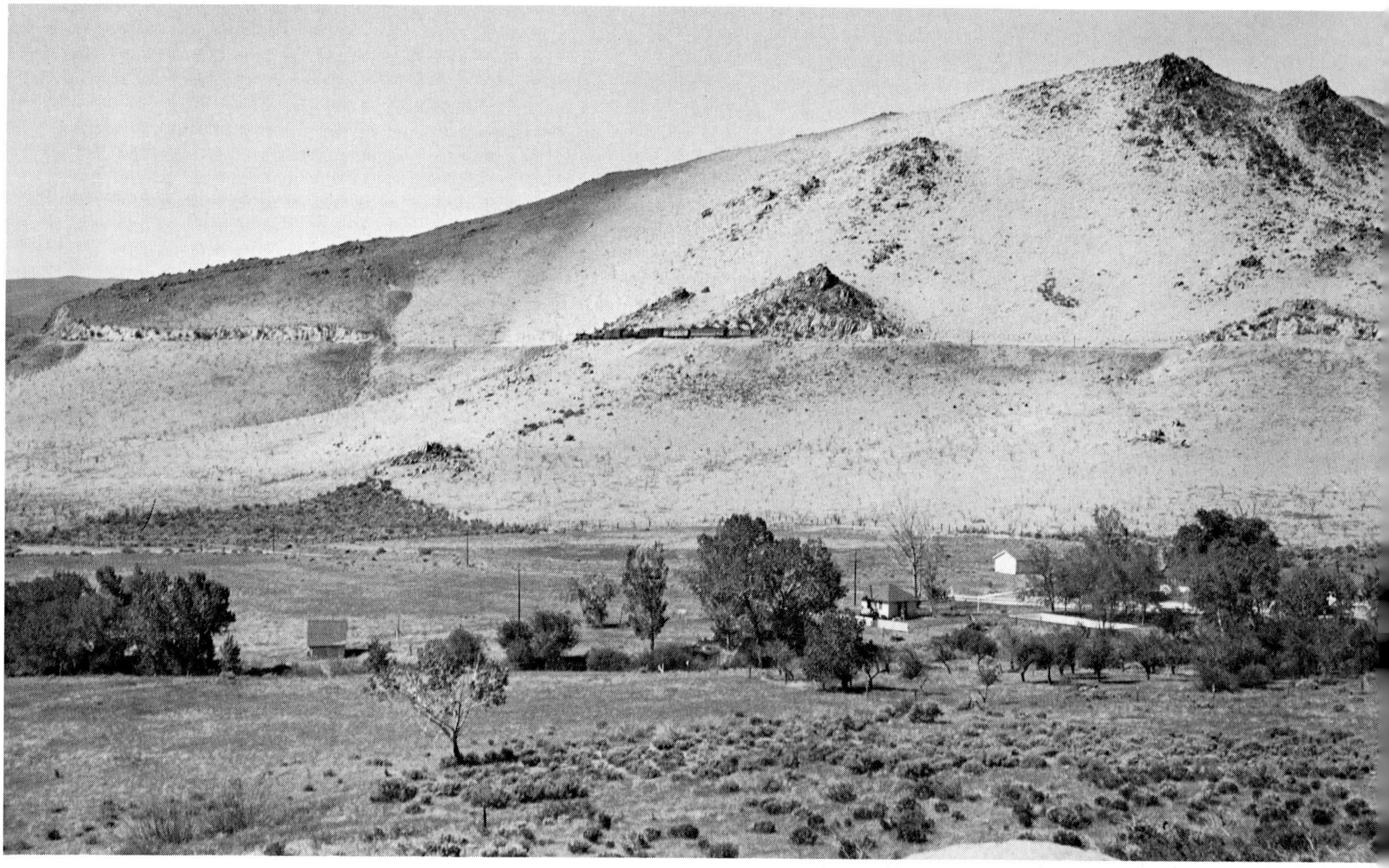

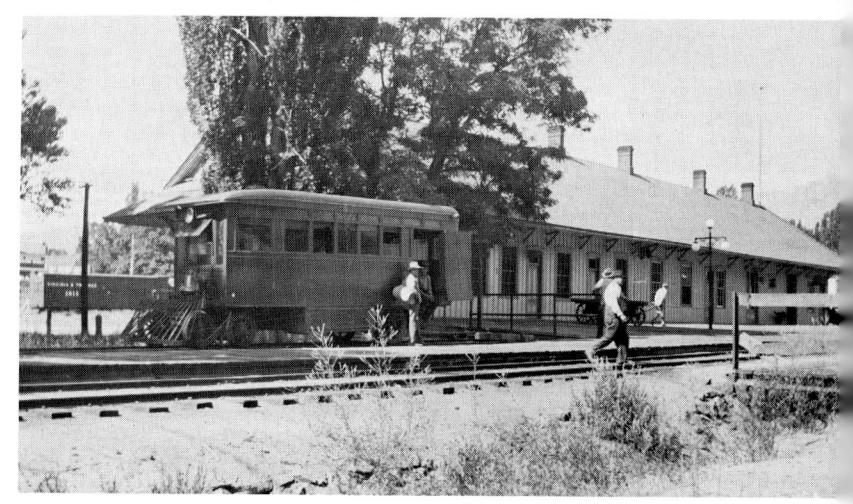
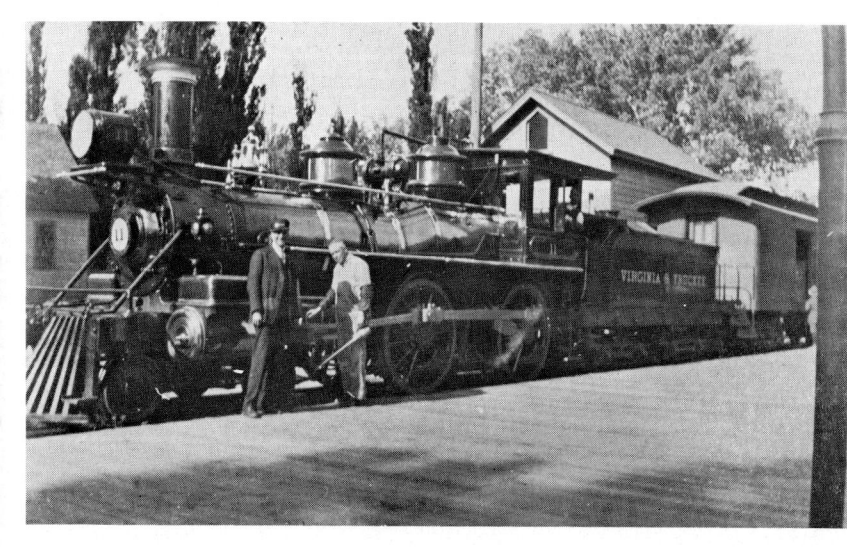

Carson City was the "home" of the Virginia & Truckee. From here it opened its original main line to Virginia City in 1870 to bring the products of the mines down to the mills along the Carson River a few miles east of town. That longer section of main, from Reno to Carson City, which provided connection with the Central Pacific, was not completed for another 2½ years. Extending south from Reno, it climbed the gentle slopes of Washoe Valley to Lakeview Summit, then dropped down the west slopes of Eagle Valley *(above, left)* to swing into town on a west-east axis. Except for the few buildings in the foreground, this train, captured on the last day of operations, might well have been the first. Tunnel No. 1 of the V&T lay just to the right out of the picture, and when it caved after the supporting timbers burned, a permanent shoo-fly was constructed around it.

The main offices of the V&T, along with the normal complement of station facilities were housed in this long, low, warmly picturesque structure surrounded by Lombardi poplars. The freight house for the alternate by-pass route on the street behind can be seen in the background, while the ornate platform lights, the horse and carriage, and the vintage auto confirm the 1914 photo dating. The V&T combine at the rear of the eastbound train was, like the railroad, ageless. In the two alternate views *(below, left)* we see the V&T's motor car whose large, lacy pilot and oversize locomotive bell belie the power of the tiny gasoline motor within. Oddly enough, it was not used on the relatively level Minden branch, but on the rugged grades of the Virginia City line. Locomotive No. 11, with its polished bell and shiny boiler appears as though it had just been reconditioned in the Carson City shops prior to taking this westbound train to Reno. *(Left, Top: Brian Thompson Photo; Center: L. J. Ciapponi Photo; Bottom: Nevada Historical Society; Right: Southern Pacific Collection.)*

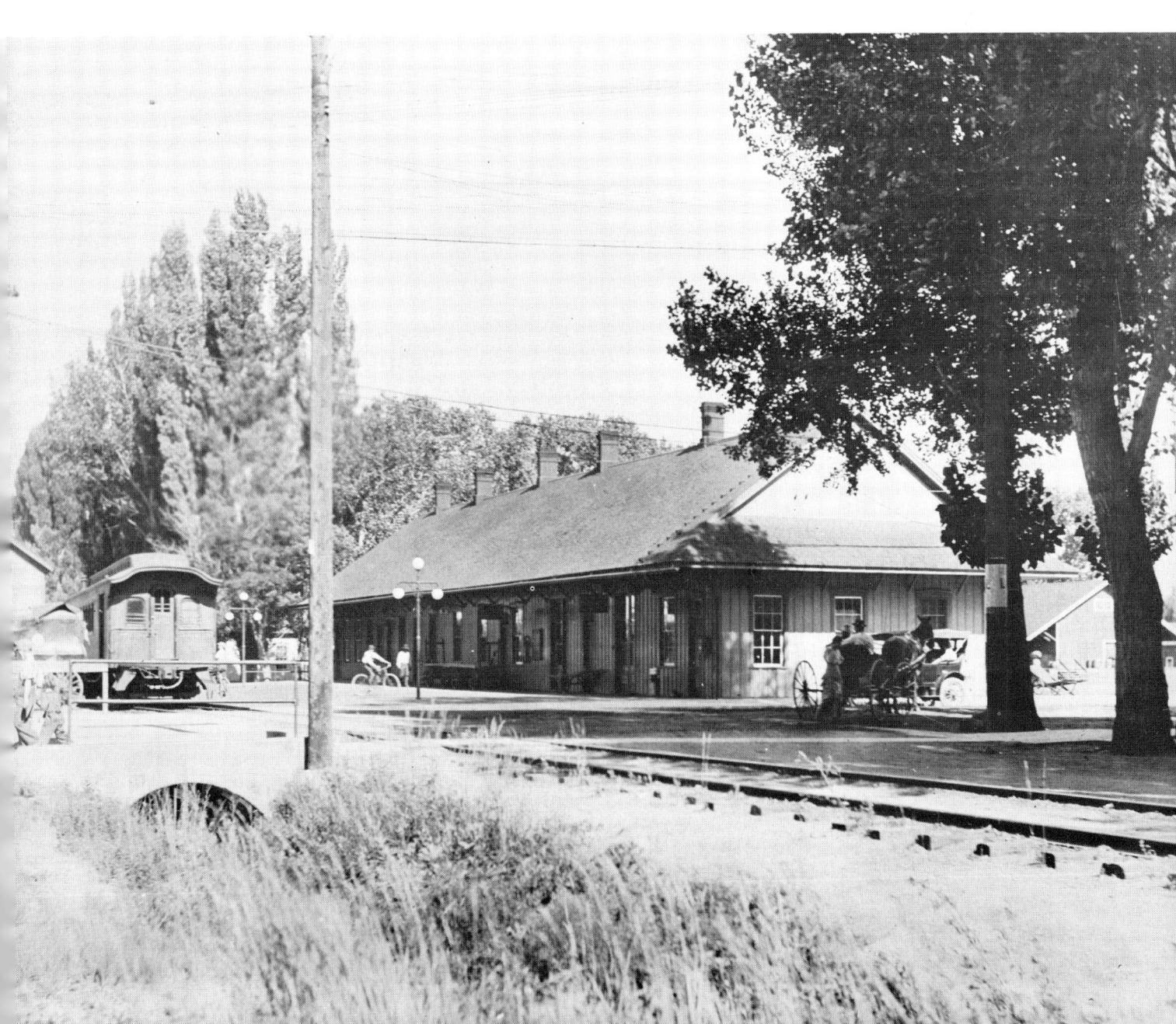

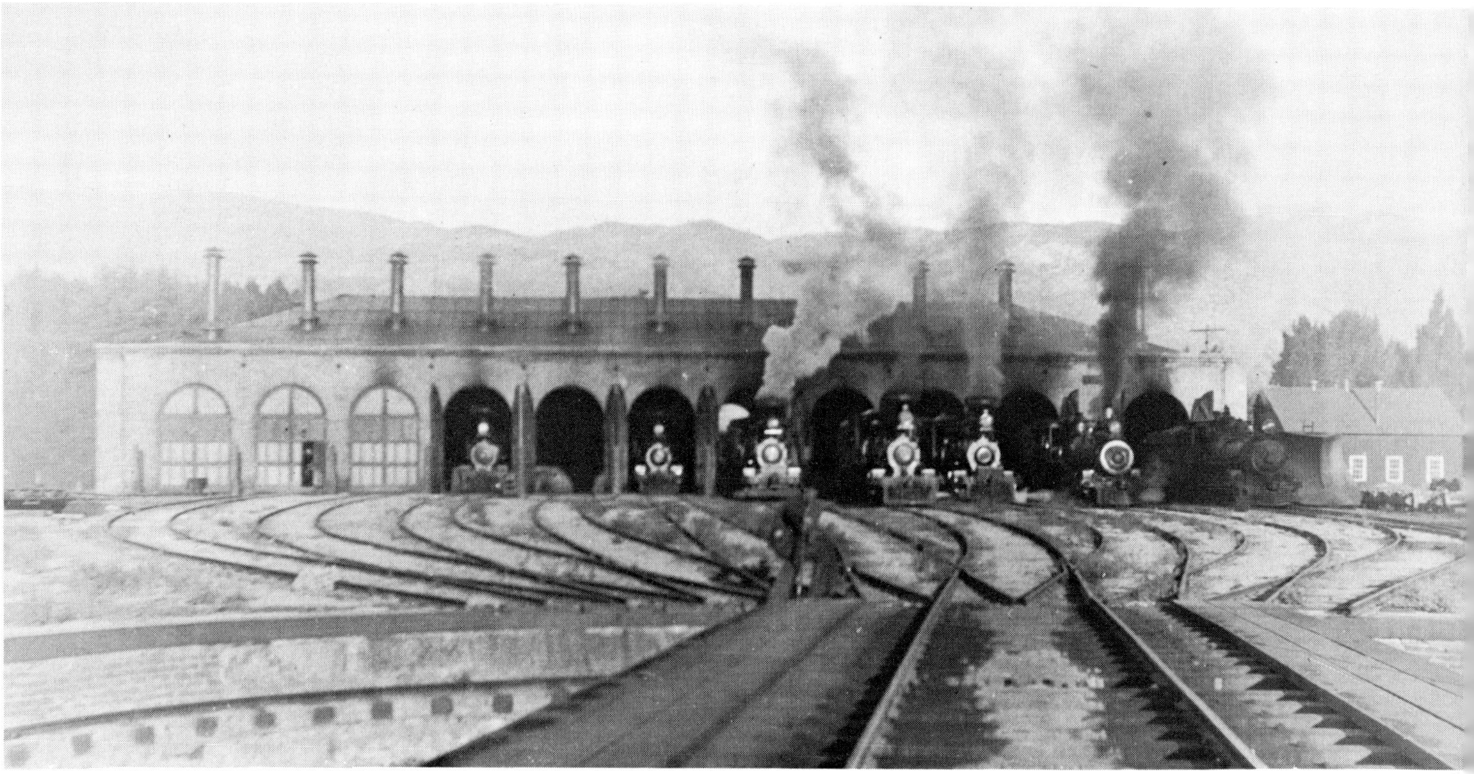

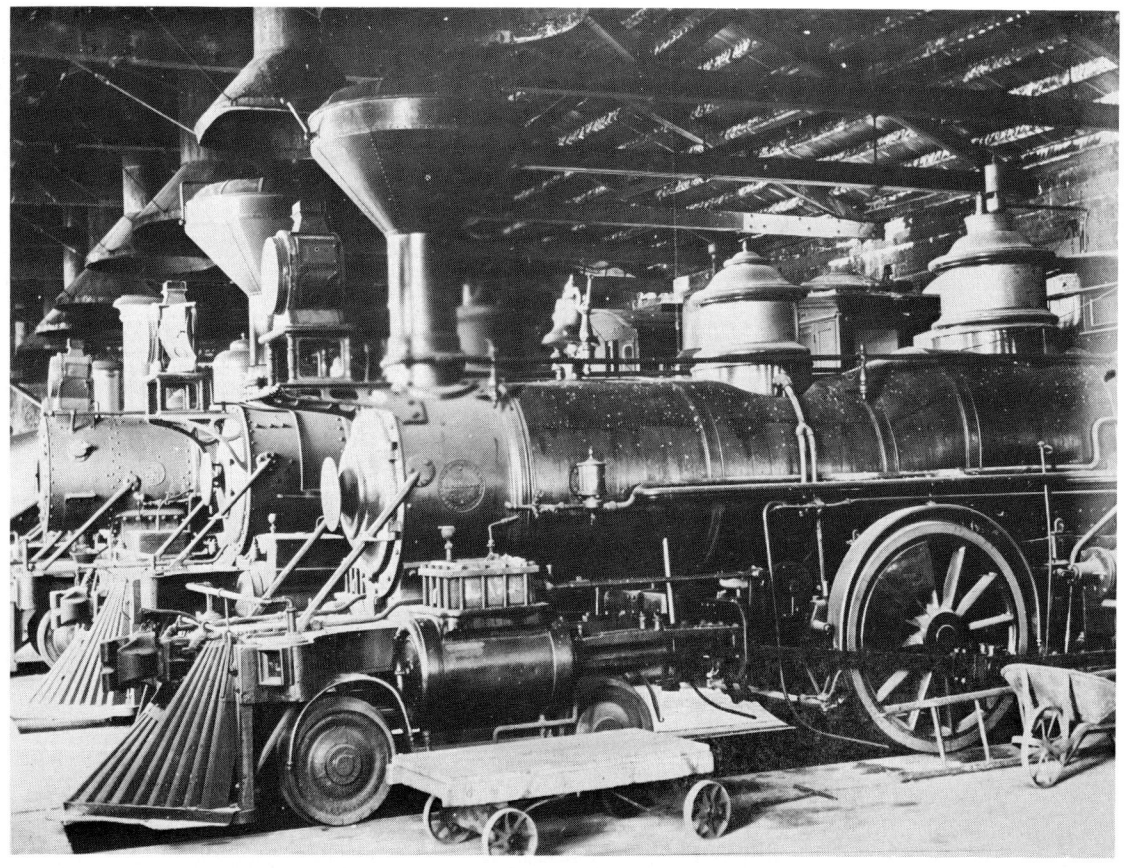

No composite of V&T shops and facilities would be complete without this impressive view of 10 tracks converging on the Carson City turntable. Although only the broad front of the engine house portion of the building is visible in the scene *(above)* or the 1914 interior, the machine, foundry and heavy repair shops extended for a block and a half to the rear. A satellite cordon of lesser buildings surrounding the area provided such auxiliary facilities as material yards, blacksmith and forging shop, power house, etc. For the V&T not only took care of its own, but it built machinery and repaired locomotives for industries and railroads throughout the countryside. On the page opposite in an early-day scene, No. 20, the TAHOE, and No. 24, the MERRIMAC, wood up in the Carson City yards with the smoke jacks of the engine house just visible in the background; while *(below)* is the contrast of the last train to Minden on the day the railroad closed down forever. The side wall of the rugged shop building may be seen immediately to left of the locomotive, and the abandoned grade of the freight by-pass crosses beneath the tender, heading toward the long-neglected precincts of Virginia City. *(Left, Bottom: Southern Pacific Collection; Right, Top: Vic Goodwin Collection; Bottom: Brian Thompson Photo.)*

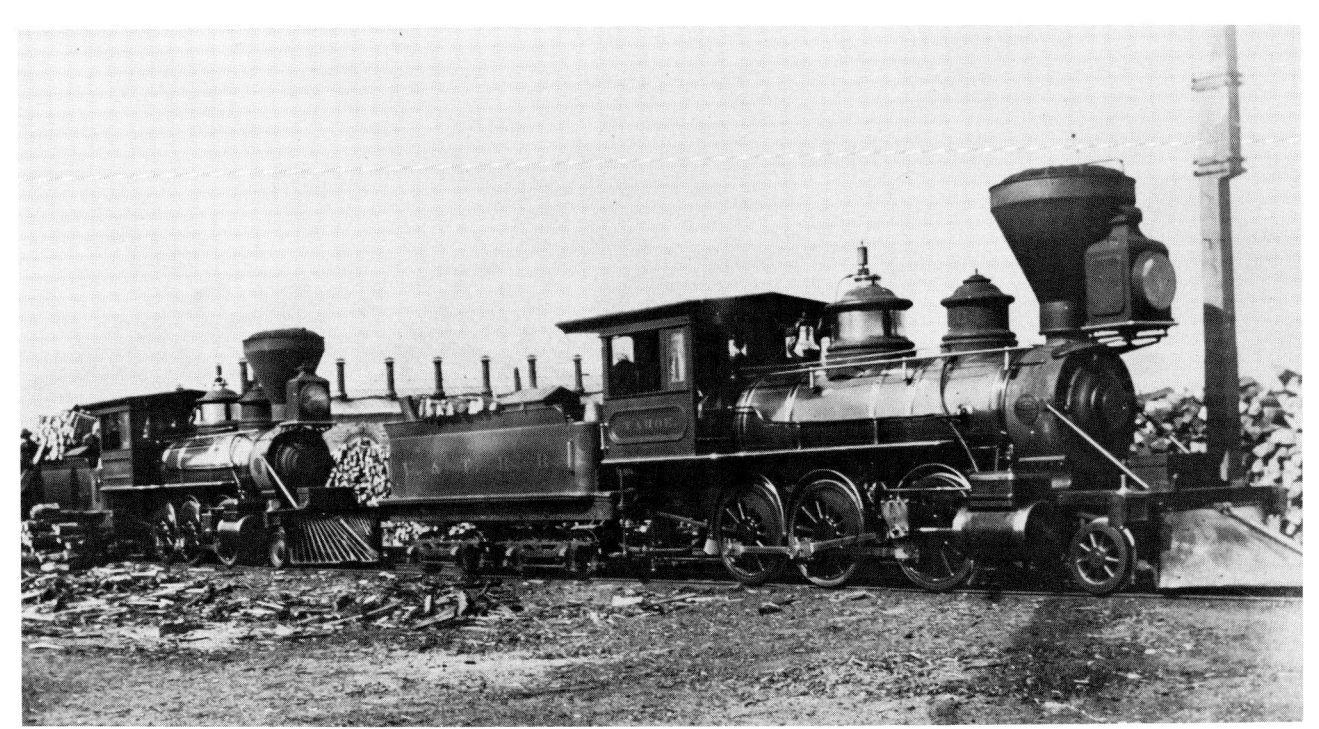

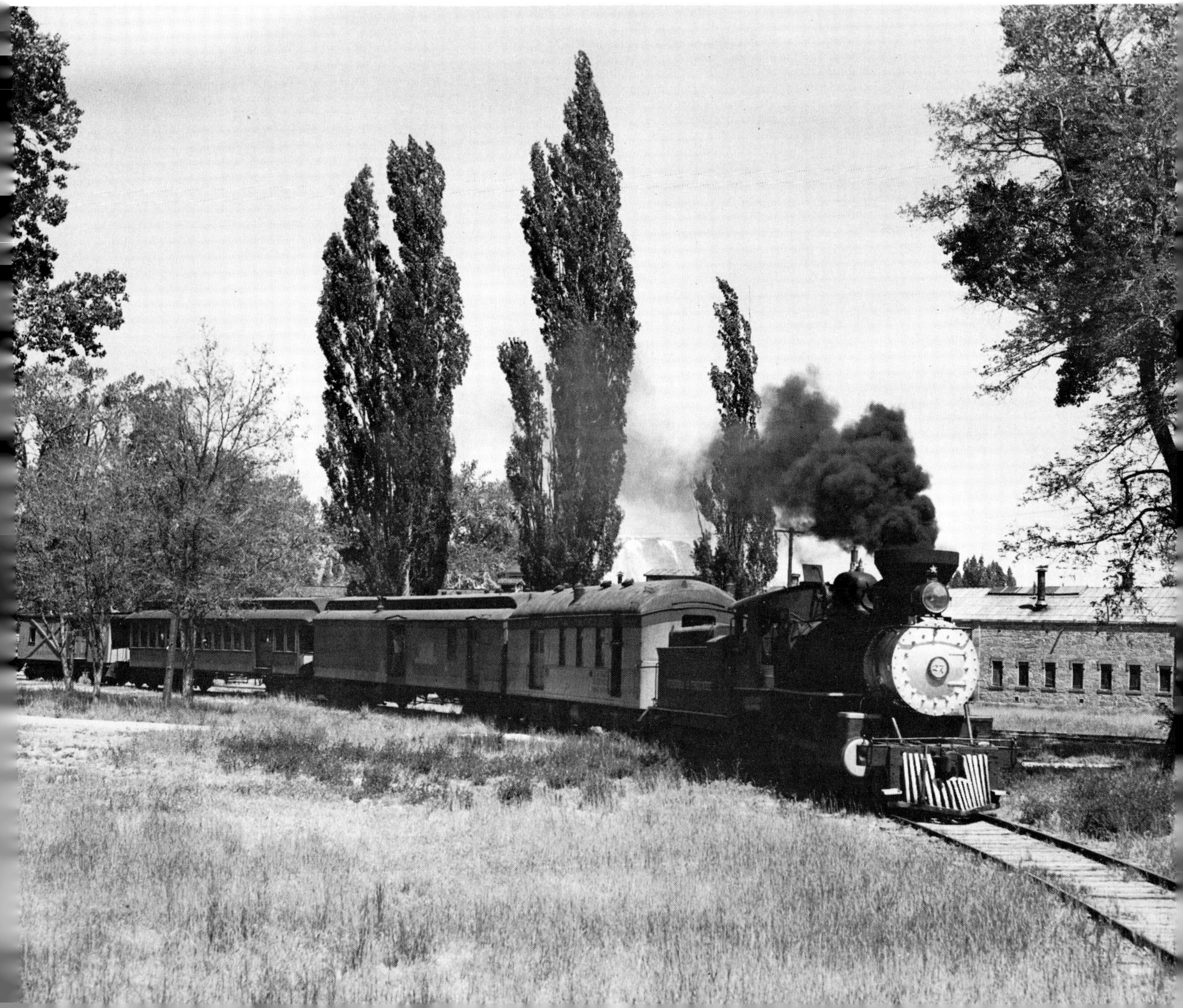

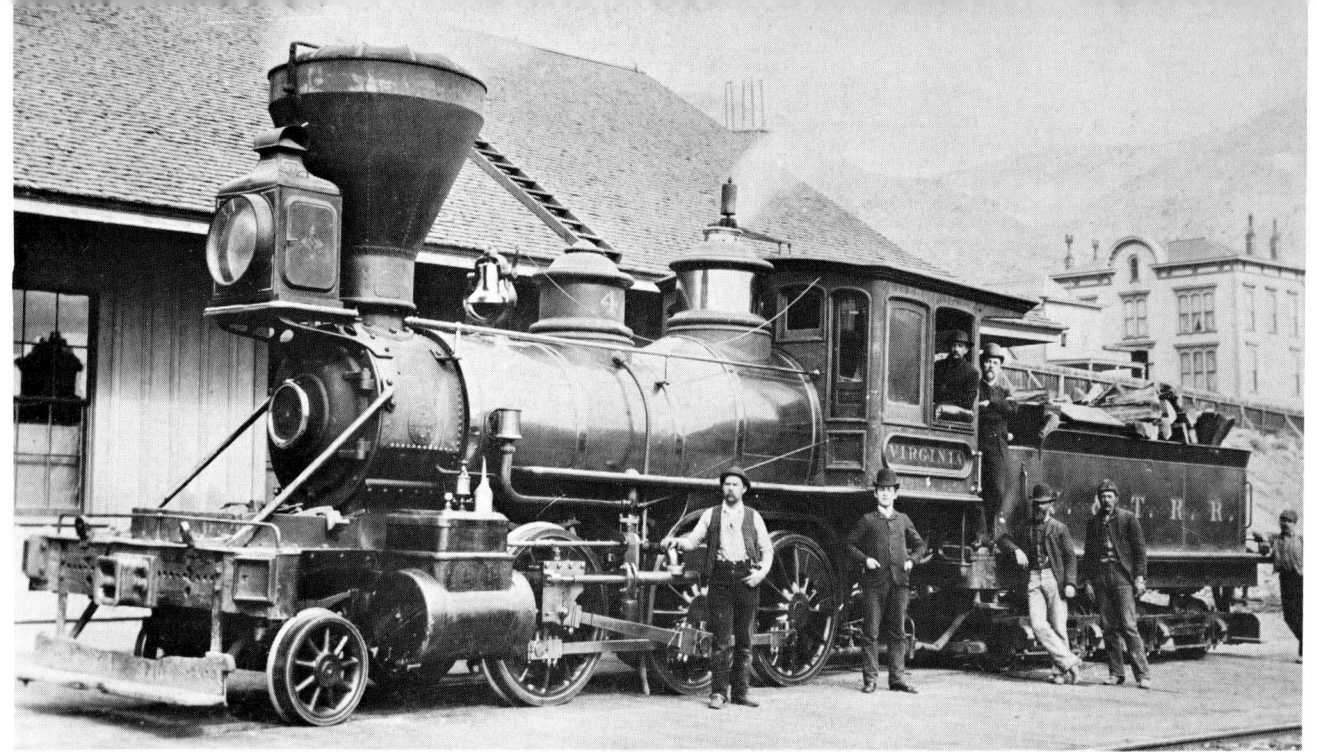

V&T motive power was picturesque and unique. No. 4, the VIRGINIA, was one of the original five locomotives purchased from Baldwin in 1869. Today, the 2-6-0 Mogul wheel arrangement appears considerably disrupted by the splash guard over only the rear two drivers nearest the firebox, while the vacant pockets on the pilot beam for the link-and-pin couplings of the period seem incongruous.

No. 11, the RENO, was both a workhorse and a *belle vivante* of the V&T. Product of Baldwin in 1872, this locomotive was used variously in freight service, snow plow duties, or pulling the road's passenger varnish. In the view *(top, right)* we see No. 11 on the point of a double-headed passenger special with No. 27 at Minden in 1941, while below *(center, right)* she rests at Scales for a moment from freight switching maneuvers under the tutelage of engineer Grover Russell in 1938.

Second No. 25 was a Baldwin 10-wheeler (4-6-0) of 1905 (replacing First No. 25, a Rhode Island American 4-4-0 of 1889 purchased from the Union Pacific in 1901 and resold in 1902). She looked resplendent *(below)* taking water at the Franktown tank (Flying ME Ranch) about 1907, and but little changed in 1955 *(below, right)* when she took part in the UP ceremonies commemorating the 50th Anniversary of the Los Angeles & Salt Lake (Salt Lake Route). *(Left, Top: Southern Pacific; Bottom: S. G. Palmer; Right, Center: Ted Wurm; Top and Bottom: Guy L. Dunscomb.)*

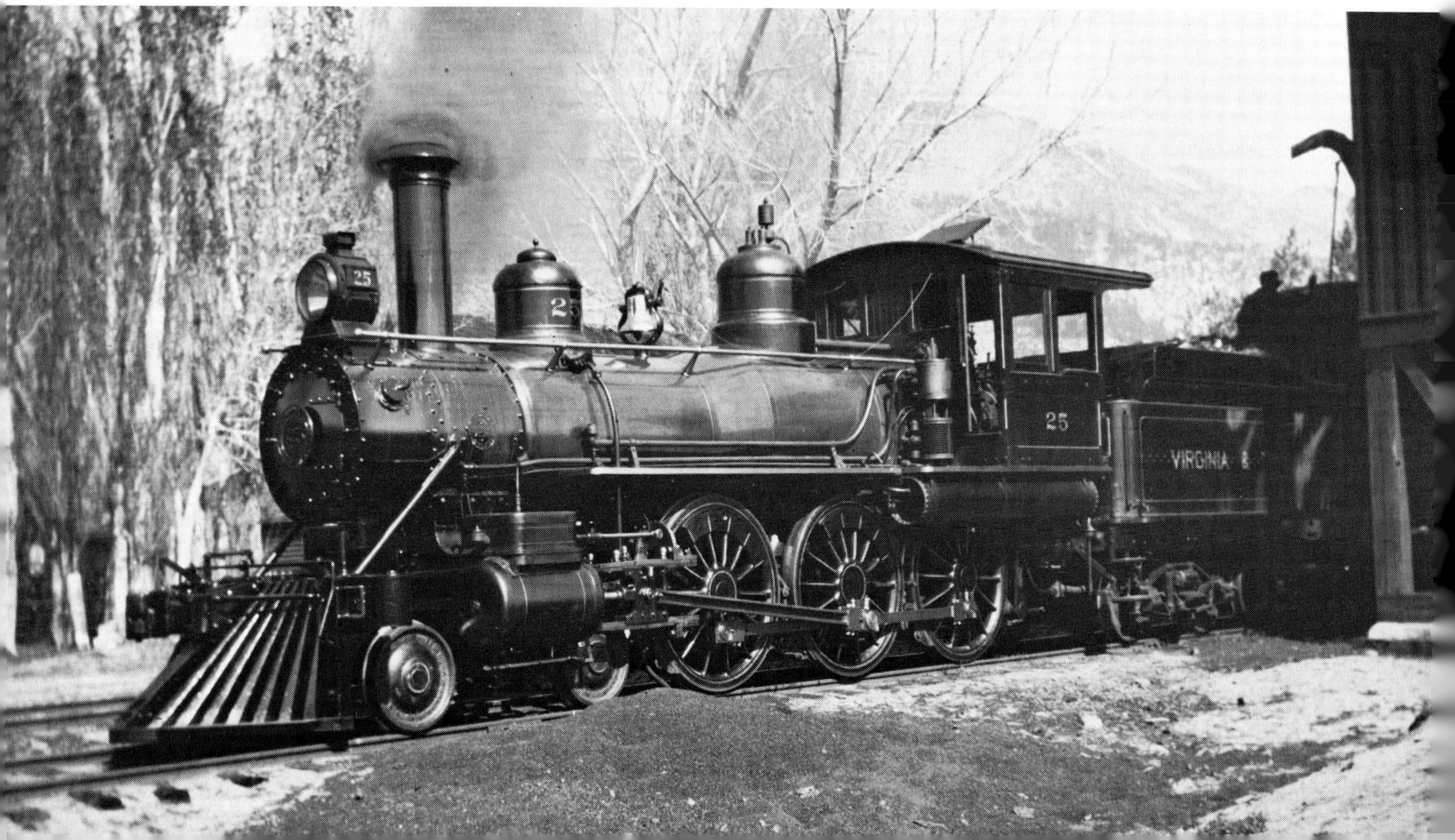

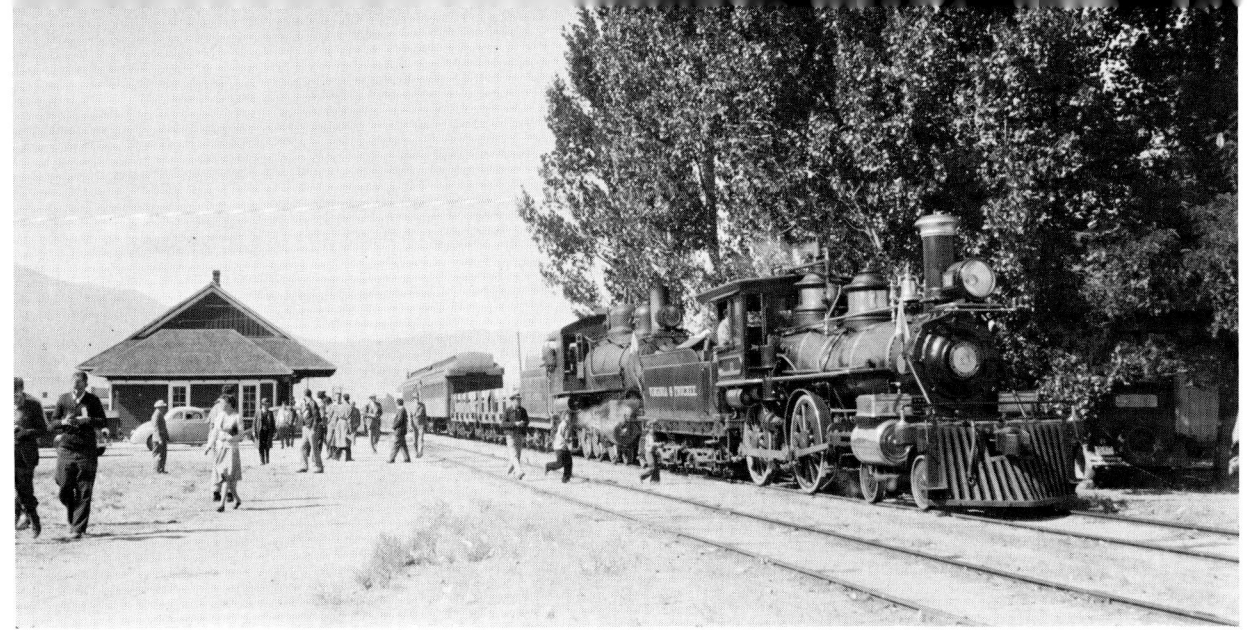

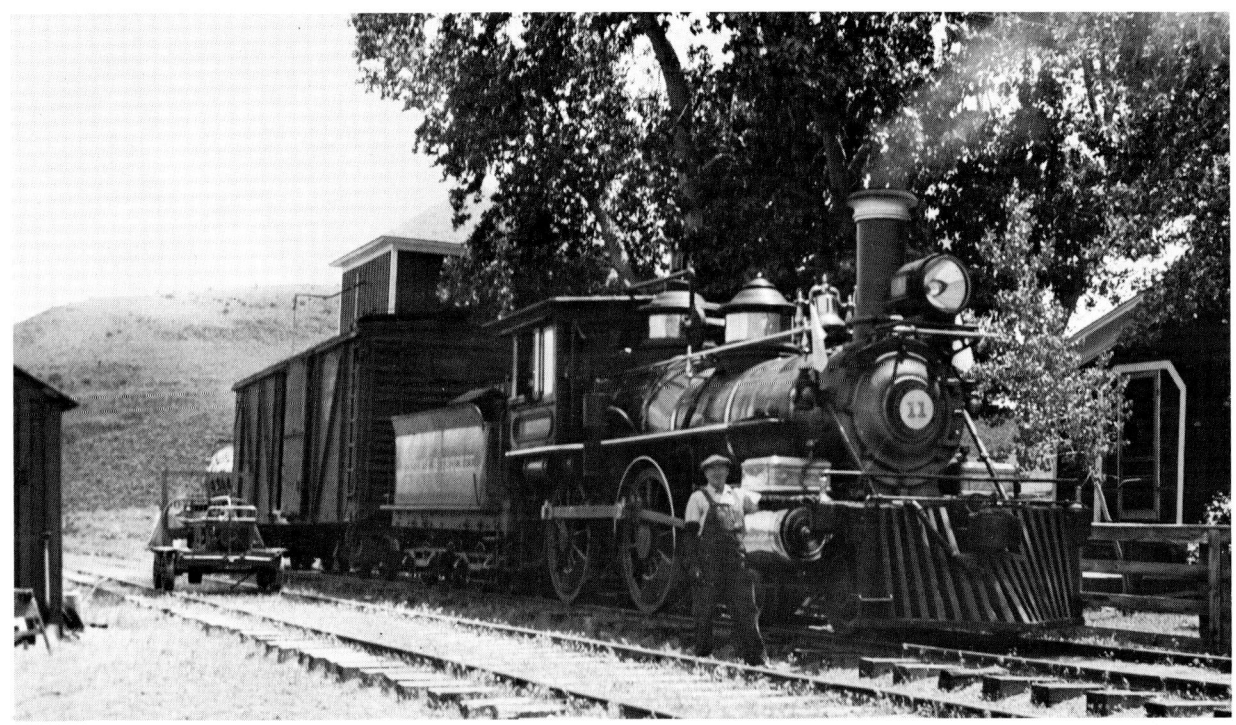

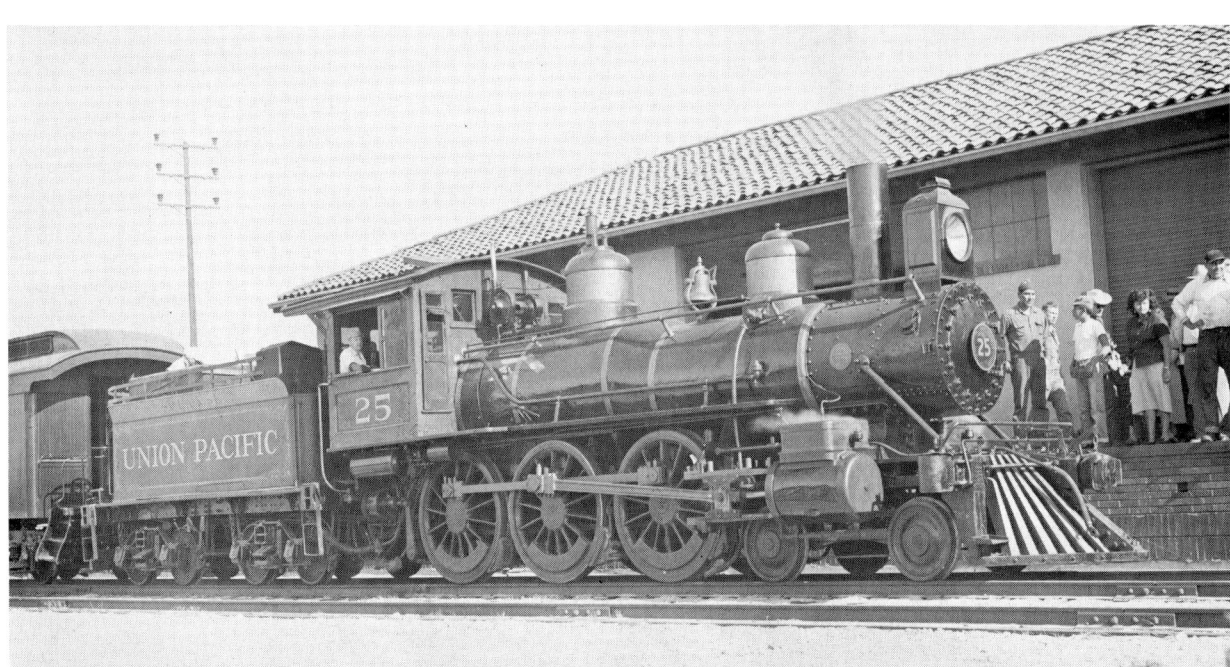

VIRGINIA AND TRUCKEE RAILROAD.

TIME TABLE NO. 1.

To take effect Monday, July 11, 1870, at 6 o'clock A. M.

For the government and information of Employees only, and is not intended for the public. The Company reserves the right to vary the same as circumstances may require.

TRAINS GOING EAST.							Distances from Carson	NAMES OF STATIONS.	Distances from Virginia	TRAINS GOING WEST.						
No. 13	No. 11 Pass.	No. 9	No. 7	No. 5	No. 3 Pass.	No. 1				No. 2 Pass.	No. 4	No. 6	No. 8	No. 10	No. 12 Pass.	No. 14
P. M. 6.00	P. M. 4.00	P. M. 2.00	M. 12.00	A. M. 10.00	A. M. 8.00	A. M. 6.00	To	Carson	21	A. M. 8.00	A. M. 10.00	M. 12.00	P. M. 2.00	P. M. 4.00	P. M. 6.00	P. M. 8.00
6.17	4.17	2.17	12.17 P.M.	10.17	8.17	6.17	3¼	Mexican	17¾	7.45	9.45	11.45	1.45	3.45	5.45	7.45
6.22	4.22	2.22	12.22	10.22	8.22	6.22	4	Morgan	17	7.38	9.38	11.38	1.38	3.38	5.38	7.38
6.28	4.28	2.28	12.28	10.28	8.28	6.28	5	Brunswick	16	7.30	9.30	11.30	1.30	3.30	5.30	7.30
6.33	4.33	2.33	12.33	10.33	8.33	6.33	5½	Merrimac	15½	7.25	9.25	11.25	1.25	3.25	5.25	7.25
7.00	**5.00**	**3.00**	**1.00**	**11.00**	**9.00**	**7.00**	10	Mound House	11	**7.00**	**9.00**	**11.00**	**1.00**	**3.00**	**5.00**	**7.00**
7.18	5.18	3.18	1.18	11.18	9.18	7.18	12¾	Silver	8¼	6.45	8.45	10.45	12.45	2.45	4.45	6.45
7.40	5.40	3.40	1.40	11.40	9.40	7.40	16½	Scales	4½	6.25	8.25	10.25	12.25	2.25	4.25	6.25
7.48	5.48	3.48	1.48	11.48	9.48	7.48	17½	Baltic	3½	6.12	8.12	10.12	12.12	2.12	4.12	6.12
7.52	5.52	3.52	1.52	11.52	9.52	7.52	18	Crown Point	3	6.08	8.08	10.08	12.08	2.08	4.08	6.08
8.00	**6.00**	**4.00**	**2.00**	**12.00**	**10.00**	**8.00**	19	Gold Hill	2	**6.00**	**8.00**	**10.00**	**12.00** M.	**2.00**	**4.00**	**6.00**
8.25	6.15	4.20	2.20	12.20	10.15	8.20	21	Virginia	To	5.30	7.45	9.30	11.30 A.M.	1.30	3.45	5.30

READ DOWN ← → READ UP

MR. H. HUNTER, Train Dispatcher, is authorized to move Trains by Telegraph or otherwise. ☞ Trains run daily.
Conductor's attention is called to Special Rules governing the movements of Trains by Telegraph.
No Conductor will leave Carson or Gold Hill without ascertaining if there are any orders, and if all Trains due have arrived.
The **FULL FACED FIGURES** denote meeting and passing places.

FROM RICHARD ENGLISH COLLECTION
COPYRIGHT, 1950, GRAHAME HARDY

H. M. YERINGTON, Supt.

---

attached, passed for the first time clear through to the terminus of the railroad near the Gould & Curry Works at Virginia City . . ." Two days later a V&T advertisement announced that, effective February 1, the passenger train would leave Carson City at 9:00 A.M. for Virginia City; returning, the train would leave Virginia City station at 2:45 P.M. and Gold Hill at 3:00 P.M. From Virginia City the fare to Gold Hill was 25 cents, while the full ride to Carson City cost $2.00. Supplementing the passenger service was a complement of four scheduled freight trains a day in each direction.

Thus the most difficult portion of the road was completed (from breaking of ground to scheduled operations) in just a little over 11 months' time. When Sharon wanted action, he got it.

The advent of the iron horse brought an immediate reduction in the cost of transporting wood of from one-third to one-half that of the teamsters' rates. With such savings being demonstrated, it was only natural that a two-mile extension west from Carson City was constructed during 1870 to reach the end of Yerington's four-mile flume in Kings Canyon. In the fall another 1½-mile branch

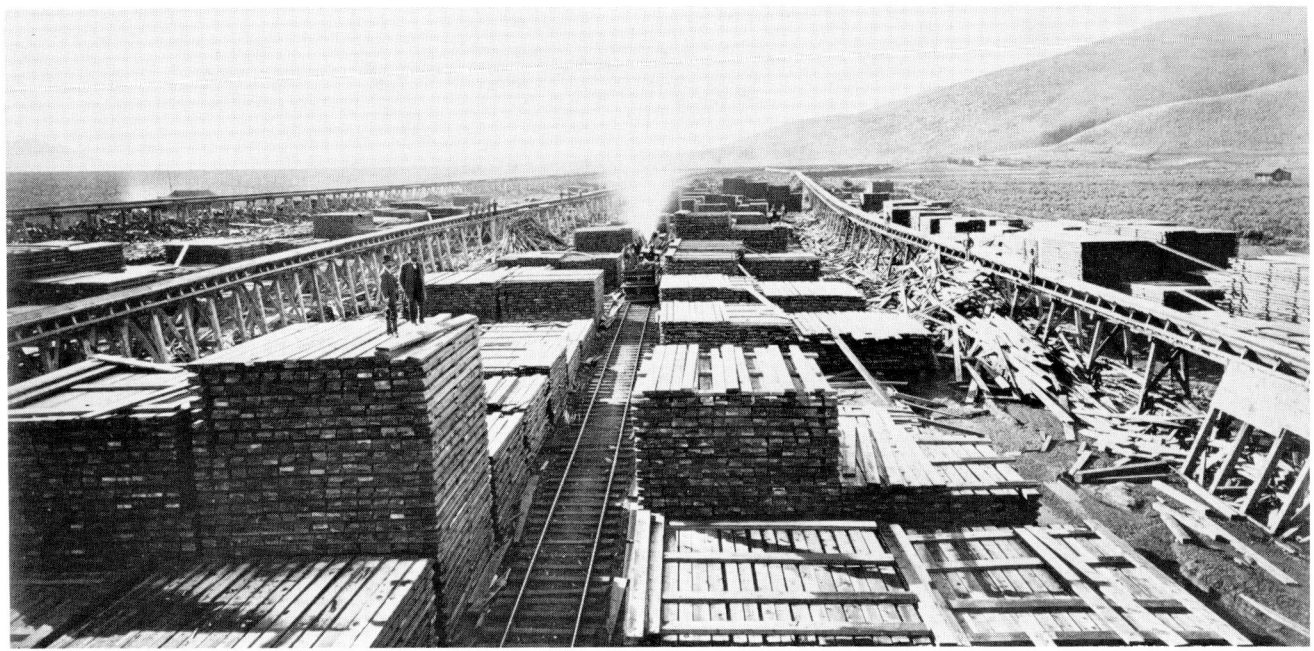

Hallmark of V&T traffic up the hill to Virginia City was lumber—boards for buildings, timbers for the mines, slab for the hungry furnaces of the various works. D. O. Mills and H. M. Yerington saw to it that the railroad was well supplied. Lumber cut in the Glenbrook mills on Lake Tahoe was hauled to Spooner's Summit of the Sierra Nevada and flumed down the mountain to the south side of Carson City. This view shows the extensive lumber yards developed on the floor of the valley with a V&T locomotive nosing in for carload business. The flume has branched into three laterals so that lumber may be handily stored over a greater area. *(Gilbert Kneiss Collection.)*

was built southward from a point near M. C. Gardner's house to the end of the Summit Flume Company's flume down Clear Creek. Gardner was also interested in a Lake Tahoe railroad, and the Clear Creek flume handled lumber originating at Glenbrook and Lake Tahoe.

In spite of the many innovations and benefits derived from V&T operations, the little road's first year was not altogether a happy one. There were a goodly number of wrecks, largely caused by new and inexperienced help, which prompted the *Reno Crescent* editor to comment that Billy Wilson's stage line made the same time as the V&T from Carson City to Virginia City without the risk of collisions. A month later, in May 1870, the Carson City correspondent tired of reporting on the two accidents that had happened within the same week and delivered himself of this diatribe: "I am told that Sharon contemplates discharging all the engineers and running the machine himself, or selling out to the employees, or as a last recourse, straightening out the curves a few." Frequent were the references to the V&T as the "Very Crooked and Terribly Rough R. R."—apparently a holdover from the initials of the old name of Virginia, Carson & Truckee River Railroad.

Had the people of Washoe County been less interested in the novelty of the newly constructed railroad and more interested in the ultimate intent of the line, they might have realized that all was not as serene as surface conditions indicated. The entire year of 1870 went by without a word as to the construction of the connecting link between Carson City and the Truckee River (near Reno). Washoe County had been authorized by the legislature to issue county bonds in subsidy providing the voters approved; but apparently Sharon was waiting for the people of Washoe County to demonstrate their generosity and donate a set of nicely engraved bonds. Since none were forthcoming, Sharon stalled.

It was Hill Beachey, the stage operator from Winnemucca (see CP), that brought the situation into focus. In February 1871 he and his associates were granted a right-of-way from Virginia City to Reno by the Nevada legislature, and a route was surveyed which partly paralleled the line of the present Geiger Grade. By June, construction of the Beachey narrow gauge road seemed "assured" and, as no Washoe County bonds were being sought, the road had popular support.

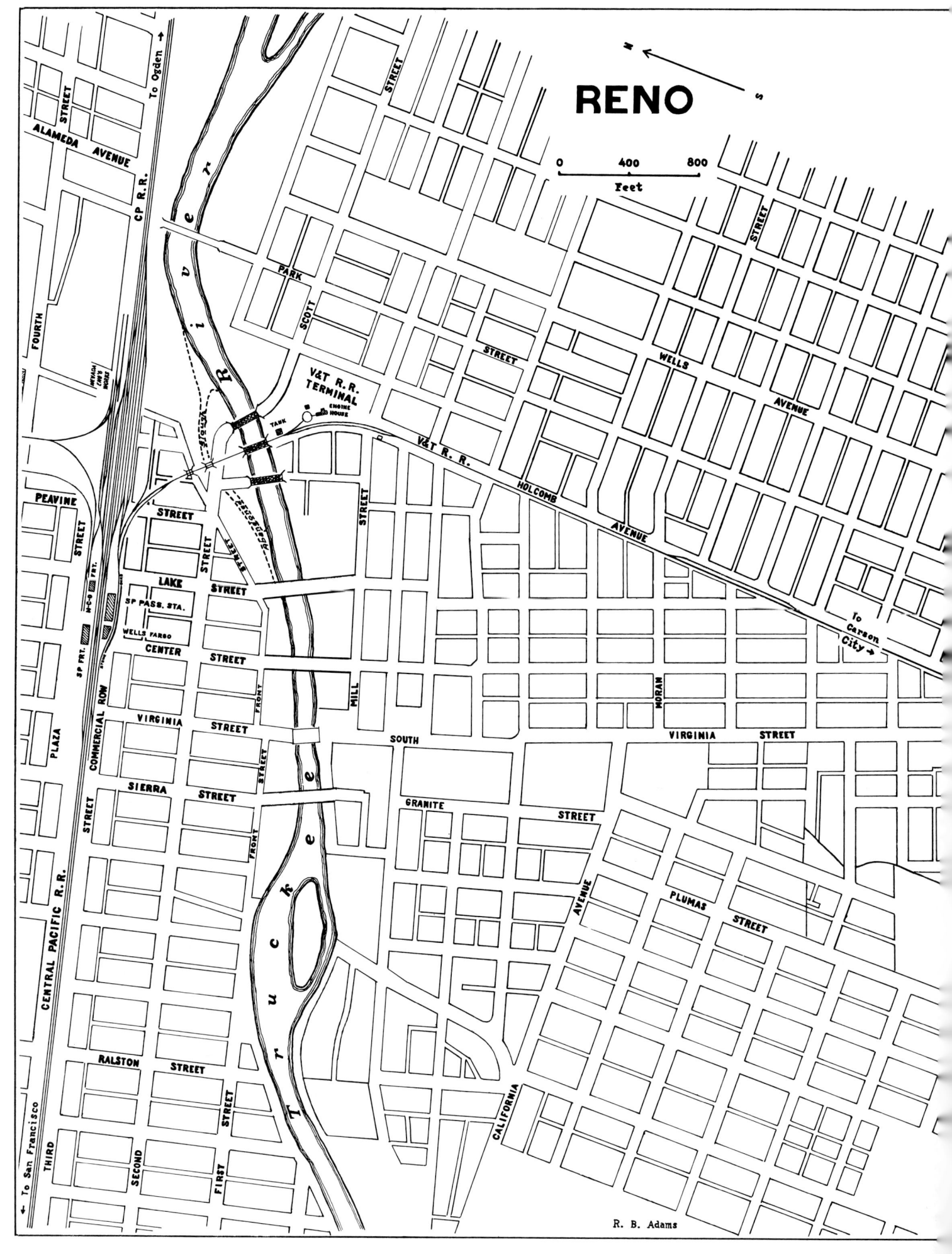

The activity finally spurred the Sharon forces into action. On July 1, 1871, the *Reno Crescent* blared out the news: "Broad Gauge Men Put in Appearance in Reno Yesterday Morning." The article went on to report that the contract for the bridge across the Truckee River at Reno had been awarded to a Mr. Thompson, the same Gold Hill contractor who had carried out the work on the Crown Point trestle. Then surveyors were sent out into the field, and actual construction work on the line started the early part of the month. By July 22 a track connection with the CP had been put in place just below the depot hotel, and a reporter enthused, "we expect the rails to be laid for some distance as soon as the bridge is built." His enthusiasm was not contagious, however, for work dragged during August and even in early September he could only report that the bridge was nearing completion.

With the bridge finally in place and supplies pouring across it, work still progressed at a moderate pace. November 11, 1871, marked the occasion of an excursion to Steamboat (Springs) on completion of the line to that point. A locomotive, two passenger cars, a caboose and two box cars comprised the accommodations for the half-hour trip which left Reno at 1:30 P.M. with many people on board. Nine more months were required before the rails finally reached Carson City and a connection with the main line to Virginia City. An enthusiastic crowd of 600 people witnessed the driving of the last spike about a mile west of Carson City on August 24, 1872, while the V&T operated its first train the full length of the line from Virginia City to the Truckee River.

The discovery of the Big Bonanza in February 1873 started the V&T on a five-year period of rushing business. From 30 to 45 trains operated over the single track line each day without benefit of such modern contrivances as ATC or CTC. Wood and lumber came through the Reno gateway, poured off the flumes at Huffaker's, Lakeview and Carson City to be loaded on waiting flat cars, or floated down the Carson River to Empire. Such business constituted upwards of 100 carloads a day in 1875. At Huffaker's alone, where the flume of the Bonanza Kings (Mackay et al.) disgorged timbers from the forests far to the west, some 35 carloads daily left the yards. Other materials—merchandise, hay, machinery, ice—accounted for another 20 to 40 carloads daily. Of such was the inbound traffic constituted, to be laboriously lifted up the hill to satiate the voracious appetite of the hungry mines and miners. Conversely, virtually all outgoing tonnage was comprised of ore for the mills in the Carson River Canyon, a sizeable 80 to 100 carloads a day. Thus with the greatest concentration of traffic on the upper portion of the line, it was altogether appropriate that four of the seven carded trains between Carson City and Virginia City carried passengers, while Reno was served with but one scheduled passenger train each 24 hours.

These were bustling, prosperous times, and the V&T frequently found itself hard pressed to keep abreast of both the demands of customers for additional services and the rapid deterioration of roadbed and equipment resulting from such severe, hard usage. Some 40 miles of spur tracks were built to various mines and mills, one extending to the Union Shaft near the cemetery northeast of Virginia City, while another was extended from the main line to a point just above the mills at Silver City. In 1874, four years from the opening of the line, the rails between Carson City and Virginia City had to be replaced with new and heavier steel rails to carry the increased traffic. Withal it was a most gratifying hardship for the little 55-mile line, considering the annual dividends of $360,000 which commenced in 1875. Small wonder the owners were sufficiently impressed to run a survey down the Carson Valley to Genoa in 1876, as well as subsequently to affiliate themselves with such other lines as the Carson & Colorado, the Bodie & Benton, the Eureka & Palisade and some of the railroads in the Lake Tahoe region. None, however, ever approached the financial success of the famed Virginia & Truckee.

The vicissitudes of mining are legion, however, and the Comstock was no exception. The years 1876-77 were the most productive; then came the slump. With it came a sympathetic, adverse reaction on the good fortunes of the V&T. In 1879 only 52,841 tons of ore drifted down the winding grade to the Carson City mills, less than one-fifth the tonnage of a scant three years previous. For 20 long years the railroad was to be maintained on a subsistence budget with greatly curtailed train service. Surplus locomotives were sold. Around 1886 the branch to Silver City was abandoned; dividends were eliminated in the 1890's; and in 1901, following an increase in the tax rate, many miles of spur tracks were removed. In 1917 a full 90 of the eight-ton ore cars were scrapped.

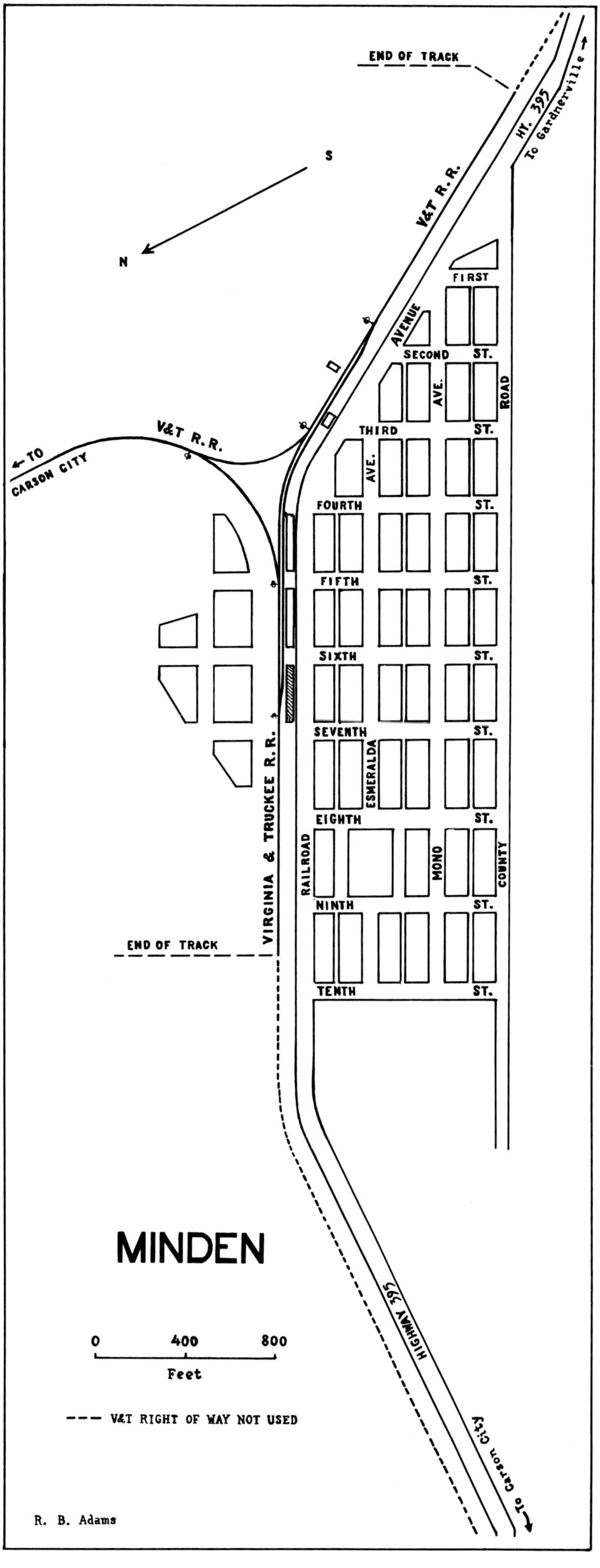

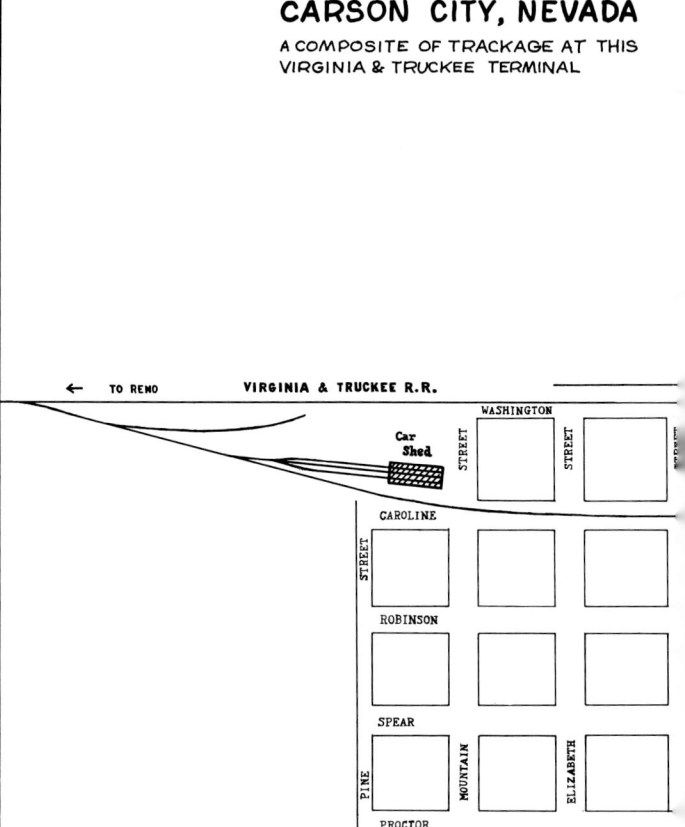

Subrogating this terrific decline of business to a moderate extent was the newly created traffic in supplies for the budding Carson & Colorado Railroad on which physical construction started at Mound House in May 1880. As the C&C directorate was closely interlocked with that of the V&T, it is quite conceivable that the stringent situation of the latter lent impetus to the former, for new sources of traffic were urgently needed. The first three years of C&C operations were profitable and considerable interchange traffic developed; then mining in the southern counties slumped and for the balance of the first two decades the C&C, like its connection the V&T, suffered terrifically in an impoverished condition.

Bright spot of dubious import on the V&T horizon was the excursion business. Even following its decline, Virginia City continued to be a major attraction, and many excursions were operated from Reno to the end of the line. One Fourth of July excursion required two sections, while the Corbett-Fitzsimmons fight on March 18, 1897, drew some 3,000 to 4,000 people to witness Fitzsimmons' victory in the 14th round. The V&T ran many extras, and the shortage of equipment resulted in permission for Southern Pacific crews to operate through trains to Carson City under V&T direction.

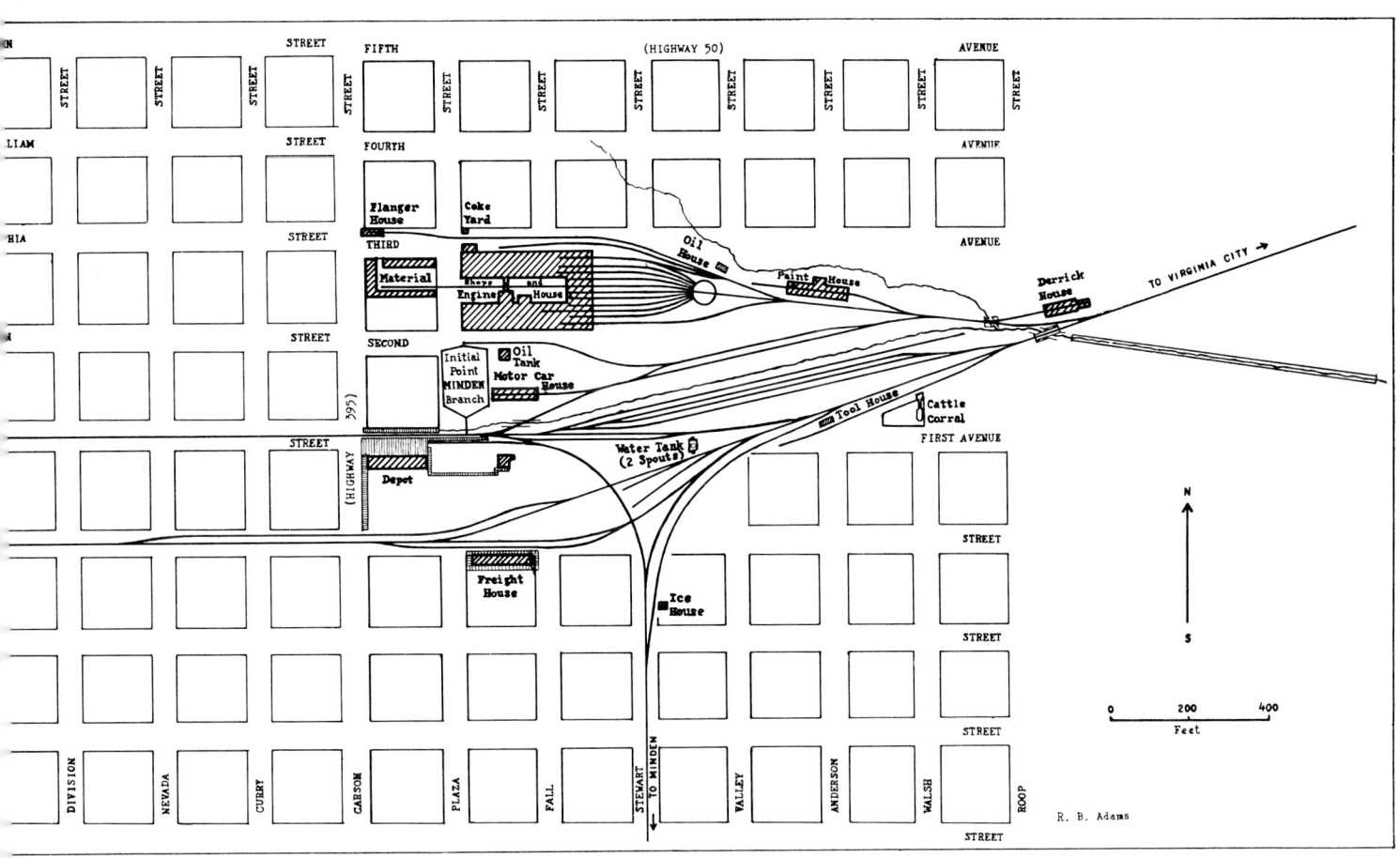

At Reno people spoke facetiously of going to the "prayer meeting," for the Christian Endeavor was gathering at Verdi the same day; but there was no question as to which event drew the larger crowd. And unlike the earlier days of Virginia City, there was no shooting following the fight.

Among the more famous of the Comstock people were Sandy and Eilley Bowers. Production from Sandy's mine in Crown Point Ravine at Gold Hill elevated him to the prominence of becoming one of Nevada's first millionaires, while the locations of his tunnels to riches were carefully plotted and directed by Mrs. Eilley Bowers through the capable assistance of her famous crystal ball. When their fortunes were high, they built an imposing edifice in Washoe Valley, not far from Franktown. Then Sandy died, and the turning tide swept the mansion away from Mrs. Bowers. It changed hands several times in the succeeding years until Henry Riter, a Reno saloon keeper, acquired and rehabilitated the property and placed it open to the public in June 1903. The warm springs were converted into swimming pools, while the old library, where Sandy had stocked the choicest literature by the yard, was converted into a haven of rest for the thirsty and weary. Bowers' Mansion became a popular resort, to the benefit of the V&T which ran many a special train to the area for picnickers and private parties.

Following the turn of the century, Nevada mining began to improve, and convulsions recurred along the Comstock. By 1903, as ore production improved, some of the mines resumed token dividend payments, and the V&T began to share in the new prosperity. More important to the railroad, however, were the developments taking place at Tonopah and Goldfield and the vast amount of traffic flowing in both directions between the Southern Pacific at Reno and the (by then) SP-owned Carson & Colorado at Mound House. All of this traffic had no recourse but to use the 41 miles of V&T rails between Reno and Mound House, transshipping at the latter point to the cars of the 3-foot C&C. Frequent V&T double headers were required over the Lakeview Summit, both for the outbound ore trains as well as the consists of merchandise inbound for the mines.

Interrupting the resurgence of traffic was a recurrence of trouble. An early morning fire on November 17, 1903, damaged the Homestead Tunnel as flames shot high in the air and cave-ins followed. Two months were required to make repairs because the rocks were slow in cooling from the intense heat.

VIRGINIA & TRUCKEE RAILROAD

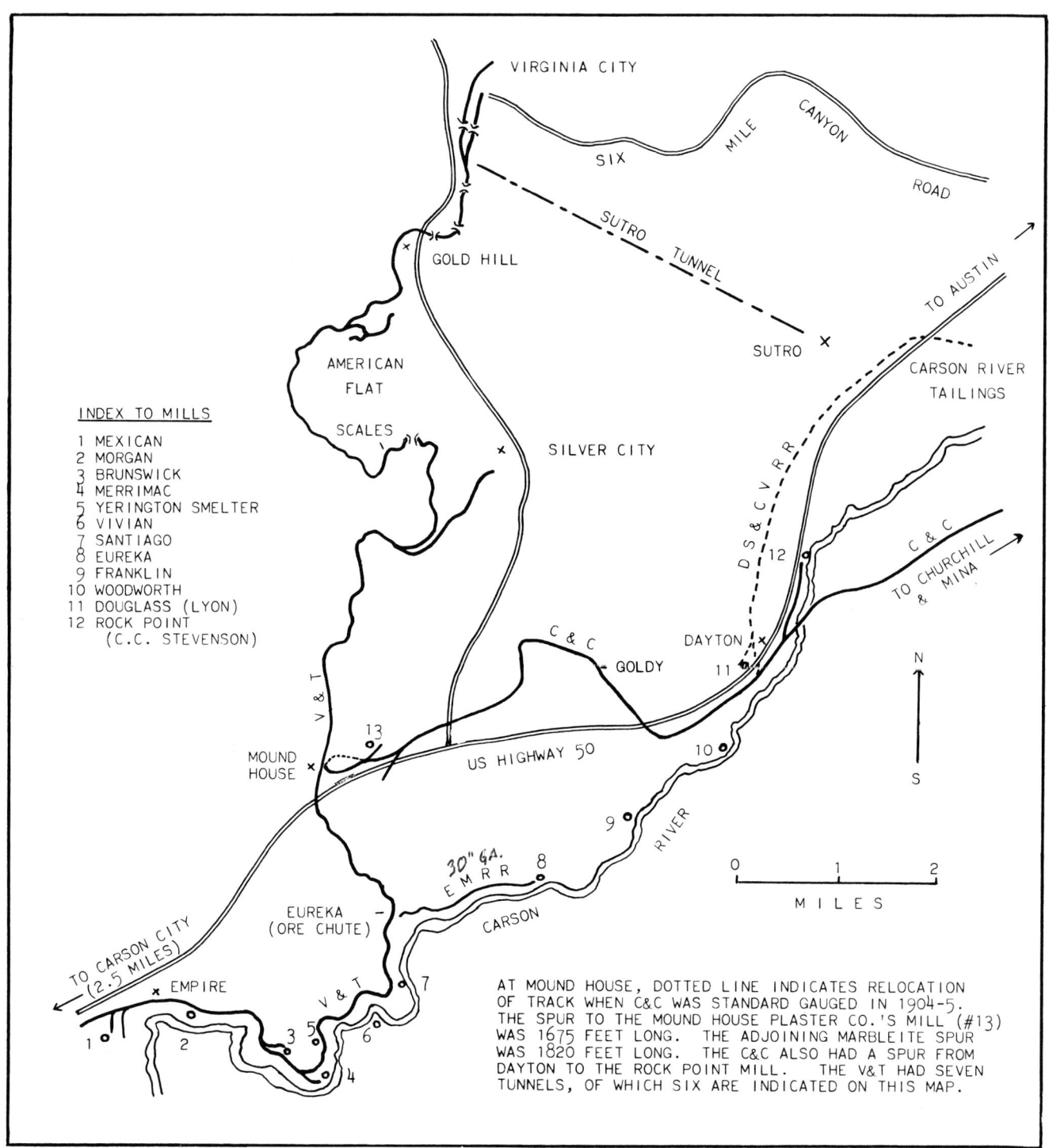

In 1904 the inevitable happened. The SP-C&C combination tired of the sharing of revenues with the V&T as well as the delays of interchange at Mound House, and started standard-gauging the C&C from Mound House to Tonopah Junction where the new Tonopah Railroad had just been completed to the mines at the new bonanza. As part of the program, pressure was applied for sale of the V&T to the SP, but when Harriman heard (what he considered) an unreasonable price, he decided to do the next best thing and arranged in 1905 for the SP to construct the Hazen Cut-Off from Churchill to Hazen on the SP's main line. The V&T's boom, born of monopoly, subsided.

"Do we hear the toot, toot of the iron horse?" asked the *Bridgeport Chronicle-Union* in April 1905. "The Nevada papers have been telling us of the extension of the V&T..." It was true; surveyors were heading southward. As early as 1901 there had been talk of extending the V&T into the Carson Valley farming area, but it was the building of the Hazen Cut-Off that gave the V&T management the impetus to start surveys all the way into Alpine County, California, where common interests held vital timber lands. On June 24, 1905, the Virginia & Truckee Railway was formed to take over the Virginia & Truckee Railroad Co. as an entity and additionally to construct any requisite extensions.

In the fall of 1905 a contract reportedly had been let for an 18-mile railroad southward to the California line. Yerington would neither confirm nor deny the rumor that the V&T would build through Hope Valley and over the Sierras to join the Santa Fe at Stockton. To add to the confusion, he did allow as how the extension might be longer than 18 miles.

During an interview in March 1906 Yerington said that the V&T would build to Aurora, then enjoying a revival, and to booming Masonic. Reno merchants were saying that Aurora should have a railroad and that, judging by the number of different surveyors (WP, SP, AT&SF and V&T), it might get one that year. More fuel was added to the fire when T. B. Rickey, a rancher and banker, threatened to build an electric line from his Topaz Lake ranch and proposed sugar beet factory to the SP at Wabuska if the V&T did not build their own line. Financial difficulties the following year absorbed Mr. Rickey's thoughts and his plans for a railroad were forgotten.

In spite of the ephemeral talk, there was a practical, concrete effort on the part of the V&T to begin construction. Grading on the 14-mile branch to Minden was instituted, and rail laying commenced in the middle of April 1906. A slight interruption was encountered when the rails reached Stewart, as the Greek track layers went on strike. Replacements were found, however, and two months later the line was finished to Minden with regular train service commencing on Wednesday morning, August 1, 1906. And there the rail stopped.

Three years later the Nevada Railroad Commission wrote to D. O. Mills to encourage him to push his line farther south to Wellington and Bridgeport, California. Just before his death Mills had surveyors out checking a possible route through Antelope and Smith Valleys to Wellington, but following his demise interest in the proposal lagged. Possibly this was due in part to the Nevada Copper Belt Railroad which was then being contemplated and which subsequently did build into Smith Valley. Whatever the reason, the V&T did no further construction except for a 2,000-foot spur to the new mill at Merrimac in 1910 and a 1.6-mile line to American Flat to serve the United Comstock Mines Company's plant during the early 1920's.

The recovery of mining in Virginia City and the development of agriculture in the Carson Valley enabled the V&T to remain in the group of dividend-paying railroads until 1924. Then red-ink operations began. Deficits were reported in each succeeding year until abandonment in 1950.

Mound House, before the coming of the Carson & Colorado Railroad, was quite a center and transfer point on the V&T. From here stagecoaches took weary travelers to Dayton or Sutro along the Carson River valley, or into the hills to such more remote mining localities as Como and Palmyra. (*Gilbert Kneiss Collection.*)

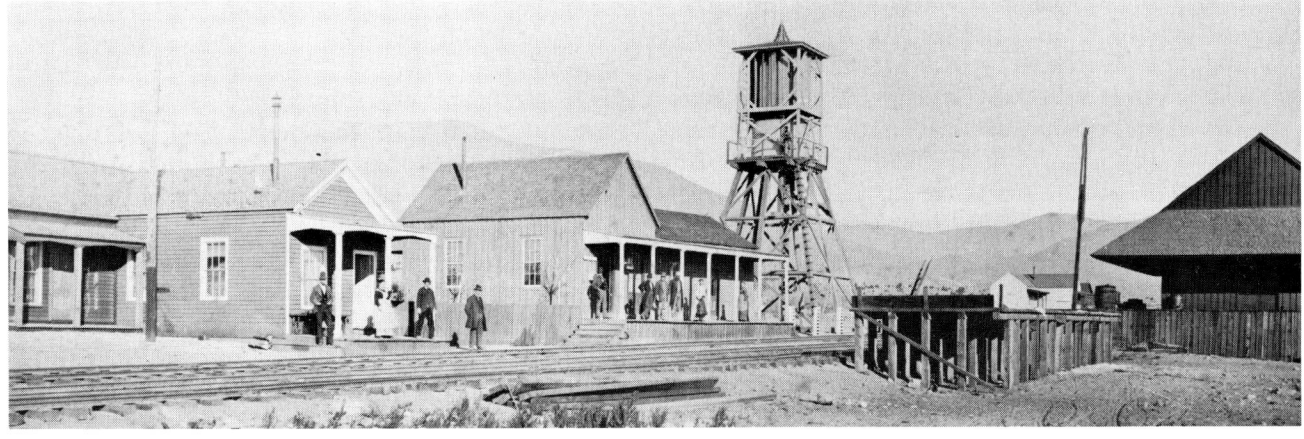

Ogden Mills acquired full control in 1933 and kept the line operating with his own personal funds until his death in 1937. Receivership followed in 1938. The next year the Virginia City portion was abandoned as the mines had become dormant. When the rails were pulled up in 1941, the scrap yielded $52,000 which provided sufficient funds to operate the balance of the line during World War II. The War did little to stimulate traffic, but the railroad provided essential transportation and carried on. Subsequently, a moderate traffic in gypsum, then in demand for agriculture, was developed from Mound House, but even this proved insufficient to support the line. In 1949 it was evident that operations could not continue much longer. The I.C.C. locomotive inspection requirements could not be met, and no money was available for repairs or rejuvenation. Following extended hearings, abandonment was approved and the last train ran to Minden on May 30, 1950, marking the end of the grand, 81-year-old railroad.

Gardnerville and Southern Railroad

When Minden, Nevada, became the southern terminus of the extension of the Virginia & Truckee Railway into the Carson Valley in 1906, the fact was hardly pleasing to the residents of Gardnerville, a scant mile to the southeast. The people made every effort to induce the V&T to extend their line the added distance, but their efforts proved fruitless. As the delays and refusals evolved into a reasonable certainty that the road would not be built, two Gardnerville men determined to take matters into their own hands.

H. H. Springmeyer, a rancher, and Arendt Jensen, proprietor of the general store, joined together to obtain a county franchise to build a line of standard gauge railroad one mile long to connect the town of Gardnerville with the town of Minden. The time was May 1909, and the *Record-Courier* was proudly pleased with the project, headlining the story, "Gardnerville on the Boom." The railroad would run from a connection with the V&T at Minden south along the county road to a terminus and depot to be constructed just back of the Odd Fellows Hall in Gardnerville. Included in the franchise were stipulations of maximum rates for freight and passengers together with other pertinent matters.

To secure local financial support, Jensen called a town meeting at which the project was thoroughly explained. The road would cost $12,000, including the price of a gasoline motor car for power. If approximately half of the required capital were contributed locally, Jensen assured the meeting that responsible parties would take over the balance of the project and complete the railroad. The townspeople responded; $5,000 was raised and the financial problem appeared to be solved.

One problem unresolved, in fact not even on the agenda, arose in an unexpected quarter. Half way along the proposed route lay the settlement of Millerville, of which Fred Dangberg was the principal land owner. It had been anticipated that two pieces of his land might be used by the railroad to avoid traversing the county road; but when the matter was put up to him, Dangberg took two weeks to make his decision and then parried the question by stating that the land was available—but at a cost of $20,000 for each piece! He softened the blow somewhat by adding that if the line were used exclusively for passengers, the lands would be available without cost; but the stipulation obviated one of the prime purposes of the line which ran counter to Dangberg's commercial interests centered in Minden.

In spite of this impasse, grading for the railroad was started on September 1, 1909, following the route surveyed by Louis Springmeyer along the county road. A dozen men with their teams were soon at work, while Jensen and Springmeyer attended to the legal technicalities of transferring the franchise to the Gardnerville and Southern Railroad which was in the process of being formally incorporated.

A month later in October 1909 all grading stopped when the V&T commenced talking about extending its own line from Minden to Gardnerville and on south into Smith Valley. The V&T, after some surveys, decided not to build the extension. By this time, however, both Springmeyer and Dangberg had become discouraged. The Gardnerville & Southern, which had begun to gain widespread prominence as one of the shortest independent railroads in the world, abruptly came to an untimely end; and the town of Gardnerville never did enjoy its direct rail connection with the outside world.

Eureka Mill Railroad

Along that portion of the route of the Virginia & Truckee Railroad which lay in the bed of the Carson River Canyon were eight important mills for the reduction of Comstock ores. Short spur tracks were laid to four of these mills from connections with the V&T main line. Near the northern end, however, where the rails climbed the steep bank of the canyon on their ascent to Mound House and Virginia City, it was impossible to construct sidings to serve two of the mills. The first of these, the Santiago, received its ores down a slide from the tracks above. The second was too far up the river to be served through any such simple expedient.

One can stand at the point where the V&T left the Carson River near Santiago Canyon and look down on a rock-based embankment extending nearly a third of a mile along the north shore of that waterway. It is the last vestigial segment of the grade of the former Eureka Mill Railroad. The EM was a short line, only 1.12 miles long, of 2½-foot gauge, and was completed in March 1872 by the Union Mill Co. to transport ore to its mill. At the western end, a 400-foot surface tramway, built on a 30 degree angle, sufficed to lower the ores down the bank from the V&T main line to rail head. Here little five-ton ore cars transported the material over narrow gauge rails to the mill.

For several years the equipment consisted of ten ore cars, two flat cars and no locomotive, all hauling being performed by horses. Subsequently the hay burners were replaced by a small steam locomotive, a product of the Porter Locomotive Works.

The first half-mile of line climbed a grade of 130 feet to the mile (approximately 2½%), but from the dam to the mill the road was laid on top of the mill's flume and had a slight downgrade. Two canyons were crossed on high trestles. In spite of the difficulties involved in construction, the total cost of the line was held to $20,000.

The Eureka Mill burned down about 1892, but the little railroad was not disturbed until some time after February 1906. Removal of the track was proposed so it could be used in the building of a spur to the Nevada Reduction Works' new mill at Rock Point in Dayton, but this was not done. The exact date of dismantlement and final disposition of the rails and equipment is unknown.

At the western end of the Eureka Mill Railroad a 400-foot surface tramway built on a 30° angle lowered the ore from the V&T's main line (on trestle above) to loading bins for the Eureka Mill. The larger picture shows one of the cable operated cars on the incline, while the smaller shows a general view of the entire operation. The horse and buggy are not waiting for a load of ore, but horse drawn ore carts took the ore to the mill before the advent of the locomotive. *(Both Photos: Nevada Historical Society.)*

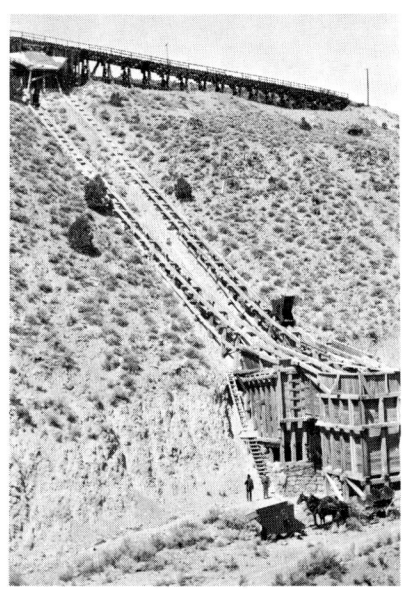
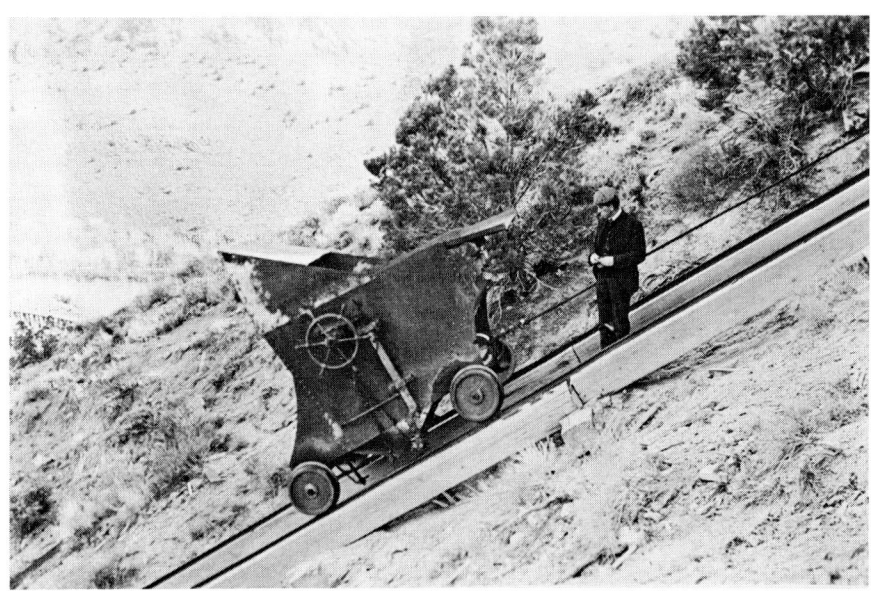

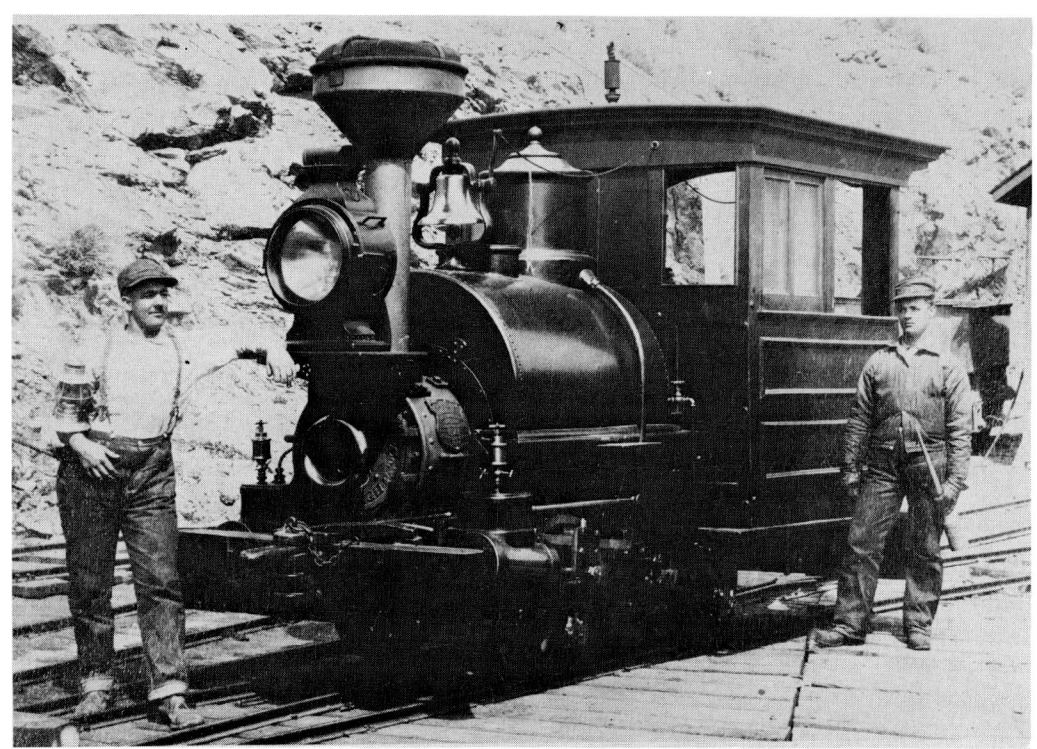

Hay burners of the Eureka Mill Railroad were replaced by this 2½-foot gauge 0-4-0-T saddle-tank switching locomotive from the Porter Locomotive Works in Pittsburgh, Pa., shown here in front of the EM's engine house facilities at the mill. The ruggedness of portions of the terrain along the line is evident in the view of one of the two high trestles *(right, above)* with the locomotive and a flat car about to cross. Graphically illustrated in the splendid panorama *(right, below)* is the EM's method of building its railroad on top of the company's flume. The main line (track nearest the river) straddles that waterway, while space for the yards and enginehouse was carved from the neighboring riverbank. Notice the cut of ore cars, with a flat car on the near end, circling behind the enginehouse on the hi-line entrance to the mill. The Carson River flows to right. *(Top Right: Grahame Hardy Collection; All Others: Nevada Historical Society.)*

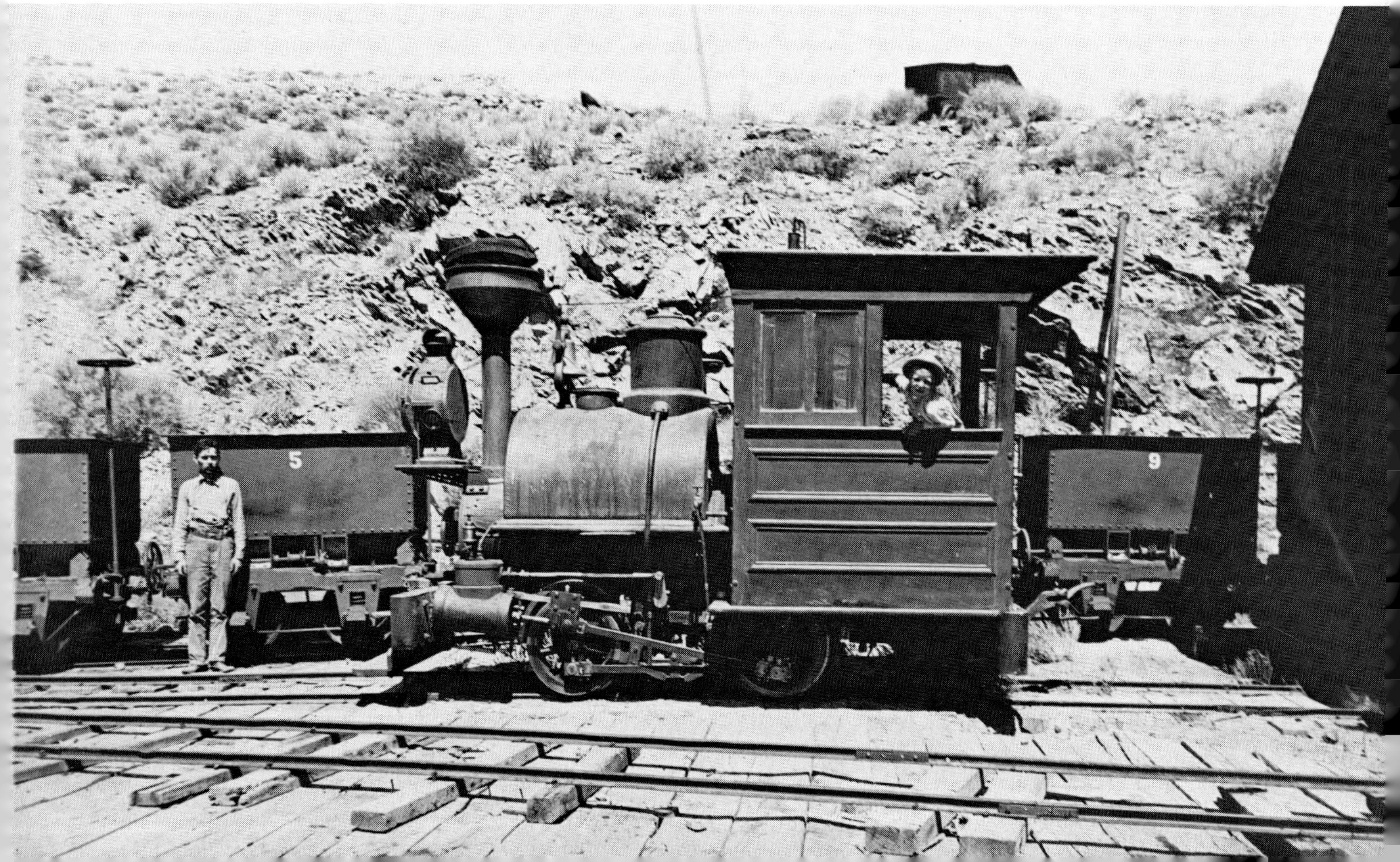

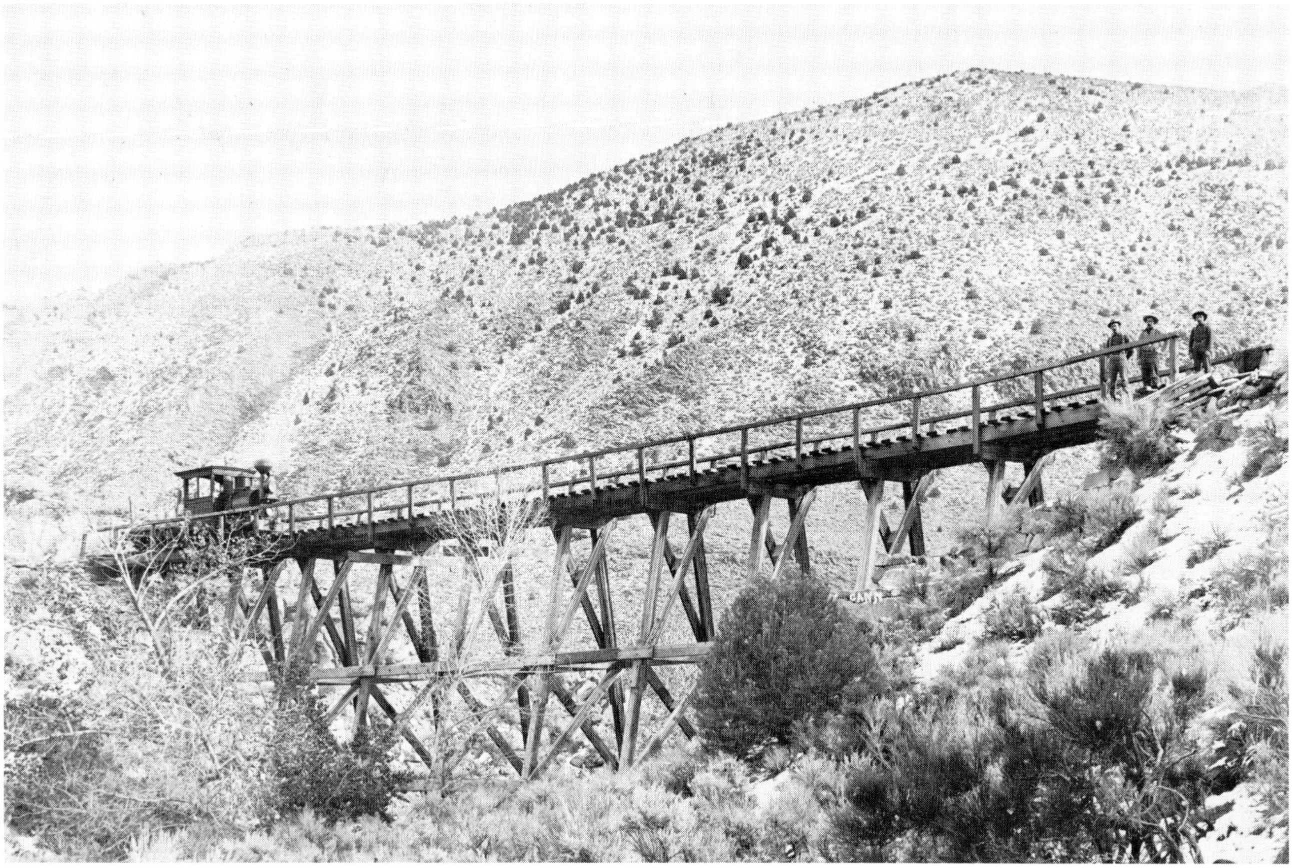

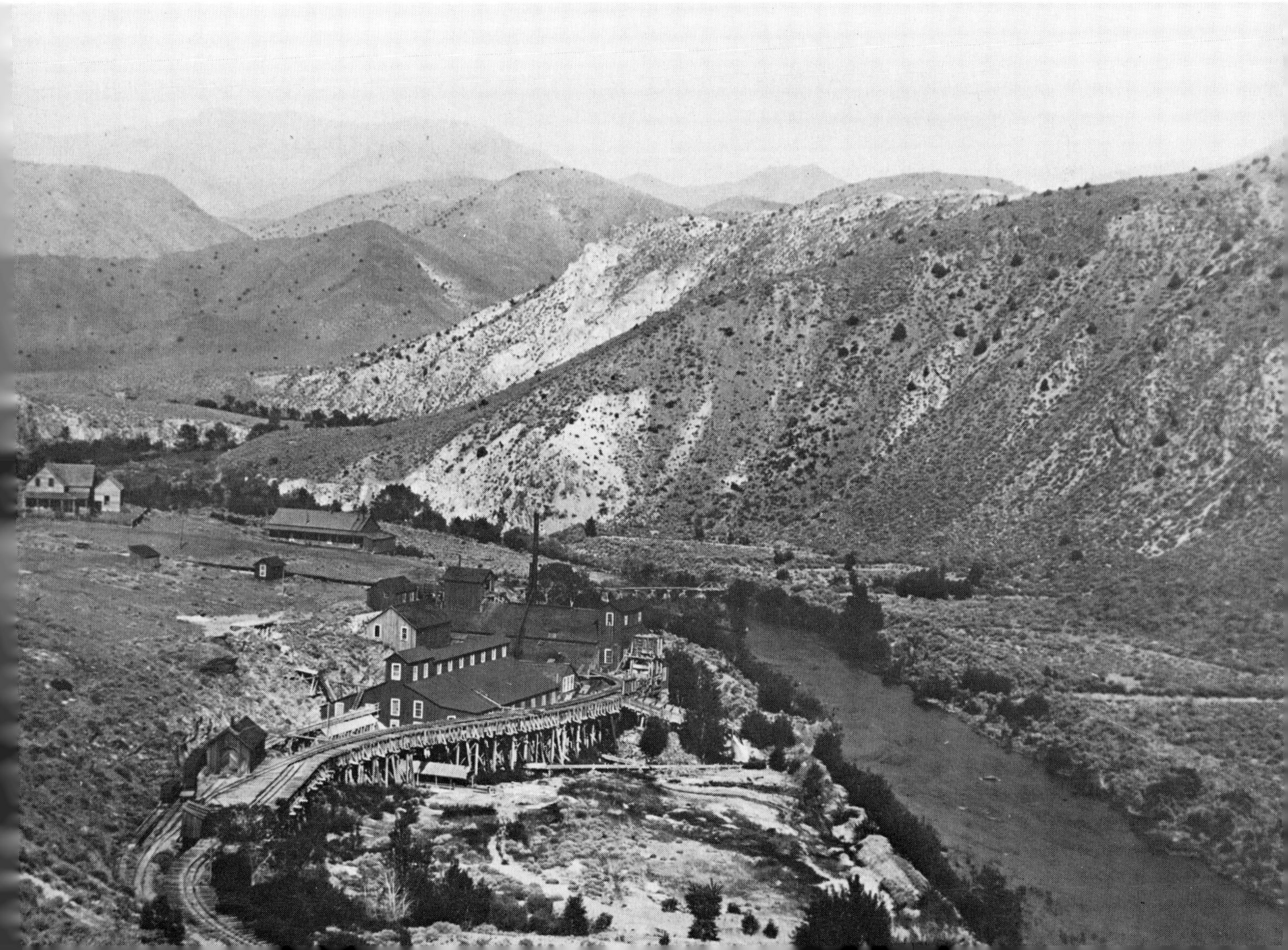

CARSON & COLORADO RAILROAD

The year 1880 was one of varying fortunes in Nevada mining. The Comstock had entered its declining period, but active mining camps stretched for hundreds of miles southward, furnishing promise of new riches to miners and fresh tonnages to any railroad ready to haul them to market.

The Comstock milling town of Dayton, for example, had declined from its peak population of 2,500 in 1865 to a mere 200 people in 1880. The Esmeralda Mining District surrounding the town of Aurora to the southeast had passed its peak in 1862-64, although explorations to greater depths were being carried on by the Real Del Monte Company with 250 men working. Farther south, the Columbus District surrounding Candelaria (60 miles southeast of Aurora) was still enjoying its boom, the Northern Belle Company having taken (to 1878) $3,754,000 from its mine alone and paid out dividends of $1,500,000. Though it produced in later years, the mine's maximum yield of $1,270,000 in the year 1877 was never again equalled. The Lida Valley District, 23 miles southeast of Silver Peak and 168 miles from Wadsworth as the crow flies, had 250 mine locations in the area, but with freight by teams costing 5 cents per pound, the activity was held to a minimum. Other districts, too numerous to mention, were being worked but lightly or else had been worked at the profitable surface levels and were awaiting better transportation to make the deeper ores available at lower cost. In addition, new claims and new districts were being developed constantly, to the extent that no one could accurately predict the possibilities for the future.

Wood and water were the basic necessities in that barren desert country, and they were largely at a terrific premium without adequate transportation into the area. On the other hand, ores needed to be conveyed from the mines to the mills and the resulting bullion transported to its market with safety from robbers, bandits, and other marauders of the public domain. Railroads had demonstrated their capabilities and their relative safety in these respects, and at a cost far lower than that of any other mode of conveyance then extant.

From the point of view of Darius O. Mills, the Virginia & Truckee had been an eminently successful railroad, increasing handsomely the already abundant wealth of its owners. The thought had been buzzing around in his head for quite some time that a railroad to the south to the newer mining areas could be a profitable venture as well as a carefully calculated risk, as any future bonanzas discovered would most likely lie in this direction. Still he hesitated. Then an independent group, subsequently organized as the N-C-O Railway, ran surveys from Wadsworth to Walker Lake with extensions to Bodie and Candelaria. The time for indecision was at an end; action was required and Mills provided it.

On May 10, 1880, The Carson & Colorado Railroad Company was incorporated to build a narrow (3-foot) gauge railroad. Among the directors were such men as H. M. Yerington (president and superintendent), D. L. Bliss, D. A. Bender, and S. P. Smith (agent for D. O. Mills). Two important Nevada rivers provided the title for this railroad, projected to run from Mound House on the Carson River (10 miles east of Carson City) to Ft. Mohave on the Colorado River at the extreme southern end of the state. Included in the plans was a branch to be built to serve the mining towns of Aurora and Bodie.

Preliminary surveys had already been made prior to incorporation, giving rise to reports circulated as early as January of that year that the V&T would extend its line in a southerly direction from Mound House to the upper end of Walker Lake. There a connecting steamer would convey passengers and freight for 31 miles to the southern end of the lake near Hawthorne. While prospects of a railroad were welcomed in most quarters, farmers in Mason Valley opposed the line because they felt it would destroy the market for their produce. Some bargaining also was required to run the survey through the Walker River Indian Reservation, but the "Bodie Extension of the V&T," as it was called, was soon surveyed to the south end of Walker Lake without recourse to that natural waterway for part of the route. In fact, it was continued another 54

For over 65 years Mound House, Nevada, on the desolate uplands northeast of Carson City, was an important outpost of the V&T. Initially it was the jumping-off place for travelers heading into the Carson River Valley for points as far south as Candelaria and Columbus. It was only natural that the Carson & Colorado Railroad should start from this same location in 1880 and build to virtually the same destinations.

When the SP purchased the Carson & Colorado in 1900, changed its name to Nevada & California and standard-gauged the northern portion of the line in 1904-05 (including the building of the Hazen Cut-Off), the importance of Mound House in the economy of the region began to wane. The panorama below, looking northeasterly up the V&T's main line toward Virginia City, was probably taken about 1910 in the waning years of the center's existence.

Three box cars (foreground) stand on the scale track of the Western Ore Purchasing Co., while a fourth car has been left on the lead just clear of the switch leading to the N&C (formerly C&C) connection to the right. Immediately beyond is the joint passenger station where two passengers stand on the (dark) snow cleared platform next to the tracks. The joint freight house is just beyond, and behind that to the right is the N&C's engine house, apparently unused since the recent snow. A variety of standard-gauge freight cars of mixed lading stand on the N&C sidings (far right, center). Two men walk up the N&C's Western Ore Purchasing Co. spur (foreground),

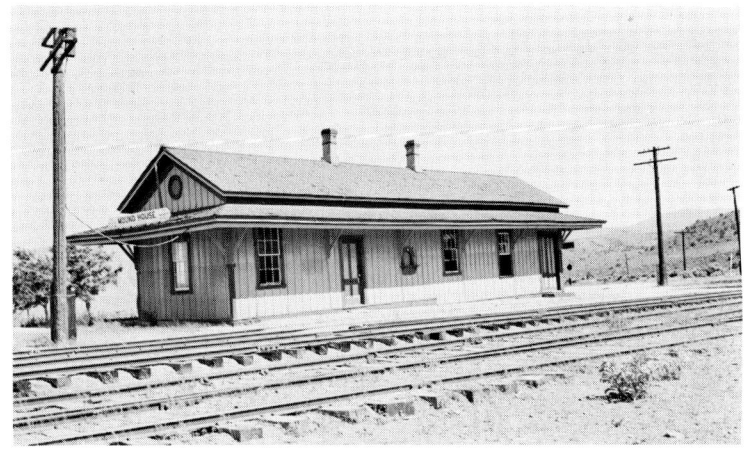

while between them and the cuts of N&C cars may be seen the embankment of the original narrow-gauge C&C loop which was reversed at the time of standard-gauging that line. Today's Highway 50 would cut across the foreground of this scene about where the stub switch stand for the scale track (right foreground) stands darkly against the drifted snow. (*Nevada Historical Society.*)

When this picture of Mound House station was snapped in June 1937, two years before abandonment of the line, the building had changed but little although virtually all companion edifices had disappeared. The now quiet tracks lead toward the Carson River to the right, and may be seen again as they skirt the bluff in the background. The station sign still lists "Keeler 293-2/10 M." and "San Francisco 285-2/10 M.", a reflection of early days when Mound House was a busy junction. (*Ted Wurm Collection.*)

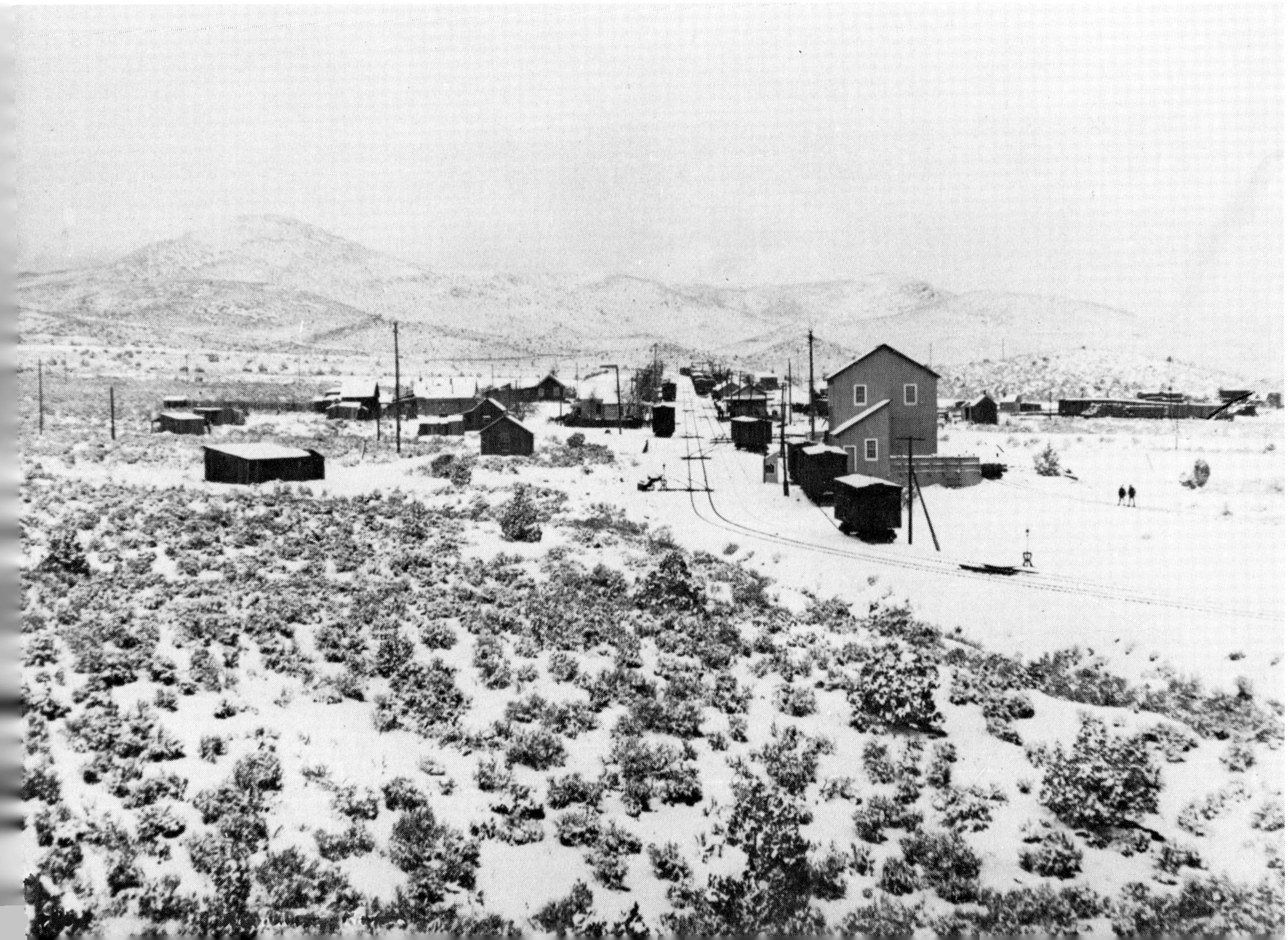

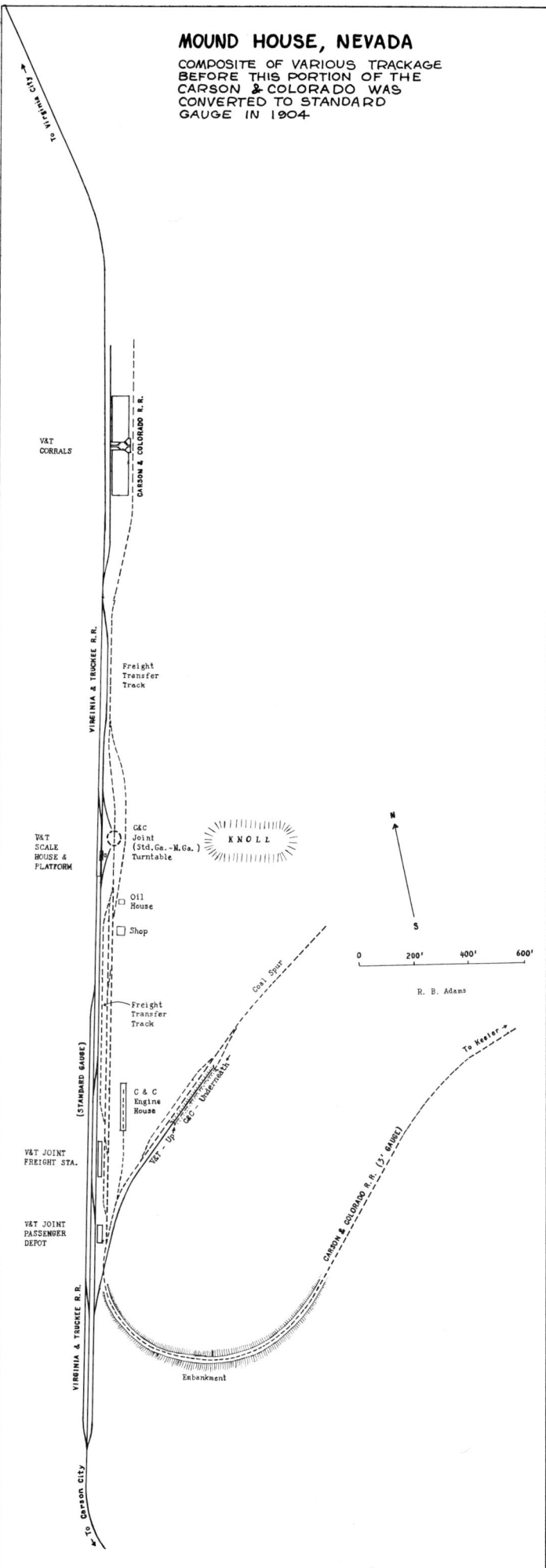

miles south to Candelaria, by far the next leading community below the Comstock.

Excitement was rampant. There was talk that a third rail would be laid on the V&T between Mound House and Carson City so the C&C could establish its headquarters there. In fact, R. R. Brown decided to call his new Carson City saloon and bowling alley the "Narrow Gauge Saloon," while the newspaper, *Virginia Stage*, went so far as to assure its readers that, in spite of the name, the beer schooners of this saloon were strictly built on the wide gauge plan. Further south, the town of Pizen Switch had just finished changing its name to Greenfield, but when the survey route passed it by 12 miles to the north at Wabuska, the name was changed once more, this time to Yerington in the hopes that the great man might be influenced to include the town on the route. Yerington failed to be impressed to the extent of altering his surveys, and the town did not get its railroad until the Nevada Copper Belt was built a full 30 years later. Even then the NCB by-passed the town a mile to the west and across the Walker River.

Actual work on the Carson & Colorado began when a special train from Virginia City brought 80 workmen (mostly unemployed Comstock miners), their foreman, a few officials, and some visitors to Mound House on May 31, 1880. At one o'clock in the afternoon Mr. Yerington walked to a point a half mile east of Mound House station where he stopped and forced a shovel in the ground. He then said: "I now in the name of the Carson & Colorado Railroad turn the first sod; may the road be carried on to successful issue." His suggestion for three cheers met with hearty response. Almost before the echoes of the cheers had subsided, a former Central Pacific roadmaster, Superintendent Robert Laws, had put the men to work, and by the time the special train departed a commendable showing had been made.

With 300 white men at work, excellent grading progress was made during the month of June. An additional 200 Chinamen were provided by a Chinese labor contractor, Ah Quong, "perhaps the slipperiest Chinaman ever exiled from far Cathay." Because of the feeling then prevailing against the use of Chinese labor, these men, hired in Reno, were taken to Churchill Canyon the long way around—east to Wadsworth and then south to the canyon.

Some of the ex-Comstock miners, who formerly had been working at $4.00 a day in the rich mines, found the prevailing pay of $1.75 a day (less 75 cents for board) far from attractive. A few of the men in Camp 3 (a half mile east of Dayton) inaugurated a strike on July 1. Others were induced to join the movement to seek an increase of 50 cents a day. Soon 100 men, armed with pick handles, were marching toward Camp 1 near Mound House. A dozen more men joined the ranks, while others quit work under threats of violence. A showdown was had with the boss—60 men were paid off on the spot and returned to Virginia City by special train while the rest entertained some second thoughts and returned to work at the old rate of pay in a more contented frame of mind.

Initial construction on the C&C started at Mound House and followed the north bank of the Carson River downstream to the east for six miles to Dayton. Here bridging carried the road first over Birdsall's Ditch and then a longer, 200-foot span across the Carson River. The line continued for 20 miles along the south bank to Fort Churchill where it left the Carson River and plunged southward for 18 miles to the vicinity of Mason Valley, a farming district. Wabuska lay at the northern edge of this farming belt on the big bend of the Walker River where its direction changed from northeasterly to southerly. Working down the stream, the road twice crossed the river in the next 38 miles to Schurz before skirting the eastern shore of Walker Lake to Hawthorne, 35 additional miles farther and four miles below the extremity of the lake.

In spite of the fact that the Western Nevada Railroad (later the N-C-O) under J. C. McTarnahan had completed surveying its all-rail route to Bodie in August of 1880, the Mills crowd did not appear to be concerned, for they had the funds for construction which the other group lacked. Supplies for the C&C began arriving in September, and by the end of the month the graders had reached the north end of Walker Lake and 250 Chinamen were discharged. Grading had been light for most of the distance, except for some annoying rock work about four miles north of Walker Lake. By the end of October the grade had been completed all the way to Hawthorne and rail laying had commenced from Mound House, where engine No. 1, the CANDELARIA, had been placed on the tracks on October 27.

Hawthorne, in October 1880, was in effect an invisible spot on a limitless waste. Yerington had said that he had selected the townsite but would not disclose its location until he was ready to build

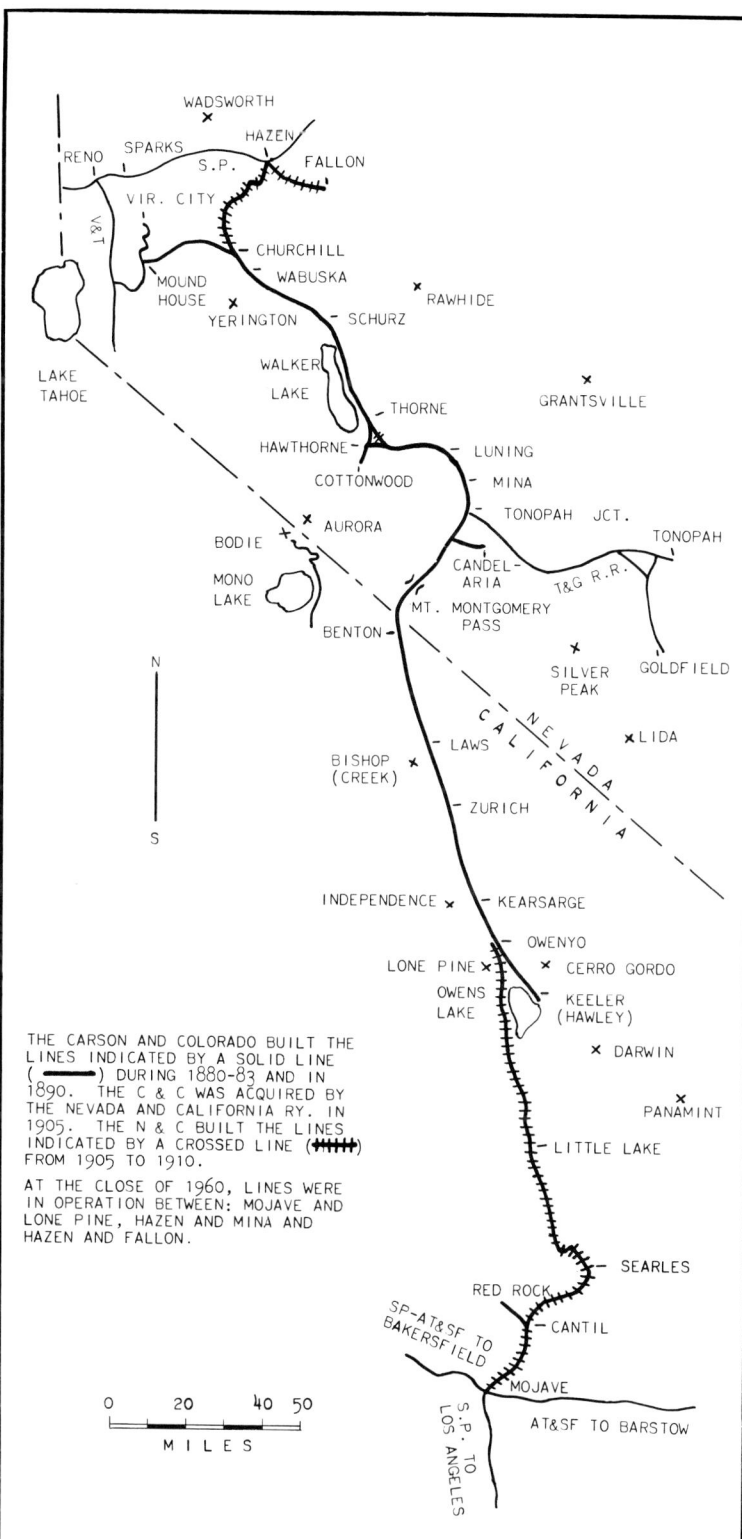

the depot. Three tents were set up in advance. Mrs. White of Belleville used one as a lodging house; Powell operated his butcher shop in another; and Jenks used the third for a general store. It was estimated, however, that once the railroad arrived, the town would zoom in importance as it would be

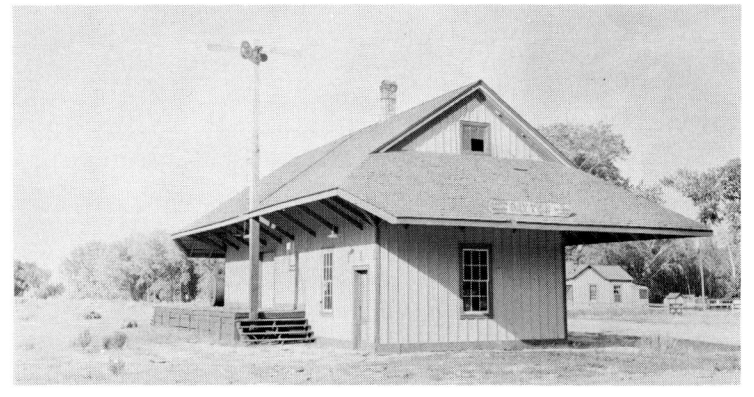

Major center on the Carson & Colorado and one of the most immediate objectives was Dayton, six miles from Mound House. Located at the foot of Gold Canyon, milling had been a primary occupation. The center photo shows an early woodburner and train approaching the station over the undulating narrow-gauge track from Mound House. To the right on the hillside can be seen faint traces of the Dayton, Sutro & Carson Valley Railroad which connected with the C&C to the west of the station.

Dayton in transition is depicted in the bottom portrait of a northbound double-headed passenger train on the broad-gauge iron of the three rail track. The time is not long after the 1905 conversion of the gauge as indicated by the unaltered station track still laid to narrow gauge and the improvised solid gravel fill over the unused rails. Lead engine, N&C 10-wheeler No. 2058, formerly worked on the SP in Arizona.

Although the Dayton trackage was abandoned in 1934, the station still stood when the picture (*top*) was taken in June 1938. The mileage designation on the station sign, "San Francisco 335-3/10 M.", would indicate a recalculation by way of Churchill and Hazen, rather than through the former outlet of Mound House. The station building was moved a short distance and converted into a residence. (*Top: Ted Wurm Photo; Other Two: Chester Barton Collection.*)

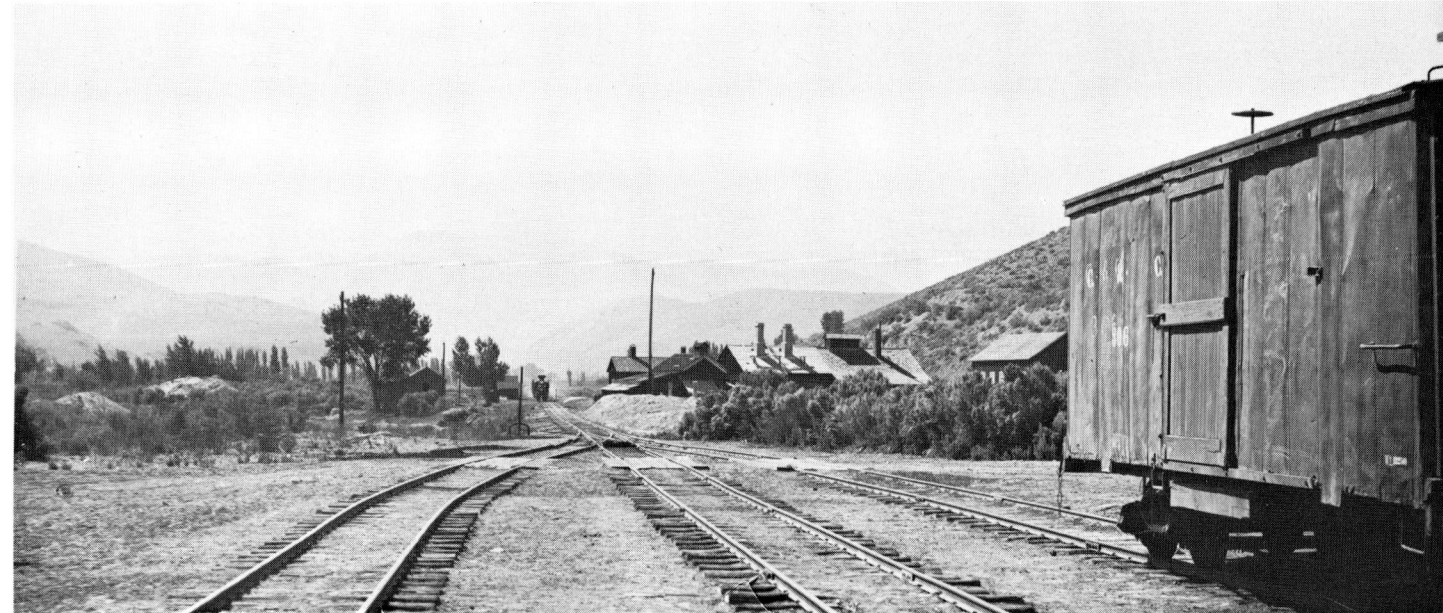

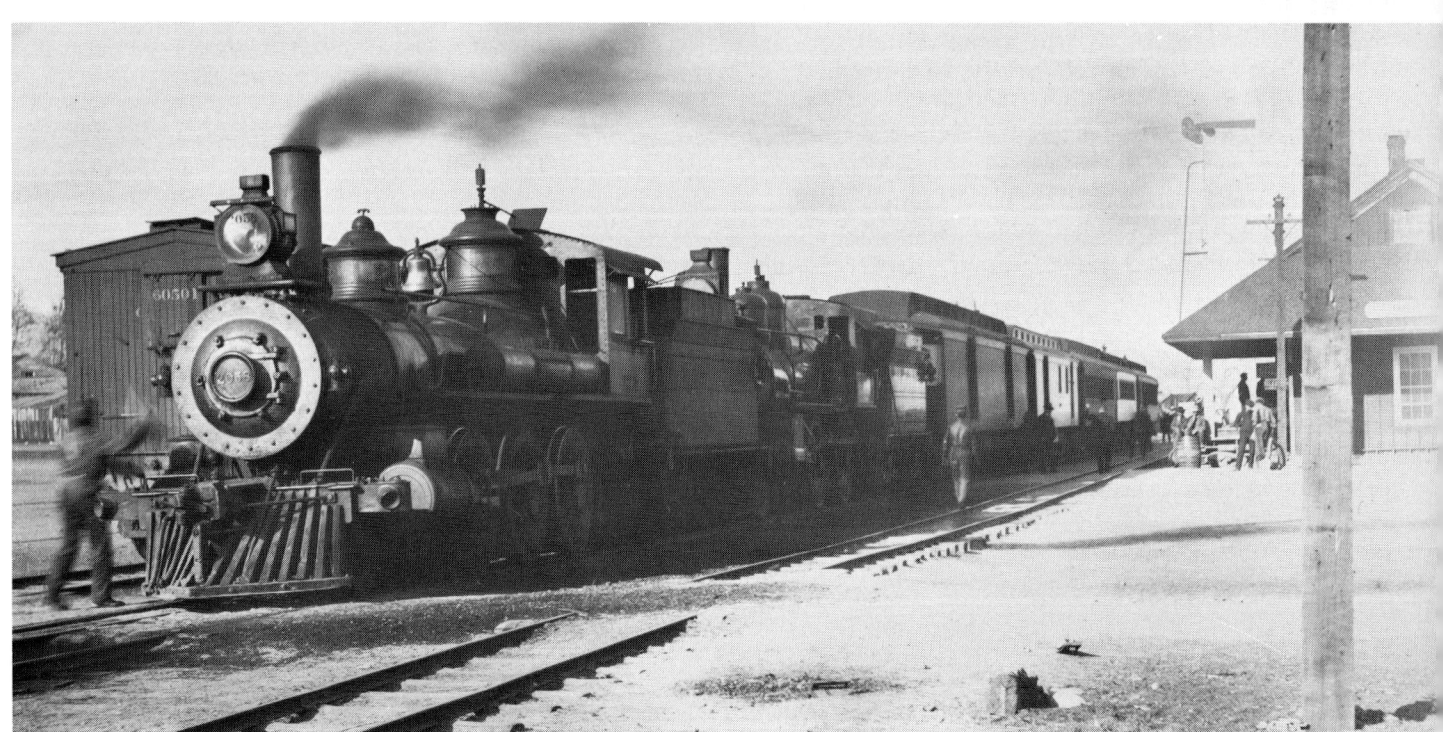

the junction of the railroad and the new wagon road to Bodie, owned by the same men who formed the C&C. "The new grade (of the wagon road) is so constructed that a railroad track could be laid down on it without much additional work. The railroad will not be built to Bodie, however. The people out there prefer to have the teams and teamsters." Whether the preference was that of the townspeople, the teamsters, or the owners of the road and railroad, was not divulged.

Rails and spikes were arriving slowly, but by December 18 the first 14 miles of track were in place. There were the usual problems, and some unusual ones too. One of the C&C contractors, Ed Reed, was settling up with Ah Sam, a Chinese labor contractor, when a misunderstanding arose. Ah Sam struck Reed on the back of the head, but Reed turned quickly just in time to knock a large knife out of Sam's hand. In Candelaria, where water was scarce until a subsequent pipeline was built, a bath cost $2.50 subject to the privilege of reclaiming the sudsy water for resale for street sprinkling purposes. The water supply failed completely in December 1880, and a few weeks later there was a threatened whisky famine. Timely corrective action was taken in both cases, however, and the town continued to look forward to the approaching rails.

The year 1881 started promisingly with two daily construction trains operating over the partly built line. On January 8 an excursion train went through to the end of track in Churchill Canyon, 22 miles below Dayton and 29 miles from milepost O at Mound House. The first public freight, consisting of supplies for Capt. Canavan's copper mine in the Naileigh District, went out on January 28.

Suddenly, two days later, a flood put Dayton under water. For 12 days the railroad was tied up while 150 men rushed repairs. But the rails did move ahead. On the evening of March 1 the engine crew reported they had seen a most beautiful sight —the reflection of the stars on the waters of Walker Lake. Nine days later the conductors began charging passengers 10 cents a mile to ride the trains.

Three locomotives were now in service—No. 1, the CANDELARIA; No. 2, the BODIE, a passenger engine; and No. 3, the COLORADO. With adequate supplies pouring in, rail laying moved ahead at a good clip. Each day six cars of rails and twelve cars of ties left Dayton for the end of track. On April 7, 1881, the track reached Hawthorne, 100

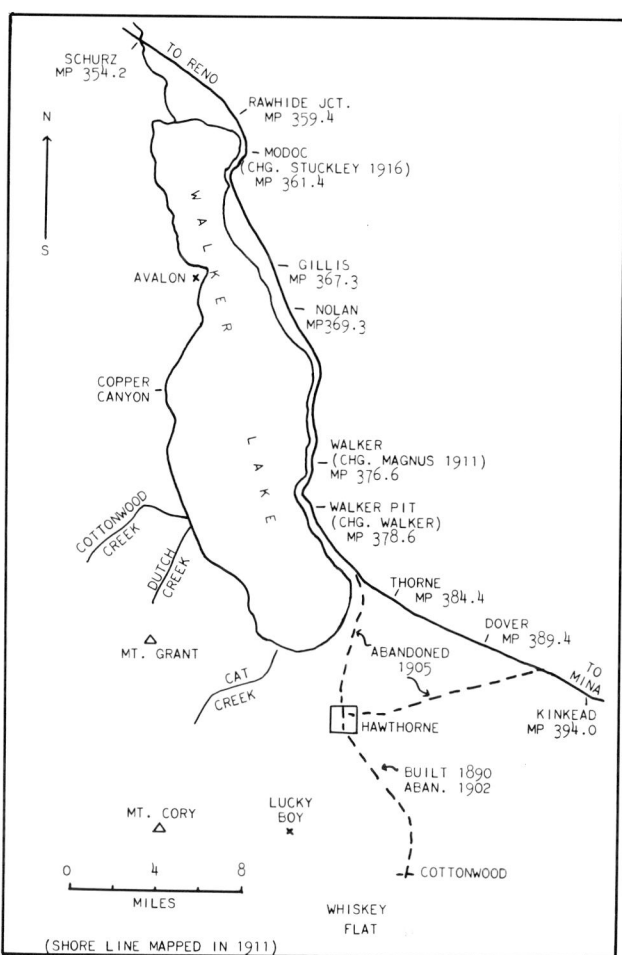

miles from Mound House, and the most immediate job was done.

April 14 was the big day for Hawthorne. Some 800 people, including Governor Kinkead, responded to the advertisements of the C&C and rode the free excursion to Hawthorne to buy town lots. A few passengers clambered aboard Locomotive No. 1, but the majority crowded themselves into or on the express car, four coaches and twelve flat cars which made up the train. On arrival at Hawthorne, considerable confusion ensued. Humorous fellows began calling, "Hotel, Sir, carriage to Palace Hotel." "Twenty minutes for dinner." "This way to the What Cheer House." A few farsighted citizens had set up tent saloons with such names as Silver Palace, Bank Exchange and Big Bonanza. One small tent saloon glorified itself with the name, The Field in the Cloth of Gold. Welcome those liquids must have been at one bit a drink, for it was a very hot day and there was no shade. What little water was available had been hauled four miles to town and was too warm to quench thirst.

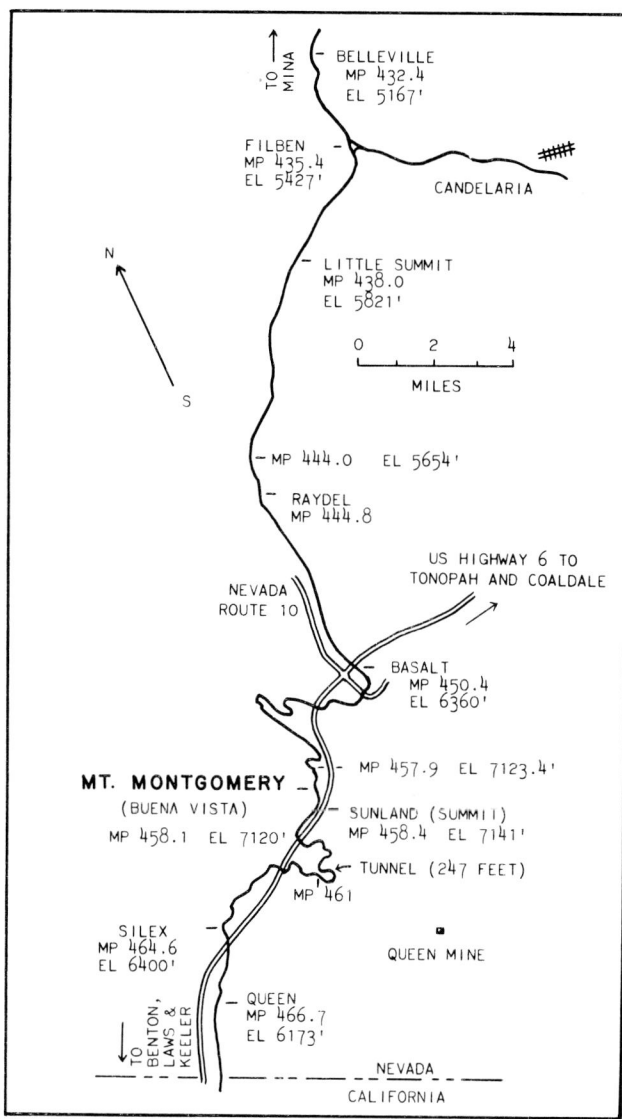

Almost before the train was unloaded a professional gambler had a "rouge et noir" game under way. In spite of this, once the auctioneer got the program started, some 35 lots were sold in a three-hour period at prices ranging from $100 to $195. Considering that this was in the middle of the desert without a permanent habitation around, the effort was considered successful, and nobody minded when a few lots went for slightly less money. Newspapermen pronounced themselves ready to start four different newspapers, though none did. The Piutes made money by selling fish, and in the excitement there was even talk of the possibility of a lynching. At three o'clock the auction was over, and fifteen minutes later the trainload of hot and weary passengers was homeward bound "with the exception of a few who had eaten too much (beer)."

The surveys and line had long been established to Candelaria, and part of the grading had been done. A few weeks after the town lot sale, activity was resumed to put the finishing touches to this section of the line, which stretched southeasterly for 11 miles across a sandy and barren waste before entering a valley floor for an additional 14 miles. By using all of the available rails, the first 11 miles were completed to New Boston Pass. There the railhead stopped, and there it remained for almost six long months.

Regular passenger trains brought ten or twelve people on each trip to Hawthorne, most of them en route to Aurora, Bodie or Candelaria. The town proper was growing, and the main line ran along F Street to the station (located at Fifth Street, where the Elks' Lodge is now), then turned east on Sixth Street to continue on toward Candelaria. An extension of the F Street line southward, plus the addition of 2 switches and a curved section of track to connect the extension with the line east on Sixth Street, furnished the C&C with a wye facility for turning locomotives at the end of their runs.

Construction languished during the hot months of 1881, but the surveyors for the rival California Central Railway were not idle. First they were reported in Lida Valley; then, working their way northward during the summer, they were last reported going over Mt. Montgomery (McBride's) Pass in October. During the same period, James Oliver, chief engineer of the C&C, paid a visit to Cerro Gordo, an early dominant silver camp in the mountains east of Keeler, California. Whether the reports of mining activity in Inyo County were responsible, or whether it was considered expedient to head off the California Central is not known, but suddenly the C&C abandoned its plans to build southeasterly through Nevada to the Silver Peak, Lida and Gold Mountain districts and instead aimed southwest over Mt. Montgomery Pass into California's Owens Valley.

In September 1881 dirt began to move once again, and rail laying started late the following month. The graders reached Soda Springs (now Sodaville), 137 miles from Mound House, while the residents of Front (11 miles from Hawthorne, the former railhead) prepared to move forward with the advancing rails. The latter part of November the tracks passed Deep Wells and approached Soda Springs, and effective December 1, 1881, scheduled trains arrived in town on a daily basis.

Deep Wells served as the western terminus of a stage line operated by Gilmer & Salisbury to the camp of Grantsville to the northeast. Shortly after the arrival of the railroad the name of Deep Wells was changed to Luning, in honor of Nicholas B. Luning, a heavy bondholder in the C&C and an investor in other railroads in California. The town of Luning enjoyed very rapid growth in the forepart of 1882, soon boasting an impressive array of saloons and other establishments. Ore from the nearby Santa Fe district was being transshipped northward to the mills at Dayton for a mere $5.00 a ton — a distinct drop from the former teamster charge of $60 a ton.

December 17, 1881, was a red-letter day. In Churchill Canyon someone piled heavy timbers and rocks on the tracks, and the first attempted train wrecking was recorded. Apparently the culprits were unsuccessful, as only guesses were hazarded that the objective was the express car of bullion regularly shipped by the mills at Belleville, which were then working Candelaria ore.

Five miles beyond Sodaville (where Tonopah Junction ultimately became located) a change was made. The original intent had been to proceed southward and approach Candelaria from the east, but in view of the decision to reach for Owens Valley and the Cerro Gordo mountains of California, the road was now swung westward toward Belleville and the climb to Mt. Montgomery Pass, 2,700 feet higher and 32 miles distant. Candelaria could be approached from the northwest as well as from the southeast.

Belleville celebrated New Year's with the advent of train service on January 1, 1882. For the next two winter months the hills echoed and re-echoed to the blasts of black powder required to finish the line to Filben (2 miles) and then lift it six miles farther and over the hump to Candelaria. Grades were steep; from Filben to the summit (approximately a mile west of Candelaria) the ruling grade was 2.26%, while outbound from Candelaria trains had to negotiate a ruling grade of 2.33%. Three miles out of Filben on the west slope a trestle 292 feet long and 50 feet high was required, while a second, lower trestle was also needed nearer the summit. Even the terminal at Candelaria presented a problem, as the station site and space for yard tracks had to be carved from the hillside above town. The first train, with the BODIE on the head end, pulled into Candelaria at 8:15 P.M. on February 28, 1882. Some 300 people, including a liberal number of ladies, scrambled up the hillside to cheer it on arrival, and waited patiently during the 20-minute delay while the locomotive gingerly negotiated the new track. Beyond the depot, the rails continued along the hillside to the ore dump of the Northern Belle Mine, and the first ore shipment was originated even though the roadbed was not complete.

An unusual accident occurred a few days later. In the middle of the night a sudden gust of wind blew the Candelaria station building over, and it rolled down the hillside. Two men sleeping in the building were shaken up considerably; the stove was broken and the contents of the building were scattered. The railroad frugally returned the building to its original site but cautiously anchored it as close to the ground as possible.

Candelaria became the terminus of the original C&C (as projected). To accommodate the change in route, two new corporations were formed. The Carson and Colorado Railroad Company, Second Division, was organized to build through Nevada to the California state line while the Carson and Colorado Railroad Company, Third Division, was incorporated in California to construct from the state line to a point "near Mojave station on the Southern Pacific Railroad."

Late in January 1882, even before the Candelaria branch was completed, 100 men started working on the 33-mile section from Filben to McBride's ranch, near the California line. The point of connection with the original main line became known as Junction, and the first four miles over Little Summit were easily graded. Aside from a small dip on the west side of Little Summit, the next 20 miles to the physical summit of Mt. Montgomery (a third of a mile west of Mt. Montgomery station) were accomplished only with the aid of 2.3% grades and some heavy curvature through rock cuts. The steepest pitch on the entire climb from Soda Springs, as revealed by the profile chart, was on the older main line just north of Belleville where a 2.776% grade prevailed.

Two miles west of Mount Montgomery station was a 247-foot tunnel, the only such bore on the railroad. It was through this tunnel that engineer Neil Ward was taking his train in August 1902 when the locomotive stalled. Gases accumulated in the firebox, exploded, blew open the door and badly burned Ward. He stuck to his post, backed his train out of the tunnel and averted a possible disaster. A week later Ward was well on the road to recovery.

On January 20, 1883, trains began operating over the 40-mile section from Junction to Benton, just over the California state line. The next 100 miles of track from Benton down the east side of the Owens Valley were quickly and easily constructed. By the middle of March the railroad was completed to the station for Bishop Creek (later Laws), where a commodious and handsome structure 20 x 60 feet was erected. Regular train service to this point started April 1, although a left-handed invitation was issued 10 days previously for all Inyo County residents to enjoy a free ride on the railroad the entire length of the line to Mound House and return. No direct public announcement was issued; rather, it was left to the discretion of the County Assessor to spread the word verbally.

Because the railroad followed the east side of Owens Valley to service the mines, the farmers and the townspeople along the way—nearly all of whom lived west of the river—were less than pleased. Public relations dipped to a further low ebb when R. J. Laws, construction superintendent, visited the newspaper offices in Independence, near the railhead. As previously reported, the C&C's route had been projected southeasterly through the valley to Panamint, Darwin and the Coso Mining District. Laws made what amounted to a public retraction of these plans by proclaiming that once Owens Lake had been reached, the route would "only be determined after actual surveys and a thorough examination and study of the country beyond." As though to stimulate additional negative confidence, he expressed surprise over the small amount of actual development then going on in the area.

Other troubles were besetting the road as well. An ore train out of Candelaria came down the hill and ran into an open switch at Belleville, disabling the engine. This and a succession of minor mishaps resulted in "a general tangling up of rolling stock" which seriously delayed materials destined for the advancing end-of-line.

In spite of these obstacles, 400 men were pushing the road ahead. Graders were stretched over a five-mile section south from Bishop Creek, and track was being laid at the rate of three-quarters of a mile on good days. An excursion train was run from Mound House to the end-of-track, then opposite Lone Pine, to bring everyone to Independence for the July Fourth celebration. Among those attending (for reasons never definitely determined) were a dozen well-dressed and gaudily painted Indians who rode down on the tender and water car from Walker Lake, returning after a quiet visit without even having joined in the local poker game.

The station at Independence was located on the old site of Bend City, so named for the large bend in the Owens River before its course had suddenly changed. Because the town of Independence (proper) lay across the river and some distance to the west, the station name was changed to Kearsarge and, for a time, to Citrus, in order to avoid confusion. Aside from the station building, there was a residence for the section boss and his family and a bunkhouse for the Chinamen, who promptly filled up the kitchen with a rock and mud furnace for their cooking.

On July 12, 1883, Darius O. Mills arrived at the end-of-track on an inspection trip in company with his henchman, Sharon. Not having seen the Owens Valley farming region to the west of the Owens River, and having viewed only the sandy, desert region along the eastern edge of the valley, quite justifiably he uttered his famous remark that the railroad had been built either 300 miles too long, or 300 years too soon. This visit settled the end of the track at Hawley, 293 miles from Mound House, as "the front" until the fall. (Actually, it was to remain "the front" until long after C&C ownership had passed into limbo.) Even though the turntable, depot and engine house were still under construction, regular train schedules to Hawley (Keeler) were initiated on August 1, 1883.

While Mr. Mills may not have been enthusiastically delighted with his new investment, his railroad was welcomed. The *Nevada Tribune,* in an article headed "Nevada's Salvation," praised the C&C for opening up new mining areas as well as for providing employment and tax money for Lyon and Esmeralda Counties. And for a while this appeared to be true. The old mill at New Boston (south of Walker Lake) was repaired. Near Luning, the Copper King Mine was showing great promise in September, 1882; other mine operators were reopening their mines; and the Melrose Smelting Company of Oakland, California, maintained an agent in Luning to control the shipment of concentrates from Downieville, 35 miles to the northeast. Responsible people report having seen pictures of the Luning station with the C&C tracks on one side and a small steam locomotive on tracks of narrower gauge on the other. Inquiry has disclosed that this was a mining railroad of many years ago, but no other details or confirmation have been found.

Soda Springs blossomed with the advent of the new smelter of the Esmeralda Copper Company whose Blue Light Mine in the Garfield District to the west showed great promise. New houses were going up in town; the C&C erected a large warehouse; and the two springs of curative waters (one hot and one cold) from which the town derived its name drew a lively business for the hotel and bathhouses of Martin Brazzanovich.

Seven miles farther down the line, Belleville boasted several stamp mills and furnaces serving the Candelaria mines in the hills to the south. A good 65 tons of ore were shipped out daily from the mines, the carloads being brought down over the grades of the C&C's Candelaria branch.

West of Mt. Montgomery Pass near Queen, the Indian Queen Mine, under the direction of John Howell, was rated a dividend-paying proposition with its five-stamp mill and furnaces. In Mono County, California, Benton station served the Blind Springs Hill, Leevining Canyon, Mammoth and Bodie mines. Farther south in Inyo County the Kearsarge Mine, high in the Sierras west of Independence, was distinguished less for its output than for its 18-inch drum-and-cable railroad running 1,809 feet from the mine to the mill. The grade varied from 28 to 60 degrees, while a passing track, 130 feet long, allowed the empty and loaded cars to transpose each other at mid-point.

Across the valley on the eastern slopes, the Eclipse Mine (later the Brown Monster and finally the Reward) also operated with a short tramway. Still farther south near the shores of Owens Lake, the rich production of the Cerro Gordo silver mine created a town of several thousand people who came and left over the short span of a 10-year period. The coming of the railroad failed to spark an immediate revival, although in 1908, during one of the subsequent active periods, the famous Cerro Gordo tramway was constructed.

At Keeler, over the years, two separate companies engaged in the extraction of minerals from Owens Lake through evaporation processes, using industrial railroads as adjuncts to the operations. The Inyo Development Company, dating back to 1885, operated approximately 2.6 miles of 24-inch gauge line along the evaporating vats as well as a segment of 36-inch gauge track of indeterminate length. The connection of the latter with the C&C's rails was broken in 1926, although the company languished for another 10 years before being dissolved. The second project, that of the Natural

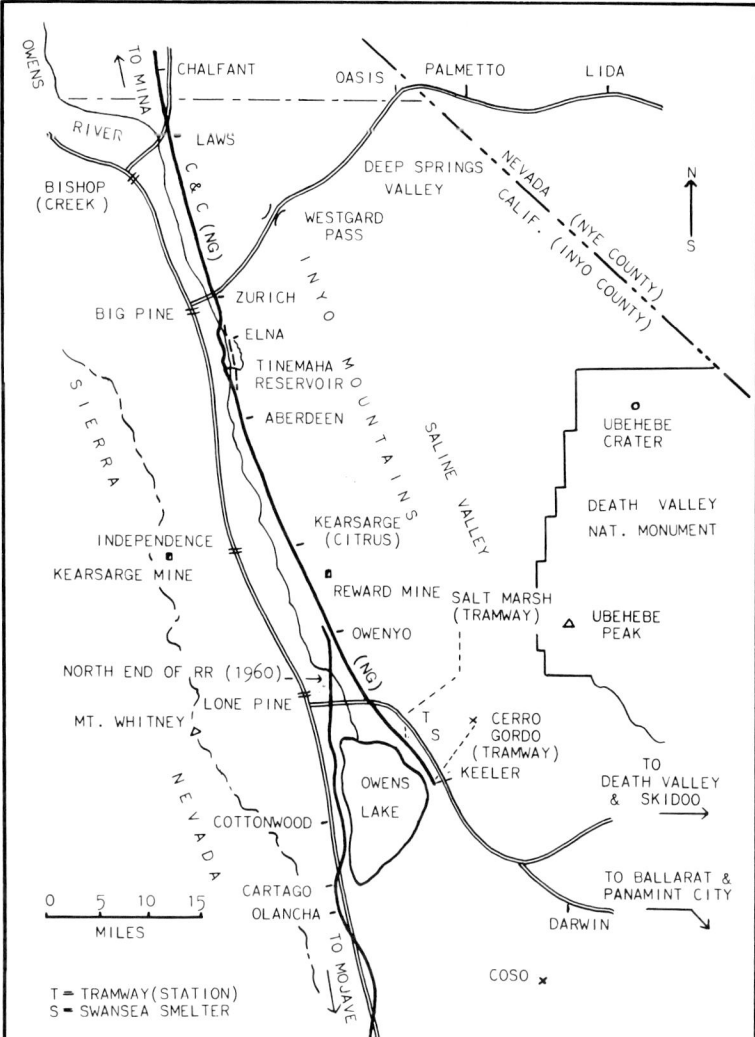

Soda Products Company, was established much later, incorporating about a mile (6,986 feet) of 36-inch gauge track in 1916. The rails remained until abandoned in 1954.

The fortunes of Owens Valley varied from year to year as new veins were found and old ones pinched out. Near Benton, the Eureka Mill at the old camp of Montgomery became active. New excitement at the Montezuma mine caused the erection of a furnace, and the C&C obligingly laid a spur to it and named the station on the main line for the mine superintendent's daughter, *Elna* Miller. Near Independence, the newspaper man, Chalfant, had the old Brown Monster mill operating in good condition in spite of its dilapidated appearance. At Swansea, a new smelter was blown in. The mill at Hawley was reopened by Capt. J. M. Keeler, who repaired the old wood flume in Cottonwood Canyon in the Sierra Nevada mountains and equipped a barge on Owens Lake so that cordwood could be floated down the flume and barged across the lake to the mill for fuel. The railroad reflected the change in management of the mill by altering its station name from Hawley to Keeler.

Such activity would lend credence to the hope for a profitable future for the railroad, for activity normally was indicative of tonnage — tonnage of supplies pouring in to the mines and mining towns, and tonnage of ores and mineral products pouring out to mill or market — and tonnage was the railroad's very lifeblood. A compilation of the figures for the early years of operation shows, in retrospect, that the period was not the beginning of an expansion but rather the end of a mild boom.

MINE PRODUCTION IN THOUSANDS OF DOLLARS

Year	Mono County Calif.	Inyo County Calif.	Esmeralda County Nevada	Total
1880	$2,990	$223	$1,206	$4,419
1881	3,685	310	1,315	5,310
1882	2,580	350	1,372	4,302
1883	2,040	128	1,205	3,373
1884	1,285	162	430	1,877
1885	574	98	855	1,527

The effect of this economy upon the Carson & Colorado is reflected in their operating results:

Year	Tons Handled	Gross Revenues	Net Income *Before **After Interest	Dividends Declared
1881	26,121	$254,066	$160,409*	$ ......
1882	56,181	442,254	111,104**	112,500
1883	70,715	441,994	46,008**	33,750

No further financial statements were made public until 1891, but it is safe to assume that with the decline in mining activity and the necessity for reorganization in 1892, the owners were somewhat less than pleased.

Candelaria had been the principal mining camp with a population of 1,500 souls amply serviced by a total of 27 saloons. When it came on unhappy times the railroad suffered too. Strife arose in 1883 when the Holmes Mining Co. sued the Northern Belle Mining Co. for $2,000,000 damages resulting from trespassing. This was an instance of David attacking Goliath, for the Northern Belle, one of the few mines developed without the necessity of assessment, already had paid some 71 dividends totaling $2,425,000 and, with ample ore in sight, was the mainstay of Candelaria. A sensation was created when, just before midnight on a Saturday night in November 1883, the jury at Carson City awarded $360,000 damages to the plaintiff.

Immediately the C&C filed suit for $10,113 for wood, salt, charcoal and transportation charges. The V&T sought $1,056 for castings. In the middle of the furor, the Mt. Diablo Mining Company (also in Candelaria) discharged most of its men while its machinery was sent to the V&T shops in Carson City for repairs. (These shops performed a wide and useful service making and repairing mining machinery for concerns along the C&C all the way down into Owens Valley.) To climax the situation, a fire on December 15, 1883, destroyed 16 buildings leaving most of the south side of Candelaria's Main Street in ruins with the exception of the fireproof Esmeralda County Bank.

Production in 1884 reflected the general chaos in Candelaria. Only $27,000 of minerals were recorded as against a bountiful $1,200,000 the year before. Improvement followed in 1885 as the Holmes took over the Northern Belle, and the mines turned out a half-million dollars of minerals in spite of declining silver prices and a strike.

The miners looked with disfavor upon a proposed daily wage cut from $4.00 to $3.00, and the mines were closed during the summer of 1885. Second thoughts during the hot, idle days apparently were more rational, and the men returned to work. In August 1890, recovery in the price of silver to $1.21 an ounce enabled the miners to bargain more successfully for a $3.50 daily wage. The situation deteriorated again in the next year when the price of silver declined. The mine owners sought to institute a variable pay scale ranging between $3.00 and $4.00 based on the price of silver; the men refused to accept anything less than the $3.50 rate; so the mines were closed on November 30, 1891, and Candelaria began a long period of depression. The miners drifted elsewhere, many men going south to try prospecting in the Tule District near Lida.

With Candelaria shut down and Bodie operating on a diminished scale, C&C revenues dropped by one-third and tonnage by one-half. The largest loss of tonnage was represented in the short-haul movement of ores from Candelaria to the mills at Belleville and Soda Springs. Although Poor's Manual for 1893 showed net results for the year ending June 30, 1892, of $84,673, this was before taxes of approximately $20,000 and interest of some $263,000. Something obviously needed to be done; the problem was what to do.

The solution devised was the incorporation on February 27, 1892, of a new company, the Carson & Colorado *Railway* Company, to take over and operate all three of the previously separate divisions. By the end of the summer this had been accomplished. The 10 stockholders of the old company exchanged their stock — share for share — for those of the new company. D. O. Mills and the Sharon Estate continued to hold three-quarters of the total stock outstanding. Mortgage debt was scaled down from $4,380,000 to $2,000,000; the interest coupons were reduced in rate from 6% to 4%, thereby bringing annual interest charges down to a mere $80,000. Mills and the Sharon Estate, being the largest bondholders, suffered the most; although the Luning Estate did not escape unscathed with its next largest holding of $200,000 of bonds. However, in spite of the improved operating and financial picture, the national economy was suffering during the 1890's, and traffic continued to decline until 1897. As a result, the reorganized company failed to earn even the reduced bond interest.

If the management and finance of the Carson & Colorado during this period appeared to be uncertain and tumultuous, the railroad's operations and personality at the public level were the direct antithesis and could best be characterized as serene and dispassionate. The abbreviated train schedules of 1894 provided a 10:50 A.M. departure from Mound House, following exchange of passengers with the V&T, thence a leisurely 10-hour-20-minute run over the 158 miles to Candelaria. Although the carded time of arrival at that southern terminus was 9:10 P.M., it is doubtful that any serious attempt was made to adhere to the timetable to obviate the numerous causes for delay. Travelers going through to California and Owens Valley perforce would detrain at Belleville and catch the next tri-weekly mixed train at 8:35 A.M. If their business carried them that far, and their constitution withstood the rigors of the trip, theoretically they would arrive in Keeler, 143 miles distant, at 6:15 P.M. The return schedule was no more energetic; apparently time was an inconsequential factor in the nomadism of the period.

A trip on the C&C was a vivid experience for many an Eastern tenderfoot. The mirages, the treeless plains, the trepidation at the sight of Indians were wondrous and fearful experiences. The southbound train was an unalloyed milk run; it picked up small cans of fresh milk at Wabuska and deposited them with inexorable regularity at the various stations all the way to Candelaria. Local residents at the wayside points would stroll down to meet the train and claim their milk cans on the station platforms. At Hawthorne, variety was interposed in the substance of a large, black dog who was trained to sniff the various containers, select the correct one, grab the hoop in its jaws and carry it home.

Liquids other than milk were also provided for the ever-thirsty desert population. Locomotive tenders were equipped with a special spigot on one side so that the Piute Indians at Rhodes Salt Marsh could draw their drinking water into buckets or jars. Also peculiar to Rhodes was the lowly box car set on a siding to serve as a temporary jail. Its impermanence was amply demonstrated one time when eight drunken Piutes were placed in confinement behind the locked doors. After yelling for an hour, they suddenly became quiet. Then, making a common effort, they burst through the side of the car, spilling to the ground in a great heap. Freedom, at the cost of a few splinters, was wonderful — until the next time.

The big question and common topic of conversation in Owens Valley and vicinity concerned the unfinished projection of the C&C from Keeler to Mojave. Following Mills' famous edict of 1883, no further construction was attempted on this final 140-mile stretch, and the Valley people found themselves living in a virtual transportation cul-de-sac. Their only means of ingress or egress lay 300 miles to the north. Of necessity, business deals were consummated in San Francisco some 500 route miles distant, whereas completion of the unfinished portion of the line would bring Los Angeles within a 250-mile trip and furnish valuable connections with the Santa Fe at Mojave in opposition to those of the Central Pacific at Reno (via V&T).

The people talked about it; the newspapers wrote about it. In fact, newspaper editors developed more conjectures than there were people to finance the propositions. Every year the subject presented itself in diverse forms, and had the price of silver held up, perhaps Mills might have been persuaded to build the line. In June 1887, D. A. Bender, Secretary of the C&C, was credited as saying that the extension would be built. A month later the directors reportedly had the matter under consideration. In August it was rumored that rail laying would start September 1. Optimism was dissipated however when a reporter finally interviewed D. O. Mills.

Reporter: "Mr. Mills, our people are very anxious to learn what prospect there is for an extension of the Carson & Colorado Railway to Los Angeles."

Mills: "Well, I cannot say. We don't know ourselves yet."

Reporter: "But isn't the matter now under consideration, and is there not a probability that the road will be completed this fall?"

Mills: "There is no doubt its extension would be a great benefit to Reno. Of course it will be extended, it is merely a question of time."

A lengthening of the railroad was accomplished that year (1887), but it was hardly the one anticipated. Allegedly to comply with charter requirements, two miles of track were laid from Keeler to Jiggerville (Boland), the former site of the old Cerro Gordo boat landing on Owens Lake.

Hopes revived again in 1888 when business picked up to the extent that double heading was required over the grades to handle the traffic. Daily train service was instituted between Keeler and Belleville, and a roundhouse and turntable were constructed at the latter location to assist in storing and servicing the concentration of motive power.

More publicity developed in 1889. The *Reno Evening Gazette* started the ball rolling with a story on March 22 that Yerington had been in Los Angeles to seek a subsidy for the extension to Mojave. Although no subsidy was obtained, some aid in the form of bonds was offered, and Yerington agreed to attempt to induce the management to build at once. A few days later it was reported Mills did not favor the extension. In August Yerington was reported as saying that, while the extension to Mojave had been abandoned, he had discussed the subject of extension with President Adams of the Union Pacific, and it was decided the C&C would build a 50-mile line from Keeler to meet the UP's projected (LA&SL) line to California. As financial difficulties halted the UP railhead at Milford, Utah, the Keeler extension died a natural death.

The subject came up once again after the death of Nicholas Luning in February 1890, for Luning had been considered the major opponent of the line. However, no action was entertained. Hope revived in 1892 when a new mortgage was recorded describing the route of the railroad as extending from Mound House to Mojave. The mortgage was duly filed; no activity resulted so anticipation subsided once again.

One final physical extension of the Carson & Colorado was made, however, but it was far from the sight and sound of Owens Valley residents. In Hawthorne, at the foot of Walker Lake, a lengthy addition to the tail of the F Street wye track was made, and it became the 7.30-mile Cottonwood Branch leading off to the southwest. Construction began on August 17, 1890, and every available, idle man was offered work. A crew of 50 were soon grading the roadbed, and the line was completed by November of that year. Immediate objective was the lumber to be found at Cottonwood, which was sorely needed for fuel for the locomotives.

In spite of the $47,751 spent to construct the line, the Cottonwood Branch was to be very short-lived. In September 1900 a program was instituted to convert the C&C's locomotives from wood burners to coal burners, the faithful V&T shops at Carson City being selected to do the work. As the conversion progressed, less and less wood came in over the Cottonwood line. Gradually it fell into disuse, and in August 1902 the rails were removed.

The capriciousness of railroad operations in the Nevada wastelands was amply characterized by the C&C's problems with moisture. Water was relatively hard to find in continuing, reliable sources for use in the locomotive boilers, while surplus water from storms and sudden flash floods was even more difficult to predict and control in the hard, arid countryside.

One station a few miles below Churchill was appropriately called "Washout" when it suffered particularly severe, heavy rains in January 1886 with the consequent loss of a half a mile of main line plus other damage along the road. A gang of 300 men was required to effect repairs. Four years later when a great series of storms tied up western railroads generally, the C&C had its share of troubles. At Dayton there were several bad washouts; at Luning an engine was off the track and badly wrecked; while another train was ditched at Candelaria. Near Independence a small bridge was washed away, and the water-soaked roadbed made several miles of track unstable. Several serious washouts were discovered over Mt. Montgomery Pass, and all idle men in Hawthorne were drafted to fix the track in that area.

At Hawthorne, a flash flood washed out part of the K&L Railroad, a "very narrow gauge" line connecting the Knapp & Laws store with the C&C freight depot. Again in March 1907 the Carson River overflowed its banks and placed four miles of track under water. Repairs were rushed, but even after several days of work, passengers still were required to step off one train, ride a hand car for two miles, and then walk around the hills to get to the other train.

Sand and wind brought additional problems to the narrow gauge operation. On a single trip in March 1904, the engineer halted his train five times so that the sand could be shoveled off the track.

Snow blockades and landslides also harassed the line. On Mt. Montgomery Pass snow would block trains frequently, sometimes for days on end. In March 1904, the agent at Mina was obliged to dispatch a relief train with food and coffee for the occupants of two passenger trains and one freight train locked in by the drifting snows.

The late 1880's and the decade of the 1890's continued to be characterized by varying fortunes. Five miles north of Keeler, Israel Luce's Inyo Marble Works developed sufficient business to warrant the construction of a long spur track to serve the works in 1887. Three years later (in 1890), a single order amounting to 200 cars of marble was placed for construction of the Mills Building in San Francisco. Farm production was given a boost when the New East Side Ditch in the Owens Valley was completed in October 1888. Up to 1891 F. M. "Borax" Smith was producing borax in moderate quantities at Teel's Marsh (near Belleville), while at the Keeler end of the railroad the Inyo Development Co. was evaporating Owens Lake water for its salines.

Indians continued to ride the freight trains almost incessantly. Their families would scramble up to the top of the box cars for a free ride to some place or other, the destination was largely unimportant. When the free rides were stopped, Johnson Sides, famed Piute Indian Chief and peacemaker, said he understood and did not blame the company, for: "Injun git drunk and pite brakeman and conductor. That business must stop. Injun no-more get drunk; then, may so, they can ride."

Following the end of the Candelaria boom in 1891, Chris Zabriskie attempted to step up business in the dull town through the medium of some personalized advertising over the door of his undertaking establishment which read: "You kick the bucket; we do the rest." Had Zabriskie been a railroad man, he might have had some business, for his appeal aptly described the trend of affairs on the Carson & Colorado. Traffic had dwindled to virtually nothing, and at the end of the fiscal year 1897 a tally of the revenues produced the astoundingly low figure of $131,096. Apathy set in among the directorate—no directors' meetings were held from May 2, 1896, until after March 1900 when the property was sold to the Southern Pacific.

The purchase of the Carson & Colorado by the SP in March 1900 came as a surprise. Up until August 1899 the CP (then under lease to the SP) was suffering financial pangs, and bankruptcy loomed large upon the horizon. Then Huntington effected his *coup de grâce* (see CP) and brought the Central Pacific under full ownership and control of the Southern Pacific making improvements and betterments of the CP property not only an expediency but a matter of necessity as well. The purchase of the Carson & Colorado by the SP represented the first step of expansion in the state of Nevada, and immediately released a flood of speculation that connecting lines at both the northern and southern ends of the narrow gauge would be built to tie it in with the rest of the SP system. There was also a rumor that the SP had purchased the V&T, but Yerington exploded the myth by declaring, "Nothing in it whatever."

In the latter part of May 1900 Collis P. Huntington, the last of the Big Four, decided to see the property that he and his SP had just purchased. Accompanied by R. J. Laws, who was retained as C&C superintendent following the acquisition, and Julius Kruttschnitt, later president of the SP, Huntington ordered a special inspection train which made the trip to Keeler in an astounding 11½ hours and returned north before local newspapermen could interview him. On arrival back in Carson City, Huntington (then 80 years old) was greeted by a committee of six including Supreme Court Justice Bonnifield. In Reno he visited with a local group and there stated that the gap between Keeler and Mojave would soon be closed. As to the northern connection with the Central Pacific he was noncommittal. Huntington died suddenly that summer, just a few days before Jim Butler made his famous discoveries at Tonopah. Thus he never realized the fortuitousness of his purchase which, within but a few years, was to be highly lucrative and profitable.

The bugaboo of narrow gauge began to plague the SP early in the C&C's operations. On February 15, 1901, R. J. Laws, Superintendent of the C&C, was reportedly surveying for installation of a third rail on the line between Mound House and Wabuska to accommodate cars destined for the copper company at that latter point. "Several cars of lumber and machinery have been shipped recently . . . (and it is) expensive for the company to have things transferred at Mound House."

Business on the C&C during the first few years of SP ownership continued at despondently low levels. Revenues in 1901 dipped to figures still smaller than those of the dull 1890's, and a small net loss was reported. The year 1902 was somewhat better; gross revenues exceeded those of the year 1891 for the first time, and a profit was reported. Improvement continued in succeeding years, but it was not until 1905 that revenues exceeded those of the earlier lucrative 1881-1883 period.

Encouraged by reports on the embryo bonanza then developing at Tonopah, the new owners commenced extensive expenditures for deferred maintenance and improvements on the C&C. Straight stacks were installed on the locomotives as conversion was completed from wood to coal burning in the fall of 1901, while SP engineers were busy along the line with their transits seeking a better alignment for the roadbed. The latter activity created considerable apprehension in Hawthorne as it was feared that the town might be cut off from the railroad. Some optimists predicted that plans called for large shops at that location which would expand the economy. Greek George, the local oracle, had some ideas too. "You want-a know what-a the rilroad do? Well, I tall-a you. He make a straight line from Carson. One beeg hill near Carson they cut-a down. They make-a one tunnel under Mountain Grant and then he make-a one bridge across Walker Lake. You maybe theenk I don't-a know nottins, but I am as smat as any o' ems, jes-a same."

May 17, 1900, was the date of Jim Butler's initial silver strike in the barren area that was to become the site of the thriving metropolis of Tonopah. Before the news spread, Butler had staked out many claims and turned the properties over to lessees to operate. Production began to climb, the ore being carted the first 60 miles to the Carson & Colorado for transportation by rail to the smelters.

The rise was rapid. In November 1901 a special train of 19 cars loaded with ore was started for the smelter at Everett, Washington. With a whole town to be built, inbound traffic swamped the station platforms at Candelaria and Sodaville awaiting the teamsters' dispositions for final movement the remaining few miles. Daily trains once again were instituted below Hawthorne, the new schedules taking effect November 18, 1901. Stages met the trains at Sodaville, and even today old-timers proudly reminisce that they were in Tonopah before the trains came.

With the rising tide of traffic, the original eight narrow gauge locomotives became heavily overtaxed. Additional SP narrow gauge engines were brought in from California. Still the problems multiplied, as well as the confusion. A carload of Montana-Tonopah ore valued at $10,000 was ignominiously "lost." Loaded at Sodaville and transshipped at Mound House, it was last seen going through Carson City. The event brought recollection of a similar situation on the CP when a car of practically pure Comstock silver rolled off the track and vanished in the Carson Sink in the 1870's. Subsequently two prospectors determined the spot, sank a shaft, and created considerable excitement with their "new Comstock" which pinched out after $25,000 of production. The effort was sufficient to warrant a short period of riotous living for the two entrepreneurs, who shortly reverted to such exalted positions as cook and mule herder.

In the early flush of excitement, railroads were projected to Tonopah from virtually every direction. Even the SP entertained the idea (see Tonopah & Goldfield). As finally built in 1904, the Tonopah Railroad was a three-foot gauge line connecting with the C&C at a point approximately one mile south of Rhodes, designated as Tonopah Junction. Operations began July 23, 1904, and in spite of heavy floods which virtually destroyed the line during the early months of service, traffic was facilitated and the congestion around Sodaville and Candelaria was relieved to a great extent, though not sufficiently to overcome the rising tide of business.

The biggest problem and greatest bottleneck of C&C operations lay at Mound House where physical interchange with the V&T was necessitated. It was not only ignominious to be obliged to use the short, bridge line's services to reach home SP rails at Reno, but there also remained the canker of transshipping all freight from narrow to standard gauge cars and vice versa. Strikes and threats of strikes by the freight handlers frequently augmented the confusion.

In 1904 special trains were occasioned solely for the rail and ties needed for the construction of the Tonopah Railroad. A new perishable freight house was built at Sodaville, while other improvements were being made all along the line of the C&C. The work was hampered somewhat when a group of Chinese laborers quit because one of their hand cars ran over a dog's tail — a certain omen of bad luck. Still the basic problem had not been solved, and when the full impact of the Tonopah business was felt following the opening of that railroad, the situation became doubly critical. Over 100 freight cars were lined up at Sparks on the SP main line waiting to get in over the V&T, while several hundred more were tied up at Mound House where all the outgoing ore was transferred by hand. Something had to be done.

Standard gauging that portion of the C&C's main line from Tonopah Junction to Mound House was a partial answer, although it still did not solve the V&T interchange problem. Work was begun in October 1904 when a carload of Japanese laborers went to work near Mound House. Two new rails were laid outside the narrow gauge tracks (the inside rails and short ties were subsequently removed) and soon four-rail track was installed for quite a distance. As the work progressed, the freight transfer point was shifted southward—to Wabuska in February 1905, then to Schurz, to Hawthorne on June 24, and before the end of July all the way to Sodaville. Several line changes were made in the process. The big curve on leaving Mound House was partially reversed; some changes were made at Dayton; and Hawthorne's apprehensions were realized when it was left completely off the line. On Sunday, August 14, 1905, the Tonopah Railroad converted its line to standard gauge, and the job was done—freight and passengers could now be routed to Tonopah on standard gauge rails all the way.

The job was not easy and the crises were many. An embargo had to be declared on the C&C as some 400 cars were clogging the side tracks and backed up all the way to Truckee on the SP main line. Express matter was allowed to go through, though at a much higher cost than that of regular freight. Wells Fargo, for example, took 2,000 bricks down to Tonopah for a mere $682, then transferred the load to teamsters for the remaining miles to Goldfield where a bake furnace was urgently in need of them. The embargo lasted for 2½ months, was lifted, only to be reinstated again on lumber traffic. These were but the first of a series of embargos as the deluge of traffic continued to plague the line.

There was little rejoicing at Hawthorne, however. Citizens watched the track forces construct the new 15.8-mile cut-off several miles to the east. To the railroad it meant the elimination of a bad curve and heavy grade plus a 6.6-mile reduction in mileage which combined to reflect a saving of nearly an hour in running time. The last trains to

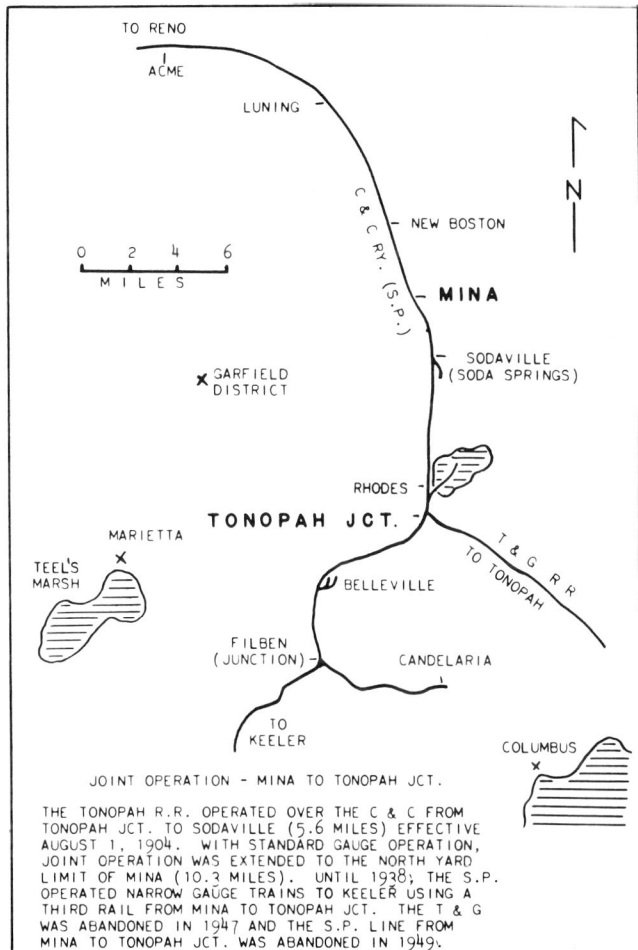

Hawthorne were operated on August 18, 1905. For a time a Chinese track crew brought the mail in by hand car over the old narrow gauge track, but eventually the operation was discontinued and the rails were taken up.

With the acquisition of control of the SP by the UP, Harriman sought to do what Huntington could not accomplish. He viewed with disdain any sharing of revenue from the Tonopah business with the V&T and sought to purchase that line to eliminate the aggravating bottleneck. When his overtures failed he decided to do the next best thing and construct his own 28-mile connection between the SP at Hazen and the C&C at Fort Churchill. Early in April, 1905, a gang of 1,000 men were set to work grading the roadbed across the flat and on the hillside above the future site of Lake Lahontan. Aside from mollifying an irate rancher over a right-of-way matter, there were no special problems involved, and the standard gauge line was opened on September 1, 1905.

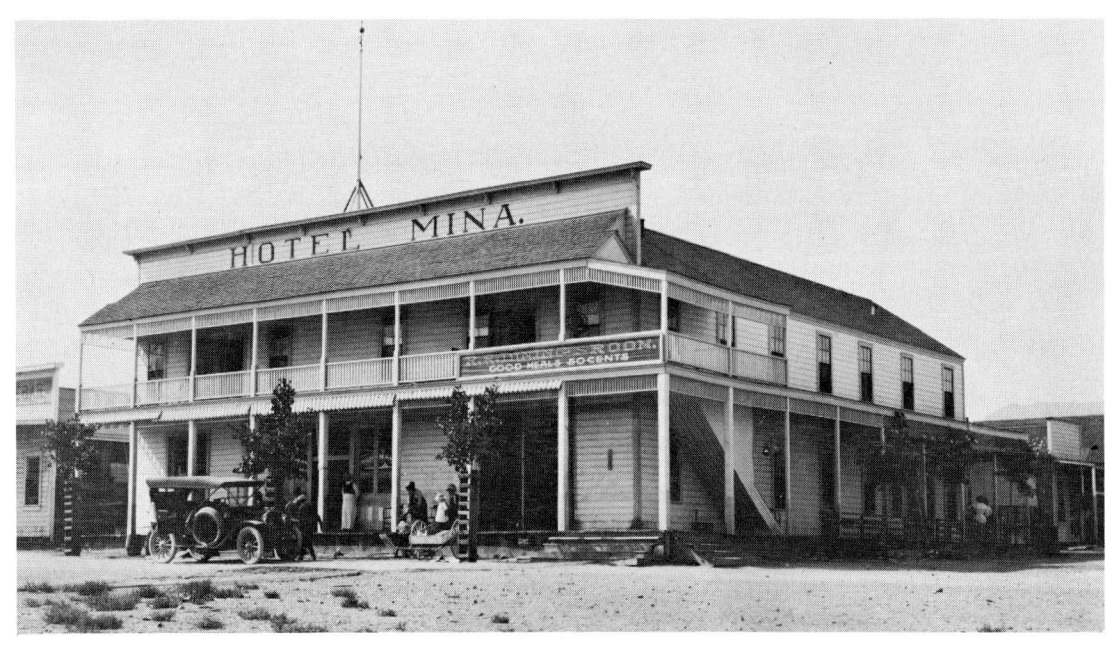

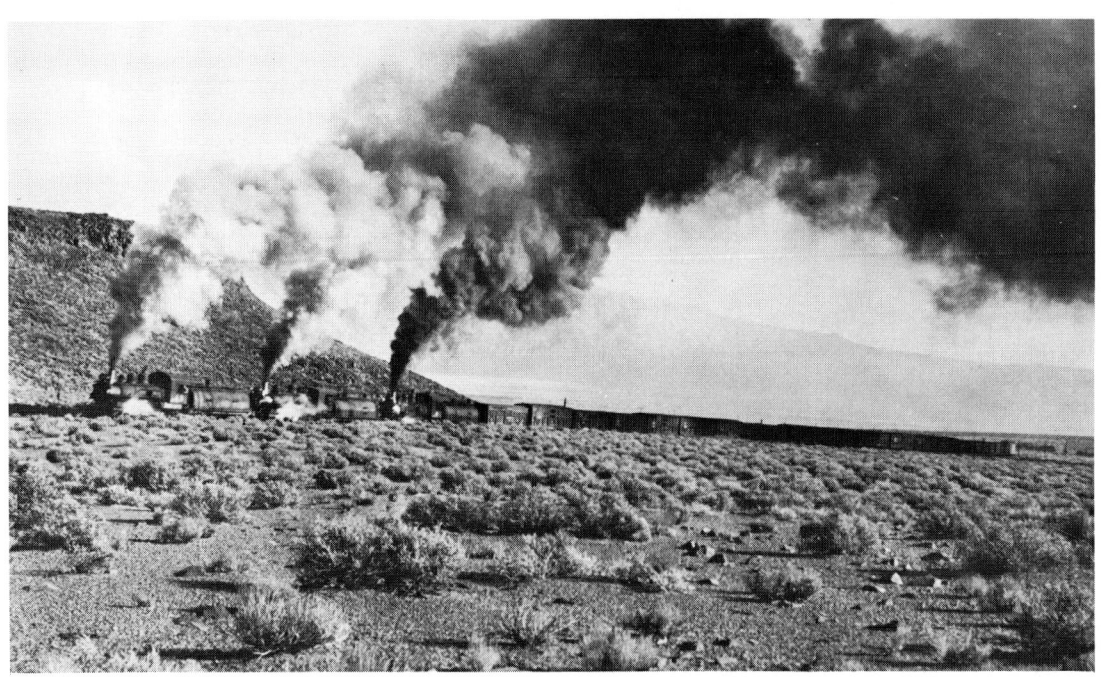

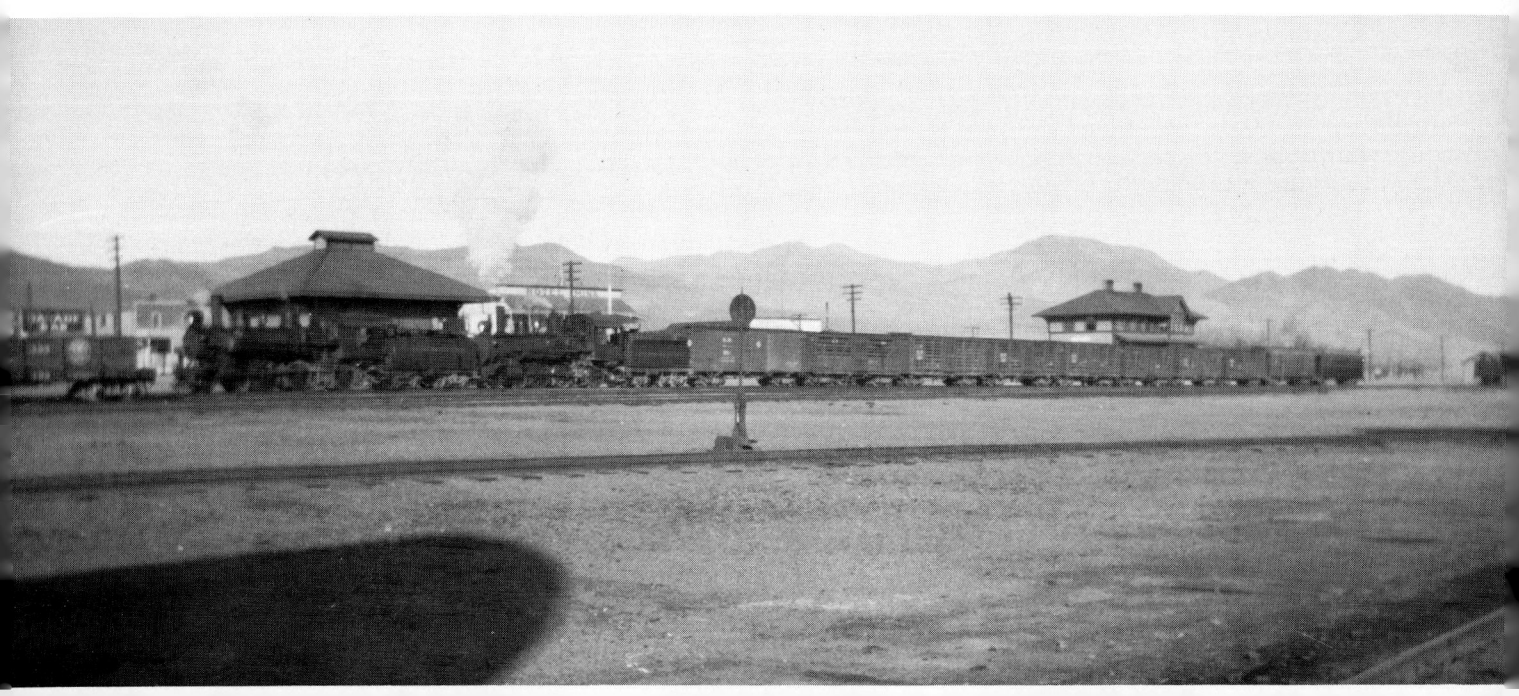

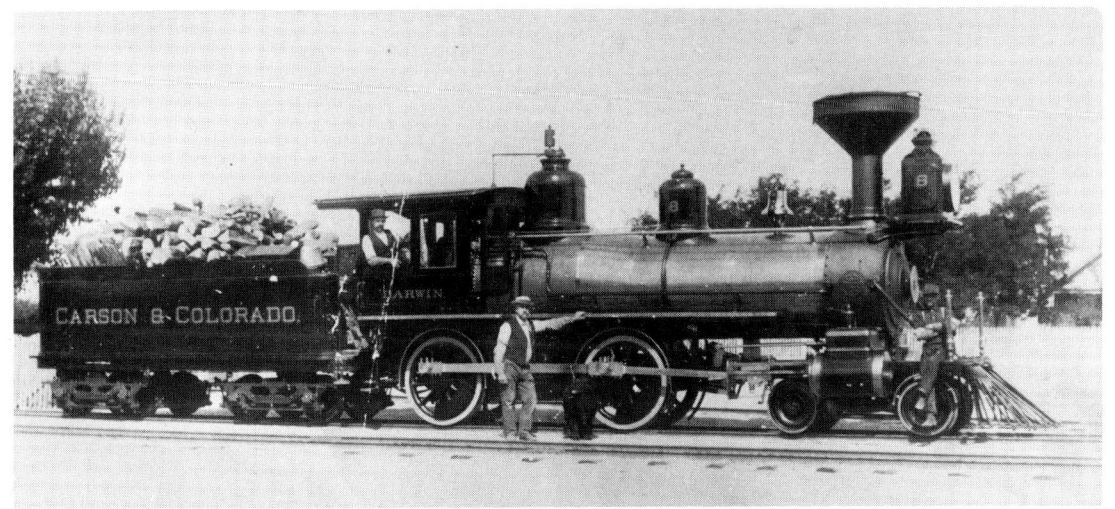

Hawthorne, 100 miles from Mound House, became the first major terminus of the narrow-gauge Carson & Colorado Railroad. It was also the junction point for the 7-mile Cottonwood branch, built in 1890 to supply wood for fuel for such locomotives as No. 8, the DARWIN *(above)*, seen standing on the south end of the wye formed by the junction of that branch with the main. Within 12 years the Cottonwood branch was gone, and the eight original locomotives of the line had been converted to coal burners, typified by No. 6, the HAWTHORNE *(below)*. By 1905, new construction accompanying conversion of the gauge to standard (as far as Tonopah Jct.) by-passed Hawthorne completely; the Carson & Colorado was consolidated with the other segments under the name of Nevada & California Ry.; and the major terminal for this new operation was located at Mina, whose hotel *(page opposite, top)* catered to N&C travelers in its "R.R. Dining Room – Good Meals 50 Cents." Internal fortification was mandatory for arduous trips over the narrow gauge in mixed trains such as the one *(bottom)* whose two oil-burning locomotives, eight high cars plus baggage and coach stretch from the freight house to beyond the station. The proximity of the hotel is indicated by the name on the facade as seen over the top of the second locomotive. Within an hour the train will be toiling up the steep slopes of Montgomery Pass, much as the triple-headed stock extra *(center)* is doing in 1938. Engines Nos. 18 and 8 are pouring forth the oil smoke. They came from the N-C-O Ry. *(Left Top: Mrs. Hugh Brown Collection; Center: G. M. Best Collection; Bottom: George D. Oliver Photo; Right Top: J. H. McBride Collection; Bottom: Southern Pacific Collection.)*

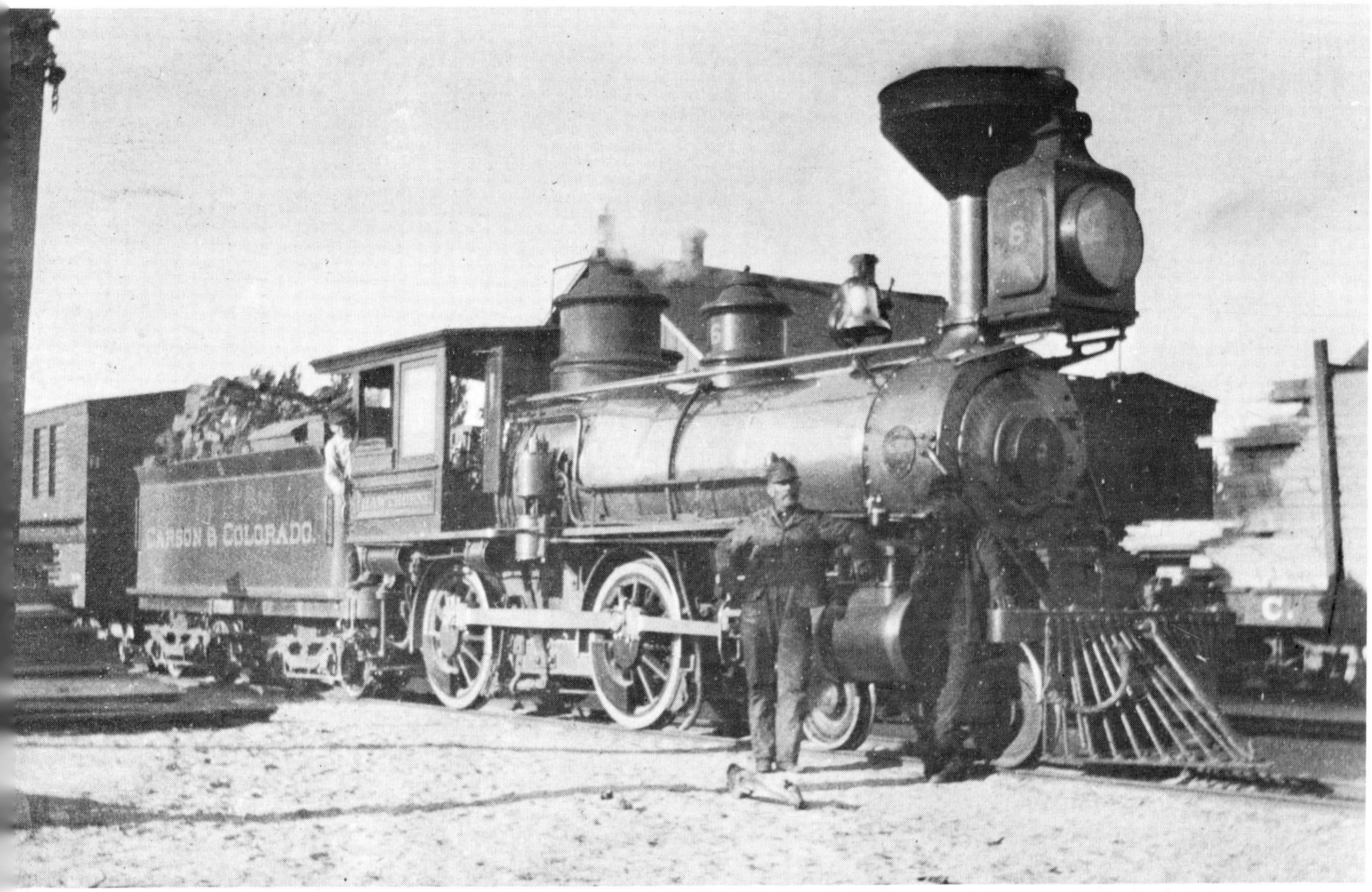

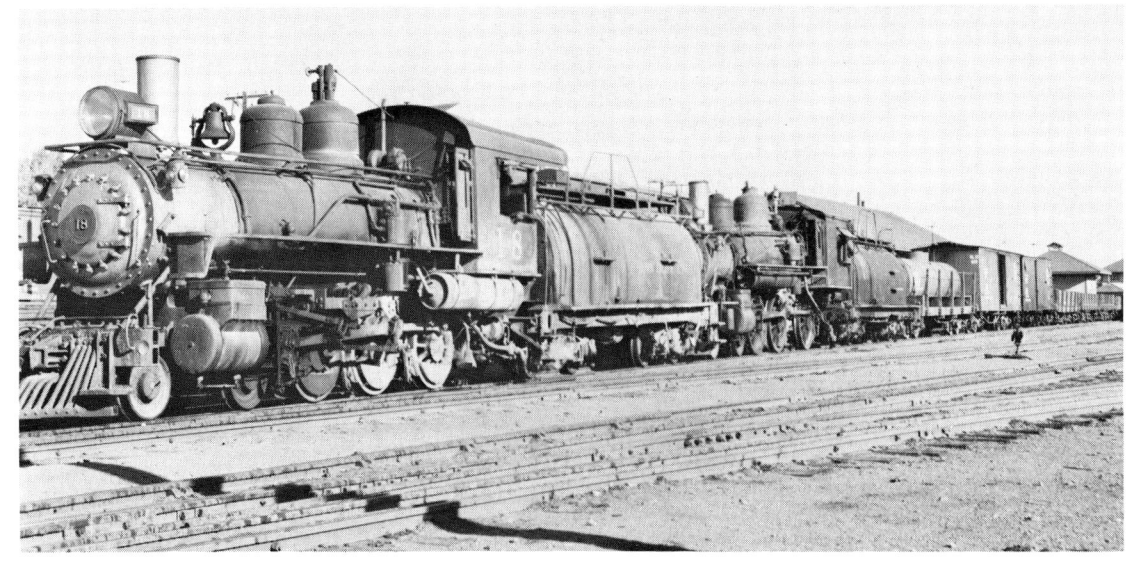
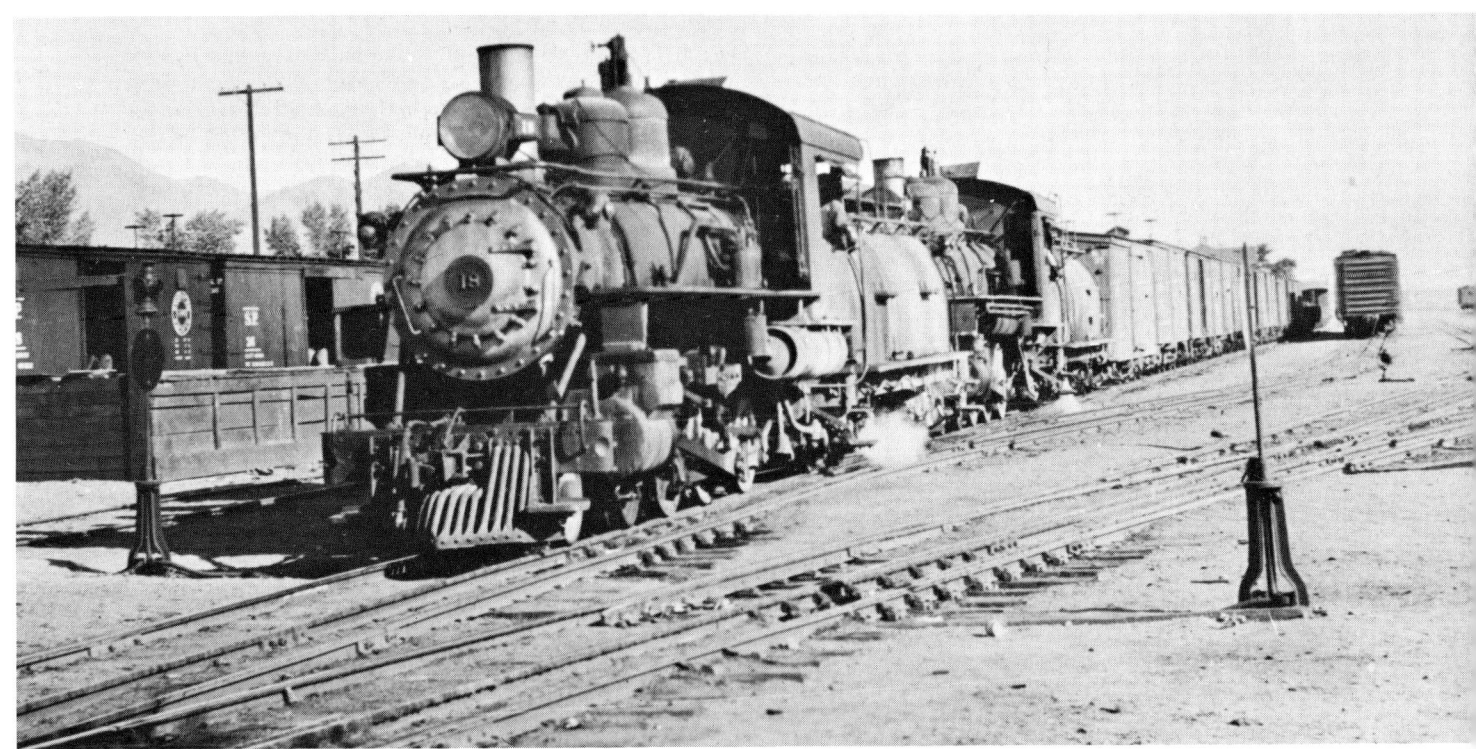
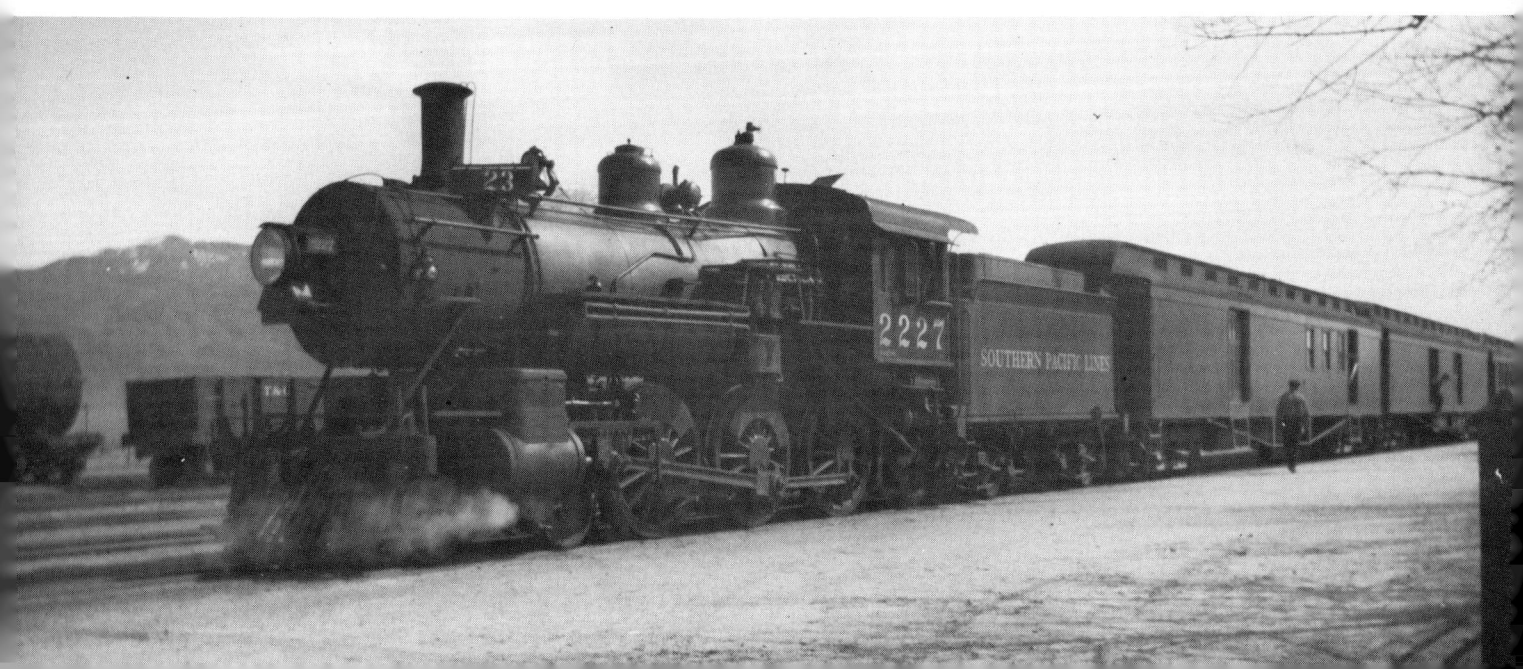

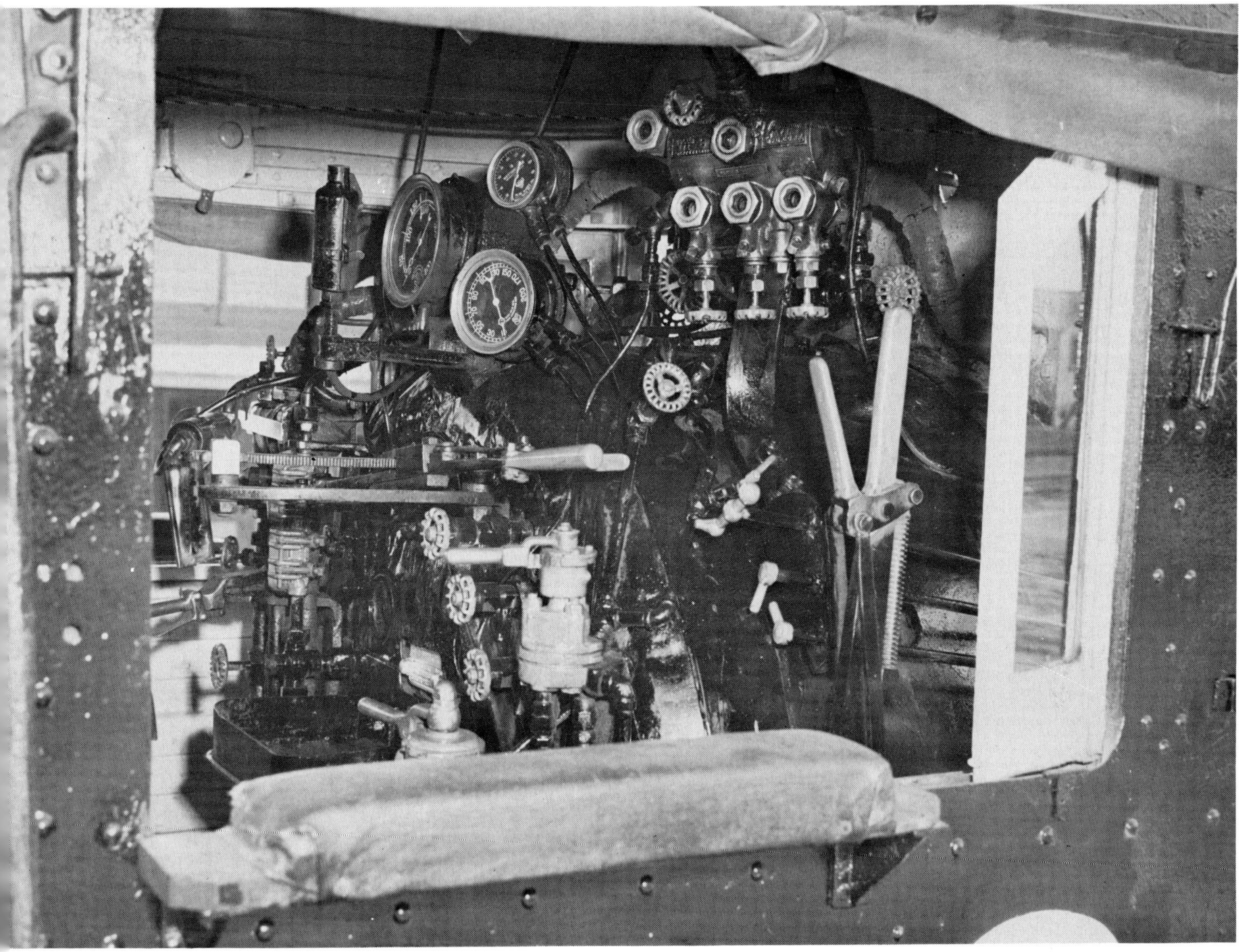

Mina as a terminal was a busy center with a wide variety of railroad interest. Double-header narrow-gauge freights arrived and left daily for the Owens Valley via Montgomery Pass. SP Nos. 18 and 17 *(top, left)* took the last train out on February 16, 1938. The previous July *(center, left)* Nos. 18 and 9 were paired in similar run. The cab of No. 18 *(above)* presented as great a complex of valves, gauges and levers as any standard-gauge engine and contrasted abruptly with the crude simplicities of American (4-4-0) No. 7, the BENTON *(below)*, of the original Carson & Colorado still operating in N&C days. Standard-gauge trains of the Tonopah & Goldfield interchanged with the SP at Mina. SP No. 2227 *(bottom, left)* stands at Mina station ready to leave with northbound train No. 23, the Tonopah Express. *(Top Left: J. H. Wright Photo; Center: Ted Wurm Photo; Bottom: George D. Oliver Photo; Top Right: Southern Pacific Collection.)*

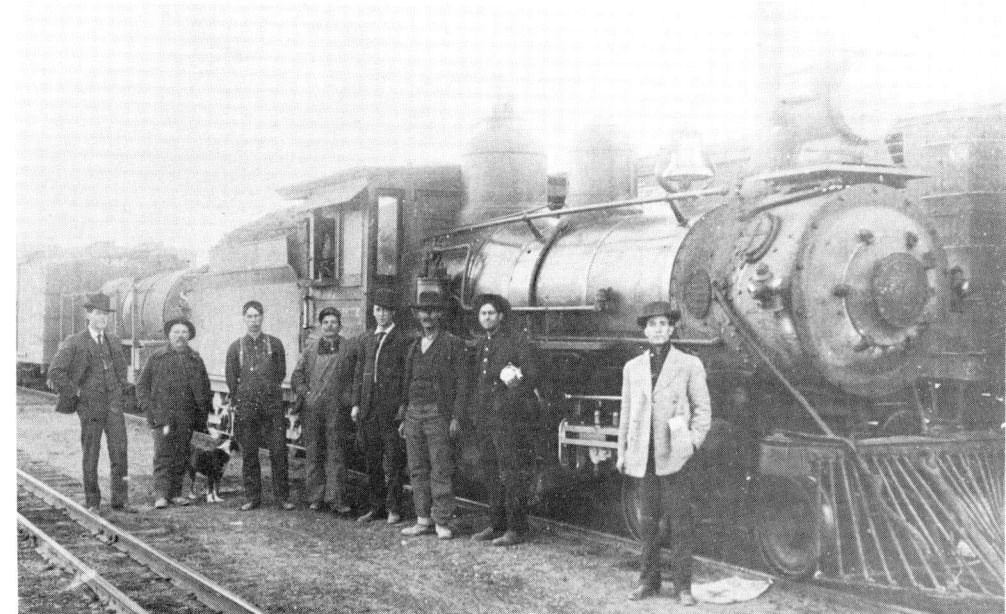

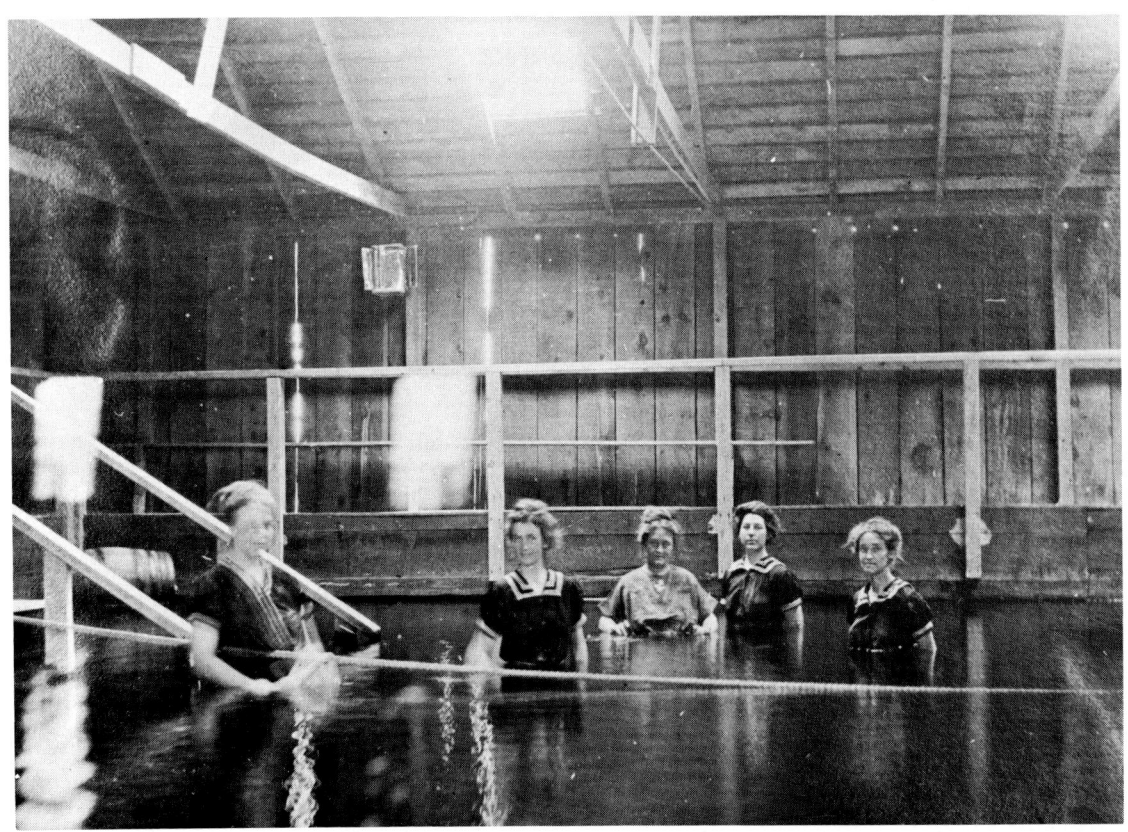

Ladies in the modest bathing suits of the period were frequent patrons of Martin Brazzanovich's hot springs baths at Soda Springs (later Sodaville). The discovery of two springs of curative waters—one hot and one cold—gave rise to the original settlement which increased in stature with the coming of the railroad on December 1, 1881, and the later addition of a smelter by the Esmeralda Copper Co. The real boom came with the discovery of gold at Tonopah and the sudden deluge of freight and passengers destined for the new bonanza (1900-05). Sodaville blossomed as a crowded terminal and transfer point, catering to weary travelers unable to obtain connecting stage transportation, and transshipping freight as fast as wagons could be found. The boom subsided on completion of the Tonopah Railroad in 1904 and ceased entirely when the Carson & Colorado (then N&C) moved its terminal facilities north to Mina. The panorama *(below)* looks east at the greatly degenerated Sodaville of 1914. The pump house and mineral baths are at the left. The railroad in the foreground continues south for five miles along the edge of the salt marsh to Tonopah Jct. *(Top: Mrs. M. Myles Collection; Bottom: Nevada Historical Society.)*

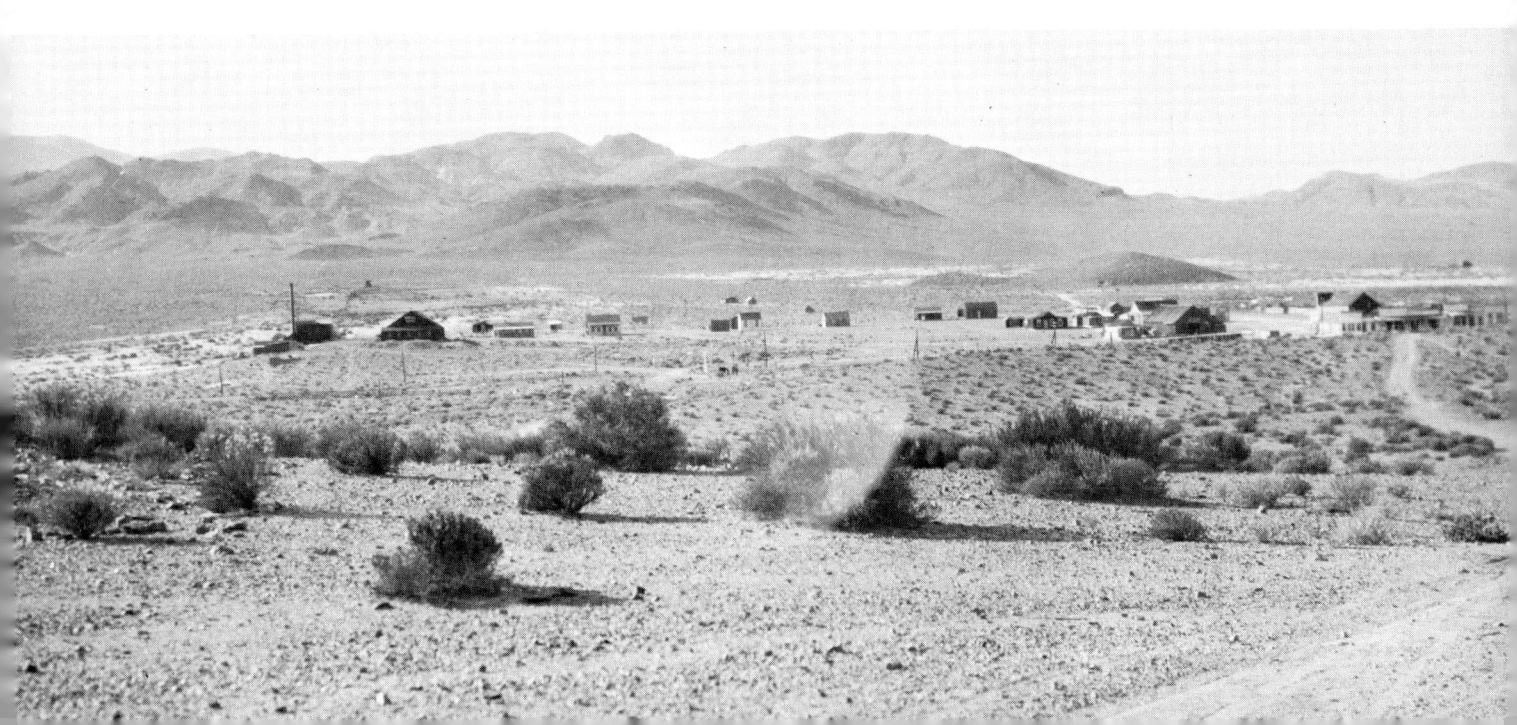

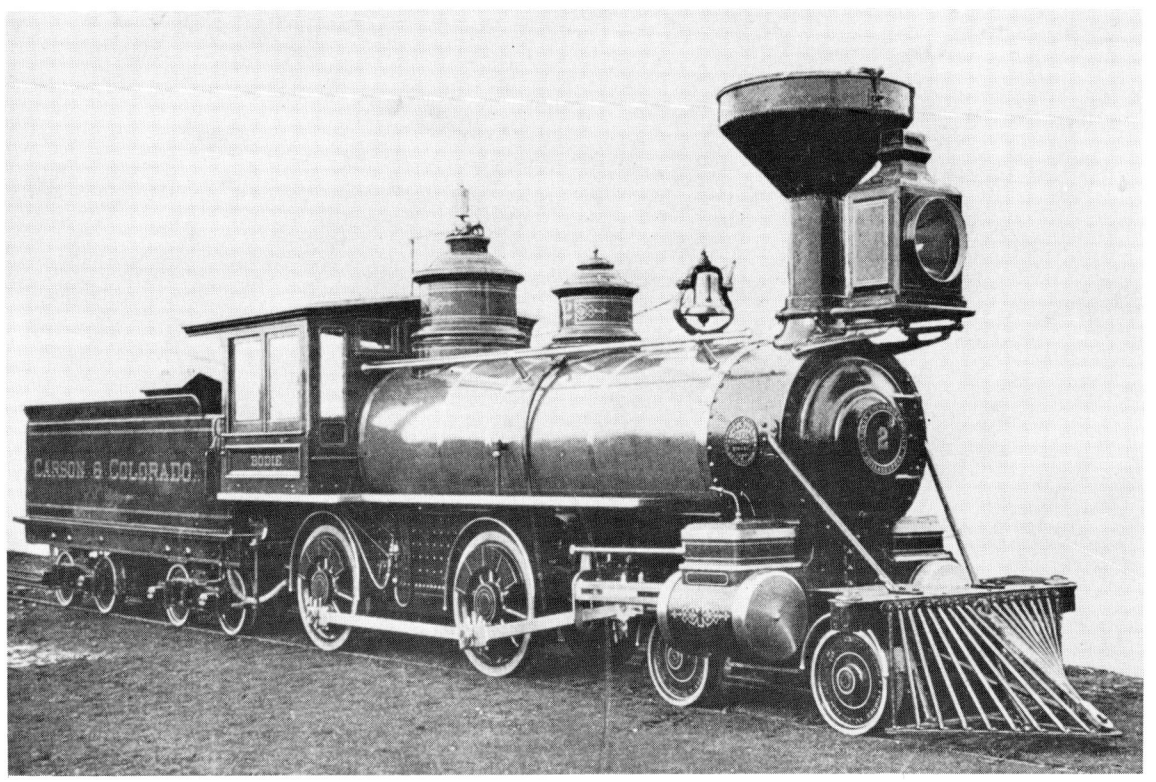

C&C No. 2, the BODIE, built by Baldwin in 1881, brought the first train up the hill from Sodaville through Belleville to the mountain terminus of Candelaria on February 28, 1882. In this view *(below)* looking south, the main street of the town is just out of the picture to the left. The railroad has climbed over the notch (behind camera) and angles downgrade along the side of the hill (right) to curve into the mouth of Pickhandle Gulch (center left). The presence of the wagon in the foreground and the extent of the mine dumps indicate that this postcard picture was taken some time around 1910. *(Top: Grahame Hardy Collection; Bottom: John M. Smith Collection.)*

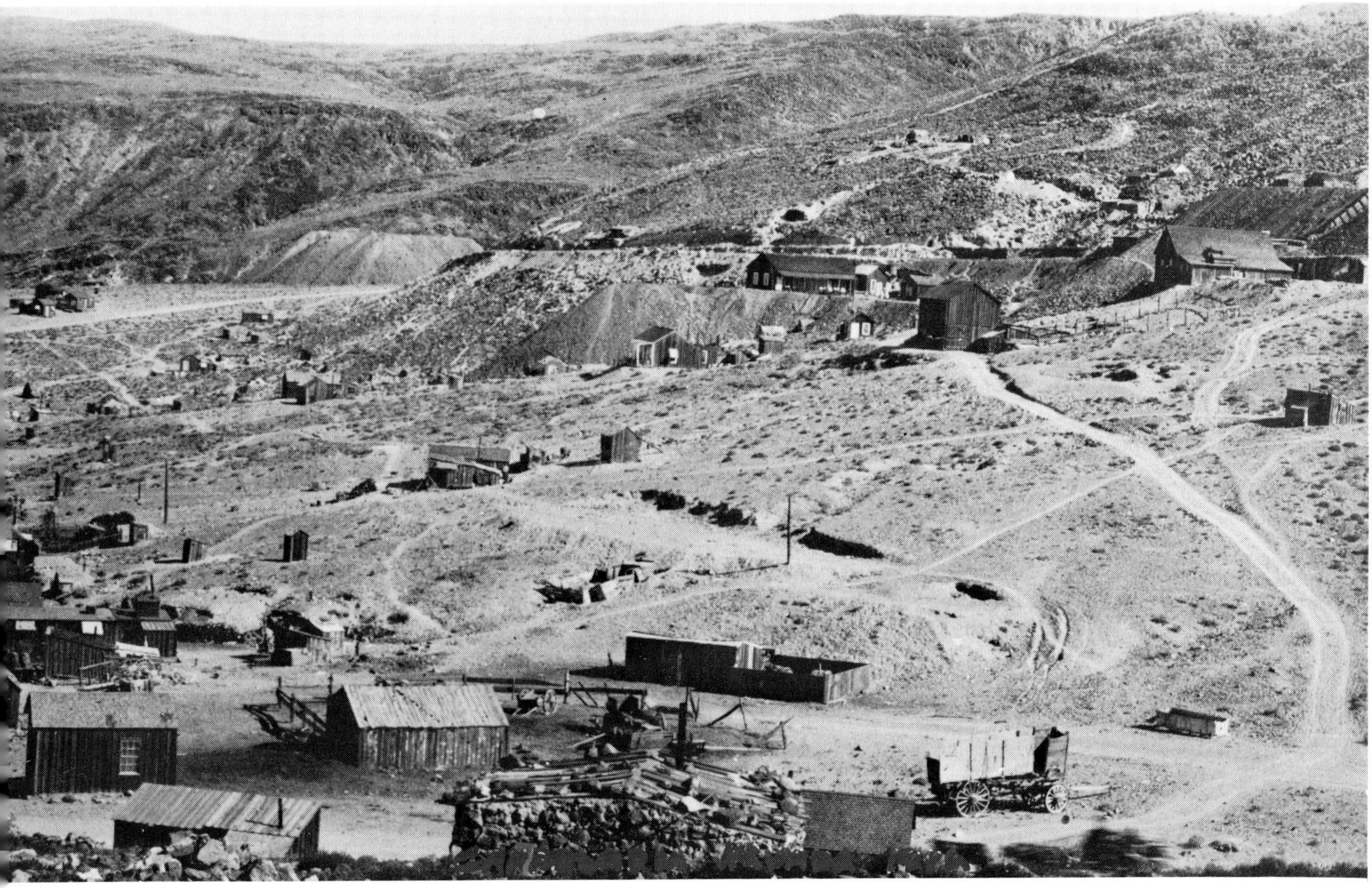

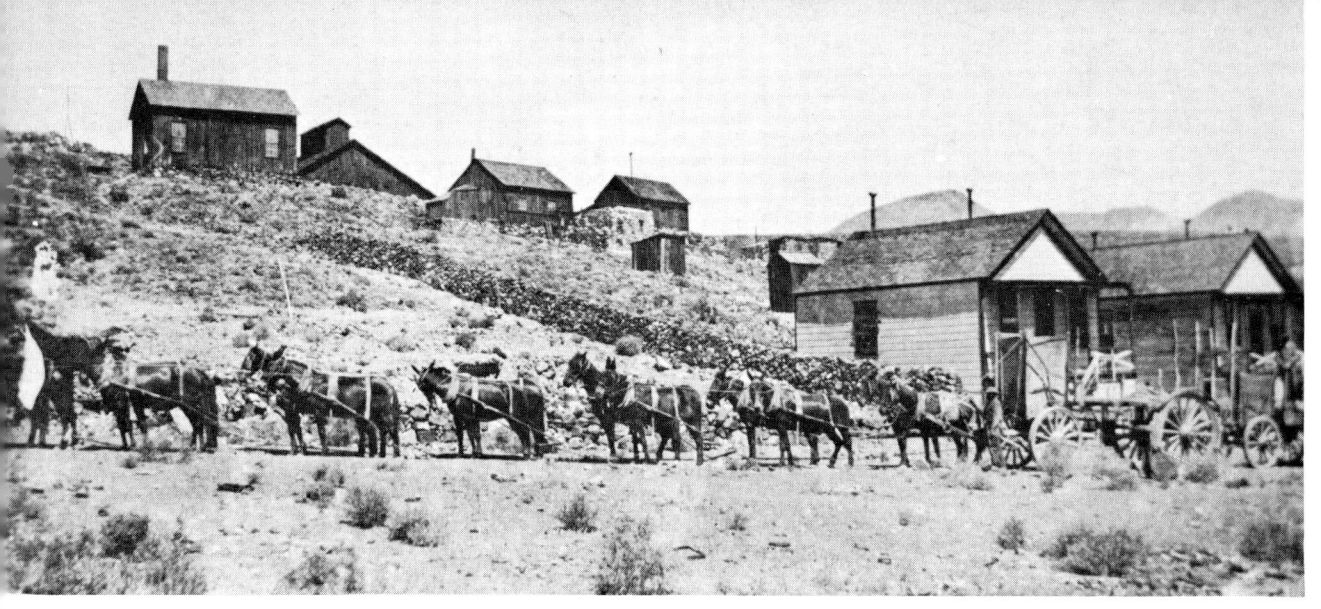

A splicing of two separate photos enables the presentation of this *(below)* panorama of Candelaria about 1910, facing to the southwest. The road from Columbus (toward Tonopah) enters in the foreground, marking the approximate approach originally intended for the Carson & Colorado Railroad before that road decided to head west for the Owens Valley via Belleville and Montgomery Pass. The town of Candelaria lies to center right, the main street running at right angles to the line of vision, stretching from the road in center foreground to the foot of the hill (right) on which the mill stands. The road then turns abruptly west and climbs around behind the hill toward the notch in the right background. The Carson & Colorado Railroad approached from Belleville and Filben, to the north through the same notch, then dropped sharply downgrade along the hillside in the background to the

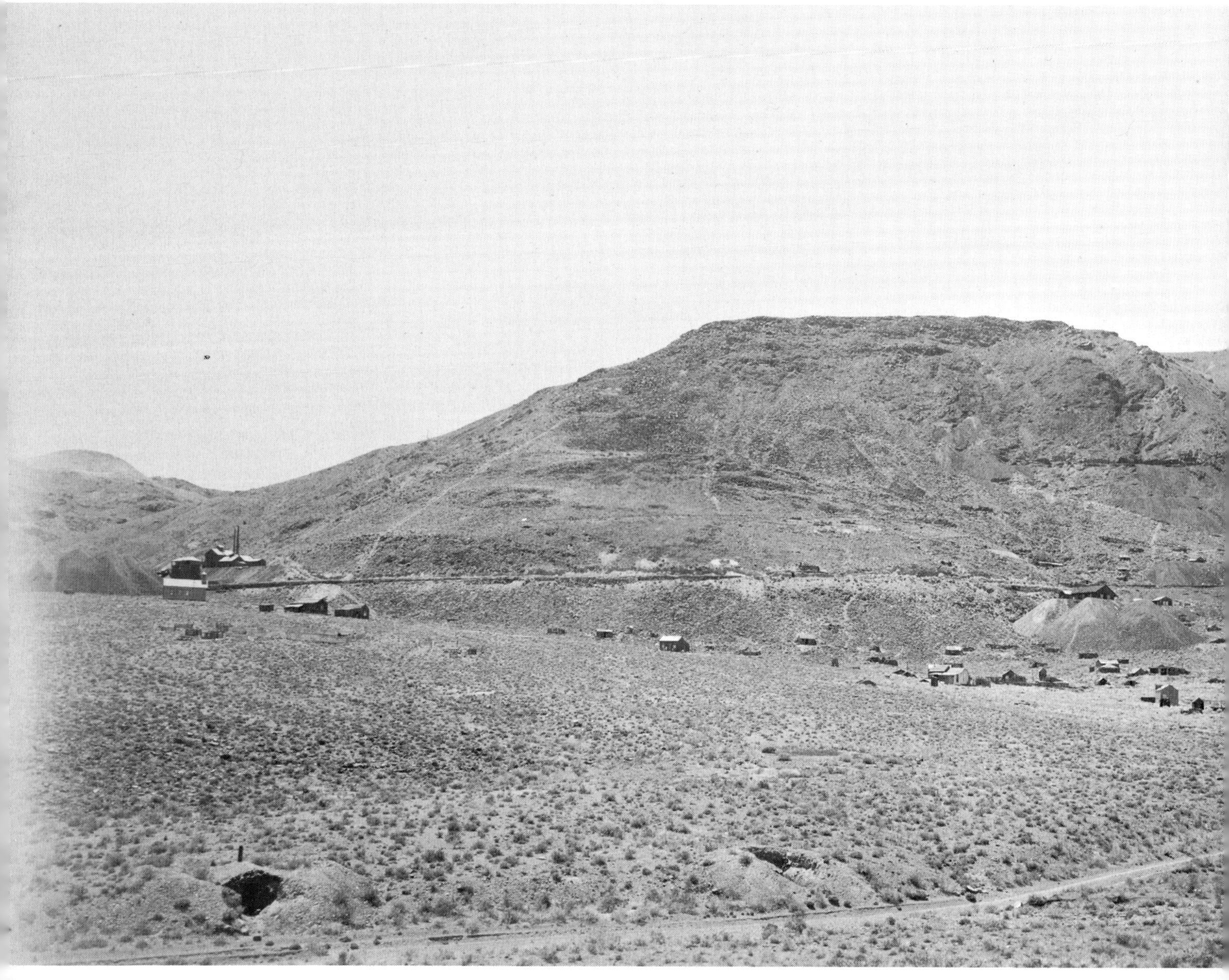

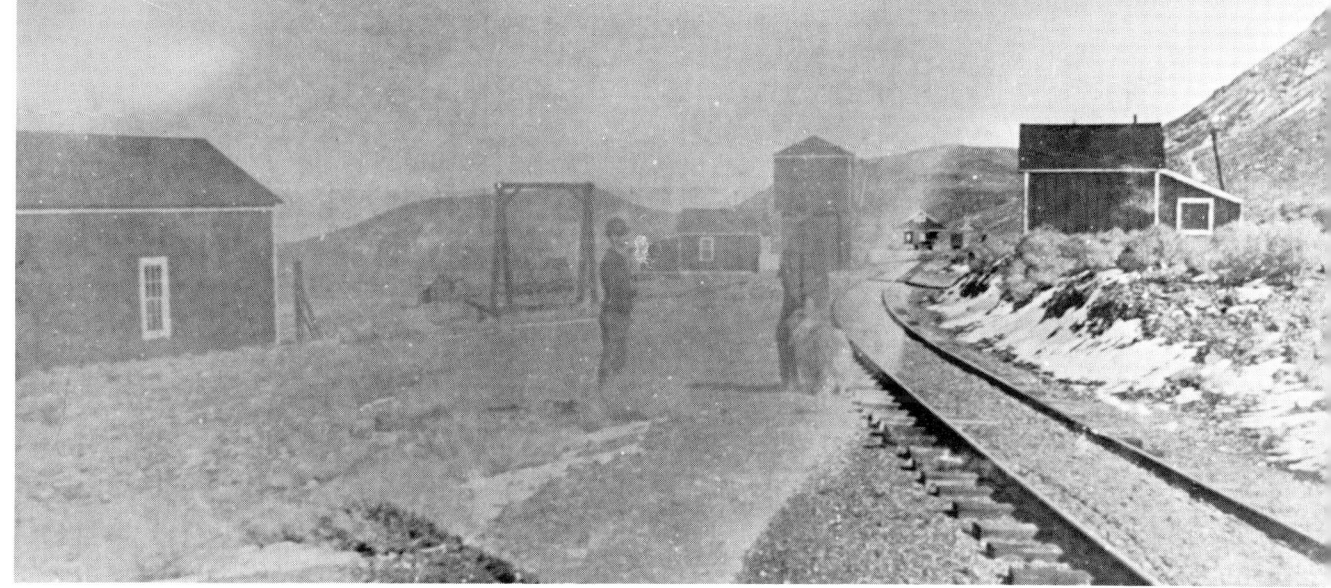

Northern Belle mine at the end of Pickhandle Gulch at far left. Lacking sufficient flat space along the hillside, the railroad located its depot and engine facilities on the north side near the notch (behind the rise on which the mill is located) where more level ground prevailed.

Unfortunately the rare view of these installations looking downgrade toward Candelaria *(upper right)* has become seriously faded and is only reproduced with great difficulty. Hauling materials from town up the steep road to the railroad could be somewhat of a chore as evidenced by the 14-horse team lined up at the north end of town *(left, above)* to move two close-coupled wagons over the grade. *(Top Left: Ben Edwards Collection (Stein); Top Right: Louis L. Stein, Jr. Collection; Bottom: D. B. Sterrett Photo, U. S. Geological Survey.)*

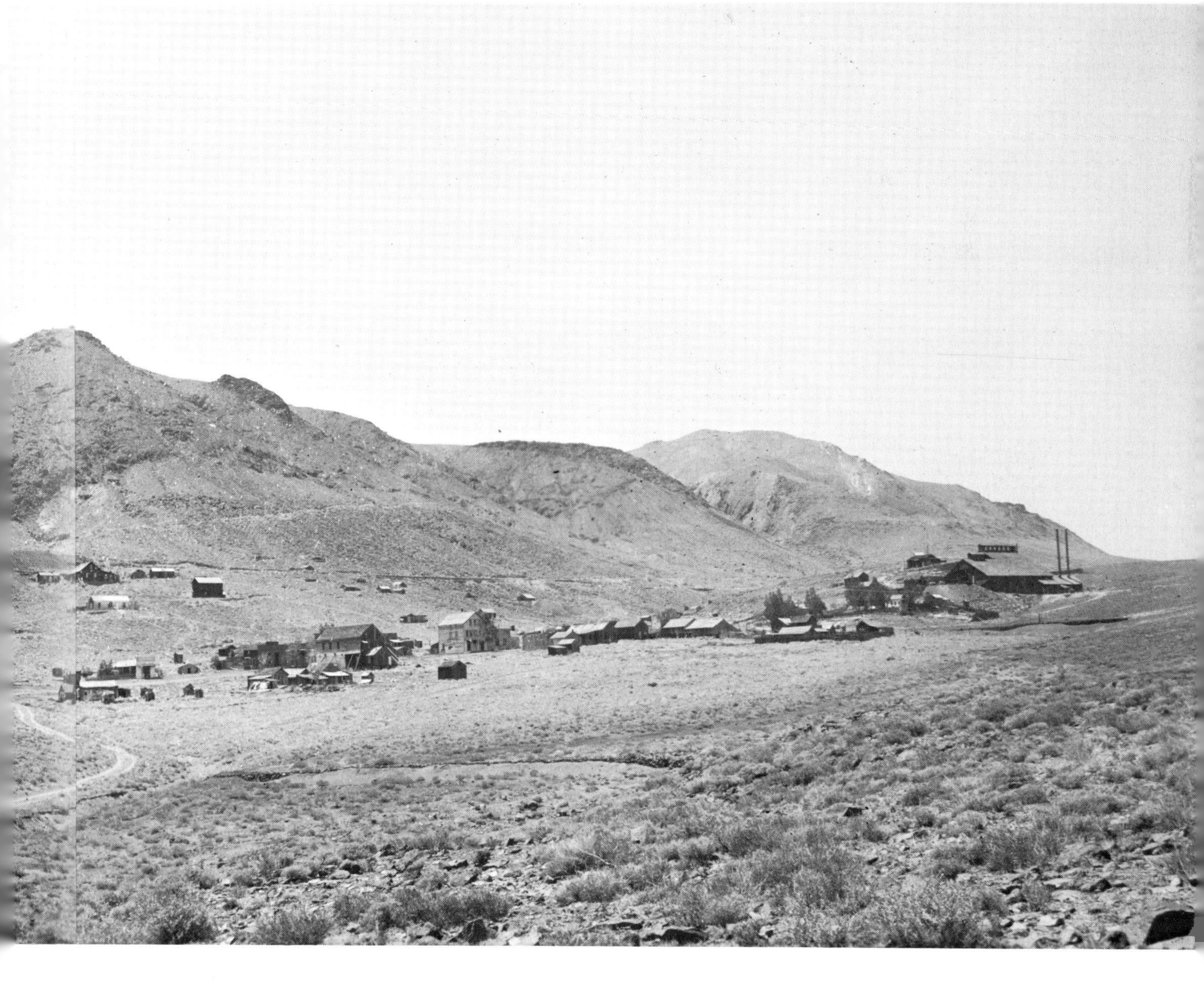

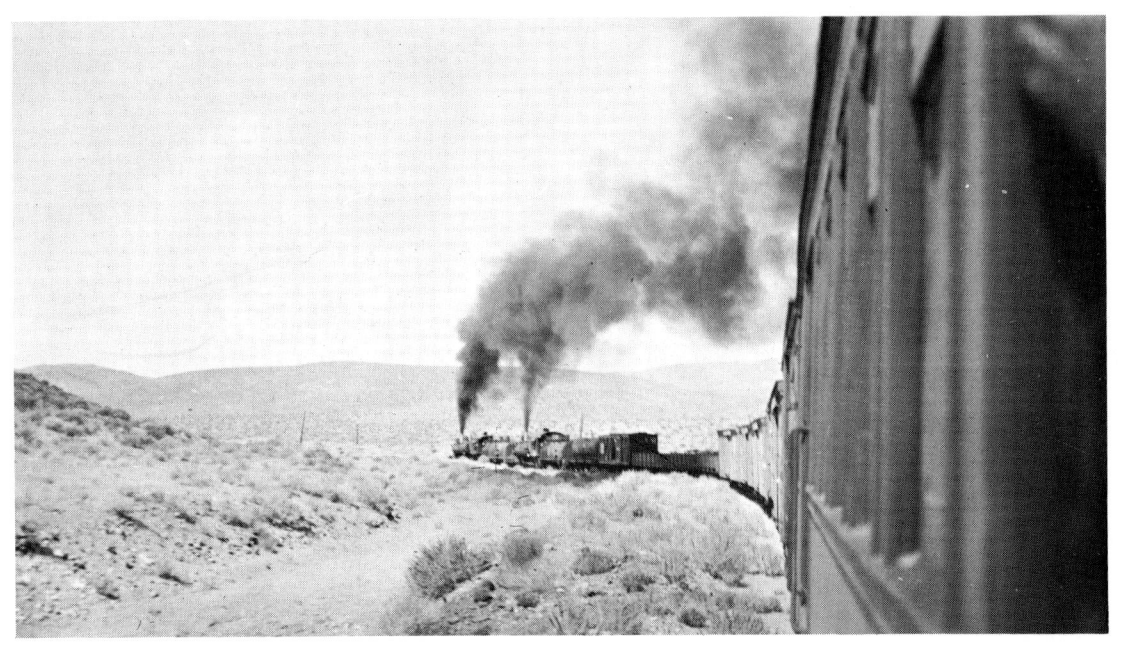
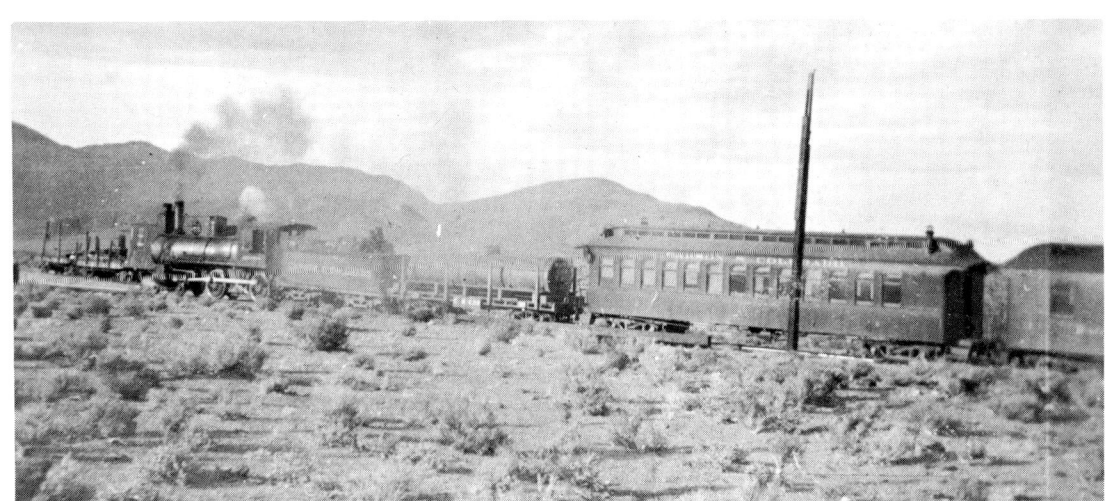

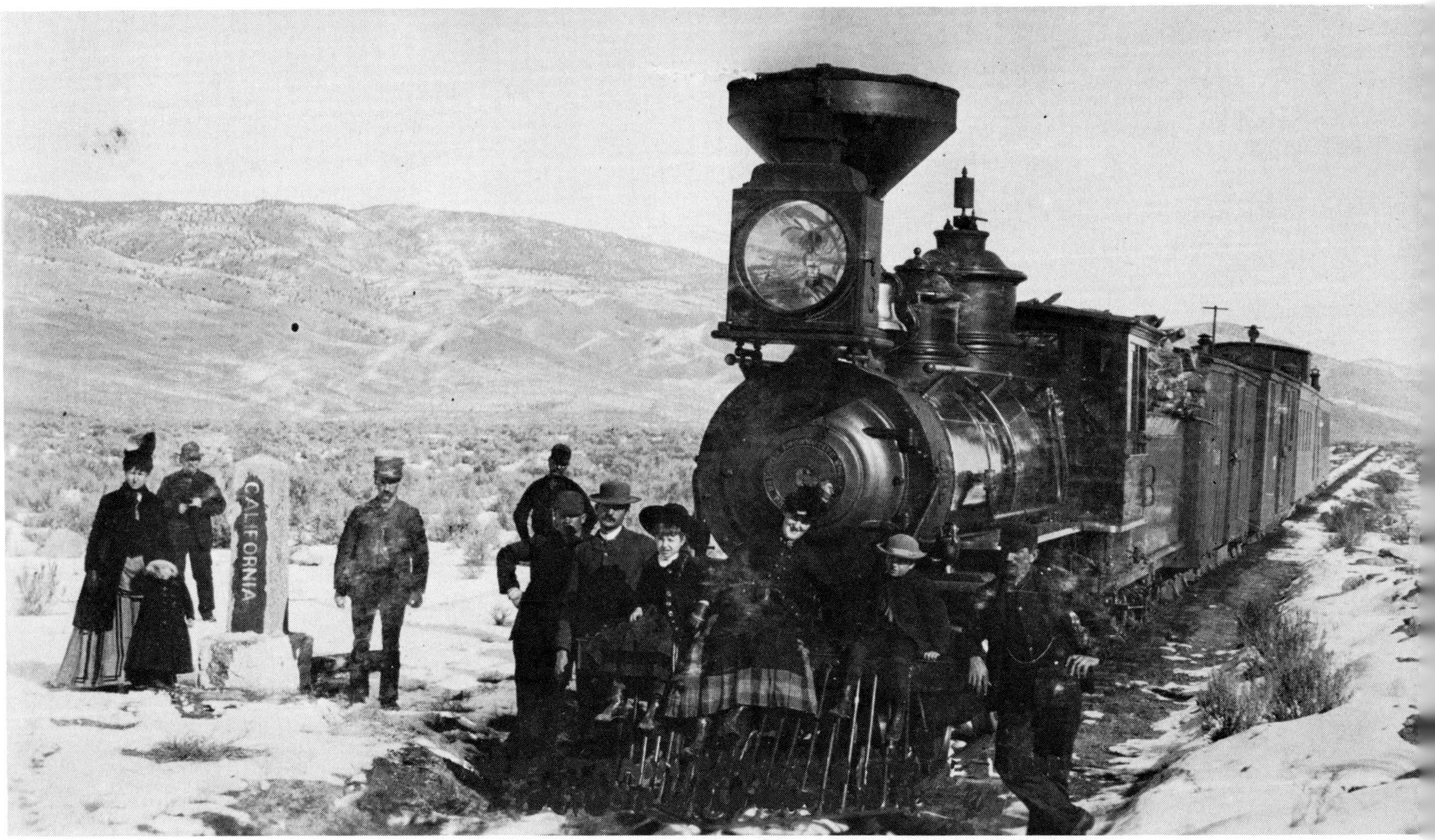

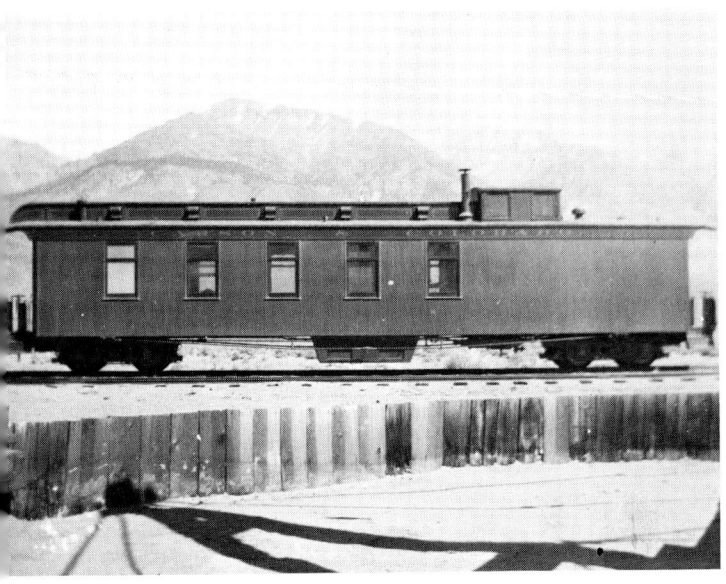
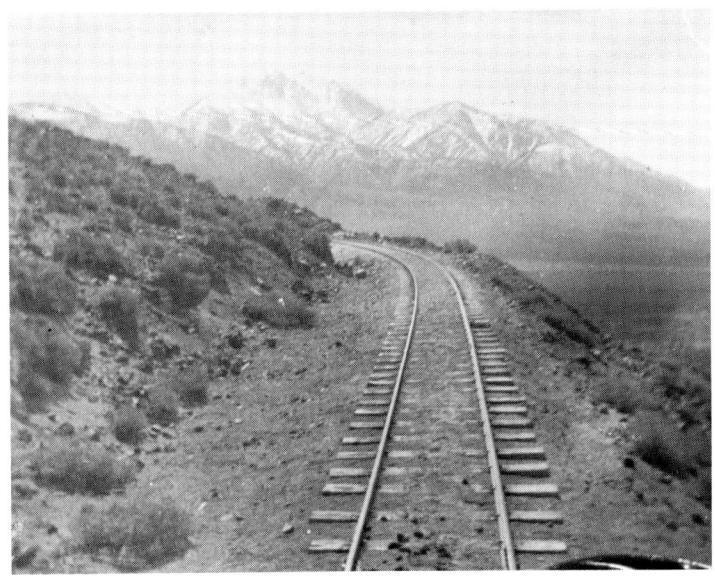

Achilles' heel of the Carson & Colorado was the long, desolate climb of approximately 40 miles to and over the summit of Montgomery Pass between Belleville and Benton. About 25 miles of 2.3% grade comprised the eastern approach, while heavy rock work, cuts, sharp curves and a tunnel were necessary along equivalent grades on the first five miles of the western lip to the Nevada-California line. SP Nos. 9 and 17 are double-heading the daily mixed on the eastern slope in the view *(above, left)* in 1938, while the earlier setting *(center, left)* shows a Carson & Colorado passenger train with No. 7, the BENTON, and an auxiliary water tank car branching off the main at Filben for Candelaria while a freight (flat cars and caboose just ahead of engine) curves to the superelevation of the main line.

Before the turn of the century the C&C had developed a form of drover's caboose *(above, left)* for use on these desert runs. Trackage on the west side of Mt. Montgomery was more spectacular *(above, right)*. Woodburner No. 6, the HAWTHORNE, and mixed train *(bottom, left)* successfully managed the descent and paused for this classic photo at the state line. Double headers Nos. 5 and 8 *(below)* didn't make it on July 3, 1923. No. 5 derailed on the curve through the rock cut a mile west of the summit, and No. 8 tried to squeeze past on the right. There were spare parts aplenty after this mix-up. *(Three Top Photos: Ted Wurm Collection; Center Left: Louis L. Stein, Jr. Collection; Bottom Left: Nevada Photo Service; Bottom Right: Southern Pacific Collection.)*

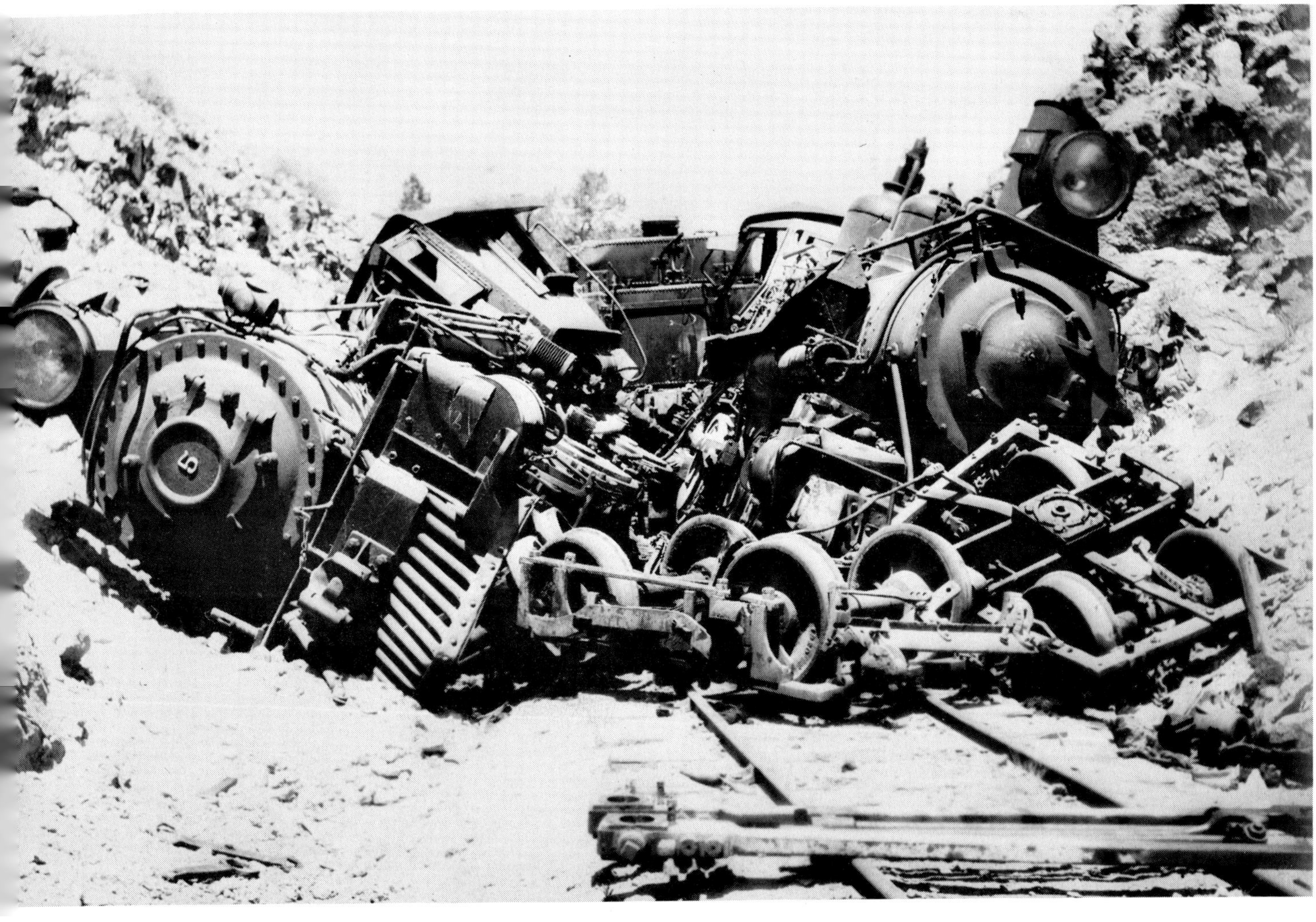

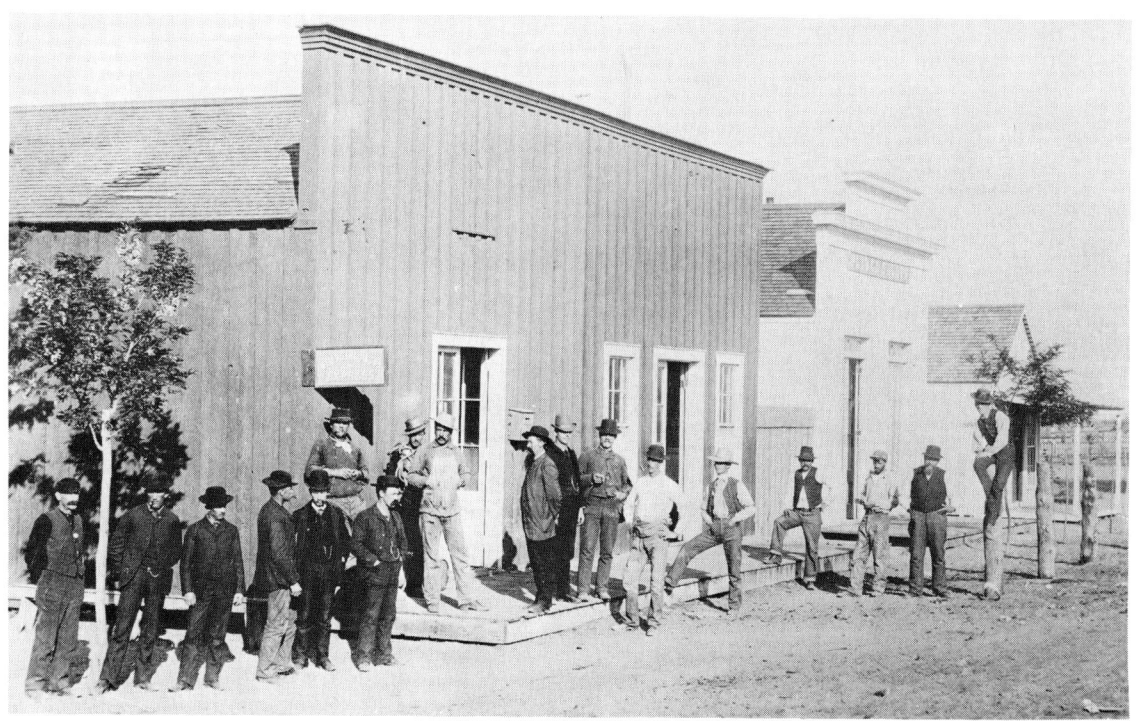

Hawley's mill on the eastern shore of Owens Lake was the southernmost point reached by the Carson & Colorado when construction stopped in the summer of 1883, and the town that grew around the railhead assumed the same name. The street scene *(above)* was taken in front of the Wells Fargo office, with C&C employees discreetly nearest the camera and not in front of the Palace Saloon on the far side. Home away from home at this desolate outpost for crews terminating their runs with little woodburners like No. 6, the HAWTHORNE, was the Lakeview Hotel in background.

When Capt. J. M. Keeler took over the Hawley mill, both the town and the railroad obliged by changing their official designations to accommodate. As late as 1949 and in spite of more modern and heavier locomotives, two of which wait on the station track *(top, right)*, Keeler still retained its original stub switch installations, a splendid example of the three-way variety appears in the foreground. Shortly thereafter standard slip switches were substituted in staggered fashion *(below)* although the longer ties remained to mark the original locations. Both views face southeast toward the Inyo Mountains. *(Top Right: Pacific Railway Journal; All Others: Southern Pacific Collection.)*

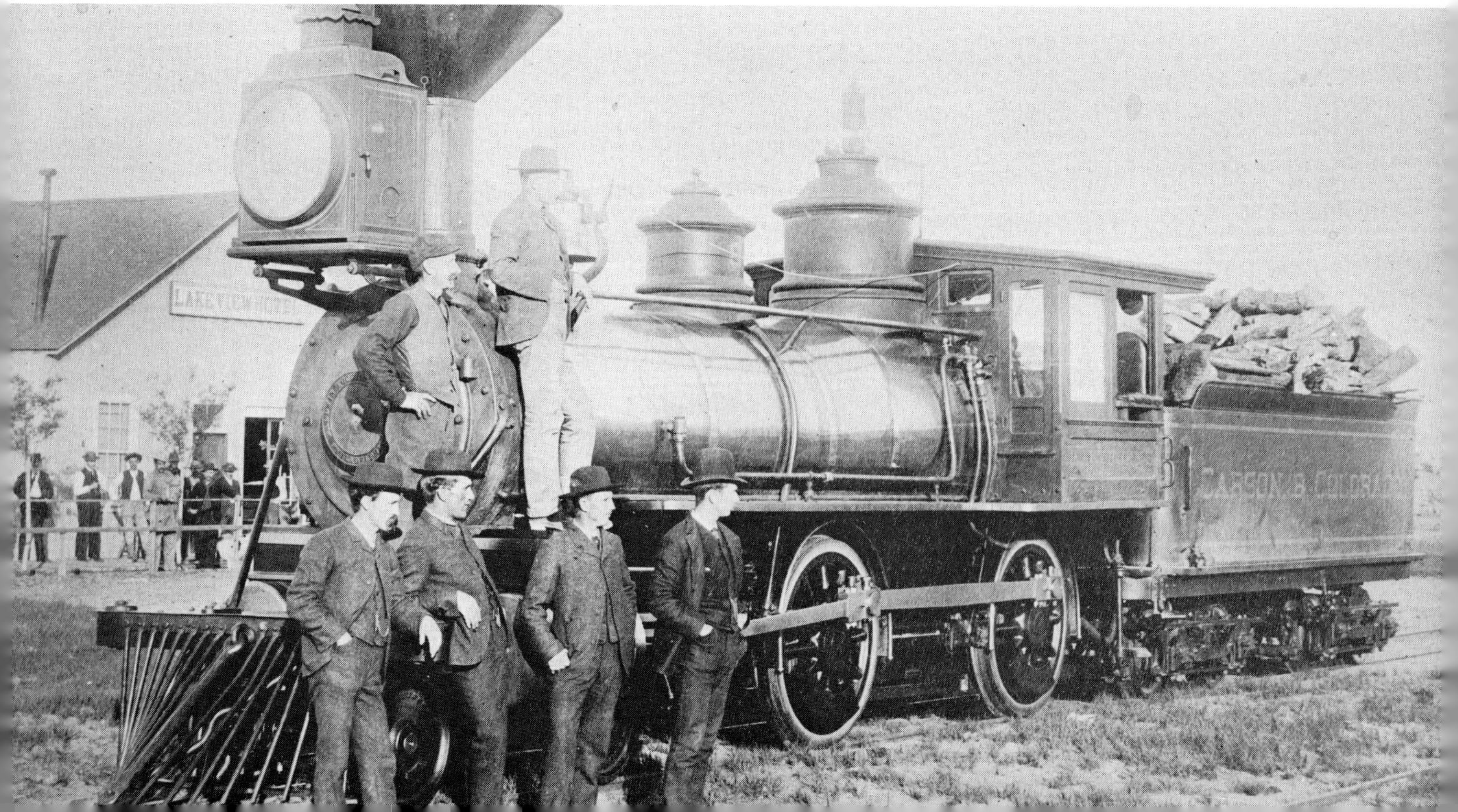

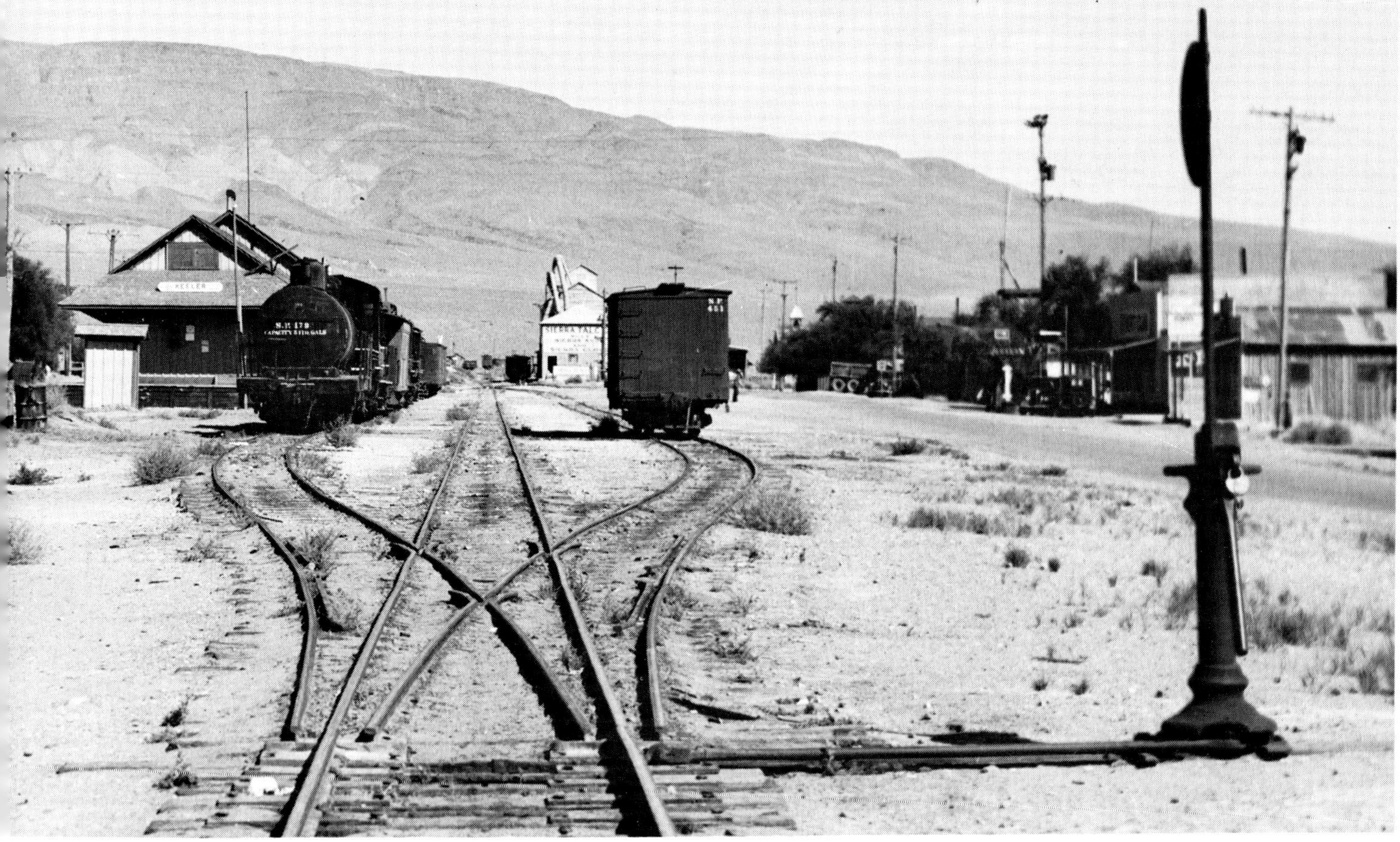

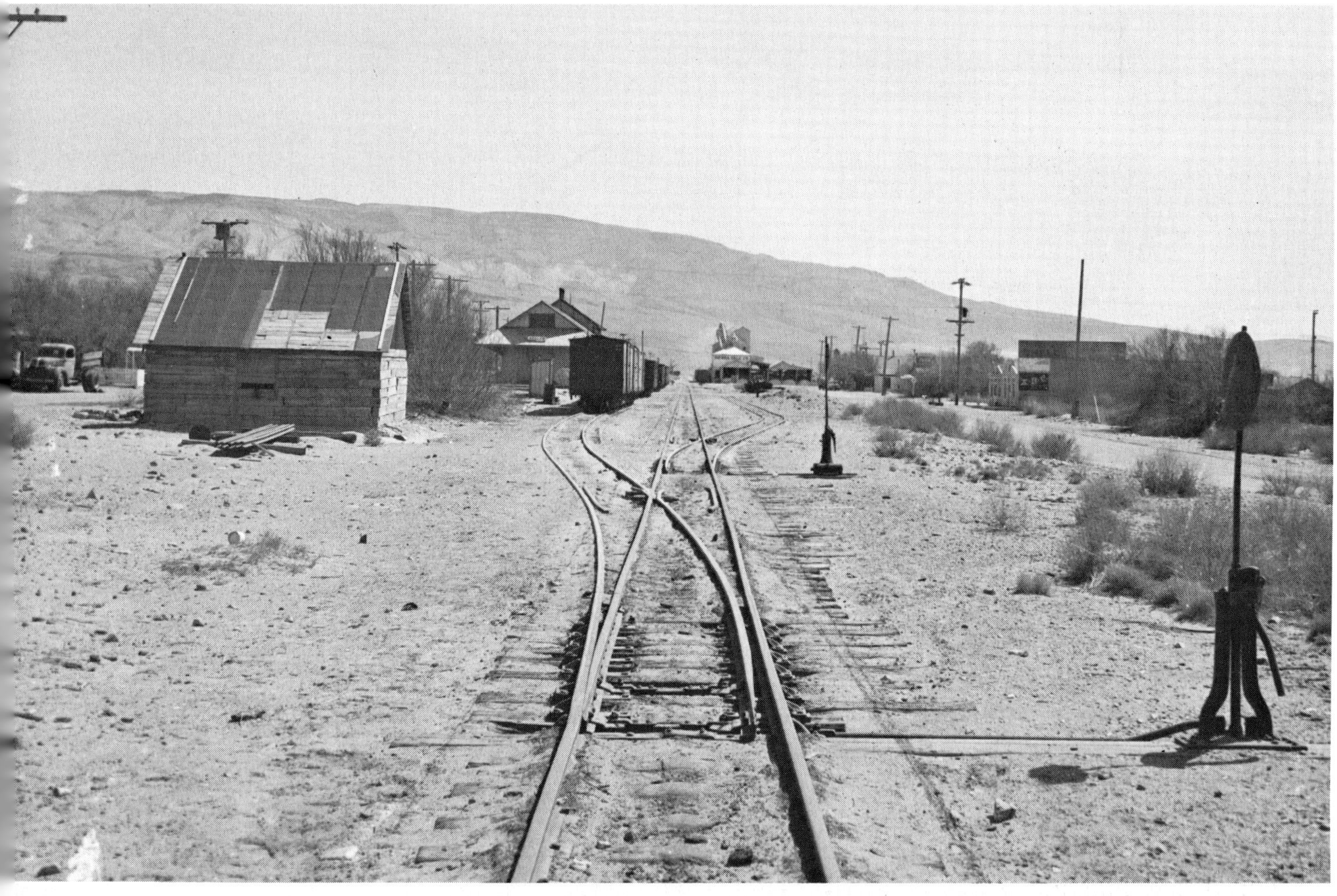

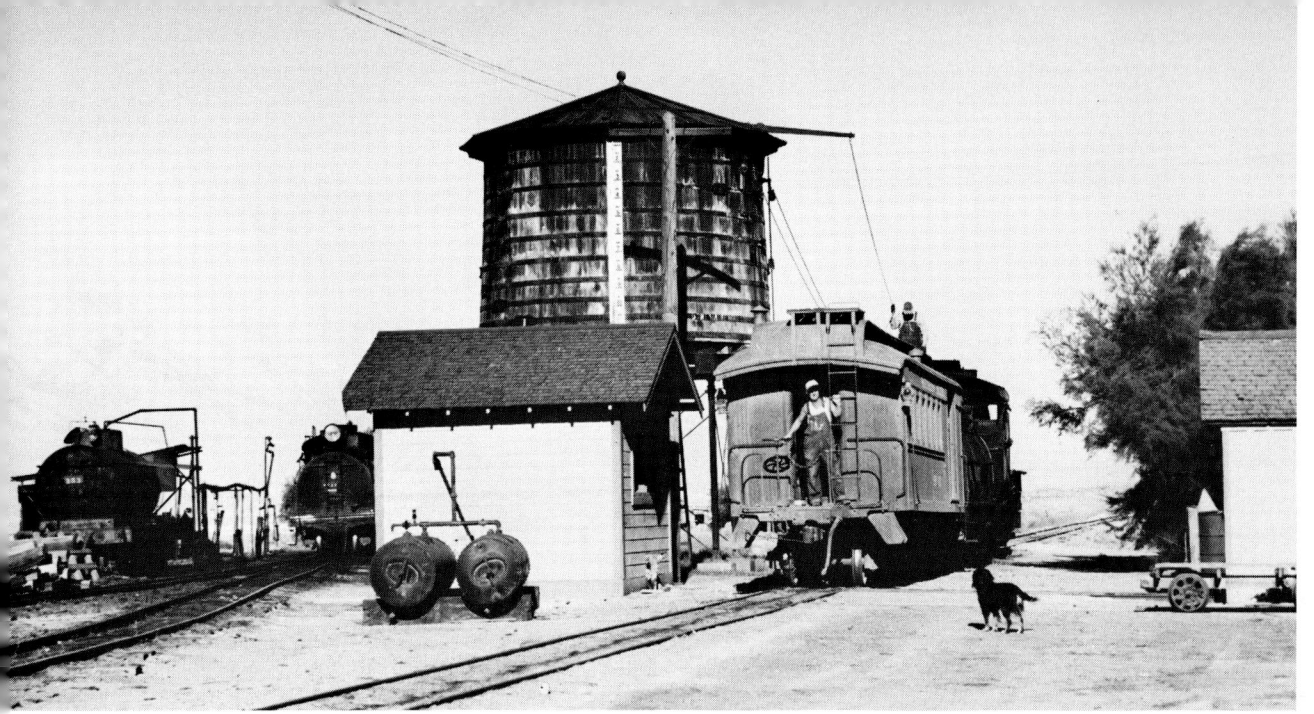

Engine facilities at Keeler were serviceable if not handsome. In the *(above)* 1949 view, No. 18 with caboose-combine No. 401 at her drawbar stands on the main for a tank refill, while No. 8 rests on the enginehouse track behind tank, where *(top, right)* Nos. 9 and 21 paused on an earlier day in 1938. What was left of Keeler in 1949 is presented in panorama *(below)* looking northwest past the station and tank across Owens Lake (dry) and the Sierra Nevada in background.

Of two large enterprises extracting minerals from Owens Lake by evaporation, The Inyo Development Company *(center, right)* was the oldest, here being serviced by C&C No. 3, the BODIE. Ultimately IDCo. obtained its own equipment *(bottom, far right)*, the No. 1 with primitive windowed box car coming from the Bodie & Benton Railroad and, judging by the freshly painted locomotive and the hillside buildings in background, probably photographed at the latter's Bodie terminus before delivery. A later view of the IDCo. plant *(bottom, near right)* indicated tracks but trains were absent at the moment this photograph was taken. *(Two Photos This Page: Pacific Railway Journal; Right Top: Southern Pacific; Center: Louis L. Stein, Jr. Collection; Bottom, Near Right: U. S. Geological Survey; Far Right: Ken Kidder Photo, Wm. A. Pennington Collection.)*

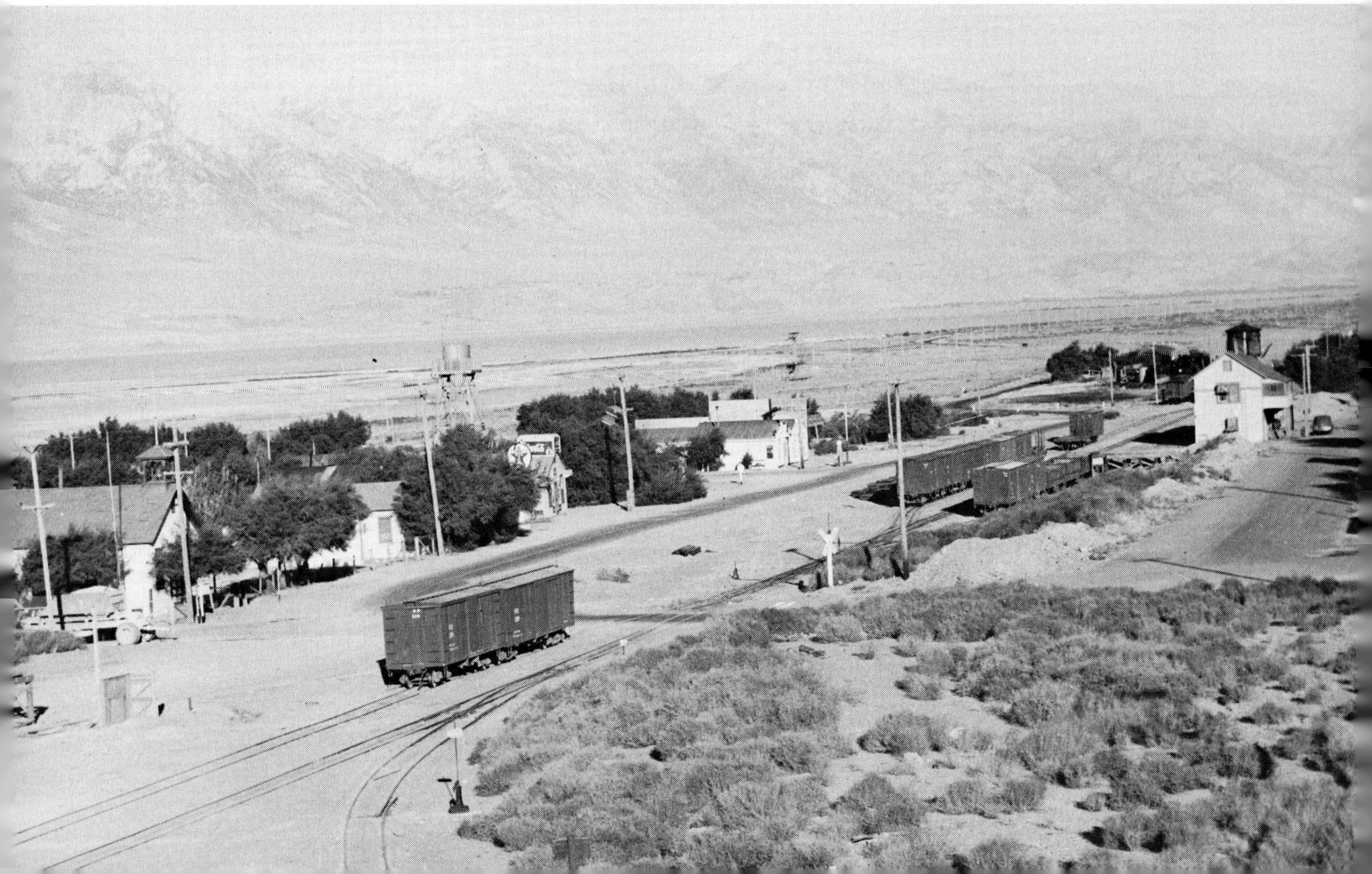

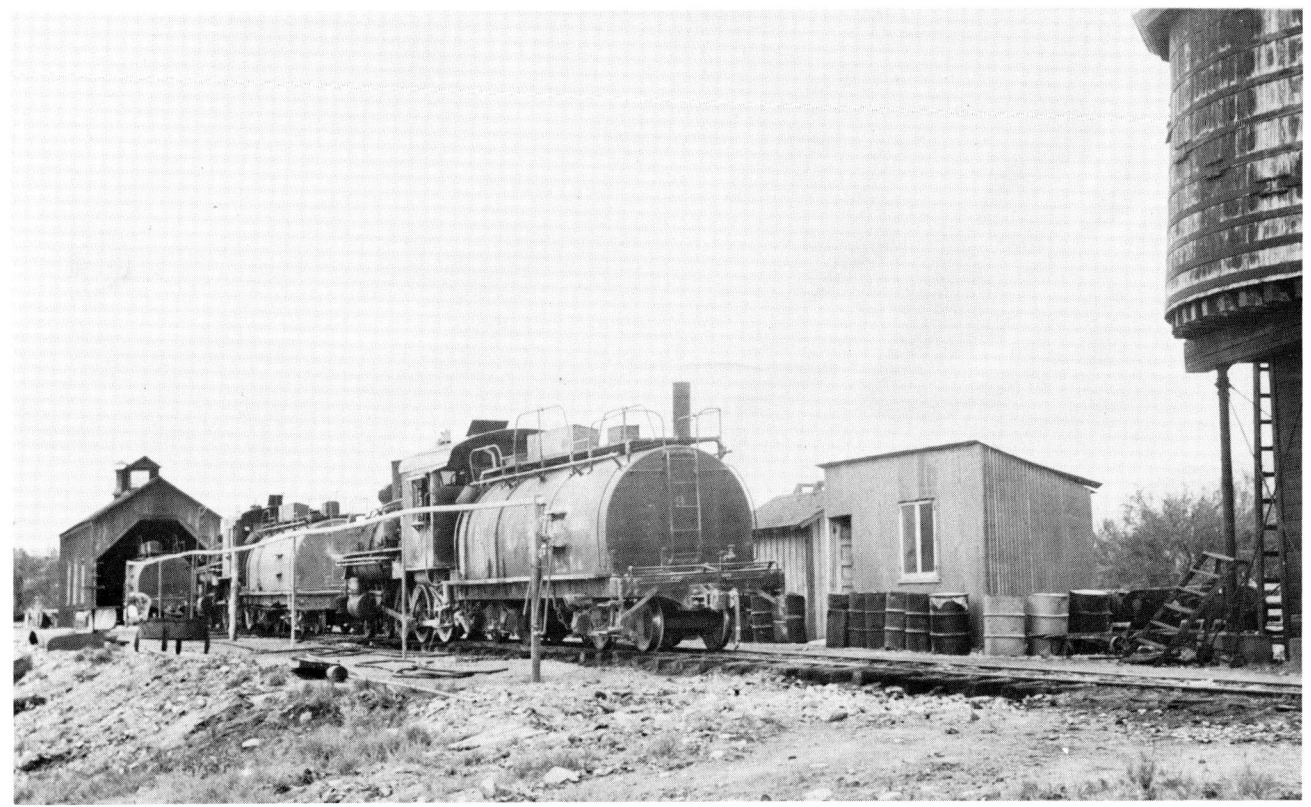

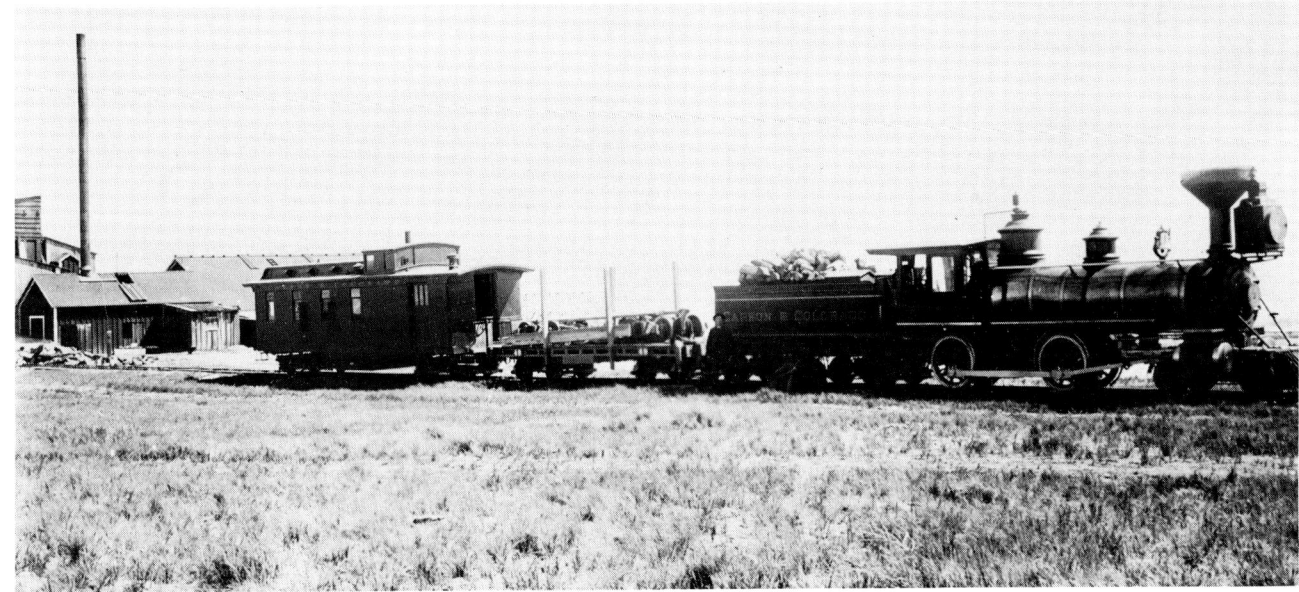

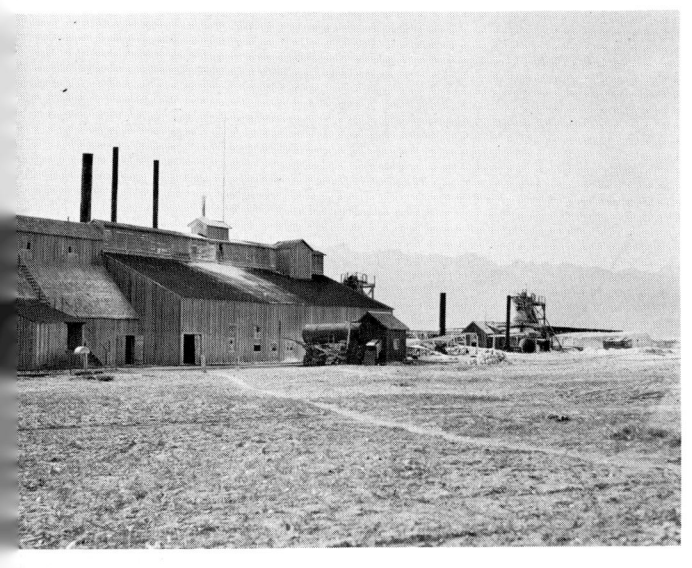
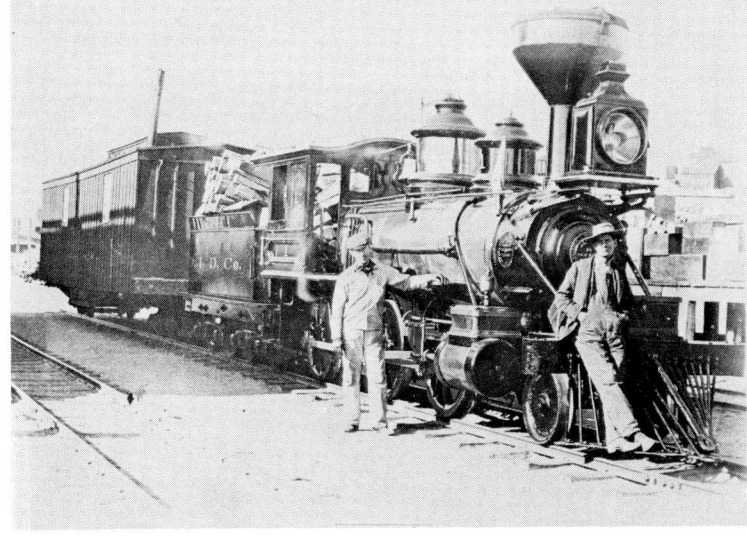

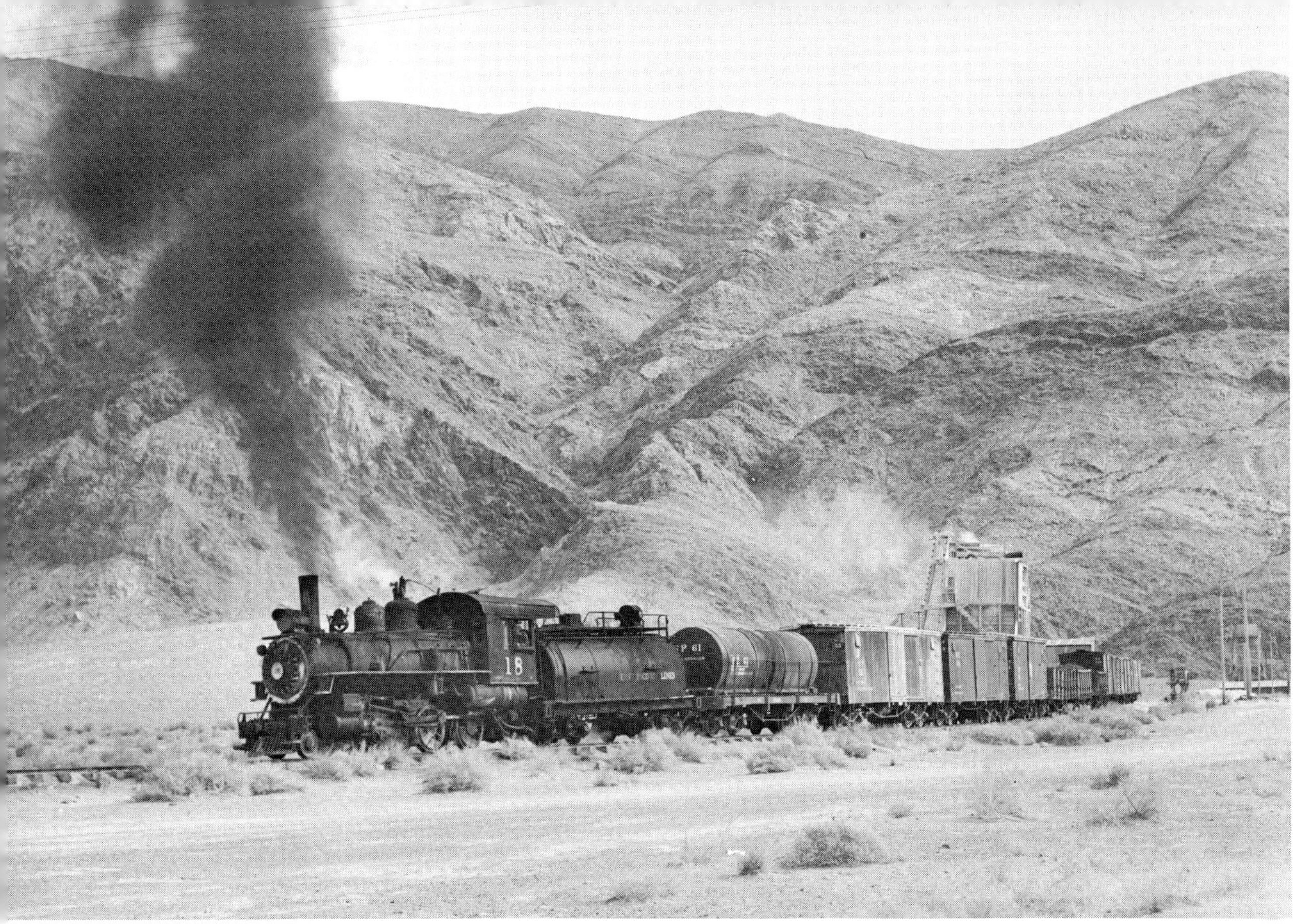

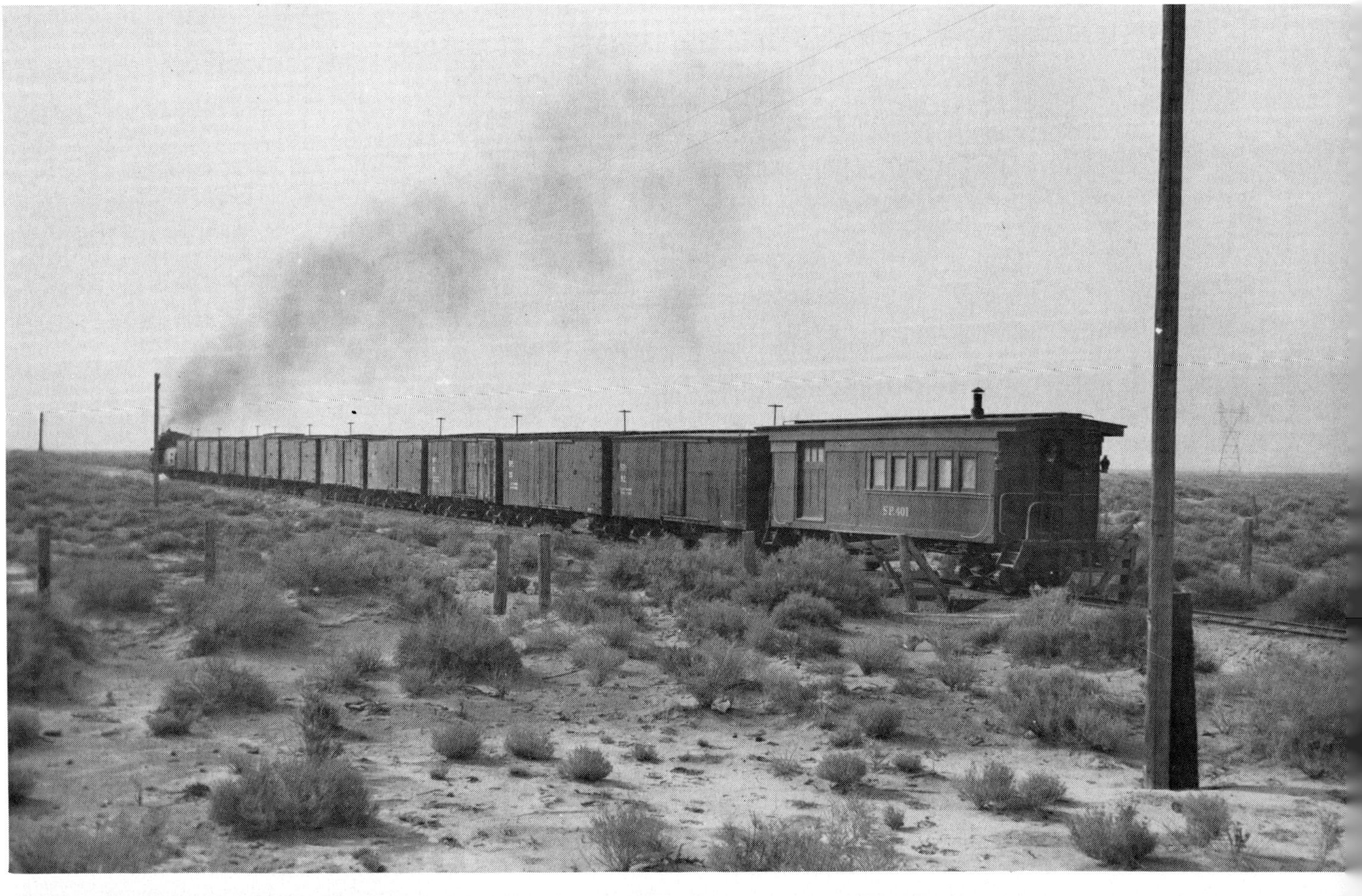

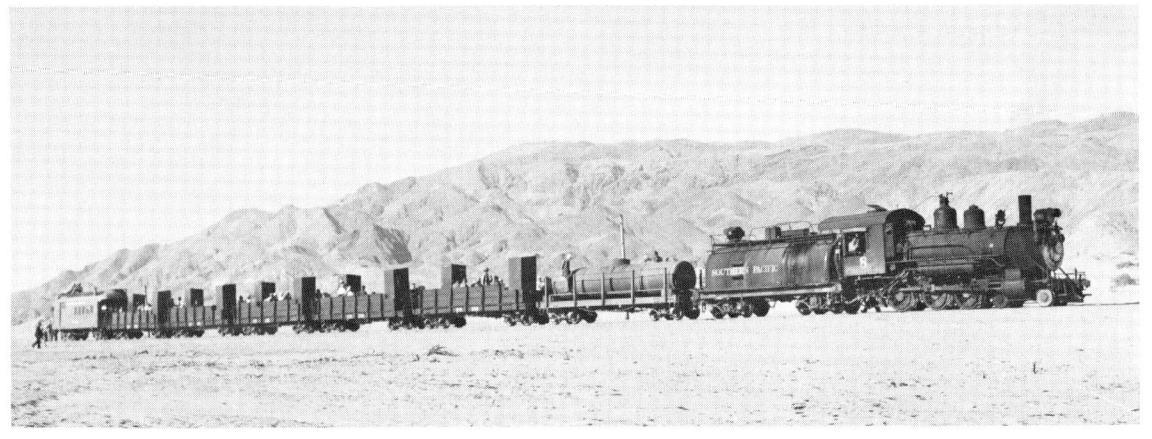

The Owens Valley at the southern end of the C&C is virtually 70 miles of flat, unbroken desert surrounded by mountains. From Bishop and Laws south to Owens Lake, the usually mild Owens River flows along the western edge, where towns and ranches are located. The railroad followed the eastern, more desolate edge to be closer to the mines in the Inyo Mountains and beyond. Traveling such an illimitable waste, where the tallest shrub is a sage brush hardly large enough to hide a jack rabbit, presents unusual problems. Those are not grain elevators on the train *(above)*, but home-fashioned "Chic Sales" mounted on stake-sided flat cars for the benefit of a group of visiting railfans. Dolomite *(top, left)*, to the south of Owenyo at the foot of the Inyo Mountains, was one of the few industrial locations to support the railroad in its waning years. On the west side of the valley the bold escarpment of the Sierra Nevada rises in majestic background *(below)*. From this point of vantage, just north of Owenyo, are visible the low-lying Alabama Hills backed by 14,042-foot Mt. Langley (left of center) and 14,495-foot Mt. Whitney (far right). SP narrow-gauge No. 18 (foreground) stands at 3,696 feet elevation. Looking along the valley floor *(below, left)* one loses all sense of time and distance in the sage-covered, sandy flat. *(Top Left, Bottom Right: Pacific Railway Journal; Other Two: Southern Pacific.)*

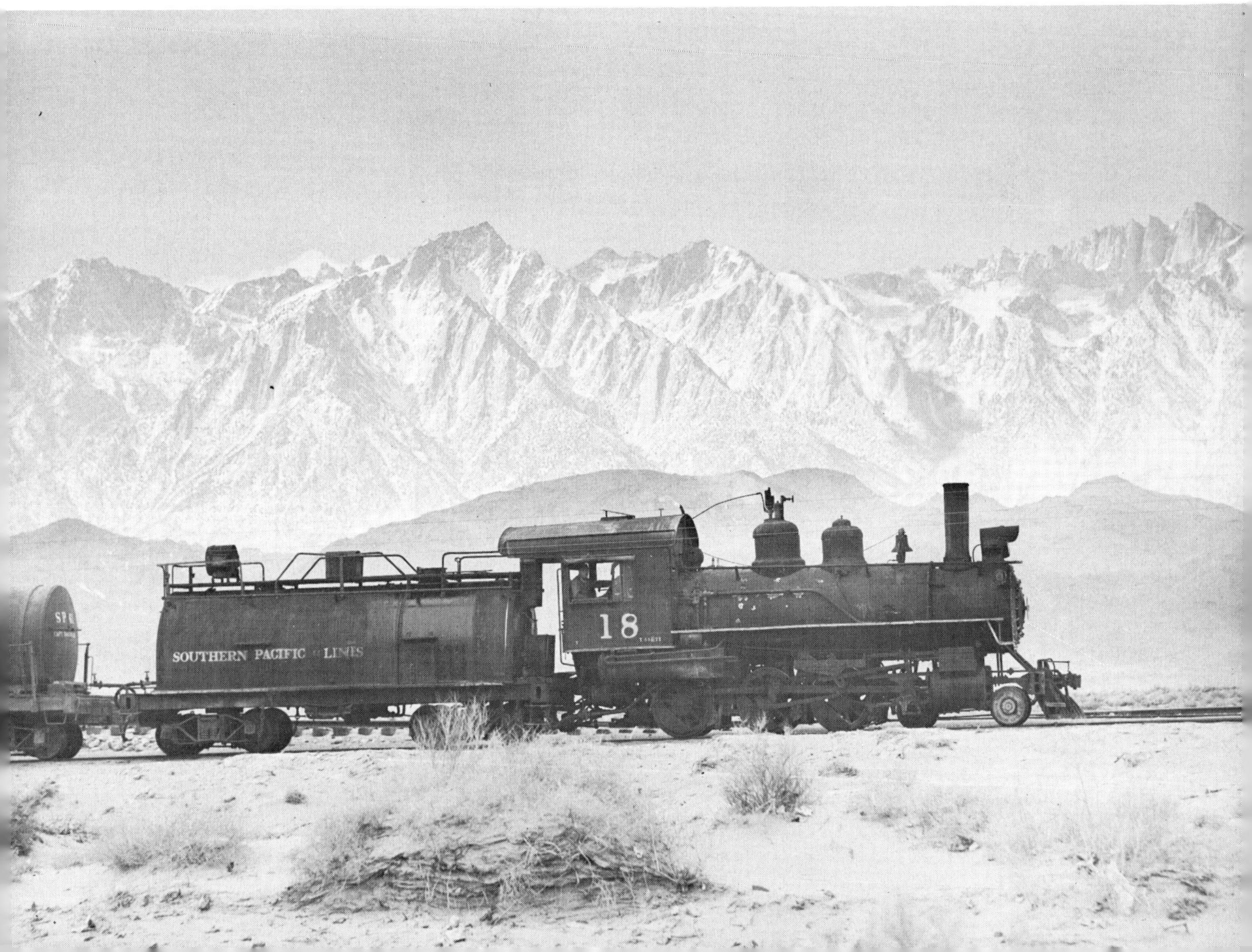

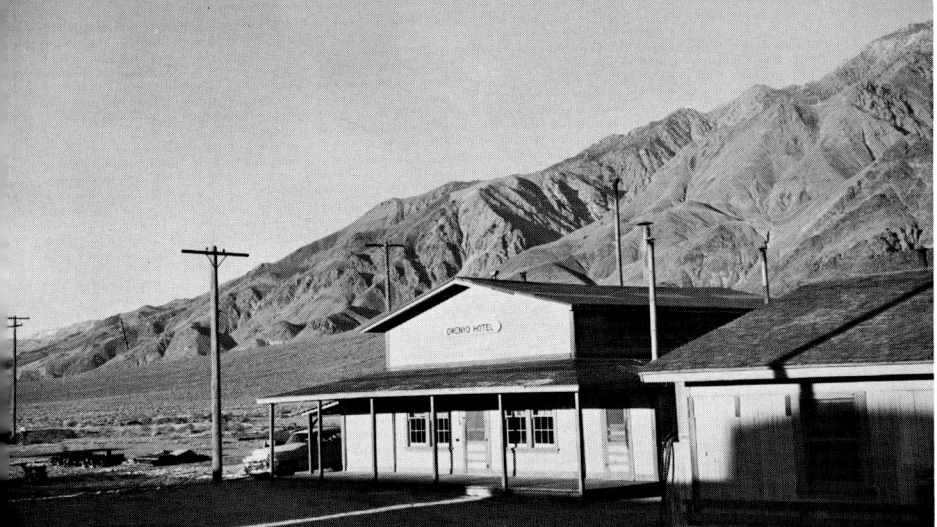

When the SP's standard-gauge, southern connecting line was finally completed from Mojave in 1910, the junction point of Owenyo on the C&C (then N&C) leaped into prominence. The Owenyo Hotel, with the Inyo Mountains in the background, provided an overnight resting place for crews. The depot *(center)* was a composite of old and new. The clock, the telegraph key and sounder on the table and the old-fashioned wall telephone are relics of a passing era contrasting sharply with the modern style telephone on the desk. In the waning years of the center's existence, a 45-ton GE Diesel handled the narrow-gauge cars to Keeler and Laws. Photo *(top right)* was taken April 30, 1959, the last day of narrow-gauge operation. Its burblings, however, could never replace the affection held for the earlier steamers as No. 9. *(Center Left, Bottom Right: Southern Pacific Collection; Bottom Left, Top Right: Richard C. Datin.)*

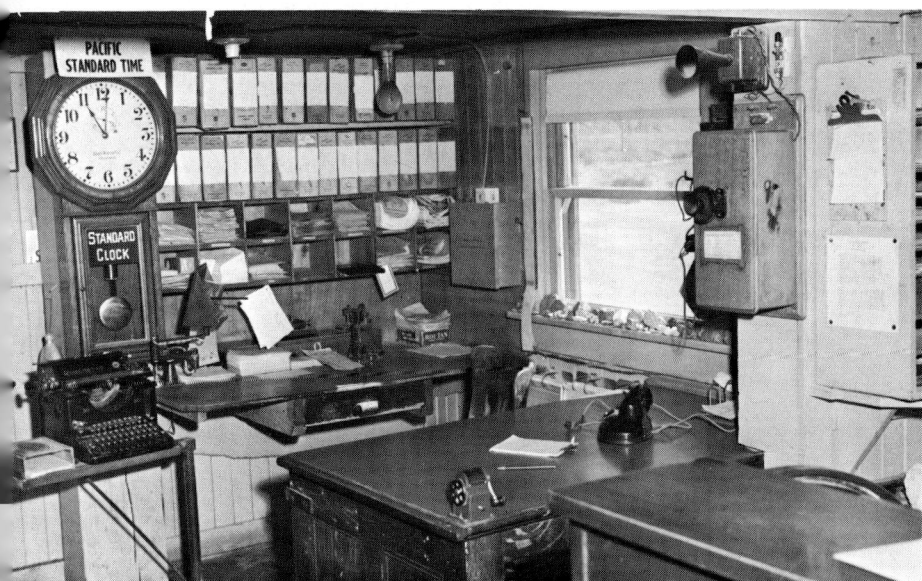

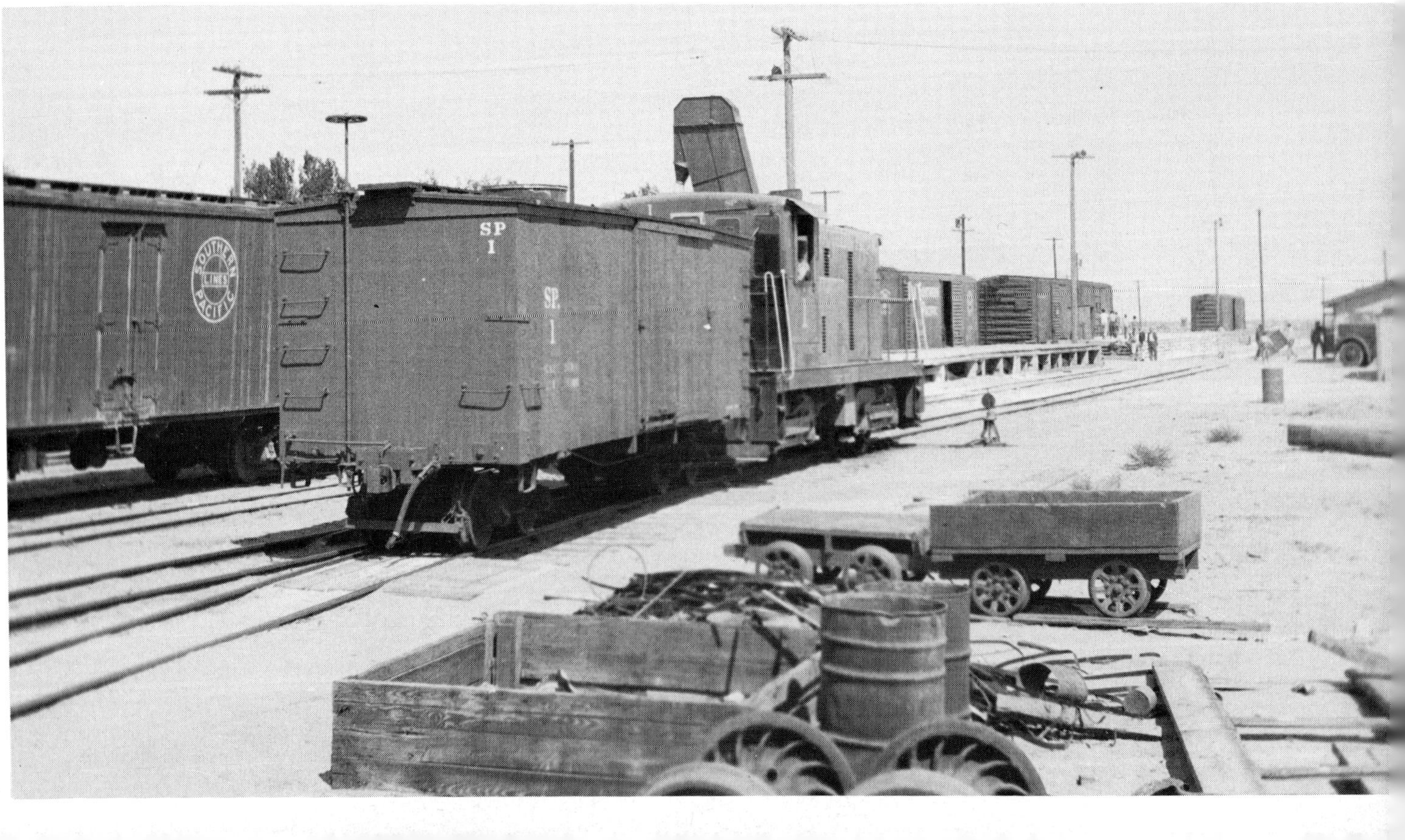

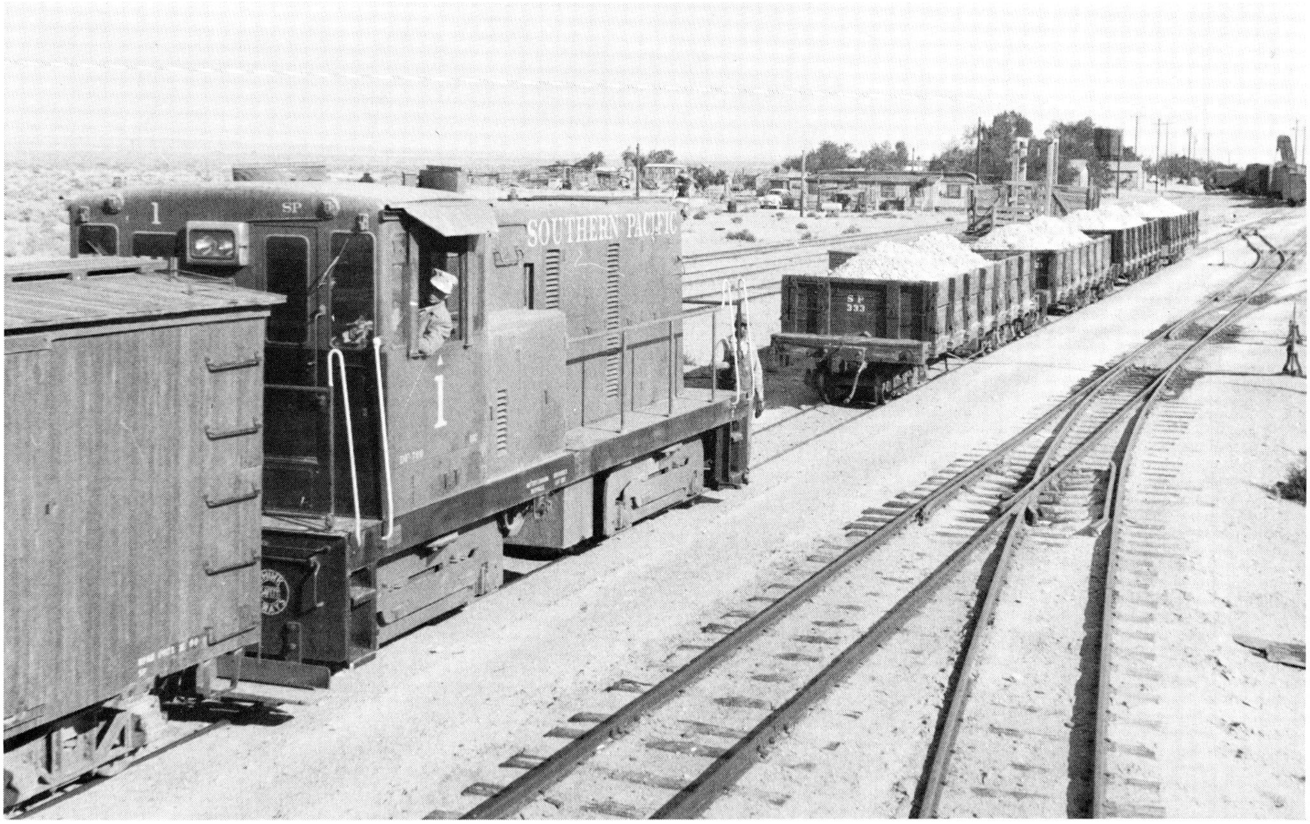

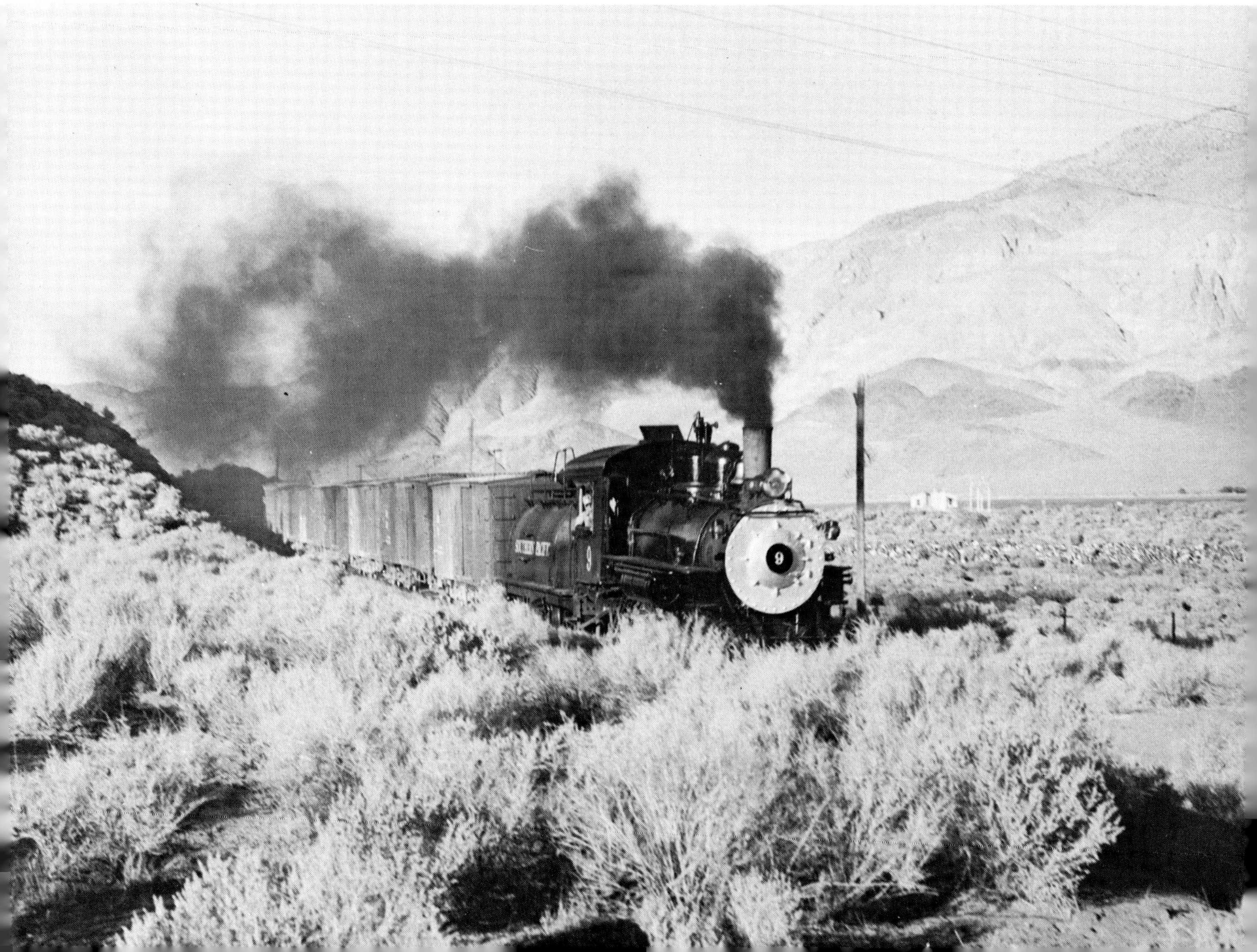

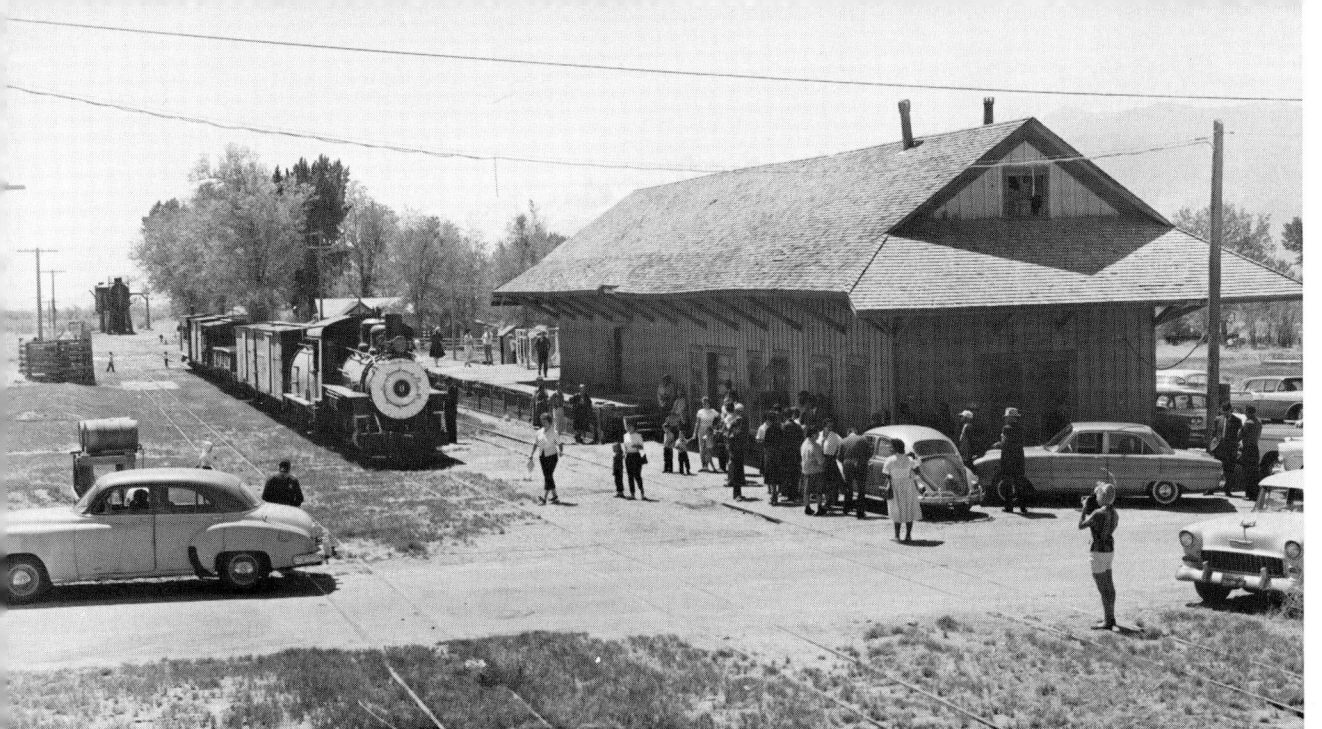

Few vestiges of the narrow gauge (ex-Carson & Colorado, ex-Nevada & California, ex-Southern Pacific) remain today. No. 9 and six cars stand at Laws, donated to the near-by City of Bishop. The "Armstrong" turntable at Laws is a fine example of one of the earliest gallows type. Two short sections of rail remain embedded, in April 1962, in the pavement of Highway 190 at Swansea, between Lone Pine and Keeler. Elsewhere the rails are gone; spikes were pulled by a tractor-mounted crane on a flat car, lifting each rail for loading and carting away. Below, the southbound train slips by the Poverty Hills and spreading sage envelops the scene. *(Top and Bottom, Far Left and Right: Southern Pacific Collection; Top Right: Richard C. Datin.)*

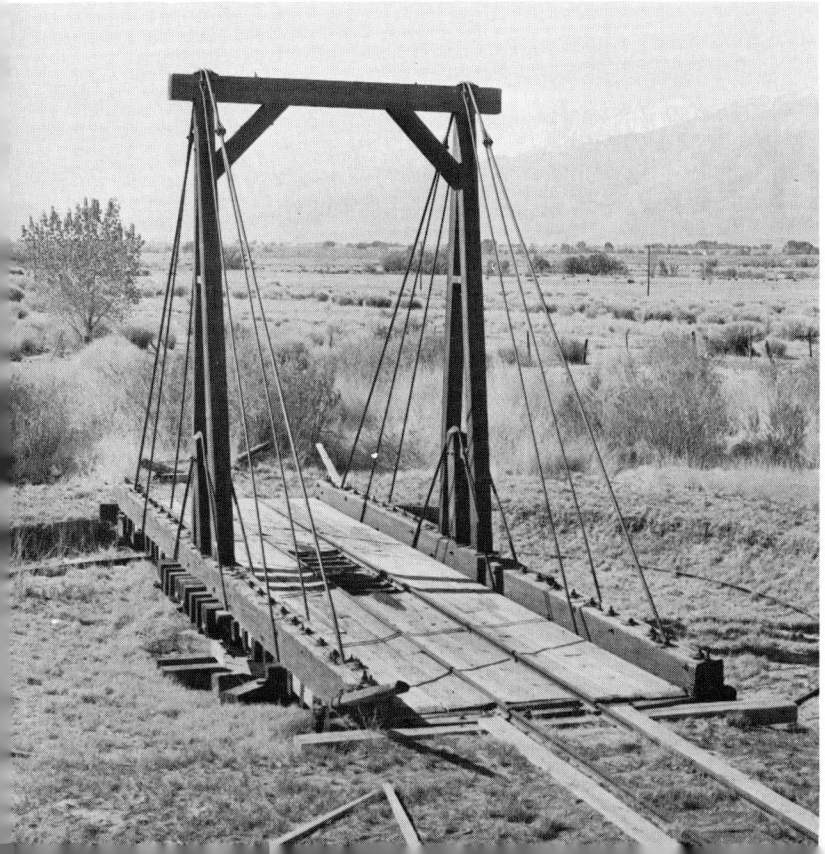

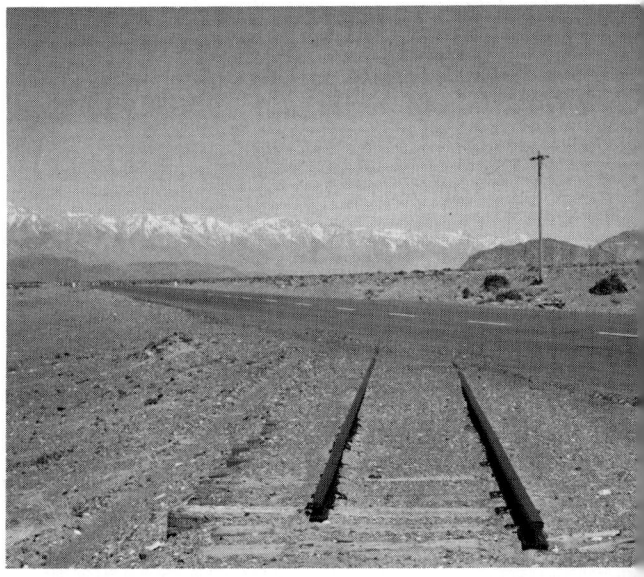

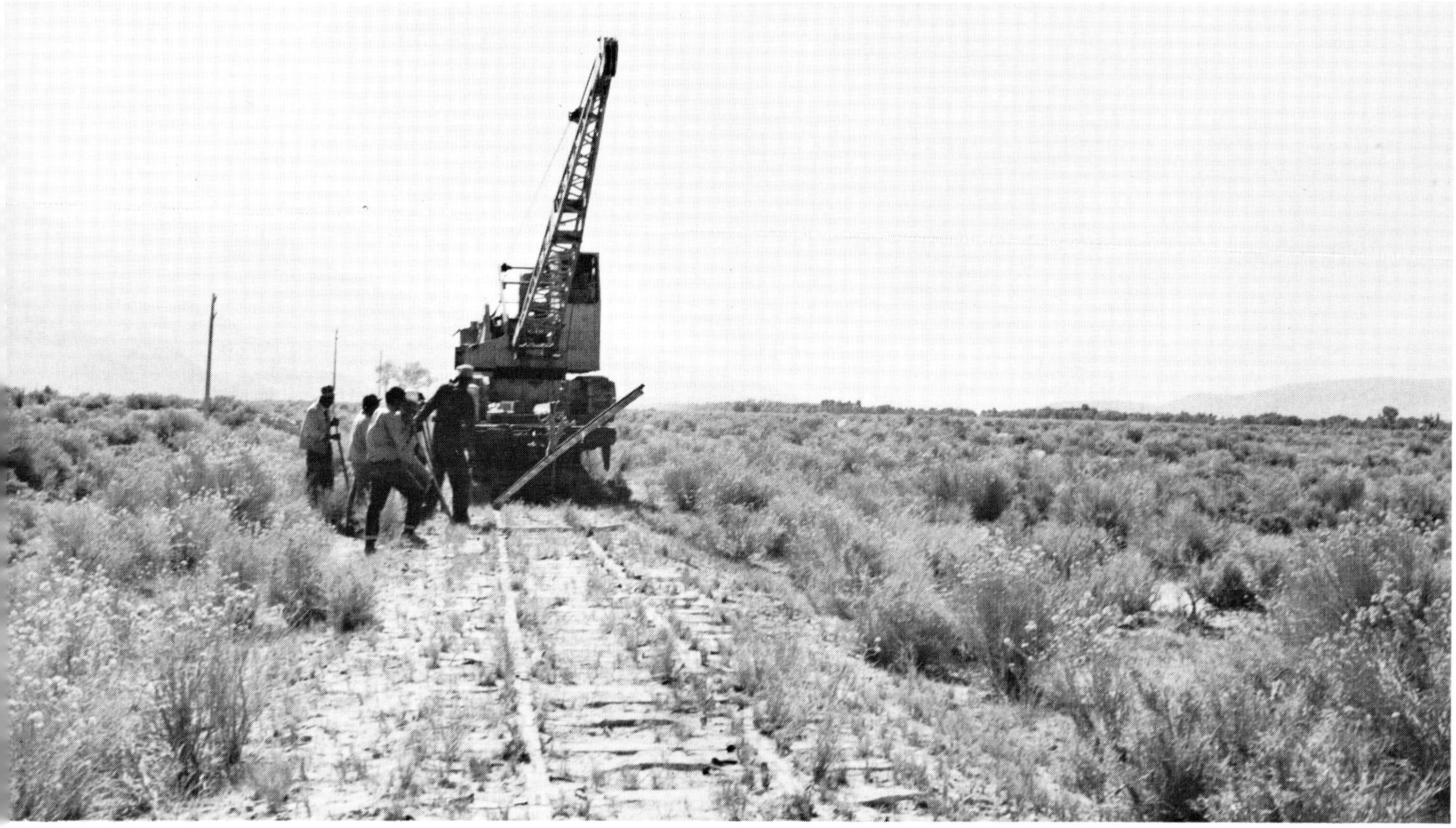

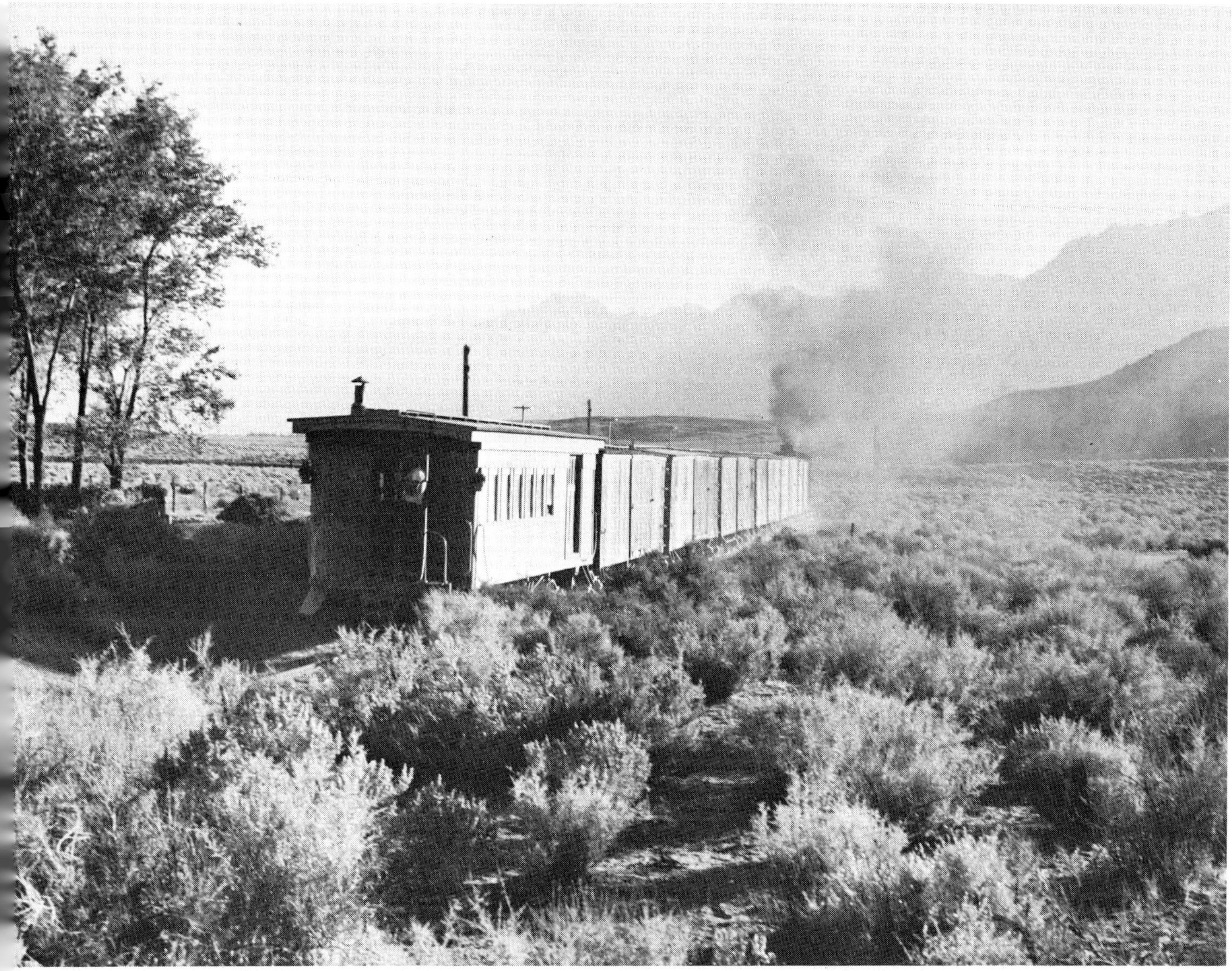

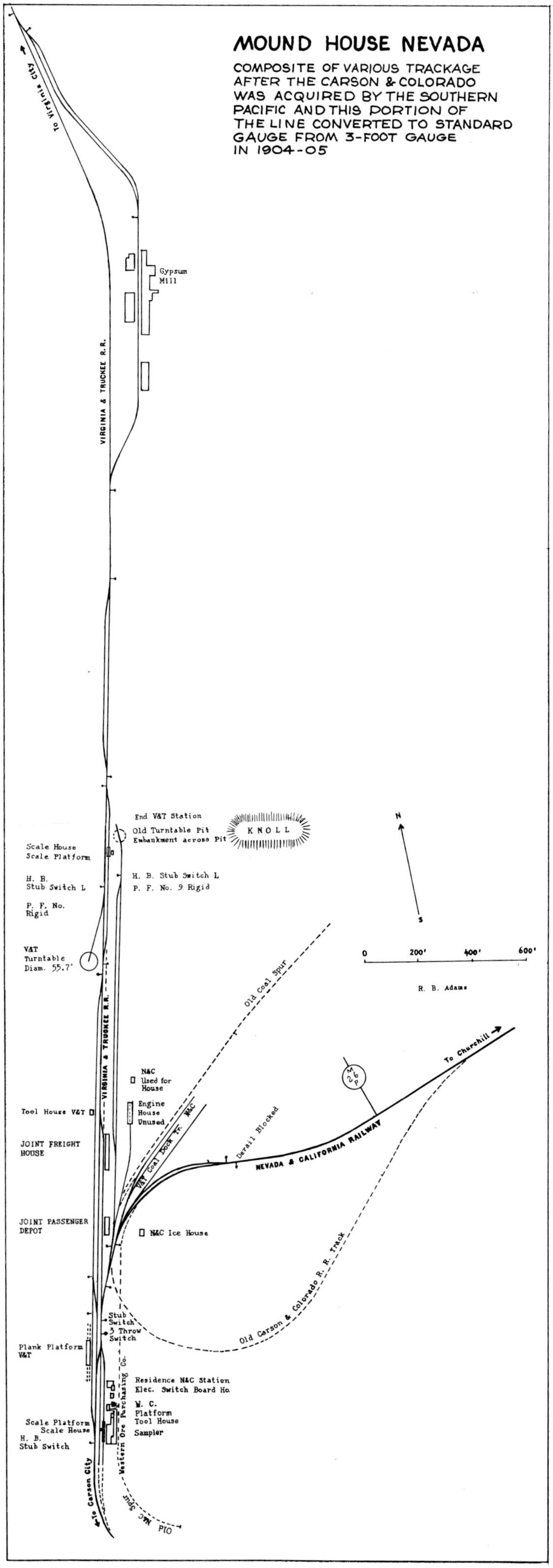

MOUND HOUSE NEVADA

COMPOSITE OF VARIOUS TRACKAGE AFTER THE CARSON & COLORADO WAS ACQUIRED BY THE SOUTHERN PACIFIC AND THIS PORTION OF THE LINE CONVERTED TO STANDARD GAUGE FROM 3-FOOT GAUGE IN 1904-05

MINA, NEVADA

When the narrow gauge Carson & Colorado Railroad was originally constructed, the southern terminal was located at Sodaville (Soda Springs). Mina was then unknown.

In 1904 the narrow gauge Tonopah Railroad was completed, connecting with the C&C at

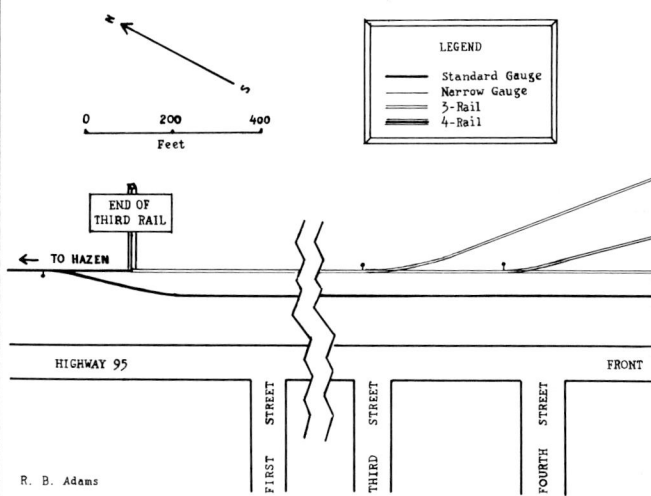

To consolidate all of these gains, the SP formed a brand new corporation on May 11, 1905, called the Nevada & California Railway. It took over all of the properties and operations of the former Carson & Colorado Railway as well as the new Hazen Cut-Off, then under construction. Additionally, it was to complete a new branch at the northern end from Hazen to Fallon, as well as to finish the extension of the southern end from the Owens Valley to Mojave. It is interesting to note that some maps of 1905 vintage also indicate a rail line between Kearsarge (Citrus) and Independence, but no verification of the actual existence of such a line has been possible let alone what (if any) connection it might have had with the N&C.

Because the SP was under UP control during this period, operations of the entire Nevada & California were placed under the jurisdiction of the UP's Oregon Short Line Railroad. That is why confusing references frequently were made (and sometimes are still made) to riding on the OSL from Tonopah to Sparks.

By the end of July 1905 the standard gauge rails were in place all the way from Mound House to Tonopah Junction, nine miles beyond the new terminal of Mina. The Tonopah Railroad was granted trackage rights over those nine miles and a third rail was installed for the accommodation of the N&C narrow gauge trains from Owens Valley, Mt. Montgomery and Candelaria.

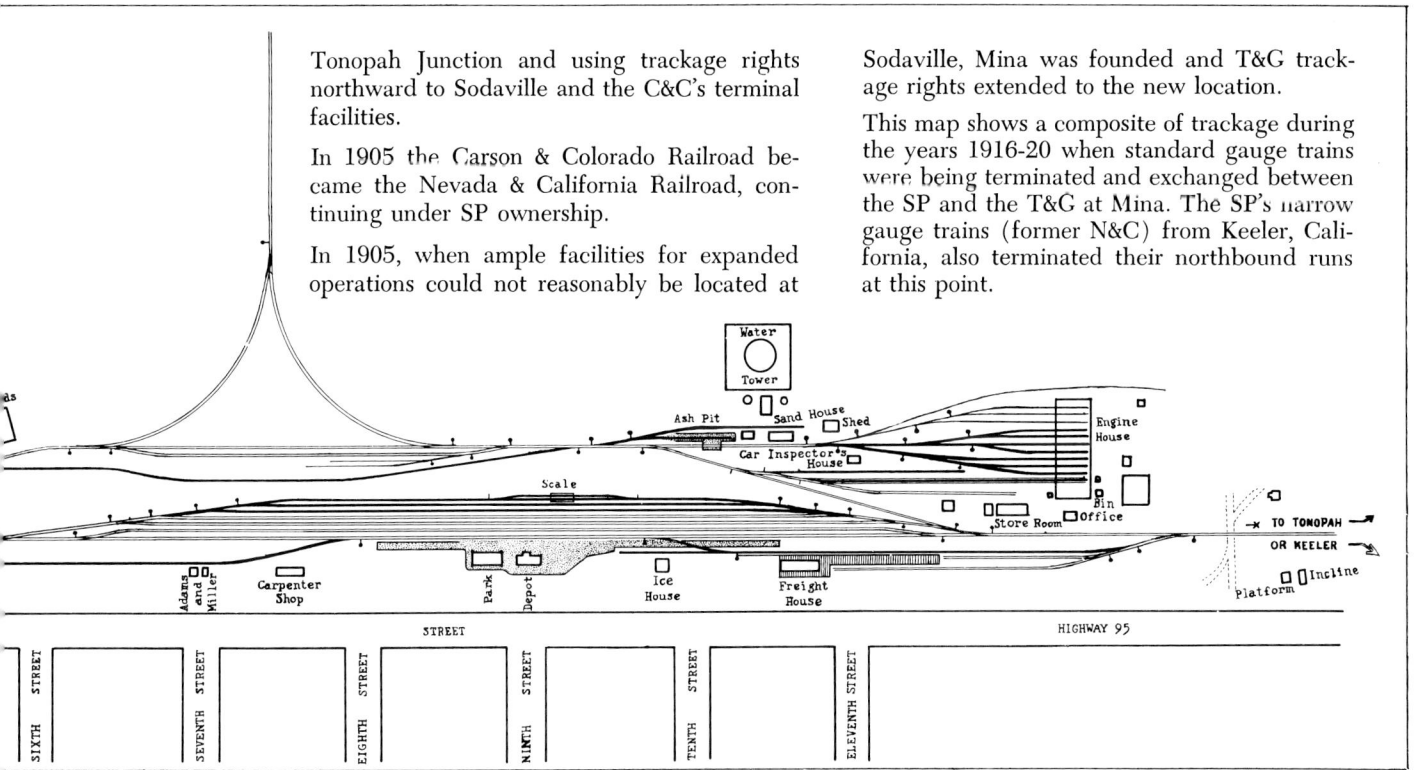

Tonopah Junction and using trackage rights northward to Sodaville and the C&C's terminal facilities.

In 1905 the Carson & Colorado Railroad became the Nevada & California Railroad, continuing under SP ownership.

In 1905, when ample facilities for expanded operations could not reasonably be located at Sodaville, Mina was founded and T&G trackage rights extended to the new location.

This map shows a composite of trackage during the years 1916-20 when standard gauge trains were being terminated and exchanged between the SP and the T&G at Mina. The SP's narrow gauge trains (former N&C) from Keeler, California, also terminated their northbound runs at this point.

Mina, as a terminal, did not just happen — it was the result of a situation. When the SP first took over the C&C, the town of Hawthorne was the basic servicing point for locomotives. It originated as a rail head with wye facilities and became a wood fueling point with the construction of the Cottonwood Branch. With the advent of the Tonopah boom, the SP installed a roundhouse, turntable and water tank at Soda Springs, bountiful in good water and end of the teamsters' lines from the mining district. When the Tonopah Railroad was completed, its trains used the SP tracks from Tonopah Junction (near Rhodes) to Soda Springs and the engine facilities at that point. As the volume of business at the Springs increased, however, a speculator sized up the possibilities and took options on the land and water rights surrounding the area from Robert Stewart, the owner. When the SP decided to expand its yard and servicing facilities at that point, the dismaying discovery was made that the speculator now valued his option at a mere $100,000. Stewart was unable to prevail upon him to reduce the price to a reasonable figure, and the SP's arguments were to no avail. Rather than pay the exorbitant price, the SP merely looked farther afield, and five miles to the north an abundant supply of water was located. With the installation of yard tracks and facilities, the town of Mina was born, and the Tonopah Railroad was granted trackage rights over the few additional miles.

Mina was a busy place. In September 1907 a count placed the number of SP employees alone at 225 people. As a town, there were the usual objections to the dance halls, but no one objected to the new school which was being built by the railroad at a cost of $5,000. Mining in the area was staging a comeback, and one mine in particular, the Blue Light Copper Mine, was considering the construction of a three-mile tramway to speed its ores to railside at the terminus.

The peak of the Tonopah-Goldfield mining boom with its accompanying frenzied speculation was reached in 1907, although mine production continued to climb to its maximum in 1910. The Nevada & California Railway which, in conjunction with the T&G, had enjoyed a monopoly as the only rail route into the area, now faced competition from two new railroads approaching Goldfield from the south (the Bullfrog & Goldfield and the Las Vegas & Tonopah). Inauguration of through service to Los Angeles on May 3, 1907, marked the beginning of the rivalry which was to last over a period of several decades with varying fortunes and misfortunes.

It was heavy traffic for which the lines were competing. In passengers alone, the N&C was carrying thousands of people. Following termination of the Goldfield strike in April 1907, some 400 people returned to the area from Reno on a single train. Two pairs of trains were operated between

Reno and the mining area to accommodate the crowds, one pair at night and the other during the day. Dining cars were a part of the regular consists. Freight traffic was even heavier. Before the mills were built near Tonopah, as many as five and six ore trains were run each day to haul the loaded gondolas consigned to the Selby smelter near San Francisco, California, or the Utah smelter near Great Salt Lake. These were in addition to the regular freights hauling all manner of machinery, products and supplies to the camps in support of their ravenous economy.

Under banner headlines reading "Schwab and Harriman will boom Nevada," announcement was made that the SP would lower its fares in Nevada by a costly 20% reduction (from 5 to 4 cents per mile or an estimated annual loss of revenue of $350,000). The move was not as philanthropic as it might have appeared, for it was made at Schwab's insistence. Schwab had invested heavily in Nevada mining (one report said $16 million, although the amount was more likely a fractional part of that magnitudinous sum), and many of the ventures were proving to be unwise and unproductive. In spite of the oft repeated colloquialism that "Charles Schwab found gold in steel," and in spite of an annual tax-free salary of $1,000,000, Schwab learned that mining gold from mere earth was a far more elusive gamble than a pay check from an affluent corporate treasury.

That chicanery was no stumbling block to Schwab's morality was amply demonstrated in many ways. The entire Nevada area was filled with so-called "mining men" looking for "opportunities." Some had money; many did not. But all were looking for any reasonable gamble on which to try their luck. It was the custom of these men to congregate on the last car of the train, and on one northbound trip from Tonopah, Charlie Schwab graciously joined the group. Everyone on board kept his ear bent to the great man's conversations, hoping to pick up a good lead to financial security; but although many hours were spent discussing mines and mining conditions, no hot tips were suggested. Just before Schwab left the train at Sparks, one man could restrain himself no longer and asked Schwab if he knew of any good prospects. "Well, I don't know," Schwab replied. "I've been down looking at a little operation at Rhyolite called Tramps Consolidated, and I think it might be interesting." During the 20-minute servicing stop at Sparks, a group of the men, including Jim Knapp, later a successful mining machinery man, dashed into Reno by street car and placed orders for the stock. Knapp purchased 1,000 shares at $1.10 a share, then went off for several weeks in the mountains. Eagerly searching the quotations on his return, he found his stock all right — at 10 cents a share. More than the men had unloaded that night at Sparks, and Schwab was comfortably free of another bad gamble.

Crimes, other than moral ones, were also committed on the railroad. Unmentioned and unmeasured was the not inconsiderable quantity of high grade ores that went out undetected in the pockets and suitcases of the travelers on each train. There were other methods, too, sometimes more dramatic. In the latter part of December 1906, armed bandits broke into the express car of the train from Tonopah to Reno. They subsequently stepped off at a convenient, desolate siding with the Wells Fargo treasure box containing a reported $30,000 in gold. Ignominiously, neither the passengers nor the crew were aware of the bandits, and the whole affair quieted down abruptly when Wells Fargo contradicted the earlier reports by announcing the loss as a paltry $200.

The vicissitudes of Hawthorne as a town and as a center continued unabated. Originally coming into existence as the terminus of the C&C, it was the prestige of the railroad that enabled Hawthorne to wrest the Esmeralda County seat away from Aurora shortly after the railroad was completed. The docket at the Hawthorne courthouse was constantly filled with cases from the tough Candelaria district, and the Hawthorne court had the reputation of trying more murder cases than any other court in Nevada although no one was ever hanged as a result of the decisions. In 1905 Hawthorne lost its railroad when the standard gauge line revision passed it by to the east. In May 1907 Hawthorne lost its county seat when jurisdiction was transferred to the active town of Goldfield. The Smith-Preston murder trial was under way at the time, and it too was obliged to move with the court. When moving day arrived, the stage line doubled its rates to $3.00, but the 30 people involved in the trial boycotted the stage line, going over to Thorne on the N&C in five private rigs and taking the train the remaining distance. Hawthorne subsided into quiescence until the Lucky Boy mining boom of 1909 revived talk of a railroad to the town and the new camp. In 1911, when Mineral County was formed, Hawthorne again became a county seat, but it was still without a railroad. Twenty more years were to go by before, in 1931, the government constructed a railroad with extensive trackage west from Thorne on the N&C main line to the U. S. Navy Ammunition Depot at Hawthorne.

With all of the furor and excitement centering largely around the Tonopah-Goldfield-Rhyolite areas, speculation and interest over the southern extension of the N&C from Owens Valley to Mojave had subsided. The SP remained cognizant of the situation, however, and as early as 1905 had surveyors running lines from Keeler to Mojave. But it was Los Angeles' crying need for water that sparked the whole program into action.

For Los Angeles had mushroomed. In 1880 it was a town of 11,000 population; by 1900 it had increased to a city of 102,000 population; by 1910 it was to treble that already staggering figure. Such a concentration of people required water, and the search for water took former Mayor Evans and Engineer William Mulholland into the Owens Valley. The story of the acquisition of that water by Los Angeles is long, bitter and controversial, and does not bear repeating here. It is sufficient to note that in 1907 preliminary work was begun on the aqueduct to carry the water from an intake a dozen miles above Independence, all the way (some 223 miles) to the San Fernando reservoir on the outskirts of Los Angeles by means of a series of canals, siphons and tunnels. Before physical construction could be commenced in September 1908 on the five-year job, transportation needed to be provided.

Preliminary talks were held with the Santa Fe, the Western Pacific and the Southern Pacific. Only the latter expressed any interest in hauling supplies under contract for the big job. Time was short. To meet the contract requirements posed by the aqueduct builders, the railroad had to be pushed — and pushed hard.

Mojave was soon bustling as a base camp and jumping-off place for the new standard gauge line. In May 1908 some 400 men and approximately 900 head of stock were on the job. The first 23-mile section to Cantil was opened on June 1. To the northwest lay scenic Red Rock Canyon, but heavy grades and the threat of flash floods caused a deviation of the line to the northeast where a temporary shoo-fly carried the rails over El Paso Summit while a tunnel was being bored. Thus Searles was reached on October 20, 1908, while the tunnel (4,340 feet long—one of the longest on the SP) was not completed until the following year. At the top of El Paso Summit a wye was built for turning the helper engines required in the shoo-fly line operation, one of an unusual number of wye tracks to be installed along the entire branch.

Although the main line was obliged to detour around Red Rock Canyon, supplies were still needed in this vital spot during construction of the aqueduct. To service the area the Red Rock Railroad was organized. From Cantil Siding on the main line, 23 miles north of Mojave, the Red Rock Railroad swung northwesterly for nine miles up Red Rock Canyon on an average grade of 3.4% to the aqueduct site. The SP carried out the construction between September 1908 and January 1909, and the line was operated for 22 months before being dismantled in December 1910. Salvage materials were sold to the U. S. Reclamation Service for use on the Lower Colorado River levees. As though to substantiate the decision of the engineers in relocating the main line, the Red Rock suffered at least one serious washout during its short span of life.

Along the main line north of Searles, in Rademacher Canyon, and again at Little Lake, temporary tracks were constructed to facilitate operation while permanent roadbeds were still under construction. The site of the reservoir at Haiwee, 104 miles from Mojave, was reached on November 17, 1909. The lake, seven miles long, was formed by erecting a dam at each end. To furnish the fill for the South Haiwee Dam, three little trains were required, each comprised of an 18-ton Vulcan locomotive hauling seven dump cars, to operate over a short three-foot gauge track.

Nearly a year passed by before the next 9-mile section was completed to Olancha. Shortly thereafter in October 1910, Owenyo was reached and connection made with the C&C's narrow gauge, thus completing the 143-mile line, commonly known as "The Jawbone," subject of so much hopeful anticipation over the years.

North of Owens Lake, the town of Lone Pine decided to celebrate. When the C&C had constructed its initial narrow gauge line down Owens Valley 27 years previously, the town had ignored the whole affair. Perhaps at that time it had felt that the line had by-passed the town, for the original route had remained on the east side of the Owens River. This new line was different; it was closer to the town; and it furnished a through outlet to the south which was most logical.

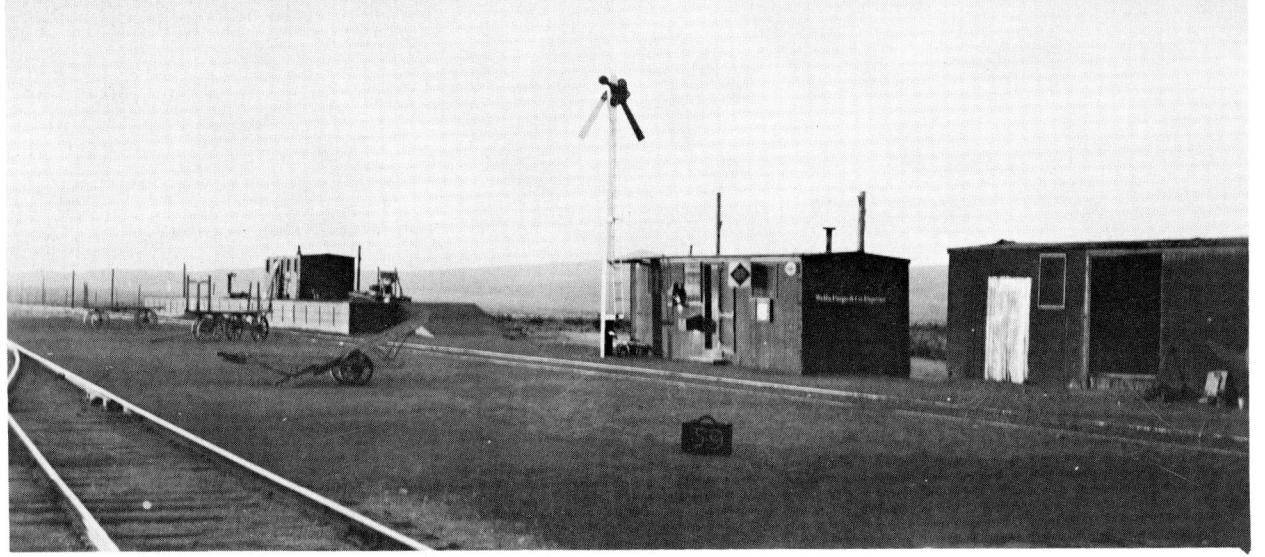

An early photo of Searles (above), 49 lonely miles from Mojave on the SP's standard gauge line to Owenyo, Searles is the junction point of the Trona Railway to Searles Lake, from which considerable traffic is derived. Freight Extra No. 2765 (below) is about to leave from the narrow gauge junction of Owenyo for Searles and Mojave where it will rejoin the SP's main line. *(Top: Southern Pacific; Bottom: Pacific Railroad Publications, Inc.)*

Two locomotives, SP Nos. 2338 and 2350 (top, right) are burrowing the hill just south of Searles with westbound freight No. 2338, while (below) an SP double-headed special leaves Searles for Mojave behind Nos. 702 and 4332. *(Both Photos: Pacific Railroad Publications, Inc.)*

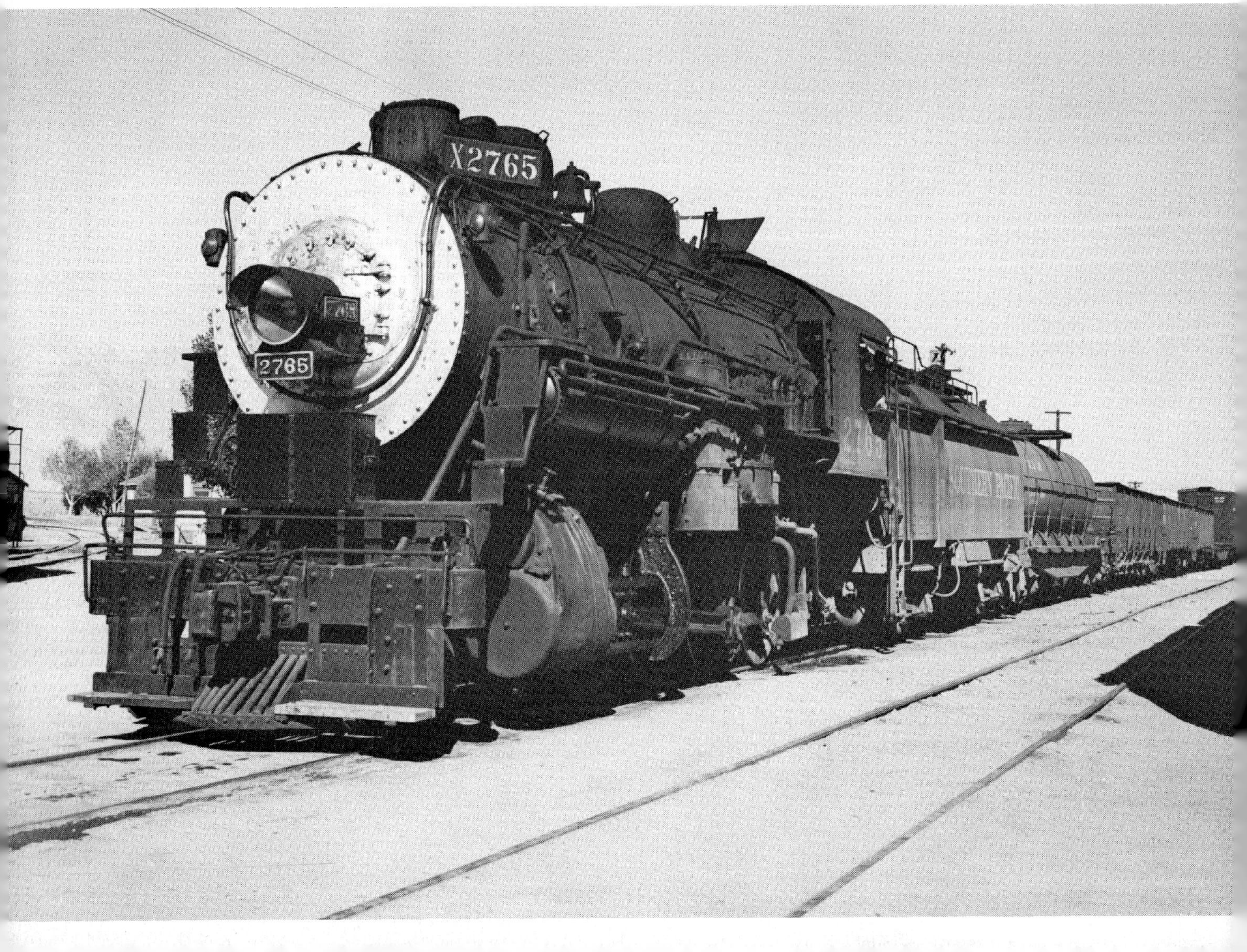

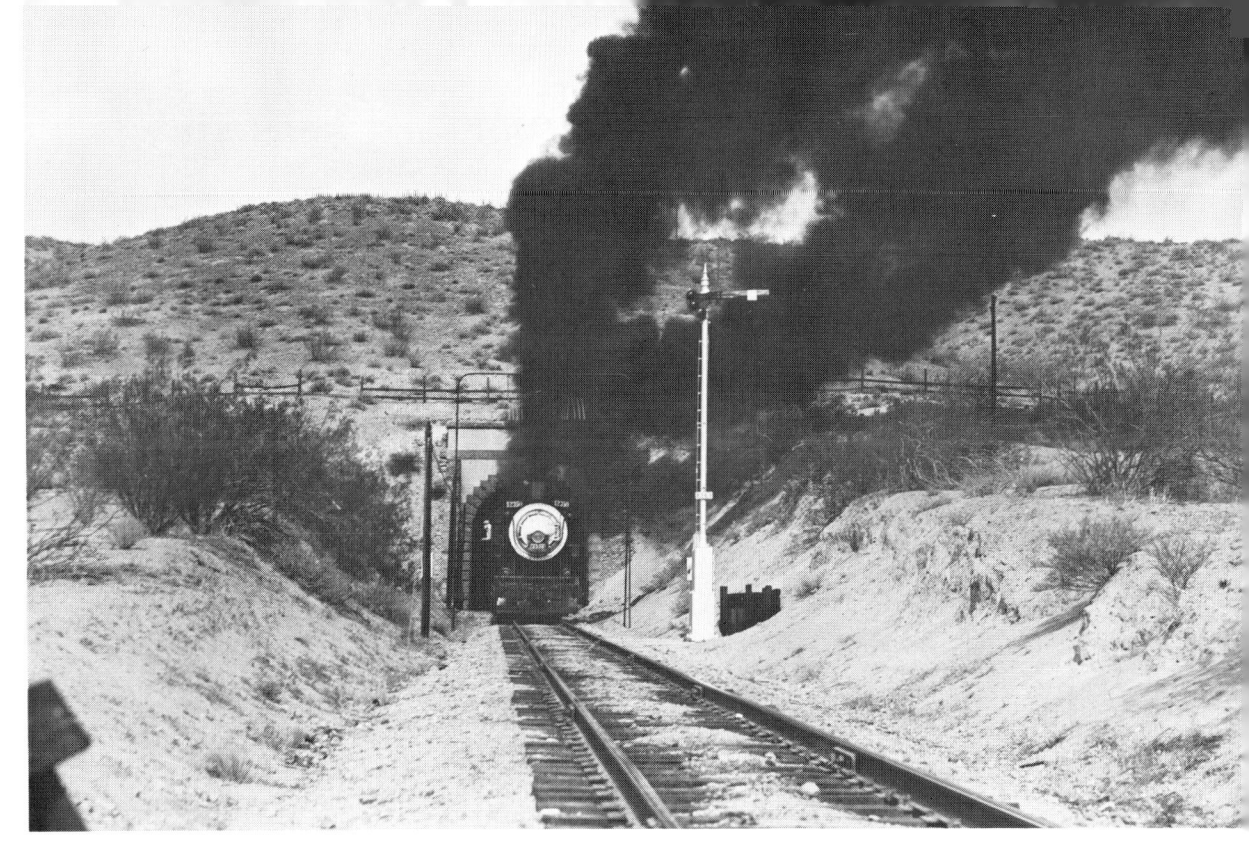

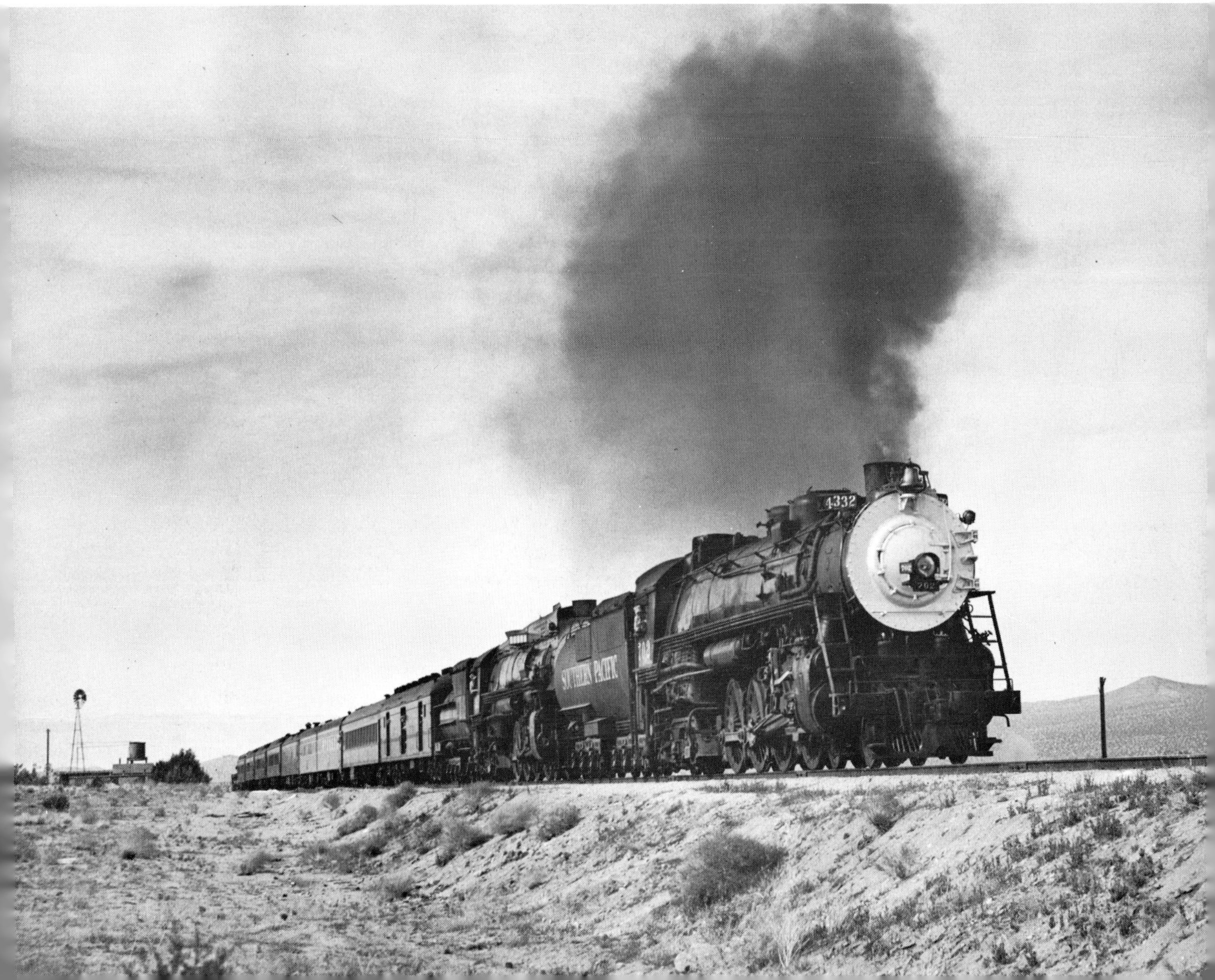

NEVADA AND CALIFORNIA RY.
MOJAVE AND SEARLES.

TIME TABLE No. 1 — Nov. 1, 1908.

Length of sidings in feet, and location of scales, fuel, water and turning and tel.ep., one stations.	Eastward — FROM SAN FRANCISCO — SECOND CLASS — 2 Mixed — Leave Daily	Distance from San Francisco	STATIONS	Distance from Mojave	TOWARD SAN FRANCISCO — Westward — SECOND CLASS — 1 Mixed — Arrive Daily	Telegraph Office hours
39,776 WFTYOP	6.00 AM	381.7	DN-R **MOJAVE** 1.3	0.0	3.50 PM	24 hours
2636	6.04	383.0	CHAFFEE 3.2	1.3	6.04	
2710	6.16	386.2	CAMBIO 4.3	4.5	3.28	
2680	6.31	390.5	TRESCOPE 4.6	8.8	3.13	
2710	6.47	395.1	PINE 4.4	13.4	2.57	
2672	7.03	399.5	CINCO 5.2	17.8	2.43	
6906	7.22	404.7	D CANTIL 5.3	23.0	2.24	7 a.m. to 7 p.m.
2708	7.43	410.0	CANEDA 4.4	28.3	2.04	
3700	7.57	414.4	GARLOCK 4.2	32.7	1.47	
2720	8.12	418.6	GOLER 4.1	36.9	1.33	
5410	8.26	422.7	RAND 4.1	41.0	1.19	
2704	8.40	426.8	TEAGLE 3.8	45.1	1.05	
4101	8.55 AM	430.6	D-R **SEARLES**	48.9	12.50 PM	7 a.m. to 7 p.m.
	Arrive Daily		(48.9)		Leave Daily	

| 2.55 | Time over District | 3.00 |
| 16.76 | Average speed per hour | 16.30 |

Westward trains are superior to trains of the same class in the opposite direction. See Rule 72.
Except No. 2 is superior to No. 1.

All trains must get clearance card before leaving Searles.

A. T. Platt spearheaded the program of the day's events for October 18, 1910. H. V. Platt, Superintendent of the SP's Southern District, was brought down the day before and was eagerly awakened at 5:00 A.M. to view the colorful sunrise on the Sierras. Later in the morning, amid whirling dust storms intensified by the freshly turned earth of recent grading, Platt drove the silver spike with unerring aim at the Lone Pine station. School children were on hand to sing "America," while a band played selected pieces interspersed among the many speeches. Everyone was buffeted by the wind which muffled the cheers following each performance, but no one seemed to care. A noon barbecue was held in town, followed by roping and bucking contests in which two Indian boys garnered the prize money. More speeches followed including some remarks by J. L. Wittenmeyer, Chief of Construction for the SP. Fireworks and an Indian War Dance rounded out the program while old-timers reminisced and reflected on the difference in appearance between today's Piute dancers in trousers and polished shoes compared with those of the old days when they were dressed in rabbit skins or nothing at all.

Regular train service over the line commenced the following Saturday October 22, 1910, with early morning departures from both Los Angeles and Owenyo for the all-day trip. Those travelers from the south intending to continue northward on the narrow gauge faced an overnight stay at Owenyo, not a very popular place. A change from day service to night service rectified the situation and eliminated the delay.

For the next few years considerable discussion was prevalent concerning an extension of the broad gauge to furnish a through route from Los Angeles northward to Ogden behind the Sierras. The SP actually had surveyors plotting a route from Keeler to Basalt, Battle Mountain and Palisade, Nevada. An alternate route was also considered to the north of Tonopah, via Manhattan but here history becomes muddled. There is record of a report that ties and rails were on the ground for the relocation and reconstruction of the western end of this line. However, before actual work could start in 1914, the project was discontinued. It is a matter of conjecture whether this was due to the start of the European War at that time or whether it was the result of the suit instituted to split the CP from the balance of the SP system which resulted in the curtailment of all major improvements on the CP. It is known that, many years later, second-hand standard gauge ties were used as replacements in the narrow gauge trackage; but other than this, no further work was done to accomplish the big objective. Speculation on the topic has remained active over the years; and even after part of the narrow gauge line was taken up in 1942, outside proposals to rebuild were made.

For many years during the 1920's an overnight sleeper was run from Los Angeles to Owenyo several times each week. This was supplemented by daily-except-Sunday passenger service over the narrow gauge northward to Laws and tri-weekly service from there on through to Mina where interchange with the standard gauge line to the north was effected. But one line change was made during these years, and this was necessitated by the construction of the Tinemaha Reservoir. Two bridges were required to carry the tracks to the west side of the Owens River, around the reservoir, and back to the original roadbed on the east bank, a seven-mile change resulting in an additional seven-tenths of a mile of trackage.

As highways improved and general economic conditions deteriorated, the Southern Pacific began to abandon many branches. On the N&C the first to go, in 1932, was the Candelaria branch from Junction to Candelaria. Operation of this line had been intermittent for the past three decades. Two years later the northern portion of the main line from Mound House to Churchill was abandoned following hearings and protests from prospective shippers which lasted for a period of over a year. At the same time the I.C.C. denied the application seeking abandonment of the 75-mile narrow gauge section from Tonopah Junction (below Mina) over Mount Montgomery Pass to Tom (five miles north of Laws) in spite of the fact that only weekly service was required to handle the traffic. Further hearings were held, and subsequently in 1938 abandonment of a smaller portion from Tonopah Junction to Benton was authorized. Because the usual covenant in the mortgage required the preservation of the continuity of the line, the rails were left in place until 1942 when the U. S. Navy requisitioned them. A year later the section from Benton to Laws was abandoned, and in 1949, following cessation of T&G operations, the line from Tonopah Junction northward to Mina was removed.

During the decade of the 1950's only two sections of the original C&C railroad were left operating. At the northern end, the 100-mile stretch from Churchill to Mina (converted to standard gauge) was connected to the SP main line at Hazen (via the N&C construction from Hazen to Churchill). At the southern end was the 71.33-mile segment of narrow gauge trackage from Laws to Keeler connected with the SP main line at Mojave by the standard gauge line from Owenyo to Mojave. In the later 1950's, trains were operated six days a week between Keeler and Elna, tying up at Owenyo each night. Three days a week trains were run through Elna all the way to Laws. Mine products were the principal commodities hauled, which included talc, perlite, pumice granules and lead. Railfans augmented the consist at sporadic intervals, one famous fan coming all the way from New York to ride this last remnant of an historic line.

Over the years, narrow gauge motive power requirements were met in many ways. The original eight locomotives handled all traffic during construction and early operations up to the early 1900's. At the time of the Tonopah boom, following SP acquisition of the C&C and organization of the N&C, several locomotives were transferred from the SP's narrow gauge South Pacific Coast Railway (from Alameda to Santa Cruz). Later, additional locomotives became available when the SP standard-gauged the northern part of the old N-C-O Railway (Wendel to Alturas), and these were transferred to the N&C trackage (the N&C ceased to be a corporate entity in 1912). For many years SP Nos. 8, 9 and 18, all former N-C-O Baldwins, supplied the needed power for narrow gauge operations. Finally in October 1954, with the narrow gauge reduced to a mere 71 miles of erratic Owens Valley operations, SP locomotive No. 1 was introduced. It was a narrow gauge General Electric 450-horsepower diesel locomotive. The old steam locomotive No. 9 was retained for standby power and was used when the diesel visited the Bakersfield shops. Old No. 8 became an exhibition piece in Carson City, while No. 18 attained the same exalted status in Independence as an Owens Valley memento.

Continuing losses finally forced the SP to seek abandonment of this last of its narrow gauge lines in 1959, together with four miles of the connecting

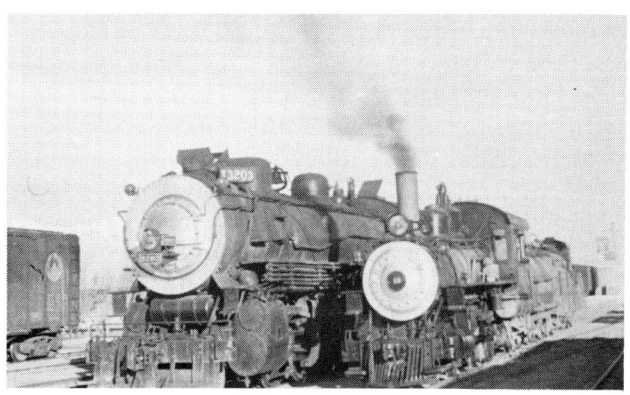

standard gauge from Owenyo to Lone Pine. Operations of the isolated segment had been difficult. Because of the original northern connection with the Salt Lake Division at Hazen, the Salt Lake seniority board controlled the personnel assignments, trainmen and enginemen being obliged to ride the bus over the 300 miles separating the rails from the division headquarters with each change of assignment. Due to the physical connection from the south at Mojave, operations necessarily had to be scheduled by the San Joaquin Division (from 1938). The resulting "split-personality" factor proved to be both an inconvenience and an expense.

Local protests arose over the abandonment petition. There was some talk of buying the line, but only one man was willing to take it over. Limited finances and other factors prevented consummation of his plans. The last train was operated on April 29, 1960. Then, at the suggestion of Senator Charles Brown of Inyo County, steam locomotive No. 9, several box cars and a caboose, together with the turntable, water tank, and a short stretch of track at Laws were donated by the Southern Pacific to the City of Bishop and Inyo County. The traveler today may still view these mementos of a by-gone era.

Dayton, Sutro & Carson Valley Railroad

Dayton, located at the junction of the Gold and Carson River Canyons, became the center for the various mills in the vicinity stamping Comstock ores. The first of these was erected in 1861 at Rock Point, about two-thirds of a mile down the river to the east. It lasted for 20 years, was removed, then others were constructed successively on the same site. Birdsall and Carpenter started another early enterprise adjoining Dayton in 1865. Theirs was the 30-stamp Lyon quartz mill which processed ores from the Chollar, Occidental and other mines around Virginia City. Four years and some 68,000 tons later, it was converted into a tailings mill for the express purpose of reworking (with improved methods) the cast-off refuse of the older mills which still contained a high percentage of recoverable ore and virtually all of which had been deposited in the common dumping ground of Gold Canyon.

Thus it was that in May 1869 Fred Birdsall constructed a half-mile, horse-drawn railroad from the mill to the tailings in Gold Canyon. In lieu of iron rails, he fabricated his own track, using strap iron (½" x 2½") placed on top of 4" x 6" scantlings. In conjunction with the railroad, the new tailings mill increased its capacity to 300 tons daily and during the next ten years produced an average annual output of 50,000 tons, greater than that of any other mill in the area. During this period the name was changed to the Lyon Mill and Mining Company with Birdsall in control.

In April 1881 the company commenced grading for a new, two-mile railroad of three-foot gauge; rail laying commenced on May 12. Starting from a connection with the Carson & Colorado Railroad, the main line ran to the mill with a side track to Ophir Flat and another line to the tailings dump at the mouth of the canyon. "The company will have its own locomotives and cars, and in everything else save the lack of timetables, excursions and free passes, will have as complete a railroad, though on a small scale, as any in the State." So read a local news item.

Construction of the railroad apparently stimulated others. Rollin Daggett, a former Congressman, projected a railroad into the Como Mountains through El Dorado Canyon which, according to his statements, would have been very easy to operate as it "was down grade both ways." Another narrow gauge railroad was projected from the Emigrant and Cherokee mines in Gold Canyon to carry ore to the Dayton mills. Neither of the roads was built, however.

Early in June, two months and $15,000 later, Birdsall's little railroad was complete. Its curvature made it quite unique. The track began about one-eighth of a mile west of the Carson & Colorado

Railroad's Dayton depot, ran north past the pan mill on the lower side, turned sharply east into the main street and, making another sharp curve, reversed direction within a lateral distance of approximately 100 feet. From here the route was southerly to the upper side of the pan mill directly over the tailings and bins. At this point various branches and spurs went to all parts of the Company's works.

Ballasting, the construction of an engine house and the arrival of two flat cars were events of record during the next few weeks. Engine No. 1, the ERNIE BIRDSALL, arrived in Dayton on July 11, 1881. A saddle-tank type with four drivers, it resembled a pet turtle running wild in search of water. The engine's peculiar shape and stunted stature excited both wonder and admiration from the small boys who saw it.

That evening steam was raised and the whistle was blown. An excursion was immediately organized. A flat car was brought up to the engine house, and a fair proportion of the youth and beauty plus a sprinkling of the old and otherwise of Dayton clambered aboard. According to the news report, virtually all of the tracks of the little railroad were traversed: to the mill, to the tailings reservoir, under waving trees, past Chinese wash houses and Indian huts. The trip was enjoyed by all, including a stop at Bender's switch for refreshments.

There was a little trouble of an unexpected nature one day. Due to restricted clearances, the low-sided cars normally were sent into the mill on a flying switch. One day a faulty brake permitted a car to continue through the south wall of the mill where no track had been laid. To prevent a recurrence, the mill roof was raised to permit the engine to accompany the cars on switching movements.

Engine No. 2, named FRED, of the Lyon Mill and Mining Co. arrived on October 18. The similarity to the first engine was strong, except for a more powerful and more compact appearance. Accommodations for it were provided by building a second engine house adjoining the first. By this time ore was coming to the mill from all parts of Nevada (the Company regularly purchased ore although it was not a custom mill). With the increased business, trains were operated regularly except on those occasions when an engine left the track. Subsequently the extreme curvatures were eased, thereby alleviating the situation considerably.

In the early part of 1882, Fred Birdsall became interested in the San Joaquin & Sierra Nevada Railroad. He sent Captain P. Dailey, who had laid the track at Dayton, to Woodbridge, California (near Stockton), to boss the work there. Locomotive No. 1 was also sent down, while No. 2 was sold to Towle Brothers for their California lumber railroad. The Lyon Mill plus the balance of the railroad and equipment were sold to J. M. Douglass of Virginia City on April 26, 1882. John Scott, the former popular superintendent, followed Birdsall to California, and when he left town the old mill shrieked a farewell whistle which echoed in the hills long after the train was out of sight.

Douglass remodeled and enlarged the mill which took his name. His superintendent, C. H. Rulison, began extension of the railroad six miles downstream (eastward) to the large tailings reservoirs at the Carson Valley Mill site. A new locomotive, JOE DOUGLASS, was fired up on September 14 with Tom Riley as its first engineer. In November, rail arrived for the enlarged and newly named Dayton, Sutro & Carson Valley R. R., and track laying was started. By the close of the month the rails were in sight of Sutro; on January 11, 1883, the first load of tailings arrived at the mill; and starting February 1, regular trips were scheduled several times daily.

The route basically followed that of the predecessor lines in Dayton. Beginning at the connection with the C&C, a heavy grade was encountered to reach town and the main line, which had been built on a trestle so that the ore cars could dump their loads into the bins. Continuing on, the track passed the old Reservoir Mill, then dropped down a short 2% grade to the crossing of the race to the old Rock Point Mill. Traversing Deadman's Cut, the line curved slightly to the north where a two-mile tangent across Sagebrush Flat carried it about 400 yards southeast of the town of Sutro. The final two miles were laid along the edge of the hillside to the tailings reservoirs.

Making up a train was a relatively simple task. Three cars, with a 10-ton load in each, constituted the full tonnage rating of the JOE DOUGLASS, which had to negotiate the 2% grade on the in-bound trip. As long as the mill operated at its full capacity of 160 tons per day, five or six trips over the little line were an indicated necessity.

The final date for the end of operations of this railroad is not known. Apparently traffic continued, probably with occasional interruptions until February 1896, and possibly for a few years thereafter.

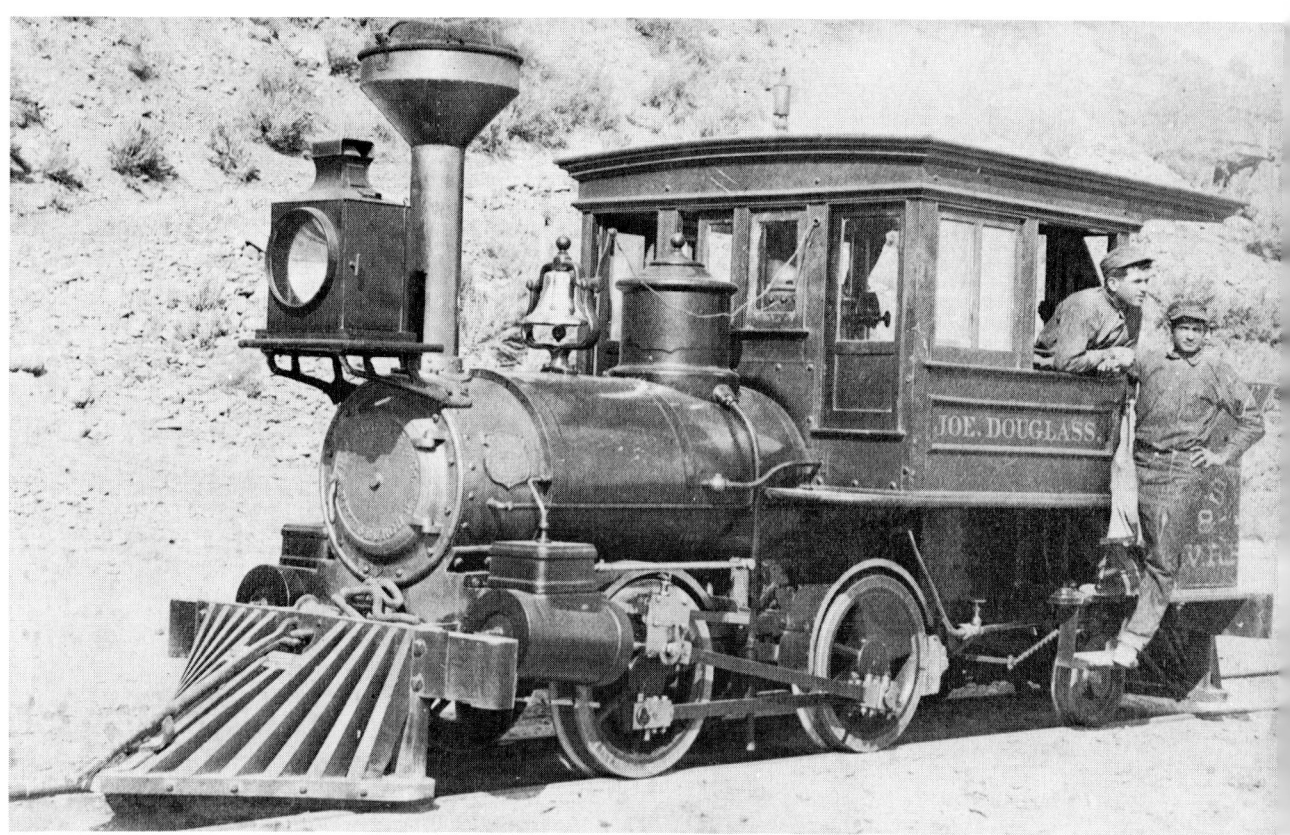

Dayton, at the junction of the Gold and Carson River Canyons, was an important center for the milling of Comstock ores in the early days. Rock Point, ⅔ of a mile east of town, was the site of the first (1861) mill which lasted 20 years. It was succeeded by several others on the same site including (Governor) C. C. Stevenson's Rock Point Mill *(below)*. A branch of the 3-foot gauge Carson & Colorado extends from the mill toward camera, while the lighter rails of the DS&CV cross in the foreground.

J. M. Douglass of Virginia City rebuilt and extended the railroad six miles to the east to the Carson Valley mill site beyond Sutro. The 0-4-2-T JOE DOUGLASS *(above)* of the newly formed Dayton, Sutro & Carson Valley was the line's only locomotive. The railroad continued operating until February 1896. Some time later an unknown photographer took this portrait *(top, right)* of the vandalized Douglass mill (on the west side of Dayton) with its broken and boarded windows and tail track of the DS&CV in foreground.

The British map of the Sutro Tunnel area in the 1870's graphically depicts the location of the various centers in relation to the early routes of commerce of the period. *(Two Photos This Page: Nevada Historical Society; Right: Chester Barton Collection.)*

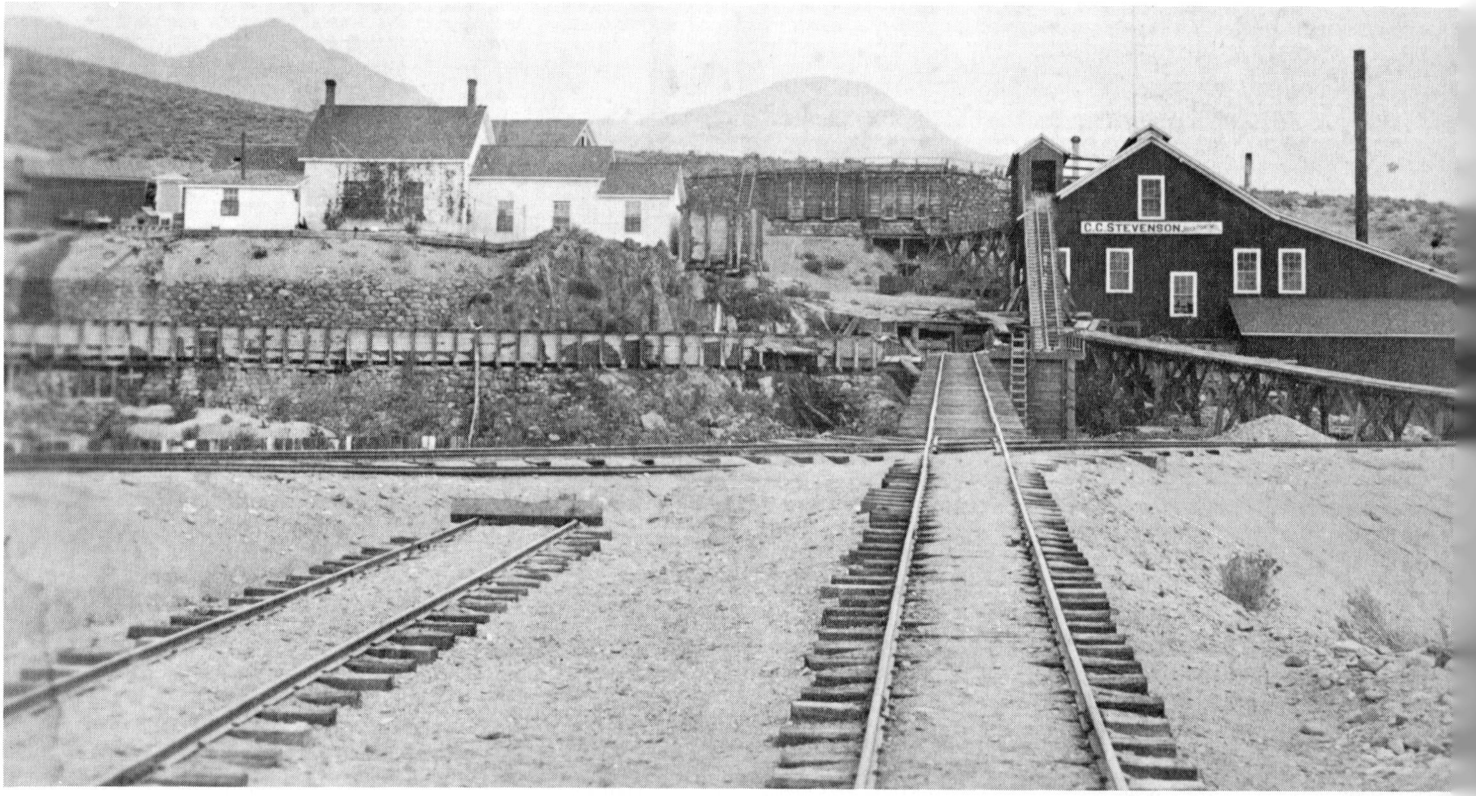

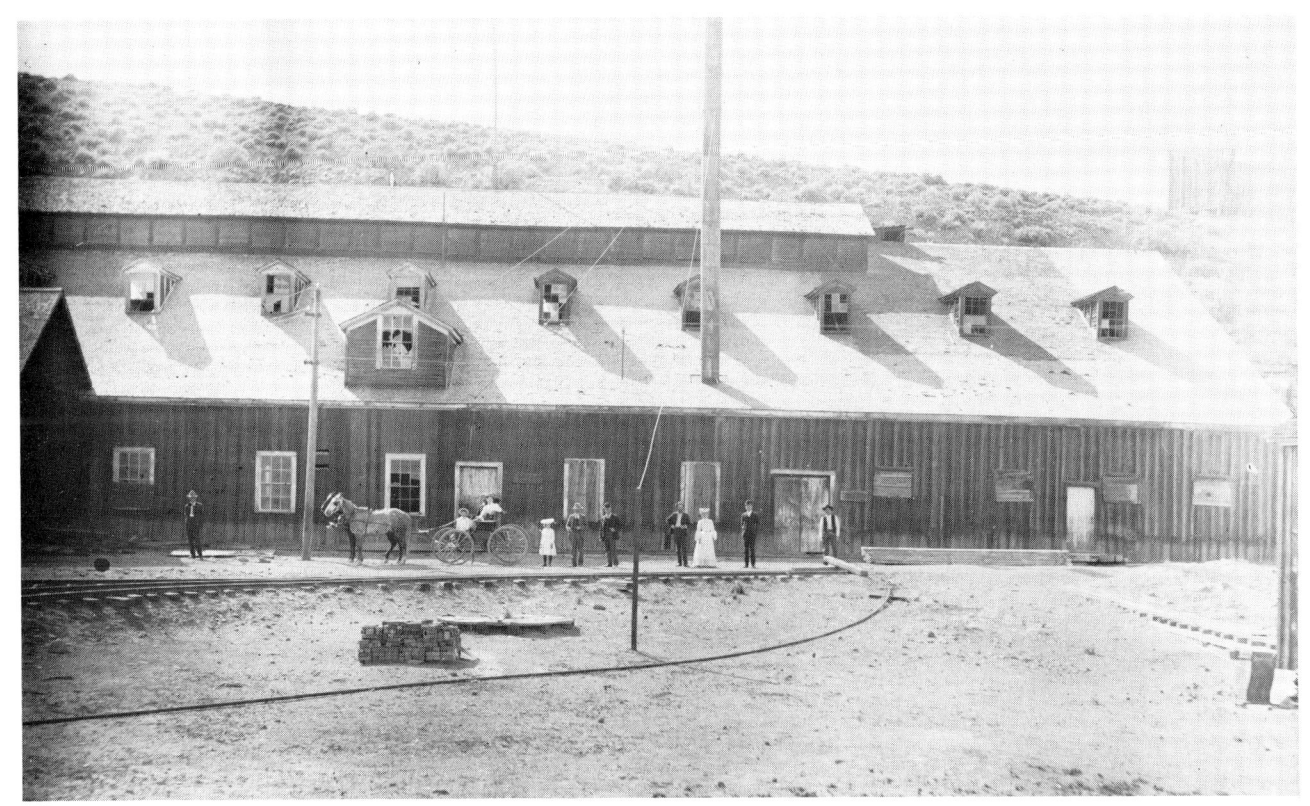

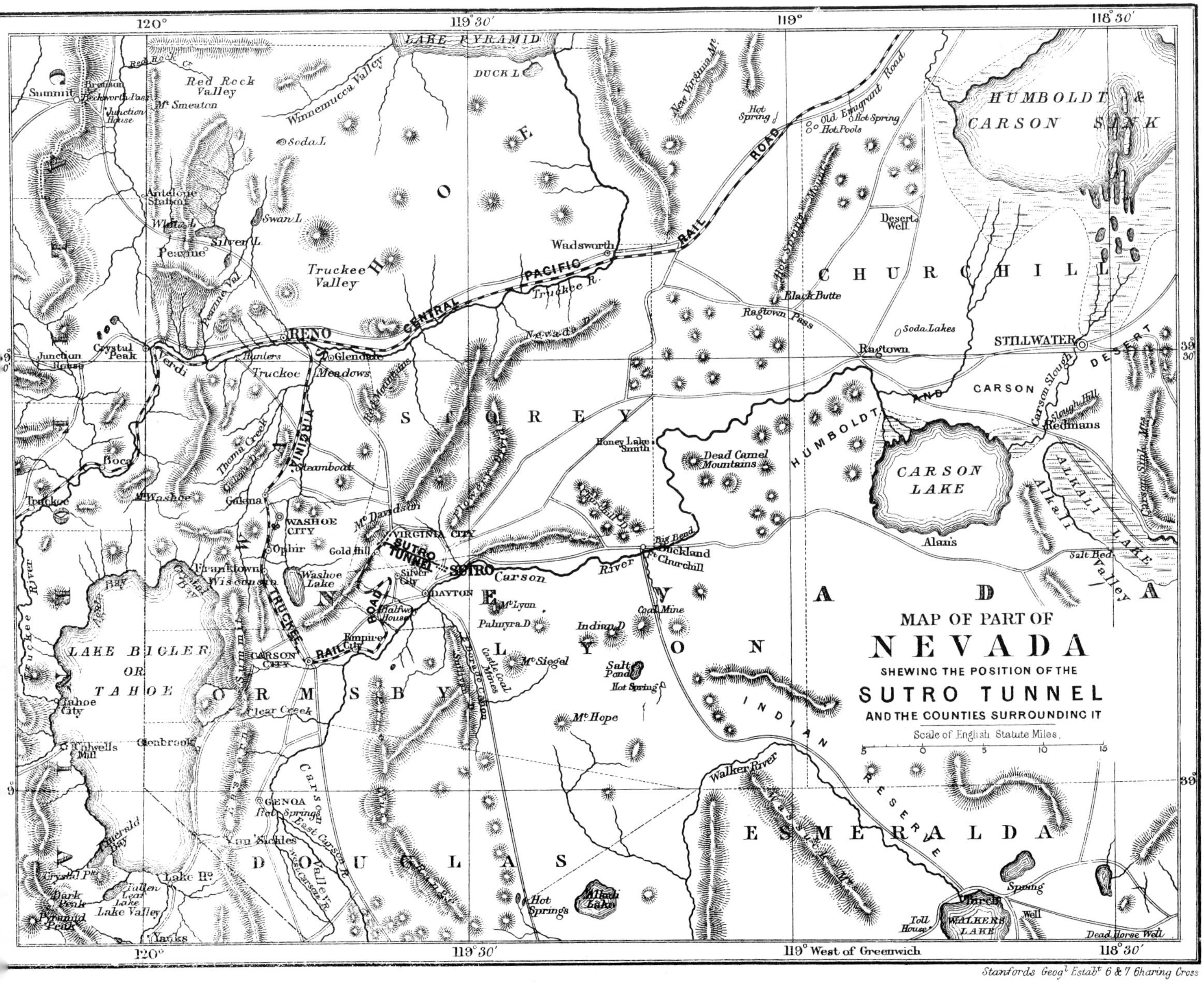

MAP OF PART OF NEVADA SHEWING THE POSITION OF THE SUTRO TUNNEL AND THE COUNTIES SURROUNDING IT

NEVADA COPPER BELT RAILROAD

Pizen Switch did not, as its name implied, have the remotest connection with a railroad; yet ironically it tried about as hard as any town could to attract a railroad right through its center.

While the origin of the name has been lost in the annals of history, Pizen Switch was not amenable to its appellation. The town fathers felt the name was derogatory and that it retarded their community's progress, so they changed it to Greenfield. Serious consequences awaited anyone sufficiently careless to allow "Pizen Switch" to escape from his lips.

But the name of Greenfield was not to fare much better. Even though it was indicative of the farming and milling community its citizens had developed, Greenfield still wanted a railroad. When its principals learned that H. M. Yerington was to build the Carson & Colorado Railroad through the valley of the Walker River, they made a desperate last attempt to attract the iron trail by again changing the town name to Yerington, in the hope that the great man would consider the compliment and include the renamed town on the route of his railroad. The flattery failed, the route of the narrow gauge remained unchanged; and Wabuska, 12 miles away to the north, became the nearest railroad station. The constancy of the status quo remained irrevocable for years until copper (not farming) finally brought the dreams of Yerington as close to fruition as the citizens were to enjoy.

Copper mining in the area dated as far back as the 1860's when bluestone (copper sulfate) was in demand for amalgamating the Comstock silver ores in the Washoe Process. A German immigrant named John Ludwig discovered the mine (that was to bear his name) on the western slopes of the Singaste Range. The site was not far from the old town of Greenfield as the crow flies, but the intervening mountain range forced the carting of ores on a northward route which obviated any benefit to the granger community. Following a number of years of moderate success, Ludwig developed sufficient finances to enable the building of a small smelter in 1881; then the tide turned against him; he became bankrupt and spent his remaining days impoverished on a chicken ranch in Petaluma, California.

Copper mining then subsided until after the turn of the century, but in November 1901 activity was renewed when the Bluestone Smelter (Mason Valley) started up with a full force of workmen. Then in September 1906, A. J. Orem put together the Nevada Douglas Copper Company, using the financial assistance of moneyed Bostonians to combine the Douglas and Casting Copper mines as a base of operations. Before the next summer arrived, Orem had added the old Ludwig mine to his agglomeration, thus combining the majority of the west slope properties into one. On the east slope of the Singaste Range near Yerington two other old properties were being reopened; the Mason Valley Mines Co. by Gunn and Thompson, and the Bluestone by Capt. J. R. DeLamar.

"You need the railroad, and the railroad needs you." That was the slogan the *Yerington Times* used during the summer of 1909 to urge local citizens to buy $50,000 of bonds of the newly organized standard gauge Nevada Copper Belt Railroad. The Nevada Douglas Copper properties on the west side of the mountain needed adequate transportation, and the final location survey for a railroad, completed in May 1909, showed that the longest way 'round was the shortest way home — it would be best to build southerly from the mines, down the west slope of the range to the West Walker River, then circle through Wilson Canyon and head north along the river to Yerington and Wabuska. A route of this devising, even though it formed a gigantic letter "J," provided better grades, passed through the Mason Valley farming area, and might be sold to the citizens of the valley to help finance construction.

The *Yerington Times* was sympathetic, commenting in a happy mood that the Nevada Douglas mines were always a consistent friend of Yerington. The town was sympathetic also. When the big pitch for money was made at a meeting the latter part of August, the bonds were being touted as a "proven gilt-edged investment" — somewhat of an extravagant claim for obligations whose only collateral represented nothing more than a survey plus a handful of incorporation papers. Nevertheless a crowd "distressingly packed" Rink Hall in Yerington the night of the meeting to hear Mayor Fred Fairbanks speak on the new railroad. With the overtures completed, A. J. Orem's son Walter was introduced to explain the railroad's financial status. Orem carefully described the solvency of the company, declaring there was sufficient money to build a 12-mile railroad from Wabuska directly southwest to the mines at Ludwig. However, he was solicitous of the people of Yerington and their needs for a railroad, and was merely asking that they loan sufficient money to the enterprise to enable the railroad to build the longer route by way of Yerington and the Mason Valley farms along the Walker River. His plan was greeted with loud applause. The people would deposit their subscriptions to the railroad bonds in the Lyon County Bank; when the NCB had finished the grade, one-third of the money would be withdrawn; when half of the track was laid, another third of the money would become available; and the balance would be used once the line was completed.

Judge Mack of Reno, in spite of his financially painful experience with the Nevada Railroad (Wadsworth to Olinghouse), analyzed the bonds and praised the valley, the mining properties, and the future potential of them both. J. E. Wilson, president of the bank, revealed that it had already subscribed the maximum of $5,000 permitted by law, while he and the other four bank directors had each taken personal subscriptions in like amounts. The display of confidence resulted in $22,000 of bonds being pledged before the meeting was over, in spite of the fact that a quick mental calculation would have revealed that someone must have reneged. The smaller investors seeking $100 and $200 subscriptions were doomed to disappointment, as the bonds were only available in $500 and $1,000 denominations.

At the end of August a contract for the initial seven miles of grading was signed with W. J. Moran of Ogden, Utah. More optimistically, nine miles of third-hand rails (rolled in 1887-96) were purchased from the defunct Nevada Railroad Company, while still others were purchased in Salt Lake City. Equipment other than the rails was obtained from points as far away as Marshalltown, Iowa.

Actual construction was started from Wabuska on Wednesday, September 8, 1909, with Captain Duncan MacVichie in charge. Grading moved along

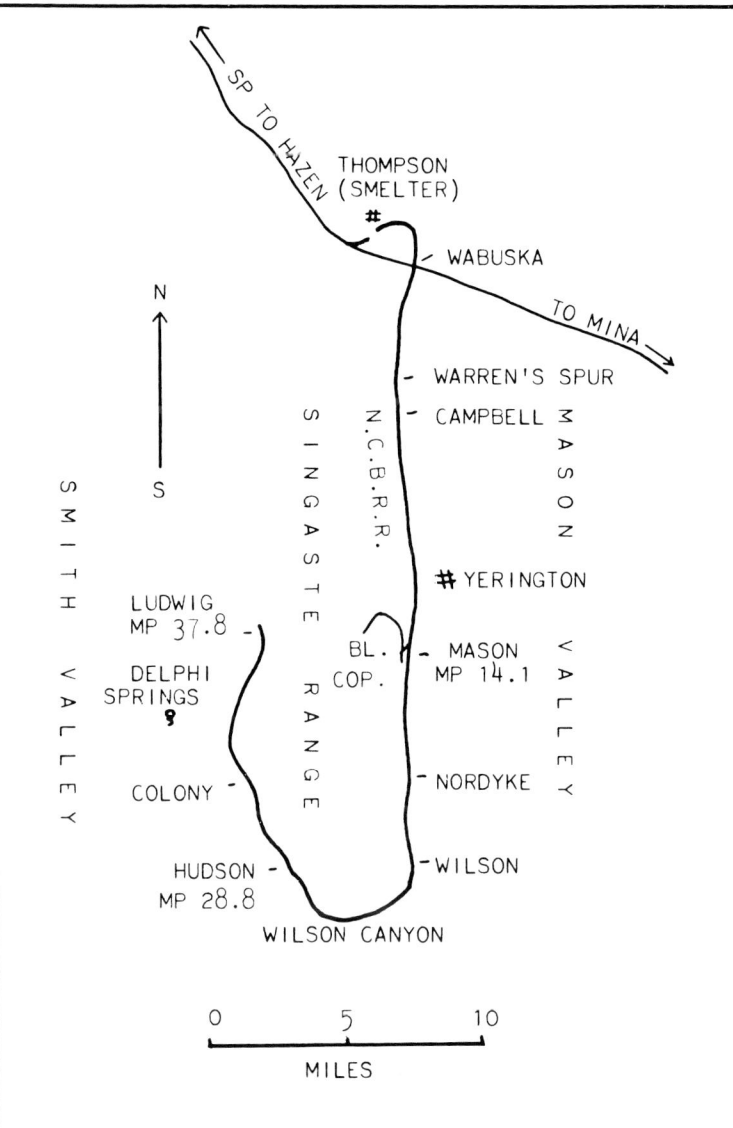

nicely, but the rails from the Nevada Railroad were delayed when the former stockholders obtained an injunction against Mrs. Mack (wife of the Judge and the sole bondholder). In spite of this Orem managed to obtain three miles of the track; most of it was released and shipped; but of that received much was sadly bent and had to be returned. Deliveries of spikes were slow, and by the middle of October only one-quarter of a mile of main line and the wye at Wabuska were completed and ready for operation. The graders, meanwhile, had completed 2½ miles of roadbed.

The first locomotive arrived the latter part of October and was immediately tried out on the three-quarters of a mile of finished track. In November the line had been extended to a point within sight of Yerington, and the locomotive was hauling supplies over five miles of finished railroad to end of track at Campbell.

January 10, 1910, was the anticipated date set for initial operations, and the railroad was making plans. Tariffs were compiled and placed in the capable hands of the *Yerington Times* for printing. An appropriately designed trade mark, consisting of a copper ingot crossbar encircled by a belt, was credited to Lois Fraizer, the 14-year-old daughter of the Superintendent. And Yerington, the town that wanted a railroad so fervently it had changed its name and raised some $40,000 in wishful anticipation, was to receive a station of calibre and distinction, fashioned of bluestone from an old mine pit along the line. Such an action might alleviate the indignation created when the railroad failed to pass through the town but remained on the west bank of the Walker River, a full and inconvenient mile away.

In spite of a shortage of ties and difficulties in hiring workmen, Superintendent Fraizer pushed the rails ahead and at 8:00 A.M. on January 14, 1910, the first passenger train pulled into Yerington Station. According to the *Times*, the engineer held his whistle cord down for a full five minutes as the cheering citizens lined both sides of the track to observe the occasion and admire the brand new coaches neatly lettered with the appellation "Nevada Copper Belt." (Elsewhere in this chapter is a picture of the first passenger train this so eloquently described.) Although pretentious for the moment, the demonstration was unwittingly portentous of the paucity of passenger travel of the future which was to occasion the languished use of a series of unprepossessing gasoline motor cars.

Grading continued to move ahead, the graders moving their camps as the work progessed—Mason to Nordyke, to the entrance to Wilson Canyon where extensive rock work would be required for the next 1½ miles. At the end of March the first Sunday excursion utilizing the newly acquired motor car was operated. To celebrate, all one-way tickets from points along the line to Wabuska were honored for the complete round trip. Obviously the gesture did not win friends with all of the people, for on April 26 two ties and two rails were placed across the track near Campbell. The motor car, en route from Yerington to Wabuska with a crew of two plus an equal number of passengers, hit the obstructions, pushed them aside, then ran into an open switch and derailed before coming to a halt. Subsequent investigation revealed that the switch lock had been broken, and both sets of circumstances were blamed on the same culprit whose identity, if known, was never revealed.

Railroad Day was celebrated in Mason City on May 7, 1910, with 2,000 people attending. A barbecue, presided over by H. D. Farris, speeches, auto tours to Yerington and the mines, and a baseball game comprised the day's activities. As a portent of things to come, Bert Lundy achieved notoriety by driving his Dorris auto from Reno to Mason City in two hours and 55 minutes, thereby cutting one hour from his previous best time.

Duncan MacVichie, formerly in charge of construction of the railroad, now became general manager of both the railroad and the Nevada Douglas mining properties in Ludwig. Not only was it necessary to rush the NCB through to completion, but a 1,600-foot tramway had to be constructed to drop ore 600 feet from the mines at the top of Douglas Hill to the end of the projected railroad. Also under consideration was the replacement of the old 30-ton Ludwig smelter with one of 100 tons capacity. However, when George E. Gunn and William B. Thompson, well-known copper men and majority owners of the Mason Valley Mines Company, revealed their plans for a smelter to be constructed immediately to the north of Wabuska, it was deemed more advisable to extend the railroad 2.7 miles to the new Thompson Smelter and process the ore from both mines in the same plant.

A telegraphic order abruptly halted all work on the smelter extension at the end of June 1910. Prevailing rumors predicted the Orems would lose control of both the Nevada Douglas and the NCB for lack of money. The *Times* expressed the common sentiment in Yerington when it commented, ". . . there is no regret expressed in Yerington. It is probable that (but) for the $40,000 raised in Yerington, the Orems could never have raised the money to build the road. In spite of this fact the railroad was not built through this city, but is across the river, a mile away. Even that might have been forgiven, but of late the Orems have been persistently and foolishly boosting Mason in their weekly market letter." Obviously the old cankers still rankled.

A month later, however, the money problem was apparently solved when work resumed on the spur. Construction was impeded by a shortage of laborers and horses, and some delay was experienced in obtaining rails from the mills near Pueblo, Colorado. The construction contract for the smelter proper was awarded to the Hughes Construction

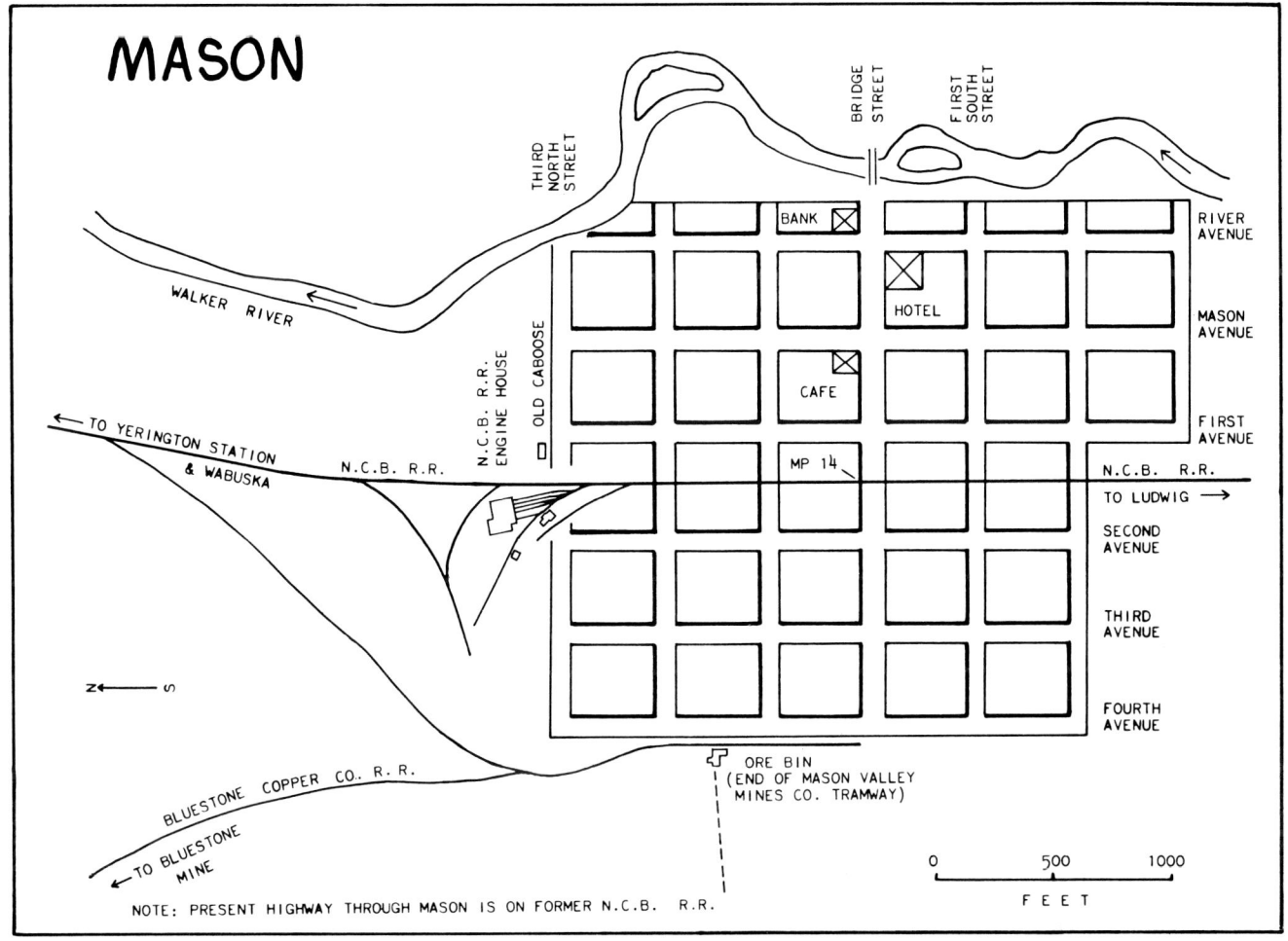

Company of Denver, and by the end of November carloads of freight were being hauled to the smelter site over the completed extension.

Work on the southern end of the line was also progressing. Rails finally reached Nordyke on November 30, 1910, although farmers had been hauling potatoes for shipment from the railhead for several weeks. The first official consignment from the station proper was made on December 8. Track laying continued all during December, the railhead finally reaching Wilson Canyon, within weeks of the death of Uncle Billy Wilson, a miner-rancher, for whom the canyon was named. December was also noteworthy for the placing of orders for a new locomotive from the Lima Works and 50 ore cars from the Pittsburgh Steel Car Company. With these signs of renewed vitality, few were surprised when New Year's Eve was celebrated on the occasion of the first annual employees' dinner. It must have been quite a liquid party, as every guest proposed an individual toast.

In January 1911 Walter C. Orem, now general manager of A. J. Orem & Co., took a second look at the progress that had been made to date and moved the completion date for the road ahead from May 1 to July 1. Relations with the press had improved during the last six months for the *Times* was now saying: "Orem is a hustler and deserves a whole lot of credit for what he has done in the district in the way of mine development and railroad building during the last two years of financial depression." Welcome indeed was the good news of the arrival of the steamer, *Rainier*, in Oakland with 8,000 hard-to-get ties for the railroad.

February was a month of progress. Starting February 12, four daily round trips were instituted over the northern extension from Wabuska to Thompson, where work continued on the new smelter. Presumably the two daily round trips to the southern end of the line were continued as before. Wabuska now boasted a new Palace hotel for the accommodation of visitors to the area. A

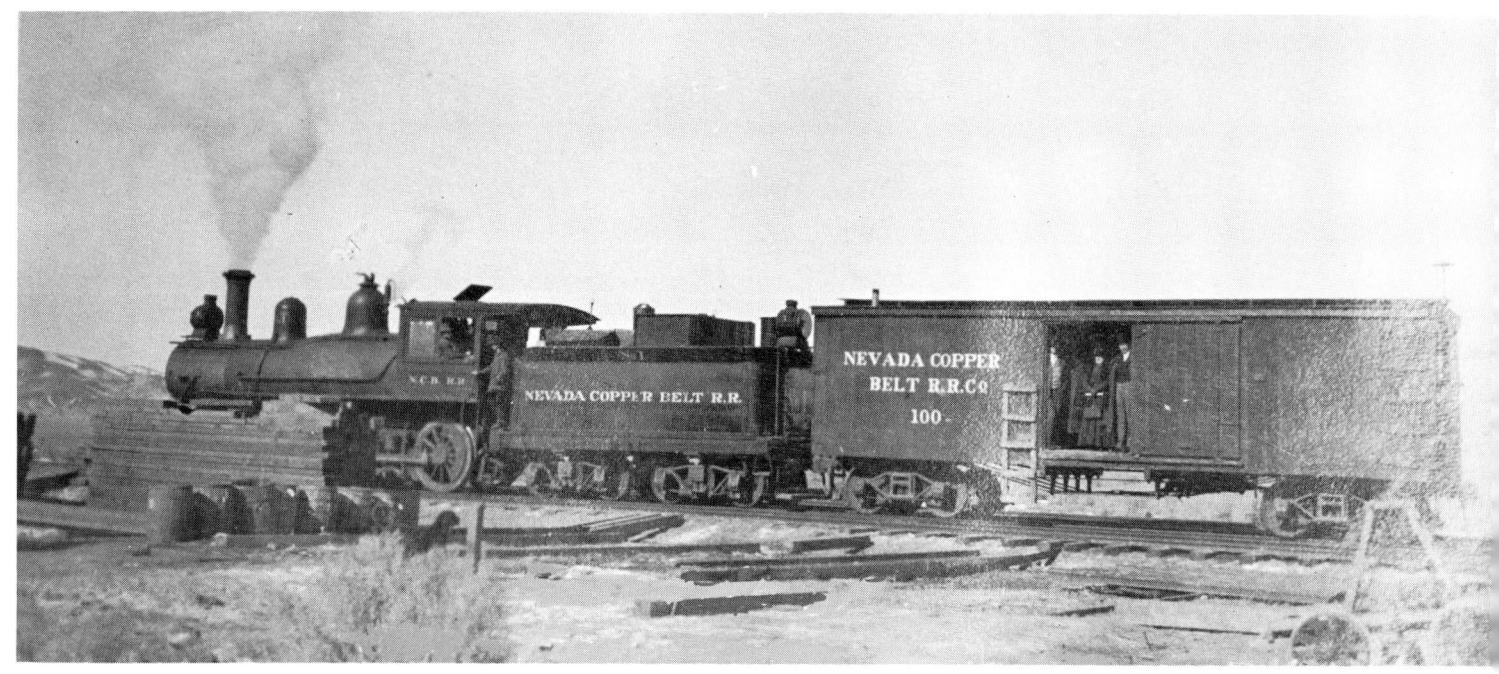

The first passenger trip over the Nevada Copper Belt from Wabuska to the end of track near Yerington was made January 14, 1910 behind locomotive No. 1 with the "side-door-Pullman" (above). Erection of the Thompson reduction works (below) just north of Wabuska furnished the vital incentive for completion of the NCB. Rails reached the location in November 1910 to bring in construction materials, but the first shipment of ore did not arrive until December 1911 and operations were not officially started until January 1912. NCB Consolidation (2-8-0) No. 3 was a handsome addition to the road's motive power, shown here at the builder's works in March 1912. A short 35 years later the steamers were gone and operations were being conducted between the squat Plymouth gas engine and tall caboose with cupola shown (below, right) in the late afternoon sunlight at Wabuska. (Top Left: Nevada Historical Society; Bottom Left: James C. Martin Collection; Top Right: H. L. Broadbelt Collection; Bottom Right: Brian Thompson Photo.)

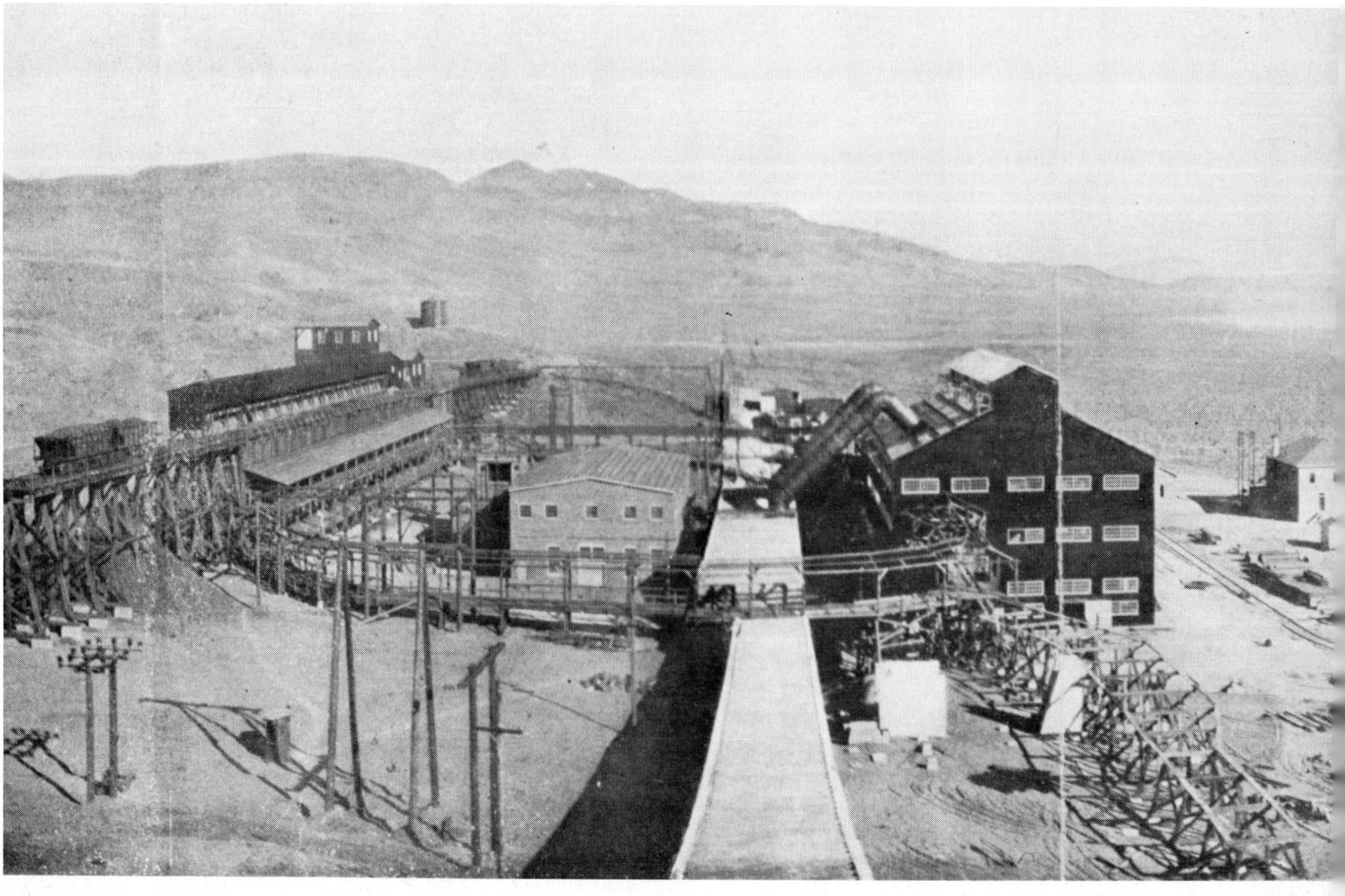

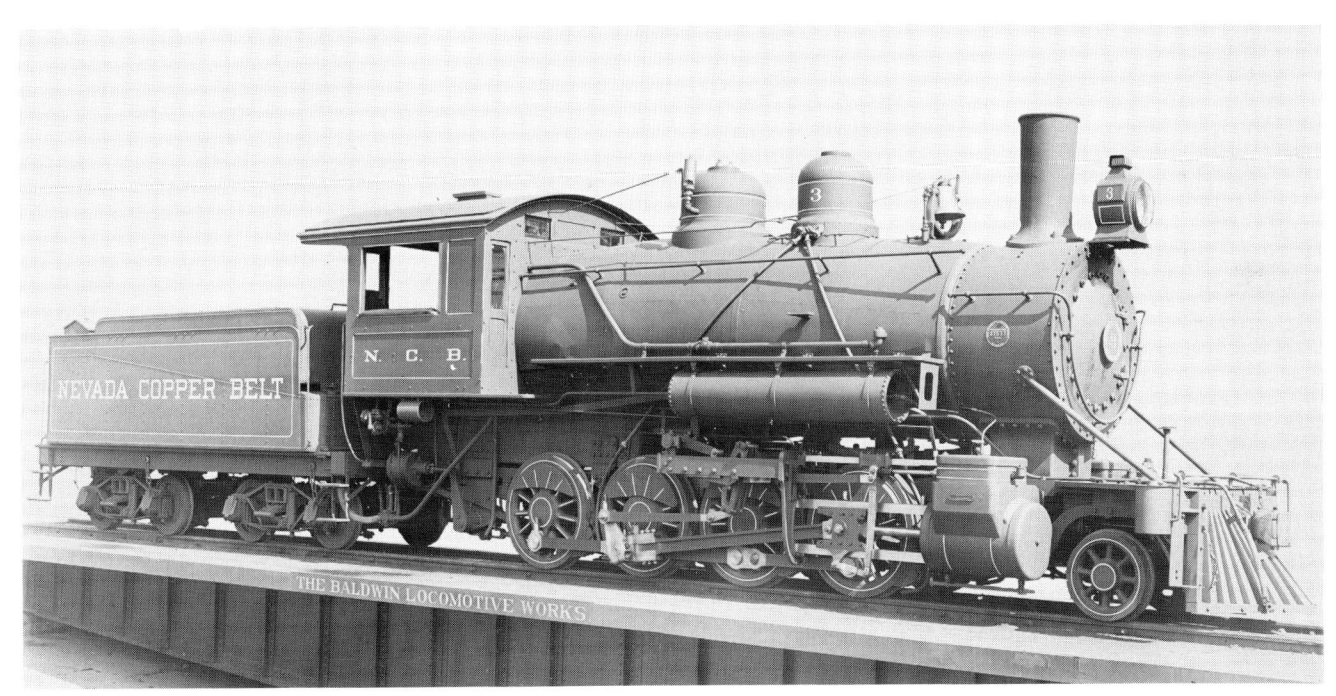

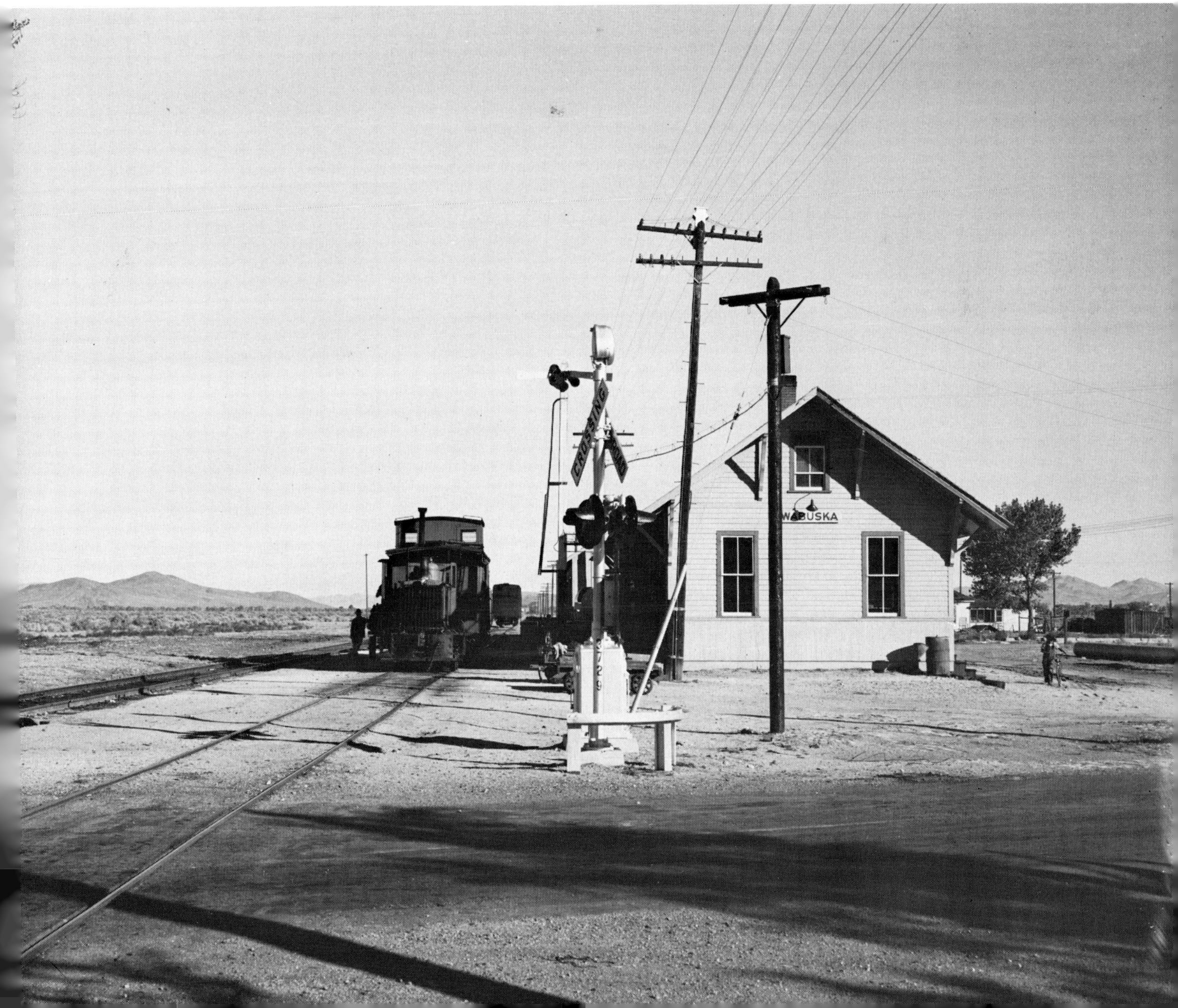

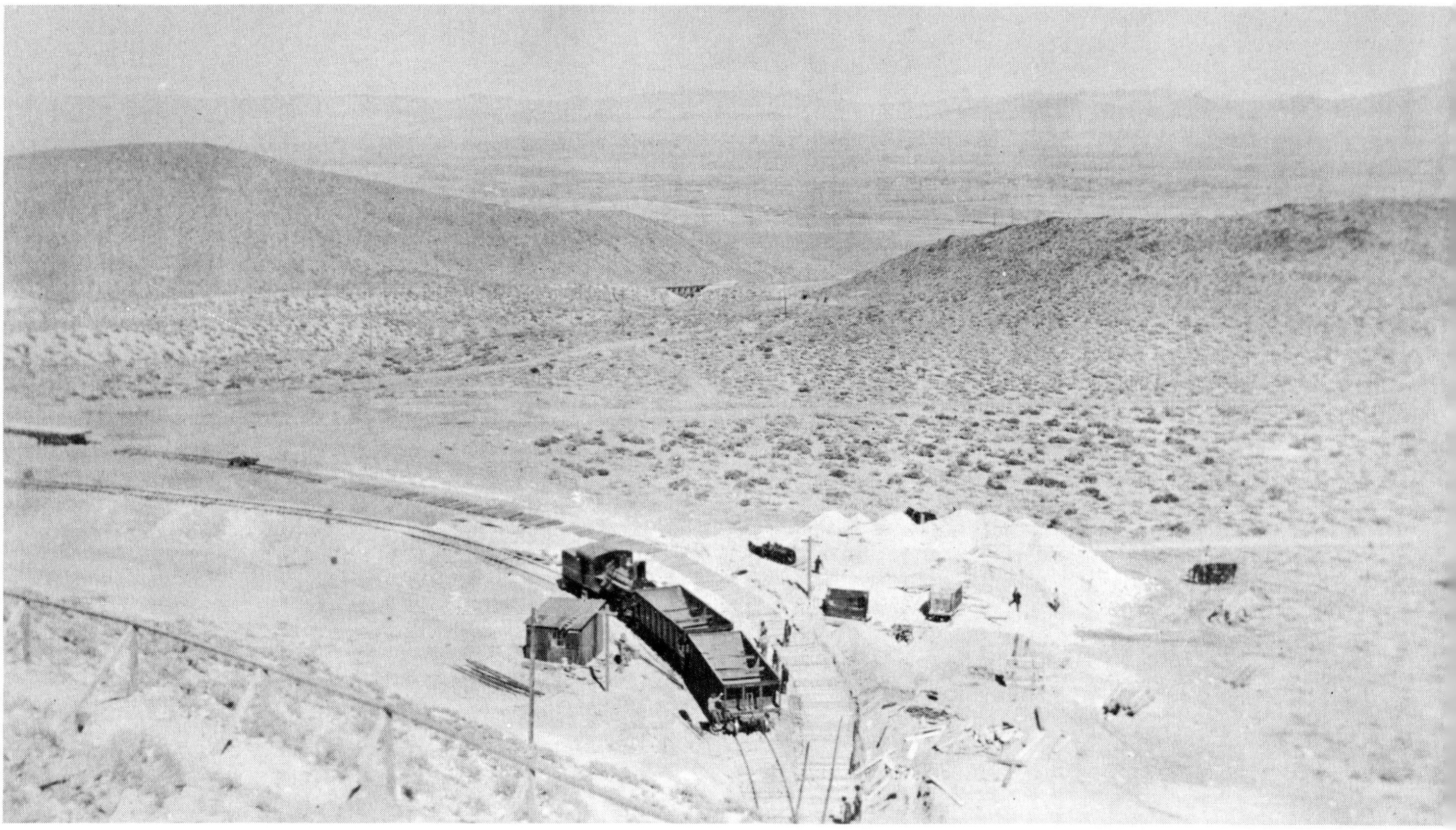

In 1917 the Bluestone Copper Co. built 2½ miles of standard gauge railroad from a connection with the NCB at Mason to its mill high on the mountain to the west. The view *(above)*, taken over the tunnel looking east shows the railroad under construction and indicates the nature of the large loop (to left) which swung back across the trestle (center) and down behind the hill (on right) to the NCB. Power for the grade was provided by Heisler No. 1, shown in close-up *(below)* under lettering for the Blake Bros. Quarry near Richmond, California, where this picture was taken on the company's pier in 1944. *(Both Photos: Louis L. Stein, Jr. Collection.)*

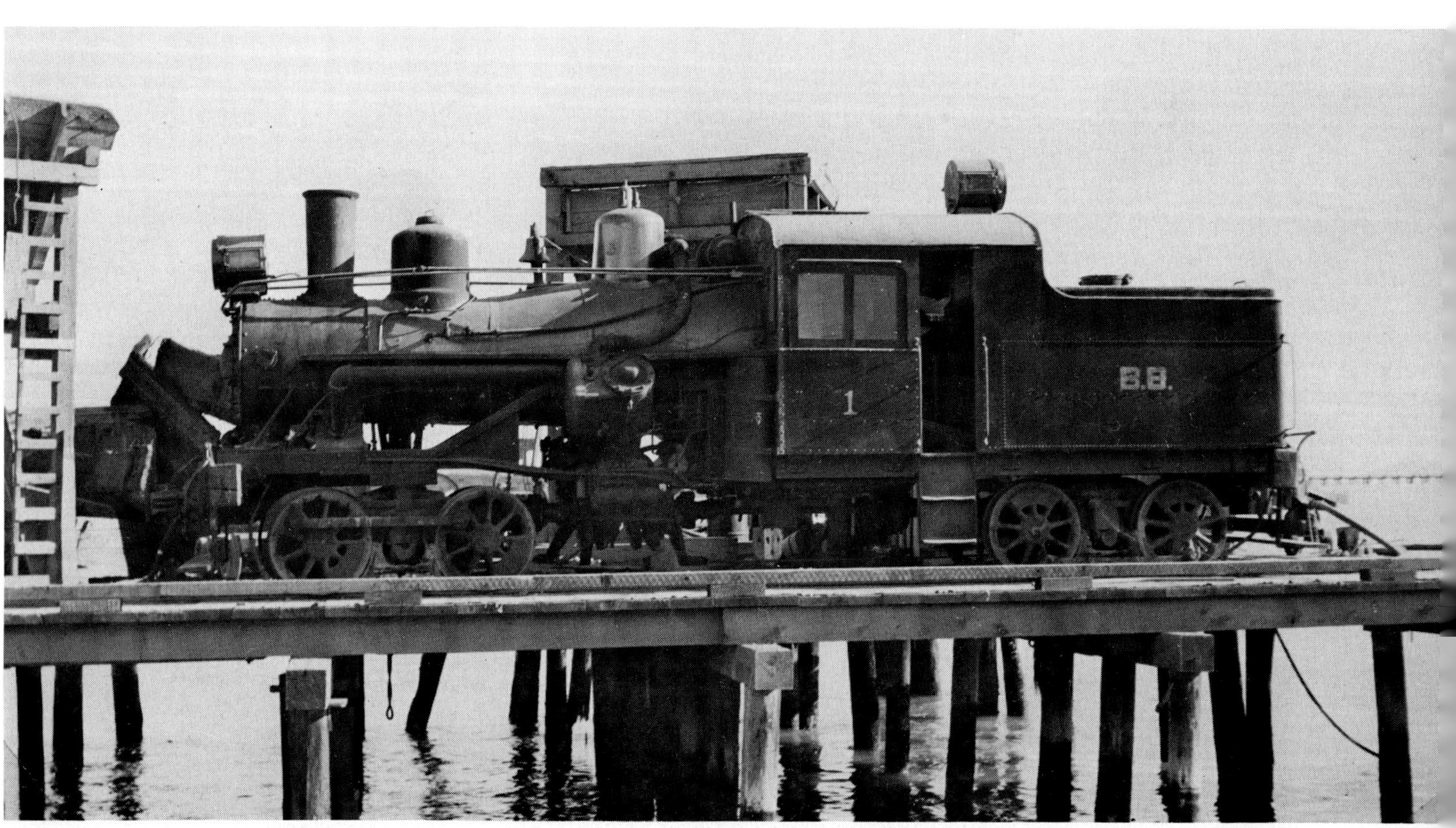

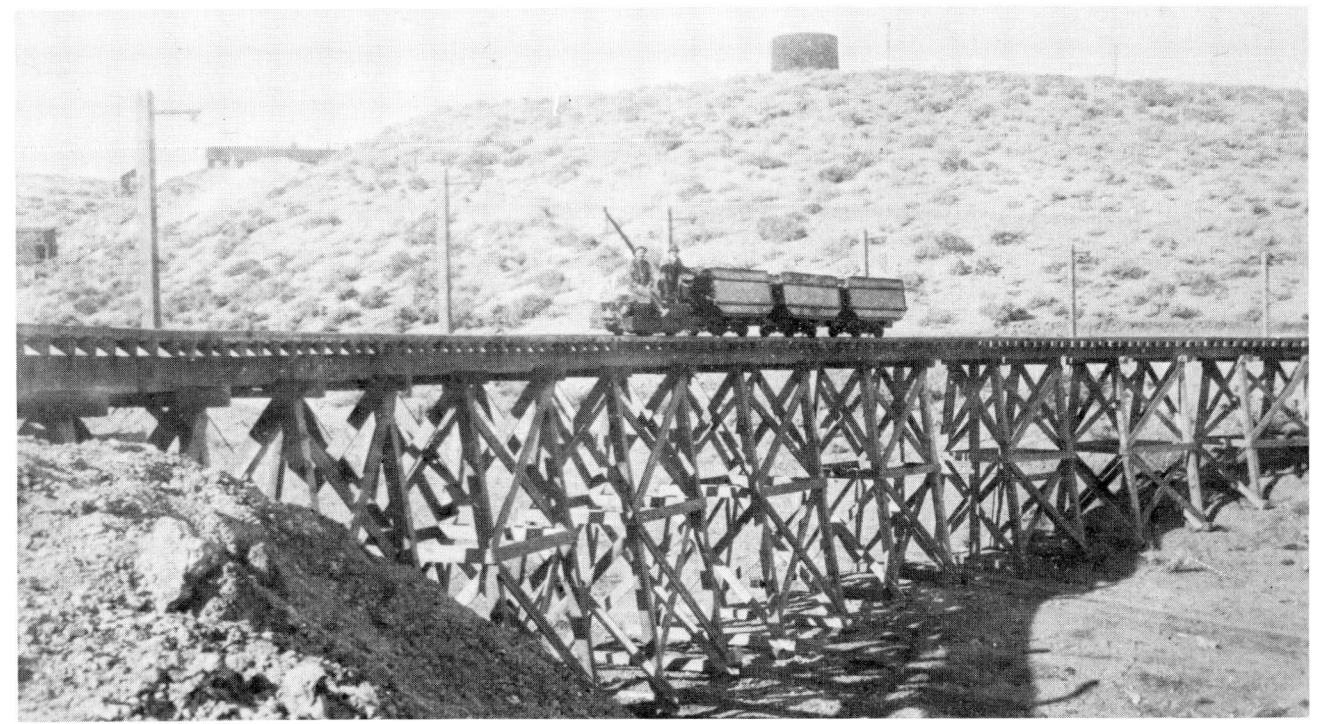

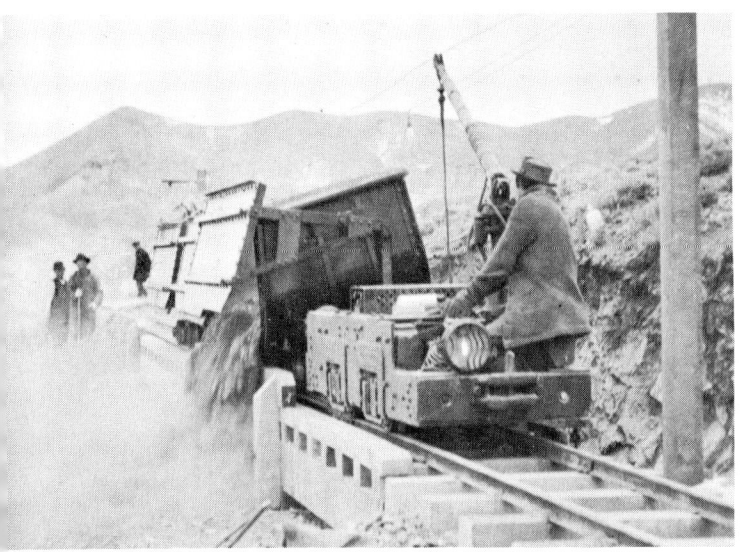

Bluestone ores were brought down the hill from the mine on a narrow gauge electric railroad *(top)* to the trestle over the mill *(bottom)* where they were dumped into the company's bins. Mine waste was used to fill in the trestles *(left)* to form more substantial earthen embankments. *(Three Photos: Louis L. Stein, Jr. Collection.)*

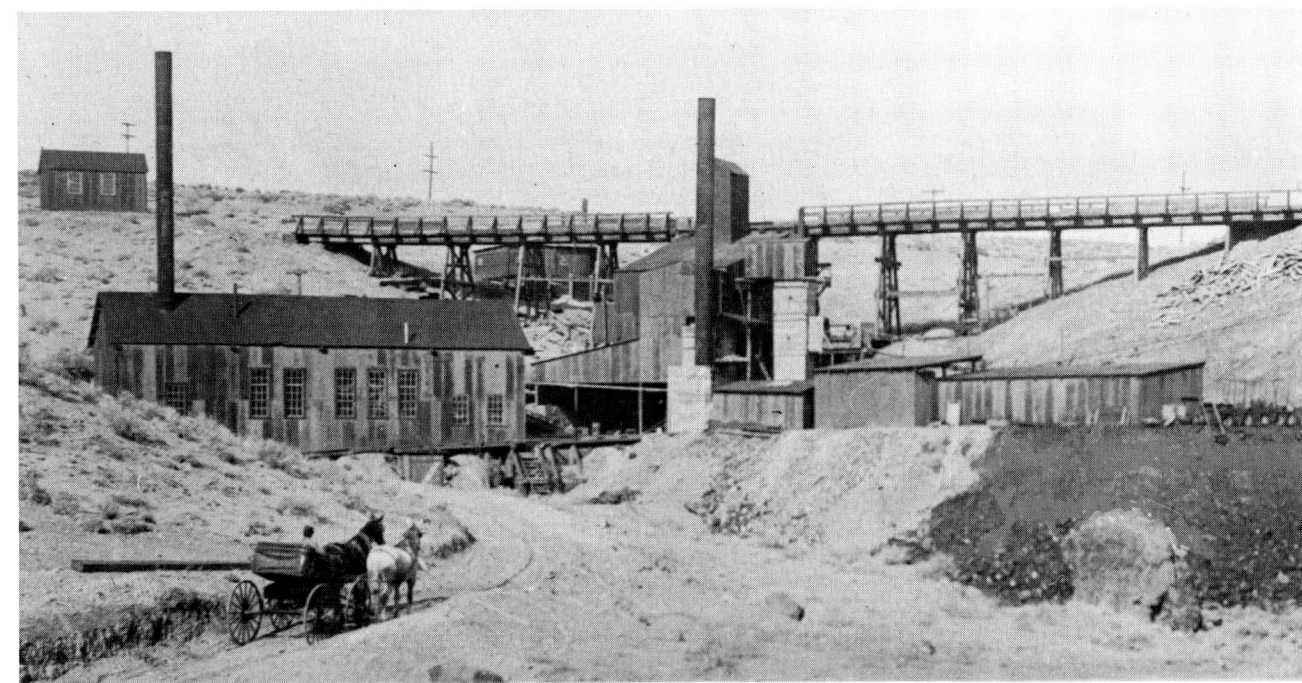

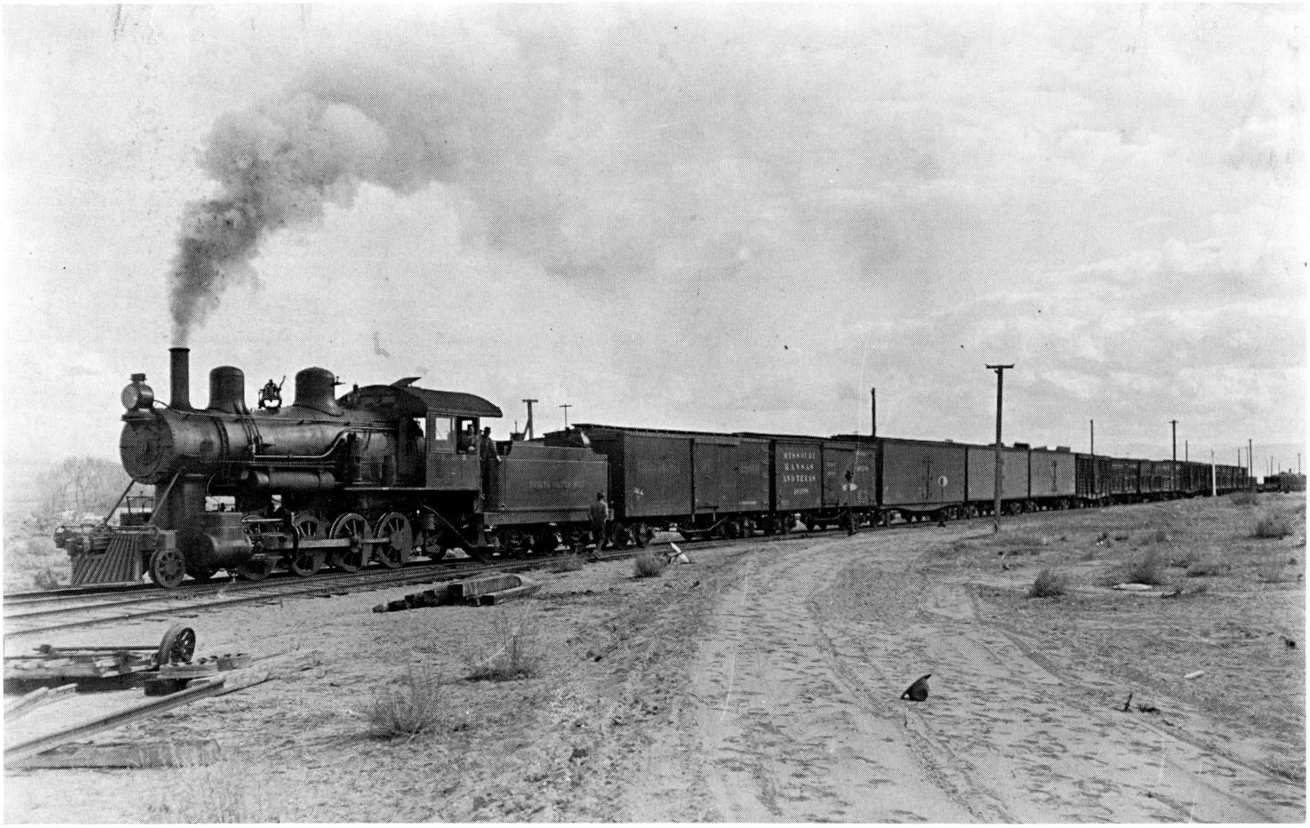

Judging by the empty hat in the foreground *(above)*, one local citizen must have deserted the territory in a hurry when NCB No. 2 arrived in Mason with the 16 freight cars shortly after completion. Much less pretentious was the later Plymouth gas engine No. 6 with the wandering NCB caboose which ultimately served on the V&T and spent its remaining days on display in Carson City. Hall Scott motor cars, such as the No. 22 shown in Wilson Canyon, provided most of the passenger service and occasionally hauled freight cars as well. By October 1946, six months before abandonment, the NCB's Yerington station *(top, right)* was showing distinct traces of neglect and disrepair, matters never adjusted in the road's remaining short history. *(Top Left: Grahame Hardy Collection; Top Right: Robert M. Hanft Photo, Guy Dunscomb Collection; Two Bottom Photos: Brian Thompson.)*

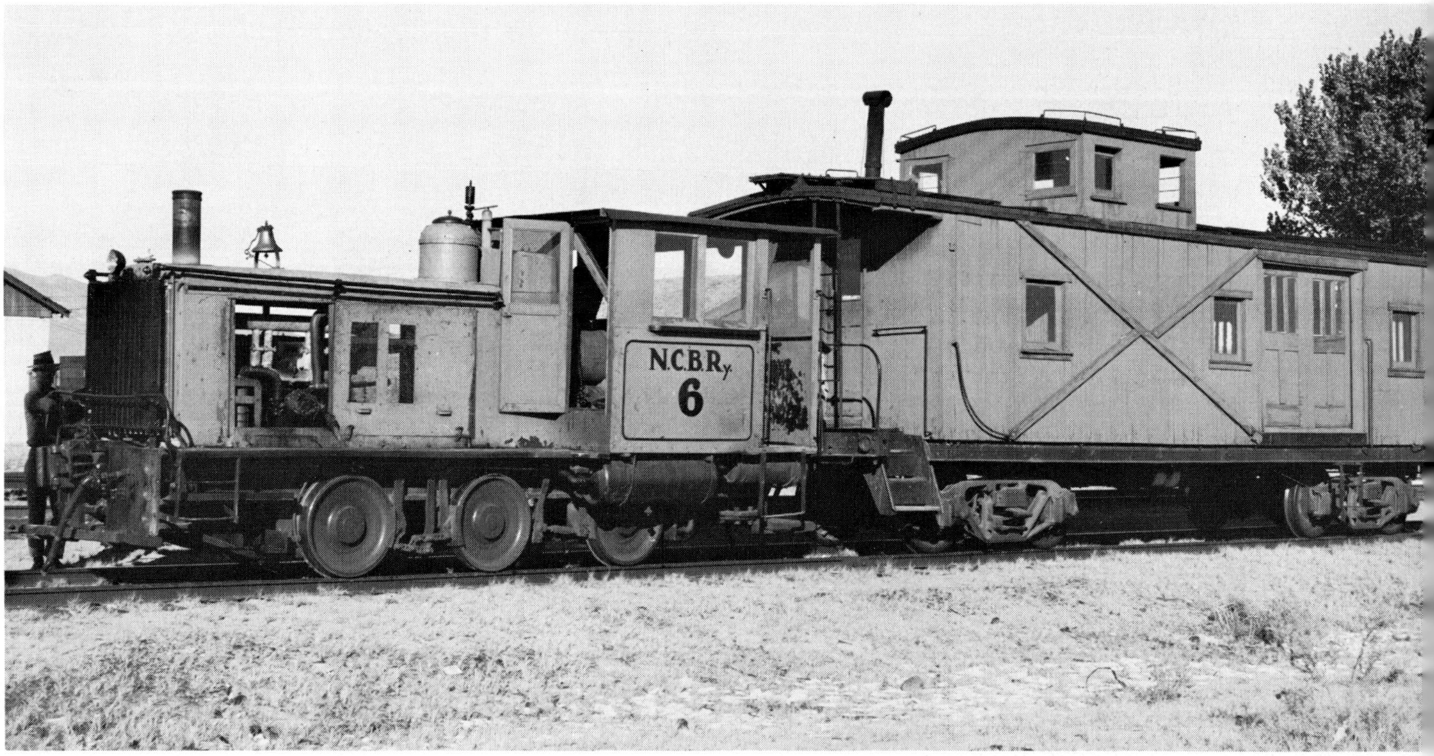

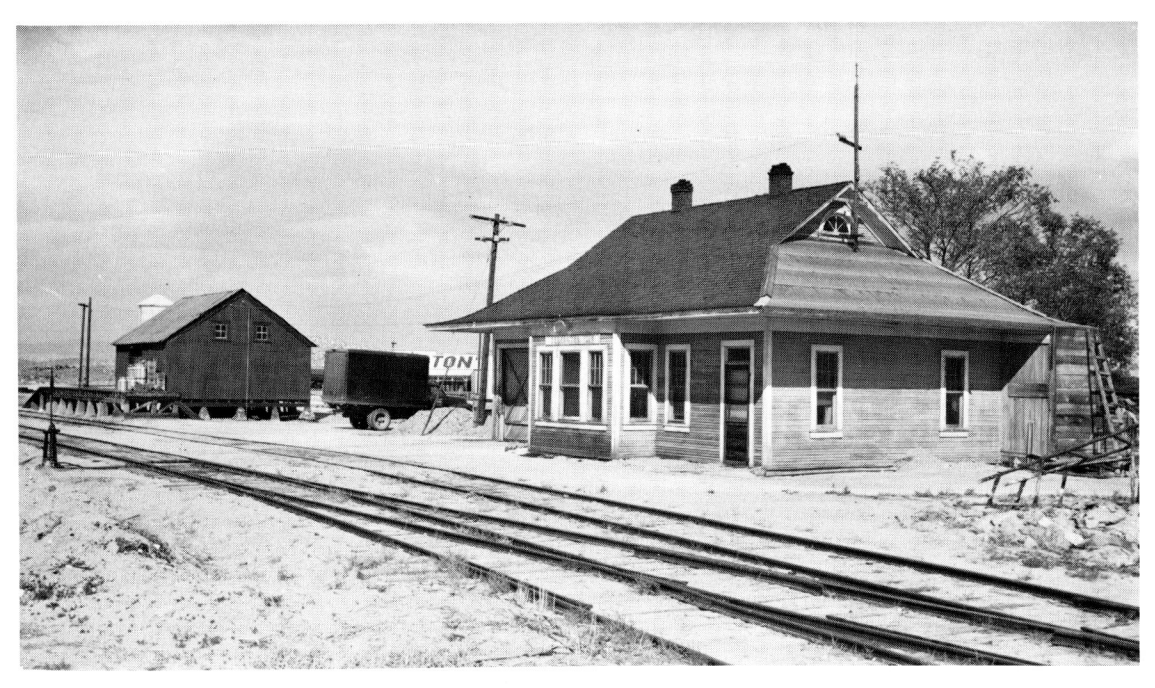

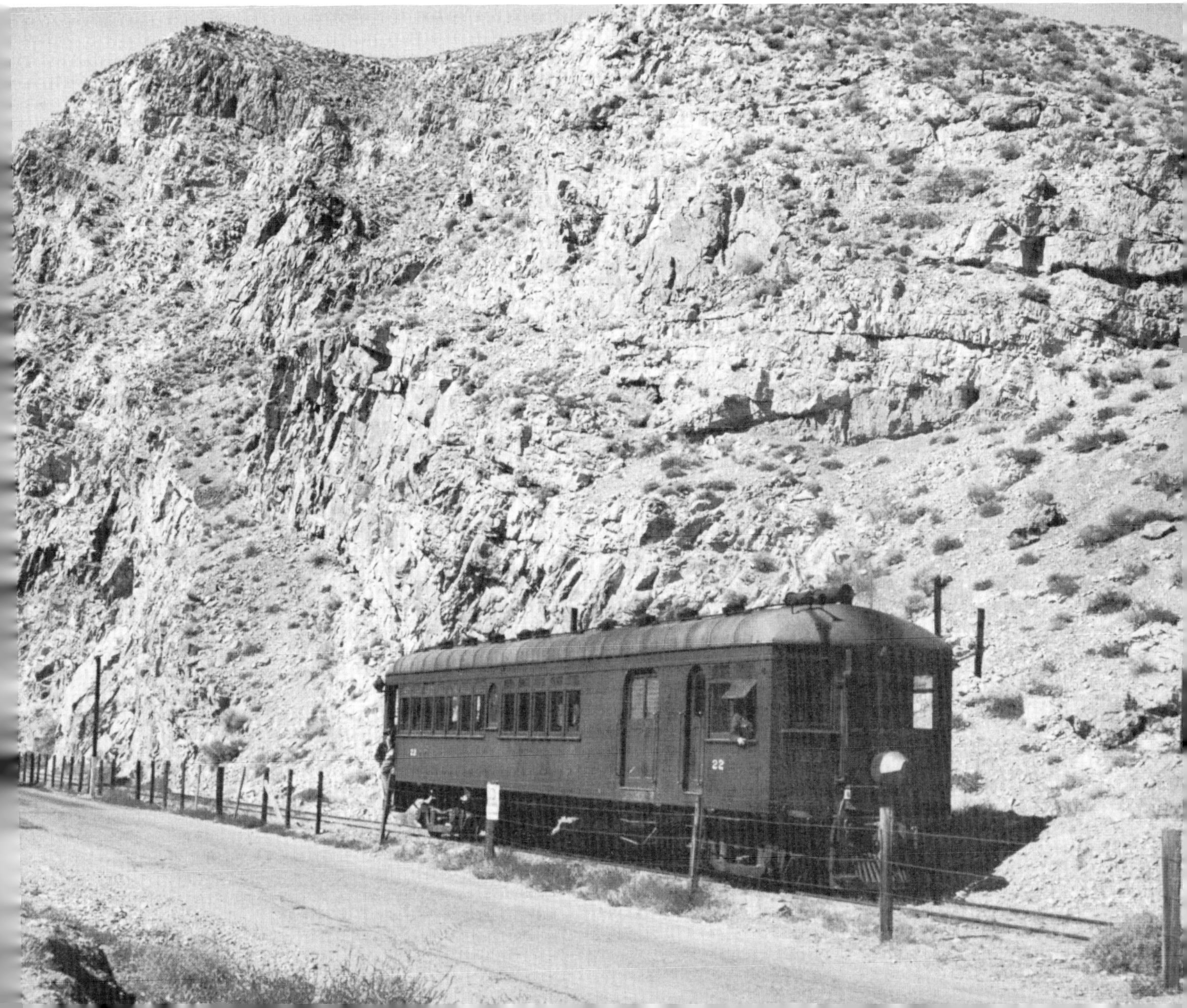

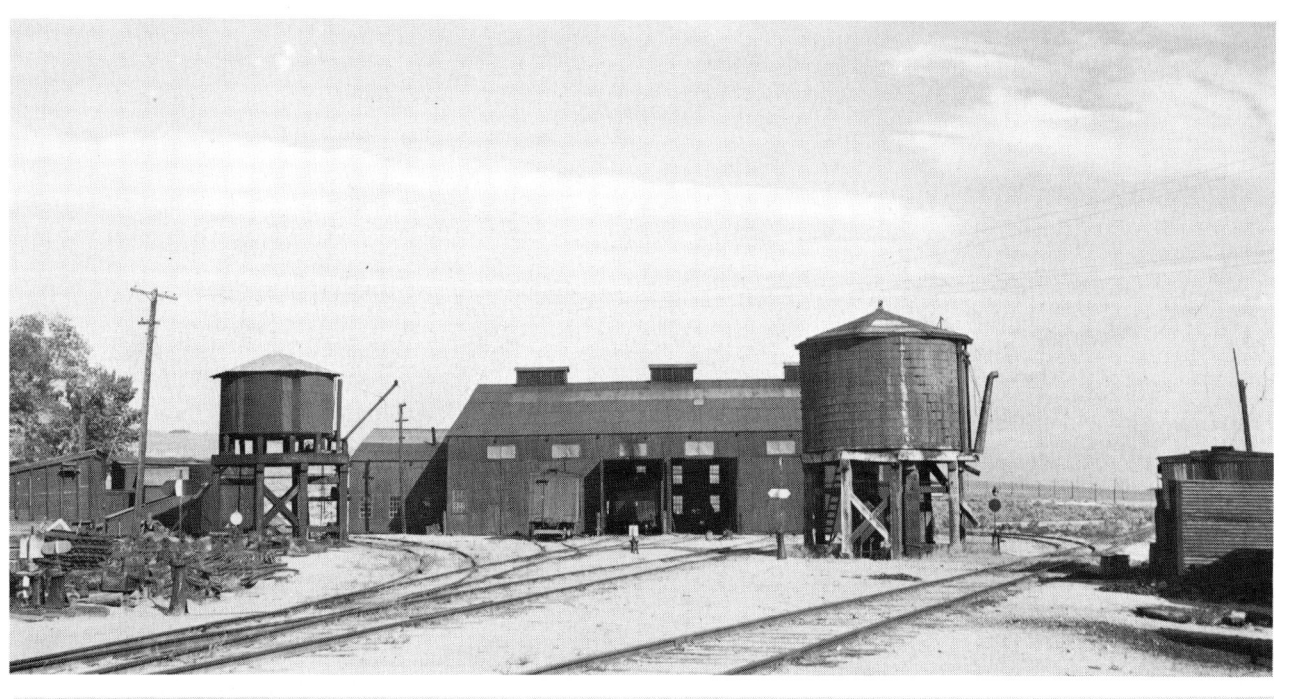

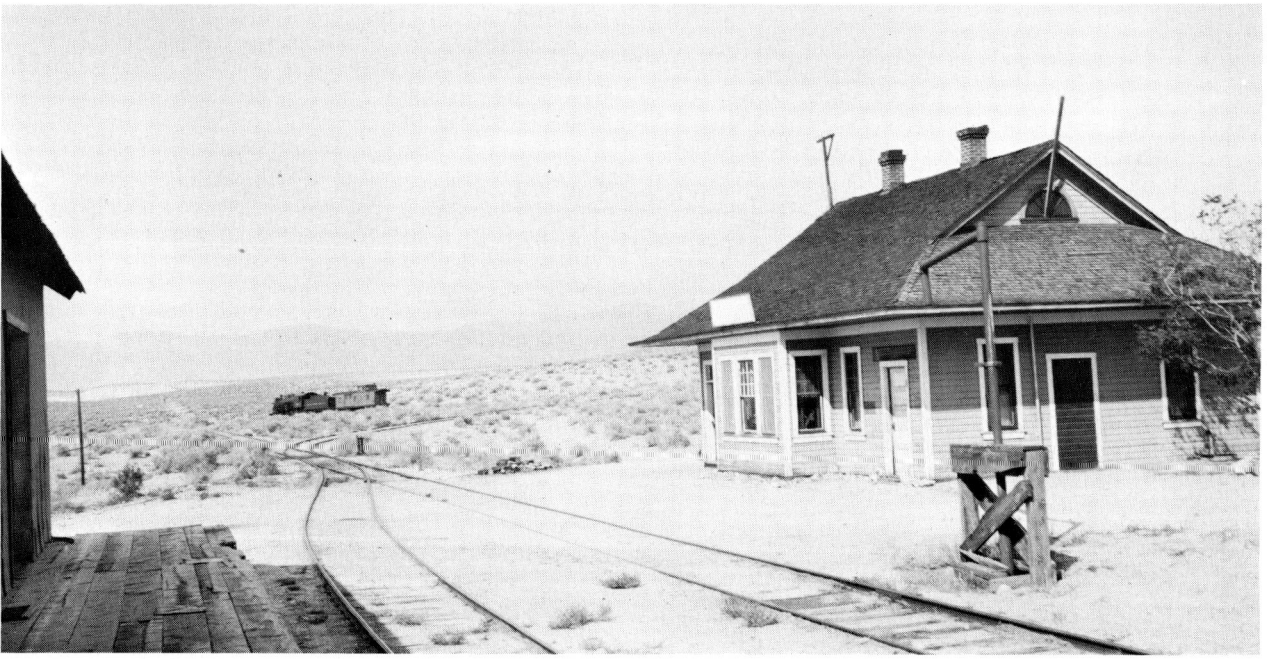

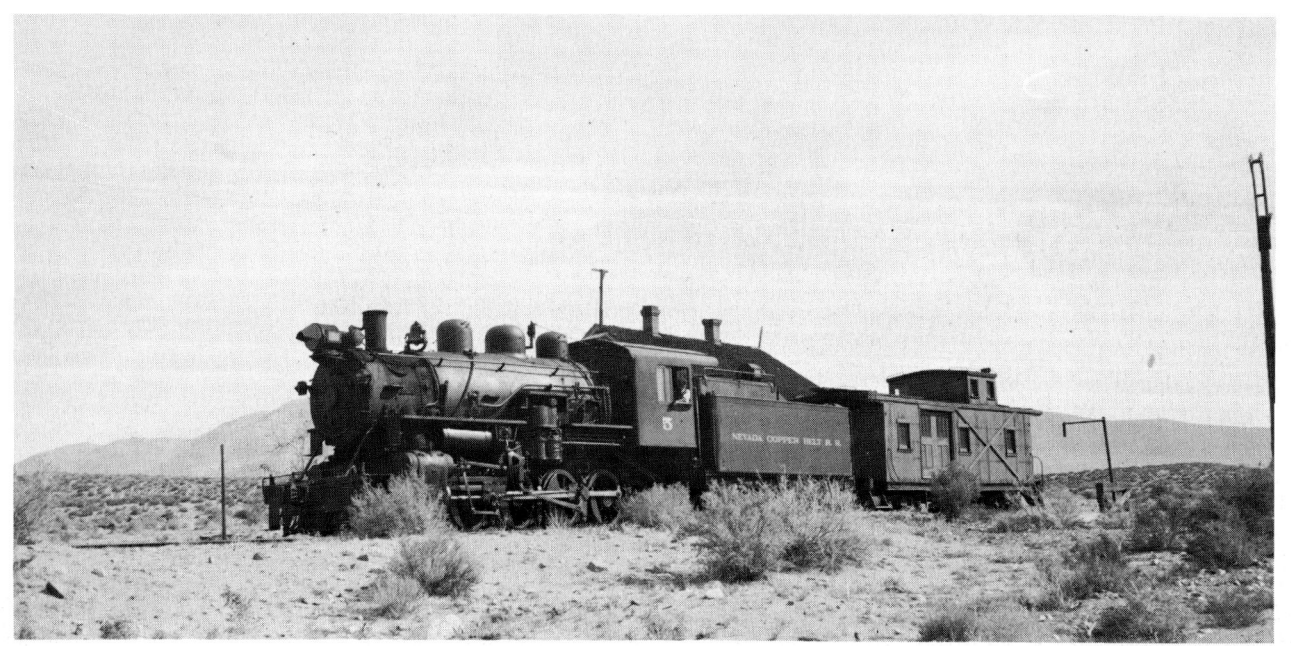

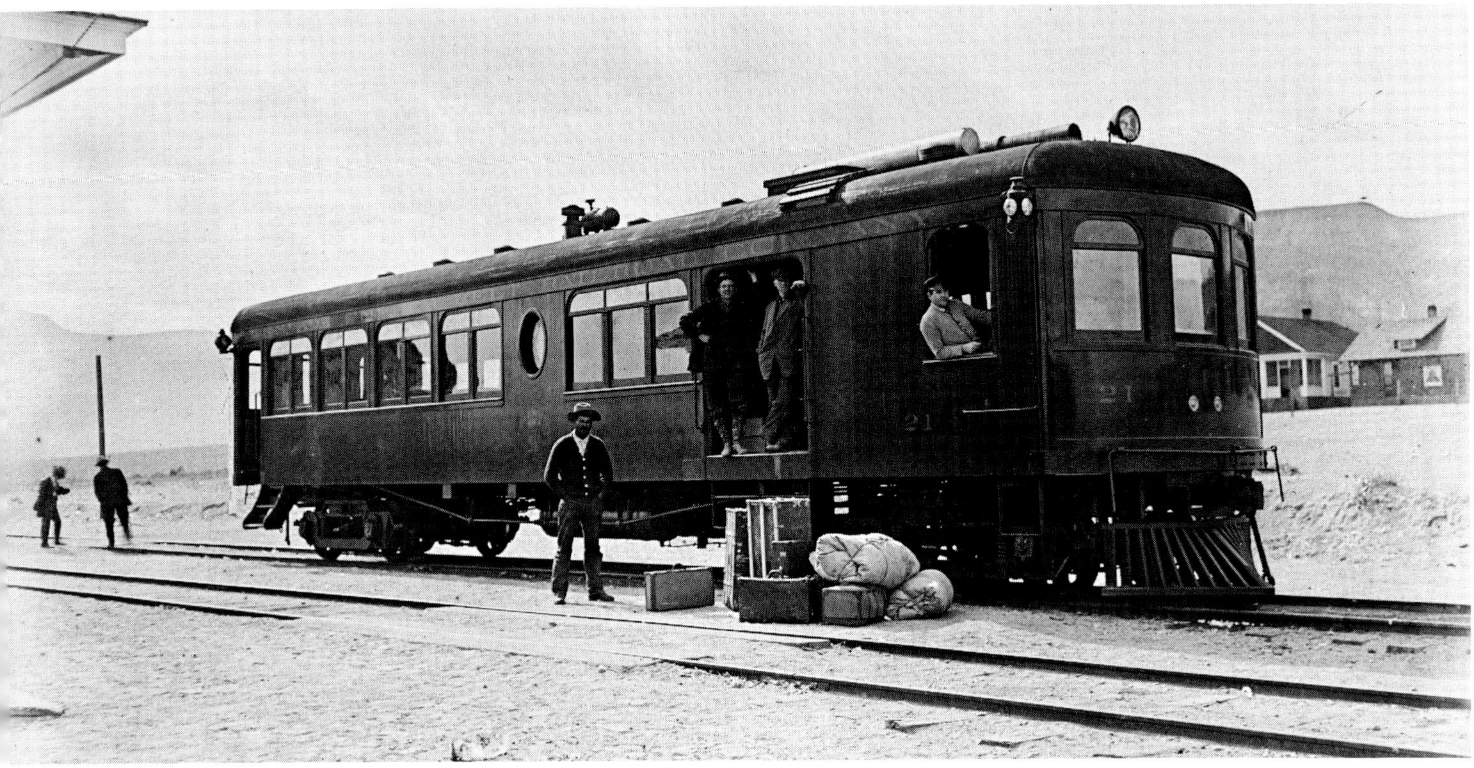

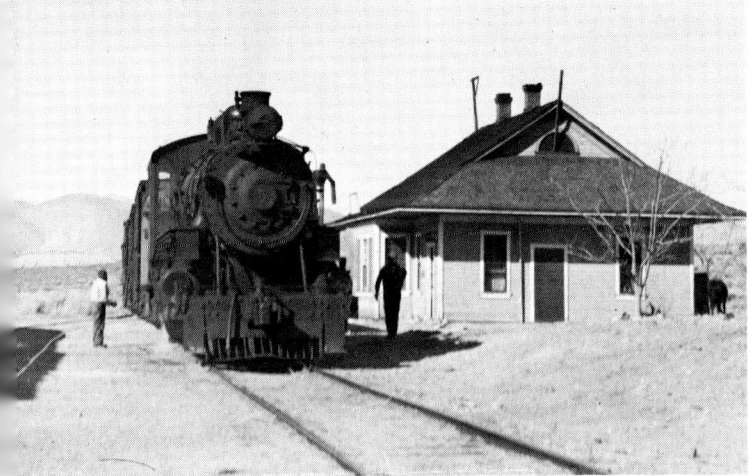

In October 1946, just before abandonment, the NCB's engine house at Mason *(top, left)* appeared deserted, and No. 5 and caboose *(left, center and bottom)* turned on the wye at Hudson without a bit of freight for the return trip to Wabuska. In earlier days *(above)* Hall Scott motor No. 21 hauled a respectable complement of baggage and head-end revenue as well as passengers, while No. 5 *(near left)* pulled a fair consist of high cars. In earliest times *(below)* even the ladies came down to see the train in, while the NCB's first (four-wheeled) motor car, behind the outfit car being switched by No. 2, went virtually unnoticed. *(Three Photos Far Left: Robert M. Hanft, Guy Dunscomb Collection; This Page Center: James Gayner; Top and Bottom: Grahame Hardy Collection.)*

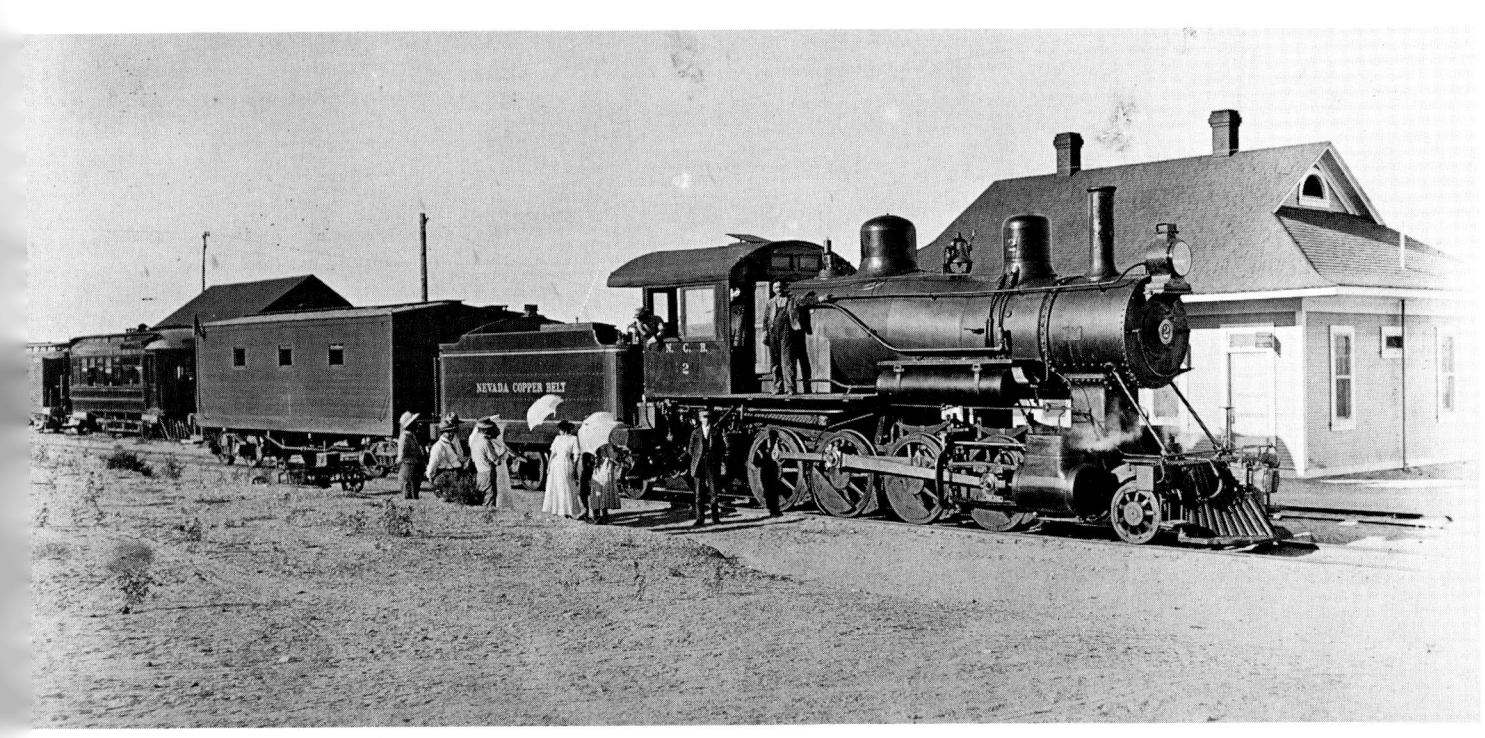

short spur was built near Mason City to the site of the lower end of the Mason Valley Mines' proposed tramway, while up on the slopes the grading for the high line at the smelter was nearing completion.

Rail laying continued through the Wilson Canyon, and on February 15 trains began operating over the extended section, turning being facilitated with the newly completed wye beyond the canyon's mouth. As this was to be the main station for farmers in the Smith Valley, it was decided to call the station Smithvale. Unexpected objections to the appellation caused a reconsideration, and when the station building was finally erected it bore the name of Hudson. W. C. Orem was busily engaged in laying out the townsite, a monumental effort considering the town's population never exceeded more than a few dozen people. Perhaps the motor car suffered from a similar malnutrition for, after having traveled 20,000 miles during the first year, it suddenly broke down and was out of service for two weeks while parts were being obtained from the factory.

The grading contract for the last section of the railroad from Hudson to Morningstar townsite (Ludwig) was awarded to Benjamin T. Tiby of Butte, Montana. Subcontracting of the work was accomplished by A. M. Fenton. Confidence in the imminence of completion of the project was demonstrated by the Nevada Douglas Copper Co. through the addition of 16 miners to the payroll at Ludwig and the ordering of 40 mine cars from the Nevada Engineering Works in Reno.

A new record of sorts was established on March 20, 1911, when the Nevada Copper Belt transported a total of 68 passengers over the line. This stimulated the *Times* to forecast that it "indicates the long-heralded business revival is with us." Further promise of good passenger business lay in the development of Hinds Hot Springs as a model health resort on the west side of Smith Valley. The NCB also had plans of its own to erect a foot bridge across the Walker River in Wilson Canyon to provide an ingress for tourist patrons to visit the petrified forest three-quarters of a mile beyond. The development of Hudson as a major terminal seemed assured with the announcement of the California Auto Transportation Co. that, starting May 1, it would provide express and light freight service between that point and the Bodie-Bridgeport area.

During the summer the graders were moved to the end of the line at Ludwig where work moved slowly as cuts were made in compact, snow-white gypsum. To close the intervening gap between the two ends of grade, the camp was then moved back to Delphi Springs. In August the job was completed. Rail laying was accomplished in September, the tracks finally reaching Ludwig late in October 1911.

Gypsum, not copper ore, constituted the first shipment from Ludwig. Two cars of the hydrous calcium sulphate mineral were routed to the Western Gypsum Company in Reno on October 28, and for some time thereafter gypsum was an important source of revenue for the new road. The first shipment of copper ore to the new Thompson smelter was made on December 1, 1911, although actual operations at the smelter were not to start until after the first of the year. Just the day previous (November 30) the new 69-passenger Hall Scott motor car had arrived to presage a new, expanding era of passenger travel. To wind the year up in grand style, Ludwig held its big railroad celebration day on December 29 with the usual complement

---

Rails of the Nevada Copper Belt reached Ludwig in October 1911. The view *(below)* looks southwest over the town across the vast upper reaches of Smith Valley. The railroad approached from the south along the eastern bank of the dry lake in left distance, then angled up the hillside to the mines and smelter. A down train can be seen in the center foreground between the mine and the mill with another cut of cars south of the mill to left. *(U. S. Geological Survey.)*

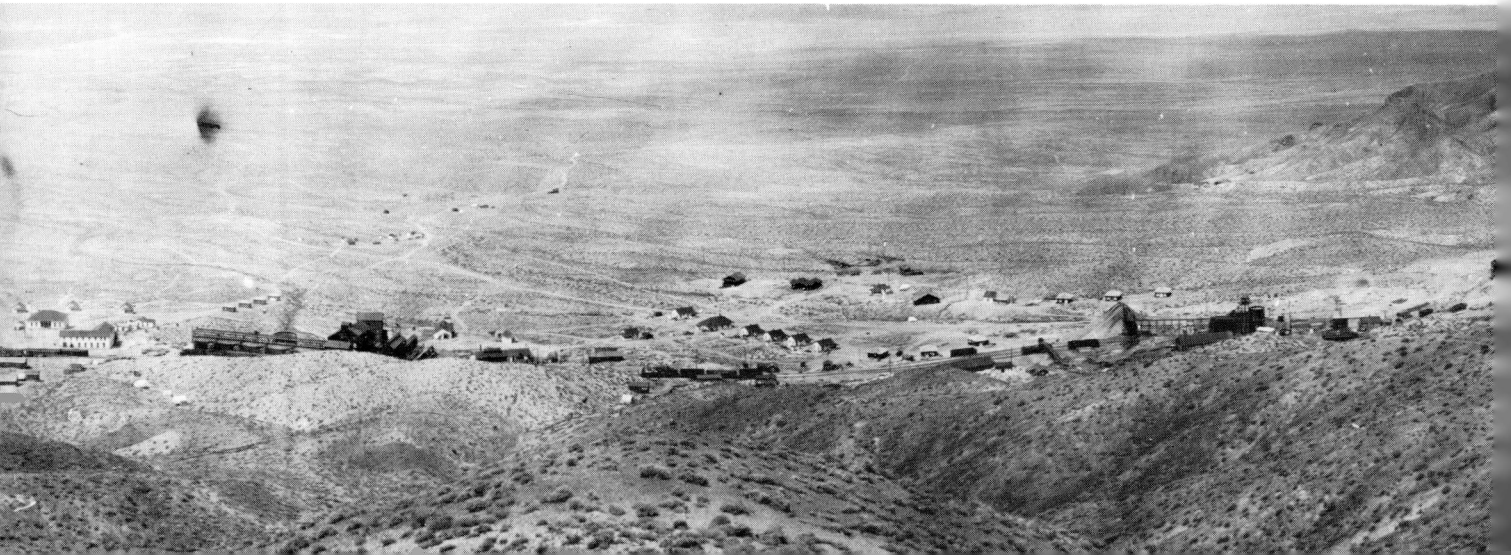

of toasts and speeches; then, two days later, the town's new store burned.

January 1912 started a new era for the Nevada Copper Belt. On New Year's Day the Thompson smelter was practically ready, though somewhat behind the anticipated schedule. A few anxious weeks had been spent the previous summer when the Pacific Live Stock Co. (Miller & Lux) had sought an injunction to prevent its operation based on the contention that fumes from the operation would poison adjoining grazing lands. The time lost in the ensuing legal wrangle obviously was well spent, as the action was subsequently withdrawn and operations proceeded. The first charge was fed into the smelter on January 6, 1912.

Almost coincidentally the Mason Valley Mines' tramway (6,250 feet long) near Mason City was placed in operation, electric mining locomotives hauling the ore in six- to twelve-car trains to the upper tramway terminal for conveyance to the railroad cars on the siding in the valley below. Built by Leschen, the tramway was capable of moving 100 tons of ore per hour in its 48 buckets with only nine men in attendance—two loaders and two brakemen at each terminal, plus one foreman. At the lower end ore was dumped into a bin for easy reloading into the railroad cars which carried it to the smelter.

With the Nevada Douglas, the Mason Valley and the Bluestone mines constituting the principal sources of traffic, the fortunes of the new railroad were inextricably linked with copper prices and production. When copper prices declined at the start of World War I, the smelter closed down on October 20, 1914, depriving the railroad of the good volume of business it had been enjoying. At the end of the war copper prices reached new highs, and the smelter was reactivated from February 1917 to February 28, 1919. Once again, during the 1920's, it was operated for a brief period when special rate concessions enabled four railroads—the Indian Valley, the Western Pacific, the Southern Pacific, and the Nevada Copper Belt—to participate in hauling Engelmine ore the 200 miles from California to the smelter. Relations between the Mason Valley Mines Co. and the NCB were not always harmonious, however, as the mining company brought several cases before the Railroad Commission of Nevada regarding rates and switching charges to Thompson and the smelter. Finally the mill was closed in 1929 and then dismantled. The Southern Pacific subsequently purchased the slag dump for a source of ballast, constructing its own spur track from a point just west of Wabuska to the dump.

Physically, the road was in good condition at the time of completion in 1912, with the exception of a bad grade extending from Yerington northward three miles to the sand hills. During that year a cut was made through the hill to lower the grade from 1.875% to .625%. The following year (1913) the new town of Hudson assumed even greater importance when 12 "auto wagons" and 14 large freight teams commenced hauling supplies to the communities of Aurora, Bodie and Bridgeport. Aurora, in particular, was enjoying one of its numerous revivals. The town had been an important producer back in the 1860's with a population of over 10,000 people; then it became a ghost town; finally the Knight Investment Co. of Provo, Utah, purchased properties there in 1912 and erected a 40-stamp mill. (The founder, Jesse Knight, was father of Governor Goodwin J. Knight of California.) Two years later the entire properties were sold to Wingfield's Goldfield Consolidated Mines Co. which operated them until 1918. During this period of activity Aurora attracted from 1,000 to 1,500 residents, and a number of new buildings were erected.

On line, the NCB also enjoyed additional activity. The Bluestone Mine near Mason City which had been owned by Capt. J. R. DeLamar since 1904, was sold to a new corporation, and by 1917 it had developed to sufficient proportions to warrant construction of a 2½-mile standard gauge railroad to connect it with the main line. Starting from the NCB spur at Mason City, the branch climbed along the hills in a northwesterly direction to the ore bins at the mine, which were kept replenished by small narrow gauge electric ore trains shuttling between the mines and the bins (the ruins of the transformer building still remain). Power for the standard gauge line was a 49-ton Heisler locomotive, which ultimately ended its days as a spare switcher for the Blake Brothers Quarry in Richmond, California.

Passenger service on the NCB was both transilient and ephemeral, and parts of it were rather highly competitive. During each school year, there was a student commutation problem in the handling of school children from Thompson and Wabuska (at the northern end of the line) to the schools in Yerington and Mason. There was a normal, sporadic business intercourse between Thompson and

Wabuska and the line stations of Yerington, Mason City and Ludwig. Then there were occasional picnic excursions — some from the end of the line at Ludwig, others from the regular on-line towns — to Wilson Canyon for a day's outing.

The railroad arranged a joint service with C. J. Monahan's auto stages for daily "all-weather" service between Wabuska and Yerington at $1.25 for the through trip. Passengers arriving at Wabuska on the N&C transferred to the NCB train for the trip to Yerington Junction (station) there to be met by the stages for the one-mile trip in to town. Competing with this arrangement were various direct Wabuska-Yerington auto stage lines of dubious integrity which operated only in good weather when the roads were clear and passable. Their solicitation of passengers detraining from the SP cars at Wabuska was forthrightly bold and resolute. The fare would be quoted at an even $1.00 for the trip. Patrons bold enough to slip by the barkers and board the waiting NCB train were promptly pursued right into the cars. The loss the stage lines suffered on the cut-rate fares was easily made up on the trips between train times when the auto fare was normally boosted, sometimes going as high as $4.00 for a one-way trip.

Finally, in 1919, the Nevada Railroad Commission found that the NCB was "forced to meet unreasonable and unwarranted competition of auto-stage carriers" between Wabuska and Yerington; that the through rate between the two points should be $1.00; and that only certain auto lines should be allowed to operate with the proviso that no auto carriers were to operate during the period from one hour before to one hour after scheduled train times. The railroad then settled on three trips daily from Wabuska to Mason with daily service from Mason on to Hudson (no passenger service ran to Ludwig at this time). The Hall Scott motor cars frequently "doubled in brass" on these occasions, sometimes hauling as many as three or four freight cars in addition to their human cargo. In October 1922 the daily service from Mason City to Hudson was reduced to tri-weekly.

From a financial standpoint, the entire NCB venture was a big disappointment. Legal complications resulting from a change in Utah laws caused the Nevada Douglas Copper Company to dispose of its controlling interest in the railroad, and in August 1913 it offered its shareholders the right to exchange their shares in the copper company for stock in the railroad company. Two years later the situation altered again, and in 1915 the copper company reacquired the majority of the railroad stock by a reverse exchange. For years thereafter the copper company held 88% of the stock.

Statistically, the net income resulting from railroad operations was desultory and varied. As a rule, the red ink flowed liberally. The greatest deficit ($124,000) was recorded in 1912 when some $90,000 of discount on securities was written off. Operations during the year 1913 showed a nice profit of $46,000, while in 1917 an even greater ($64,000) profit was enjoyed. Some $20,000 was earned in 1918, but in 1919 the same figure was marked down in red ink. The loss in this latter year was most untimely as the $622,000 First Mortgage Gold Bonds fell due on July 1, 1919.

Losses could not be helped in the operations of a railroad so greatly dependent upon mining activity for its very existence. Gross revenues fluctuated widely; those for the five years from 1916 to 1920 (expressed in thousands of dollars) were $97, $251, $310, $107, $73, respectively. With declining copper prices and an erratic earnings record, the bonds could not be refunded and so were allowed to run. The bondholders took over in November 1923; J. I. Wilson was appointed receiver on April 2, 1925; and the road continued to be operated by the receiver until it was sold to the Parr Terminal interests of Richmond, California, effective April 21, 1942.

Various portions of the line ceased to be operated or were abandoned over the years as the necessity arose. That portion of the railroad from Hudson to Ludwig had been out of service since July 13, 1933 and was written out of the accounts in 1936. The track from Wabuska north to Thompson had been out of service since August 20, 1935. Formal approval of these abandonments was obtained from the I. C. C. in June 1942.

Although business did increase during World War II, not one of those years of war-time operations was profitable. Under the Parr management, revenues for the *four* years to September 30, 1946, totaled $270,000, but expenses and taxes exceeded this amount by some $75,000. Passenger service was continued until 1945, and freight service was provided on a twice-daily basis to Mason and tri-weekly to Hudson. Finally, highway competition and the dim traffic future caused the owners to seek abandonment of the line on August 21, 1946.

Protests, including some from the Lyon County Farm Bureau and the Smith Valley Rotary Club, were voiced at the hearing in November, but the Public Service Commission of Nevada concluded that there was "no prospect of a profit with the amount of traffic available," and on December 30, 1946, authorized abandonment of the line. March 24, 1947, was the last day of operation; then the wheels ceased to turn; and another short line became but a scar of abandoned grade and a group of memories in the minds of those who "knew the railroad when."

Rawhide Western Railway

"This church is closed. God has gone to Rawhide."

According to legend, it was Tex Rickard who nailed this sign across the doorway of an unused church in Goldfield as a means of publicizing Nevada's newest mining camp. Neighboring Rhyolite proved that its promotional efforts could be equally as cogent when the wife of E. S. Hall, Sr., agent for the Las Vegas & Tonopah Railroad at Rhyolite, awoke with a shock one morning to find that the "For Rent" sign in front of their unused Presbyterian Church had acquired an addendum reading "*Christ* has gone to Rawhide."

The year was 1907. The decline in the price of silver had affected Tonopah; labor troubles were disturbing Goldfield; and the mines in Rhyolite were not proving to be as productive as was at first anticipated. Dull times were causing men to look elsewhere for employment or a chance to make a stake. Glowing reports from Rawhide gave promise of a personal resurgence of riches for anyone interested — and thousands of people were.

Credit for the initial ore discovery at Rawhide has been given vicariously to a number of people. Two ranchers living near Fairview, named Wasson and Schaedler, are reported to have made their discoveries on December 5 and 6, 1906. Other strikes were made by C. C. Dunning, T. A. Roseberry, C. A. McLoed and Jack Davis in February 1907, and on the 17th of that month the Regent Mining District was formed. When a local rancher attempted to organize the postal delivery by nailing a tin can and a cow's tail to a post with the notation to the postman: "Drop mail for Rawhide here," he established a town name that was to survive in history.

In July 1907, word of the new discovery reached the four Grutt brothers of the state of Washington, then visiting in Reno. They had already inspected the properties in Olinghouse and were about to leave for California in search of lucrative gold properties when they learned of the discoveries in the new district. Dan Snowgoose, their mining engineer, had already preceded them and wired that the new district looked promising and should be inspected personally. The first look was enough to satisfy, and the brothers began buying up claims. As fast as titles could be cleared, individual mining companies were organized for each claim, the lessor performing the actual work on the lease. To establish continuity of identity, names were established in a uniform manner including Rawhide Victory, Rawhide Consolidated, Rawhide Grutt Mining Co. and several others.

By September there were over 300 people in the new camp, and the Rawhide Townsite Co. was busy selling lots. The rush was already under way. Before the end of the year, W. W. Booth of Tonopah had established the *Rawhide Rustler* newspaper as the "Pioneer of the Greatest Gold Camp in the World." Two other papers were established in short order, but one of the weeklies and the daily were soon merged.

By the early part of 1908 a new water system had been installed, replacing the Dead Horse Well Water Company which had delivered water to any part of town at $2.50 per barrel under the proud contention it was "The only water that has stood the test." (Just what constituted the *test* was never explained.) A telephone system was placed in operation, and the Rawhide Light & Power Co. began completion of the installation of a power plant and distribution lines. Power was furnished by two 80-HP Fairbanks-Morse engines acquired from the old Rhyolite plant. Three banks in the town were reduced to two through the expedient of a merger, then to none when two successive bank runs left Rawhide without any banking facilities for several weeks. The last run had been caused by a false rumor that the president had suddenly left town with the deposits, an incident of previous happenstance in Goldfield.

The cultural aspects of town life improved as plans were made for an opera house. On the distaff side, the displeasure of the community was sufficiently aroused to compel 200 men to meet, march over to a "house," and bodily move it out of the business district. Some months before, a similar but less organized attempt to move a tent serving as a "house" was successfully rebuffed when one of the girls let it be known in some rather choice language that she did not wish to be disturbed, emphasizing her remarks with a shotgun.

Reports of rich finds were frequent and staggering. (Fred Grutt, one of the four Grutt brothers, has kindly indicated the more nearly correct figures which have been placed in ( ) following each item.) A strike on the Happy Hooligan assayed $79,000 to the ton ($50,000). Ore from the Truett Lease was worth $168 per pound ($100). Grutt Hill Coalition was sacking ore assaying $211 per pound ($10). These and other newspaper statements were eagerly seized upon by promoters to assist in selling mining stocks of something less than doubtful value to people all over the country. Publicity flowed from the boom town, and the news of strikes commanded attention far and wide. People came to Rawhide and neighboring Bovard and Nugent by the thousands; if they could not come in person, they frequently sent their dollars to represent them.

Four people initiated the publicity for Rawhide town. George Graham Rice, whose L. M. Sullivan Trust Co. blew up financially in Goldfield leaving thousands of small investors skeptical of mining stocks, managed to persuade the former actor, Nat C. Goodwin, to serve as a front for a new company. To boost selected stocks, Rice established the *Nevada Mining News,* and the information published therein was widely disseminated. Tex Rickard was another promoter. Driving from Goldfield to Rawhide in one day, he spent $8,000 for a choice lot and quickly built another Northern Saloon, duplicating the successful pattern established in Goldfield. Then there was Mrs. Elinor Glyn, whose novel *Three Weeks* was enjoying good sales (it had just been banned in Boston). She came to Rawhide for adventure, found it, and told. But it was the funeral of Riley Grannan that capped the climax. Riley had just established a gambling hall in Rawhide before his demise, and it was the splendid oration of an unwitting and unfrocked minister that brought the greatest and most lasting fame to the town. Thousands of copies of W. H. Knickerbocker's oration have been printed — the twelfth printing was made no later than 1957.

Rawhide is approximately 25 miles east and slightly north of Schurz, the nearest railroad connection on the C&C. It is located on a gently sloping plain surrounded by Grutt Hill, Hooligan Hill and Balloon Hill. To the northeast of town is Stingaree Gulch, at that time a popular resort area. Service to Rawhide was frequent and varied. An auto stage furnished a choice of conveyances east from Schurz, passengers riding in six-cylinder Chadwick Racers or Thomases. A similar service operated southward from Fallon at the end of the SP branch from Hazen, Peerless automobiles being provided for the comfort of passengers. Slow but dependable horse-drawn stages were operated by Kimball Brothers out of Luning, south of Walker Lake, via Bovard to the Ross Hotel in Rawhide. Too, there were Day & Como's six-horse Concord stages to provide a generally reliable way, also from Schurz. There was an occasion, one summer day at Bluff Rocks, when the reliability wavered as road agents asked for the Wells Fargo box. The box was surrendered graciously; the passengers were not molested; and the highwaymen were apprehended cautiously in Rawhide the very next day.

A railroad connection between Rawhide and the outside world was becoming more imperative daily. Finally, in February 1908, Jim Sword of Salt Lake City made the first overtures with his announcement that he would build a 150-ton stamp mill at Schurz (on the N&C) and an electric railroad to Rawhide, utilizing power generated by the Walker River. His pronouncement, "Work to start in 90 days" was the last ever heard of this project, but interest was easily transferred to another scheme which proposed a railroad south from Fallon on the SP. As planned, the line would start out eastward from Fallon, pass the Grimes' Ranch and proceed to Rock Springs. At that point one branch would continue east another 10 miles to Sand Springs, while a second line would reach southward for 21 miles to Rawhide. In spite of the authenticity conveyed by the naming of the surveyor and contractor, no further reports were made by this railroad either.

Next to take the limelight was another electric line, projected to run from Mason Valley (Yerington) through Schurz to Rawhide. Then a Mr. F. T. Torpey planned to include Rawhide on the route of his Nevada Cable Traction Co. Some talk also persisted that the Nevada Central Railroad (from Battle Mountain to Austin) would swing westward from Austin to Rawhide with branches to Fairview and Wonder. For a town of dubious distinction and possibilities, Rawhide's homespun promotions were generating a maximum of interest.

Early in March 1908, just before the Rawhide boom began to subside, positive action was taken to bring a railroad into town with the formation of the Rawhide Western Railway. Fred Grutt was named president, A. G. Renfro general manager, and Judge Crump counsel. E. W. King and Tex Rickard were among the directorate. Grading contracts were signed with the California Construction Co., who underwrote the majority of the stock. Local subscriptions, however, were being accepted on the basis of 25% down, 25% in 30 days, and the balance to become due when the line was completed. In true Rawhide promotional style, the local press pointedly called its readers' attention to the profits reaped by the stockholders of another nearby mining railroad, the Tonopah & Goldfield.

The Rawhide Western was to be a very modest railroad, 28 miles long and of standard gauge to match the revised gauge of its N&C connection. It would start from a point to be known as Rawhide Junction, one mile north of Modoc and a few miles east of Schurz. The first 16 miles would be tangent with a nominal grade of 1%; the remaining 12 miles would hug the foothills south of the auto road and gradually curve around so as to approach Rawhide from the northwest. The way the editor of the *Rawhide Press-Times* stated the proposition, it was confidently expected that the first train would swing around the curve and pull up at the Rawhide depot some time the early part of June 1908. To clinch the argument, final surveys were made and the right-of-way acquired. Holders of mining claims were very considerate, and not one dollar was demanded for crossing the claims.

There was a delay in obtaining the grading outfit. Charles W. Reed of the Reed Teaming Company, subcontractor, had to finish the job on the Sacramento Southern (SP) in California and did not arrive on location until April 27, 1908. Grading began the following day at Rawhide Junction.

When general manager Renfro returned from Sparks, following negotiations with the SP for necessary side tracks at the Junction, he revealed that two locomotives had been ordered from Baldwin along with "a string of coaches and flat cars." Most of the rails and some 50,000 ties were ordered at the same time. Conceivably most of this material was surplus from the T&T which was having a severe set-back following the decline of activity in Goldfield. Renfro frankly stated that "the T&T had more steel rails, more ties, more passenger cars, and more locomotives than it could possibly use. We got them for less than their actual cost. We saved time by the deal as well as money."

Greatest of the construction problems was that of obtaining sufficient water for the men and particularly the teams on the job. And the further the work progressed, the greater the problem became. Finally Tex Rickard's drilling machine was obtained to see what could be done. Wells were drilled at points 8 and 16 miles from the Junction, tapping water at 418 and 285 feet, respectively. The contractors were most fortunate; Rickard had drilled another well to the north of Rawhide and gone down 1,200 feet without success.

The grading force of 50 men and 90 animals was under the charge of G. S. Gamble. Progress was being made, although at times it appeared to be so little the impression was created that the work had ceased. When someone asked Superintendent Reed if work had been discontinued on the railroad, he replied: "Yes, we discontinue every evening at five o'clock until eight in the morning." He then went on to assure the questioner that work was going on each day. By the middle of June, 12 miles of grading had been completed (an elapsed time of 1½ months), and plans were under way for a gala Railroad Day. Although the big day was moved ahead from July Fourth to Labor Day, interest was sustained with the announcement that "several distinctive features were being considered."

Grading continued during July and August, sometimes at the expeditious rate of a half a mile a day. Grading forces could be seen from the hills west of town, and subsequent additional gangs were set to work starting from Rawhide westward. To add to the confusion, Rawhide enjoyed some unusual weather when sleet fell in town on July 13.

In the middle of August, Joel W. Hicks, secretary and treasurer of the railway, rendered the encouraging report that excellent progress was being made — the grade was practically in town. True, there was a minor gap of from three to four miles between the east and west sections of grade, but that would be closed rapidly just as soon as rails were laid from the Junction. It was necessary to wait for this phase of the operation, he explained as the daily cost of watering the mules (rumored to be running as high as $3.00 for each mule) would then be materially reduced. Once the first rails were laid, the intention was to secure a locomotive and water car from the SP, which would facilitate and reduce the cost of water delivered on the job.

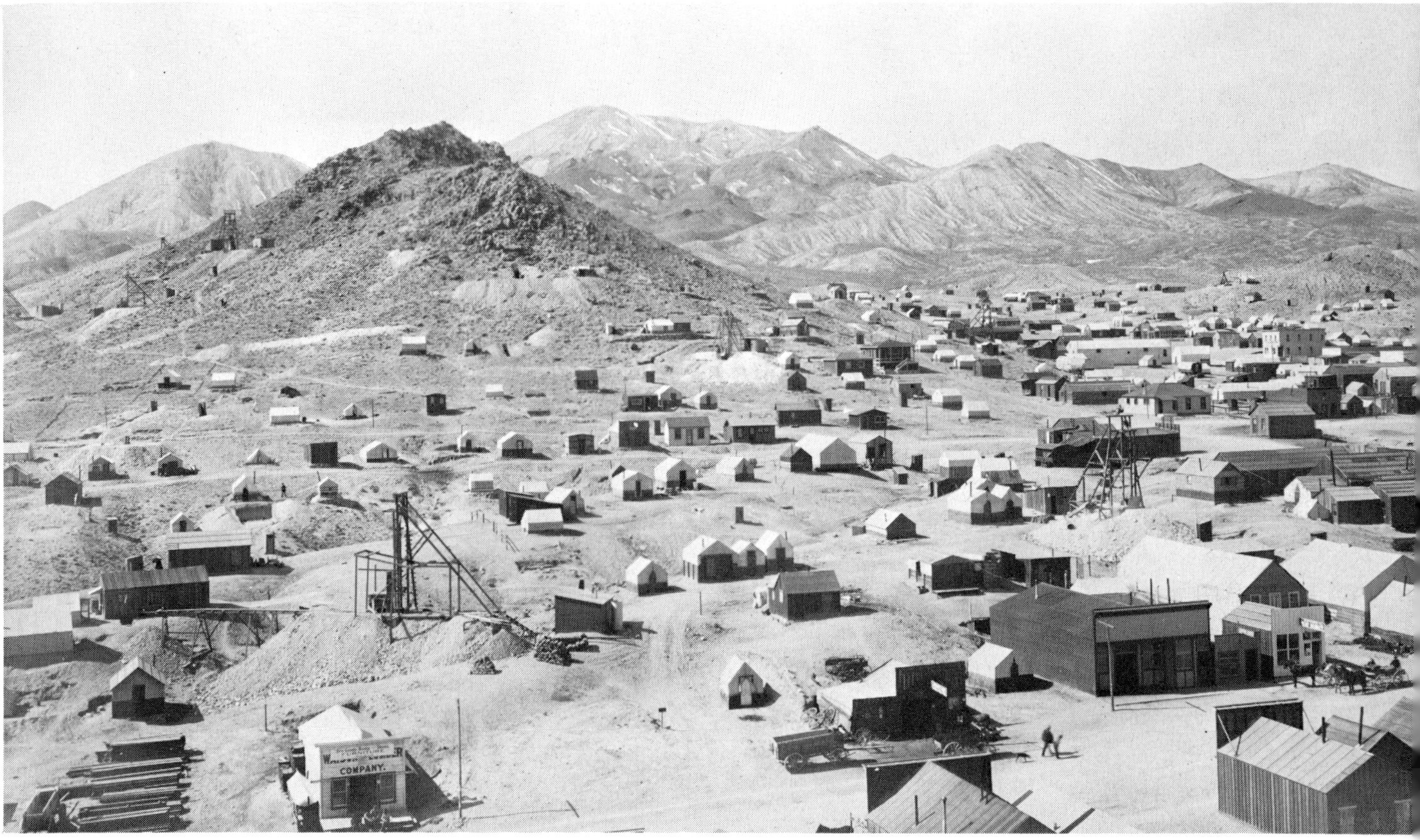

Rawhide boomed in 1907-08. The town proper clustered along Nevada Street on the floor of a gently sloping valley along an approximate southeast-northwest axis. The view *(above)* faces southwest with Hooligan Hill in the upper left. The town proper extends out of the picture up the valley to the right.   *(Sewell Thomas Photo.)*

Stingaree Gulch *(below)* was Rawhide's "amusement center" and branched off the main stem in a generally northerly direction. On the left is Grutt Hill and on the right, the sloping bank of Balloon Hill. Between the two and just to the left of the top of the mine headframe can be seen grade of the Rawhide Western Railway which approached from behind Grutt Hill and terminated at the foot of Balloon Hill. Behind the base of the same headframe is "Tex" Rickard's Northern saloon and farther up the same street (to left) is the Yellowstone Bar. Two buildings to the right is The Barrel House of Geo. Goeppert & Son. *(U. S. Geological Survey.)*

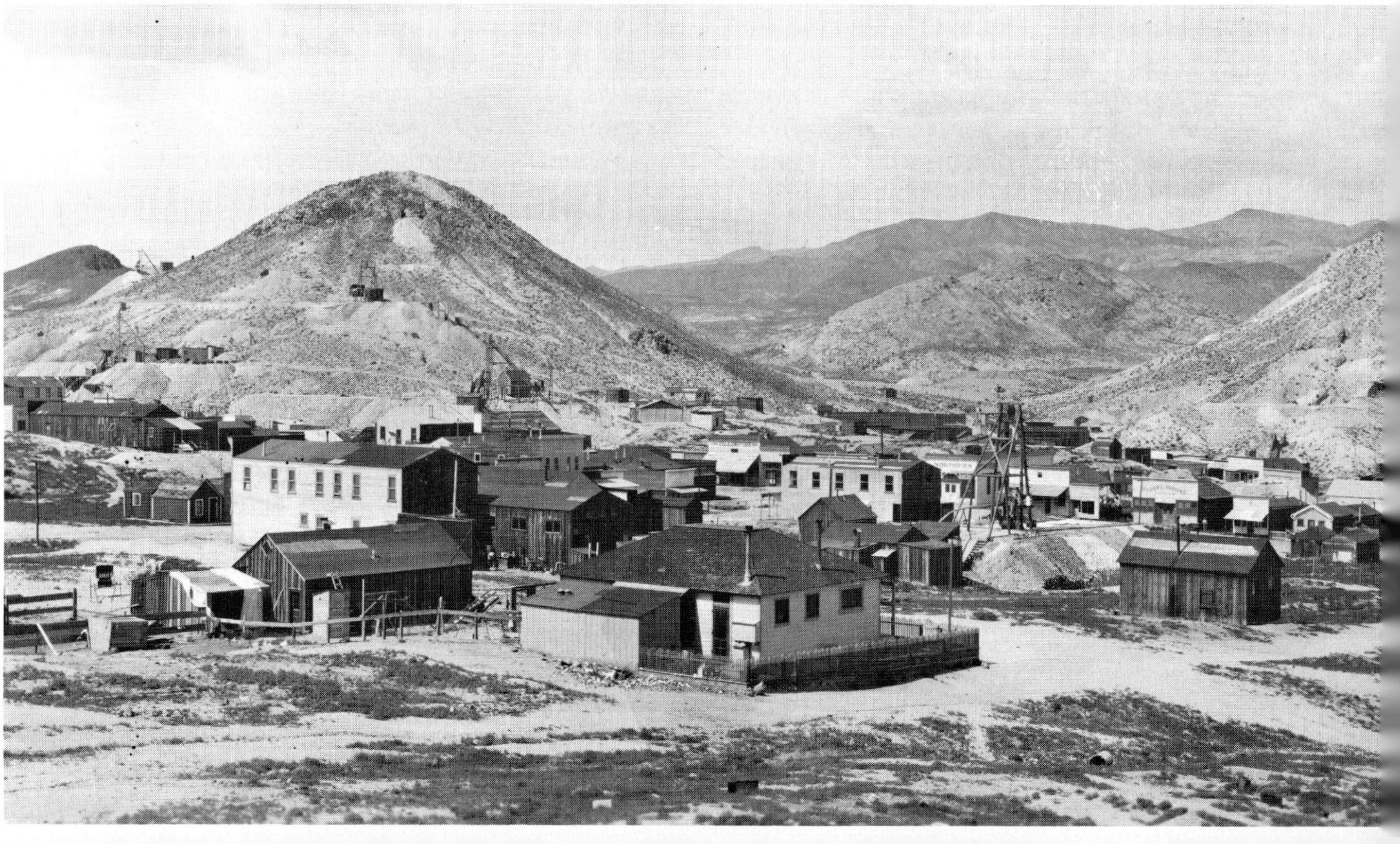

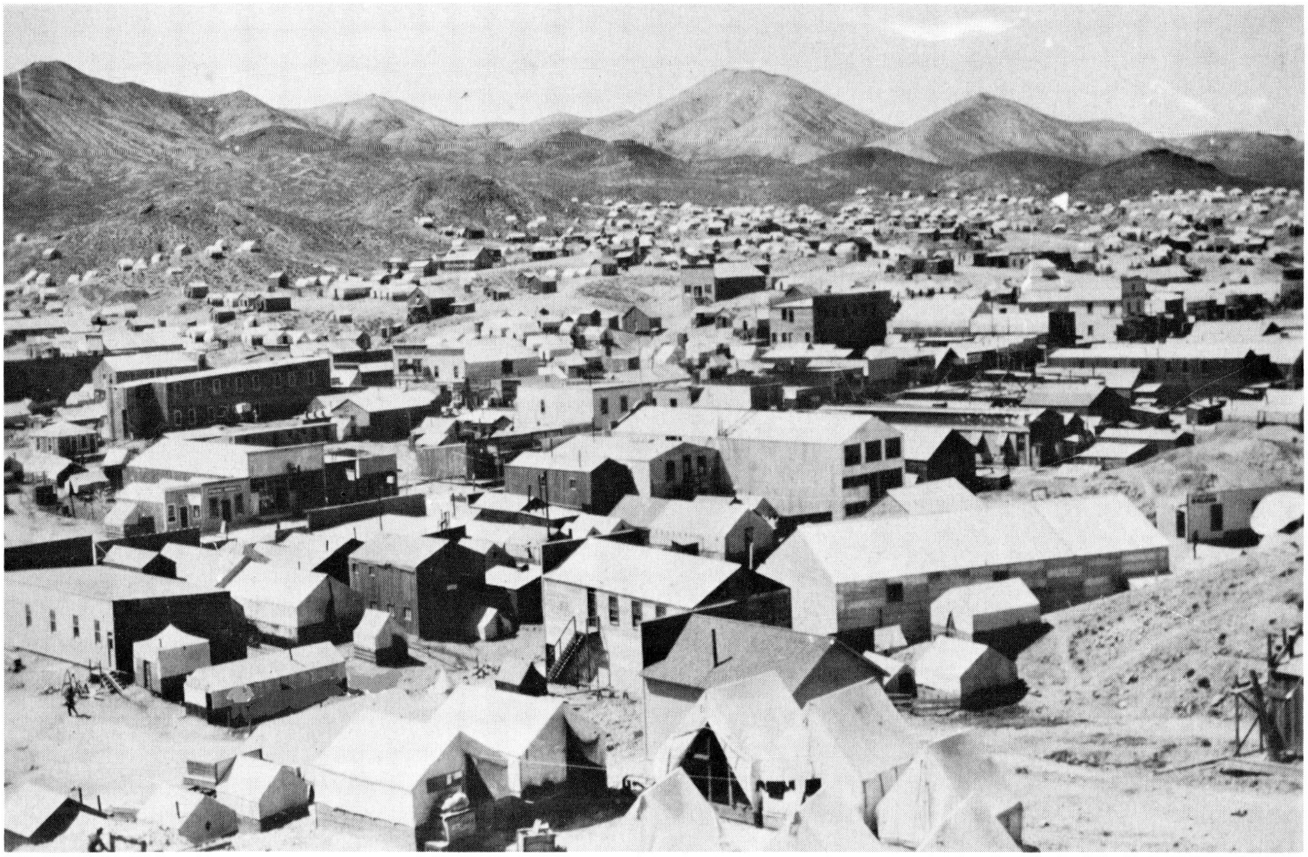

The picture *(above)* almost forms an extension of the one on the facing page, being taken from a vantage point slightly farther to the north and looking more directly south across town. The tie-in with the mountains in the background and the row of houses along the low ridge at upper left is clearly indicated. The heart of Rawhide lay along Nevada Street which cuts diagonally through the center of the picture. *(Nevada Historical Society.)*

Rawhide's economy went up in flames in the great holocaust of September 4, 1908. The view *(below)* is taken from virtually the same spot and in the same direction as the one above, and graphically depicts how rapid and thorough destruction of Nevada mining towns by fire could be. *(Nevada Historical Society.)*

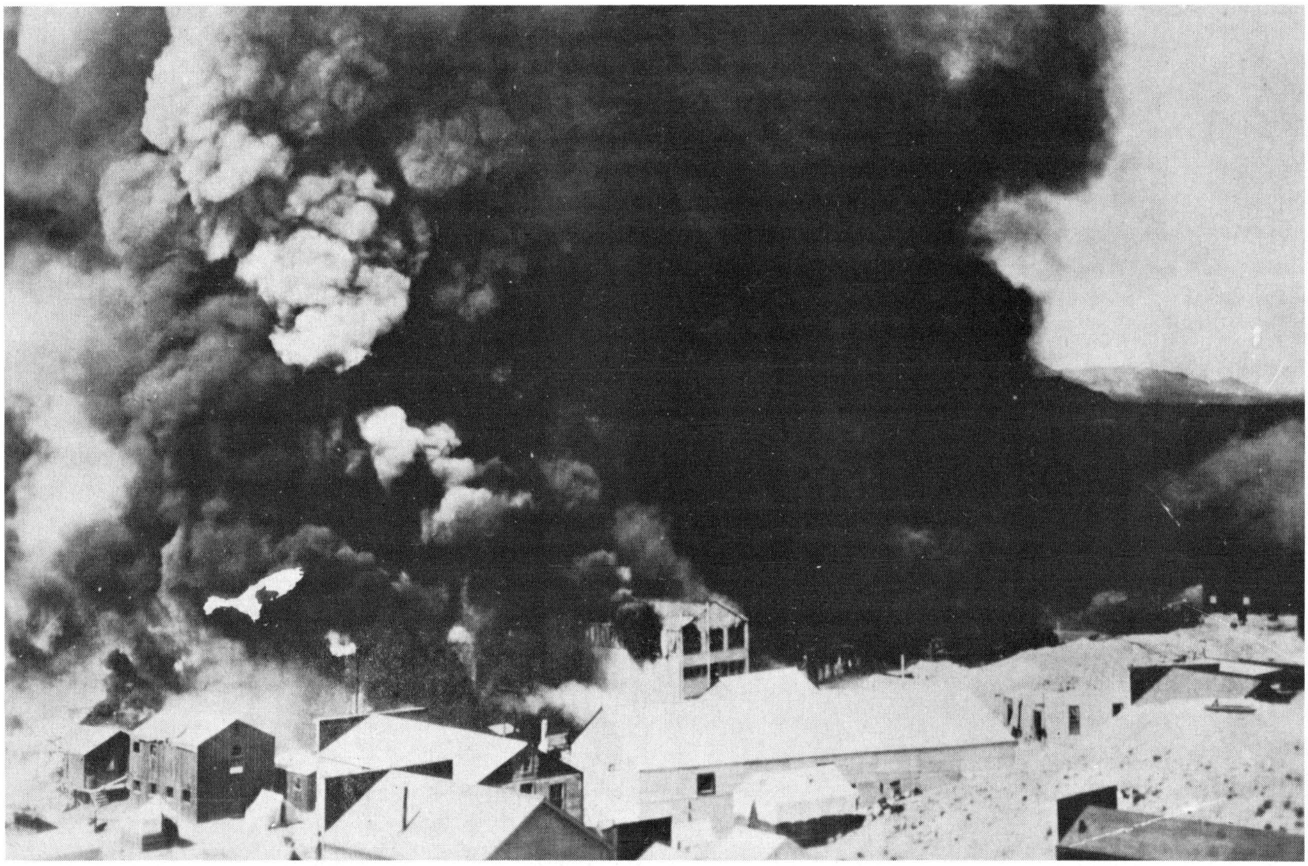

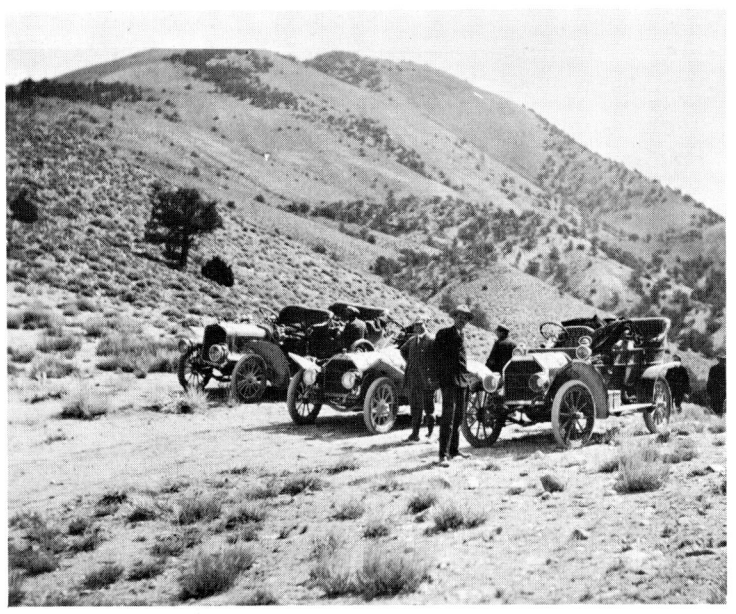

Transportation to Rawhide from Schurz and Luning on the west and from Fallon to the north was furnished by six-cylinder Chadwick Racers, Thomas and Peerless autos. Three of these early, high-wheeled machines paused at the summit of the pass between Luning and Dead Horse Wells in April 1907. *(Sewell Thomas Photo.)*

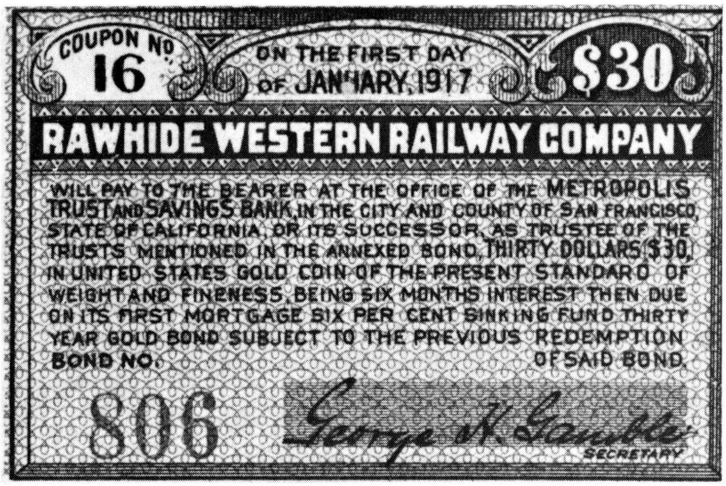

Lack of suitable transportation instigated several proposed railroad projects culminating in formation of the ill-fated Rawhide Western Railway Company whose bond coupon No. 16 was never to be redeemed on its due date of January 1917. *(L. J. Ciapponi Collection.)*

The only known photograph of the Rawhide Western Railway under construction is this view of some dozen and a half teams preparing the sub-grade. *(Grutt-Weight Collection.)*

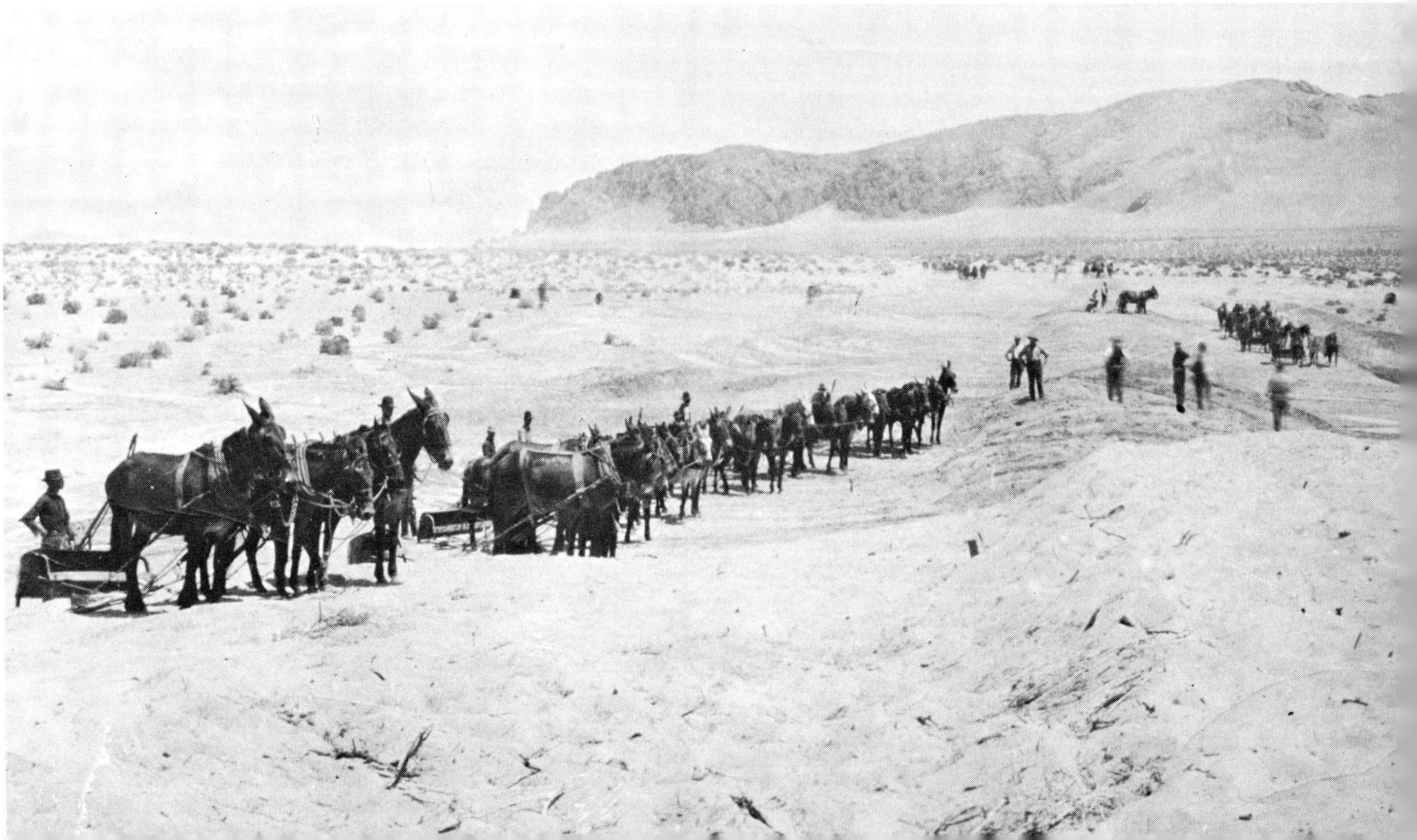

The railroad grade wound its way into Rawhide from the northwest, terminating in the back of Stingaree Gulch. Plans anticipated that the terminal would be located on the ground of the Rawhide Northern Mining Company in the North Rawhide Addition. With completion of the line to a point within sight and reason, sales of town lots proceeded at a brisk rate, and Sacramento wholesalers were busy acquiring land for warehouses.

Then it happened. Fire swept through the main part of town on the morning of September 4, 1908. Dynamite was used to stop the flames, but nine business blocks were razed before the blaze was brought under control. Reconstruction was started immediately after the fire and a great deal accomplished; but with money tightening all over, the spirit was gone and the boom was over for Rawhide.

The directors took another good look at the railroad. In one meeting following the fire, two of the directors forgot *Robert's Rules of Order* and after a short and ugly word there was a right to the jaw and the battle was on for a few minutes. Tex Rickard managed to separate the two fighters at the expense of covering himself with blood, while the two combatants were described as "not handsome."

Sufficient work was accomplished virtually to complete the grade in October. A subsequent report stated that rail laying would commence immediately and that trains would be due in Rawhide before Christmas. Technically, the laying of rails did commence, but only sufficient trackage to complete a supply track at Rawhide Junction. Grading for yard tracks at Rawhide was never completed, although the grade for a single wye track was ready for the track force. One newspaper report, later corrected, stated that carloads of ties and rails were at Schurz and that several hundred Japanese were at work. Another report quoted the railway as refusing to accept 60-lb. second-hand rails from the SP and T&G which were readily available, as they preferred to wait for the heavier 80-lb. rail. A telegram from Reno early in October reported that sufficient money was on deposit in New York to enable completion of the line. The next week a reliable report revealed that the mortgage was virtually arranged in New York and that the bonds would be sold later on when market conditions were more favorable. The following week the news leaked out that the bonds had not been placed at all.

Actual ore production at Rawhide during the first year did not amount to more than $1,500,000—no accurate figures are available, for apparently the leasers were too busy extracting the high grade ores to bother reporting. True, there were some rich assays, but the ore was found in small pockets and not in large ore bodies. The disappointing production figures convinced the railroad directors that the best policy would be to allow the project to die quietly without spending any more money on it.

The boosters of the town, however, would not give up. Reports were circulated that big financiers were in town ready to buy up the partially completed railroad, the unfinished Truitt mill at Schurz and certain other mining properties in a package deal. Some question of a commission on the sale delayed the transfer, and eventually the parties lost interest.

In the spring of 1909, Augustus J. Tilden, engineer of the Rawhide Western Railway, said that eastern capitalists were due in town to examine the mines and buy the railroad grade. Although Malcolm McDonald, one of Charles Schwab's mining agents, was seen entering the office of Charles W. Reed, then president of the railway, no news emanated from his office following the meeting, and nothing further developed as a result of it.

Toward the latter part of August 1909 Rawhide suffered a flood, though probably not as severe as was first reported. People became disappointed in "the camp of a thousand failures," (as one newspaper aptly described it in July 1911), but some production did continue during the ensuing years. The Nevada New Mines Co. took over the Rawhide Queen and Coalition (promotions of George Graham Rice) and managed to contribute some recorded production in 1913-16. Even the Grutt Brothers returned in 1928 and shipped some ore from time to time until their efforts ceased in 1941.

A few people still live in Rawhide today, and when the scheelite mines were operating a few miles to the east, some of the workers lived in the town. A number of the buildings are still in reasonable condition, and the stone jail is as solid as ever, ready to be of service if needed. One of the "variety houses" on the edge of Stingaree Gulch is still standing with its fancy wallpaper on the ceiling. One can imagine the activity there in the old days when Rawhide was a booming mining camp with a claimed population of 10,000 people and a brand new railroad almost at its door.

TONOPAH & GOLDFIELD RAILROAD

When Jim Butler's burro became lost on May 17, 1900, the renaissance of Nevada began. The amazing chain reaction touched off by this minor incident created mining communities and mining history, made men's fortunes, and drastically altered the railroad map of the state of Nevada. Seldom had such a profound effect been derived from such an obscure cause.

The situation at the turn of the century was ominous. The once fabulous Comstock mines at Virginia City had been declining from their peak lavish productiveness for the past 20 years, and with their wasting had come a diminution of the economy of the land and a dissipation of the population. Added to this was a drastic decline in the price of silver which made the outlook most importunate.

Then one innocent occurrence altered the entire picture. A town was born which boomed into prominence as the fabulous bonanza of Tonopah. Satellites Goldfield, Rhyolite and Bullfrog came into being, together with a galaxy of lesser lights which became illumed and as quickly extinguished. Four major railroads stretched their ferrous arms over 500 miles of new gradient, generating parasitical short lines of dubious unique distinctions. Of them all, the Tonopah & Goldfield Railroad was to start the earliest, subsist the longest and be the most lucrative for its progenitors.

I — THE TONOPAH RAILROAD

It was the report of the finding of promising ores in the (Southern) Klondike District that started Jim Butler on his famous trek. Heading southward from his ranch (some 40 miles north of Belmont) Butler was still a dozen miles short of his destination when night overcame him on the trail. On breaking camp the following morning, he discovered one of the burros had strayed during the night and needed to be rounded up. The operation was elemental — a well-aimed rock on the rump was sufficient encouragement to bring the animal in line. But the rock Jim picked up was an eyecatcher demanding closer examination. Thinking it might be something special, he gathered more samples and took them along to Klondike on the recalcitrant burro. The local assayer refused to do business on other than a strictly cash basis, scorned Jim's offer of a quarter interest in the claim in return for an assay, and discarded the samples as worthless. (Interestingly enough, the assayer later learned the value of Butler's strike, managed to locate the samples, assay them and claim his quarter interest. Although under no obligation to do so, Butler generously gave him a fractional interest in the ground.)

On his return trip from Klondike back to Belmont, Butler again located the find and took more samples with him. Back home in the (then) Nye County seat, he took the samples to Tasker L. Oddie, a promising young lawyer who was later to become Governor of Nevada and a United States Senator. Oddie accepted Butler's proposition and arranged for an assay. When the ultimate report showed values of $300 per ton of ore, Oddie dispatched an Indian runner to the Butler ranch with the news. But Jim Butler, being of an apathetic disposition, was not particularly concerned and allowed several months to go by before he finally located the ground with Mrs. Butler on August 27, 1900. The timing was close, for news of the assay had leaked out and many prospectors were already seeking valuable ledges in the undefined area.

Primitive living was required to explore the possibilities of the new claim. The difficulties of camping on the barren Nevada hillside were augmented by the increasingly colder fall weather and the necessity of hauling all water from a source a good three miles distant. The effort was not without its reward. The Butlers, Wilson Brougher (Nye County Sheriff) and Tasker Oddie managed to mine two tons of ore, haul it the 50 miles to Belmont, and place it in the hands of regular freighting teams for transport over the next 70 miles to Austin. There it was placed aboard the cars of the narrow gauge Nevada Central Railroad for the 93-mile trip to Battle Mountain where further transshipment to standard gauge cars of the Southern Pacific facilitated ultimate delivery to the smelter near Salt Lake City. Time passed, and anxiety grew during the period of waiting, but finally the answer arrived—a check for $500. It was a jubilant moment for all concerned.

Attempts have been made repeatedly to ascribe a preordained knowledge of the Tonopah situation on the part of officials of the Southern Pacific who made the decision to purchase the inauspicious Carson & Colorado Railroad in March 1900. Whatever surreptitious SP motivations may have prevailed, no intuitive perception on the part of its directors could have pertained to Jim Butler's find, although it is interesting to speculate on the different course history might have taken had Butler's initial discovery been made just a few months earlier.

Following the initial Butler development, the ground was turned over to leasers, and the new camp of Tonopah was born. In 1901 Butler sold his claims, including the Mizpah, to the Tonopah Mining Company which had been formed by a group of Philadelphia investors including Arthur and John Brock, C. A. Higbee and Governor Charles Miller of Delaware. Sale of the Butler claims was conditioned upon the leasers working the mines for the balance of the year, and every effort was made to secure maximum production in the limited time remaining. Tonopah was beginning to grow, although of interesting comment is the fact that mail continued to be addressed to "Butler Post Office" until March 1905.

Immediately attending the founding of Tonopah with its resultant agglomeration of prospectors, miners and engineers around the veins and outcroppings of the region, there arose the problem of transportation. People needed a means of ingress and egress; freight and general merchandise were required on location for construction, housing and sustenance; freshly mined ores demanded conveyance to smelters before profits could be realized. Passengers to the area usually stepped off the SP trains at Reno, took the connecting V&T local to Mound House, then transferred to the narrow gauge cars of the C&C for a six-hour ride to Hawthorne. Here an overnight layover was mandatory before catching the morning train south to Sodaville or Candelaria where stage coach connections were available for the remaining 60-odd miles to Tonopah. Freight was handled in large wagons pulled by teams of horses over either of two routes. That via the C&C was usually hauled to or from Sodaville on the main line, although some perishables were routed via the Candelaria branch for several years. Other shipments took the longer

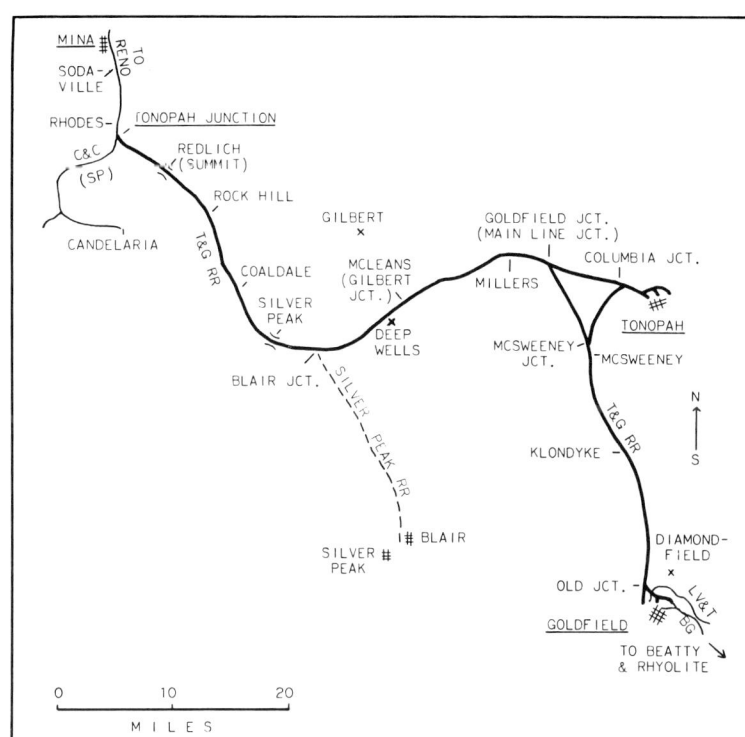

wagon route northward through Belmont to Austin, southern terminus of the narrow gauge Nevada Central Railroad. In either event, delivery of ores at the Selby, California, smelter was a long and costly process and any ores assaying less than $100 a ton were not shipped but rather routed to the mine dump. Railroad connections were called for in long and loud voices, but investors with a knowledge of previous short-lived mining booms were leery of any projected railroad to embryonic Tonopah.

But Tonopah continued to grow. In 1902 its population reached 1,300; a newspaper was established; and although a pneumonia epidemic took severe toll of the population in January of that year, more people moved in and the town continued to expand. One most welcomed newcomer was Wyatt Earp, the famed marshal of Tombstone and more recently of Nome, Alaska, whose announced objective was the opening of a new saloon on lower Main Street called "THE NORTHERN — A Gentleman's Resort." Concurrent with the population explosion, a multiplicity of transportation problems arose. Supplies moving in to Tonopah now required the services of 400 horses in teams of 12 to 20 horses each. Stage coach routes and services multiplied, along with the hazards of travel from both natural and sociological origins. For example, in May 1902 the crowded stage on the 12-hour run from Sodaville struck a rut in the road near Crow Springs and tipped over, landing on one of its roof-riding passengers with fatal results. At a later date about

10:30 of a summer evening, "Curly Dan" Robins was held up on his California, Oregon & Idaho Stage in one of the boldest robberies in years. The location was somewhere on the Candelaria route; the Wells Fargo Box was the expendable item; and by curious coincidence, there were no passengers to attest to the veracity of the occurrence.

In spite of the stringency of risk capital for railroad construction, there was definitely no dearth of promoters and others with a multiplicity of schemes such as would rival the contents of Pandora's box. One of the earliest and possibly most sincere projects was that proposed by Simon Bamberger to broaden the gauge of the existing Nevada Central Railroad from Battle Mountain to Austin and use it as a base for a new Nevada Midland Railroad to continue construction over the 120 miles from Austin to Tonopah. The project was initiated in 1901 and extensive surveys and organizational work were accomplished before its demise in the early part of 1902 (see Nevada Midland Railroad).

Hardly had the news been circulated of the NM's demise than Eureka jumped into the fray in June of 1902. The Eureka & Palisade Railroad was lethargic, having just gone through bankruptcy, while Eureka's town proper was suffering from dormant mines and needed new life. The loyal editor of the *Eureka Sentinel* promoted a Eureka-Tonopah railroad so enthusiastically and so arduously that finally even editor W. W. Booth of the *Tonopah Bonanza* was moved to comment: "The *Eureka Sentinel* has about three miles of rails on the new railroad laid from Eureka to Tonopah. The roadbed will be ballasted with hot air cinders from the Salt Lake papers, which are now telling their readers that Salt Lake capital is interested in the road. If it is, the road will never be built."

Although the editorial battle may have been of dubious consequence, it is certain that developments at Tonopah were attracting attention. At the instigation of E. H. Harriman (who at this time had acquired working control of the Southern Pacific) a special SP representative, W. H. Holabird, arrived in Tonopah and caused the following statement to be published under the dateline of June 30, 1902:

"The Southern Pacific Company will build and operate a Standard Gauge Railroad from a point near Rhodes Station on the Carson and Colorado Railway to Tonopah, beginning construction by — 1902, and diligently continuing the same until final completion:

"Provided, that the mining and sundry interests of Tonopah subscribe and bind themselves to pay upon completion of said Railroad the sum of Two Hundred and Fifty Thousand ($250,000) Dollars to the said Southern Pacific Company. The Southern Pacific Company will also add a third rail to the Carson & Colorado Railway between Rhodes and Mound House, thus enabling freight to move in unbroken bulk to and from destination."

Had editors been capitalists, the project would have been well received. The *Tonopah Bonanza* was naturally opposed to subsidies, but in this instance approved because the Tonopah Mining Company was only being asked to subscribe to $200,000 while the smaller companies could unite in subscribing to the additional $50,000. The *Yerington Times* was even more liberal, commenting that if Tonopah did not pay the $250,000 in full then all of the counties should chip in because the cattlemen along the line of the C&C would likewise benefit from the use of standard gauge livestock cars. That the editors did not have the confidence of their readers is evident, for the money did not materialize and the proposal joined the other unsuccessful plans in dormancy.

More official recognition of the Tonopah situation was accorded by Eureka in September 1902 when Mark Requa, president of the Eureka & Palisade Railroad and a prominent mining man, spent a week in the new bonanza town. The activity and the prospects were obviously impressive, for surveyor Edward G. Tilton was dispatched to project a roundabout route from Eureka via Copper Flat (near Ely) and Tybo to Tonopah. The solicitation was made that if the Copper Flat mine owners would participate in the cost of the line, the railroad would be constructed. Unfortunately Copper Flat was experiencing adverse difficulties with the miners (a wage cut became a necessity), and lacking financial support, the project died.

At least two other proposals were to gain recognition before the year 1902 passed into limbo. According to one report, the California Midland "was assured" of completing its line from Oakland to Tonopah and Pioche via the conveniences of the Fresno River basin (east of Madera) and Mammoth Pass (20 miles south of Yosemite). The assurance obviously was all in the mind of the wishful newspaper author. Still another report contended that the SP would take up the old rails of its South Pacific Coast Railway to Santa Cruz and use them to extend the more recently acquired C&C to

Tonopah. The refurbishment of the SPC to standard gauge was eventually accomplished in the year 1906-07, but the rails thus released were never to see a Nevada sunrise.

It was in February 1903 that the first faltering steps were taken on a project which ultimately was to result in a railroad to Tonopah. At the risk of waggish connotations, the undertaking might be said to have been a "lemon" from the very beginning; for C. S. Lemon was the instigator, but C. S. Lemon sustained a reputation for being successful in all of his undertakings. Concurrently with the placing of surveyors in the field to map a railroad from Rhodes (4½ miles south of Sodaville on the C&C and one mile north of the future site of Tonopah Junction) to Tonopah, Senator Thorn of Esmeralda County introduced a bill in the Nevada legislature granting Lemon a 200-foot right of way for the line. The bill became law with the affixing of Governor John Sparks' signature on March 12, 1903, and provided that construction must begin within four months and be completed by 15 months from that date. The gauge could range variously anywhere from 36 to 56½ inches.

Results were not long in forthcoming. The survey fixed the line at 62.39 miles in length, starting from M.P. 143 on the C&C (later designated as Tonopah Junction) and continuing to Tonopah over grades not exceeding 2½% and curvatures of 6°. The total estimated cost, including a branch to Silver Peak, was fixed at $1,050,000. A total of $165,000 was reportedly on hand to cover immediate expenditures, while an additional $400,000 had been pledged by local mining companies. Lemon, indeed, was putting the squeeze on all and sundry.

In Tonopah, the McNamara Mining Company presented the railroad with a strip of ground for its new depot, a gift that was hotly contested by two lot jumpers who set up their tents before the property could be enclosed with a fence. Clyde Jackson, one of the McNamara's principal owners, resented the intrusion for, as later recorded, "Jackson and ye scribe happened along about this time and told them to vacate. They demurred. In two minutes round one was won by Clyde. The other trespasser then told Jackson that if he would remove his glasses he would pummel him in splendid style. Clyde removed his glasses; round two was on in a jiffy; and Clyde won that one too." The lot jumpers were thoroughly trounced, and the depot grounds were saved in a manner to prove that Tonopah justice was sometimes earned the hard way.

Such a positive, direct approach to the railroad's problems was not always possible. It took a lengthy, chain-reaction deal to secure a satisfactory, yet essential traffic agreement with hesitant SP dignitaries over interchange at the T&G's only outside connection, Tonopah Junction. Harriman of the SP had to be favorably impressed, and it appeared that a convincing letter from his friend, John Scott of New York, would be the best approach. Lemon turned the problem over to another of the T&G's originators, John C. Gilmore, President of the Colonial Trust Company of Philadelphia. In turn, Gilmore contacted a friend of his, railroad bond salesman Augustus Mellier, who was a personal friend of John Scott. Mellier explained the situation to Scott who agreed to write the desired letter to Harriman. The situation was almost anticlimactic. By the time Harriman was reached, the "little giant" was convalescing from appendicitis at his Hotel Netherlands suite immediately before leaving for Europe, so the matter was referred to J. Kruttschnitt, then an SP vice-president in San Francisco. The net results of the efforts were favorable, however, for the return wire stated that if the parties were thoroughly responsible, a satisfactory agreement could be made as the SP decided not to build to Tonopah.

July 12, 1903, was the deadline for the commencement of work on the line under the terms of the Nevada bill. Even though all arrangements were not entirely completed, Lemon protected his rights by starting a small force of workers at The Narrows, several miles east of Rhodes, just a few days before the expiration date. His announcement of the moment indicated that the railroad would be of narrow (3-foot) gauge, although wide gauge ties would be used in the roadbed to permit easy conversion to standard gauge when the SP's C&C trackage was broad gauged. The announcement ended on a hopeful note with the statement that only a few minor details needed to be arranged before large construction forces would be instituted. For reasons unascertained, McCarthy of the *Walker Lake Tribune* at Hawthorne was antagonistic toward the new line and facetiously reported: "The working force consists of three men, and each has a pick. It is reported that a small boy will be added to the force next year, but the report is discredited."

Although it was generally accepted as far back as March of 1903 that the Tonopah Railroad Company had been formally organized, the minute book reveals that the official organizational meeting did not take place until July 25, 1903, in Philadelphia. Andrew J. Maloney was named president and John F. Braun treasurer. Augustus Mellier set about the task of organizing a construction company, while John Braun and John Gilmore (of the Colonial Trust Company) undertook the solicitation of funds. When Gilmore failed to produce his quota of moneys, Braun induced C. S. Lemon to call on John W. Brock and Richard H. Rushton, the former the head of the Tonopah Mining Company and the latter the president of the Fourth Street National Bank of Philadelphia. Brock and Rushton had the money and were ready to take over. Actual transfer of the organization and its franchises was accomplished at the next meeting of the board on September 1, 1903. Brock became president and director, while others on the board included Clyde A. Heller, Richard H. Rushton, Thomas M. King and William Jay Turner. From this point on the destiny of the railroad lay with these men whose offices were in Philadelphia's Bullitt Building and whose connections were close with the Fourth Street National Bank.

Brock immediately journeyed to Tonopah and San Francisco to initiate work on the railroad. On October 12, 1903, it was announced that Paul Iglehart (formerly with the B&O and N&W) would become the locating engineer and that R. W. Fairbanks, surveyor for the Tonopah Co. would meet him and conduct him over the proposed route. In picking up the threads of construction left by the departing C. S. Lemon, Iglehart (who was described as a man of perfect charm but entirely without knowledge of desert cloudbursts) utilized most of Lemon's work in the final survey except for moderate revisions of certain grades and curves. Believing, as did many Easterners, that no rain fell on the desert country, Iglehart limited the grading to a minimum of 330,000 cubic yards for the entire line and provided only narrow culverts as a further gesture of economy. His shortsightedness was to be deeply regretted almost immediately following the opening of the road.

Procurement and expediting of materials was placed in the hands of Alonzo Tripp, the Tonopah Railroad's first superintendent and a former employee of both the B&O and the Southern. Under his direction, narrow gauge ties and other materials were ordered in San Francisco; 50-pound, second-hand rail from the SP's Wadsworth cut-off was purchased; and three Mogul (2-6-0) locomotives were ordered from the Baldwin Locomotive Works (two reconditioned, one new).

The Tonopah Mining Co. undertook to build the narrow gauge railroad for the Tonopah Railroad Company under a contract dated December 30, 1903. Payment was scheduled to be made in $500,000 of First Mortgage 5% Bonds plus $500,000 par value of capital stock. Obviously Iglehart's economies (which also included abandonment of plans for the branch to Silver Peak) were calculated to reduce the cost of the road well below the original $1,050,000 estimate. On January 2, 1904, at noon all bids were opened, and the organization of McLean and McSweeney was awarded the subcontract for their (Scotch-like) low offering.

Time was fast running out on the franchise and speed of action became essential. A second-hand Consolidation type (2-8-0) locomotive was purchased from the Nevada-California-Oregon Railway (one which had been found to be too cumbersome for the light roadbed and sharp curves of the former line.) J. Hammond in San Francisco became the recipient of an order for 15 freight cars. Clarence Oddie (Tasker's brother) and John T. Overbury started moving dirt in initial grading operations on January 25 near French's Wells immediately following receipt of the telegraphic "start work" order from Philadelphia. Utilizing 60 men at $2.00 a day plus board and 80 horses and mules pulling sulky plows and Fresno scrapers, work progressed rapidly. Favorable dry weather helped in the making of a little money on the subcontract as well as the low wages for laborers. McLean and McSweeney together with Collins and Young were likewise grading individual sections of roadbed, and by the middle of February the completion of 16 miles of grade could be tallied. First rails for the 1,000-foot siding at Tonopah Junction (near Rhodes) were spiked in place on February 19, 1904, in anticipation of the arrival of Engine No. 3 (formerly N-C-O No. 4) which was due the following week. By early March the locomotive was in operation over the first mile of track. The Baldwin locomotives, all Moguls (2-6-0), were shipped from Philadelphia the previous February 7, but were the last to go into service on the line.

Transportation problems multiplied when a shortage of livestock disrupted normal stage operations to Tonopah. Already overtaxed by the influx of visitors to the area, stage coach service became an extreme luxury with the reduction in frequency to one a day. Thus when 28 passengers disembarked from the morning C&C train at Sodaville, a "reservation system" was placed in effect which assured a full complement of stage passengers for several days' trips in advance.

Graders began to join completed sections, and as each unit was finished the grading outfits moved on to other locations. A big rock cut 1½ miles west of Tonopah created the greatest difficulty, for only 15 feet of headway per day could be accomplished with the crude hand methods of excavation employed. On March 7 a track laying machine was placed in operation, and track layers gained a half-mile each day over grading operations. The first station, Coal Wells, was scheduled to be established on April 15.

Actual train service to Coal Wells, though only for construction supplies, was inaugurated two days later. Passengers still used the crowded stage coaches for the full distance from Sodaville. One exception was conceded by the railroad when steel magnate Charles M. Schwab arrived in a private car over rails of the C&C. Schwab had become interested in Nevada mining, and arrangements were quickly made to demonstrate hospitality by operating the first revenue train over the 20 miles of completed rails to Coal*dale* (a more euphonious name substituted for the original designation of Coal Wells). A personal letter of appreciation to Superintendent Tripp was subsequently penned by Schwab from his private car *Loretto*.

During the first week of May 1904 regular train service was instituted to Coaldale, and trains were met by O'Keefe stages for conveyance of passengers to and from Tonopah. Track laying came to a frustrating and abrupt halt when the inventory of rail stacked at Rhodes became depleted. Sufficient rail for the job had been ordered, but it was temporarily delayed at Mound House pending ability of the C&C to deliver it to location. The situation was merely a precursor of even more stringent times to come.

As the bottleneck was broken and steel again became available, track laying proceeded. On May 28, 1904, the rail head reached Deep Wells, 41 miles from Rhodes; in June it jumped to Kelsey's; and on July 1, Goldfield Junction became the end of track, where connecting stages took passengers the remaining 30-odd miles to that new mining area.

Then work stopped again, as rails became scarce. The time was the Fourth of July, and Carson City was staging a monster parade replete with floats, bands and all the paraphernalia attending a large civic holiday celebration. Crowds deserted Tonopah to witness the major event, and all C&C rolling stock was conscripted to handle the surfeit of pleasure seekers. Possibly worthy of mention, but of somewhat dubious distinction, was the first prize earned by the Tonopah float. The citation likely made the trip appear worth while to the participants, but the diversion of locomotives to a fatuitous passenger service obviated their usage in helping to clear up some of the freight congestion. Thus the needed rails rested comfortably for several more days at outlying Mound House.

Monday through Wednesday, July 25-27, 1904, were officially set aside for the big Railroad Days Celebrations at Tonopah. Basic plans for the occasion were formulated at a mass meeting the previous June when W. W. Booth, now postmaster as well as newspaper editor, was elected president of the celebration committee. A bang-up program was outlined pending completion of the railroad by the appointed hour.

When the C&C finally delivered the deadlocked rail, work on the Tonopah Railroad was resumed. With the end almost in sight and the Celebration Days almost at hand, the track laying forces attempted to take advantage of the situation by making unreasonable, last-minute wage demands. It was a misjudgment on their part. Without a moment's hesitation, "green" construction hands were assigned to finish the job, and the narrow gauge track crept into town on Saturday afternoon, July 23, 1904. The job was completed within an elapsed time of just over four years from the date of the initial ore discovery by Jim Butler and his burro, and the town was ready to tell it to the world.

The first train over the entire new line to Tonopah was an extra which arrived on Saturday night bearing that important adjunct to the forthcoming celebration, the Carson State Band. Another excursion extra arrived on Sunday to swell the already bursting ranks of revelers. Finally, on Monday morning, the first regular train pulled into town to signify the start of the celebration. Many people waited up all night to greet it on arrival, although of those that did, there appeared to be some question as to how many were capable of casting a discerning eye over the equipage or noting with

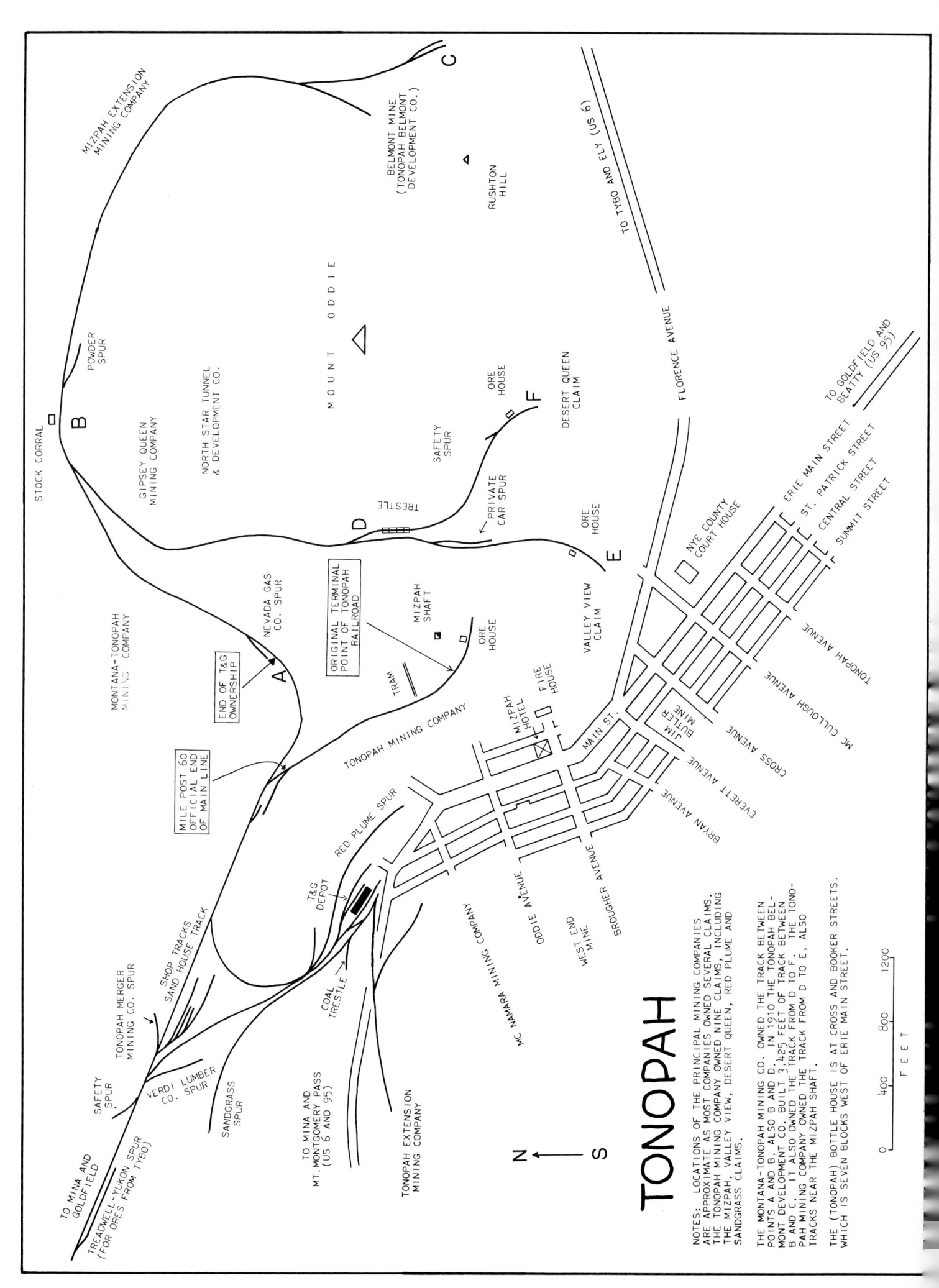

understanding that the locomotive was burning Nevada coal from the recently developed mines of the Nevada Fuel & Manufacturing Company at Coaldale.

Miss Belle Pepper (later Mrs. Zeb Kendall) was crowned Queen of the Celebration Days. Governor Sparks and beaming Jim Butler were prominent figures in the big parade. Alonzo Tripp, now general superintendent of the Tonopah Railroad, drove a specially cast silver spike in good workmanlike style, following it with a "short but pithy speech" wherein he looked to the future and expressed the premature hope that he would soon drive the last spike at Goldfield (the new mining community to the south). The Tonopah Dramatic Club wound up the evening by presenting a capital play entitled "My Friend from India."

Tuesday was a day of contests—foot races, rock-drilling contests, and a baseball game between Tonopah and Reno nines—topped off by a grand ball in the evening at the opera house. The final day's events on Wednesday included a foot race to the top of Mt. Oddie and return, an Indian parade headed by Jim Butler, and a disappointing bronco bucking contest in which there was a sad lack of any horses with sufficient "go" to enable scoring on the usual point basis. In a kangaroo court, "Judge" Ole Elliot fined Jim Butler $20.00 for having too much money; and when Butler became "judge" in turn, he had Ole arrested and fined $20.00 for incompetency. Yet, mixed in with the horseplay and hilarity, there was withal a serious side to the celebration. Some 300 people visited the Montana-Tonopah mine, and a large crowd witnessed the formal presentation by the citizens of Tonopah of a handsome gold watch and chain to Contractor McSweeney as a mark of recognition for his timely assistance in bringing his own staff to take the place of the striking workmen. But little recognition was given to the Railroad Day Committee which was left without assistance to struggle with the $1,000 deficit resulting from the celebrations.

In the construction of the Tonopah Railroad vicissitudes and misfortunes of normal frequency occurred and were taken in stride. Before the rails reached Tonopah, the first wreck occurred near Deep Wells on Sunday, July 17, 1904, when spreading rails dropped flanges to the ties and a passenger train landed in the ditch. Although no one was reported to have been hurt, Zeb Kendall from Goldfield and all of the other passengers were both tired and hungry when, by the end of the day, they had only reached Sodaville on the C&C.

Immediately following the Railroad Days Celebration, a series of cloudbursts and thunderstorms unparalleled in number and severity burst upon the woefully unprepared forces, spreading destruction and ruin. On Saturday, July 30, 1904, the track was washed out at Coaldale on the TRR and at New Boston on the C&C. Repairs were rushed and restoration of service accomplished. Then from August 13 to 18 the Tonopah Railroad was completely out of business. The track was washed out all the way from Rhodes (on the C&C) to Summit (Silver Peak); what was worse, it was swept away a second time the moment it was restored. Further, a cloudburst over Ray Flat destroyed the track at the stage connecting point of Goldfield Junction, while at the other extreme another cloudburst over Silver Star Canyon wiped out the C&C trackage three miles out of Sodaville. Repairs again were rushed, and traffic was restored with 22 cars of ore leaving Tonopah and a trainload of passengers and mail arriving, the first activity following four days of suspended service.

With Goldfield coming into prominence, some preliminary surveys were made for an extension of the Tonopah Railroad to the new mining bonanza, but it was prudently reported that any extension of the existing line would not be seriously considered until the mines had proved themselves by going to the 500-foot level. Goldfield's Combination mine was not yet down 300 feet, while the Jumbo and the January were each operating at the 200-foot level.

On Monday, August 22, 1904, more rains came. Five miles of the Tonopah's roadbed vanished on the desert floor. When the waters receded, the track was discovered to be in far worse condition than originally anticipated. Restoration was rushed, but the gesture was unavailing. A week later on August 29 a train ventured out from Sodaville and shortly became enveloped in a cloudburst. Before ground of respectable elevation could be reached, the track behind as well as ahead of the train was washed away, leaving the locomotive and cars completely isolated. Then the very rails on which the equipment was stranded became undermined causing the train to fall on its side and inflicting minor injury to one of the passengers from broken glass. Some 15 miles of roadbed dissipated on the barren desert that day; passengers from the stricken train were returned to Sodaville; and stage coach service

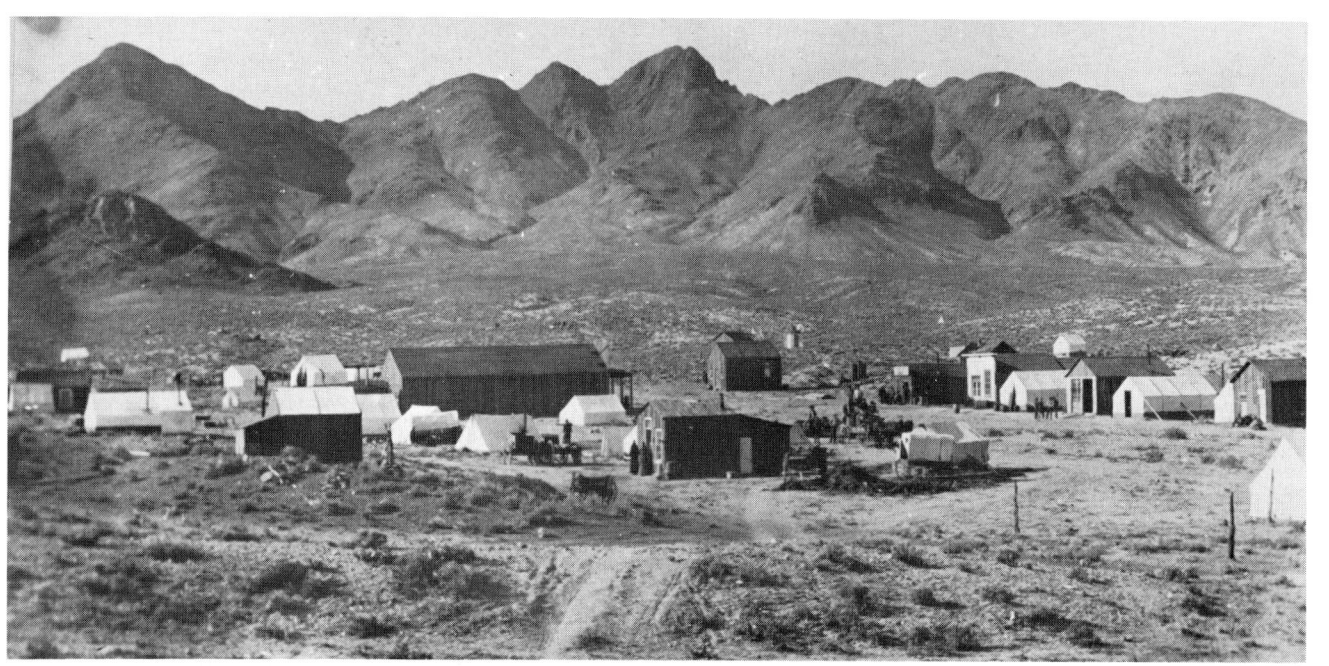

On May 1, 1901 Tonopah *(above)* was only six months old and just beginning to get its first frame buildings intermingled with the tents. Mt. Butler (named for Jim Butler, discoverer of Tonopah) appears in center background with Brock Mountain at left and Heller Butte in front. The latter two were named for officials of the Tonopah Mining Co. who later were important figures in the Tonopah & Goldfield Railroad. Productivity of the Cutting Lease in 1901 *(below)* is demonstrated by the sacks of ore against which H. C. Cutting (1) leans while Mr. and Mrs. Jim Butler (2 & 3) and W. A. Ingalls (4) join in the picture. *(Top: Mrs. R. T. Norris; Bottom: Mrs. Hugh Brown.)*

The entire population of Tonopah turned out for the photograph *(above, right)* taken early in 1902. Probably later in the same year photographer E. W. Smith posed in front of his own camera on a windy day *(right, below)* for this panoramic view of Tonopah looking to the southwest. In the center background is prominent Mt. Brougher with the rounded dome of Siebert Mountain to the left. Wilson Brougher, associated with Jim Butler and Fred Siebert, an early manager of the Tonopah Mining Co. provided the names for these mountains. *(Bottom: Mrs. Hugh Brown Collection.)*

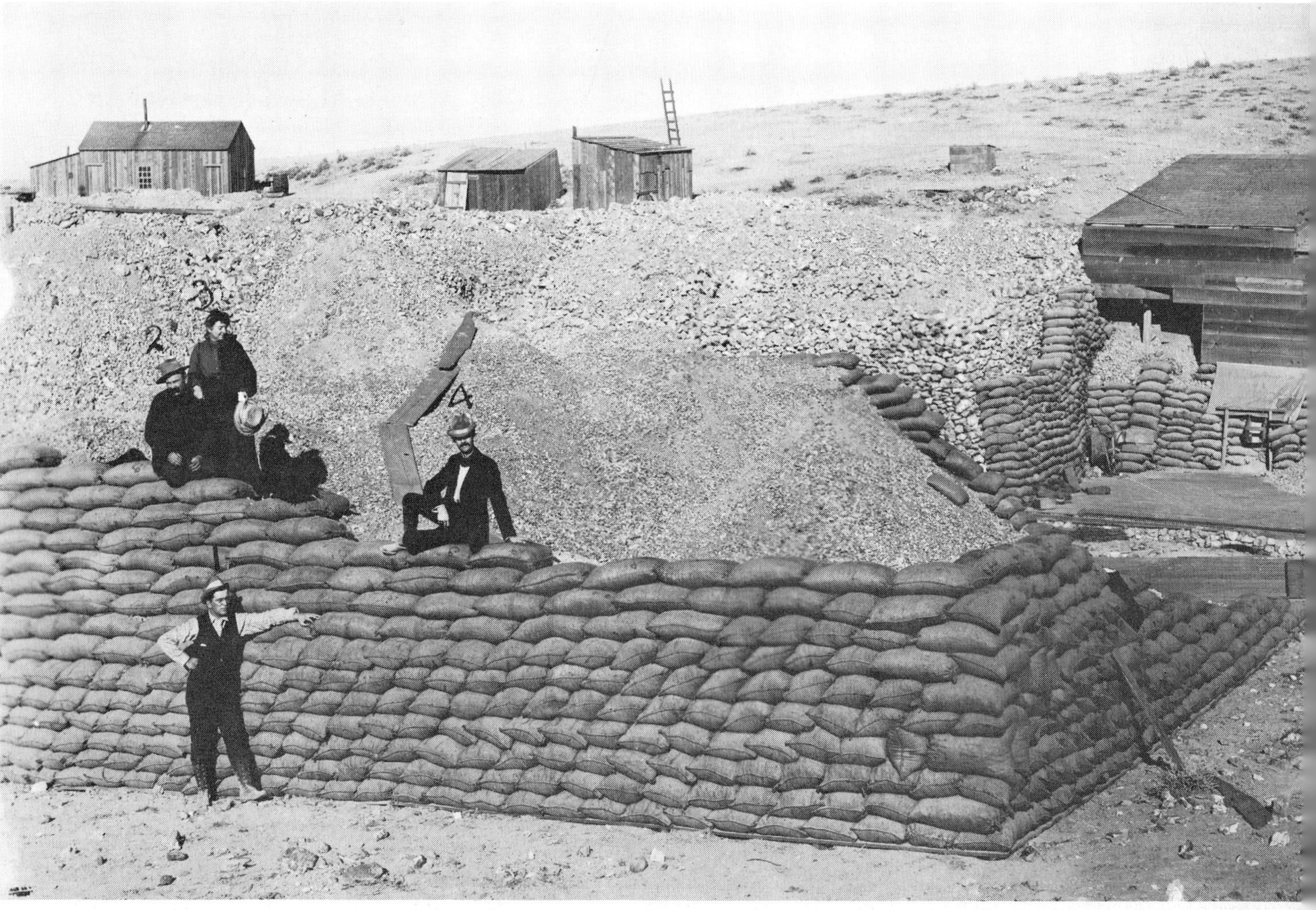

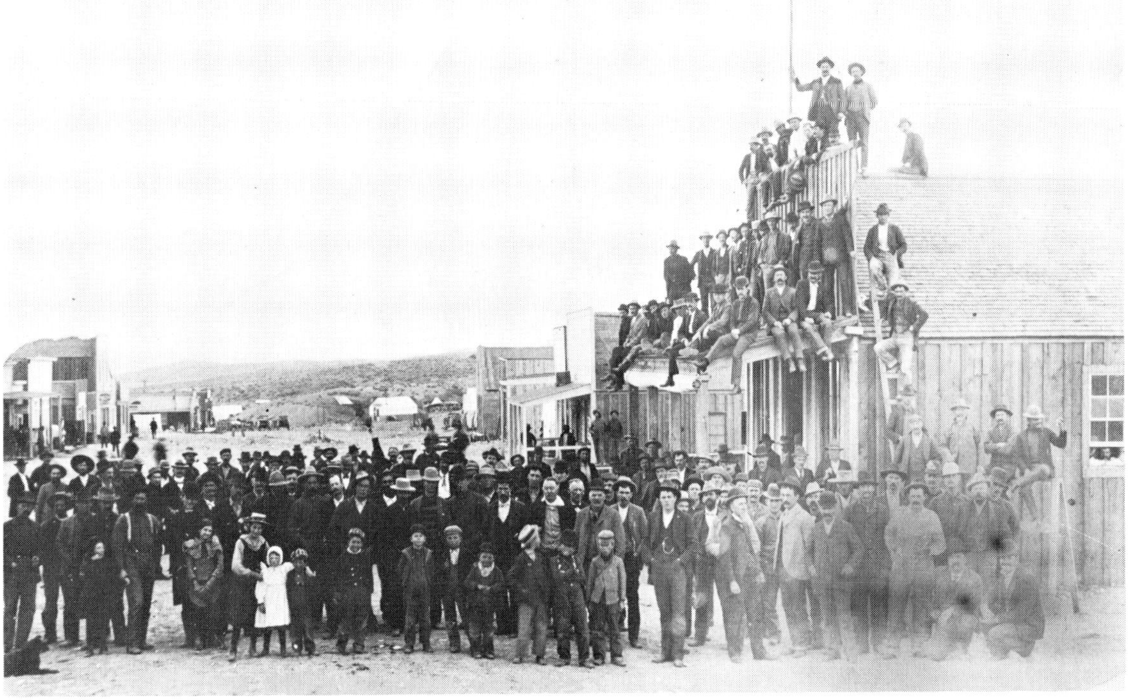

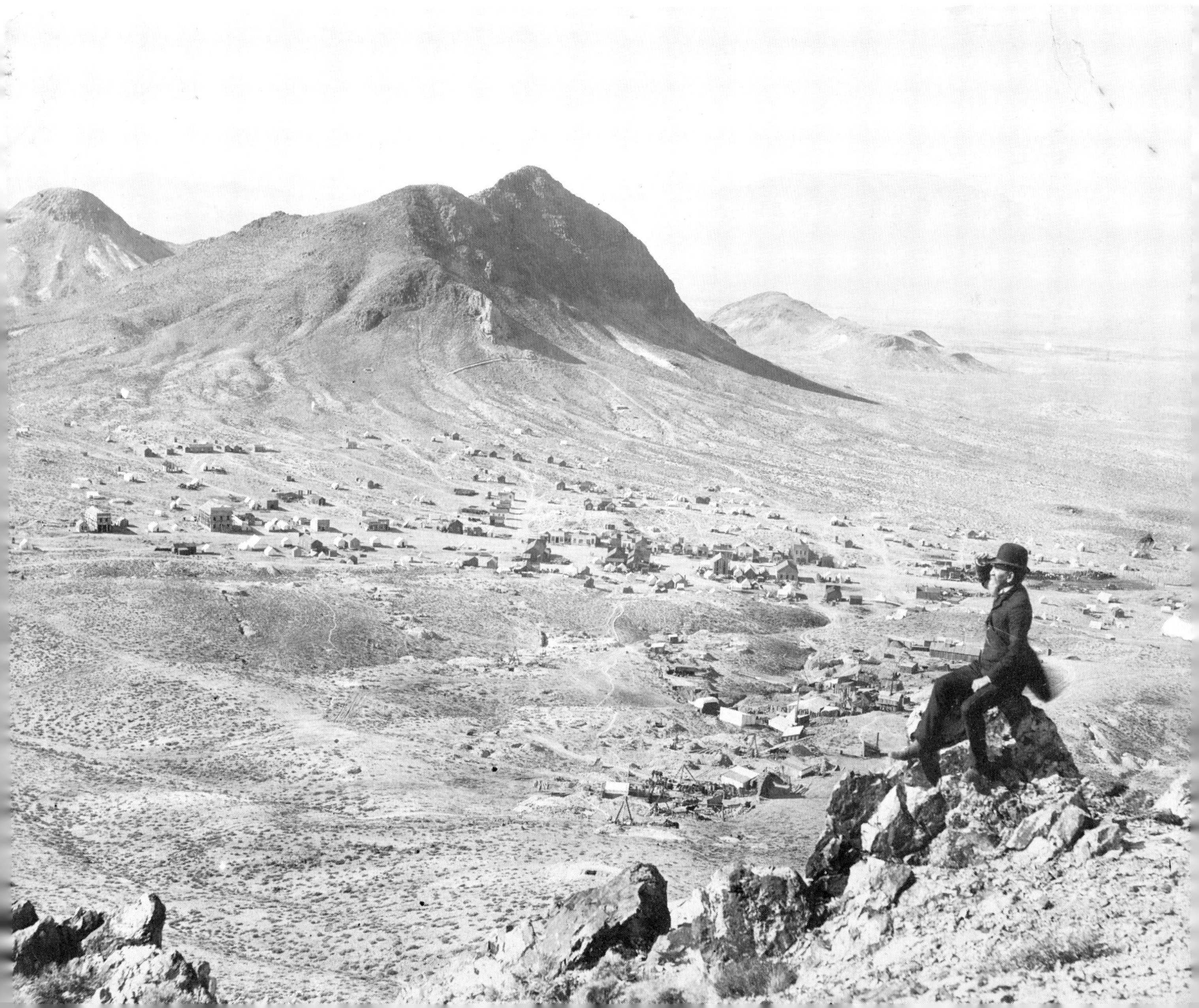

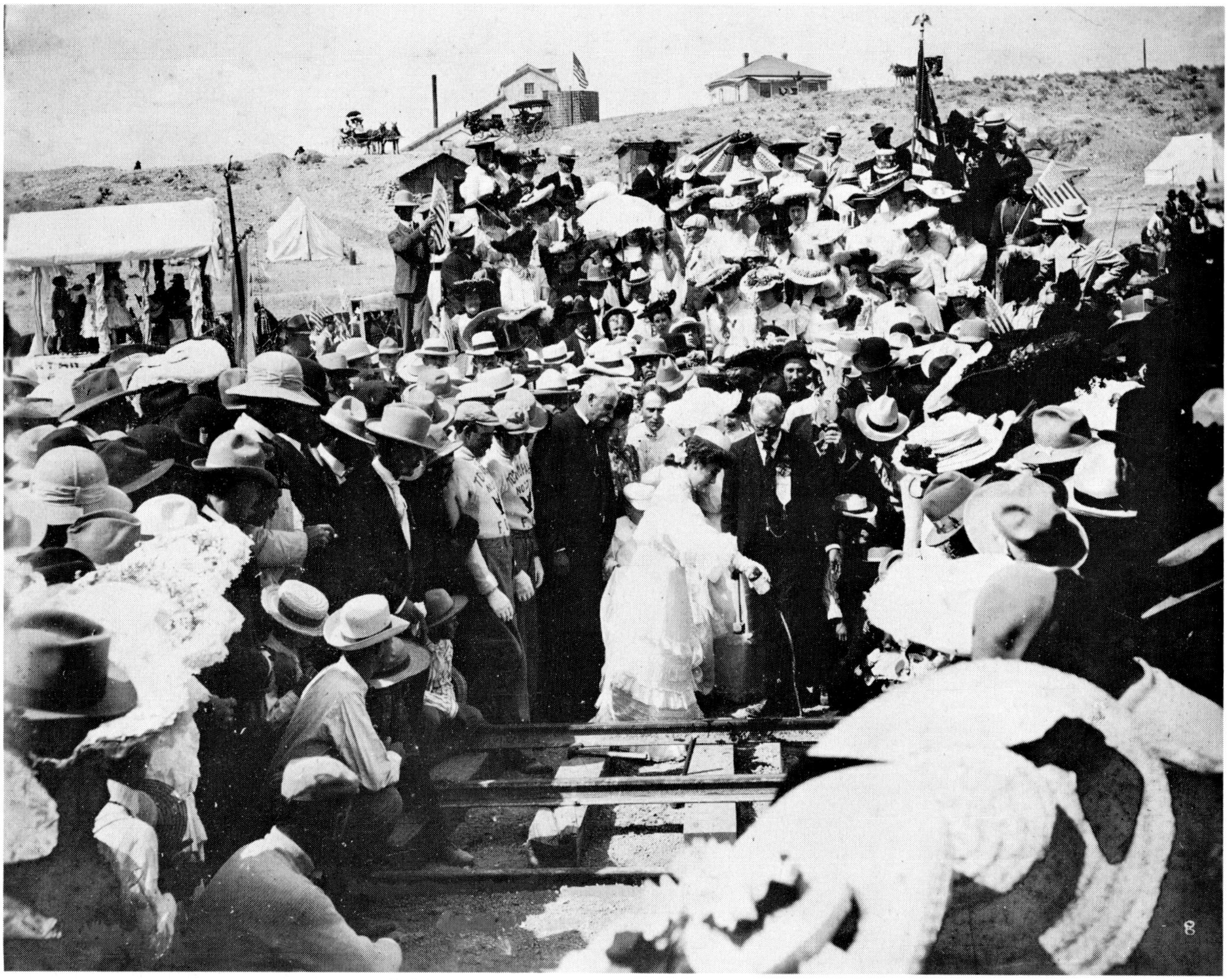

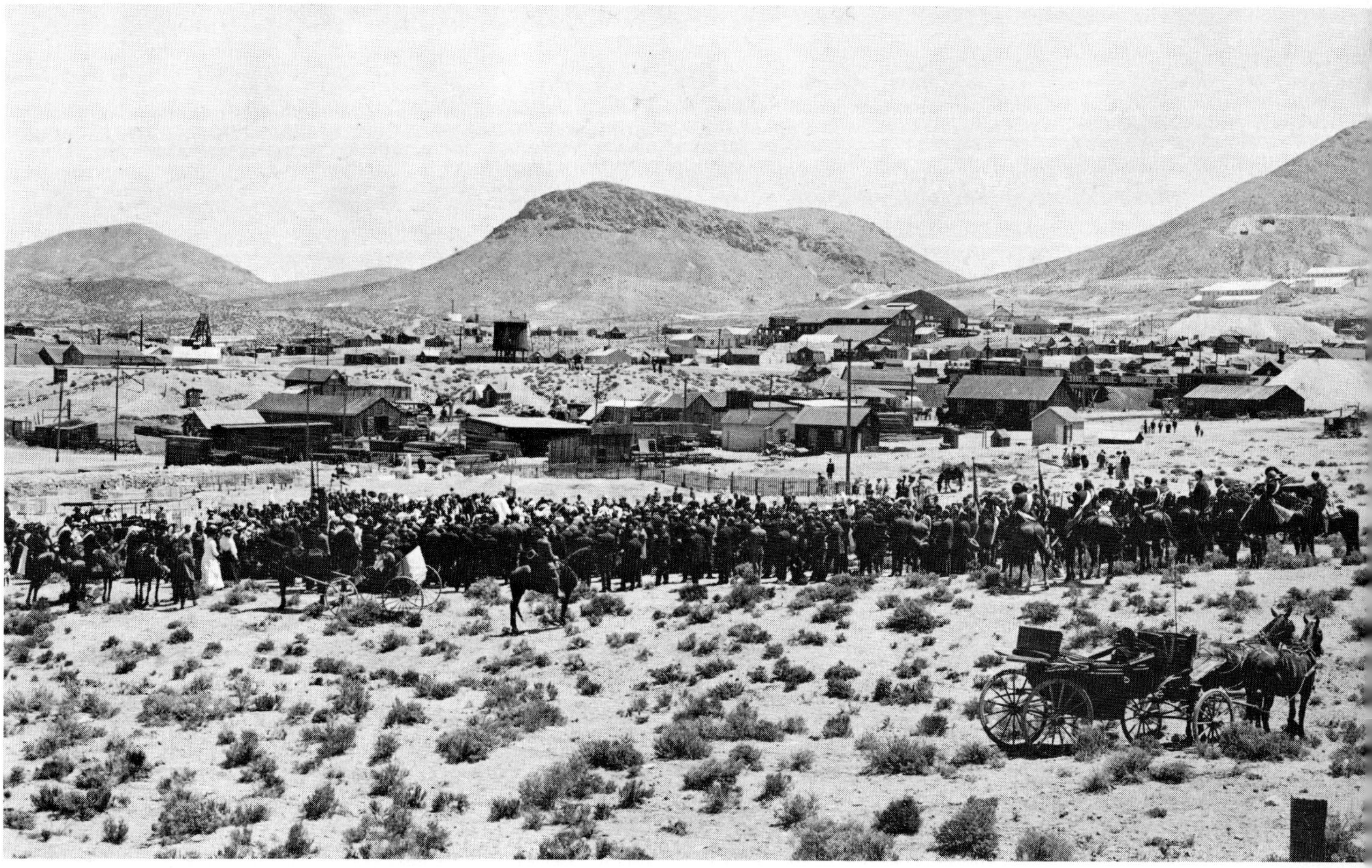

Tonopah Railroad Company

Office of General Superintendent

Tonopah, Nevada, July 9, 1904.

Mr. G.D. Flint
San Francisco

The Tonopah Railroad Company requests the honor of your presence at the Celebration of the completion of its line into Tonopah, to be held on July 25th, 26th and 27th, 1904.

Alonzo Tripp,
General Superintendent.

John W. Brock,
President.

Railroad Days for Tonopah, July 25, 26 and 27, 1904, were a gala event to celebrate completion of the narrow gauge Tonopah Railroad. Engraved invitations were sent out; Miss Belle Pepper (later Mrs. Zeb Kendall) was crowned Queen of the Celebration Days and is shown *(far left)* christening the silver spike while Col. Tripp (to her right) looks on. Decorative floats *(below)* boosted the proposed extension of the railroad to Goldfield and propounded the wealth of the Ridge and Curtis Lease— "30 Tons of Ore $45,000!" At a later date *(bottom, left)* a big parade again lined up east of town. *(Top Left: Mrs. Herbert A. Tripp Collection; Bottom, Left and Right: Mrs. Hugh Brown Collection.)*

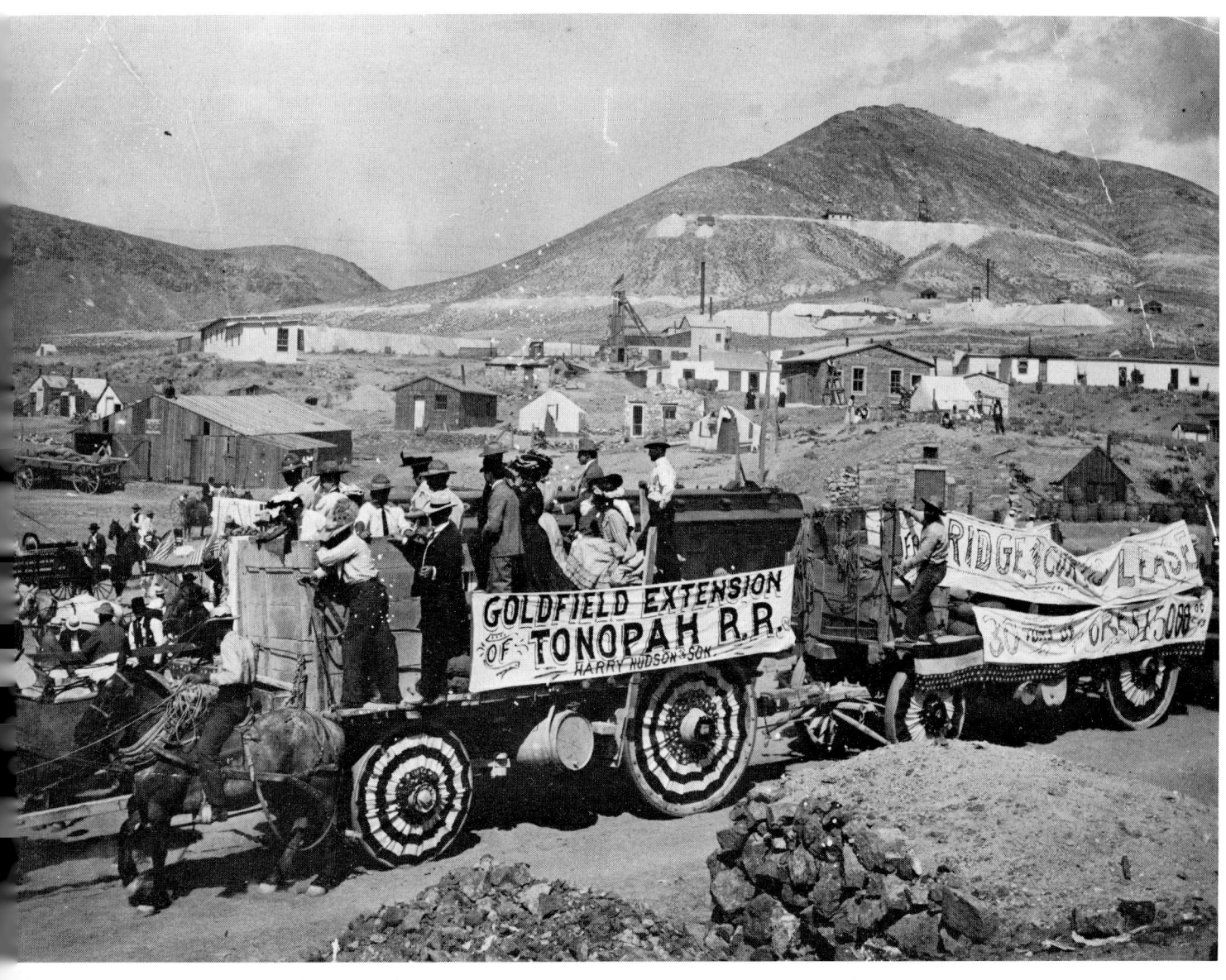

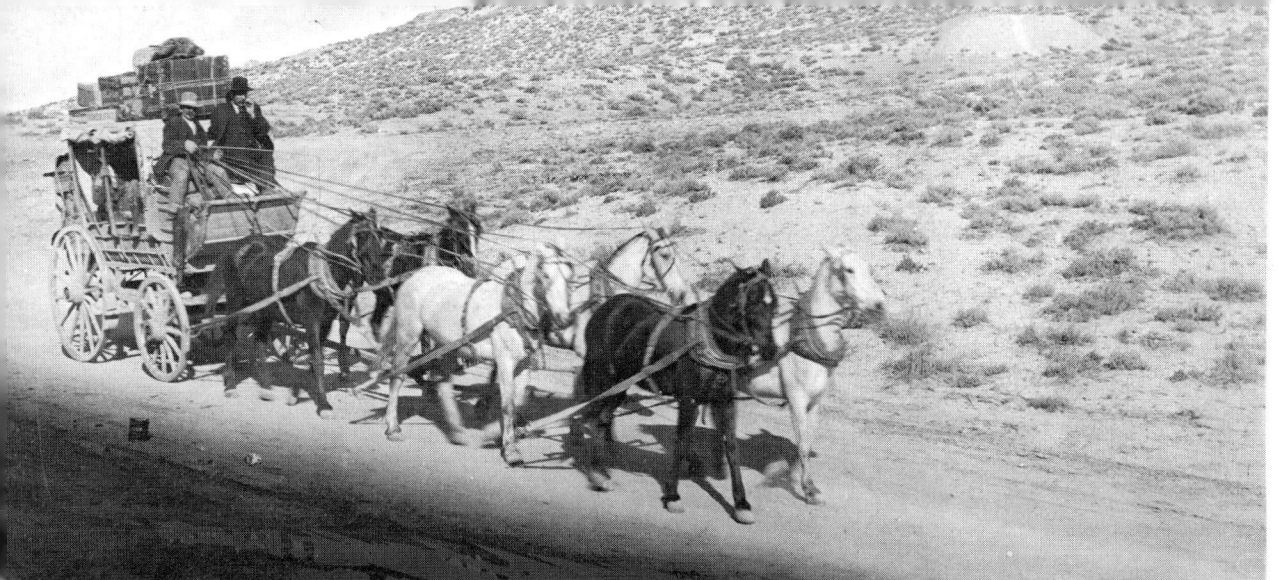

Various areas lay tributary to the Tonopah channels of commerce. Manhattan, to the north, was served by the daily stage coach *(above)* of the Tonopah & Manhattan Stage Line which terminated its run at the Merchant's Hotel *(below)* on Manhattan's muddy Main Street. Early cars as well as pedestrians in February 1907 found the going difficult in the sudden thaws. Several rail lines to Manhattan (including one by the T&G in 1906) were proposed, but none was ever built. *(Top: Lambatucci Collection; Bottom: Mrs. Hugh Brown Collection.)*

When Gilbert, 25 miles west of Tonopah became active in 1924-25, the T&G advanced $500 toward construction of an independent railroad which never materialized. Ore was brought to Tonopah by truck *(top, right)* under armed guard. The town of Gilbert *(center)* was hardly imposing. The large mill *(bottom)* was that of the Desert Power and Mill Co. at Millers on the T&G, which processed the ores of the parent Tonopah Mining Co. *(Top and Center: Mrs. Hugh Brown Collection; Bottom: Fourteenth Annual Report, The Tonopah Mining Company of Nevada.)*

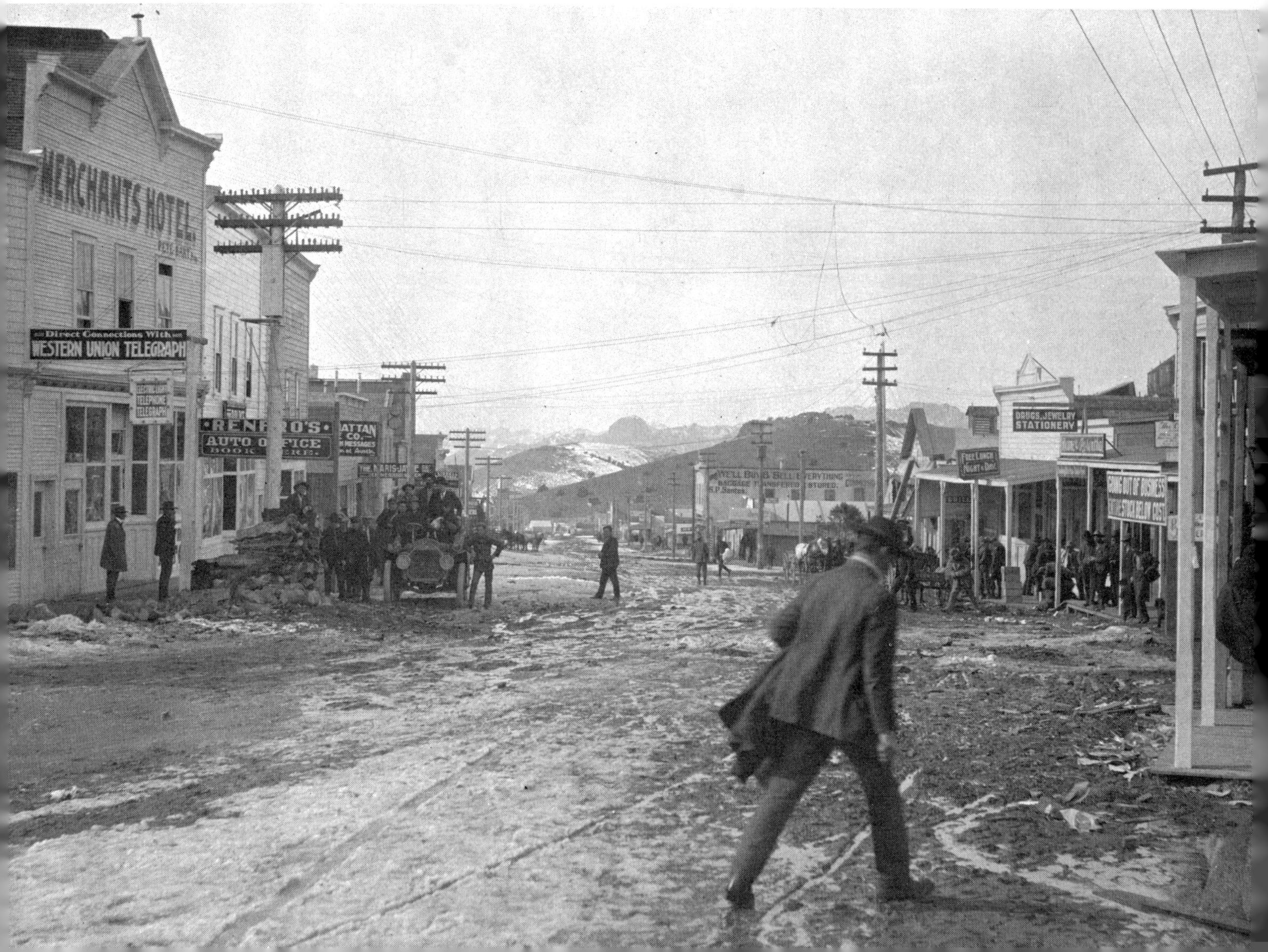

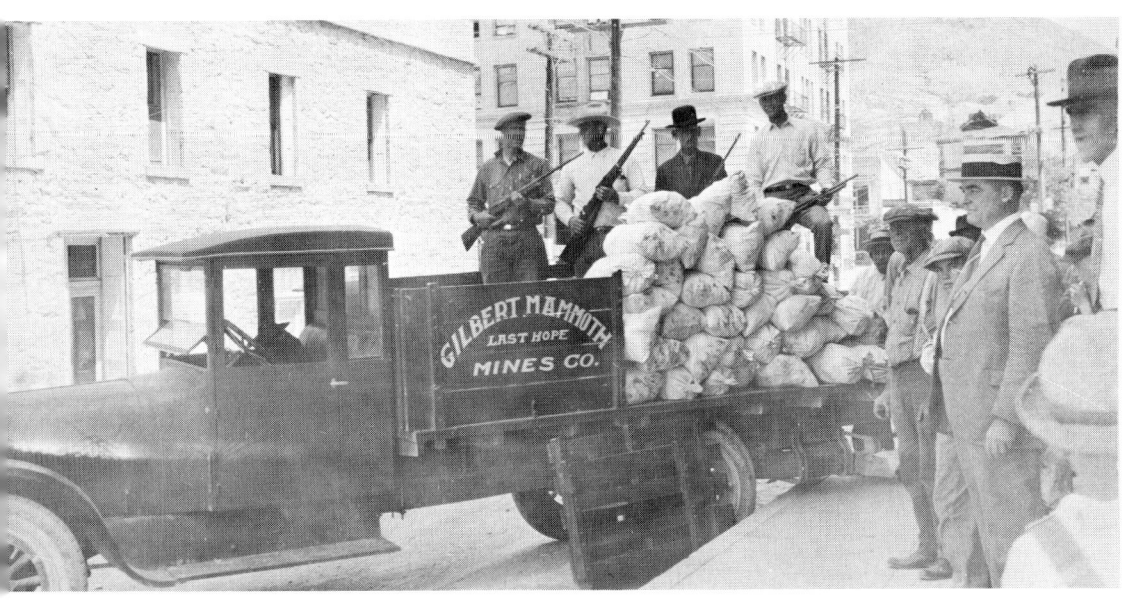
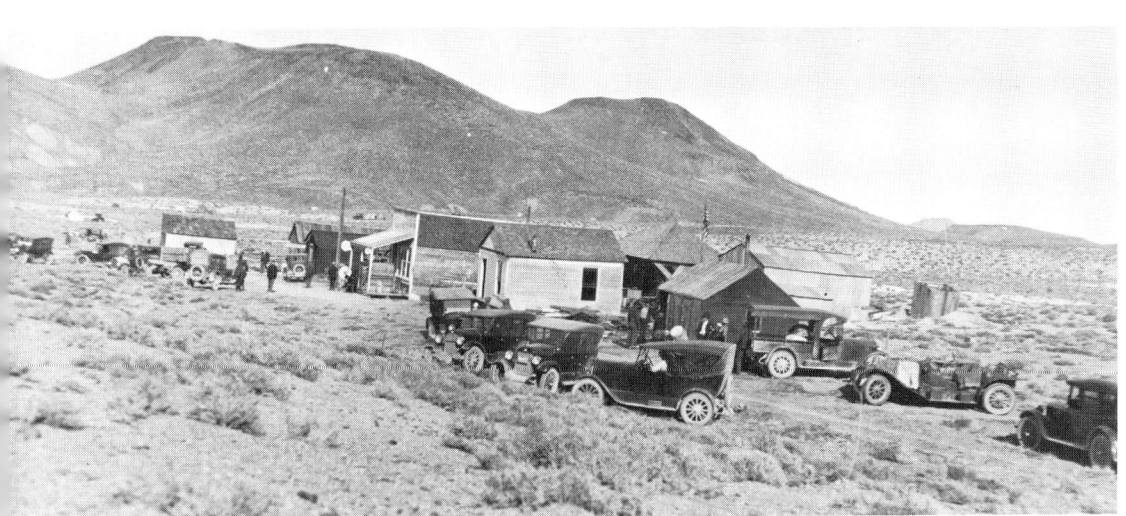

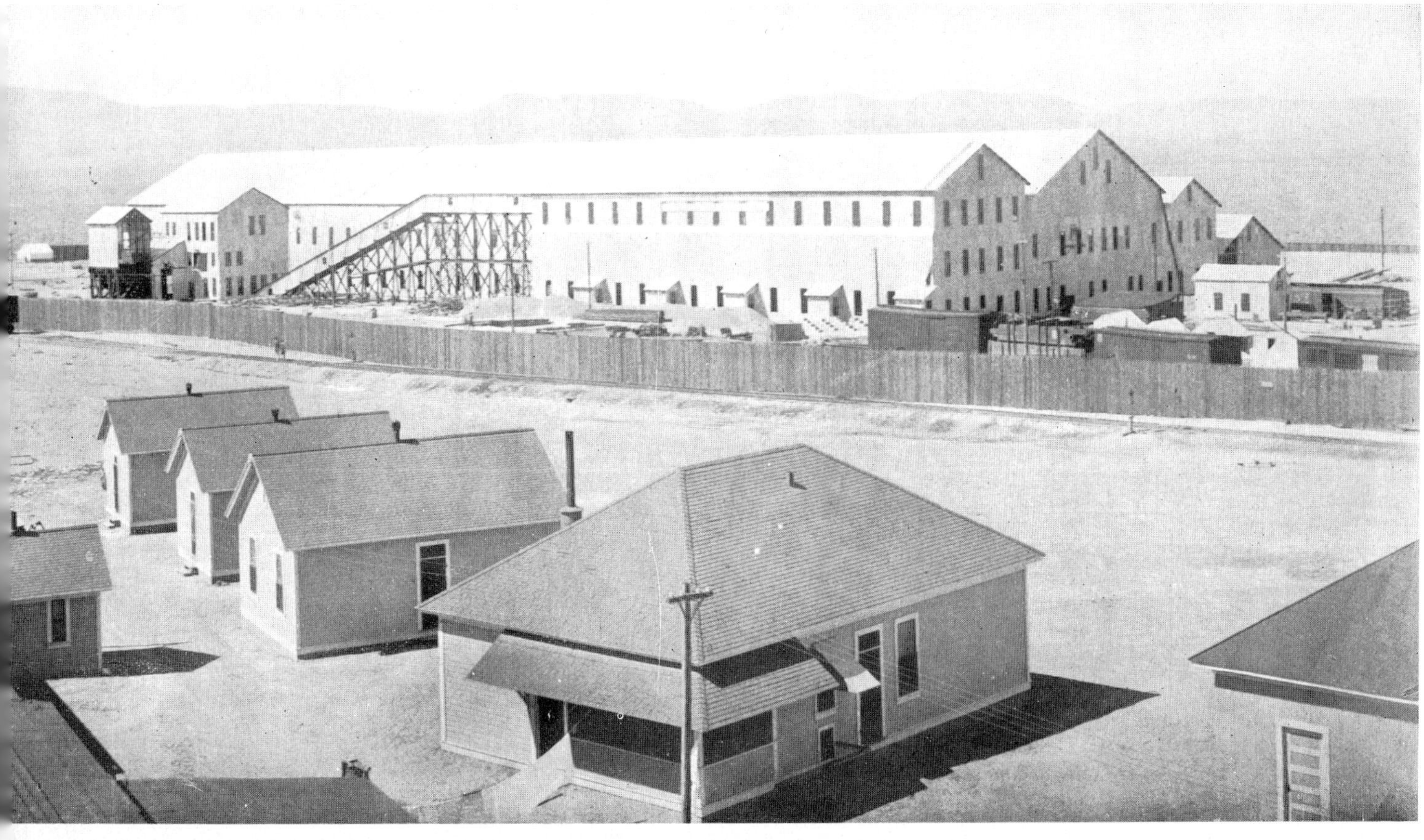

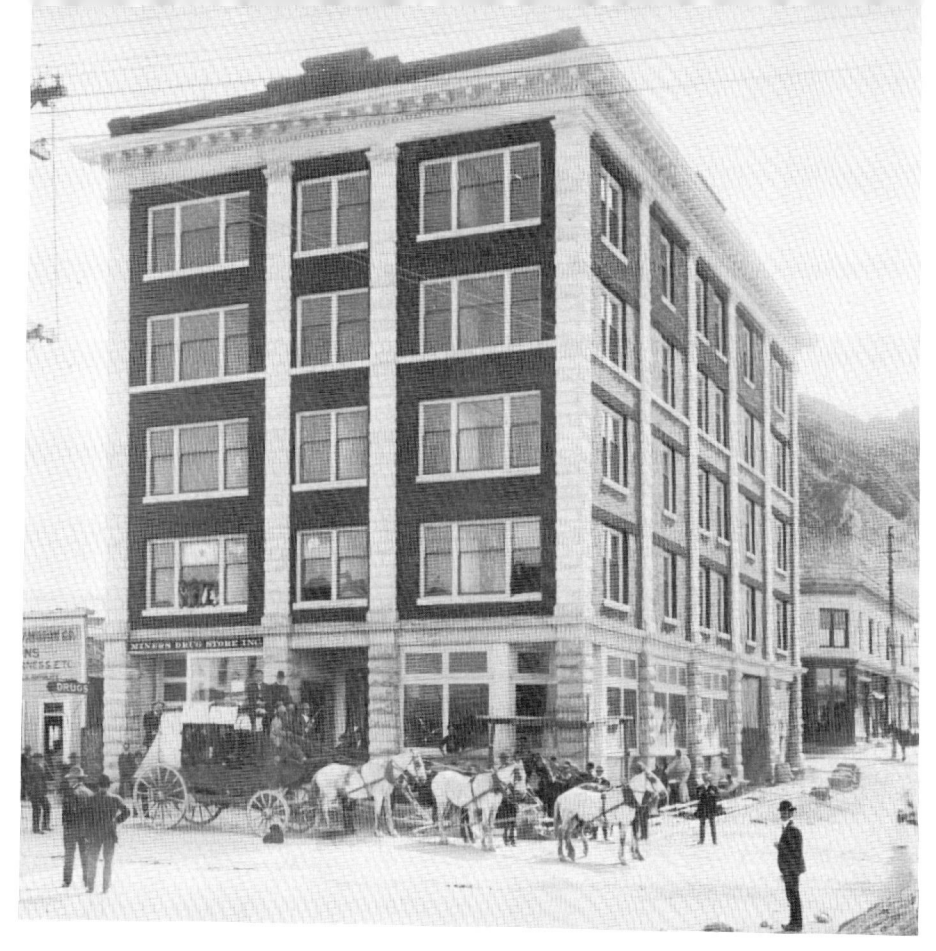

Tonopah grew rapidly. The panorama *(right)* appears to have been taken about 1903 looking northwest from the slopes of Mt. Brougher. Most all buildings are still of frame construction. Headframe of the famous Mizpah shaft is visible near bottom right, a close-up of which appears immediately below. *(Both Photos: U. S. Geological Survey.)*

Landmarks of 1905, following arrival of the railroad, were the stone masonry buildings of T. B. Rickey's State Bank & Trust Co. *(top, left)* with the Goldfield stage coach just ready to leave, and the Mizpah Hotel *(bottom)* which towered above its neighboring Tonopah Banking Corporation building and offered heavy competition to the earlier Merchants Hotel (foreground) of Casey & Arden. *(Both Photos: Mrs. Hugh Brown.)*

When the directors of the Tonopah Belmont Development Co. elected to build this mill *(below, right)* on the east side of Tonopah in 1911-12, the Tonopah & Goldfield Railroad lost the revenues from daily shipments of substantial ore tonnage to the company's older mill at Millers. It was a severe blow to the railroad. *(U. S. Geological Survey.)*

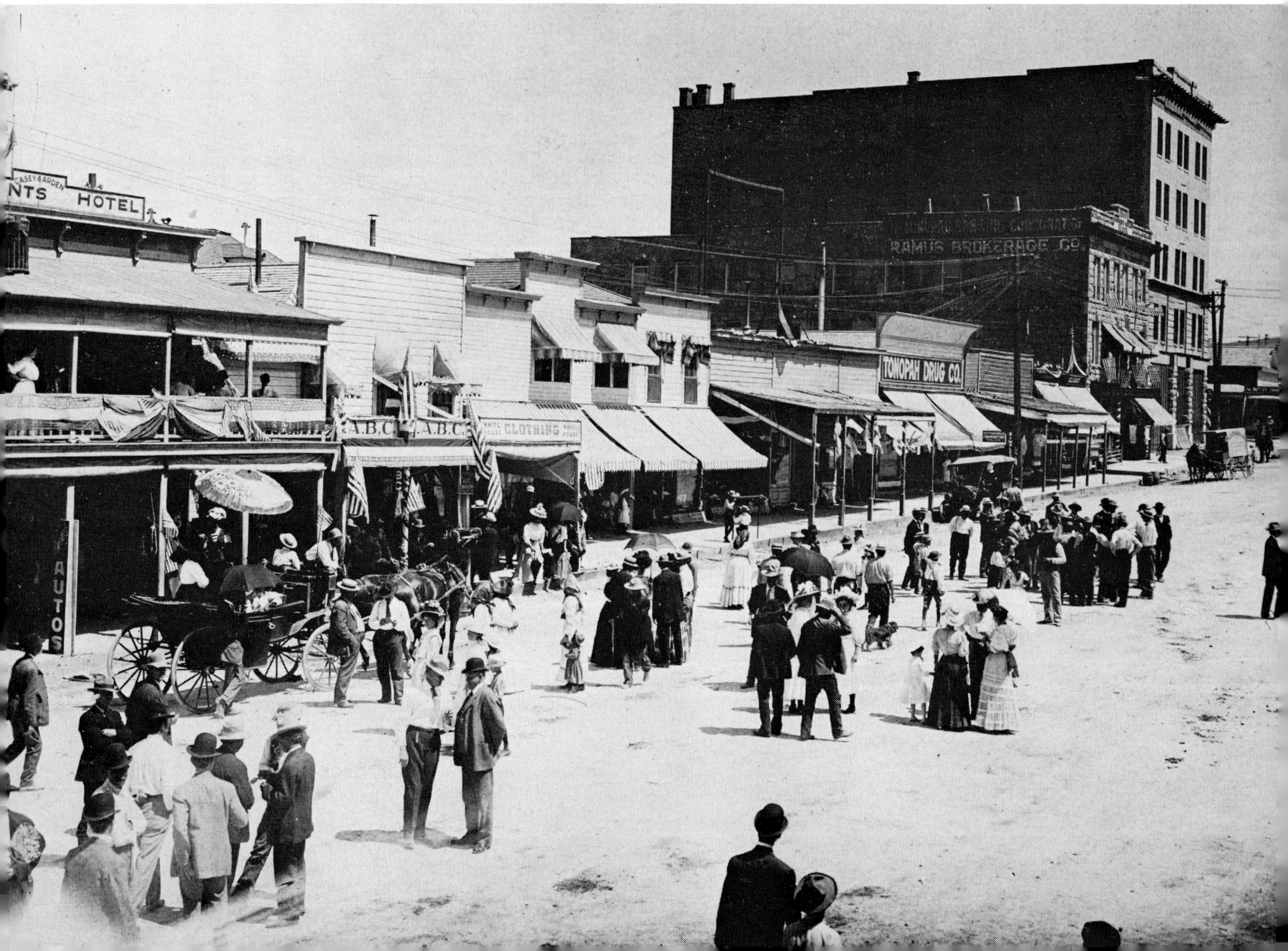

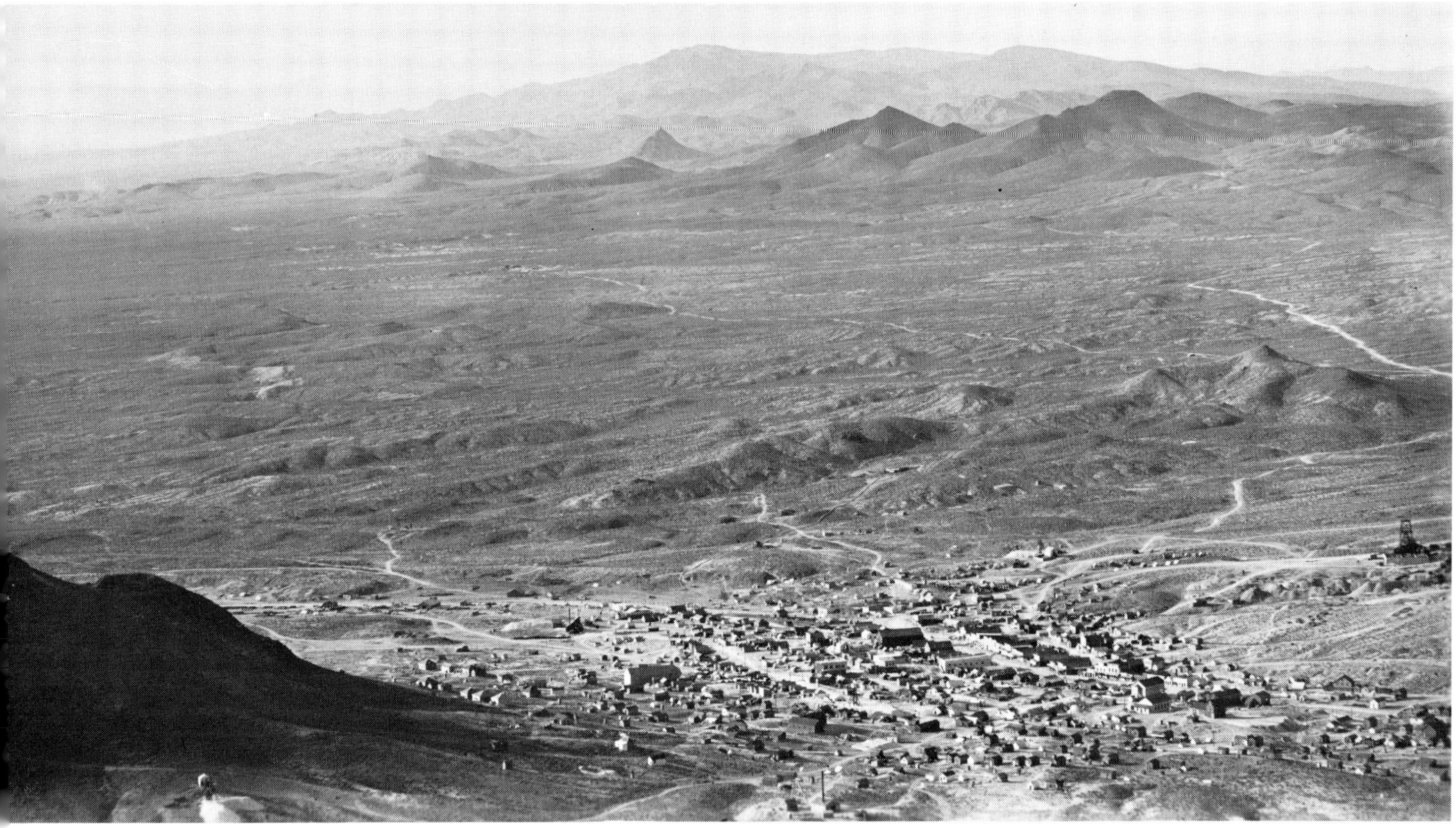

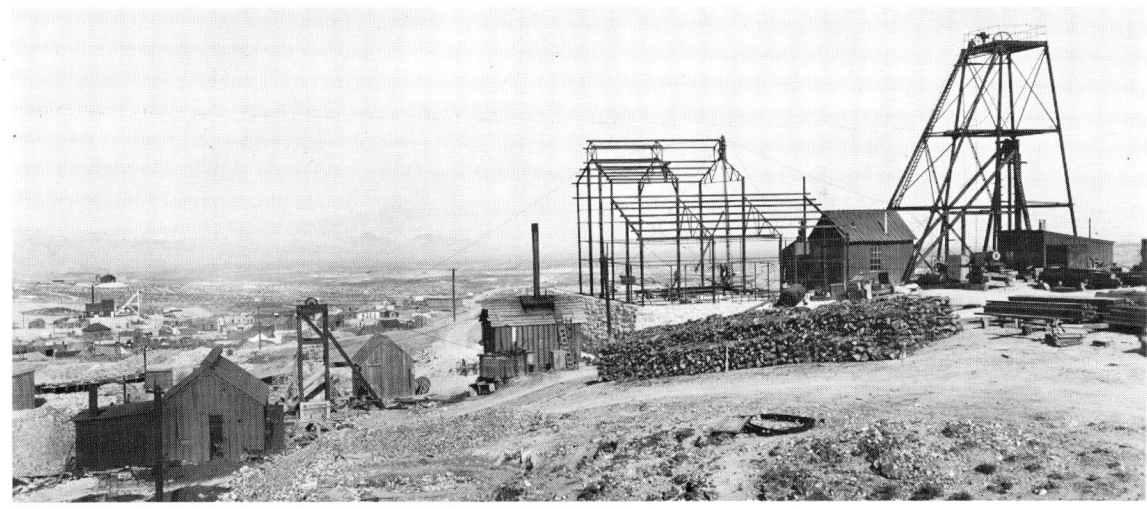
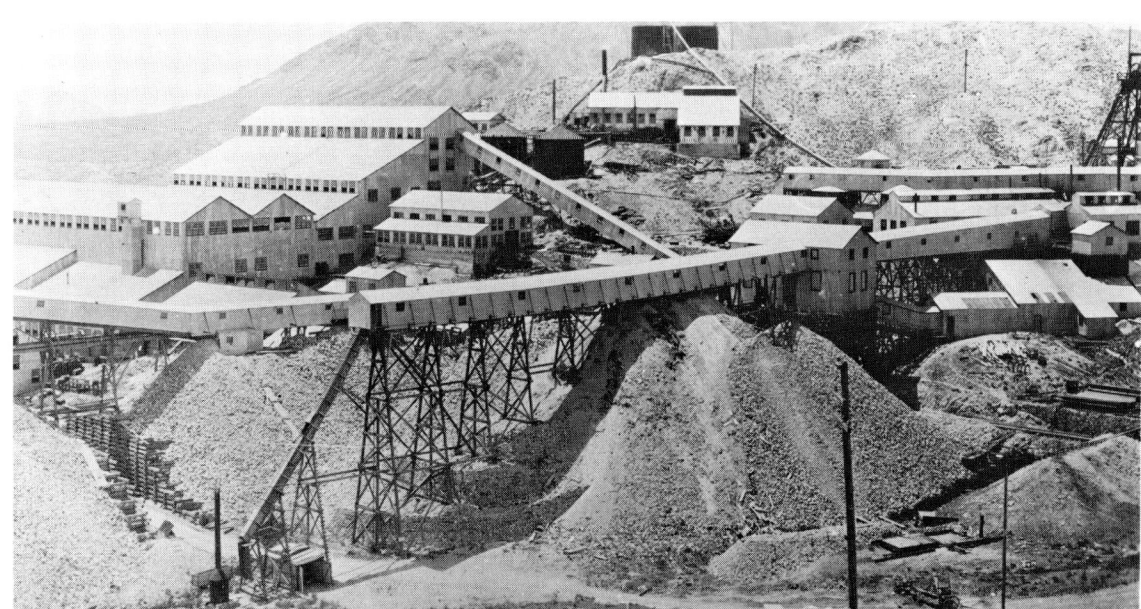

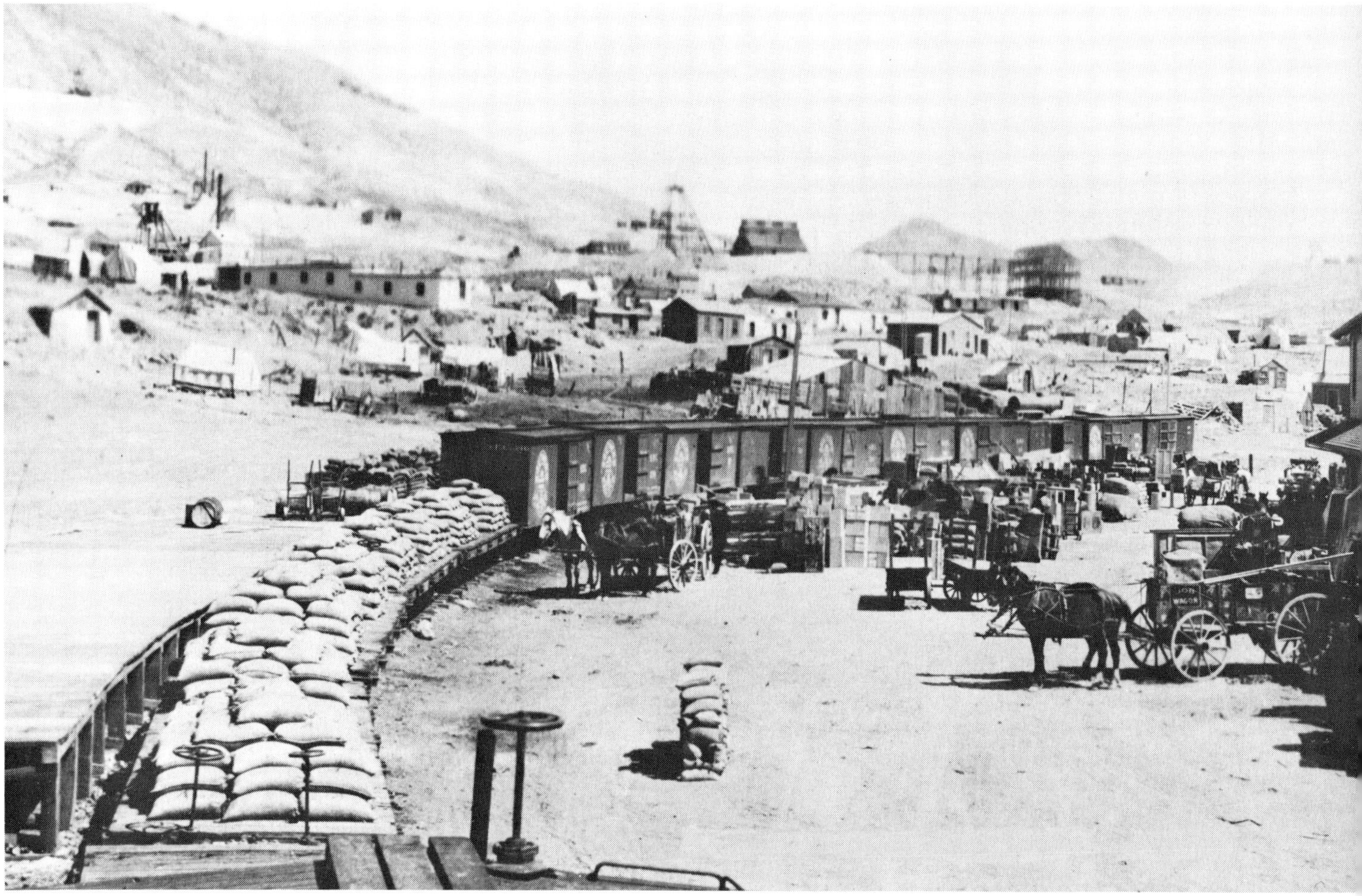

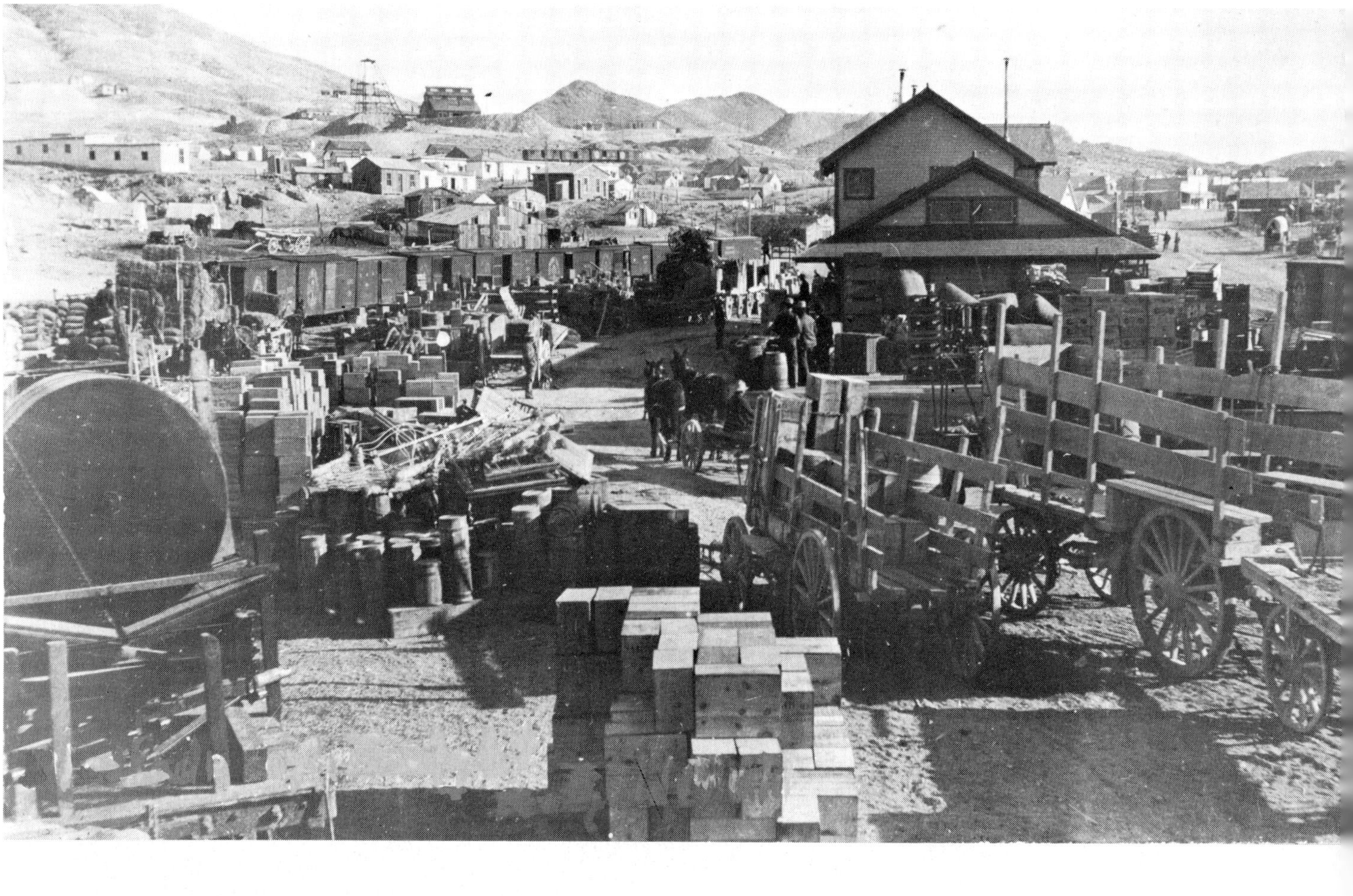

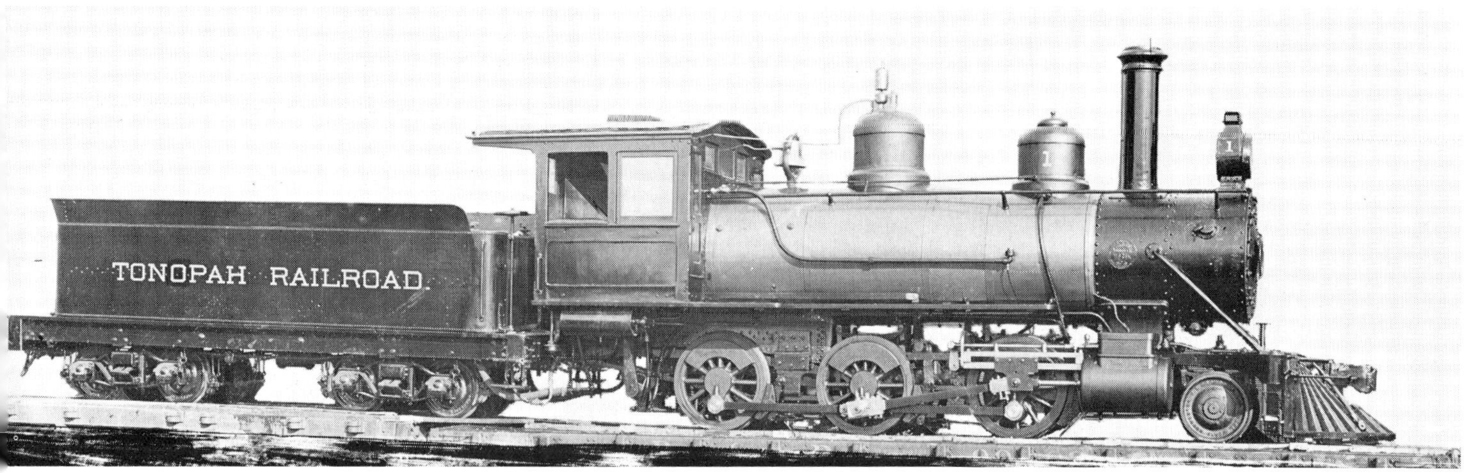

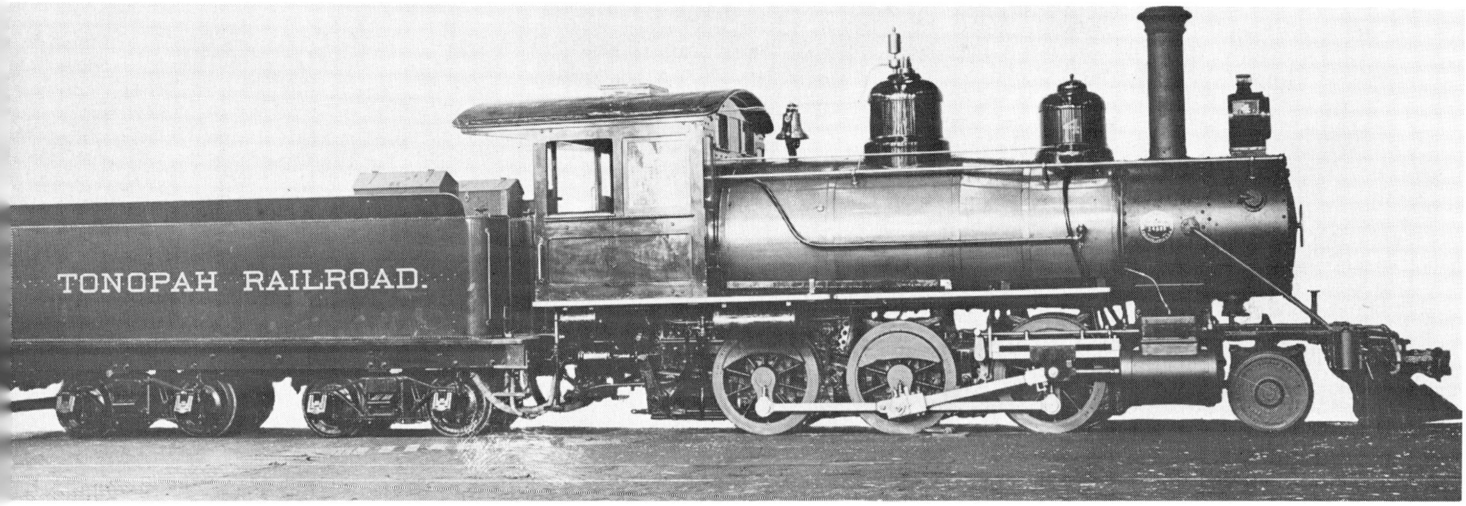

Narrow-gauge days on the Tonopah Railroad (first train July 23, 1904, last train August 14, 1905) boomed from start to finish. Little Moguls (2-6-0) like the No. 1 and No. 4 *(above)* hauled loads of ore and empty box cars *(top, left)* out of town, while inbound chattels *(bottom, left and right)* swamped cars, tracks and platforms alike. Every available 3-foot gauge box car (largely from the SP's South Pacific Coast Railway between Oakland and Santa Cruz, California) was pressed into service, and still the demand could not be met. Miracle of the age was the fact that a sizable proportion of the glut of materiel eventually found its way to the proper owners in spite of rough handling, thefts and vandalism. *(Two Photos Top Right: H. L. Broadbelt Collection; Bottom Right: Mrs. Hugh Brown Collection; Bottom Left, Oro Parker Collection.)*

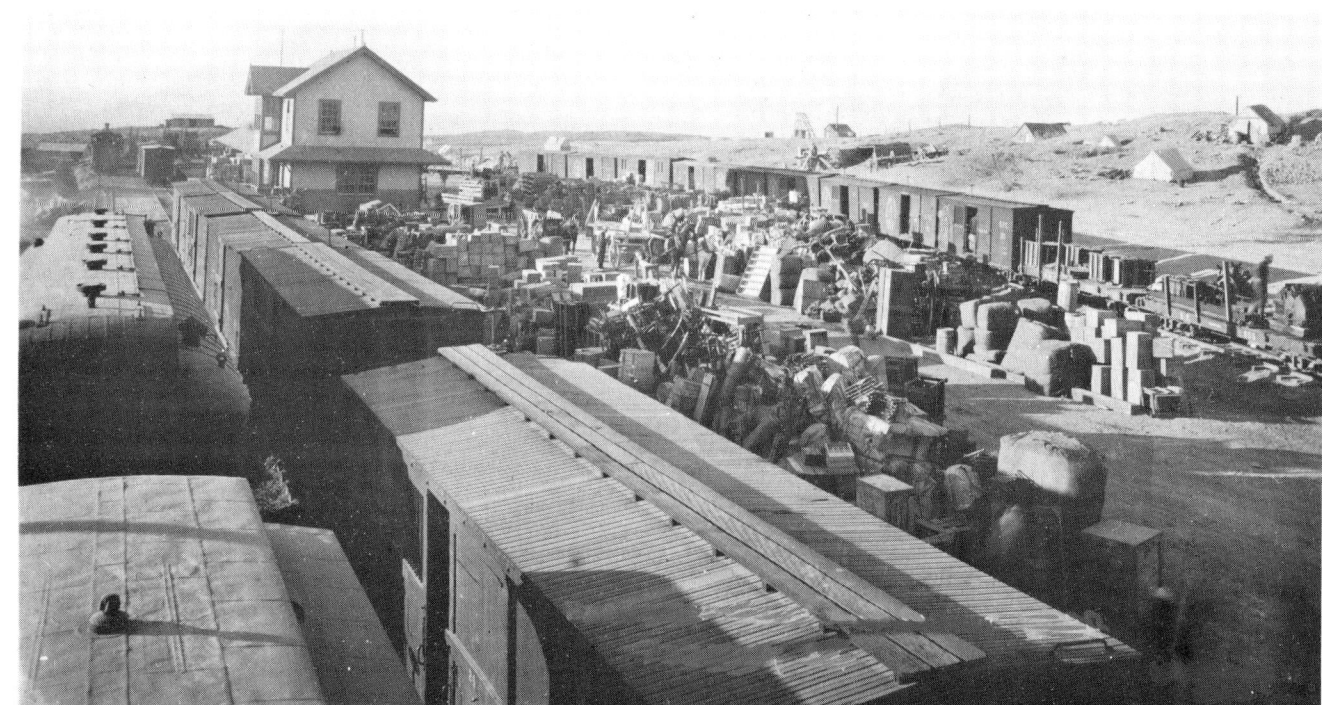

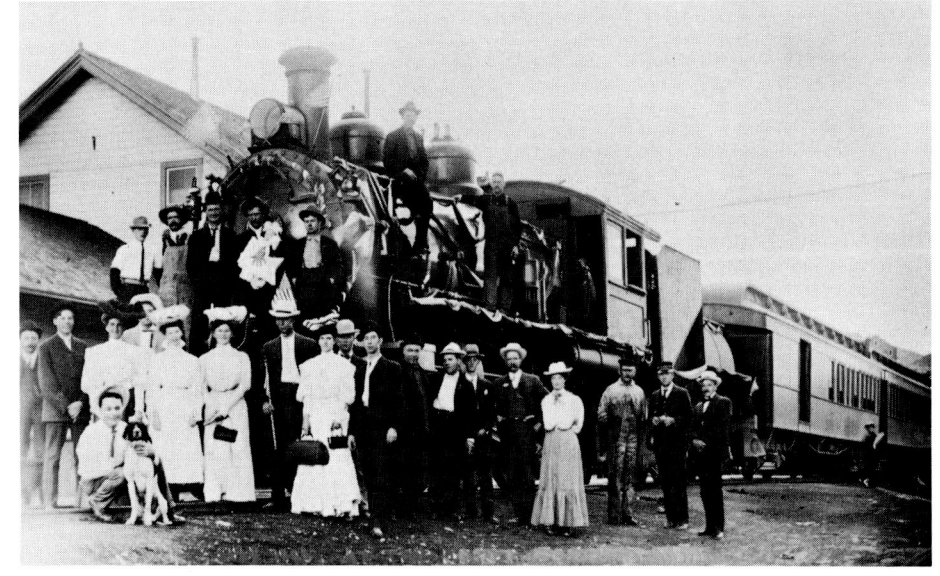

The press of business did not abate for almost two years after the Tonopah Railroad was converted to standard gauge in August 1905. Several times in 1906 embargoes had to be placed on the line until cars could be unloaded and worried back over the single track main around the inbound freight. Elimination of the transshipping blockade at Mound House merely allowed the cars to pile up that much faster. Still the people found time for occasional relaxation, such as the group posed in front of their gaily bedecked engine on July 4, 1906, or the crowds that necessitated lengthy 10-car passenger trains *(left, center)*. Gauge conversion ultimately did help win the battle, and pandemonium subsided as evidenced in the more prosaic scene at Tonopah *(below)* with cars from the west coast Southern Pacific, the central states Chicago & Northwestern and the easterly New York Central. *(Top: Nevada Photo Service; Bottom: Mrs. Hugh Brown Collection.)*

By 1910, when the expansive map and timetable *(right)* appeared in the Railway Guide, the T&G was examining all possible avenues for increased revenues and apparently had quiet and mysterious plans to construct on east from Tonopah to a connection with the Nevada Northern at Ely and the smelter at McGill. No one can be found today with any recollection of the project, and no formal discussions were ever recorded in minutes of the meetings of the Board of Directors. *(Nevada Historical Society.)*

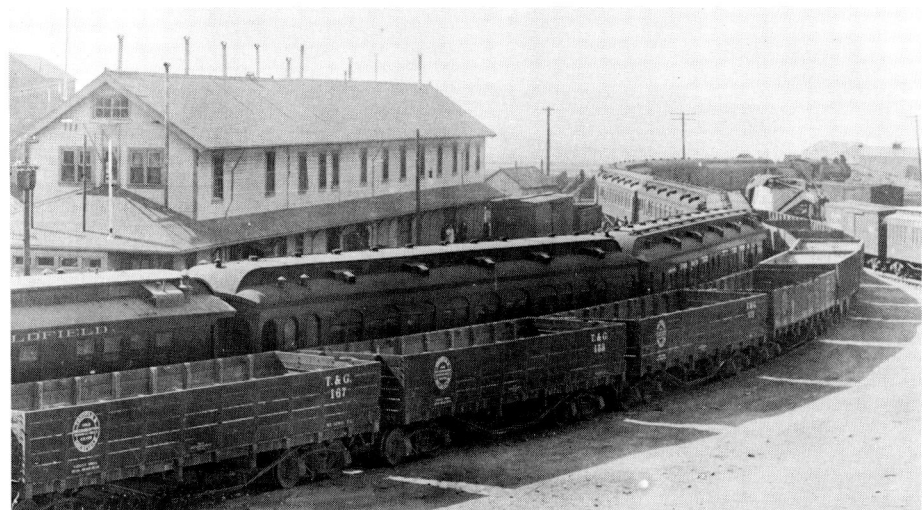

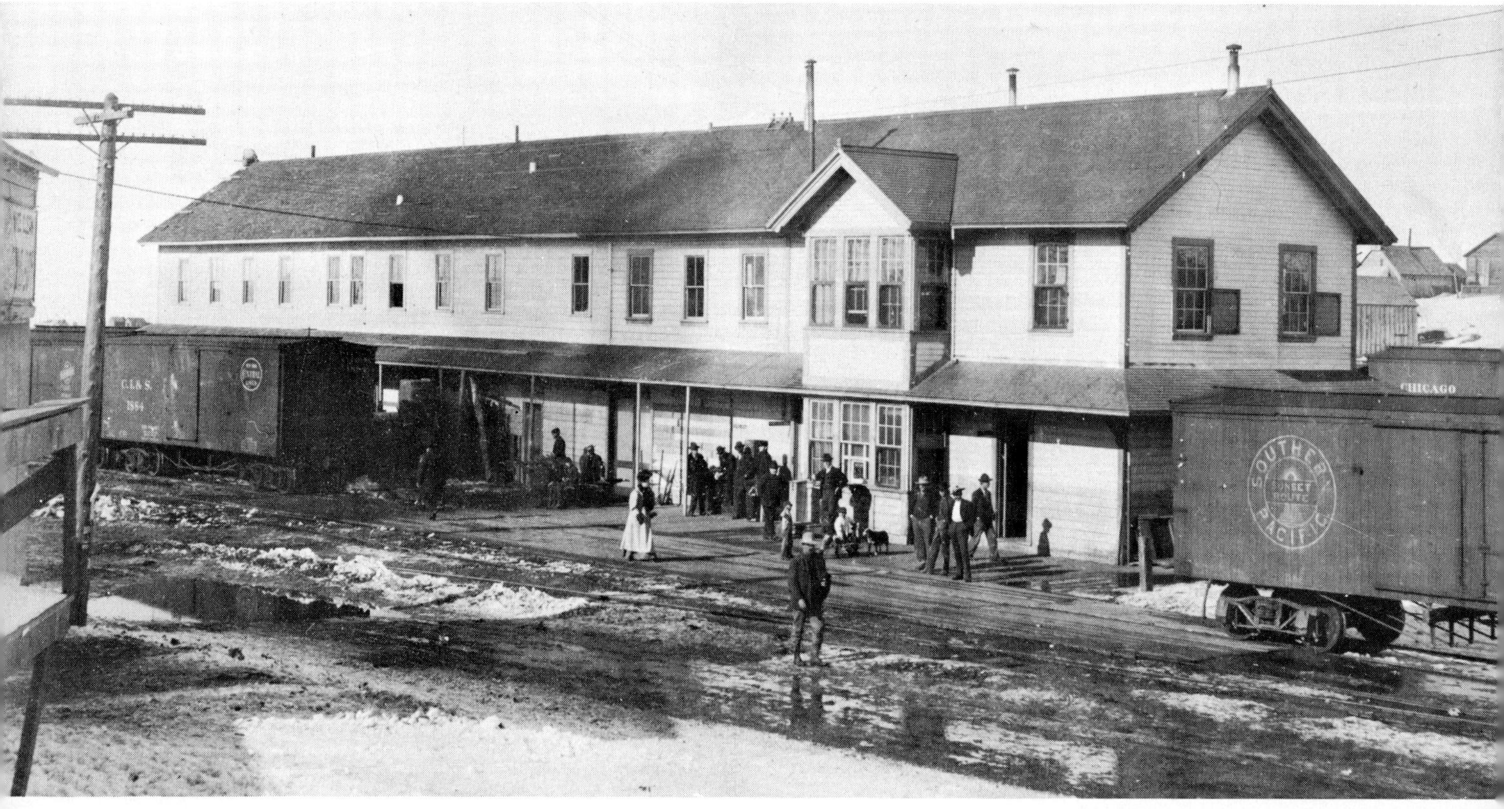

Tonopah & Goldfield Railroad Co.

THOS. M. KING, Chairman of the Board, Philadelphia, Pa.

E. H. RUSHTON, 1st Vice-Prest. and Treasurer, Philadelphia, Pa.
JAMES S. AUSTIN, 2d Vice-President, "
WM. F. HENSHAW, Assistant Secretary, "
H. E. HANLIN, General Superintendent, Tonopah, Nev.
W. D. FORSTER, Traffic Manager, "

A. J. LYON, Auditor, Tonopah, Nev.
W. W. CHARLES, Assistant Treasurer, "
A. B. PHILLIPS, Superintendent of Motive Power, "
F. T. MOORE, Trainmaster, "
F. T. ARMISTEAD, Engineer Maintenance of Way, "
D. A. BROUGHEL, Car Accountant, "

GENERAL AGENTS.

H. R. GRIER, Goldfield, Nev.
J. E. HOGAN, Tonopah, Nev.
MATT. CLARKE, Sheldon Building, 461 Market Street, San Francisco, Cal.

PHILADELPHIA OFFICES—571 BULLITT BUILDING.

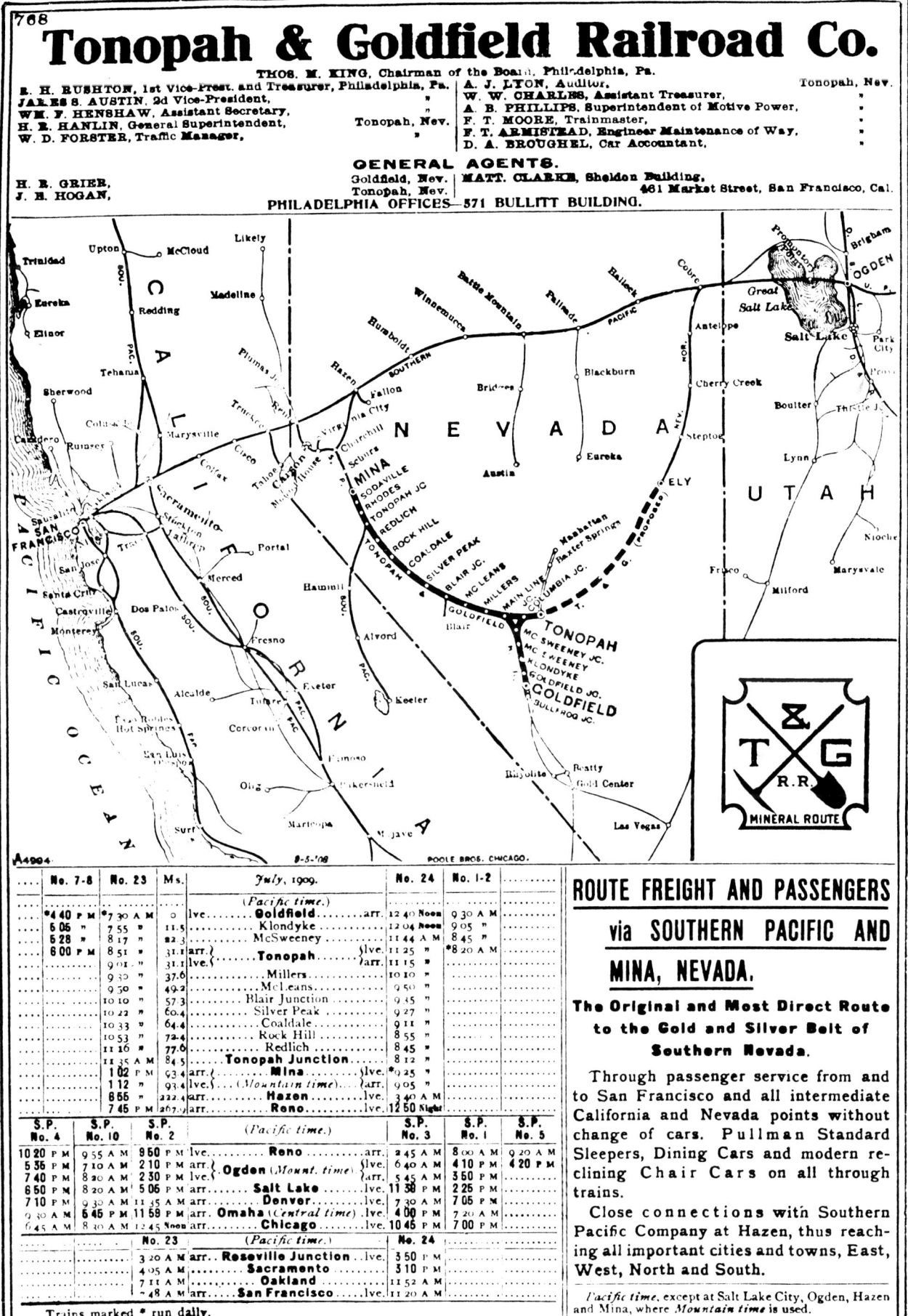

	No. 7-8	No. 23	Ms.	July, 1909.	No. 24	No. 1-2
				(Pacific time.)		
	*4 40 P M	*7 30 A M	0	lve......Goldfield......arr.	12 40 Noon	9 30 A M
	6 05 "	7 55 "	11.5	......Klondyke......	12 04 Noon	9 05 "
	6 28 "	8 17 "	22.3	......McSweeney......	11 44 A M	8 45 "
	6 00 P M	8 51 "	31.1	arr.} Tonopah {lve.	11 25 "	*8 20 A M
		9 01 "	31.1	lve.} {arr.	11 15 "	
		9 30 "	37.6	......Millers......	10 10 "	
		9 50 "	49.2	......McLeans......	9 50 "	
		10 10 "	57.3	......Blair Junction......	9 35 "	
		10 22 "	60.4	......Silver Peak......	9 27 "	
		10 33 "	64.4	......Coaldale......	9 11 "	
		10 53 "	72.4	......Rock Hill......	8 55 "	
		11 16 "	77.6	......Redlich......	8 45 "	
		11 35 A M	84.5	......Tonopah Junction......	8 12 "	
		1 02 P M	93	arr.{ Mina {lve.	*6 25 "	
		1 12 "	93.4	lve.} (Mountain time){arr.	9 05 "	
		8 55 "	222.4	arr......Hazen......lve.	3 40 A M	
		7 45 P M	267.9	arr......Reno......lve.	12 50 Night	

S.P. No. 4	S.P. No. 10	S.P. No. 2	(Pacific time.)	S.P. No. 3	S.P. No. 1	S.P. No. 5
10 20 P M	9 55 A M	8 50 P M	lve......Reno......arr.	2 45 A M	8 00 A M	9 20 A M
5 35 "	7 10 A M	2 10 P M	arr.} Ogden (Mount. time){lve.	6 40 A M	4 10 P M	4 20 P M
7 40 P M	8 20 A M	2 30 P M	lve.} {arr.	5 45 A M	3 50 P M	
6 50 P M	8 20 A M	5 05 P M	arr......Salt Lake......lve.	11 30 P M	2 25 P M	
7 10 P M	9 30 A M	11 45 A M	arr......Denver......lve.	7 30 A M	7 05 P M	
9 30 A M	6 45 P M	11 59 P M	arr......Omaha (Central time)......lve.	4 00 P M	7 20 A M	
6 45 A M	8 30 A M	12 45 Noon	arr......Chicago......lve.	10 45 P M	7 00 A M	

	No. 23		(Pacific time.)	No. 24		
		3 20 A M	arr......Roseville Junction......lve.	3 50 P M		
		4 05 A M	......Sacramento......	3 10 P M		
		7 11 A M	......Oakland......	11 52 P M		
		7 48 A M	arr......San Francisco......lve.	11 20 A M		

Trains marked * run daily.

ROUTE FREIGHT AND PASSENGERS
via SOUTHERN PACIFIC AND
MINA, NEVADA.

The Original and Most Direct Route to the Gold and Silver Belt of Southern Nevada.

Through passenger service from and to San Francisco and all intermediate California and Nevada points without change of cars. Pullman Standard Sleepers, Dining Cars and modern reclining Chair Cars on all through trains.

Close connections with Southern Pacific Company at Hazen, thus reaching all important cities and towns, East, West, North and South.

Pacific time, except at Salt Lake City, Ogden, Hazen and Mina, where *Mountain time* is used.

was peremptorily reinstated. With such complete and obvious devastation staring them in the face the Tonopah Railroad forces determined to abandon Iglehart's routing and to relocate the line as reconstruction proceeded. Still the elements frustratingly thwarted the project. Even as repairs were being accomplished at various locations, cloudbursts were washing out the track in other areas. Between Deep Wells and Goldfield Junction alone, flash floods at 26 different places destroyed the road. With 225 men and 80 horses diligently applied to the project, Alonzo Tripp was still sadly disappointed with the progress. Finally, after 16 days of effort, the first train crept through to Tonopah on September 7 at 3:00 P.M. to the cheers of the milling crowds of residents lining the hills.

Shortly after restoration of service, a new luxury was afforded patrons of the narrow gauge Tonopah Railroad. Sleeping car service was instituted direct from Mound House via the C&C. Although the schedule provided for an ultra-early morning arrival at Tonopah, compensation for the inconvenience of the hour was provided through the exclusive privilege of sleeping aboard the standing car until 7:00 A.M. before debarking, an uncommon pleasure for wayfarers of the times. With some 400 people arriving in town each week and approximately half of that number departing, only a small minority could participate in this latest convenience.

In the latter part of October 1904 the C&C commenced laying standard gauge rails outside of its narrow gauge tracks over that portion of the line from Mound House to Mina, Sodaville and Tonopah Junction. At the same time, the Tonopah Railroad made plans for conversion of its line and placed orders for ties and eight new locomotives from Baldwin. Freight for transfer from standard to narrow gauge cars had backed up at Mound House to such an extent that four months were required to work off the congestion. By March 1905 the C&C's standard gauge rails reached southward from Wabuska, and the Tonopah Railroad was taking delivery of the new, long ties for the conversion of its line. In May the Tonopah started 200 men on the task of inserting the standard gauge ties in the roadbed preparatory to the changeover. By the end of July the C&C's standard gauge rails reached all the way to Sodaville, and the Tonopah prepared for its big conversion.

On Wednesday, August 10, the last narrow gauge freight train arrived in Tonopah, and it was announced that the last narrow gauge passenger train would leave Tonopah for Sodaville at 1:00 A.M. on Sunday morning, August 14, 1905. In spite of the early hour, the last train was crowded to capacity with some 300 workmen for the big conversion, groups of men being dropped off at 1½-mile intervals. The big shift began promptly at 6:00 A.M., and by 8:00 P.M. the job was completed. Promptly at 2:30 A.M. on Monday morning the first regular standard gauge passenger train pulled into the Tonopah depot, and a new era had begun for the little line.

This also was the period of the C&C's problems over land and water rights at Soda Springs. With traffic booming and expansion of facilities most urgent, a land speculator had grabbed and was holding the desirable properties under option, demanding an exorbitant price for their release. Rather than accede to the avidity of this modern Scrooge, the C&C moved its entire yard and terminal facilities a few miles farther north where abundant water was located, and the town of Mina was born. As an accommodation the Tonopah Railroad's trackage rights, which formerly extended four miles from Tonopah Junction to Soda Springs, were extended to include operation over the entire nine miles from the Junction to Mina, increasing the railroad's ton-miles of freight proportionately.

II – THE GOLDFIELD RAILROAD

Immediately following the initial excitement at Tonopah, mining men and others began to spread out into the surrounding hills in search of overlooked or possible new ore discoveries. Results were not long in forthcoming. Late in 1902 "float gold" was discovered by Harry Stimler and William Marsh on Columbia Mountain some 25 miles to the south of Tonopah, and on December 2 the Sandstorm Lode was located at a site called Grandpa on the west side of the same mountain. A short-lived rush to the new location ensued, to be followed by the usual disappointment and return of the prospectors and miners.

The following year newspapers picked up the story of the discovery of the Combination Lode by Al Myers and Bob Hart in the same general area, and by the end of 1903 the Tonopah papers were singing the praises of the new bonanza of Goldfield. The population of the embryo location jumped to the thousands by the forepart of 1904, and on April 29 of that year the *Goldfield News* appeared in print with the confident, first-issue slogan: "All That's New and True in the Greatest Gold Camp

Ever Known." Editor James O'Brien filled his paper with glowing accounts of activity designed primarily to attract readers from without the area. Specious reasoning was a commonplace, as when he was pleased to report that John Brock (president of the Tonopah Railroad) had written to a friend that the railroad would be extended to Goldfield after it had reached Tonopah. "Not bad for a seven months' old camp," he crowed. The effect was not lost, however; one optimistic broker wagered a new suit that trains would be running to town by the end of the year. Additional headlines were made when the first auto arrived at the new camp, covering the approximately 30 miles from Tonopah in an elapsed time of just under three hours, including many anxious moments incurred when the driver became lost on the desert.

Some consideration was being given to the question of a railroad to Goldfield. Preliminary surveys were run during the summer of 1904, and the matter was formally presented to the Board of Directors of the Tonopah Mining Company (principal owner of the Tonopah Railroad) on December 29, 1904. It was the considered opinion of the Board that the Tonopah Mining Company had no interests in the Goldfield area and therefore should not invest their stockholders' money in any railroad project to reach it, either directly out of the mining company's funds or indirectly from funds of the Tonopah Railroad Company. Of more immediate necessity was the retirement of an issue of mining company preferred stock, a requirement before the declaration of any dividends on the common stock of the company. The restriction was satisfied by payment of the remaining $299,300, permitting complete recall of the issue.

The official position of the board in no way detracted from the interest and enthusiasm of its members as individuals or of the company's stockholders. As a matter of record, 11 of them had joined with nine other men the previous October 7, 1904, to form what was termed the Goldfield Syndicate. Each man of the group had pledged $25,000 to a pool of funds, and a new corporation had been organized called the Goldfield Railroad Company. When the Tonopah Mining Company declined to build the connecting line of railroad, the Syndicate arranged to go ahead on its own. To avoid right-of-way troubles, several routes were surveyed with particular emphasis on one through Diamondfield (immediately to the north and east of Goldfield) which would be most likely to ward off speculators and troublemakers from the selected line.

In spite of precautions, difficulties arose. It had been intended to locate the Goldfield Railroad terminal close to the center of town. However, an unctuous land grabber named Phenix, whose wife had recently attained distinction by attempting to kill an imposing squatter, refused to cooperate in the venture. Placations being unavailing, it was reported that one night in some mysterious manner the Phenix residence went sailing into the air assisted by a box of giant powder and that subsequently Mr. Phenix moved to a town in California "where times are not quite so strenuous."

Bids for the grading of the new railroad were turned in on February 11, 1905, at the Pacific Construction Company's office in Tonopah. No particular problems were encountered for the route; the ground from Goldfield Junction to Goldfield was on a gentle slope most of the way. Facility of travel over the proposed area was amply demonstrated one Monday morning when employees of the Goldfield Bank and Trust Company opened the doors to find that the organization's officers, wearying of mundane banking practices, had unexpectedly departed over the weekend with $78,000 of the bank's cash resources, leaving a thoughtful $21.05 with which to commence the new business day.

By the middle of March three miles of roadbed had been graded. On July 24, 1905, grading had been completed and rail laying commenced at Goldfield Junction (later Main Line Junction) to the same standard gauge to which both the C&C and Tonopah railroads were preparing to convert. Anticipation ran high in August with the erection of the Goldfield station alongside a right of way devoid of rails, and plans were set in motion for a gala Goldfield Railroad Day. As a feature of the occasion, scheduled first-day shipments contemplated two solid trainloads of ore, each worth $100,000, a prospect undoubtedly contributing to the report circulated as far east as Denver that the Goldfield Railroad used gold and silver for ballast — assays running as high as $18 a ton in the 30 miles of ballasted track.

At 12:43 A.M. on September 12, 1905, the first passenger train pulled into Goldfield station over the new standard gauge railroad. Over 300 people cheered the five-car special on its arrival direct from the Oakland Mole, California, via the Hazen Cut-Off at top speed all the way. P. D. Pyne handled the throttle of Engine No. 1; A. A. Peterson stoked the coal; while Sam Parker collected the tickets from the 50 passengers in the four coaches plus the Pullman *Zerbino.* "We had a great trip," Parker enthused, "free from mishaps of any kind, and although we did not break Scotty's record, we were sure going some."

Two days later the "last spike" ceremony was held. Heading the celebration was Milton Detch, a Goldfield attorney who had worked hard to secure the right of way for the new line. The spike was fashioned from gold ore donated by the Red Top Mining Company, a feature of publicity which might have been a factor in the abnormal rise in value of Red Top stock to four times its price at year opening. Alonzo Tripp spoke in reference to the silver spike ceremony of the Tonopah Railroad the year previous and his hope, expressed at the time, of driving the last spike in Goldfield; now, by golly, here he was!

Goldfield's celebration of Railroad Days included a parade down Crook Street to the depot, led by Queen Charlotte Putnam. Fraternal organizations joined in the march as did the Goldfield News Boys Union, No. 555, and the Goldfield Fire Department proudly escorting its new chemical engine. Of the 2,000 visitors on hand for the two days of fun, the children particularly enjoyed the carnival spirit; many wore masks and blew tin horns. Gambling was virtually forgotten, and street fakers were notably absent, although "Bosco, the man who eats 'em alive" was ready to devour rattlesnakes for a small fee. Open house prevailed at the Montezuma Club, and the governor was on hand to lend authority and prestige to all important gatherings.

Through the medium of a subsidiary company, the Tonopah Railroad attempted the operation of a line of auto stages from Tonopah to Goldfield. According to the *Virginia Chronicle,* the trial trips were decidedly not indicative of successful operation. One vehicle became engaged in an unsuccessful altercation with a locomotive, while the other succeeded in splitting its gear case wide open and spewing the contents over the ground. When the astonished chauffeur failed to close the steam valve in the ensuing excitement, 10 passengers hit the desert floor in a climactic cloud of dust, to be followed in anticlimactic fashion by the filing of several liability suits.

No sooner had the railroad been completed to Goldfield than shippers began expressing dissatisfaction with the rail rates of both the Tonopah and the Goldfield Railroads. Although far less than those formerly charged by the teamsters, they were still viewed as extortionate. Businessmen in Tonopah petitioned the Sierra Railway to build over the mountains from California. Considerable interest was expressed in J. G. Phelps Stokes' revived plan to extend the Nevada Central Railroad from Austin to Tonopah. The boss of the January mine in Goldfield flatly stated he would not ship any ore until the rates were reduced, contending it cost $7.00 a ton for the haul to Mina, $10.00 more to forward it to the smelter where a $1.00 sampling fee and a $10.00 smelter charge were imposed. The problem had already received cognizance at the time of his statement, and the rates were readjusted.

III — THE TONOPAH & GOLDFIELD RAILROAD

The subterfuge of the Goldfield Syndicate in organizing and constructing the Goldfield Railroad was quickly outmoded. In February 1905 the Tonopah Mining Company had accomplished retirement of its vexatious issue of preferred stock which freed both it and the subsidiary Tonopah Railroad for reasonable expansion. Backers of the Syndicate and of the Mining Company were largely the same individuals; Alonzo Tripp and other key personnel were directing the affairs of both railroads; and as construction of the Goldfield Railroad progressed, it became increasingly evident that two short-line railroads (one of 60 miles and one of 30 miles) serving the same interests were impracticable. Development of the Goldfield area was strengthening as the mines began to prove themselves, and merger of the two railroads was a natural eventuation.

Discord was rife as to the *means* to the end. The Tonopah Railroad had had the benefit of a year of operating experience and demanded the larger slice. A frequent story still circulates that the line paid for itself in its first year of operation to Tonopah, apparently based upon Tripp's answer (to a direct question) that the line only cost about $550,000. This cannot be wholly confirmed. At October 31, 1905, the total investment on the books was $1,476,399; it is claimed that the cost of standard gauging the line (alone) amounted to approximately $600,000. As a matter of record, the net income from the first 15 months of operations amounted to a neat $611,481.

William J. Turner and Louis Teller, minority stockholders in the Tonopah Mining Co., contended that the terms of the proposed merger were highly unfair. Teller protested that the cost of the Goldfield Railroad of $505,000 was exorbitant in the extreme and that the members of the Goldfield Syndicate (John Brock et al.) had enjoyed superior personal profits from the construction venture. The contention was vigorously denied, though apparently without conviction. A plan to lease both railroads to a new company to be formed in New Jersey failed of accomplishment when counsel advised that this would conflict with Nevada statutes. Teller then challenged the merger in the U.S. Circuit Court in Philadelphia in October 1905, adding to the foregoing a further contention that the Goldfield Railroad was a new line with unproved earning power and therefore was not entitled to one-fourth of the new issue of T&G stock.

In spite of the action, the merger became effective November 1, 1905, and the Tonopah & Goldfield Railroad was created. An agreement ultimately was reached on the adjustment of the distribution of stocks and bonds involving the Tonopah Mining Co., and Teller withdrew his bill of complaint on March 16, 1906. A T&G bond sale, which had been postponed, was resumed and completed.

Plans were instituted in December 1905 to construct a line from Old Junction (on the main line, a mile north of Goldfield) southeastward toward Milltown and the Jumbo and Florence mines near the Combination Mill in the central part of the mining area. Three months later construction was started on the T&G spur, with the intention to continue it on to Milltown to the east. However, when the graders reached the Combination claim they were ordered off the grounds. The Red Top and the Florence mines likewise flatly refused permission to cross. The impasse arose from the fact that the railroad had secured its permission from the leasers of the properties and not the owners, and until the matter could be resolved, construction on the route was halted at the smelter of the Columbia Sampling and Ore Company. Rumors concerning the situation spread rapidly, including one that the mine owners were retaliating against the high freight rates.

Another extension, considerably longer, was considered by the T&G. In February 1906 surveys were made for a 50-mile branch northerly to Manhattan; but no action was ever taken as a result of the surveys, and no construction was ever accomplished. A connecting feeder line was built, however. In July 1906 grading started on the independent 17½-mile Silver Peak Railroad and trains were running by October 16 of the same year.

From the very beginning, business boomed on the Tonopah & Goldfield Railroad. The demand for lumber supplies and luxuries completely overtaxed the line's ability and capacity to handle the volume of freight required of it. Several times it was necessary to invoke embargoes in attempts to alleviate the situation. In December 1906 the SP's Salt Lake Division reportedly held some 1,105 cars on sidings destined for the boom area, while the yards and sidings at Tonopah and Goldfield were jammed with cars waiting to be unloaded. A stiff $10 a day demurrage charge proved not to be the answer for many of the merchants lacked the cash to pay the freight bills, a vital prerequisite before unloading. Even when unloading was accomplished, merchandise was subject to the most rapacious thievery. Freight on the station platform had a way of disappearing so fast it was essential to have a minimum of three watchmen on every shift, and in spite of these precautions a large mining A-frame disappeared into thin air from in front of the Tonopah station.

For these and other reasons the T&G found it necessary to replace Superintendent Alonzo Tripp, the man who had worked so hard to build and to restore the line after its first bouts with desert cloudbursts. Money had been pouring out of the coffers in various ways. Payrolls were padded with the names of dead men; checks were sent out to the section gangs to be endorsed with an "X" or a signature and then cashed by the foreman at the nearest saloon; seven masked men held up two watchmen at the Goldfield freight station one midnight and threw them, together with the telegraph operator, into a box car while they dynamited the office safe and walked away with an undetermined amount of valuables. John F. Hedden, former superintendent of the Central New England Railway, succeeded to the joint position of superintendent of the T&G and BG Railroads, but even his tenure in office lasted less than two years.

Nevertheless, the T&G made money. In the first year of the merged company's existence (ended November 1, 1906), a net income of $377,000 was reported and a 7% dividend was declared in celebration. The narrow gauge locomotives had been sold, and the 50-pound rail in the Tonopah's main line (left over from narrow gauge days) had been replaced with more substantial 65-pound rail.

Goldfield boomed, too. In the one month ending November 7, 1906, the combined market values of a dozen-odd Goldfield mining stocks advanced a staggering $30,000,000. Stockholders were jubilant. So too were the robbers who successfully doped the coffee of the guards at the Frances-Mohawk mine and helped themselves to some $20,000 in high grade ore.

The big event of 1906 was the Gans-Nelson prize fight which Tex Rickard, owner of the Northern Saloon and promoter *extraordinaire,* had staged to put Goldfield on the map. Thousands of people swarmed into town on special trains to witness the fisticuffs and see Gans be declared the winner of the 42-round bout held in the ball park immediately to the east of the site of the future LV&T depot.

Another big event, unplanned and unpromoted, occurred on November 17, 1906, when the second Goldfield Hotel burned spectacularly at a loss of $100,000. Unfortunately, the master of ceremonies, Fire Chief Claude Inman, was en route out of town by train to San Francisco when the conflagration commenced. On seeing the fire from afar, Inman asked the conductor to have the train return but the request was denied as the U. S. mails were being carried. Although Inman returned on the next train back from Tonopah, he was too late to be of service. A new and larger hotel was erected on the site which still stands today as an empty and forlorn monument to previous glory.

Shortages were severe in the oasis that was Goldfield. Corner properties were at a premium. Shortly after the fire, the northwest corner lot (100' x 30') at Columbia Street and Ramsey Avenue sold for $15,000, while the southeast corner lot (100' x 90') at Columbia Street and Crook Avenue commanded the same price.

The scarcity of wood for fuel was particularly severe as the winter months approached. Telephone poles developed a surprising way of vanishing suddenly; 18 of them disappeared in one night in the tenderloin district to become firewood. Trains were annulled as the coal supply dwindled, and the T&G considerately turned over 4,000 cross ties to the citizens of Goldfield for firewood.

Congestion in the Goldfield yards increased as lumber became harder to procure. The sidings were filled with 59 cars ready for unloading, but no teams were available to haul their contents away. Some lumbermen with teams were unable to get to their cars; others resorted to the practice of unloading at distant points and hauling the lumber in by wagon. Some mine shafts closed from the lack of timbers, and the railroad was blamed when 200 men were laid off. Vengeance was thrice expressed when incendiarism was discovered at the T&G depot and among the cars at Goldfield.

Withal the vicissitudes, the lucrative Tonopah-Goldfield area was a tidy little package which John Brock and his Philadelphia associates had tied up, using the ribbons of T&G rail for a string. Quite understandably, any advancements by other roads which might siphon so much as a modicum of traffic from the T&G were taken with umbrage. The only other foreseeable (and unavoidable) calamity to which their minuscule cartel might be subjected was the possible collapse of the very bonanza which had originally created the boom. It so happened that, with the inexorable passage of time and circumstance, both contingencies transpired.

Two railroads attempted to invade the Tonopah-Goldfield area; both approached from the south toward the exposed southern flank; while a third (of T&G sponsorship) was pushed southward to head them off. Primal stimulant to the increased activity were the new discoveries at Bullfrog and Rhyolite in the late summer and fall of 1904. What were believed to be rich extensions of the Tonopah-Goldfield veins excited the miners and prospectors, but posed terrific problems for the T&G protagonists. The Tonopah Railroad was just getting its standard gauge legs and had hardly had time to learn to walk; the Goldfield Railroad was still in the throes of completion and commencement of operations; merger of the two lines was in the offing; and neither Brock nor his cohorts wished to be involved in the consideration of another major (gambling) investment in a railroad to a bonanza which might or might not materialize. The wisdom of their thinking was amply demonstrated in the next few short years.

F. M. "Borax" Smith initiated the progression in July 1904 with his first abortive effort to provide transportation between Las Vegas and his then-developing new borax operations at the Lila C mine in the mountains just east of Death Valley. When troubles over connections (with Clark's SP, LA&SL) at Las Vegas developed, Smith stopped work entirely on the Tonopah & Tidewater and shifted his base of operations to Ludlow on the Santa Fe, starting construction all over again. The delay was both the downfall and the salvation of the T&T, for it was the last railroad to reach the gold region; it never penetrated beyond the southern extremity at Gold Center (near Beatty); yet it survived the longest of all three of the southern roads before final abandonment.

Concurrently with Smith's setback at Las Vegas, Senator Clark organized his own Las Vegas and Tonopah Railroad in 1905 to accomplish virtually the same objectives. Taking advantage of the T&T's preliminary grading, Clark pushed construction hard and reached Beatty and Rhyolite before the end of 1906; then pressed on into Goldfield by the fall of 1907.

At the same time (summer of 1905) Brock and his associates reluctantly organized the Bullfrog Goldfield Railroad to build south from Goldfield and head off the two upstarts. However, with their hands full of T&G problems and finances, and with the value of the Bullfrog-Rhyolite bonanzas still undetermined, the Brock group failed to organize construction of the BG until March 1906. The project was then further delayed when obstreperous T&G stockholder, Louis Teller, effectively argued against a proposed T&G guaranty of BG bonds. It was over a year later before trains started running to Beatty—too late to be effective—for the collapse of the mining boom coupled with the general business slump of 1907 automatically put an end to further railroad construction or expansion. As a railroad entity, the BG was always under the domination of one of the other three lines, the T&G being the first to assume its operation under a contract for the six-month period from January to June 1908.

Thus for a time (from 1904 through 1907) the Tonopah & Goldfield reigned supreme, and Goldfield was proving to be a most affluent kingdom. Certain of the mines were pouring forth immense treasures, showering the lucky shareholders with their flowing riches. The whole town, approaching an approximate population of from 20,000 to 25,000 people, was developing ways of sharing in the general prosperity. T&G freight rates and passenger fares were high (passenger fares were 10 cents a mile for some time); merchants charged high prices to the miners; but even the miners discovered a way to supplement their usual $5.00 daily wage. "Picture rock" surreptitiously found its way out of the mines and into illegally operated "assay offices" through a clandestine routine called "highgrading." Estimates of the mine operators' losses through this process ran as high as $2,000,000 in one year during the peak of Goldfield operations. With some 2,500 men on the mine payrolls at this time, obviously a goodly number were indulging in the "sport" and enjoying such luxuries as were obtainable from the town's limited offerings.

Labor turnover on the T&G was particularly high, approximating 150% annually. Many of the men set their own rules, not to mention their compensation. Switching crews extracted an extra share of the prosperity from consignees through a form of "payola" amounting to $25 for each car spotted on sidings. The practice was not without its unusual incidents. One yardmaster received an unexpected $90 check from the perplexed foreman of a lumber yard who confided under questioning he understood the usual fee was $6 a car and was there something wrong? "Not at all," the yardmaster had replied as he silently recalled the mixed trainload of 15 cars which had plugged the main line one day, and in order to get rid of them he had ordered, "Shove 'em on the lumber spur."

Life could be both pleasant and stringent. When Eugene Rebarb resigned an $80 a month stenographic job on the Santa Fe to take a similar position on the T&G at $150 per month, the only housing available was with two other men in an old engineer's cabin. Home life was greatly improved when the bar from the old narrow gauge private car was installed, but reaching the office in winter necessitated an old pair of shoes for walking through the mud and slush while a clean pair protruded from the hip pockets to be donned on arrival.

Train operations in the Tonopah area were interesting. A local ore train left Tonopah regularly with ore cars for the Desert Mill at Millers (named for Charles R. Miller, one-time governor of Delaware, a staunch investor in streetcar lines, and a director of the T&G for over 20 years). While switching was being accomplished at Millers, the inbound freight from Mina (on the C&C) passed by on its way to Goldfield, dropping any cars for Tonopah at Main Line Junction (formerly Goldfield Junction). The Goldfield freight then swung off to the south, while the returning ore local from Millers picked up the inbound cars at Main Line Junction and brought them up the hill to Tonopah. Because the grade approaching the Tonopah station was particularly steep, train crews quickly learned to pull straight through into the mining spur and then back down the east leg of the wye to the station. Even this facility was rendered impotent during a strike of the railroad workers when someone thoughtfully greased the rails.

Westbound out of Tonopah and immediately below the station wye a safety track was located, following an incident with a runaway car. The switch was normally set for the safety track, and the trainmaster's daughter dutifully attended to its operation upon receiving the customary whistle signal from approaching engineers. One day, when an unattended engine drifted silently down the grade without blowing the usual imperious command, the confused girl asked her father for instructions. "Do nothing," he replied, and the runaway locomotive was allowed to run harmlessly up the safety track.

Not all critical situations were so easily avoided. In October 1906 a runaway ore car crashed head-on into the locomotive of the inbound passenger train at a spot eight miles west of Millers. Although the engineer of the passenger train had been warned and was traveling slowly at the time, the impact damaged the engine and covered it with rocks which required removal before the train could be hauled into Tonopah. Although women and children in the cars were frightened, there were no casualties except in the dining car where food and liquids danced about and one man in a white vest was decorated with coffee and gravy.

Although speed was not indigenous to the T&G, it was not totally unknown. Mine leasers were constantly working against the deadlines of their leases and anxious to obtain the maximum production while in possession of the properties. Frequently materials would be needed in a hurry. One such incident involved a trainload of lumber and machinery from Denver for the Hayes-Monnette lease in Goldfield. Special running rights were acquired, and the train established some unofficial records, beating the time of the Overland Limited over the same route. The cost of the venture was $4,000, but with timely expansion of a limited lease with a $30,000 daily production involved, such expense could be justified.

Passenger service in May 1907 consisted of four daily trains each way between Tonopah and Goldfield, two of which went on to Mina, Hazen, Reno and return. At times traffic was so heavy that seven cars were required and all seats would be filled. Connections to the south were made at Goldfield with the two daily Bullfrog Goldfield Railroad trains from Rhyolite, a service but recently inaugurated by the Amargosa Construction Co., builders and operators of the line. Three additional T&G local trains shuttled back and forth on the round-trip circuit from Tonopah to the mills at Millers.

The fiscal year ending June 30, 1907, was the greatest in the history of the Tonopah & Goldfield Railroad. Operating revenues of the 90-mile line soared to $2,387,000 while a comfortable $843,000 of net income was recorded. Unwise, extravagant dividends of 30% were paid on the common and participating preferred stock; more locomotives were ordered from the Baldwin Locomotive Works; new repair shops were erected at Millers, the old, narrow gauge shop at Tonopah having become too small and the terrain too limited to permit their enlargement. It was a fantastic economy—too good to last — and it didn't.

HARD TIMES

The general prosperity shrank rapidly as the Panic of 1907 swept across the land. Banks closed their doors in October. On November 27 some 1,900 Goldfield miners went on strike over their method of payment and to protest against attempts to halt highgrading. Federal troops were called in to preserve order and this action caused considerable discussion for many years. The strike continued long after the troops were withdrawn and was not finally settled until April 1908.

The T&G was particularly full of unrest. At the labor level, demotion of the Goldfield yard foreman to switchman in August 1907 resulted in a short strike until promises were made to review the matter. Other difficulties were brewing, but when a conductor in Tonopah was fired for refusing to take his train to Millers with but two brakemen instead of three, the trainmen went out on strike in October. The Goldfield Chamber of Commerce wired the newly formed Nevada Railroad Commission that there was only sufficient food on hand in Goldfield to last for 48 hours and please to do something. In return the Commission wired T&G's manager Hedden to please reach an agreement as they had no legal authority to do more than that. This was most unsatisfactory news for a mass meeting in Goldfield. Even though the union ordered the men to go back to work, they refused to return, causing the national brotherhoods to condemn the strike and threaten to revoke the local charter. Again in January 1908 a third short-lived walkout took place following a cut in the wages of the section forces.

T&G management was equally turbulent. When it was found that the shops at Millers had cost far more than expected, the president was moved out of the way, and C. K. Lord succeeded John Brock to that post on November 1, 1907. Unfortunately, Lord's effectiveness was seriously impaired by sickness most of his short term, and he was forced to rely upon J. W. Reinhart. In April 1908 John Hedden resigned as superintendent, to be replaced by H. R. Hamlin; then on July 1, C. K. Lord resigned the presidency, to pass away shortly thereafter. His position was left vacant for over a year, during which period Thomas M. King, a director, held the title of Chairman. Finally, in October 1909 M. B. Cutter became president to complete the slate of officers once again. These were difficult transitions to accomplish, particularly considering that from their very beginning the T&G was faced with another rival for Goldfield business. For the LV&T had crept into town on October 26, 1907.

It was J. W. Reinhart who really saved the T&G from bankruptcy. A railroad consultant and one-time president of the Santa Fe, he was brought in with the titles of Assistant to the President and Comptroller. The T&G being the terminating carrier on interline freight and the originating carrier on passenger movements, large sums of money were collected for division among the participating railroads. Had settlements been made currently as was the normal practice, all would have been well, but with delays resulting from consignees' slow payments and general confusion, this was not done. Thus large cash balances accumulated which, with a handsome net income, lured the Board of Directors to celebrate with generous dividends and appropriations for property improvements. When the time for interline settlements ultimately arrived, the Board was suddenly faced with the horrible realization that there was no cash in the till.

Reinhart solved the problem by arranging for the T&G to issue notes for past due interline settlements and short-term notes for working capital, using unissued bonds as collateral. Long hours and hard work were necessary to carry out the plan, and Reinhart never stinted of himself. Following a full day's work, he would return to his apartment on the top floor of the Tonopah Mining Company building at Tonopah to handle correspondence and dictate the day's reports. Here in the privacy of his quarters Rule G was overlooked, and in the eyes of his overworked secretary one of Reinhart's great feats was his ability to step into the adjoining bathroom, mix and down a drink, without so much as disturbing the even flow of his dictation.

The program brought results. By hounding the Bullfrog Syndicate for the money it owed the T&G, sufficient cash was obtained to pay off the loans. On June 15, 1908, the T&G divested itself of the onerous BG operations, and Borax Smith's T&T assumed the paternalistic role of connecting carrier. For the fiscal year ending June 30, 1908, the T&G showed a profit of $199,000; by the end of August the financial crisis was over; and Reinhart left with a vote of thanks from the Board of Directors for his good work over the last nine months.

For the next two years the status quo of the T&G remained relatively stable. Operations were profitable, but net income was too small to suggest dividends. Further economies were reflected late in 1908 through the gradual depletion of coal reserves and the conversion of locomotives to oil burners. Fuel costs per locomotive mile dropped from $1.53 to 42 cents, a not inconsiderable saving.

On September 30, 1908, Charles Knox presented a proposal to the Board of Directors for construction of a branch to connect with the Mono Lake Railway and the mines at Bodie (see Bodie and Benton). Innumerable committees and extensive surveys later, the project was discarded. In 1909 an additional survey was made for a short branch from Tonopah eastward to Ellendale, but the mining excitement at that location was over before more serious consideration could ensue.

Mike Donahue was knocked to the floor when he attempted to pull the fire alarm switch at the T&G shops in Tonopah on June 28, 1909. Mysteriously, the switch had been grounded, and the origin of the blaze itself assumed something of the occult. "Tonopah's worst fire" burned rapidly as hoses were stretched 2,000 feet (nearly one-half mile) to reach the flames. The effort was futile; the shops were destroyed, and locomotives Nos. 11, 56 and 101 were severely scorched.

Hardly had the embers ceased to glow than Goldfield commenced making attractive overtures to persuade the T&G to relocate its shops there. Following extensive negotiations an agreement was reached whereby the Town of Goldfield donated the shop grounds and the railroad consolidated its facilities in the one center. Clearing the site was accomplished early in 1910, and construction was started. The Casey Hotel became headquarters for the general offices on June 11, 1910, the first floor being utilized for office space while the upper floors provided sleeping quarters for the single men. By August the new $132,000 shops were ready and the railroad moved in, following which the shops and turntable at Millers were retired and any useful equipment from there and from Tonopah transferred to the new site.

New discoveries of promising ore divided the directors of the Tonopah Belmont Development Company into two opposing camps in 1910. Those directors with some financial interest in the T&G favored a continuation of the current routine of shipping ore to the Tonopah Belmont mill at Millers. Those without such ties supported a proposal to build a new, more elaborate, more efficient mill at the Belmont property just east of Tonopah, thereby eliminating a transportation charge of 50 cents per ton on the ore. Even as discussions were going on, the Belmont mine made headlines when an underground fire on February 23, 1911 took the lives of 17 men and the T&G obligingly arranged special excursion fares so men from Goldfield and Millers could attend the funeral. Whether the incident spurred decision will not be known, but in June 1911 authorization was granted for the new, 500-ton (daily) reduction plant. When it commenced operations in July 1912, the T&G ore tonnage suffered a compensating reduction.

Dividends Again—For a While

Under president M. B. Cutter the T&G rapidly trimmed its operations to the new, lower level of business prevailing at the time. Surplus rolling stock was sold; unused spurs were abandoned; water lines and the original old freight and passenger station at Goldfield were eliminated from the list of properties owned. Negotiations were instituted with Senator William Clark and his brother, J. Ross Clark, for possible sale of the T&G to the LV&T or other railroads. No stone was left unturned.

The program began to produce results. Operations turned profitable; net income began to improve. When J. Ross Clark turned apathetic toward the negotiations for sale of the road, following the sinking of the *Titanic* in April 1912 and the consequent loss of his son, negotiations were allowed to lapse. By late 1912 dividends were again restored to the stockholders, though at a considerably more conservative rate.

The year also witnessed the culmination of another bit of unresolved T&G business from more prosperous days. The Goldfield Railroad's famous gold spike, driven by Alonzo Tripp on that eventful September 14, 1905, was redeemed from the bank by President Cutter who arranged to have it properly inscribed and presented as a permanent souvenir to the Goldfield Commercial Association. Apparently someone had resolved a financial problem by using the spike as collateral for a bank loan; the railroad's cost of redemption was $250.

Two events of notable interest marked the normally placid operations of the T&G in 1913 — one was mental, the other, physical. During the summer a proposal was received and given studied consideration for leasing of the BG Railroad (then under operation by the T&T). For a time the prospects looked favorable; the T&G directors authorized an advance of $5,970 with which the BG met its July 1 interest payment; but ultimate agreement was not reached and the matter was dropped.

Then unexpected excitement arrived. On September 13, 1913, floods came. "Two Hundred Lives Lost in Goldfield Flood" screamed the Tonopah extras on the basis of early reports. Heavy rains started at 11:00 A.M., followed by hail and lightning. A distant roar announced the opening of a great, black cloud, and water fell to the hills in torrents. At 2:15 P.M. Rabbit Springs Canyon resounded to the press of turbulent waters and spewed forth a flood which swept away 50 cabins before it flashed through the red light district and rolled on to tear up the T&G yards and strew debris over a 12-mile course to Dry Lake. It was true — people were drowned — but the number was 2, not 200. All three railroads were damaged; though not as severely as at first reported, and trains were operating on a regular basis within a few days. The T&G shops were filled with mud and much of the stores were washed away, particularly a quantity of small, heavy brass castings which floated away "contrary to the laws of gravity."

Matters were not easy for any of the railroads serving the Goldfield area; there was scarcely sufficient business for one line, let alone all three. The T&G fought for its share of the traffic with a deliberate local appeal advertised in the Goldfield papers: "The Goldfield Road with the Goldfield Payroll—Route your business our way!" The appeal obviously was not completely lost, for in June 1914 the LV&T and the BG showed signs of suffering by getting together in an arrangement to combine the best portions of both lines between Goldfield and Rhyolite and eliminate excess trackage. Senator Clark (LV&T) tried unsuccessfully to interest President Cutter of the T&G in buying the surplus

BG terminals in Goldfield. Terminals without business were of no consequence to Cutter, but the first 1.25 miles of old BG main line continuing southeast (from E.S. 117) through Milltown were of interest. The alignment could be useful in the event of mine cave-ins, and the rails could be used for relayers. To obtain the facility, the T&G parted with $5,000; Goldfield became a two-railroad town.

Five houses previously built for T&G employees in Tonopah were sold in 1915. In the same year the T&G assumed operation of the Goldfield Consolidated Milling & Transportation Company's short railroad.

Notwithstanding a general contraction of the mining boom in Goldfield and a corresponding diminution of traffic on the railroad, the T&G continued to make money. Economy of operation was uppermost. Careful husbanding of earnings had built up a healthy cash balance so that dividends were again warranted beginning in 1912; an operating ratio of only 53% was favorably reported in 1913; 7% dividends on both the common and preferred stocks were the rule (through 1918), although a surprising 10½% was paid in 1915. During the years of World War I, U. S. Liberty Bonds were purchased while the company paid off the last of its own bonds, thus eliminating the annual interest expense. In the same period the first of the southern roads (the LV&T) was cast out by the U. S. Railroad Administration and was abandoned months later.

Following the war, but before normal mining conditions could be returned, new excitement was created by an ore discovery in the Tonopah-Divide District a few miles southeast of Tonopah. However, with the expiration of the Pittman Silver Purchase Act, the price of silver plummeted and wage cuts became an economic necessity. A six-week strike in 1919 was but a prelude to the four-month walkout in April 1921 in ineffectual protest over a 75-cents-a-day wage reduction. Mine operators attempted to alleviate the situation for the workers through organization of a Tonopah-Divide Mercantile Company to furnish the necessities of life at reduced prices, a tangible though largely unappreciated assistance.

In spite of reduced production by the mines and reduced traffic for the railroad, the T&G managed to carry on. Improvements were made; a gasoline motor passenger car was purchased for $8,150; a new telephone system connected all stations west from Tonopah; shopmen received an increase in wages following the pattern of Class I carriers. A 19-mile branch from Coaldale into the Fish Lake Valley was surveyed in May 1921, and the Board of Directors sanctioned its construction subject to approval of the president and the executive committee. Apparently the latter were undecided, for no work was done on the branch although the T&G did advance part of the cost of some oil drilling on the part of the Fish Lake Merger Oil Company, whose dry wells were abandoned at 3,200 feet at a loss to the T&G of $26,000. Whether the road was unconvinced or desperate for new traffic is unknown, but subsequent similar advances were made to the Coaldale Merger Oil Company for equally unsuccessful efforts but with more fortunate recovery of money on sale of the oil rig. The effect upon the stockholders of these non-railroad participations and declining revenues was a complete suspension of dividends during the years 1921 and 1922.

July 6, 1923 is best remembered in the area for the holocaust at Goldfield. Fortunately but two lives were lost — one man was burned to death; another suffered a heart attack—in spite of the fact that the whole center of the business district was ravaged and gutted. The explosion of a private still in the rear of a shanty during the early morning hours started the conflagration, and the fire rapidly spread to the Brown-Parker Garage where one man, in an effort to rescue his car, calmly drove it right through the garage door which still remained locked from the close of business the previous day. A total of 16 autos were consumed by the flames, including the fateful car of a prospector which contained 50 pounds of dynamite. The resulting explosion smashed the windows of the monumental Goldfield Hotel across the street and hurled a red-hot piece of metal into a bedroom, setting the bed on fire. The occupant of the room probably can be credited with saving the hotel, for he promptly extinguished the blaze without the aid of firemen. An early rising wind propelled the flames from one building to another, while citizens with cars and wagons hauled loads of furniture and belongings out of danger to dump them and return for more. As the flames spread, the salvaged possessions had to be moved again to points even farther afield. The old J. S. Cook Bank building and the T&G offices were easy victims of the blaze, and virtually all of the railroad's records were lost except the general books of account in the Auditing Department. Dynamite was finally used to level abandoned

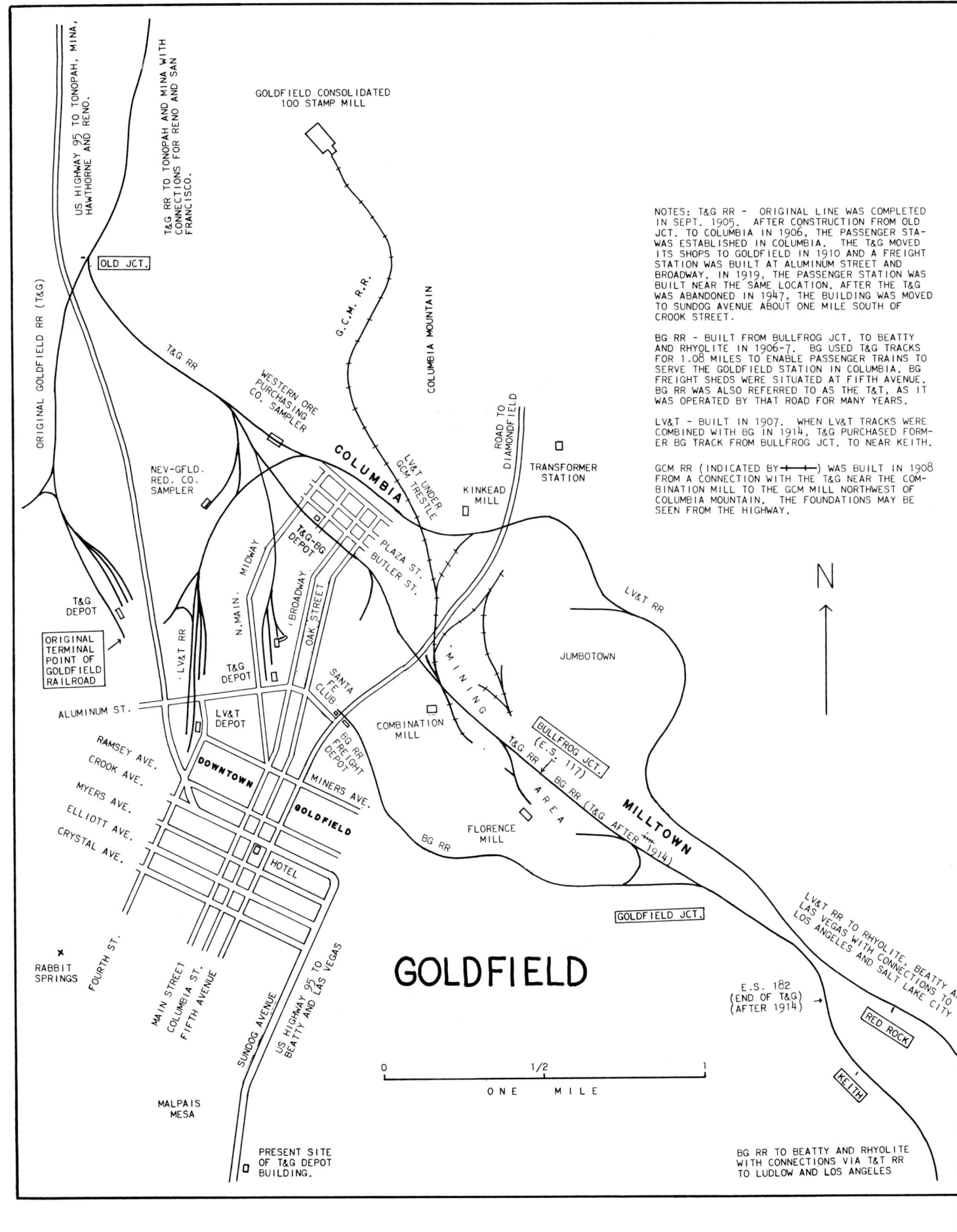

buildings; the blaze was brought under control; and five hours after the initial explosion the fire was out.

Goldfield licked its wounds. The Brown-Parker Garage was rebuilt on the same site and is still operating today; the site of the old T&G building was donated for an Elks' Home; a new J. S. Cook Bank building provided sufficient office space for the T&G; while R. W. Cattermole, then chief engineer for the T&G, was credited with protecting the railroad's shops and terminals with an efficiency that enabled them to escape the flames. In a depressed economy, the results were not achieved without effort and sacrifice.

When the Mammoth Copper Company offered a bonus for low grade ores for fluxing purposes in 1924, the area responded with some 20,000 tons of silicious ore. The T&G hauled it to Mina where the SP took over for the balance of the trip to the smelter at Kennet, in Northern California. In spite of the relief afforded by the additional business, the picture was not particularly encouraging and several officers, including W. D. Forester, V. P. and Traffic Manager, left the company. Even President Cutter, with his many years of service, showed concern for the future but still managed to secure a three-year contract as manager at an annual stipend of $15,000 to be paid irrespective of any possible sale of the line or election of a new president.

The saving grace for the road during this difficult period was its strong cash position, and what remuneration stockholders received was largely supported by this resource. In 1923-24 the last dividends were paid on the common stock; from 1923-26 the preferred stockholders received full dividends, then none thereafter.

Curtailed operations at Tonopah and disappointing developments at Manhattan, Round Mountain, Tybo and Gilbert (feeder territories) were responsible for a loss in 1926. Two years previous, Gilbert had been booming and the T&G had donated $500 as a start toward construction of an independent railroad from Gilbert to Gilbert Junction (formerly McLean's) where a small station had been built. Now Gilbert had subsided with only one property operating. Net loss for the year, first in the railroad company's history, was $12,577.

One of the worst washouts in T&G history occurred near Redlich in 1927, causing a four-day shutdown of operations and a threatened food shortage in Tonopah. Repairs to the area took a neat slice out of the budget, as also did the expense of replacing the rails on Tonopah Hill which had become worn out. To alleviate the situation it was decided to take up the long unused track on the McSweeney Cut-Off to Goldfield from Main Line Junction to McSweeney Junction. Application to abandon the 6¾-mile line was approved by the I.C.C. in December of that year. A partial offset to these outlays was obtained through the sale to the Nevada Copper Belt Railroad of 10 old wood gondolas with steel lining previously operated by that

---

FOLLOWING PAGE:

Goldfield, Nevada, on August 3, 1908, was a very impressive city when an unknown photographer climbed to the Malpais Mesa and faced his camera to the north. Main Street, Columbia Street and Fifth Avenue (left to right in center) stretch in boulevard style toward Columbia Mountain in center distance. The gold of Goldfield with its picturesque ores attracted far more mining companies resulting in a greater number of office buildings than did the more richly productive silver ores of Tonopah to the north, as attested by the size and quantity of office buildings in the broad belt across the middle of the picture, the center of the business district. That famous landmark, the Goldfield Hotel (still standing today), is the first tall building nearest the camera on the right hand side of Columbia Street. The large square building two blocks to the right (also still standing today) is the school. The diagonal streets beyond the business district leading off-center to the left background ran to the industrial area known as Columbia. The major mining area lay to the far right and extended on east (out of the picture to the right) almost to the summit of the notch near Milltown.

Both the Bullfrog Goldfield and the Las Vegas & Tonopah railroads used this notch to approach Goldfield from the south. The BG dropped directly down a steep grade to its freight terminus near the present day Santa Fe Club on the far reaches of Fifth Avenue (center right). The T&G built its extension from Old Jct. to Columbia (cars on track extreme upper left) and on to the Combination and Florence mills and to Milltown where connection was made with the BG. The latter road terminated its trains at the T&G's Goldfield (Columbia) depot. Although the LV&T was adjacent to the BG coming through the notch near Milltown, it swung its tracks on a more circuitous but easier grade along the slope to the northeast (upper right) and then down in front of the base of Columbia Mountain, reaching its terminal in Goldfield on October 24, 1907. The smoke of the departing east and southbound LV&T train is plainly visible (center, rear) as it curls over the large trestle of the Goldfield Consolidated Milling & Transportation Co.'s railroad extending 1.87 miles from a connection with the T&G (cars on track upper right) northwesterly along the face of Columbia Mountain to the large 100-stamp mill on the western shoulder (two trestles and buildings top left). The foundations of the mill are still plainly visible from Highway 95 on the north side of Goldfield. (Sewell Thomas Collection.)

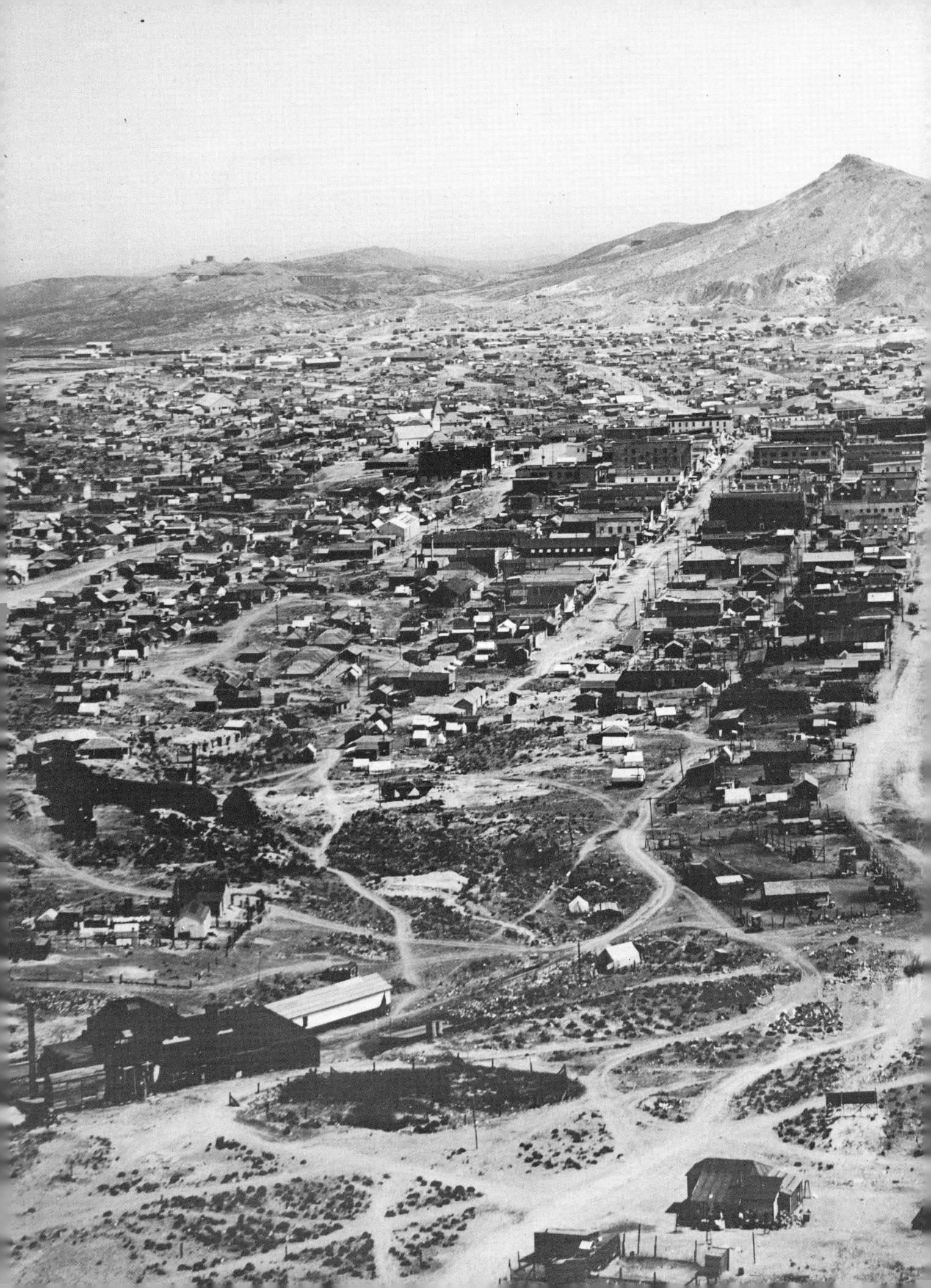

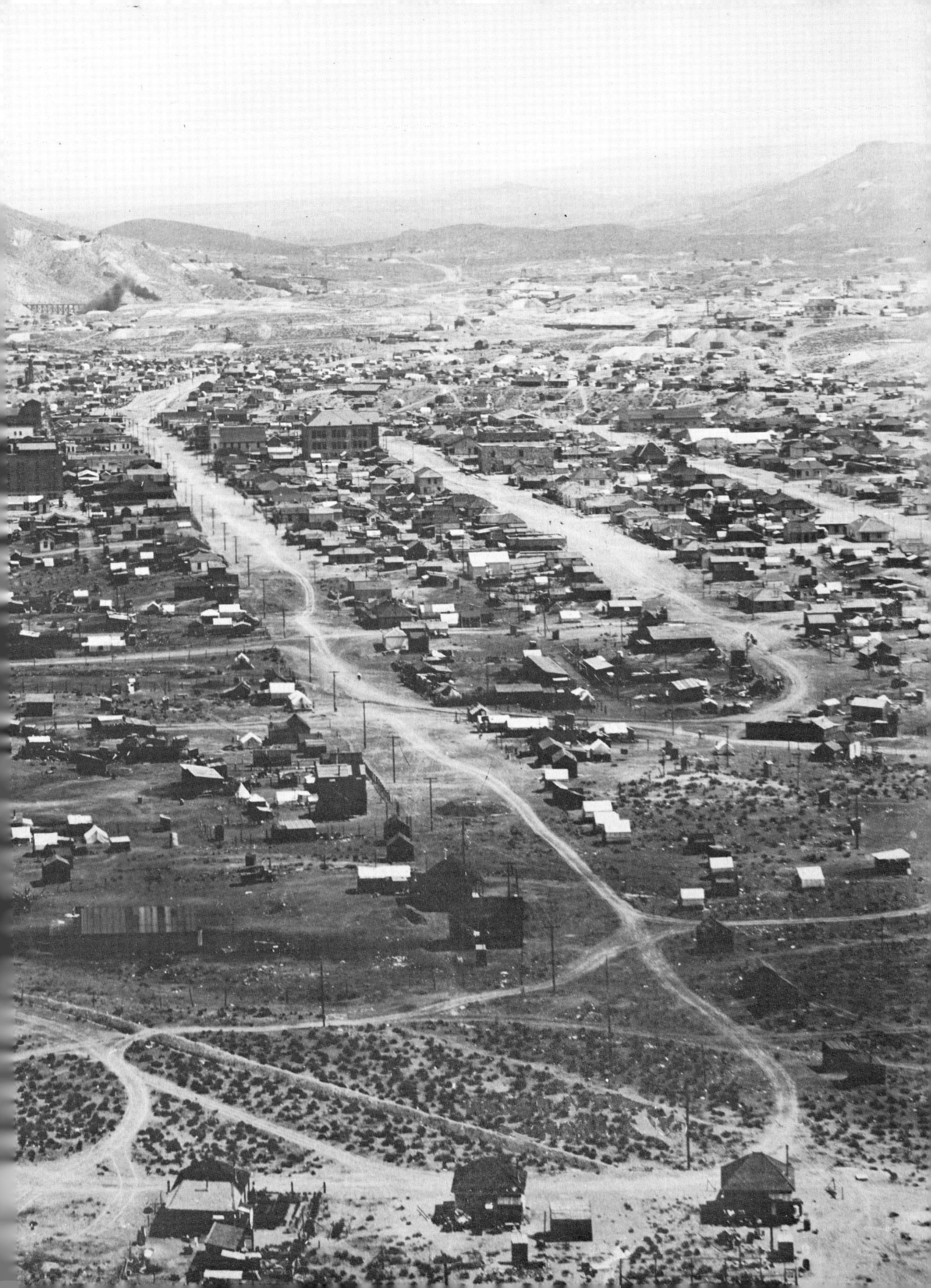

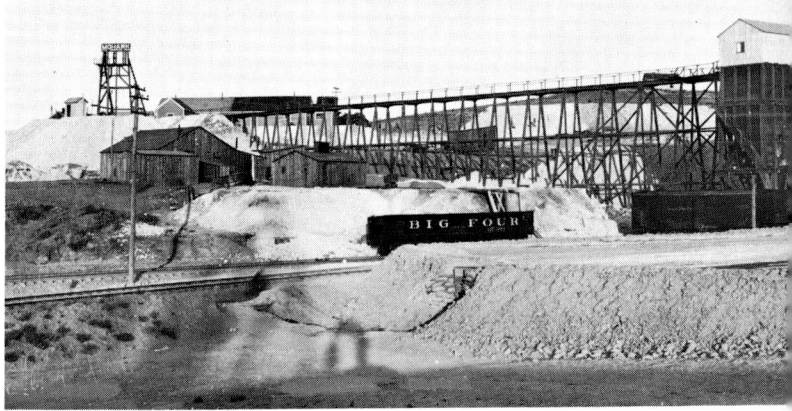

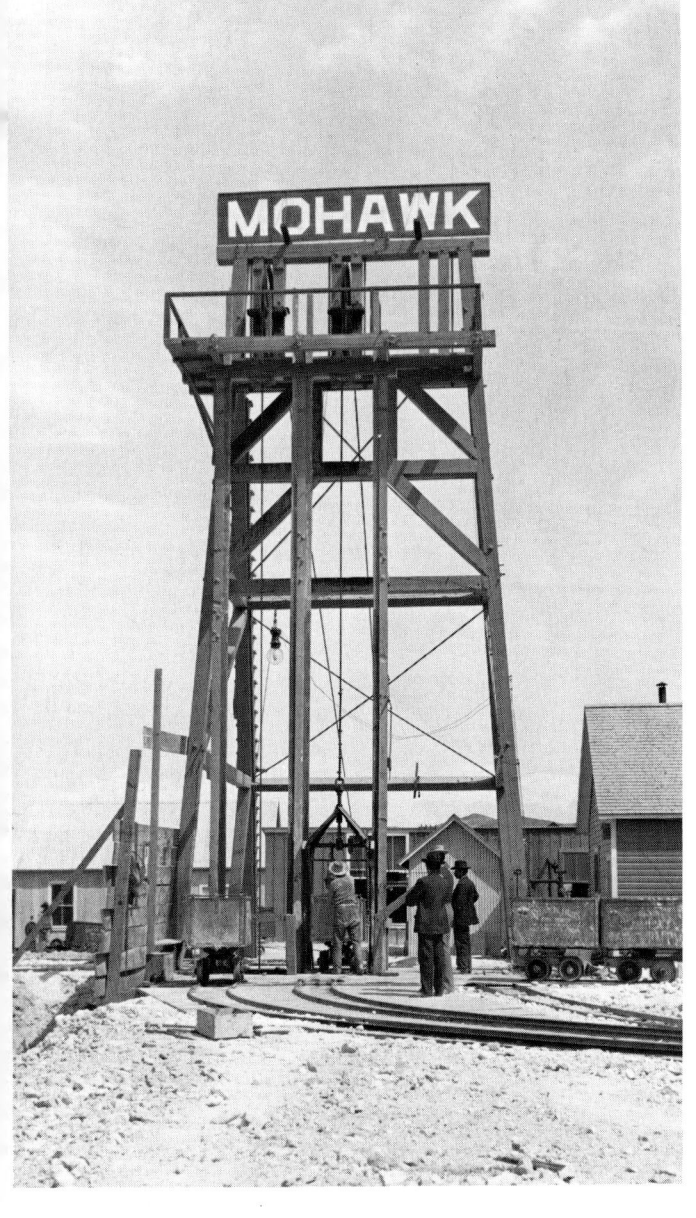

Most prolific of all the mines in the Goldfield area was the fabulous Mohawk — Hayes and Monnette, lessees — which in one year produced over $4,000,000 in gold ores and from which a total, cumulative take in excess of $27,000,000 was tallied. Two compartments of the shaft *(left)* accommodate cages as indicated by the cables and sheaves above. An empty mine car is being positioned in the cage for return to the subterranean depths for reloading. Tracks in the foreground lead to the company's ore bins *(above)*, on the siding for which two box cars and an empty gondola have been spotted. *(Top: Sewell Thomas Collection; Left: S. G. Palmer photo.)*

But few mines in Goldfield could begin to approach the Mohawk's prosperity, although many put on a hopefully bold front and emblazoned their headframes with names which frequently smacked of plagiarism. In the center of the view *(below)*, taken before the Goldfield Consolidated Mines Company's railroad was scarred across the base of Columbia Mountain in the background in 1908, are visible (left to right) the Jumbo Annex, the Higginson, the Frances-Mohawk, and the Mohawk Ledge Mining Co. *(S. G. Palmer Photo.)*

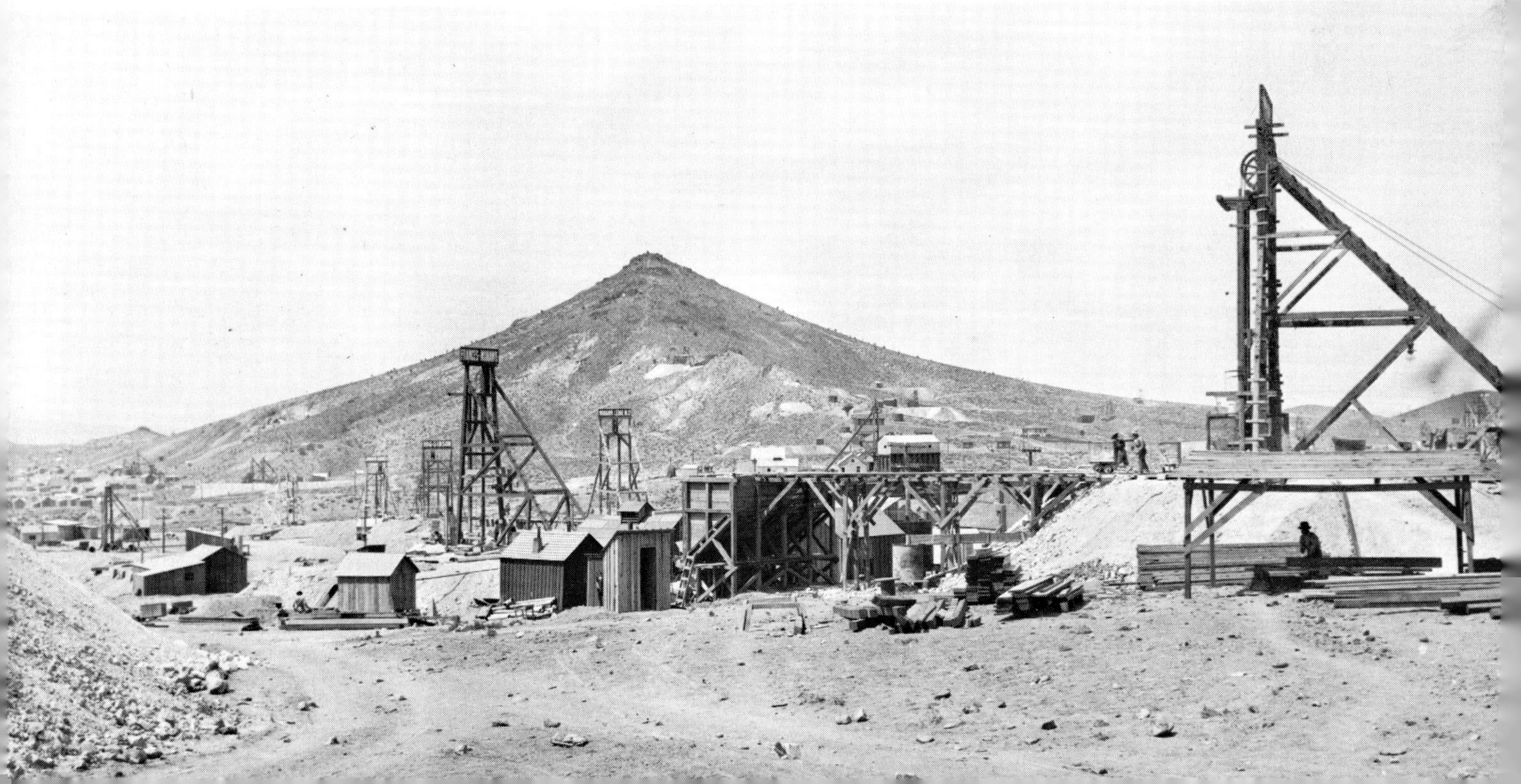

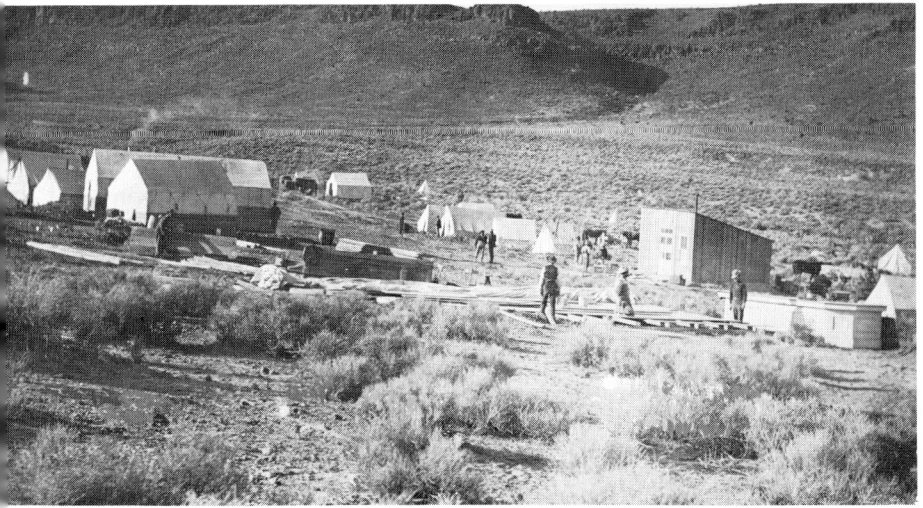

Goldfield had its humble beginnings as a tent city, shown here in November 1903 looking south toward the Malpais Mesa in background. *(Sewell Thomas Collection.)*

By 1905 Goldfield had expanded considerably. Looking north up Main Street from the corner of Myers Avenue, the heart of town can be seen clustered around the Hotel Esmeralda, terminus for the Bullfrog Stage Line (Wm. Kitchen, Prop., whose coaches departed daily at 6:30 a.m. for Bullfrog, Rhyolite and Beatty), The Overland Stage Co. operating to Tonopah, and one or two lesser lines whose names cannot be ascertained in the melange of signs. Almost directly across the snow-covered street are the offices of the Sodaville Tonopah Telephone & Telegraph Company and the ubiquitous Wells Fargo & Company Express. *(Sewell Thomas Collection.)*

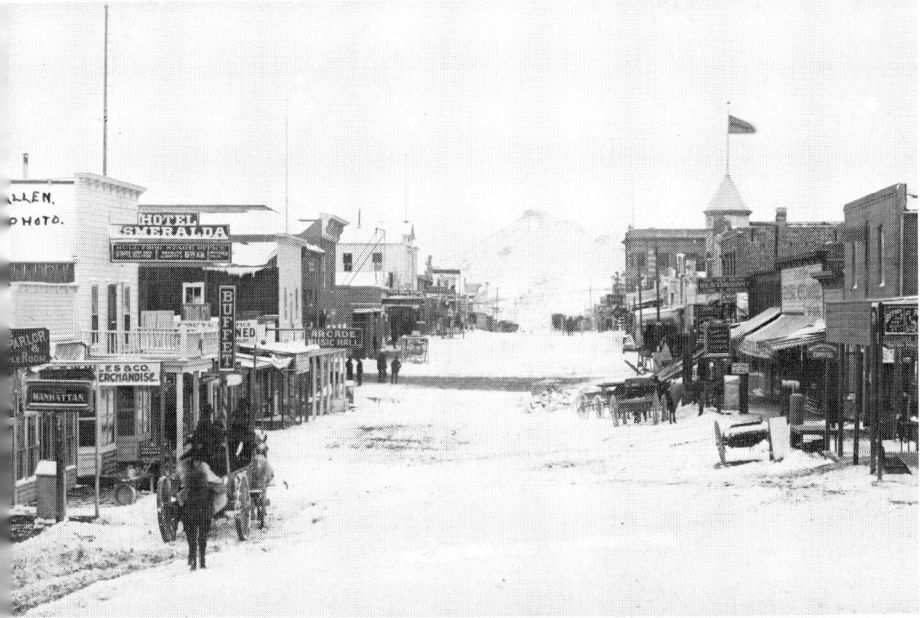

Three blocks farther north, at Broadway and Miner Streets *(below)*, is the Assay Office of the Downer Bros. In this early morning view in 1907, the street sprinkler has made his first sweep of the day to settle the dust for the morning traffic, while an early riser stuffs the last hard boiled egg in his mouth as he crosses the street following a stiff brace of beer at the Rathskeller. *(S. G. Palmer Photo.)*

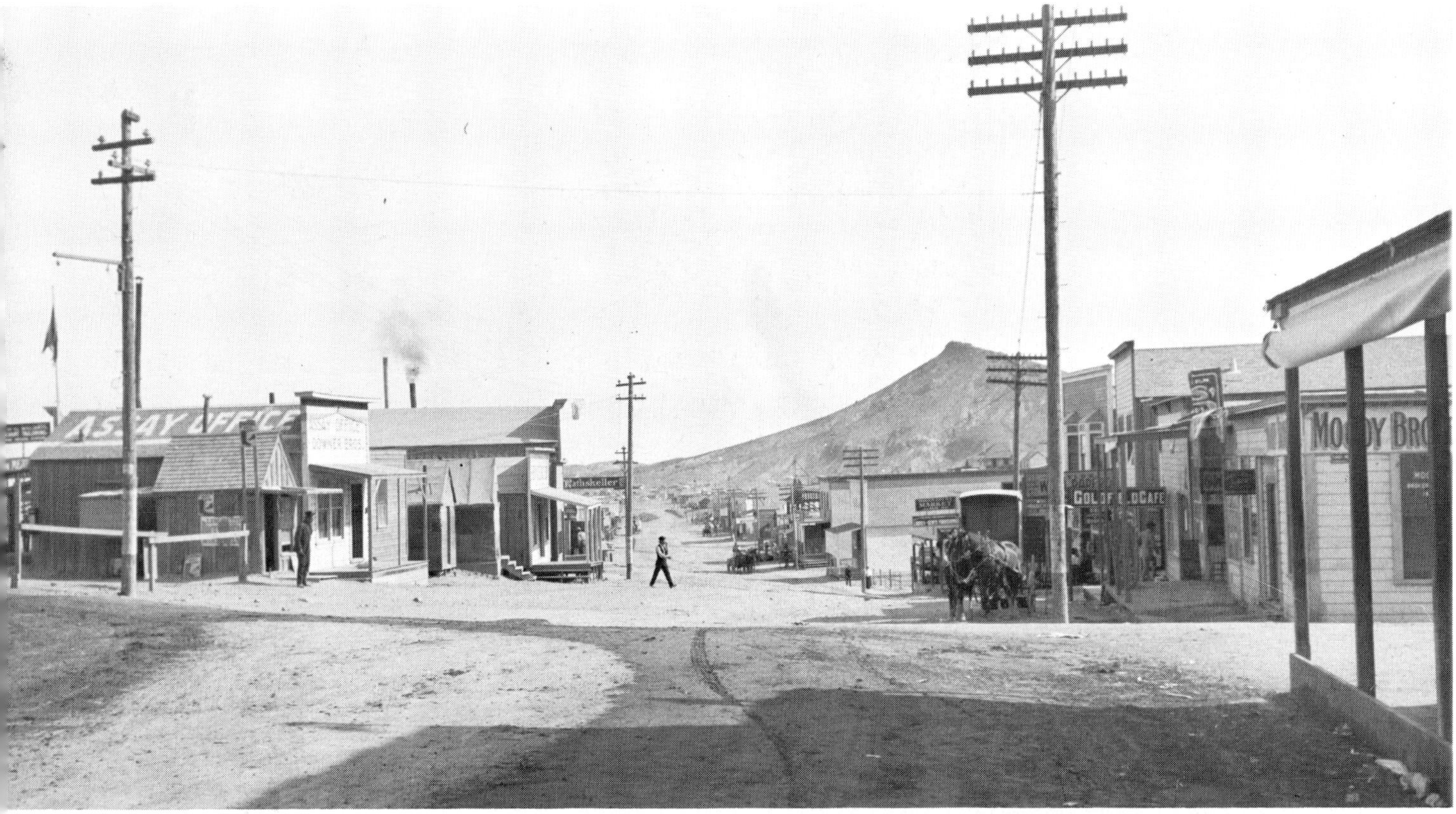

Two-man rock drilling contests, such as this one at Tonopah Railroad Days celebration, were a popular feature of all holidays and celebrations throughout the Nevada mining country. Goldfield was no exception. *(Mrs. Herbert A. Tripp Collection.)*

Initially the Goldfield Railroad had its own equipment and used the original depot on the northwest side of town. The road merged with the Tonopah Railroad on November 1, 1905, and the combined Tonopah & Goldfield planned and, starting in March 1906, built the extension from Old Jct. to a new depot in the Columbia section of Goldfield. The rare view of Goldfield Railroad coach No. 13 (*below*) was taken at Tonopah as the men on the platform load machinery and parts for a 10-stamp mill into the wagons in foreground. The water barrel fastened to the wagon was for emergency use only, normal refreshments were obtained after the job was done at "Columbia Saloon and Board," across the tracks behind the coach, where wine, liquors, cigars and Williams Lager Beer were plentiful. *(Mrs. Hugh Brown Collection.)*

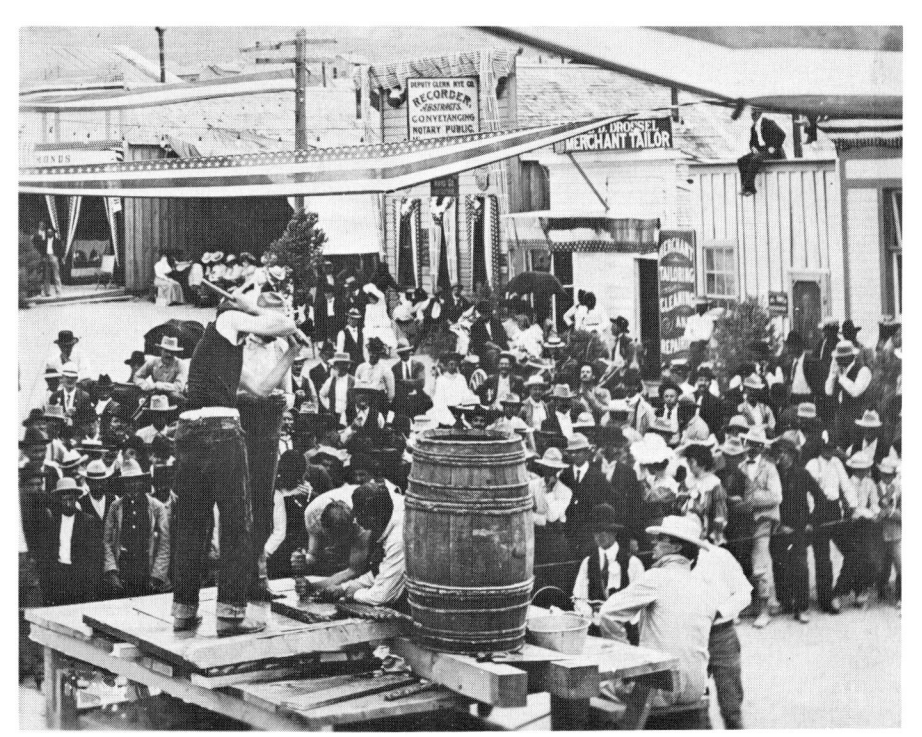

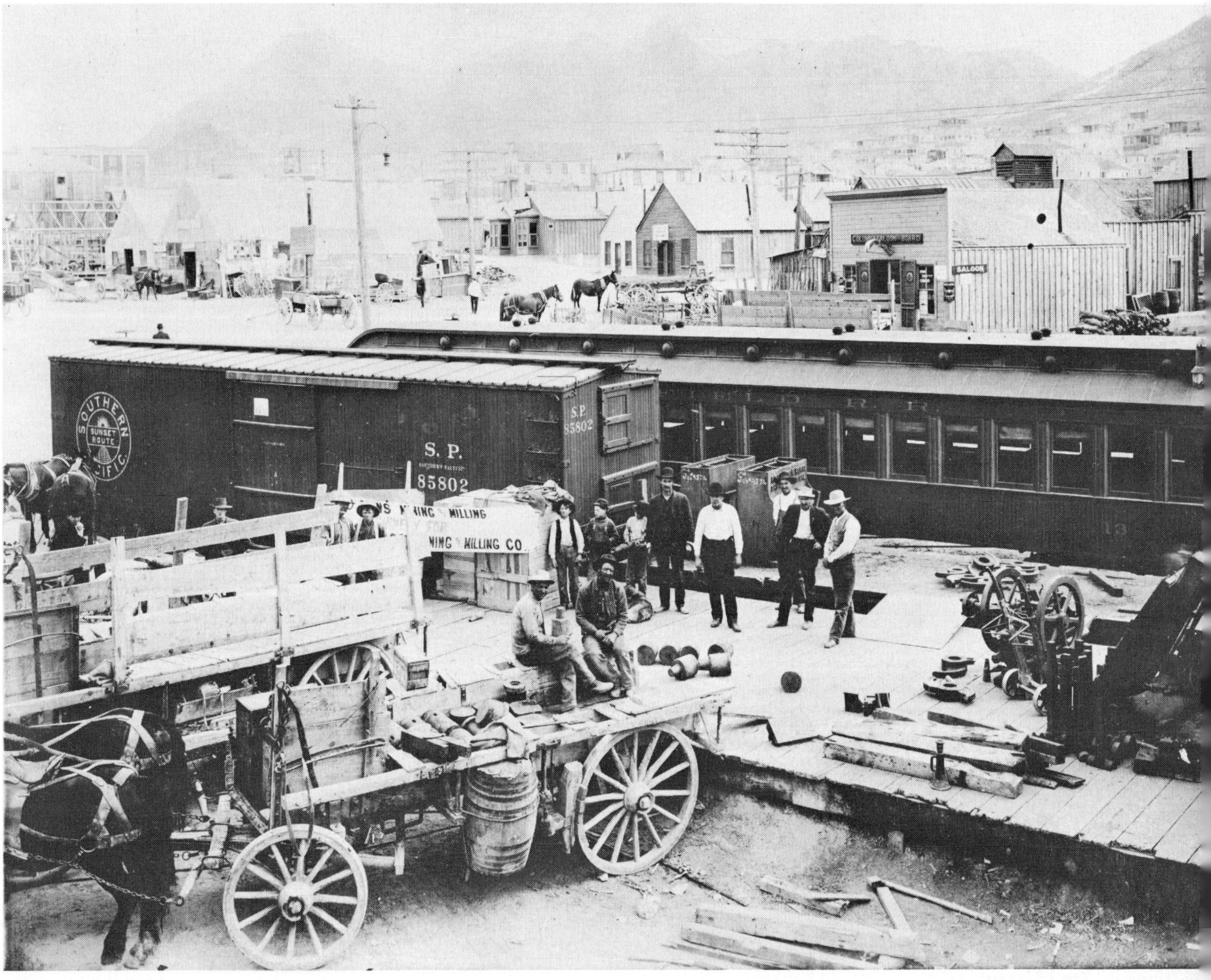

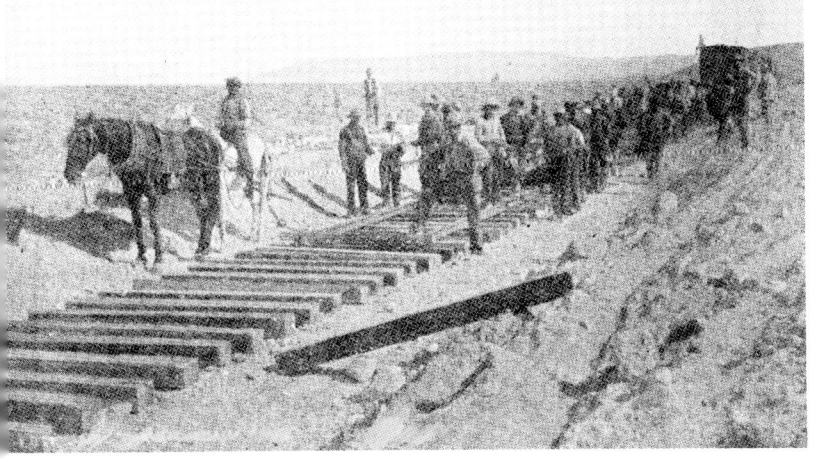

Building the Goldfield Railroad south from Tonopah presented no difficult problems other than obtaining the physical labor necessary to perform the task in the hot desert sun. Flat cars of rails were pushed to the end of track where horses pulled the individual rails into position for spiking. *(Illustration from* GOLDFIELD NEWS.*)*

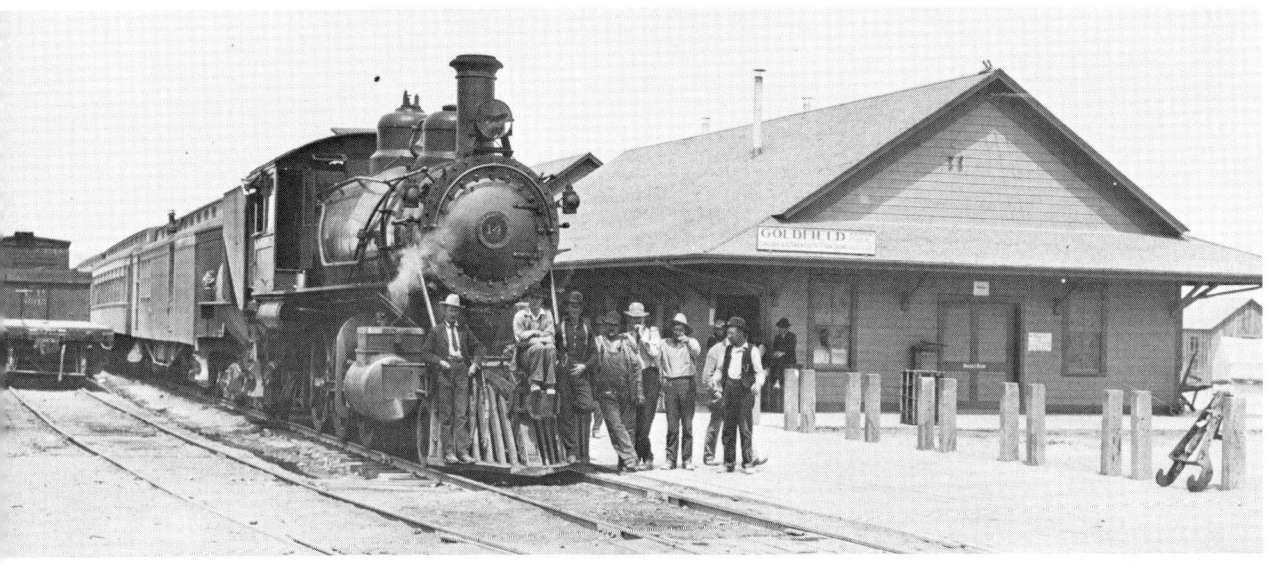

The T&G's Goldfield station at Columbia (Elevation 5,700 feet; Tonopah 28 M.; Reno 271 M.; San Francisco 515 M.) was also used by the Bullfrog Goldfield Railroad, whose locomotive No. 14 and passenger train here stand ready to depart southbound for Beatty and Rhyolite. No. 14 later was renumbered 12 and subsequently blew up near Beatty. *(S. H. Palmer Photo.)*

In a later day *(below)* at the Goldfield freight station, the main line northbound appears to be devoid of business, but three separate locomotives work quietly on the sidings. *(Hendrick Collection.)*

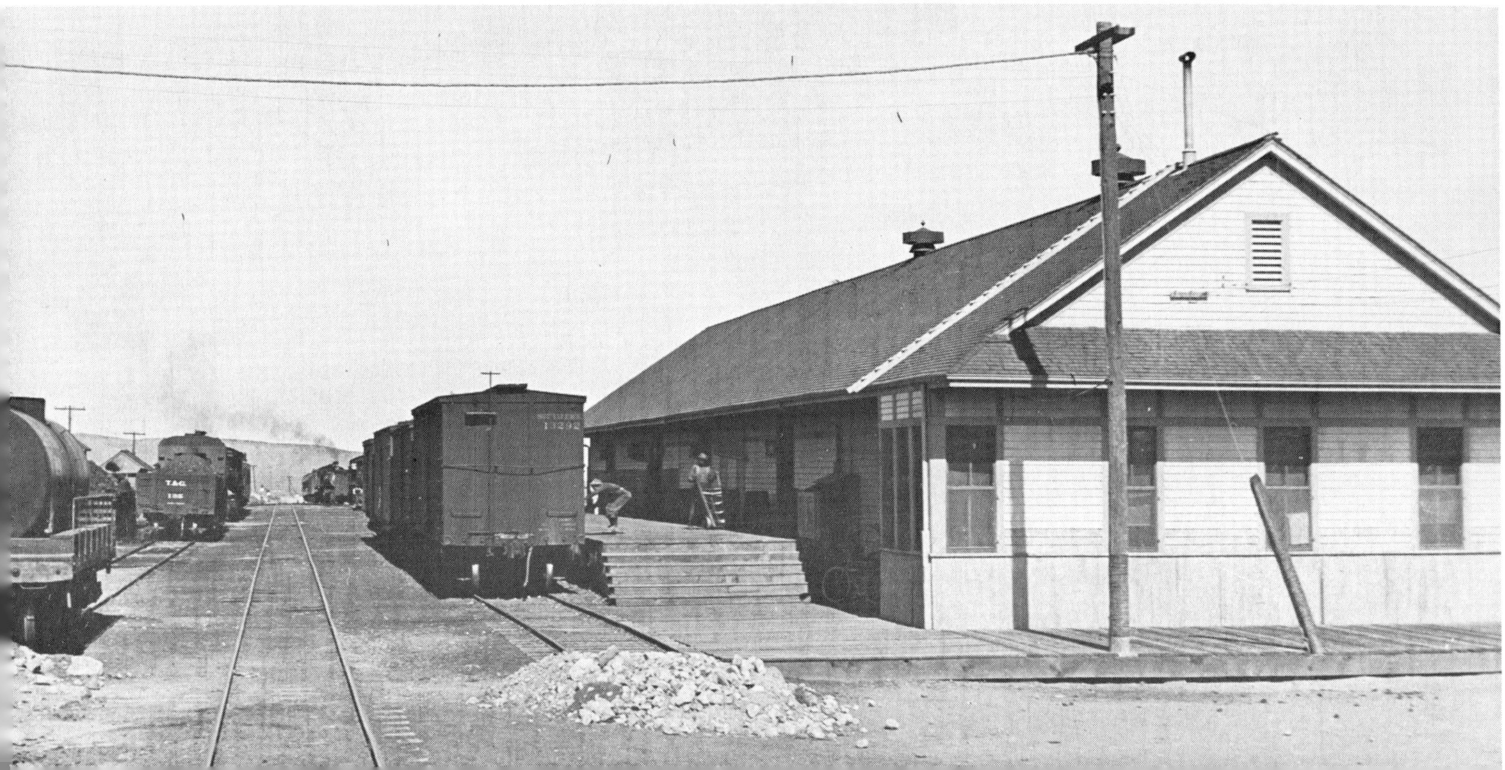

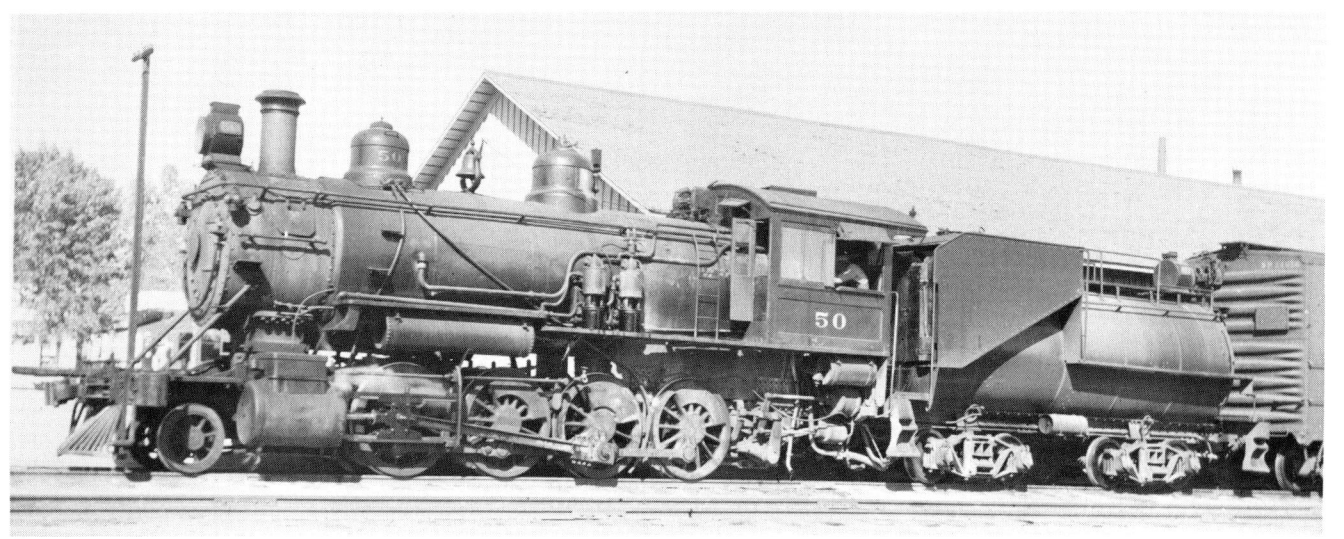

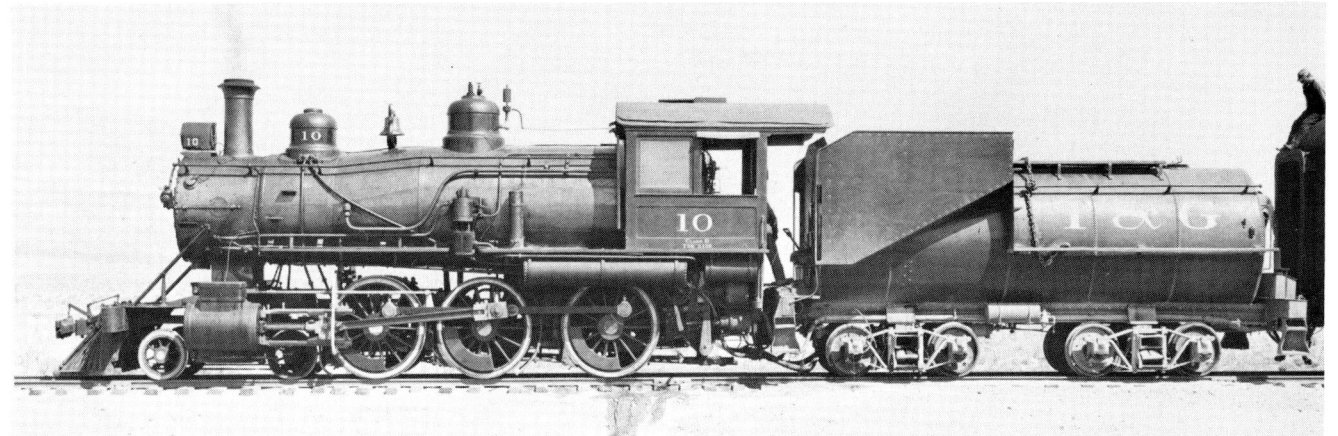

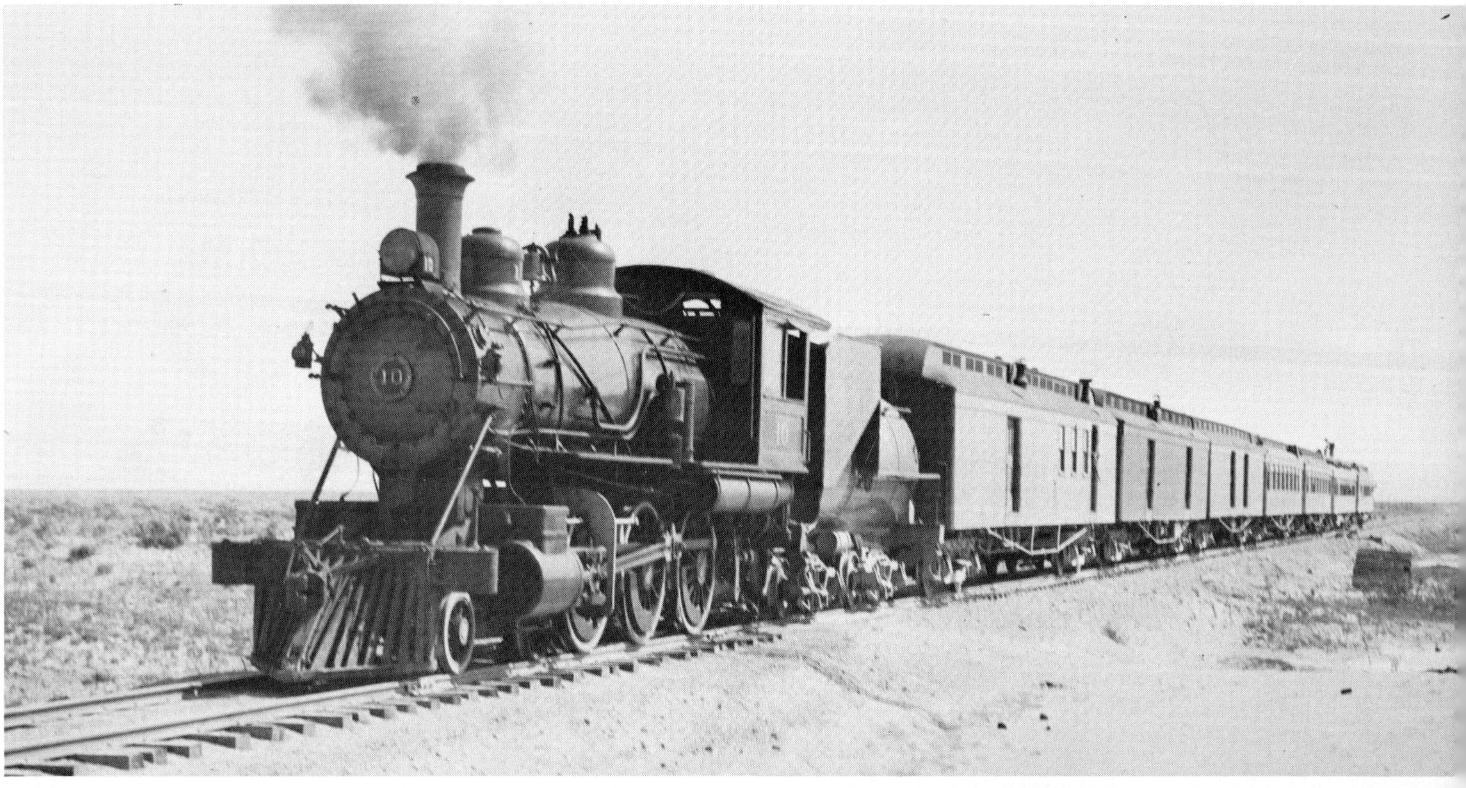

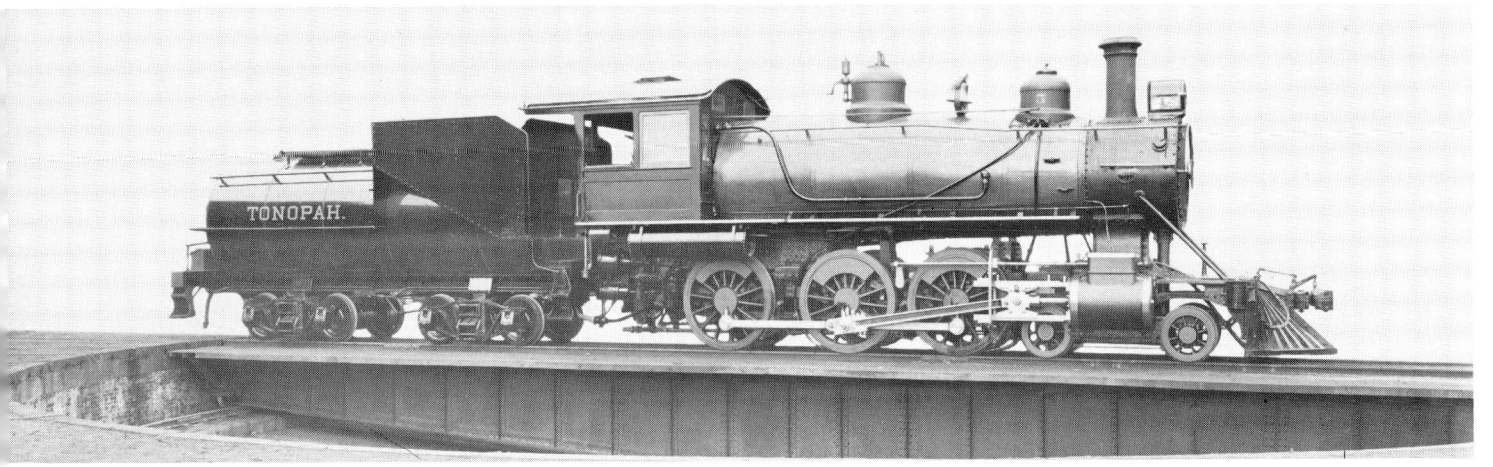

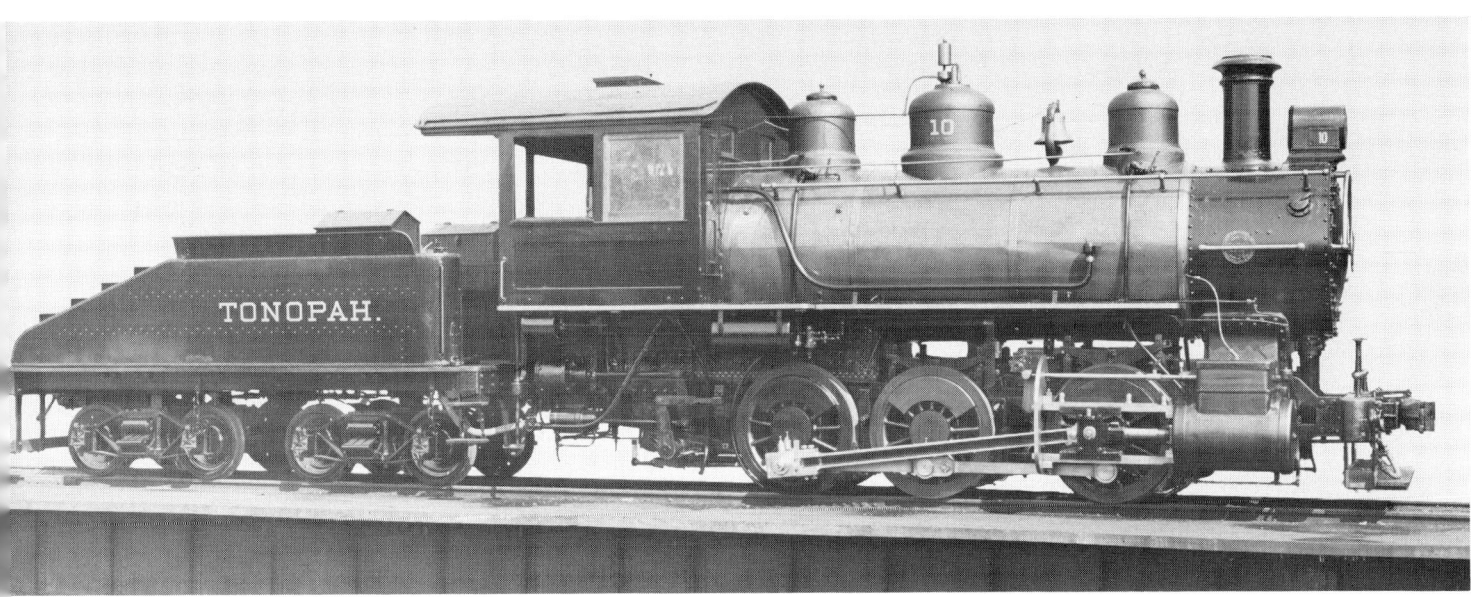

T&G locomotives did not stay as meticulously groomed as they appear on these pages, for sand and desert storms rapidly took their toll. The two locomotives *(above)* were original Tonopah Railroad equipment when that line was standard-gauged on August 14, 1905. The 6-wheel switcher No. 10 was the only switcher ever owned by the road; and in the reshuffling following merger of the Goldfield Railroad with the Tonopah on November 1, 1905, switcher No. 10 became T&G No. 1, while the Goldfield Railroad's (4-6-0) 10-wheeler No. 1 *(center, left)* became No. 10 on the combined Tonopah & Goldfield roster. In the general view *(left, below)* No. 10 has stopped its train on the desert about 25 miles north of Goldfield in the summer of 1907 so that a small fire in the vestibule of the rear Pullman could be extinguished. *(Top, left: Al Rose Photo; Center and Bottom: Stanley Palmer Photos; Three Photos This Page: H. L. Broadbelt Collection.)*

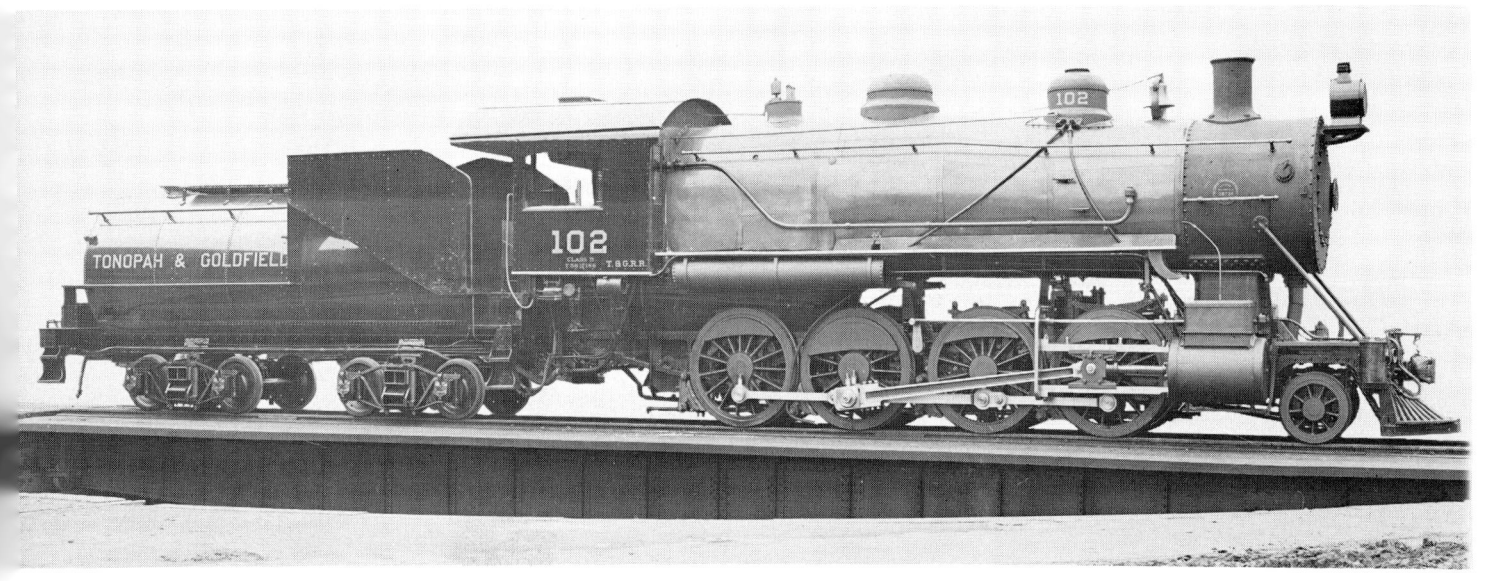

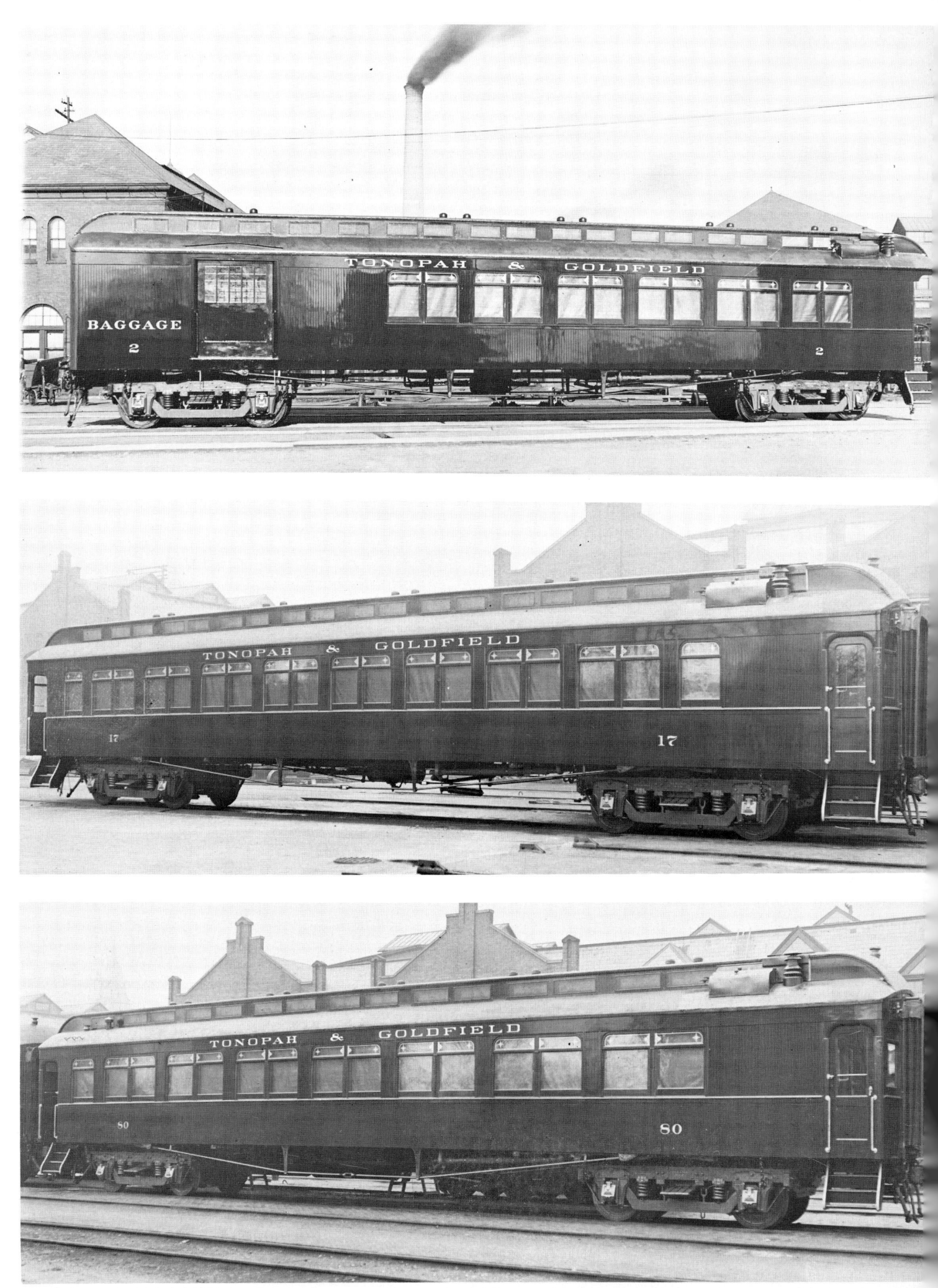

The beauty and craftsmanship that went into the T&G's standard-gauge passenger equipment are clearly evident in the three photos *(left)* taken before delivery of the cars in January 1907. *(Pullman-Standard Car Mfg. Company.)*

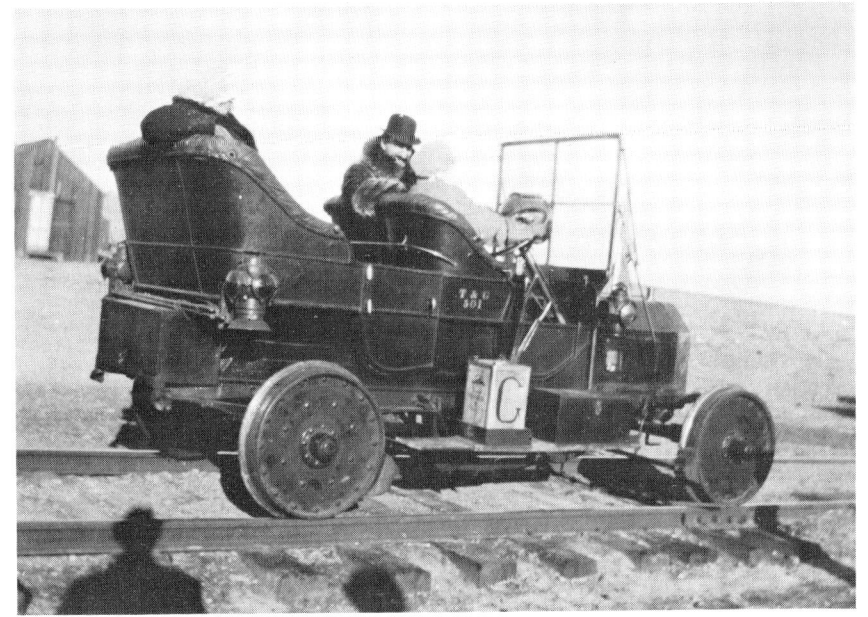

The number "501" does *NOT* indicate that the T&G operated a fleet of 500 rail inspection cars such as is illustrated *(top, right)*. Abundantly equipped with four marker lights — two each fore and aft — a four-square windshield and four-wheel brakes, this converted tonneau touring car with right-hand drive, outboard gear shift and a huge spot light for night driving appears to be giving the gauntleted lady driver a bit of trouble as it heels to the curve in the tracks at Coaldale. Or does the trouble stem from the attentive, raccoon-coated gent in the front seat or the well bundled lady in back? There's no denying the extra five-gallon can of petrol anchored on the running board will assure their crossing the desert to Tonopah before reaching short supply. *(Grahame Hardy Collection.)*

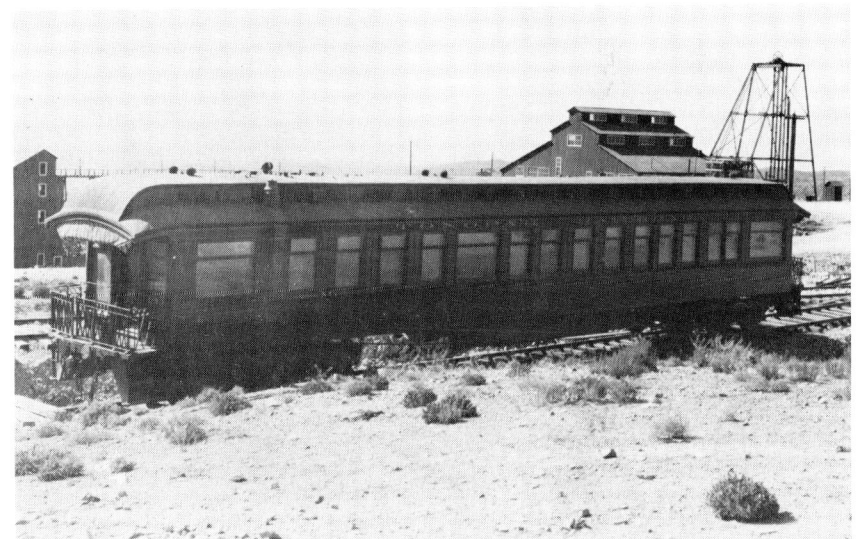

Built for the Tonopah Railroad before its merger with the Goldfield, the luxury appointed, double observationed *Janet (center, right)* was the pride of the road. It is pictured here at Tonopah on the private car spur near the Valley View Claim with the Mizpah Shaft and mine buildings in the background. *(Clarence M. Oddie Photo.)*

Another self-propelled car was Motor M-103 shown here at Millers with a trailing baggage car. In April 1948 when this picture was taken, only the most modest passenger accommodations needed to be provided for the occasional wayfarer. *(W. A. Pennington Photo, Guy Dunscomb Collection.)*

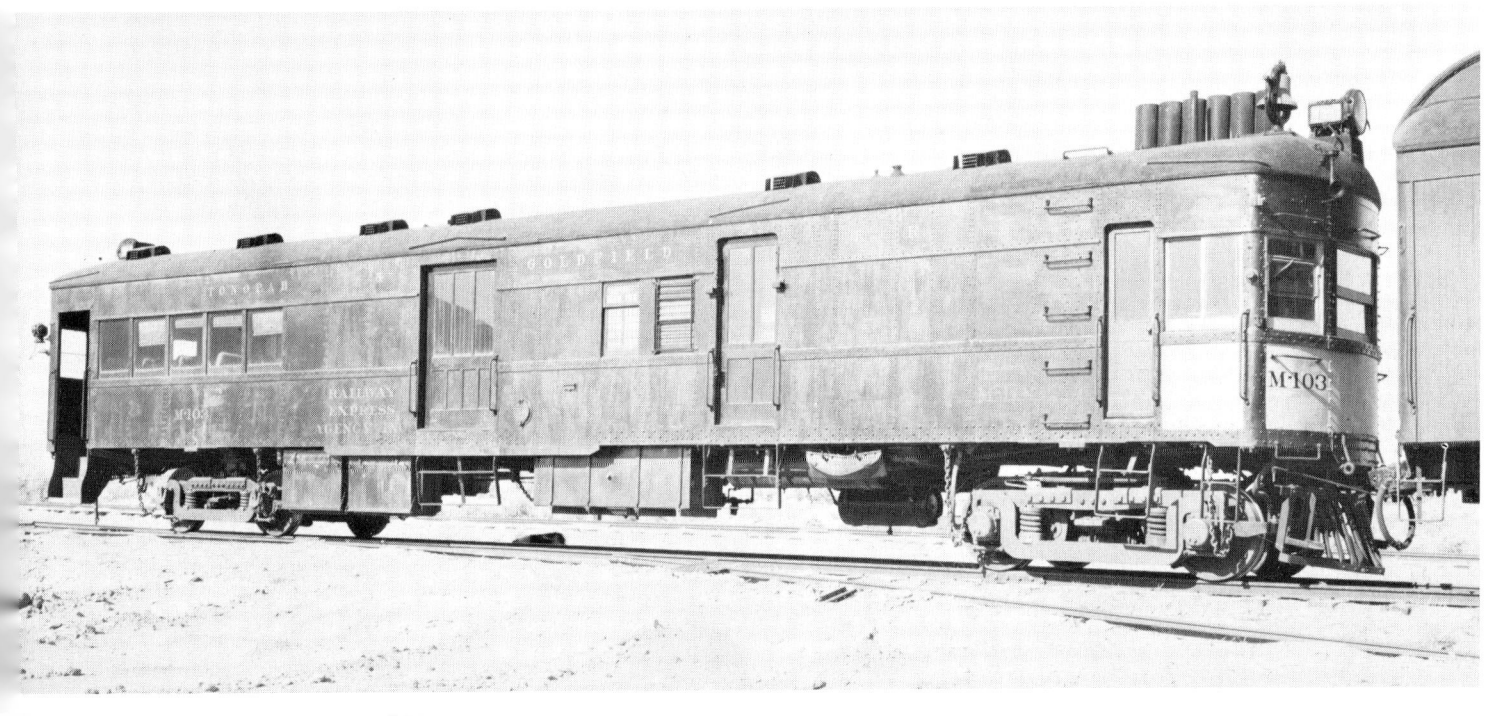

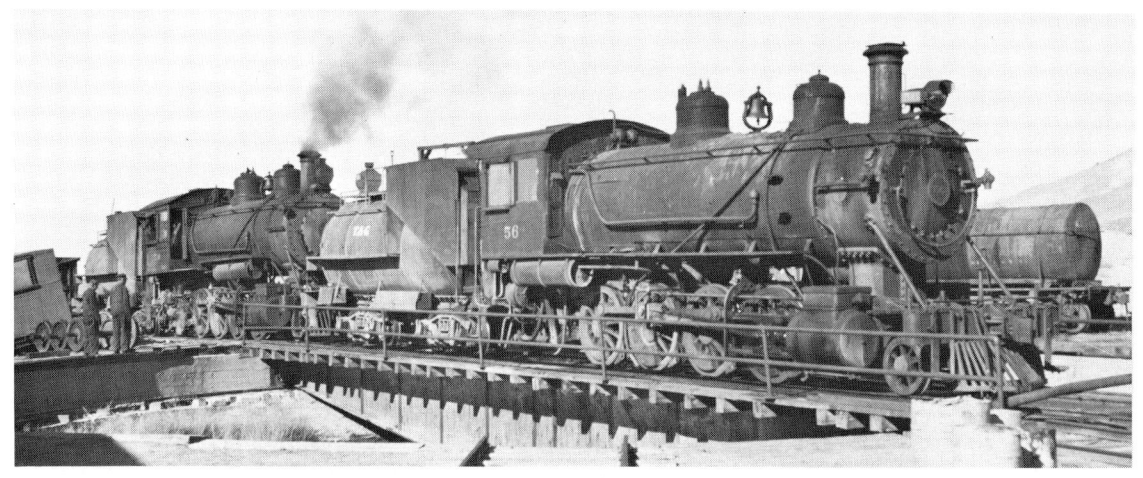
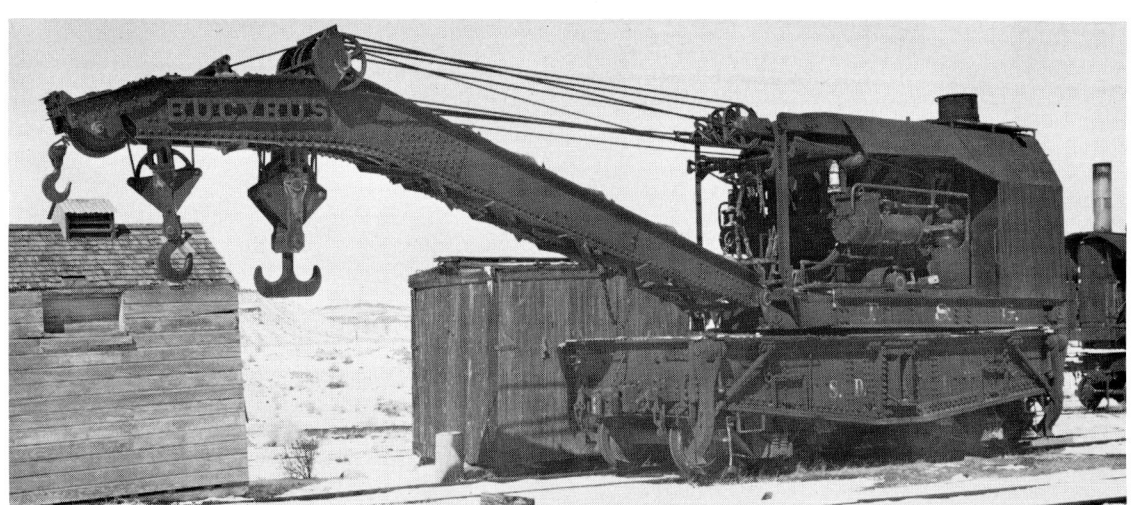
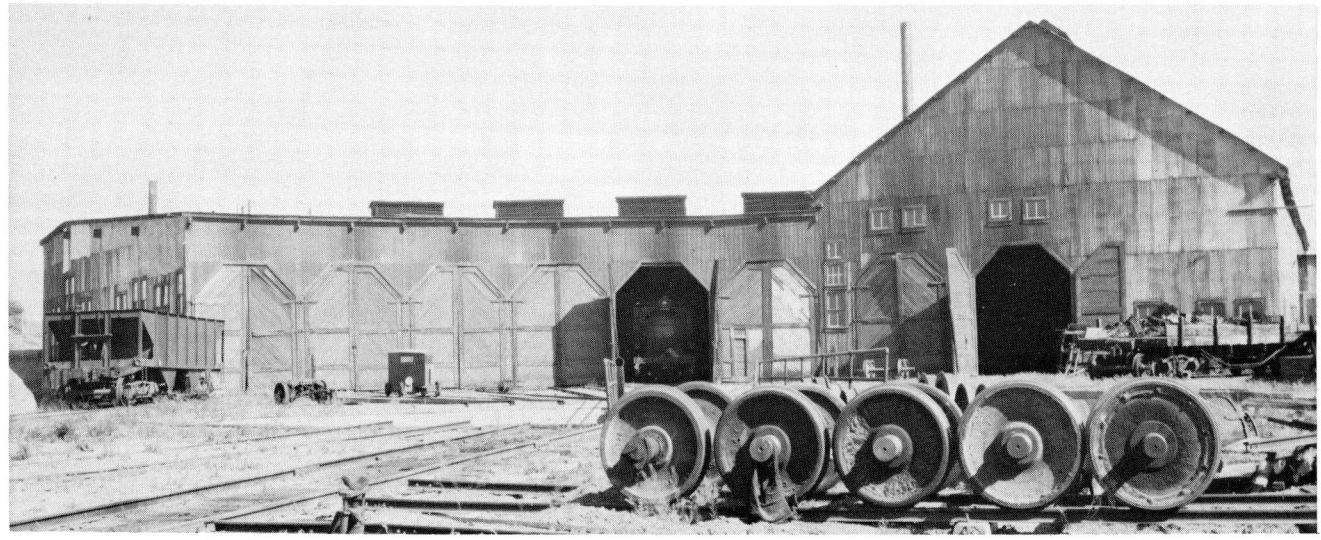
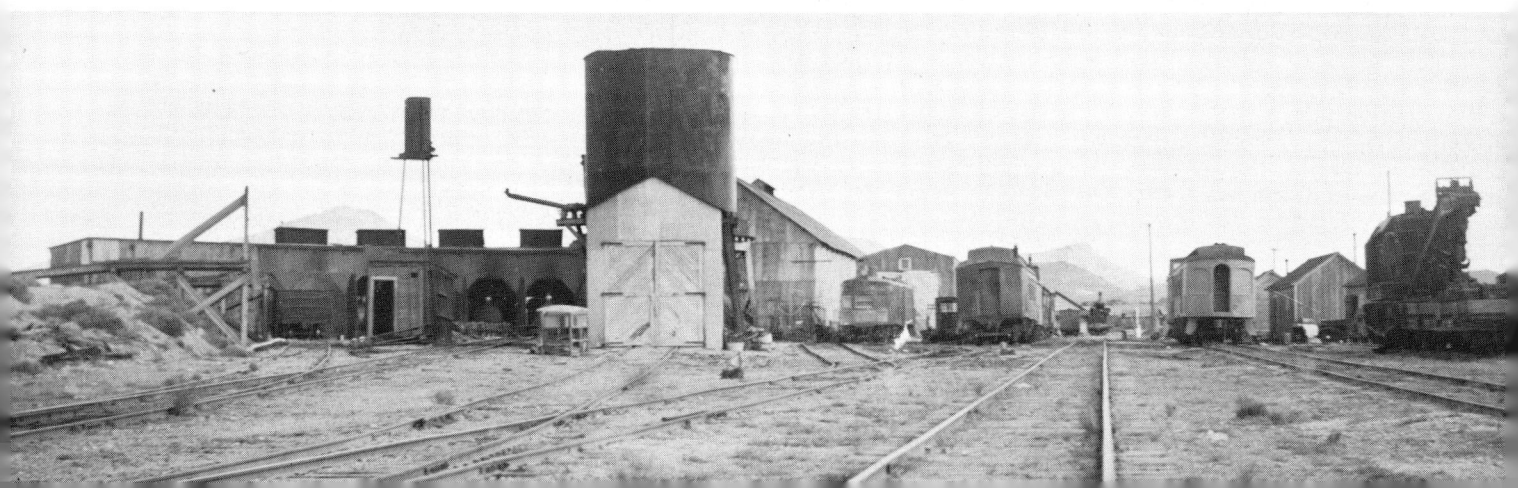

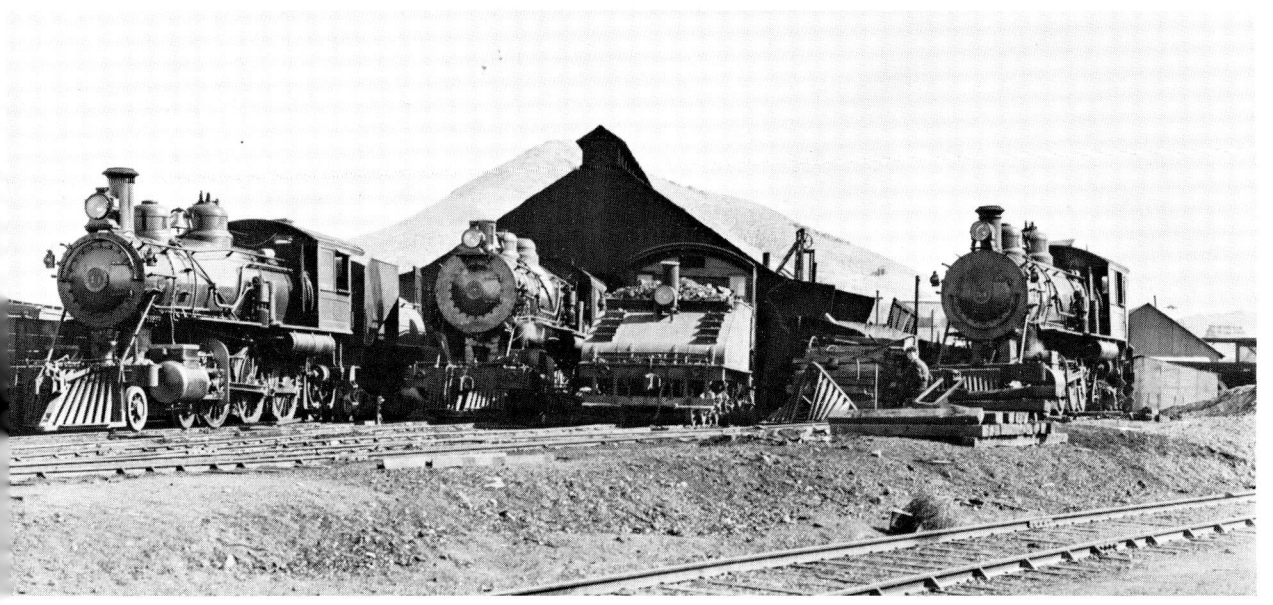

When the T&G's shops in Tonopah went up in flames in 1909, Goldfield seized upon the opportunity and offered to donate a section of land between North Main Street and Broadway if the railroad would relocate its shops in town. All pictures *(left hand page)* were taken at this Goldfield location in the 1940's, about the time Dulien Steel Products, Inc. of Seattle took over operations. In contrast, *(above)* are the former facilities at Tonopah with Mt. Oddie in the background. *(Top, left: Al Rose Photo; Others: Guy L. Dunscomb; Above: Clarence M. Oddie Photo.)*

With white flags flying, this one-car special of the Tonopah Railroad *(below)* was obliged to pause on the desert for minor adjustment and repair in spite of its small contingent of prominent mining men who came forward to watch the progress of the work. They are Frank Keith, Chas. R. Miller, W. W. Satterwait, John T. Overberry and W. W. Keith. The Tonopah Railroad's No. 6 became T&G No. 12 following the merger with the Goldfield Railroad in 1905. *(Clarence M. Oddie Photo.)*

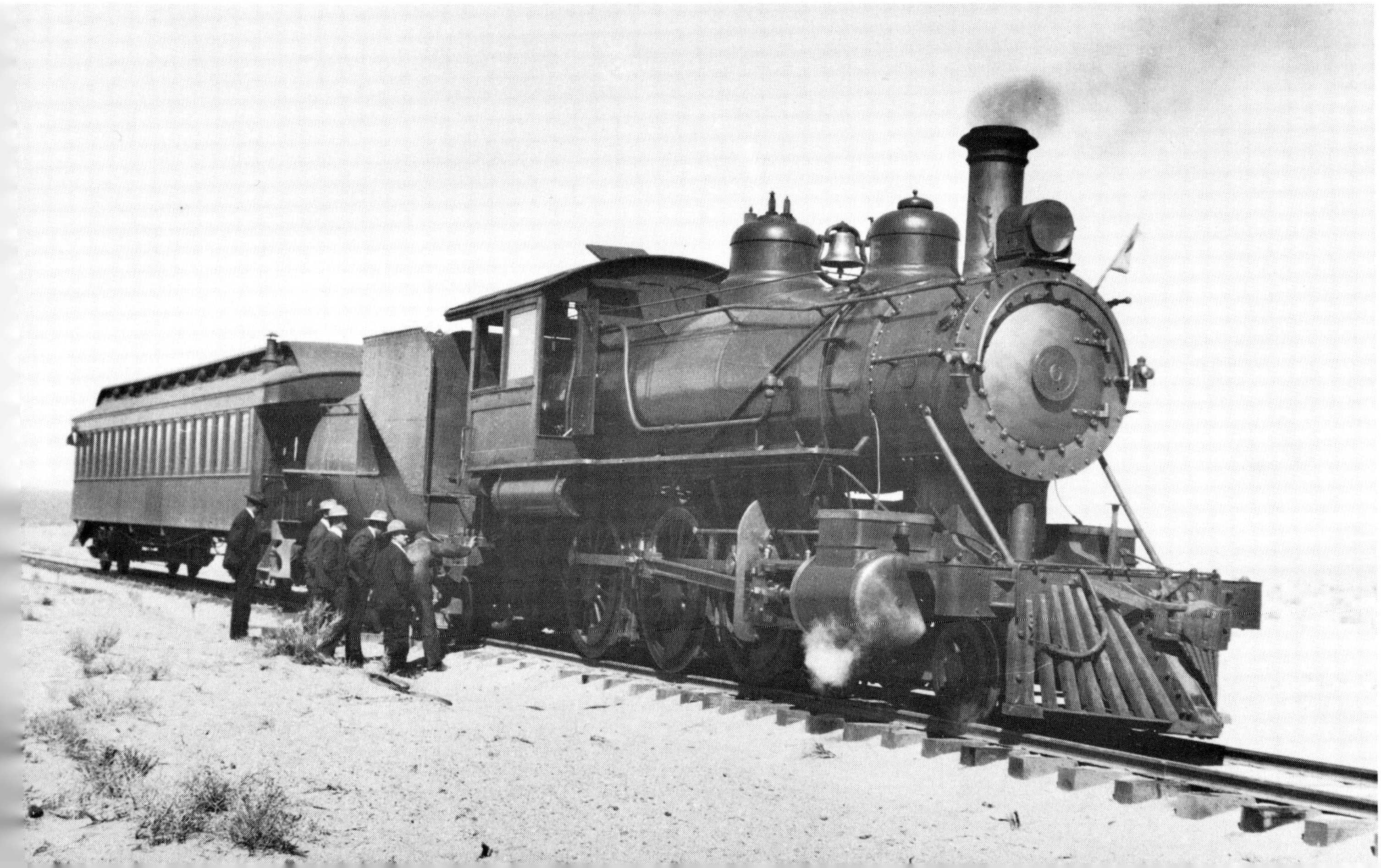

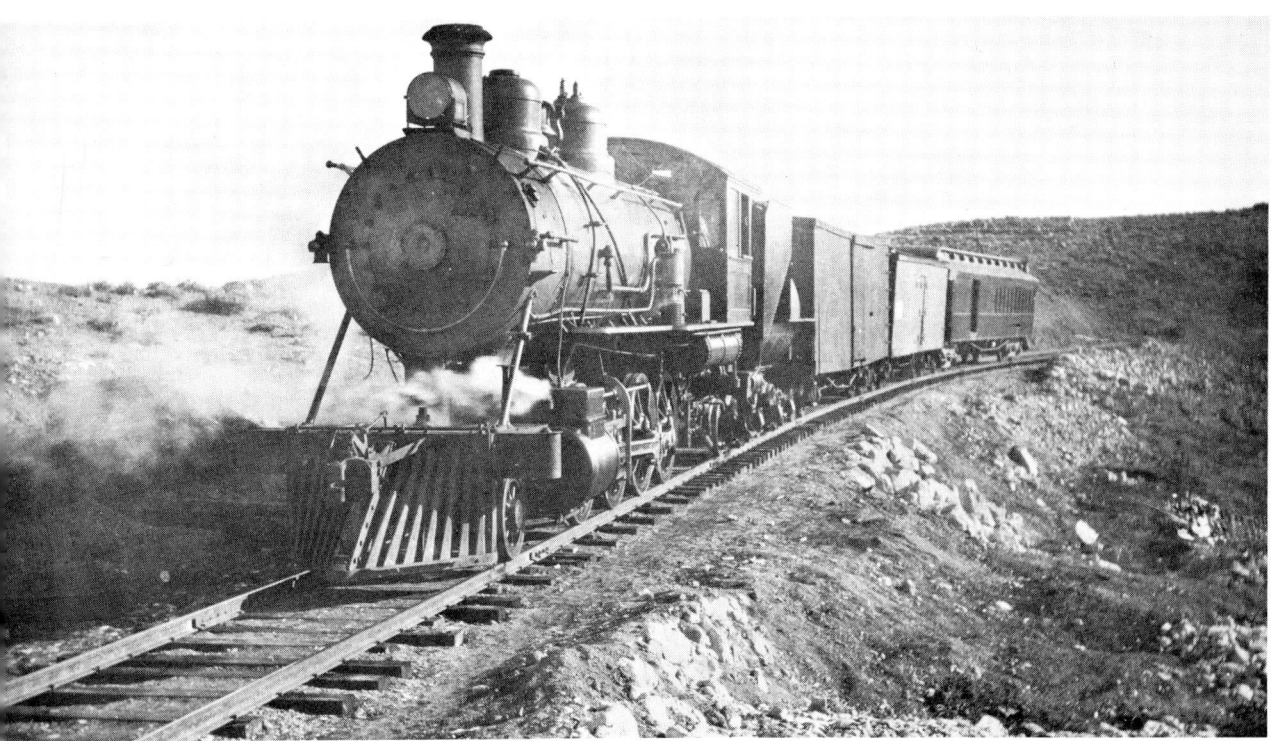

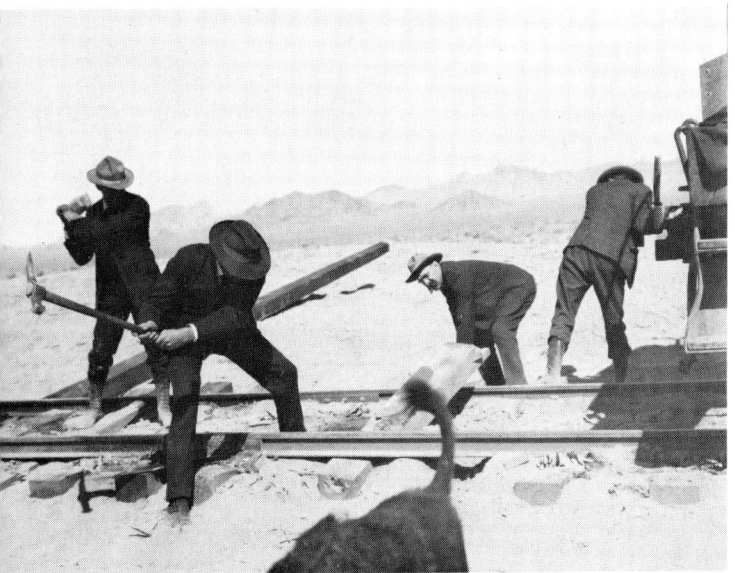

The frequent appearance of short, narrow-gauge ties beneath the rails indicates that this picture of Tonopah Railroad No. 9 and mixed train drifting down the hill from Tonopah was taken shortly after the line was converted to standard gauge on August 14, 1905. *(E. V. Dodge Photo.)*

Trains did stop on the desert for a variety of reasons, usually minor troubles. Here the railroad's owners were caught by the camera as they indulged in a bit of horseplay, the destruction more comical because of their patently city attire. *(Center: Clarence M. Oddie Photo; Bottom: Stanley Palmer Photo.)*

Man's strange devisings are illustrated *(right)* in the form of home-made Motor No. 1 and its equally confusing trailer shown standing on the SP's three-rail tracks at Mina in the early 1930's. *(W. A. Pennington Photo.)*

Tonopah Railroad No. 5 *(center)* bedecked with white flags, ran as a light extra out of Reno for delivery at Mina. After the merger it became No. 11 on the T&G. Gasoline for the Tonopah Air Base *(bottom)* was important traffic in World War II. *(Center: Stanley Palmer; Bottom: Al Rose Photo.)*

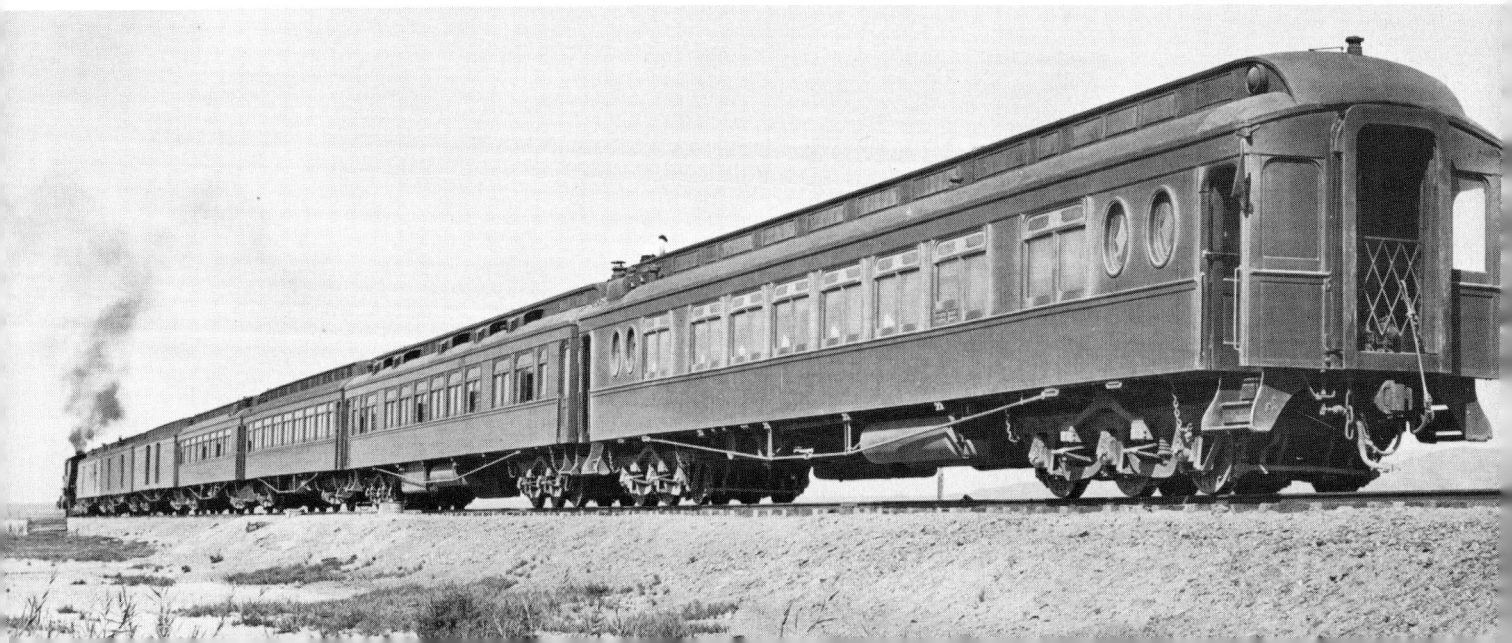

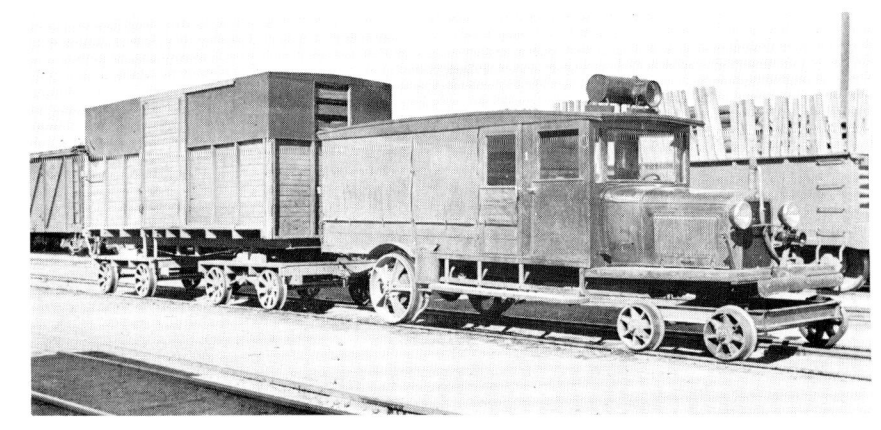

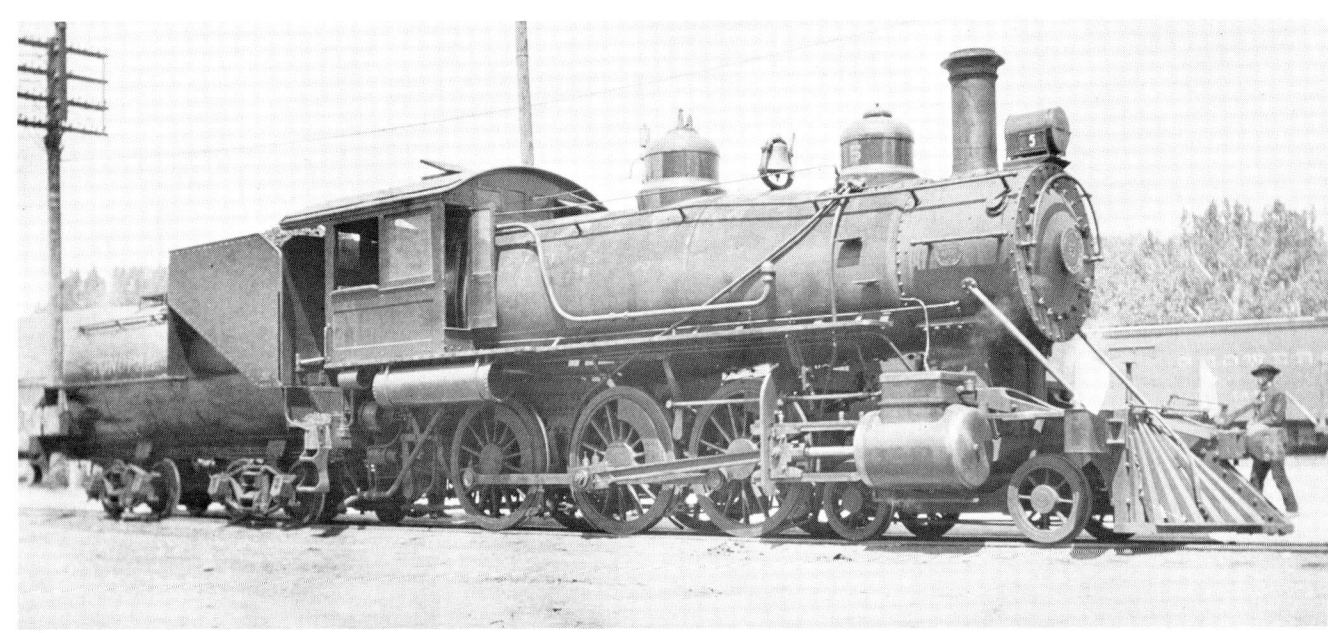

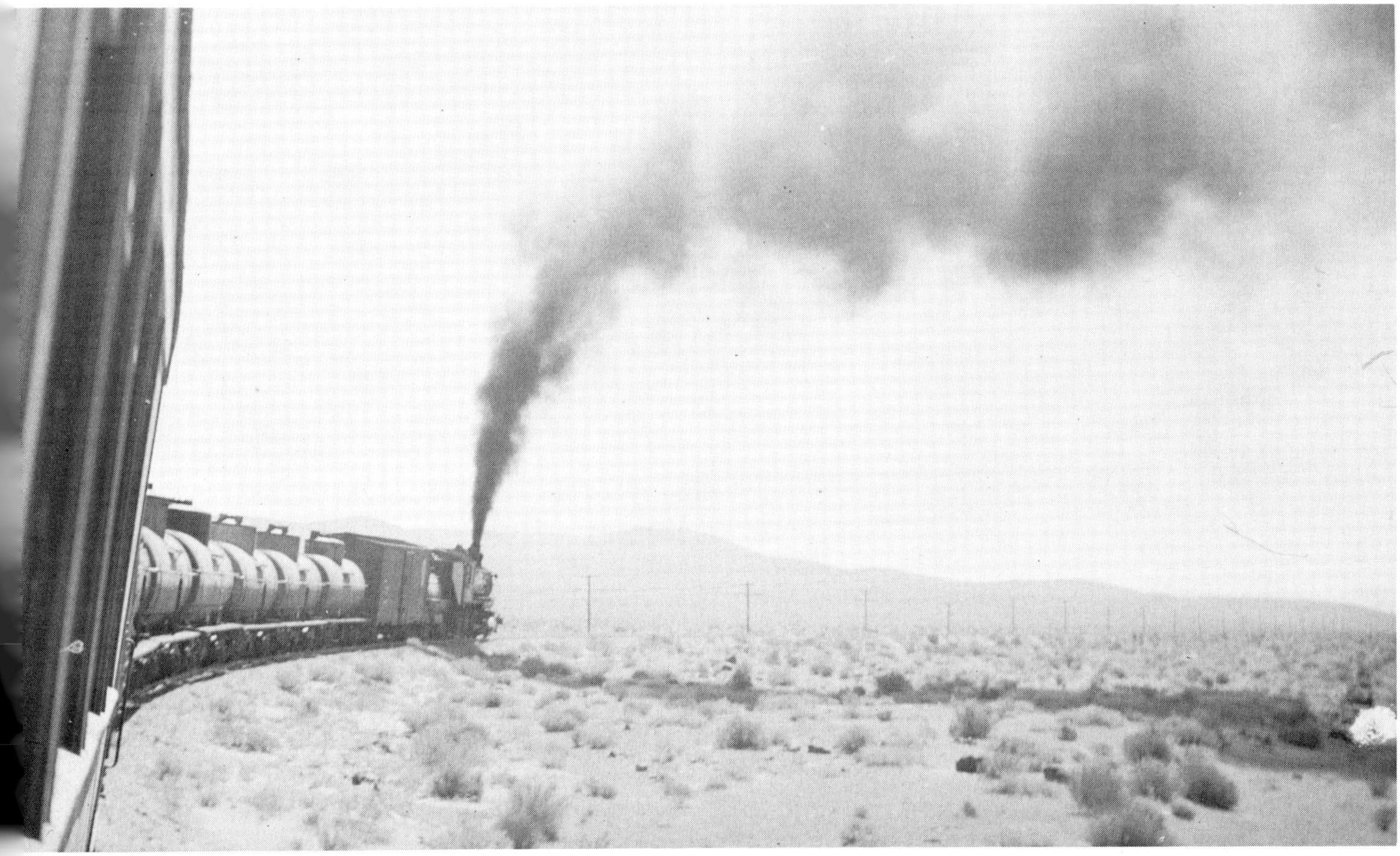

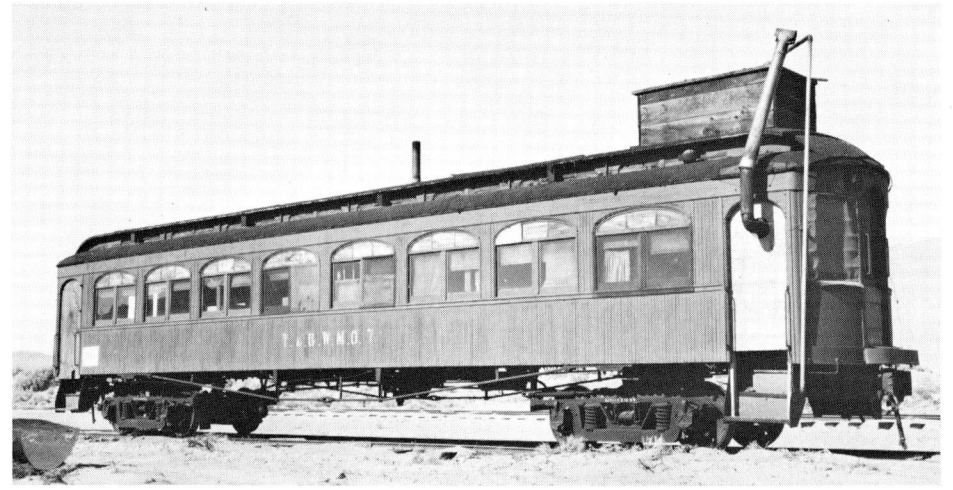

Final days on the T&G may be amply characterized by these views of a weathered coach on the siding at Millers *(top, left)*, the once proud *Mizpah (center)* in custody of the Walker-Hovey Lumber Co. at Canby in northern California, and the late afternoon train out of Tonopah *(below)*, powered by a borrowed U. S. Transportation Corps Diesel in October 1945. Activity at Tonopah has diminished; the rails, which once encircled Mt. Oddie (right of center, background) to serve the Belmont and other mines, have been withdrawn; solitude and loneliness pervade the scene. *(Top: W. A. Pennington Photo; Center: Ted Wurm Collection; Bottom: Al Rose Photo.)*

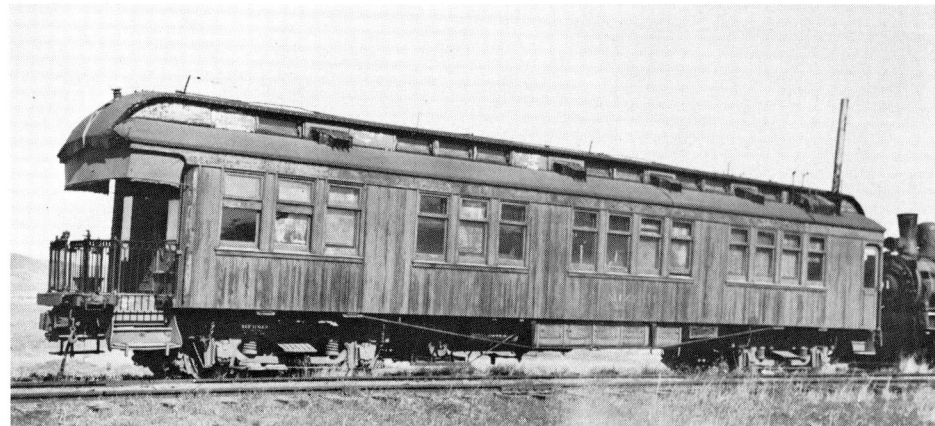

At Goldfield the passenger station has been moved to a point of vantage along the highway where, with no rails approaching it, it is used as a bar. It is located *(top, right)* one mile south of Crook Avenue on the way to Beatty, and the whistles of approaching trains *(bottom, right)* will no longer be heard as they cross Highway 95 to the north. *(Bottom: Walter Averett Collection.)*

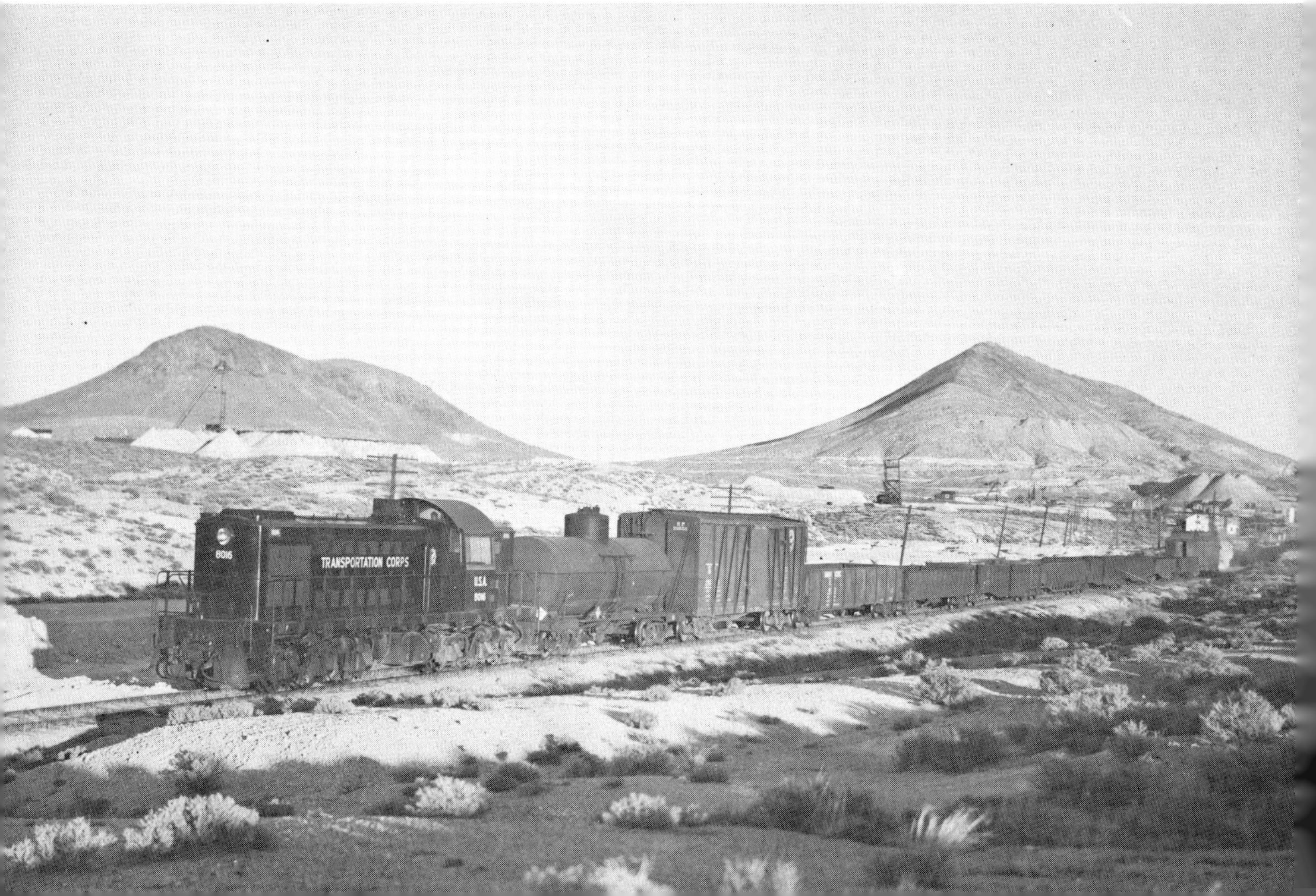

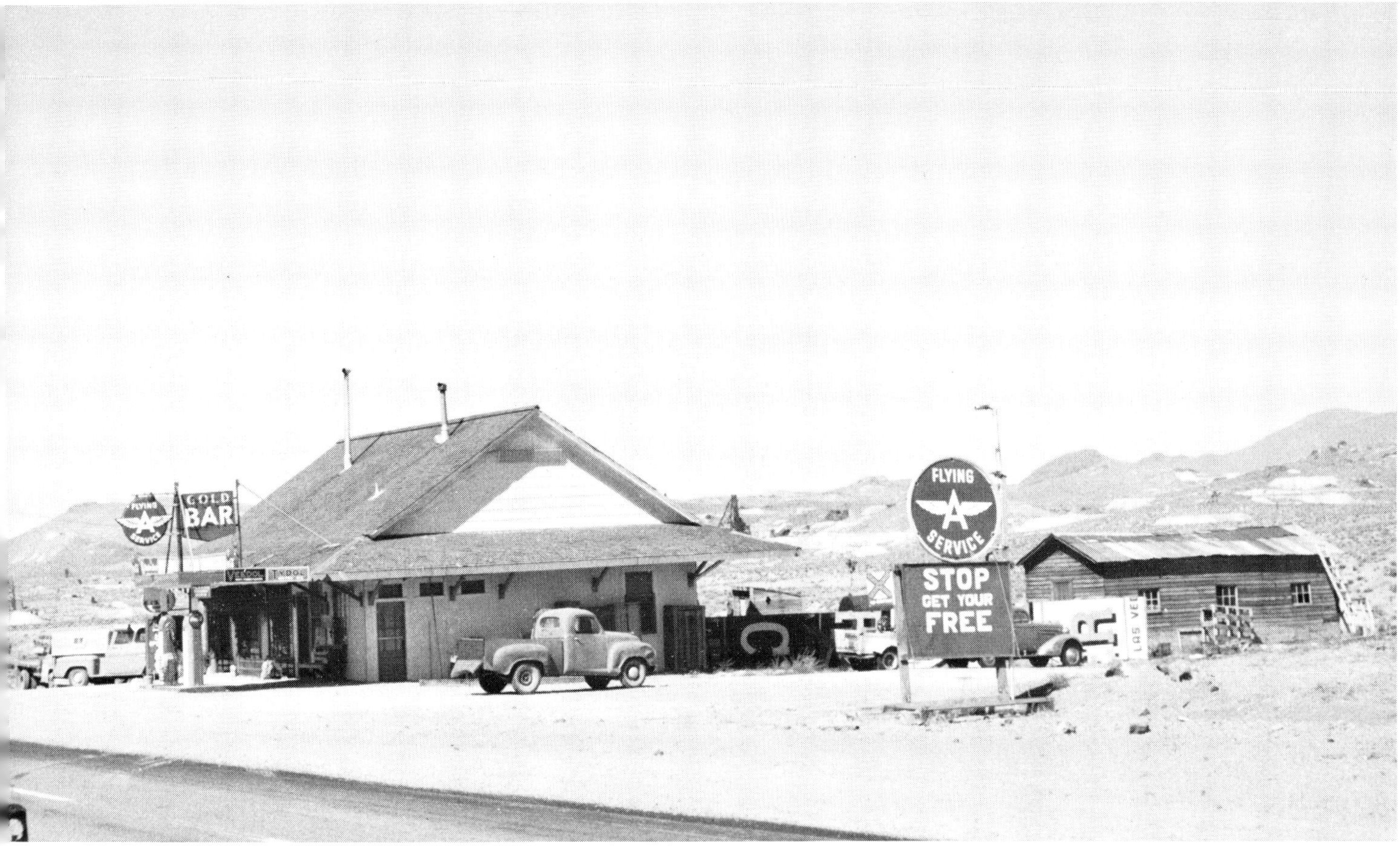

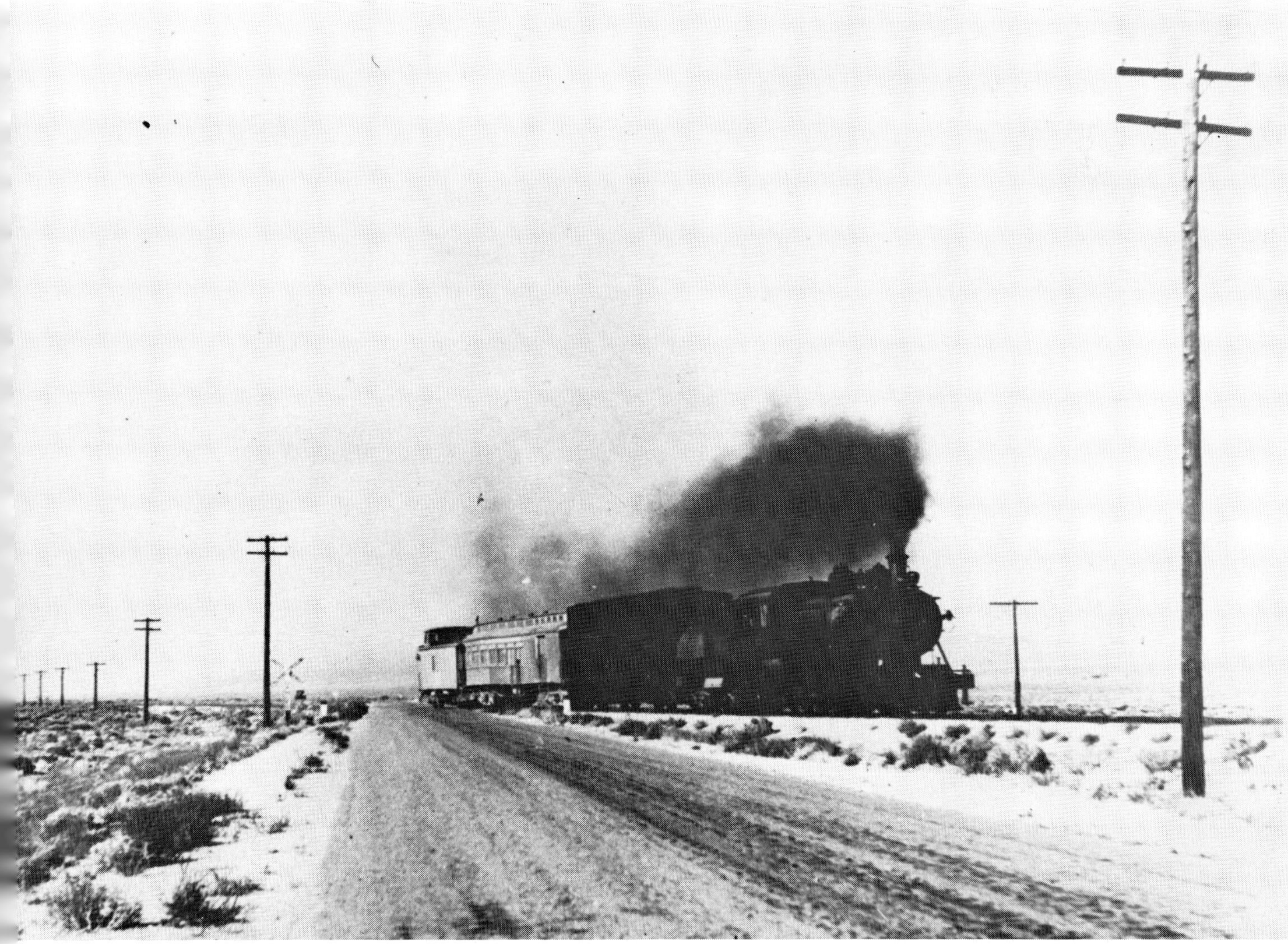

road under lease. At the same time the Board also authorized the sale of a steam shovel and three worn-out passenger locomotives.

The T&G's strong cash position had been running around $400,000 in cash, marketable securities, Liberty bonds and demand loans. Late in 1927, following a new Nevada statute permitting such action, $250,000 was appropriated to buy in all of the preferred stock at half price, in lieu of using such "excess funds" for dividends. With the exception of 62 shares in the hands of one stockholder, the entire issue was thus retired.

Dull times persisted, however, and took their toll of the competition. In January 1928 the second of the southern roads (the Bullfrog Goldfield) ceased operations and was abandoned. With the removal of its rails, the T&G had the area — at least what was left of it — all to itself. The only remaining southern line, the T&T, reached only to Gold Center and Beatty to the south.

The first major accident in 20 years of T&G operations occurred on September 22, 1928. A brake beam dropped and derailed the mixed train. Two passengers were injured in the wreck, and the track and equipment were extensively damaged.

The following year was one of crisis. Reduced earnings continued. Passenger revenues amounted to a meagre $14,000, a sharp drop from those of 10 years previous in 1919 when $96,000 was recorded or even more dramatically, the heyday of 1907 when $572,000 was paid for transportation over the line. The trend was reflected by sale of the private car, *Mizpah,* for $800 and one of the passenger cars for $500. Motor Car No. 99 and 10 gondolas also changed ownership to complete the tally of equipment reductions. Of the 2,471 freight cars handled during the year, over 70% (1,777 cars) carried ores and coal, yet accounted for less than a third of the freight revenue. The most lucrative traffic comprised the 694 carloads of food, gasoline, general merchandise and other supplies. Total revenues for the year amounted to $291,000 (approximately an eighth of that of the boom years), yet by shrinking operations to fit the available business the road was able to show a profit of $24,000, including a 20% pay cut President Cutter delegated to himself.

The market crash of 1929 only served to heighten the crisis. Six weeks after it happened the Executive Committee called its demand loans and used the proceeds to purchase "such high grade securities as may be readily marketable." By this means stocks of 11 different railroads were acquired at a cost of $186,385, and in March of 1930 they were sold at a profit of $11,410. The T&G then decided to buy in its own common stock at lowest possible prices, not to exceed $35 per share or a total of $175,000. As a result of the offer, 6,049 shares were purchased at an average cost of $29 per share, but the effort depleted the strong cash position which the Company had maintained for so many years. Following the program, cash on hand amounted to a mere $10,000 while the portfolio of marketable securities which had cost $47,000 was still steadily declining in value. The future looked bleak indeed; and it was.

Each month until September 1930 the T&G operated at a loss. In October M. B. Cutter stepped down from the presidency, and W. L. Haehnlen (pronounced Hanlon) moved from vice-president into the top job. One of his first actions was to cut his own salary from $500 to $300 per month, but money was still so tight it was necessary to borrow $10,000 by the end of the year to pay the taxes. Further economies were planned including some drastic reductions in service.

When the Tonopah Extension Mining Co., one of the larger shippers, closed down early in 1931 train schedules were revised even more drastically than previously anticipated. Steam trains were reduced from three to two a week, and a Ford truck, converted to rail use, was purchased from the Brookville Locomotive Co. to be run on the days the regular trains were not operating. Service under this schedule was instituted on March 27, too late to affect the net loss shown for the first two months of the year of $10,000 or to prevent the borrowing of $3,000 from the Tonopah Mining Co., still the principal stockholder. Official salaries were cut again, the president's being reduced to $200 per month; more money was borrowed to meet the second installment of 1930 taxes payable in 1931 of $14,370; expenses were subject to more rigid controls than ever before. By July 1931 operations just showed in black ink for the first time.

Then came more trouble. A late summer cloudburst in August damaged the roadbed. In October mining operations at Tybo, an important source of business, closed down. One encouraging sign on the horizon was a new talc operation 50 miles south of Goldfield. In December, steam train service was cut to one train a week, the rail motor car providing substitute facilities on all other days. For a time experimental runs were made with a McKeen rail car rented from the SP, but the results were not satisfactory.

Although itself hard pressed, the Southern Pacific acceded to the T&G's request to cut in half the rentals for the joint track and terminal facilities at Mina. T&G benefits from this action were more than neutralized when the Tonopah Mining Company demanded return of its $15,000 by May 16, 1932, or they would petition the U. S. District Court to appoint receivers. With an empty treasury and $11,000 in taxes due on June 6, the T&G directors instructed the Mining Company officers to join with them on June 2 in a petition seeking appointment of a receiver. (Receivership would assure continued operation of the property, whereas without it a creditor might attach a local bank account needed for payrolls and operations would cease forthwith.) On June 27, 1932, in keeping with the usual practice of appointing former officers, Haehnlen and Cattermole became receivers of the property, qualifying on July 19. Had it not been for local taxes and costly cloudbursts, the road might have squeaked through the 1930's. Most railroads were faced with the difficulty of meeting interest requirements on their bonded debt; the T&G was in a far more favorable position, having retired the last of its bonds in 1917.

The Reconstruction Finance Corporation turned a deaf ear to pleas for help in 1934. One major washout had set the T&G back some $7,000, and an additional $25,000 was sorely needed to finance rebuilding of 50 ore cars to bring them up to AAR standards for interchange.

A surprising net profit of $25,507 was earned in 1935. The costly expense of a second gas-electric car was offset by other economies including the purchase from the receivers of the Tonopah Banking Corporation of their three-story stone office building in Goldfield, including all fixtures, for $3,029.35. The building provided low-cost office space for the railroad, while additional income was provided through the lease of extra space to others. All in all, it was a nice performance for a receivership road in a depression year.

Gold and silver prices moved upward in 1936, bringing with them a revival in mining and an upsurge in shipping via the T&G. Although gross revenues boomed to approximately $200,000 (almost double the 1939-41 revenues), net income was about one-half of that reported in 1935. The following year the red ink appeared again on the ledger when the Treadwell Yukon property at Tybo, the second largest producer of lead and zinc in Nevada closed down. A net loss of $2,600 was reflected on the railroad's books when this and other factors affected the economy. Truck competition increased as more franchises were granted by the PSC, while management casualties took their internal toll. The Chief Engineer, Cattermole, was killed when a tire blew out on his auto near Walker Lake; then his successor, R. S. Titlow, fell from a cliff into Walker Lake, apparently a victim of poor eyesight.

In spite of the difficulties, the internal economies of the road improved sufficiently so that, on July 31, 1937 the receivership was terminated and the property returned to the stockholders. Many problems still prevailed. The passenger business was subject to so much competition the comment was elicited that "revenue from this source is rapidly approaching the vanishing point." Shutdown of the Eastern Exploration Co. at Goldfield in September caused a further reduction of revenues, although somehow the railroad had again built up a relatively strong cash position.

Finally, even the Tonopah Mining Co. began to tire of its stepchild. In 1939 the statement was made: "The problem of continued operation of the railroad is becoming a very serious one for the Company." The next year two of the six serviceable locomotives were retired. Finally, in November 1940 a group of minority stockholders headed by William Fogarty of Philadelphia brought suit in Carson City, demanding that a receiver be appointed and that necessary applications for abandonment be filed. The group's aim was to scrap the property promptly and liquidate the assets before further losses were incurred. Abandonment was avoided, however, when the U. S. District Judge dismissed the case the following summer. As the war in Europe progressed, it was anticipated that ore shipments would increase. Then President W. L. Haehnlen died. For years he had felt a great loyalty and love for the railroad and treated it as a pet project. His heirs, not having any sentimental interest, arranged for the Tonopah Mining Company to sell its controlling interests to Dulien Steel Products, Inc., of Seattle. The price was $226,768.40 or $29 per share (the same price at which the T&G purchased its own shares in 1930)—the date, October 13, 1942.

Although the T&G was unaware of it, the next five years of its existence were to be its last. They were hectic, topsy-turvy years, full of surprises and reversals largely created through the exigencies of World War II. Their analysis abounded with the factors of which abandonments are made, and the T&G was to be no exception.

Even as Dulien Steel Products took over the railroad, the infamous War Production Board Order L-208 had gone into effect causing most of the gold mines in the area to shut down in April 1942. Ore tonnage over the railroad virtually ceased with the exception of shipments from the Tonopah Mining Company. Its property was being operated by leasers, and the silicious content of the ore made it desirable as a fluxing agent in copper smelting. Dulien, on the other hand, was not anxious for the business for it had acquired the railroad in the anticipation of realizing a profit from its salvage. Before anything could be done, however, the Army Air Force established its Air Base at Tonopah, and traffic began to soar.

From an economic standpoint, 1945 was the peak year of operations with revenues reaching $493,000, four times those of the pre-war level. Freight constituted the principal source of revenue, and most of the inbound traffic consisted of tank cars of aviation gasoline. Passenger revenues, which had averaged less than a dollar a day in 1940, increased 100-fold, due in great measure to heavy troop movements. Significantly, even this large volume of business resulted in profits in only two years (1942 and 1945) while all other years, particularly 1944 and 1946, ended with heavy losses. In 1946, the first full post-war year, business sank to a depression level; motive power difficulties forced the placing of an embargo on all traffic; the Public Service Commission of Nevada issued a suspension order for a period of 60 days from October 1, 1946; hearings were held at the courthouse in Tonopah the first week in October; and the facts began to come out.

Admittedly the difficulties were the result of bad management. Captain Walter Rowson, attorney for the line for years, told of the many problems connected with wartime operations. In large measure, much of the trouble stemmed from poor superintendence. The initial incumbent, Superintendent Jack Peck, had been with the road for a number of years and was then not in the best of health. He had relied quite extensively upon assistance from H. A. Johnson, president of the Tonopah Mining Company (and a protestant at the hearing). When Peck resigned the position in December 1943, Dulien brought in Colonel Kruttschnitt, a retired Army officer whose qualifications included railroad experience and a father famous in SP history.

Kruttschnitt had expensive tastes and ran the railroad accordingly. One famous extravagance was the replacement of 17 wooden trestles with concrete at a cost of from $3,000 to $4,000 each. Another involved his lavish use of labor. Men were difficult to find during the war years, so Kruttschnitt would call Captain Rowson in Reno with the demand: "I need 75 men." Rowson, in turn, would contact the U. S. Employment Service and the War Labor Board in an effort to fill his request, and such men as could be recruited were sent down. The majority represented floating labor for whom such items as bunkhouses, mattresses, pillows, sheets, etc., were furnished by the railroad. The turnover of labor, particularly during 1944, was abnormally high, and for months efforts to obtain Mexican Nationals to replace the winos were fruitless. Suddenly in the summer of 1944 Kruttschnitt announced his intention of transferring to the U. N. Rehabilitation Administration, another not inconsiderable expense for he had to be retained on the payroll pending his appearance as a witness in an I. C. C. hearing.

Dulien next found Bernard Yates, formerly with the Copper River & Northwestern Railroad in Alaska, to succeed to the superintendency vacated by Kruttschnitt. In spite of keeping two managers on the payroll, it was anticipated that the new talent would shortly solve many of the prevalent problems. Unfortunately, as Captain Rowson explained, "Mr. Yates' management was nothing short of tragic. He was a spendthrift. While Colonel Kruttschnitt had been with a Class A railroad and also with the Army where the budget is usually inflated, at least he had made efforts to put on the brakes. I don't think Mr. Yates put on any brakes at all. The sky was the limit. The payroll increased by leaps and bounds. Some help was brought all the way from Alaska—high-priced men." The statistics reflected the results—maintenance of way expenses jumped to $187,000, over three times the figure for 1943. Shopmen increased in number; some individual monthly paychecks were as high as $1,100.

In December 1944 Rowson tried to interest J. M. Hiskey, formerly with the Nevada Central Railroad and later with the O. D. T., in taking over the job, but Hiskey turned it down. Ultimately Dulien located James Loftus in February 1945, and once again there were two managers on the payroll for a time. However, results were forthcoming. Where

Yates had moved the offices from Goldfield to Tonopah and spent a lot of money leveling off a site for the shops at the Victor Shaft in Tonopah (under lease at $150 per month), Loftus quickly abandoned the project and found a suitable site near the rear of the Tonopah depot. In the one year under Loftus' rule the T&G showed a profit of almost $69,000, whereas the year before the loss aggregated nearly $64,000. "In my opinion," Captain Rowson explained, "if we had been fortunate enough to have obtained the services of Mr. Loftus a year earlier than we did, we would not today be present for any hearing on abandonment."

Unfortunately, Loftus resigned the position in November 1945, and C. A. White, formerly with the Magma Arizona Railroad, took charge until formal abandonment late in 1947.

The lack of good management was felt in many other ways. From 1940 to 1944 the serviceable fleet of the road's locomotives remained at four in number; in the latter year two more were added to the roster. Inexperienced engineers caused many of the locomotives to be sent to the shops far ahead of normal expectancy, and at such times additional locomotives would be leased for short periods from the SP. In 1943 the entire fleet of 50 ore cars were retired, making the road completely dependent upon outside sources for car requirements. During 1944-45 the equipment was pounded to death, running night and day with two and frequently three engines on a single train. In the shops, men worked 16-hour shifts to keep the wheels turning. Finally, in September 1945 with six steamers badly in need of repair, the T&G leased two diesels from the U. S. Army and figuratively threw in the sponge.

No attempts were made to rebuild or repair the aging steamers; rather, those shop forces not specifically required were dismissed. Use of the diesels likewise rendered useless the maintenance of water and other facilities. When the pump house at Klondyke burned down and new tanks were needed, nothing was done toward replacement. Veteran roadmaster Emil Peterson declared that the tank at Millers "leaked so badly you can't keep any water in it"; then he went on to describe the condition of the bridges and trestles and drew a laugh from the group by declaring that anyone who ran a train over them ought to be decorated with a medal.

With the end of the war, economic conditions changed rapidly. One month following the cessation of hostilities the Tonopah Army Air Base was deactivated. Then the long anticipated backlog of ore production and its movement to the smelters failed to materialize due in part to the inflated cost of mining and in part to the strike-bound closing of the principal Utah smelter from December 1945 to July 1946. With business at a depression level in 1946, and with the road's equipment and facilities at their lowest ebb, it took but one little act to upset the scales of balance.

The crisis was precipitated when the Army asked for the return of its diesels. The initial request for the first of the two was placed in February 1946, but procrastination on the part of the T&G delayed the return until July 3. Then on August 28 the Army asked for delivery of the remaining unit by October 1. That was the final blow. On September 3 an embargo was announced on all traffic to become effective October 1, 1946. A few days later the T&G filed a petition for abandonment, to be followed by a suspension order from the Public Service Commission of Nevada postponing action for 60 days from October 1 so that hearings could be arranged in the Tonopah courthouse during the first week in October. At 9:30 P.M. on the stormy night of October 1 the last diesel was turned over to Lieut. Noel Wilson at Mina as cloudbursts threatened the dilapidated roadbed of the T&G's meandering mileage. Then, even as the hearings were in progress, the remaining piece of equipment, the old motor car, was derailed near Millers while hauling its consist of mail and express.

The record developed at the hearings was a long and critical one. The transcript numbered 533 pages. Admittedly bad management had existed, and the road was without the necessary funds to resume steam operation. The poor condition of the road was emphasized, which caused the PSC to claim that many of the statements were made with abandonment in mind. The traffic outlook was discussed by Ross Morris who found little encouragement for the future.

The opposition felt that the resumption of mining depended upon a railroad to haul the ores to the smelters as truck rates were too high. Representatives of the various mines hoped to ship out a few cars each month once they were able to resume production. Overlooked was the fact that wages and other mining costs were much higher than in the late 1930's, while the prices of gold and silver were at about the same levels. Also overlooked was the cold, hard fact that the railroad could not exist on sporadic ore shipments moving at low rates while the trucks skimmed the cream of the traffic.

As it could not operate as a railroad, the T&G applied for and secured temporary authority to handle its mail and express by truck.

The I.C.C. held hearings in Reno in November 1946, and on January 22, 1947, the Commission issued its order authorizing abandonment of interstate operations which constituted approximately 90% of the road's business.

The Public Service Commission of Nevada, as a result of its hearings, issued a lengthy decision on January 31, 1947, denying the T&G the authority to abandon the intrastate phase of its operations. It said in part: "This Commission is primarily concerned with the welfare of the people engaged in mining . . . For many years . . . the railroad has been of great service to these people, and it has been reasonably shown that it may continue to be of such service as the country once more gradually returns to normal. In the interests of these people, the company should be required to continue service."

The Nevada Commission then petitioned the I.C.C. for a reconsideration of its decision. When this was denied, the T&G's interstate operations ceased, although intrastate operations were still required. The T&G then filed a complaint in the First Judicial District Court in Carson City to have the PSC order set aside. Hearings commenced on May 21, 1947, and at their conclusion the Court returned the entire record to the PSC for further review and consideration.

On June 29 the PSC issued its opinion again denying abandonment. Back to the court the matter went for argument, and on August 28, 1947, the District Judge, Clark J. Guild, issued his decision setting aside the order of the PSC. Abandonment was finally realized.

Judge Guild, a man with mining experience who had spent his young manhood in the area was sympathetic with the need of the industry for low-cost transportation for their ores. He explained: "It is with considerable of a heartache that this writer has had to reach a conclusion contrary to that of the Public Service Commission in this case . . ." Then he went on to point out the cold facts that only 83 cars of ore were shipped off-line during the first eight months of 1946, and that there was nothing in the record except hopeful speculation that shipments were destined to be increased in the near future. Continued deficits and a bankrupt company left only one answer — abandonment.

Effective October 15, 1947, the T&G was formally abandoned. There had been some previous talk of its possible purchase and operation by local interests. A group headed by Charles Cavanaugh had expressed interest in November 1946. On another occasion Mark Bradshaw, an early Western Pacific Railroad surveyor and a Tonopah mining man, made an effort to acquire it, because he envisioned the T&G an important link in a possible north and south railroad. However, no sale materialized; salvaging operations commenced the last week of February and were completed in September of 1948.

Thus the Tonopah & Goldfield Railroad, a bonanza institution of 45 years duration, perished. Its only traces are a few scars on the Nevada landscape plus a few weathered buildings at scattered and sometimes remote locations. The fame of Tonopah as an historic place has been immortalized — not by the fabulous railroad which bore its name — but by an innocuous picture postcard depicting Jim Butler and his burro under the blithe caption "Me and Jim Butler founded Tonopah." From such asinine situations does history develop.

Goldfield Cons. Milling & Transportation Co.

Most Nevada mining booms followed a standard, somewhat inexorable, pattern—an immediate rush to an area, followed by a tremendous surge of mining claims and prospects out of which arose a large number of incorporations, a smaller number of producers, and finally a mere handful of mining properties of the caliber which made men rich. The boom in the Goldfield area was no exception to this pattern, for many producing companies emerged but only one was to reign supreme.

The Goldfield Consolidated Mines Company was a composite of the richest producing mines in the area and succeeded in extracting some $50,000,000 in ore (as compared with the Goldfield District's total production of $87,000,000). Its nearest rival, the Goldfield Mohawk, achieved a mere $9,000,000 of recorded production.

Two men, George Wingfield and George Stuart Nixon, became fabulously wealthy through their large ownership in the Goldfield Consolidated Mines and their influence on Nevada's mining, banking and economic life was widespread. Unfortunately their complete story will never be known, for Nixon died in 1912 and Wingfield, though he lived until Christmas 1959, steadfastly refused to divulge his own story. Besides having owned the Riverside Hotel in Reno, his connections included directorships of both the T&G and the N-C-O.

This much is known, however, Nixon was born in Newcastle, California, and in his youth worked as a telegraph operator at various places including Candelaria, Nevada. Subsequently he shifted into banking, first in Reno and later in Winnemucca. He was a member of the Nevada legislature, active in the Silver Party, and ultimately became a U. S. Senator from 1905 until his death.

George Wingfield was a young livestock man from Arkansas. Down on his luck, he dropped in to see Nixon at the bank in Winnemucca. Tonopah was just opening up at the time, and Wingfield wanted to go there and explore the possibilities if Nixon would grubstake him. Any profits from the venture were to be shared on a 50-50 basis. Nixon agreed, and the balance of the story of the partnership history is one of accumulating wealth.

Operating the Tonopah Club (which still serves drinks across the bar to this day) and dealing in mining stocks, Wingfield invested the partnership funds wisely in a variety of mining interests. They backed the Mohawk mine in Goldfield which was just beginning to make good showings. In January 1906 the Mohawk property was leased to various parties (including Hayes and Monnette), and three months later beautiful ore was uncovered. Then additional rich ore was discovered on the adjoining Frances-Mohawk lease, and the news spread like wildfire. People flocked to Goldfield; its population multiplied; and gold began to flow from the ground. By September 1906 the daily production from the Hayes-Monnette lease alone was running around $30,000, and when the lease expired the following January 11 over $4,000,000 had been extracted, virtually all in gold ore.

The owners of some of the adjoining properties filed suit in an attempt to claim ownership of the vein. Acting on the advice of counsel and using the financial aid of Bernard Baruch, partners Nixon and Wingfield bought up the adjoining properties and formed the Goldfield Consolidated Mines Co. on November 13, 1906. The Jumbo, Laguna, Red Top and Mohawk mining properties (subject to existing leases) were then merged into the new company a few days later. In January 1907 the Combination and the January mine of the Goldfield Mining Company were acquired. Goldfield Consolidated had crested the peak.

Development of the properties was immediately begun in spite of serious labor problems (the I.W.W. was running wild in Goldfield at the time) plus the nationwide business slump which closed the doors of innumerable banks and created a distinct shortage of money. Work was started on an $800,000 stamp mill on the old Sandstorm Claim on Columbia Mountain about two miles north of Goldfield (the old foundations may still be seen from the highway). To service the mill a standard gauge railroad was projected, and on January 24, 1908, work commenced with 100 men rushing the road to completion. Perhaps they rushed just a little too much when setting off the larger blasts of powder, for unwelcomed by the residents of Columbia were the showers of rocks which riddled the roofs of houses. A 25-pound rock fell through the roof of a house and missed a 12-year-old girl by a scant six inches. Work proceeded, however, and $93,000 later, on April 2, 1908, George Wingfield drove the traditional last spike.

The "main line" of the railroad extended a full 1.87 miles from a connection with the Tonopah & Goldfield Railroad, up and over the recently laid LV&T tracks, and on up the mountain to the mill. A connecting track to the LV&T in Goldfield plus 2.09 miles of spurs serving the mines provided facilities for transportation of the ore to the mill and thence to market. Equipment consisted of one locomotive and six steel hopper cars. Initial operations consisted of hauling construction materials to the new mill site.

The following year, in August 1909, a separate company called the Goldfield Consolidated Milling and Transportation Company was formed to own and operate the railroad, milling and water properties. Virtually all of the stock was held by the parent company which continued operation of the mining properties.

In June 1910 the GCM&TCo began reporting its results to the Railroad Commission of Nevada, and an interesting report it was. No revenue passengers were carried; the only traffic consisted of ore hauled from the mines to the mill. In 1912 the transportation of 364,226 tons provided freight revenue earnings of $91,056. With an operating ratio of 31.8% it was a profitable little venture—the reported net income for the year was $2,566,689 while the dividends paid amounted to a staggering $3,284,-

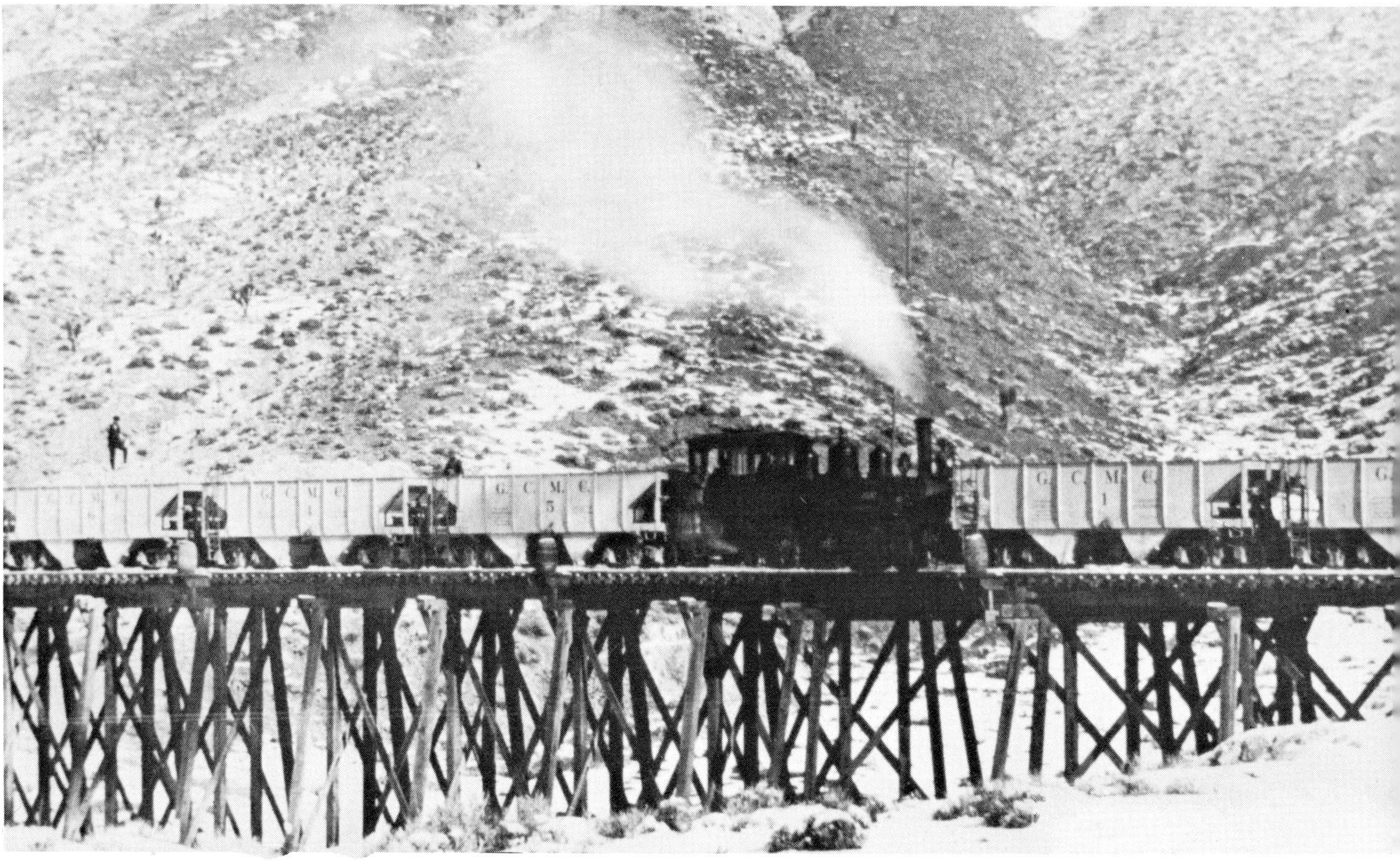

Goldfield's fourth railroad was a local industrial line designed to bring ores from the mines up the slopes of Columbia Mountain to the large 100-stamp mill *(bottom, left)*. The road was completed in April 1908 under the aegis of the Goldfield Consolidated Mines Company, as may be noted from the initials on the ore cars *(above)* or the name on the tank locomotive, No. 1 *(top, right)*. In August 1909 a separate company, the Goldfield Consolidated Milling & Transportation Co., was formed to own and operate the railroad, and locomotive No. 2 *(center and bottom, right)* carried this altered designation. In 1915 the T&G assumed the road's operations; in 1916 the mill was closed; but the railroad continued to operate vaguely until 1931 and remained in place until some time subsequent to 1942. *(Above: Bob Weaver Collection; Below: Sewell Thomas Collection; Top Right: Baldwin-Lima-Hamilton Photo; Right Center and Bottom: Tolford Collection.)*

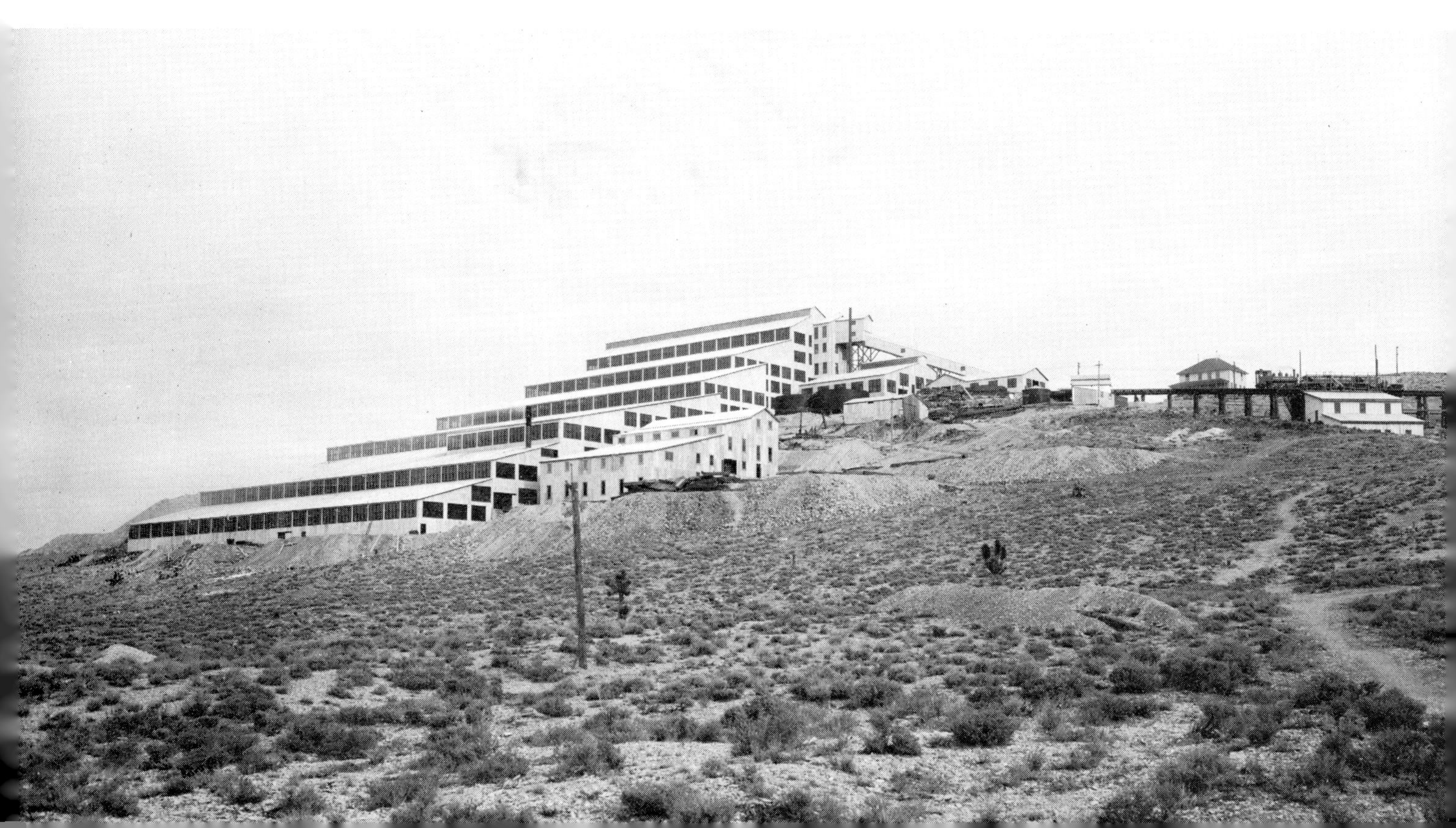

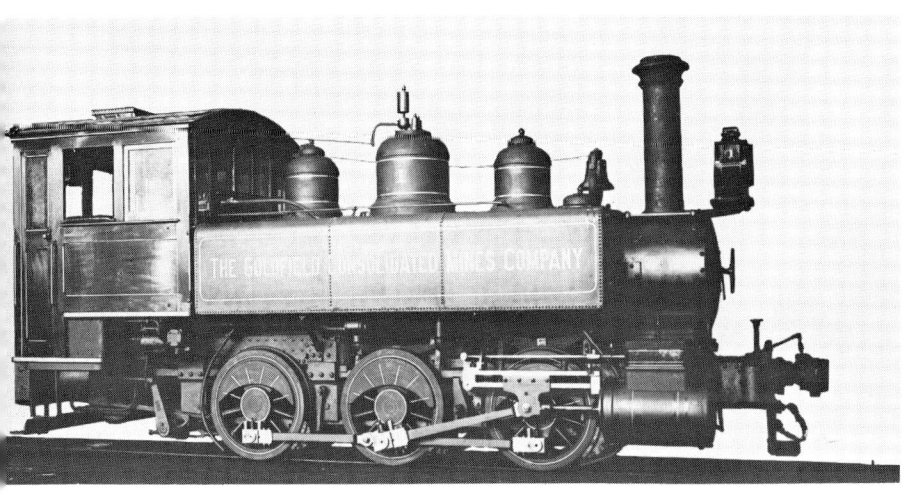

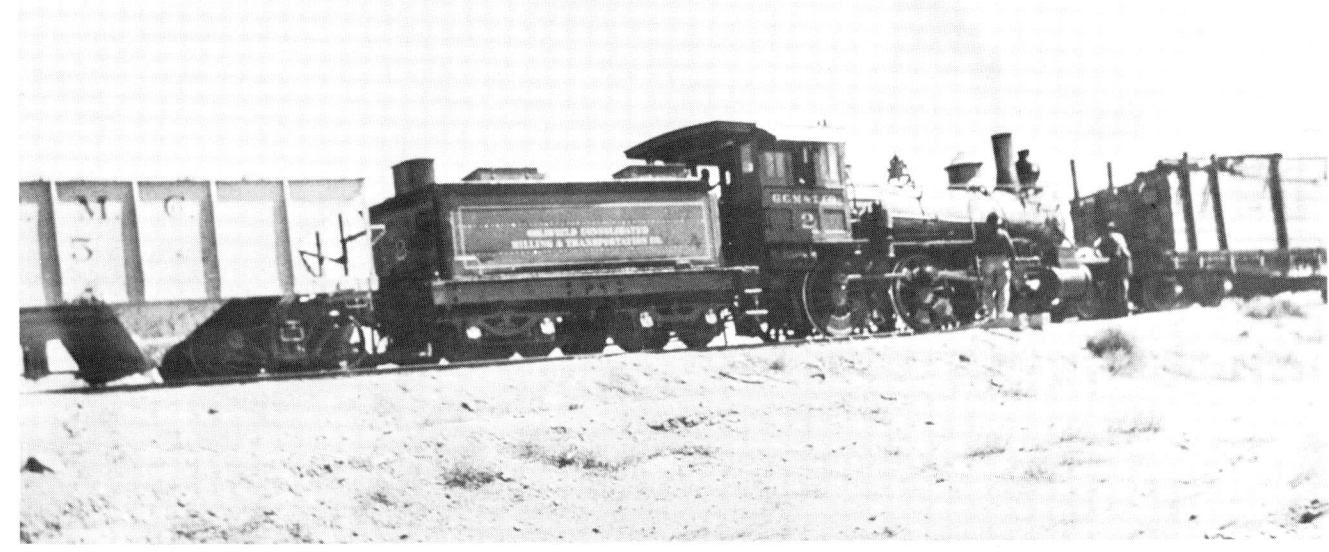

— 291

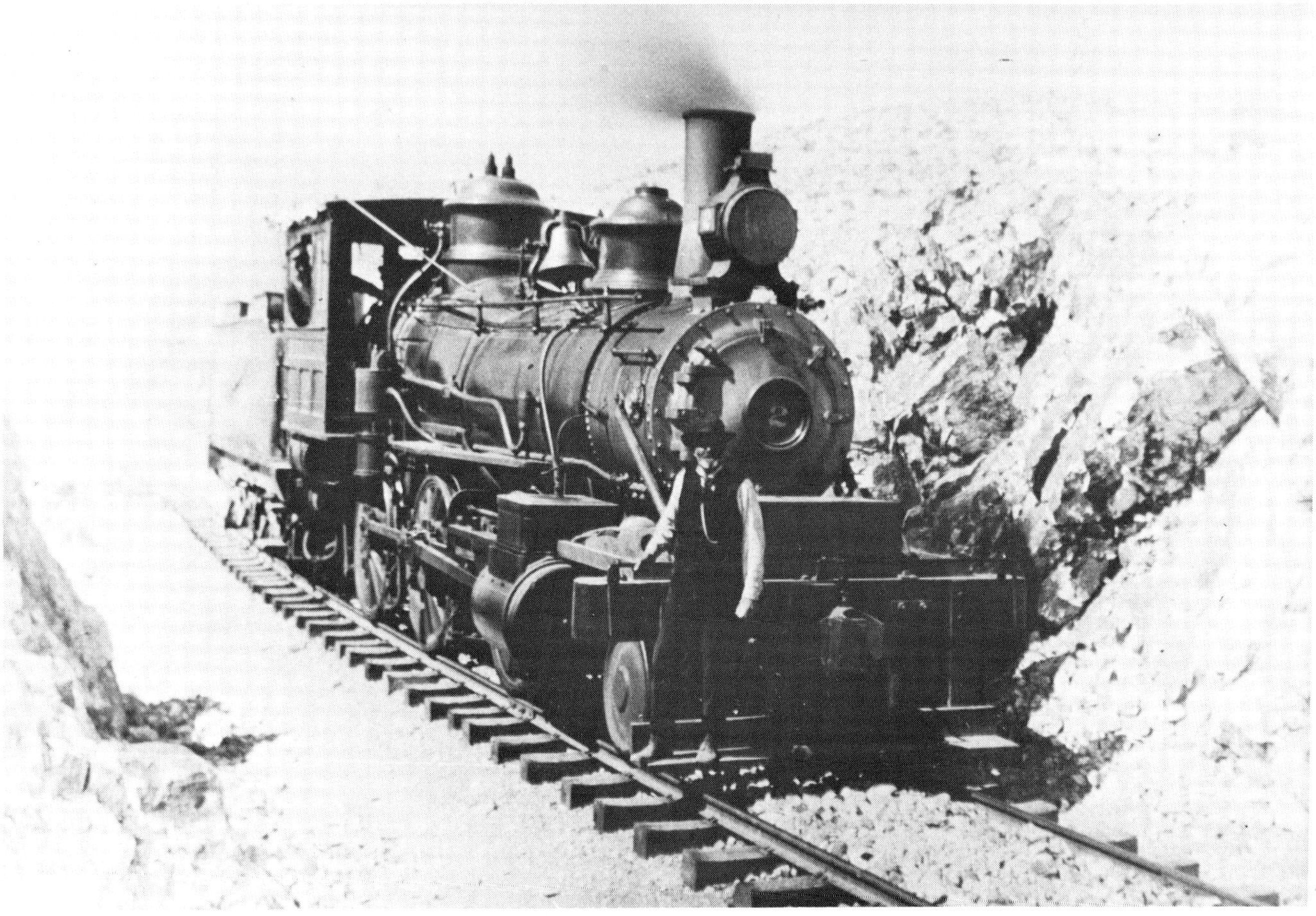

163. The apparent discrepancy was accounted for by a small item of "miscellaneous revenue" in the amount of $3,586,128 representing milling charges to customers. In other words, what appeared at first glance to be a normal railroad with a milling background was actually an unusually large milling operation with an incidental railroad. Unusual too was the railroad's engineer of the moment, for incidental intelligence reports he had but one arm.

Prosperity did not last forever — Goldfield's ore reserves began to dwindle. The railroad became a costly plaything, and finally under an agreement dated September 29, 1915, the T&G took over operation of the little line. When the T&G men attempted to bring the tank locomotive down to their shops for overhaul, they discovered that the air brakes had become inoperative, and the locomotive jumped the track.

The big 100-stamp mill on Columbia Mountain was closed down in 1916. Subsequently it was dismantled and sold for scrap. The T&G continued to operate the railroad until 1931; then it was reported as "not in operation"; and in 1942 it ceased to be reported at all.

The Goldfield Consolidated Mines Co., however, continues to be active in Nevada mining even today. In March 1962 it announced its affiliate, Getchell Mines, Inc., expected to resume gold mining and milling operations northeast of Winnemucca. And its interest in transportation has obviously been modernized as the same announcement included word that the company had bought control of Frontier Airlines, a scheduled air carrier serving the Rocky Mountain States. It's a far cry from the days of the early prospectors traveling with their burros, or the later single track railroads which brought the ore down out of the hills.

Silver Peak Railroad Company

Most of the early (nineteenth century) mining activity in Nevada was concentrated in the northern part of the state where railroads, water and water power were generally available. The southern part of the state was largely uninviting to most prospectors, being remote, unexplored and basically lacking in water and transportation. Few mining districts developed in this area. There were exceptions, however, and Silver Peak was one.

Situated on the edge of an ancient lake bed approximately 40 miles south and east of Candelaria and about 30 miles west of the future site of Goldfield, Silver Peak registered its initial production in 1863. The following year the Great Salt Basin Mining and Milling Co. was organized to develop the area. Three years later, two miles of grading had been completed for a proposed eight-mile railroad to connect the mines with the mill. The plan was discarded, however, in favor of a 1½-mile surface tramway along the Drinkwater Trail whereon loaded cars drifted by gravity down to an ore bin, and mules hauled the empties back to the mine. From the ore bin at the base, enormous wagons (said to be the largest ever used in Nevada) transported the ore from the bin to the mill.

John I. Blair (wealthy banker and railroad financier of New York and Blairstown, New Jersey) became interested and took over the property. In 1870 all hands were suddenly discharged. According to legend, Blair had heard that his superintendent had been cheating him; and instead of hiring a new superintendent, Blair "followed the extremely logical course of shutting down the mine." His interest in Silver Peak had declined.

During the next three decades the property was sold to impecunious souls who shortly defaulted on their payments; then it was leased from time to time. One leaser, John Chiatovich, is reported to have cleaned up $150,000 from a single ore pocket and to have considered the building of a railroad from the mine to a mill site on his ranch where water was available. A second thought apparently reversed this scheme, and it was decided to run a water pipe to the mine and erect the mill at the mine site.

Silver Peak was the announced goal of a number of projected railroads, including the famed Carson & Colorado and the California Central. None ever actually reached the area, however, and rail transportation, when it finally arrived, was conceived and constructed by Pittsburgh interests.

Following John Blair's death late in 1899, his estate set a price of $750,000 on the property at Silver Peak. For some fortunate reason, it was decided to have the famed mining engineer, John Hays Hammond, look the property over before selling. When Hammond submitted a bill for $60,000 for his services, instead of being incensed, the executors paid the fee without a murmur and promptly increased the price of the properties to $2,000,000 on the strength of the report.

By 1906 eastern investors were ready to buy Nevada mining properties, and when Martin L. Effinger, a Salt Lake City promoter, went to Pennsylvania he found a receptive audience to his proposals. A group of Pittsburgh men including William Flinn, newspaper publisher and state senator, and George T. Oliver, steel magnate and U. S. Senator, purchased the property and organized a new company in May 1906 called the Pittsburg Silver Peak Gold Mining Co. to acquire the assets. A month later rail transportation was decided upon, and the Silver Peak Railroad Co. was organized, the initials of which (SP) on maps frequently created confusion with those of the Southern Pacific.

The story of the Silver Peak Railroad is very unlike most railroad construction stories. Money was ample and grading was easy. Water was scarce, but the problem was solved. The original location survey was made on horseback by surveyor Orlando McCraney who sighted a hand level perched on the brim of the hat of his assistant some distance away. Only on curves was a transit required, and curves were relatively few and far between in the flat valley land. The final survey for the 17½-mile railroad was completed in June 1906. The proposed route extended from a point on the T&G at the end of the Big Smokey Valley called Blair Junction, traversed a dry lake, then crossed over a broad pass to the mill site at the edge of Clayton Valley.

The mill site was determined by economics. Since land speculators had gobbled up all the land around the town of Silver Peak, a new townsite two miles farther north (and nearer to the T&G) was surveyed secretly at night, thereby shortening the railroad and leaving the greedy speculators to the problem of their own devising. After some discussion the name of Blair was given to the new location, and the mill was built on a sloping hillside immediately above the town, thus permitting the gravity flow of ore so necessary to the operations. Enigmatically, water was close at hand in spite of the panoramic view of the dry lake bed in Clayton Valley where two islands projected above the desert floor named Goat and Alcatraz — probably named by some homesick San Franciscan.

The Silver Peak Railroad's construction contract was awarded to McLean and McSweeney, contractors for the Tonopah and Goldfield Railroads. Grading began the latter part of July 1906 with Garfield Logan in charge of a dozen grading teams,

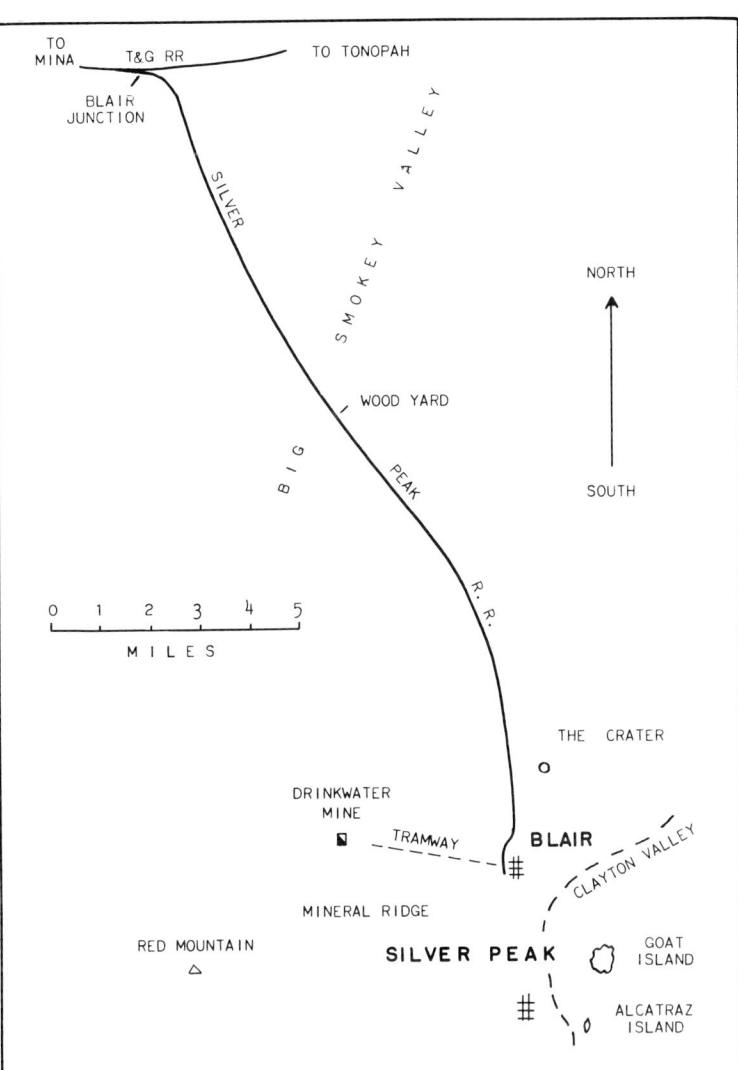

each consisting of a man with two horses pulling a plow or a Fresno scraper. No particular difficulties were encountered, as the only rock work on the entire railroad consisted of one or two cuts on the hillside in the last half-mile of roadbed.

By early August six miles of grade were ready for the ties and rails. Track laying began the latter part of the month, utilizing the second-hand T&G 50-pound rail left over from narrow gauge days on that road. Rails and ties were moved to the advancing rail head on push cars motivated by hand power, as the first locomotive for the line did not arrive until September. There being but few culverts, it was not necessary to halt rail laying while trestles were constructed. By September 20 at least one-half of the track was in place and all but four miles of grade were completed. On October 15, 1906, the work was done, and the following day the first train pulled into Blair with a welcome load of lumber.

With the railroad completed, lumber for housing and machinery for the mill were easily available.

A building boom ensued, and a month later Blair boasted 100 frame buildings and a population of 700 people. J. G. Crumley began construction of his new hotel (which ultimately burned in an unfortunate fire in July 1910); two newspapers were started; and more saloons appeared on the scene than were considered necessary. The intensity of the activity engendered grandiose plans, including talk of extending the railroad on southward to Lida.

Most of the values in the Blair-Silver Peak area were in gold. Principal mine was the old Drinkwater, located on the opposite side of the ridge from Blair. On the near side, the Mary mine was in an excellent position to feed ore to the mill by tramway. Thus development commenced with the drilling of a 3,800-foot tunnel to connect the Drinkwater with the Mary mine. Electric locomotives then brought trains of 10 side-dump, 2½-ton ore cars from underground loading stations in the Drinkwater, through the tunnel into the Mary mine, and on to the ore bins at the mouth of the Mary mine. Here a crusher reduced the rock to more manageable size, whence it moved on to another bin for loading on the 14,000-foot tramway. The site for the aerial tramway was one of four under consideration. The mechanism was built by Leschen and consisted of 124 buckets attached to a cable which dropped the ore 1,600 feet to the mill in 56 minutes. All in all, it was quite an efficient operation.

Initially, water was a major problem. No water could be found at Blair, so McCraney sank a well at Silver Peak and located a good supply — so successfully in fact, that the well promptly drained all the other wells in the Silver Peak area. With the Silver Peak-Blair relations already strained as a result of the location of the new townsite, there were many strong feelings about McCraney over this latest development. The day was saved, however, when, in blasting out the bottom of his own well, McCraney hit a new underground spring which lavishly increased the flow of water to all the wells.

For milling purposes, water was obtained by sinking caissons made of wagon wheel tires into the dry lake bed. The water thus obtained was quite brackish, but appeared to improve with the pumping operation and was quite suitable for washing the cyanide tanks after the ore had been treated.

With an ample supply of water assured to the town of Blair, it was suddenly discovered that there was no appropriation in the budget for fire hydrants. Seeking a solution to the problem, the construction engineers decided to draw on their own resources and put on a minstrel show, proceeds of which would be used to purchase the needed hydrants. Although the acting talents embodied in the small group of volunteers were of dubious distinction, a case of whiskey donated by a local merchant bolstered the morale of the individual performers so greatly that one of the actors missed the stage completely and soared off into space. One father, visiting a member of the cast, commented that "the show was so terrible it was entertaining." The piano playing of Garfield Logan, construction boss, probably saved the show which was a financial success, references to its quality notwithstanding.

Water also presented its problems in the railroad operations for a time. Filling the tender at Blair normally provided sufficient water for the round trip to the Junction and back. On warm days, however, with heavy inbound shipments for the big mill then under construction, the locomotive frequently used up its supply and the train would grind to a halt midway in the desert until an emergency ration could be procured. To eliminate this problem, a well was sunk at Blair Junction and a pump was ordered from Allentown, Pennsylvania. Due to the congestion along the connecting railroads at that time, freight service was so uncertain the Silver Peak ordered the pump shipped in its own "private" express car. Delivery was accomplished, and following installation of the pump the water difficulties were over.

Six days a week the little train left Blair at 8:15 A.M. for the leisurely 45-minute trip down to the Junction where connection was made with the T&G trains. The return trip left the Junction about 10:45 A.M. after picking up inbound passengers from the T&G. Such was the service provided in 1908-09.

Not many people rode the train. In 1912 the average number of passengers per trip was three. Perhaps the high passenger fare was a discouraging factor; it cost 10 cents a mile to ride the train, or $1.75 for each trip. Business was boosted temporarily in 1908 during a placer gold rush in Cow Camp, a dozen miles south of Blair. Occasional special excursions were reported, the most outstanding probably being that for the Fourth of July celebration at Goldfield in 1911 when special reduced rates applied.

For several years two Italian brothers gathered firewood in the mountains northwest of Blair and

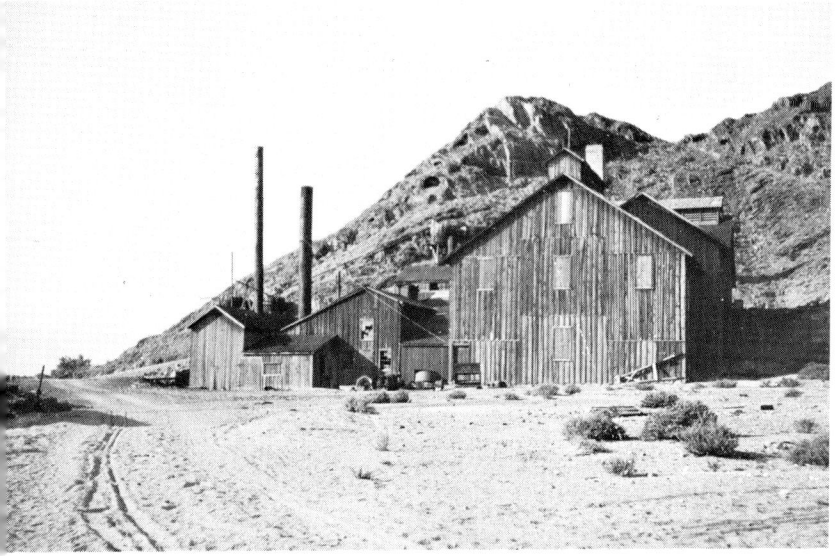

Silver Peak, on the south side of Mineral Ridge from the later town of Blair, registered its initial production as early as 1863. The old Silver Peak mill, built in 1867 and here photographed about 1903, was said to be the oldest in Nevada. *(U. S. Geological Survey.)*

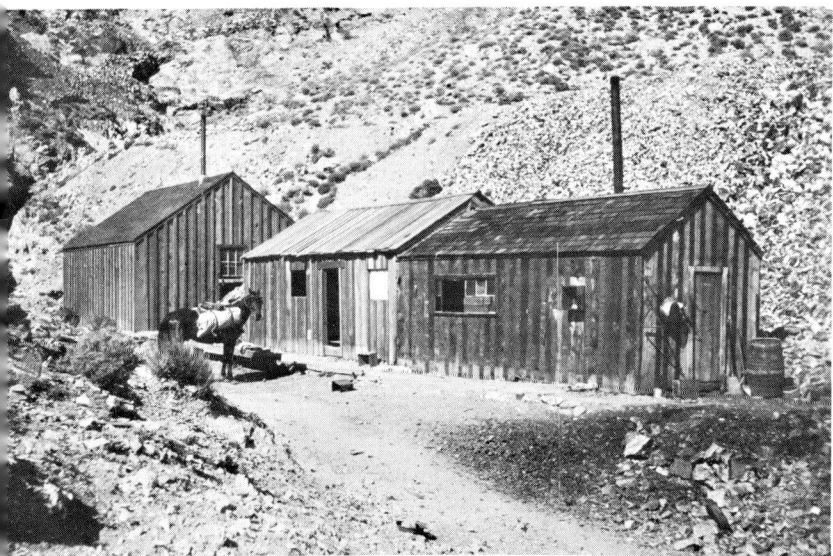

This photograph *(left)* of the buildings of the Drinkwater Mine, west of Blair, demonstrate the simplicity of this early mining operation. *(U. S. Geological Survey.)*

Looking east over the town of Silver Peak *(below)* with the dry lake in the background, in 1912. To avoid land speculators, the town of Blair was located two miles to the north (to left in picture) on the other side of Mineral Ridge behind camera. *(U. S. Geological Survey.)*

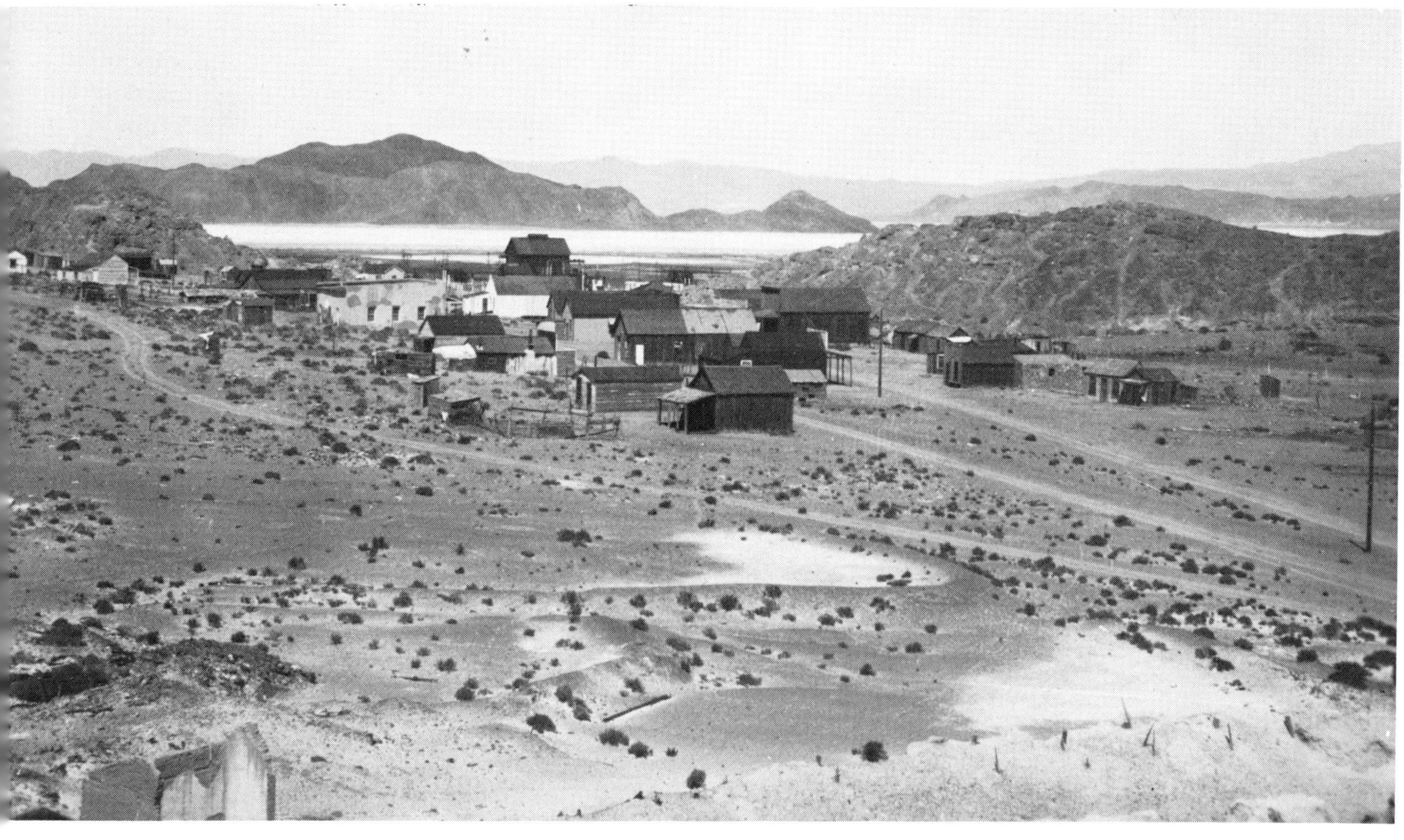

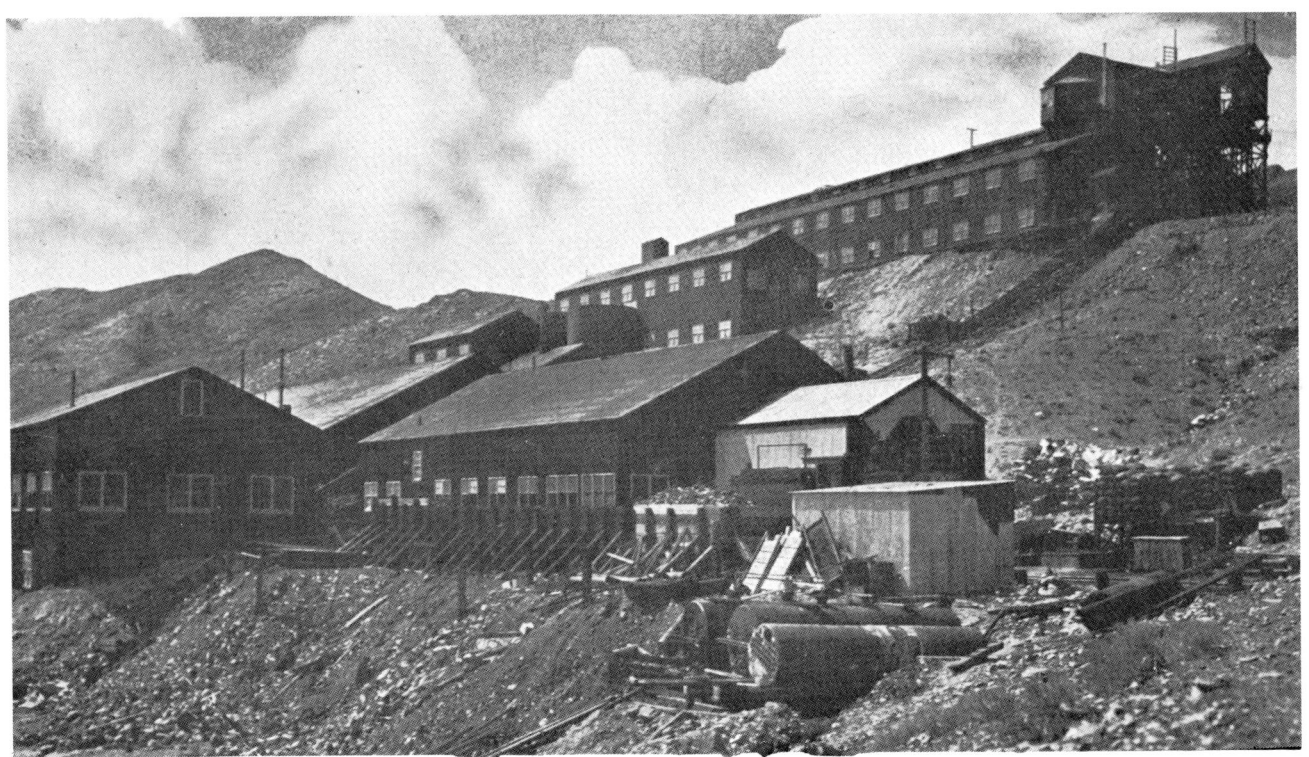

The 120-stamp Silver Peak Mill *(above)* was the largest in Nevada in its day, but it was operated only 10 years. In the 1907 view *(below)* looking north, the mill buildings are under construction. At the foot of the hill are the frames for the warehouse and the shop buildings astride one track of the Silver Peak R.R. on which three "Silver Pk" flat cars stand. Behind these lies the town of Blair, the white building is the Blair Hotel. The track of the Silver Peak R.R. approaches from the north past the western side of the large, dark cinder cone in background, and can be seen as it swings in a broad S-curve toward the mill forking near the water tank into two legs. *(Bottom: Mrs. Hugh Brown Collection.)*

Photographs of Silver Peak Railroad equipment *(page opposite)* are rare in the extreme. The railroad's name still appears on the McKeen Car, (photographed at Westwood, California, on later owner Red River Lumber Co. premises), but the original name "Mary" has been obliterated from the nose and the number "12" substituted. Engine No. 1 is seen at Blair *(center)*, but No. 2 has had her rods removed preparatory to being scrapped at South San Francisco. *(Top: Al Rose Photo, Guy L. Dunscomb Collection; Center: Gilbert H. Kneiss Collection; Bottom: Ken Kidder Collection.)*

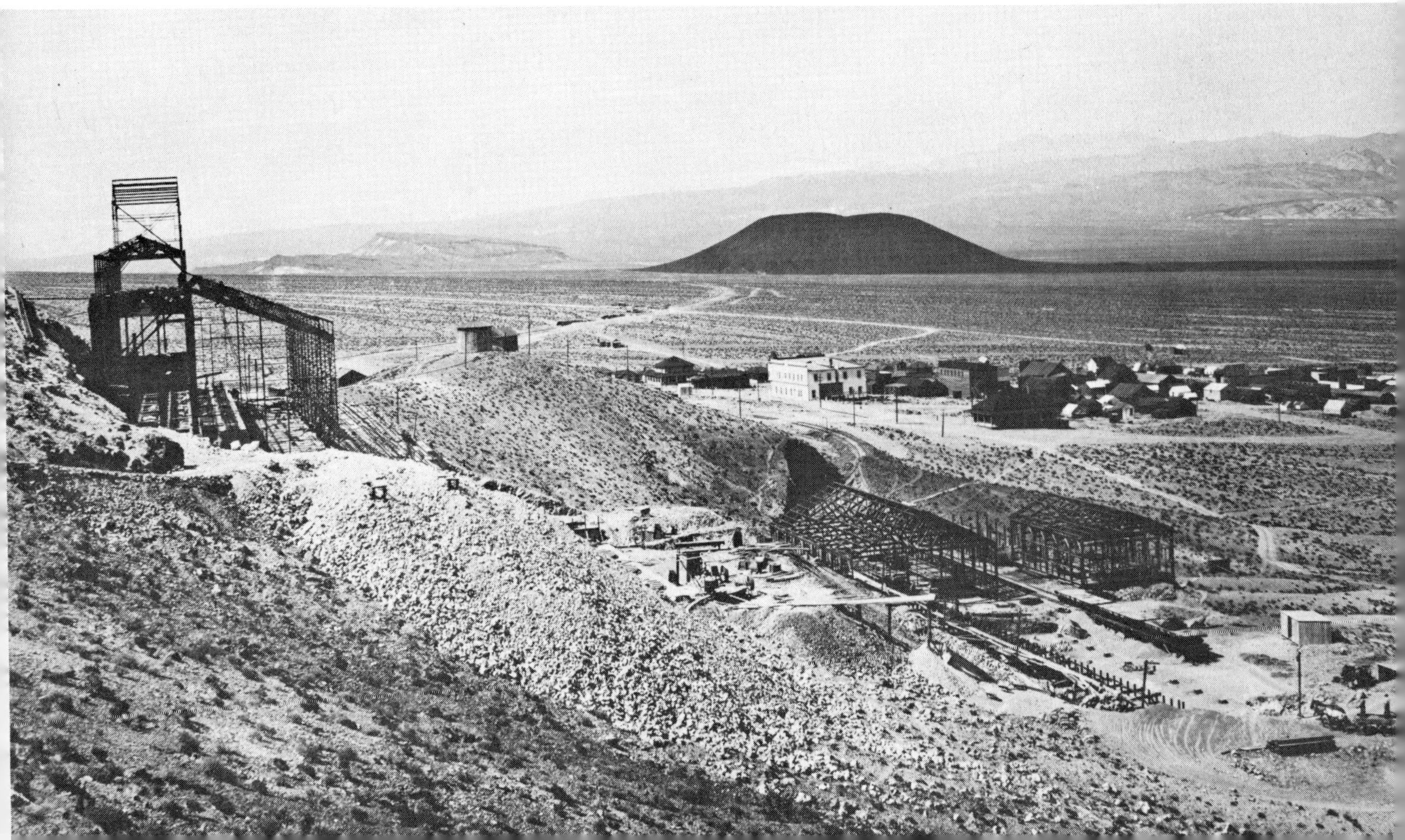

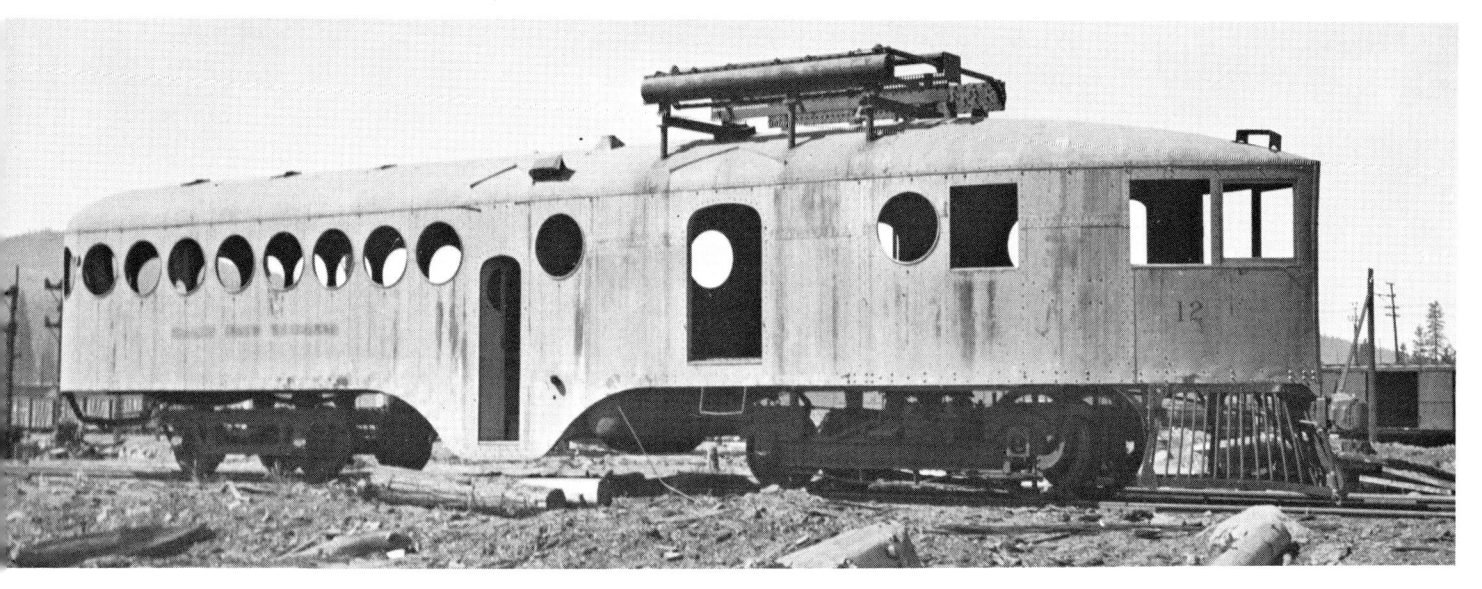

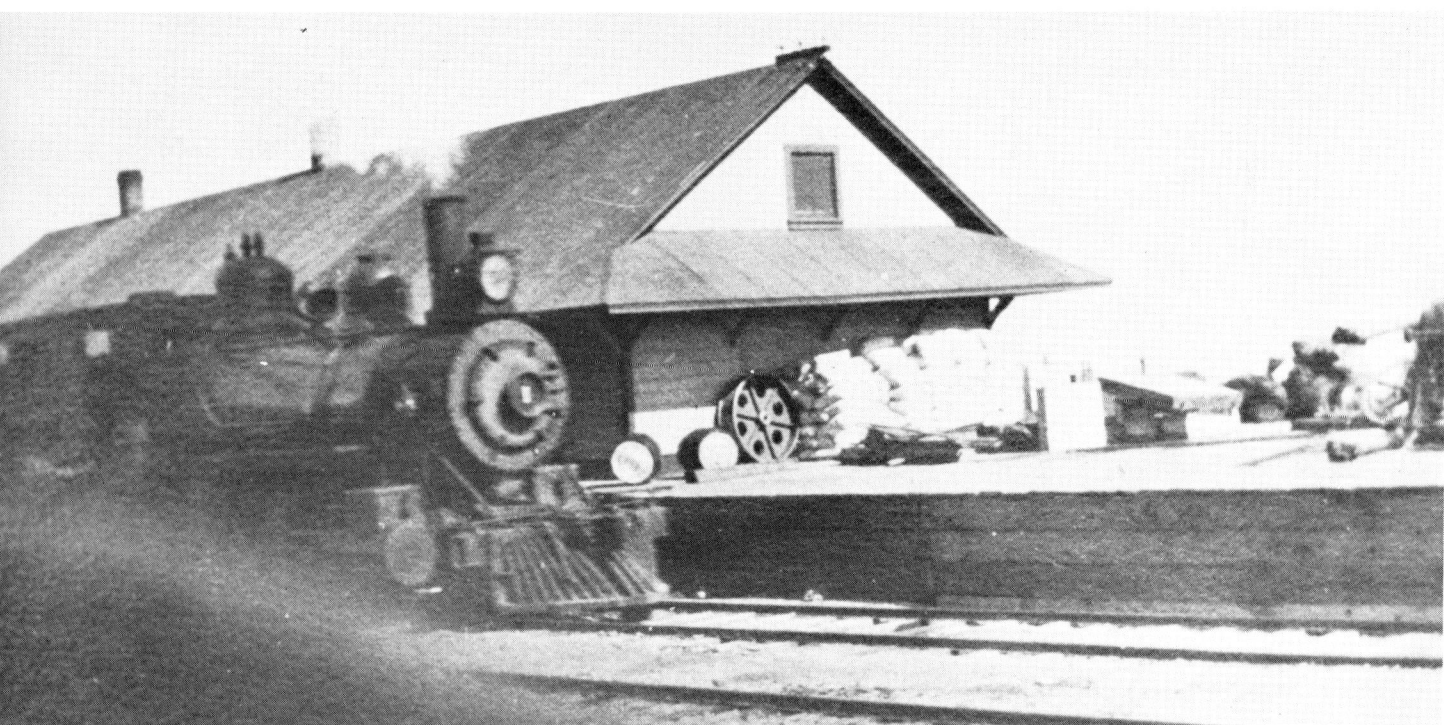

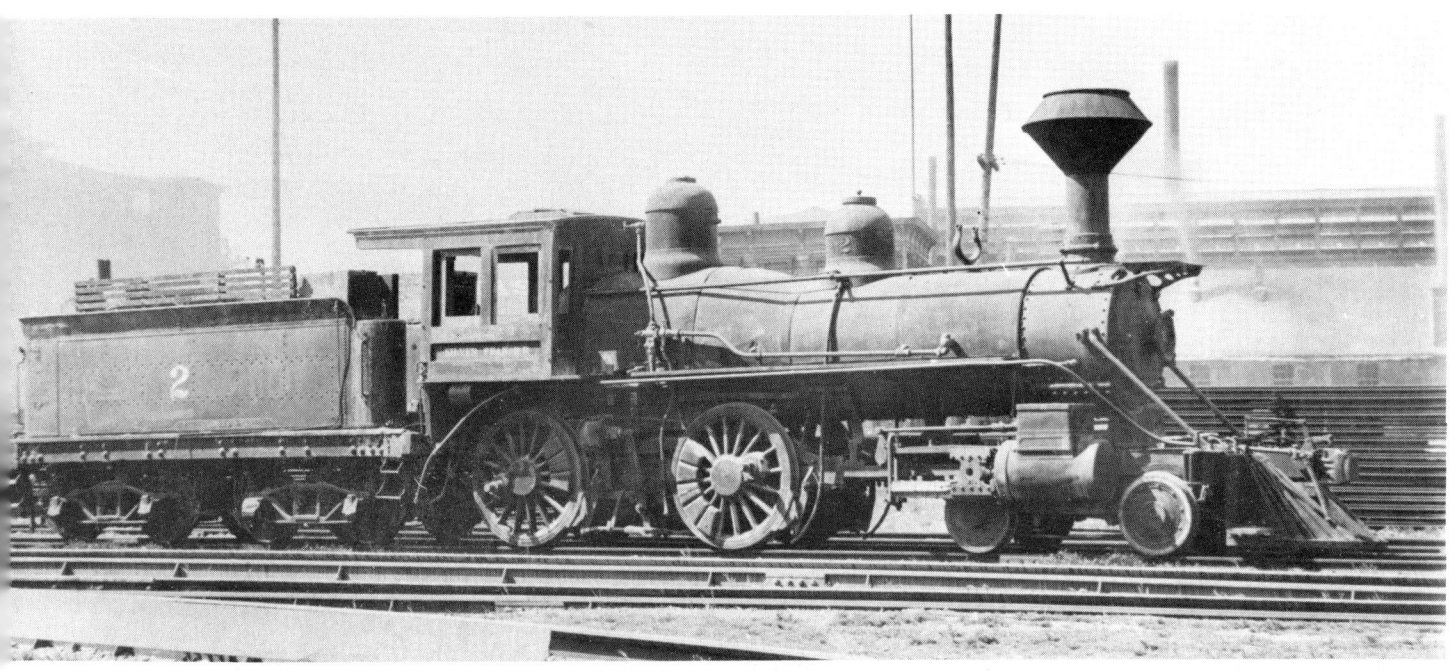

brought it in to town. In 1913 the railroad established a new station called Wood Yard at a point about 10 miles north of Blair and provided special rates and fares to this point. The following year wood products constituted one-third of the railroad's tonnage.

Being a short-line railroad, the Silver Peak's freight rates were unusually high, averaging approximately 19 cents per net ton mile or about 16 times that of the average of the larger railroads. Traffic consisted of coal, some ores, lumber, steel products, cement and merchandise. The total tonnage handled only amounted to about 3,000 to 4,000 tons a year, roughly equivalent to that hauled by one good, modern, mainline train today.

The Silver Peak Railroad had only one primary purpose for existence — to serve the mines, mills and town at Blair. Its whole economy was wrapped up in that one big operation. The first part of the big mill was placed in operation on October 26, 1907, when Senator Flinn, one of the owners, was on hand to assist in the ceremonies. The following April the number of operating stamps was increased to 100. In 1910 the firm acquired the Silver Peak-Valcalda mine and added 20 more stamps to the mill, making it the largest in Nevada at that time. A year later a mine railroad, partly surface and partly underground, was constructed to connect the two mining operations. By October 1915 the big mine was considered worked out and dismantling of the mill began the next year. Its equipment was sold piecemeal to various mine operators in Nevada and California. One former employee recognized certain equipment when it was delivered to the White Caps mine in Manhattan, Nevada. By 1918 there was little left of the original operation, and the town of Blair was practically deserted.

The fortunes of the railroad followed a similar pattern. In 1909 revenues topped $22,000 for a peak, then quickly fell to $14,000 and continued on downward in ever decreasing amounts. The early years were the profitable ones; after 1911 losses were the rule. Operations were conducted with a minimum of employees. By 1916 these had been reduced to an agent, engineer, fireman, conductor and two "general officers," all of which were part-time, except for the engineer. The general officers drew only $50 a month, yet the total wage bill amounted to $5,000 or 83% of the revenues for that year.

By May 1918 word had circulated that the railroad was ready to fold up. The citizens of the county filed a protest with the Commission. A hearing was held. The railroad management pointed to the recurring losses and explained that present business was largely comprised of hauling parts of the dismantled mill out of the area. Business from other mines in the area was less than $1,300 in 1914, although it constituted 20% of the total. To make matters worse, the water supply was about to give out, forcing discontinuance of the semi-weekly trains. Equipment was down to one oil-fired locomotive and a single flat car. Except for people dismantling the mill, Blair was practically deserted and little business could be expected from the other mines.

Abandonment was authorized, and by the end of 1918 the little railroad was gone.

Amazingly, from 1906 to 1920 some $6,000,000 practically all in gold, was produced from the Silver Peak District, and Blair in particular. Mining is still going on in the area, and the town of Silver Peak can still support two bars — the Black Mammoth and Cleary's. Two miles to the north at Blair nothing is left except the skeleton of one building and the foundations of the mill. In the afternoon sunlight, one must look sharply to see the Blair townsite, deserted in the sage, a half mile west of the highway leading to that other deserted spot, Blair Junction.

Bodie & Benton Railway

As a railroad, the Bodie & Benton was a complete paradox. It began on a barren hilltop and ended in a forest; it never served the town proper of the first of the habitations in its corporate title and never reached the second; it never had a single railroad connection with the outside world (although proposals were made to connect with three different lines); yet it operated successfully for nearly half a century. To understand the anomaly, one should understand Bodie — that is, if one can understand an enigma.

Bodie. The name had almost as many connotations as there were people to talk about it. It meant millions in gold to the fortunate, poverty to others; a California camp of tremendous possibilities, or

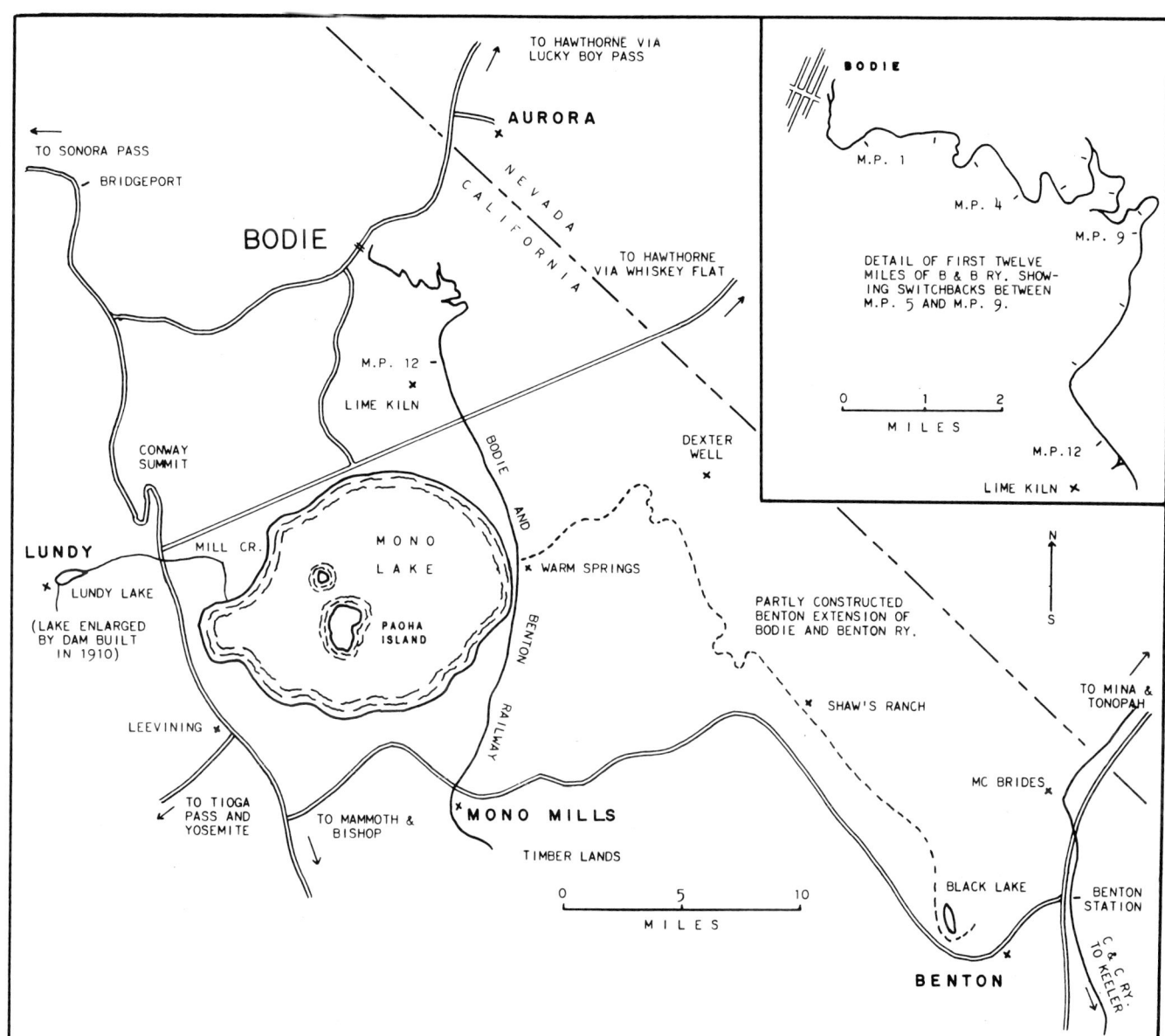

a wretched windswept mining town on a barren waste; a place of fun or of sorrow; one in which to prey or be preyed upon; a heaven or a hell.

William S. Bodey gave the town its name following his discovery of gold in the surrounding hills in 1859. Like so many of the pioneer prospectors, he never shared in the ultimate $30,000,000 yield from the veins of his find, for only a few months following the initial discovery he perished in a snowstorm. Production at Bodie was exciting in the early 1860's but was overshadowed by the output of the neighboring Aurora mines, then at the first of several peak productive periods. And Aurora, aside from its tremendous production and the fame of being one of Mark Twain's home towns, also enjoyed the unique distinction of being the county seat for two different counties (Esmeralda and Mono), each in a different state. The distinction went unrecognized for some time until finally a boundary survey definitely placed Aurora over the line in Nevada.

PAGE FOLLOWING:
This panorama was taken from a point just north and behind the Standard Mill looking southwest. The Standard Mill is in the immediate foreground, and Main Street extends from the lower right corner diagonally across the picture. On the far side of the street (center of picture) the first big two-story building with the false front is the I.O.O.F. Hall. To its right is the Bodie Miners Union with the flag pole in front. The whole area on the right side of the picture was devastated in the great fire of 1932. *(Grahame Hardy Collection.)*

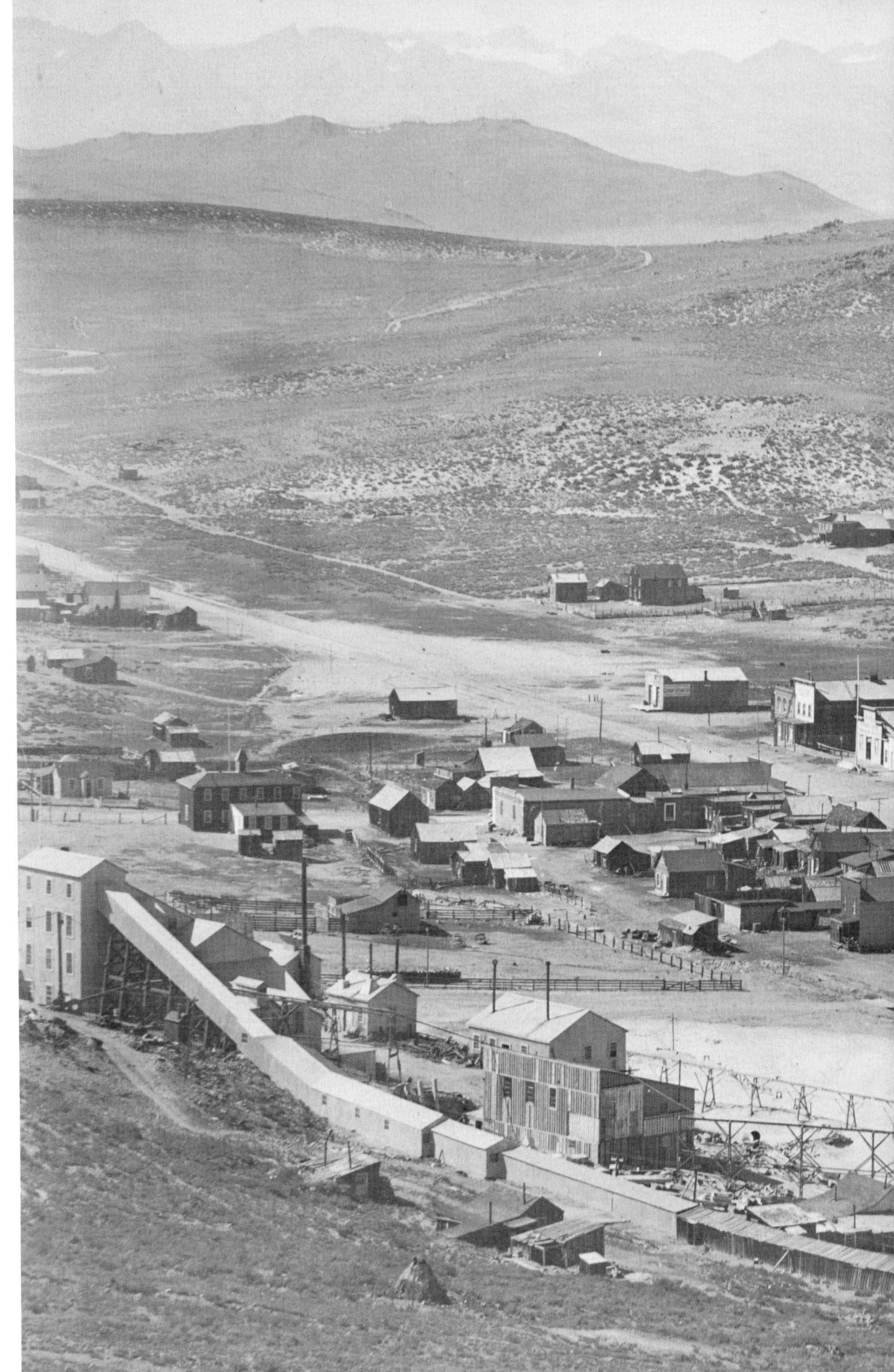

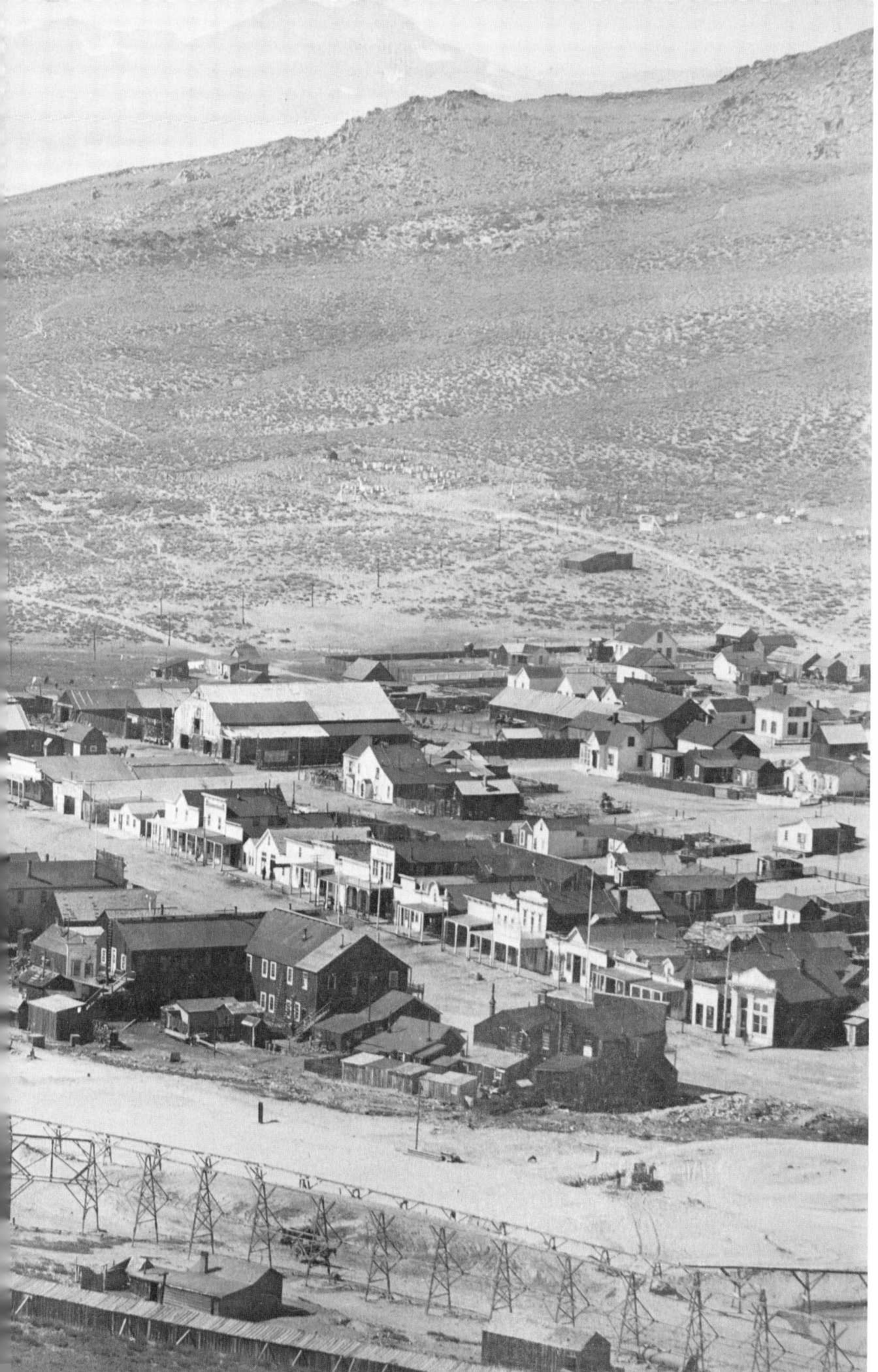

MAP OF THE BODIE MINING DISTRICT.

A Birdseye View of the Mining District and the Town of Bodie, Mono County, Cal.

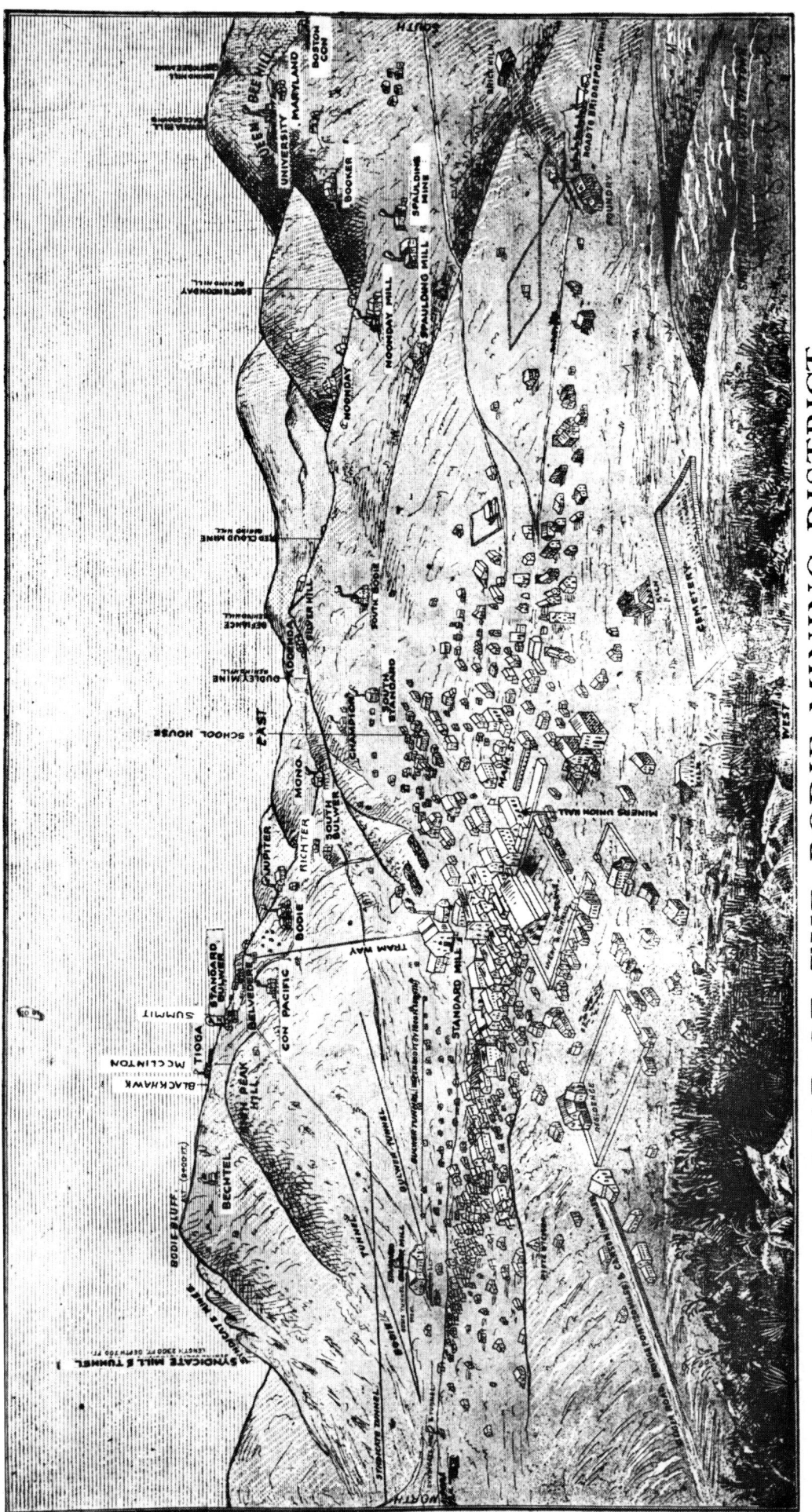

This sketch is a very accurate one, being specially drawn for THE DAILY STOCK REPORT by H. F. Sanford, of Bodie, in November, 1879. It was taken from a point looking east, and shows the three or four bluffs and hills containing the ore channels of the district. These hills are topographically very distinctly defined, being almost surrounded by what was once a grassy valley, affording a fine townsite throughout the entire circuit. The town of to-day is centered in the larger valley west of High Peak and Silver Hills, and spreading both north and south. The Booker Flat, under Queen Bee Hill, is a large site in itself and is building up rapidly. The sketch shows the hoisting works and mills better than the town, which, however, is sufficiently set forth in detail to afford the reader an excellent idea of everything appertaining. The outlines of the main hills and those in the background are nearly perfect. The Syndicate and Bodie mills cannot be shown in a side view; the first is located at the extreme north end of Bodie Bluff—the Bodie at the northeastern base of same.

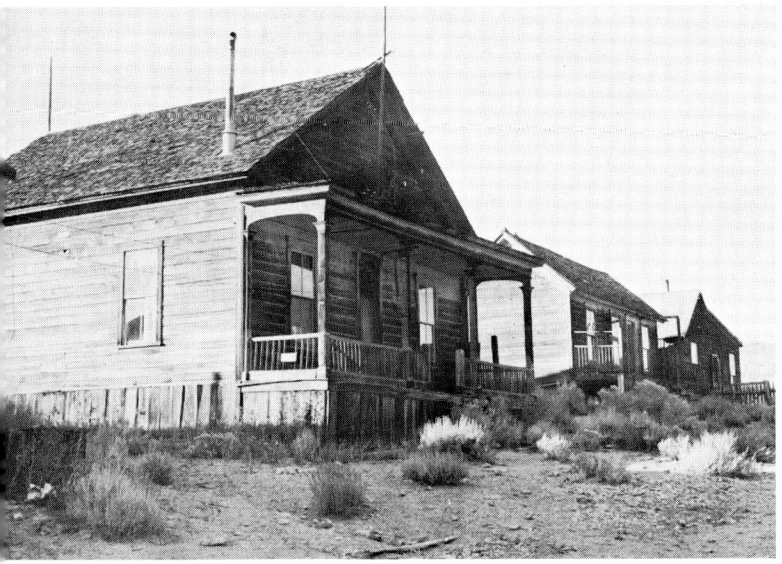

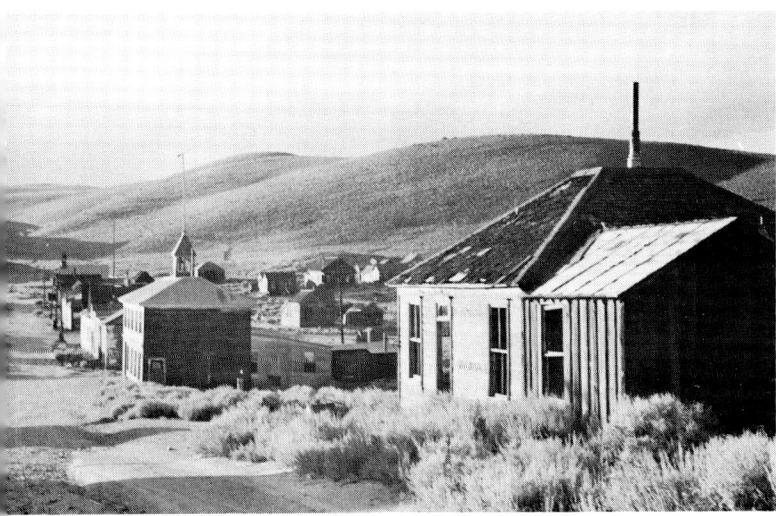

The map of Bodie *(page opposite)* was drawn in 1879 and was published in *The San Francisco Daily Stock Report,* so great was the productivity of the area and the interest of miners and speculators therein. The view faces directly east and identifies all of the major mines and mills. Just beneath the word "East" on the horizon is the Mono shaft which was the starting place of the Bodie & Benton Railroad. Halfway up the rise to the left is the Standard Bulwer mine from which an aerial tramway extends down to the Standard Mill on the edge of town.

The two small pictures on this page show Bodie in 1961. The panorama *(below)* is diametrically opposed to that of the map, being taken in 1952 from a point on the hillside near the Mono shaft and looks slightly north of west up the road to Bridgeport. *(Facing Page: Bancroft Library.)*

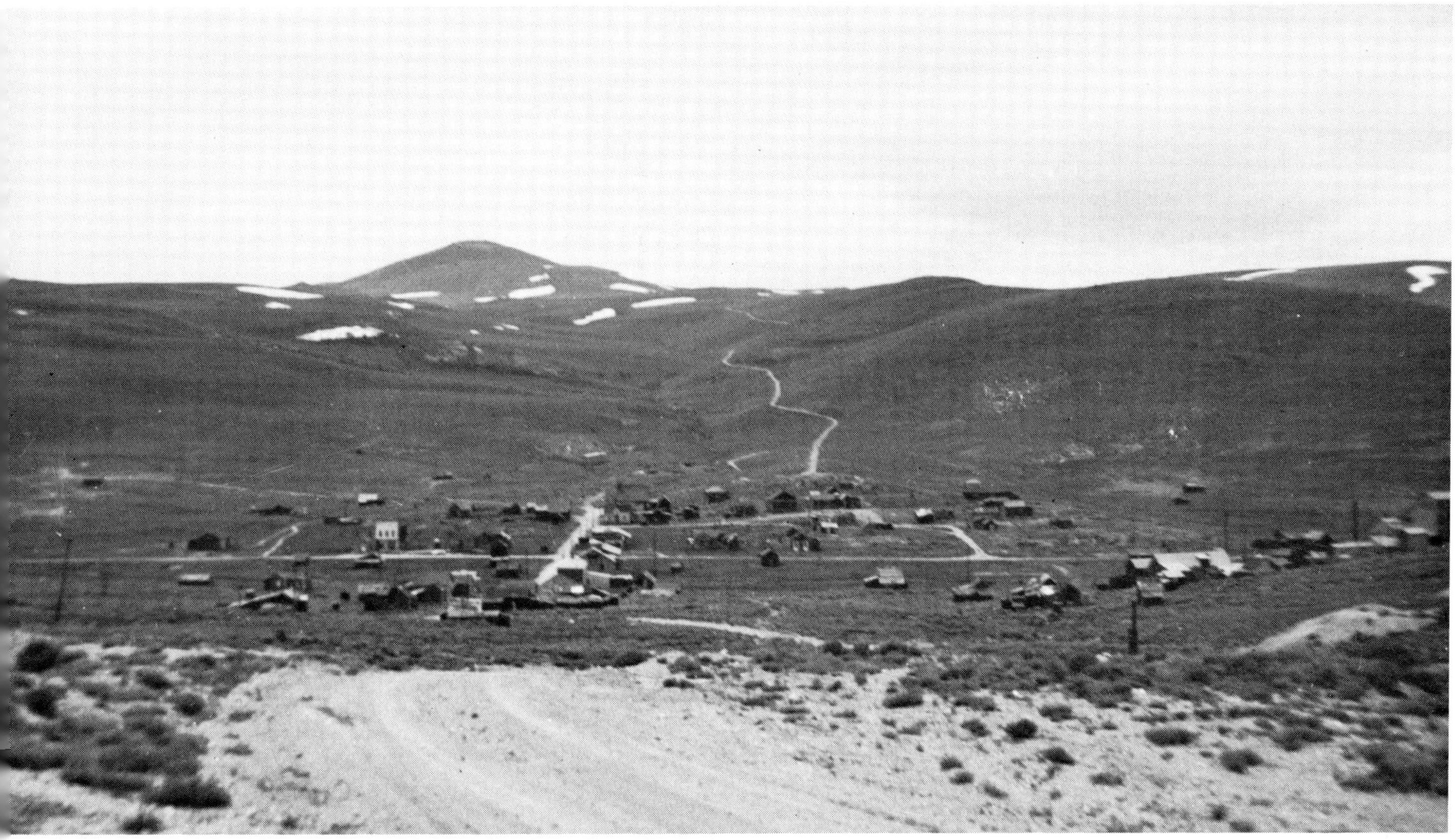

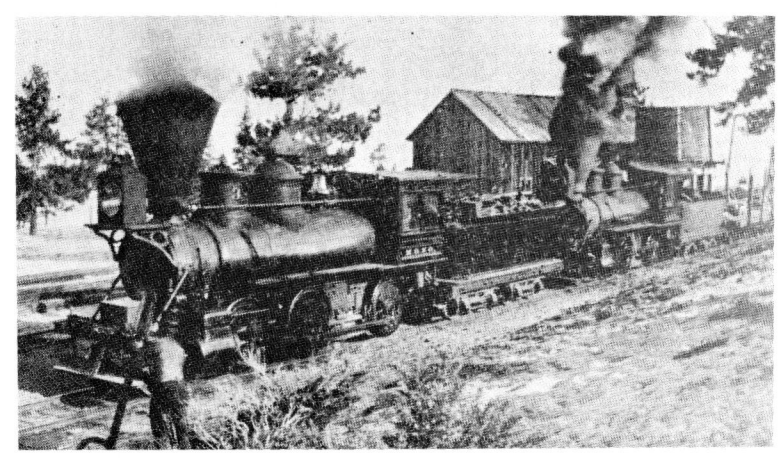
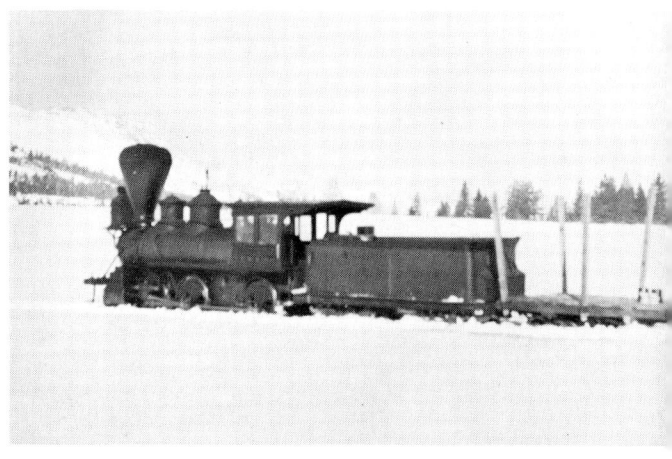

Three little (2-6-0) Mogul locomotives — the MONO, the INYO and the TYBO — constituted the bulk of the motive power of the Bodie & Benton Railway. The double-headed train *(above)* has No. 3, the MONO, on the point. To the right, the INYO negotiates the sandy flat north of Mono Mills on a wintry day. *(Left: Ted Wurm Collection; Right: E. W. Billeb Photo.)*

In 1907 a roving photographer pictured the (0-4-2-T) saddle-tank monstrosity *(top, facing page)* at Mono Mills. Its origins have been lost in obscurity. Not so the portrait of the INYO *(center)* at Bodie in 1909. The consist of the train comprises one of the earliest, western "piggy-back" operations on record, for the flat cars behind the locomotive hold three cars of George Wingfield and a party of Goldfield residents who motored to Bodie for the trip to Mono Mills. In another scene *(below)*, in the Bodie yards, the INYO stands posed for a group of adults and adolescents. Note the extra width of the tread on the blind center driver to compensate for sharp curvature and the whiskey bottle on the tool chest behind the man sitting on the pilot — it might contain valve lubricant for the hand oilers over the cylinders, or it could be stomach lubricant for convivial companionship. *(Top: L. J. Ciapponi Collection; Center: Olive Redman Wilson; Bottom: E. W. Billeb.)*

All that remains of the Bodie & Benton Ry. today is the Railroad Office *(left)* with its adjacent water tower constructed after the railroad closed down. On the plains near Mono Lake *(below)* the ruins of the old lime kiln may still be seen, monument to an era long gone. *(Bottom: Nevada Historical Society.)*

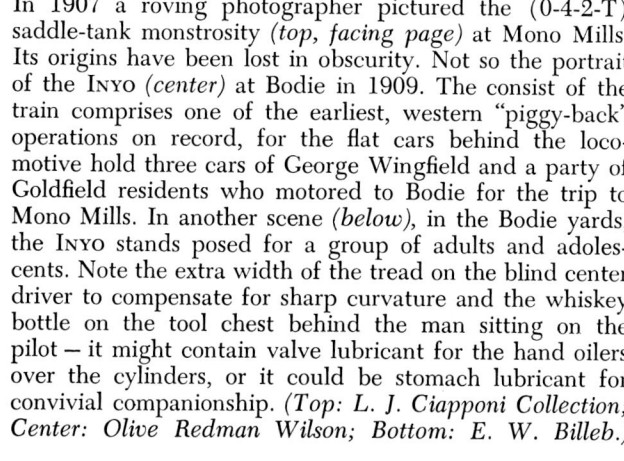
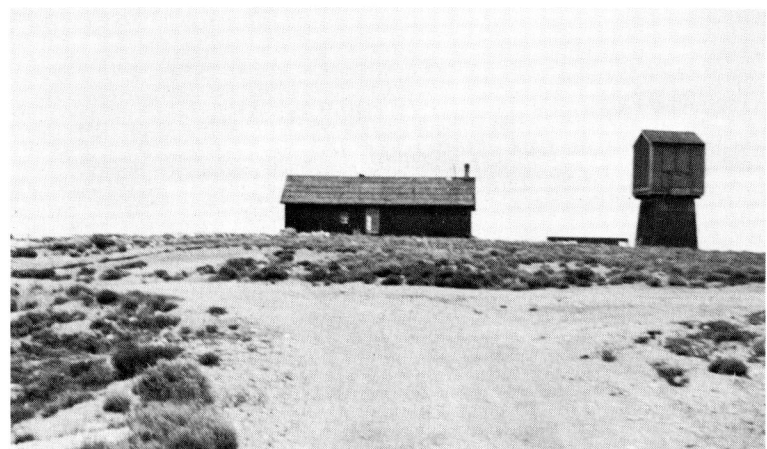
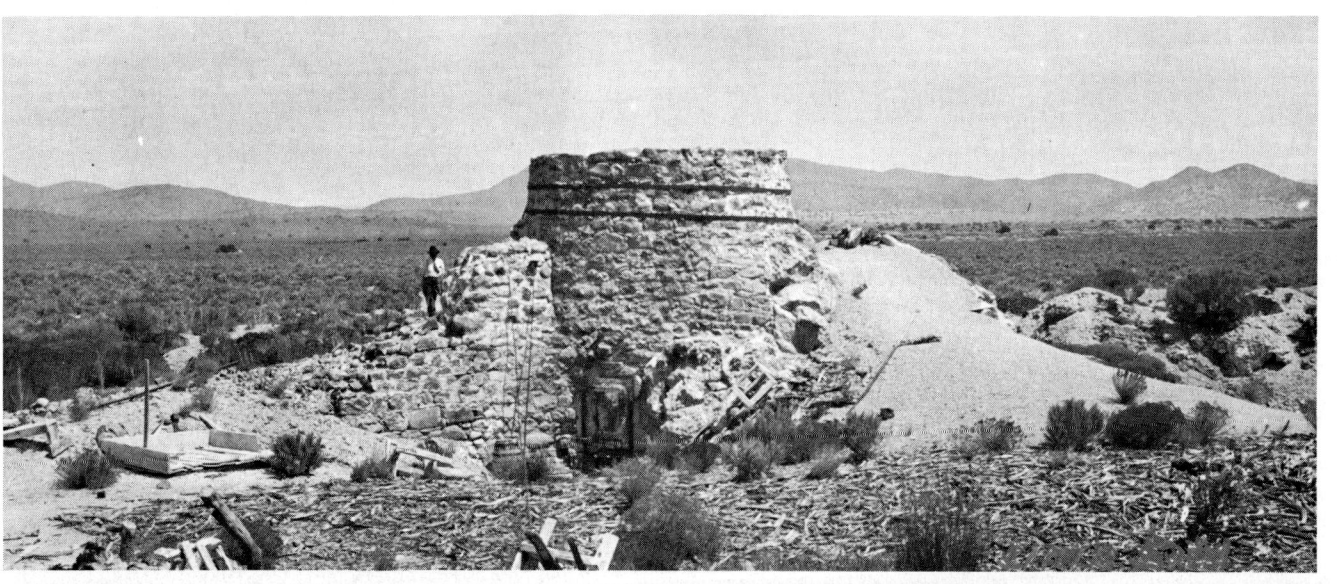

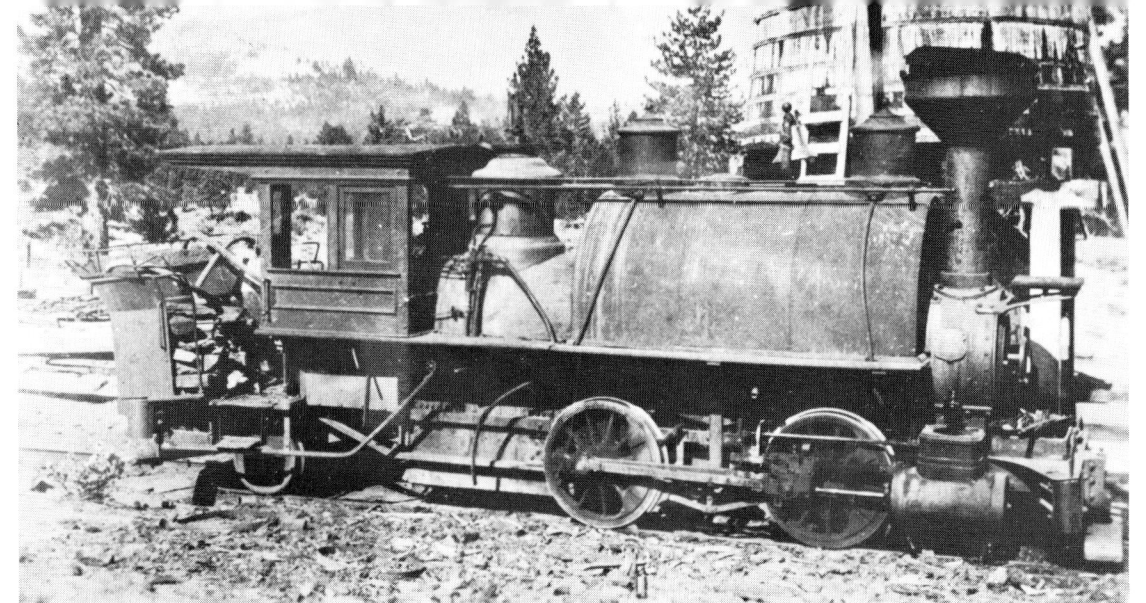
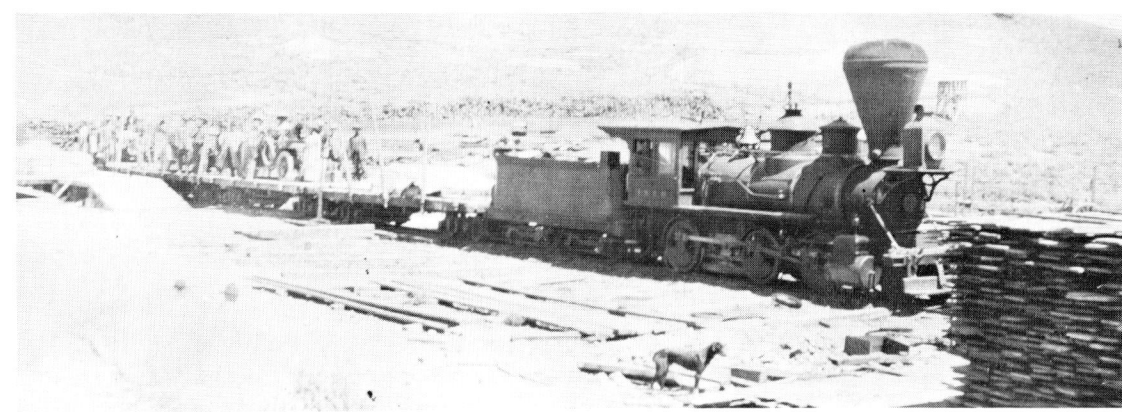

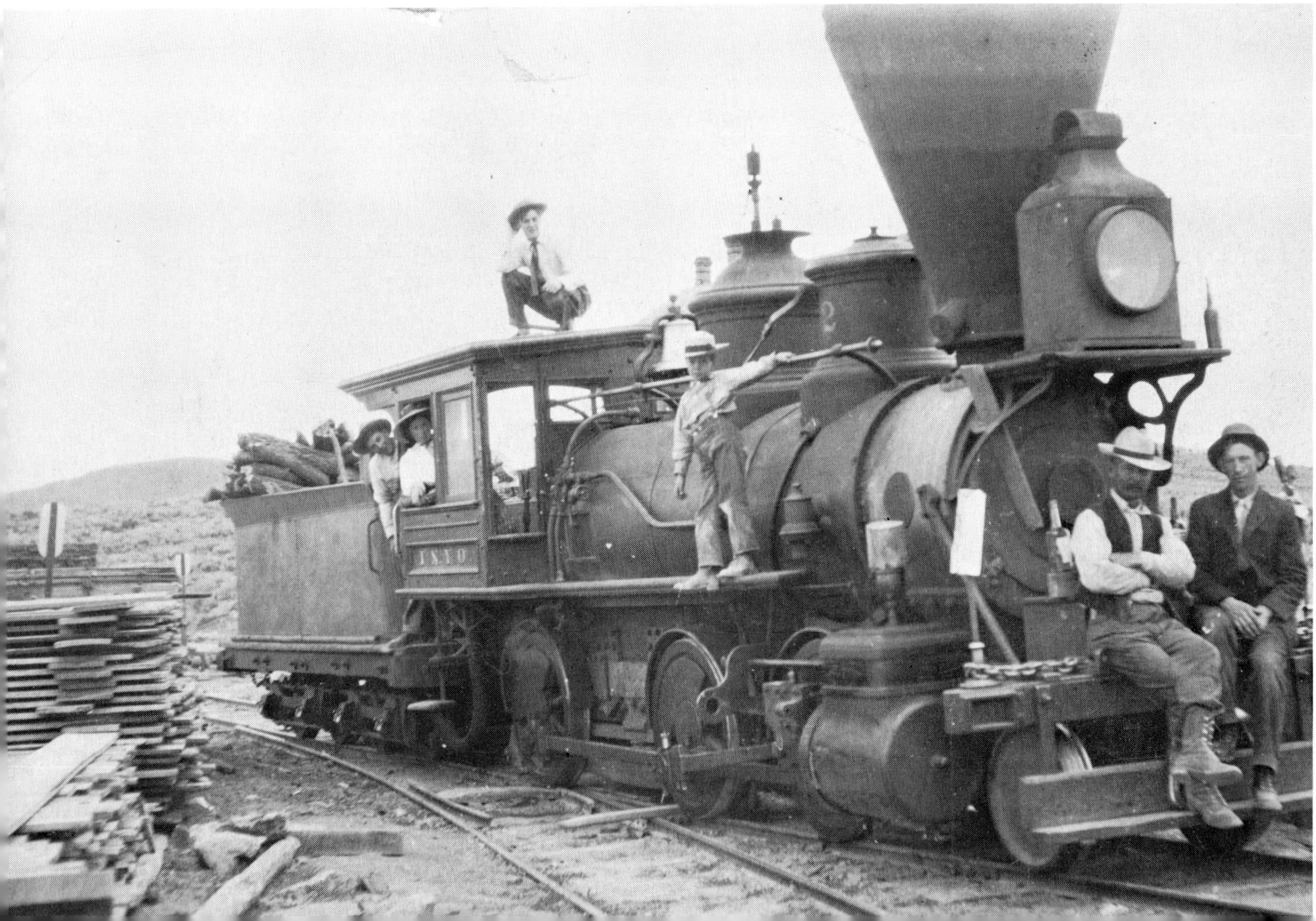

A bar of gold shipped from the Standard Mine in April 1877 (the first in four long years) signified the start of the period of greatest prosperity lasting for a few climactic years. Miners arrived in hordes — from the declining Comstock region, from the ostensibly exhausted Aurora, from other less promising areas both far and near. At the maximum, a reputed 12,000 persons congregated near the tunnel mouths, many more than the number of jobs available.

Miners were leaving the Comstock and stages to Bodie in the summer of 1879 were so crowded it was necessary to book passage days in advance. Bodie became filled with idle and destitute men, and visitors were urged to keep a sharp lookout for garroters. Stages were frequently stopped. Two men, Jones and Sharp, held up seven stages in four months. At Sweetwater Station, in the early part of June 1880, a stage was held up, the Wells Fargo box was taken, and five passengers were relieved of their valuables. A week later the same men held up the same stage at the same place and Charlie Cambridge, the driver, on recognizing the men told them he would appreciate the return of his watch because of its sentimental value. Although the return was promised, no record was ever made of the physical delivery of the property.

Thus Bodie's reputation as a rough and wicked town developed. Killings and holdups became commonplace, and it was not without justification that Eastern journalists supplied their readers with sensational and frequently gory diatribes on the carnage that was Bodie. The editor of the Bodie *Free Press* was disturbed by the reputation developed and put forth a plea for tolerance and understanding when he wrote, "To be sure, here is something of a shooting gallery, and there is a man for breakfast not infrequently, but what are we to do? . . . Times are dull, inexpensive recreation is needed, six shooters are of no account unless used, and coffins will warp if left in the undertaker's room. In India mothers throw their children in the river . . . but in Bodie, when things are crowded and a man is put out of the way to make room for a new arrival, we are called a 'hard crowd'." Regardless of pretense or facetiousness, the stark fact remains that in all of Bodie's criminal history up to 1881 only one murderer was sent to San Quentin and only one man was hung—an unfortunate Chinaman. No wonder people celebrated the New Year 1881 by jumping some 40 claims! Such was the grim side of Bodie life.

There was a humorous one, too—for example the problem of flooded streets in the downtown area due to the action of gravity on water pumped from the mines farther up in the hills. With tongue in cheek, it was suggested that Commodore Bob Love had purchased the steamer *Rocket*, then in use on Mono Lake, to ferry school children and pedestrians across Mono Street. Drier streets returned with the construction of flumes to divert the mine water.

In 1880 mining production in Bodie was relatively steady, but still insufficient to accommodate the abundance of people in the town. Times were rough with many mines closed and "coin was scarce and folks feel blue." By the middle of August hundreds of people were leaving town yet it was said that the mines never looked better and that only the drifters had departed (largely via the stage as opposed to the coffin).

By early 1881 there were 23 mines operating, but most of the production was concentrated in the Standard Consolidated and the Bodie Consolidated. The local daily paper pointed with pride to the fact that the Standard Consolidated distributed more in dividends in 1880 than any other gold and silver mine in the country, and that its dividends that year exceeded those paid by all the mines on the Comstock Lode. Such mines as the Bulwer Consolidated, Noonday, North Noonday and the Bechtel were small producers, though contributors to the general welfare.

Arrivals and departures at the Bodie Hotel and the Grand Central were duly noted in the daily press. Board and lodging at the Bodie House could be obtained for $10 a week while the Occidental insisted that it was "the only first class house in town." Due note and mention were made of the demise of Mammoth City (today a lively ski resort area) which only a year previous had boasted a population of 1,500 "and still growing." It had had a reputation for being the roughest place outside of Mexico, which appellation apparently applied to the bitter end, for when the Wells Fargo office was closed, an observant stage robber met the outbound stage and with the priority of firearms helped himself to $800 being sent out with the office ledgers. Then the town was abandoned to the coyotes.

Bodie's town proper was situated in a broad, arid valley in the high country east of the Sierra Nevada Mountains. At an elevation of 8,374 feet, it was subject to severe winter storms and deep snow. Little vegetation could grow, yet an abundance of wood and timbers were required to feed the boilers of the hoisting works and for use as shoring timbers in the mines. Every cord and board foot was carted in by teamsters from points many miles away, lining the pockets of the teamsters and creating economic havoc for the mine operators. Finally, Seth and Daniel Cook, principal shareholders in the Standard Consolidated and R. N. Graves, a mining investor, joined forces with H. M. Yerington of the V&T and others to combat the menace.

On February 18, 1881, they organized the Bodie Railway & Lumber Company in San Francisco with the avowed purpose to build and operate a narrow gauge railroad, to be used exclusively for the carrying of freight, to run from Bodie south to the timber lands owned by the Bodie Wood & Lumber Company some 40 miles to the south. Additionally, it was to have the right to cut timber, operate saw mills and purchase timber lands, especially those of the Bodie Wood & Lumber Company.

Within a week of incorporation J. T. Oliver, the man who engineered the Carson & Colorado, arrived to make a survey for the line. On March 16 the job was done. Surprisingly, the projected route passed southward along the east shore of Mono Lake to Mono Woods, whereas the line originally had been contemplated as passing along the west side of the lake so as to be close to, and be able to serve, the mining town of Lundy.

Lundy was the principal community of the Homer Mining District, but probably its greatest claim to fame was as the home of Captain J. W. E. Townsend's *Homer Mining Index*. According to another well-known newspaper man of the times, W. A. Chalfant of the *Inyo Register*, "Lying Jim" Townsend not only reported the news in his own inimitable style but continued his talented efforts to the point of creating advertising for Lundy stores and establishments of phantom existence plus schedules of arrivals and departures of ghostly trains over a trackless railroad. The veracity of such accusations are somewhat questionable as incomplete files of the *Index* presently available do not reveal the challenged inconsistencies. Transportation available in the area consisted of boating on Lundy Lake, the usual complement of stages, plus several tramways in nearby canyons. One tramway, 3,500 feet long, extended from the lowest level of the May Lundy mine down to the floor of Lake Canyon where the ore was loaded into wagons for the five-mile haul to the mill. A few years following the closing of the May Lundy mine in 1884, the tramway was swept away by snowslides.

Construction on the Bodie Railway was pushed as rapidly as possible. President R. N. Graves named Thomas Holt superintendent in charge of construction, and by the middle of May 1881, 10 miles of rails had been purchased in San Francisco and the balance placed on order. A (2-6-0) mogul locomotive of Baldwin descent, the Tybo, was purchased from the Eureka & Palisade Railroad to initiate operations while three additional locomotives were ordered from the firm of Prescott Scott & Company in San Francisco. Of the total estimated investment in the completed railroad of a half million dollars, approximately $180,000 purportedly represented freight charges on inbound equipment and supplies, including teaming from the rail terminus at Hawthorne which the Carson & Colorado Railroad had just established a few weeks before.

Before work could begin, Holt ran into labor difficulties. An initial advertisement in the paper sought 200 white men to build the road at a daily wage of $1.25 plus board, work to start on Wednesday, May 25, 1881. A late snowstorm the day the ad appeared delayed response, and of those that did apply, many were Chinese. Discretion being the better part of valor, Holt hired a few gangs of Chinamen to work on the alkali flat at the south end of Mono Lake where the white men refused to work. The word got around. A protest meeting was held nearly filling the Miners Union Hall the night of May 24. With mine wages at $3.00 to $4.00 a day (when work was available), the miners looked with disdain on the low wage offered by the railroad and with disgust on the hiring of Chinese "barbarians" in preference to white men. Before the meeting adjourned to the next night, a resolution was passed to compile a list of volunteers to drive the Chinese out of camp.

Wednesday morning arrived; the Chinese went quietly to work on the Mono Lake alkali flats; and official grading began as scheduled on the eastern slope of Bodie Ridge, a short distance southwest of the Dudley Hoisting Works. Approximately 50 white men started work that morning, and any others applying for work during the day were added to the force. A large crowd witnessed the commencement, some of whom obviously were present to check on the possible employment of Chinese labor. Although the day's work went smoothly enough, still the men were not satisfied.

That night, at the continuation of the meeting adjourned from the previous night, a positive statement was sought from Holt that he refrain from hiring any "Celestials." On Holt's refusal and upon learning of the group of Chinese already working the alkali flats, some 40 men (believed to be egged on by disgruntled timber teamsters) set out at 1:00 A. M. Thursday morning for the Chinese camp a good 30 miles away. Using teams, horseback, and some even walking, they arrived on the scene to find the Celestials had been removed with a month's supply of food to Paoha Island in Mono Lake, about six miles from the shore. The *Rocket,* the only steamer on Mono Lake, had been engaged from Captain Annas for this event. There being no other boats available except one or two rickety rowboats, all the men could do was make faces at the Chinese who were cooking gulls' eggs in the hot springs on the island.

The Bodie *Free Press* took a stand against the miners and their inciters, publishing an editorial condemning the action of the group. An anonymous letter to the editors threatened to drive them out of the country along with the Chinese. Meanwhile local Chinese merchants raised $300 in one hour to help their brethren and were prepared to take the matter to court.

In their rush and enthusiasm to get to the Chinese camp, the men found they had neglected to bring blankets, food, or firewood with which to sustain themselves against the rigorous climate. Arrangements finally were made with Louis Sammann to eat at his ranch, but by Friday even this source of sustenance was in jeopardy for lack of pay.

Out on the island the American flag could be seen flying over the Chinese camp, named Fort Conroy in honor of the old miner in charge of the Chinamen. The *Rocket* was making regular trips on signal, while the protesting workmen watched in the hope of seizing the ship, putting all 47 Chinamen in barges and driving them from the country.

Still farther south of the Chinese camp, Tom Sharp had 21 men at work grading the wagon road leading from the proposed terminus of the railroad into the timber areas. When the protestants attempted to enlist the aid of these 21 men in ridding the area of the Chinese, they were met with a prompt rebuff as the latter preferred to remain on the job. Sheriff Showers came down from Bodie to read the men the riot act. If necessary, he planned to utilize Sharp's men in the formation of a posse to arrest the group. Friday afternoon two buckboards loaded with food and whiskey were dispatched to lend encouragement to the strikers, but late that night they drifted home, disheartened, and the two-day protest was over.

The first hurdle had been surmounted. Following a week's work, good progress could be reported. At the northern end near Bodie, the grade extended from a point near the Mono Mine down as far as the Defiance Hoisting Works near the eastern base of Silver Hill and was ready for the track. A boarding house was being built four miles out from town near the railroad. At the southern end below Mono Lake, work progressed on the wagon road into the timber while the stone foundations for the sawmill were set in place. Then came more trouble.

The grading force had been increased to 115 men by this time, and more were being hired as they applied for work. A new man in town, on the morning of his first day of employment, worked up a strike among the others for daily wages of $2.00 instead of the prevailing $1.25. Superintendent Holt paid off the 56 men who demanded their time, subsequently reinstated 36 who changed their minds as dinnertime approached. The other 20 continued their efforts to foment revolt through public meetings that night and coercion on the job the next day. Law officers sent to the scene of trouble warned the strikers, and the band was gradually dispersed.

In spite of these disruptions, work on the railroad moved ahead. At the end of four weeks of effort some nine miles of grading were completed; 200 white men and 100 Chinamen were constantly employed; the wagon road to the timber was finished; and the boiler and engine for the yet incompleted sawmill had been shipped. Anticipation ran high in Bodie. The editor noted strong indications of a boom when he saw a dog fight, a stray cow, an empty horse dray and an express wagon with an empty trunk in it on Main Street, all at the same time. Individual prosperity could rise and fall with singular events. When a man lost a $20 gold piece in the plank sidewalk, willing hands promptly tore up the boards in an effort to be helpful. Josiah Brown marked the Fourth of July by opening his new hotel on Green Street, just east of Main on the way up to the depot, and proclaimed it the largest in Bodie. By contrast, the Bodie Hotel fell upon dull times and was offered for lease the following month to anyone willing to take his chances.

By the end of July 1881 the railroad graders had completed 22 miles of roadbed and, with two more miles being graded, only eight miles were yet unworked. Superintendent Thomas Holt took the

Free Press reporter on a trip over the railroad grade. The resulting report in the paper stated that the line started near the old Mono Shaft, ran along the eastern slope of Silver Hill to a point between the Red Cloud and Defiance Shafts, then turned and crossed the flat before heading southward on the western slope of Nevada Hill. It then turned easterly and followed the old Syndicate Mines wood road for a long distance to the intersection of the Noonday Mine wood road, four miles out from Bodie. Thus far the grade was light, not exceeding 70 feet to the mile (1.3%), but in the next seven miles the grade increased to a steep 200 feet to the mile (3.8%) with sharp curves.

Five miles out was Camp No. 2, consisting of a plain board dining room and kitchen surrounded by a scattering of white walled tents, the temporary home of Ben Drum and his crew of 35 men. A mile farther on was Camp No. 3 wherein were housed Thomas F. McMillan and his crew of 25 men plus the commissary headquarters maintained under the supervision of H. C. Tichnor. A half-mile beyond, the first switchback reversed the direction of travel for the next 1½ miles whence a second switchback once again set things to rights. Camp No. 4 with its 200 men was located at the second switchback, a full two miles away from Camp No. 3 by railroad yet only three-fourths of a mile distant as the crow flies. Much heavy grading was required to bring the line down the hill. Many cuts were dug, some 25 feet deep; a 260-foot trestle, 50 feet high, was also constructed. Beyond the trestle, another camp of 68 Chinese was busy grading the next two miles, leaving only five miles of route over the plains east of Mono Lake on which work was not in progress. No difficulties were anticipated in the construction of this last easy section.

South of Mono Lake, the big sawmill, larger than the mill at Glenbrook, Lake Tahoe, was completed during August 1881. By the end of the month wagons were bringing in a disassembled locomotive, a tender and some rails from Hawthorne on the C&C. The first rails were spiked down south from Warm Springs, early in September, and shortly thereafter the locomotive was running over a mile of completed roadbed. The final five miles of grading were completed during the month, and the new mill was kept busy turning out ties for the railroad.

The *Free Press* reporter took a second trip over the line on October 7 and noted that the boarding house was now located at Warm Springs station on the eastern shore of Mono Lake. From this point southward for 10¼ miles to the mill the track was completed, though somewhat insecurely, for when traveling over it "a little jar was now and then experienced as the track was not yet lined and surfaced." A twenty-minute ride (at 15 miles per hour) brought one to the mill and "the sweet odor of pine, and the aroma of fresh sawdust reminded one he was a long way from Bodie."

Mono Mills, the southern terminus, was described as prosperous if not large. The two-story sawmill was advantageously located in a ravine so that logs, on entering the mill at the top, were converted in a matter of 20 minutes into ties through the medium of 54-inch saws and a crew of 25 men. Mr. Wedge, the foreman, reported a 10-hour daily cutting of 2,816 ties, size 6" x 8" x 7', sufficient to lay one mile of track. Total production for the month of September amounted to 29,000 ties.

Gilchrest and Sharp had just completed their general store. Mrs. McConnell, formerly of Bodie, ran one of the two boarding houses. Six small houses were located on the street from which could be seen the 40 mules used to bring in the wood and the two large ox teams engaged in hauling logs to the mill.

Warm Springs was the hub of railroad construction. Initially, teams hauled the rails and supplies from the C&C railhead at Hawthorne to the north shore of Mono Lake. They were then barged to Warm Springs and distributed to the track layers. When a storm kicked up heavy swells on Mono Lake, the little steamer *Rocket* was tied up and the barges did not move. Severe storms in October almost swamped the craft and caused a four-day delay. A week later another storm swamped the railroad's barge. Frequently, there was trouble among the sailors.

The first track laying proceeded southward to Mono Mills and the source of ties. Later it extended northward toward Bodie from a point three miles north of Warm Springs. Each mile of track required 352 rails 30 feet long. Under Mr. P. Canning, an experienced track layer, a crew of 46 men were laying approximately a mile of track each day subject, of course, to numerous delays. On the more level ground 35-pound rail was used, but on the heavy grade and switchback 40-pound rail was deemed more expedient. Storms took their toll on this phase of the work as well, for along the east side of Mono Lake sand piled high on the track in some places and drifted from under the ties in others, once almost causing the ditching of a locomotive.

November 8, 1881, was a notable day for Bodie. For the first time the sound of the locomotive whistle was heard in town, causing the editor to write that the town had become terribly quiet, one never heard a gun go off any more. As though in refutation of his contention, the railroad horse team became frightened the same day and ran away down the hill toward town. On the way down the team hit a wagon and finally was stopped by an awning post on the sidewalk in front of the Humboldt Beer Hall, causing 16 men to dive for the entrance.

The last spike was driven at 3:00 P.M. on Monday, November 14, 1881. Before the end of the day the first train rolled in with two cars of lumber for the Standard Mine, then employing 147 men including 60 miners. To celebrate the occasion, Superintendent Holt arranged a big turkey dinner for all BR&L personnel plus selected guests. Conviviality reigned, and numerous congratulations were offered, not undeservedly. For great credit was due to Holt for the vigor with which he pushed the road. Not only did he have labor troubles, but rail was difficult to obtain as American sources were sold out for months in advance. One ship with a cargo of rail for the line was wrecked, and it was only by borrowing from the Central Pacific and the C&C that a sufficient quantity was procured to enable completion of the BR&L's main line. Rail for the side tracks at Bodie and for the incline to the new Standard shaft was not available for some time to come.

As the editor of the *Free Press* was saying, and rightly so, Bodie was now "the terminus of an important railway system." The schedule called for a train to leave Bodie at 6:30 A.M. daily, arriving at Mono Mills at 10:00 A.M. Returning, it left the mill at 2:00 P.M. and arrived in Bodie four hours later. Since each train of necessity had to be broken into three sections to negotiate the big grade and switchbacks, the number of arrivals and departures at the Bodie end were multiplied.

Completion of the railroad brought with it increasing signs of prosperity for the Bodie area. The Standard Consolidated paid its 53rd monthly dividend in December of 75 cents a share together with an extra dividend in the same amount. Bulwer Consolidated and the Bodie Water Co. announced initial dividend payments, though admittedly small. The renewed vitality of the area resulted in many uncalled-for shootings which caused the editor to complain that it disturbed those with normal sleeping hours. Additional rail was finally procured, and the tracks were extended to the Standard Mine and along Bodie Bluff with the expectation that all the wood yards would soon have spur tracks. Frank Bell built a telegraph line along the railroad to the sawmill. Every day four trains arrived in Bodie, each consisting of six flat cars loaded with cord wood, this in spite of a post-Christmas snow storm and high winds which required a large force to keep the tracks clear.

Early in January 1882 the sawmill closed down for the winter. A private excursion (the BR&L never operated any formal passenger service) was organized for January 7 to mark the last train of the season. To accommodate the crowd of 25 people, an enclosure was constructed on a flat car body to provide protection from the wintry winds. Oil cloth was spread on the floor, and benches were placed around a stove. With these crude precautions, the train left Bodie, and passengers saw teams hauling lumber from the stacks along the railroad to the mine shafts as rails to the mines could not be laid until spring. Puffing switch engines were shuffling cars in the yards and on sidings. Then the train started down the grade, negotiated the switchbacks, and proceeded across the flat to Lime Kiln Station, 12 miles from Bodie. Five miles farther, at Warm Springs, the *Rocket* was observed, pulled up on the shore for the winter. At Mono Mills, 10 chilling miles farther, it was found that the sawmill had been shut down even though 100 men were still busy cutting logs in the woods.

The guests were greeted by Charles Gilchrest and Thomas Sharp, proprietors of the general store, who "threw open their establishment from garret to cellar—more particularly the cellar," and treated them well. The telephone line (operated in connection with the telegraph line) was kept busy as Pixley and Lyman sang "Larboard Watch" to their enraptured friends 30 miles away. Raymond Holmes and Walker, visiting the mill, sang "Treasures of Memory" which Pixley, in Bodie, pronounced excellent. A delicious lunch was served by Joe Stow.

An extra passenger was provided on the return trip when Sheriff Jim Showers mixed business with pleasure and brought back, for incarceration in the Bodie jail, a man charged with an old murder in Alpine County. No problems were encountered, and R. K. Colcord, superintendent of the Bodie

Syndicate Mine and later Governor of Nevada, proposed a vote of thanks which was "tendered with three cheers and a tiger."

There was little news of railroad activity during the next few months as snow drifts covered the tracks and the cars of the BR&L. The railroad's organizers, however, had time to digest and review the results of the efforts of the preceding year, and the picture looked good. In January 1882 (as the C&C was starting its construction from Filben over Mt. Montgomery Pass to Benton and the Owens Valley), these same men organized The Bodie & Benton Railway & Commercial Company to take over their existing line and build a branch from Warm Springs on Mono Lake to the C&C near Benton. Moreover, a second rail connection with the outside world appeared likely as the California & Nevada Railroad was working its way through the hills behind Berkeley and was headed for Bodie.

The mild winter of 1882 belied the unexpectedly severe spring weather which followed. On March 9, 1882, a heavy snowstorm dropped over three feet of snow, and strong winds pushed it into drifts as high as 15 feet. Holt returned from his vacation to find the railroad quite thoroughly covered with snow. He was still optimistic, however, and announced that the extension to Benton would be completed in October, with work to begin on May 1. This was the earliest that rails could be delivered (possibly not until later); then 60 days would be required to lay them.

Spring fever ran high in 1882. The B&B moved its offices from Main Street in Bodie to the depot at the top of the hill pending construction and completion of its own office building. By the early part of April the snow began to melt; the men cleared the tracks; and the trains began operating for the new season at hand. However, late snowfalls and drifts severely hampered operations. With May only a week away, the snow banks on the side streets were still three feet high. Then the Bodie Bank (one of two in town) voluntarily closed its doors and liquidated its assets. No one was particularly incommoded; its building became a shoe store; and the old vault went to the railroad. Another finger appeared in the citizen pie when the railroad, already largely in the wood business, started advertising delivery of pine wood around town for $12 a cord.

May 12 marked the commencement of grading on the extension to Benton. Almost at the same time work began on a spur track from Mono Mills into the woods to bring the timber nearer to railhead. Superintendent Holt arranged for a series of five excursions from Bodie to the woods to acquaint the people with the operations being performed at that end of the line. On May 19 the first excursion, primarily for "practical miners" (although some ladies were among the 400 people on the seven-car train), went to visit Mono Mills and see the woods. A few days later a group of 60 people and a band made the trip, with the usual stops at Lime Kiln and Warm Springs. On arrival at Mono Mills it was found that Gilchrest's store had been cleared for dancing. Lunch was served in the engine house, following which the guests witnessed logging operations. It was reported that no social event in Bodie had ever been more thoroughly enjoyed. The last excursion was run on May 25 for the members of the YMCA, who found riding on the open cars of the B&B a bit chilly because of the unexpected snowstorm that day.

June was notable as the month of a "new arrival," a switching locomotive. Previously, in March, the *Inyo Independent* had editorialized at length about the railroad and quipped: "The engines on the Bodie and Mono Lake Railroad are named MONO, INYO and TYBO. Now let them complete the extension and put on the COMO, COSO, YOLO and three or fomo'." The suggestion was not heeded, however, for the new locomotive was assigned the proud name of BODIE, reflecting the activity of that town, and of the railroad which had extended its tracks to the Standard Hoisting Works and was busy hauling tremendous quantities of wood to the Standard and Bulwer mills.

Work on the proposed connection to Benton was progressing nicely, with grading completed to within 15 miles of Benton. Suddenly on July 10, 1882, all work was halted, and 25 white men and 100 Celestials were laid off. Adequate reasons for the abandonment of the project never were stated publicly by anyone in authority, but local sages had their expressed opinions. Some contended that the Carson & Colorado was to blame, as its failure to obtain rails delayed the extension of their line over Mt. Montgomery Pass to Benton, and there was no incentive to rush a B&B connection to an unfinished railroad. The majority favored the reasoning that, because the C&C proprietors were also in the wood and lumber business, they would not welcome fresh competition for outside markets from the large Mono Mills on the B&B. It can be speculated that a high freight tariff on B&B lumber shipments over the C&C would have effectively eliminated any competition from the Bodie lumber people. Since R. N. Graves, president of the B&B, was in New York at the time, possibly he visited D. O. Mills (principal backer of the C&C) and was rebuffed with the suggestion of the futility of the project. Mills had been known to have done this in another instance (See N-C-O Railway).

Bodie continued active and prosperous throughout the summer and early fall of 1882. The smaller mines were busy, necessitating a constant supply of wood which, in turn, kept the B&B's locomotives activated and the rails shiny. Then, in November, the Noonday and Red Cloud mines suddenly closed down. Noonday payroll checks were protested in San Francisco and many men, in order to establish their lien, refused to accept a check because a receipt would have been required. Both Mono and Inyo counties had been outstanding for California mining production in 1882, but the recent closings were discouraging and men drifted away to seek employment elsewhere. Standard Consolidated, which had been the mainstay of the Bodie camp, halted dividend payments early in 1884. On May 1 their noon whistle sounded and all hands were discharged summarily. At nearby Lundy, the Gorilla tramway was still hauling ore from its mine to Wasson Meadows, but the sheriff closed the nearby May Lundy mine in August. One happy event was the finding of a small body of rich ore in the Bodie Consolidated which enabled resumption of dividend payments for a few months.

From 1885 to 1887 the output of the Bodie district never greatly exceeded $500,000 (one-sixth of the 1880-81 figure), most of the production coming from the Standard Company. Matters went from bad to worse in 1888 when production slumped to $126,000. Of the 162 mill stamps, only 15 were in operation; of the 50 mines, only three were operating and but one, the Standard, was producing ore. The population of Bodie had shrunk to 500. In 1890 the 2,800-foot tramway from the Standard mine to its mill in Bodie, long the pride of local residents, was dismantled. With the mines closed, there was no wood to haul and the B&B Railroad ceased operation.

For three years Bodie was dormant. Reorganization followed in 1893 when the Bodie Railway & Lumber Co. (virtually the original title) was formed. Two years later the railroad began its annual stint of two months of summer operation to supply wood and lumber to the mines which had by then resumed operation. In 1897 four additional miles of track were built into the woods near Mono Mills, bringing the total mileage to 37. A visitor to Bodie that year found 600 people living there with no less than 265 of them working for wages of $4.00 per day. Farmers were receiving spot coin for their produce, and there seemed to be any amount of money in circulation. Eight saloons and gambling houses plus 12 stores were in operation excluding those in the Chinatown area. A new water pipe was being laid, and some 140 children attended the local school. Three mines—the Standard, Syndicate and Bodie Tunnel—were going full blast. In October 1898 the Standard 20-stamp mill burned, but the prevailing mining prospects warranted its rebuilding.

For a few years the railroad was leased to an operator named E. L. Reese. Then, late in 1906, Charles E. Knox, organizer and president of the Montana-Tonopah Mining Co., became interested in the property. After inspection he purchased the BR&L together with the 7,600 acres of timber lands at Mono Mills on December 23, 1906, for a reported $200,000. The name was changed again, this time to the Mono Lake Railway & Lumber Co. The following June the timber lands were augmented by the purchase of an additional 15,000-acre tract, and an ambitious construction and expansion program for the railroad was outlined.

To obtain connections to the east (where the Tonopah and Goldfield booms were under way), the MLR&L proposed to build from Warm Springs on Mono Lake eastward to Basalt, Nevada, on the N&C, a distance of approximately 45 miles. From Basalt, trackage rights over the N&C would carry the trains to Mina (also the terminal for the Tonopah & Goldfield Railroad). Expansion to the west was anticipated to start from Bodie and run northwesterly past Bridgeport to a point near Sonora Pass. Here, pending a two-year delay to bore a four-mile tunnel under the crest of the Sierras, stage coaches and freight wagons would close the gap to a connection with the Sierra Railway, thus forming an independent route to tidewater via the Sierra and Santa Fe railroads. According to the newspaper report, Contractor McLean would bring his entire force of 400 men from southern Nevada to work on the line to Basalt, which was scheduled for completion no later than November 1, 1907.

In July 1907, a month after the announcement of the new rail link, Knox contended that if the SP relocated its (N&C) line from Mt. Montgomery Pass to Whiskey Flat, a possible alternate route, only a dozen miles of new construction would be required from Warm Springs. In August, Mark B. Kerr, engineer in charge, stated that the Mono Lake Railway with its five miles of grading (probably referring to the 1882 grade to Benton) was at a standstill until the SP declared its intentions. Meanwhile the Mono Mills, following repairs, were turning out 50,000 feet of lumber daily for Bodie, Aurora and other camps. The railroad was being extended southeasterly into new lumber territory.

Having made no real progress in 1907, Charles Knox, who was also a member of the Board of Directors of the Tonopah & Goldfield RR, invited T&G participation in his scheme at that Board's meeting on September 30, 1908. Following the usual T&G practice, a committee of three other board members was appointed to review the matter. A month later the T&G Board agreed to subscribe to stock in the Mono Railway (the railway and lumber operations having been separated) to an amount equal to the value of T&G surplus rails, ties and equipment. Salable to the Mono Railway the equipment consisted of three T&G locomotives, 27 flat cars, eight box cars and passenger coaches. The total amount of Mono Railway Company stock authorized was $1,500,000, and there was provision in the agreement that the balance other parties would subscribe for in good faith.

Apparently the necessary subscriptions were not forthcoming, for a year later Knox was back with a different proposition. This time the T&G would be given a six months' option to participate in the construction of the railroad. Again the matter was referred to a special committee with instructions to render a report before the expiration of the option on May 15, 1910. To determine practicability, the committee instituted a survey at T&G expense. Under R. W. Cattermole, subsequently Vice-President and General Manager of the T&G, a party started out from Tonopah Junction on January 8, 1910. When a mere 12 miles out, the surveyors ran into grades of 3 and 4 per cent. There was so much snow on the ground that at times the surveyors were unable to determine the grade. The effort was abandoned, and the situation reviewed. Then a second preliminary survey was attempted. Backing up the T&G right-of-way to Coaldale, the party attempted to make a new start and run its line through the hills via Basalt, there to tie in with the previously proposed line from Warm Springs. Again difficulties were met, and the route did not appear promising. The committee's report in April decided the T&G Board to leave the matter of financing a possible third survey and extending the option up to the discretion of President Cutter.

Knox was not one to take defeat lying down. On April 16 he told a reporter in Mina that his line would start at Mina and proceed 2½ miles to Mina Canyon. Then, passing the F. D. Qualey copper properties in the Excelsior Mountains, his road would go through Whiskey Flat to Mono Lake. Whether this was intended to impress the SP or the T&G is difficult to determine. The SP failed to raise an eyebrow, while President Cutter and the T&G lost interest in the project, and the scheme died.

Following 1912, mining activity in Bodie declined, and with it came a decline in the demand for lumber and wood. In 1914 the Standard closed down thus ending its second era during which it had paid $750,000 in dividends. With the closing of the Standard, the Mono Railway lost its biggest customer; and as the cutting of any additional timber would require another extension of the railway to new locations, an application was filed with the California Railroad Commission to abandon the entire line. On September 6, 1917, approval was granted and subsequently the road was dismantled.

To paraphrase on the Bodie & Benton's initials, it might be said that the road was "born & booming" then "beaten and busted." However, for a strictly commercial operation, it had served its purpose well.

Owens River Valley Electric Railway Co.

The town of Bishop, located in the northern part of the Owens Valley in eastern California, wanted public transportation to the outside world. The town of Laws, four miles to the east, was quite adequately served by the narrow gauge Nevada & California (SP) Railroad, or at least it had a better mode of transportation than slow horseback or buggy travel could provide. Any community, in the modern year of 1910 needed adequate transportation.

The desire was not new. Several years before, certain local citizens—C. F. Wildasinn, Charles E. Johnson and White Smith (of the Saline Valley Salt enterprise Smiths)—had managed to interest George C. Carey of South Omaha, Nebraska, in the construction of a similar project, but somewhere along the line the plans failed to materialize. Johnson picked up the franchises and turned them over to a new company, the Owens River Valley Electric Railway Co., chartered November 17, 1910, which was sparked by Harry Shaw as president and H. N. Beard, general manager. Shaw was also president of the Owens Valley Bank, veteran of a full seven months' banking operations.

With the railroad's organization accomplished it was appropriate that, early in 1911, plans were announced for a four-mile electric railway between Bishop and Laws, on the N&C. To avoid demeaning comments about the length of the line, the projectors included in their announcement tentative plans for a 12-mile extension northwestward to Round Valley and a 16-mile southern extension to Big Pine. For the moment, however, every effort was to be concentrated on the four-mile line to Laws.

In the middle of February 1911 surveys were started. Initial plans contemplated a narrow gauge road to match the prevailing trackage of the N&C with ample allowances for conversion to standard gauge with the minimum of difficulty should the SP decide to standard gauge its constituent. Offices were opened in the Johnson Building on East Line Street in Bishop, from which emanated a two-page advertisement for publication in the *Inyo Register* offering stock in the enterprise to the public. It was a combination deal—for each share of railway stock subscribed a bonus would be given of one share of stock in the Aqueduct Lands and Orchards Co., a Beard organization contemplating development of a 1,300-acre apple orchard in the Sunland District near Bishop. To acquaint the public with the project, a promotional booklet entitled "The Big Red Apple—The Money Tree" was issued, from which local wags derived and spread the railway's nickname, "The Red Apple Route." Four subsequent advertisements promoted the sale of stock during the ensuing weeks, the size diminishing with each publication.

Late in March 1911 the surveys were completed. Then no further progress was reported until June, when it was announced that all of the right-of-way had been acquired except one small portion across the Leary property. The route selected would enter Bishop on East Line Street and terminate at Main Street where a 548-foot frontage had been acquired.

The grading contract was signed with Herbert Francisco and Neil McLean on June 10. (McLean was an old hand at Nevada railroad grading, having done the work on the T&G some years before.) Work was to start within 10 days, and the 4¼-mile line was to be ready for ties and rails in 90 days. A fill, 600 feet long and 17 feet deep at the maximum point, was required as well as a long cut, 11 feet deep. Aside from these two problems, the route was largely over level ground.

A celebration was planned to mark the initial construction. W. L. Rowan would render an oration, and there would be "free lemonade galore." The *Inyo Register* announced that President Shaw "will delve into the soil with a shovel decorated for the occasion (the shovel will be decorated, and not Mr. Shaw) and the first shovelful of dirt will be thrown into the winds . . ." When the big celebration finally took place on Saturday, June 16, 1911, the stores were closed for two hours in the morning while 25 horseless carriages passed in parade. Musical entertainment consisted of two impromptu solos for the featured fife and drum corps failed to put in an appearance. Somewhere in the lengthy harangues of the local orators it was revealed that sufficient stock had been subscribed to enable completion of the line.

Actual work began the following Monday when 32 men and 60 horses tackled the big cut near the Owens River. A month later it was finished. Four narrow gauge carloads of pipe arrived over the N&C for use in construction of the 39 culverts required for the line. The site for a sawmill was purchased by the electric railway at Andrews Spring in Black Canyon, in the White Mountains east of Owens Valley. By early August the graders were working on the big fill near the north branch of Bishop Creek, and the sawmill was completed. At month end the grading was virtually finished, although operations at the sawmill appeared to be somewhat less than satisfactory as there were frequent delays in cutting the logs. It was whispered that initial operations on the railroad might be instituted using gas motor cars; then came a positive announcement that the line would be an overhead electrical system after all. November 1911 arrived, and with it came the proclamation that no further work would be done on the railroad until the following spring except some fencing along the right-of-way.

Winter passed, then the spring of 1912 came and lapsed into summer. Still there was no progress or promise of progress on the railroad. Finally, in

June, Harry Shaw made the last public pronouncement. "Large plans are maturing, looking to work on the road in the near future," he reported. Just what the plans were, or why they were not instituted, was never revealed. The secret remained with the individuals involved, and they are now deceased.

The diversion of the Owens River water to the Los Angeles Aqueduct in 1910-11 caused many hardships in the Owens Valley. The proposed apple orchard and the unfinished electric railway lost investor confidence and gradually subsided into ignominy. Many people in Bishop today have never heard of the project; some doubt it ever existed; others do remember the building of the grade; and one man recalls seeing pictures of the types of passenger cars on order with the builder at the time. To add to the general misunderstanding and confusion, a visitor to the area around 1912 thinks he recalls going to Bishop over the Owens River Valley Electric.

Although nothing more than a grade was built, the "Red Apple Route" left its mark on the Bishop Quadrangle map of the U. S. Geological Survey (1911) as a completed electric railway. Portions of the grade can still be seen today by traversing the sometimes sandy back roads of the area between Laws and Bishop, using that map as a guide.

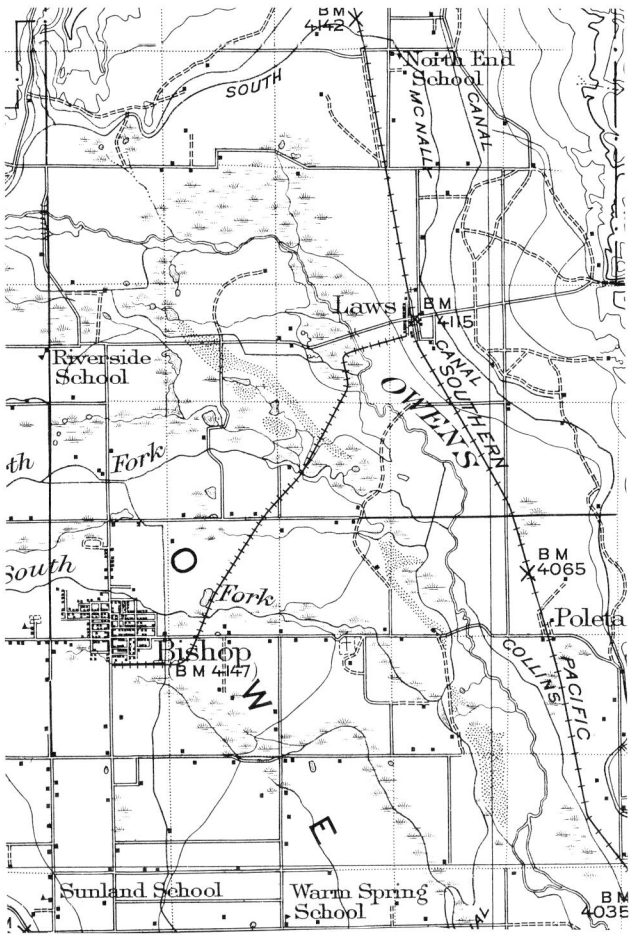

A section of the Survey map of 1913 shows the line. Pièce de résistance is the view of grading gangs hard at work in the summer of 1911. *(Bottom: Mr. and Mrs. Frank Merril Photo, Arthur D. Haig Collection.)*

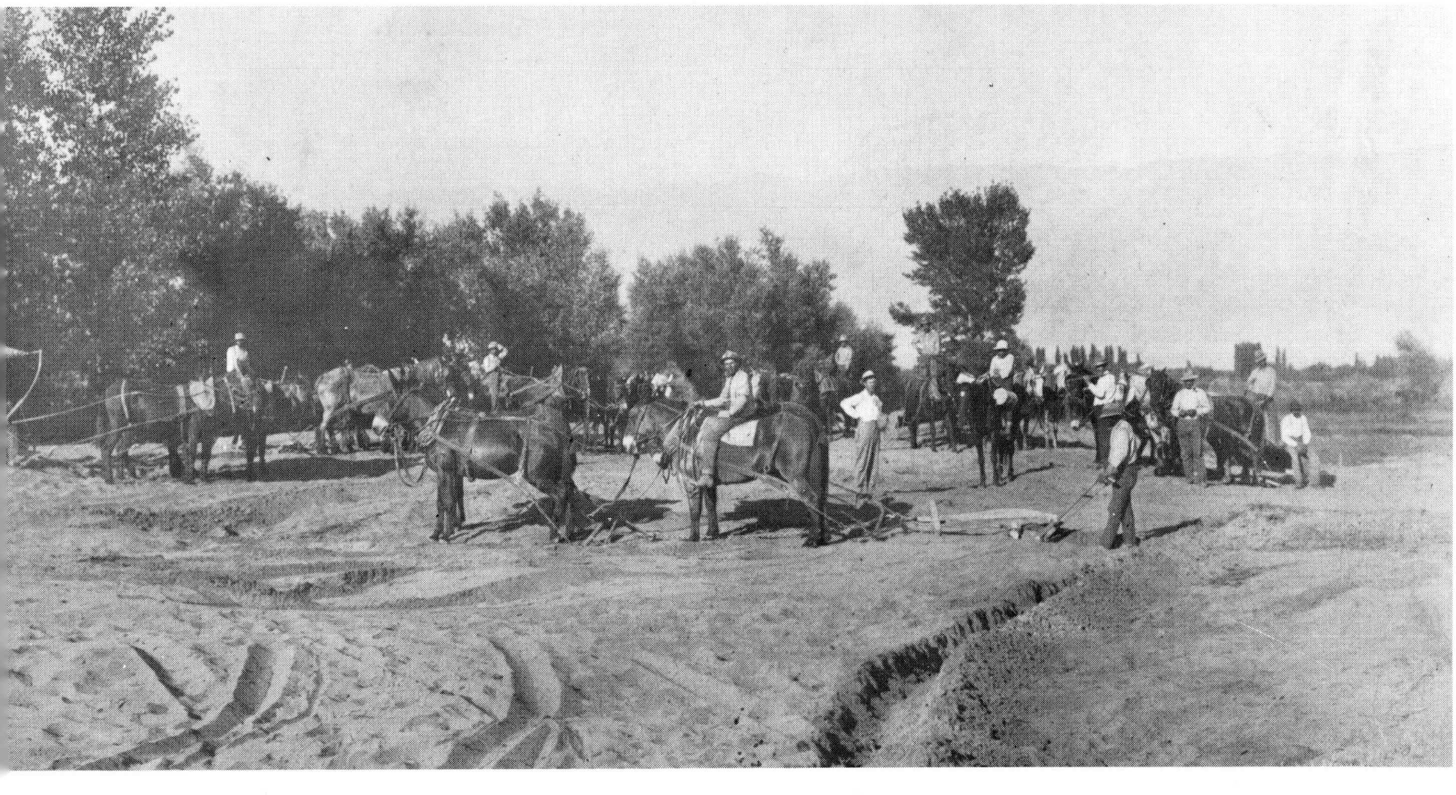

WESTERN PACIFIC RAILROAD

To the Western Pacific goes not only the glamorous title of "Most Recent of the Transcontinentals," but also the unique distinction of being one of the longest pieces of new railroad construction in this country in the twentieth century. With the advantages of more modern construction equipment, techniques and planning, the development of the railroad also entailed additional possibilities that errors, when made, could be equally modern and more costly.

Extending for 924 route miles between Oakland, California (a ferry took passengers and freight cars to San Francisco), and Salt Lake City, Utah, the Western Pacific came to enjoy maximum grades of but 1% in spite of its several mountainous crossings, yet it traveled a minimum of 150 extra miles (when compared with the Southern Pacific's route to Ogden) to do so. Construction was speeded and simplified by the presence of many earlier railroads all along its route, for supplies could be delivered at numerous centers and work could proceed on as many as four sections simultaneously. However, the bankers who had seen the funds of other railroads unjudiciously squandered on non-productive branches forced a restrictive clause in the WP's mortgage which provided that no branches could be built, thus creating, in effect, a railroad bridge route between terminals with but little on-line traffic. This restriction became the WP's Achilles' heel and was not eliminated until after the first reorganization some five years after operations commenced.

Formal incorporation of the Western Pacific Railway took place on March 6, 1903. The actual backers of the railroad were shrouded in mystery, but George Gould was the No. 1 suspect. His father, Jay Gould (1836-92), had compiled a partially complete, coast-to-coast system terminating at Ogden, Utah, at the western end of the Denver & Rio Grande and had had his eye set on the Central Pacific for the connection from there to the shores of the Pacific. However, the CP went under firm SP control in 1899, subsequently became dominated by the Union Pacific when the UP bought a controlling block of SP stock in 1901.

George Gould, the son (1864-1924) was watchful and waited. He became vice-president of the Rio Grande as well as president of the Missouri Pacific, and he took a seat at the director's table of the UP, which automatically placed him on the board of the SP as well, in 1901. With his finger on the pulse of western railroading, he still hoped to fill the gap between his own roads and the golden state of California. In fact, there was some talk that George might join Senator Clark's projected (LA&SL) railroad from Salt Lake to Los Angeles, but the Senator's brother, J. Ross Clark, told newsmen in April 1902: "I have not received any direct information concerning a combination with Mr. Gould. It would seem probable that such a connection at Salt Lake would give Mr. Gould the long-sought outlet to the Pacific Coast, but I can't enlighten you now." Since this was the time that Clark (LA&SL) and Harriman (UP) were about to join forces in the Salt Lake Route project, Gould lost out again.

In view of these frustrations and other considerate matters, it became apparent that construction of a new line of railroad would be the most expedient, although more costly, method of reaching the Pacific Coast. Harry Adams, then handling traffic matters for the Goulds and later to become one of the eight presidents of the Western Pacific, recalled that there were two alternatives under serious consideration. The first was to construct a line from Utah through Idaho to the Pacific Northwest, roughly paralleling the Oregon Short Line (UP); the other was to build to California generally following the Central Pacific route. Prospects for heavy tonnage hauling from the Tesla coal fields (southwest of Stockton, California) plus anticipated diversion of traffic from the Southern Pacific largely determined the selection of the present route.

Even as the incorporation of the Western Pacific was announced in 1903, rumors floated around that the WP was a myth; that the SP was behind the surveys and activity. Two years later the San Francisco *Call* had a story that the WP was being financed by Mrs. Collis P. Huntington and others who wanted to build a great system and have the

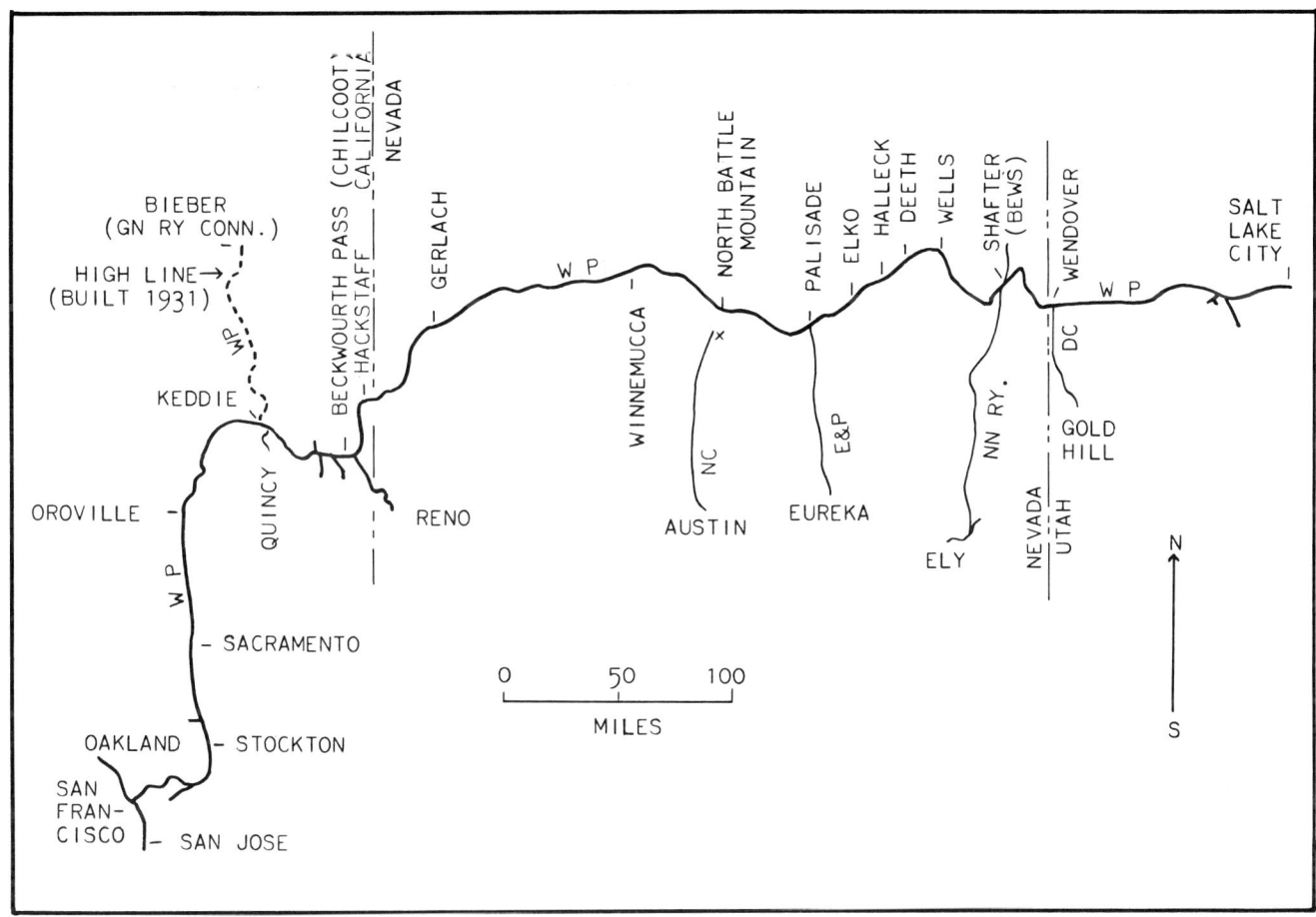

famous Huntington name again conspicuously identified with western railroading. According to the *Call*, the Gould holding was only nominal. It was not until October 1905 that the full truth came out when George Gould who by then had resigned his directorships of the UP and SP, wrote to Governor Sparks of Nevada asking support for the WP railroad project.

Once the Western Pacific became a matter of public record, the shell of secrecy surrounding the project began to crack open. Preliminary negotiations for financing were undertaken; old surveys were reviewed; alternate routes were plotted, particularly across the state of Nevada. Virgil Bogue, who had laid out lines for the Union Pacific in the late 1880's, was retained as chief engineer, and no possibilities were ignored. One route, strongly considered, entered eastern Nevada from the Dutch Mountains (near Gold Hill, Utah) and bore westward to Ruby Lake on a maximum grade of 1½%. Skirting the southern fringe of the Ruby Mountains, the line cut across the ranges to bisect the Eureka & Palisade Railroad at Narrow Gap (Garden) Pass, crossed the Reese River at Jacobsville (near Austin), then continued to New Pass and on to the north side of Carson Lake. Fallon, Nevada, hoped to be a division point for the western sector, which would cross the SP at Wadsworth and head for the grades of Beckwourth Pass and the Feather River Canyons.

A little work was done at Beckwourth Pass in December 1904. The effort was probably expended to hold the location as a right-of-way which was granted on the condition that a station be established in the vicinity of Chilcoot where Richard Martin maintained a roadhouse. Mrs. Martin became very excited the day she first discovered WP surveyors in her chicken yard. It was not the chickens about which she was concerned; she was afraid they might dig up the $45,000 carefully cached in the ground for safekeeping. The money was safely rescued before excavations commenced.

In April 1905, two years after incorporation, the bonds were floated. The mortgage had some annoying covenants. One stipulated that the grade of the railroad could not exceed 1%, a provision which obviated most of the alternate routes through Nevada and forced the road to parallel the SP right-of-way along the Humboldt River for 177 miles in order to avoid the numerous mountain crossings necessitated by any other route. Harriman (of the UP-SP) was not inclined to make things easy for Gould by allowing the WP to use part of the SP right-of-way, with the result that the WP's projected roadbed required 12 crossings of the SP to negotiate the tortuous mileage. A dispute developed, and was settled only after arbitration, with Governor Sparks of Nevada acting as the neutral member of the committee. Ultimate arrangements finally limited the crossovers to a single, unavoidable one at Palisade, but the delays attending the wranglings prevented final location of the central Nevada mileage until May 1907.

As fast as money became available, work began from both ends of the line toward the middle. On January 2, 1906, the first spike was driven on the western end in Oakland, California. A few weeks later 100 Japanese were sent to Beckwourth Pass to start preliminary work at that location, but they were found to be too light for the job and many were discharged. Other men were located, and soon 500 were employed near booming Clairville while an additional 200 were spotted between Keddie and Portola at Spring Garden. At that time Portola had not yet received its name, but houses were being erected rapidly in the general vicinity of Mormon where it was anticipated the WP eventually would build a depot. Spring Garden attained its distinction in a different manner. Early surveys down the Feather River revealed that any grade down either the North Fork or the Middle Fork, individually, would be too steep, but that by combining the advantages of both river forks, a good route could be located within the railroad's restrictions. The 7,343-foot Spring Garden Tunnel solved the problem by connecting the two forks of the river, and it became the longest tunnel on the Western Pacific Railway. The 6,002-foot Chilcoot Tunnel beneath Beckwourth Pass was the second longest and these, together with 32 shorter tunnels along the Feather River Canyon constituted such a terrific volume of rock work, construction was slowed considerably.

It is interesting to note that the whole upper Feather River area was reasonably remote from civilization and transportation at that period. True, the N-C-O had picked up the previous Sierra Valley & Mohawk narrow gauge and was operating it as a subsidiary branch line over Beckwourth Pass and down as far as Clairville and Clio, but the service was tremulous and somewhat uncertain. And there was the relative newcomer, the standard gauge Boca & Loyalton, whose stubby little fingers of rail were stretching greedily into the timber to the north. Although neither road could be considered a vital force in the area, the WP's parent, the D&RG, acquired a controlling interest in the B&L on September 6, 1905, with the primary intent of keeping outsiders away from the territory pending completion of the Western Pacific. The fact that the B&L might profit from haulage of WP construction equipment and supplies was purely incidental.

Progress at the eastern end of the Western Pacific was faster and easier. The first rails were spiked in place at Salt Lake City on May 24, 1906, and a year later on May 14, 1907, tracks had reached the Utah-Nevada state line. The first engine poked its nose over the boundary on May 18, 1907, while the first (unofficial) passenger train was run two months later with recumbent Agusta Andres. A boulder had crushed his skull while working near Deykes, and fellow Greek laborers had stopped the train and pleaded with the crew to take him to the hospital. With the conductor on the cowcatcher waving a warning lantern, the engine and single caboose dashed 60 miles through fog and the early dawn to Salt Lake City.

About 4½ months later Bews (Shafter), Nevada was reached, 164 miles from Salt Lake City. Here a vital connection was made with the Nevada Northern Railroad servicing the copper belt at Ely to the south. Although the rails were pushed a few miles farther west, they stopped abruptly at the mouth of the 5,676-foot Flowery Lake Tunnel under the Pequops, third longest on the system. It was to be more than a year before the barrier could be pierced.

Although physical connection with the Nevada Northern was accomplished on October 3, 1907, the first train over the new line arrived on October 8 and passed on through to Ely. The first passenger train operated was a special for Ely copper tycoon, William B. Thompson, who tested the route on October 21.

Construction across the state of Nevada languished during the early part of 1907 pending outcome of the dispute with the Southern Pacific over the right-of-way. Boring of the Flowery Lake Tunnel through the Pequops was started in February, but the tunnel was not opened for traffic until November 1908. To facilitate the movement of supplies and assist in the progress of track work on the western side during the later stages, a temporary track was laid over the summit of the range. It was used for a period of four months, then removed.

Most of the work in Nevada was performed under contract by the Utah Construction Co. During the summer of 1907 progress was made on the grading between Deeth and Winnemucca on the Humboldt River stretch. Desperadoes hung around the grading camps, holding up the workers and (on one occasion) the paymaster. This attempt was foiled and not repeated. Near Winnemucca, two workers fought over a girl friend (all Negroes), and one man died in the shooting. At the western end, a trestle collapsed at Chilcoot (on Beckwourth Pass) injuring some men, and five men were blown to bits in an unpremeditated explosion at Beckwith in the Sierra Valley.

By the fall of 1907 the job was running well behind schedule in spite of a force of 7,772 men. The Flowery Lake Tunnel in eastern Nevada, the series of tunnels in the Feather River area and others (totaling 43 tunnels in all), were obdurate obstacles to overcome. Too, the banking crisis of October and November 1907 presented a problem of hard coin. Work stopped at Chilcoot when the storekeeper refused to cash the men's paychecks when he found that San Francisco banks would not accept them. For a time it appeared that all work across Nevada might be affected in the same manner, but the problem was solved and construction continued. Others in the area faced a similar difficulty. The Glasgow & Western (Golconda & Adelaide) met its payrolls with coin shipped all the way from the home office in Scotland. The Nevada Northern, perhaps in a public relations move, paid its White Pine County taxes of $6,704 in shiny $20 gold pieces.

Regular operations to Bews (Shafter) commenced on November 9, 1908. By the end of that month tracks extended all the way from Salt Lake City to Halleck, Nevada, on the Humboldt River 240 miles to the west. The next 23 miles to Elko were finished and trains were running to that center just before Christmas 1908. In April 1909 track laying started westward out of Winnemucca, and by early summer a total of 722 miles of road was ready, having been built in four separate sections. Only 202 miles remained to be completed.

Finally, on November 1, 1909, the last spike was driven (unceremoniously) at the Spanish Creek Bridge (at Keddie) a few miles west of Quincy, California, and the job was done. Following brief cleaning-up operations, regular freight service was instituted the first of December, and passenger service the following August (1910).

Whether in celebration or retaliation, Nevada's Humboldt River went wild in the big storm of March 1910. The town of Palisade was flooded; miles of track of the SP, WP and even the tiny E&P were completely washed out. With the experience and facilities of years of operation, the SP made repairs and started running trains again within 12 days of the event; the WP, by detouring over the SP, was able to resume service 20 days later; the narrow gauge E&P required two years, a bankruptcy and a complete reorganization before operations would be reinstated.

Because of the Western Pacific's onerous mortgage restriction prohibiting the construction of branch lines, traffic trickled slowly to the new system. Over the next dozen years the Feather River country began to develop, and a number of independent logging railroads were constructed to bring logs to sawmills near the route, thereby providing some outbound traffic in the form of finished lumber. The Quincy Railroad built a five-mile road from Quincy Junction (Hartwell or Marston) to Quincy, the seat of Plumas County. The Indian Valley Railroad was built from Paxton to the copper mine at Engel, 21 miles away (to the north).

However, basically, but little on-line traffic could be generated; in spite of the numerous interchange points with the SP, considerably less traffic was diverted than anticipated; and the volume of business between terminals was insufficient to support the road. There was constant talk of connecting lines and/or acquisitions of connecting roads. Possibly, if the cost of the WP had been closer to that of the original estimates, money might have been available and some of the projects realized. Press reports frequently discussed a proposed connection to the V&T and south from that road to Los Angeles via the Black Hills and Owens Valley. In fact, during WP construction days, stories of the sale of the N-C-O or the V&T to the WP occurred with such regularity they became monotonous. Finally, after one such repetitious reporting, an N-C-O spokesman unburdened himself with the comment: "I think it is about time for us to report that *we* intend to buy the Western Pacific. That would be something new, whereas the rumor that we have been absorbed is decidedly lacking in novelty."

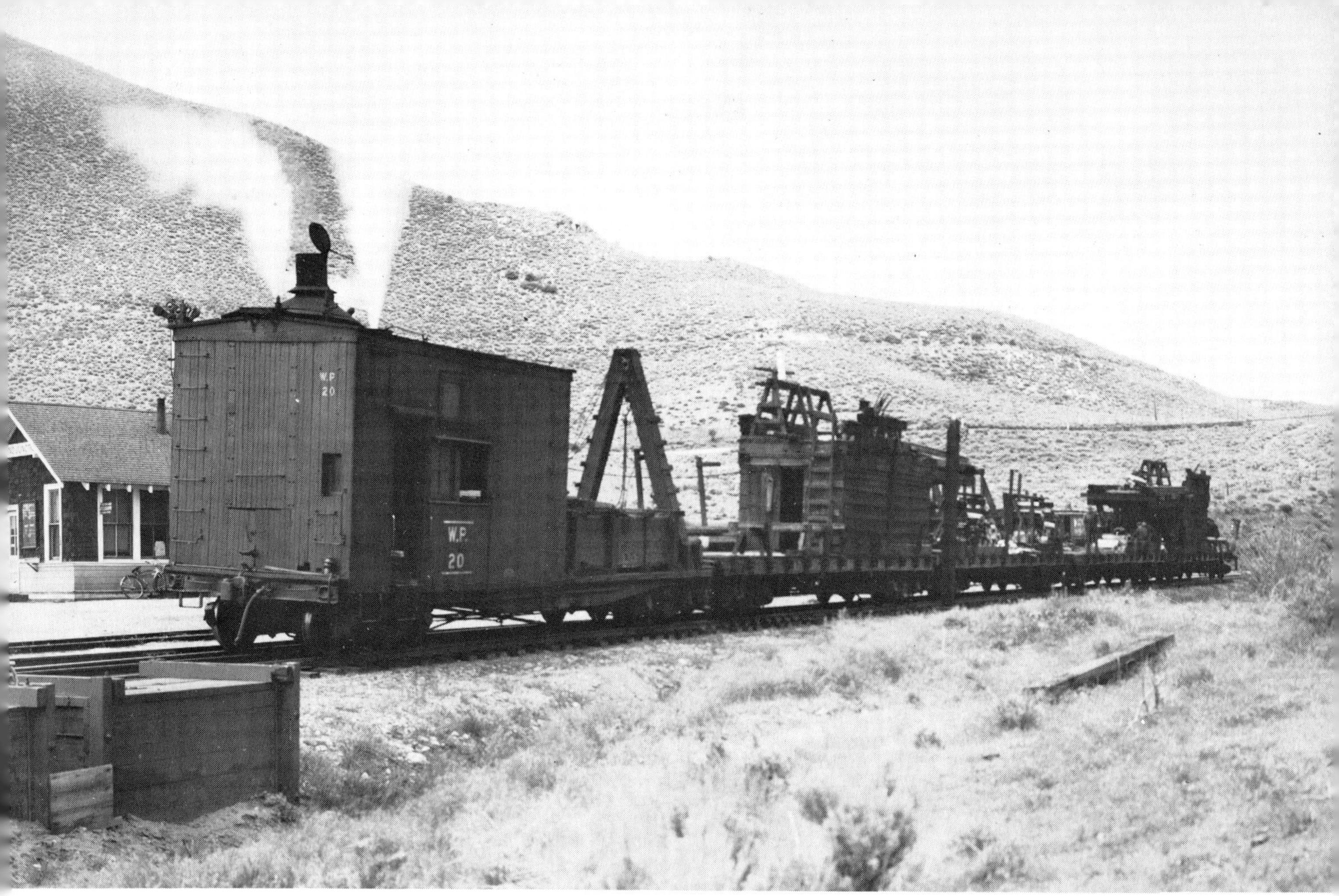

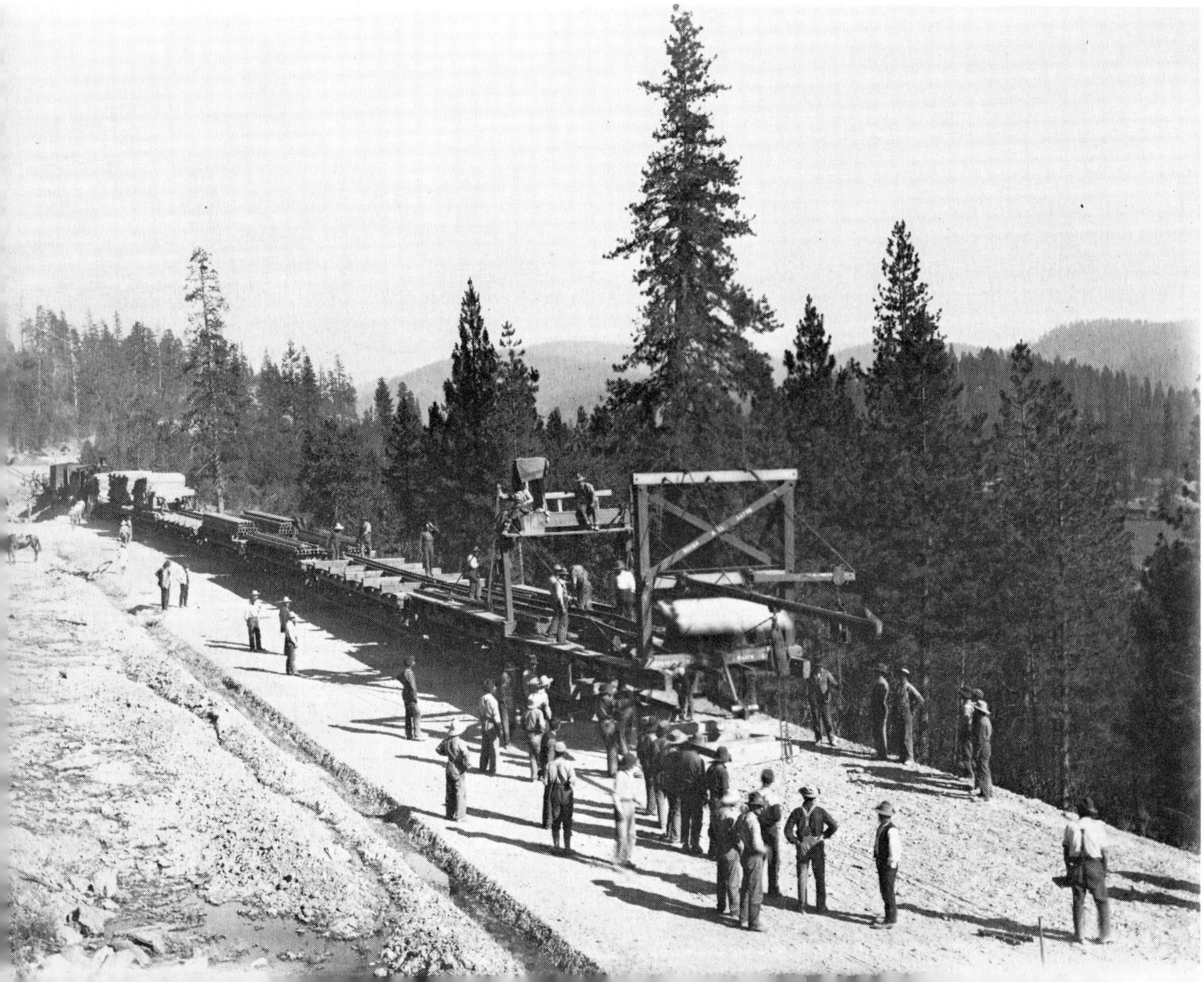

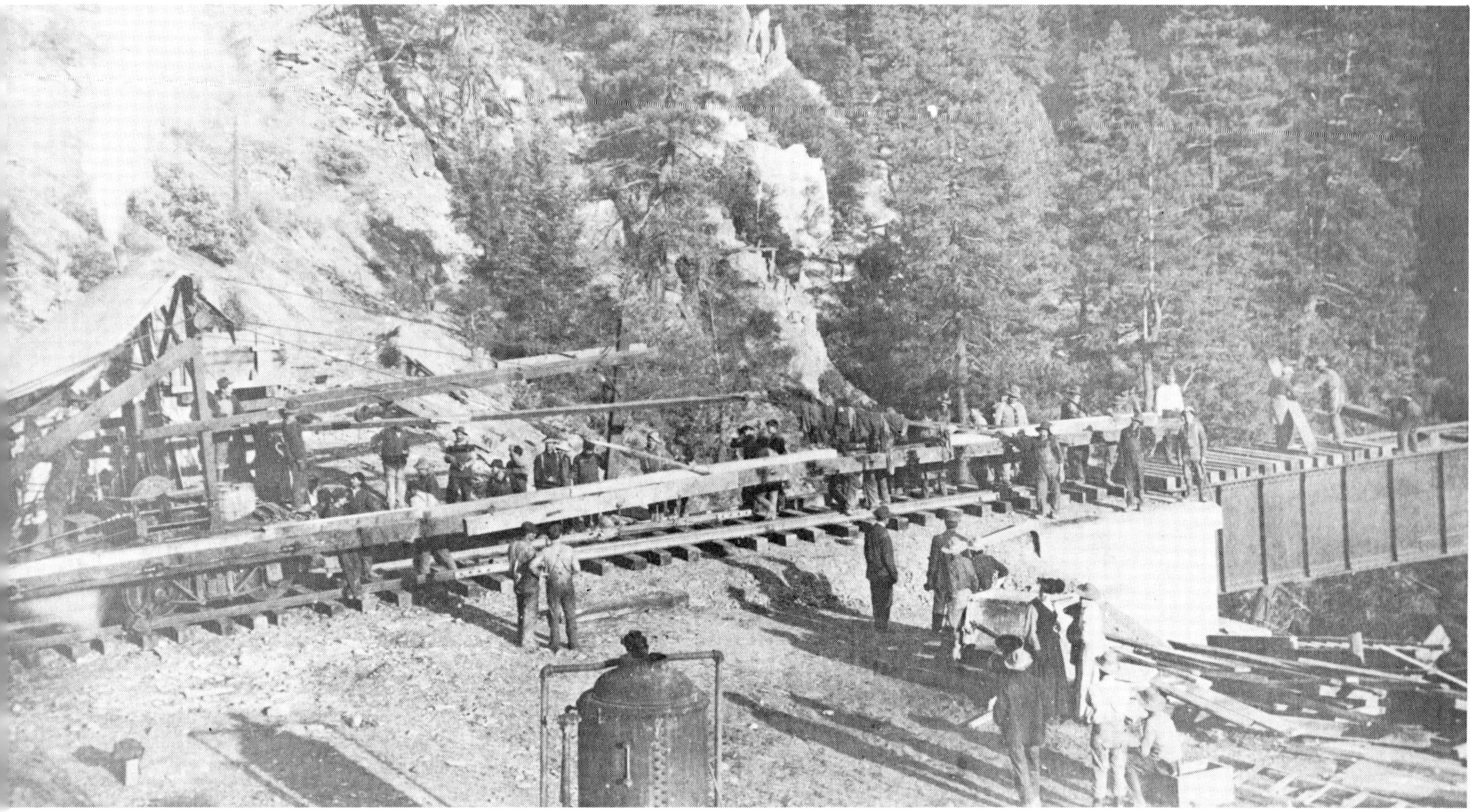

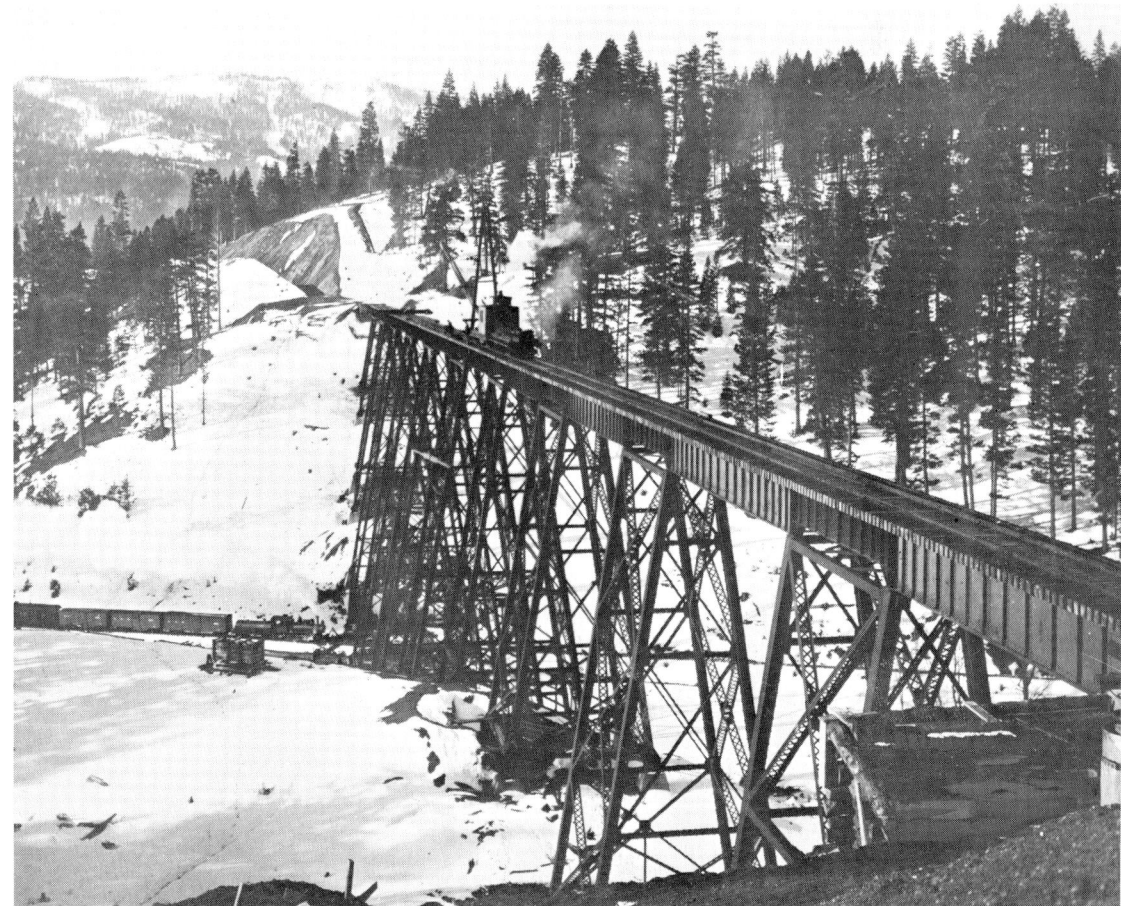

The work train at Reno Junction (top, left) stands on a siding at the eastern portal of the Chilcoot Tunnel under Beckwourth Pass. The grade part way up the slope in the background is that of the highway; that nearest the top, the roadbed of the Sierra Valleys Railway, absorbed by the N-C-O in 1915 and purchased by the Western Pacific in 1917 for dismantlement.

Heavy construction is indicated by the view of the Harris track laying machine (bottom, left) near Clio and the tremendous Willow Creek Viaduct (bottom, right) still in process of completion with a Sierra Valleys narrow-gauge train climbing the canyon beneath. The last rail (above) was laid at the Spanish Creek viaduct near Keddie.
(Top Left: Louis L. Stein, Jr. Collection; All Others: Western Pacific Collection.)

—321

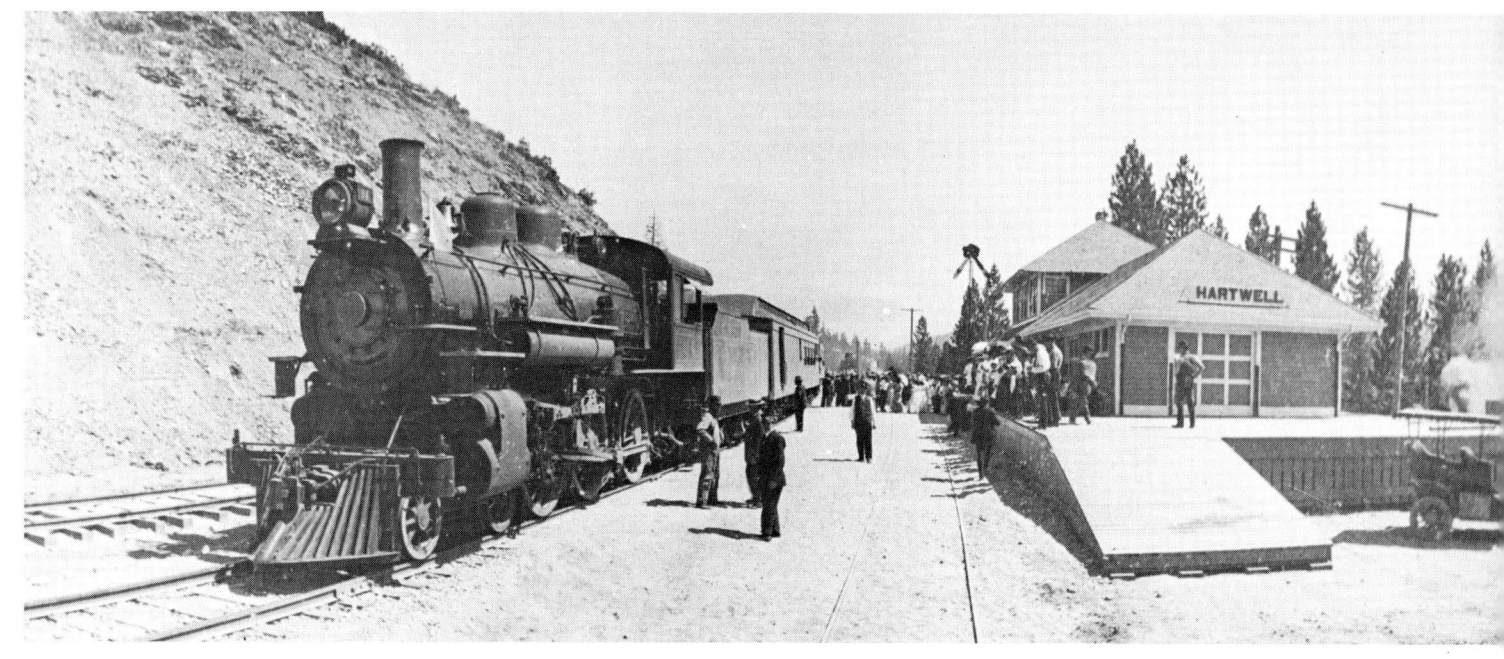

Operation of the Western Pacific's first passenger train on August 22, 1910, was an important and well photographed occasion. As the station stop for Quincy, the county seat of Plumas County, Hartwell (*above*) held appropriate greetings. In the same year the Quincy Western Railway (now Quincy Railroad) built its five miles of connecting line from Hartwell (now Quincy Jct.) to Quincy. (*Western Pacific Collection.*)

Passengers on that first train caught glimpses of wooden trestles (*upper right*) used over canyons which later could be filled with earthen embankments, and steel trestles such as the Willow Creek Viaduct (*lower right*) which were permanent installations. At Portola (*next below*) the train paused while a fresh locomotive was attached. The third car in the train, center right foreground behind the group of three men, was a special library car. Pullmans in the consist were specially named "Golconda," "Belleville," etc., for places famous in Nevada mining history. Another engine change was made at Elko (*bottom*) where construction crews were still working on side tracks and other facilities. (*Below Center and Bottom: Louis L. Stein, Jr. Collection; Right Top: California State Library; Bottom: Western Pacific Collection.*)

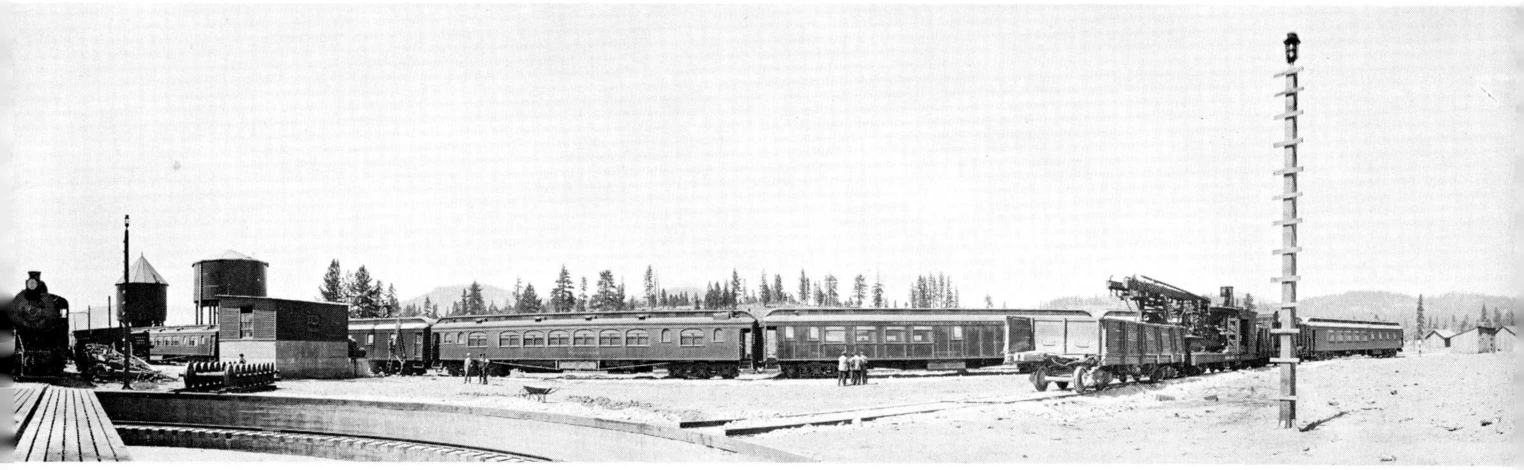

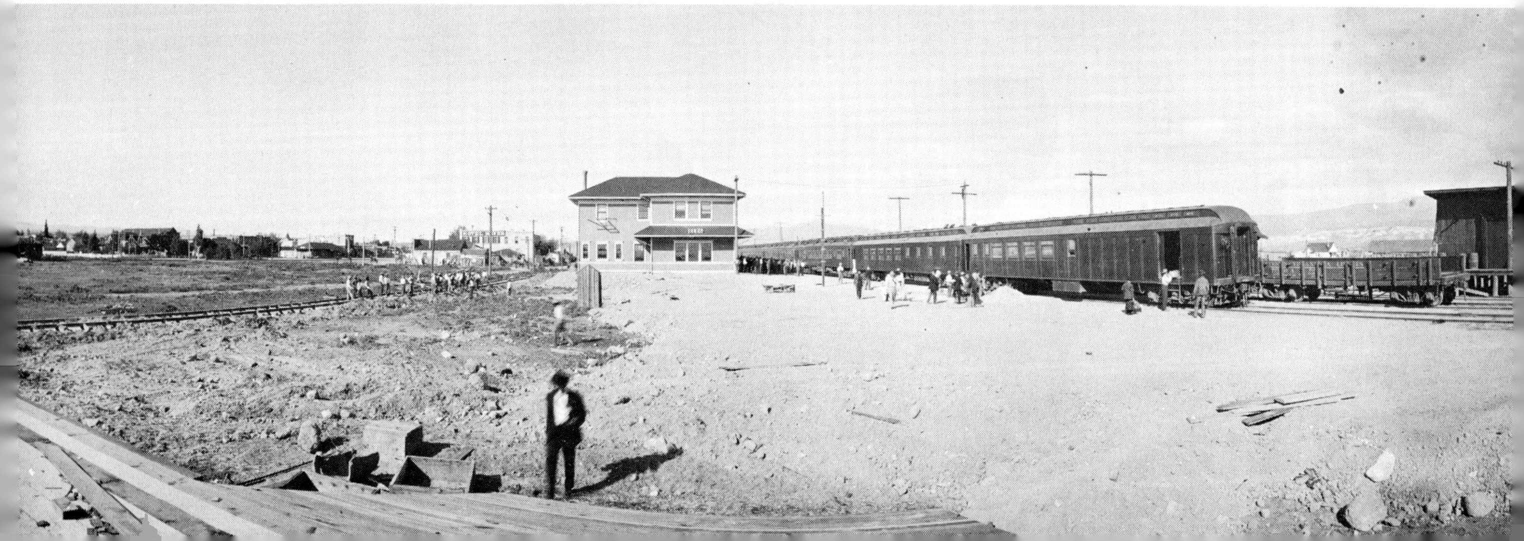

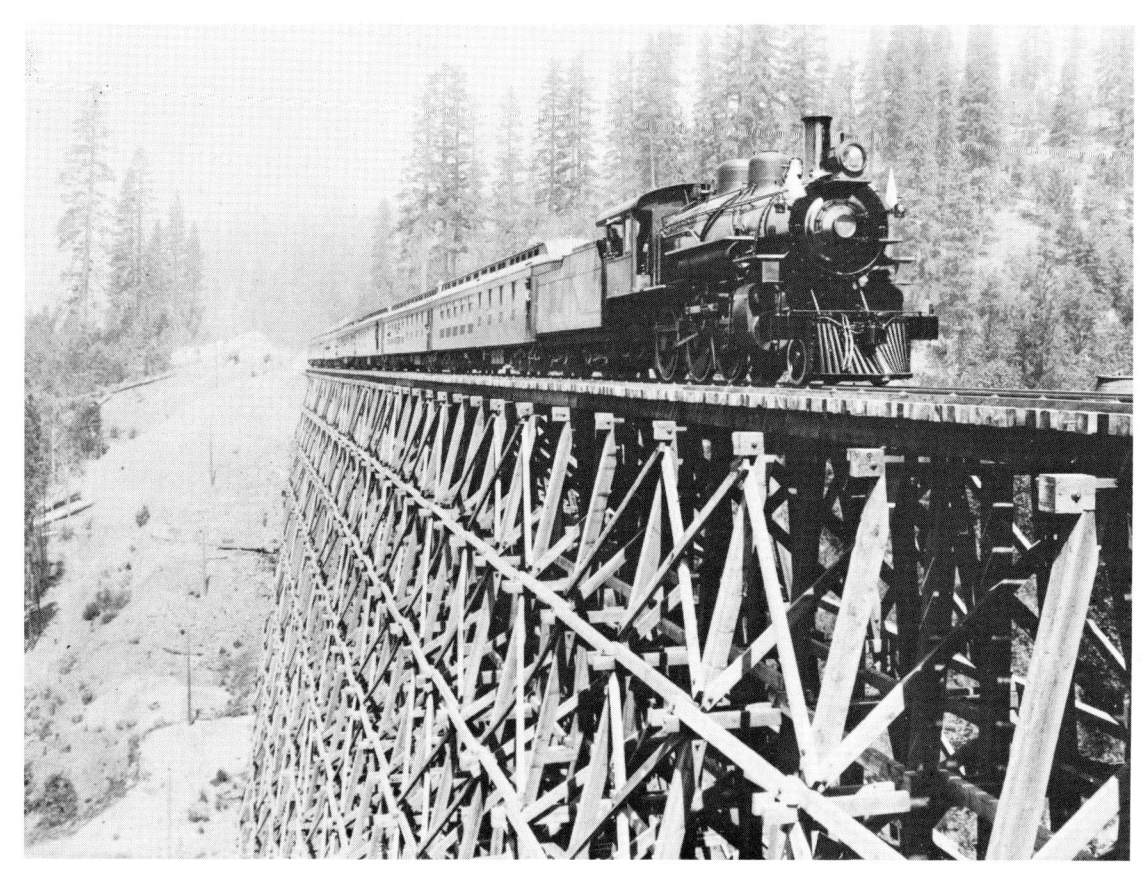

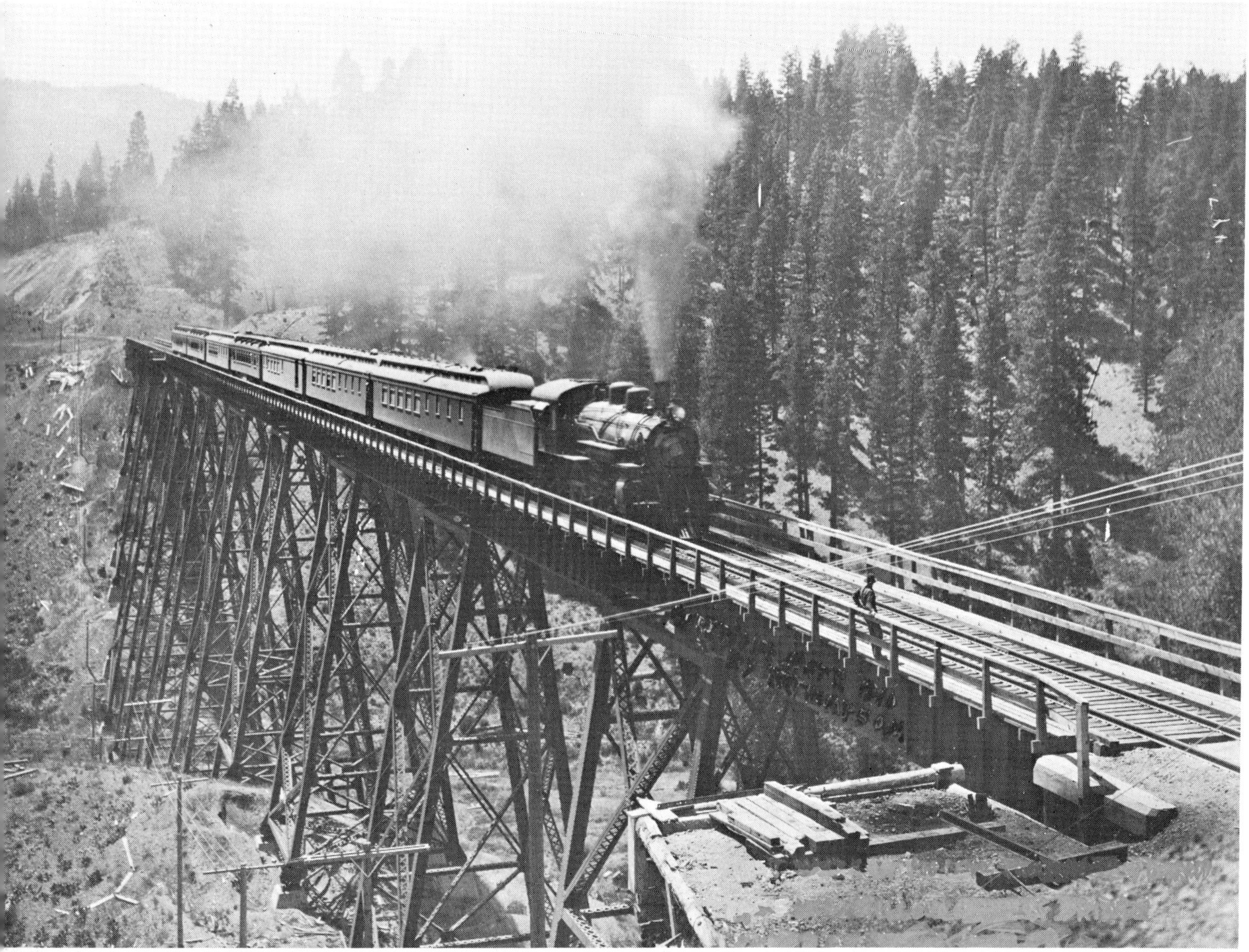

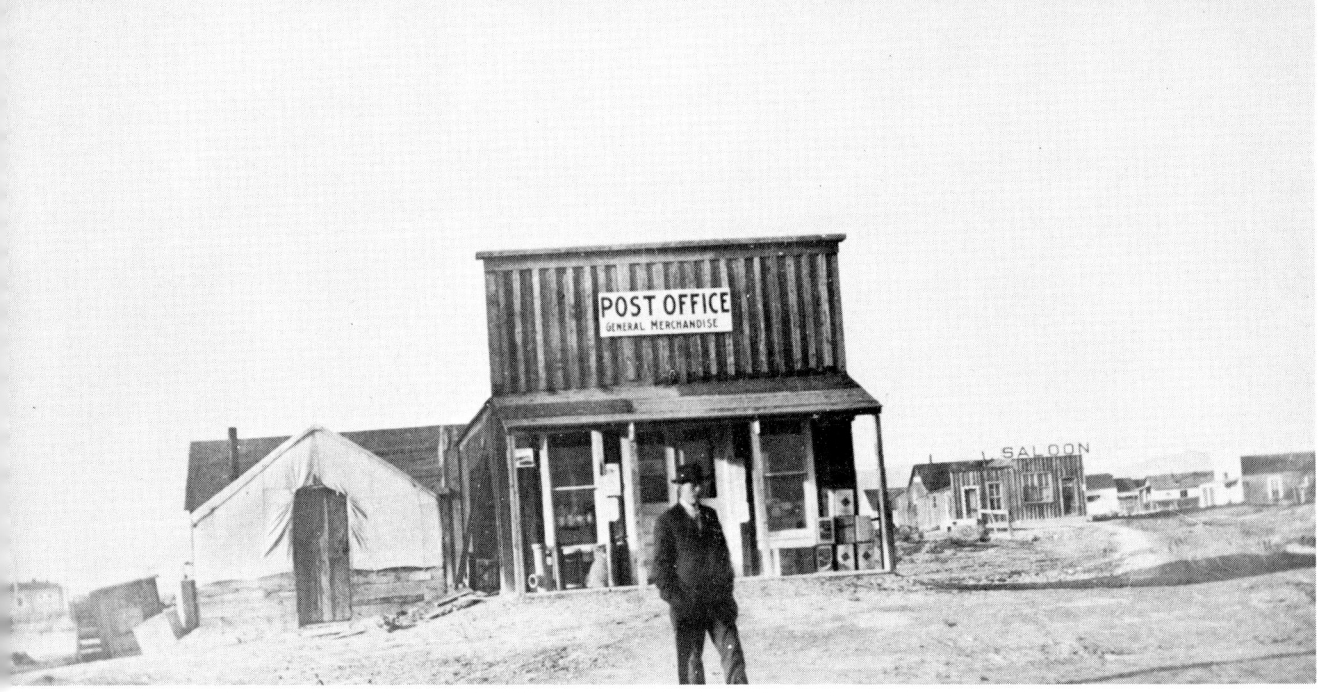

Earliest days on the Western Pacific are depicted in the photos on this page. Gerlach *(top)* still retained traces of its tent town status during the WP's construction days, and the proprietor of the saloon hadn't concluded yet that it would be better to move closer to the tracks. Near the eastern end of the line, Wendover, Utah *(below)*, was very much of an embryo. Although thousands of cross ties were stacked along the spur tracks leading out from the engine terminal and yard, the railroad was already in business as the stock loading chute in the center indicates. A passenger train waits in the yard for its engine to be changed, a routine undoubtedly completed in ample time for the meet with the freight train approaching in the background.

The Western Pacific was maturing when the track gangs *(upper right)* put the finishing touches to a section of relocation of the N-C-O's former line to Reno, following purchase of that portion of the line in 1917. The old narrow-gauge roadbed lies to the left from which the rails have been removed and relocated between the broad gauge of the WP's rails. After the last N-C-O train left Reno on January 30, 1918, the slim-gauge rails were removed.

Many windows characterized the WP's enginehouses as at Elko *(center right)* or Gerlach *(bottom)* where the stud of iron horses has been nosed toward the turntable for this impressive view of steam in its heyday. *(All Photos: Western Pacific Collection.)*

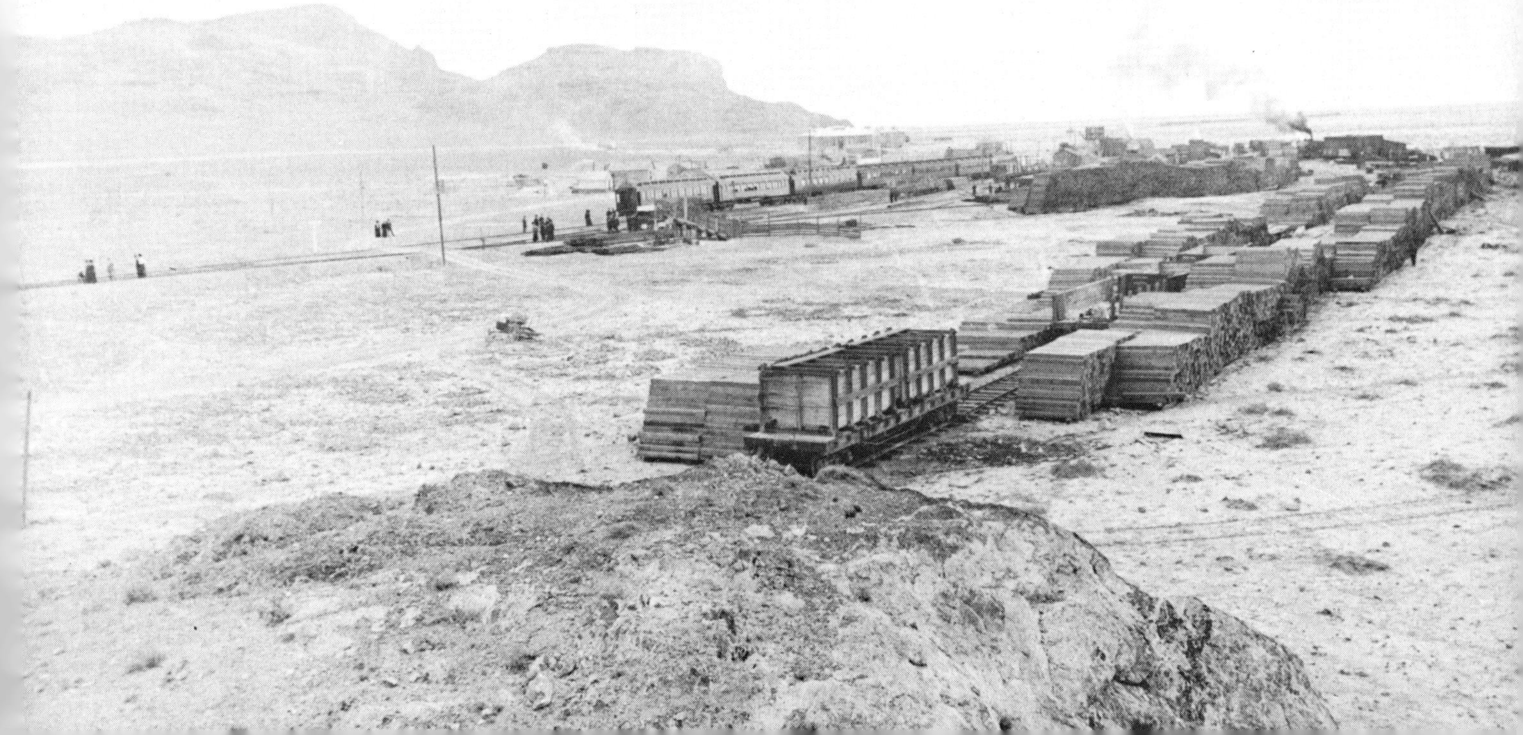

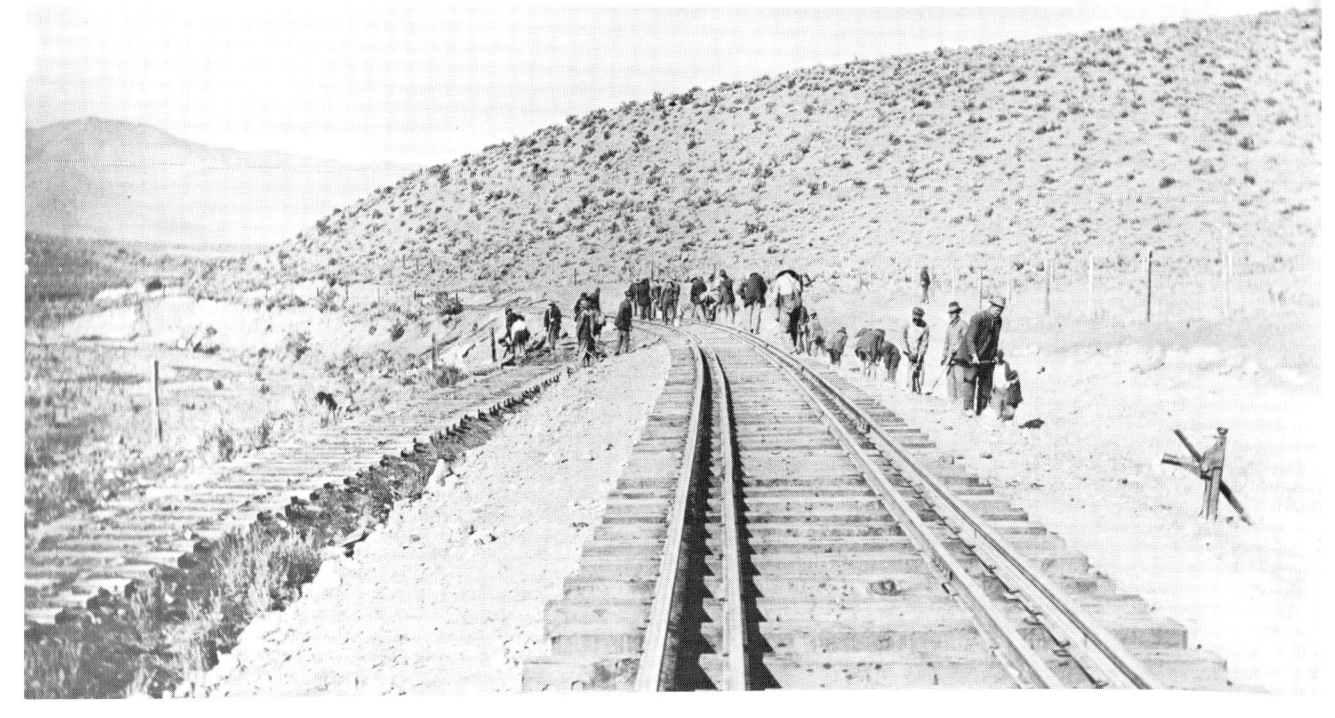
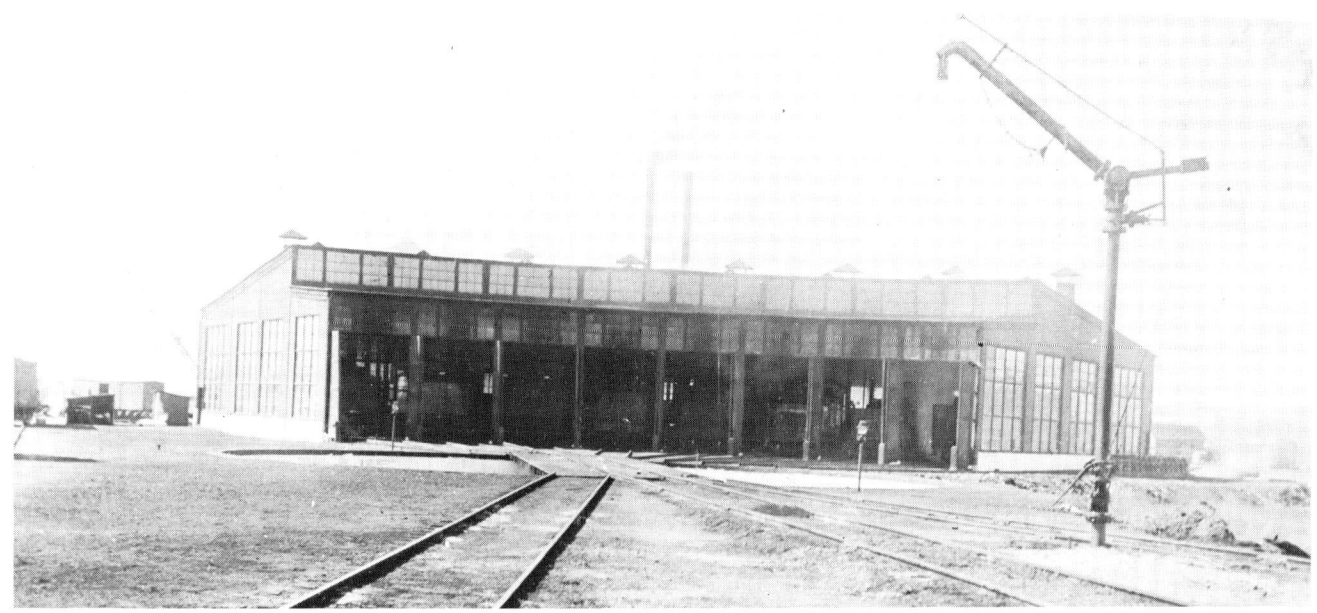

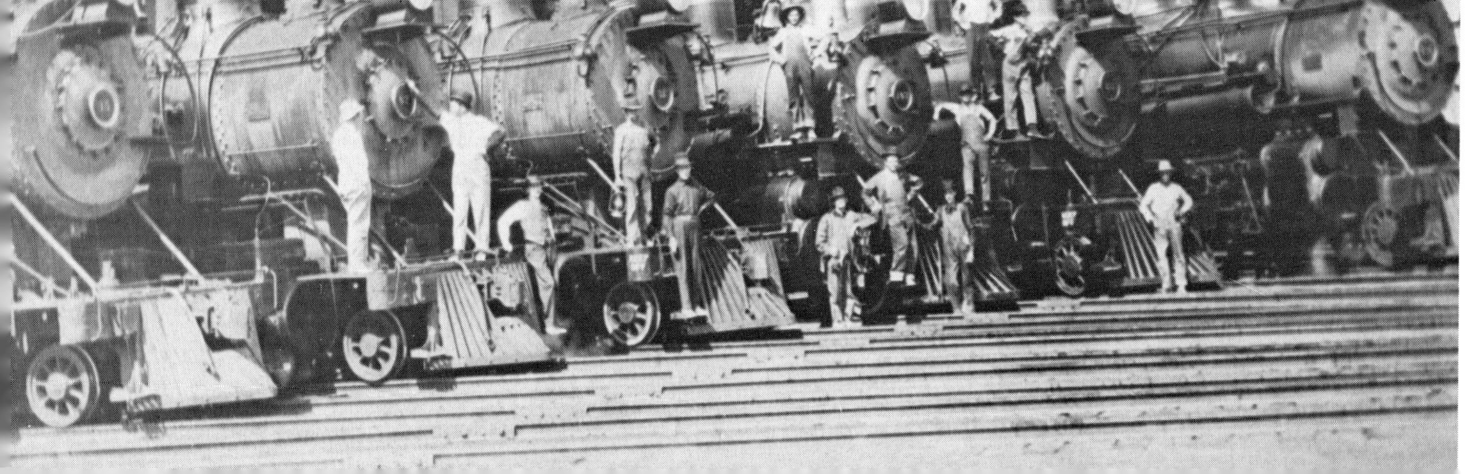

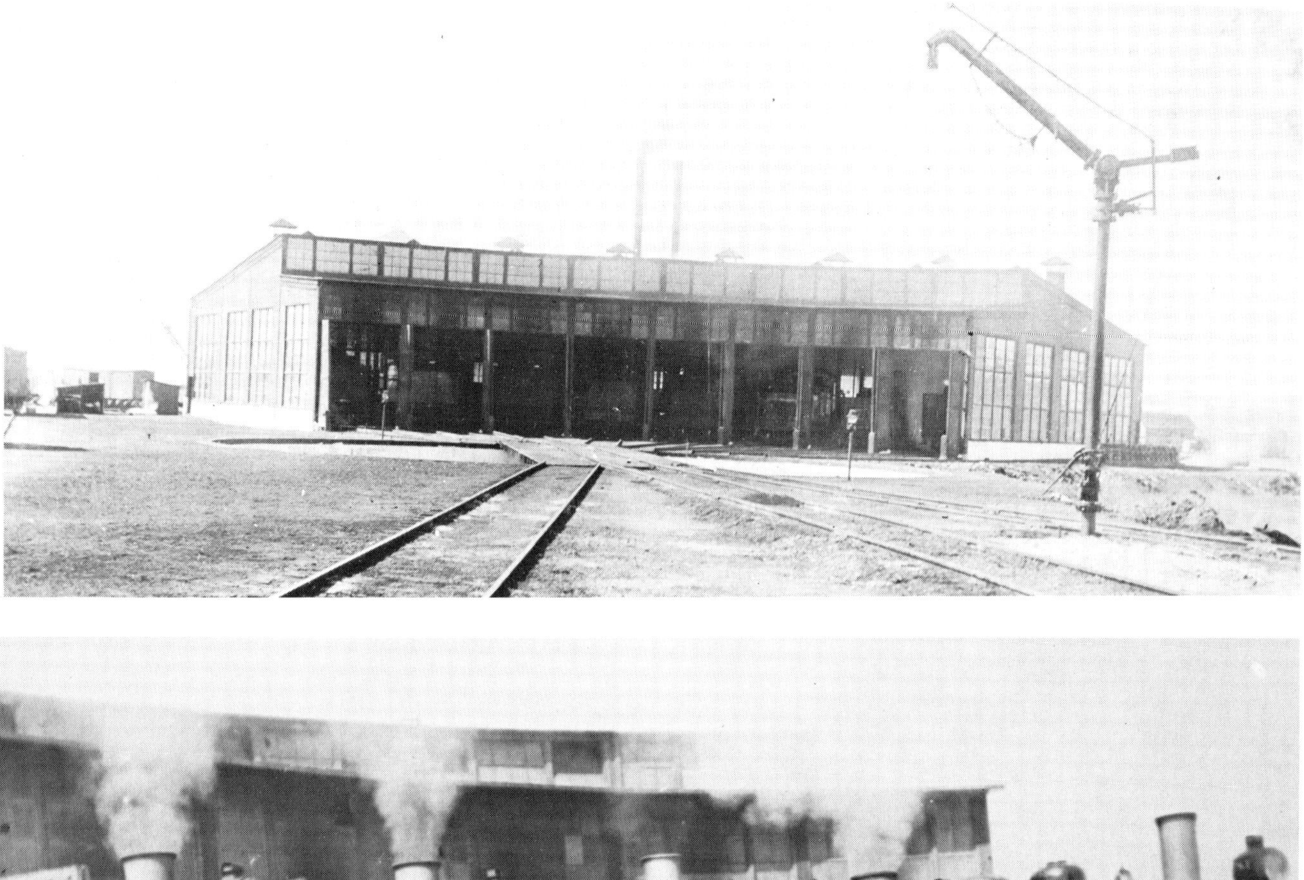

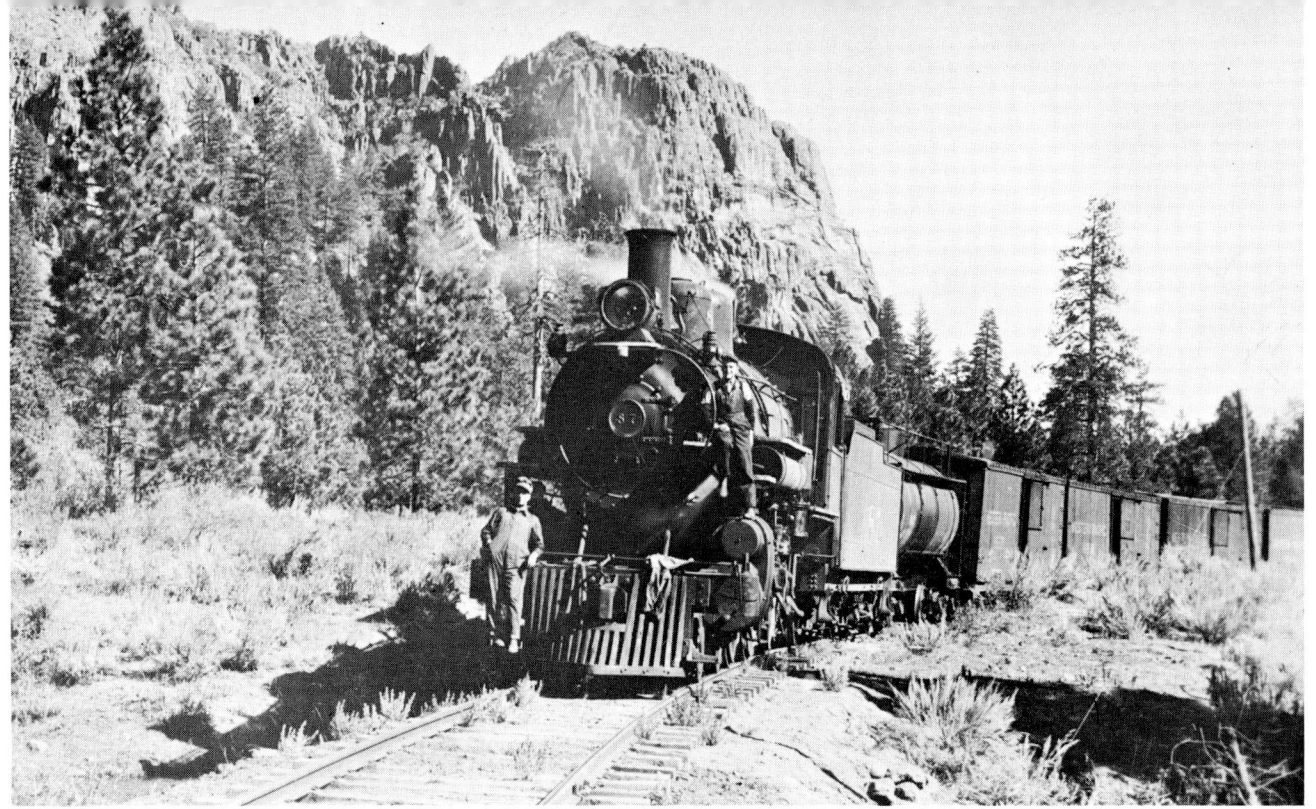

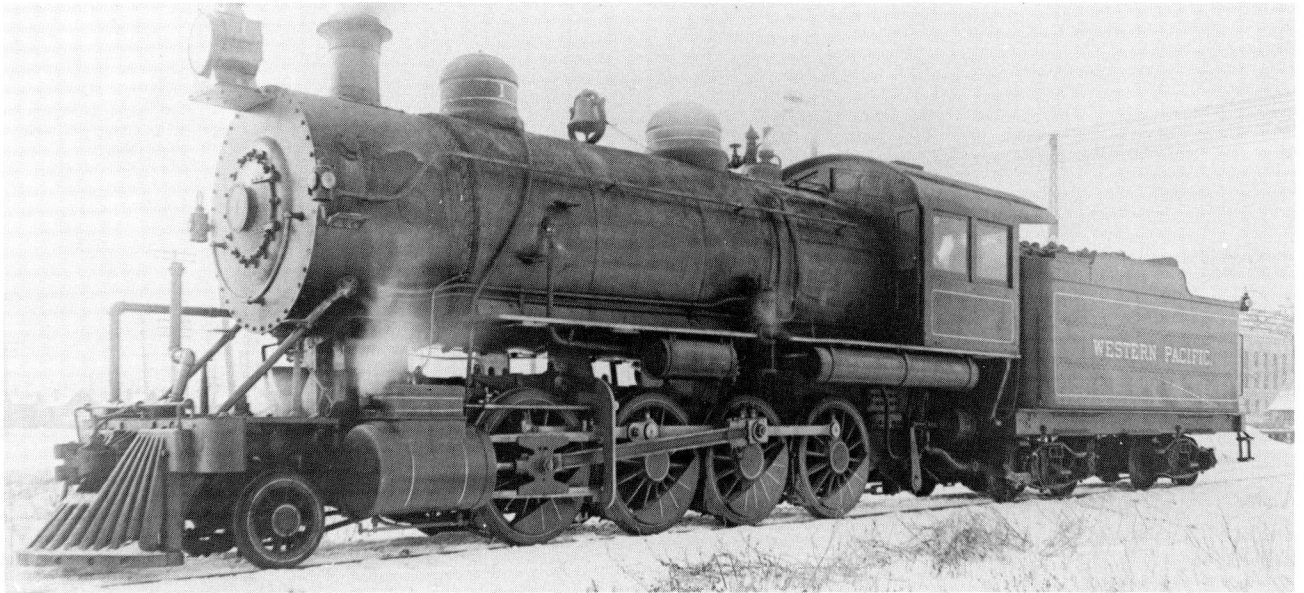

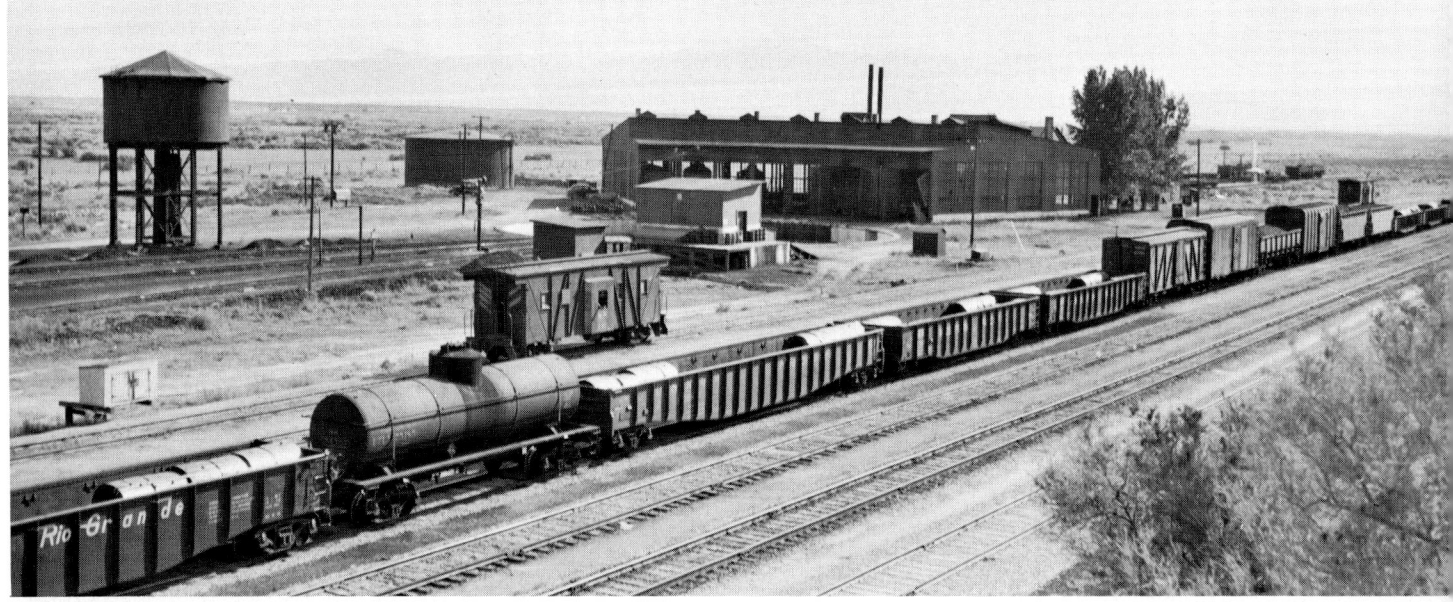

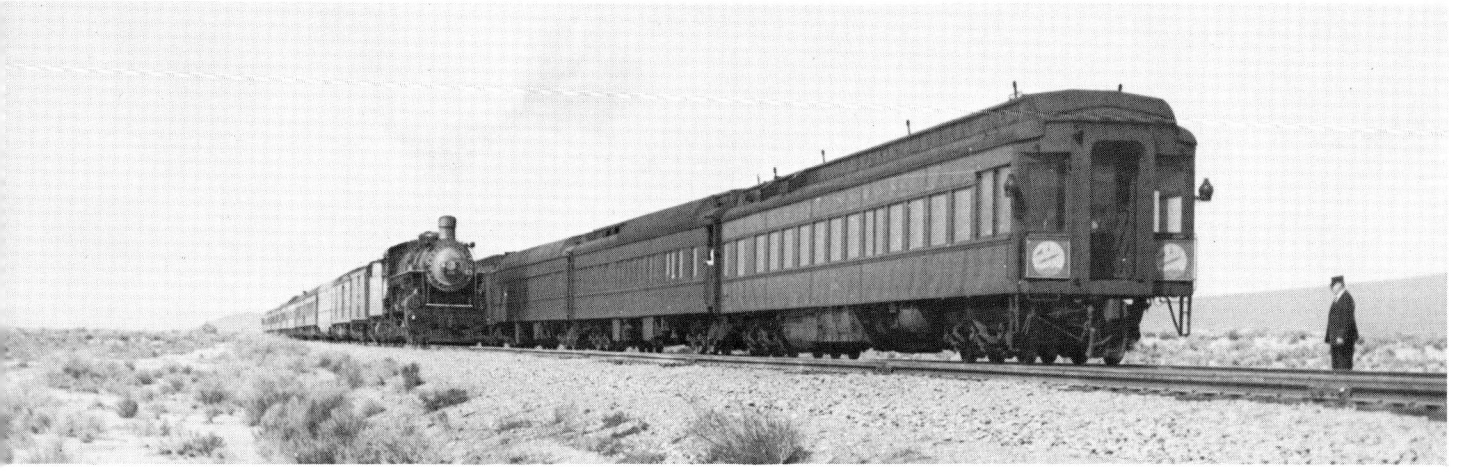

Western Pacific operations ranged from the rustic, light freights typified by 10-wheeler No. 87 and train on the Calpine Branch in the 1920's *(facing page, top)*, to the huskier (2-8-0) Consolidations such as No. 1 *(center)* which performed yeoman service during construction days, then turned to line-haul work with freight manifests as shown *(bottom)* passing the Winnemucca engine terminal. *(Top: W. A. Pennington Collection; Center: Western Pacific Collection; Bottom: Guy L. Dunscomb.)*

Varnish hauls sometimes waited in the heat of the desert for meets with opposing passenger trains, as the "Exposition Flyer" *(this page, top)* is doing in 1942 at Jungo, Nevada, before completing their runs and rolling into terminals in fashion similar to the "Royal Gorge" *(center)* approaching Salt Lake City in 1948. Most spectacular stretch of the Western Pacific's trackage in Nevada lies along the Palisades of the Humboldt River *(bottom)* where a paired trackage arrangement with the Southern Pacific enables the trains of both roads to use the tracks of the other in prearranged one-directional movement. *(Top and Center: Arthur L. Lloyd; Bottom: Louis L. Stein Collection.)*

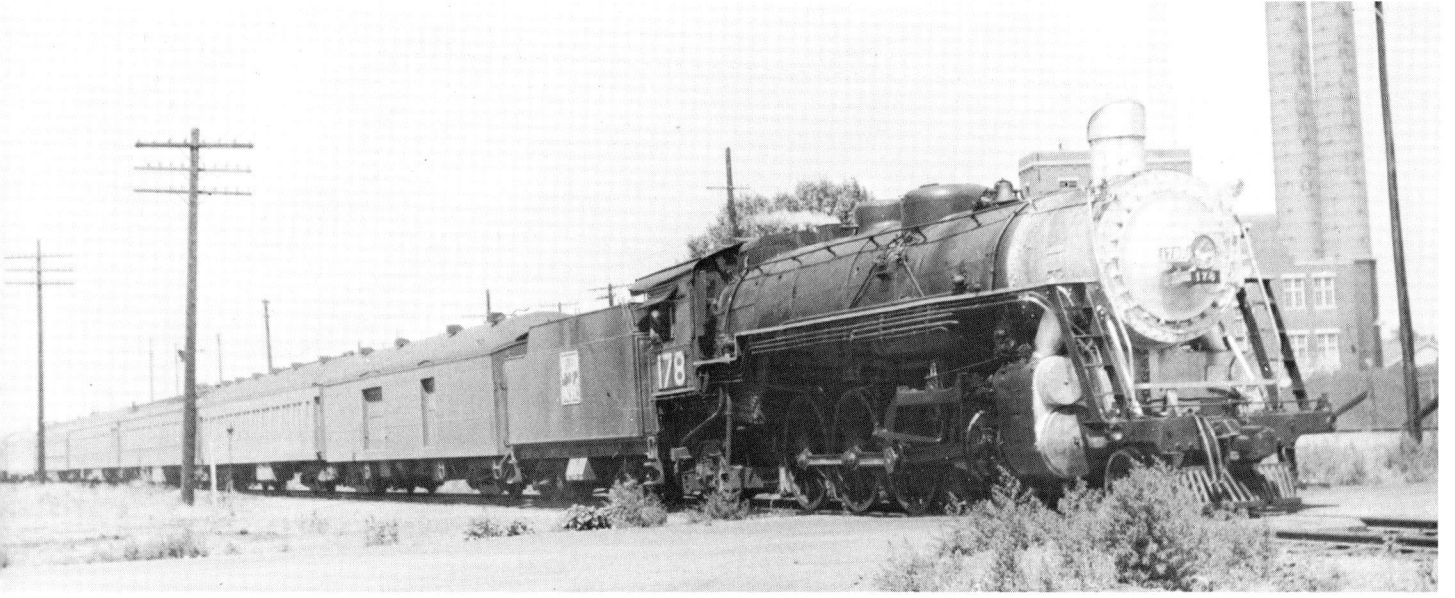

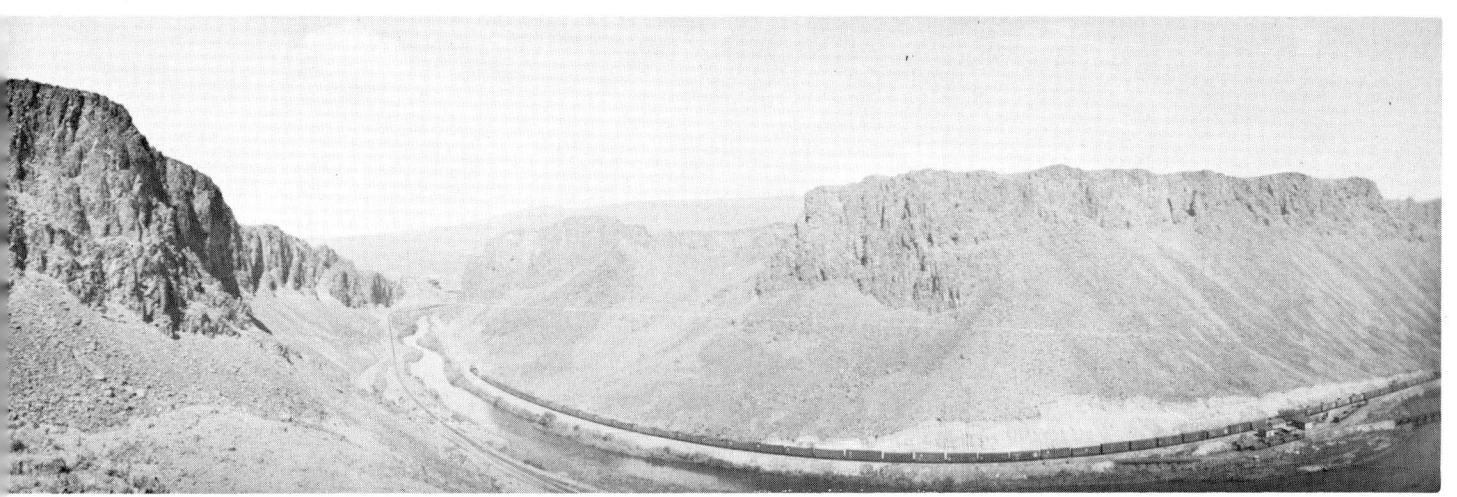

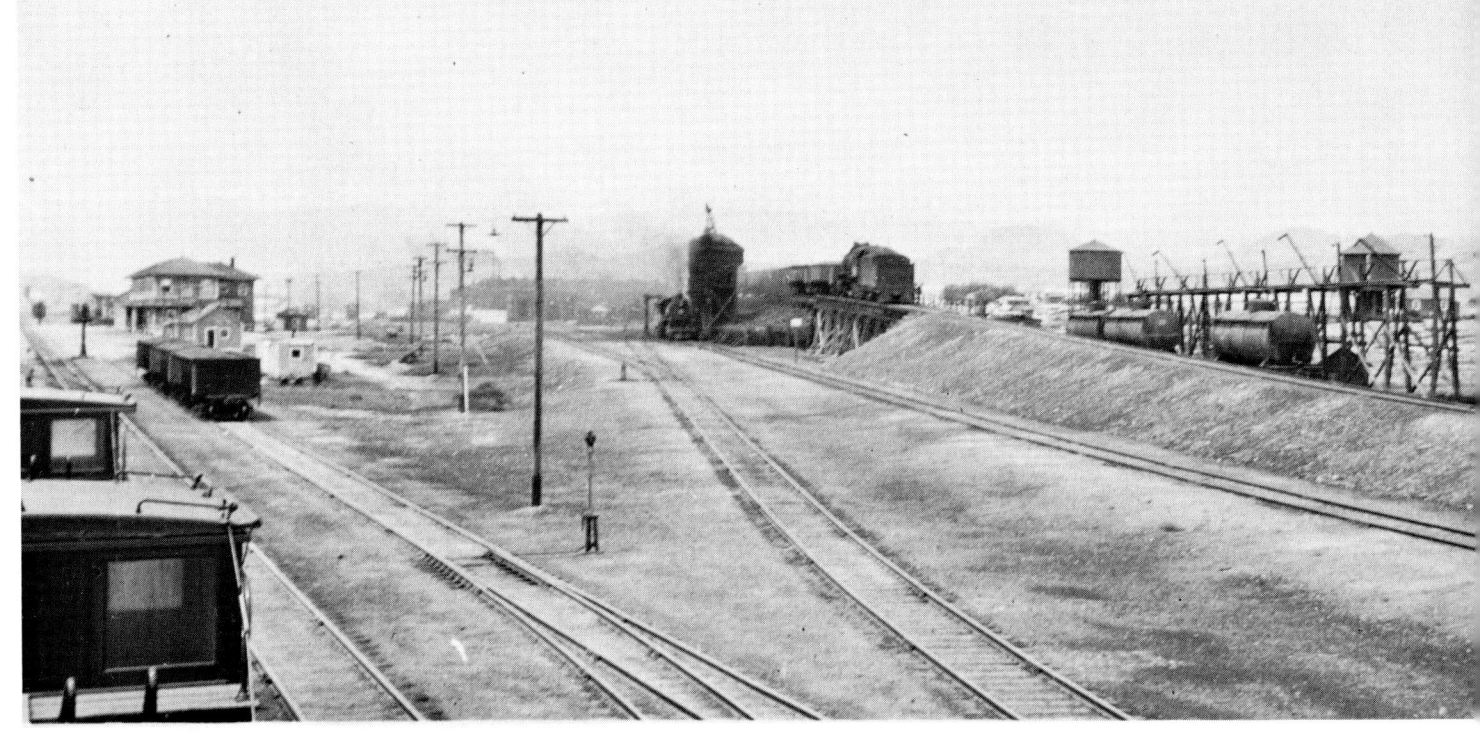

Snow flurries were just beginning to fall when the westerly view of Wendover, Utah, *(above)* was taken. Hardly two decades had passed since the similar scene presented earlier was photographed, but already the age of steam was drawing to a close. A tired Consolidation is nursing a cut of coal cars on the trestle above the coal bin, while a road locomotive stands waiting for its supply at the foot. Behind, in the gathering storm, additional locomotives stand on the ready tracks. *(Louis L. Stein Collection.)*

Western Pacific No. 407 *(below)*, a 4-6-6-4 simple articulated, carried 265 lbs. steam pressure to spin her high 70-inch drivers and represented over 500 tons of handsome machinery in her 120-foot length. Alco built her in 1938; she ran for something less than 13 years until November 1950; then was sold for scrap in 1952. Cost when new was in excess of $180,000; price on disposition — less than $14,000. Shown here leaving Wells, Nevada with a diminutive train, she was still performing far more useful work than any two Cadillacs of comparable value. *(Guy L. Dunscomb.)*

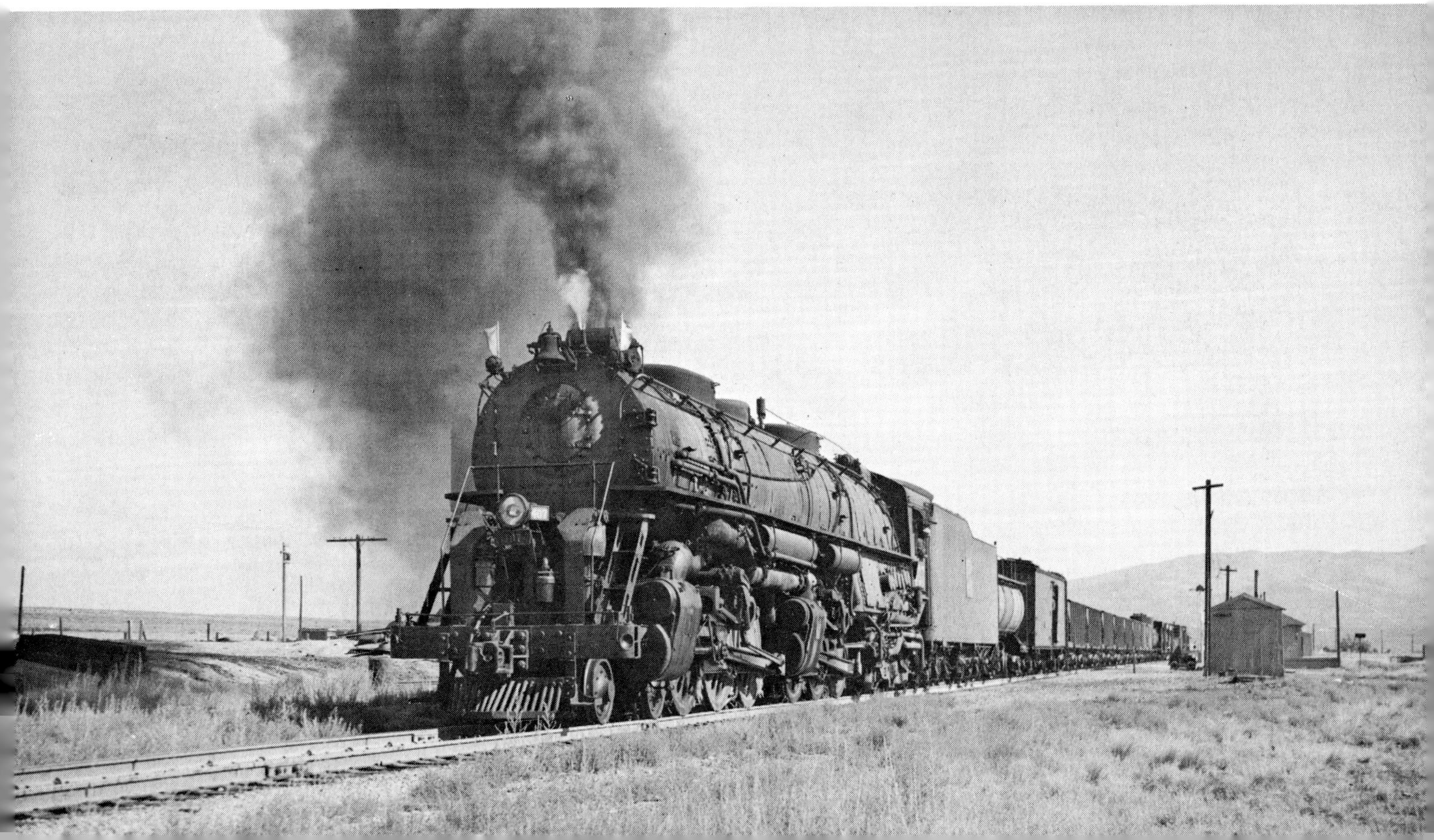

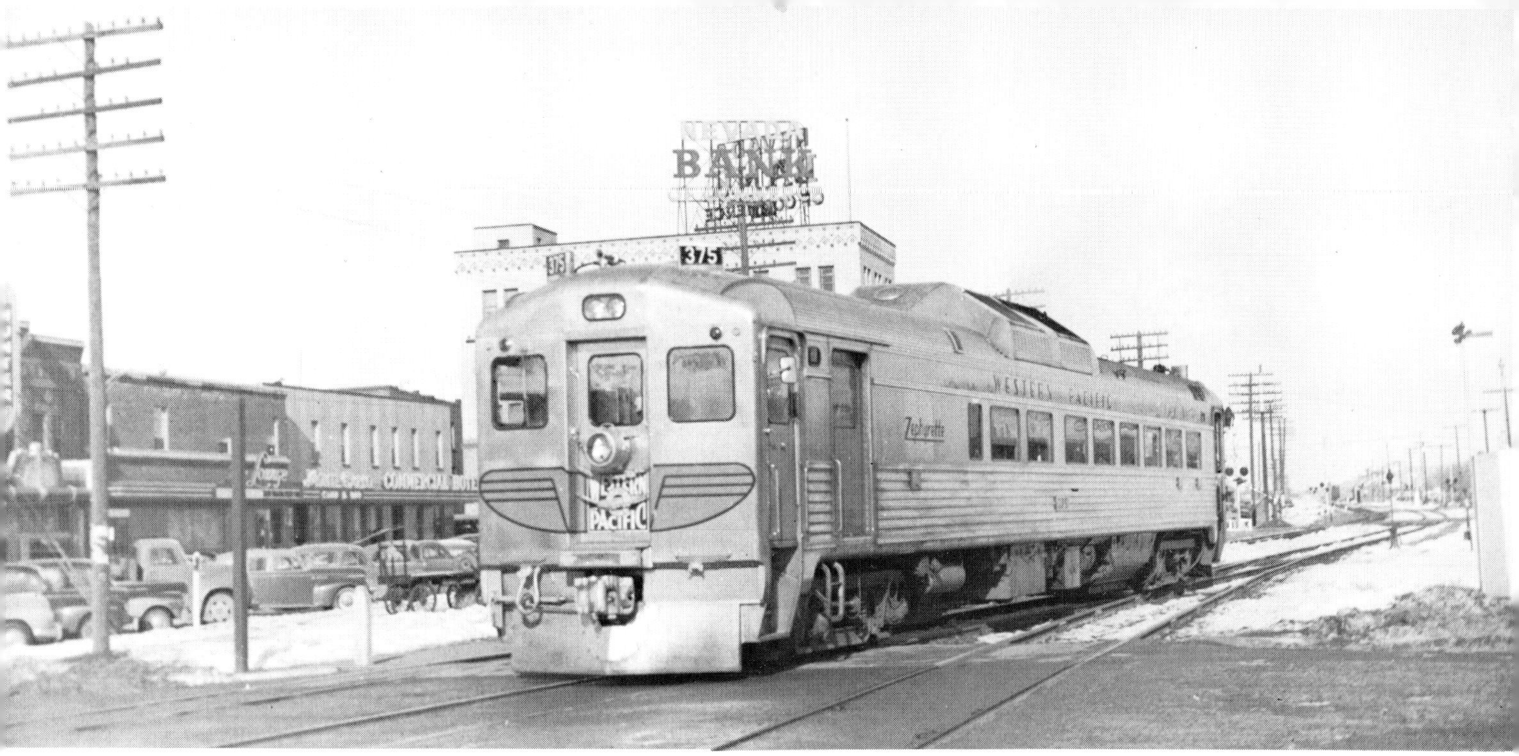

On September 15, 1950, the Western Pacific commenced operation of two Zepherettes (Budd RDC cars) on a tri-weekly schedule to supplant the former conventional steam train, the "Royal Gorge." They lasted a little over 10 years and were discontinued on October 2, 1960. Zepherette No. 375 is shown *(above)* westbound at Elko, Nevada, on a wintry afternoon and *(at right)* surmounting Silver Zone Pass in the Pequop Mountains of eastern Nevada. *(Top: Western Pacific Collection; Right: Al Graves Photo.)*

Steam devotees might argue that no self-respecting articulated would ever need eight additional helpers to move the eastbound freight *(below)* out of Portola — and they would be right. But neither is a nine-unit Diesel necessary, as appears at first blush to be the case. The first four units are being deadheaded to the eastern end of the system to balance the WP's power load. *(Al Graves Photo.)*

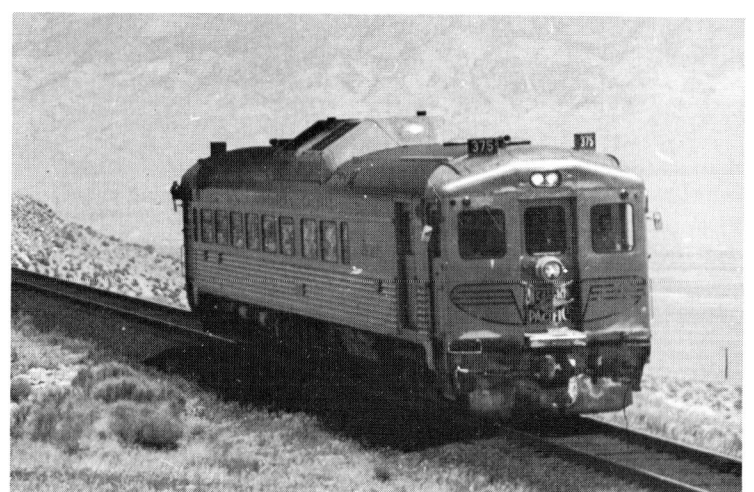

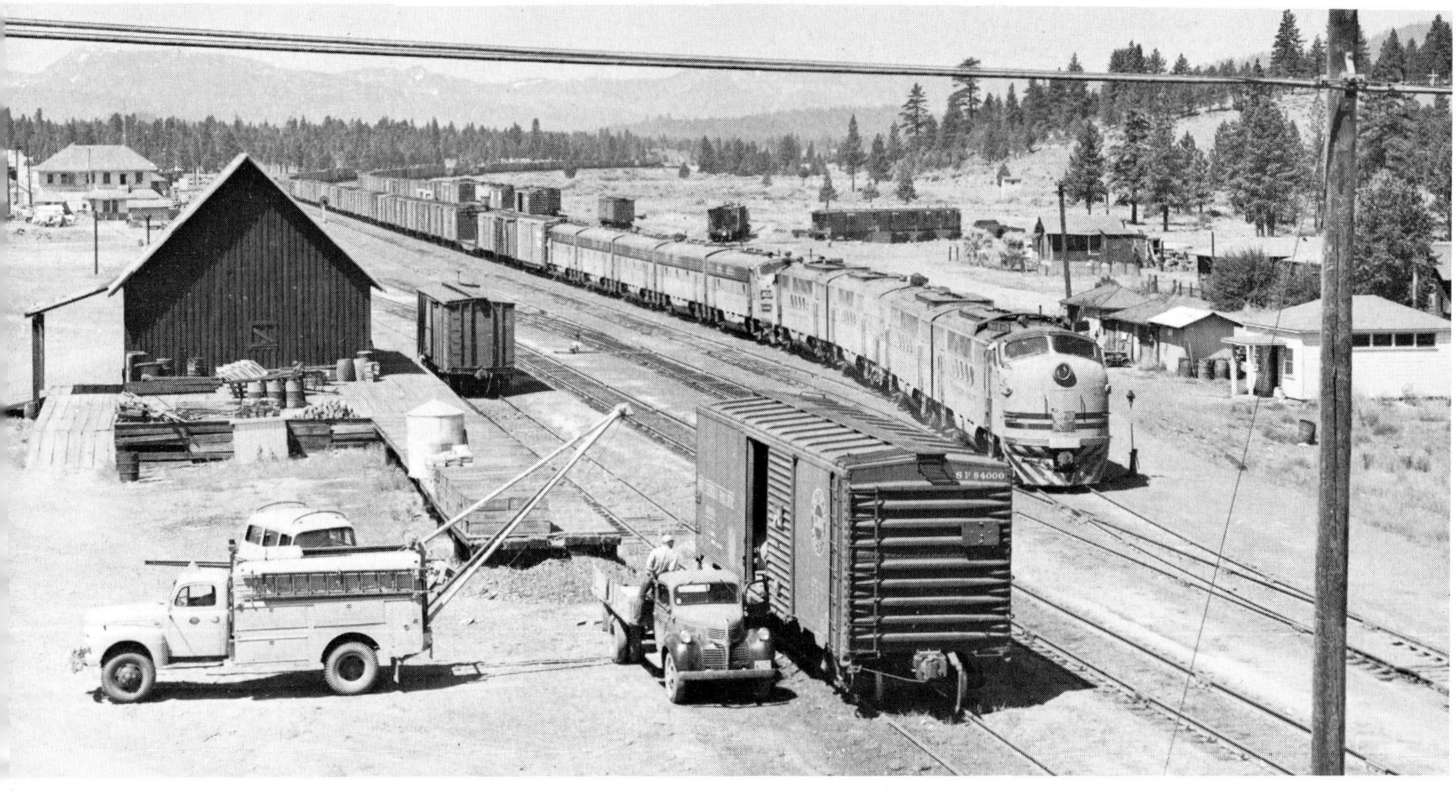

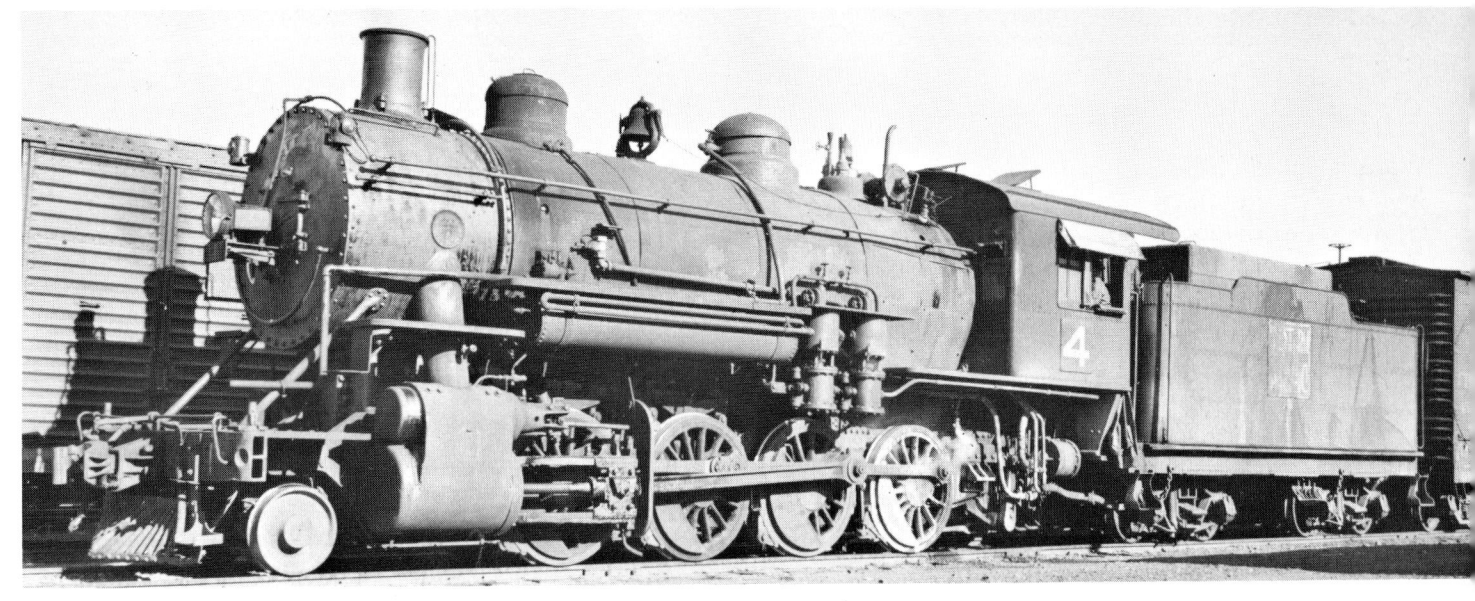

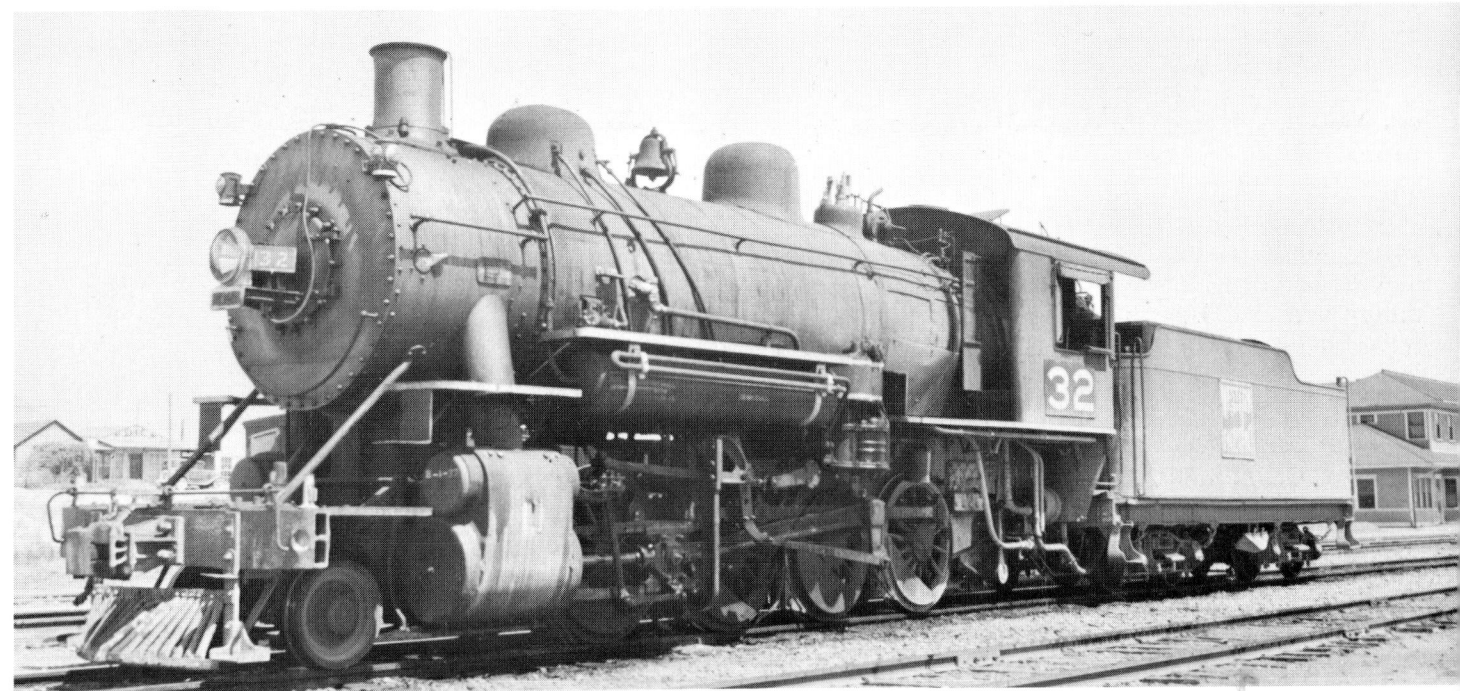

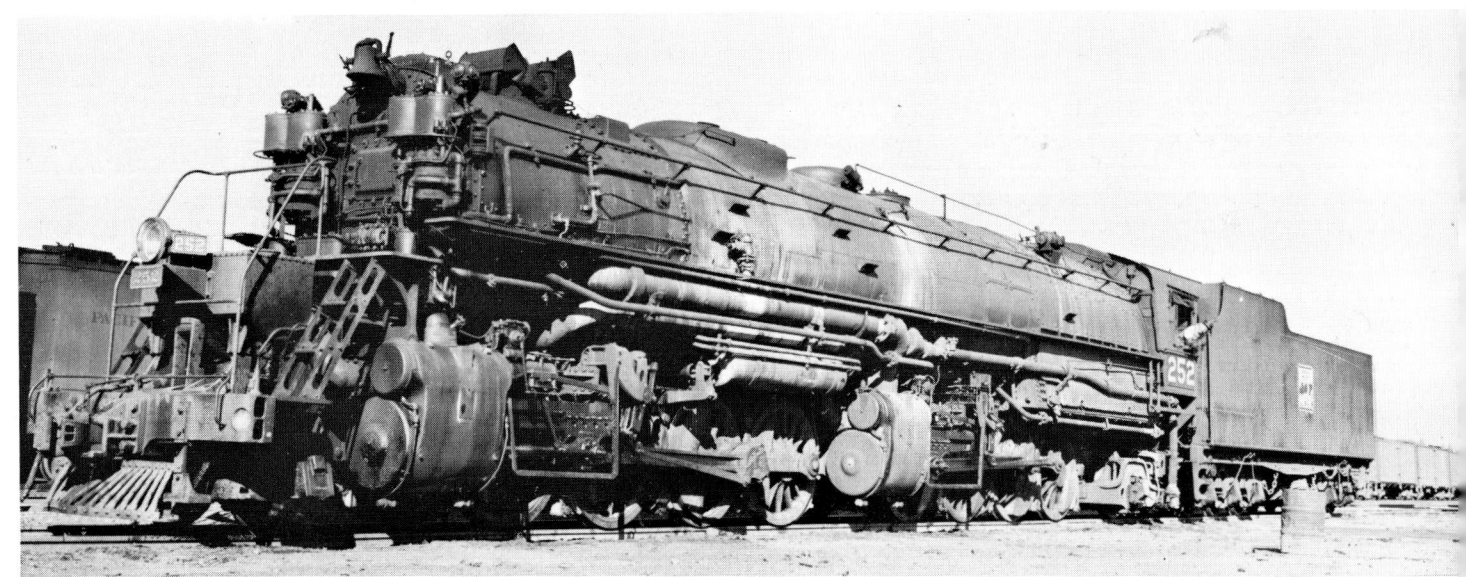

The Western Pacific's first locomotives were Consolidations numbered 1 through 20, built by Baldwin in 1906. A second group, Nos. 21 through 65, were purchased from Alco in 1909. Articulated No. 252, a 2-8-8-2, was one of a lot of six engines built by Baldwin in the depression year of 1931. *(Three Photos: W. A. Pennington.)*

There was other rumormongering as well. The Western Pacific's name was tied with that of the Nevada Central Railroad out of Battle Mountain to Austin, and reports were even circulated that WP was interested in the traction lines in Reno, Nevada. One optimist even predicted the extension of the lines to Wonder, Fairview and Rawhide.

Momentarily, the only actual construction that took place was the result of necessity and not of desire. A fire broke out in the Chilcoot Tunnel toward the end of May 1912, completely consuming the timber tunnel lining and so overheating the rock walls and ceiling no repairs could be made until the earth and rock had cooled. To get traffic moving, a temporary shoo-fly track was thrown over Beckwourth Pass in a short matter of 10 days, but nearly a year elapsed before the tunnel was restored and train schedules returned to normal.

One other line revision was also required in eastern Nevada where a temporary 3% grade between Arnold and Proctor on the east approach to Silver Zone Pass was replaced with a longer, more circuitous 1% grade, known as the Arnold Loop. The project might have escaped the public's attention, had it not been that two men were killed in the unfortunate incident of a runaway train almost before work could begin. Construction of the new line was accomplished between July and December 1913. From December 14 of that year to April 7, 1914 the new 1% grade was used for all eastbound movements, while the 3% grade was used for westbound trains. After April 14, 1914, the 1% grade was used in both directions, the 3% grade being retained as auxiliary trackage only for a period of a few years.

The big 5% interest on $75 million of bonds issued was the major item in the Western Pacific's undoing. With relatively light through traffic and no branches to feed nourishment to the main trunk, the road could not earn sufficient revenues to carry the load. In 1915 the line succumbed to receivership, emerging a year later as the Western Pacific Railroad with a far more realistic $20 million debt and without the obnoxious restriction on branch line construction. Over the next 15 years, some 230 miles of new lines were projected and built, and other railroads were added by acquisition.

With but minor exceptions, the first and foremost of the feeder lines was the branch to Reno, Nevada. Since the narrow gauge N-C-O Railway had long possessed the most feasible route through the hills, initial discussions entertained the thought to lay a third rail over its roadbed from a connection in the vicinity of Beckwourth Pass to Reno. Subsequently it was agreed that the WP purchase for $700,000 the entire N-C-O line (including the Plumas Branch) from a point just south of the WP – N-C-O crossing at Hackstaff (now Herlong) to and including the Reno station building, roundhouse and shops. The sale was consummated on June 11, 1917, and the work of conversion begun immediately.

At the northern end, a 2.2-mile connection was constructed from a point known as Reno Jct. (just east of the Chilcoot tunnel) to the N-C-O near the site of (old) Chat. From that point southward, standard gauge rails were laid outside the 3' gauge trackage over those portions of the N-C-O roadbed used by the WP. This permitted narrow gauge trains to continue servicing the area during the conversion operations. From Chat, 8.2 miles of the N-C-O line were used to Peavine (formerly Purdy), then 13.4 miles of new construction were instituted along the northeastern slope of Peavine Mountain to improve upon the six miles of extra trackage Thos. Moore had originally built into the N-C-O with its large loop in that area. Connecting again near Summit, dual gauge roadbed was installed for the rest of the 9.3 miles to Reno, the twisting route being adjusted for curvature and graded for standard gauge operations. The 39.4-mile Plumas Branch to Davies Mill in the Mohawk Valley was abandoned in its entirety, as was the segment of main N-C-O line north from Chat to a point 2,000 feet short of the crossing at Hackstaff. Total cost of the Reno Branch rehabilitation came to $453,713, and on February 1, 1918, the first WP train left Reno at 7:00 A.M. The last narrow gauge N-C-O train had left town the previous day.

Of the other branches projected or constructed, the WP gave serious consideration to the possibilities (prior to 1917) of a light-traffic branch from Reynard, Nevada (22 miles west of Gerlach), northwest through Buffalo Canyon to Surprise Valley in the vicinity of Cedarville, California. Down in the Sierra and Mohawk Valleys in California, it purchased the Boca & Loyalton Railroad lines when that road was sold at foreclosure on September 18, 1916, formal title being transferred on December 1 of that year. Following abandonment of unwanted portions of the B&L, the balance of the system became the 12-mile Loyalton Branch. The 2-mile Gulling (Grizzley Creek) Branch, was abandoned in 1940 following the cessation of the natural ice

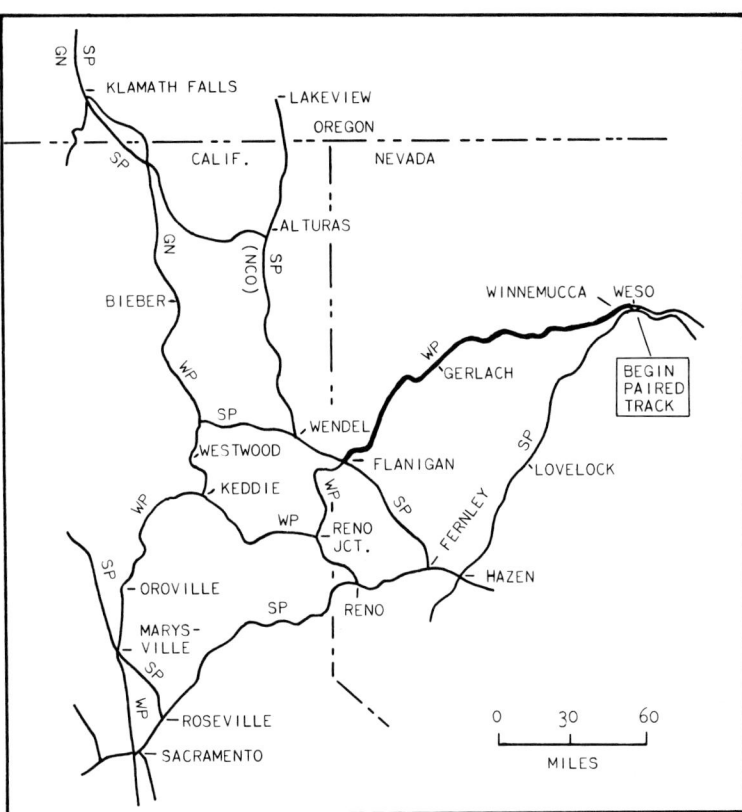

In 1929, Southern Pacific completed its Modoc Line between Klamath Falls, Oregon, and Fernley, Nevada, to open up new country and provide a short-cut for transcontinental traffic from Oregon. By agreement of June 18, 1962, the Western Pacific granted Southern Pacific operating *bridge* rights over its railroad between Flanigan and Weso, Nevada, a distance of 151 miles (heavy line on map). The agreement, approved by the I.C.C. in September 1962, provides for the payment by SP of a fixed annual rental plus a monthly rental based on car miles and a share of the maintenance expenses. The route through Gerlach is 54 miles shorter than through Fernley and Lovelock and will save SP two to three hours running time of freight trains.

Forest products from the SP lines in Oregon are the prime eastbound movement; westbound movements are largely non-compensatory as most trains are returning empty cars. Photographs of regularly scheduled SP freight trains passing through Gerlach will not be possible until sometime in 1963 as track connections are to be built and details resolved.

---

harvesting activities. In September 1917 the WP opened a 1-mile branch from Blairsden to Davies Mill at Graeagle to serve lumbering operations there which were active until the mid-'30's. A similar operation of the Davies Johnson Lumber Co. instigated construction of the 12-mile Calpine Branch which was opened in January 1922 and abandoned in 1940 when the mill closed. At Wells, Nevada, a 6,000-foot link with the Rogerson Branch (OSL) of the Union Pacific was placed in operation on December 5, 1928. New trackage was needed to service the Stead Air Force Base, north of Reno, in 1942. The WP's portion of the line amounted to 738 feet and work was completed on June 20. The Base was inactivated in 1945, but reactivated again on April 14, 1948.

In the years of World War I (1917-1918), the WP and the SP tried out a plan of paired track operation along the Humboldt River whereby the rails of one road were used for all eastbound movements and the other for westbound. Following the war, each road reverted to its original, independent status, but the idea in retrospect looked good. Finally, on August 1, 1924, both roads entered into an agreement whereby WP tracks would be used for all eastbound trains and SP rails for all westbound. Automatic block signals were installed along the 177.7 miles of WP trackage between Weso (near Winnemucca) and Alazon (near Wells), Nevada, to match the previous SP signalling (installed in 1906-10) along its 182.7 miles between the same points. Thus since all traffic was one-directional on either line over this mileage, there was no need to include such trackage in the WP's program to install C.T.C. on the Nevada line during the period for 1949 to 1952.

In August 1935 hard times forced the WP into bankruptcy, but when it emerged in December 1944, the road's condition was vastly improved both physically and financially. On March 20, 1949, the Western Pacific leaped into the public fancy with the inauguration of the joint WP-D&RG-CB&Q California Zephyr streamlined transcontinental train between Oakland, California, and Chicago, Illinois. With a daylight scheduling over the most scenic portions of the route and upper level domes from which to observe the spectacular countryside, the six trains comprising the fleet have created an outstanding record for popular appeal and profitable operation. They are, indeed, a fitting tribute to this "Newest of the Transcontinentals."

As this book goes to press, a new phase in the turbulent history of the Western Pacific is in progress. Following several years of unsuccessful SP-WP negotiations for joint use of certain parallel lines, the Southern Pacific Company decided to seek stock control of the Western Pacific. On October 12, 1960, the Far West was startled with the announcement that the SP had purchased almost 10% of the stock of the WP and that it was filing an application with the Interstate Commerce Commission to seek authority to acquire control of that line. There was an immediate flurry in the stock market as heavy trading developed in Western Pacific stock, but the buyer was a mystery. The SP was suspected, but on October 25 the identity of the real purchaser became apparent when the Santa Fe Railway announced that it had purchased 20% of the WP's stock and that it, too, sought I.C.C. approval for control of the line. The Santa Fe's action was endorsed by the directors of the Western Pacific a few days later when the WP Board voted to support the Santa Fe's proposal.

Other proponents then joined the fracas. Late in 1960 the Great Northern Railway, although very busy with its own plans for merger with the Northern Pacific and the Burlington, picked up 9% of the WP's stock and announced that it would support the Santa Fe's position. On the other hand, in January 1961, the Union Pacific purchased 10% of the WP's stock and stood in favor of the Southern Pacific's application. Thus approximately one-half of the Western Pacific's stock became held by four railroads, and both sides began lining up an impressive array of star witnesses in support of the individual arguments.

Speakers from the railroads involved traveled the territory extensively expounding their individual positions in efforts to gain the endorsement of various civic and governmental bodies. The SP preached the necessity for elimination of duplicate and parallel rail facilities in order to compete more effectively with other forms of transportation. On the other hand, the Santa Fe and the Western Pacific attacked the SP's plan as a railroad monopoly. Charges and counter charges flew in every direction prior to the hearings which began on July 17, 1961 before I.C.C. Examiner Paul C. Albus in the Gold Room of San Francisco's famed Sheraton-Palace Hotel. The Santa Fe was supported by the Great Northern and the Western Pacific, all partners in the Bieber Gateway or "Inside Route" from California to the Northwest, and reassurances were expressed that the famed slogan "Santa Fe all the way" would not result in traffic diversions and short hauling of the WP's eastern connections. The arguments fell upon the skeptical ears of the D&RGW, the Rock Island and the Missouri Pacific which joined with the Union Pacific in support of the SP's application.

During the weeks of hearings, hundreds of witnesses appeared and before the record was closed, the transcript numbered 9,500 pages plus extensive exhibits. Top executives of the railroads involved were in regular attendance, and the newspapers filled their columns with lively quotations from the more outspoken witnesses. At the same time, quiet meetings were being held leading to an arrangement for joint use of certain SP-WP tracks. Agreements were reached on some proposals which had been cited in the hearings, and other proposals (such as the joint use of the WP's line from Flanigan to Weso (near Winnemucca, Nevada), continued under discussion.

Concurrent briefs (if 400 pages can be called "brief") summarizing the principal points expressed by the applicants were filed with the Interstate Commerce Commission on May 1, 1962. At the moment that is where the situation rests. No decision can be expected from the full Commission for at least another year.

Ironically, when the Western Pacific's annual report to stockholders for the year 1961 was issued in March 1962, a strange disclosure was made. In seeking a higher return of income on some $3,000,000 of working capital which could not immediately be used, the Western Pacific pulled a reverse play by purchasing 53,800 shares of Southern Pacific stock to which additional shares were subsequently added to bring the total to 100,000 shares. In order to avoid playing favorites, the Western Pacific also bought 100,000 shares of Santa Fe stock for the same basic reason. Some people find such transactions confusing; some are entertained; while still others exhibit no more than a wry smile.

Oregon Short Line (Idaho Central)

All across the northern part of the state of Nevada and the adjoining southerly areas of Oregon and Idaho lies a vast, relatively undeveloped territory which, over the years, has served as a constant inhibitor to railroad construction and advancement. The scarcity of business and of industry has left little incentive for moneyed men to invest their dollars, for the hope of adequate financial return has been nebulous in the extreme.

True, a few abortive lines stretching north from Nevada's Humboldt River arteries did attain various stages of development or construction (more notably the N-C-O, the early Nevada Northern, and the ill-fated Metropolis branch of the SP), and numerous others were seriously propounded

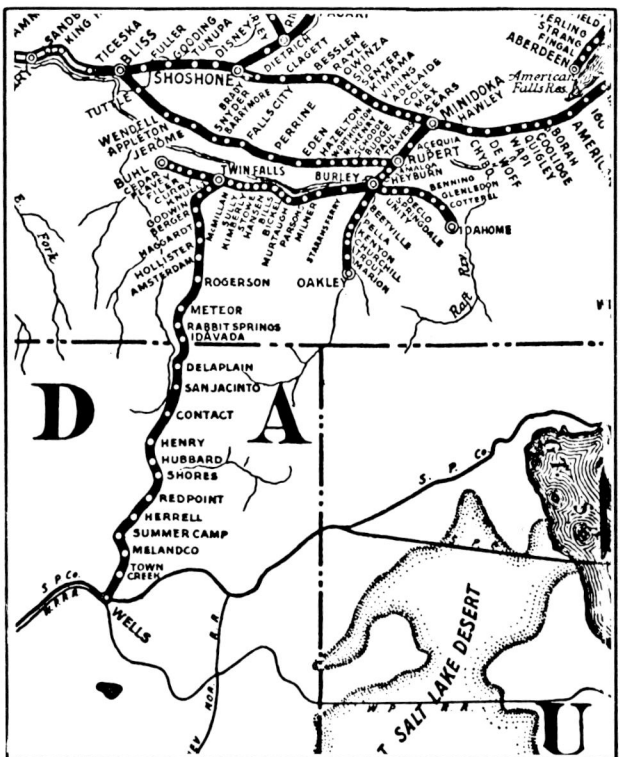

at one time or another (from Winnemucca, Battle Mountain, Carlin, Elko and Wells); but it was an Idaho railroad reaching southward to the transcontinental trunk lines in Nevada that finally accomplished connective fruition, and then not until the 1920's. It was the last major railroad built in Nevada.

Around the turn of the century, Southern Idaho became the locale of a number of reclamation projects in the Snake River area; and the Oregon Short Line (a UP subsidiary), sensing new sources of traffic, determined upon extensive branch line construction southward from Minidoka to Rupert and Burley, then westward to Twin Falls and Buhl. A feeder line was also plotted to Rogerson, and the possibility of extending it all the way south to a connection with the SP near Wells, Nevada, was not overlooked. Construction of the Buhl branch was inaugurated under the name of the (affiliated) Minidoka & Southwestern Railroad, and the main line was pushed the full 74 miles to Twin Falls and Buhl with regular trains operating by October 1, 1907. The business slump of the period forced a halt to further expansion at that time.

As economic conditions improved, work on the Rogerson branch line was resumed. On April 29, 1909, graders were started at Twin Falls, and by the following spring the job was essentially completed. On July 1, 1910, regular trains steamed into Rogerson, 28 miles to the south. Then a hush fell over the area as all work on the line halted at that point. The silence deepened when the Minidoka & Southwestern disappeared that fall, absorbed by its parent, the OSL. Ten long years went by, and although several independent companies were formed in futile efforts to carry on with the extension of the line, no celebrations were held and no shovels were recorded as turning first sods.

In 1920 a spark of life appeared. An ambitious group of men from San Francisco, California, and Twin Falls, Idaho, incorporated the Idaho Central Railroad (the last of several such organizations with the same name) to bridge the 90-100 mile gap between Rogerson and Wells. Joseph L. Stewart of San Francisco and Thomas McDougall of Twin Falls were the principal promoters, and according to the provisions of the recently enacted Transportation Act of 1920, they applied to the I.C.C. for authority to build the line. That august body then requested the regulatory commissions of Nevada and Idaho to hold public hearings and forward the evidence, together with their recommendations.

At the public hearings held in September 1920, witnesses expressed a strong desire for the railroad. Around Twin Falls, farmers wanted the 300-mile shorter route to decrease shipping costs of produce to San Francisco markets. Traffic in cattle from the extensive ranches along the proposed line, and alfalfa from Twin Falls for their winter feeding, were important considerations. Mine operators at Contact, Nevada, a mining district dating back to the 1870's, told of increased activity since 1915 and went on to insist that the mines "have now passed the experimental stage of their development and only rail transportation is needed to assure success." It was claimed that 20,000,000 tons of low grade copper ore were waiting to be mined—a broad statement carefully qualified by the admission that only a small part of the vast ore body "is now technically in sight." Mining spokesmen did not hesitate, however, to point to the growth of Ely and its copper mines as a result of the advent of the Nevada Northern.

Citizens of the area demonstrated their desire for the railroad by pledging $500,000 to be paid to the promoters through individual subscriptions upon completion of the railroad. Elko County was authorized to donate $50,000 to the cause, the

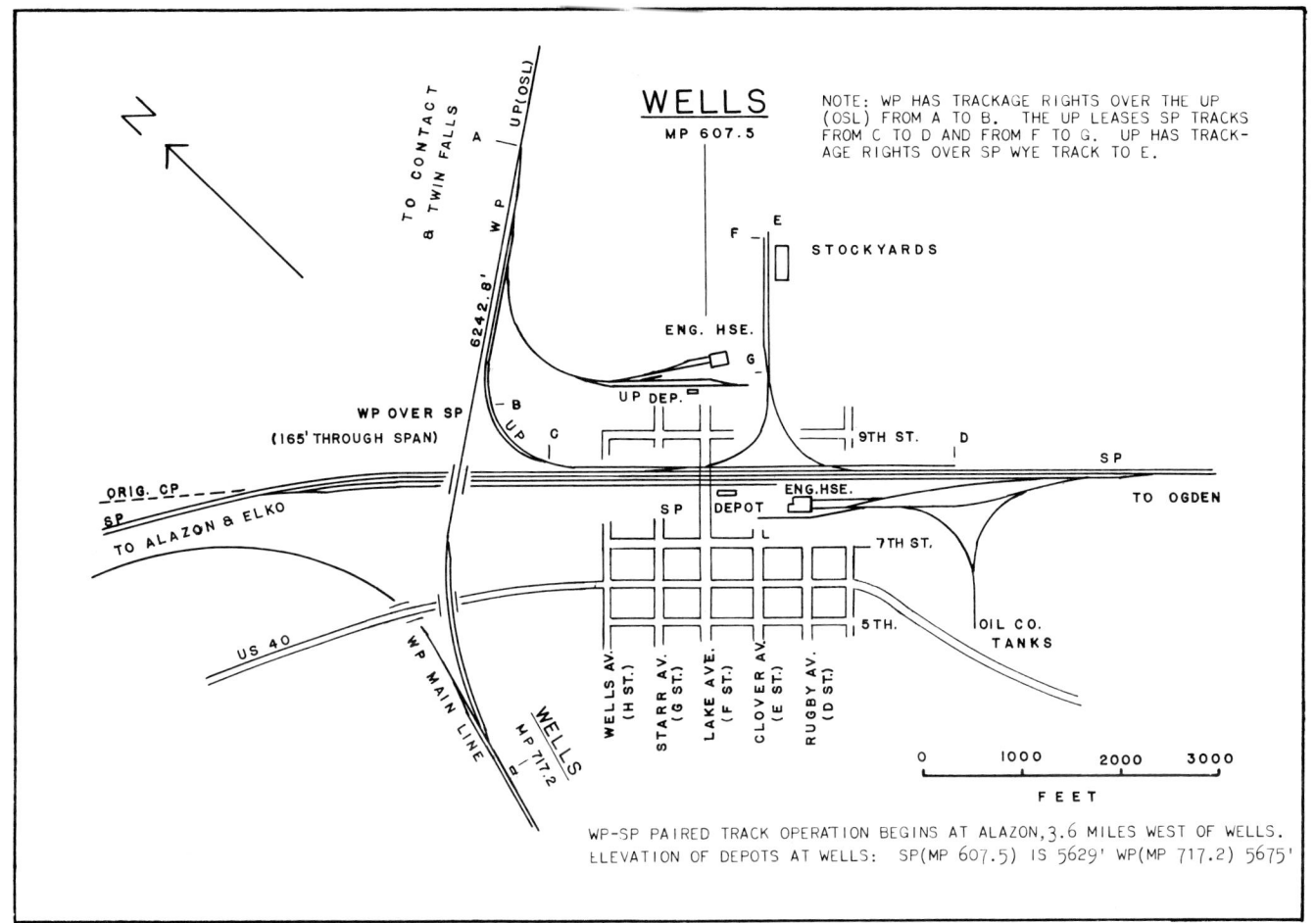

money to be raised by a general property tax. Weakest link in the chain appeared to be the lack of personal funds which the promoters of the railroad had available for the project.

The I.C.C. reviewed the results of the hearings with mixed emotions. The local need was obvious; the project had the blessing of the two state commissions which sensed the political pulse of the public; but the reasonableness of the estimated net railway operating income (before bond interest) of $310,000 in the first year was not fully convincing. In fact, there were serious doubts as to the projected earning power of the railroad at all. In face of the odds, the I.C.C. acquiesced and granted its approval on July 28, 1921. However, conditions were imposed—the Idaho Central was to explain to the I.C.C. the sources of its financing, and the job was to be completed by the end of 1923.

Preliminary surveys were immediately arranged by the Idaho Central, and an unsuccessful effort was made to raise the $3,500,000 necessary to build the road. Without funds, construction was impossible; the futility of raising such a sizable amount became increasingly evident; finally the towel was thrown in. On April 24, 1923, writing from their office in the Claus Spreckels Building in San Francisco, Stewart and McDougall addressed a letter to the railroad committees in Twin Falls, Contact and Wells offering all rights, stock and other assets of the Idaho Central upon payment of $25,000.

Welcome indeed was the interest manifested by the Union Pacific Railroad in completing the project. President Gray visited Twin Falls in his private car early in May 1923 and told local committees that the UP would build the line. The local committees responded by raising the necessary $25,000 with which to buy the old rights of the Idaho Central, thus paving the way for faster action on the part of the next builder, and also arranged to donate the right-of-way and terminal lands in Wells.

Two weeks later the UP filed its application in the name of the Oregon Short Line Railroad. Figures submitted on the application showed that, instead of a profit for the first year, a $60,000 loss was expected; moreover it was anticipated that the loss would be repeated in each of the first five years of operations. The cost was higher, too—now $5,094,000—but it was estimated that the new traffic generated would benefit the entire Union Pacific System sufficiently to warrant the increased expenditure. Apparently relieved by the decision of the Idaho Central directors in requesting the cancellation of their certificate, and by the substantial financial strength of the new applicant, the I.C.C. granted the appropriate authority to the OSL on July 21, 1923.

The OSL did not wait for the favorable I.C.C. decision before taking action. Shortly after President Gray's visit, surveyors were placed in the field. John Paul Elliott was the engineer in charge of construction, and Jack (as his friends called him) possessed an almost uncanny ability to traverse a new, wild country casually on a reconnaissance survey and still spot the proper curves and elevations. Experience demonstrated that his locations were usually accepted with but little deviation by the field men who followed him with their instruments.

The Utah Construction Co., builder of so many Nevada railroads, also took this line under its wing. The route passed by a number of ranches the construction company then owned, permitting the use of the ranch houses as headquarters. As a matter of expediency, when actual construction began in the spring of 1924, portions of the job were subcontracted to others. With the OSL-UP treasury behind the work, financial problems were obviated.

The work of grading was largely carried out with mule teams, Fresno scrapers and elevators. The rolling country was (and still is) wild—one field engineer, Dick Weske, got the surprise of his life when he saw a huge, hungry timber wolf just outside of Rogerson. Day-off entertainment for the engineers consisted of fishing in Goose Creek or hunting sage hens. The men learned by experience to avoid the large birds due to their over-abundance of sage flavor. The Mexican laborers normally celebrated their weekends with camp brawls on Saturday nights, but by and large they were normally back on the job when Monday morning rolled around.

Heavy snows retarded the work during the two winters of construction, but early in 1926 the last of the new 90-lb. rails finally were spiked down at Wells, Nevada, and a Railroad Celebration was in order. Railroad Day, the last of so many held within the state, was scheduled for February 15, 1926, and on that day the line was officially opened. Because the regular train schedule, dictated by connections at Twin Falls, Idaho, provided for a 9:15 P.M. arrival at Wells (too late to service the celebration), a special train was operated to bring the people from Twin Falls over the 124 miles to Wells.

The double-headed special—consisting of seven Pullmans, two private cars, a chair and a baggage car—set a noisy pattern as it pulled into town at 3:00 P.M. on Monday, February 15, 1926. Engineers Joseph Phillips and Fred Dodge tied down the whistle cords of both locomotives as they swung their train through the switch to continue on SP tracks. Wells was in a joyous mood to greet the visitors. Some 1,500 people, including 200 who had journeyed over from neighboring Elko, witnessed the arrival, while willing hands at the SP roundhouse blasted the siren and pulled the whistle cords and rang the bells of the five locomotives standing on the ready tracks.

Judging by the reports in the Wells' *Nevada State Herald* and other papers, everybody had a good time; nobody could pay for a thing, everything was free. Not only was the town now served by a new railroad involving 94.6 miles of new construction, but that day, for the first time in three years, the town's high school basketball team trounced its counterpart from Metropolis, a small farming community 10 miles to the northwest. Metropolis had suffered a previous loss, for it had once been the terminus of an SP branch line, but the rails had been torn up the year before, and in spite of efforts on the part of the townspeople to attract the new OSL line past its doors, no cognizance was taken of the pleaded necessity.

That evening the ladies of Wells prepared a magnificent dinner. Railroad officials, state and local politicos from the governor on down, gave forth with the expected words of praise normally heard at such occasions. Those wishing to avoid the blustery speeches were invited to witness continuous free movies at the Wells Opera House where colored movies, then very much of a novelty, repeatedly packed each performance. There was "just enough comedy, love and thrills to be entertaining." By 10 o'clock the banquet was over, and the gymnasium floor was cleared for dancing to the music of the Wells Hoot Owls, a feature event which lasted continuously throughout the night until train time early the next day. It was a tired but well entertained group that departed for Idaho the next morning. At Contact, on the return trip, the train was stopped for an hour while guests were showered with sandwiches and offers of auto rides to the copper mines.

For a time the railroad's new branch offered a tri-weekly passenger train to accommodate the riders, but eventually this gave way to a six-day-a-week mixed train. The first freight shipment to Wells arrived a week after the celebration, consisting of a carload of lumber from Oregon. Although the initial track connection at Wells had been made with the SP (as the WP tracks were some distance to the south), the situation was corrected about two years later. Following I.C.C. approval, the Western Pacific constructed a 6,000-foot connection to the UP's OSL, placing the extension in operation on December 5, 1928.

The copper development at Contact, predestined to become another Ely, has yet to reach such an exalted realization, but the branch-line railroad has managed to continue its landfarings down through the years regardless. In 1962 the southbound traffic largely consisted of flour and livestock while northbound cargoes included such items as automobiles, plaster board, roofing material and canned goods. For the rail fan, this line has a tremendous distinction — it schedules the only "mixed train" in Nevada in regular operation in 1962.

Other Northern Nevada Short Lines

Of the multifarious short line railroads projected or constructed in Northern Nevada, some were promotions of short duration; others were part of the corporate families of larger railroads; still others were adjuncts to the mining or miscellaneous activities of various corporate enterprises. Of those reaching a state of tangible actuality, the following are worthy of mention on these pages.

The DEEP CREEK RAILROAD was primarily a subsidiary projection of the Western Pacific Railroad in the state of Utah, to reach from Wendover (on the main line) to Gold Hill, Utah, to service the Deep Creek and Ferber gold mining districts. The 46-mile, standard gauge line hugged the Utah-Nevada boundary for the first 17 miles, being just 30 feet east of the state line. Inclusion of the road in this history of Nevada railroads is justified solely by a circumstance of nature — to avoid a slough, a half-mile detour was made which brought the tracks over the line into Nevada. Construction commenced late in 1916, and the road was opened on March 12, 1917. Immediate, widespread fame attached to the line a few months later when bandits held up the train and made off with considerable treasure. In less than a quarter century, Deep Creek (an old mining district once thought to be a part of Nevada) became played out, and the railroad ceased operations on July 31, 1939.

The PACIFIC PORTLAND CEMENT CO. operated plants at various locations in northern Nevada and elsewhere. Among these was a gypsum processing plant at Empire, six miles south of Gerlach, Nevada. To service the facilities, a standard gauge industrial railroad was constructed between the two points, control passing to the U.S. Gypsum Co. upon purchase of the properties in 1948. Still in operation from a connection with the Western Pacific, the motive power, formerly steam, is now, since April 1954, a light diesel locomotive.

The NEVADA MASSACHUSETTS CO. operated the largest tungsten mine in the United States at a spot just eight miles north of Mill City, a station on the Southern Pacific Railroad 27 miles west of Winnemucca. Connecting the mines with the crushing plant was a narrow gauge railroad of several miles in length, powered by midget gasoline locomotives. Declining prices of tungsten forced a closing of the mines in 1957, and kept them closed as the railroad suspended operations. Although the tracks remained until 1962 in mute testimony to the enterprise, all mining machinery, buildings and equipment were then sold and the mines allowed to fill with water.

CORTEZ MINES, LTD. operated another isolated mine-to-mill railroad near Tenabo, approximately 30 miles southeast of Battle Mountain. A solitary steam locomotive shunted its cars over a track less than a mile long up until the time the property was abandoned many years ago.

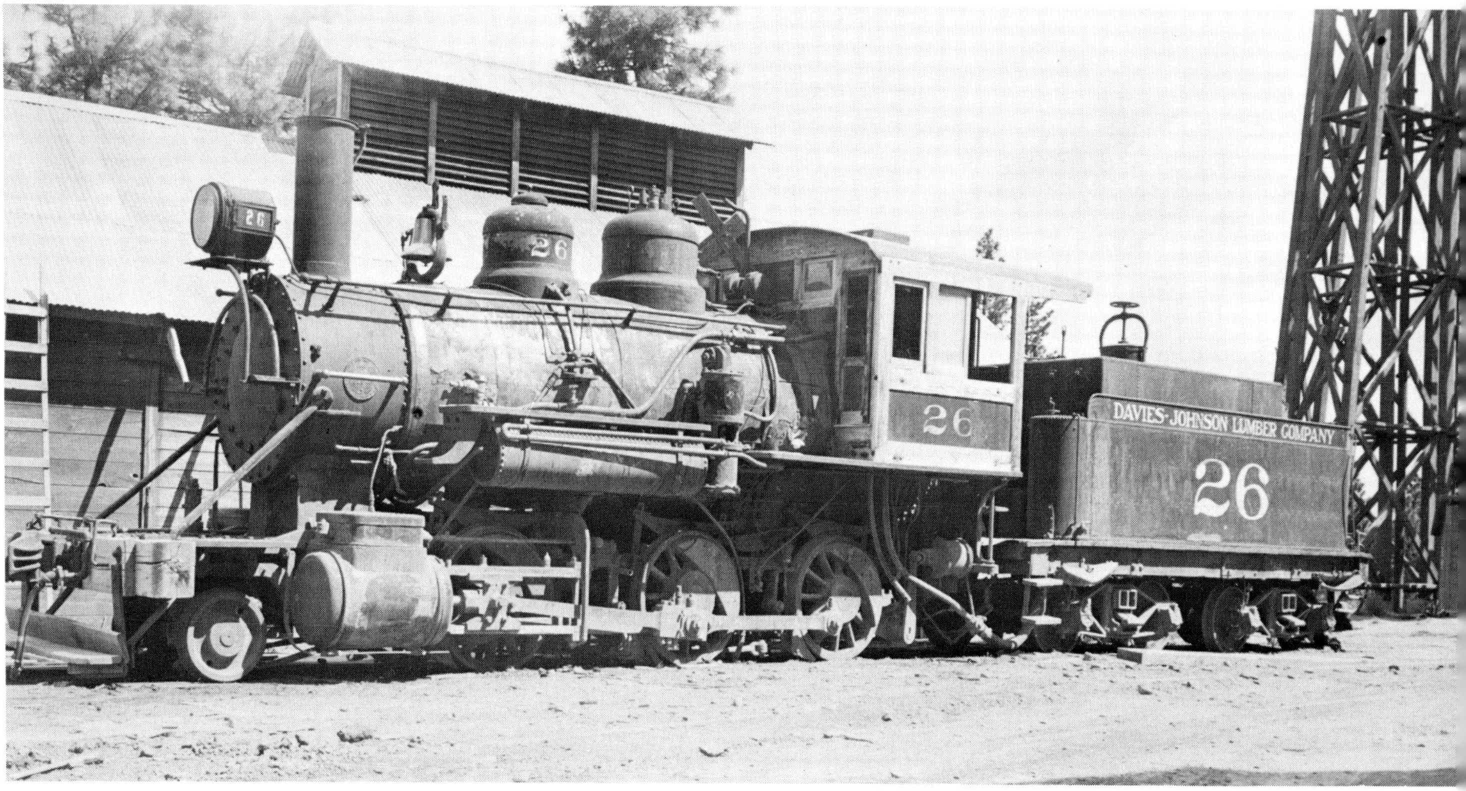

Various were the connecting roads to the Western Pacific and strange was their equipment. Locomotive No. 26 *(above)* stands at the Calpine connection of the Davies Johnson Lumber Company's railroad in May 1938. No. 5 *(below)* is the mine-to-mill motive power of the Pacific Portland Cement Co.'s six-mile line south from Gerlach, Nevada, to Empire. The picture was taken at Gerlach in 1947 just seven years before a light Diesel locomotive usurped the No. 5's duties. *(Top: Guy L. Dunscomb; Bottom: Robert Gray Photo, Guy Dunscomb Collection.)*

The Deep Creek Railroad *(page opposite)* was primarily a subsidiary projection of the Western Pacific from Wendover on the main line 46 miles south to Gold Hill, Utah, along the Nevada border. Consolidation No. 2, shown here at Wendover, was the road's mainstay in 1938, but her career ended July 31, 1939 when the railroad ceased operations. Dismantlement was immediate, as evidenced by the piles of ties stacked in the middle of Gold Hill in the March 1940 view *(center, opposite)*. The building to the left of Main Street is the hotel, and on the hillside (far center background) is the tungsten mine which gave the town sustenance. *(Top: Ken Kidder Photo; Center and Bottom: Guy L. Dunscomb.)*

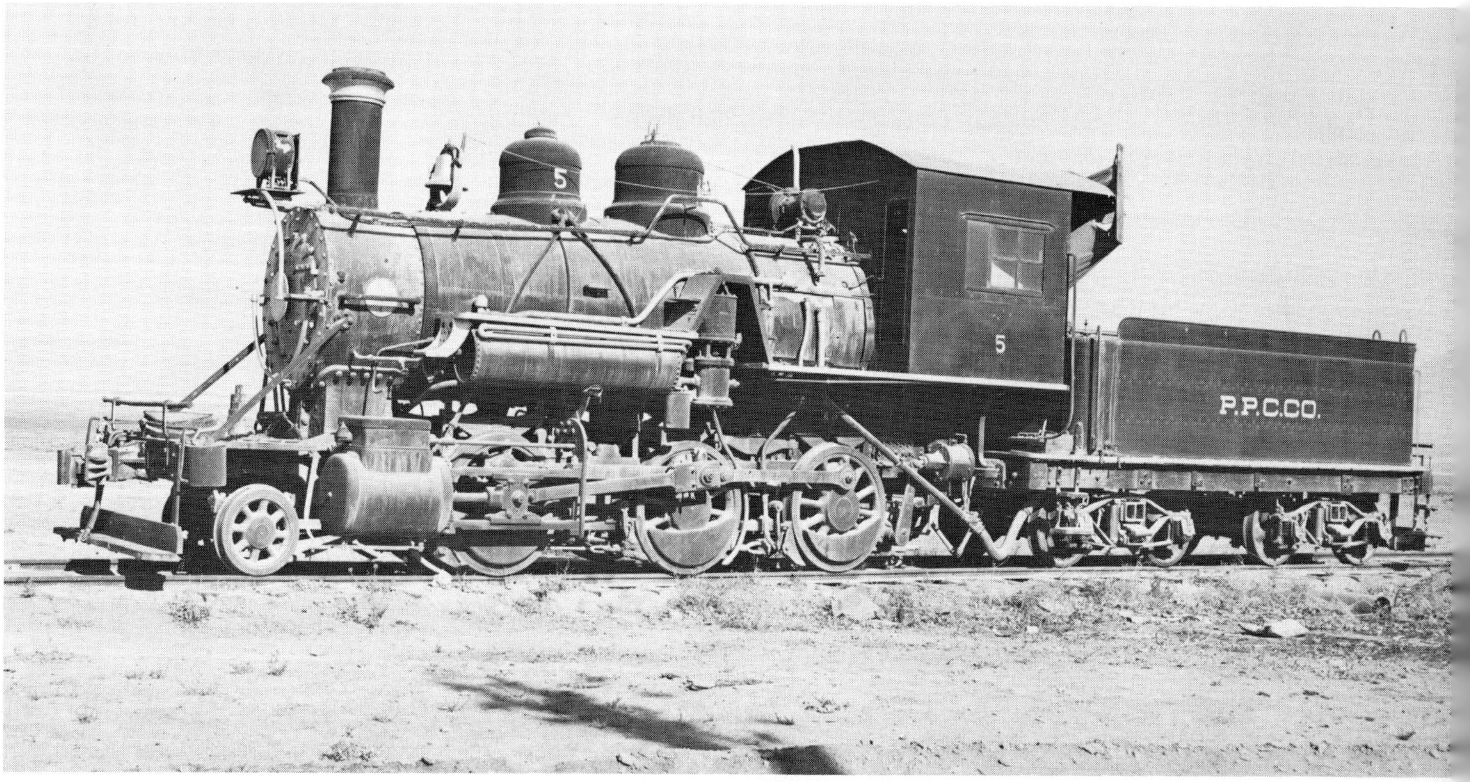

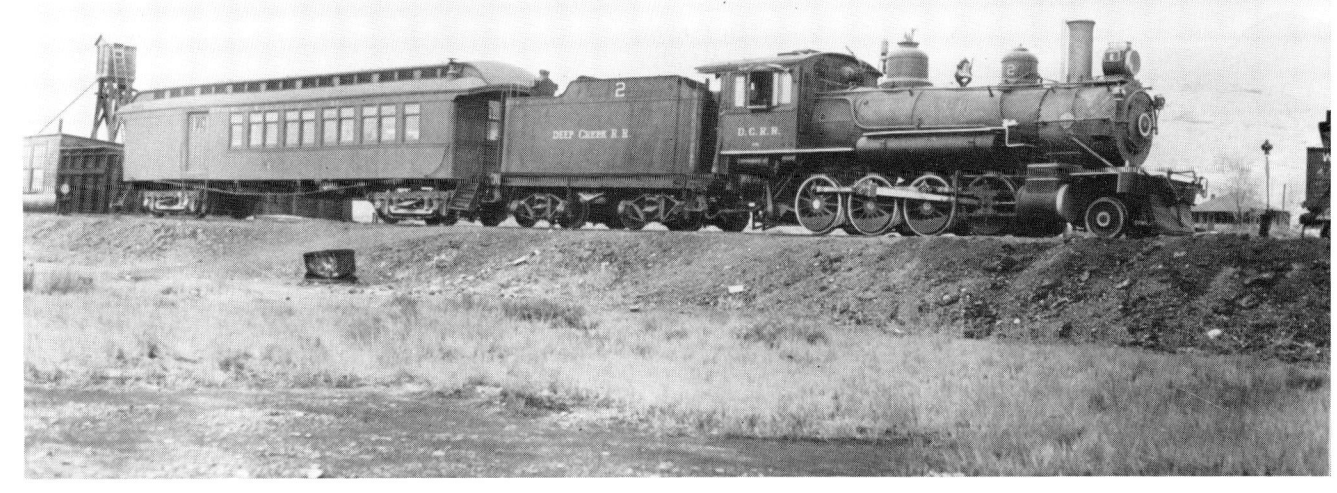
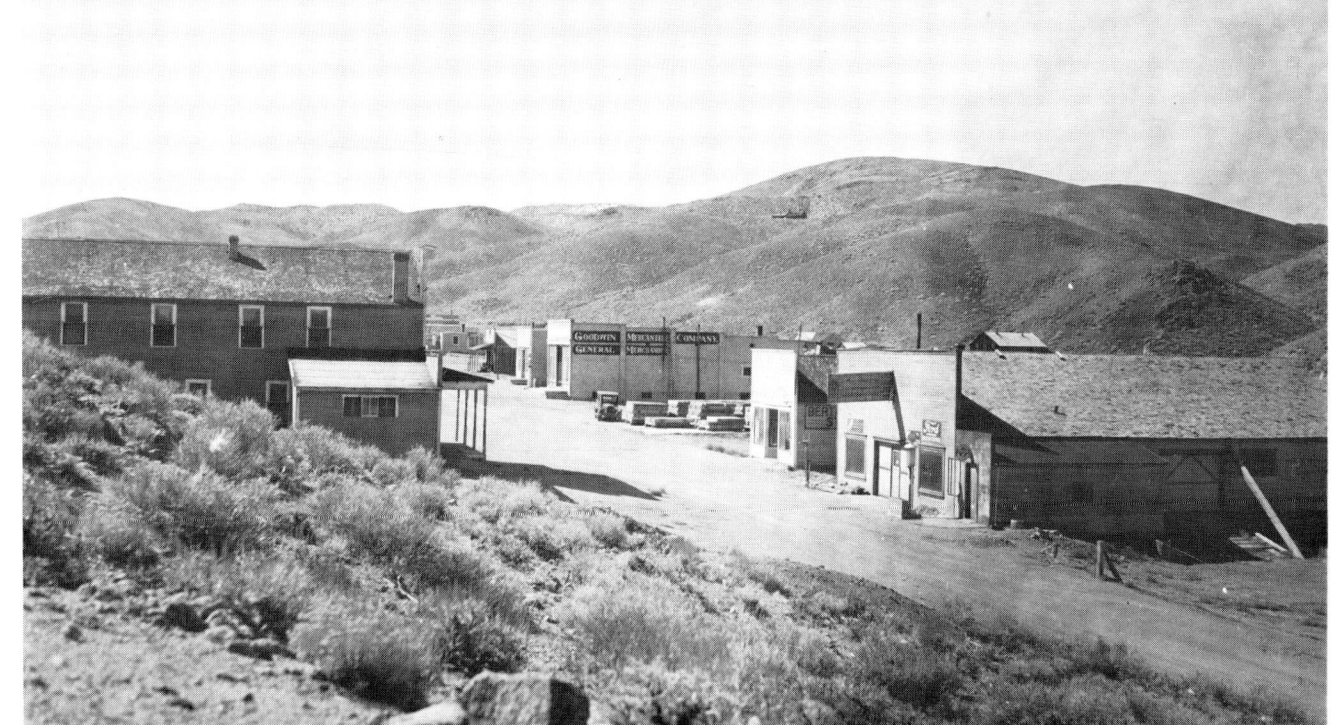

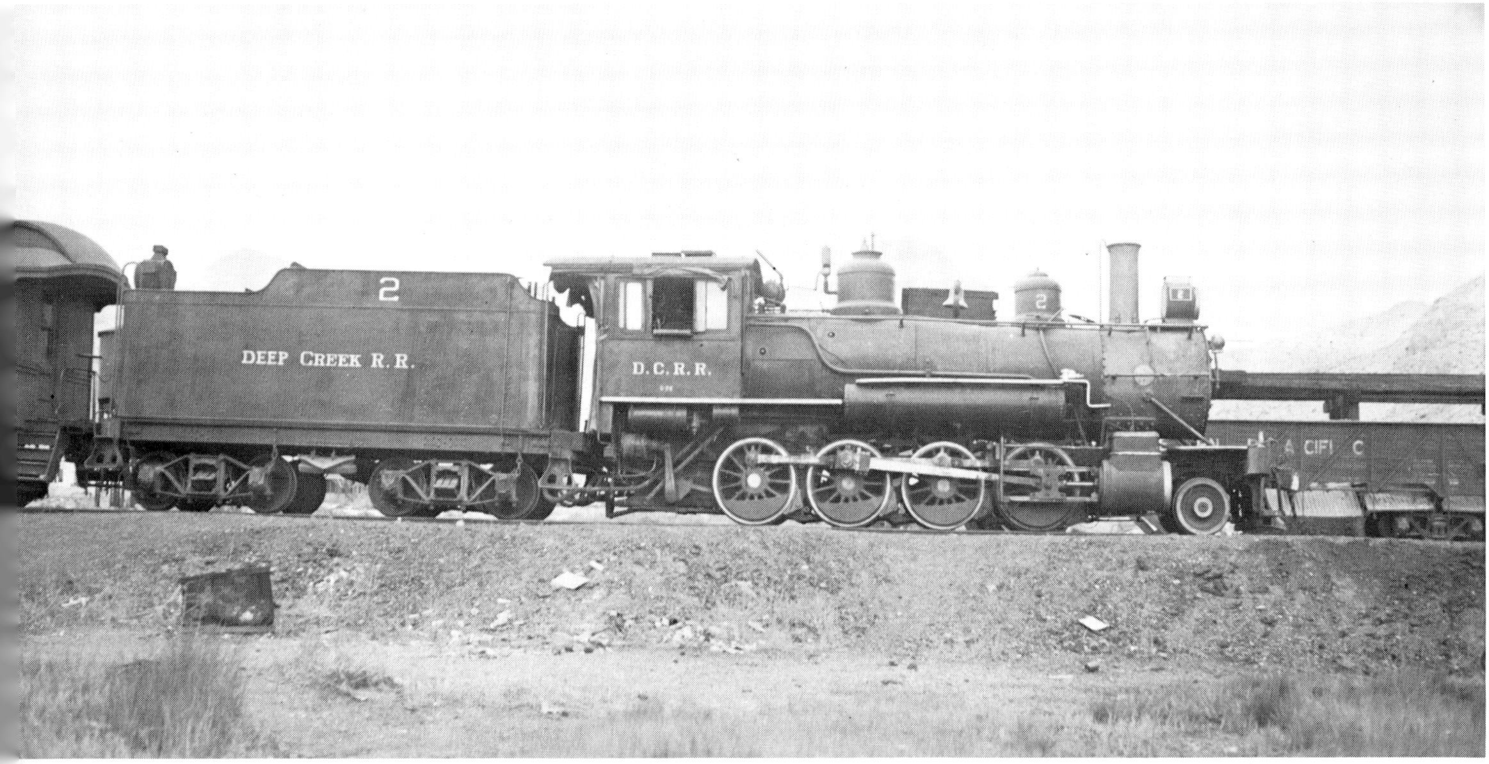

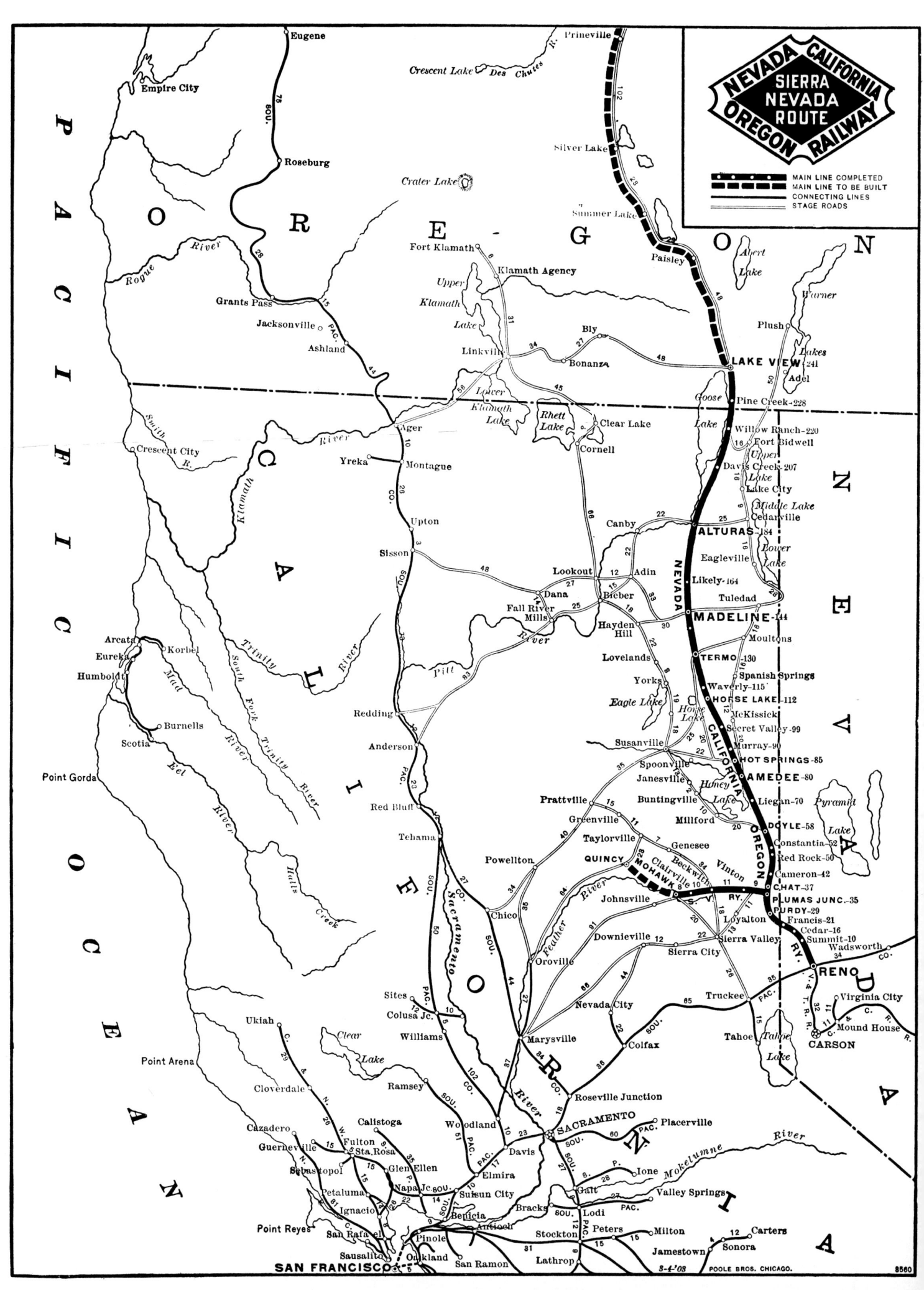

NEVADA-CALIFORNIA-OREGON RAILWAY

The Nevada-California-Oregon Railway was one of the most contrary railroads ever to appear on the Nevada scene. It was originally planned to run south, not north; it was to start at Wadsworth, Nevada, not Reno; it wrangled its way through five changes of title; yet over a period of 50 years it grew from a dream to become one of the twentieth century's longest narrow gauge railroads (275 miles), and segments of it eventually formed important standard gauge links in two of the country's major railroad networks. All factors considered, the performance was quite impressive.

In 1879 Wadsworth, Nevada, was an important jumping-off place for the southerly mining camps of Belmont, Ellsworth, Grantsville, Candelaria and Belleville, the last named being some 133 miles distant. A total of 16 freight teams made regular trips south from Wadsworth, hauling in supplies to the region and returning with ores and salt for the refining of Comstock silver. John T. Davis of San Francisco was visibly impressed by these surface manifestations of activity and investigated further. At the offices of the Central Pacific he learned that a good 44,000,000 pounds of freight were shipped south from Wadsworth each year. Then, visiting the (A. J.) Rhodes Salt Marsh nine miles to the east of Belleville, he discovered equally emphatic statistics on the volume of salt consumed in the refining of Comstock silver. A railroad was definitely indicated; in fact, Rhodes promised Davis daily shipments of 100 tons of salt if such a line were made available.

Davis looked further. The Virginia & Truckee appeared to be content with its line from Reno to Virginia City and was making no overtures for expansion or extension. True, the Nevada Central was constructing southward from Battle Mountain, but it was a long way from completion to its announced destination of Austin, let alone any possible continuation. No competition appeared to be in sight, so in December 1879 Davis formed the Western Nevada Railroad Co. to build south from Wadsworth, Nevada, 55 miles to Walker Lake, including branches. With him in the venture he enlisted the aid of A. J. Rhodes, Silas M. Holmes, a San Francisco business associate, James McMecham, a real estate note broker, and George L. Woods, a former governor of two states — Oregon and Utah.

To raise necessary funds, Davis went to New York in February 1880. Frank F. Fowler, a capitalist, became interested, and when Davis revealed that he could raise $100,000 in California and Nevada, Fowler's enthusiasm increased. Assurances were given that the balance of the funds could be found in New York without difficulty. Fowler then arranged an introduction between Davis and Col. Thomas Moore of Elizabeth, New Jersey, a railroad contractor. With no sense of foreboding, a preliminary agreement was reached between the two men, and the Colonel arranged to make a trip west to examine the route.

Sitting in his New York office, Darius O. Mills (of the V&T) learned of Davis' project and figured its effect upon his own undeveloped plans for a railroad south into the same general area. Thoughts rapidly crystallized into action; a meeting was arranged with Davis wherein Mills outlined his plans to build to Candelaria; and a telegram was dispatched to the V&T's H. M. Yerington to commence work immediately on the Carson & Colorado Railroad. Thus Davis' spark ignited the powder, and the resulting explosion echoed across Nevada.

In April 1880 Colonel Moore came west, and in the company of John C. McTarnahan, a wood man and surveyor, went over the proposed route of the Western Nevada which Davis had now amplified to extend to Bodie and Candelaria. The results of the reconnaissance survey were favorable; Moore was acquiescent; but McTarnahan was dissatisfied and did his best to prevail upon Moore not to build to the south. The Carson & Colorado already was springing into action and a second railroad, the Nevada & Arizona, was contemplating construction of a line in very much the same location. To assess the situation, Moore went to Reno and spent three days meeting local businessmen and discussing the various possibilities. He left for New York convinced that Reno would be a more logical starting point, although still undetermined as to point of direction.

Actually affairs in Reno were rather dull and listless, and the outlook was not particularly attractive. A fire the previous March had destroyed most of the downtown section of the city, leaving 100 families homeless — a proportionately large segment of the population considering the 1880 census tallied only 1,302 people. The bank had failed; grasshoppers had taken over the crops; and declining mining activity on the Comstock had filled Virginia City and the nearby territory with unemployed men. A new railroad would be an important asset to the city, heavily involving the lives of its citizens.

In the light of Moore's revised recommendations and report, Davis abandoned his original scheme and organized a new company on June 1, 1880, called The Nevada and Oregon Railroad Co. (not to be confused with an 1875 company of the same name which did no construction). The railroad was projected to run in both directions from Reno — to the south of Aurora, and to the north to the California-Oregon line at the "Western Shore of Goose Lake." John McTarnahan had won his point, and he and two others joined the group of organizers. At a public meeting in a Reno theater, both Governor Woods and McTarnahan outlined the proposal which had a terrific local appeal because it would make Reno the major rail junction for traffic to the Northwest. (It should be noted that until 1883 there was no direct railroad from Chicago to the Northwest, and that until 1887 travelers bound from California to Oregon or Washington faced a perilous sea voyage or a rugged stage trip of as much as a week's duration.)

The new Nevada & Oregon lost no time in getting organized. A few days later two separate parties of surveyors started out, one in each direction. Davis, with McTarnahan as a guide, began at a point in Reno just east of the V&T (a little south of its bridge) and worked southward toward Carson City, thence on down the Carson and Walker Rivers, reaching Bodie in the month of August. McTarnahan spoke to a crowd in front of the Bodie Bank, made numerous promises, and predicted that wood and vegetables would be cheap and everyone would benefit from the new railroad.

The northern survey was placed in the hands of a newcomer to the organization, A. J. Hatch, Nevada Surveyor General. On July 6 Davis reported that Hatch's party was in Long Valley, California, after "having scaled the summits of the 'everlasting hills' north of Reno with a grade that falls below 100 feet to the mile, thus securing an easy outlet for the iron horse." Obviously pleased, Davis continued, "As this was the greatest obstacle to overcome, we are happy to say that we have been disappointed in a very pleasant direction."

At its meeting in Carson City on August 26, 1880, the Board of Directors was divided (the first of many such situations to come). The majority favored the building of the northern segment first; the minority felt the southern leg would be the most advisable. Apparently the minority prevailed, for an agreement was drawn up with Moore providing for construction of the railroad as stock subscriptions were made, in the following pattern: The Carson Division from Reno to Carson City (30 miles) with a 20-mile branch from Washoe Summit to Virginia City would be built as soon as subscriptions of $250,000 were realized; the 31-mile Reno Division to Beckwourth Pass would be next in line for construction; then the 105-mile Bodie Division would follow to complete the line. It was estimated that net income, after all charges, on the completed road would amount to some $350,000 annually.

John Davis, the organizer, was furious. He not only refused to sign the contract as drawn but resigned as president and director in protest, returning to his pulverizing and grinding business in San Francisco. General Hatch, the surveyor, assumed the presidency and affixed his signature to the agreement.

Subscription books were opened in Reno and surrounding towns, but nobody rushed to make any large pledges. Nobody could; no money was available. E. V. Spencer of Susanville managed to obtain a few, sporadic pledges, but doubtless even these failed to materialize. Frank Fowler's New York financing was contingent upon local subscriptions; and obviously none were to be had. It was only because General Hatch, with great zeal, advanced some $14,000 of his own money that any progress was possible. Two engineers worked night and day in the railroad's new office opposite the courthouse in order to finish the engineering details before Moore returned from New York, for Moore's arrival was to signify the beginning of construction.

Late in November Colonel Moore finally returned to Nevada, but illness confined him to his room for the first several days. Early in December a number of meetings were held, and two new contracts were finally drawn and signed with Moore on December 4, 1880, providing for many reversals of previous plans. Included were provisions that the 31-mile section from Reno to Beckwourth Pass would be the first to be constructed; work would start when the contractor was satisfied that $100,000 in stock subscriptions would be realized; then the company would pay Moore the $500 cash which Davis had promised when Moore first came west, plus another $20,000 upon the shipment of 1,000 tons of rails and splices. When these rails arrived in Reno, Moore was to receive as compensation a portion of the Company's bonds and stock. After shipment of the balance of the rails needed for the first 31 miles, Moore would then have received a total of $310,000 of N&O First Mortgage Bonds plus $450,000 of the $600,000 of stock outstanding.

Bad weather (the Susanville stage was stuck in three feet of snow at the summit north of Reno) and various business arrangements in San Francisco delayed the breaking of ground until the afternoon of December 22, 1880. On Evans' field opposite Brookins' house, George Woods made a long speech dealing with the plans of the railroad — how it would eventually extend to the Columbia River with one branch through Linkville (Klamath Falls) to the Rogue River Valley and another branch to Eugene. He expressed explicit (if misguided) faith in Colonel Moore, then went on to say that the area to be traversed was hidden from the outside world, "but now, by the talismanic touch of railroads, the curtain will be pulled aside and its beauties and excellencies revealed." Following Woods' speech, the Rev. W. R. Jenvey invoked the Divine Blessing on the work, following which Colonel Moore broke the ground, throwing the first shovelful of earth over the crowd by way of baptism.

That night, before Moore left on the train for New York to raise additional money, contracts were signed with H. L. W. Knox for the first three miles of grading and with John Sturgeon for the necessary trestlework. Knox organized his work quickly and a few days later commenced grading operations with a force of 20 men in order to take advantage of the moist and frost-free ground. Sturgeon also started on his phase of the operation, contracting with Katz and Henry's sawmill to cut the timber for the N&O trestles. By January 28 men were completing the heavy fill behind Evans' slaughterhouse while Sturgeon was fitting up timbers for the trestles, the first one a mile and a half from town.

The job was well along on the third mile when Knox suddenly suspended work on February 21, 1881, and filed a lien for $5,328. Under the terms of the grading contract, February 20 was the date established for the first settlement, and neither Moore nor his money had put in an appearance when due. The men had an expectant attitude toward their pay, and the Reno *Gazette* said that the "N&O remains in a state of suspended animation" — a polite way of saying that they were broke.

Basically the trouble stemmed from the lack of local stock subscriptions. Money from this source, or from temporary bank loans, would have to finance the first five miles of finished railroad. Then, using the completed portion as security, 8% bonds could be issued at the rate of $10,000 per mile (a total of $50,000) which Moore had arranged with Moran Brothers, New York bankers, to discount at 80% of par. Such a transaction would have brought some $40,000 into the till.

In Reno money was tight, however, as only about $400 in actual cash had been paid in stock subscriptions to that time. Following Moore's departure for New York the previous December, President Hatch tried his best to raise money to keep the work progressing. Paxton, Curtis & Co. had refused a loan; and Hatch, who had already advanced some $14,000 on his own, did not want to put up his home for a greatly needed $6,000 more, although he did hypothecate his salary at a considerable discount to keep the surveys going.

In January 1881 Hatch wrote to Moore that he was becoming embarrassed financially and that unless something were done, he would attach the property (which only consisted of a mile of grade, some maps, profiles, and survey stakes). Moore replied: "If attachment must come (which God forbid), save my interest." (It is interesting to note that up to that time Moore had not put up so much as a single dollar.) Moore then went on to say that the company must finance itself from subscriptions and that it was an outrage to call on him for money when the company still owed him the initial $500.

Then George Woods went east to join Moore in New York, and in February Hatch began receiving communiques: "$80,000 subscribed here"; "$25,000 in bank"; "Moore has purchased the iron"; "Moore is coming back heeled with coin to go on with the work." They were most encouraging advices; unfortunately they were not true.

Finally Woods and Moore in New York signed a contract establishing February 20 as a cut-off date and providing that all expenditures prior to that date be paid from the $20,000 anticipated receipts from stock subscriptions (this in spite of the poor results already demonstrated). In addition, stock subscriptions after the February 20 date would go to Moore on his contract, and Moore would also receive $450,000 in stock and $310,000 in bonds as soon as the certificates were engraved.

When it came time for the directors in Reno to ratify the agreement, President Hatch refused, feeling that it would preclude any chances of recovering the $30,000 due himself and others for actual cash advanced. The Board did ratify the contract, however, at a meeting held in the back end of a caboose standing on a siding near the Depot Hotel. This and other events convinced Hatch that he should resign the presidency, following which (in April 1881) he attached the maps, profiles and drawings of the road to secure payment of the money due him. Two prominent Reno hardware merchants, A. J. Manning and W. F. Berry, went on bond to secure the release of the attachment. Later, when Hatch won his suit against the railroad, much to their sorrow these two men learned that they had unknowingly assumed liability for the $13,000 judgment and had to dig up $5,000 for the initial installment due in September 1882.

Governor Woods and Colonel Moore, apparently fortified with funds of undetermined origin, returned to Reno on April 7, full of placations and saying that everything would be satisfactorily adjusted. Woods became the new president, and the *Gazette* facetiously remarked: "A good strong pull, altogether, would now set the ball to rolling finely; but Reno people never have pulled together, and it looks as if they never will."

The *Gazette* appeared to be correct. One group of Reno people felt that Moore would never build the railroad; so they made plans to take over the project and resume construction. Moore's friends moved faster; on April 25, 1881, they organized a new company called (simply) Nevada and Oregon Railroad Co. (the initial word "The" being omitted) with essentially the same principals still in control. A newcomer, Judge E. D. Wheeler of Oakland, California, joined the group and subscribed to 3,000 shares. That same morning the directors of the old company met and deeded all rights over to the new company.

Immediately Knox put his graders back to work, although men were hard to find. Even Ah Jack could not fill all his requests for Chinese labor. By the middle of May, 240 men including 80 Chinese were pushing the grading along. Two miles of roadbed were ready for the laying of ties and rail, and deliveries of these items were expected momentarily.

For once good fortune had come to the aid of the harassed undertaking. Moore had persuaded the Pacific Rolling Mills of San Francisco to take his order for the initial five miles of track at a total price of $18,000. Furthermore, considering the risky circumstances under which the N&O was being constructed, Moore had accomplished the spectacular feat of obtaining credit for $10,000 of this amount. Cash for the remaining $8,000 balance was advanced by Hugh J. McMurray, a San Francisco wholesale grocer, who also became a stockholder in the new railroad. As soon as the first five miles of rail were laid, Moore would be in a position to secure the first $50,000 of First Mortgage Bonds for which the Moran Brothers had agreed to give him $40,000 cash. This money could be used to pay off the obligations, and construction could continue.

May 28, 1881 was a red-letter day. E. C. McClellan, N&O civil engineer, drove the first spike, following which a gang of 75 men started pushing the rails forward. By June 11, three miles of track were in place, and in spite of delays attending trestle construction the first five miles were virtually completed by June 13. This triggered the release of the bonds, and on the strength of that fact it was reported that Moore had purchased the first locomotive for use on the line. Excitement was in the air, and as Moore headed east to cash in the bonds, the N&O hands headed for Reno and a strenuous, well-earned, pay day celebration. The following morning Reno streets were strewn with manly graders, while "one found a sleeping apartment in Loomis' show window."

When another new stockholder, Daniel W. Balch of San Francisco, joined the ranks in June 1881, the railroad project finally seemed to be getting under way. The added strength to the company lent credence to the optimism of two directors who talked of a branch line westward into Plumas County, California, and even inspected a possible route as far as Quincy.

By July, when Moore returned from the East, approximately 400 men were on the job and some 15 to 20 kegs of powder were being used for each blast in the stubborn rock cuts. A dispute between Superintendent Holmes and a gang of Chinese laborers resulted in a lively skirmish, following which the Chinamen went out on strike for a short period.

Then the first rolling stock arrived — five narrow gauge flat cars from the Lake Tahoe R.R. (Glenbrook). Early in August the SANTA CRUZ, a second-hand locomotive from California, was delivered, looking for all the world like a boy on horseback as it sat perched up on a flat car. It made its first trip on August 8, pushing the five flat cars loaded with men and boys anxious to participate in the historical event. Sam Hilliard filled the post of engineer while Nate Kendall fulfilled the duties of conductor. Two days later another trip took the directors and friends out to the sixth mile where a celebration was held to the accompaniment of the "usual champagne ceremony."

Beyond the seventh mile, Moore suddenly changed the location of the route from that originally surveyed along the northeastern slope of Peavine Mountain (which the Western Pacific uses today) to one that was six miles longer and worked around to the northeast before swinging back in a large loop to Purdy. The result of the change was that a 37-mile railroad was necessary to reach the base of Beckwourth Pass where formerly it would have been 31 miles. Coupled with the elongation of the route, Moore sought to conserve his funds by stinting on the quality of the work; the cuts and embankments were made smaller than originally provided, thus subsequently creating operational hazards, particularly during winter snow storms.

Labor continued to be a problem. It was most difficult to get men and virtually impossible to satisfy them once they were hired. Various of the directors received threatening letters from time to time. John Sturgeon, the bridge contractor, received this anonymous warning:

August 21st, 1881

"Mr. Sturgeon.—Sir: as a friend of yours & do not want to see Eny foul happen to you but would say to you if you do not quit hireing a Lot of Strange men as you are and Let the carpenters Lay of that has famely in Reno you will be Roughly dealt with I am afraid yours truly A. Friend."

By September 8 progress was evident. A full 10 miles of rails had been laid (thus releasing the second $50,000 of bonds), and some 21 miles of grading had been completed. Beyond the rail head the roadbed stretched out across Lemmon Valley "as smooth and pretty as Harlem Lane." Several teams were busily engaged in taking water to the grading gangs from the few available springs. Four miles from Cold Springs, a new camp was set up to accommodate the men doing advance work on the project.

On the surface, the picture looked good. True, there was a general division of feeling about Moore in Reno. Delays in paying the workmen and local suppliers had left a poor impression, but other people favored Moore's accomplishments. Charles Moran, the New York banker, came out from the East and appeared to be satisfied with the progress of the work.

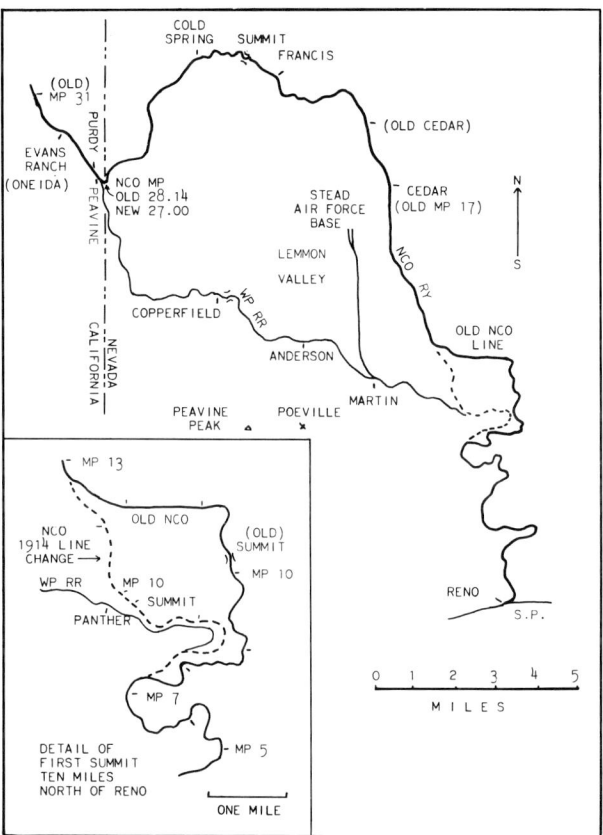

Underneath the surface, however, Moore was not getting along very well with the directors. Moore's eastern education and his devotion to small details constantly rankled the westerners. What was worse, no attempt had ever been made by Moore to account properly for any of the moneys he had received, let alone to reveal where they had been spent. None of the advances made by the directors had been reimbursed. Over the months the antagonism increased, and the grumblings grew into loud complaints. Although Moore really controlled the company through his prospective holdings of a majority of the stock, he was powerless to take any action in the situation until a set of by-laws were written for the company specifying the terms of the directors. As matters stood, the directors could remain in office until removed by the stockholders.

Frank Fowler, the New York capitalist who originally introduced Moore to Davis back in 1880, was still very much interested in the project. He, together with his friends in New York, had subscribed to $80,000 of stock (800 shares), paying for it by installments. When Fowler came out to Nevada from New York, he was shocked to discover that, after five months of operations of the new company, no by-laws had been written for the corporation. Together with Moore, he called a meeting of the stockholders for September 27, 1881, to remove and replace the present directors.

The directors, however, had no intention of taking the situation lying down. A special meeting of the Board was called for September 25, two days preceding the stockholders' meeting, to determine a course of action. For some unexplained reason, Squire C. Scoville, Secretary of the company, was conspicuous by his absence. To obtain the Company's books from the safe, the directors found it necessary to call in a locksmith. When opened, the safe was bare; Scoville, acting on behalf of Moore, had taken the books to San Francisco. This still did not deter the anti-Moore faction of the Board led by Judge Wheeler and James McMecham. Being in the majority at the meeting, they were able to issue themselves 50,000 shares of stock. Since Moore and his friends only held something like 5,000 shares, the balance of voting power for the forthcoming meeting was completely reversed.

Moore promptly obtained an injunction from a Nevada Court restraining the Wheeler faction from transferring or voting its stock at the special meeting. Judge Wheeler retaliated by obtaining an order from the Federal Court modifying the injunction, thus permitting the stock to be voted.

The afternoon of the stockholders' meeting, a number of graders reported to the railroad's office, ostensibly to get their pay, but in reality to render physical support to Moore's program. When the Wheeler party showed up, Moore allowed as how they were not stockholders and suggested that they leave. Wheeler and McMecham did not take kindly to this idea, and when efforts were made to eject McMecham by force, wild shooting commenced. Daniel Balch and Squire Scoville (Company secretary) were hit. Great excitement ensued; people came down from Virginia City and up from Carson City to learn the details of the incident. Scoville died six days later, leaving behind a widow and two small children. (His widow later established a kindergarten and subsequently a young ladies' school in New York City.) Balch recovered from his wounds, and became president of the company a few weeks later. For some months after the shooting there were two boards of directors, but Moore's board eventually re-established control.

The inquest went on for ten days and was dutifully recorded in the Reno *Gazette*. A reading of it impresses one with the innocence claimed by each of the parties involved. During the inquest, every man carrying a gun that day made it a point to say that ordinarily he did not go about armed, but that on that particular day he thought it might be a good idea to stop in at Parrott's to have his gun checked "just in case." One of the most baffling aspects of the situation was that after the shooting there were only three empty gun chambers, yet eight bullets were located. "This would indicate cool work on the part of the combatants," commented the *Gazette*.

The grand jury considered the testimony but adjourned after three days, not finding sufficient evidence to warrant hope of conviction. Their action was approved by the *San Francisco Post* and the *Carson Index*, but down in wicked Bodie it was roundly condemned in the *Free Press*. "The Reno railroad wreckers or murderers, whatever they may be called, have all been discharged and the disgusting affair has been settled. Not even a tar bucket is to be used. Let some poor tramp steal a pail of slops or a loaf of stale bread and see how quick the outraged community will rise up."

Following the gunfight, the names of Moore vs. Wheeler, McMecham, Sunderland, Coffin, et al. echoed in Nevada and New York courtrooms for several years. Wheeler's group charged that Moore had not lived up to his contract, one example being that a new, not second-hand, locomotive should have been furnished. They also accused Moore of appropriating $12,000 for his personal use to which Moore retaliated by slapping a $500,000 defamation-of-character suit on them. The original modifying order permitting the voting of the 50,000 shares of stock was vacated in November 1881, thus endorsing the election of Moore's directors. The suit was carried to its conclusion, and Judge Sabin ruled that the issue of the stock was fraudulent and void. His reaction, as reported by the press, was: "The case was one of the most outrageous that ever came under his notice. There is no shadow of right or decency in it. He characterized the offers of the interested parties to sell out for large sums of money as utterly corrupt and such as no honest men would think of." A prominent Carson lawyer said that every one of the Ten Commandments had been violated but one. Asked which one, he said: "The seventh. There is nothing to *show* that they committed adultery."

Money continued to be scarce in the N&O household. Time after time McMurray was prevailed upon to help the struggling line. Before the shooting he advanced $1,000 to salve the pleas of the field engineers who, not having been paid for months, did not have enough money to buy so much as a meager loaf of bread. Now, in the fall of 1881, Moore and Fowler approached him again for an additional advance of $22,962 to finance the purchase of the next seven miles of rail. Apparently McMurray could not refuse; the money was forthcoming; but this time he bought the rail himself, taking a lien for $22,962 on the property as security.

By November a few new freight cars and one new passenger car, built by Carter Bros. of Newark, California, arrived along with the first shipment of the seven miles of additional rail. The grading for the 31 miles of road was nearly completed, bringing it past the David Evans' ranch in Long Valley, California; the forces were dismissed, most of them went south to work on the C&C. The ranch became the terminal for the railroad and was variously referred to as Oneida, Antelope, and Evans. It is interesting to note that, years previously, in this same ranch house which typically doubled as an inn (burned about 1950), the planning took place for the famous Verdi train robbery of 1870 (see Central Pacific).

In mid-November a climax was reached. Creditors were hounding the doorstep; there was no money in the till; no accurate accountings had been furnished by Moore to show what moneys had been received or how they had been spent; even director McMurray had not been repaid for his $22,962 advance. With full pressure brought to bear upon him by even his former friends, Moore finally threw in the sponge, broke his contract, and on November 17, 1881, he left for the East for the last time. The burden of completing the road was shifted to Fowler, and later to Balch and McMurray.

A large party made a 15-mile inspection trip to the end of track late in November and reported that the curves in the first 10 miles of road to the summit rivaled those of the world-renowned, curvacious V&T.

Work ceased in December 1881. A total of 17 miles of track had been laid; then the money ran out. Rails had to be paid for immediately, as well as labor, or liens would apply. There was not a dollar in the treasury, and interest was coming due on the bonds. This time Daniel Balch responded, advancing sufficient funds to meet the most pressing obligations, but he could not finance everything. Locally the feeling was hostile. As many supplies as possible were purchased from local merchants on credit; then payment was forestalled as long as possible. The result was a general and constant clamoring for payment. Manning & Berry was the concern most severely affected, for they had supplied the majority of the picks, shovels, blasting powder, etc., which went into the construction of the road.

The directors were obliged to hold innumerable conferences, both among themselves and with the creditors. "One time I remember we were in session, and a lot of fellows came in there and wanted to hang us," Balch recalled at a later date. Also outstanding in retrospect was the time spent in securing releases from liens (88 were on file at one time). Every holder had to be "interviewed probably from one to fifty times, and they had to be treated with liquor; they had to be gone over." Balch's constant hope was that the firm would be in funds, but it never was. The only inducement he could hold out to creditors was the hope that when the road was finished and a going concern, enough cash could be generated to pull through and settle properly all creditors' bills.

For the local merchants, dealing with Moore had been complicated. Some items he had ordered charged to the N&O; others had been charged to himself; still others had been charged to a "construction account." Moore's personal account with Manning & Berry tallied a modest balance of $15,000 — credit extended on the representations of Hatch and John Sunderland, then the president and treasurer of the N&O, respectively. On top of everything, Moore considered the locomotive and flat cars his personal property, and Moore had skipped the state. Manning & Berry suffered the most. Not only were they left holding a large unpaid account, but they also had the liability for the costly Hatch judgment for which an initial $5,000 installment was coming due in September 1882. On February 18, 1882, the personal property of Thomas

Moore was sold by the sheriff. Manning & Berry successfully bid $3,000 for the locomotive SANTA CRUZ and the 15 cars, and promptly leased them back to the N&O from June 1, 1882, to February 1, 1883, at a daily rental of $10.

Included in the sheriff's sale were 2,720 shares of N&O stock owned by Thomas Moore. On the basis of a judgment held by McMurray against Moore, the stock was sold for $4,000, and the money used to pay a portion of the sums owed to McMurray.

Meanwhile, back in New York, Fowler and Balch were attempting to resolve the major financial problems between Moore and the N&O. According to Moore's estimates, it would cost about $145,000 to complete the railroad although only 17 miles of rails were down and approximately 32 miles of roadbed graded. Through these representations Moore had been able to sell 210 bonds to the Morans, leaving 100 bonds to finance the balance of the first section of the railroad. On April 26, 1882, an agreement was drawn up providing for the issuance of 100 bonds in small amounts at 75% of par instead of the former 80%. Included was a provision that the last $22,200 of the $75,000 proceeds would not be paid until McMurray had agreed to release his $22,962 lien on the seven miles of rail. In the best of good faith, and relying on promises by Balch that the company would reimburse him in some way, McMurray did sign the release, but he was never repaid as Balch was helpless to accomplish any payments.

The N&O proposals for settlement of outstanding accounts were not well received in Reno. The company had no credit; McMurray had lost his entire fortune. Still it was decided to go ahead with the construction anyhow. By pledging his home in San Francisco, McMurray succeeded in raising the necessary $7,000 from the Pacific Bank with which to buy two miles of iron. Work began on May 22, 1882, after a lapse of five months. With the first two miles laid, the bonds were released to the Morans, and from the proceeds of their first draft, the bank was repaid and a portion of the creditors' liens satisfied. With each two-mile interval, the process was repeated and the work continued. Ties on which to lay the rails were supplied by Lonkey and Smith under the same basic arrangement.

By August 7, rails had reached the 25th mile post. A 10% deposit was made on a new locomotive from the H. K. Porter Co. based on promised financing by the Pacific Bank; but when the time came for delivery of the equipment, the bank reneged and McMurray lost another $937. By late September rails were down all the way to Oneida, 30 miles from Reno, and grading was being extended for an additional two miles beyond. Two weeks later, winter weather forced suspension of construction for the season.

TRAINS OPERATE TO ONEIDA — AT LAST

Regular trains to Oneida began operating on a 2½-hour schedule on October 2, 1882. There, Meylert's connecting stages provided transportation as far as Susanville. The combination service was important to Nevada and Oregon, and if Meylert's stage was late on its southbound journeying, the N&O's train obligingly waited for several hours.

A crowd of nine people made the inaugural run on the first day of service. The comforts of the new passenger car were greatly appreciated, particularly that October which was one of the rainiest months in the past 30 years. Patronage improved; Uncle Jake McKissick, a Long Valley pioneer rancher, helped fill the coach to capacity one trip; and other people of note began riding the cars. One morning, after the well-filled train had been on its way for a few minutes, it was stopped and backed to the Reno station again while someone sought out a missing passenger who had overslept. The individual who climbed aboard with eyes looking like boiled chestnuts was none other than A. W. Keddie, the Feather River surveyor.

Quite understandably, freight service was not overlooked in the scheme of things. The first carload of lumber originated at Bragg & Schooling's new mill in Long Valley, was floated down a four-mile flume and then teamed to the railroad. The first freight losses were bound to occur — and did. One morning it was discovered that some whiskey had been stolen from the Oneida freight shed; the barrel was there, but minus part of the contents. Investigation revealed that some person had crawled under the building, found a crack in the floor, and carefully tapped the whiskey barrel. On removing the desired quantity, the hol had been thoughtfully plugged, perhaps in anticipation of a subsequent indulgence. The driller was never identified, but the following day there appeared a suspiciously large number of drunken Indians.

The railroad's first excursion was run on a wet, chilly November evening when 60 people left Reno for Dave Evans' hotel in Oneida to partake of his good food and enjoy a bit of dancing to the music of Roff's band. Others began to discover new and different uses for the road's facilities; hunters found to their amazement that there were plenty of deer all along the winding N&O route. In Reno, local pride for the road was increasing and not to be taken lightly; when a stranger referred to the locomotive SANTA CRUZ as a grasshopper, he was promptly knocked down.

By the turn of the year, passenger business had declined and the *Gazette* was unconscionably naming each daily passenger. Not much space was required — one day only four people entrained for the trip north, but this was still a big improvement over business on the V&T — which had only one passenger, and he was a deadhead. Some relief was afforded in January when Phi Bates shipped the first carload of beef over N&O rails, but the innovation was not repeated with regularity. During the last three months of 1882 *gross* revenues had only amounted to $2,173, a far cry from the optimistic annual *net* income of $350,000 projected by the incorporators. On January 29, 1883, the last trains were run, and the line was closed down, ostensibly to effect some needed repairs to its only locomotive, but more practically for financial reasons.

In his report to the California Secretary of State on February 1, 1883, Balch had an opportunity to express his personal feelings, and he took complete advantage of the situation. After advising that the books, vouchers and accounts had been lost, stolen or mislaid by the former officers, he went on: "In consequence of the chronic impecuniosity of the corporation it has not had enough funds to comply with the laws of the State in relation to keeping of account books, as required by law, as the officers have received no compensation since they were connected with the company, and have been compelled to find for themselves and work for nothing.

"No dividend has ever been declared by this accursed corporation, and it is a safe bet that none ever will be. . . . The net profits of the road have been nothing, as the corporation was conceived in iniquity and born in fraud. Every honest friend of the enterprise has been swindled and robbed, and disaster has overtaken all persons who have been connected with it in any capacity." They were harsh words, but quite understandable, for even Moore had gone back on him.

When Charles Moran came out from New York to look over his investment, represented by 310 bonds of $1,000 face value with 8% interest payable semi-annually, he was perturbed. Four semi-annual bond coupons had not been paid, he contended, so he had instructed the Trustee to file suit. Then he received a big surprise. Although he held only bonds authorized to be issued, it developed that there were 147 more bonds outstanding of equal $1,000 face value. When Moran then filed a new complaint to declare the extra 147 bonds to be null and void, the facts began to come out. Apparently the Board of Directors, in desperation at trying to meet the obligations of the virtually bankrupt railroad, had formally requested the Union Trust Company to turn over the remaining bonds the previous November (1882). Then, in February 1883, to settle the outstanding debts with the creditors (including those of Manning & Berry and director H. J. McMurray), the 147 bonds were issued in lieu of cash at the same discount rate of 80¢ on the dollar that Moran had obtained. Without recourse, Manning & Berry temporarily became insolvent until matters could be adjusted.

The ensuing investigation was long and protracted, with considerable testimony taken by special examiners. The contracts were cited, and the difficulties under which the railroad was built were explained in detail. In the fall of 1883 the case was submitted to the U. S. District Court in Carson City; in May 1884 Judge Sabin found that the 147 bonds had no value, pointing to the understanding and agreements that limited the issuance to $10,000 per mile of completed road. McMurray et al. filed an appeal with the U. S. Supreme Court in 1886, which was accepted for review two years later. On March 3, 1890, the decision was rendered, splitting the holders of the 147 bonds into two groups — those who knew of the restriction on issuance, and those who did not. As Manning, Berry, and McMurray had all been members of the Board of Directors, they were considered to be informed and their bonds were ruled to be invalid. Entitled to share in the trust estate were 31 bonds, while the claims of the remaining 20 bonds were dismissed with the statement that each claim would depend upon the individual circumstances. Charles Moran made cash settlements with the holders of those bonds ruled valid; McMurray was disappointed again.

In spite of legal wrangles (which frequently take years in the processing), railroading must go on, and Jerry Schooling provided the spark which put life back in the defunct N&O. Jerry wanted to ship lumber from his Long Valley mill; so a plan was evolved whereby the railroad was leased to Judge Webster who felt that it could be operated for $20 a day, barring accidents and wear and tear. The SANTA CRUZ was sent to the V&T shops in Carson City for repairs, and on June 22, 1883, the locomotive began making regular trips. In fact, so much lumber had piled up at Bragg & Schooling's mill that two round trips a day were necessary for a time. Two summer specials were also run to add to the revenue—a ladies' picnic special and what was called a "country special" which brought people to Reno to see John Robinson's "3 Strictly Moral Circuses 3."

On September 3, W. L. Berry, former partner in Manning & Berry, fulfilled an ambition of long duration when he took over operation of the N&O. Among other things, he arranged with Dave Evans for the quartering of teams of patrons from the north at Oneida so the people could proceed to Reno by train. Regular newspaper advertising was instituted; business picked up. Grain as well as from three to five carloads of lumber daily began to move by rail. One Saturday 400 boxes of apples were shipped. When Nate Kendall was called for jury duty, Berry took over as conductor, and the trains continued to roll.

Fall dissolved into the white of winter, and a snowplow plus two stiff splint brooms were attached to the pilot of the SANTA CRUZ. Its snow performance was surprisingly good. When it came to cuts filled with snow from three to five feet deep, "the little puffer flew into them with 120 pounds of steam, seemed to enjoy the sport, throwing snow over the passenger car and giving the passengers the impression of a small-sized avalanche." The next day it did not do as well, became stuck, and was finally dug out two days later. Then it was derailed while bucking the snow, and an all-night job was required to get it back on the track. To clear the road, 50 men were required; even then, normal operations were not resumed until two troublesome weeks later. (The Central Pacific was having its troubles too; 10 engines were required out of Truckee to push a snowplow through the drifts.) Once back in operation, the N&O handled its first shipment of livestock—a buggy horse—and a few days later undertook another shipment of perishables—28 cases of Sierra Valley butter. When a group of 46 Reno people wanted to join an equal number of ranchers at Dave Evans' hostelry for an all-night dancing party, the railroad was the logical means of transportation even though the festivities did not end until 4:00 A.M. with the train returning to Reno at 6:30 A.M.

In compliance with court orders, the N&O property was sold on the steps of the Reno courthouse by a U. S. Marshal on April 17, 1884. Moran Bros. were the only bidders, and for $372,-534.21 found themselves the owners of a railroad of rather dubious distinction. Not included in the sale was the equipment, which A. J. Manning quickly remarked belonged to him (being rented to the railroad on a daily use basis.)

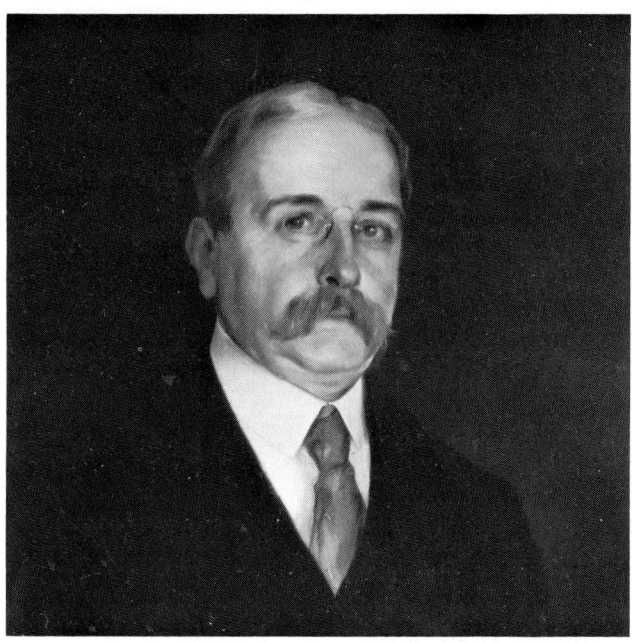

Amedee Moran (1811-1895)

Railroading was not a venture foreign to the nature of the banking firm of Moran Bros. Charles Moran (1811-1895) had started the organization when he came to this country from Belgium as a young man. Originally engaged in the dry goods business, he subsequently took in a partner and operated as an importing house under the name of Moran & Iselin until 1852. Then, with his brother Theodore, he founded the firm of Moran Bros., and because of his successful floating of the Erie R.R. loan in 1856, he became president of that road for two years. Theodore retired shortly after Charles returned to the banking business, and Charles' two sons, Amedee Depau and D. Comyn, entered the firm. The present Charles Moran, whose career included writing and a term as naval attaché in Peru, joined his father (Amedee) and became a partner in 1908. In 1915, following Amedee's death, the partnership was dissolved. At other times the firm of Moran Bros. was interested in other railroads including the Texas Central and the Toledo, Peoria & Western.

A report of a trip on the N&O in May 1884 started with genial manager Berry saying to his fireman, "There, there, that's enough of that chin music"; and to his passengers, "Get aboard and go out with us." And away they went, up and out of the meadows, over long, wooden trestles, climbing the first ten miles with ease. A fine view was noted as they crossed Lemmon Flat, a dry lake area which

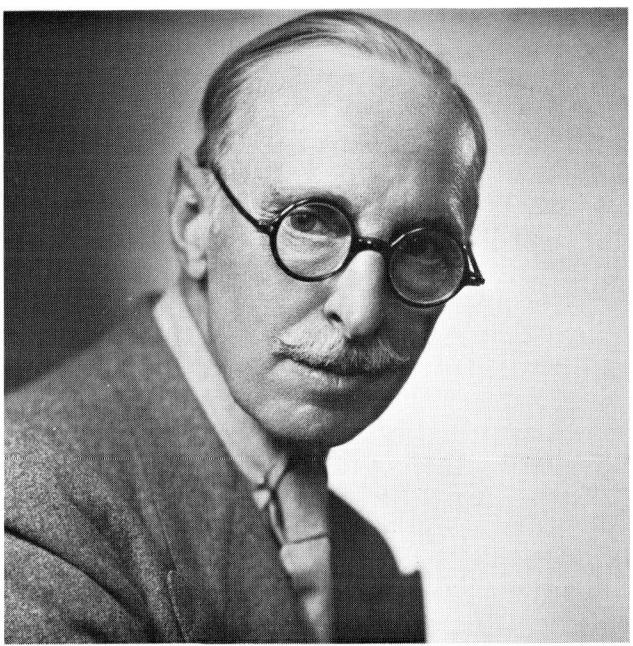

Charles Moran II, last president of the N-C-O.

two weeks before had been a 2,000-acre pond, the waters of which had almost evaporated completely. Across the way was Fielding Lemmon's fertile ranch, fed by springs from Peavine Mountain. A stop for water was made at Cold Springs before proceeding on across the state line into California to the terminus at the old Antelope Ranch (Oneida) where Dave Evans had 55 acres planted in wheat. The 30-mile trip normally took about 2-2½ hours, but was still an improvement over an even longer and bumpy stage ride.

A few weeks later, on June 11, 1884, operations were again halted and a last train run. The SANTA CRUZ had been running for a year without shopping, and there was no other locomotive to take her place.

Under the law, the N&O stockholders had six months from the judicial sale (April 17, 1884) in which to redeem their property. Realizing such a step was financially impossible, they accepted the invitation of Moran's attorney to turn the road over in July, and Edgar L. Heriot, a man with experience on various southern roads, was placed in charge that same month. Heriot made a number of inspection trips with Berry as co-pilot; some lumber was brought in; a church excursion was run; but no regular service was offered the public. Grading was started on a new five-mile extension on October 1, and the contract for the work was given to J. J. Holmes. Shortly afterward, track laying followed, and ties were supplied by Bragg & Schooling's saw mill. On December 8, 1884, the rails reached Junction (House), thereby bringing the total trackage to 37 miles.

In January 1885 Heriot was busy putting the railroad in first-class shape. The name was changed to Nevada & California Railroad, but ownership was still vested in Moran Bros. A depot was built in Reno, and a new passenger car arrived from the East. The old coach was converted into a combination baggage-smoking car. The straw color with dark trim outside contrasted pleasantly with the inside oak paneling which was painted an alternate black and white. Two new Baldwin locomotives arrived in do-it-yourself kit form, the pieces filled four flat cars. In spite of their complexity, they were promptly set up. Then the SANTA CRUZ, the N-C-O's pioneer locomotive, was sold to G. W. Chubbuck, a Lake Tahoe lumberman.

Regular trips from Reno to Junction, at the foot of Beckwourth Pass, began on March 2, the first return trip bringing in $60,000 in bullion from the Plumas-Eureka mine. At Junction (soon renamed Moran and still later Cuba P. O.) a depot, complete with waiting room and office, was erected and John Sumpter placed in command. Additional facilities included a warehouse, a store, and an office for the D. W. Earl and Meylert joint stage agents.

A short distance south of the N&C depot was Junction House where Chat Roberts hosted. The Roberts boys were considered a tough lot; Chat, the father, was in the Verdi train robbery; other members of this family burned R. N. Smith's lumber mill three times. A number of shootings took place in the bar—two of Smith's sawmill men died from bullets in February 1887. On the railroad, Junction became known as Chat's and finally just

Chat. The name stuck even though Chat sold out to his son Bedford early in 1889 to go into the cattle business. Later that year, when the life of the N&C agent was threatened by the Roberts boys, the railroad moved the Chat station buildings almost two miles to the north. A happy event resulted from the change; the agent married his new neighbor's daughter, the couple later moving to Southern California.

In the fall of 1885 a news butcher became a regular fixture on the N&C trains. At the same time, construction was started at a point near Junction on the 3-foot gauge Sierra Valley & Mohawk Railroad, an ill-fated lumber project to run westward up and over Beckwourth Pass and down the Middle Fork of the Feather River to near Mohawk. Although not foreordained, the N&C ultimately was to acquire full control of this connection 15 years later.

Bad weather set in in January 1886. An unusual 36-inch snowfall lasted for two days, followed by an unseasonably warm rain which flooded all the valleys. The N&C was undermined in 52 places, and all traffic suspended for 21 days. In the great swale in Lemmon Valley, 14 miles from Reno, track was under three feet of water, and one mile of it was completely washed out. Heriot rushed repairs and business was resumed, with traffic showing substantial gains as the year progressed. Receipts in August were twice those of the preceding year with lumber becoming an important traffic item. Truckee (to the south of Reno) had ceased to be a great wood camp, and people were looking more and more to the northern country served by the N&C for lumber and many other needs. Monday became known as "butter day," with three or four tons going as far south as Virginia City for the week's early markets.

The N&C was again challenged by snow during the early months of 1887. For a time the track was kept open by running double-headers, but even this expedient was not sufficient at one point, and 50 Chinamen were sent out with shovels to get the trains rolling.

When the hot springs at Brubeck's ranch on the east shore of Honey Lake were sold and the name changed to Heriot's Place, citizens of Susanville (to the northwest) saw in the action a portent of things to come. Bad feelings and resentment toward the N&C increased over the obvious inference that the railroad would build northward along the east shore of Honey Lake, thus by-passing Susanville, rather than along the southwestern shore directly into town. One citizen openly proclaimed that the railroad must prefer the patronage of the Piutes over that of the ranchers and businessmen of Susanville. At a town indignation meeting, Judge Spencer attempted to simplify the railroad's problem by explaining, "If we go there, we can't get out." The townspeople thereupon proposed to find a way out, but if they did the railroad was not convinced. It was felt in railroad circles that even if the route were allowed to diverge to the west of Honey Lake, no more business would be forthcoming than obtained at the moment. As Erasmus Gest, the next manager of the N&C, wrote to Moran, "It is a waste of money to build 20 miles merely to reach that 'noplace' and there stop." Bad feelings prevailed among the Susanville merchants which even John Fulton, master of transportation, could not pacify. Supplies were carted by teams all the way from Chico to the west, in preference to using the facilities of the N&C. Statements in Susanville's *Lassen Advocate* became so critical the railroad sued for libel —but lost. As viewed by later management, Gest's by-passing of Susanville was considered to be "one of the most monumental blunders I have ever known a supposedly sane man to commit."

In April 1887 work started on the next extension northward (and to the east of Honey Lake as Susanville had feared). Great stimulus to the construction, no doubt, were the number of irrigation projects initiated in the 1880-1890 era encompassing Long Valley and Honey Lake Valley. The largest was a plan for using Eagle Lake water for irrigation by constructing a mile-long tunnel. To meet the challenge, the N&C put 500 men to work on the first six miles of grade; then suddenly the work was halted and the men discharged. Also discharged was Heriot, who had proceeded to grade across ranches arbitrarily without securing permission for the right-of-way. Loud protests resulted.

Erasmus Gest, a man with railroad experience gained in Ohio, was selected as Heriot's successor. No formal announcement was made, which puzzled the local press. The inquisitive reporter, seeking the facts, found the assignment discouraging:

Reporter: "Mr. Gest, it is rumored that there is to be a change in the superintendency of the Nevada & California Railroad. Is there any foundation for the rumor?"

Mr. Gest: "I am very busy here now attending to my correspondence and haven't time to talk to you. You must excuse me, please."
Reporter: "But Mr. Gest, at this time this is of special interest to the public and besides the *Gazette* must make some comment on the rumor already published in the morning paper."
Mr. Gest: "Well sir, I have nothing to say. You must see someone else; see Mr. Knox, grading contractor—he is one of Heriot's men."
Investigation revealed that Knox was out of town, but the reporter noted that Gest, not Heriot, was signing the checks.

Four months later, in August 1887, work was resumed; but because of the difficulties with the terrain at the big bend of Long Valley Creek, progress was slow. Condemnation suits also hampered the work. A. E. Ross owned the most prosperous ranch situated about 16 miles above Chat. He objected most strenuously to having the railroad cross his land and kept the matter in litigation for 18 months in spite of the fact that the railroad built through. It was Ross' contention that the railroad, being owned by individuals, did not have the usual power of condemnation ordinarily vested in a railroad corporation. Moran's (railroad) view was upheld by the California Supreme Court and a new point of law was established.

The year 1888 was a busy one for the N&C in virtually every department. Gest was anxious to push the road north as fast as possible, for he feared invasion of the Modoc country by Jay Gould building down from Huntington, Oregon, or the proposed routes surveyed by the C&NW (Chicago & Northwestern) through southern Oregon, or the line the Donahues were building up from San Francisco Bay. In preparation for the expanded economy of the line, the Morans formed the Nevada-California-Oregon Railway Company to take over their property operated in the name of the N&C, but in the light of the pending litigation over the N&O bonds, complete transfer of the assets was not made until January 1, 1893.

On March 1, 1888, the railroad continued northward in Long Valley, moving its northern terminal to Camp Ham (45 miles from Reno), then to Doyle (57.75 miles) on June 6. Picnic excursions to Red Rock, near M.P. 48, were so popular that summer that the railroad considered making the area a permanent picnic resort. Liegan (originally 70 miles) became the railroad terminal on September 10, 1888, and Mac Sample moved up from Doyle to take over the agency.

Repairs and improvements were also on the agenda. Gest advocated the replacement of decaying trestles with fills, and considerable effort was devoted to widening the cuts where winter snows had given so much trouble in the past. A steam shovel was acquired for that specific purpose. A new route over the first summit north of Reno was also recommended, to follow the southern slope where winter suns would help melt the heavy snow which the present route protected. Too, it would also avoid one particularly troublesome cut—500 feet long, 30 feet deep, and on a 16° curve. Winds were so strong at this location, a passenger car was once blown off the track. To remedy the situation, a precautionary speed restriction was placed in effect during such inclemencies.

New Year's Day 1889 was noteworthy for the unusual excursion which carried 40 people to the end of the line in Liegan to view the total eclipse of the sun. Variety was injected into the return trip when a stop was made to inspect the new steam shovel. The year 1889 might also be called the year of the fires. The Reno station burned and was replaced by a brick edifice of character and distinction. Then someone shot and tried to turn "Bodie," the Chinese cook, and his outfit car, into a funeral pyre; but the fire went out.

Big snows hit the little railroad in January 1890. For 10 days all hands valiantly fought the drifts to keep the line open. Total cost of the operation came to $3,876, over half of which was paid to transient snow shovelers.

Work on a further extension to Brubeck's ranch began in August 1890, and late in October the last rails were laid. Scheduled service began November 17 over the 79 miles between Reno and the new terminal of Amedee established on the Brubeck ranch property. (Line changes and remeasurements caused the Reno-Amedee mileage to vary from 77 to 80 miles.)

The newly formed Amedee terminus grew to a population of from 300 to 400 people, boasted a three-story Amedee Hotel (torn down in 1949), a second, smaller hotel, a restaurant, barber shop, butcher shop, blacksmith, several residences and the usual complement of saloons. There was even a newspaper, *The Amedee Geyser,* to record the local happenings.

For a number of years Amedee was a busy place. Stages and teams from the north and west connected with the railroad. Cattle and sheep from Senator Flanigan's ranches were brought to corrals at the railhead. Lumber from the west was rafted across Honey Lake for routing over the N&C. Honey Lake also offered boating and bathing to Reno people and the railroad responded with a special round-trip fare of $4.50 for the long, scenic ride.

Greatest novelty of the area were the hot springs and geysers which erupted from the soil. Initially the N&C tried to use the natural water supply for its locomotives, but sediment deposited in the locomotive boilers discouraged the practice. However, commercial use for the hot water was found in a sheep-dipping plant as well as an experimental chicken hatchery. Even the geyser was harnessed for a novel purpose—Amos Lane invented a clock which moved ahead exactly 38 seconds with each spurt of the water, thereby keeping perfect time for sightseers to follow. By 1901 Dr. Wilhelm Schmitt was advertising the beneficial effects of the hot springs.

For 10 years the railhead remained at Amedee while the financial economy of the area and of the country fluctuated. On January 1, 1893 the N-C-O Railway officially took over the entire railroad and the N&C passed out of existence. The panic of 1893 took its toll, as did a blight of Spanish mildew which struck the Honey Lake area. When Amedee Moran sent a flag to the town in 1893 along with his best wishes, he wrote Gest that everything was blue on Wall Street—money was impossible to raise. The despondency of the times was reflected in causticism—one inebriated individual spotted the letters N-C-O on a box car and proclaimed that it meant "Narrow, Crooked & Onery," a nickname that stuck throughout the lifetime of the road, although at times "Northern California Outrage" was also used.

"THE GREAT NORTHERN"

In January 1899 work began quietly on a northern extension of the N-C-O, but no one would say where it was headed. At Hot Springs (5 miles north of Amedee) a hotel was erected in anticipation that the railroad would stop there, but the rails pushed right on by. Climbing the hill to Mud Flat, the line passed through Secret Valley, then followed the route of Snow Storm Creek in the ascent to Madeline Plains. Here, 50 miles from Amedee, it stopped on a great dusty plain filled with low sagebrush and without a shrub or a blade of grass to be seen. An enormous freight house was constructed (178' x 48') with a concrete floor; and this, together with a few barns and some recently constructed cottages, comprised the railhead that was Termo. No one could understand why the track was not continued on to Madeline, while the warehouse was considered by many to be a monument to Mr. Gest's "$50,000 Folly on the Desert."

To service the new extension two new Baldwins arrived late in 1899, and several passenger cars were built by the Reno Mill and Lumber Co. In Reno, the N-C-O shops were enlarged and a force of 45 men were employed full time. In fact the impact of the more impressive corporate title plus the renewed vitality expressed by activity on the road made Reno far more cognizant of the importance of the N-C-O, and it began to think and refer to the line as its own "Great Northern."

On June 1, 1900, the entire line to Termo was placed in operation, and the first mail and passenger train was met by Van Loan's stages to take passengers on to Alturas, 50 miles farther to the north. Then, in October, Gest retired at the youthful age of 80, and was succeeded by T. F. Dunaway, formerly with the Colorado & Southern Railway. One of Dunaway's first acts was to use the telegraph for train operations, explaining that he did not believe in running trains by shadow and smoke. In addition a small depot was constructed near the Henry Butters ranch (formerly owned by A. E. Ross) which became known as Constantia.

Good neighborliness was expressed by the N-C-O on March 14, 1901, when it acquired control of the Sierra Valleys Railway. The connecting carrier had run into difficulties with various creditors; so to preserve the line and its traffic the N-C-O paid the judgment and settled the liens, subsequently making the road a direct subsidiary.

An additional 14 miles of new trackage was also constructed that same year. Termo lost its significance as the northern railhead when George Bailey stepped out of his role as a rancher in the Modoc Land & Livestock Co. to tackle the grading contract for an extension to the new town of Madeline. Clearing the sagebrush was begun with a crew of 40 Indians in July 1901, and the grade was finished before fall. Deliveries of new rail were delayed due to a steel strike, but in January 1902 the track was in place and ready for the spring traffic which commenced on April 1, 1902, after the new roadbed was considered properly settled.

The town of Madeline assumed a considerable importance as the new terminus of the railroad. It developed into a large livestock shipping center, while the Madeline Meadows Land and Irrigation Co. under the leadership of J. Noble Jones attempted to colonize and develop the fertility of the area for many years. Postcards were roundly circulated depicting orange trees growing along a local irrigation ditch, while a box of "locally grown oranges" was always on display at the hotel. To accommodate the visitors (and the curious), Van Loan completed a new, two-story hotel offering 32 cozy and sunny sleeping rooms. Unruly visitors were housed in a wooden jail on the west side of the tracks.

Reno, at the southern end of the road, was not overlooked in the program for extensions and improvements. Late in 1901 an addition of 1,500 feet of new track connected Flanigan's warehouse with the main line, bringing added revenues. Then, in June 1903, a branch line was built right up the middle of Fifth Street and Alameda Avenue to the Fair Grounds. Instigator of the innovation was the Reno Wheelman Club which objected to the livery charge of 50¢ for the short trip. Through arrangement with the N-C-O, it was agreed to build the rail line and charge but 25¢ for the convenient transportation. The line was laid in four days in spite of the howl of liverymen; Sunday crowds used the train to the Fair to watch Reno win the 50-mile bicycle relay race; then, four months later the track was removed.

Additional revenue was also derived from the new subsidiary, the Sierra Valleys Ry. Sunday excursions were operated over the branch line to Clairville and Clio (near Mohawk) which proved to be popular attractions. Normally 100 passengers could be counted upon to make the weekly pilgrimage, but in 1903 when a timber cruiser discovered some rich quartz near Mohawk, the patronage suddenly jumped to 400 passengers.

Floods attacked the N-C-O in February and March 1904, causing cessation of operations for some 15 days. Considerable damage near Cameron (about three miles north of Chat) was created, a not unusual occurrence. Previously, in 1900, undermining by swollen waters of Long Valley Creek in the same area had resulted in a freight car diving into the waters and a consequent shifting of the track. The necessity "for a new line to avoid Long

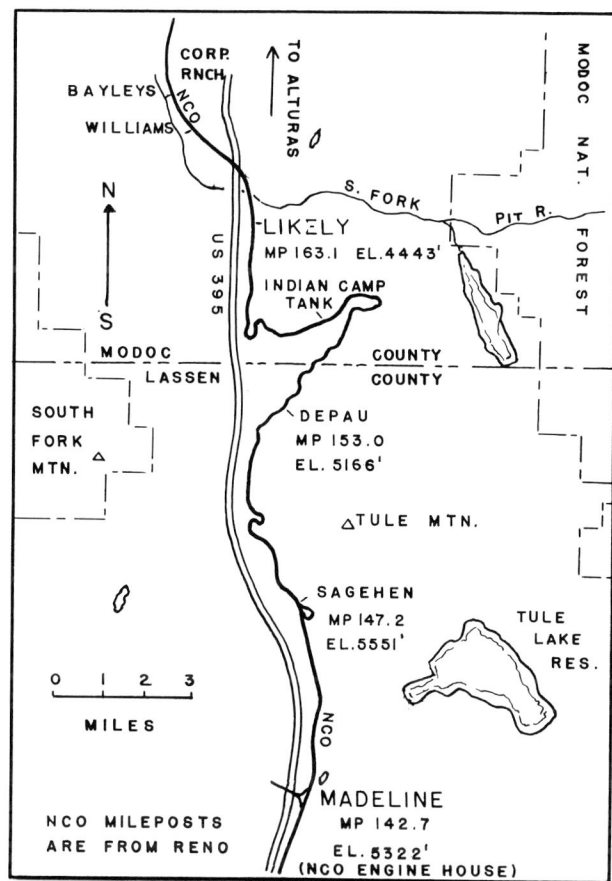

Valley Creek" was indicated. Spring floods were a concomitant circumstance, however, which the N-C-O faced each year. In March 1907 near Plumas Jct. a mile of track was under water for several days; no sooner was the damage repaired than two more storms struck, and the work had to be done all over again.

The advent of June 1906 signified the start of the next push northward. The segment was the 20-mile stretch from Madeline up and over the 200-foot hill to Sage Hen, thence a drop of 1,100 feet to Likely. Construction was more difficult and progress slower than on some of the previous sections, with the result that trains did not start operating over the new line until October 1, 1907. While the grades were sufficiently difficult in themselves, twenty feet of snow in 1916 demonstrated that severe weather conditions could make them worse. Witness the curt message to the dispatcher from one snowbound crew which stated briefly: "Am stuck on Madeline Hill!" To which the dispatcher tactfully and promptly replied: "Well, marry the girl and come on in."

The station at Likely failed to live up to the promise of its name, and the N-C-O paused only long enough to consolidate its gains before pushing on to Alturas (originally Dorris Bridge), 20 miles farther to the north. The route followed a tributary of the Pit River, passed the Corporation Ranch, and halted on the outskirts of town where a portion of the right-of-way was presenting difficulties. The problem was solved by constructing the line on a Sunday when no court actions could be filed, and the people of Alturas took advantage of the occasion to ride on the construction trains as the track was being laid. Regular service to that Modoc County seat started on December 1, 1908.

The next extension carried the line 20 miles farther north to Davis Creek at the foot of Goose Lake. Here passengers for Lakeview, Oregon, could embark by boat for the balance of their journey, pending completion of the 34 additional miles of trackage. Rails ultimately reached Lakeview, 238 miles from Reno, on January 10, 1912, and this remained the northernmost terminal of the N-C-O in spite of the fact that the corporate charter had been previously amended in 1910 to provide for a possible extension onward to The Dalles, Oregon, on the Columbia River. One off-rail, truck extension of service was instituted briefly in 1913 from Alturas eastward over Cedar Pass to Cedarville, California, but the operation was disappointing and the service discontinued.

Financially the N-C-O had struggled through the years with about the same measure of success that it had obtained construction-wise. For the 25 years from 1889 through 1913 (including the depression year of 1893 which sounded the financial death-knell of many roads), there was an unbroken record of profits, however modest. By and large these were plowed back into the road in the form of construction or improvements. In the more lucrative years from 1906 to 1912, the preferred shareholders participated in the profits, but the full 5% preferred dividend was paid only three times in 1908-09-10. Common shareholders received less consideration in accordance with their rank, receiving dividends of 1% only in the years of 1909 and 1910. From 1914 on, deficits were almost universally the rule as expenses, particularly maintenance, increased. These years were to be the most discouraging period in the railroad's history.

For one thing, the competition was increasing. The Western Pacific Railway was completed in 1909, and its main line climbed the North Fork of the Feather River, then crossed to the valley of the Middle Fork to parallel the entire length of the N-C-O's Sierra Valley Branch from Mohawk to Beckwourth Pass. From Beckwourth the WP swung north along the N-C-O's main line for another 27 miles before crossing it at Hackstaff grade and heading east. To add insult to injury, in June 1912 the SP's Fernley & Lassen Railway started construction to its line from Fernley and Wadsworth, Nevada, to Susanville and Westwood, California, to tap the Red River Lumber Company's new interests near Westwood. In spite of their lower costs of construction, the N-C-O's narrow gauge rails and equipment were at a big disadvantage in competition with the standard gauge, transcontinental carriers.

Unprecedented rains during the first three months of 1914 badly disrupted traffic on the N-C-O. Repairs were effected, however, and the line struggled on. In fact an improved crossing of the first summit just north of Reno was completed in June, 1914, which, together with other minor adjustments, shortened the main line by a little over a mile, making the distance from Reno to Lakeview 236 miles.

Major shifts in management personnel also occurred when Charles Moran succeeded his uncle, D. Comyn Moran, as president. Ramsey M. Cox, formerly superintendent of the Texas Central, was made general manager in place of Dunaway who had served the road for 14 full years. Just as Dunaway had brought in his friends from Colorado when he had assumed charge in 1900, so Cox followed the same practice at the time of the inauguration of his duties by bringing in men from Texas to operate the line. Among them was Alex "Dad" Hawkins, the famous N-C-O conductor.

In an attempt to build the on-line territory, Cox tried to arrange for the settlement of lands near Ravendale, just south of Termo. To handle the program he hired a Russian named Kelso who succeeded in relocating 25 Russian families in the area. Rabbit drives became a regular winter occupation, whole carloads of meat being shipped via N-C-O to a tamale factory in San Francisco. Whether the rabbits were not as virile as generally reputed, or whether the winter harvest was insufficient to support the families on a year-round basis, has not been determined; it is known that the Russians apparently tired of rabbit meat and gradually drifted away, leaving Ravendale to its solitary sage.

Two locomotives, three passenger cars, two mail and express cars and 78 freight cars were added to the roster of equipment in 1915. The total cost of the entire group of rolling stock was only $22,750 plus freight (a distress price) for the famous Florence & Cripple Creek Railroad in Colorado was ceasing its narrow gauge operations. Not such a bargain was another acquisition in the same year — the Sierra & Mohawk Railway. Actually, the N-C-O had controlled and operated the line since 1901, and its absorption into the parent company was largely a matter of convenience.

Severe blizzards ushered in the year 1916. In northeastern California the temperature stood at zero with winds of 60 miles per hour. Blowing and drifting snow forced trains to a halt, then covered them in its blanket of whiteness. For 22 days no trains moved on the line, while the Plumas (S&M) branch remained closed for a full seven weeks. Of the 14 locomotives, only two were operating; one was in the Reno shops; all others were immobile in the snow — off the track and generally on their sides.

The year also was notable for the emergence from receivership of the Western Pacific Railroad, minus its previously onerous restriction that no branches were to be built or acquired. Growing pains immediately became evident. The road wanted and needed a line into Reno, and to this end discussions were held with the N-C-O about laying a third rail on its roadbed from Chat to Reno. On the other side of the fence, the N-C-O was facing hard times with the loss of considerable traffic to both the WP and the SP. Bondholders were becoming restless; some wanted to throw the company into receivership, while others — personal friends of Moran, M. Charles de Wendel of the French family of Maître de Forges, and particularly the (toothpaste) Colgates — held large blocks of N-C-O bonds and accorded considerable cooperation during the difficult times.

Faced with the possibility of a duplicate line to Reno the N-C-O decided to sell the Western Pacific the 64 miles of main line from the Hackstaff crossing (named for the family of Charles Moran's wife — subsequently changed to Herlong) to Reno, together with the 39-mile Plumas Branch to Davies Mill, plus the station and shops at Reno. The agreement was signed June 11, 1917; the price a badly needed $700,000, which was used to retire some of the N-C-O bonds coming due two years later.

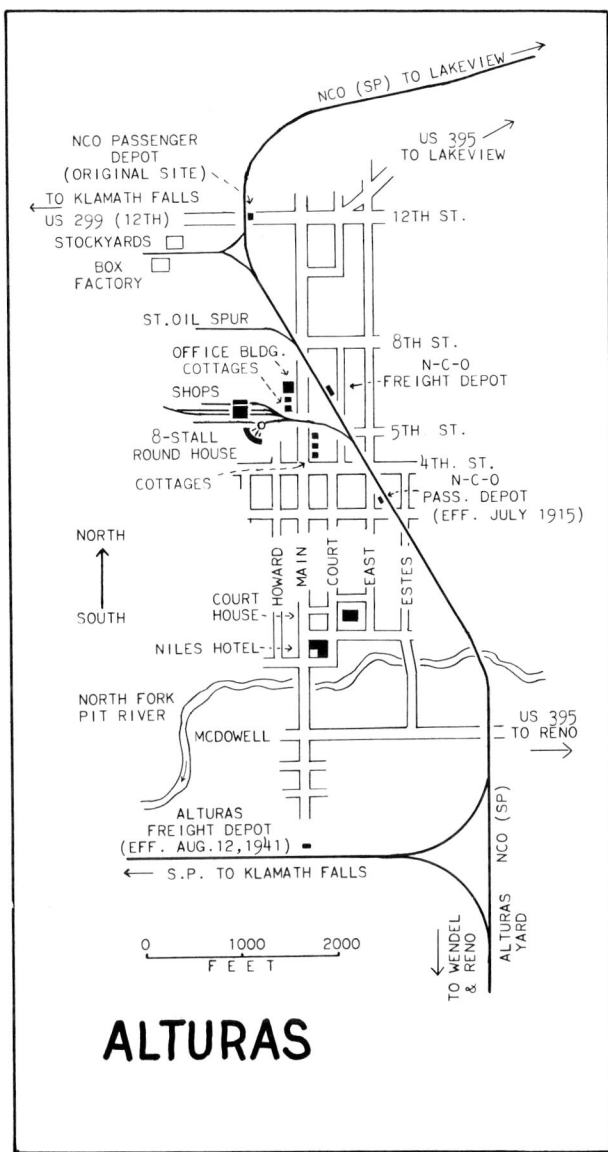

ALTURAS

To effect the change of ownership, considerable major work needed to be undertaken. Alturas, the only major habitation of any size near the midpoint of the abbreviated N-C-O operation, invited the 171-mile railroad to establish its headquarters there. To emphasize the point, it backed its welcome with a gift of town lots and a cash contribution of $10,000. The N-C-O responded by erecting in Alturas an imposing two-story stone edifice for its general offices as well as an eight-stall roundhouse and general shops. Four cottages were built and two houses purchased for the use of the employees (title being held in the N-C-O Realty Co., a subsidiary).

At the south end of the line, the Western Pacific commenced laying new and heavier rail outside the slim gauge of its predecessor, readjusting the alignment of the roadbed in numerous places, particularly between Purdy and the Summit (north of Reno) where Moore had uncompromisingly added six miles of irrelevant trackage in the early days of construction. In addition, the signboards and other indicia on the brick Reno station, the shops and the roundhouse (burned in 1940) were changed to conform to the new ownership.

Seven months later, at 10:00 A.M. on January 30, 1918, the last N-C-O narrow gauge train left Reno with four passenger cars and 10 freight cars in tow. Two engines were required to haul the tonnage up the hill, for the last 50 N-C-O employees were bringing everything movable with them. As the train left the yards, WP crews began tearing up the narrow gauge tracks. When the dismantling crews reached Plumas Jct. at the northern end, they continued to remove the rails on the old main line from that point to Hackstaff as well as those on the entire Plumas branch to the west which no longer served any useful purpose as a duplicate facility.

Thus the N-C-O became an isolated feeder railroad, beginning in the wilds of southern Oregon and terminating in the wilds of eastern California. Its outpost shops at Alturas became largely dependent upon repairs and improvements of their own devisings, and many were the strange and wonderful fabrications of the track and shop forces. Several times the Superintendent of Bridge, Building and Water Service, H. E. Gasaway, was called upon to execute the movement of water tanks along the line; each time he managed to transport them on the proportionately tiny, narrow gauge flat cars without untoward incident. When the freight station at Alturas burned in 1915, the most expedient method of replacement was to "borrow" the depot at Surprise Station and bring it to Alturas, nine miles to the south. Again Gasaway came to the rescue, but unlike the previous operations, he first dismantled the building into sections before having it transported and reassembled.

When the imposing belfry of the general office building in Alturas needed a set of bells which the railroad could ill afford, Charles Chapman met the challenge by turning dummies of wood on the company's shop lathe. One metal bell was installed, and this was used by general manager Cox to summon his colored boy, Jim. At one time, at an uptown meeting, Cox found that he had left his wallet in the office, and he sent for Jim. Instructing him to fetch the wallet, Cox cautioned in a voice that all could hear to give it proper care as it had $80,000 in it. Jim returned with the wallet, only to inform his boss, and incidentally those present, that it did not contain $80,000 but merely 80¢. "I know," he said, "I looked."

Basically, the N-C-O was dependent upon cattle, sheep and lumber for most of its business. These commodities comprised better than 50% of the tonnage, although petroleum products, wool, grain, hay and l.c.l. shipments contributed importantly to the revenues. Each fall's cattle rush required three, daily, 20-car stock trains with double crews, creating a mad scramble in the labor market for men of any kind to fill the required quota. Shop forces were depleted; men were taken off the streets of Alturas; even boys in their teens were approached with the regulation minor's release form to take home for their mother's signature so they could report for work.

In the wintertime, when snow covered the range lands and blocked the roads, hay for the cattle became an important item. The railroad, being the only operating link with civilization during the long winter months, became the lifeline of the territory it served. P. S. Dorris, a Modoc pioneer, recalled that the N-C-O frequently was the only salvation for stockmen, particularly during the spring of 1917 following an unduly severe winter when the carloads of N-C-O hay kept 90% of the stockmen in business.

Unlike other Nevada railroads, the N-C-O was but little concerned with mining activity in that largely mineral state. The Antelope Mine near Purdy, the mines at Poeville on Peavine Mountain, and the minor activity in the Diamond Mountain District near Doyle contributed no business to the narrow gauge. The High Grade District in the Warner Mountains east of Fairport had some excitement around 1905-10, creating one of the few man-made incidents ever to mar the N-C-O's normally placid existence. It was customary for the southbound passenger train to bring in a goodly amount of gold bullion from the High Grade, and apparently the news leaked out. At Hot Springs near Amedee one day, two men rode up on horseback, dismounted, and proceeded to a high trestle where they anchored a steel rail in such a position as to wreck the southbound train on arrival. Fortunately, a trackwalker discovered the obstruction in time to flag the train, thus saving the occupants. Ironically, no credit could be taken for saving the gold shipment as there was very little coin on board on that particular trip.

There was a frivolously light, pleasurable side to N-C-O railroading, too. For example, a dollar would place one aboard the Alturas-Fairport excursion of a summer's day where swimming, a ride on the Goose Lake steamer, or a stay in a hotel, said to be the finest between Reno and Portland, could be had for the selection. Also on the agenda were the intense sporting rivalries between Alturas and Lakeview teams. Special trains to accommodate the visiting rooters were a normal part of each event.

When J. H. Mahan went to Alturas as traffic manager of the road, he immediately became active in promoting all business possible. At the outset, his curiosity arose over the difference in cash receipts reported by each of two conductors over virtually the same route. Sam Phelan normally turned in substantial receipts for his runs, occasionally amounting to several hundreds of dollars; the other conductor invariably collected but $1.50 each trip. When confronted with the facts, the guilty conductor quietly vanished and was never heard from again.

The N-C-O's two private cars — the *Fairport* (later CP #20, the *Esmeralda*, on the Mina-Keeler run) and the *Lakeview* — were both ex-Union Pacific conveyances. A colored porter is credited with the conflagration in the *Fairport* one day which did extensive damage to the car and its contents. Apparently the porter went off on a personal errand, forgetting that a fire had been left burning in the stove. When he returned, the blaze was beyond control. His reaction was both immediate and sensible — he saved the whiskey; to which the railroad took exception as to the method utilized — he tried to consume it as fast as he could pour it down.

Of particular interest were the two little buffet-sleeping cars — the *Alturas* and the *Madeline* — which had come from the Tonopah Railroad following the standard gauging of that road in August 1905. For years they brought up the rear of the Pullman-green passenger trains, then later the mixed — first out of Reno; subsequently from the abbreviated terminus of Hackstaff. While the necessity of the sleeping facilities on the long, 16- to 17-hour daylight runs from Reno to Lakeview might be questioned (except on occasions of forced layovers during winter blizzards or spring floods), there is little doubt as to the efficacy of the buffet-dining compartments on the train's lonely landfarings through the barren wastelands.

The years from 1910-25 were ones of sad statistics. True, the operating revenues were running

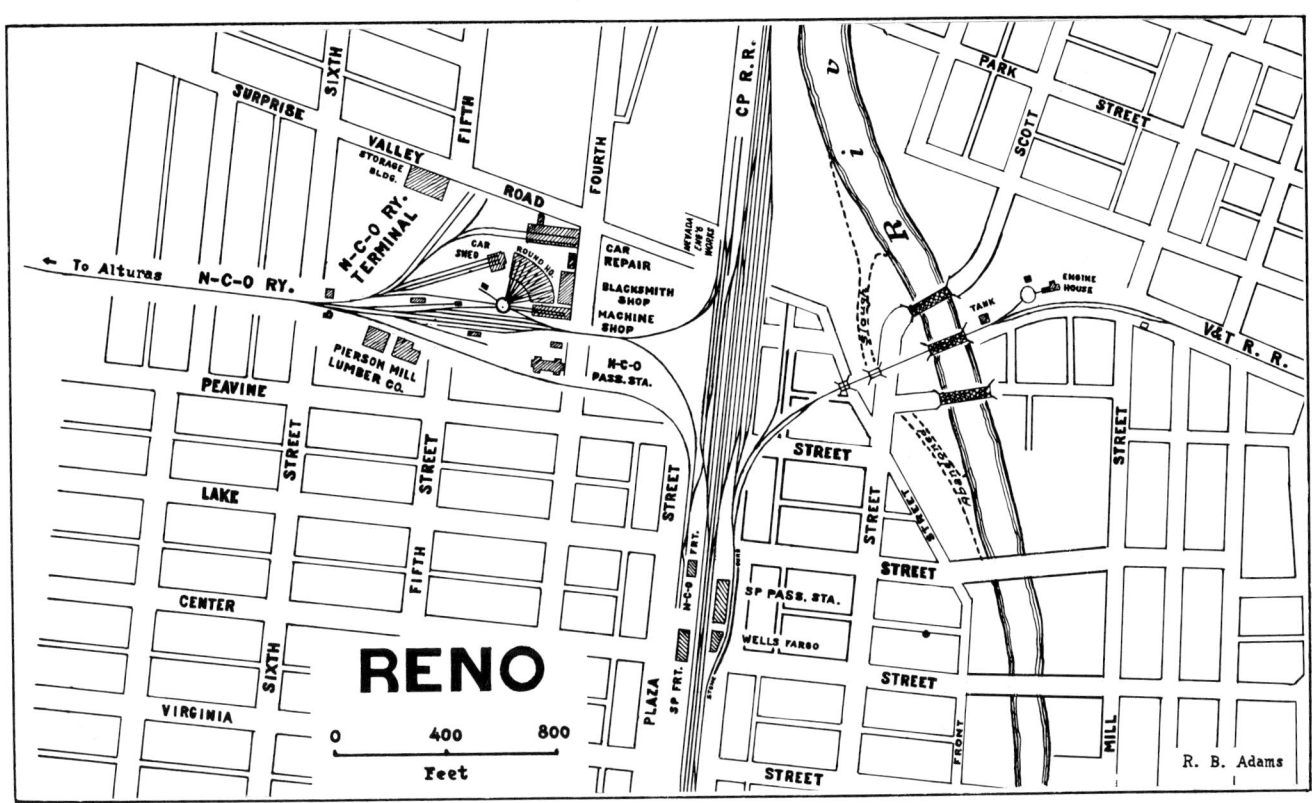

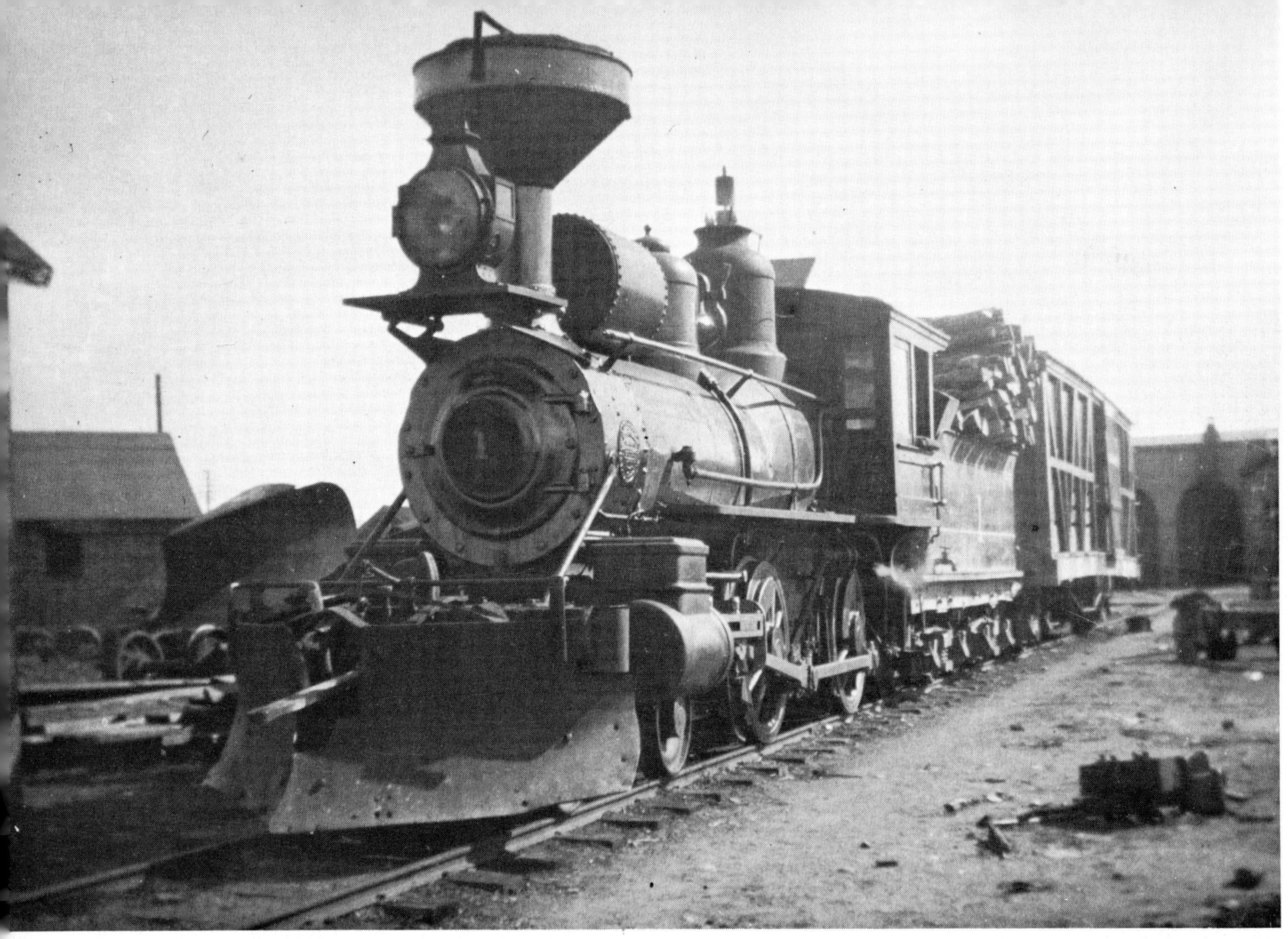

The engine *(above)*, shown at the Reno roundhouse in 1900, is Baldwin-built, narrow-gauge, woodburner No. 1 of the N-C-O (ex-No. 1 of the N&C). A pilot plow for early winter snows has been fashioned around its link-and-pin coupler, but the full-sized wedge plow in the left background will be brought into play when the snows deepen. The air tank atop the boiler is obviously a later addition when compared with the portrait of the same locomotive *(below)* in N&C service with its passenger train ready to depart from the Reno depot in the late 1880's. The view looks north across the Central Pacific's standard-gauge rails with the N&C's wooden station visible at left before it was demolished by fire in 1889. *(Top: Stanley Palmer photo; Bottom: Charles Moran.)*

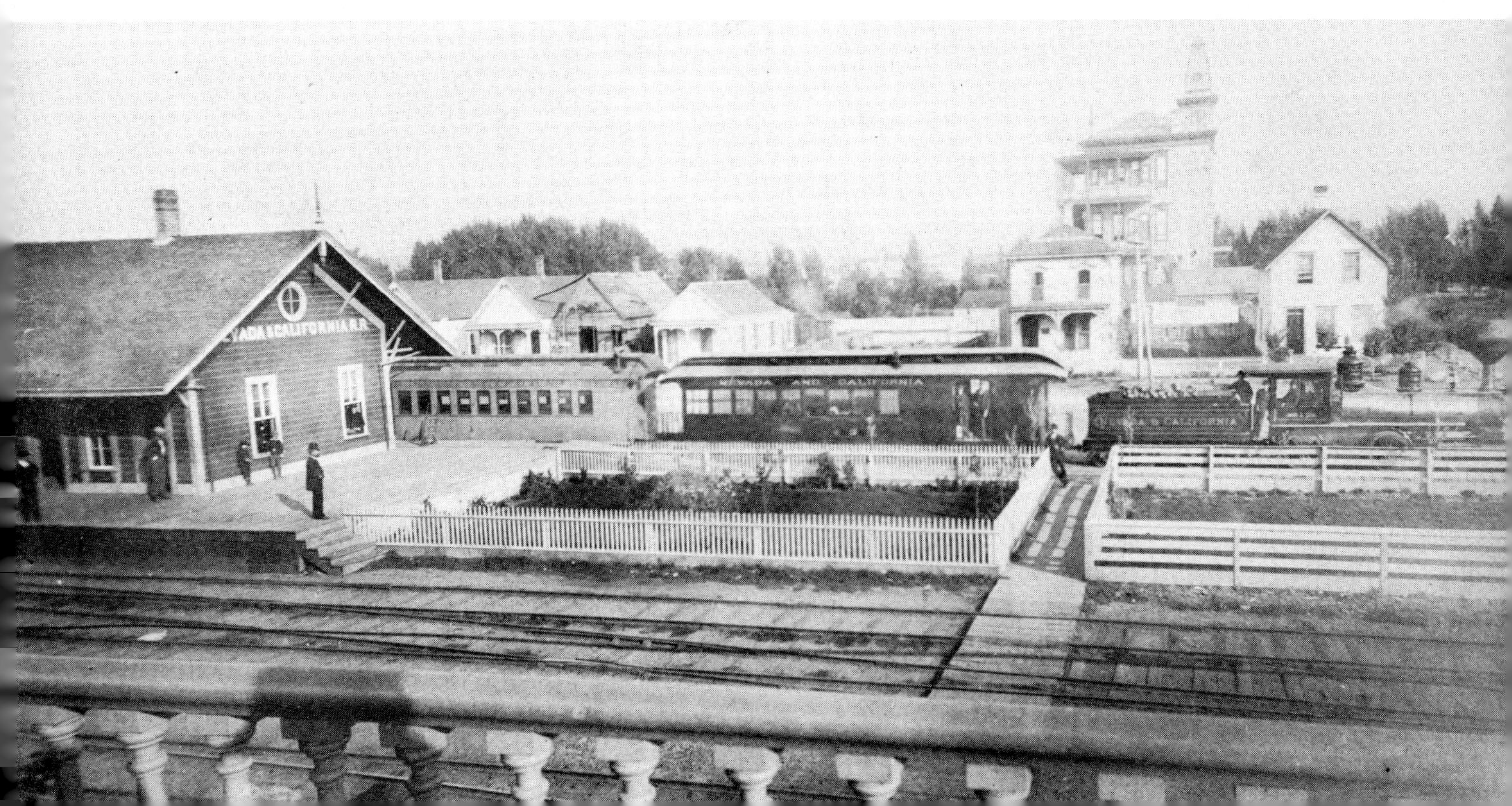

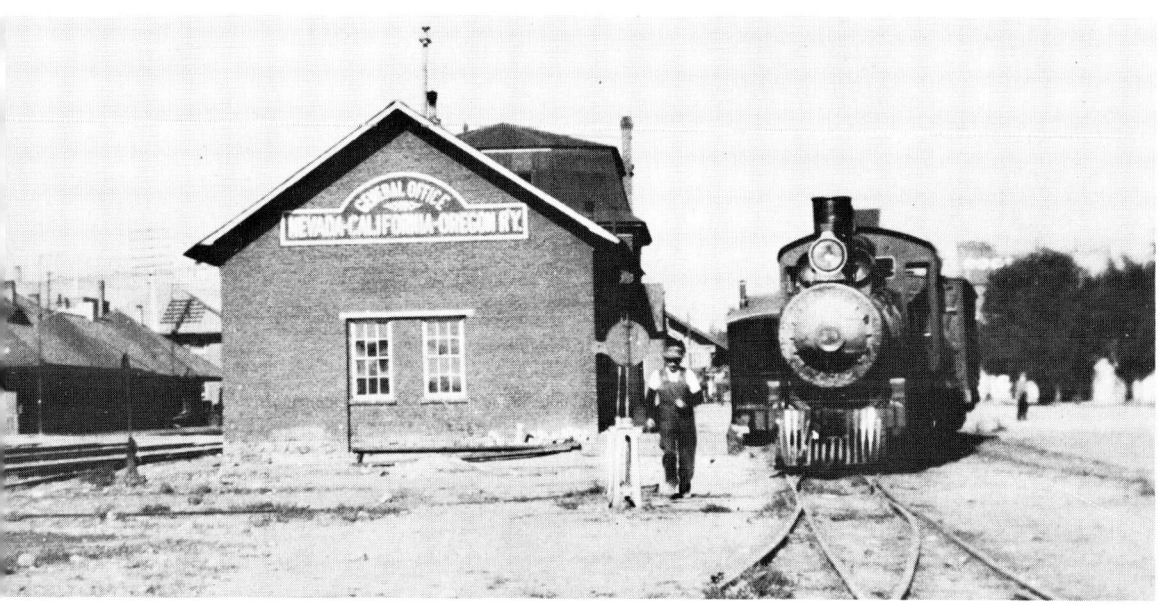

The brick structure (above) replaced the N&C's wooden station after the latter burned. In this 1905 picture, the SP tracks and passenger station are visible at left with the roof of the SP freight station jutting out past the N-C-O's General Office toward the narrow-gauge coach to right, which has been left on the siding while the balance of the mixed train is sorted for spotting on the various sidings and yard tracks. (Stanley Palmer Photo.)

Continuing extensions of the N-C-O in the early 1900's brought more business, required more equipment and necessitated expanded facilities. The old station next to the Southern Pacific's tracks became outgrown, thus a new and considerably larger and more imposing edifice (below) was erected on Reno's Fourth Street, adjacent to the N-C-O's terminal facilities. The day is June 9, 1910; the "hay-burner taxi" of the Riverside Hotel has just deposited its load of departing passengers and is ready to return empty to the hotel; the last late arrivals are scampering aboard; and the N-C-O's first train from the new depot is about to depart for all points along the 207-mile route to Davis Creek, California, at the foot of Goose Lake astride the Oregon state line.

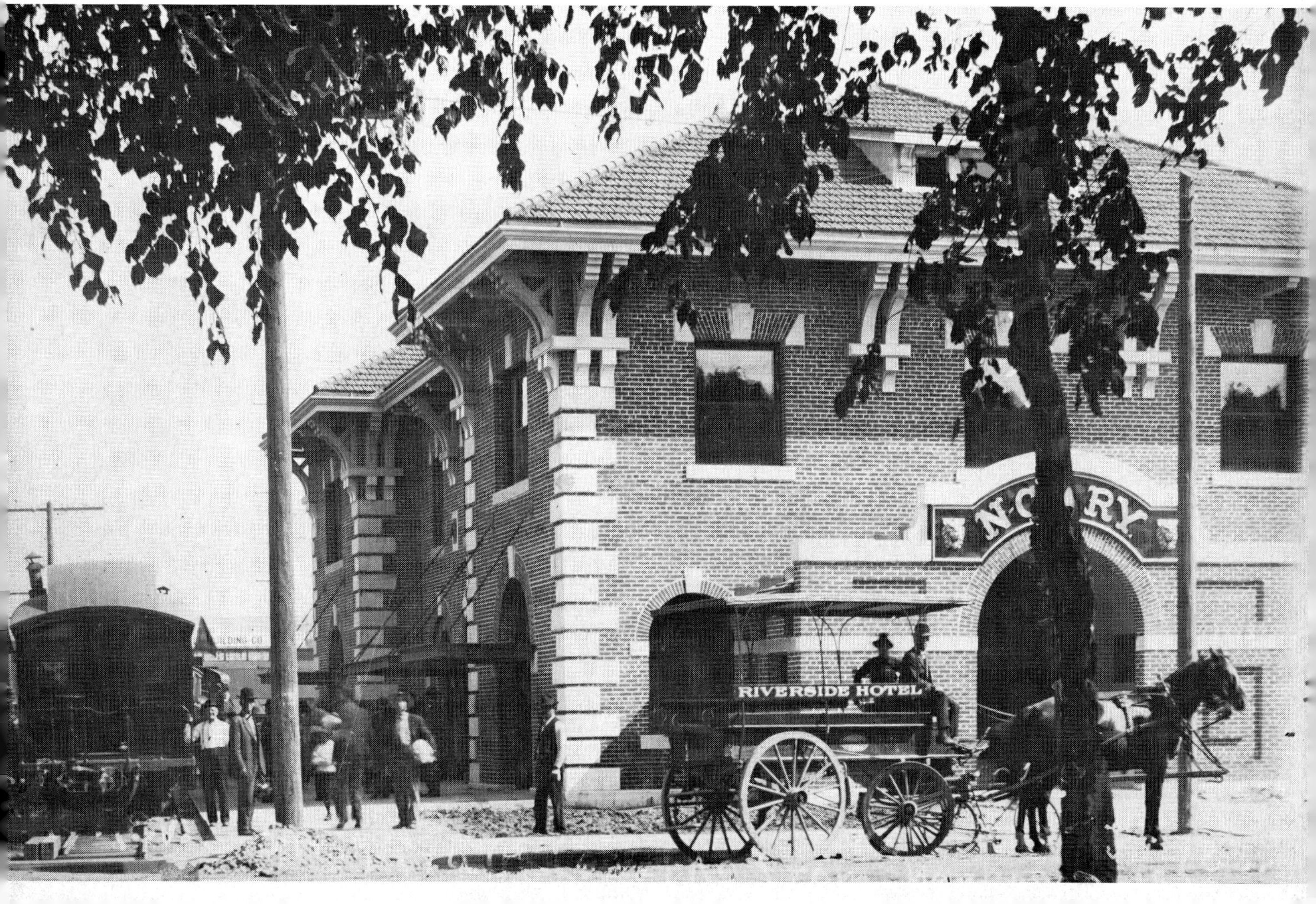

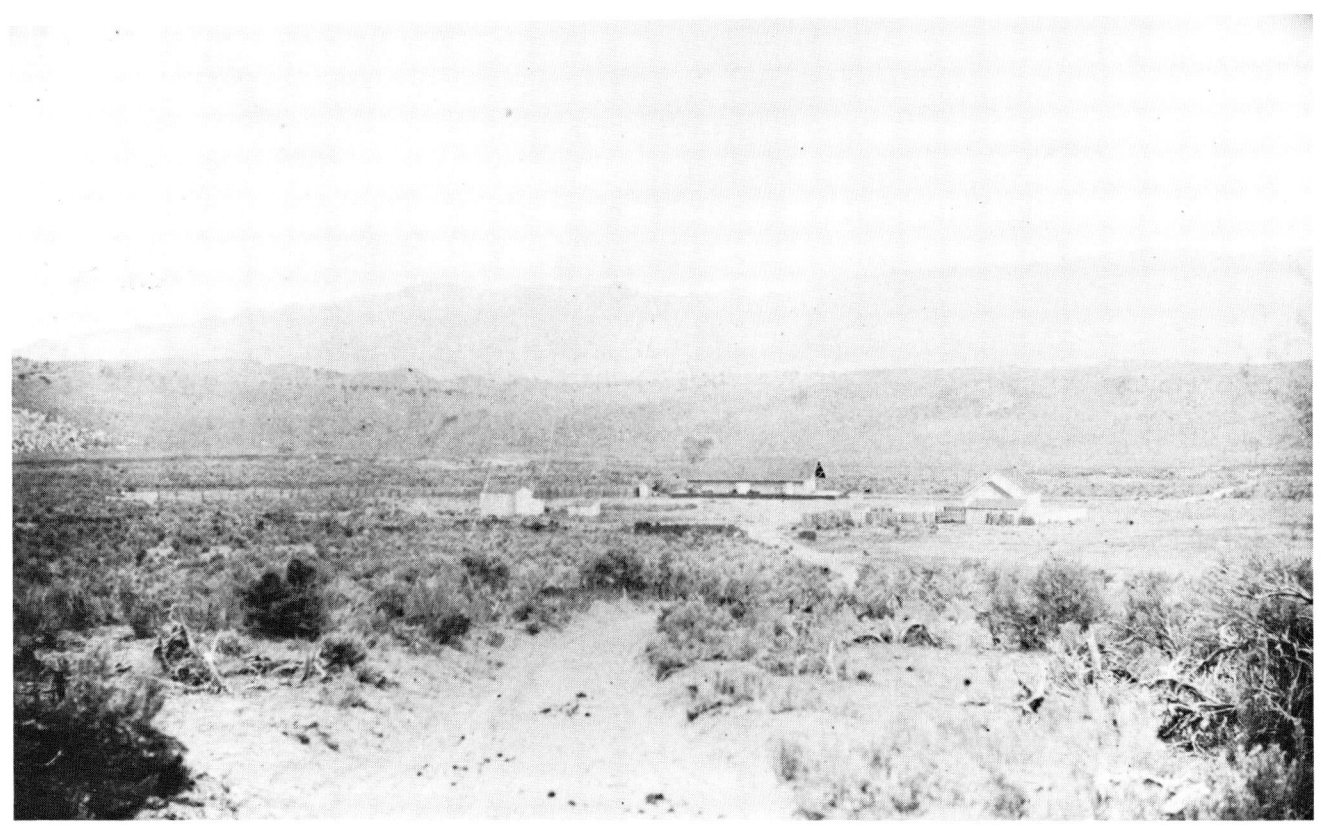

Chat Station on the N&C in 1897 (*above*) was two miles to the north from the original location of Junction (House), first reached by the narrow gauge on December 8, 1884. The depot, warehouse, store and stage office personnel at the railhead were constantly in jeopardy from casual shootings exercised by the Roberts boys whose father, Chat, had been involved in the famous Verdi train robbery of 1870 and at this time operated the famous Junction House to the south of the station. Although an effort was made to redesignate the location as Moran, and much later as Cuba Post Office, the name of Chat still stuck in common usage, even after the moving. Today, over 60 years later, it is almost impossible to find the site of the former activity. (*R. F. Ramelli Collection.*)

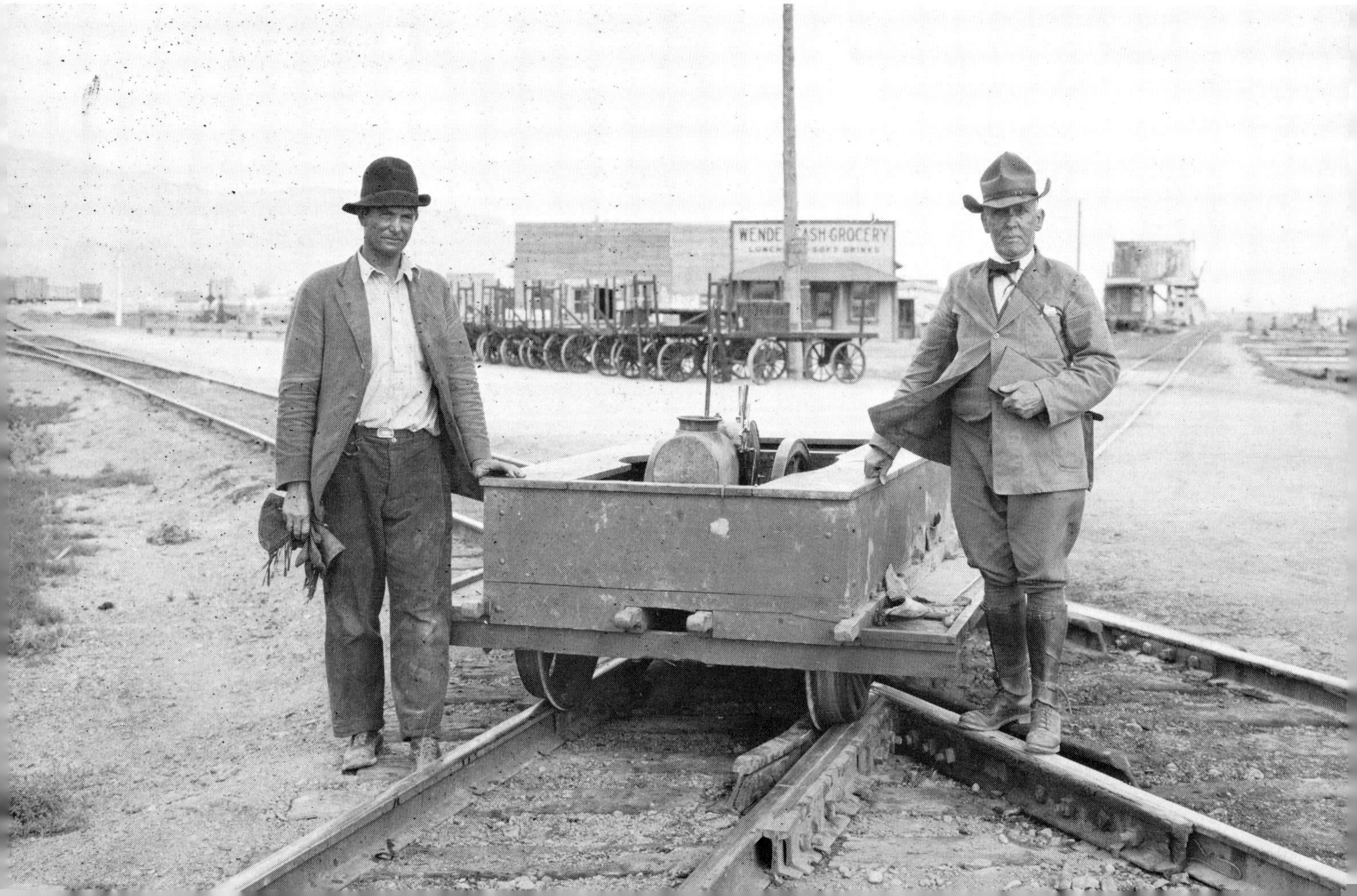

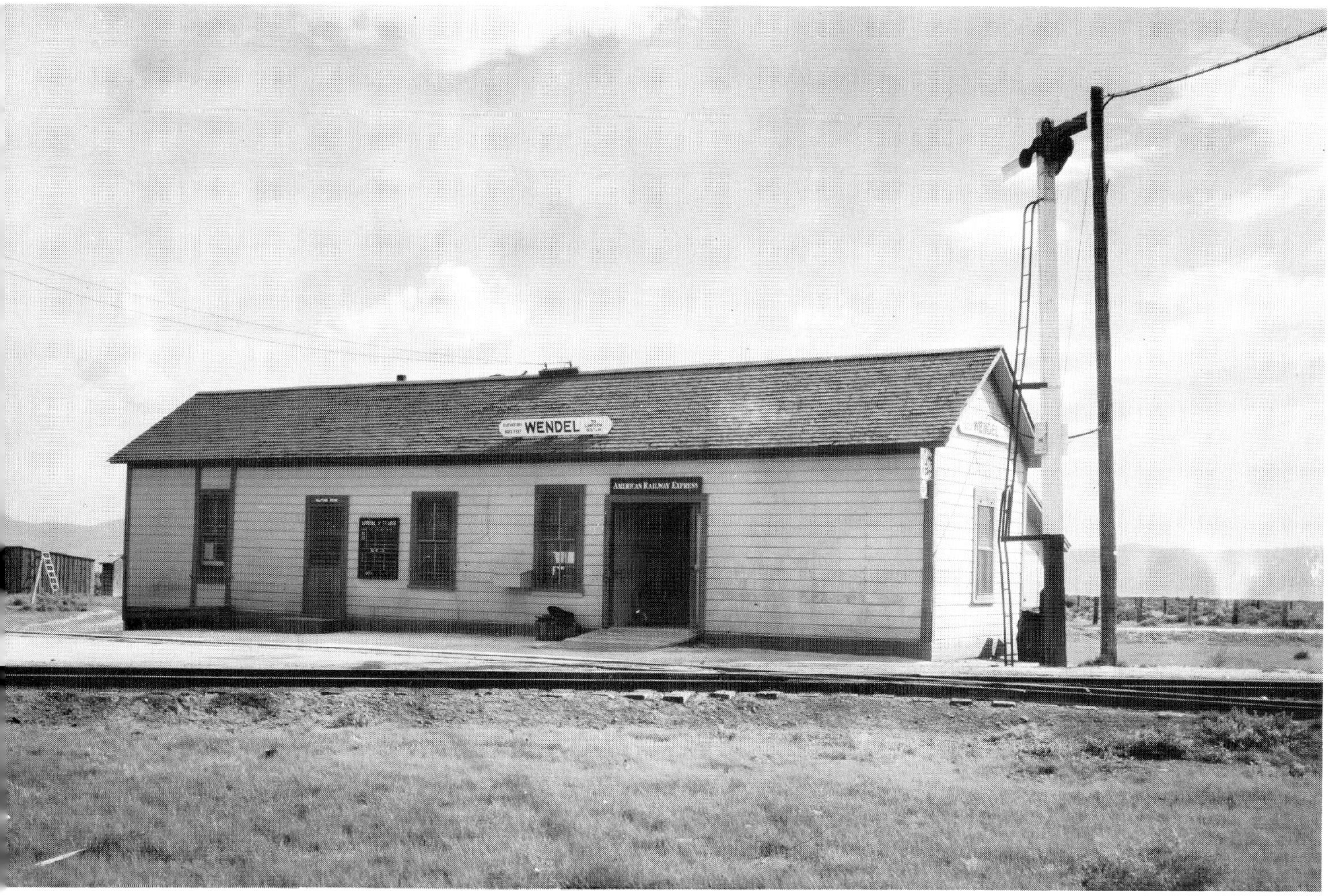

Wendel sprang into prominence in 1913 when tracks of the SP's Fernley & Lassen Railway reached and crossed those of the N-C-O at that point. In 1890 the Nevada & California had bogged down at Amedee, immediately to the south. Before construction was resumed in 1899, the name of the railroad underwent the change to Nevada-California-Oregon Railway, more facetiously known as the "Narrow, Crooked and Ornery" and sometimes as the "Northern California Outrage."

The Wendel station ("Elevation 4,012 feet; To Lakeview 153⁶⁄₁₀ M.; To San Francisco 358⁷⁄₁₀ M.") was operated as a joint facility of the SP and the N-C-O, and stood in the southwest corner of the crossing (above). In the southeast corner (left) was the Wendel Cash Grocery, handy to stranded passengers or such railroad employees as (left to right) H. E. Gasaway, roadmaster of the N-C-O, and Wm. L. Gould, the line's chief engineer, here posed with their home-made, single-cylinder, gas-powered section car. (Both Photos: Southern Pacific Collection.)

In preparation for operations at the new junction point, the N-C-O's 50,000-gallon water tank (below) was slung over the end trucks of two narrow-gauge flat cars and moved north to Wendel at the rate of two or three miles an hour. At left is the tank about in position for unloading and at right in its final location ready for action. (Left: H. E. Gasaway; Right: Southern Pacific Collection.)

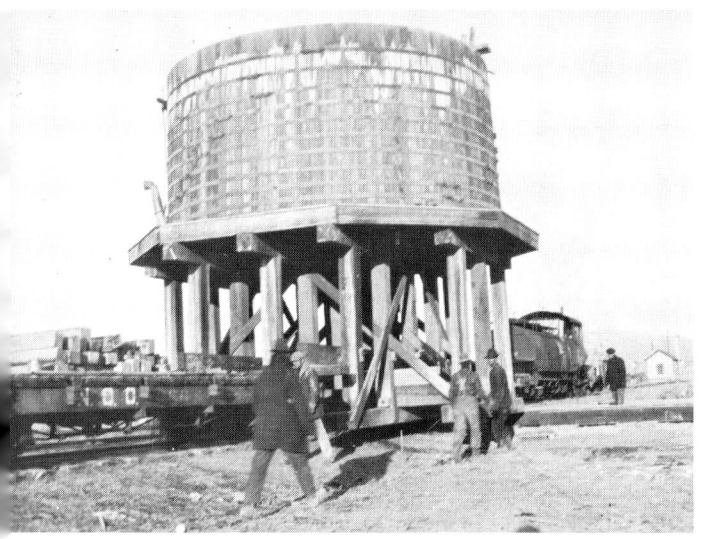
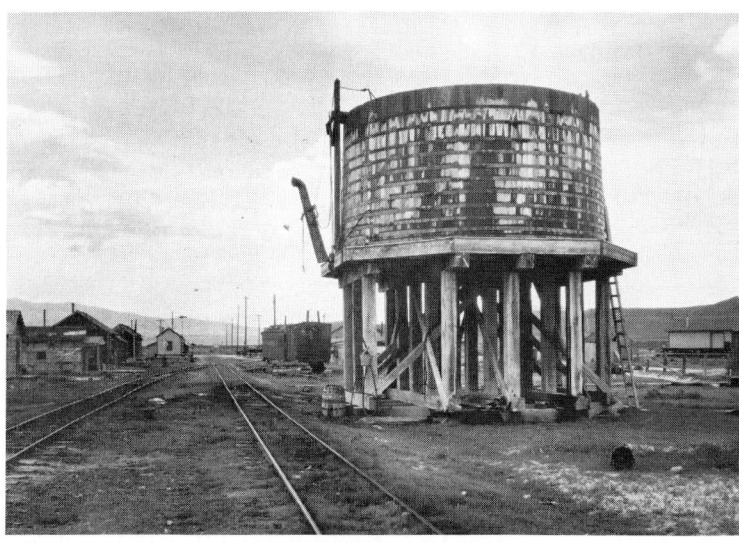

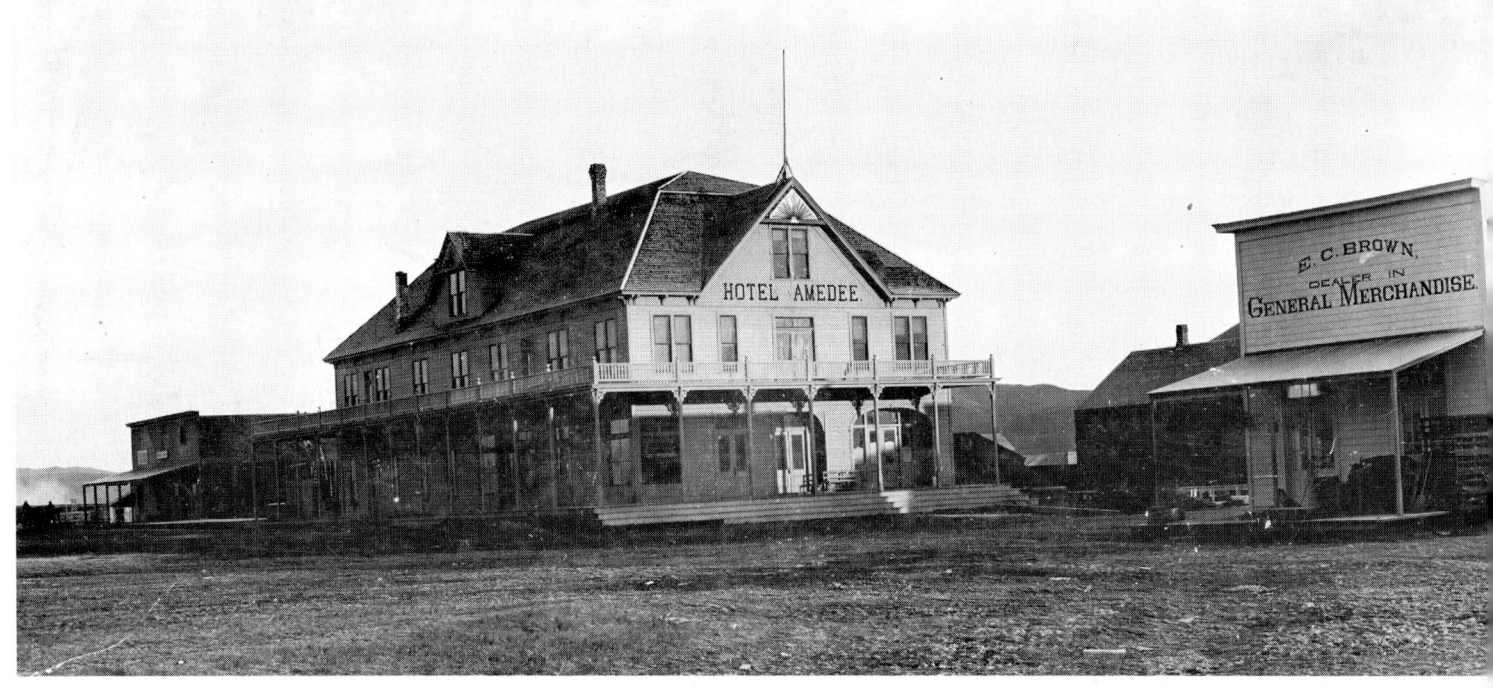

Amedee (named for Amedee Moran, a principal figure in the railroad's history) was originally part of the Brubeck Ranch when the N&C first began operations to that location on November 17, 1890. In the 10 years it remained the terminus, the town grew to a population of from 300 to 400 people, supported the three-story Hotel Amedee *(above)*, another smaller hotel, numerous local merchants, a newspaper, and the usual complement of saloons. The hotel was finally torn down in 1949. *(Nevada Historical Society.)*

Big event in 1899-1900 was the big push to extend the N-C-O another 50 miles to the north; big wonder was why the line terminated at Termo *(top, right)* where this large warehouse was built on the empty, dusty plain populated only by sagebrush. As a railhead, Termo lasted but one year. *(Southern Pacific Collection.)*

From Amedee the line climbed the hill to Mud Flat and paused for water at Karlo *(right, center)*, whose only other claim to fame was its Post Office. The bleak station building at right bore the notice: "To Shippers: When any freight to ship, hang white flag up here and train will stop and load it. If flag is not up trains will not stop." *(Southern Pacific Collection.)*

Between Karlo and Termo lay the water tank, station and yards at Horse Lake *(below)*, shown here about 1926. Back in earlier times when the daily mixed consisted of from seven to ten cars of freight, trains stopping for water would leave their "varnish" sitting way out on the desert, as in the April 1, 1915, view *(bottom, right)*. The R.P.O. clerk is nowhere to be seen, but the Wells Fargo Express agent is at the door; a curious passenger leans out from the steps of the coach behind; and the white-jacketed porter guards the platform of the combination diner-sleeper at rear. *(Left: Southern Pacific Collection; Right: H. E. Gasaway Photo.)*

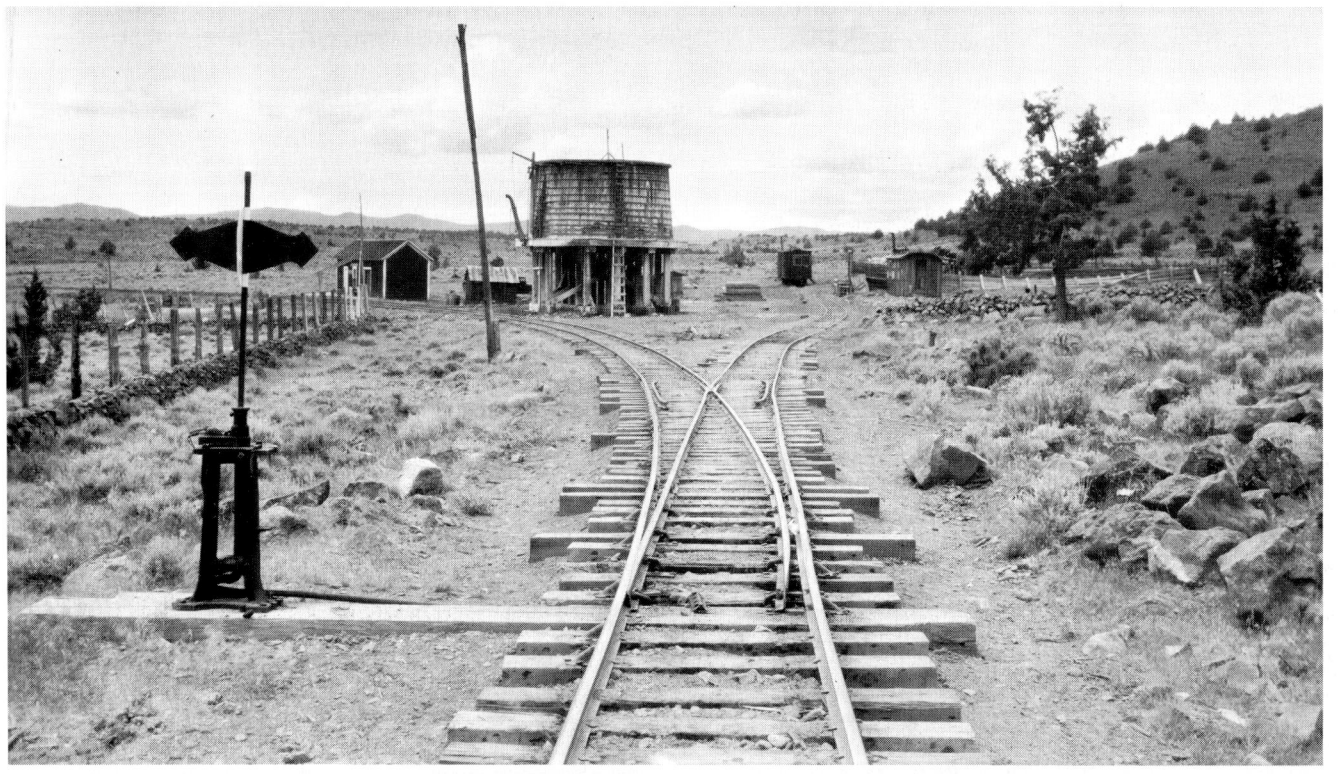

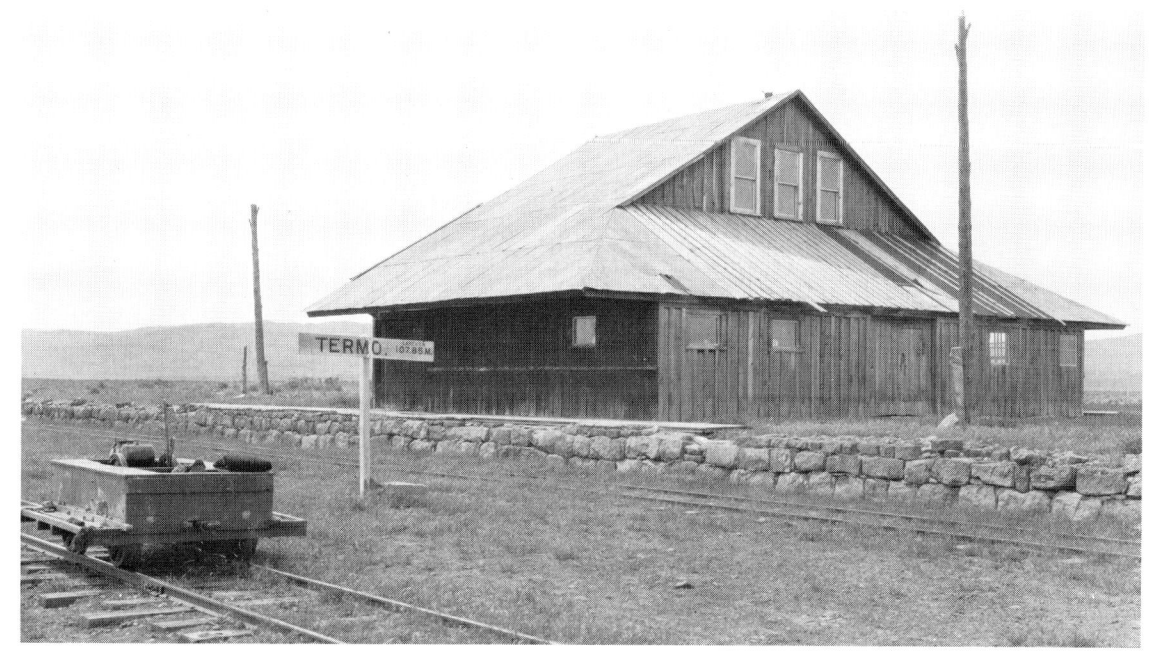

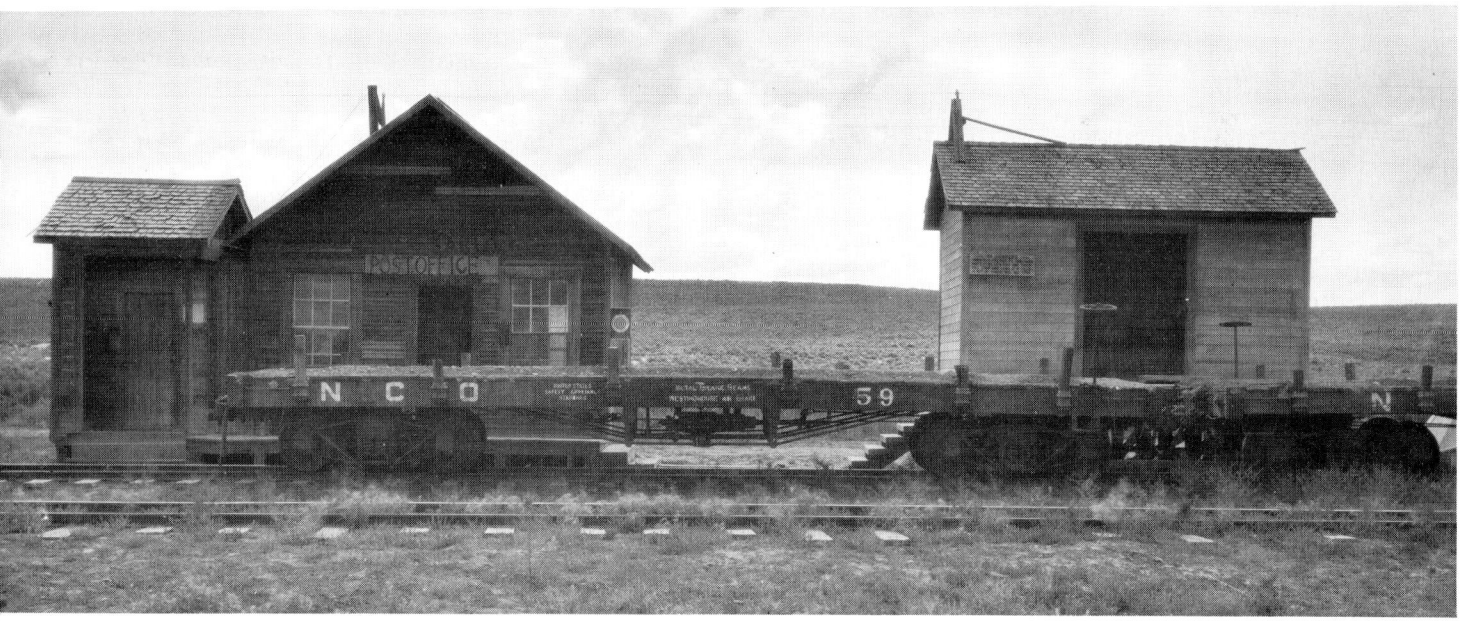

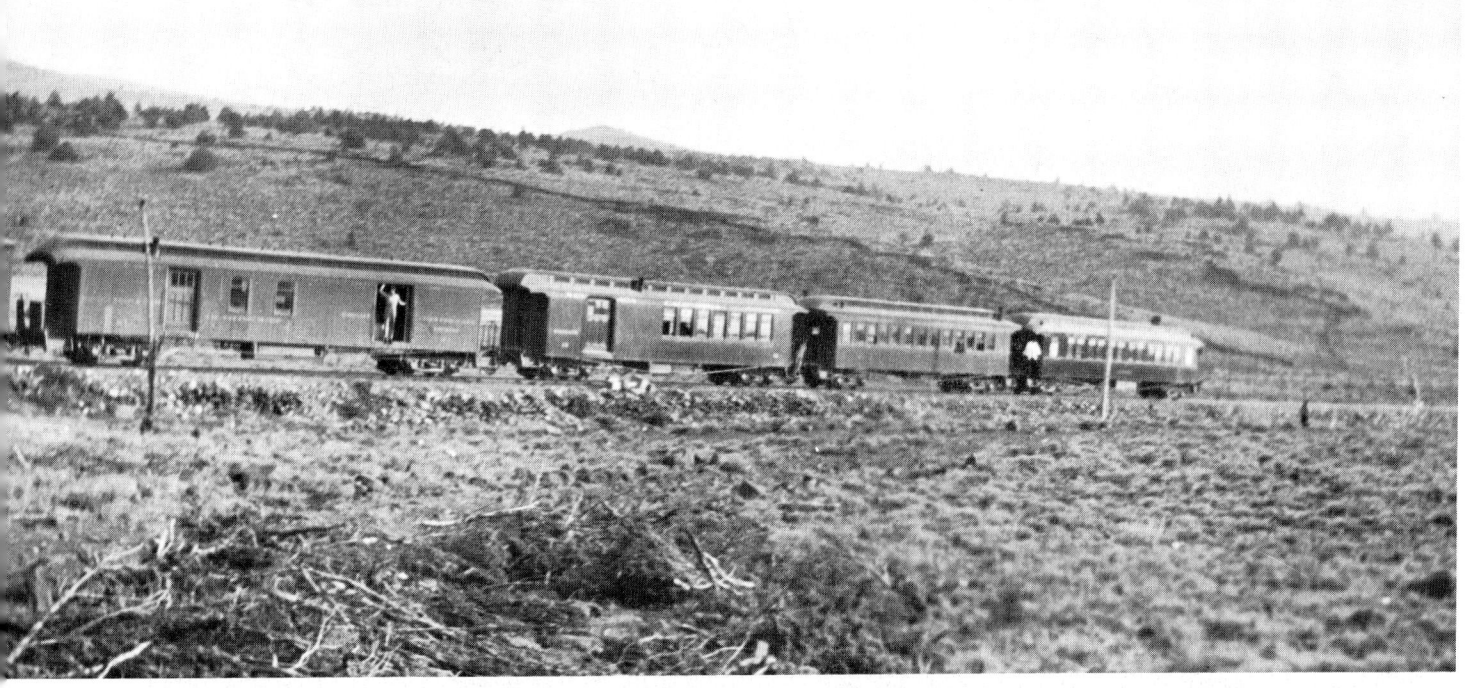

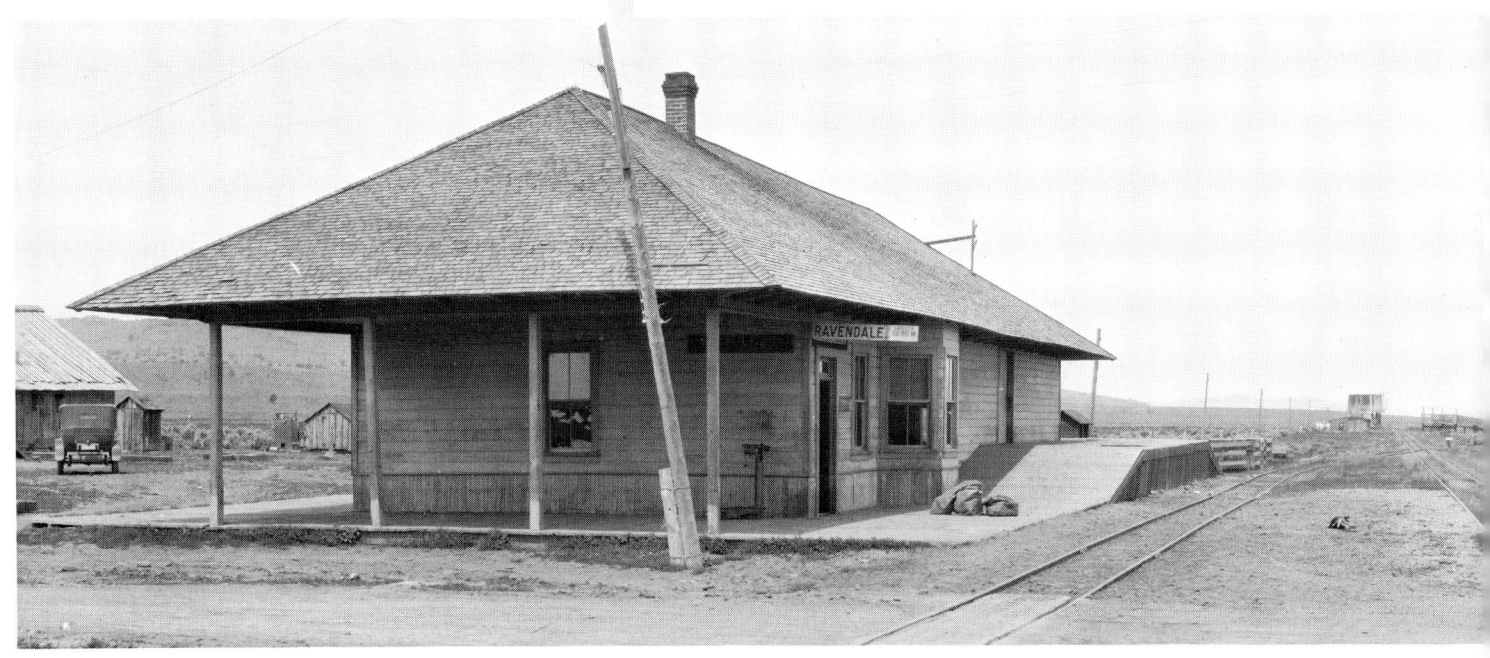

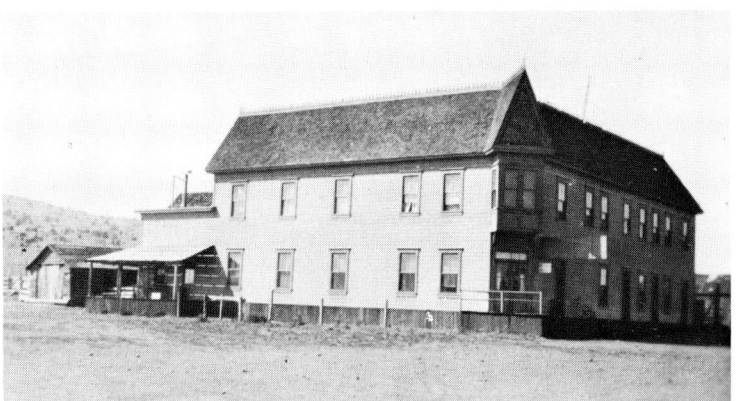

Ravendale *(above)* lay five miles to the south of Termo, but did not assume importance until 1915, long after Termo had withered. Russian families were imported to the area in an attempt to build on-line business. They shipped carloads of rabbit meat via N-C-O to a tamale factory in San Francisco. *(Southern Pacific Collection.)*

Tracks reached Madeline *(below)*, 14 miles north of Termo, early in 1902 and the town remained the railhead for the next four years. The Madeline Hotel *(left)* promoted the "locally grown" orange groves through continuous display of boxes of fruit in the lobby for the benefit of visitors to its cozy and sunny sleeping rooms. Most transients, however, were more concerned with the livestock trade, for which Madeline became a large shipping center. *(Center: Maud Miller Collection; Bottom: Southern Pacific Collection.)*

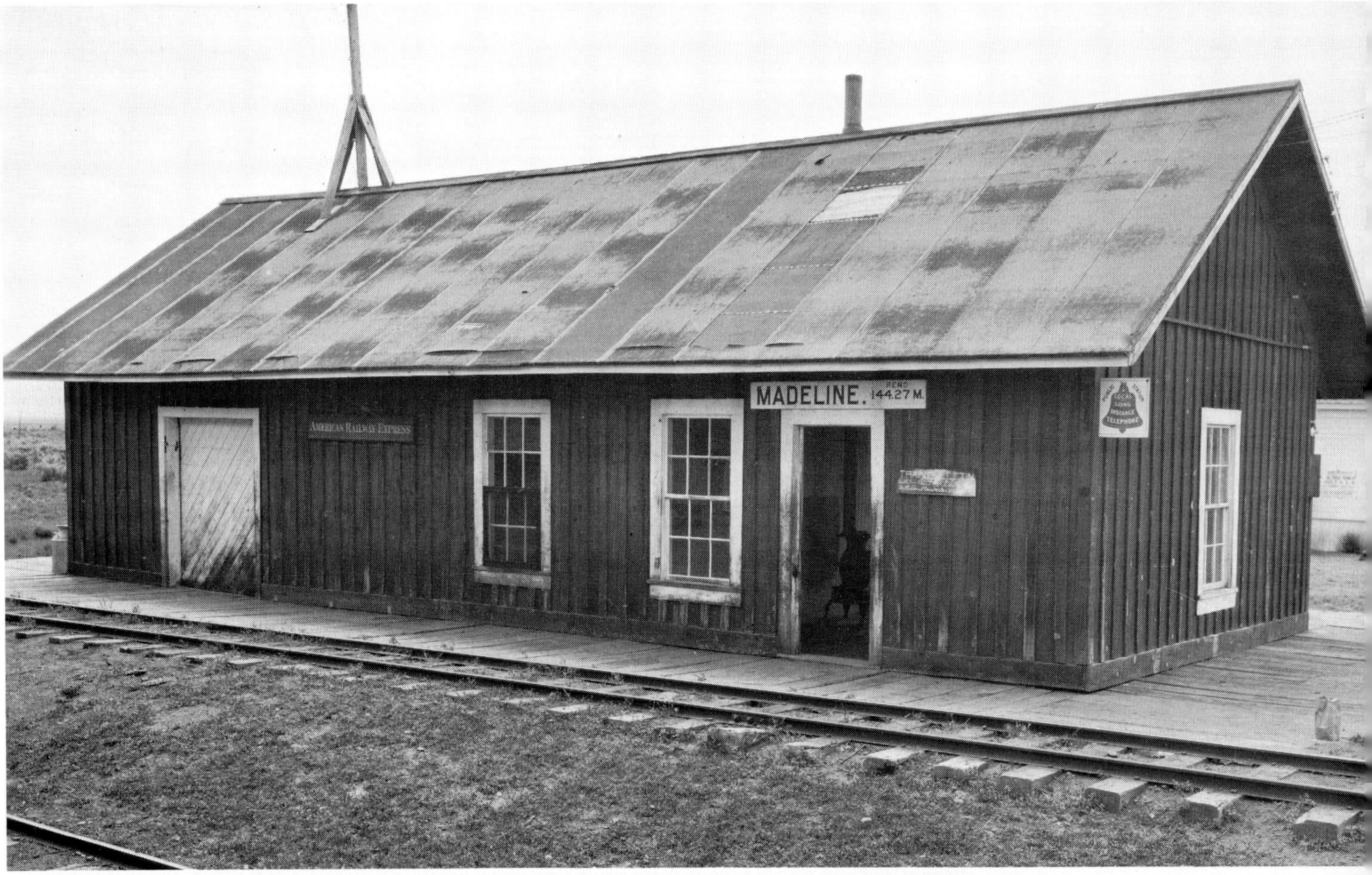

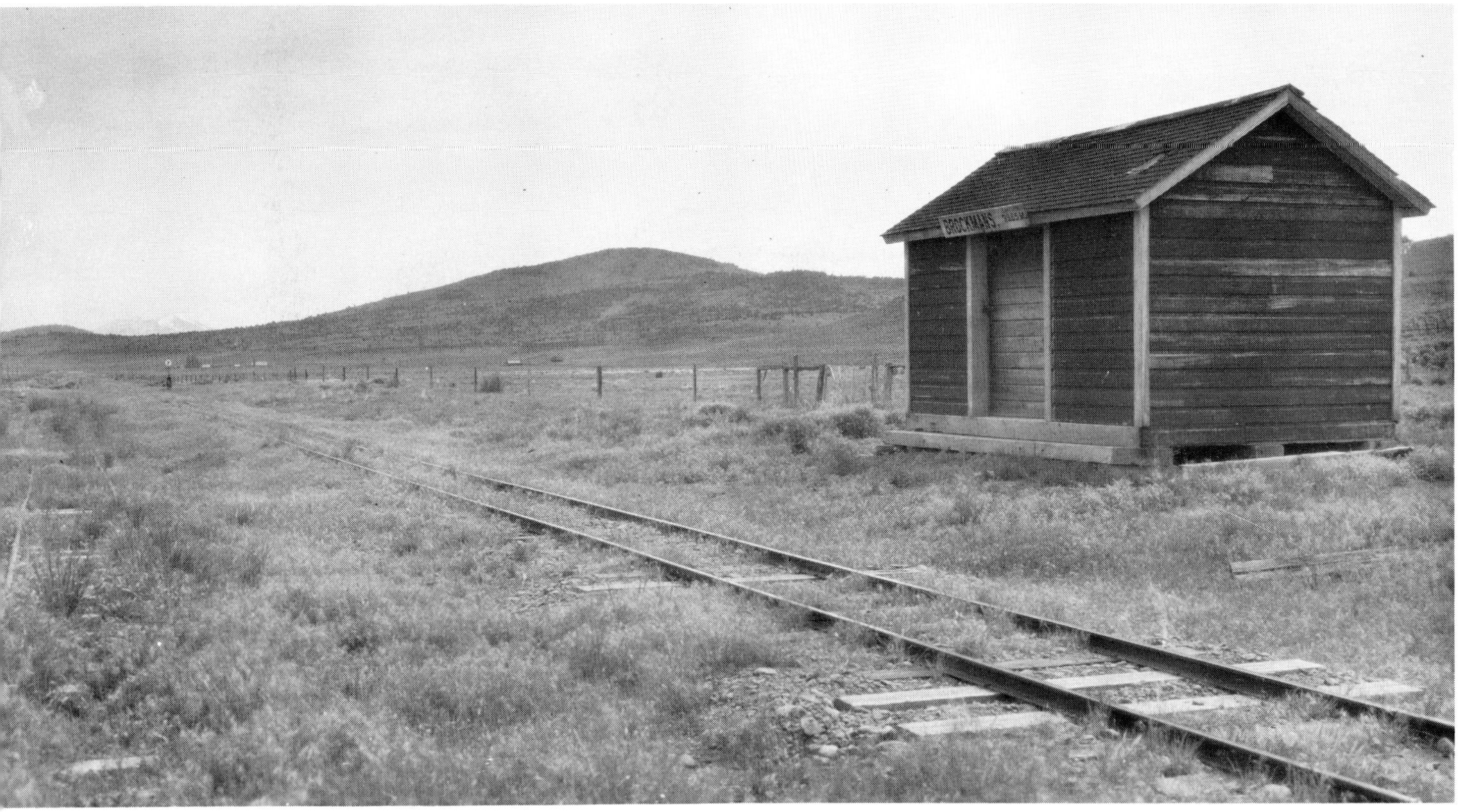

Brockmans *(above)* was but a siding in the wilderness approximately half way between the former railhead of Termo and Madeline. Judging by the fenced-in rangeland, carloads of cattle were originated from this point. *(Southern Pacific Collection.)*

In 1906-07 the N-C-O pushed on from Madeline for the 20 miles up and over a 200-foot hill to Sage Hen, followed by a drop of 1,100 feet to Likely *(below)*. The town failed to live up to its name, and most trains paused just long enough to have their picture taken, as was done with northbound No. 7 *(right)* in June 1919. The next 20 miles to Alturas were placed under construction almost immediately, and through service to the Modoc County seat started on Dec. 1, 1908. *(Right: H. E. Gasaway; Bottom: Southern Pacific Collection.)*

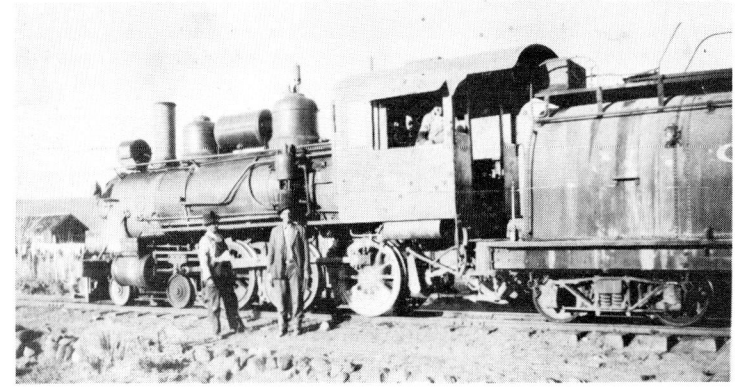

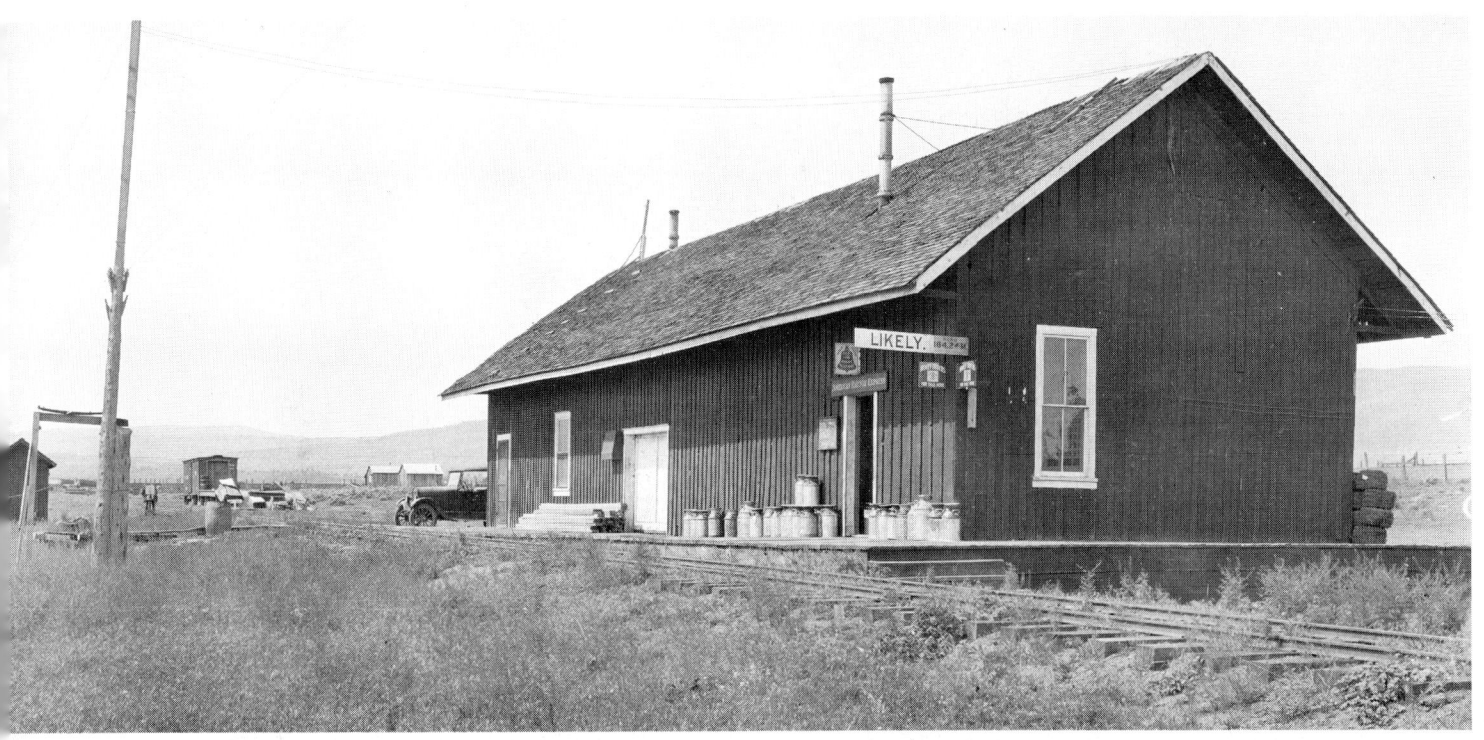

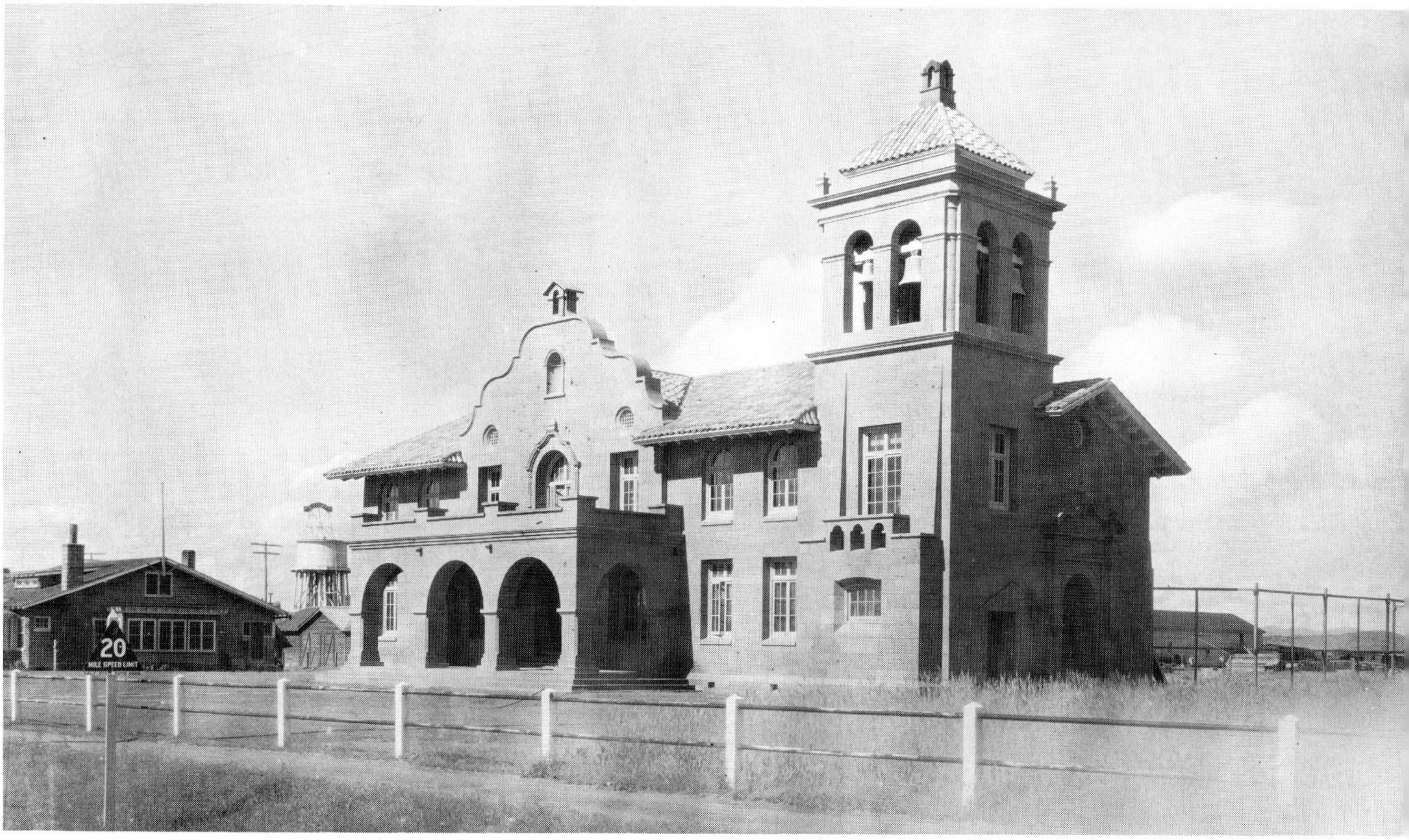

Although Alturas was stimulated when rails of the N-C-O first arrived in 1908, its economy boomed when the shops and headquarters of the road were moved from Reno in 1917-18, following purchase by the Western Pacific of the southern portion of the line from the WP's Hackstaff crossing to Reno. An imposing new, two-story general office building *(above)* was erected, complete with belfry and (wooden) bells turned on the company's lathe by Charles Chapman. New shops and roundhouse completed the facilities and can be seen from rear *(top, right)*, from in front *(center)* and from above *(bottom)*. The entire project lay on land donated by the town of Alturas just to the north and west of the N-C-O's Alturas station *(below)*. *(All Pictures: Southern Pacific Collection.)*

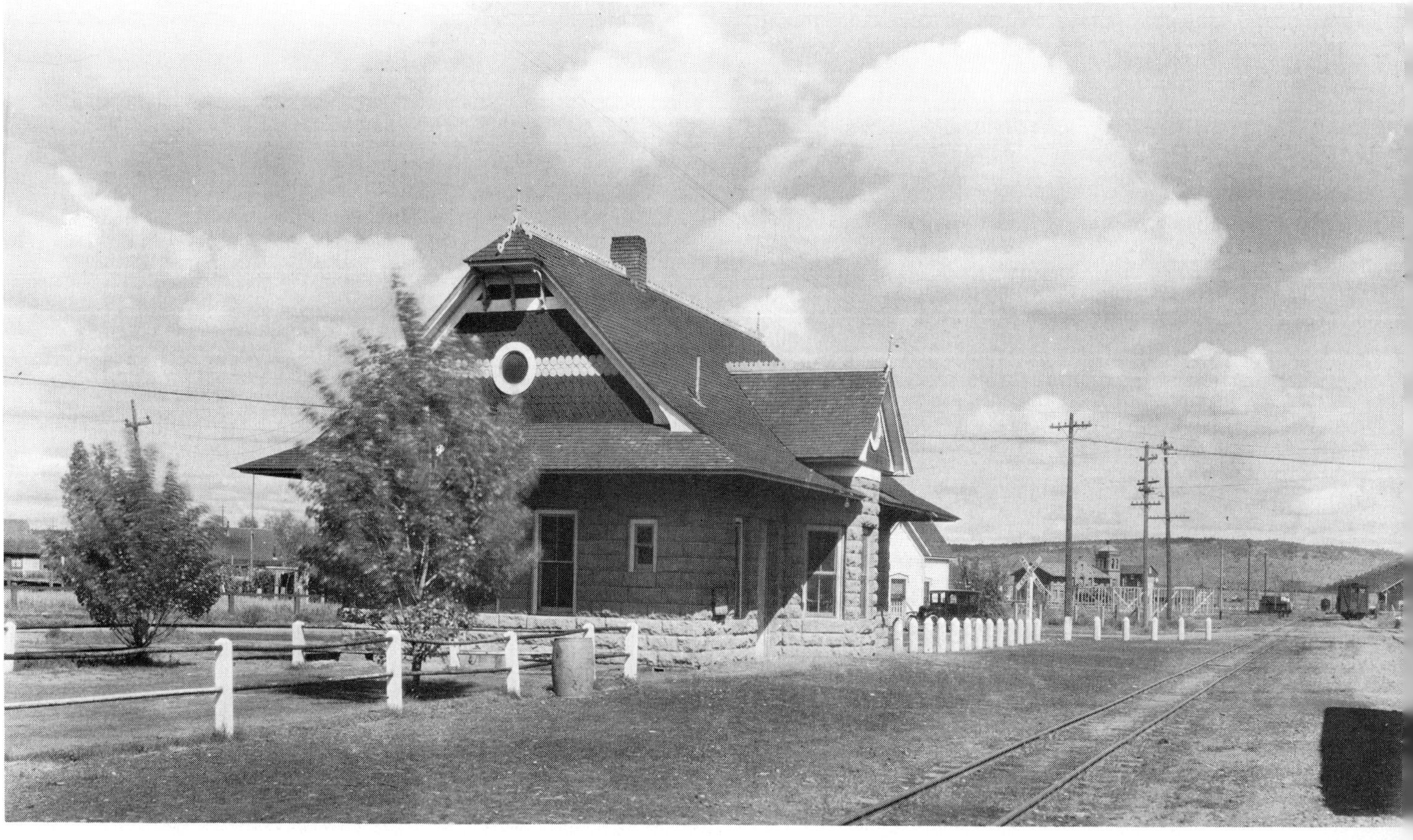

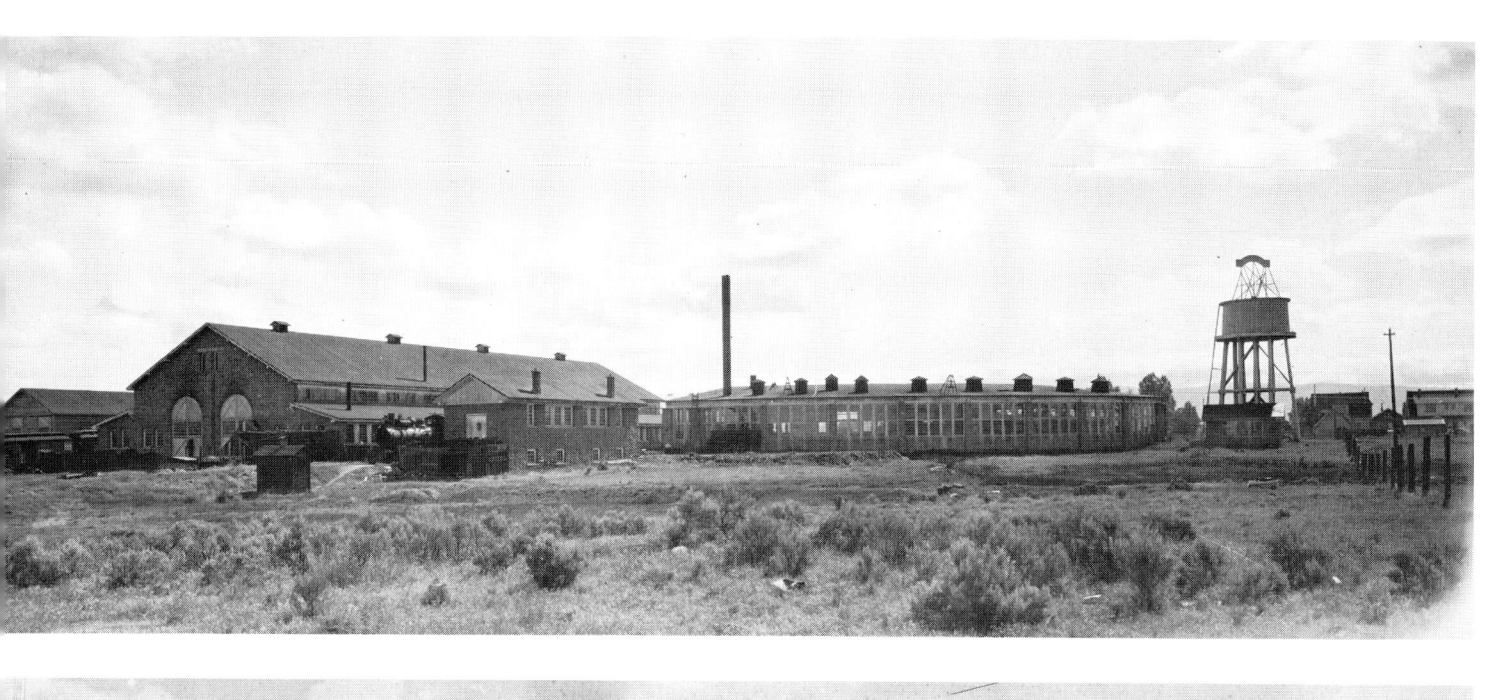
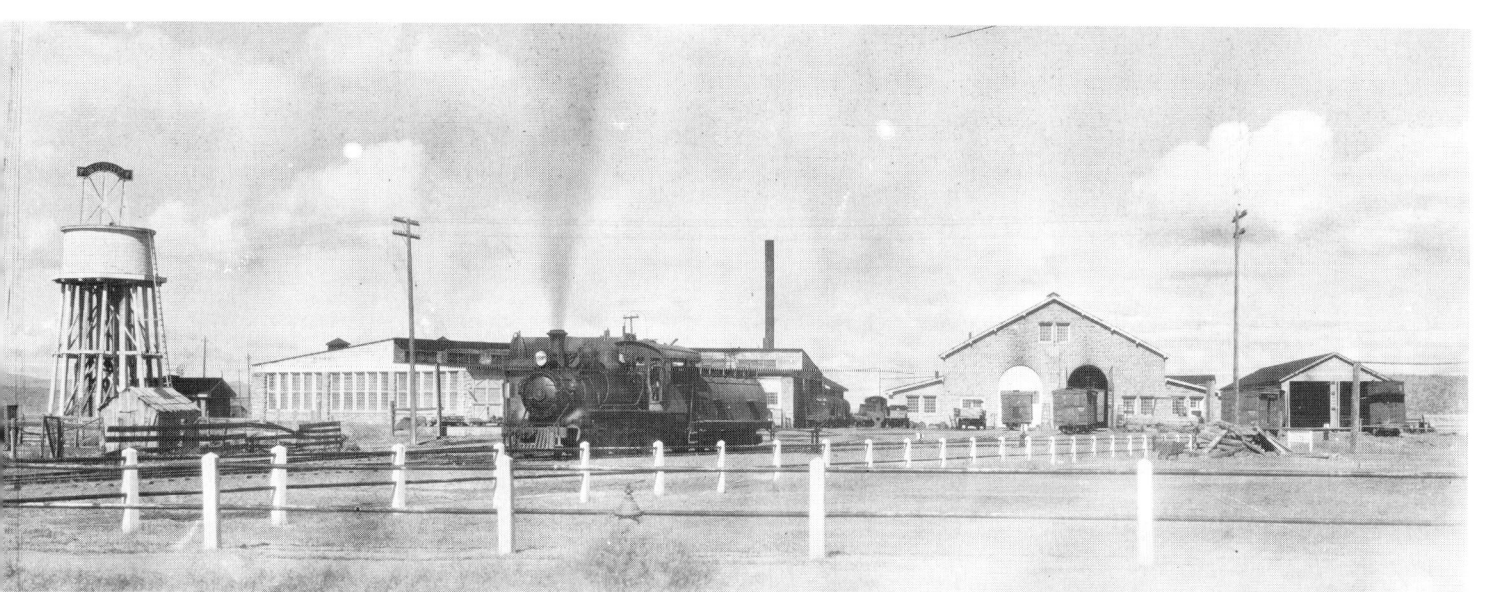

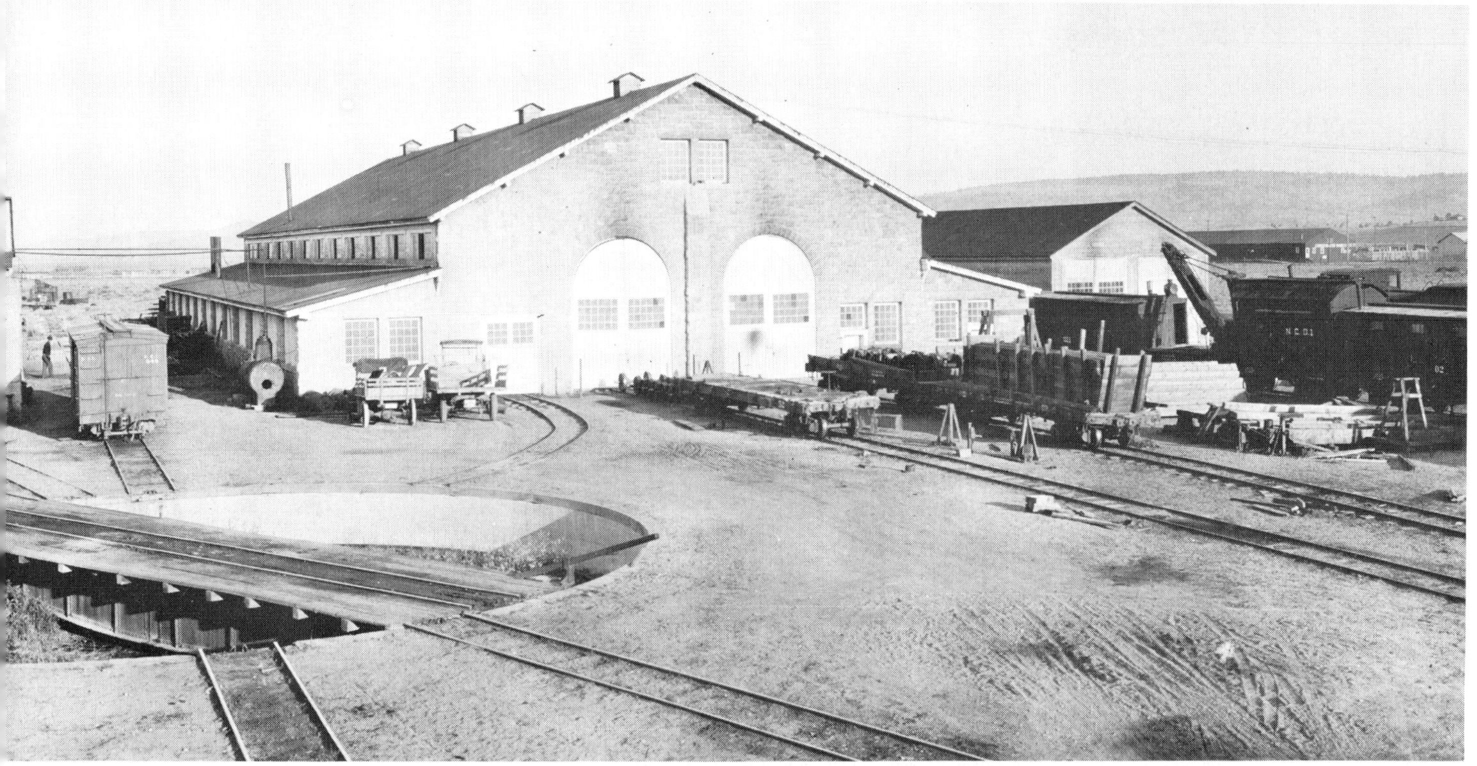

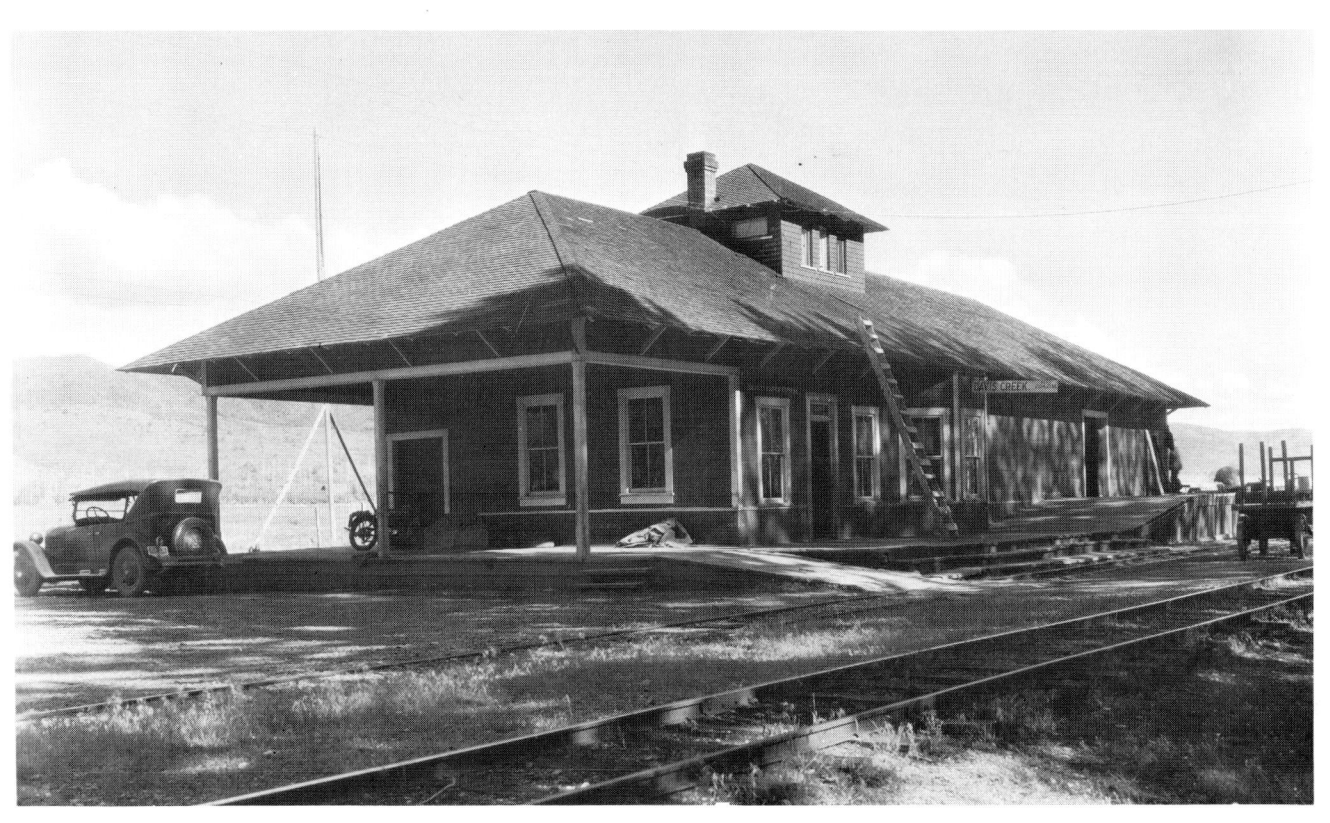

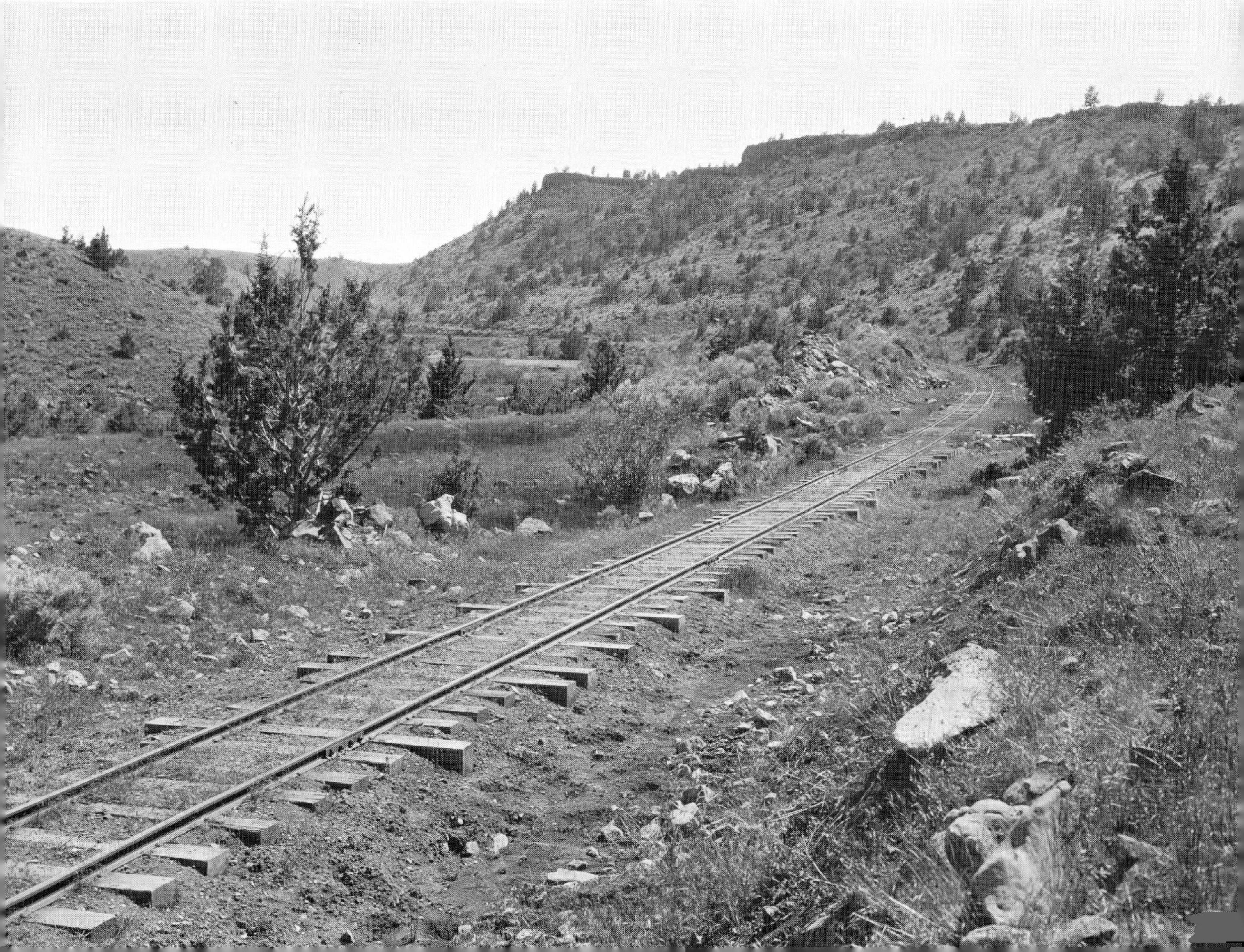

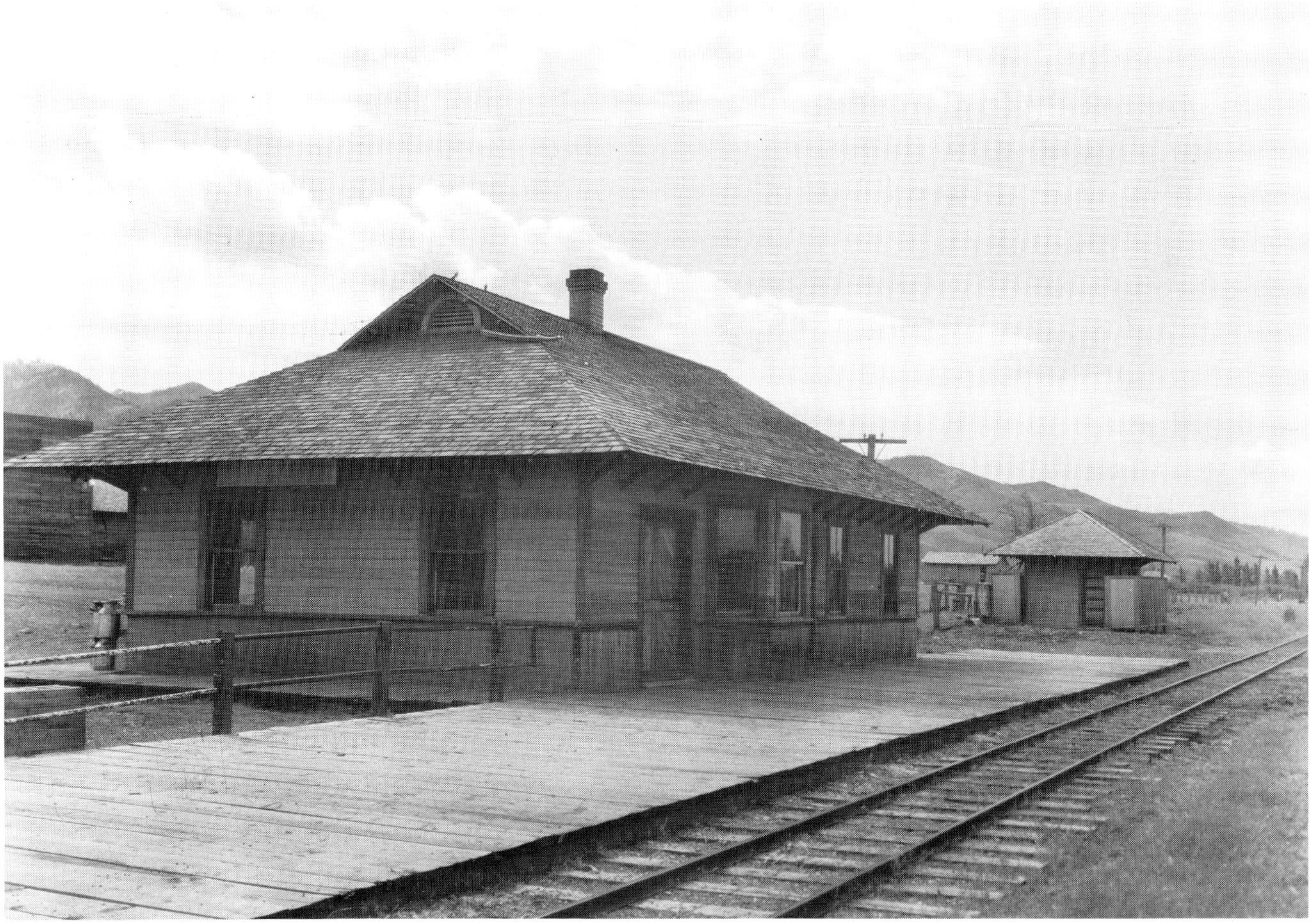

Davis Creek *(top, left)*, where passengers could embark by boat on Goose Lake for Lakeview, Oregon, was the next objective of the N-C-O. The 20-mile approach from Alturas mostly lay along the banks of the Pit River *(left, below)*, wherein the presence of standard-gauge ties in the roadbed dates this picture about 1926-27 just prior to the line's conversion to standard gauge. *(Both Photos: Southern Pacific Collection.)*

The only mining rush in the area occurred near Fairport *(above)* whose station sign, in lieu of the formal name, carries the faded legend: "High Grade Gold Camp 10 Miles." Along the way, the N-C-O built through Willow Ranch *(below)* which lay seven miles to the south. *(Both Photos: Southern Pacific Collection.)*

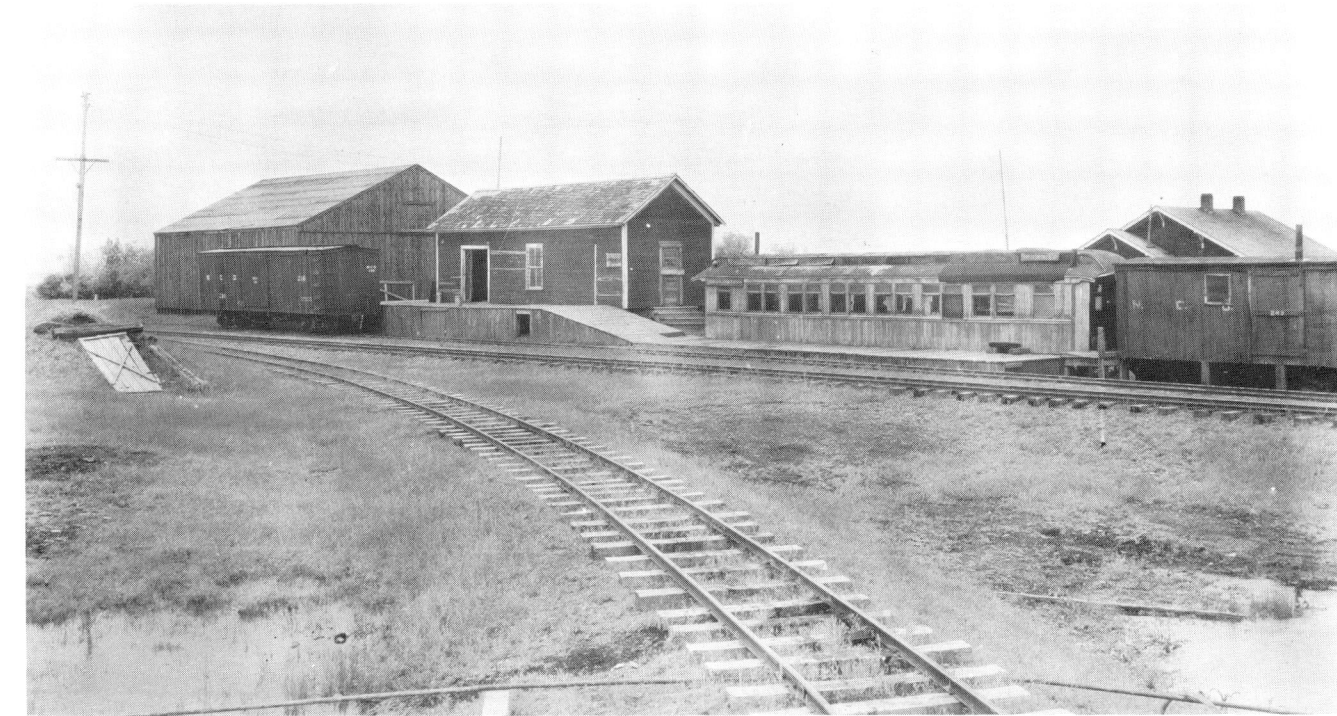

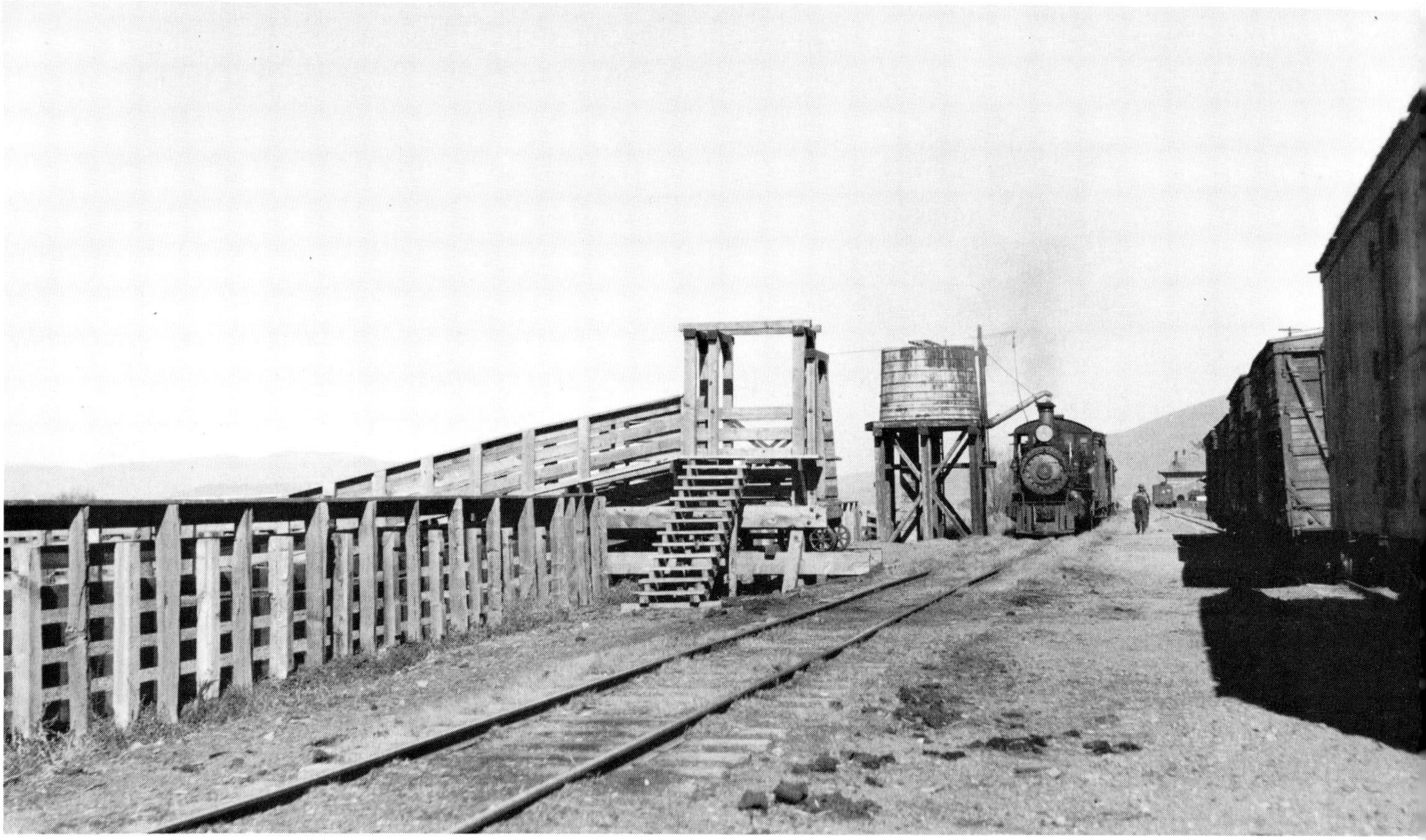

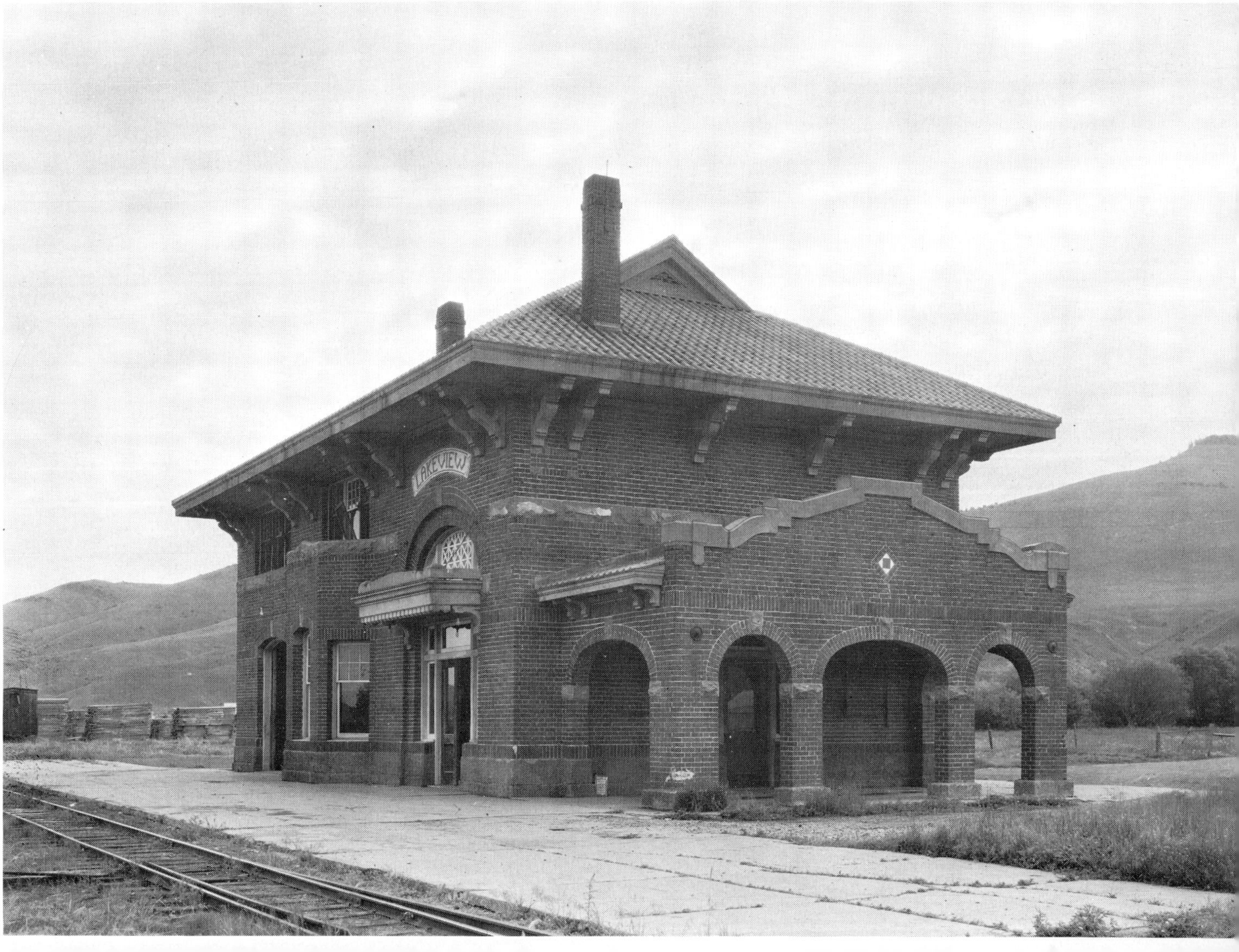

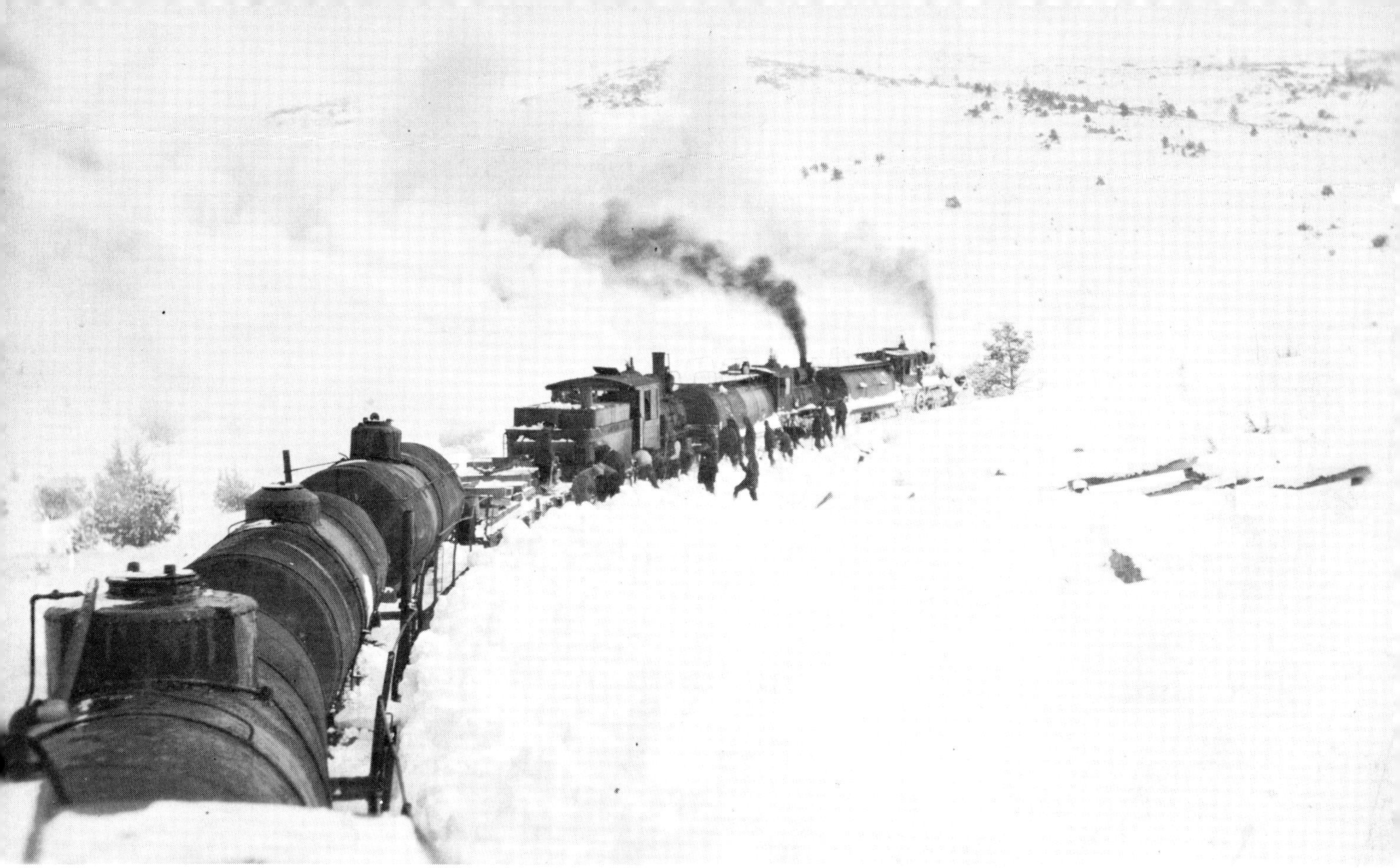

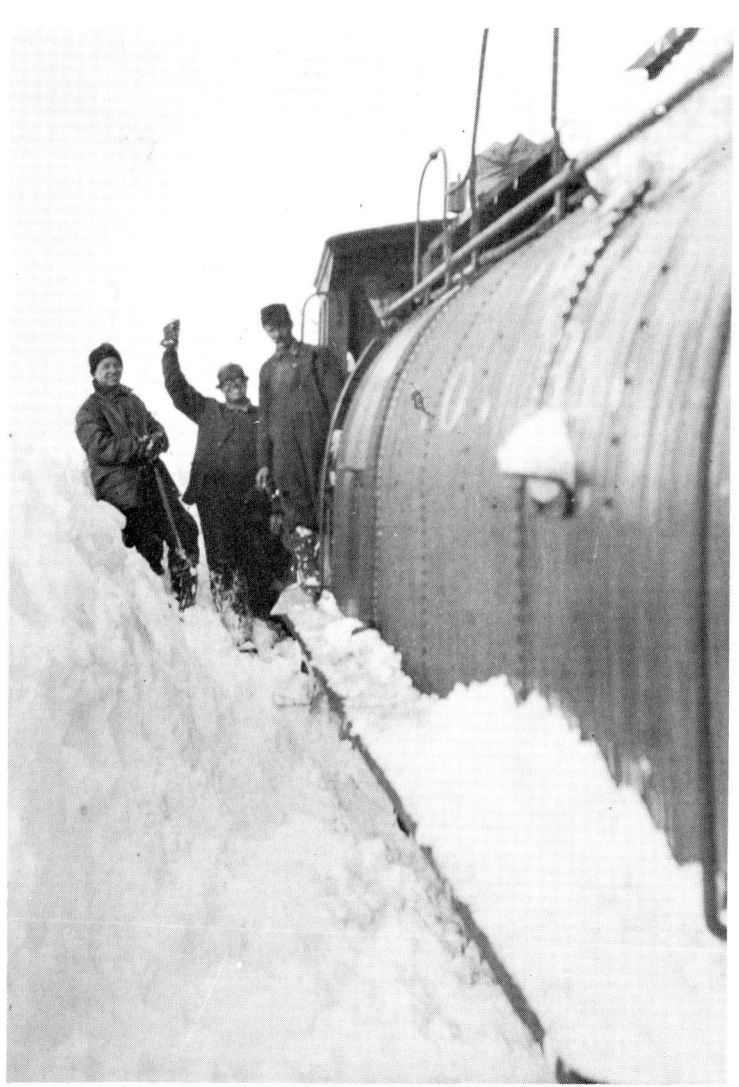

The cattle yards at Lakeview, Oregon *(above, left)* constituted but one of the objectives for extending the N-C-O to this remote location, which was finally reached on January 10, 1912. Lumber provided another major source of traffic, and there was always the ultimate hope of extending the railroad to The Dalles on the Columbia River so the road could become a real through route. In the photo, No. 5 has just finished taking water as the dripping spout attests, and the trainmen are about to uncouple the caboose and coach so the morning mixed may be made up. Behind and to right of locomotive is the Lakeview station, shown in close-up *(bottom, left)*, which was modeled after the main brick depot built in Reno in 1910. *(Top: Stanley Borden; Bottom: Southern Pacific Collection.)*

Severe blizzards ushered in the year 1916. Temperatures dropped to zero and below. Winds of 60 miles per hour drifted snow and forced trains to a halt, then enveloped them in its blanket of white. The main line became blocked for 22 days. Of the 14 locomotives on the line, only two remained in operating condition and one was in the Reno shops; all others were off the tracks and immobilized. The triple-header *(above)*, with locomotives Nos. 3, 5 and 22 at the head end, had started down the hill from Sage Hen to Likely in an early storm on January 4, 1916, when No. 5's tender left the rails. Every available man is desperately trying to dig to get a rerailing frog in place before the blowing snow and biting cold immobilize the train. Five days later on January 9 Engineer Sam Boney of No. 10 *(right)* waves a greeting as his plow train, momentarily halted, tries to clear the line. *(Both Photos: H. E. Gasaway.)*

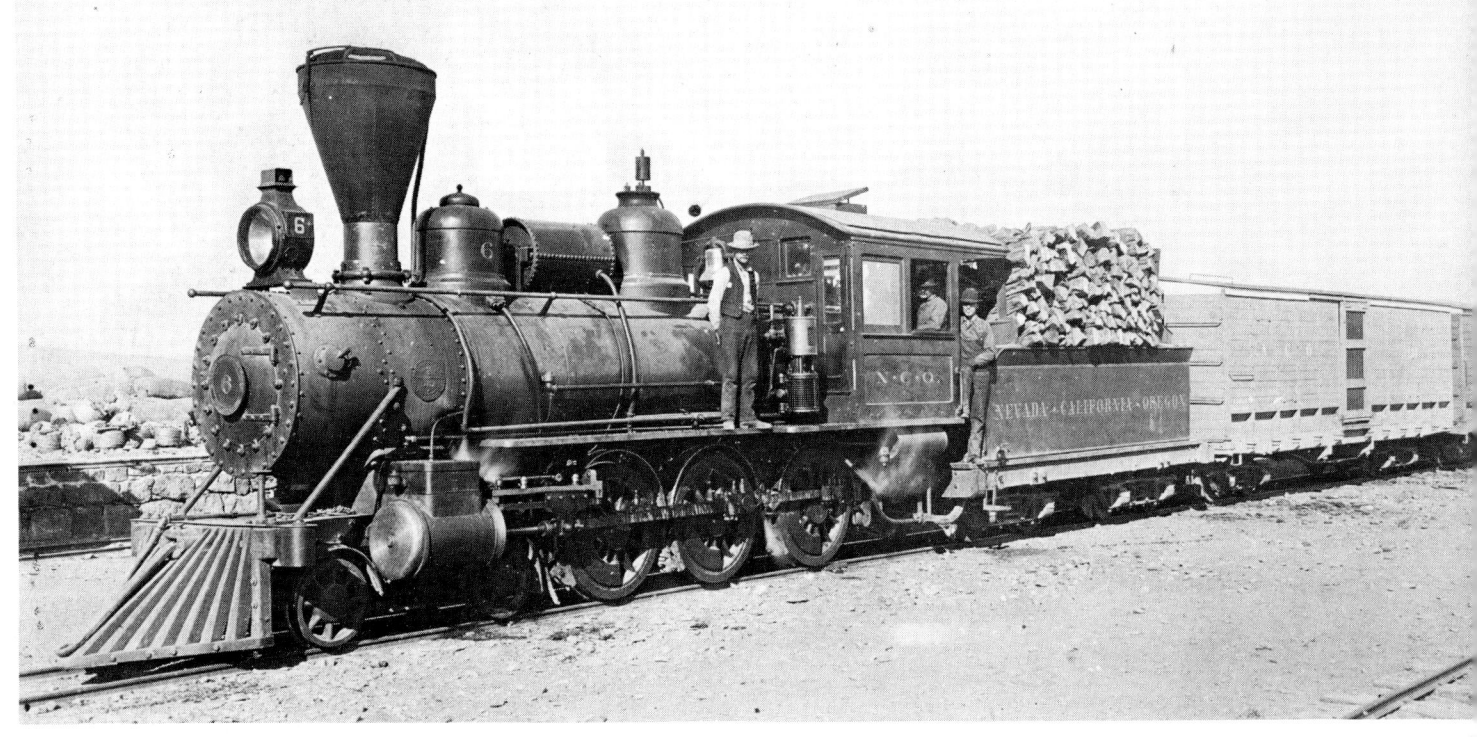

Baldwin 10-wheeler (4-6-0) No. 6 was obviously still a woodburner and still used link-and-pin couplings when this picture *(above)* was taken in the early 1900's. *(Stanley Palmer Photo.)*

The coal-fired, steam-powered ditcher *(below)* attracted considerable attention and admiration when first acquired. It could travel the N-C-O's narrow 3-foot rails or operate on broader 6′ 4½″-gauge track over soft ground as the occasion required. *(Southern Pacific Collection.)*

Passenger Motor Cars Nos. 101 and 102 *(right, top)*, pictured at Davis Creek station on their trial run in May 1921, were intended for operation between the Western Pacific connection at Hackstaff, California, and Lakeview, Oregon. They proved to be unsatisfactory in regular service and were returned to the builder. The home-made, elongated touring-car-bus *(center)* of an earlier era did a much better job. In spite of these innovations, the light steam passenger power they were intended to supersede continued to roll merrily on. American (4-4-0) No. 3 *(bottom)* is seen here in July 1929 at Wendel. *(Top: H. E. Gasaway; Center: Maud Miller Collection; Bottom: D. S. Richter Collection.)*

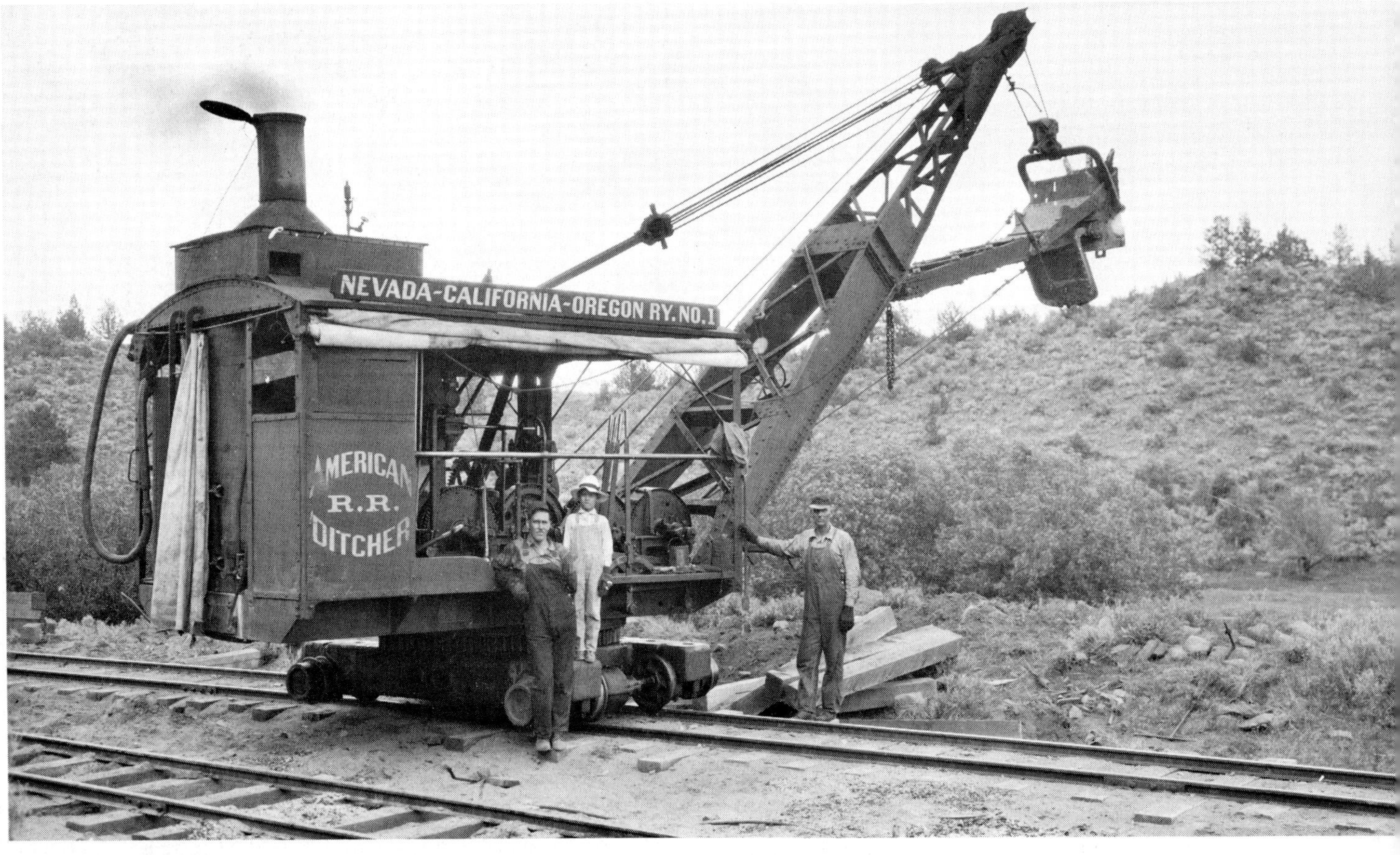

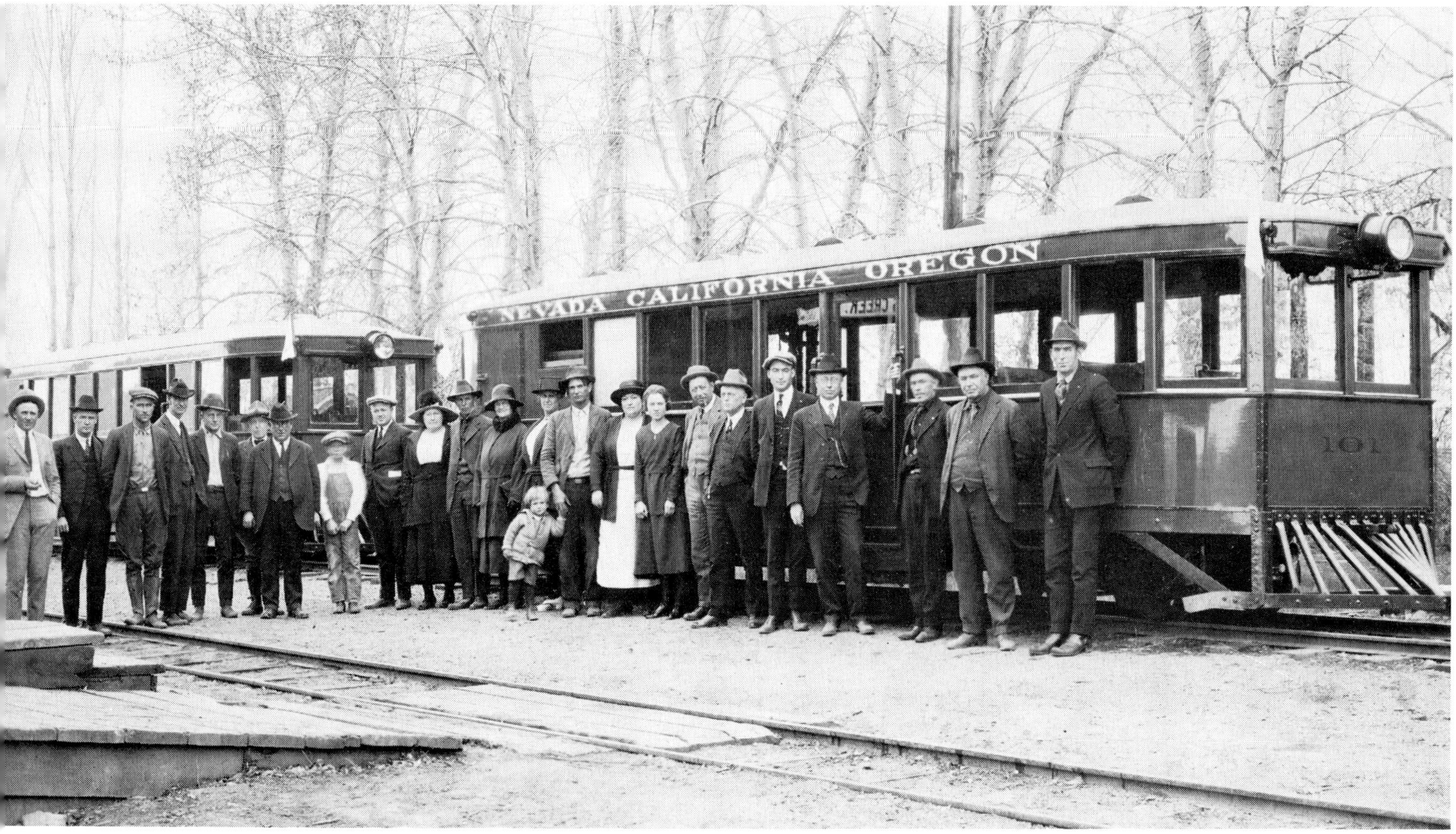

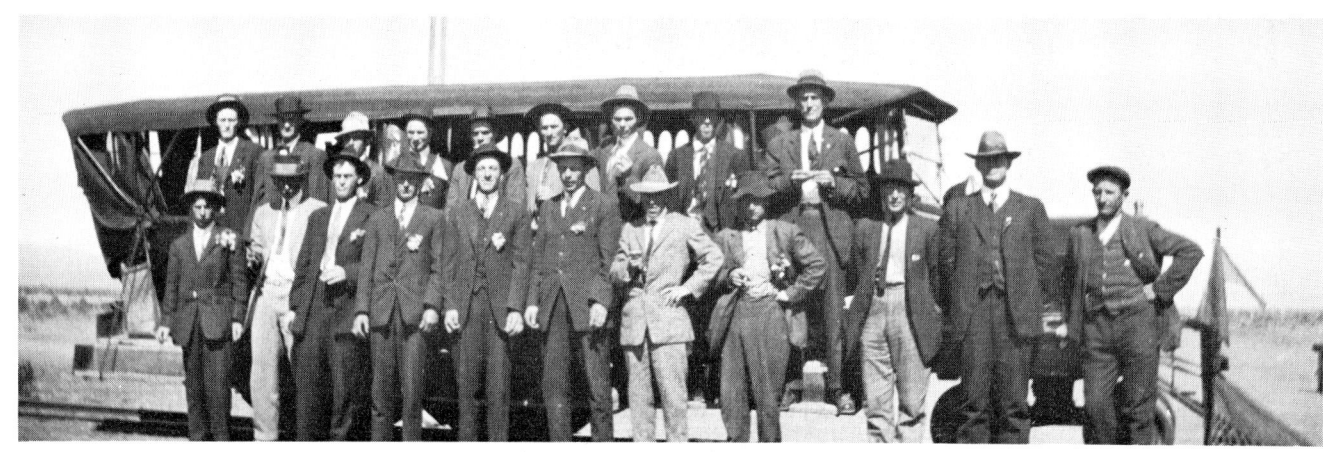
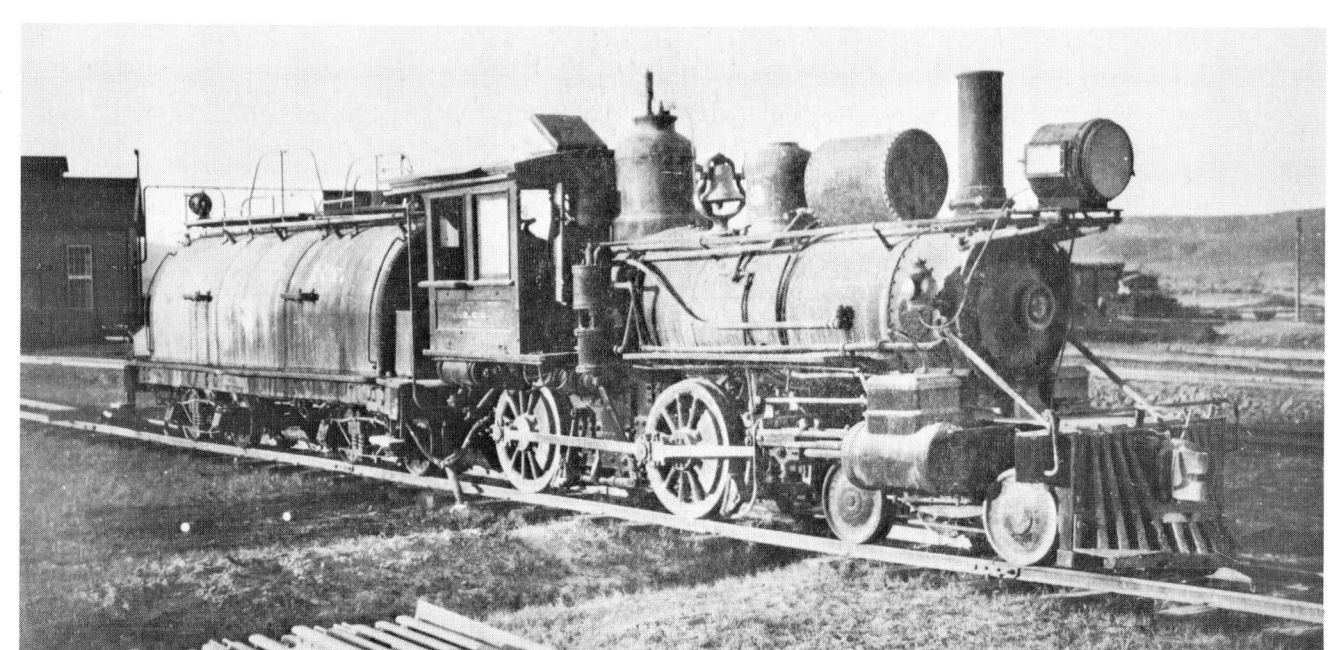

-375

around $400,000 annually, but every year after 1914 regularly recorded deficits, except one wherein a special accounting adjustment was made. Compared with 1899 when the gross revenue was a mere $44,622 but the operating profit was $12,330, the results left a great deal to be desired. And losses continued to mount as more money was advanced for operations by the Morans and by the local banks. In 1916, and again in 1920 and 1921, efforts were made without success, to sell the entire line to the Western Pacific. In 1921 a proposed 14-mile extension from Lakeview into the Thomas Creek country with a six-mile spur along Camp Creek, was contemplated to bring substantial new lumber traffic. When the WP refused so much as to lease the necessary rails, except under onerous terms, the N-C-O began to consider the possibility of removing the 16 miles of track south from Wendel (the SP connection) to Hackstaff (the WP connection). Since this trackage was being operated primarily for the benefit of the WP, the N-C-O felt it might benefit more by taking those rails and extending its line into the new timber area, relying on the SP connection for its only interchange. However Baldwin, the WP attorney, had insisted on a preferential traffic interchange clause in the 1917 agreement of sale for the Reno portion of the line, and this clause precluded the elimination of the Hackstaff connection.

Difficulties in handling lumber on narrow gauge cars pointed to the need for conversion of the line to standard gauge, but since only one lumber company indicated any interest, the expense could not be justified. With these bleak portents coupled with the already overburdening losses, the N-C-O decided to abandon *operation* of the line. Hearings were held at Alturas in February 1922 with people in the entire area deeply concerned. Greatest argument for preservation of the road revolved about the livestock business which had grown with the 36-hour service to San Francico. Transfers of livestock were made at Wendel or Hackstaff, day and night (under sputtering arc lamps); but as S. H. McCartney, vice-president and general manager advised, the revenues from this business were offset in large measure by the heavy return movement of empty stock cars, and the fact that 75% of those same cars lay idle for eight months out of the year.

The California Railroad Commission heard the case for the I.C.C., which weighed the testimony and found that the railroad was needed to serve the people in the area. However, it did authorize the abandonment of the 16 miles of track between Wendel and Hackstaff (last train was operated October 31, 1922), and it increased the N-C-O's share of the division of the through rate on freight traffic interchanged with the SP. The WP filed a threatening law suit, but their action was thrown out of court.

For several decades the Southern Pacific had been looking for a short route to the east from Oregon. Acquisition of the Nevada-California-Oregon Railway plus construction of a connecting line from Klamath Falls southeast to Alturas (on the N-C-O) would provide a through route all the way to Fernley, Nevada, where it would tie in with the Overland Route (the SP's main line to the east). Thus it was that when Moran returned from a trip to Europe, he found a memo on his desk in New York asking him to call the SP. William Sproule, SP president, made what Moran considered an eminently fair first offer, and an agreement was signed on April 30, 1925, for the purchase of all of the bonds and stock of the N-C-O (Moran and his three sisters held all of the stock), payment to be made in bonds of the Pacific Electric Railway, an SP subsidiary. Following I.C.C. approval, the SP formally acquired control in October 1926, even though Moran did not convey the preferred stock until March 22, 1929, as allowed under the agreement.

On July 1, 1927, 17 outfit cars were parked at Wendel, and SP forces began the project of widening the N-C-O trackage to handle the larger and heavier equipment. The roadbed was reworked; standard gauge ties were inserted under the rails (many had already been installed as replacements during the previous two years); then the wide gauge rails were spiked in place, largely outside the two narrow gauge rails although in places three-rail track was employed. The multiplicity of rails frequently created confusion, particularly during night switching operations, and many times yard engines ended a movement on the ties.

With 800 men at work, the project moved along swiftly. Regular operations to Alturas over the standard gauge commenced October 24, 1927, whereupon the narrow gauge railroad mileage of the nation immediately dropped 7%. On Armistice Day a big celebration was held, the crowds being augmented by special trainloads of people until the attendance was estimated at 5,000. Cattleman "Doc" Hordon undertook the task of feeding the multitude by cooking 500 pounds of Modoc red beans in a series of large buckets, all at one time.

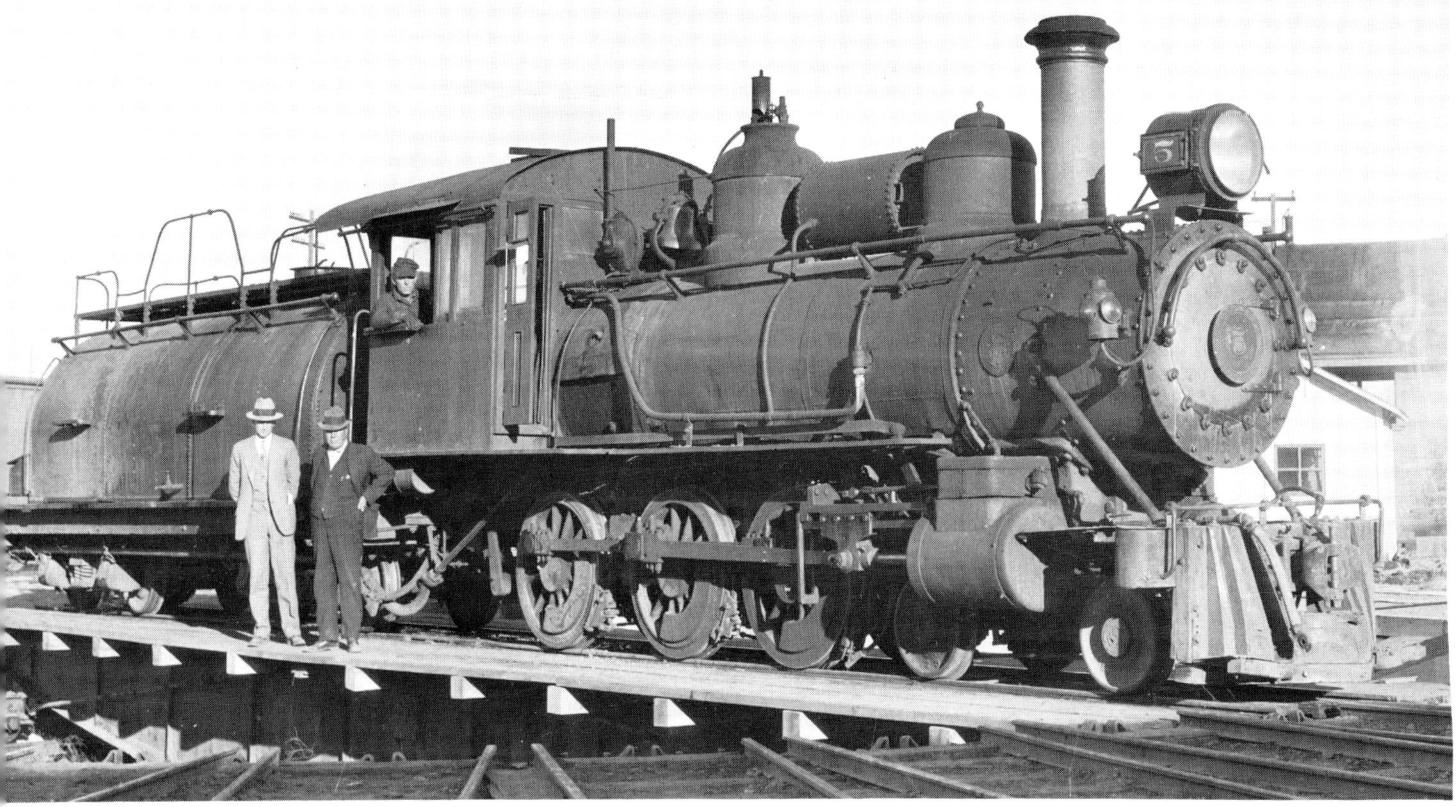

N-C-O Baldwin-built 10-wheeler No. 5 *(above)* at Alturas. Harold Mahan, traffic manager and Ed Smith, master mechanic are standing; T. Allie Smith is in the cab. No. 11 of a later date *(center)* had two air tanks behind the stack and a heavier pump installed by the builder before delivery. Consolidation (2-8-0) No. 14 *(bottom)* was delivered in 1914 and outfitted in the same manner. *(Top: Southern Pacific Collection; Center: H. L. Broadbelt Collection; Bottom: Baldwin-Lima-Hamilton Corp.)*

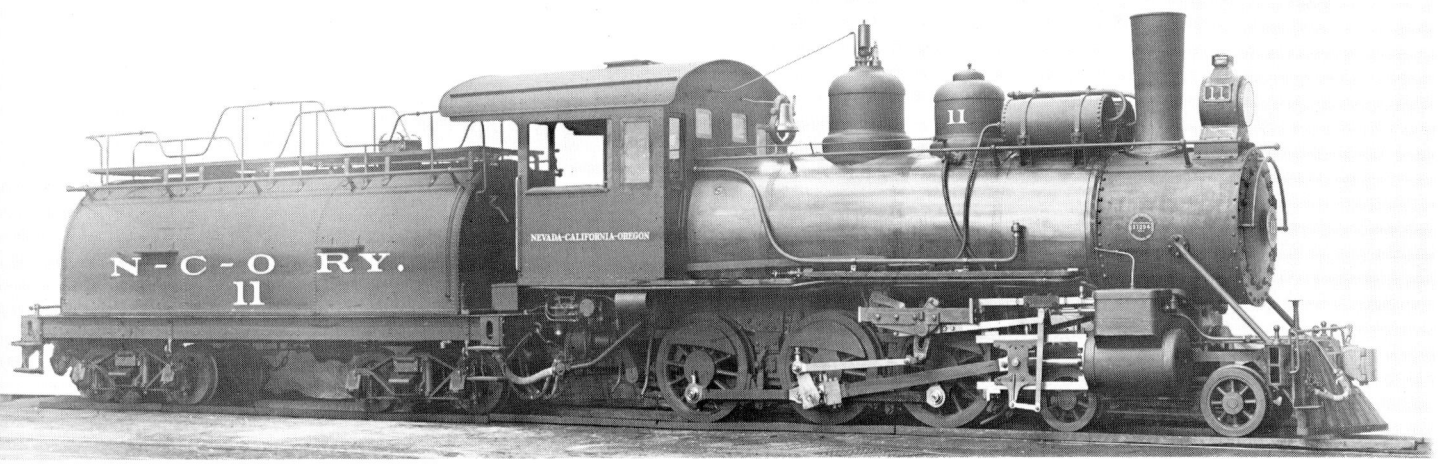

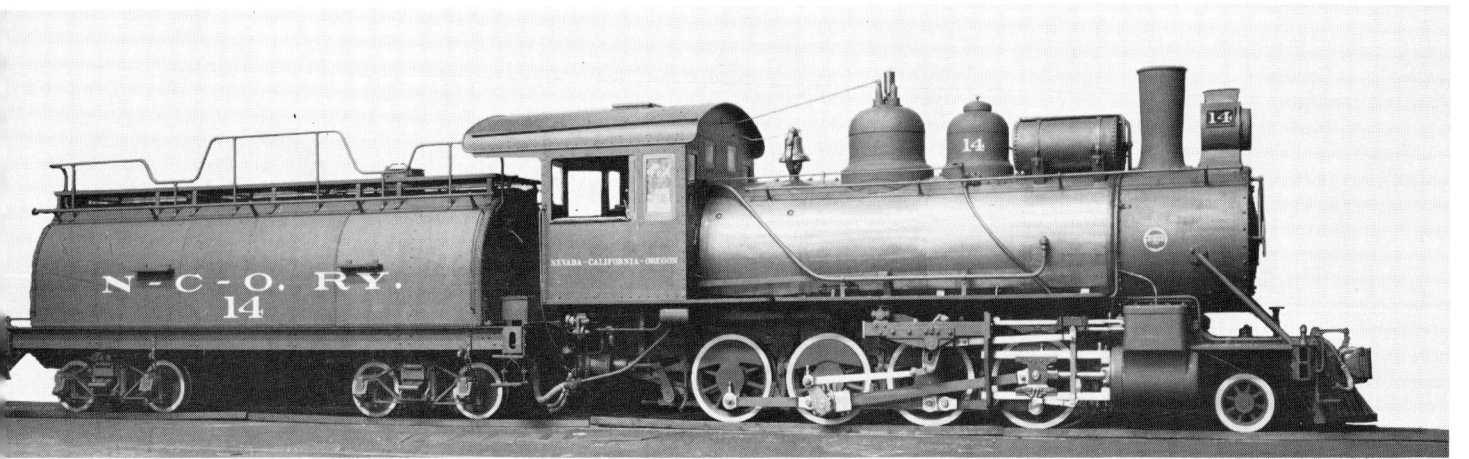

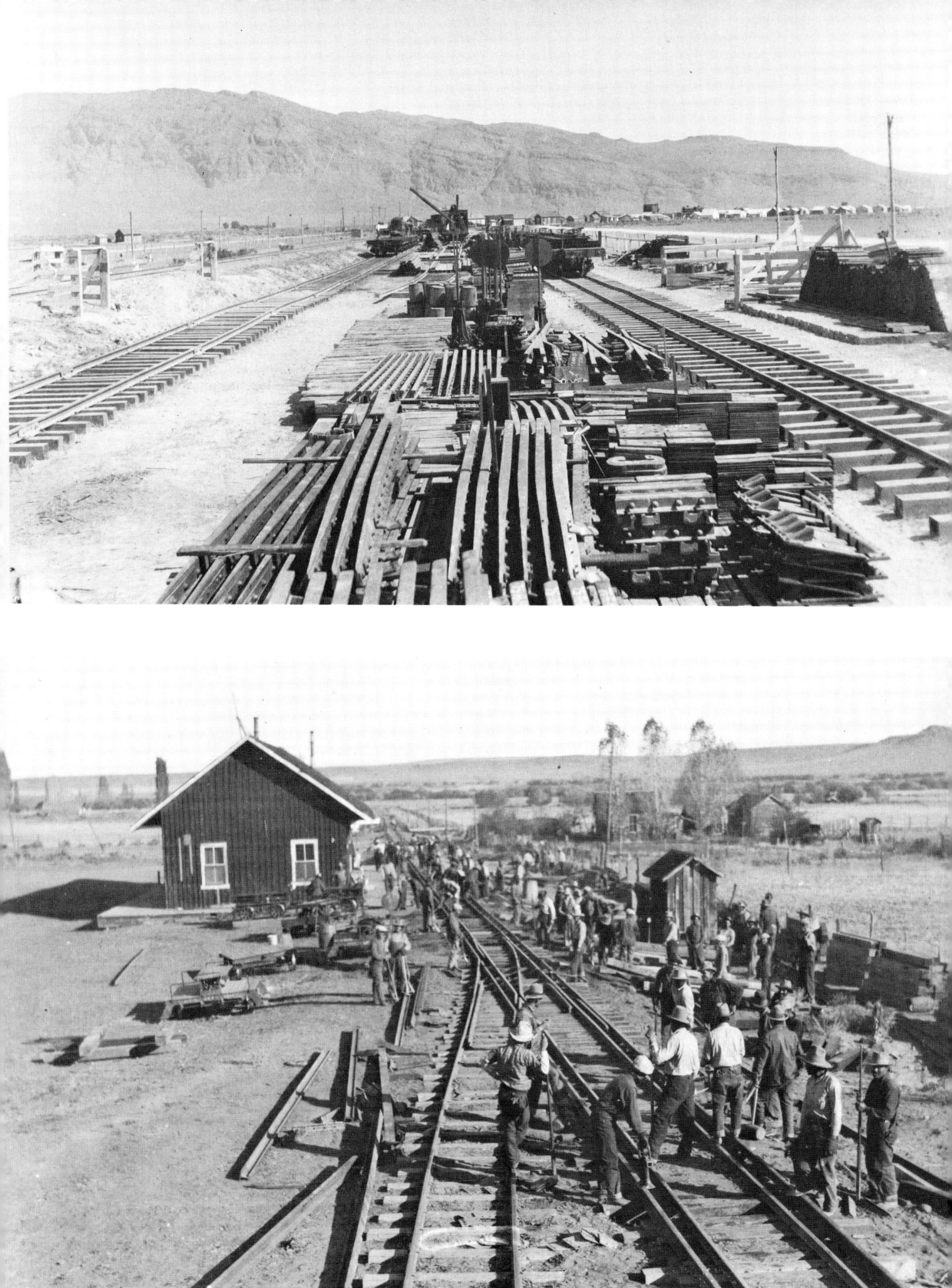

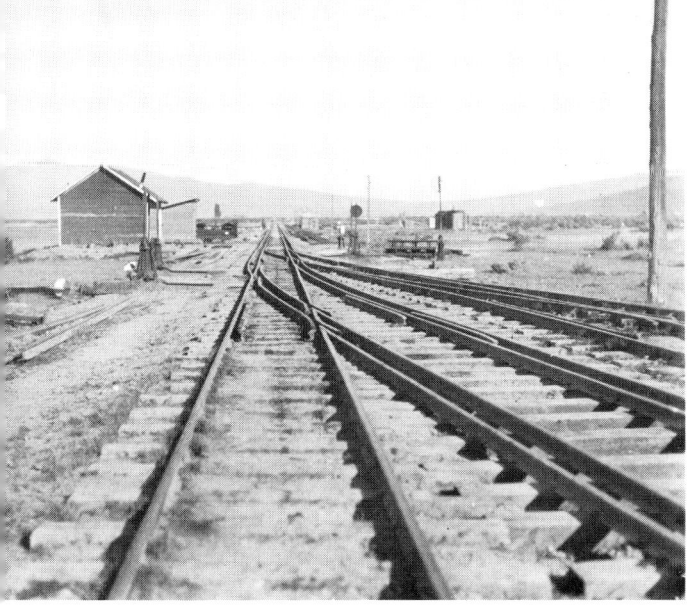 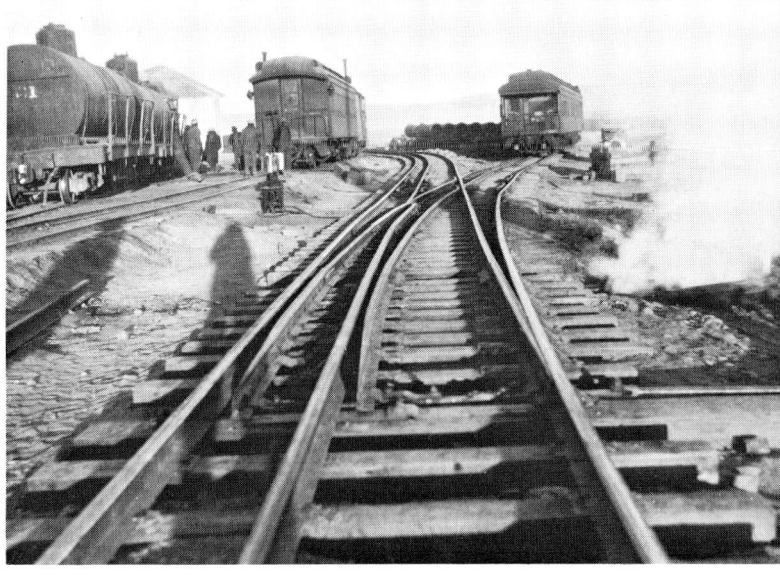

Widening the gauge on the N-C-O in 1927 was a laborious task. Work started at Wendel *(left, above)* where fish plates, rail joiners, switch points, frogs, rails and ties were stacked in profusion. Note the standard-gauge track on the left and the narrow-gauge track at right laid on standard-gauge ties to facilitate the loading of cars of either dimension. Four rails were laid on the main line, the two narrow inside the two standard, as shown *(directly above, left)* heading north from Wendel and again *(left, below)* at Likely where intricate switch work was being installed. A change was made at Alturas *(above, right)*, and three-rail tracks were used resulting in some confusion, particularly in night yard switching when engines unexpectedly wound up on the ground.

North from Alturas to Lakeview the slim gauge rails continued to prevail until the following year, which accounts for the presence of this narrow-gauge train *(below)* with the N-C-O's business car *Fairport* in tow as late as October 18, 1927. The long ties distributed beside the right-of-way foretell the imminent fate of this last segment of the narrow gauge. *(All Photos: Stanley Borden Collection.)*

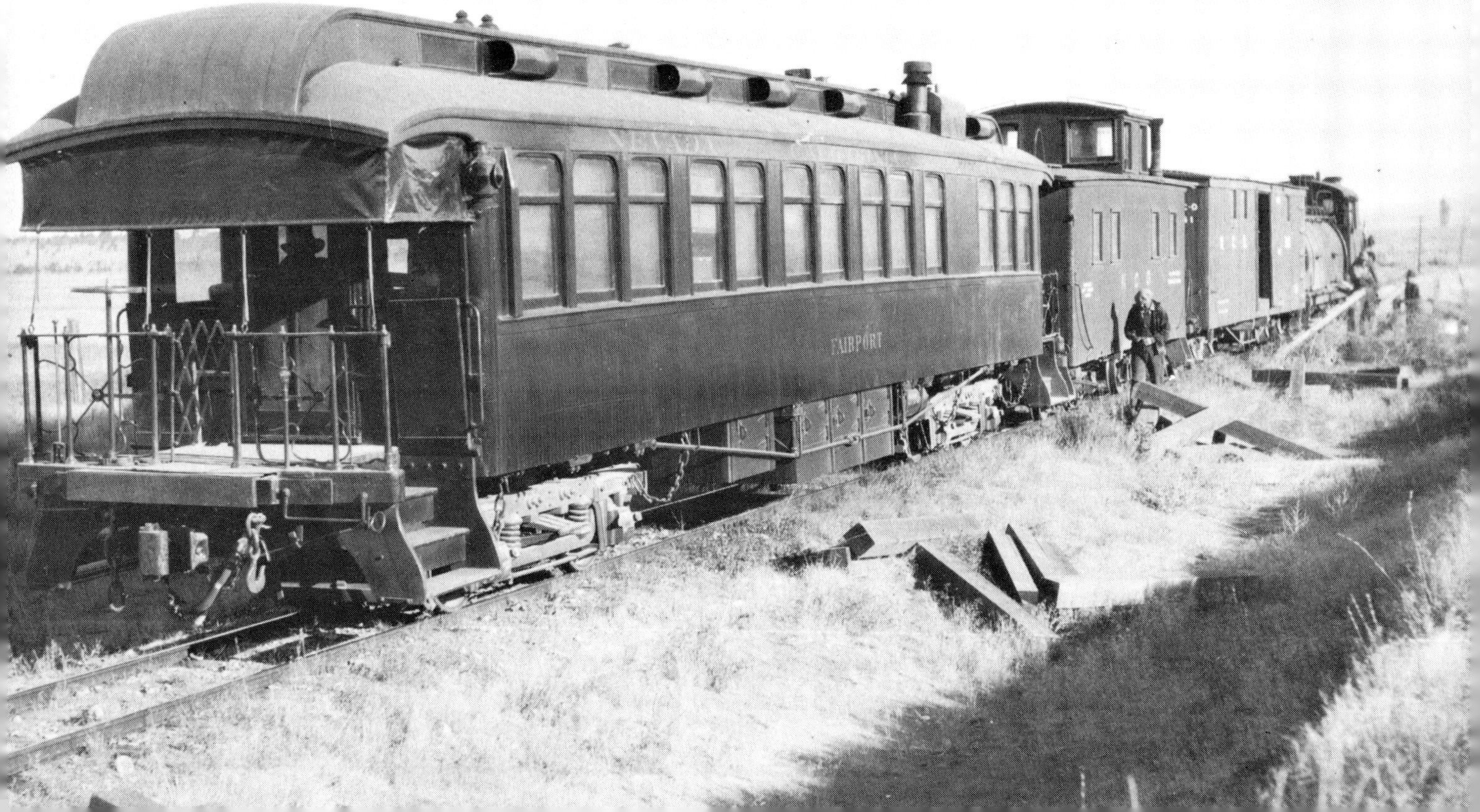

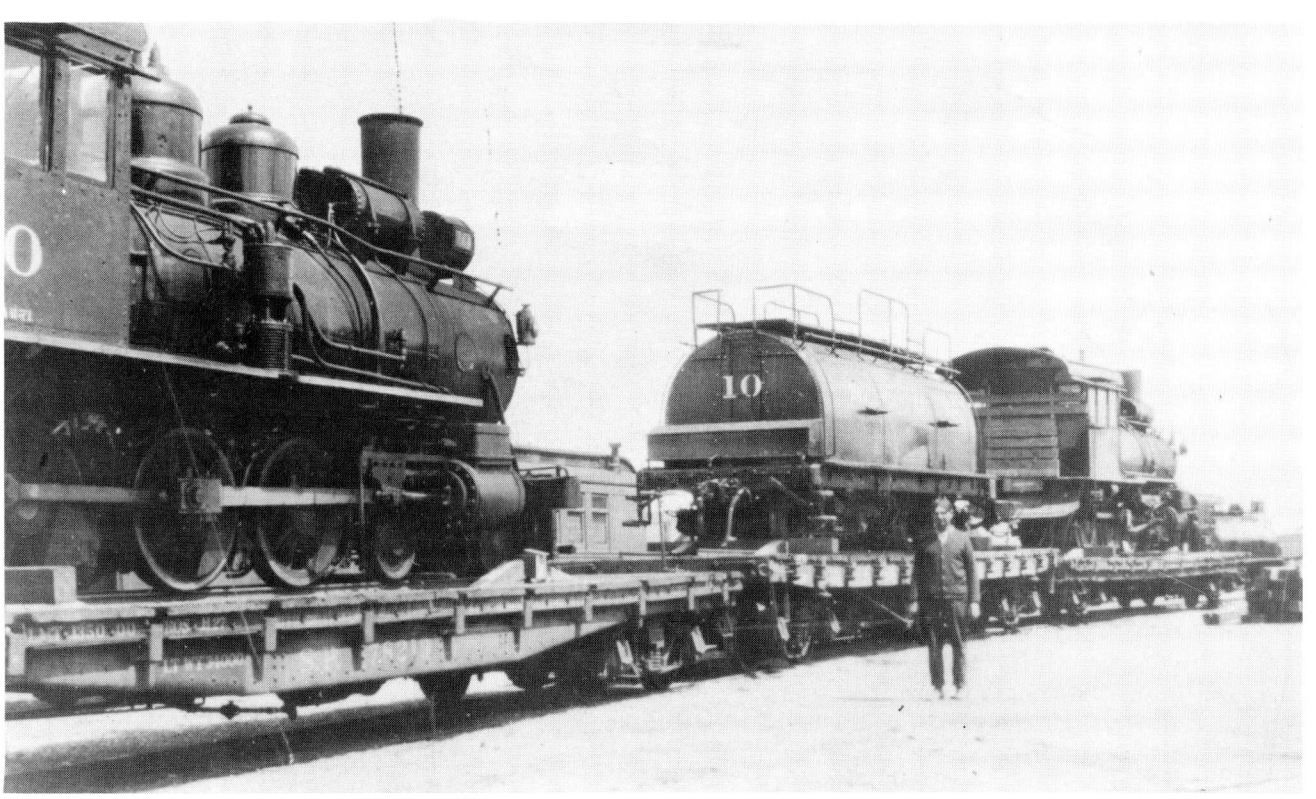

In the fall of 1927 the N-C-O began to dispose of its little narrow-gauge locomotives, shipping them out on flat cars *(above)* mostly to the remaining Carson & Colorado trackage out of Mina, Nevada. Standard-gauge operations to Alturas commenced on October 24, 1927, the first train being shown *(top, right)* as it leaned to the curve approaching Sage Hen, on the hill just south of Likely. *(Above: H. E. Gasaway; Top Right: Stanley Borden Photo.)*

Conversion of the balance of the N-C-O line from Alturas to Lakeview was completed on May 27, 1928, but the event was not celebrated until the time of the town's Annual Roundup on September 1 *(bottom, left and right)*. Little realized is the fact that, to accommodate the road's traffic during the period of conversion and before operation was taken over by the Southern Pacific, standard-gauge SP cars and locomotives were acquired and relettered for the N-C-O and operated from July 1927 to September 1929. Following this, the line became a formal part of the Southern Pacific. *(Both Photos: Southern Pacific.)*

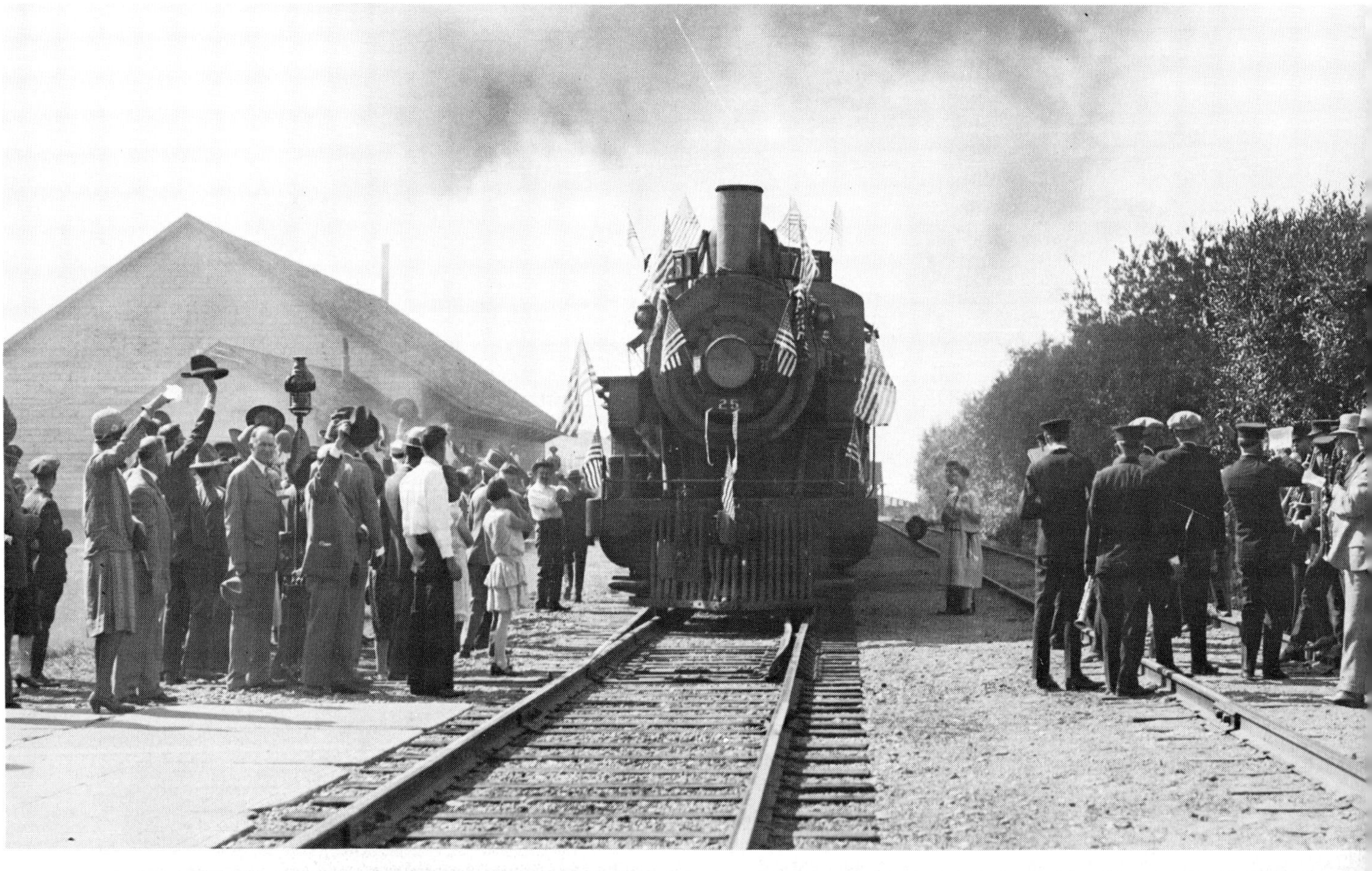

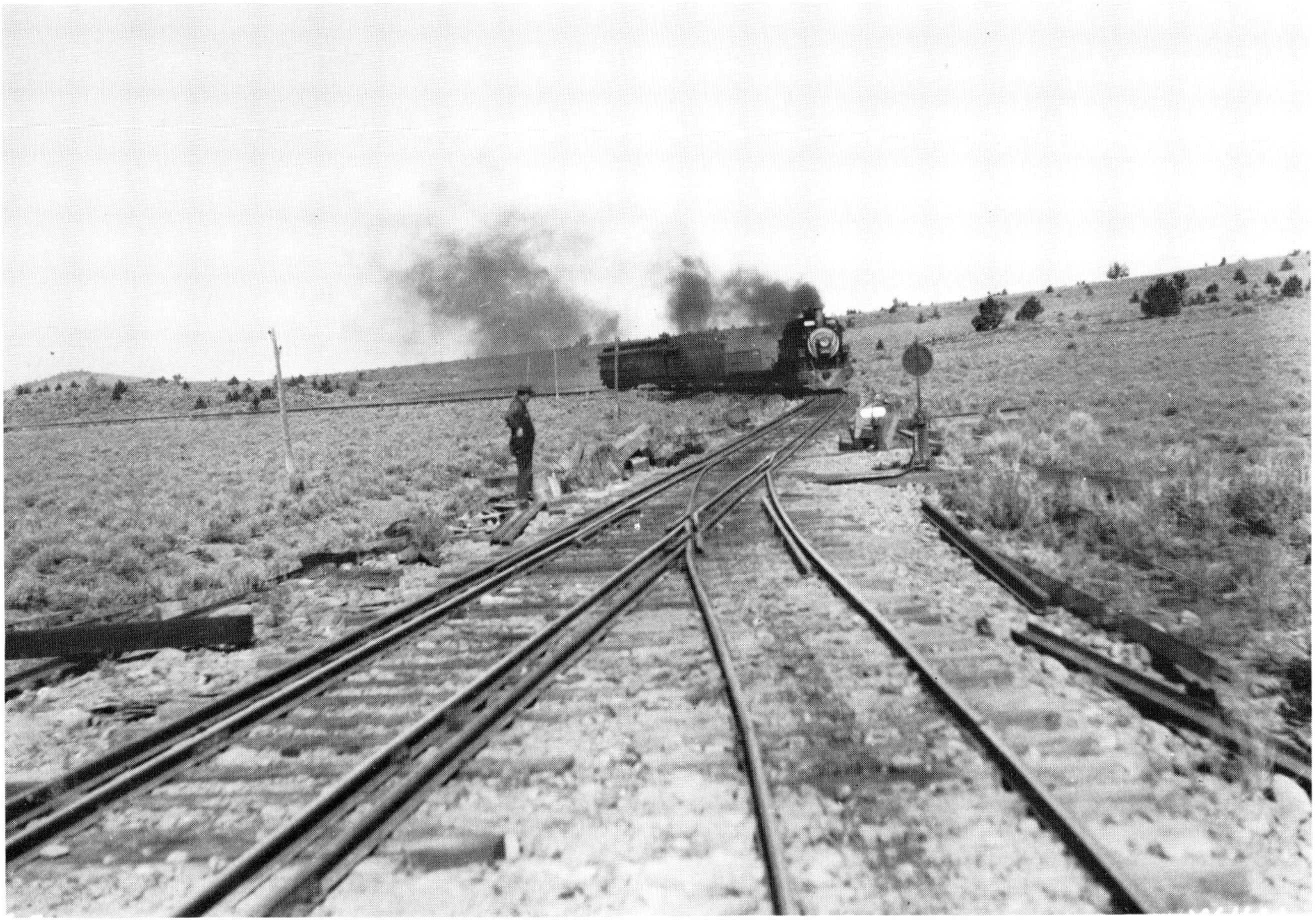

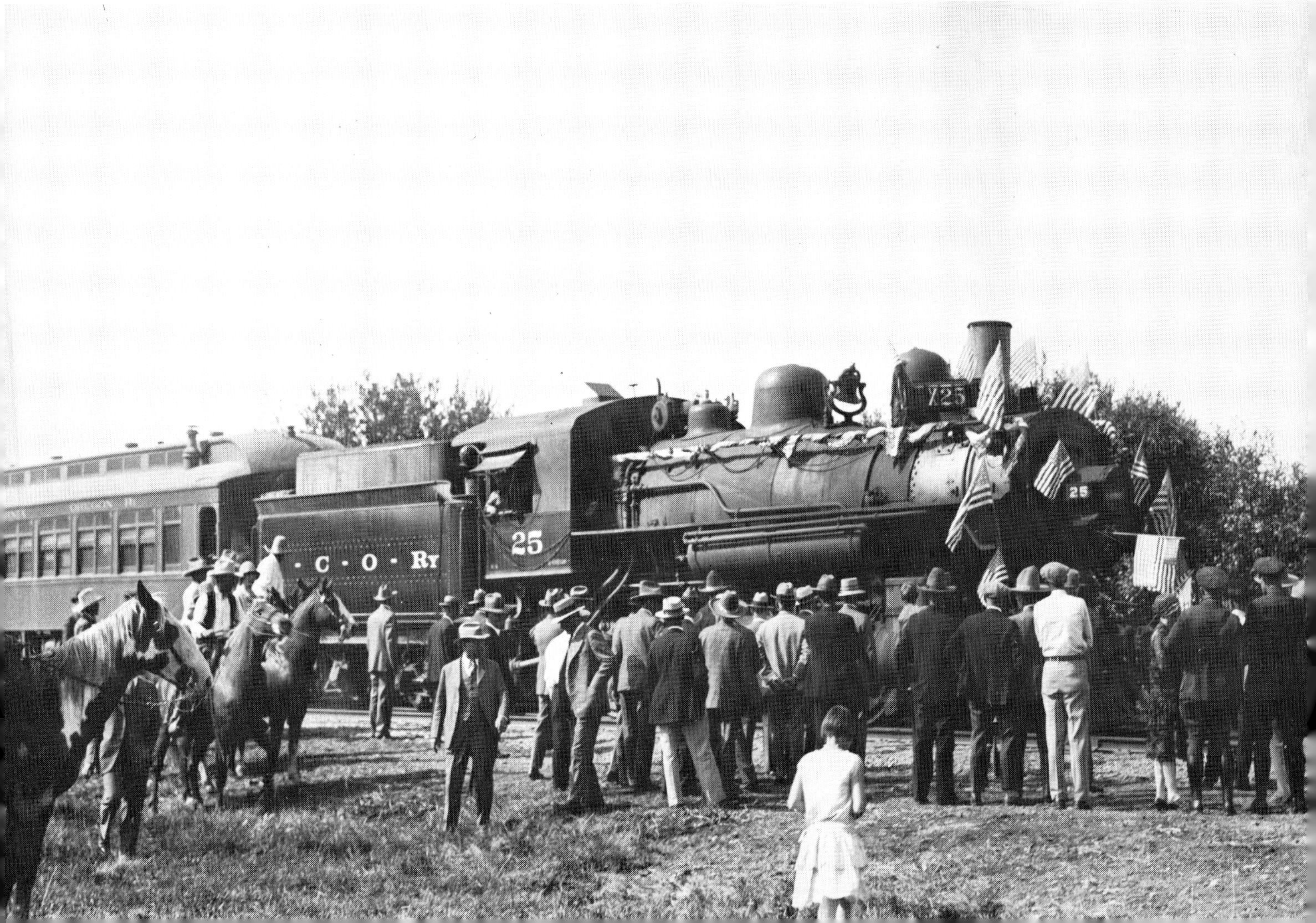

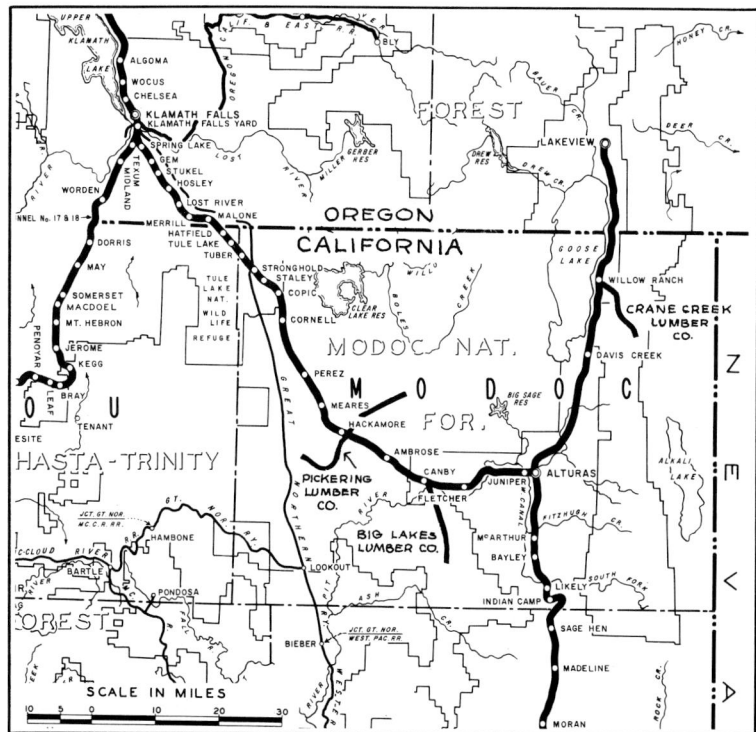

That evening, while a select 600 people attended a wild duck dinner in the town hall, those less fortunate dined on beans, following which they had their choice of attending any one of the five separate dances held in as many different halls in Alturas. Around midnight the dance floors were suddenly deserted as waves of people became ill. "Doc" Hordon, who had a reputation for practical jokes, was roundly accused of spiking the beans with croton oil; although it was subsequently determined that, in scalding the buckets in preparation for the cooking, the hot water had acted on the flux in the solder in the buckets.

By the end of 1927, when work was suspended for the winter, 10 more miles of track had been widened. The balance of the line was completed between March 16 and May 27, 1928, and Lakeview, Oregon, celebrated the event (without the same results) at their Annual Roundup on September 1.

But little known or realized is the fact that, during the N-C-O conversion period from July 1927 to September 1929, the former narrow gauge continued to maintain its corporate identity in spite of SP control. A series of SP standard-gauge locomotives and cars were relettered for N-C-O service and were used exclusively in that road's operations. On September 1, 1929, this arrangement ceased, and the N-C-O properties were operated as an integral part of the SP system, being divided between the Salt Lake and the Shasta Divisions.

To complete the job, 31 line changes aggregating 13.6 miles were made in 1929 and early 1930, thereby reducing the total distance one mile and curves from 16° to 10°. The roadbed was widened, passing tracks were lengthened and wye tracks installed at Waverly and Likely. Built for the section forces were ten badly needed houses and, at Likely, a two-stall engine house was built for the helper locomotives necessary to boost loads up Madeline Hill to Sagehen where a balloon track was laid to facilitate the return of the light power.

Simultaneously with the widening of the gauge of the N-C-O, the SP went to work on its new, long-contemplated, 95.4-mile standard gauge Modoc Line from Alturas to Texum (Klamath Falls). The name Modoc came from the Modoc Indians living along the line. As part of the general authority for railroad development in eastern Oregon, the I.C.C. approved the construction of the line in 1926; grading began on June 13, 1927, but work was suspended after a few miles because of the uncertainty surrounding the Great Northern's construction in southern Oregon. Then, with a contract awarded to the Utah Construction Co., work was resumed on July 17, 1928, and rails joined the two terminal communities on July 13, 1929.

The new line was not turned over to the operating department until September 15, 1929, the day after the big celebration at Hackamore, 36 miles west of Alturas. Five special trains brought the celebrants to town, swelling the crowd to 3,000 and including a sprinkling of star performers — such as Indians in full dress, pioneers with long beards, and railroad officials with large, standard gold watches. To climax the celebration, SP #2775 crashed through a "last barrier" purposefully set up to commemorate the event. One facet of new service made possible by the opening of the line was a through Pullman car operated from Portland to Ogden via Klamath Falls, Alturas, and the former N-C-O.

Lumbermen were delighted with the new standard-gauge facilities provided. Shortly after the Alturas-Klamath Falls line was completed the Pickering Lumber Co. built two lumber railroads each about 10 miles long. Both extended into the woods from Hackamore — one to the northeast and the other to the southwest. With a Heisler locomotive for power, the lines were operated for only a very short time before succumbing to the depression of the 1930's.

At Canby (a station formerly called Ghent), 21 miles west of Alturas, another standard gauge lumber railroad stretched to the southeast. Principals behind the undertaking were Walker and Hovey, who joined forces in 1936 to build a mill at Canby and a 13½-mile logging line to tap the necessary timber. Before the two men could get the mill into operation the following year, the entire property was leased to the Big Lakes Box and Lumber Co. which operated the property for years, extending the railroad mileage proportionally as the cutting area moved southward. At some undetermined date the railroad (sometimes referred to as the Canby Railroad Co.) plus the sawmill became operated by the Ralph L. Smith Lumber Co. until 1948 when a dramatic and fatal event suddenly closed the line. Old No. 91, a three-truck Shay, blew up. Without a locomotive, and apparently without the means or desire to obtain another, the Canby Railroad ceased operations and was abandoned shortly thereafter.

On the now standard gauge N-C-O at Willow Ranch, California, 34 miles north of Alturas, the Crane Creek Lumber Co. constructed a standard gauge railroad late in 1928. It followed the southeasterly course of Lassen Creek for 6½ miles to the sawmill, then continued for approximately 10 more miles into the woods. A second-hand Lima Shay, the only motive power, negotiated the maximum grades of 7% and minimum 24° curvature. No sooner had operations begun in August 1929 than a disastrous forest fire swept through the timber, destroying the logging operations and indirectly the railroad as well. Within a short time the line became idle.

Withal, the SP had acquired a rather unusual railroad in the N-C-O. Personnel-wise, one of its top officials was a lady — corporate secretary Maud Miller — while physically, the line of road crossed numerous mountain ranges without any tunnels and crossed a variety of water courses without any major bridges. Along its entire 275-mile route, it connected with no independent logging or mining railroads (save that of the aforementioned Crane Creek Lumber Co. built after the narrow gauge days were over), and what little industry there was could be counted on the fingers of one hand. Quite obviously its greatest value lay in the role of a bridge line, and this the SP was determined to exploit.

For a time following the absorption, passenger service was continued — on one occasion it was exceptional. Just before Christmas 1932, the southbound train was running late and the passengers were becoming unhappy over the possibility of missing the connecting train to San Francisco. Pestered so much by one particular lady, one conductor fabricated a story that if the connection were missed, the SP would surely run the Alturas train right on through over the SP rails to the Bay at San Francisco. The conductor's wife, riding on the train and overhearing the conversation, was highly critical of her husband's fanciful appeasement, but the situation was miraculously saved when the train with its heavy load of passengers did miss the Reno connection and the SP authorized its continuance over the hill to San Francisco.

Passenger service did decline, however, and was abandoned entirely at the close of 1937. Inversely, early freight traffic over the line was modest until World War II. Then, with the housing boom stimulating the development of the Oregon lumber industry, the volume of business soared and the Modoc line resounded to the roar of passing freight trains. A three-mile line change to reduce the grade and curvature between Ravendale and Crest was placed in operation on April 5, 1960, thus lifting an onerous speed restriction of 20 m.p.h. up to 45 m.p.h. in that area.

Today, the old order has been changed completely. Amedee, the once busy metropolis and namesake of a founder, is gone; the entire townsite was sold for back taxes in 1950 for a paltry $32, and the poplar trees which once surrounded the Amedee Hotel, are all that remain to mark the site of the former habitation of from 300 to 400 people. To perpetuate the name of the guiding hand of N-C-O affairs, one of the SP's new sidings, (established in 1953) has been titled with the proud, pioneer name of Moran, thus preserving a continuity of influence which has extended over three-quarters of a century of trials and tribulations.

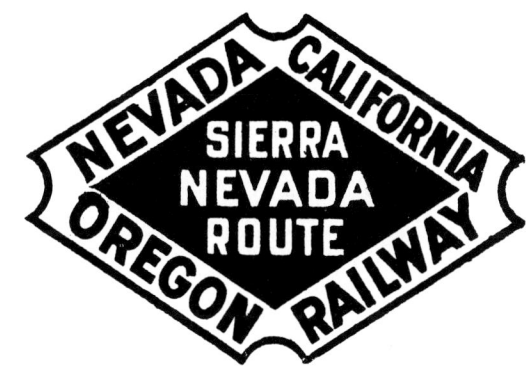

SIERRA VALLEYS RAILWAY

North of Reno, Nevada, and immediately west of Beckwourth Pass, lie the Sierra and Mohawk Valleys in Plumas County, California. A legendary but elusive "lake of gold" attracted the earliest settlers to the area, but it was the green gold of the forests which proved the more lucrative over the years.

In the fall of the 1849 Gold Rush, an exhausted man named Stoddard struggled back into civilization with the convincing tale that he was the sole survivor of a party of three men which had been attacked by Indians just as they had found a fabulously rich gold lake. The following spring, a small party of prospectors organized to relocate the bonanza site, but the news spread quickly and they were joined by an additional thousand uninvited but eager fortune seekers. Once out on the trail, and with Stoddard to guide them, the days and the miles began to accumulate; but as the landmarks diminished in number, they also became more confusing to the party's mentor. Finally an ultimatum was delivered: one more day to find the golden lake — or else. Stoddard, not wishing to be swung from the end of a long rope, quietly vanished the next night leaving his tormentors to their own devisings. Reportedly the episode was incorporated into the nomenclature of the region — Last Chance Creek commemorating the event, Humbug Creek designating the location of his departure, Gold Lake naming a small Alpine body of water and indicating the hopes and aspirations of the group.

In spite of the disappointments, the trip was not without a happy ending for some of the participants. On the return trek, placer gold was discovered along the Feather River, and above the Mohawk Valley near Johnsville, California, the famed Plumas-Eureka mine was started, to become a steady producer for many years. During a portion of its productive era, it operated a ¾-mile railroad from the mine to the mill, cars drifting downgrade with their loads of ore while horses hauled the empties back to the mine.

Other industries also developed. With timber abounding, it was only natural that lumbering

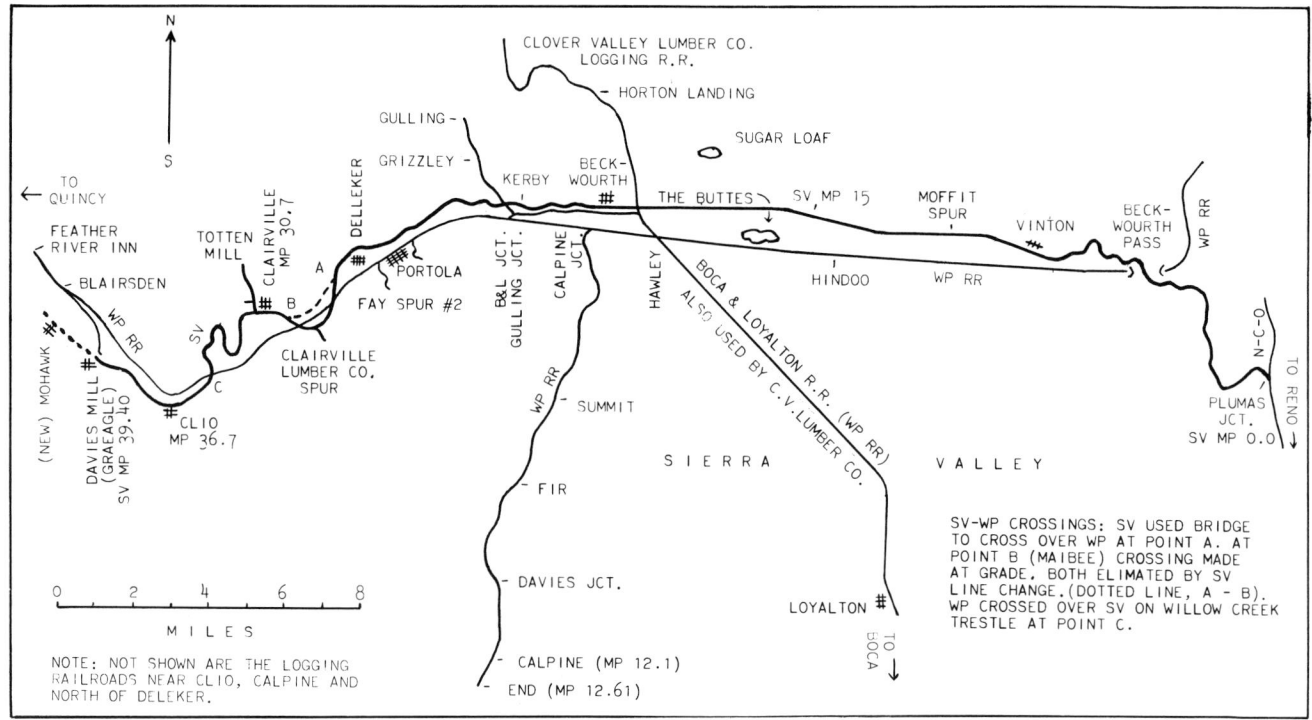

should become a major industry of the area, and Swiss ranchers who settled in the Sierra Valley produced fine crops when grasshoppers did not beat them to the harvest.

Beckwourth Pass (elevation 5,218 feet) immortalizes the name of Jim Beckwourth, trapper and scout, who first discovered the notch between Nevada and these California valleys in 1851. Settling in the northern end of the Sierra Valley, he erected a cabin the following year (still standing) and lived there for 15 years until Alex Kerby arrived and purchased it from him in 1866. The town of Beckwourth also honors the name of this pioneer, although for years the name of the town was incorrectly spelled when a postal clerk confused Beckwourth's name with that of Lt. E. G. Beckwith, the railroad surveyor. The correction to the postal department's records was not finally and formally made until 1932.

The heavy industries of mining and lumbering cried out for an adequate means of transportation, and agitation for a railroad to the area began as early as the 1870's. Various proposals were made, some to connect with the Central Pacific at Truckee. Then the Sierra Iron Co. obtained a railroad franchise which it later transferred to an affiliated company, the Sierra Iron & Quincy Railroad. The line was projected to start at Quincy and run eastward to a connection with the Nevada & Oregon (N-C-O), which itself was merely in the talking stages. A branch to the south would tap the iron mines near Gold Lake and continue over the hills to Downieville on the North Fork of the Yuba River. San Francisco people were the incorporators of the project, A. T. Nation was the local attorney, and Arthur Keddie was the chief engineer. Financial assistance was sought in Boston, and due to the current (1881) interest and enthusiasm for the two-foot gauge Billerica & Bedford Railroad in Massachusetts, serious consideration was given to the possibility of using that gauge for the line. Some right-of-way was acquired from a point west of Mohawk to the present C. A. Lundy ranch, where a one-story building with 18 offices was constructed (later demolished by fire about 1900). The railroad scheme ultimately became dormant when, in spite of Baron von Richthofen's favorable geological report, the Gold Lake iron mining project was never activated. It is interesting to note that the idea still lives and that exploitation of the mines continues to be advocated from time to time.

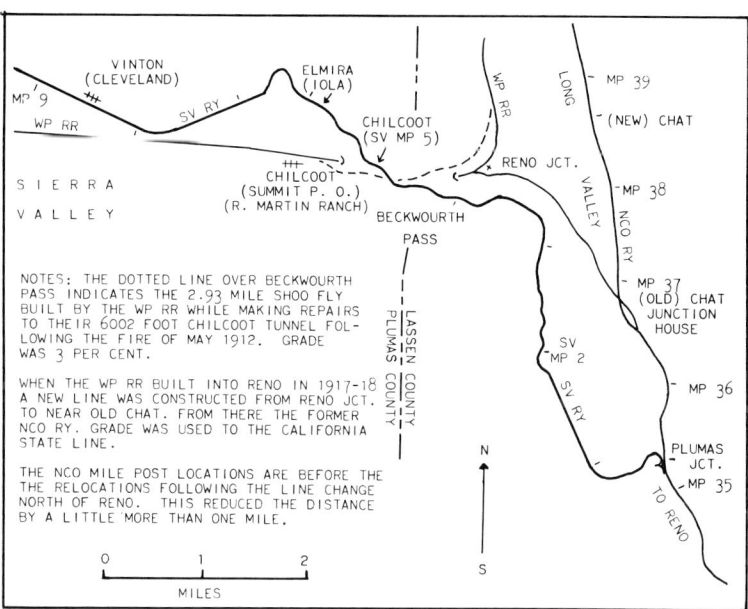

The demand for railroad transportation was not to be denied, however, and the California Land and Timber Co. was the next to take up the cudgels. With considerable timber lands in the area, a sawmill at Mohawk, a band mill under construction at Kerby, cattle and hay ranches in the American and Mohawk Valleys, plus a retail lumber yard in Reno, it wanted and needed an outlet for its products. Consequently, on October 1, 1885, the CL&TCo in conjunction with some of the men from the previous Sierra Iron & Quincy Railroad effort, formed a new organization known as the Sierra Valley & Mohawk Railroad to build to a connection with the N-C-O (then known as the Nevada & California). Since it was anticipated that this would be a connecting line, the same track gauge of three feet was adopted.

Work began a few days later on the eastern end at Plumas Jct. with Knox and Holmes handling the grading contract. Labor was scarce, and the Chinese labor contractor, Moy Foot, supplied his fellow countrymen. This caused an outcry in Sierraville at the southern end of Sierra Valley, although it was pointed out that the 12 men gathered at a saloon to look for work refused employment when it was offered.

By January 1886 a mile and a half of track had been laid along Dinwiddie Creek, and the graders had moved up and around the side of the mountain to Beckwourth Pass, 4½ miles from the Junction. In their wake was a roadbed incorporating some 20° curves and 2% grades to gain the 5,218-foot summit. Then bad weather set in — two to three feet of snow, followed by an unseasonably warm rain. The N&C was washed out for three weeks, and the consequent lack of supplies delayed

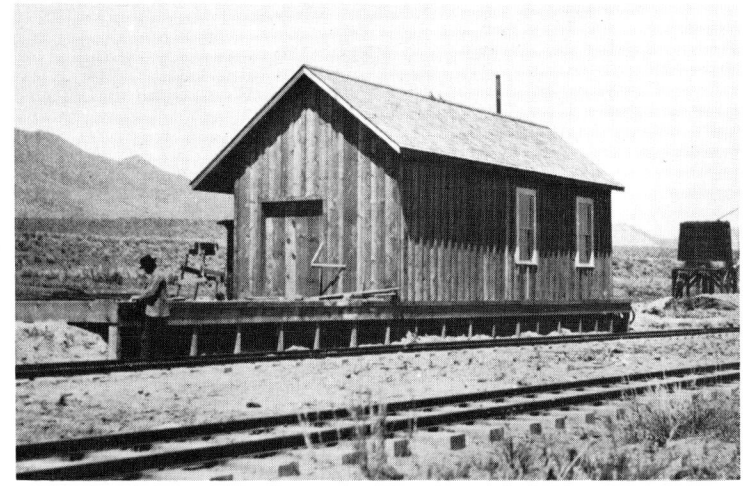

Plumas Junction *(left)* was the starting point of the original Sierra Valley & Mohawk Railroad on October 1, 1885. The route followed Dinwiddie Creek across the plain in the background, then climbed 2% grades and went around 20° curves to the 5,218-foot summit atop Beckwourth Pass, 4½ miles away to the northwest (behind station).

Westbound trains invariably stopped for water at this tank *(right)* just short of the summit where passengers frequently amused themselves by shooting at the hundreds of jackrabbits which collected around the dripping base.

In the winter of 1894-95 the name of the railroad was changed to Sierra Valleys Railway under the ownership of Henry Bowen and two second-hand locomotives were acquired from the SP. Sierra Valleys No. 2 *(left, center)* is shown here pulling into Plumas Jct. where all freight was transferred to N-C-O cars, no interchange of equipment being permitted.

Despite appearances *(center, right)* the Sierra Valleys never operated regular passenger trains as such. On this particular day the PLUMAS had no freight cars to sandwich between its tender and the combine as it started west from Plumas Jct.

Taking water in winter was sometimes a difficult task when ice plugged the drains and froze the connections of the tank spout firmly in place. Fortunately the train *(bottom)* is eastbound down the hill and could coast to Plumas Jct. if necessary.

Porter-built, woodburning SV No. 1, the PLUMAS *(bottom, right)* was a photogenic (2-6-0) Mogul with its large oil headlight, diamond stack, fendered drivers, crosshead-actuated pump, and wood-racked tender with link-and-pin coupling.

(All Photos: Mrs. Vinton Bowen White Collection.)

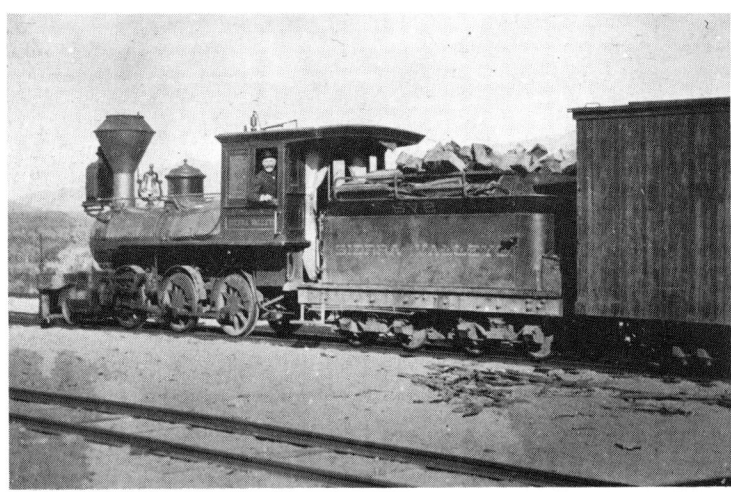

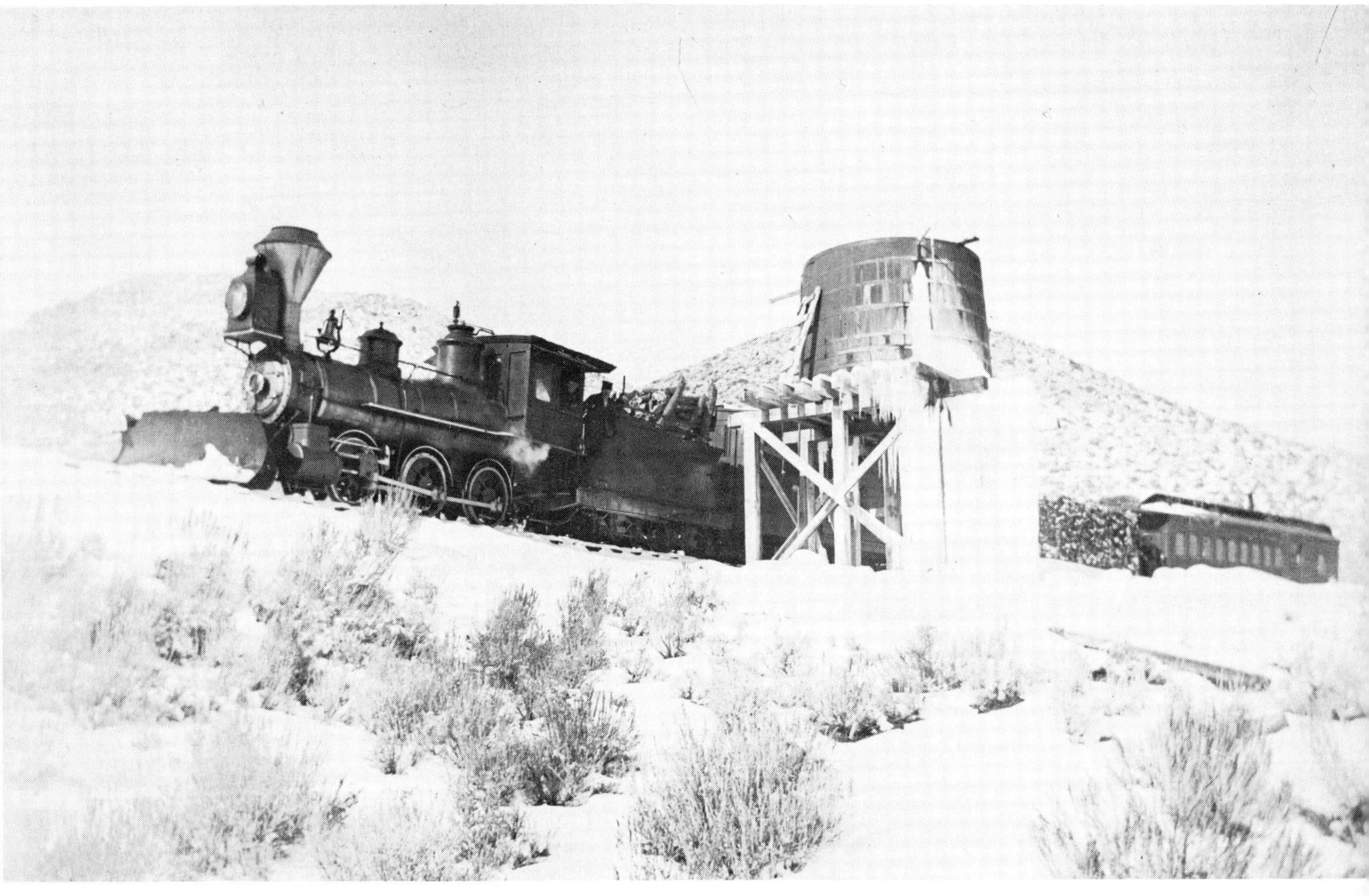

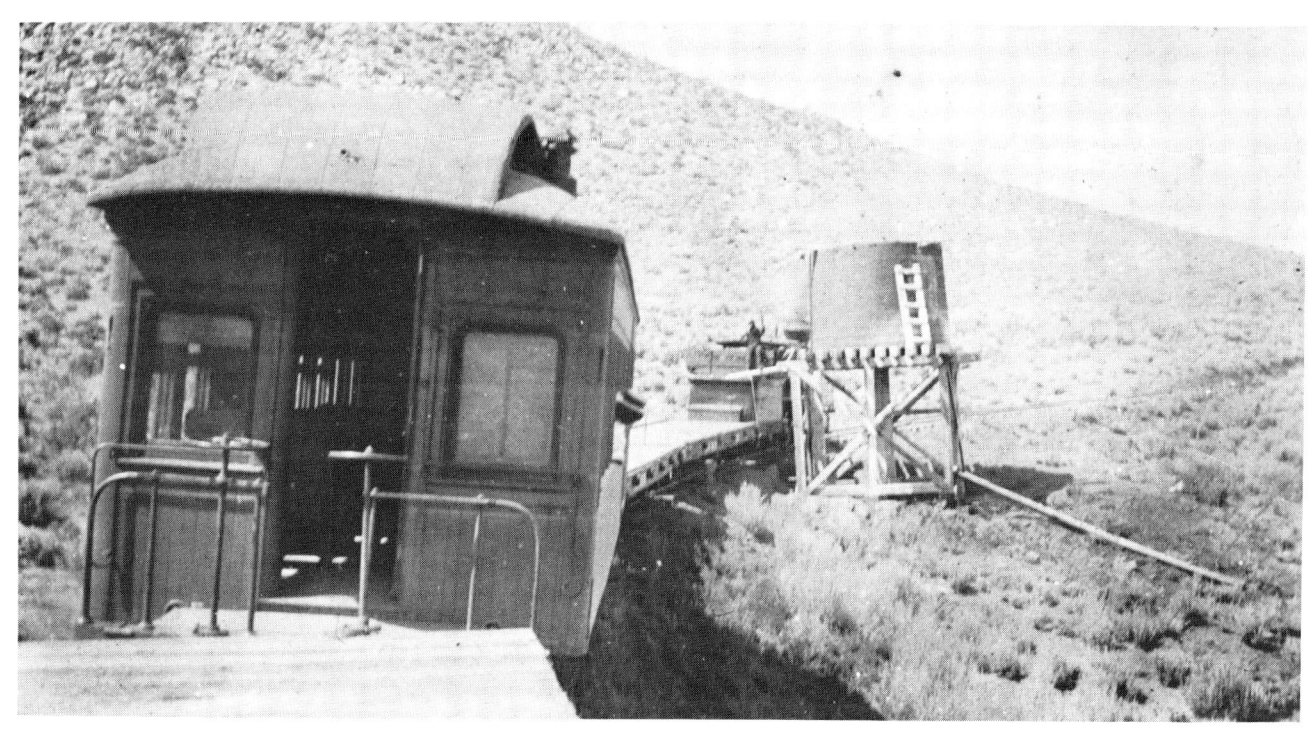

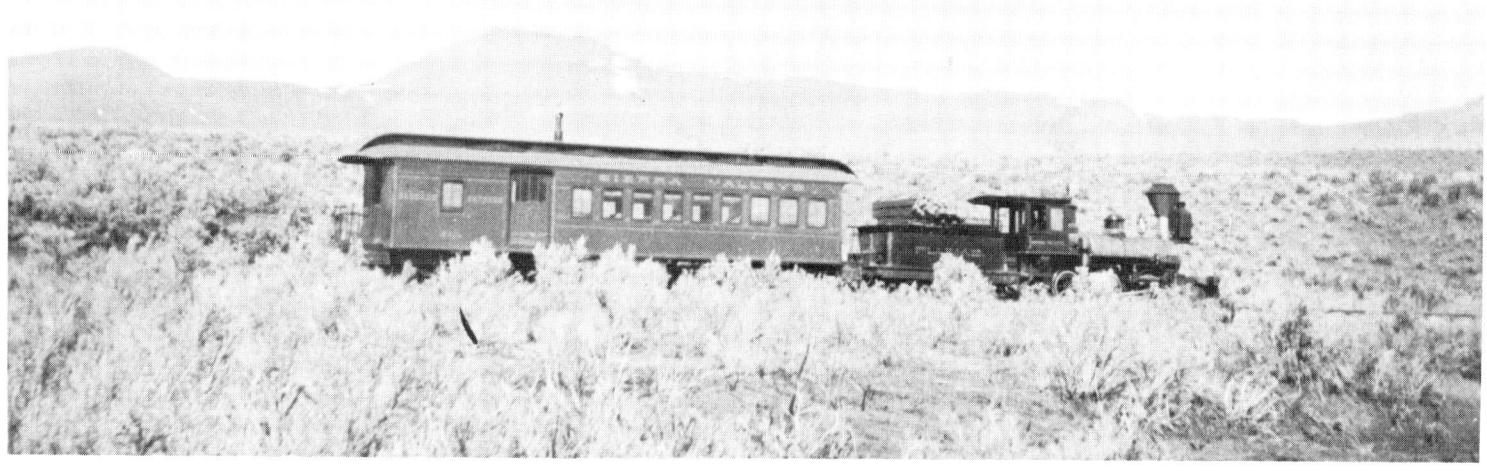

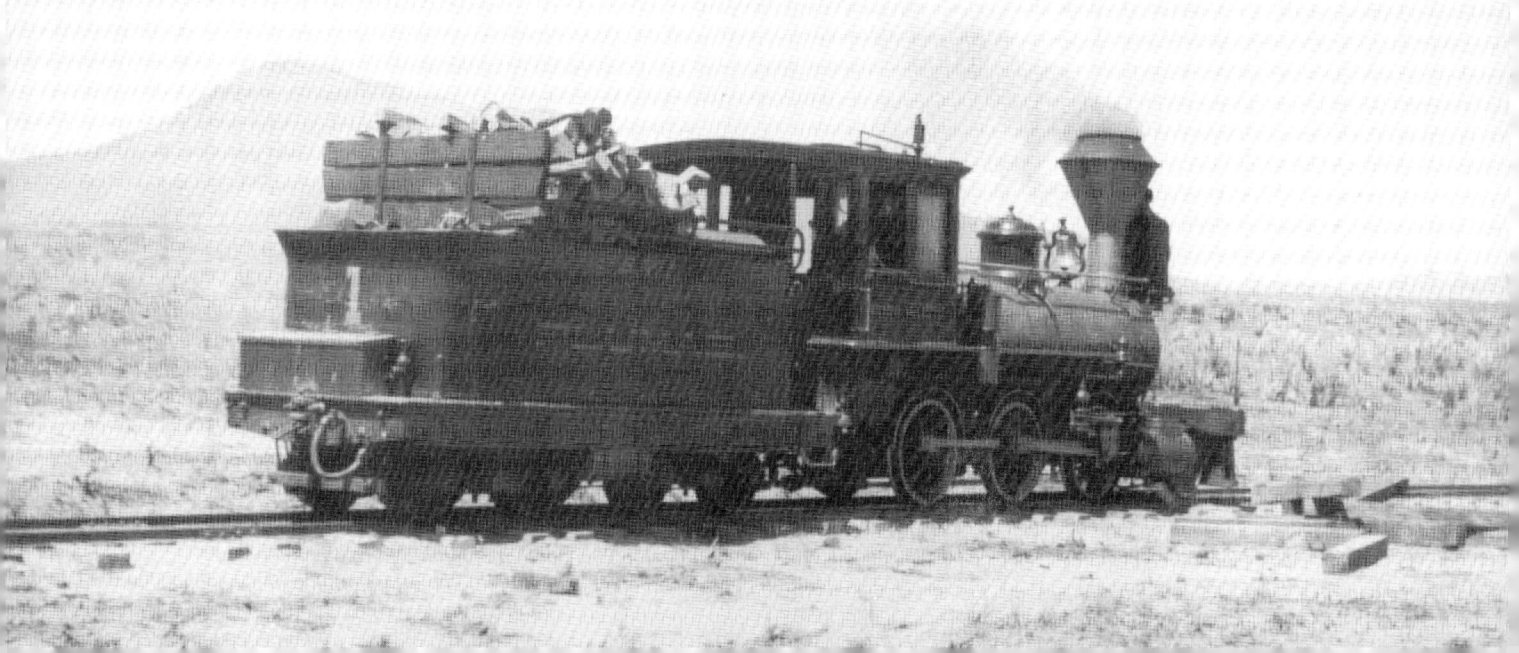

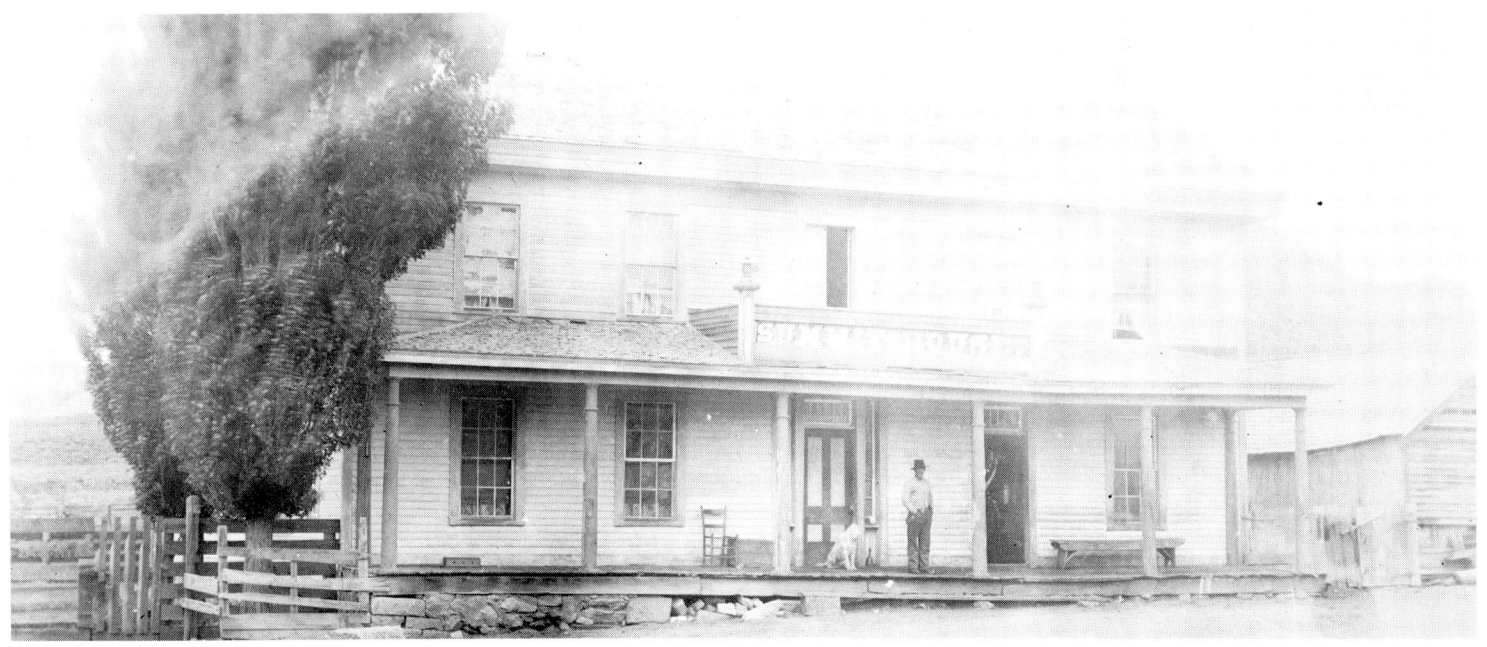

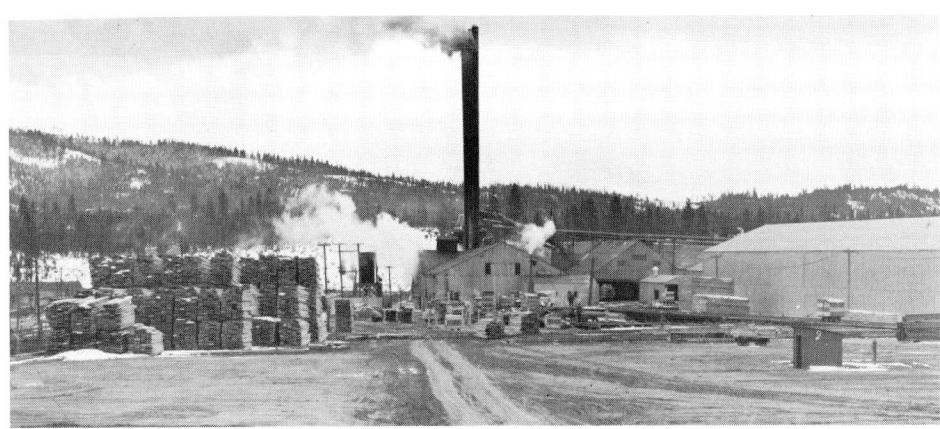

Summit House (top) was across from the Chilcoot store (in ruins today) near the top of Beckwourth Pass and was a welcome stop for meals.

The big mill at Delleker (center) was a later innovation in the valley served by the SV, whose construction train loaded with ties and timbers (below) was probably photographed about the time of the 1895 extension to Clairville. (Top and bottom: Mrs. Vinton Bowen White Collection.)

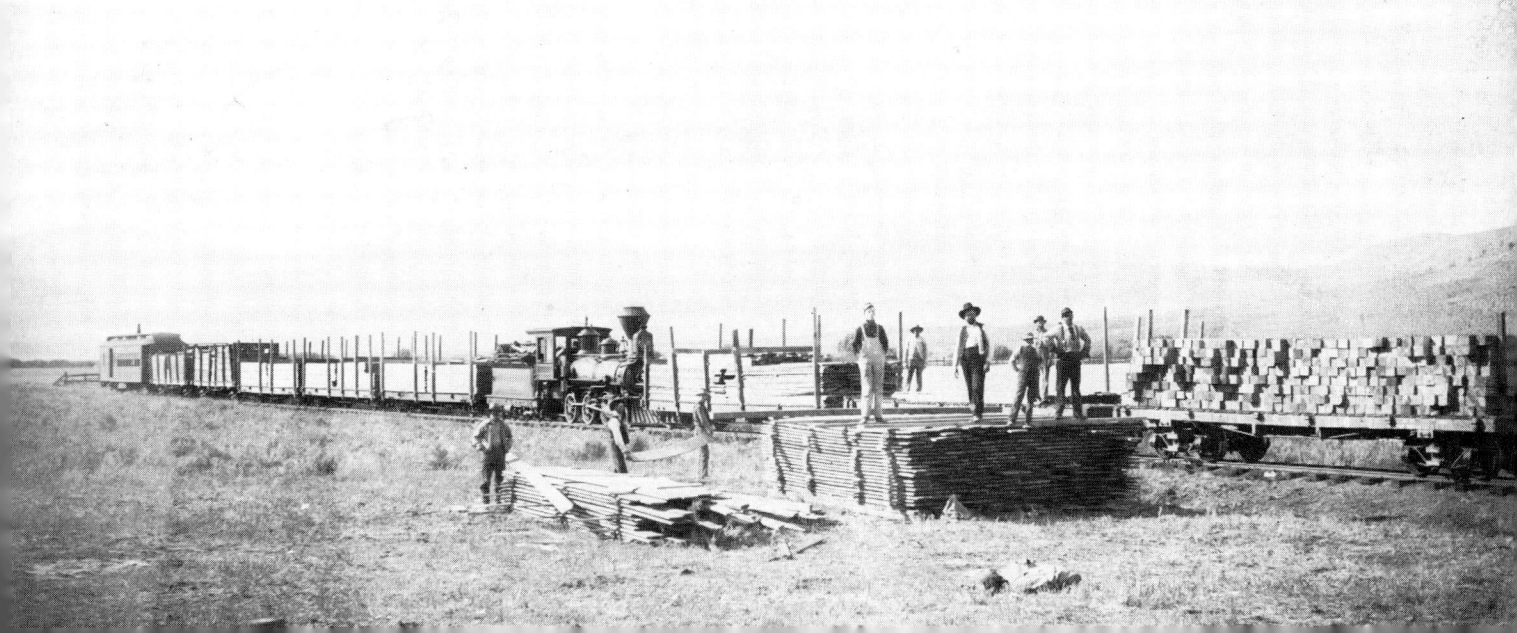

construction still more during the first few months of 1886.

With the advent of better weather, work did resume. The rails crept up and over the summit of Beckwourth Pass and down along the headwaters of the Middle Fork of the Feather River. Cleveland (later Vinton) was passed, and the Buttes came in sight. By September the graders had passed Kerby, 23 miles from the junction, and were heading down the canyon toward Mohawk, which they hoped to reach by the end of the year. R. W. Harden, superintendent, had shopped around for a construction locomotive and had sent his 26-ton purchase to the V&T shops for conversion to the slim gauge. Bearing the name MOHAWK, it was on hand and ready when physical track connection with the N&C was effected in November 1886. Six carloads of rails were delivered together with six flat cars, two track cars and one hand car. By the end of the year 11 miles of track were in place (two miles beyond Cleveland), and Beckwith (subsequently changed to Beckwourth) was only nine miles from end-of-track. A total of 30 miles of grading had been completed (past Kerby to Clairville) leaving only 11½ more miles of construction to finish the line to Clio and Mohawk.

Beckwith was then enjoying a boom, and Marion Bringham was busily engaged in enlarging his Beckwith Hotel which he had opened a scant five years earlier. But in spite of the times and the activity of construction, there was still a touch of the Old West to be experienced. When Col. Day, superintendent for the California Land & Timber Co., took the stage to Mohawk on one of his frequent trips, bandits halted the ride a mere four miles from the terminus with the usual order to throw down the Wells Fargo box. Although the order was obeyed, the nervous gunman shot the Colonel in the hip, was subsequently arrested and incarcerated in San Quentin for three years.

The band mill at Kerby attracted considerable attention when it began cutting timber in January 1887. A contract for cross ties for the railroad was one of the earliest jobs, but its value was seriously questioned when, at the end of February, the advance Chinese grading force went into winter quarters in Reno. Some people suspected that the railroad was facing a period of financial stringency, a fact that was indirectly confirmed when Moy Foot filed a labor lien in the month of May. The company attempted to raise additional funds by means of an assessment of $10 a share on the stock subscriptions in July, but the inefficacy of the effort was attested by the number of names of prominent people on the list of delinquents. Some money was raised, however, as evidenced by the dozen men sent out at the end of July to finish laying rails under the old contract. When work finally ceased in August 1887, 15 miles of track (to a point just east of The Buttes) and 14 miles of additional grading had been completed, but other than construction trains, no regular service had been provided over the line.

The end came in sight when Sheriff Dean began selling the personal property of the railroad to satisfy judgments. Among the items going at auction were 65 picks @ 25¢ each, 60 long-handled shovels @ 5¢ each, and 14,954 cross ties (products of the Kerby band mill) @ 8½¢ each. Eventually all of the property of the railroad and of the land company was sold, although collusion might have been charged for it appeared that several of the principals of the railroad purchased a substantial portion of the property. Local opinion held to the theory that funds which should have been used in construction had been squandered on the erection of superfluous, ancillary buildings, facilities which should have been deferred until after completion of the line.

For several years the railroad lay dormant. Hopes continued that some means would be found to place it in operation, but there was no activity except for the regular payment of taxes on the property.

As early as 1891 Henry A. Bowen became interested in the property. His father's associate, Jacob Goldberg (in the San Francisco grocery business of Goldberg-Bowen), had been a director of the railroad, and Bowen had been a stockholder. Through his attorney, Henry Bowen bought the railroad and band mill at Kerby for $20,000 in April 1894. The band mill was soon sold, and Bowen voiced the opinion that "The Mohawk road is certainly worth what I paid for it, if only for the steel rails and other portable material attaching to the property. As yet I cannot say what will be done with it."

It was an unfortunate decision for Bowen that he did not salvage the rails, for his efforts to continue construction and operation of the line brought nothing but misfortune in the seven years to come. Although not immediately apparent, it started with H. L. N. Knox's initial contract to restore the 14 miles of original railroad (one mile less

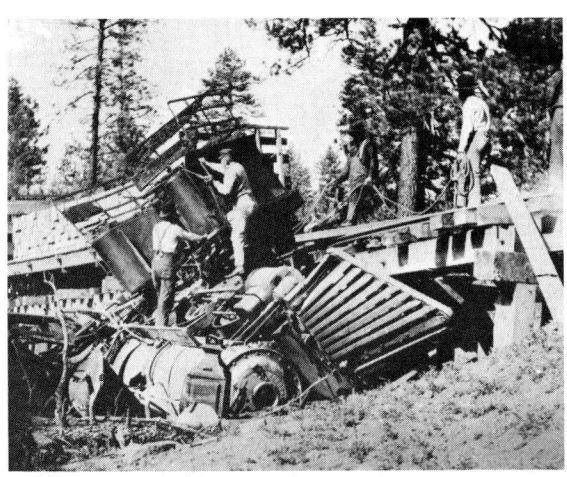
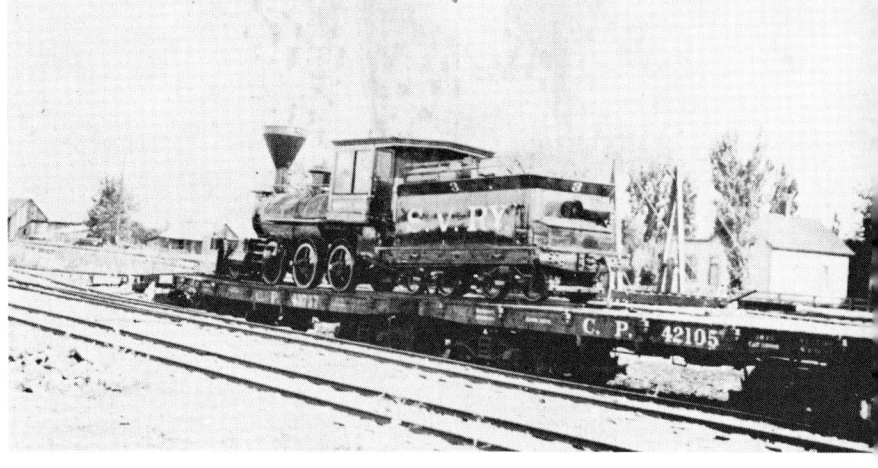

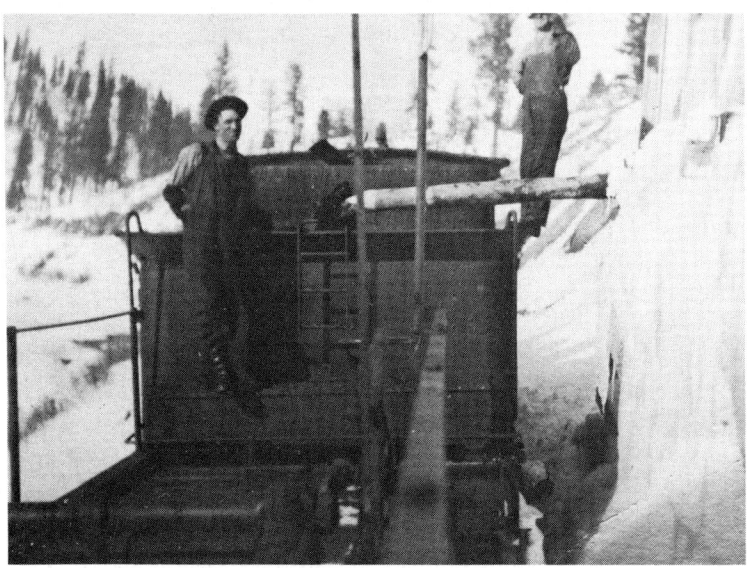

When a cow became wedged in a trestle, engineer Chambers was unable to stop his train in time and was killed in the resulting wreck *(top, left)*. Following this calamity another locomotive was obtained from the SP. No. 3 *(above)* is being delivered at Reno. The inclined track at rear will enable her to be run off the standard-gauge flat cars onto 3-foot N-C-O rails at Reno, from which point she will be hauled to Plumas Jct. for delivery to her owners. *(Both Photos: Mrs. Vinton Bowen White Collection.)*

West of Beckwourth toward Clairville, Supt. J. M. Engle poses while the train stops at the water tank (filled by diversion of waters from a stream through a flume) *(below)*. Any excess dripped harmlessly over the edge to the ground — until winter's cold created a clearance hazard from thickening ice *(center, left)*. *(Left: Al Graves Collection; Bottom: Mrs. Vinton Bowen White Collection.)*

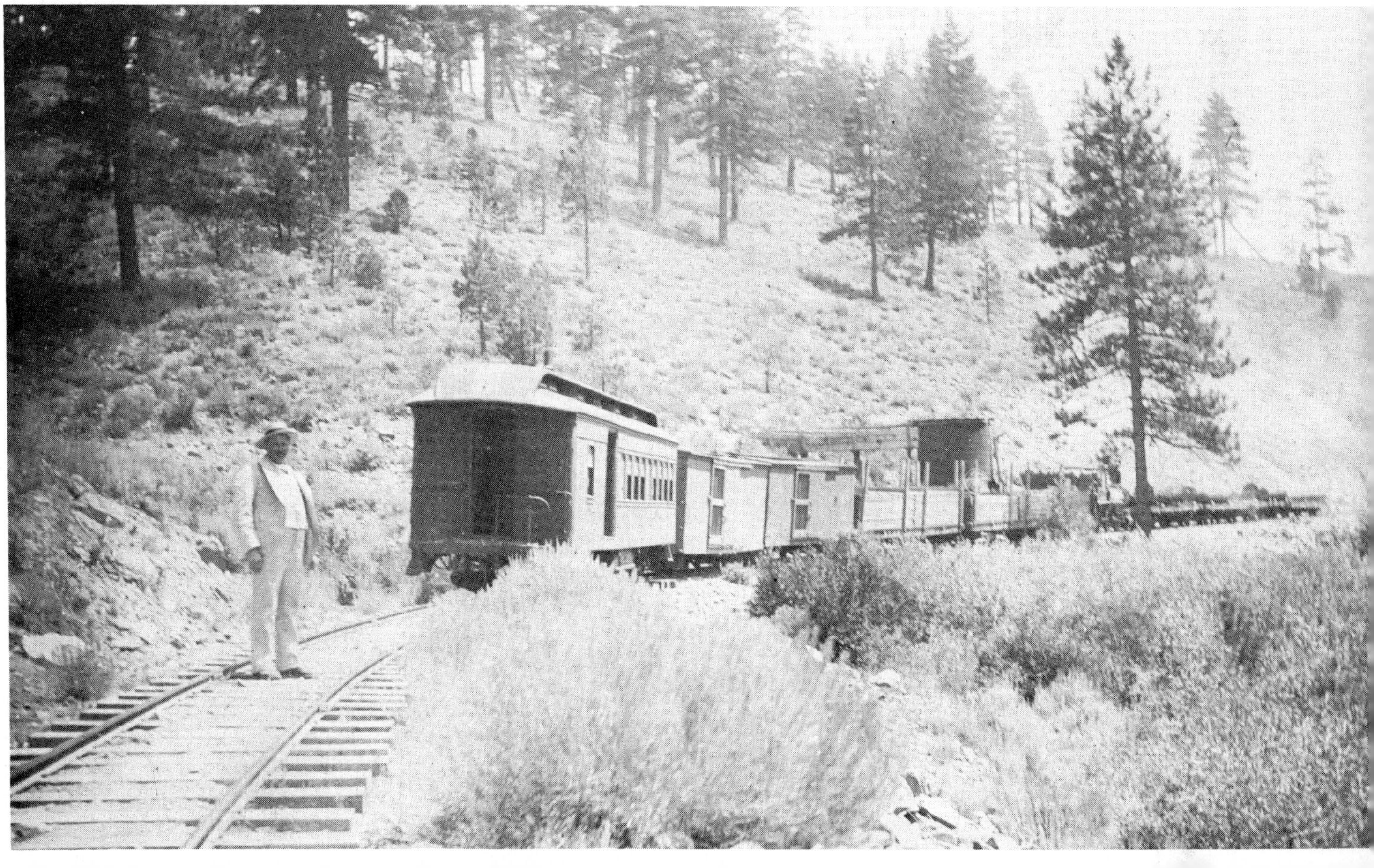

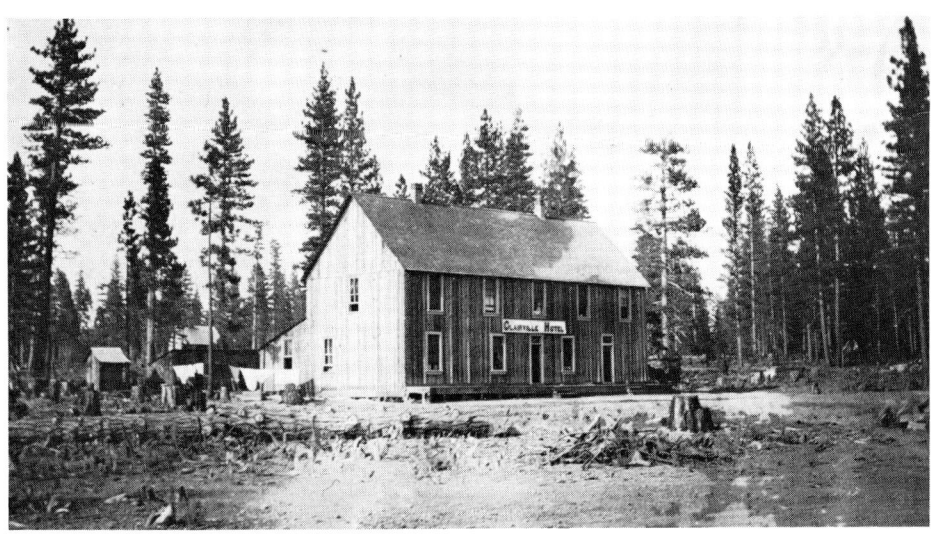

Regular operations over the extension of the SV to Clairville commenced in June 1896. The air of affluent activity attracted the notorious Chat Roberts who built and operated the Clairville Hotel *(top, right)*, an uncommonly tough place with lots of gambling. This hotel burned but was replaced. Directly across the square was the Clairville depot, *(below)* with SV No. 3 standing "wooded up" and ready to leave on the morning's run. Although Henry Bowen started work on an extension to Clio *(center, right)*, six miles farther down a winding canyon grade, his failing finances forced timely intervention by the N-C-O, and the line to Clio was not completed until May 1903 under the latter's ownership. *(Top and Center: Mrs. Vinton Bowen White Collection; Bottom: Southern Pacific Collection.)*

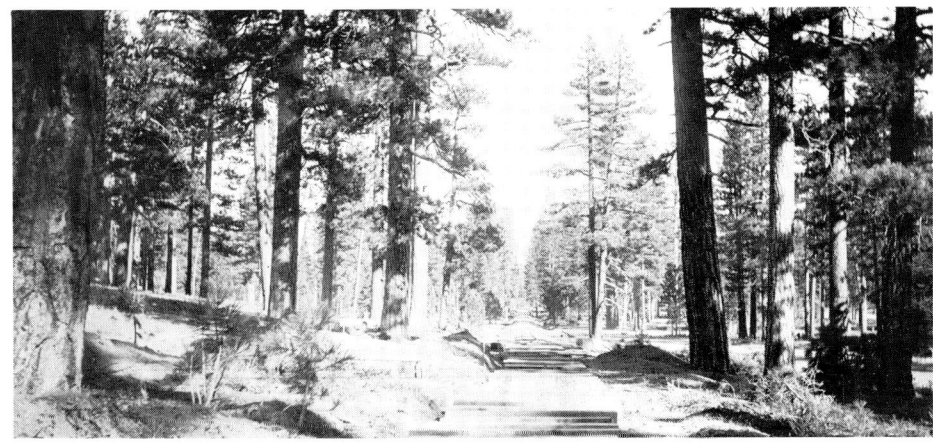

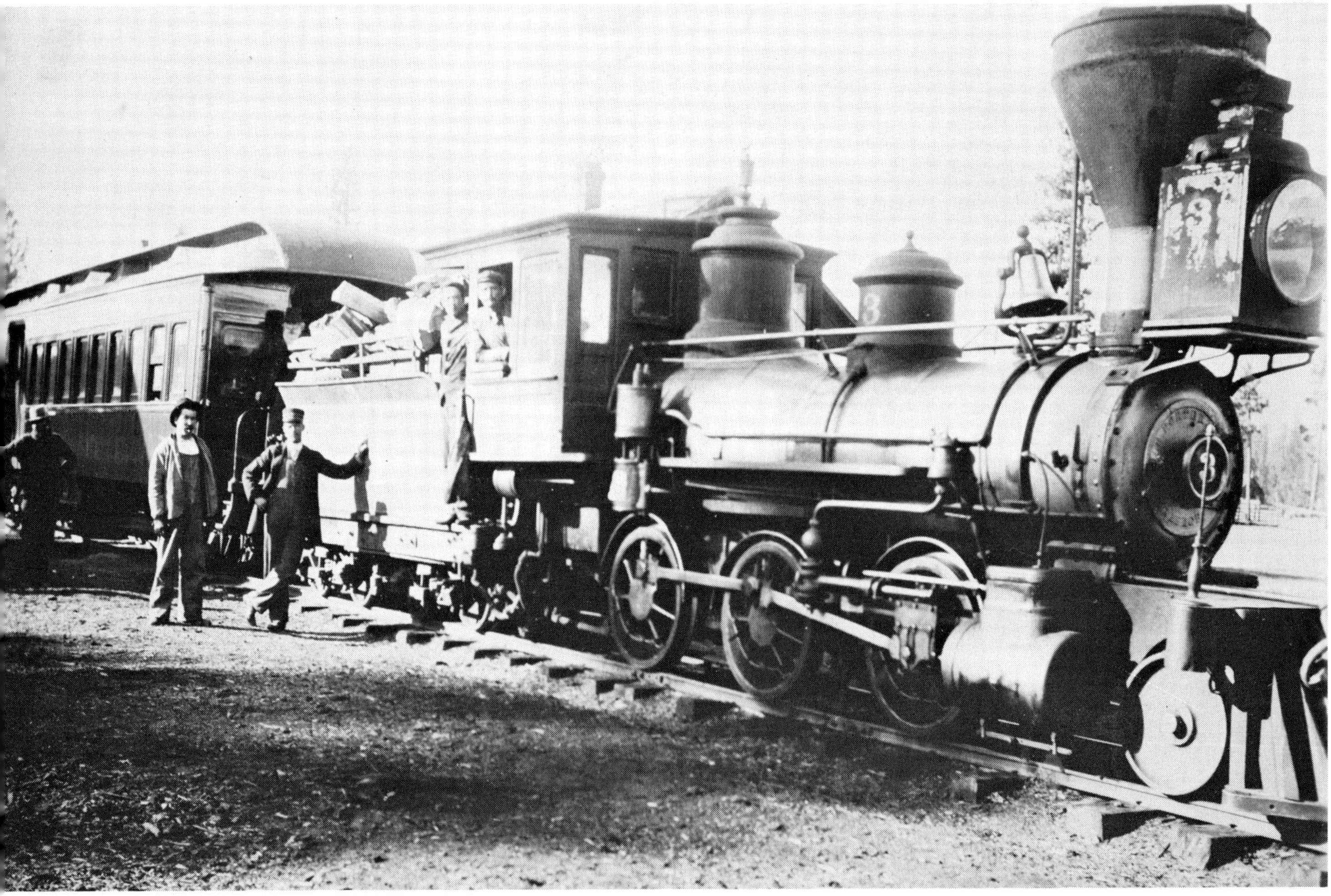

than reported as laid down in 1887) including the clearing out of sagebrush and installation of new ties where necessary. In addition, nine miles of new track were to be laid over the former graded roadbed (which had become a wagon road since cessation of activity in 1887) to the Rock Quarry a few hundred feet west of Kirby Mills (for which the spelling had been changed at this time). The contract also called for new side tracks at Plumas Jct., Beckwith and Kirby Mills, while the old wood spur about two miles west of the junction and the engine house spur were to be removed.

By November 1894 Marion Bringham had a crew cutting ties in the Mohawk Valley while the first locomotive, the PLUMAS, was put through its trial runs. C. H. Clark, a local agent, and his friends celebrated the event with wine and cake.

Inevitably, winter storms delayed construction, but down in San Francisco Bowen was busy with the paper work of incorporating his Sierra Valleys Railway to take title to the railroad and reduce his personal liability. The scope of the project was expanded to include a line from Reno to Quincy, 100 miles, and some consideration was given to the possibility of adding a third rail for both narrow and standard gauge operation.

Better weather arrived in March 1895, and the PLUMAS began making daily trips to bring in supplies. The people of Beckwith watched the approach of the railroad around the north side of The Buttes, and the town began taking on new life. On April 22, 1895, with the railhead but three miles distant, Bowen operated the first passenger train to take his family and friends to Plumas Jct. On May 1 regular passenger service commenced from a temporary depot erected at the same site, and Conley's stage carried the mail and passengers to Beckwith and on to Quincy. On June 3 the rails had reached town and regular service was started without benefit of the 130x36-foot depot which was erected the following month.

In July 1895 the rails were extended another three miles to Kirby and, after doing other miscellaneous work, Knox announced that he had completed his job and would Mr. Bowen please remit. Mr. Bowen retorted that the job was not complete and that he would not be making the final payment until he was satisfied that it was. Knox thereupon marched out about a mile east of Beckwith and brought matters to a head by tearing up a dozen rails. Trains were halted that day, and the U. S. Mail and all unfortunate passengers were transported to Chat by stage. Bowen immediately wired the district attorney to proceed with the sheriff and keep the trains moving. Knox was forcibly removed from the premises, the damage to the track was repaired, and trains commenced operating the next day.

A Stockton, California, contractor signed a new contract on August 21, 1895, to pick up the loose ends of uncompleted work and to refurbish the grade and lay the rail on the remaining eight miles of line to Clairville (M.P. 30.7), where the Lloyd Bros. had recently constructed a sawmill. The line followed closely along the north bank of the Middle Fork of the Feather River, and although Portola did not exist as a community at the time of construction, a station was subsequently erected to service the area. By the end of October the road was virtually completed, but again a misunderstanding arose with the contractor as to what constituted a completed railroad, and train movements over the extension were not started until June of 1896.

Henry Bowen was not above injecting family personalities into his railroading. Clairville, at the western extremity of the road, was named in honor of one of his two daughters, so to make matters even, Cleveland (M.P. 9.18) near the eastern end of the line, was renamed Vinton in honor of the other. But Clairville was Bowen's favorite. It was Bowen who laid out the townsite and offered lots for sale at $25 and up; it was Bowen who purchased timber land in the area in 1896 and erected a mill just east of town; it was Bowen who completed Clairville's facilities as a fitting terminus for the Sierra Valleys Railway by installing a roundhouse for the locomotives in 1897. The Clairville Lumber Co. was an important industry for the area, and to service it properly a quarter-mile spur was constructed from a point a mile east of the Clairville station.

Others came to Clairville, too. Chat Roberts, who already had a nefarious station house to his credit on the N-C-O, took a lot across the square from the depot and erected the Clairville Hotel, which apparently followed his usual style as it is recalled as being a tough place with lots of gambling. In addition to a number of residences and saloons, there was a school and even a Chinatown, which impiously burned in 1903 as a result of delirious carelessness on the part of an aged Chinaman smoking opium. Teamsters, loggers and railroad men sought entertainment in the red light

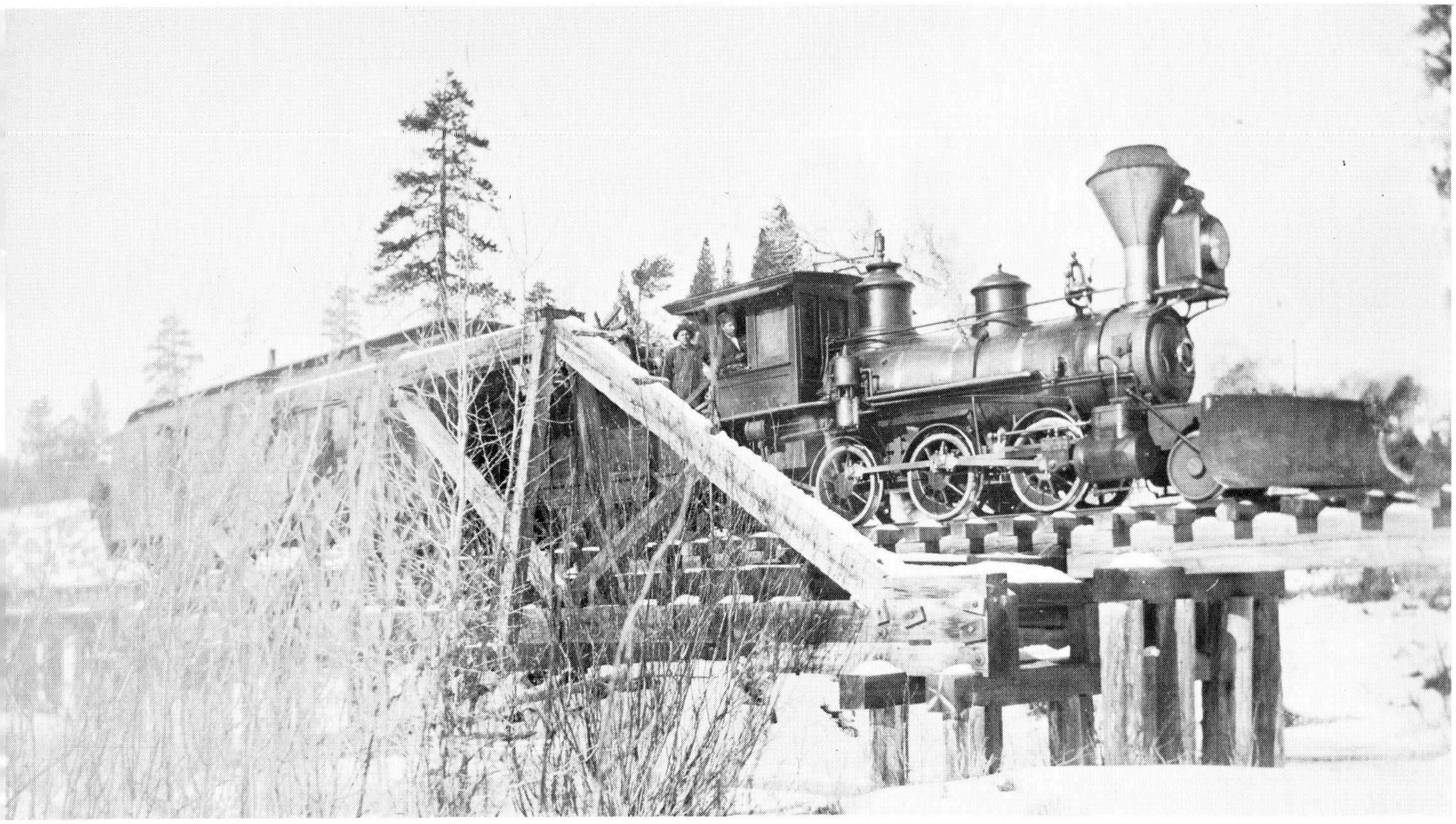

Engineer Chambers holds the time-honored cab position in the view *(top, right)* of No. 2 and the mixed train's combine on the very trestle which ultimately caused his untimely death. *(Mrs. Vinton Bowen White Collection.)*

Lack of a load of wood on the tender together with the casual air of the hostler and his dog suggest that the lead engine *(below, right)*, pilot-plowed No. 2, is about to go to the engine yard for servicing before the day's activities. No. 3 (to the rear), all "wooded-up" and raising a cloud of wood smoke, is about ready to depart with the morning mixed. Note the steam hose coiled on the forward end of her running board, probably used for thawing stubborn, frozen switches as sidings are worked en route to the Junction. *(Mrs. Vinton Bowen White Collection.)*

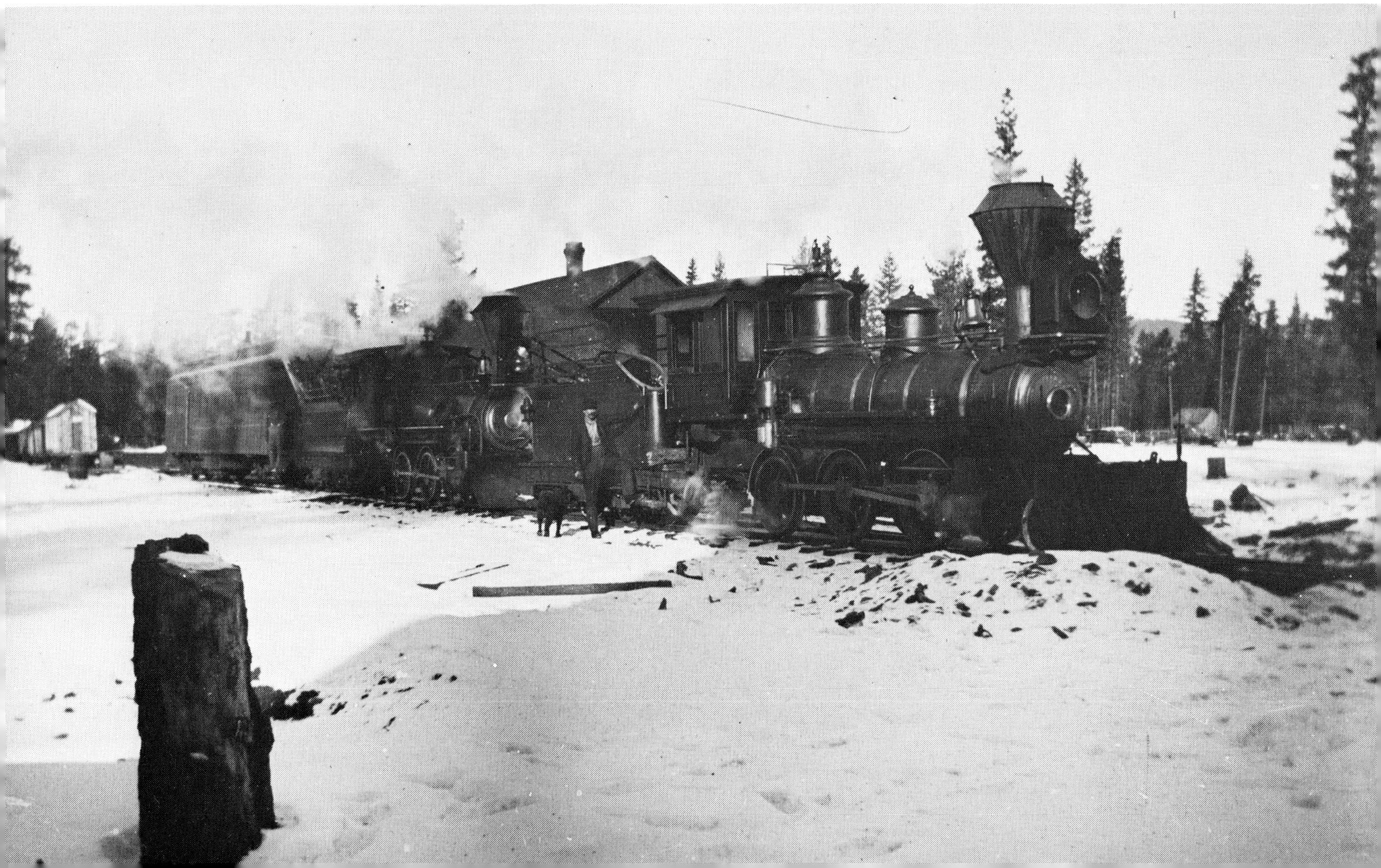

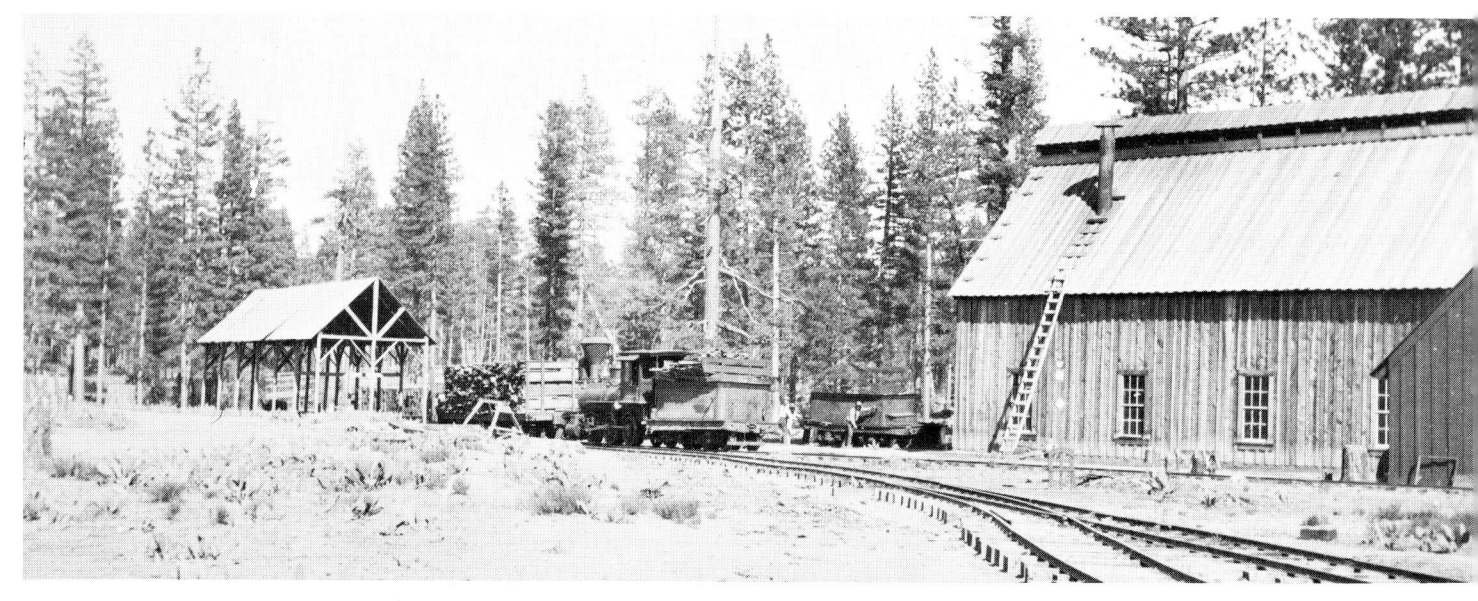
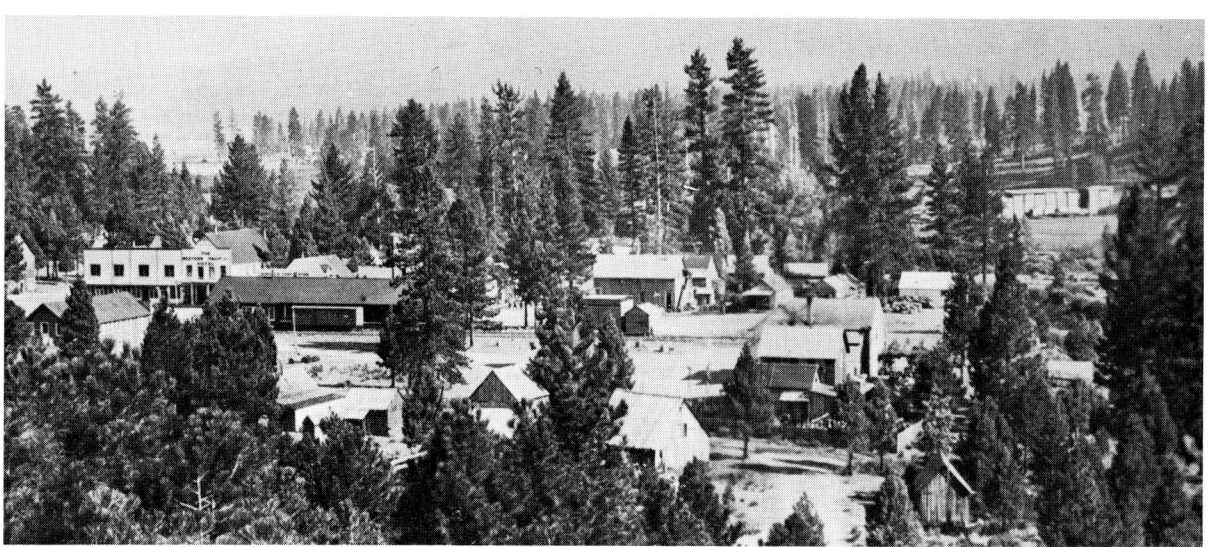

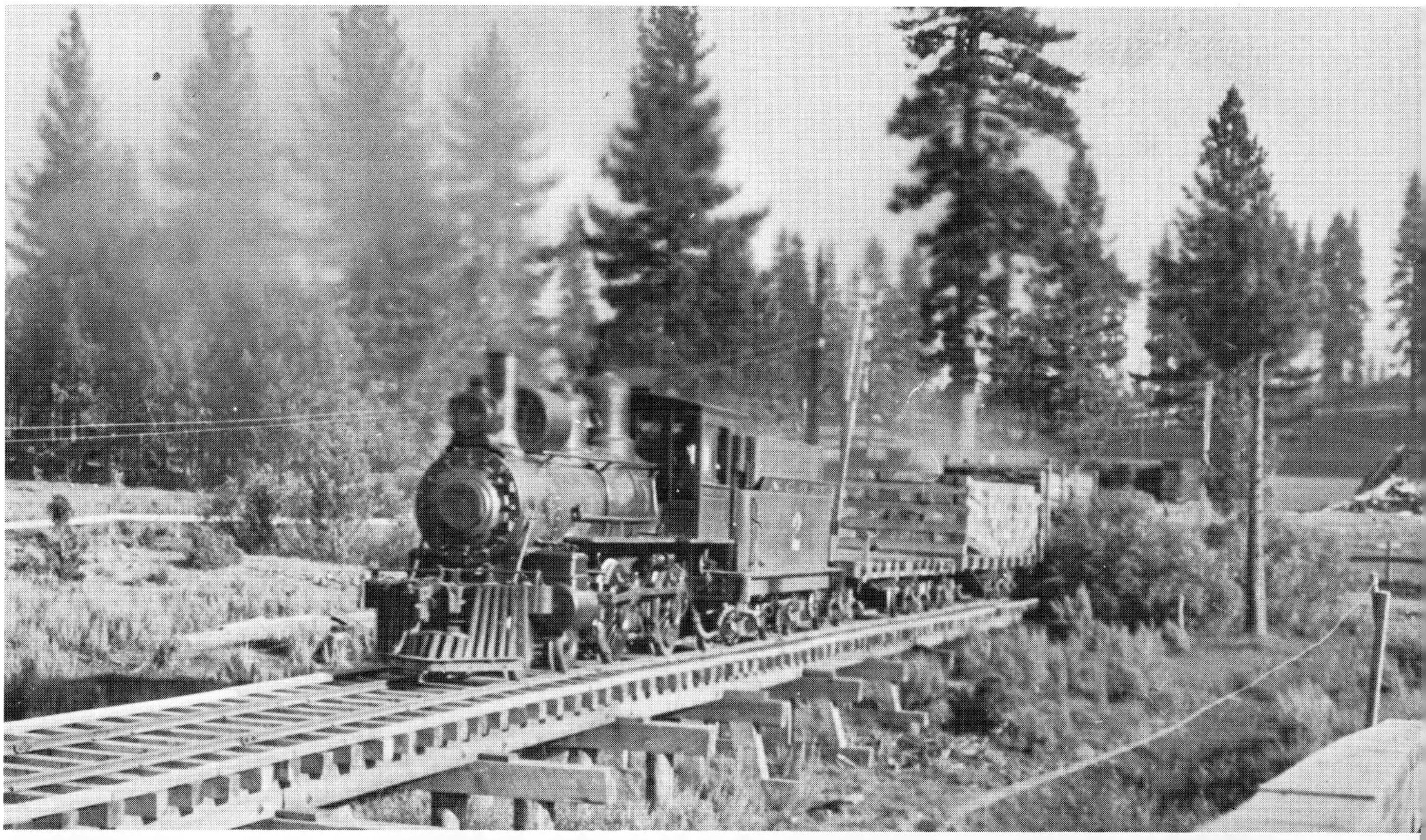

district and in the saloons, frequently ending their evenings in fights, drunk or robbed. Following one reported shooting, the *Plumas National* was moved to comment, "Pistol practice in that town seems not to be a very uncommon entertainment...."

Above all else, lumbering was the principal activity in the Clairville area. Pedrini & Ramelli succeeded to the Lloyd Bros. original mill, while to the north of town the Totten Mill (Feather River Lumber Co. No. 2) was reached by an 11,200-foot spur of the railroad. Sierra Valleys Railway superintendent J. M. Engle did all he could to encourage the lumber industry and ultimately, in 1899, he went into the timber business himself; but during the period from 1896 to 1899 he had his hands full of problems in operating the little line.

Primarily, equipment to handle the lumber was insufficient; the track was in poor condition; wrecks were not infrequent; and the N-C-O was unwilling to interchange equipment with the SV so that all wood and lumber had to be transferred to N-C-O cars at Plumas Jct. Moreover, the Bowen girls were considered a jinx; whenever they rode the trains, something happened. One time a car jumped the track; another time a fire started in the wood in the tender. Most of the bad luck seemed to occur when locomotive No. 2 (the Porter mogul) was on the head end.

A trip on a Sierra Valleys train inevitably was an adventure. Frequently, when the lumber load was heavy, "doubling" would be required up the hill. This would mean an hour or more delay while the locomotive took half of the train to the summit before returning for the other half. Male passengers usually seized upon the occasion to entertain themselves by shooting rabbits, which were plentiful around the dripping water tanks. Invariably there was a luncheon stop at Chilcoot near the top of the pass where, in one emergency, the cook was called upon to assist in the birth of a baby. On another occasion the engine stalled in the heavy snow at the summit; the wood supply became exhausted; and two days elapsed before a sleigh could reach the stranded party with a load of wood from Beckwith.

The year 1898 was known as the year of the fires. In March a conflagration in Vinton consumed the saloon of the late Mr. Lompa (who had been killed in a gun fight two months earlier) along with a butcher shop and a blacksmith's shop. Later, in July, sparks from a SV locomotive set the Beckwith depot aflame, the blaze spreading rapidly, first to the hotel, then subsequently enveloping the whole town. Only the church and the school escaped, all else was in ashes. Although rebuilding started immediately, it was many months before life got back to a more normal keel. Then suddenly on October 21 five lives were lost as a fire of mysterious origin swept the Clairville Hotel. Among items not found in the ashes was the gold for the lumber company's payroll of which Pompey Pedrini was custodian. It was a case of triple jeopardy; for not only did Pedrini lose his life and the lumber company its payroll, but the men were never paid. Other victims of the fire included the owner's mother-in-law, while seven other people had near escapes by jumping from second story windows. Although the hotel was rebuilt, its patronage was somewhat reduced.

The following year (1899) was filled with misfortune, too. On June 21 a special train left Clairville for Beckwith at 6 o'clock in the evening. A mile out of town the engineer came upon cattle grazing along the track. Shrill blasts from the whistle startled the animals into movement, and they all dispersed except one which ran down the track onto a trestle and became stuck between the ties. Engineer Chambers immediately applied the air brakes but was unable to stop in time to avoid hitting the cow. Although the other members of the crew jumped to safety, Chambers stuck to his post; the engine was thrown off the bridge; Chambers was badly injured and died a few hours later. His widow was awarded a $3,000 judgment which the railroad could not pay, but nevertheless

---

At the Clairville enginehouse *(top, left)* SV No. 2 shifts a load of wood out of the way preparatory to pulling the abandoned tender of PLUMAS No. 1 back on the rails. Four men with a heavy chain stand ready to couple up for the movement. *(Mrs. Vinton Bowen White Collection.)*

When the N-C-O completed the Sierra Valleys extension from Clairville to Clio, it also refurbished the balance of the line. At Clio *(center, left)* the SV facilities were maintained in the long dark building with the narrow-gauge box car in front, just left of center in the photo. Behind that building and to the left is The Western Pacific Hotel where WP construction forces stayed. In the clearing at upper right can be seen a portion of the stacks of lumber of the Burkhardt & Grassie Mill, from the siding of which N-C-O No. 2 is shown emerging *(bottom, left)* to cross the light trestle over the Feather River to the main line. *(Two Lower Photos: W. A. Pennington Collection.)*

over the ensuing years she continued her efforts to collect.

That fall Henry Bowen was injured in a track motor car accident, and shortly afterward (January 2, 1900), he suffered another. On this occasion he had taken a locomotive out from Clairville in anticipation of meeting the regular passenger train at Kirby. For some unknown reason the latter train was on time (a most unusual occurrence), and the two locomotives met on a sharp curve not far from Clairville. Although personal injuries were slight, one engine had to be sent to the V&T shops for major repairs, while the other was out of service for several days as local crews mended her broken parts.

Whether this series of misfortunes tipped the scales of the delicate balance of finance is difficult to determine in retrospect. Certain it is that the road was conceived in poverty, born under difficulties, and nursed to adolescence on the leanest possible formula of hard work and whatever adversity the pioneer district could provide. When resuscitation was first started back in 1894, Bowen had borrowed the money (to improve and extend the road) from the Southern Pacific through the offices of his good friend, Collis P. Huntington. The Sierra Valleys' two locomotives had also been purchased from the SP, notes being issued for all of these advances. By March 1899 the notes were long overdue, and legal proceedings were started to enforce their collection. Bowen had anticipated he could obtain money in England, and Henry A. Butters (of the Butters Mill in Virginia City) had cabled that the money was in hand. Then the Boer War struck, and the promises of money evaporated into thin air. To cap the climax, Huntington (then 80 years old) died in the summer of 1900, and following his passing the SP procured a judgment against the SV late in 1900. By that time finances had reached such a low ebb the rolling stock was attached for back wages, and all trains were halted for a while.

At this point the neighboring, connecting N-C-O stepped into the picture. While it may have been distrustful of the SV's dilapidated equipment and refused it access to N-C-O rails, the traffic from the Sierra and Mohawk valleys was a most welcome augmentation to N-C-O revenues, and worthy of a helping hand in distress. To get trains rolling, the back wages were paid and the liens released. Next the N-C-O purchased the $97,000 judgment from the SP, and on March 14, 1901, it acquired control of the Sierra Valleys Railway, continuing to operate it under the same name as a subsidiary company.

All was not to be serene, however, for competition reared its ugly head. From the southeast, the Boca & Loyalton Railroad came racing across the marsh lands of the Sierra Valley to reach the center of Beckwith in October 1901. From there the main line subsequently turned down the valley on the south side of the river as far as Mormon (later Portola), while another branch left the main at Horton Jct. (near Beckwith) and headed to the northeast toward Clover Valley over a hotly disputed grade crossing with the Sierra Valleys. (See B&L.)

While the SV could do little about the invasion of its territory by the B&L, it was not to be caught entirely flat-footed. Bowen's earlier enthusiasm, in spite of his financial difficulties, apparently had not been dampened; for even as he lost control of the SV, work had been started on a six-mile extension from Clairville to Clio, down in the Mohawk Valley. This work the N-C-O pushed through to completion, and operations over the line commenced on May 4, 1903. The road formed a large letter "S" in reverse as it dropped down the hill and followed the bed of Willow Creek. Just before reaching Clio, a single-stall engine house and a water tank were installed at the end of a wye track.

The town of Clio proper boasted 14 saloons and a variety of names. Wash Post Office had moved there from a nearby ranch; other names—Newtown, Boozeburg, and New Mohawk (some maps show it as Mohawk)—were applied at various times. The principal industry to which the town looked for subsistence was the Feather River Lumber Company's mill No. 3, which the railroad served by means of a short spur track.

The railroad suffered from heavy snow blockades in the winters of 1902 and 1903, and there were ominous rumblings on the horizon as the Western Pacific Railway was incorporated in 1903. If scant attention was paid at that time, the matter was more forcibly impressed upon the minds of the N-C-O directors when some preliminary WP work was performed on Beckwourth Pass in December 1904 in order to hold the location.

Local business continued to increase during the period of 1905-06-07; the years 1906 and 1907 showed profits, probably for the first time in the history of the road. Revenues and profits hit a peak

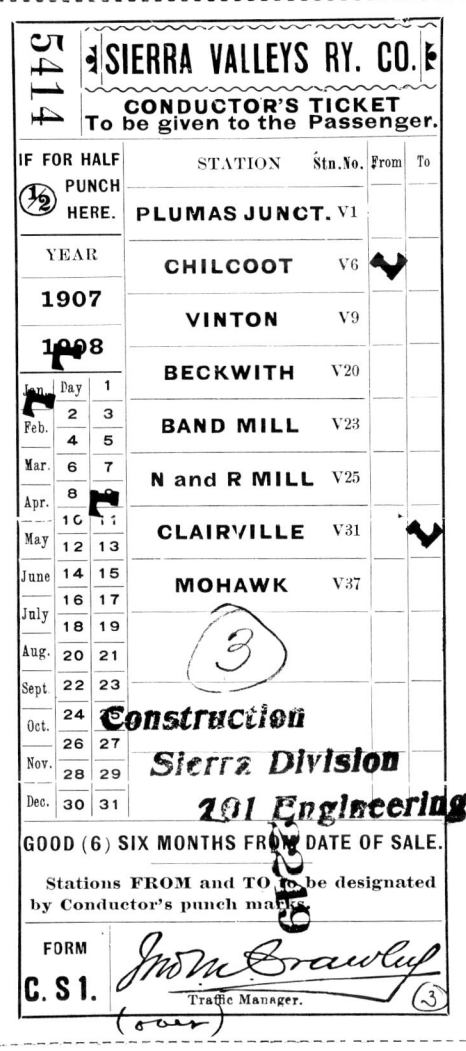

during 1908-09 while the Western Pacific Railway construction was concentrated in the area; then a decline set in in 1910, following which losses again became the pattern. 1906 annual revenues were approximately $25-30,000, soaring to $93,700 in 1909. With an operating ratio of 33%, the 1909 net income was a whopping $47,000 for the little line.

In 1911, following some financial and legal settlements, Bowen's Sierra Valleys Railway was reorganized as the Sierra & Mohawk Railway, the new company still remaining as an N-C-O subsidiary. But even a new name and a new start could not erase the dead hand of the indigent past. Long dormant and entirely forgotten, the widow Chamber's $3,000 judgment (following the death of her husband in the wreck of 1899) was converted into a lien. Some years later the property was attached and sold at public auction and the widow Chambers, bidding at the auction, found herself a railroad owner. Since the N-C-O held the property as a subsidiary company, it had to buy its own railroad back from the widow in 1912.

The Sierra & Mohawk Railway was absorbed into the N-C-O on January 1, 1915, to become known as the Plumas Branch. Daily the "Sagebrush Limited" continued to ply its way out of Plumas Junction, up and over Beckwourth Pass, down the Sierra Valley to Beckwith, Kirby and Clio. Clairville had become uninhabited by 1913, and winter snows had caved the roofs of several residences. Near the site of the former Clairville Lumber Company's plant a double grade crossing, where the Western Pacific's new line crossed and then recrossed the S&M's tracks, posed operating problems for both roads. In 1915 the S&M tracks were relocated to the north, the route was shortened by ⅝ of a mile and the crossings were eliminated.

At the western end of the line, a 2.69-mile extension was started in April 1916 to carry the tracks out of Clio, across the Feather River, and on down the waterway to the Davies Mill where extensive yard trackage was installed. First rails reached the mill in the middle of July, and another month was required to finish the yard facilities. Although corporate authority had been given to extend the branch another mile to Mohawk, no work on this segment was ever undertaken. The N-C-O, however, did considerable rehabilitation work on the whole of the Plumas Branch to make it safe for the heaviest locomotives and trains.

A scant two years later, in 1917, the Plumas Branch was sold to the Western Pacific as part of the N-C-O line purchase (see N-C-O), and on April 16, 1918, the road was abandoned. In the Mohawk Valley, the old grade was rejuvenated for a time when the Graeagle Lumber Co. used the old roadbed for a portion of their logging lines built in the 1920's. The activity was short-lived, however, and the tracks were taken up about 1935.

Many miles of the old Sierra Valley & Mohawk railroad can still be viewed today. Much of U.S. Highway Alt. 40 is constructed on the old railroad grade between Vinton and Delleker. The site of the former Portola station is now occupied by a gasoline station on the south side of the highway near the old bridge. Of the former town of Clairville nothing remains except a few excavations, while to the north pine trees with 10-inch trunks grow between the rotting ties of the once-busy branch to Totten Mill (Feather River No. 2). Another era has ended.

BOCA & LOYALTON RAILROAD

When the Central Pacific Railroad Company of California flung its tortuous roadbed over the crest of the Sierras and down along the Truckee River in the late 1860's, the junction of the Little Truckee and the Truckee Rivers was just one more small wilderness hurdle to be surmounted in the great eastward push. Some men, however, stopped to look—and to think. The Central Pacific needed ties—hundreds of thousands of ties representing millions of board feet of timber—and each new settlement opened up along the route would require lumber for building, timber for the mines, and wood for fuel. A vast market for forest products was being created, and the hills surrounding the Truckee River were well forested. Here was an industry made to order; so here they stayed to found the lumbering center of Boca.

But timber was a static product. As the hills along the river became denuded, men necessarily worked farther and farther back into the mountains, the hardiest going deep into the woods to found new settlements and build new mills. Transportation to and from these more remote outposts was an eternal problem.

Of such pioneer stock were the three Lewis brothers who, around 1886, joined forces with two Peck brothers to build the Lewis mill, 17 miles north of Boca in the wilds of Smithneck Canyon. To reach the location, one followed the valley of the Little Truckee River to the point where that stream turned westward, then continued on up Sardine Valley to the 6,370-foot summit and thence down Smithneck Canyon to the camp. The alternative, shorter, though more circuitous route climbed the reaches of Dog Valley out of Verdi, passed over Dog Valley Summit down to Merrill, then joined the trail from Boca up Sardine Valley as before. In spite of the two summit crossings, Verdi, being the handier location, was more favored. In 1887 the Lewis brothers established a box factory at Verdi, the same year that the Pecks left the firm.

Obscure today are the reasons why John H. Roberts joined the Lewis' organization in 1888. Roberts had been a Sacramento River steamboat captain, and he brought with him to the wilderness a fleet of steam "wagons" (or traction engines) which he had formerly used in connection with his river boat business. They were ponderous machines, weighing as much as 29 tons, and resting on huge, six-foot driving wheels with a single center-front driving wheel. In operation, they chuffed and clanked along the forest roads like prehistoric monsters, belching forth great clouds of black smoke as they towed their trains of lumber wagons from the mill to Verdi and return. Farmers' horses along the route were terrified, and the farmers objected most strenuously to the fire-breathing demons. When a proposal to build a new road on the opposite side of the canyon failed to appease the situation, W. S. Lewis arranged for a big family picnic for all concerned. To the gathering he explained his aim to provide year 'round employment for people in the area as well as his desire to help the farmers market their produce. An amicable solution to the problem was finally arranged whereby the horse-drawn wagons would use the road during the day-

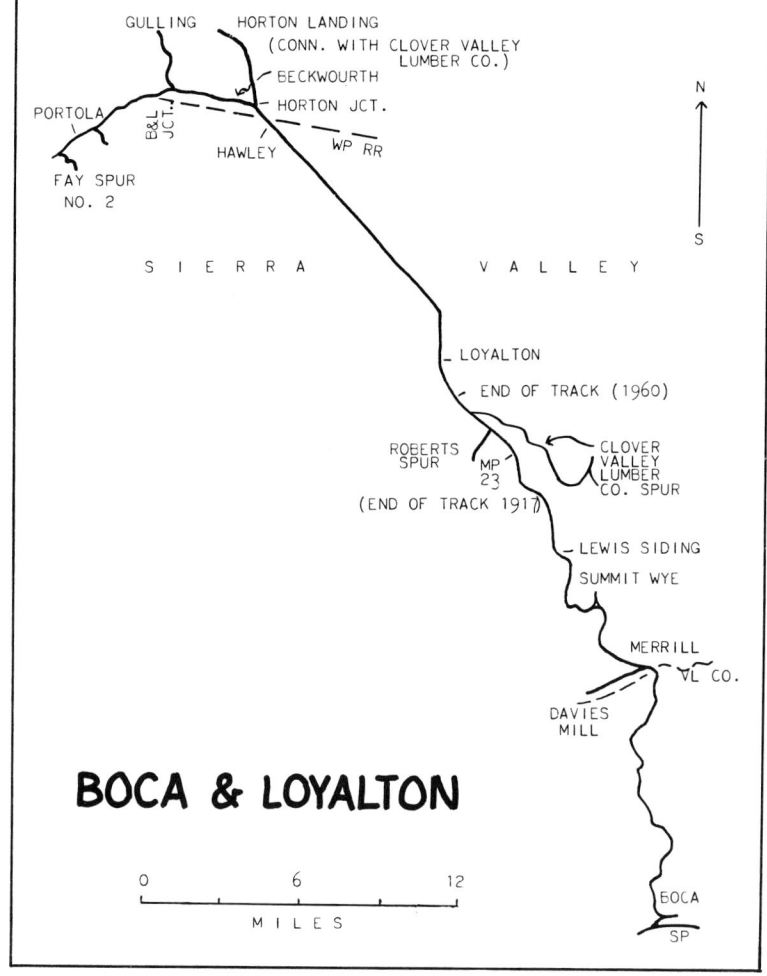

time, and the steam-driven monsters would roam only at night.

Down in the Truckee River valley, Boca was having its growing pains as well. In 1888 the Boca Mill & Ice Company (started in 1867 by L. E. Doan to cut ties for the CP) built a dam to form a large pond for natural ice. The business developed so nicely, a year later they built a second ice pond a short way up the Little Truckee River, servicing the new facility by means of a short, two-mile railroad. However the combination of the railroad and the products of the Boca Brewing Company proved to be a lethal liability to the population of the center, for so many drunks were run over by trains it was found necessary to close the saloons. This move provided but a temporary solution, for Roddy McClellan laid out a town immediately across the river, called it Rodyville, and installed two large saloons to accommodate the thirsty.

By 1900 Messrs. Lewis and Roberts had tired of their nocturnal, lumbering steam wagons and determined upon a railroad to provide the faster, more efficient transportation required. Moreover, to avoid the costly second summit of the route to Verdi, the new line would run north from Boca, up the valley of the Little Truckee, and would extend beyond the Lewis Mill, down Smithneck Canyon to Loyalton on the southern edge of the vast Sierra Valley.

Loyalton had originally been called Smith's Neck in honor of its pioneer settler and miner, but the name had been changed about the time of the Civil War due to the large number of volunteers who entered the conflict. From an industrial standpoint, it was an ideal location for lumbering because of the long drying season existing in the Sierra Valley. Not only could the lumber be dried, but also the employees — for the Lewis family had passed strict laws prohibiting saloons inside the city limits, then had pushed those limits far out into the surrounding countryside to discourage such trade anywhere near the populated area, thus making Loyalton one of the largest cities (area-wise) in the state of California. The strictness of town morals was amply demonstrated in 1902 when 25 ladies were arrested for indulging in a quiet game of whist.

The Boca and Loyalton Railroad Company was incorporated on September 25, 1900. Work on the line commenced in the fall of 1900 and was carried forward until bad weather forced suspension of activity early the following year and 116 men were

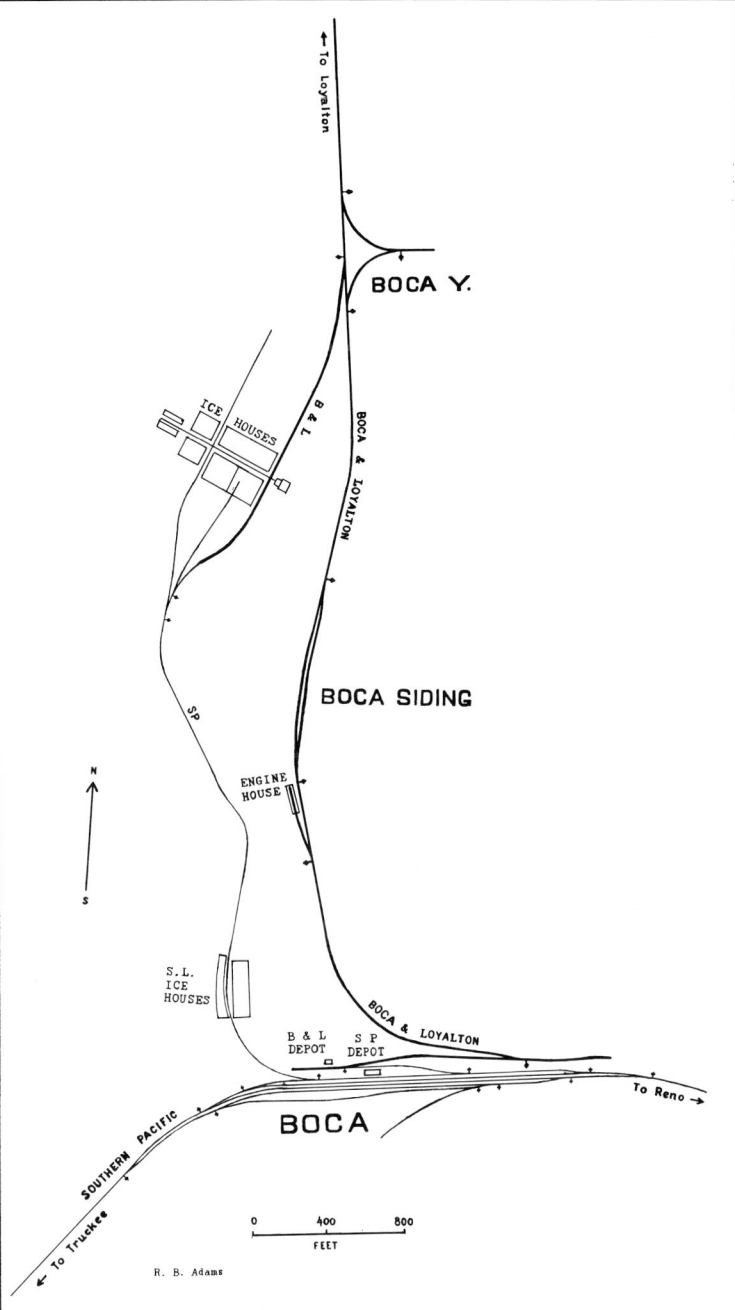

laid off temporarily. By March 1901 the road was completed to Lewis Mill, and several cars of box shook were being shipped daily to Boca, 17 miles away. Some 50 men were still occupied with the ballasting operation, while job applicants were welcomed to start on the next section of nine miles to Loyalton on which work would be rushed as soon as the snow cleared away.

By the summer of 1901, the railroad was completed, and the population of Loyalton (which had consisted of 50 people) began to increase as new arrivals crowded the B&L's coach to apply for work in the galaxy of mills being constructed at the edge

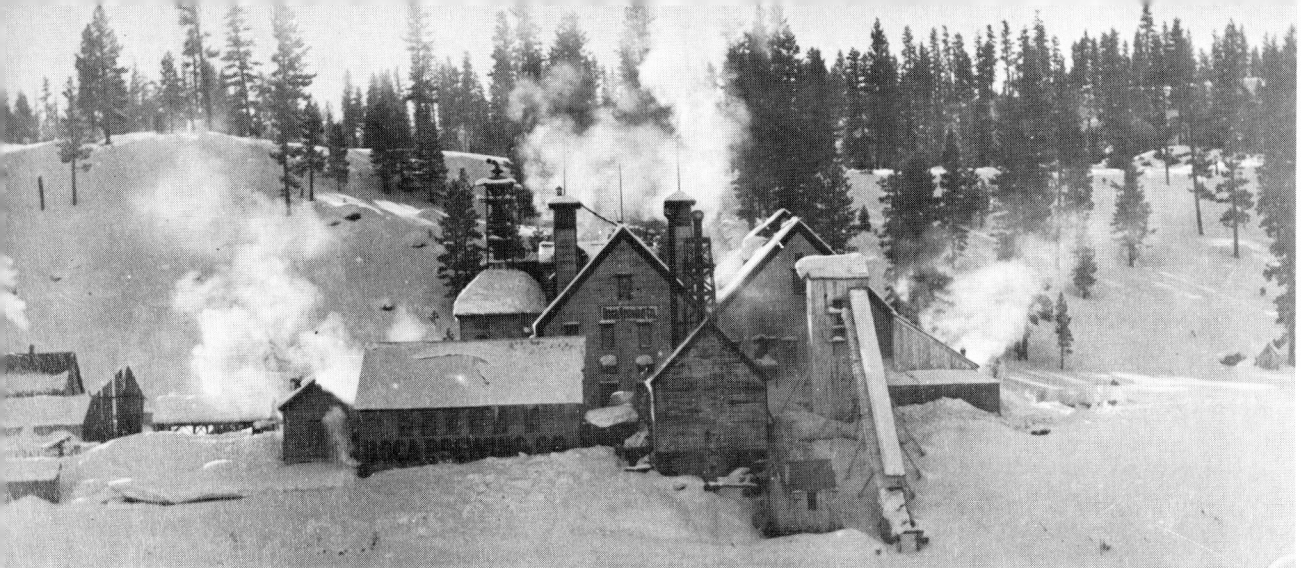

The combination of good, clear mountain water and thirsty lumberjacks in the nearby woods contributed to the success of The Boca Brewing Co. *(above)*. Boca Beer was widely known in years gone by. *(Southern Pacific Collection.)*

In the early 1900's Boca was a busy junction. The view *(below)* looks east along the Truckee River Canyon. The Boca & Loyalton Railroad swings in from behind the town along the canyon wall to the point where the woodburning locomotive is standing. Here a short steep switchback leads down toward the camera to the Southern Pacific station. Behind and just to right of the station an SP engine is switching a cut of cars; another stands in front of the large warehouse of the Union Ice Co. *(Grahame Hardy Collection.)*

Early days of logging are typified by the Best steam traction engine *(top, right)* which hauled lumber prior to the building of the railroad; B&L woodburner No. 7 *(center)* with a new combine on the occasion of a local outing; and another woodburner and older combine *(bottom)* which were pressed into service near Portola during construction of the Western Pacific in 1908. Virgil Bogue, vice-president and chief engineer of the WP stands on the platform at left with W. S. Lewis, B&L superintendent in doorway at center. *(Top and Center: Al Graves Collection; Bottom: Western Pacific Collection.)*

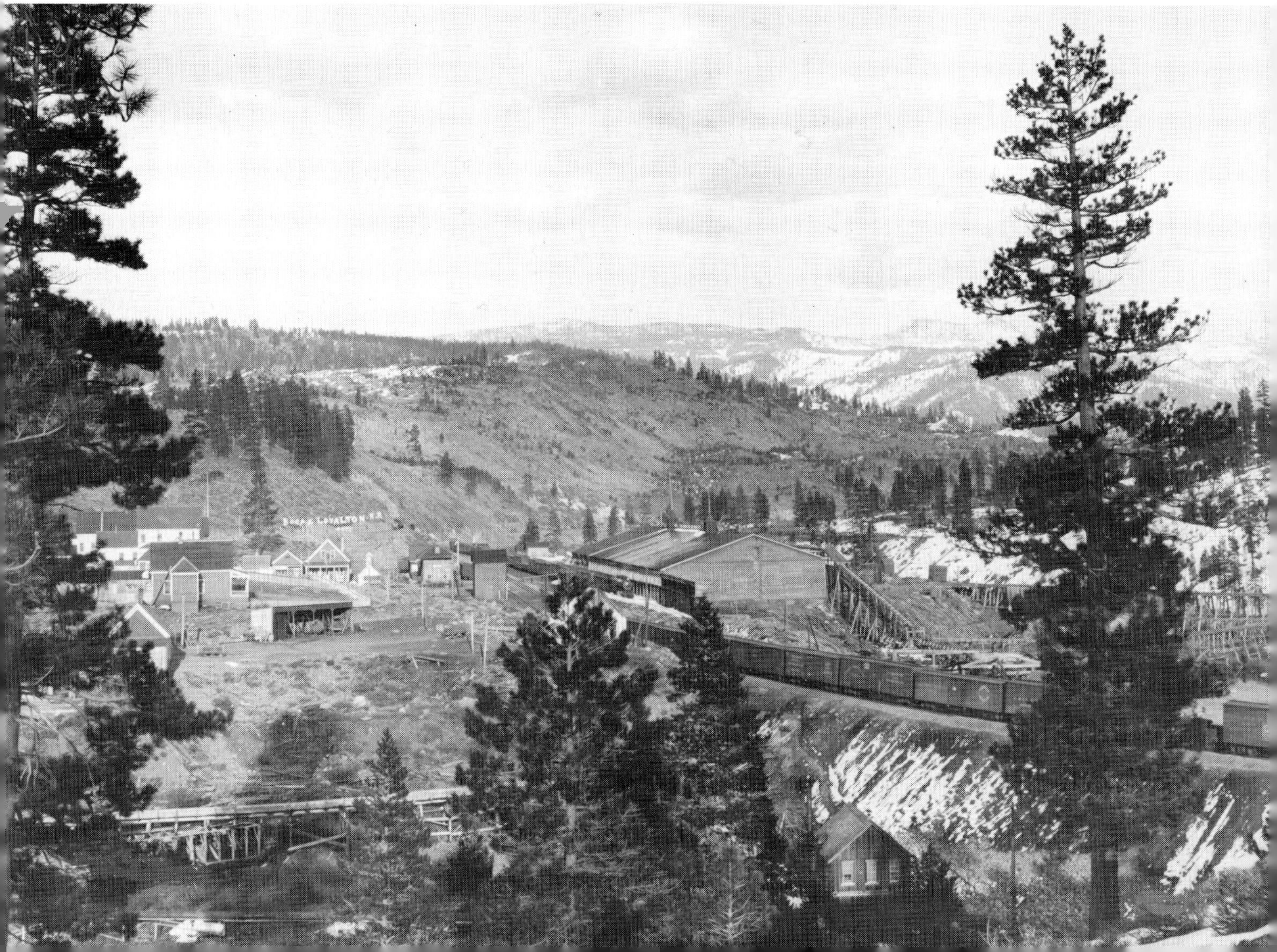

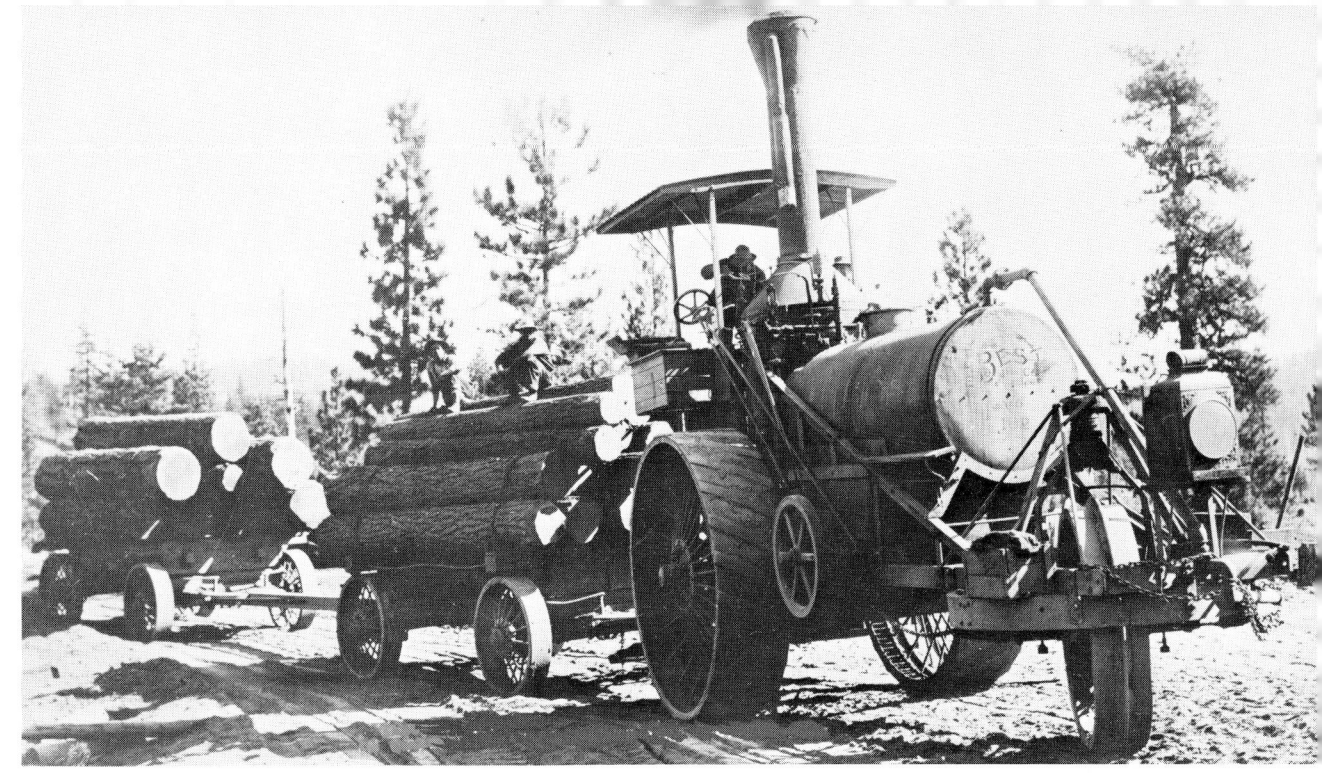

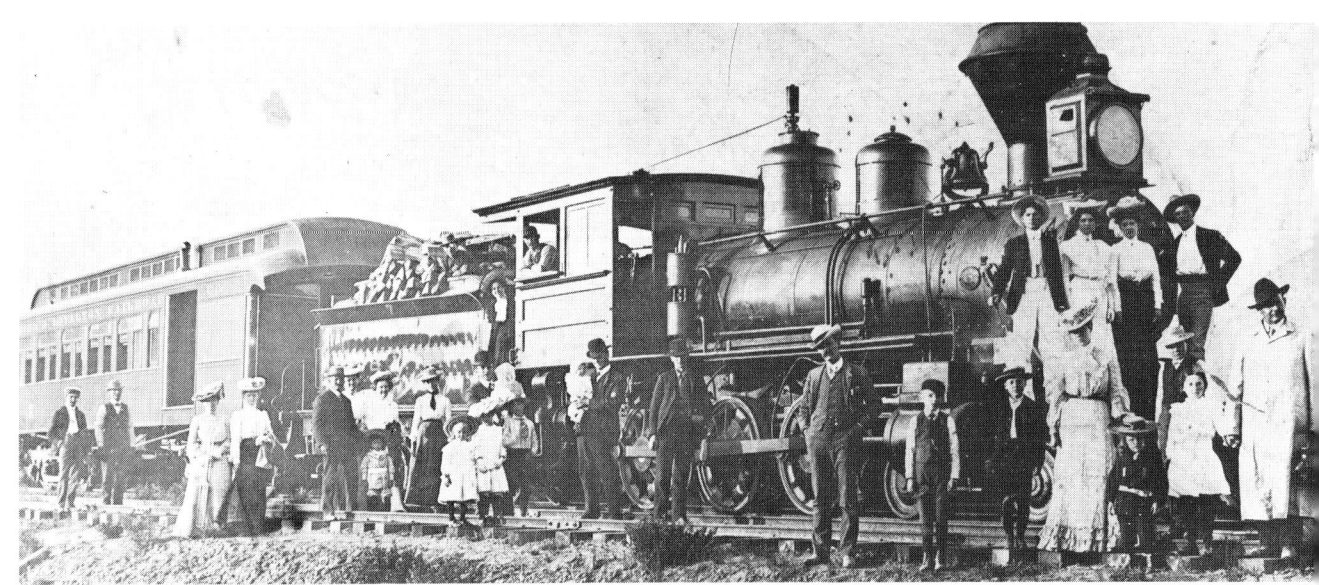

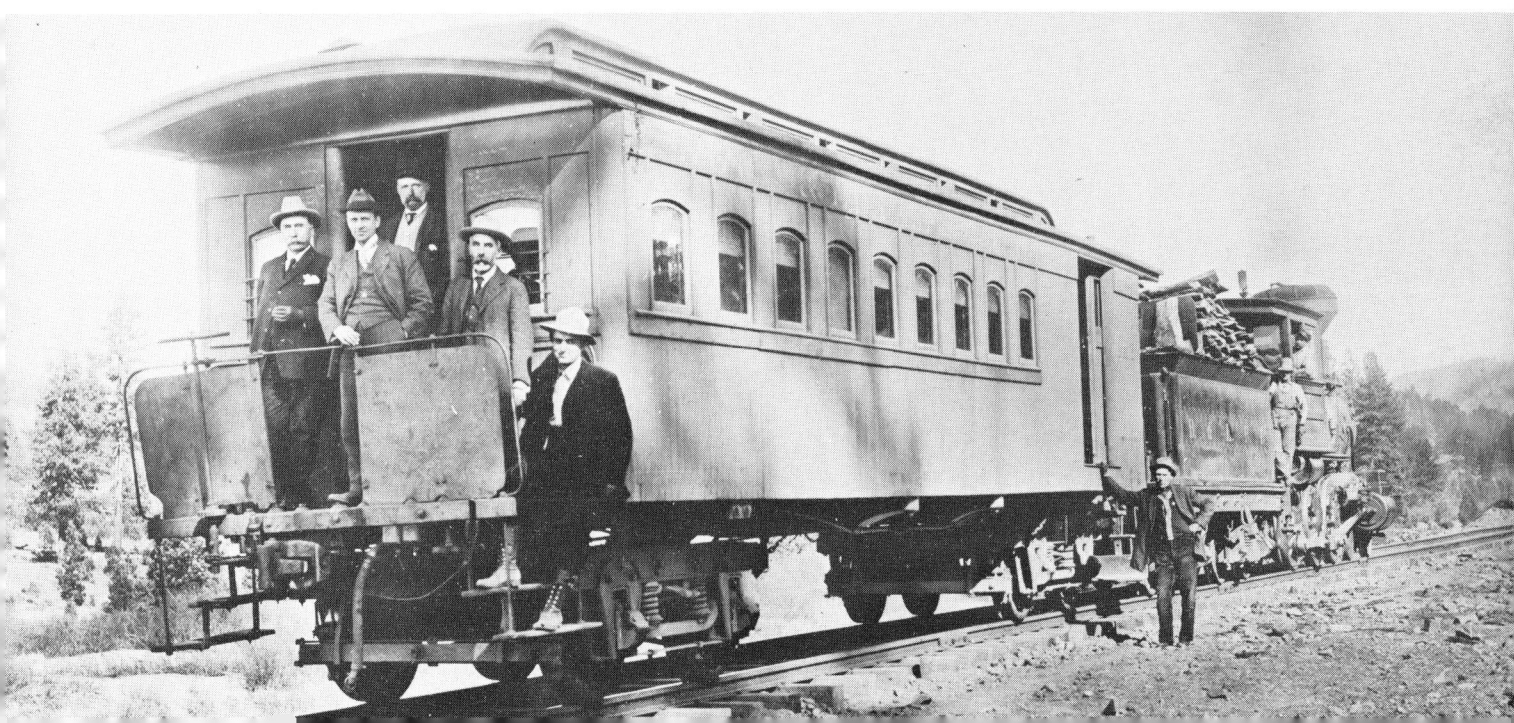

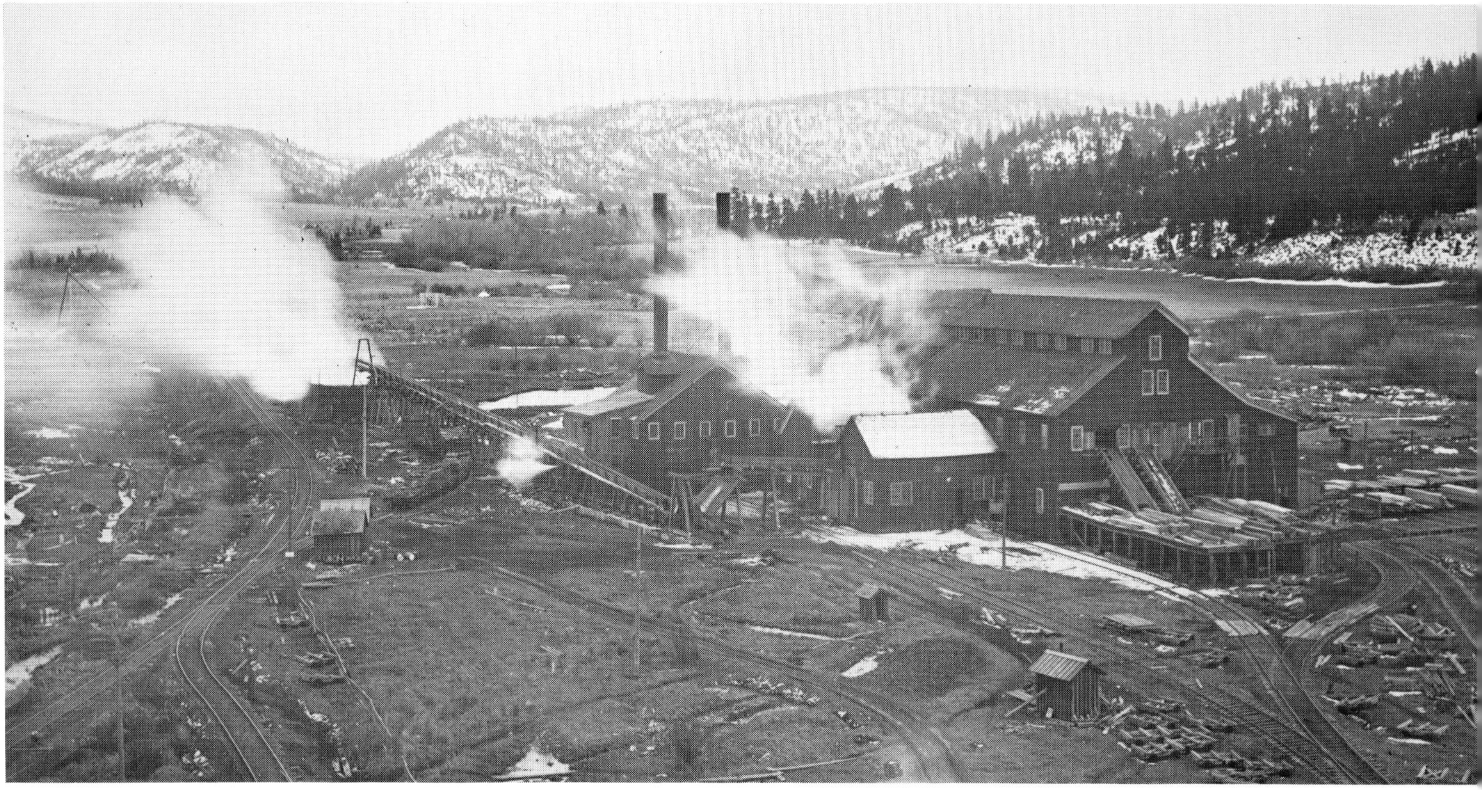

In the view *(top)* facing south are the extensive mill and facilities of the Roberts Lumber Co. whose logs were stored in the millpond behind. The main line of the B&L is at the left and passes the smoking burner as it heads for Smithneck Canyon at the end of the valley beyond. *(J. F. Conklin Collection.)*

The cordwood being hauled behind the B&L's trim Consolidation (2-8-0) No. 5 *(below)* was a by-product of the slab cuttings and waste from such mills as the Roberts and Lewis Mill *(top, left)* which was a pioneer in the Loyalton area. *(Both Photos: Stanley Palmer.)*

Loyalton about 1908 was an important place. In the view looking north *(bottom, right)* the Roberts Mill is in the lower right corner between the trees. Behind it are the car shops and wye of the B&L with the main line extending from the tree trunk on north past the 3-story gabled station with car in front to cross the long tangent of the Sierra Valley toward Beckwith and Portola. In the center foreground is the Plumas Box Factory, to the left of which (in quick succession) are the tall stacks of the power house and box factory of the Roberts enterprise. At far left is the Reno Mill Co. and millpond. The town of Loyalton proper lies behind this industry, dominated by the white 3-story school on North Second Street. *(Grahame Hardy Collection.)*

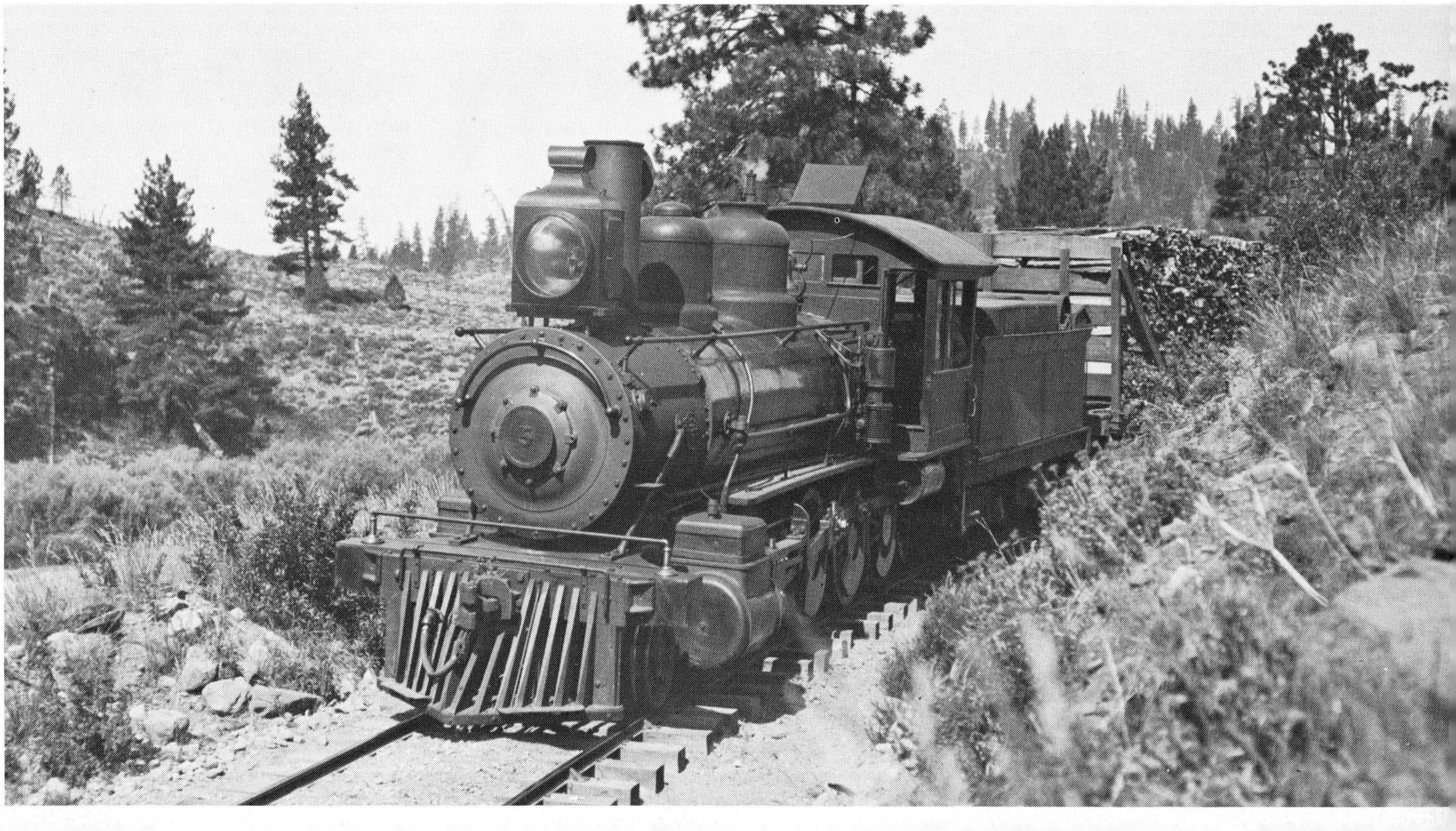

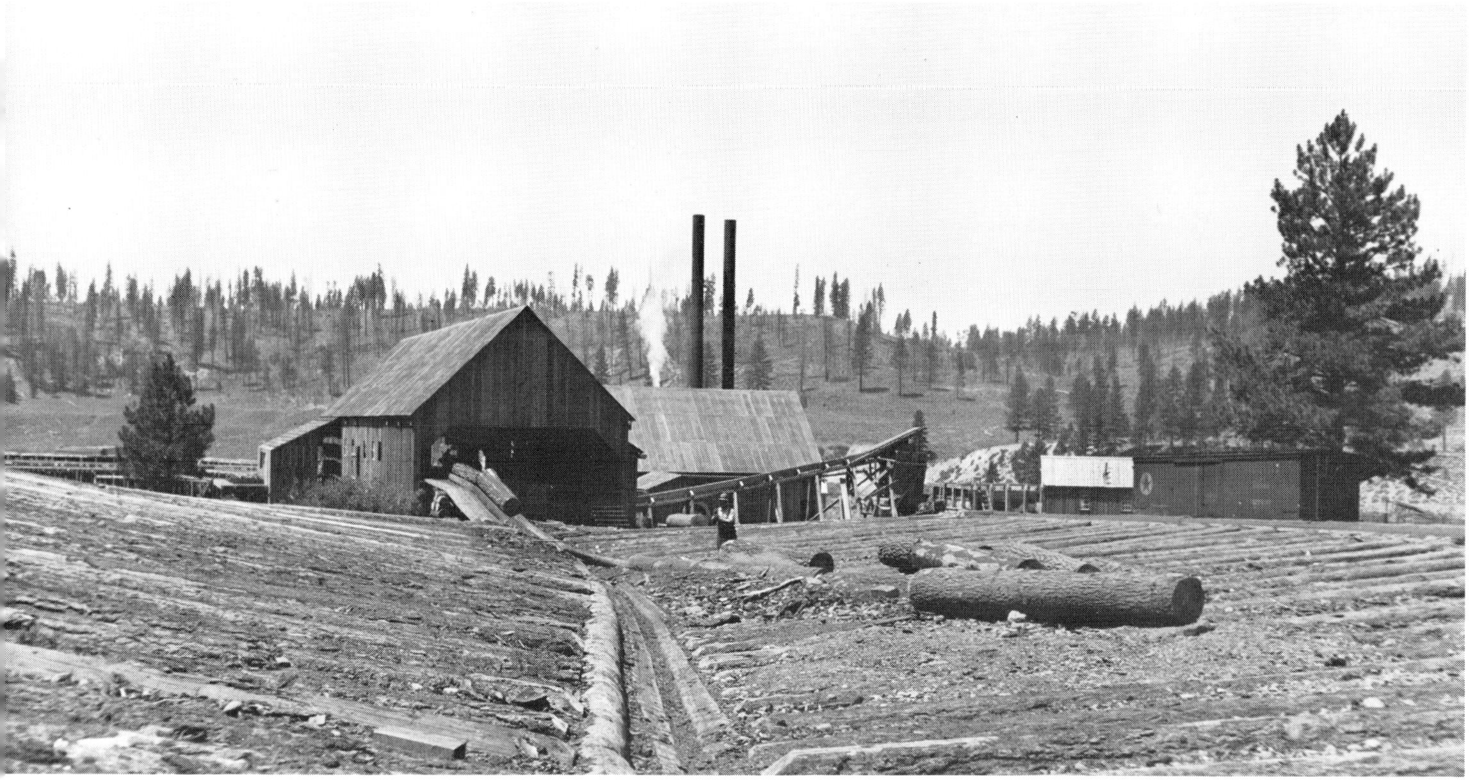

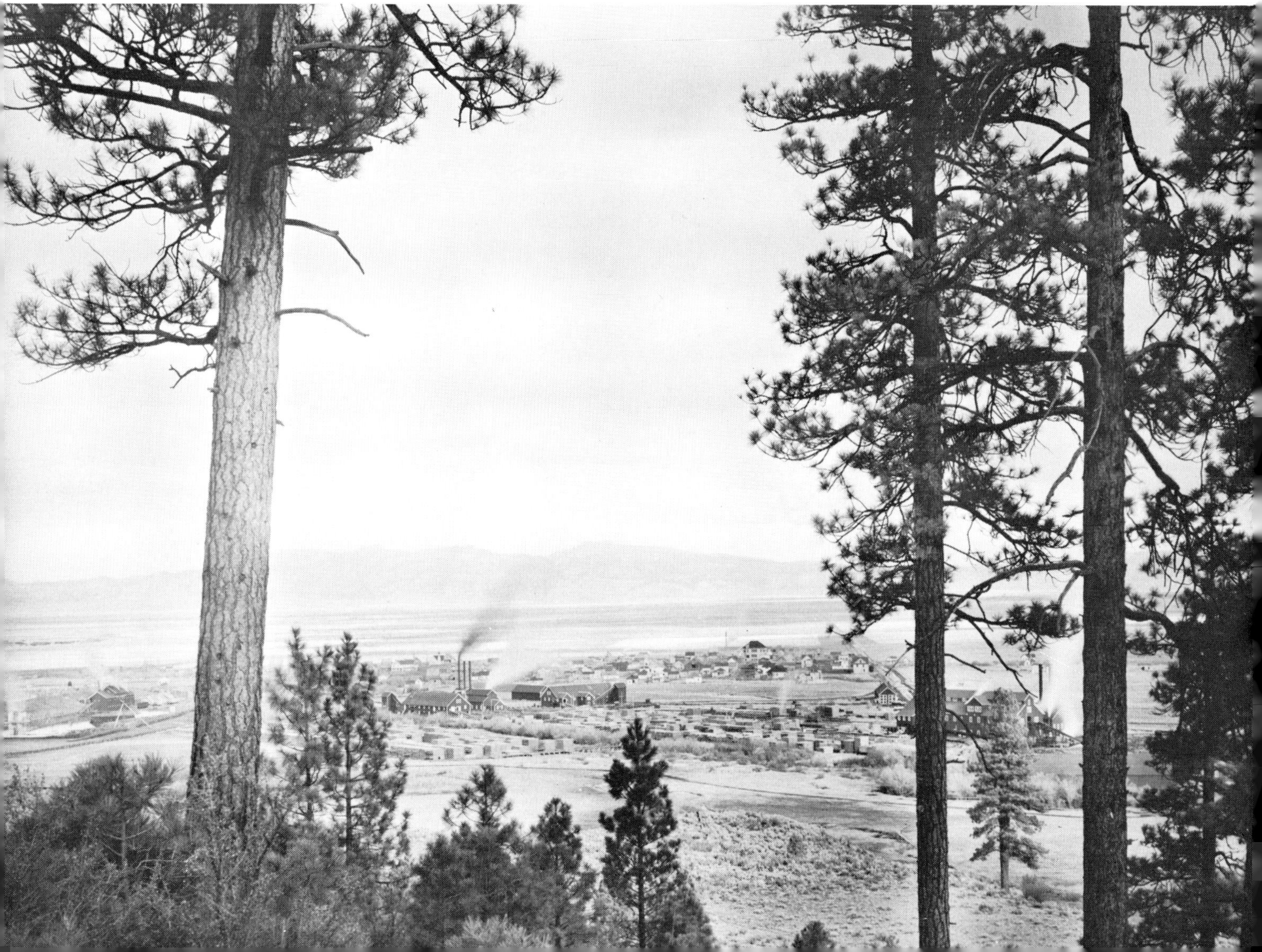

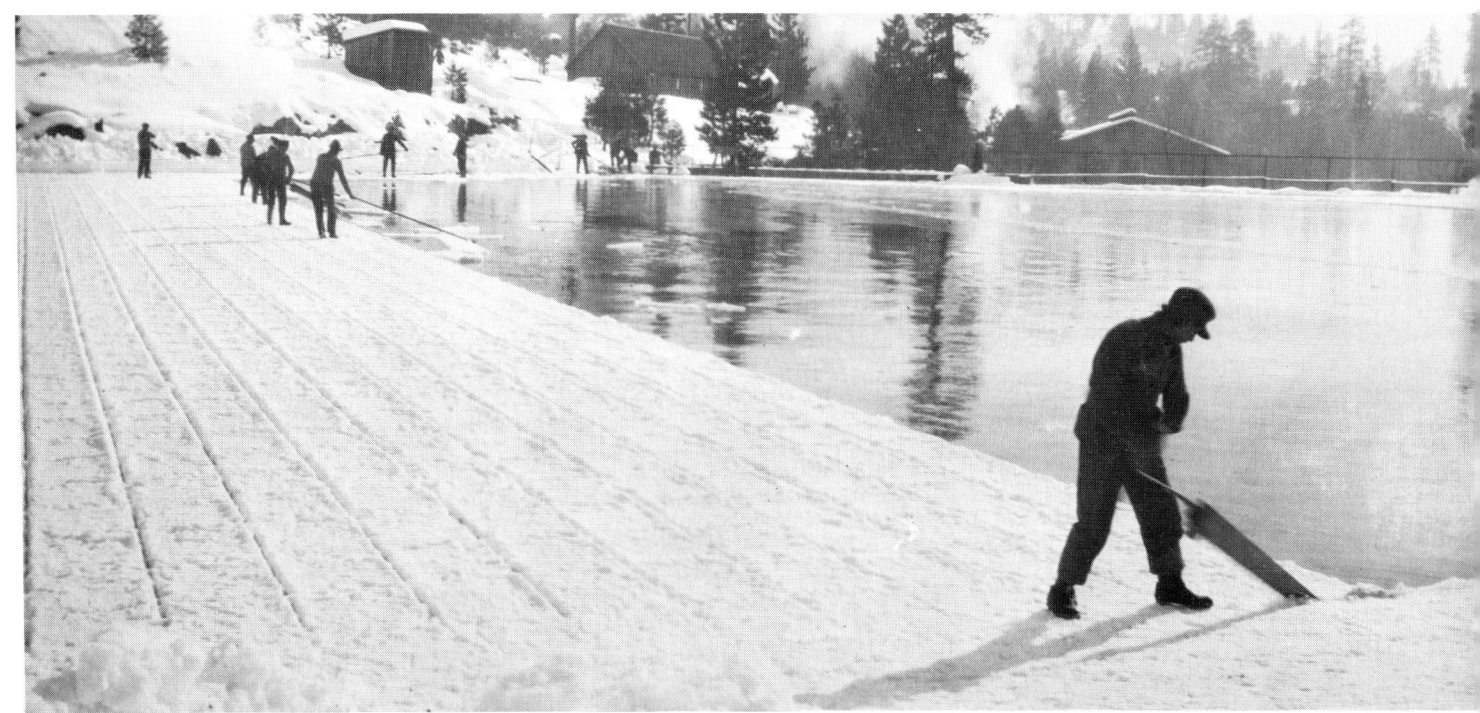

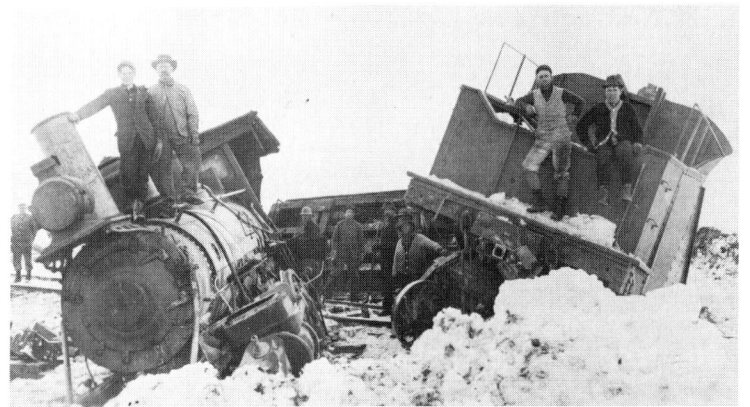

Snow and ice were both the doing and the undoing of the Boca & Loyalton. Harvesting ice at Gulling on Grizzly Creek *(above)* meant revenues for its coffers, but wrecks *(left)* from ice on the rails and the constant winter job of clearing snow from the main with push plow *(below)* or rotary *(below, right)* were a serious drain on the finances. As a result, engines were immobilized and stored at Loyalton *(top, right)* until better weather prevailed. *(Top Left: J. F. Conklin Collection; Center: W. A. Pennington Collection; Bottom: Vinton B. White Collection; Top Right: Al Graves Collection; Bottom: Louis L. Stein, Jr. Collection.)*

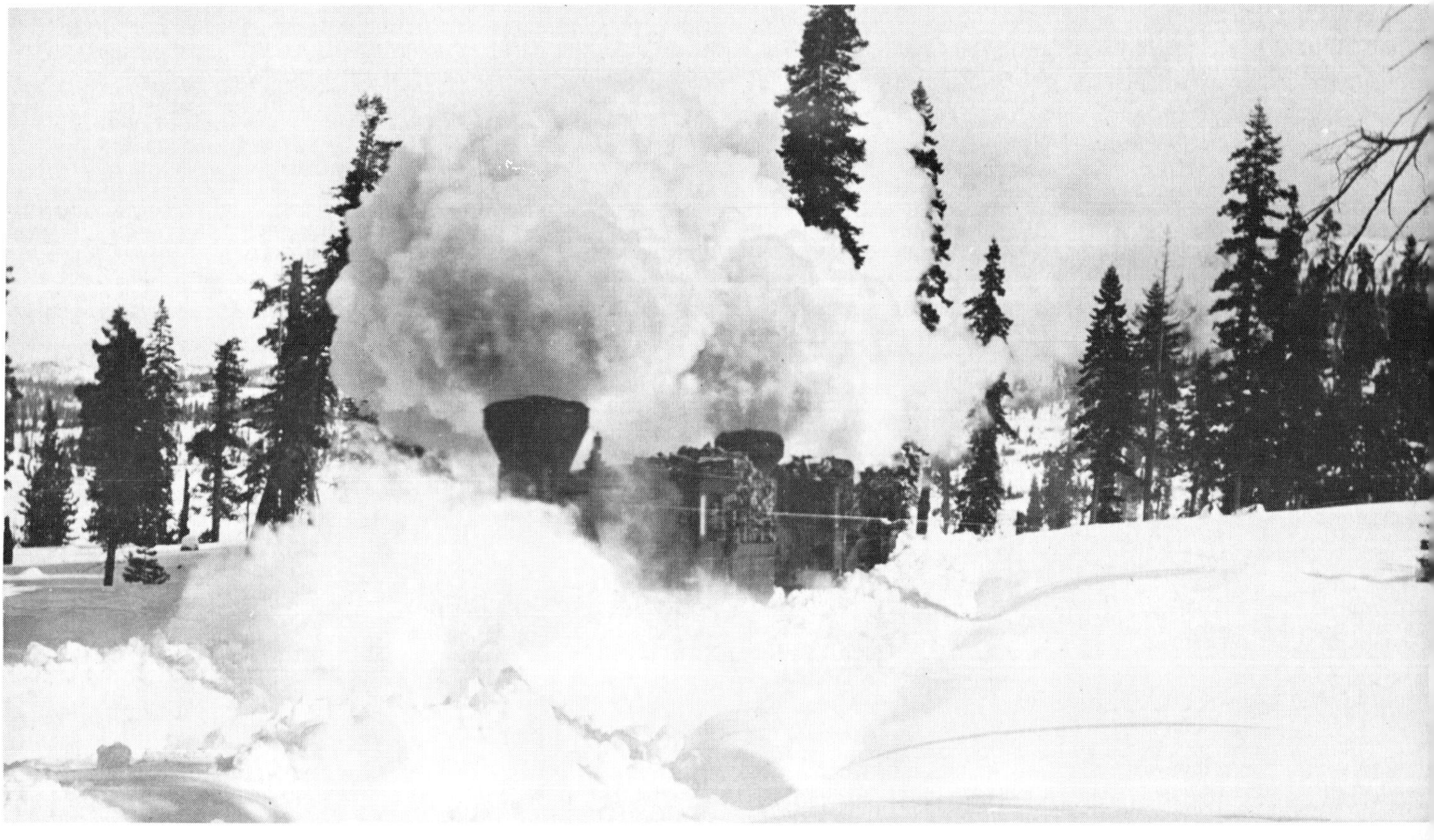

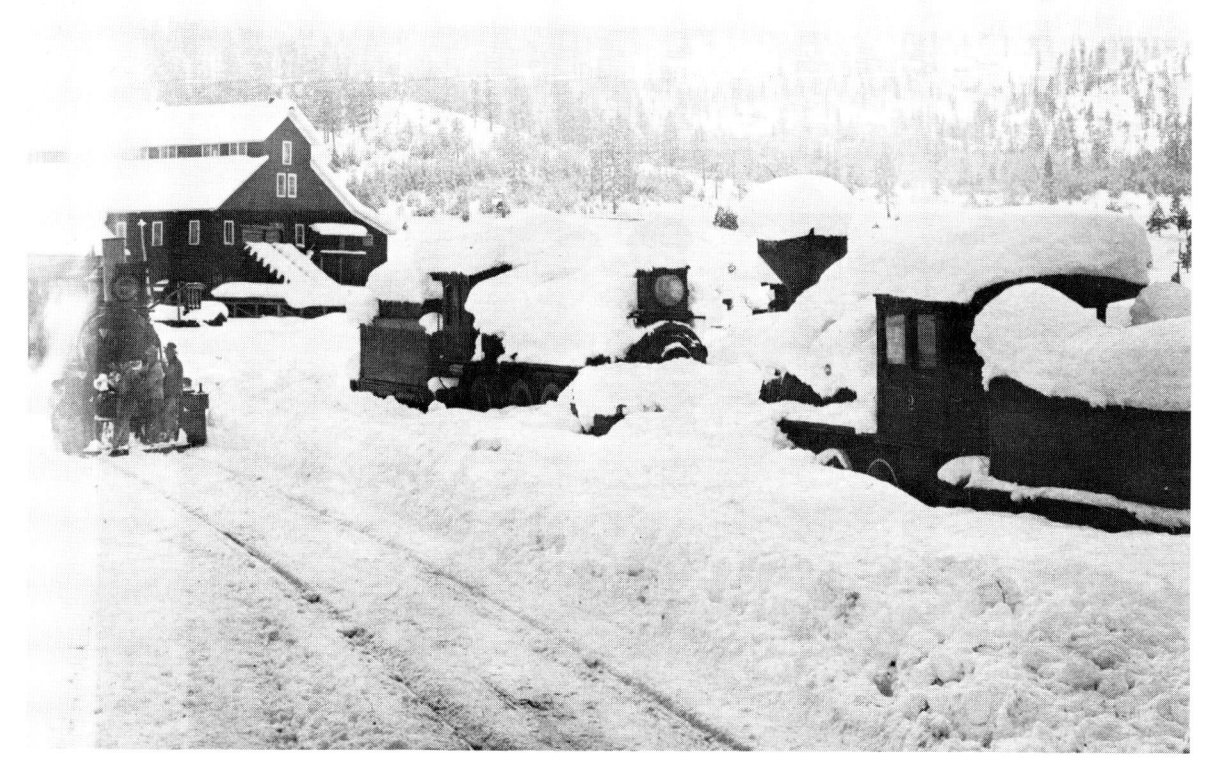

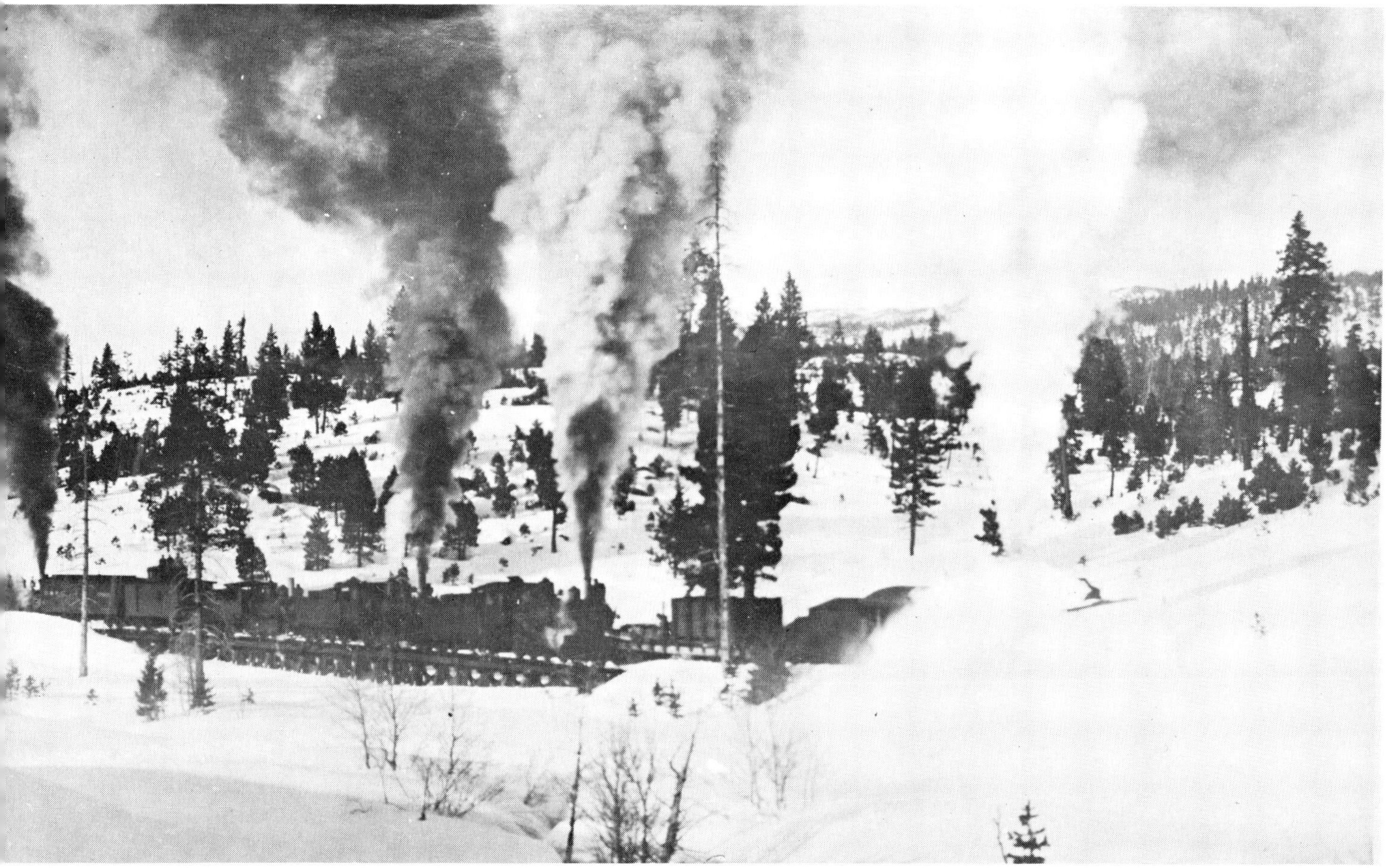

of the plains. The Roberts Lumber Company sprang into being, purchasing two ranches as a site for a mill while Captain Roberts scoured the countryside for available timber lands at $1.25 (script) per acre. Horton Bros. moved their mill from Clover Valley to Loyalton and added a box factory to their operations. Turner Bros. (primarily a planing mill), the Reno Mill & Lumber Co. (Charles Gulling, prop.) and the California White Pine Lumber Co. also moved to Loyalton to enjoy the superior advantages of the Sierra Valley climate. It was here also, that the B&L installed its engine house and shops, using a wye to turn the locomotives.

The rapid expansion of industry in the area automatically indicated the need for extension of the railroad, and work on the line never stopped as the road pushed due north for three miles, then swung northwest over a 10-mile tangent across the marsh lands of Sierra Valley. In October 1901 it reached Beckwith (Beckwourth), and over the next several years various moderate extensions were made. The main line was swung to the west, crossed the Middle Fork of the Feather River, and proceeded down the south bank to Mormon (Portola); a major extension of many miles was contemplated to the Diamond Match Co. plant at Chico, but this was never built, probably due to the projection of the Western Pacific. About 3 miles east of Mormon a branch was constructed northward for 1½ miles along Grizzly Creek to tap a timber area, while another branch left the main just east of Beckwith at a point called Horton Jct. and proceeded northward into the timber area toward Clover Valley.

The line to Clover Valley involved a grade crossing with the N-C-O's narrow gauge Sierra Valleys Railway, and an almost constant battle raged in the courts and sometimes on the ground from 1903 to 1907. The first altercation occurred in June 1903 when the B&L sent 150 men on a Saturday night (and in violation of a court injunction) to cut the SV line and install the crossover. With the physical deed perpetrated and the crossing in place, they then sought legal protection through a counter injunction against the SV to restrain it from tearing up the crossing! Whereupon the California Safe Deposit and Trust Co. stepped into the picture as trustee of the SV Railway bonds and filed suit, in November, 1903, in the Lassen County Superior Court claiming that the B&L crossing, forcibly built, invaded their rights and asked that it be removed. Judge Kelly agreed with the plaintiff and ordered the removal. The case created some interesting speculation as the leading attorney for the Trust Company was W. J. Barnett, also president of the newly formed Western Pacific Railway which, some held, had plans to acquire the narrow gauge line.

The crossing was removed by the SV under the watchful eye of the B&L, but eventually it was reinstalled. Then, three years later in 1906 (when the B&L and the WP were both under D&RG [Gould] control), the SV once again yanked the crossing out on the reported contention that they wanted $10,000 for the crossing privilege. Loyalton furnished an armed force of 200 men (probably a goodly number were mill workers laid off due to the difficulty), and the crossing was replaced. The ensuing legal battle raged from court to court, but ultimately the crossing was allowed to remain.

Fire, snow and floods plagued the B&L's short line. In April 1904 Boca had its worst fire since 1885; the SP's fire train from Truckee was called to help out; the hotel burned; and the B&L depot caught fire several times, the blaze being extinguished in each instance. Three years later, another fire destroyed the B&L roundhouse, a locomotive, and several freight and passenger cars. In January 1906 a blizzard dropped 12 feet of snow on Boca and four feet at Lewis Mill; the subsequent thaw and freezing deposited nine miles of ice on the rails which had to be chopped away before the road could be operated. Floods at Merrill and in the canyons frequently disrupted operations. A general storm in April 1907 badly washed out the line. On another occasion the bridge at Grizzly Creek was washed away and subsequently was found in the middle of the stream; in other places high water floated the ties and rails right off the roadbed, leaving them hanging in the trees when the waters subsided.

There were human crises, too. On one occasion a lovers' quarrel resulted in the girl's suicide on the train as it approached Beckwith. Again, in November 1902, the cook for the B&L's survey party, a burly Negro, suffered a swelling in his throat, closing off his air passage. The crew boss telephoned the 20 miles to Loyalton to obtain a special train, but the only locomotive available was stone cold and waiting to be scrapped. Nevertheless, in the emergency, willing hands built up steam and the locomotive rushed to the camp to bring the man back to Loyalton. Within three minutes of his arrival he was placed on the operating table, but un-

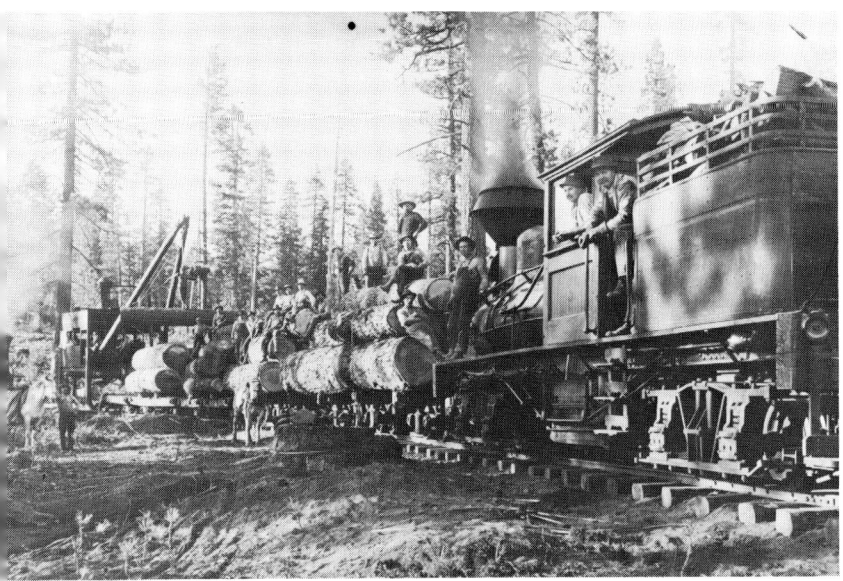

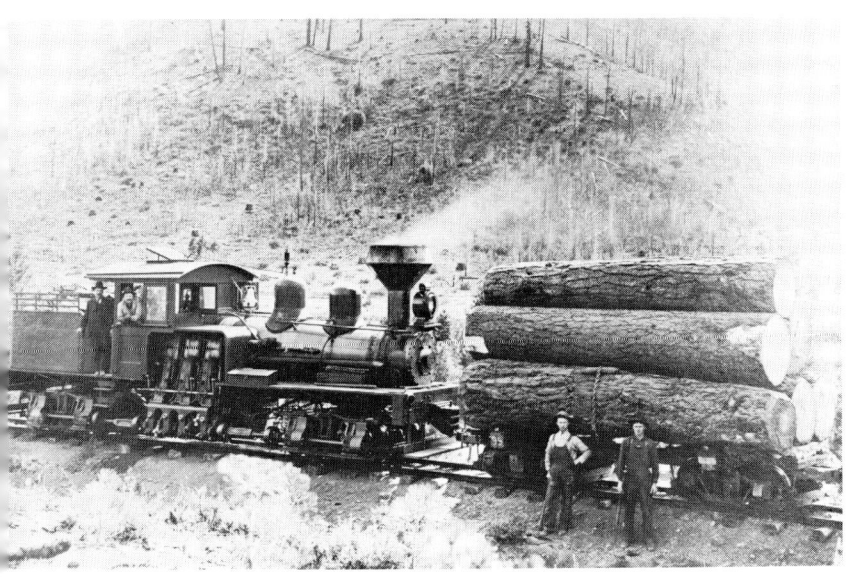

Feeder lines connected with the Boca & Loyalton near Horton Jct., just east of Beckwourth. The pioneer was the Marsh Lumber Co. *(top and center)*, to be followed later by the extensive Clover Valley Lumber Co., whose 2-6-6-2T compound articulated No. 4 *(below)* eventually went to a lumber mill just west of Reno for stationary boiler service, following the demise of the CVL. *(Top and Center: Al Graves Collection; Bottom: Guy Dunscomb Photo.)*

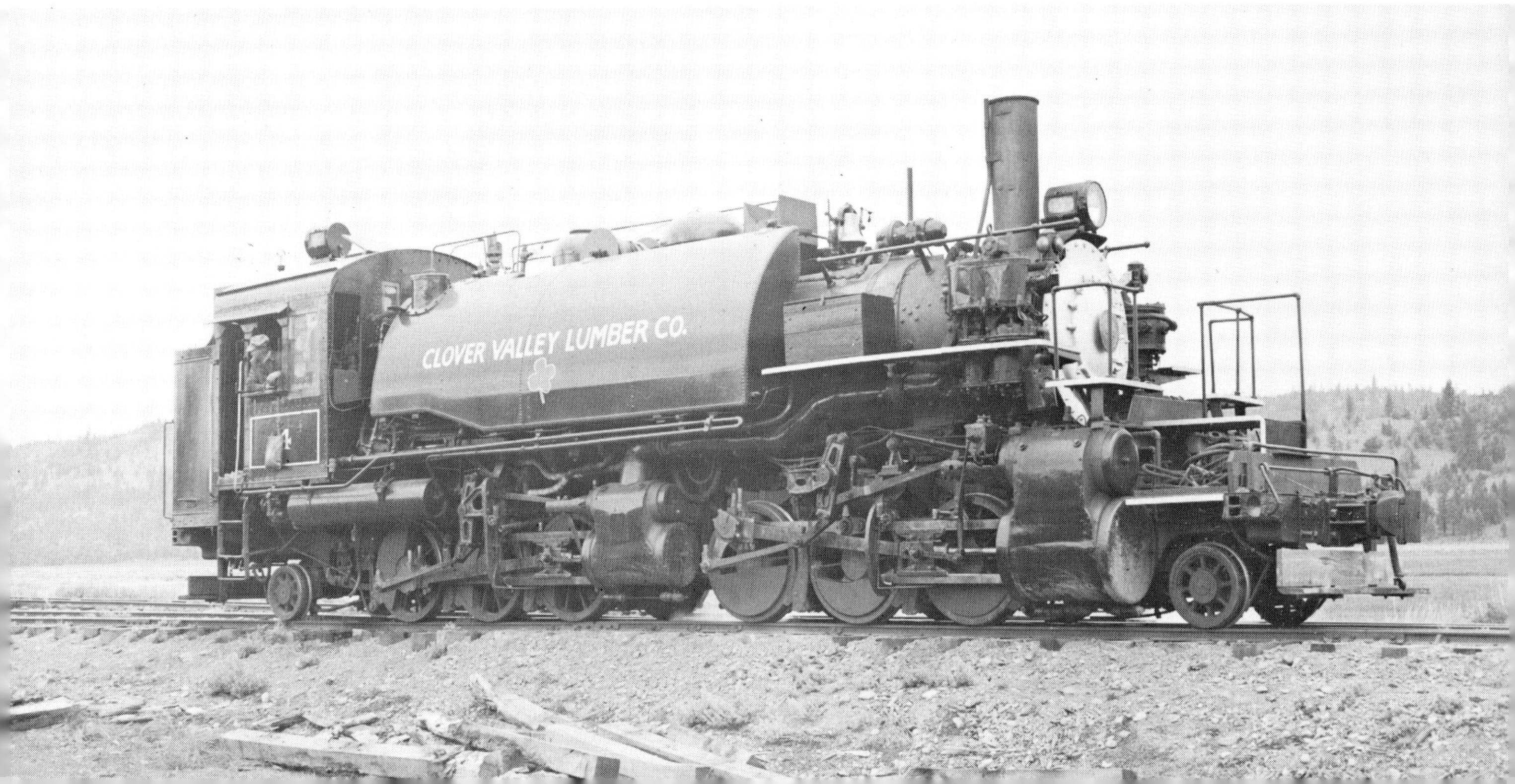

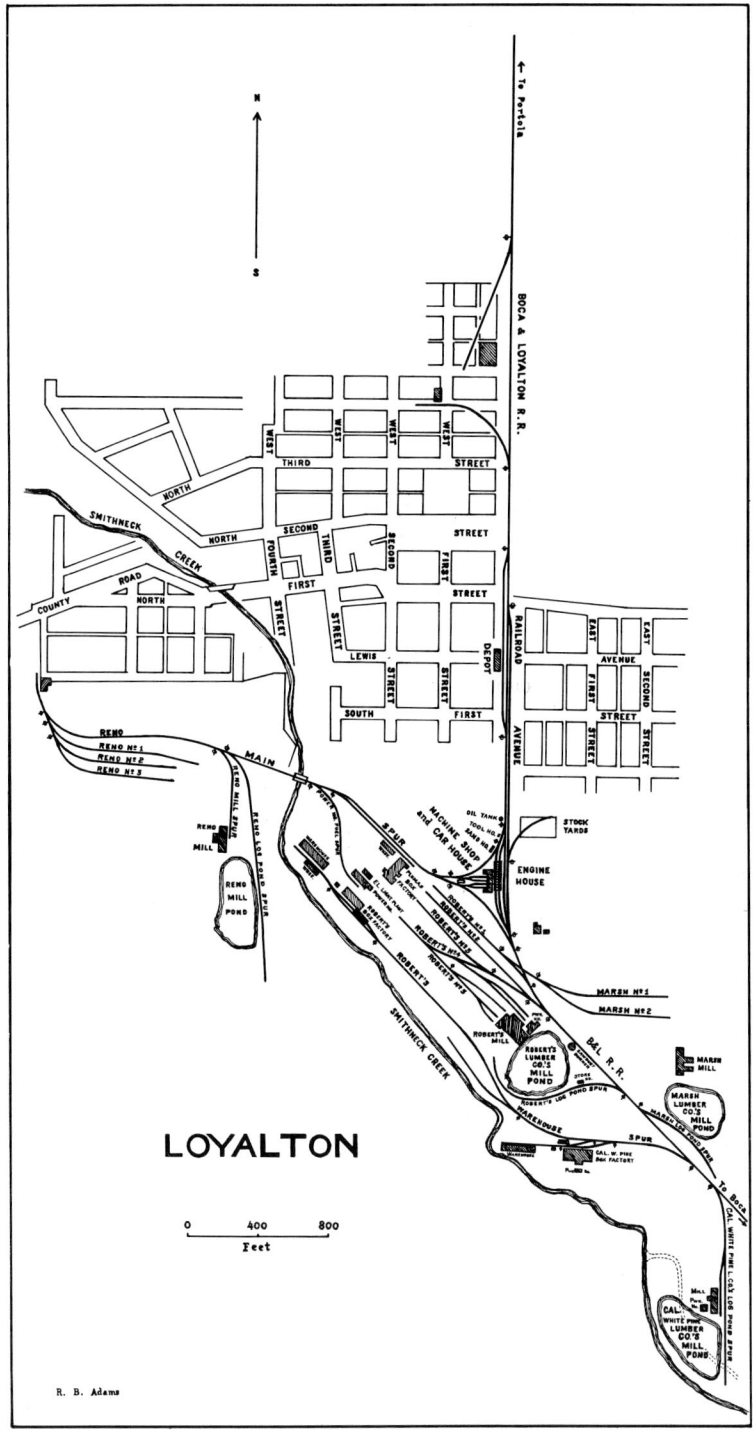

opened the throttle of the switch engine and raced northward over the straight track of the Sierra Valley, "starting a race with death," as lumberman Charles Gulling later described it. For a while the errant car gained on the low-wheeled locomotive, but finally the engine pulled away and the car slowed sufficiently to be caught and brought in. On the other occasion four loaded logging cars and one empty got away at Marsh on the line to Clover Valley. Charging down on the B&L crossing of the SV at an estimated 60 m.p.h., a number of stationary cars at Horton Junction were instantly reduced to kindling wood.

By 1907 four sawmills and three box factories were keeping the economy of Loyalton in a high state of preservation, all fed through the lifeline of the Boca & Loyalton Railroad. Many spurs served the mills, while others ran into the timber where lumber camps supplied the raw material to fill the pipelines of industry. Between Boca and Loyalton, alone, there were 15 such tentacles reaching into the trees. The embryo Western Pacific's parent, the D&RG, had had its eye on the area, and had acquired a 51% controlling interest in the B&L as far back as September 6, 1905, to keep rival interests out of the territory. However, by 1907-08, the timber lands south of Loyalton had largely been cut over and the road was in need of a new source of business.

This it found, temporarily at least, in the big movement of construction materials and supplies for the Western Pacific, which concentrated its efforts in the Feather River district in 1908 and 1909. Seven locomotives appeared on the roster, and 133 employees were listed on the payroll, as train after train blasted its way up from Boca to construction sites along the Feather River. But the "good neighbor" policy was to backfire when the Western Pacific gobbled up that portion of the western extremity of the line from Mormon (Portola) 2.6 miles to a point west of Beckwith to be known as B&L Jct. The grade was straightened and curves were eased, and by considerate agreement the B&L was granted the right to use the realigned trackage to Portola in perpetuity.

It is interesting, though ineffectual, to note that 1908 was the year the Verdi Lumber Company extended its railroad west over Dog Valley Second Summit to Merrill where connection was made with the B&L. Ultimately the line was extended many miles beyond as timber operations reached farther and farther into the hills. Had the B&L

fortunately died before two waiting doctors could help him.

No mountain lumber railroad could operate without its share of accidents, and the B&L was no exception. Two runaways occurred in 1907. A carload of lumber from Smithneck Canyon careened wildly into Loyalton one day threatening the engineer of a switch engine working on the main track. Realizing there was not enough time to get down and throw a switch to a side track, the engineer followed the path of its steam traction engines and constructed to Verdi in accordance with the early traffic, its story might have been different. But that would be second guessing.

The big movement of construction materials for the Western Pacific ceased in 1909, and late in that year the nation's newest transcontinental route was opened for traffic, becoming a competitor of the B&L for what little business remained in the area. The facts are well substantiated by the figures. Gross revenues for 1908 amounted to $215,000 with a reported net loss of $8,680; in 1909 and 1910, although the gross revenues declined, the road showed profits of $19,667 and $9,743, respectively, probably the only two profitable years in the line's history. By 1912 revenues had dropped to $101,000, and in 1916, the last year of operation, revenues were only $28,000. Net losses during this period ranged from $41,000 to $52,000 annually.

The Grizzly Spur, three miles west of Beckwith (which later became part of the WP Gulling branch), was an important feeder to the B&L. In addition to tapping a timber area, it also served a natural ice plant, the Grizzly Creek Ice Company, established by Charles Gulling in 1912. The ice plant subsequently was acquired by the Clover Valley Lumber Company which used it to supply ice for refrigerator cars on the WP and, prior to the abandonment of the B&L, the Southern Pacific. A wagon road also furnished connections with the Walker copper mine.

From 1910 to 1915 the B&L defaulted on the sinking fund requirements of its bonds, and on June 9, 1915, Charles L. Hovey was appointed receiver for the road. One of his earliest acts was to request permission from the California Railroad Commission to suspend operations from January 1 to May 1, 1916, in order to save the expense of wintertime operations. After the hearings, limited service was authorized from Loyalton to Beckwith, while no service was provided south of Loyalton toward Boca — apparently nobody cared.

The service was short-lived. On September 8, 1916, the railroad was sold at foreclosure. Topping a junk dealer's bid by $100, Alexander R. Baldwin, attorney for the Western Pacific, purchased the line for $35,100. Following another hearing, complete abandonment of the Boca-Loyalton segment was approved, as was the sale of the remainder to the WP. Title was transferred on December 1, 1916, and the B&L ceased to exist.

Under Western Pacific control, the segment of the B&L's old main line from Horton Jct. to B&L Jct. was abandoned in 1920. The only portions of the old line that remain in operation today are the 11.86 miles from Loyalton north to Hawley (which, until railroad operations were discontinued in 1957, were also used by the Clover Valley Lumber Company), and the former Grizzly Creek line which became a part of the WP's Gulling branch until abandonment in 1940. Smithneck Canyon and Sardine Valley today lie silent in the wilderness, mute testimony to the evanescence of man's efforts.

It's a sunny summer day in 1908; automobiles are virtually unknown; and the squat drivers of Boca & Loyalton No. 5 whirling effortlessly and endlessly along the winding twin ribbons of rails clinging to the hillside furnish the fastest and most pleasant travel into the high country surrounding the summit of Smithneck Canyon. Hope that trestle holds solid 'til we're past! *(Stanley Palmer Photo.)*

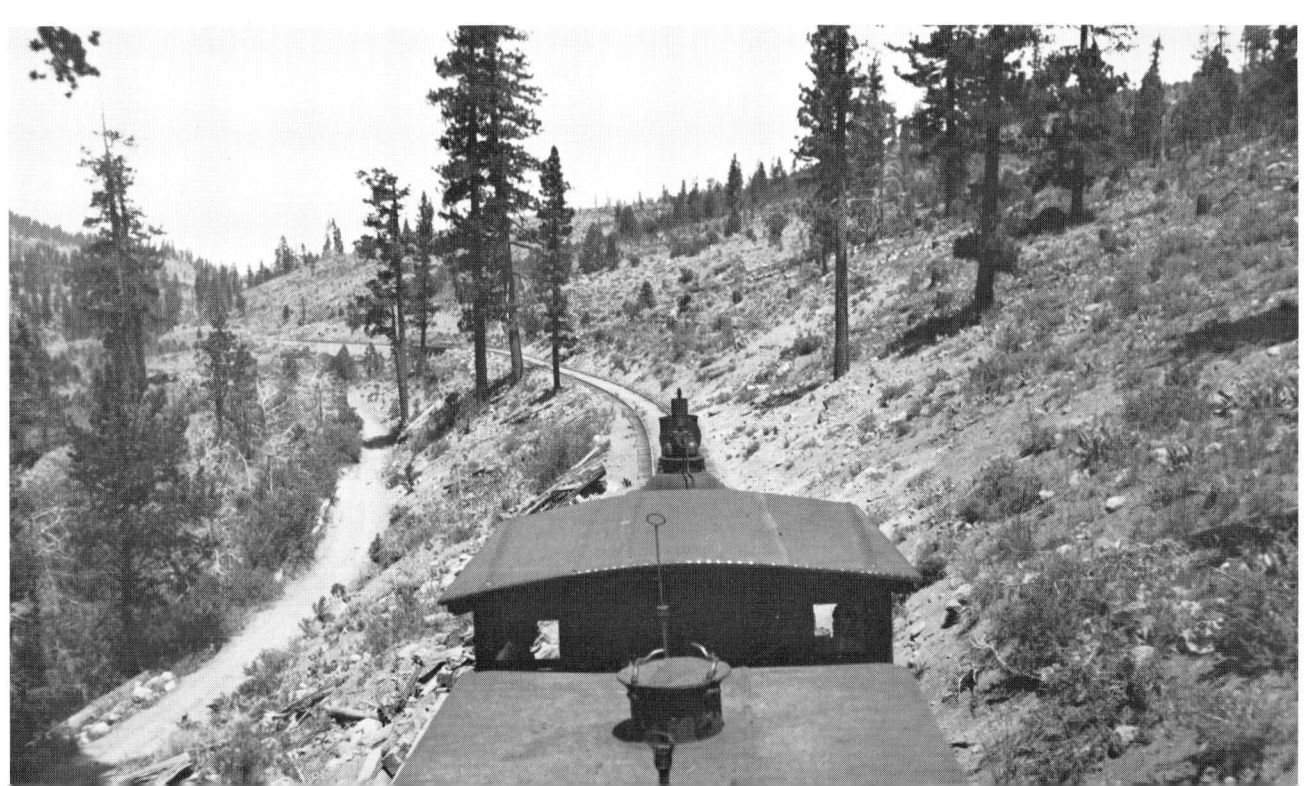

VERDI LUMBER COMPANY

Verdi, at the western edge of Nevada, is located on the Truckee River approximately 10 miles west of Reno. Like most of the Truckee River towns, it came into being as an active lumbering center for the primary purpose of supplying ties to the Central Pacific Railroad when that line built across the state in 1867-69. Cross ties continued to be a major product of the area as the Southern Pacific Railroad reached across Arizona in the early 1880's. When the nearby timber was cut, the loggers worked back into the hills to the west of Verdi and entered the Dog Valley country of eastern California, creating a problem in logistics to supply the timberman as well as a problem in transportation to bring the fallen timbers to the mills.

A five-mile flume was the first effort to solve the problem. It was partially completed by the time Katz and Henry purchased the Crystal Peak Lumber Co. in March of 1879, together with its sawmill located to the northwest in Dog Valley. Four years later the property changed hands again, to become part of the Truckee Lumber Company, one of the largest producers in the area. But the signal honor was not to last.

Although there were other sawmills in the vicinity of Verdi, as well as ice ponds and even (subsequently) a branch of the Inyo Marble Company, it was Oliver Lonkey's auspicious Verdi Mill Co. that was to lend impetus to the region. Lonkey had operated a planing mill and box factory in Truckee, before moving to Verdi in 1888. This mill was incorporated into the Verdi Lumber Co. in 1900 which Lonkey formed in conjunction with J. F. Condon and J. H. Roberts (of Boca & Loyalton fame). When the new company acquired a large stand of timber in Dog Valley from the Truckee Lumber Company, the news traveled swiftly. Members of the Reno Improvement Club were particularly pleased to learn at a meeting that the lumber company planned a 12-mile standard gauge railroad from Verdi into the timber, an event of general community welfare and consequence.

The decision for the railroad once made, grading commenced immediately as two crews started work late in 1900. M. J. Curtis, the Reno architect, was retained to direct the construction of the railroad's bridge across the Truckee River. Seven cars of rails arrived in Reno in February 1901, but their advent proved somewhat premature as a scarcity of workmen in Verdi delayed progress more than anticipated. However, by August of that year, five miles of railroad had been completed up the steep acclivity of Dog Valley Creek, two switchbacks being used to overcome the abrupt change in elevation.

In May 1902 a visitor to the area reported that Verdi was a "lumberman's paradise." Some 45 men were at work in the box factory; 40 more were employed at the band mill; while an additional 50 were working in the woods and on the railroad, now seven miles long. A crowd of 300 people from Reno responded to the offer of a Sunday excursion in June, including a day in the woods, a baseball game between the Floriston nine and the Reno Wheelmen (in which Floriston defeated the Wheelmen by a score of 17 to 16), plus a ride over the new and spectacular "Verdi Scenic Railway." The latter was so successful one passenger was overheard to remark: "A ride over this road is a pleasure long to be remembered," and numerous requests were received for repeat performances.

As a town and lumbering center, Verdi was to remain active for another quarter century despite its record of many fires. In August 1902 the box factory burned and was rebuilt four months later. The following April 1903 a whole city block burned, and another serious fire occurred in July. Although the box mill was ultimately sold to the California Pine Box and Lumber Company, it continued to be operated under the former management.

The Verdi Lumber Company railroad transported logs to the Verdi sawmill over the years, pushing its tentacles into the woods whenever and wherever needed. In 1904 it was extended northward, then eastward to Port Arthur, 11 miles north of Verdi. In 1905 an even longer branch pushed northward to Long Valley Canyon near Purdy, 13 miles from Verdi. The lower portion of this line constituted a relocation of the old main and incorporated a switchback near Lazy Station to alleviate the steep grade of the original roadbed. At the upper end between Lakeview and Long Valley a continuous series of five switchbacks were necessary to surmount the abrupt change of elevation. Because of the steep grades and sharp curves, Shay geared locomotives operated into the woods, making two round trips daily.

The year 1905 also brought about another significant change. Dog Valley timber was becoming exhausted, and new sources of supply were needed. Verdi Lumber set its sights westward, and surveys were made for a 12-mile extension of the railroad from a point near Lazy Station in Dog Valley, over Dog Valley Second Summit and on to Merrill in Sardine Valley where connection would be made with the Boca & Loyalton Railroad. Apparently the project was stillborn, for no construction was attempted during the next three years.

In 1908 A. L. Revert, using profits from his prosperous Tonopah Lumber Company (a retail outlet serving the entire Tonopah-Goldfield area), purchased the Verdi Lumber Company and operated it until its final dissolution. One of his first acts was to commence construction of the extension of the railroad, and over the succeeding years the rails were pushed up the switchback to Dog Valley Second Summit and on to Merrill where the B&L was crossed without stopping and trackage continued along Davies Creek into the mountains. In contradiction to the experience on the Port Arthur branch, a 1912 relocation of the main line on the east slope of Dog Valley Second Summit eliminated the switchback on that section of the line, but the device was not to be discarded. In 1917, after the north side of Davies Creek had been logged, the railroad built a spur with a series of switchbacks using grades up to 13% to climb into the hills above Bear Valley. Cutting proceeded there for the next year, following which the railroad branched out again, this time westward from Davies Creek to the hills on the south side of Lemon Canyon. Logging continued at this point for another five years, to be followed by a switch to the north side of the same canyon for several years more.

Misfortune came often to the Verdi Lumber Company's railroad. Big storms in March 1907 washed out the truss bridge over the Truckee River, completely halting operations to the mill. The next year Verdi suffered another fire; and that summer a flash flood damaged the railroad's roadbed, washed away some cars, and drowned the superintendent's daughter at Camp Pixley in Long Valley in spite of

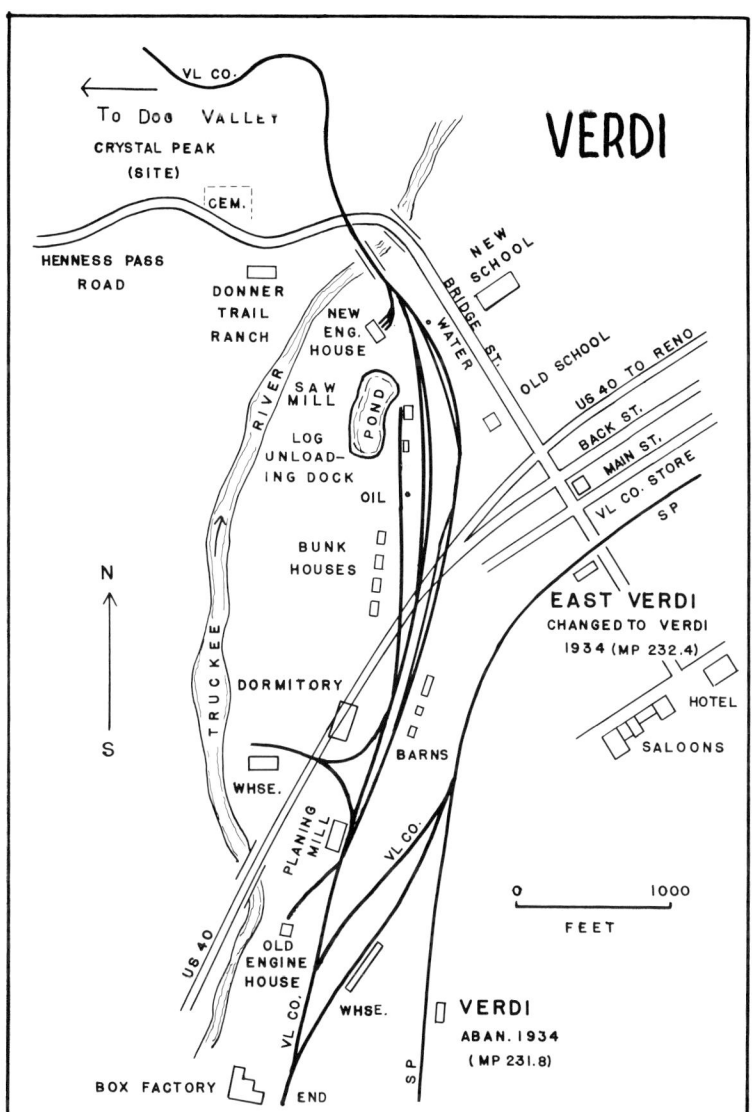

the heroic efforts of two men to save her. 1916 was the year of the big fire in Verdi; a strong wind blew sparks from the mill over the town, and in about an hour some 42 homes were burned, only the mill surviving. The following year the roundhouse burned, but it was rebuilt at a new location.

In common with many a lumber line, the Verdi Lumber Company's railroad is remembered as one which skimped on spending money for roadbed maintenance, thereby making a trip over the line an adventure in rough riding. With heavy grades (including five sets of switchbacks), there were the anticipated number of wrecks as well. Moving a logging camp was always an experience, and the occasions were frequent. Cabins were hoisted aboard flat cars for their perilous ride to the next site. Once, when an old, drunken logger refused to vacate his premises, the boss had the cabin placed aboard the flat car anyhow. Coupled into the train, the cabin made rough riding over the poor track,

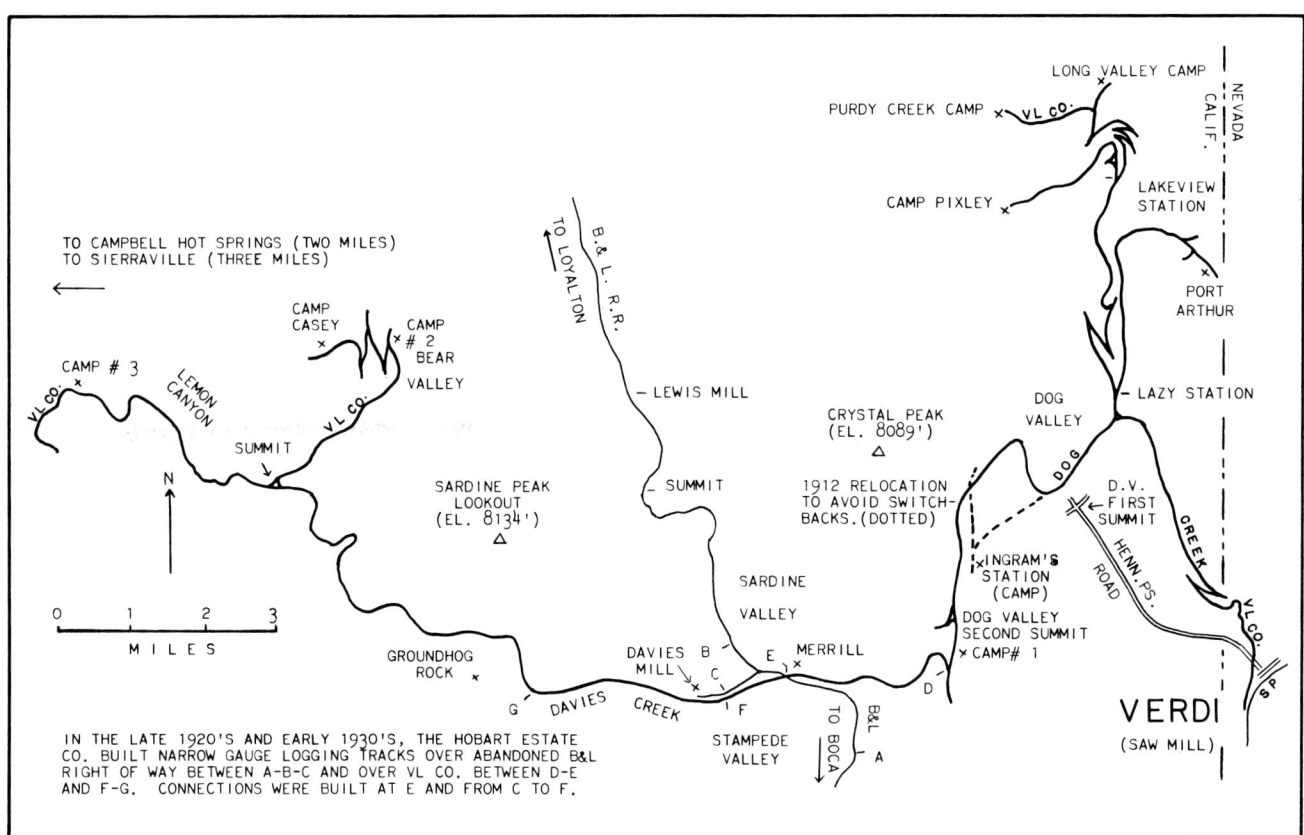

IN THE LATE 1920'S AND EARLY 1930'S, THE HOBART ESTATE CO. BUILT NARROW GAUGE LOGGING TRACKS OVER ABANDONED B&L RIGHT OF WAY BETWEEN A-B-C AND OVER VL CO. BETWEEN D-E AND F-G. CONNECTIONS WERE BUILT AT E AND FROM C TO F.

so our man consumed an additional quantity of alcohol to ease the jolting. Finally all of the cabins left the train on a particularly bad curve, the occupied cabin rolling to the bottom of a small hill. Still drunk but unhurt, the logger crawled out of his smashed quarters to hurl most uncomplimentary remarks about the engineer's handling of the train over that rough stretch of track.

Two Shays and one rod locomotive kept operations moving over the 28-mile line in 1916. By 1924 additional branches and extensions brought the trackage to 32 miles, while a big forest fire that year threatened Verdi and scattered hot embers over Reno. The threat became a fact two years later when, in May 1926, the sawmill, storage yard and round house were burned. (It might be noted that the company was not affected by the July 1926 conflagrations which imperiled Floriston and Carson City, for the Verdi Lumber Company's timber had already been reduced because of decades of cutting.) A smaller sawmill was erected on the site of the former mill, but the roundhouse was never rebuilt. Financial difficulties stemming from the sawmill fire plus the exhaustion of its timber resources at Bear Valley and Lemon Canyon (the most westerly operation), brought the activities of the company to an end. Scrapping of the railroad began shortly after the mill was closed. By May 1927 virtually all of the rails had been removed, then dismantling of the sawmill began.

A large portion of the Verdi Lumber Company's railroad is still visible as an abandoned roadbed today. The more adventurous may drive over long segments of the route as it winds its climbing, tortuous way among the verdant hills. Although second forest growth is beginning to hide the scars of a former generation, it will be many years before the vestigial traces of the Verdi Scenic Railway disappear from the landscape.

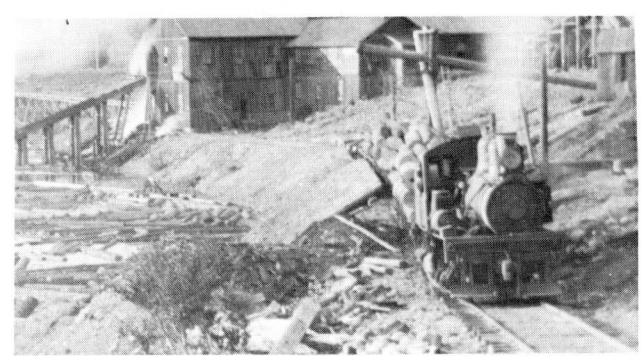

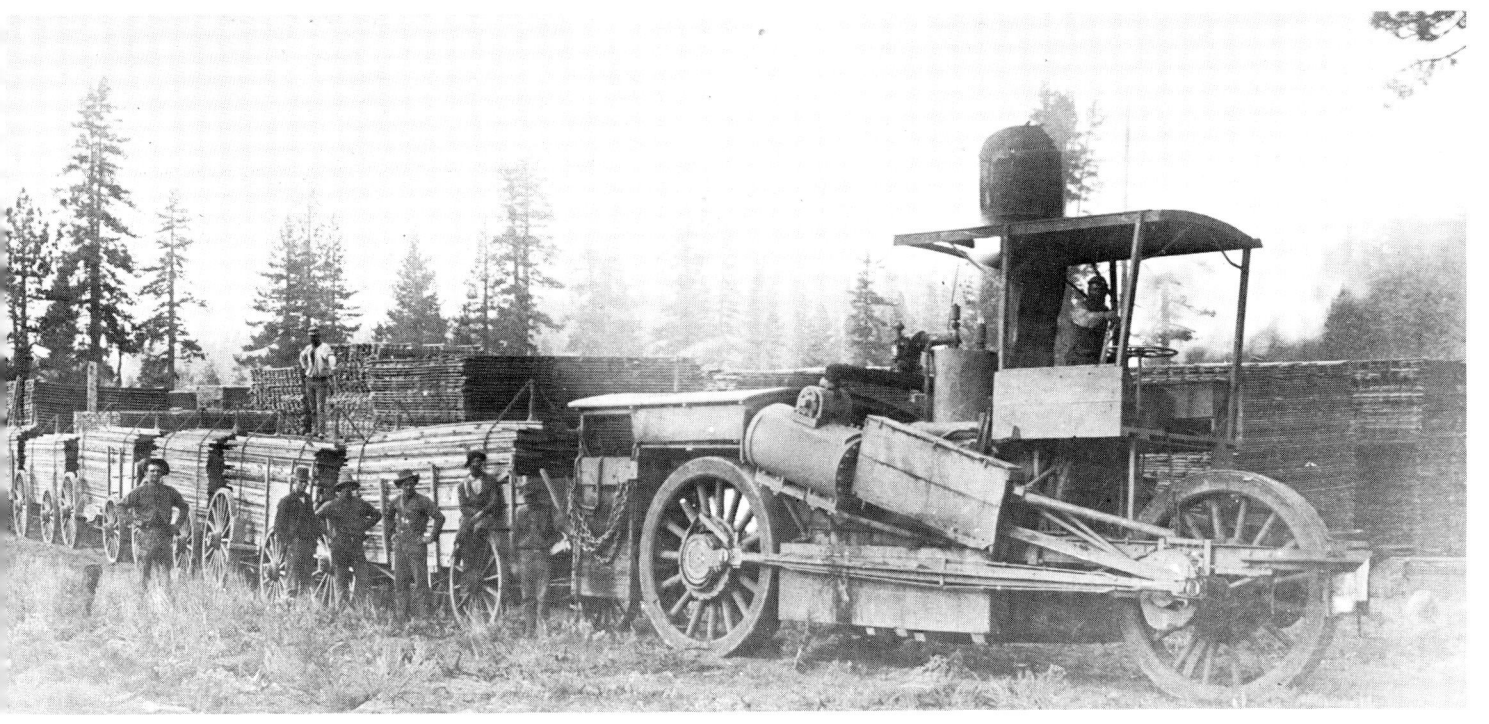

Before rails reached into the woods, Verdi, Nevada, was the major terminus and shipping point for such "trains" of lumber as this one *(above)* shown leaving the Roberts & Lewis pioneer mill in Smithneck Canyon about 1895 behind a Doan Steam Wagon. *(Henry Hunken Photo.)*

Seven years later the Verdi Lumber Co. had extended tracks into Dog Valley and was hauling lumber behind trim, woodburning Mogul (2-6-0) locomotives such as No. 1 *(below)* paused with its crew at Lazy Station on September 1, 1904, while waiting for a connecting train from the Port Arthur branch. Left to right: Orrin Barton, brakeman; "Tubby" Grignon, fireman and Ed Lonkey, engineer. *(Henry Hunken Photo.)*

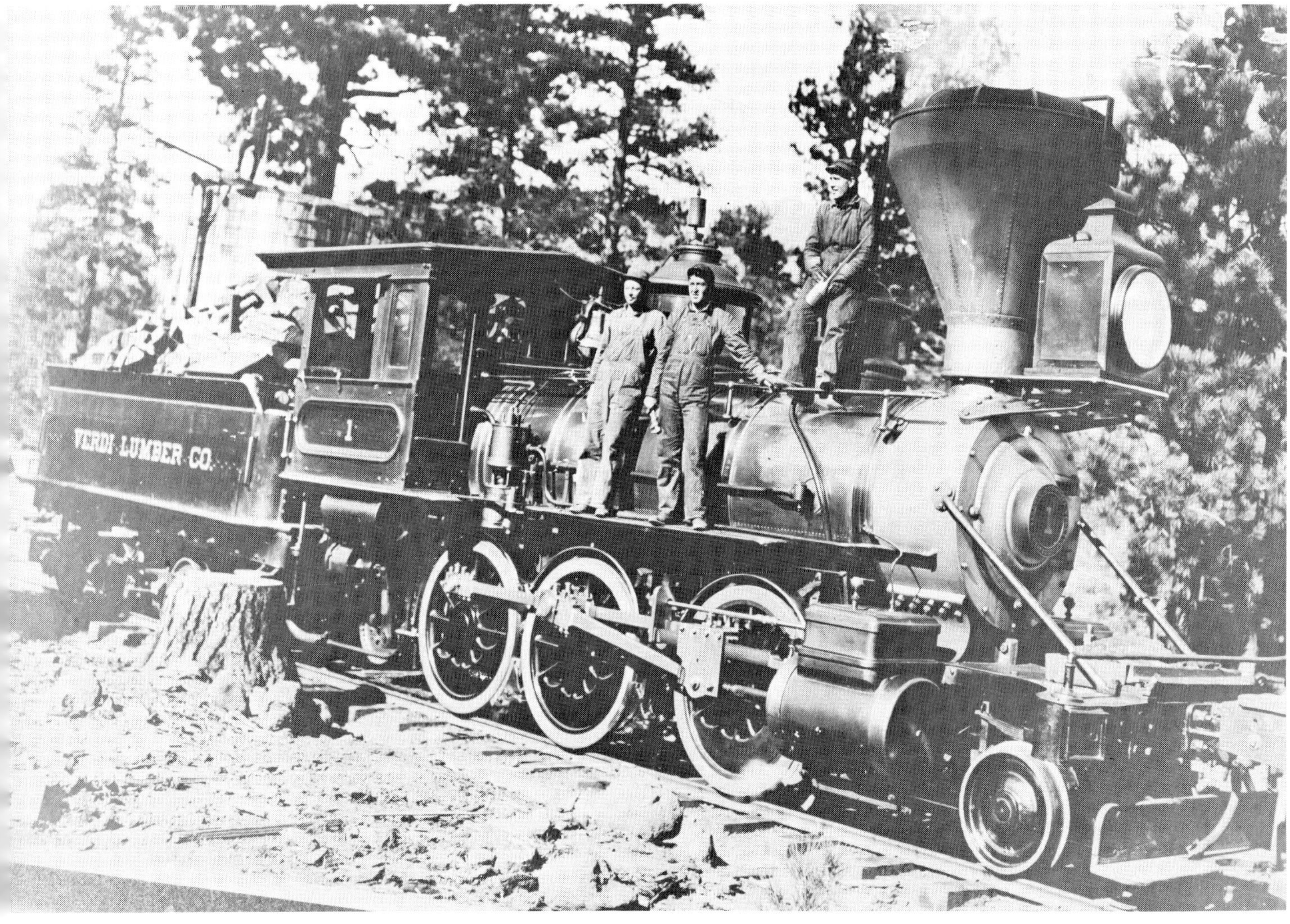

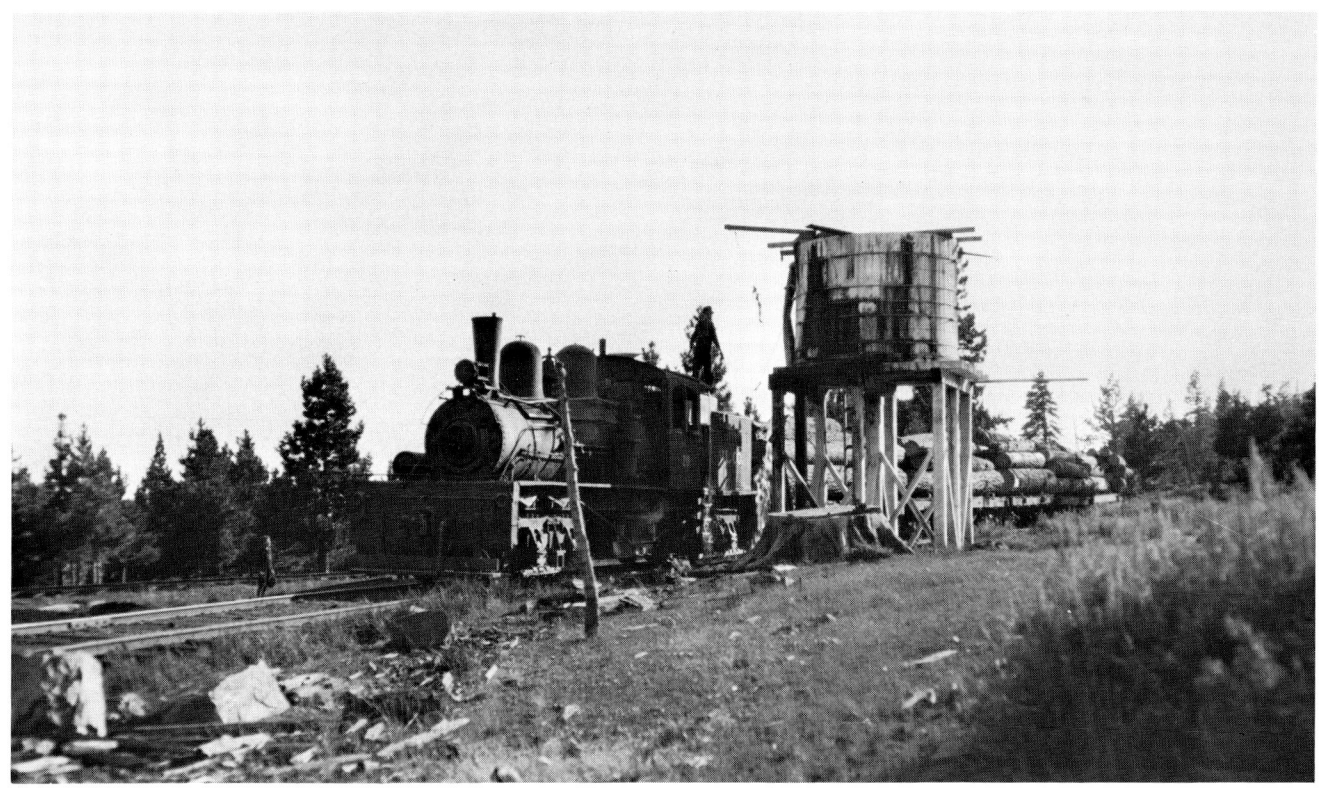

Shay locomotives were required for the steep grades, sharp curves and heavy loads of the Verdi Lumber Co. Railroad's outer reaches. Shay No. 20 (above) has just finished taking water at Dog Valley Second Summit, while the little boy at left with hat in hand is gazing bewilderedly at the complex of cylinders, cranks and rods comprising the mechanism invariably affixed to the right hand side. (Stanley Palmer Photo.)

The light rails and undulating track of the Bear Valley branch in 1921 (below) could still sustain the heaviest loads at a Shay's slow speed. Verdi Lumber's side-door caboose No. 1, on train at right, is today in the service of the Quincy Railroad in Plumas County, California. (Henry Hunken Photo.)

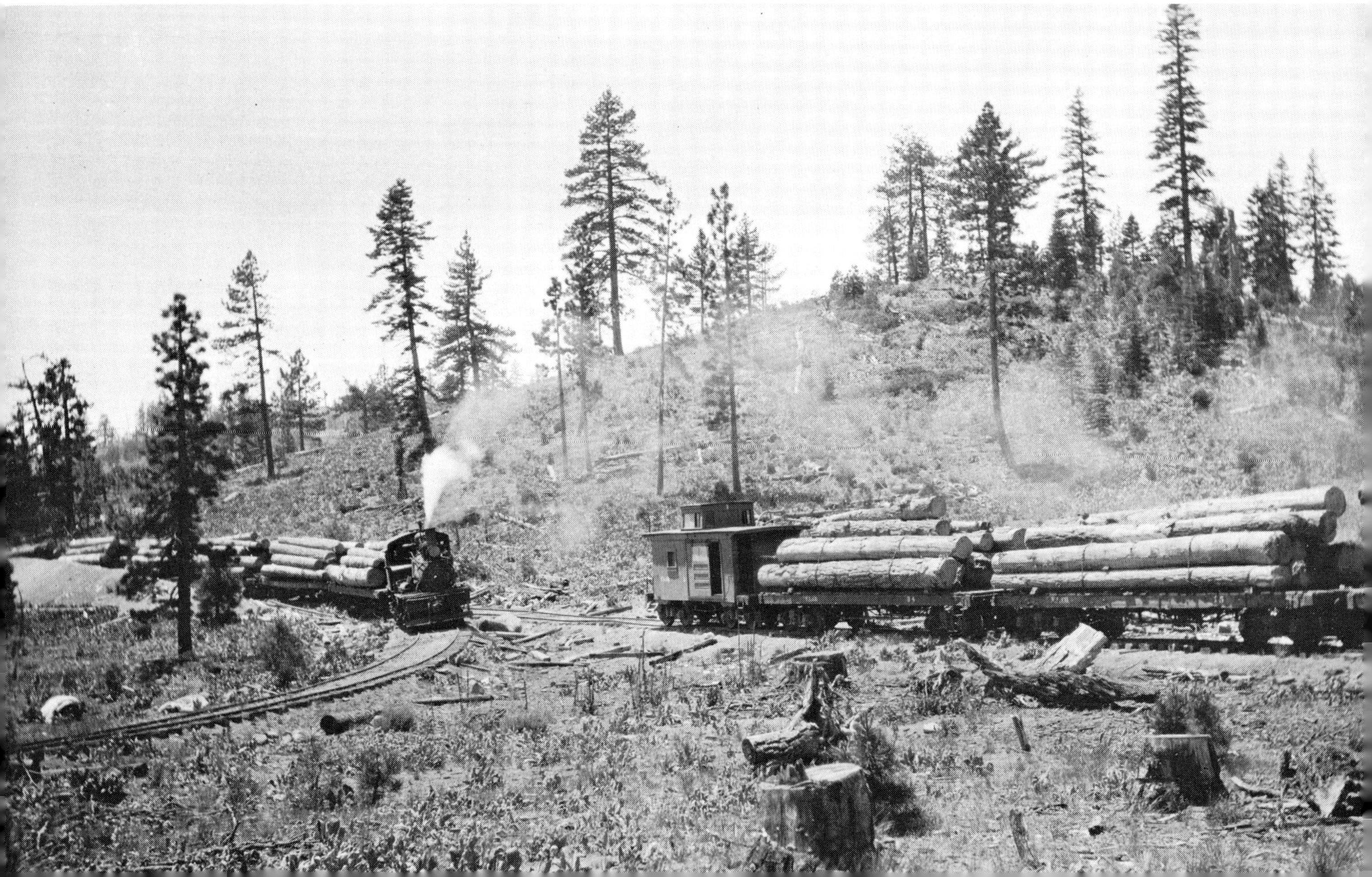

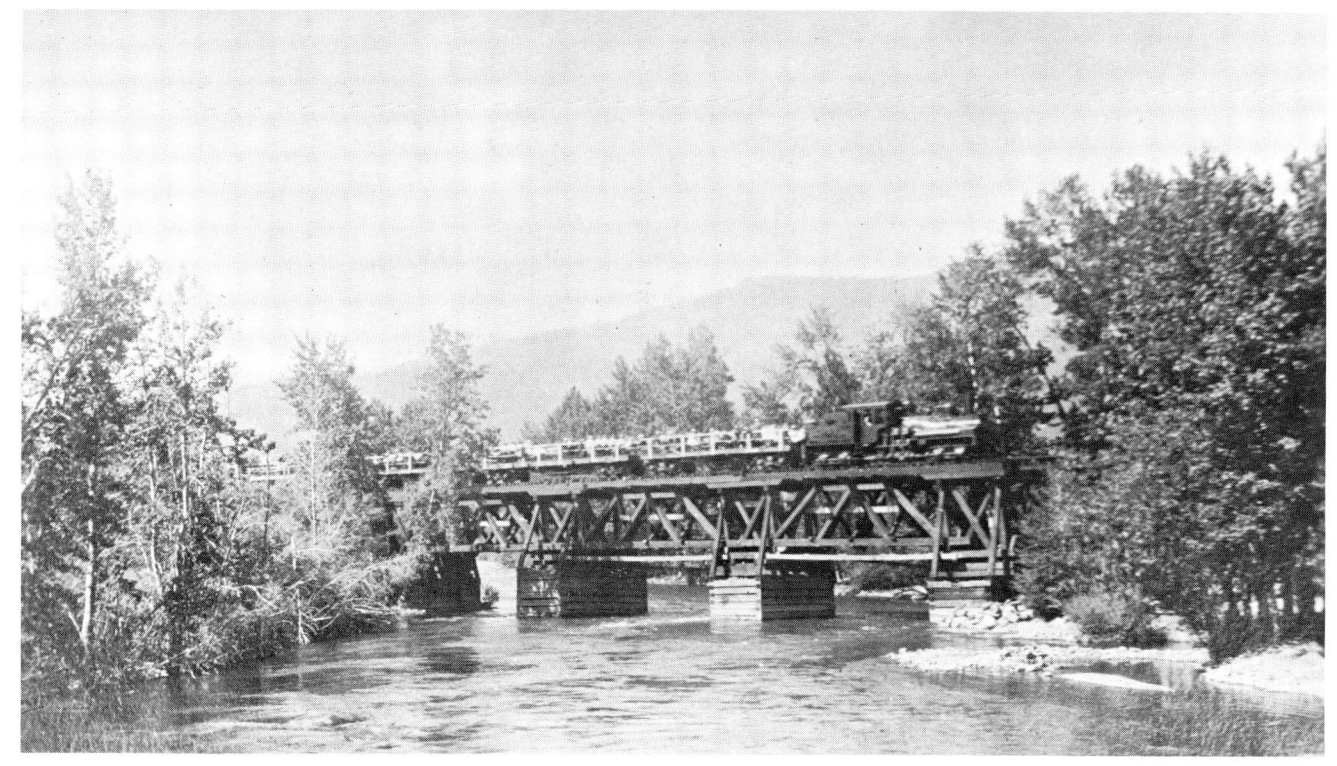

On July 4, 1916, this crowd of happy excursionists *(above)* was riding a "picnic train" in true railfan style — on open benches affixed to flat cars. Shay No. 2 is leading the way home across the bridge over the Truckee River. *(Henry Hunken Photo.)*

The devastation wrought by Verdi Lumber's disastrous roundhouse fire of May 1926 is being examined by the small group of men *(below)* standing near the remains of Shay No. 3 at left. (The enginehouse exhaust stack has settled on the locomotive.) No. 2, to right, was not unscathed in spite of her appearance. Verdi Peak Ridge lies in the background of this view looking west. *(Henry Hunken Photo.)*

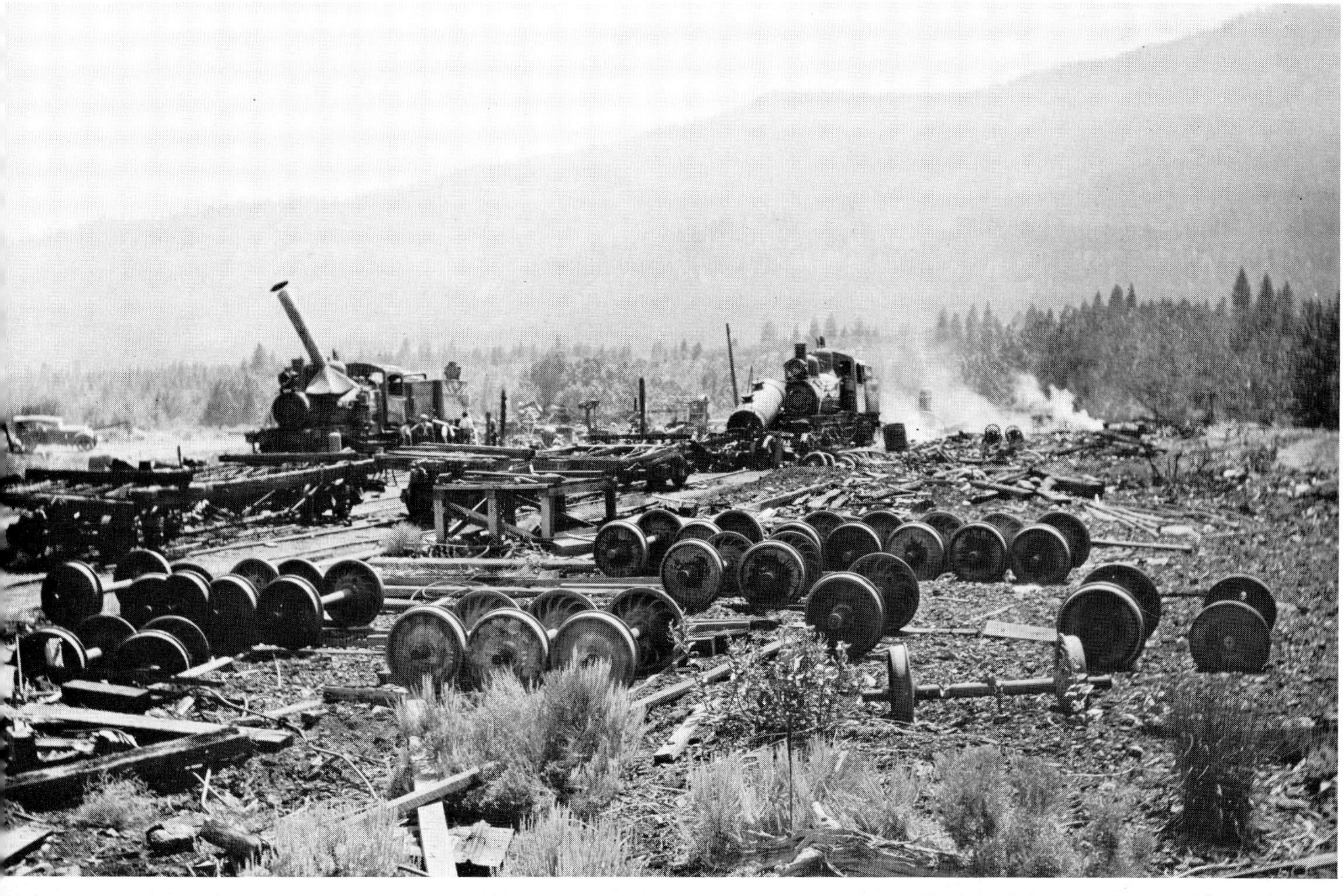

Logging Railroads—Lake Tahoe & Truckee River Basin

Timber was one of the first and foremost necessities of the pioneers who settled in the Washoe Valley of Nevada and along the banks of the Truckee River. Timber supplied the firewood with which these early settlers cooked and heated their cabins; it provided the lumber with which their later houses were constructed; and, following the advent of the Comstock discoveries, it served in the construction of the stores and mill buildings, and additionally provided the requisite supporting timbers lining miles of tunnels deep within the mines. Wood was the fuel with which water was heated in primitive boilers to furnish steam to drive the engines powering the hoists, pumps, stamp mills and many other power-operated devices; and steam, generated by wood-fueled fires, powered the early railroad locomotives.

Nowhere in the state of Nevada was wood as abundant as along the eastern slope of the Sierra Nevada near the California-Nevada border and, handily for the Comstock, possibly the greatest stands of timber were concentrated in the vicinity of Lake Tahoe and the Truckee River to the north. Although the mountains posed a barrier which was difficult to surmount, the pioneers found ways to overcome the obstacles with improvisations which were spectacularly crude yet effective.

The earliest sawmills were established in Washoe Valley by the Mormons at Franktown (later a station on the V&T) prior to the discovery of the bonanza Comstock lode. Timber cutters nibbled at the trees fringing the valley at the foot of the mountains which were handy of access and relatively easy to transport. However, in 1857 they abandoned their holdings and returned to Utah, heeding the call of Brigham Young to defend their way of life. Forced to dispose of their sawmills and other property at ridiculously low prices, they caused a curse to be cast upon the purchasers for all time. The inefficacy of the malediction was amply demonstrated when the discoveries on the Comstock a few years later boomed the demand for lumber and wood of all kinds to the extent that both the productive capacity of the mills and the carrying capacity of the agencies of transport were completely overtaxed.

As the felling of timber reduced the immediately accessible supply, cutting operations extended back to the foot of the mountains and deep into the valleys, then up and over the slopes of the mountains themselves. A. W. Pray established one of the earliest sawmills on the shores of Lake Tahoe in 1861, one which became the forerunner of the extensive Glenbrook properties of a decade later.

Lake Tahoe, headwater of the famed Truckee River, lies high on the eastern edge of the Sierra Nevada at an elevation of 6,225 feet. It is one of the most scenic and largest mountain lakes in the world, approximately 21 miles long and ranging from eight to eleven miles in width, and belongs in part to two different states, for the Nevada-California state line runs through it on a north-south axis for most of its length. Completely surrounding the

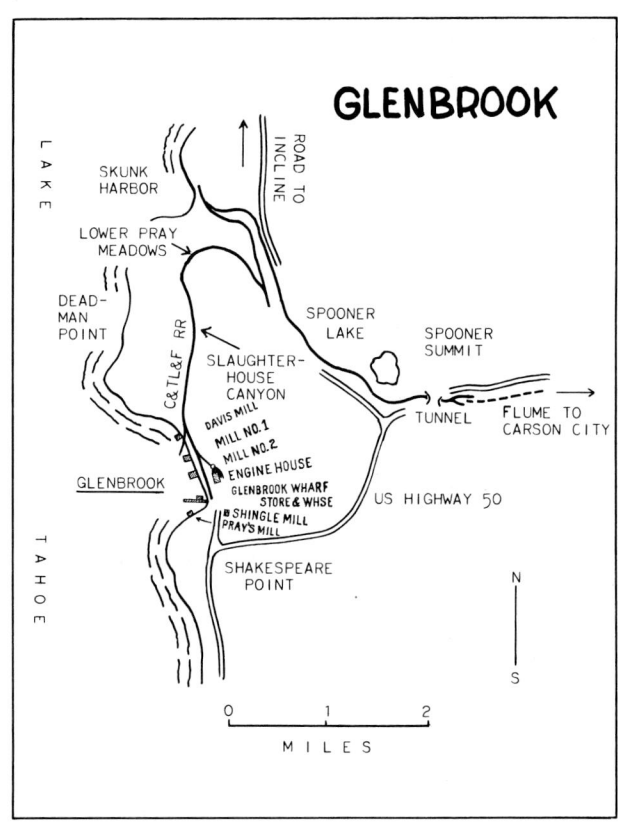

lake are prolific stands of timber surrounded by mountains reaching to elevations of from 8,500 to over 10,000 feet. Within this natural bowl (a scant 23 air miles from Virginia City), during the last half of the nineteenth century, two large lumber and milling companies developed, operating in five separate localities, each utilizing some form of railroad transportation. The companies competed with each other and with operators from other areas to the north and west of Reno for the timber trade of the voracious Comstock. The majority of these enterprises were born, flourished and died before the turn of the century, following which the Lake Tahoe area fully blossomed as a resort area.

Carson and Tahoe Lumber and Fluming Company

Oldest of the Lake Tahoe lumbering operations was the Carson and Tahoe Lumber and Fluming Company, for its antecedents dated back to A. W. Pray's pioneer mill of 1861 located at Glenbrook. Others followed Captain Pray and additional mills were erected in the vicinity. Teams were used to haul the cut boards and timbers up and over Spooner's Summit (used by Highway 50 today), down to Carson City and onward to Virginia City. The operation was slow, cumbersome and expensive; it needed improvement.

The Summit Flume Company provided the most immediate answer to the problem. Construction of an 11-mile, V-shaped flume from Spooner's Summit eastward down the Canyon of Clear Creek to a point just south of Carson City provided a facility which not only delivered the loads of lumber with greater rapidity, but eliminated the necessity for teams and wagons to return up the mountain to obtain successive loads. The operation was eminently successful for its time.

After the Virginia & Truckee Railroad was completed between Virginia City and Carson City, a branch line was built late in 1870 south from Carson City to connect with the Summit Flume Company's terminus facilities at that point. Hauling timbers by rail to Virginia City was a further improvement in the transportation chain from Lake Tahoe, which reduced costs and improved the service.

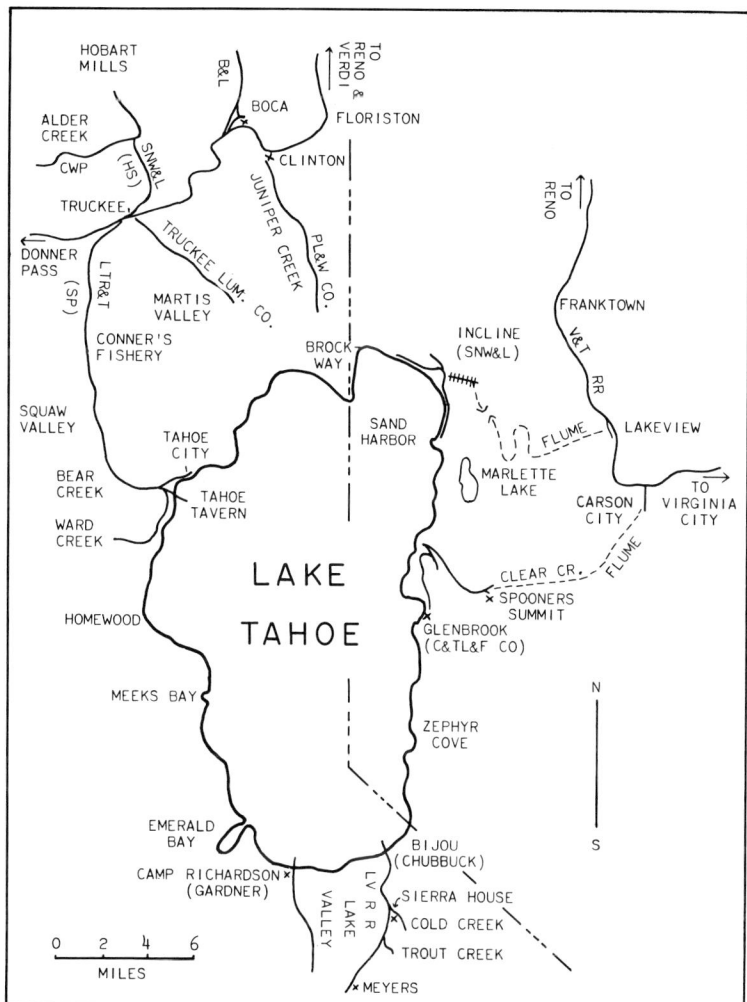

In 1873 D. O. Mills and H. M. Yerington, both prominent in the V&T's affairs, joined with banker Duane L. Bliss to form the Carson and Tahoe Lumber and Fluming Company. The purpose of the organization was to acquire the various sawmills and lumber interests at Glenbrook and secure to themselves the source of supply of Virginia City lumber. Included in the properties acquired was the Summit Flume Company, which gave them complete control of all operations from forest to destination at the mines.

One of the first acts of the new owners was to mechanize the last animal-power link in the transportation chain — that uphill stretch from the mills to Spooner's Summit at the head of the flume. It is doubtful that the Mills-Yerington-Bliss combine was concerned about the welfare of the teams involved in the hauling; their previous experience in operating the V&T had soundly demonstrated that a railroad could haul greater loads per trip and do it with greater frequency and economy — and almost regardless of weather. Thus Bliss proceeded with arrangements for a survey for a railroad which,

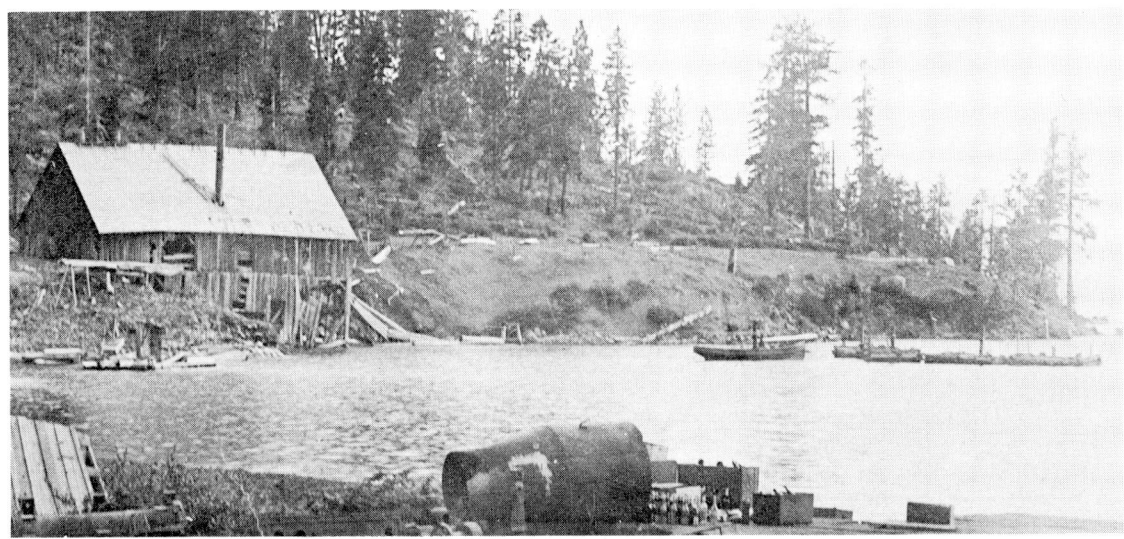

Pioneer operation in the Lake Tahoe area was the mill *(above)* of A. W. Pray, built in 1861 on the cove at Glenbrook. Note the small steam launch to right which was used in light towing service. *(Nevada Historical Society.)*

Shakespeare Point towers 800 feet above this view of Mill No. 1 *(bottom)* of the Mills-Yerington-Bliss combine, major successor to the Pray operation at Glenbrook. Southeasterly to the right of the mill can be seen the cupolaed peak of the Lake Shore House (still used today as an employees' residence), and beyond that the large main store (near the pile of stacked cordwood on the location of the present Glenwood pier). Behind the mill are two tall trees which still stand today to mark the site, while strung out below are the wires and poles of one of the pioneer telephone systems in the West. In the foreground a spur of the C&TL&FCo. railroad runs out over the log pond area to facilitate the dumping of logs brought in from the hills above, while at left center is the steeply pitched roof and smokejacks of the engine house on the bank. *(Grahame Hardy Collection.)*

The impressive height of the three-stall engine house is dramatically emphasized *(above, right)* when compared with the size of the men in front or the locomotive TAHOE at right. One end, tie rod and push bar of the manually operated gallows turntable serving the unit are seen in foreground. *(Grahame Hardy Collection.)*

The TAHOE *(bottom, right)* stands on the engine house lead at the head of a maximum tonnage consist of lumber for the grades to the summit. The engineer, fireman and conductor are grouped around the locomotive, while boss C. T. Bliss, in straw hat and vest, leans against the tender. The brakemen on the loaded cars to rear will have their hands full going up the switchbacks at the north end of Lower Pray Meadows. *(Grahame Hardy Collection.)*

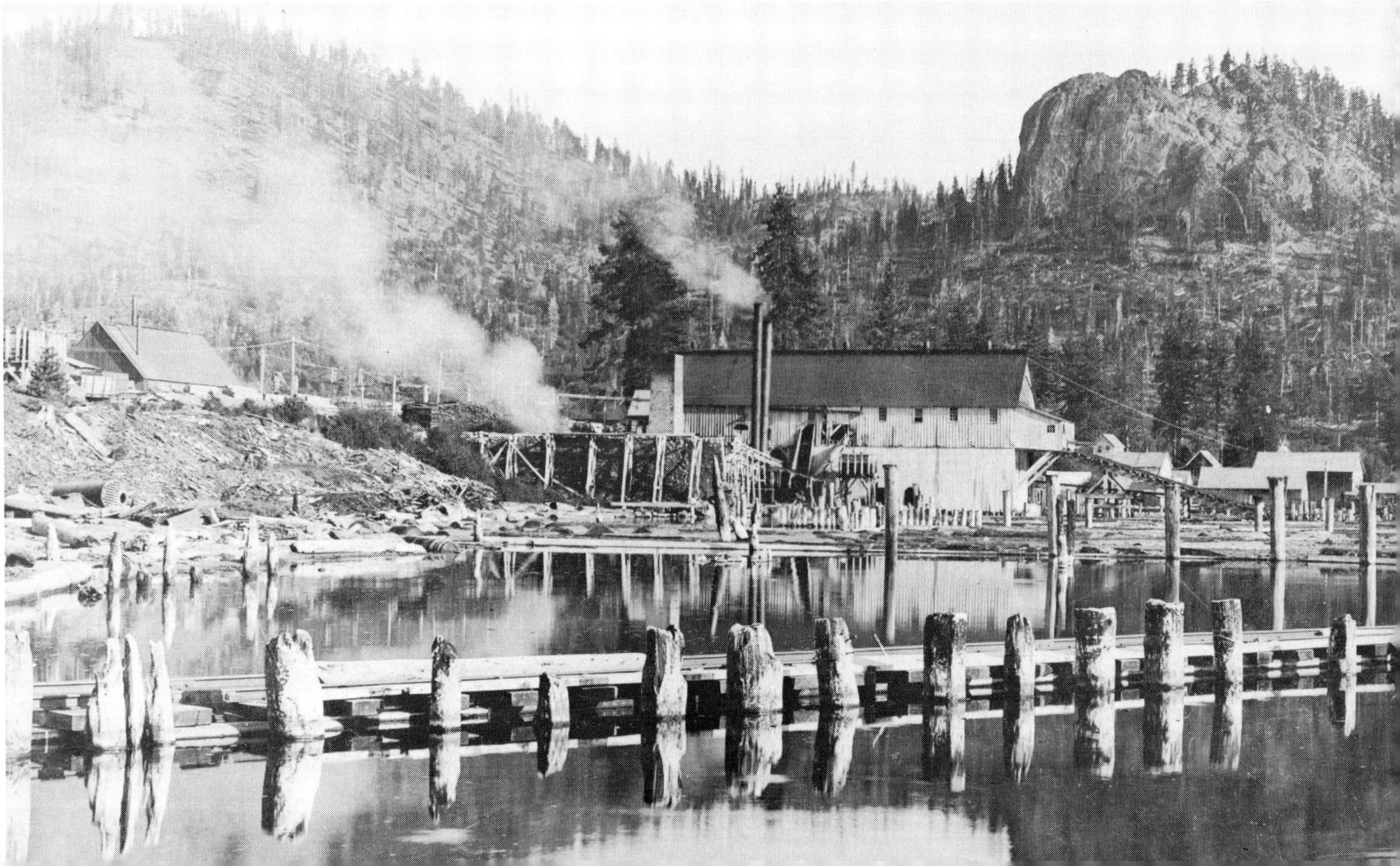

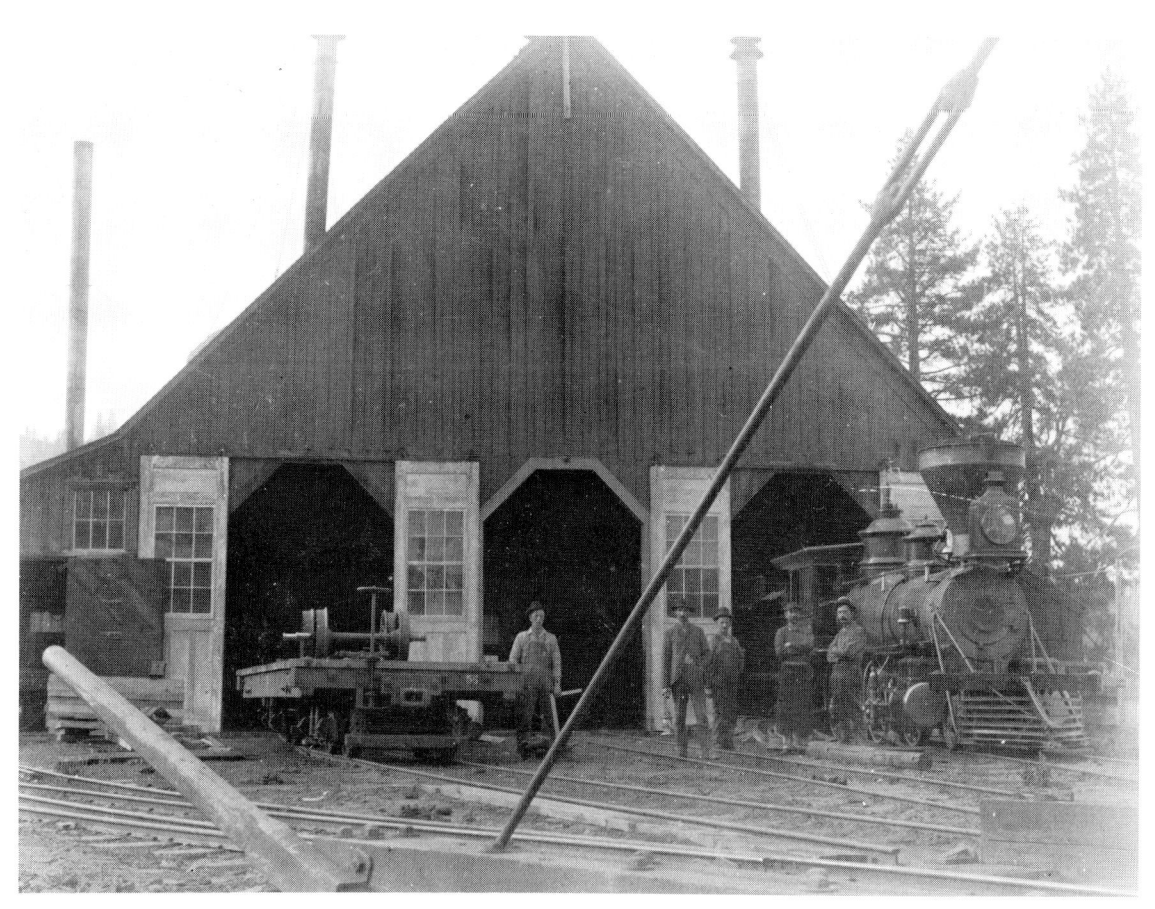

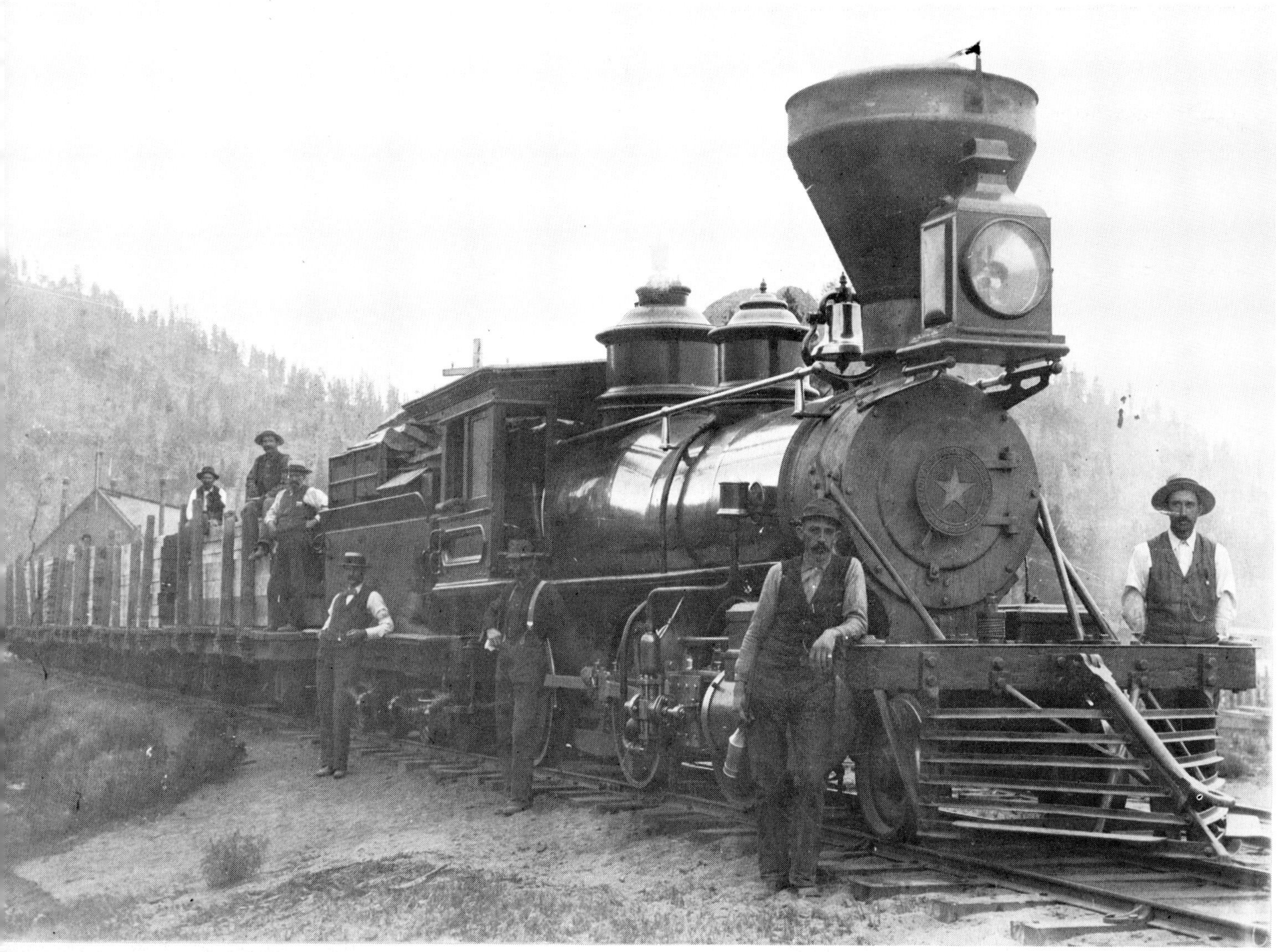

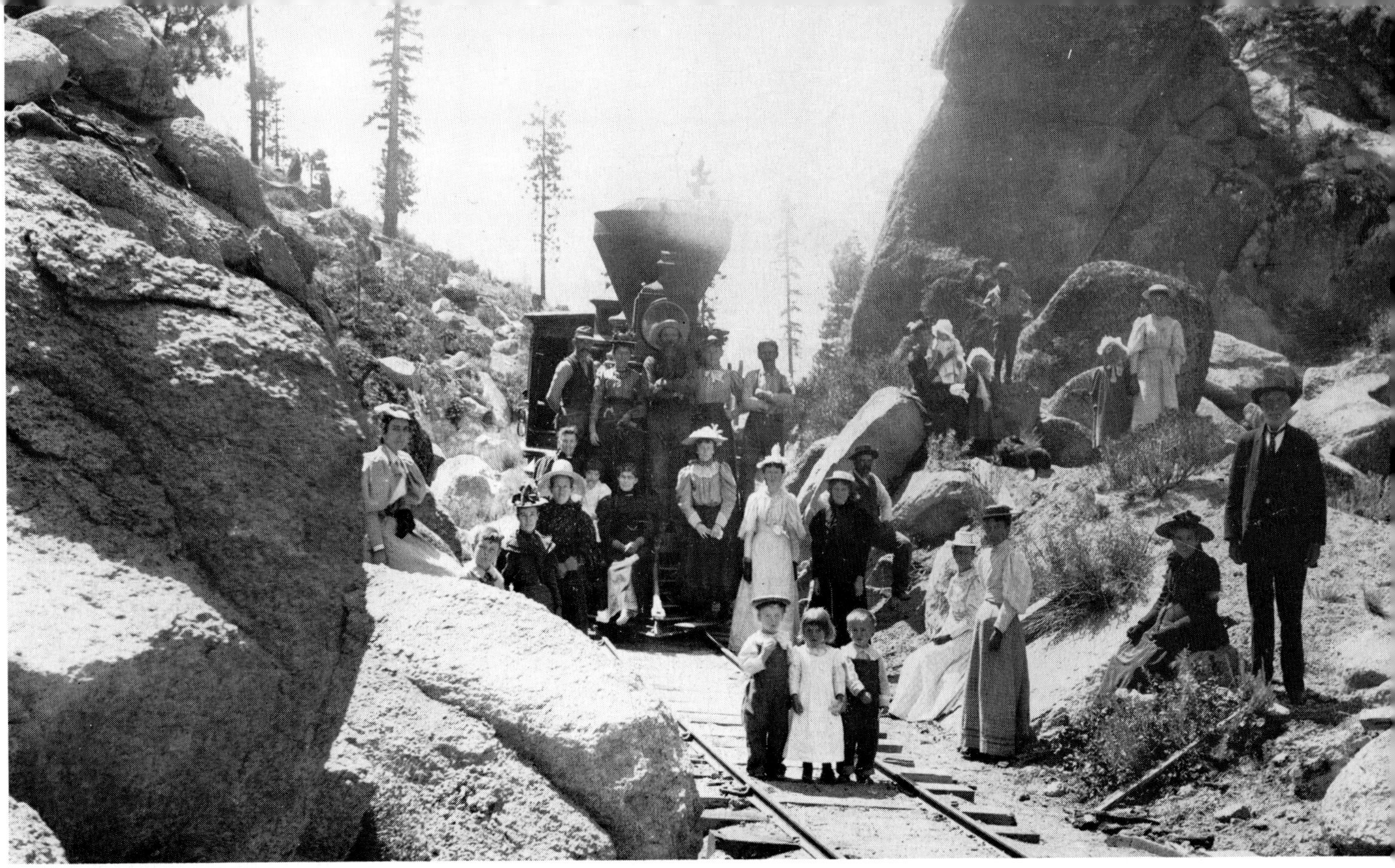

Sunday picnics via train were a real treat for people employed in the Glenbrook operation. Of all the 29 people posed in the photo *(above)* taken above Lower Pray Meadows, the three children in the foreground steal the show. *(Grahame Hardy Collection.)*

Weekdays it was business as usual. In this 1891 view *(below)* the TAHOE crosses a low trestle as it charges the grade approaching the switchbacks while *(bottom, right)* on another occasion, it is shown posed on the unloading ramp at Spooner's Summit. *(Bottom Left: George D. Oliver Photo; Right: Grahame Hardy Collection.)*

The picture *(above, right)* appears to have been taken on the occasion of a slight contretemps on the upper leg of the switchback. Judging by the position of the cars behind the TAHOE on the left hand track, a derailment has occurred which has nearly fouled the right hand main. The engineer of the GLENBROOK, however, has attempted to pass and is watching carefully for signals from the rear in the event of trouble, ignoring the spinning drivers as the locomotive slips on the superelevated grade. Behind the TAHOE's train the conductor can be seen peering between the cars to check the clearance as the trains pass. *(George D. Oliver Photo.)*

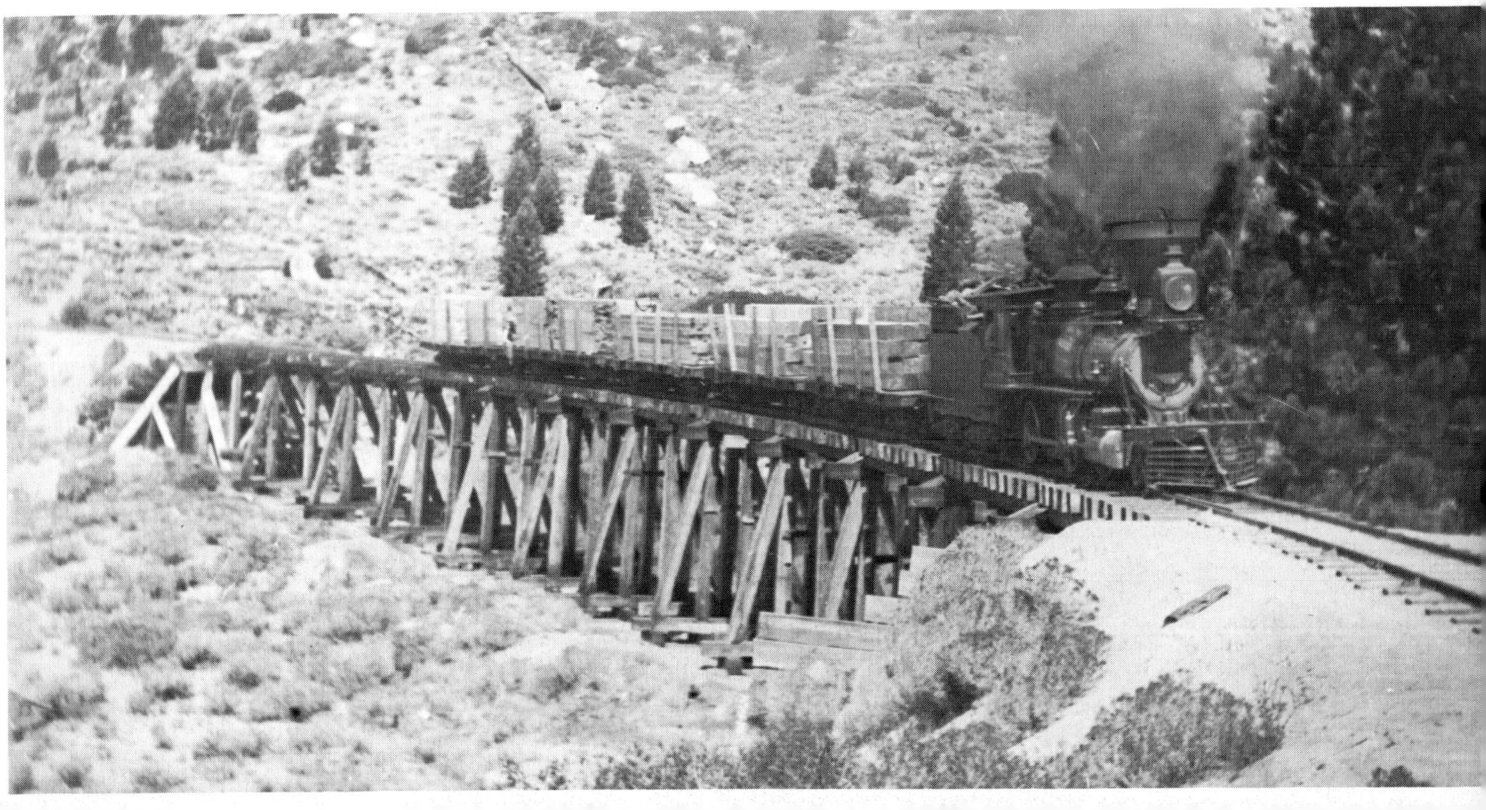

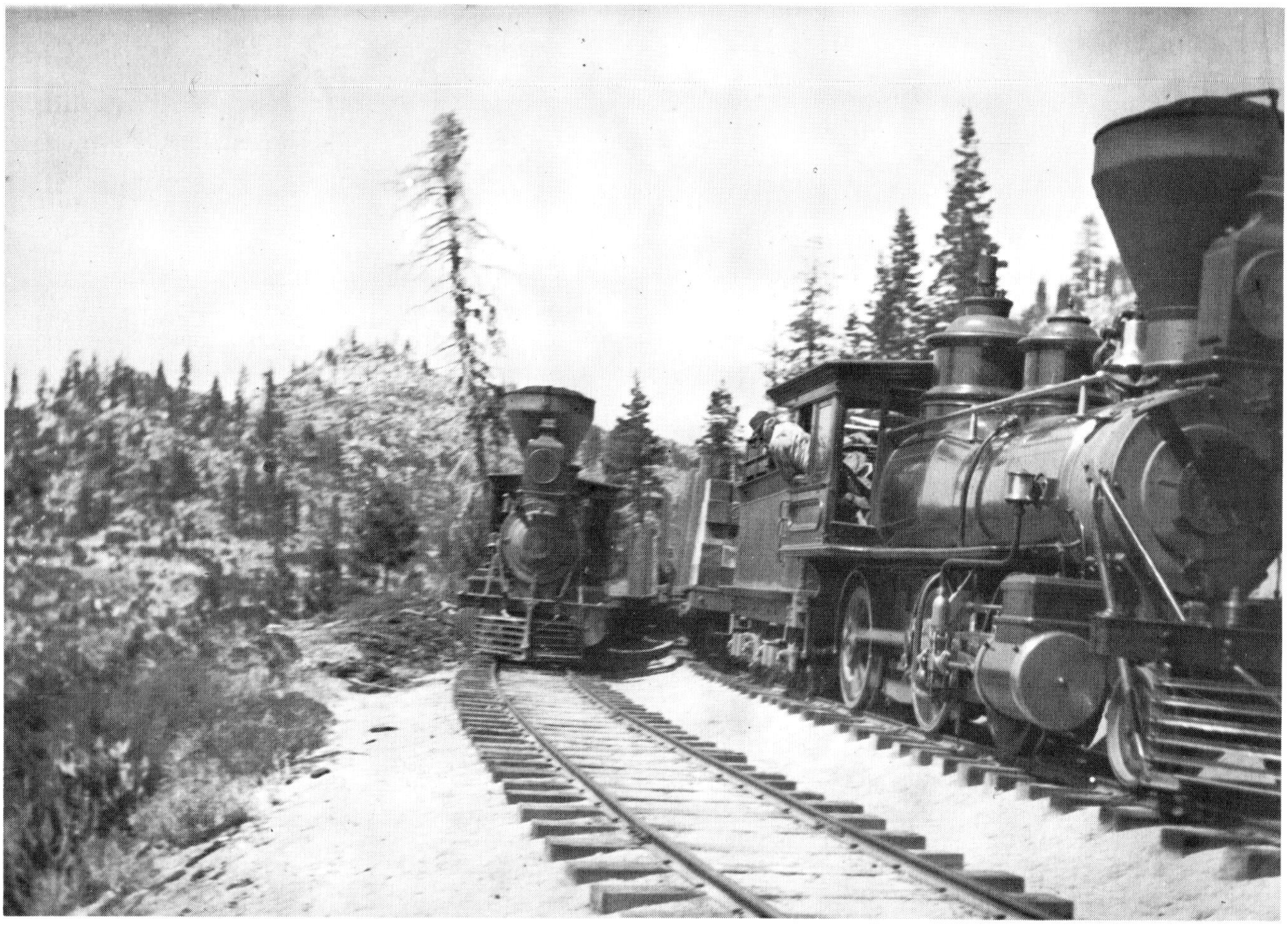

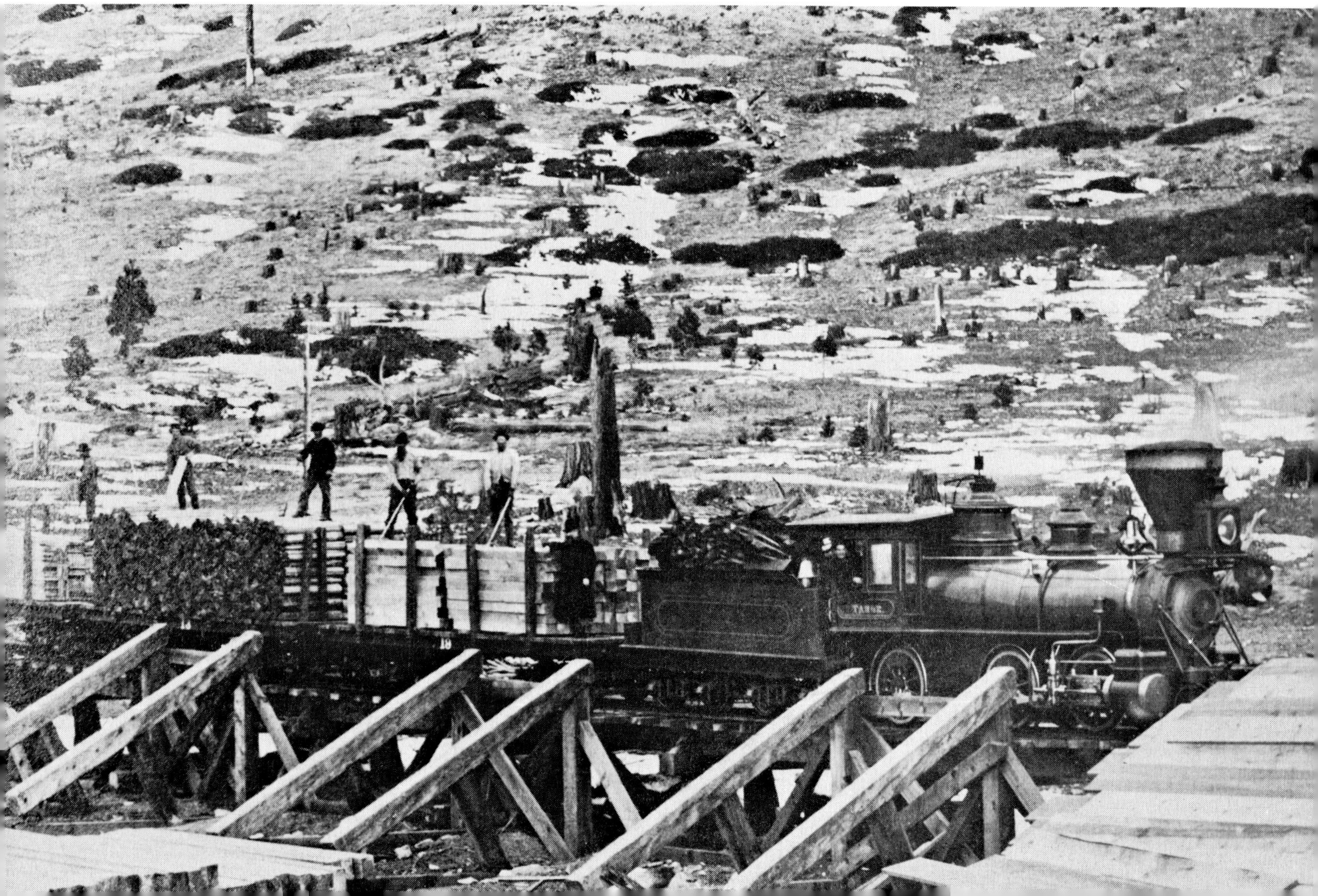

though a company operation, became more commonly known as the Lake Tahoe (Narrow Gauge) Railroad.

The job was not easy. The terrain was difficult; the grades were steep; one portion of the route was so troublesome the surveyors were obliged to work suspended by ropes. It was July of 1874 before the job was done, so construction was postponed until spring of the following year.

Work on the line was started on April 19, 1875. Two weeks later on May 2, Hank Monk passed through with one of Benton's stages on his way over the summit to Carson City and told a reporter that times were lively in Glenbrook with railroad grading under way. A large force of 250 men under construction boss Jule Holmes made rapid progress. Graders were strung all the way from the summit down to the lake, while another crew attacked the 487-foot tunnel at the Summit. Large boulders caused problems — one, 15 feet in diameter, was moved only after being persuaded by 20 kegs of powder. Time and labor were the essential ingredients required in the erection of 11 trestles for the 8.75-mile mountain climbing line; timber for their fabrication was available for the taking.

At the end of June, just after the first mile of track had been spiked in place, the locomotive GLENBROOK suffered its first collision at a crossover. Pushing some flat cars, it sideswiped a string of mill cars moving under the tutelage of the TAHOE on the adjacent track. Fortunately damage was relatively minor and no one was injured.

The tunnel was holed through in the middle of July, as the trackwork was pushed up the slope. A month later rail laying was finished, and on August 21, 1875, the road was pronounced "complete." Formal operations, commenced two days later, consisted of six daily trips to the Summit for each locomotive with a tonnage consist of six cars of lumber measuring approximately 25,000 board feet. Thus the capacity of the new line approximated 300,000 board feet of lumber per day, a far cry from the results of team hauling.

The increased facility of the railroad enabled greater productiveness in the mills as well, which in turn increased the demand for logs from the forests. To fulfill the demand, logs were brought from various parts of the Lake Tahoe area. The company owned timber lands at Emerald Bay (a portion of which now comprises the D. L. Bliss State Park), while other holdings were leased to contractors. Gardner and Chubbuck became important operators at the southern end of the lake; Smart & Sons of Carson City logged near the Upper Truckee River; others included such well-known personages as Duff Morris and Henry Martin.

With the Glenbrook operations in full swing, the area became a mecca for students of lumbering, businessmen and sightseers. The latter were particularly delighted with their trips over the narrow gauge railroad, though the line was primarily a lumber hauler without passenger accommodations. However, the trip offered rewardingly spectacular views of the deep, blue waters of Lake Tahoe as well as a chance to share in the thrills of mountain railroading. Regrettably, one man became so overawed with the view in 1877, he was killed in a fall from a car.

A ride over the line commenced at the mills at Glenbrook, where a diamond-stacked, wood-burning Mogul locomotive headed up its train of six loads of lumber. Passengers could select whatever timber they wished to ride upon, but preferably one with few splinters. Following a blast of the whistle, the train left camp, heading upgrade to the north through Slaughterhouse Canyon to Lower Pray Meadows, where a loop of track reversed the train's direction and ended in the first of the switchbacks. Backing upward to the next level, the tail track of which ended on a trestle high on a steep bank above Lake Tahoe's waters, the train reversed again and proceeded up the steep grades which averaged 2% in most instances with some stretches reaching as high as 4%. The roadbed followed a stream to the tunnel at Spooner's Summit, a short distance beyond which the rails fanned out into a yard at the head of the flume and came to an end. A little grove of aspens now marks the site of the east portal of the tunnel. The original length of the line was 8.75 miles, although subsequent additions in later years brought the total to 10 miles.

The Glenbrook mills continued to be an important factor in the economy of the Lake Tahoe region until the lands were logged out near the close of the nineteenth century. The mills were credited with sawing more lumber than any others in Nevada at the time of their closing following the end of the 1898 cutting season. The sawmill machinery was used again at Carters in Tuolumne County, California, and the mill buildings were dismantled and brought to Truckee for use in rebuilding the mill of the Truckee Lumber Company which burned in May 1902 and again in 1903.

The railroad to Spooner's Summit was dismantled soon after the mills were closed in 1898. All rails and equipment were taken across the lake to Tahoe City (on the northwest shore) for use in construction of the next Bliss narrow gauge line, the Lake Tahoe Railway & Transportation Company, running between that point and Truckee on the Southern Pacific. The mills at Glenbrook, the old roadbed in Slaughterhouse Canyon and the switchback at Lower Pray Meadow returned to an ephemeral solitude to await the coming of the tourist and the resort builder.

M. C. Gardner (Camp Richardson)

As previously noted, M. C. Gardner of Carson City became one of the lumber contractors for the Mills-Yerington-Bliss combine, operators of the Glenbrook properties. (It is interesting to note that Gardner's daughter was the wife of Squire Scoville, Secretary of the N-C-O Railway, who ultimately was shot and killed at the infamous N-C-O directors' meeting of 1881.) Gardner's contract stipulated the production and delivery of 60 million board feet of timber over a six-year period; the territory assigned lay along the southwest shore of Lake Tahoe, a few miles west of Bijou.

To fulfill the terms of his contract, Gardner planned a railroad to haul logs from the forests to lake shore where they would be dumped into the water, assembled into booms, and towed by tug to the sawmills at Glenbrook. The road was to be of standard gauge (the only such railroad at Lake Tahoe until 1926), and in March 1875 arrangements were made with the V&T to lease its locomotive No. 2, ORMSBY, together with nine flat cars. The purchase of the equipment was an easy arrangement to make; not so the delivery. Some 50 years later, in recalling the terrific efforts his father expended in hauling the locomotive up and over Spooner's Summit to Glenbrook, James Horace Gardner recounted: "The locomotive was loaded on two trucks coupled together and hauled to Glen-

---

M. C. Gardner operated the only standard-gauge railroad in the Lake Tahoe area at Camp Richardson. Power for the line was the second-hand ORMSBY, originally No. 2 on the Virginia & Truckee, shown here at work in the Tallac Woods with an assorted crowd of lumbermen and their families. *(Louis L. Stein, Jr. Collection.)*

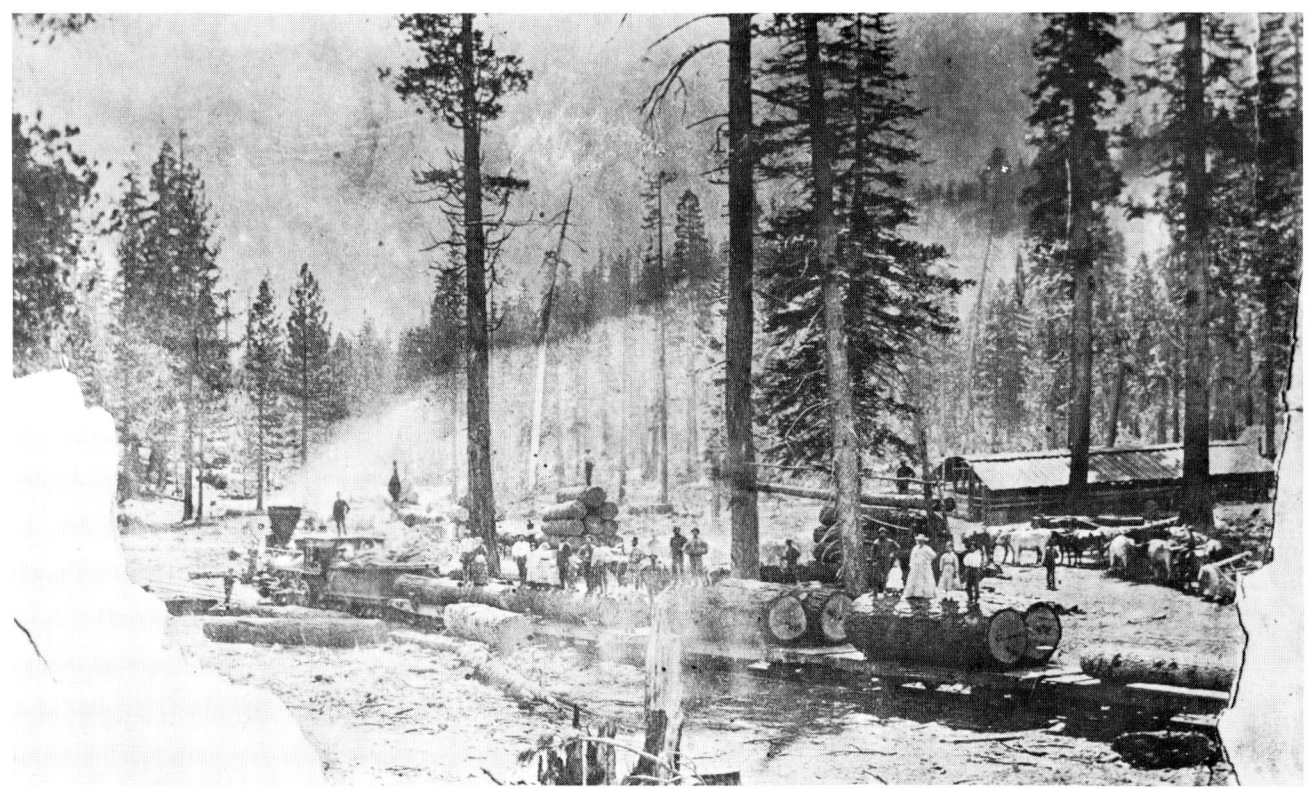

brook from Carson. It took six weeks to move it 14 miles. On straight roads it was pulled along with oxen, but when it came to the short curves of the summit, block and tackles had to be used." Once on the shore of Lake Tahoe at Glenbrook, the rails and rolling stock were loaded on barges and towed across the lake to their destination.

Construction of the railroad began in May 1875. Starting from the pier at Gardner's Camp (now Camp Richardson), the right-of-way proceeded along the west side of Lake Valley for approximately five miles to the base of Twin Peaks, then appropriately known as Gardner Mountain. The first half-mile of track was quickly completed, as the beautiful country offered no grading problems for several miles. At the end of July, the *Gold Hill News* reported that "One mile of track is already laid, and in a few weeks the ORMSBY will arouse the feathered denizens of the forest with its shrill shriek." No specific date of completion is recorded, for a logging railroad is never "finished." The tracks were moved many times over the years as logging operations were transferred to new stands of timber.

For approximately a decade the ORMSBY shuttled back and forth bringing its loads of logs to the water where they were dumped into a protected harbor. Once a week the *Emerald* or the *Truckee* would visit the camp and tow away the accumulation to the mills at Glenbrook. Ultimately financial difficulties beset Gardner, forcing suspension of the operations, and the railroad was abandoned some time after 1885.

G. W. Chubbuck— Lake Valley Railroad

Another of the Mills-Yerington-Bliss combine's lumbering operations centered at Bijou near the southeast corner of Lake Tahoe. The work was contracted with G. W. Chubbuck under a procedure similar to that followed by M. C. Gardner— namely, a railroad would be constructed to bring the logs from the woods to the lake where log booms would be formed for towage to the Glenbrook mills.

The project was organized with Bijou as the terminus of the G. W. Chubbuck narrow (3') gauge railroad. The SANTA CRUZ, pioneer locomotive of the N-C-O Railway, was purchased and sent to the V&T shops in Carson City during the summer of 1886 to be reconditioned. At the same time, rails were purchased and hauled in by teams from Truckee. In September the locomotive arrived, and by late November the four-mile railroad ex-

G. W. Chubbuck's lumbering operations centered at Bijou near the southeast corner of Lake Tahoe. To power his narrow-guage railroad, a locomotive was obtained from the Carson and Tahoe Lumber and Fluming Company, probably No. 3. *(Ted Wurm Collection.)*

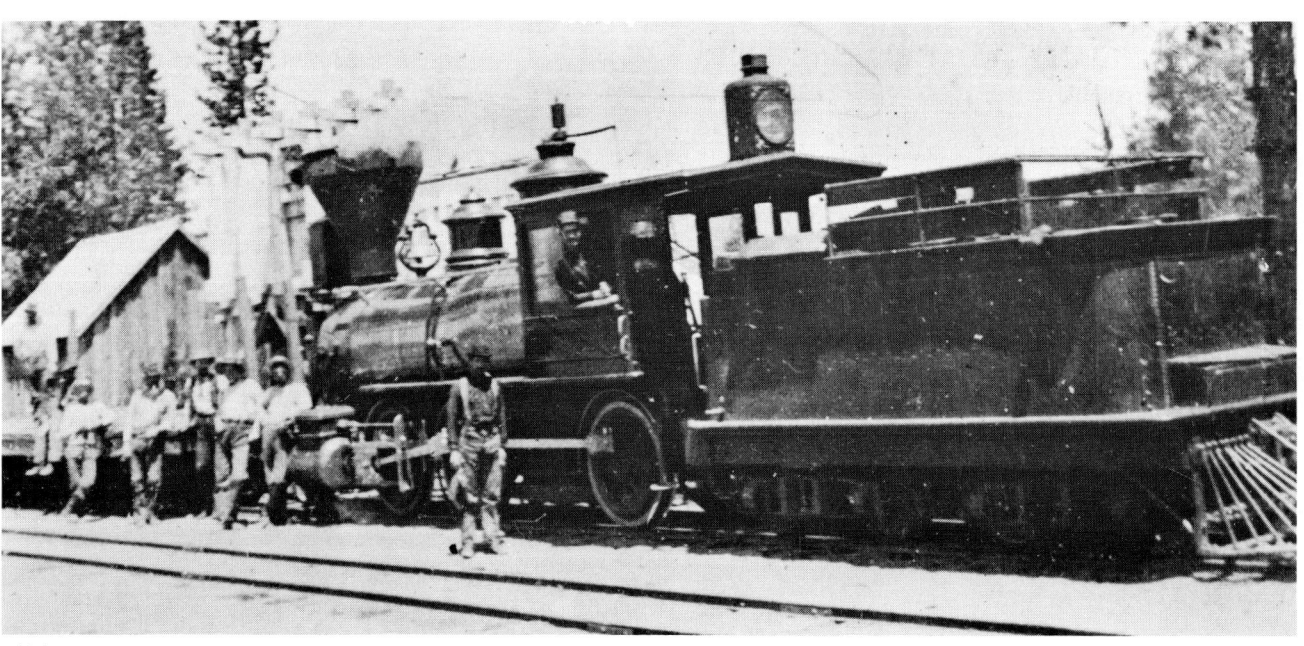

tending up Cold Creek Canyon was reported to be "nearly completed." Chubbuck, however, ran into financial problems about this time, and the property came into the hands of the Carson and Tahoe Lumber and Fluming Company (Glenbrook).

The Glenbrook interests continued to operate the property, and late in 1887 an expansion was deemed necessary. A new company was incorporated by allied interests called the Lake Valley Railroad, and a five-mile extension was constructed from a point near Sierra House (about a mile short of the terminus of the Cold Creek line) to Meyers in Lake Valley. One additional branch was projected near the mid-point of the new line to run approximately a mile up Trout Creek. In 1893 the total trackage was recorded as 10.50 miles.

At least one serious accident occurred on the line. In July 1891 a stray cow wandered onto the track and wrecked a logging train. Four Chinese loggers riding the consist were killed, and many others were injured.

Following the pattern of early logging procedure, the timber land ultimately became cut over and operations ceased. The railroad was torn up during the summer of 1898, and all salvageable materials and equipment were pooled with those from the Glenbrook operation and taken to Tahoe City for incorporation in the Lake Tahoe Railway & Transportation Company's line to Truckee.

Sierra Nevada Wood and Lumber Company

You will find no trace on modern maps of one of the most spectacular early operations in the Lake Tahoe area, and even the nomenclature of the region will appear confusing and misleading to students of this primal enterprise. However, ample evidence of the once famous incline railway of the Sierra Nevada Wood and Lumber Company, operated by the Hobart interests during the last quarter of the nineteenth century, does still remain.

The intrepid, seeking tangible proof of the existence of this vast engineering project, will face a jeep ride along a treacherous mountain trail to a point high in the northeast corner of the Lake Tahoe area. There, standing out boldly against the skyline, are the giant 12-foot bull wheels of the former cable railway, still resting in their foundations, a vital memento of a pioneering enterprise. Although large trees now block any view of the downward course of the tramway, the bull wheels, the heavy beams, and parts of the platforms still remain.

The name of Incline Creek will be a complete misnomer for those seeking the site of the former Hobart mill at the foot of the incline. Instead, look for Mill Creek (about ¾ of a mile southeast), where the mill was located near the foot of the hill up which the cut lumber would be shipped. The old lake shore railroad grade (on which the present highway is largely built) looped inland at this point to cross Mill Creek about ⅓ of a mile upstream from the present highway bridge, and it was here the Hobart engineers erected their mill and flung the double-track tramway directly up the face of the escarpment to the head of their flume which ran down the east slope of the Sierra Nevada to Lakeview. The little cars of lumber were pulled up the mountain (and empties lowered) by means of cables strung over the giant bull wheels in the machinery building at the top.

W. S. Hobart, in conjunction with S. H. Marlette, initially started in the lumbering business in Little Valley, just west of Franktown at the foot of the eastern slope of the Sierra Nevada. Their Excelsior Mill was turning out timber for Virginia City as early as 1876, but within two years they decided to move the sawmill to Crystal Bay on Lake Tahoe's northeast corner where timber was more plentiful and operations could be expanded. More money was needed, and Alvinza Hayward (a San Francisco capitalist) and others joined with Hobart in the incorporation on April 22, 1878, of the Sierra Nevada Wood and Lumber Company with a capitalization of $5,000,000. J. B. Overton, superintendent of the Virginia City and Gold Hill Water Company, doubled as boss of the lumber company.

Broad vision and large-scale planning were primary requisites in development of the new company's interests. There had to be a smooth, logical flow of material from woods to mills to consumer. Logs cut in the woods were to be hauled to the lake, to be towed to a harbor, there to be transported by logging railroad to the mill at Mill Creek. Branches of the railroad extending into the woods north of Crystal Bay would furnish additional logs direct from the woods. Finished lumber

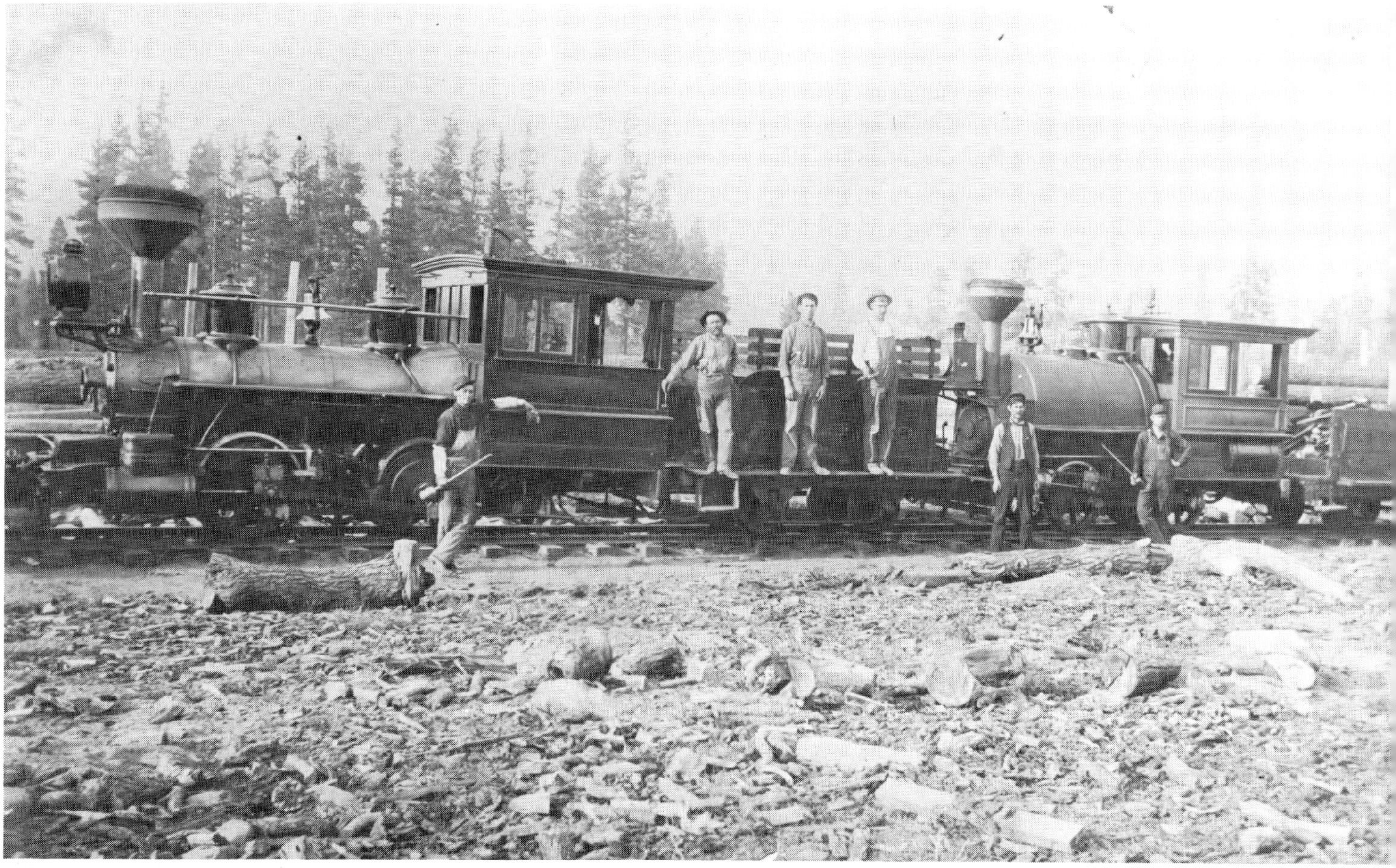

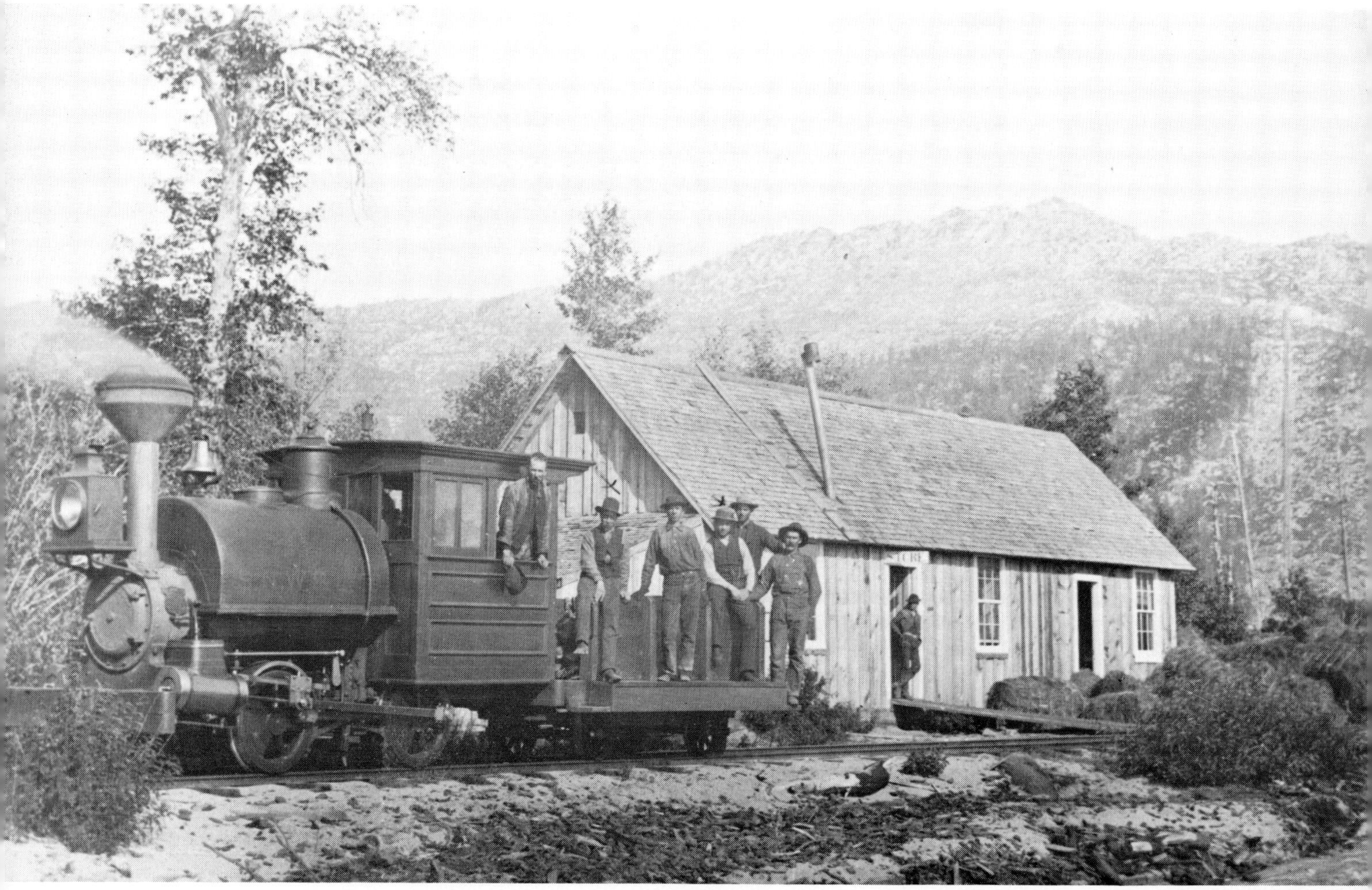

The entire motive power of the Crystal Bay Railroad which served the mill and famous incline of the Sierra Nevada Wood & Lumber Co. is shown in the view *(top, left)* taken some time after the 1889 delivery of the lead locomotive, No. 2. Note that saddle tanker No. 1 trails a full fashioned 4-wheel tender, an item not available when the earlier view *(bottom, left)* was taken in front of the Marlette & Folsom store on the shore of Lake Tahoe whose waters are just visible in the foreground. Behind and to right of the building the pathway of the incline can be traced up the side of the mountain, of which a more detailed view appears at *top right*. Combinations of cordwood and lumber were hauled over its 4,000-foot length.

All that remains of the spectacular operation today are giant bull wheels *(bottom, right)* standing against the sky near the top and jumbled timbers *(bottom)* which once formed part of the trestle at the upper end of the incline. Trees obscure the right-of-way down the slope, but the location can be spotted by a sharp eye from Highway 28 along Crystal Bay in background. *(Top Left: George D. Oliver Photograph; Bottom Left: Mrs. P. R. Evans; Top Right: Louis L. Stein, Jr. Collection.)*

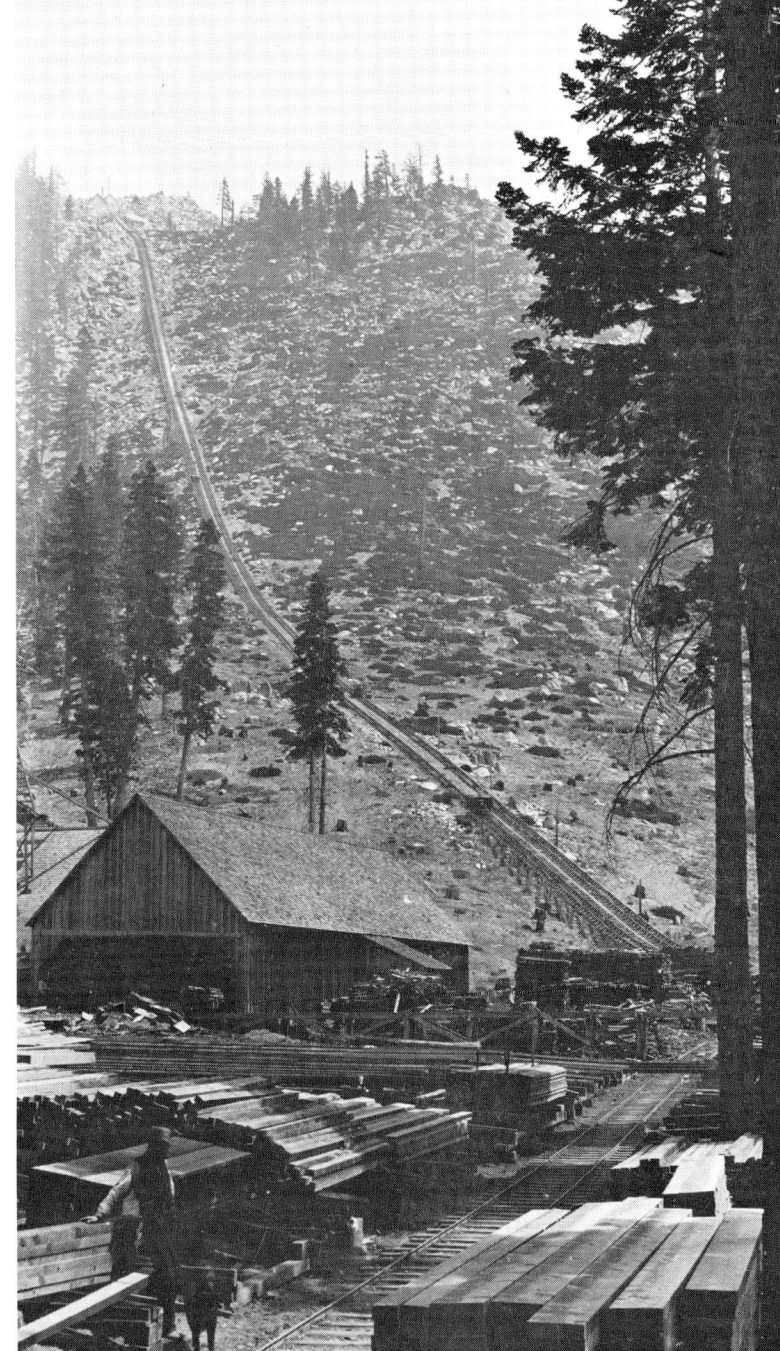

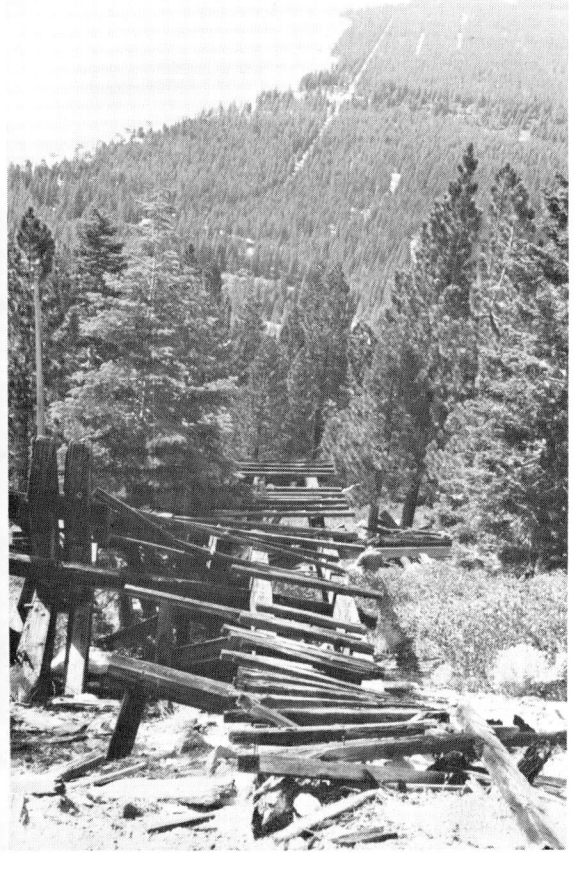

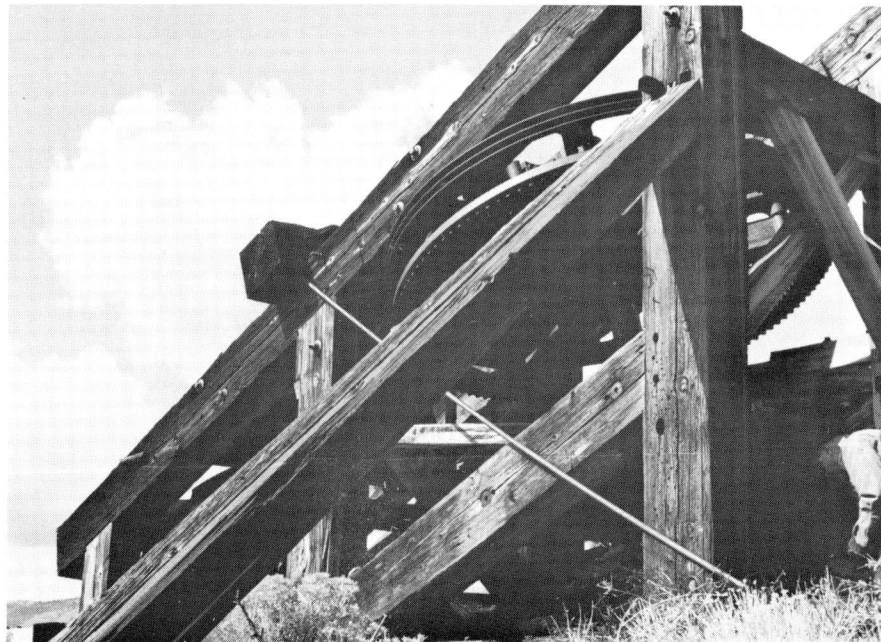

from the mill would be taken up an incline railway to the head of a flume at the top of the mountain and there floated down the east slope of the Sierra Nevada to Lakeview in the Washoe Valley below. Railroad transportation would then convey the lumber to consumers throughout the Carson City-Virginia City district.

By 1880 the project had become a reality. The most prominent feature of the works was the steep, double-track, cable-powered incline railway. Starting at the base near the steam sawmill and soaring up the mountain for a distance of 4,000 feet, it overcame a 1,400-foot increase in elevation, and served to bring the lumber direct to the head of the flume to Lakeview. A 40 h.p. steam engine at the top of the incline turned the large 12-foot bull wheels, around which the cable (over an inch in diameter) was wound. The cars were constructed with their floors at an angle sufficient to compensate for the steep grade of the incline, which ran as high as 66% in some places, and were attached to the cable by a clutch (or grip) similar to that employed by the San Francisco cable cars. Thus they could be engaged or disengaged from the cable for loading, unloading or shifting at either end of the line. Since the cable traveled in a constant direction, loaded cars were hauled up the mountain on the north track and returned light on the south track.

Even before the incline was completely finished in October 1880, two loaded cars took off without notice. A streak of fire was all that could be seen during the mad dash downward. When the excitement was over and the smoke had cleared away, it was found the cars were completely wrecked and the wood splintered into matches. One board escaped destruction by sailing aloft and wedging itself into a tree at a point some 20 feet above the ground. Following several more runaways and the loss of seven cars, a cog and ratchet system was devised which limited the slippage of any one car to a four-inch span.

The company's flume, from the top of the mountain to Lakeview also embodied an unusual feature, due largely to Hobart's allied interest in the Virginia and Gold Hill Water Company. Following the Virginia City fire of 1875, the water company had extended its gathering lines all the way west to Marlette Lake, and to obtain a downward flow to the Washoe Valley had bored a 4,000-foot tunnel through the crest of the mountain. Since the tunnel was seven feet high, and since relations between the lumber and water companies were on the friendliest of terms, it was an easy matter to obtain permission to run the flume through the tunnel under the mountain immediately over the open water on the tunnel floor. Thus the lumber flume was continuous from the top of the incline, and boards could float uninterruptedly for the full distance to Lakeview in the saddle between Carson City and the Washoe Valley.

At Lakeview, as a protective measure, the lumber company had a survey run for an 18-mile narrow gauge lumber railroad which skirted the southern edge of Washoe Valley and climbed to Virginia City. With Comstock production declining the effort was needless, and satisfactory arrangements were made with the V&T (owned by the Mills-Yerington group which also operated the Glenbrook interests on Lake Tahoe). All cartage was thus performed by that standard gauge carrier, which by then was glad to have the additional traffic.

Initial timber cuttings by the SNW&L Company were made about a mile north of Crystal Bay. To service the area a 1½-mile narrow gauge railroad was constructed in the spring of 1881 from the mill to the shore of Lake Tahoe and on northward into the timber. The first rails were delivered by the CP at Truckee, hauled to Tahoe City, then loaded aboard the *Minnie Moody,* a chartered sailboat under the direction of Captain Powell, and landed at Crystal Bay. The three narrow gauge cars followed a different route. Unloaded from the CP at Clinton (on the Truckee River), they were hauled to the top of the bluff and placed on the rails of the Pacific Lumber and Wood Company's narrow gauge railroad (see separate section). Approximately seven miles farther, at the end of the line, they were transferred to sledges and hauled through the forests to the shore of Lake Tahoe where barges brought them the rest of the way to Crystal Bay. The locomotive was a new one from the works at Pittsburgh, Pennsylvania, but unfortunately its delivery route was not considered sufficiently newsworthy to record. It has been determined, however, that by July 1881 the little railroad was in operation.

For a long time the one small saddle-tank locomotive did all the work, although a second locomotive was procured in June 1889. The fireman became the first casualty of the line, even though his injuries were not sustained in the line of duty.

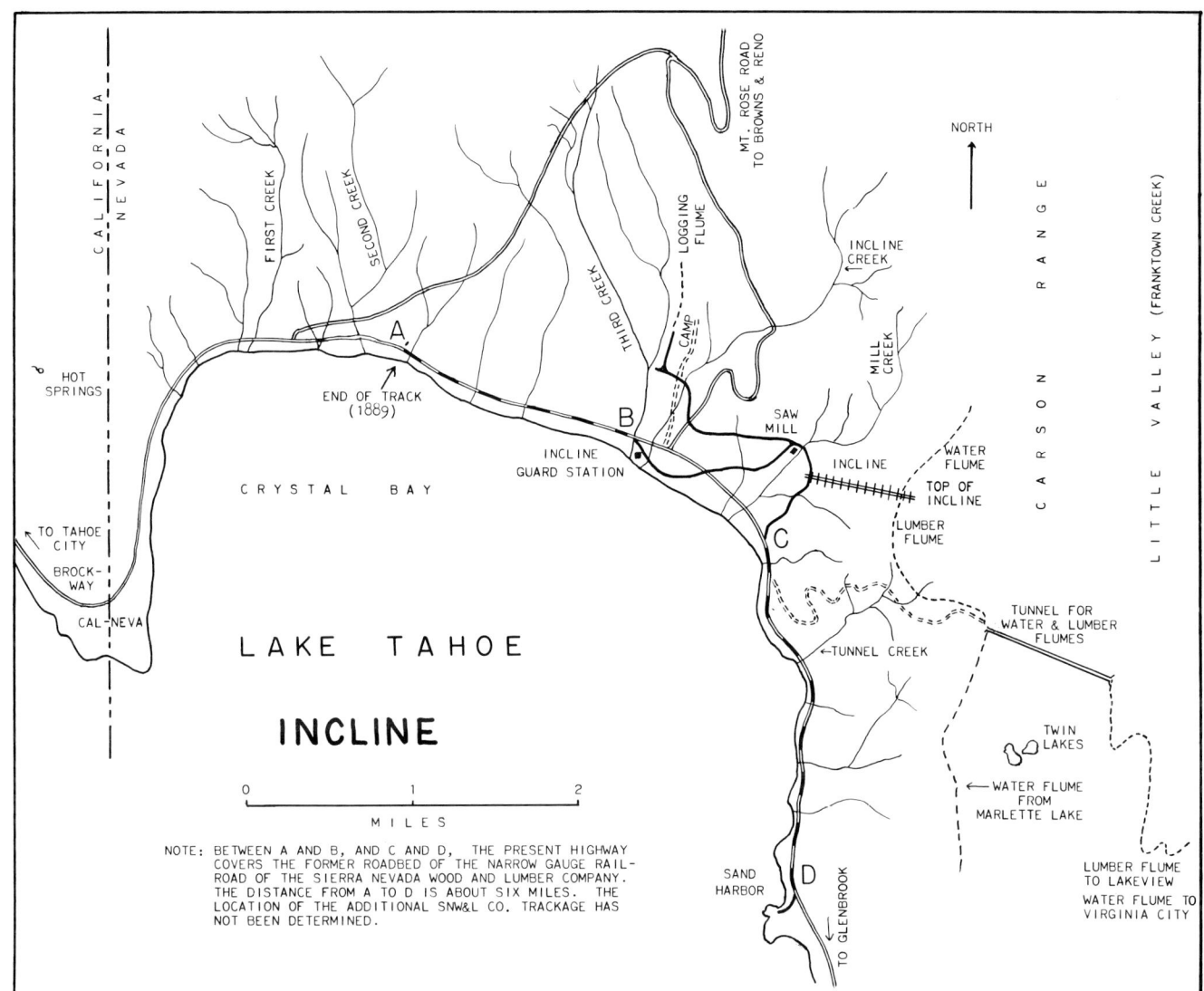

During a fight at a picnic, he had a knife blade stuck into his hand.

The length of the Crystal Bay Railroad (its colloquial name) appears to be as uncertain as the logging operations it served. Reports filed with the I.C.C. indicated its length to be 9 miles in 1888, 13 miles in 1889-92, and 10 miles in 1893. On the other hand, the report of the Surveyor General of Nevada for 1891-92 ascribed to it 8 miles of line extending from Sand Harbor to Incline; yet various maps of the region indicate that this distance would not exceed 3 miles. Most of the trackage lay along the shore line of the lake (currently covered by the present paved highway) except where the tracks swerved inland to loop past the sawmill. There is evidence to indicate a short spur was constructed along the east side of Third Creek (near Incline Creek) for approximately one-half mile to a V-flume and lumber camp, and some early maps show tracks extending farther westward along the shore of Crystal Bay to within a half mile of Second Creek.

In June 1891 a visiting reporter noted the bustle of activity at the camp where a total of 200 men were sometimes employed, and commented on the train which ran south to Sand Harbor (tracks extended in October 1888) where logs were received from other parts of the lake. Each day the engine brought back several cars with immense logs, he related, winding "in and out of the thickly wooded forest with the lofty hills on one side and Tahoe on the other, whistling and puffing as loud as an overland passenger engine. The little wood cars on the incline move slowly along with their loads, three going up full and as many coming down empty."

As the available timber supply began to diminish, plans were laid and lands acquired to the north of the Truckee River to continue operations (see SNW&L Co.—Hobart Mills). By the middle of the 1890's the forests were almost logged out, and preliminary steps for the big move were taken. The last major season appears to have ended in the fall of 1894, and the railroad was abandoned shortly thereafter. The road was dismantled and all rails and equipment were taken to Overton (Hobart Mills) for incorporation in the narrow gauge lumbering lines fingering northward from the mill into the woods.

Lake Tahoe Railway and Transportation Company

First (and undoubtedly best known) of the twentieth century Tahoe-Truckee area common carriers was the narrow gauge Lake Tahoe Railway and Transportation Company's miniature line between Truckee (on the SP) and Tahoe City on the shores of Lake Tahoe. It was a project of the Bliss interests (Glenbrook mills), and utilized existing rails and equipment from the abandoned Lake Tahoe (Narrow Gauge) Railroad at Glenbrook, the G. W. Chubbuck narrow gauge railroad at Bijou and its connecting Lake Valley Railroad from Sierra House to Meyers. Collectively, there was more than sufficient material to iron and power the new 15-mile line.

The idea for a railroad to Lake Tahoe from the west or north was not new. Two surveys from the west were run at various times—one from Placerville in 1888 and a second, subsequent, aborted effort around 1910 by the Sacramento & Sierra, which gave up after constructing a few miles of road out of Sacramento. As far back as 1879, a railroad from the north at Truckee had been projected over virtually the same route as that followed by the LTR&TCO, and in December of that year the enthusiastic residents of the area fully expected the line would be constructed the following summer at the absurdly nominal cost of $70,000. However, since tourists and tourism as big volume business were virtually unknown at that time, and since the primary interest in the whole Tahoe area initially centered around the production and transportation of lumber to the markets in Virginia City, all efforts were directed toward eastward connections and not ones to the north or west. It was not until depletion of the available timber supply forced a change of venue that any alternate routes were considered practical.

Members of the Bliss family incorporated the Lake Tahoe Railway and Transportation Company in December 1898, although the board of directors was soon increased to include such famous and capable personages as W. S. Tobey and Mark Requa. Among the first acts of the new organization were the purchase of the property of the Lake Tahoe Transportation Company (a Bliss company owning various lake vessels, wharves and machine shops) and the acquisition of the salvaged railroad material from Glenbrook and Bijou. By contractual agreement with the Truckee Lumber Co., a right-of-way was secured across their lands in the Truckee River basin, and construction of the road commenced in April 1899. Work continued during the summer and fall of that year, then was suspended during the winter months. In the spring the job was finished, and on May 1, 1900, the road was formally opened, thus meeting one of the requirements of the lumber company's contract.

Unlike previous railroads in the Tahoe region, the LTR&TCo's new line was a tourist railroad right from the beginning. It was operated during the tourist season (from May 15 to November 15, annually), and tourists comprised the bulk of its business. Of the freight hauled, there was little except forest products. The Truckee Lumber Company was the largest customer with major operations at Ward Creek and later Squaw Valley, and there were some independent contractors working private or Bliss holdings of timber, but by and large it was the great American tourist who became the mainstay of the line. At Lake Tahoe, trains ran out on a long pier so passengers could be delivered right at boat side; then the graceful and stately steamer *Tahoe* would ply the waters for pick-ups and deliveries at the various resorts along the shore line. In its early days, trains also made short side trips down the branch to Tahoe City, a hop-skip-and-a-jump north of the famous Tahoe Tavern.

At times, when the weather seemed favorable, the seasonal period would be extended, but almost inevitably difficulties with snow would be encountered. One early season trip created big head-

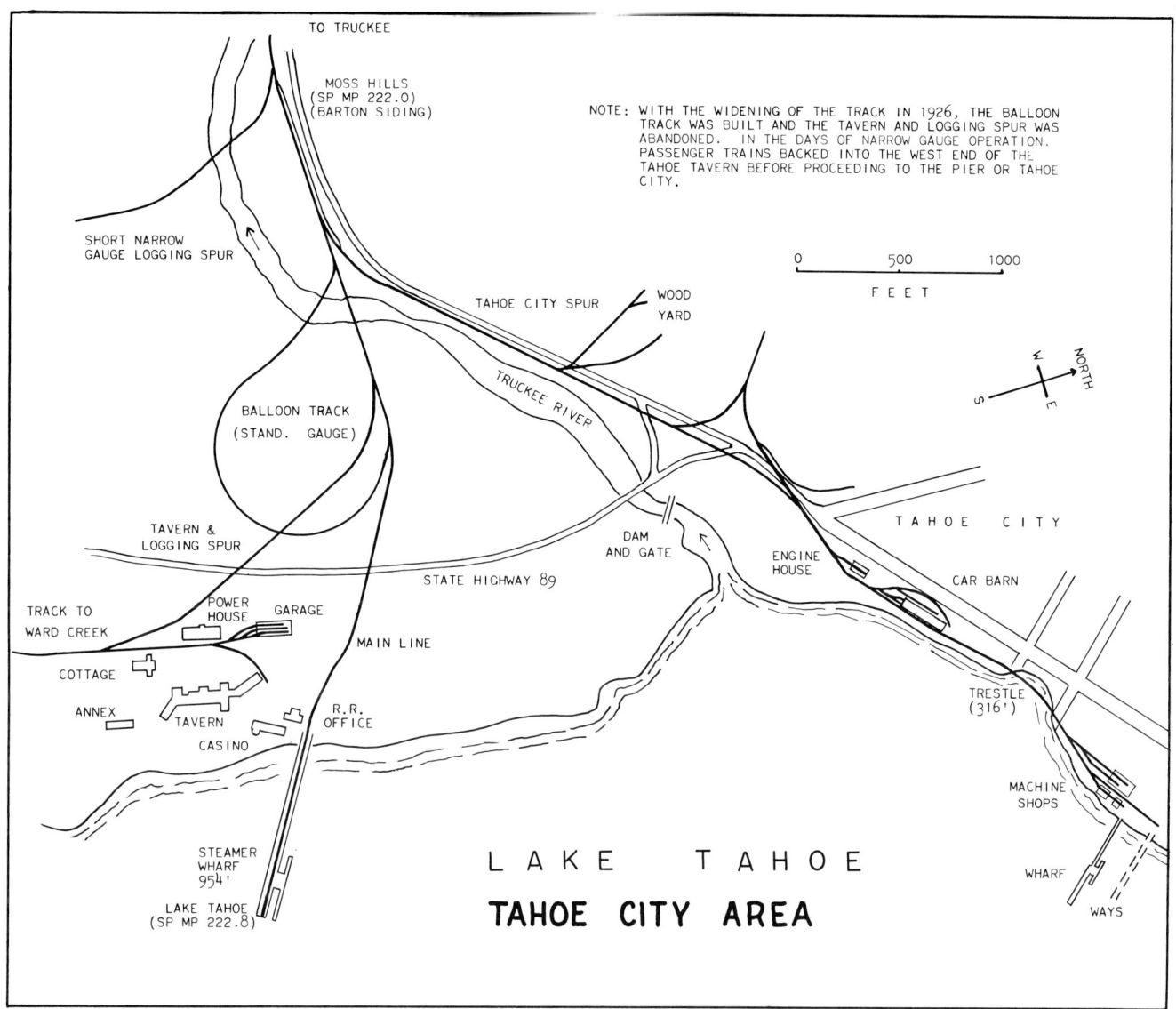

lines on April 1, 1903, when the train became lost. It had left Truckee at 3:00 P.M. the previous afternoon, and nothing had been heard since that time. People became alarmed; snow was on the ground, a storm was brewing, and the Truckee River was swollen with spring freshets. Grave fears were felt as to the probable fate of the train with its 12 people aboard, including two ladies from San Francisco. Searching parties were organized and started out on snowshoes, one from each end of the line, in an attempt to locate the missing train and its occupants. They found it sitting peacefully in a cloud of smoke and steam in the midst of a big snow drift about 10 miles from Truckee, the passengers comfortably ensconced inside while the storm raged.

In addition to the problem of heavy snow, the railroad also suffered occasionally from high water on Lake Tahoe. A particularly severe storm in June 1907 caused considerable damage to the road's facilities at Tahoe City.

In 1903, when the Truckee Lumber Company started cutting timber on Ward Creek, about four miles south of Tahoe City, the lumber company built a branch line down the shore and up Ward Creek. The LTR&TCo supplied the rail and hauled the logs to their main line for 28¢ per 1000 board foot measure. Later, when the camp was shifted over into Squaw Valley in 1909, another lumber spur was constructed to service the new area. It is interesting to note that the Ward Creek spur became an issue before the I.C.C. in 1914

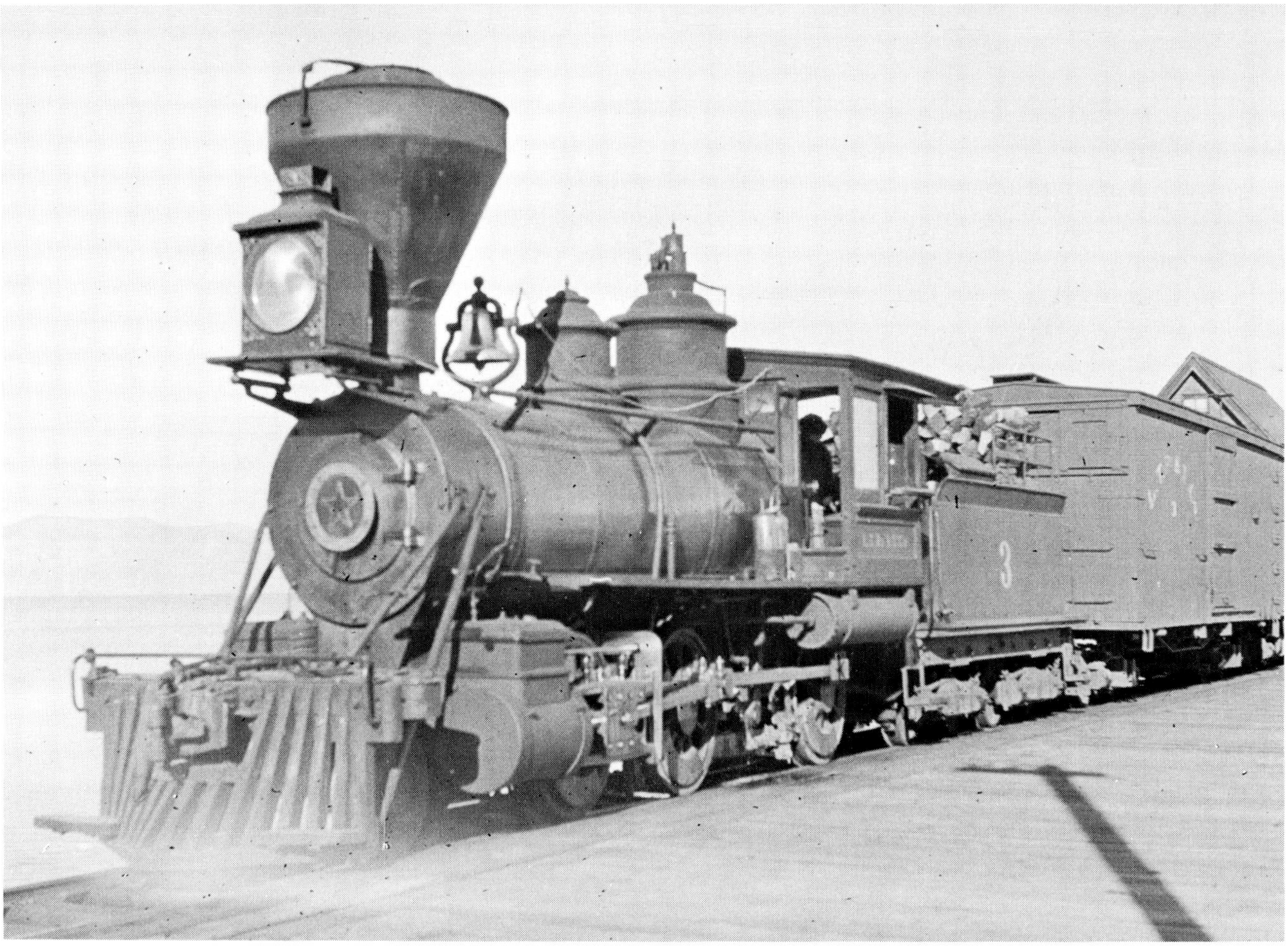

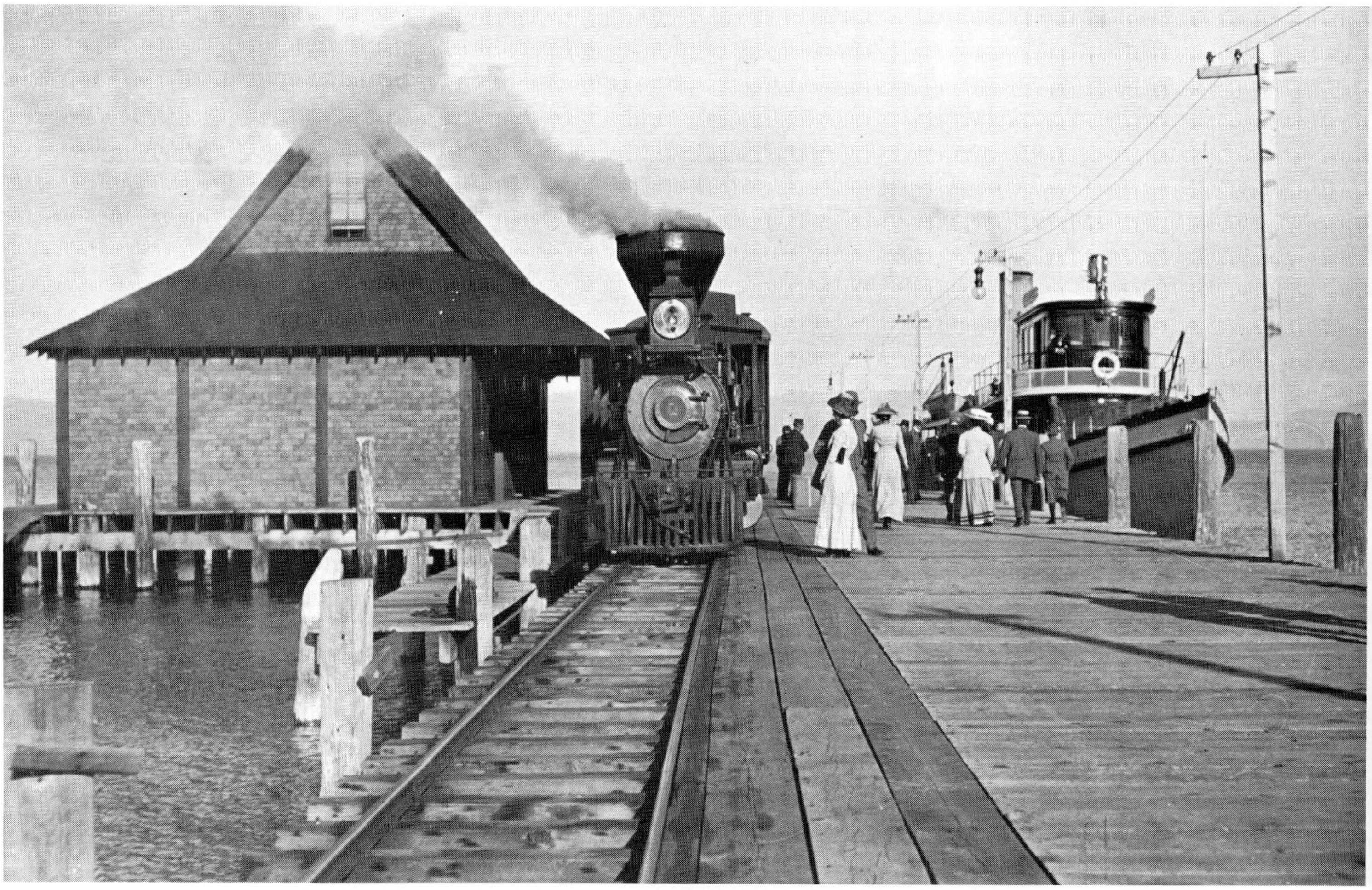

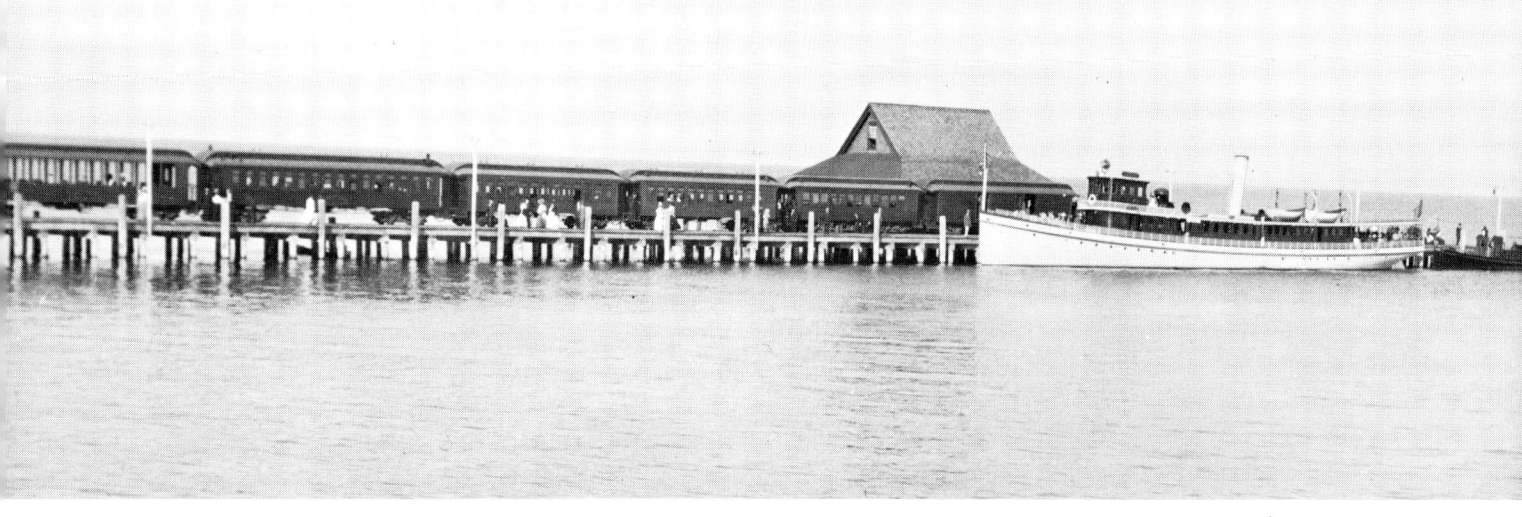

The Lake Tahoe Railway & Transportation Co.'s narrow-gauge railroad between Truckee and Tahoe City was primarily a tourist hauler from the very beginning. A modicum of freight and some traffic in forest products rounded out the road's utility. To facilitate interchange of passengers, baggage, trunks and valises from train to boat for the further voyage to individual lake ports, the railway was extended onto a long wharf near Tahoe Tavern, where these pictures were taken about 1908.

At *top, left*, No. 3 stands ready to depart as soon as homeward bound passengers have completed the transfer, as also is No. 4 *(bottom, left)* which has met the *Tahoe*, Lake Tahoe's largest and most luxurious passenger steamer. In reverse procedure, an inbound 6-car train has just arrived *(above)* while the *Tahoe* waits to pick up the stragglers. Note the open observation car at rear, a feature summer attraction while riding through the spectacular Truckee River Canyon. The clanging bell of highly polished No. 3 *(below)* indicates that she is just pulling out on the pier to end her run, while the little boy in the foreground races the engine to her stop. (Above: *Bob Stein Collection;* All Others: *Stanley Palmer Photos.*)

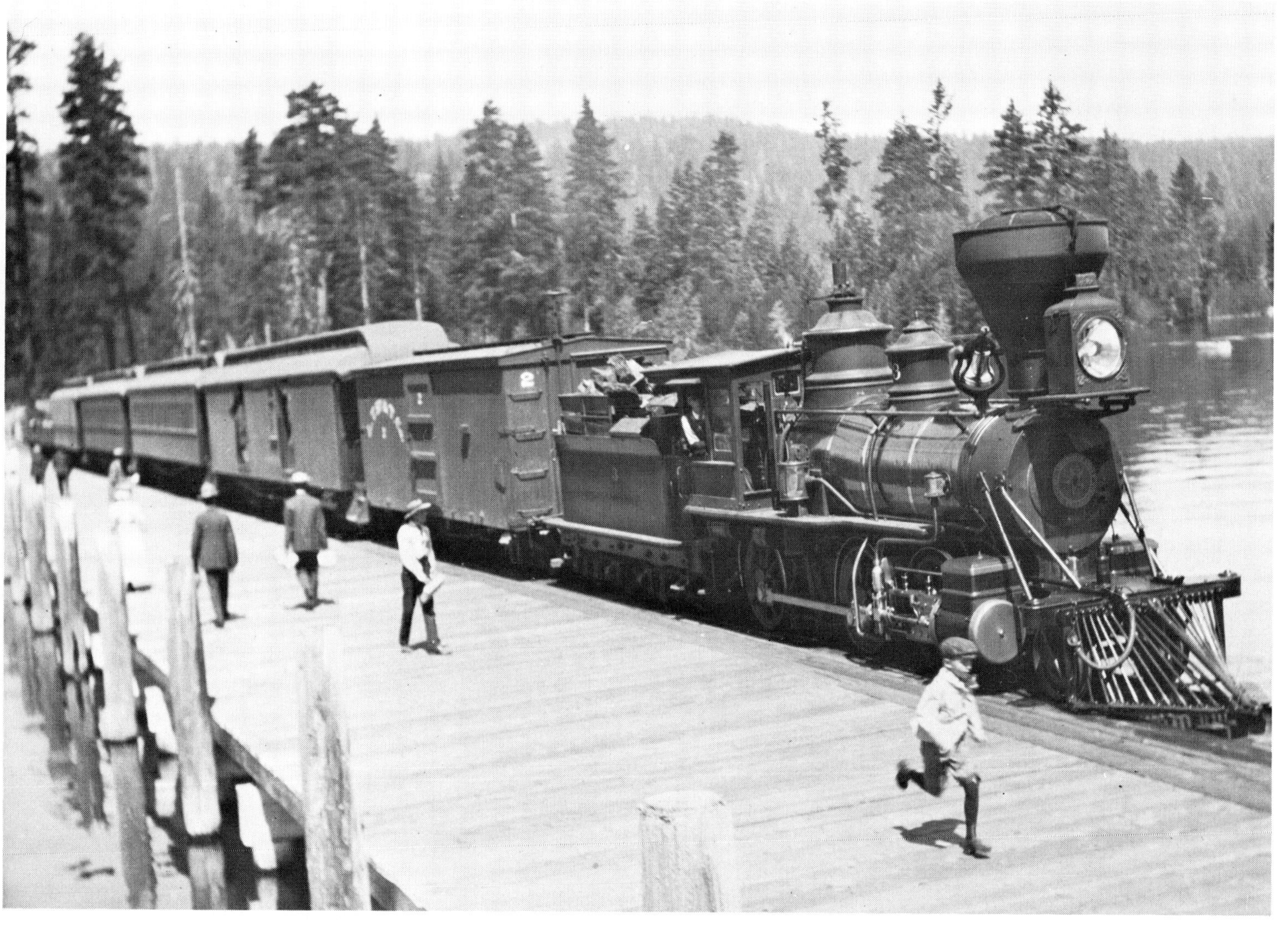

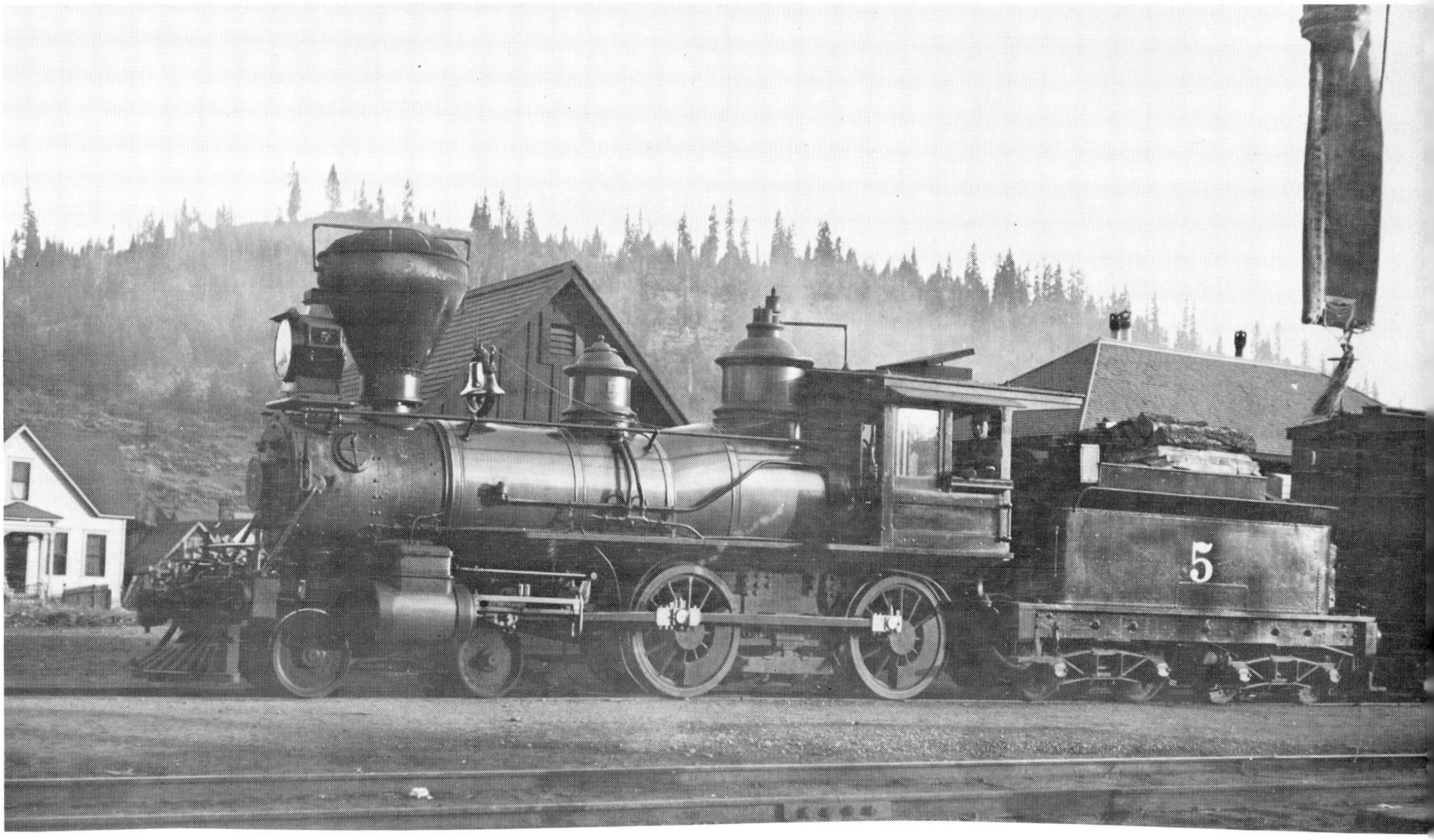

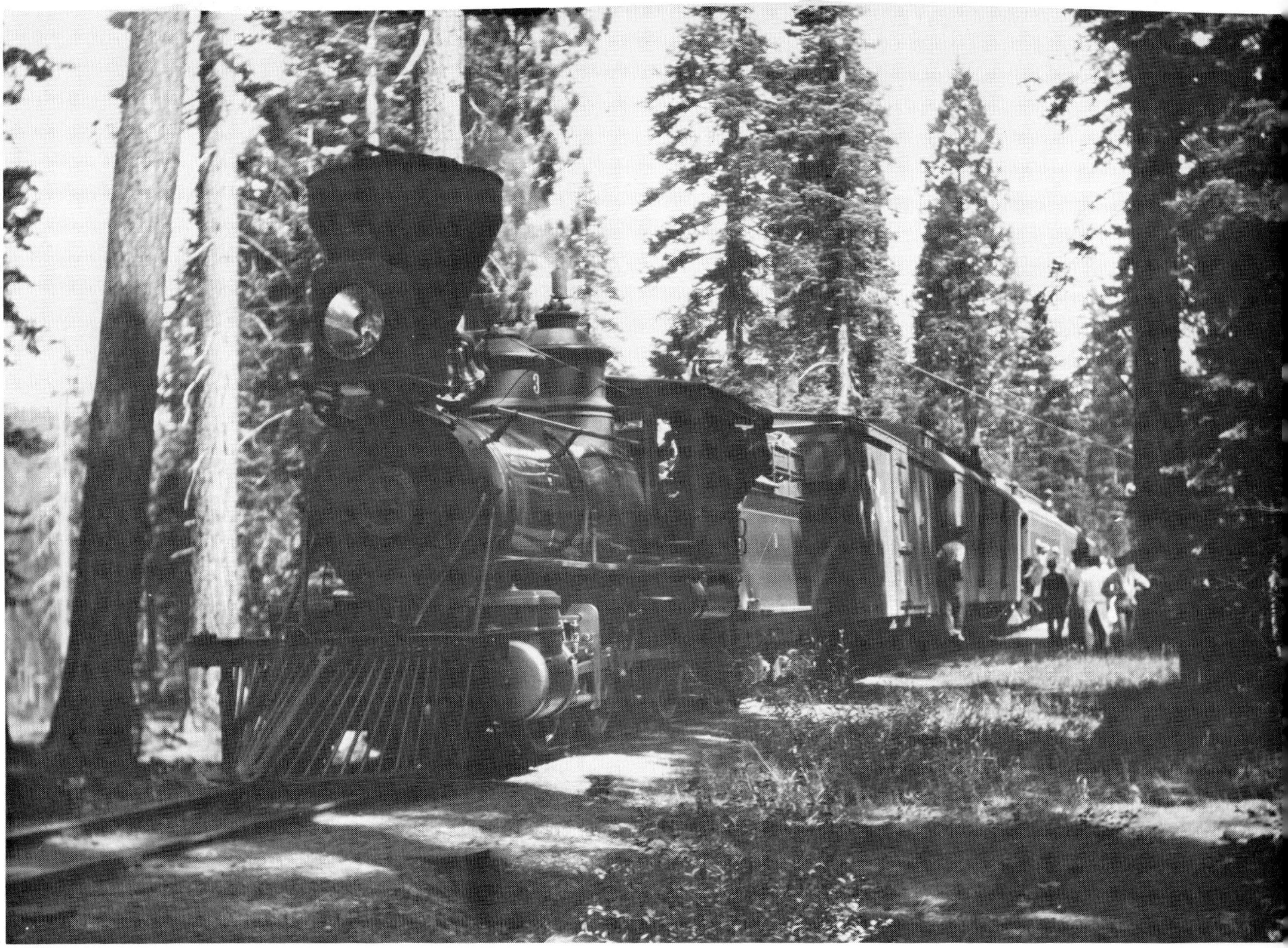

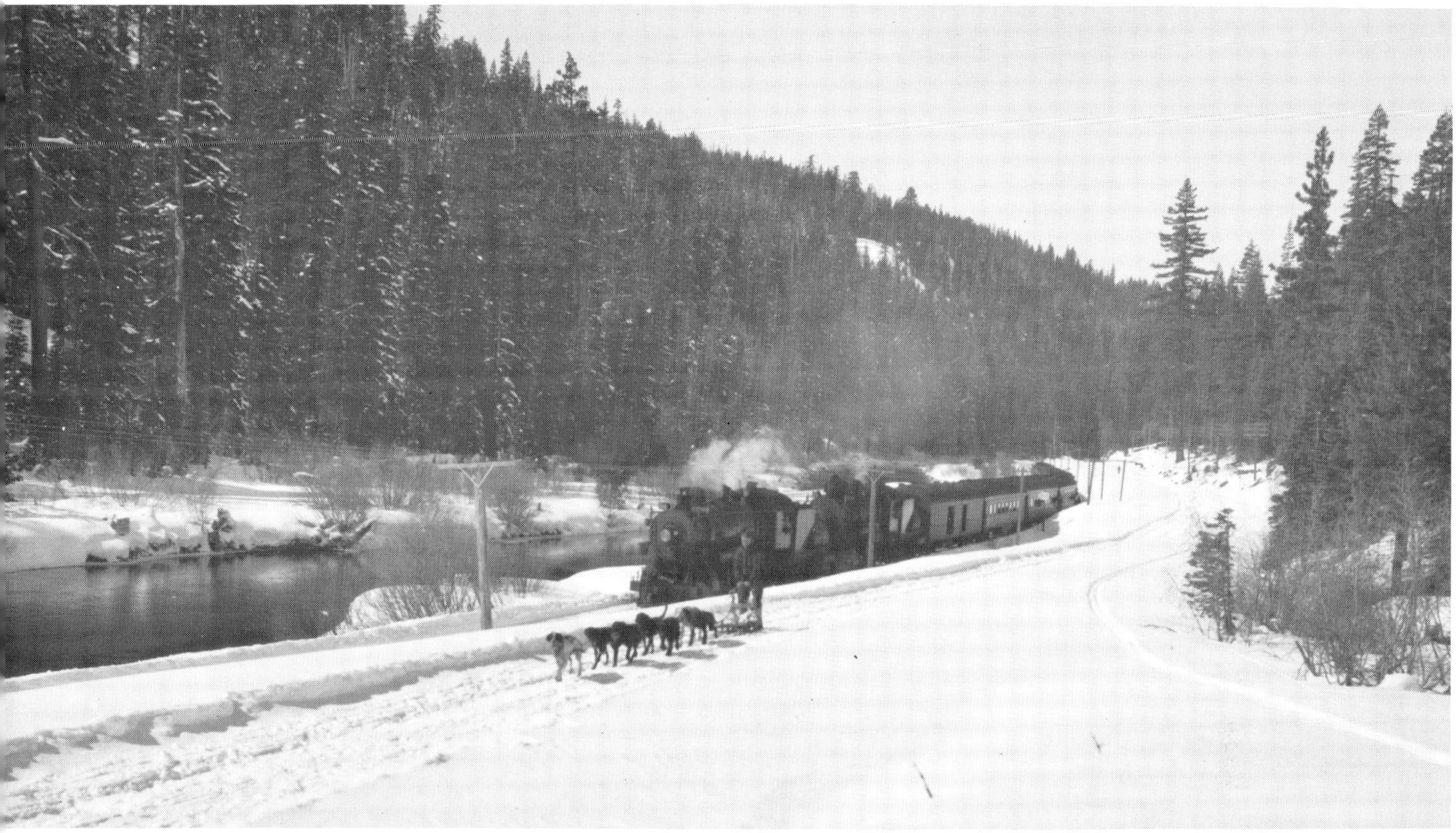

The canvas covered spout of the water tank dangles in the foreground *(top, left)* as LTR&TCo. No. 5 awaits the moment of departure from Truckee station in the year 1908. One hour later and 15 miles distant she will pull into the Tahoe Tavern stop, near which *(left, below)* No. 3 has stopped with her train in a wooded glade. In the early days of the railroad's operations, trains continued on to Tahoe City *(below)* where the company's engine house, car barn and shops were located. *(Two Left Photos: S. G. Palmer; Below: George D. Oliver Photo.)*

In 1925 the railroad was leased to the Southern Pacific, and in 1926 Pullmans operated over the newly widened tracks. In the wintry view *(above)* in 1928, a double headed SP winter sport special and dog sled were posed by the Truckee River. *(Southern Pacific Photo.)*

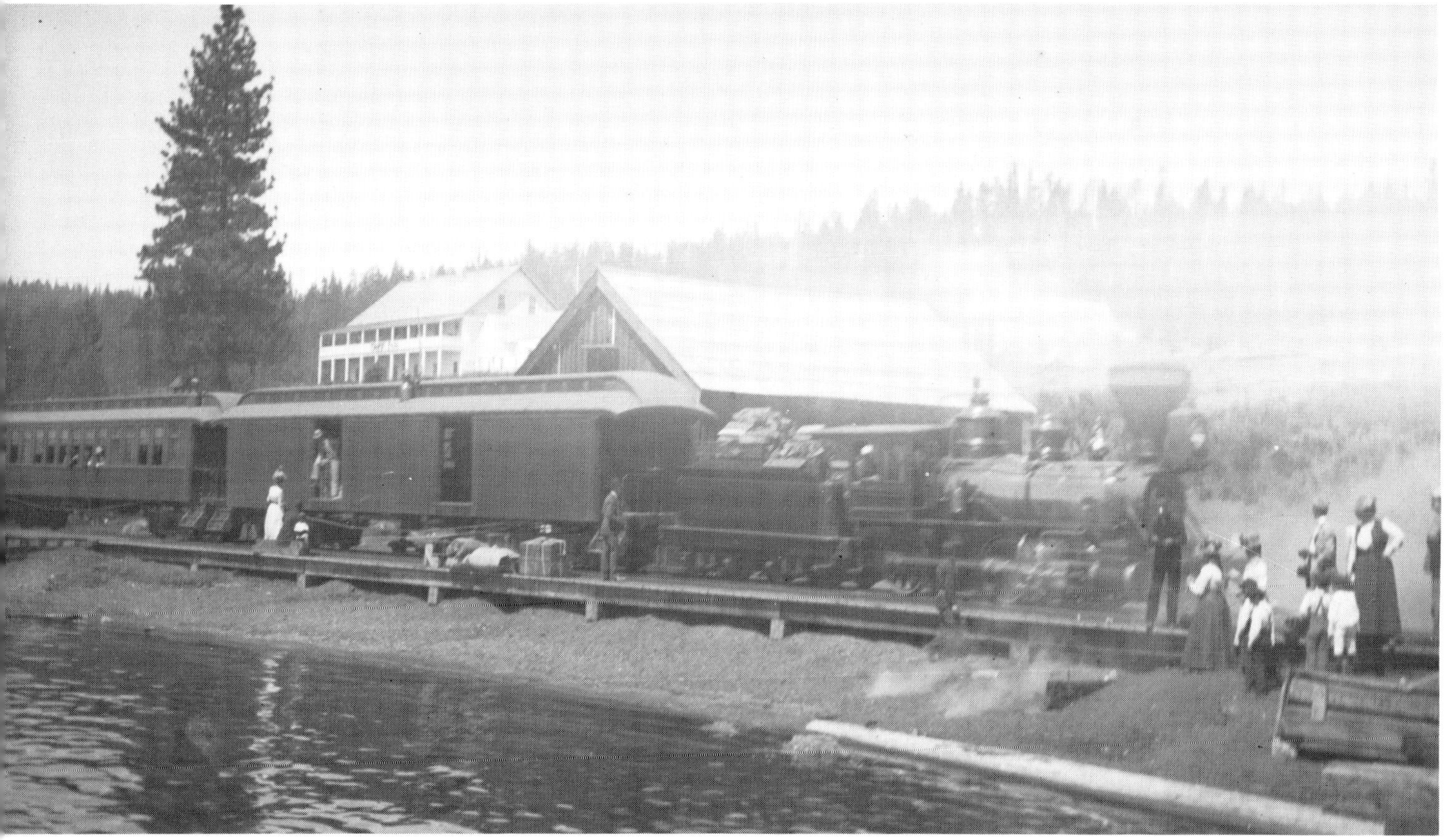

while that body was conducting a general investigation of railroad-owned steamship lines in competing transportation. When it was pointed out that the spur was used only for hauling wood for fuel to Tahoe City, that the steamer did not serve any point reached by the spur, and that there was no question of parallel service by each facility, the I.C.C. authorized continued ownership of the boat line as an extension of the railroad.

Passenger business rapidly increased until the advent of improved highways in the area. During the summer of 1915 there were four carded round trips daily; by the 1920's these were cut to three. Excursions were always a popular pastime; many were operated from Reno during the 1900's, and by May 1923 a circle tour was evolved at an advertised price of $7.25. Starting from Reno, the tourist took the SP to Truckee, rode the narrow gauge to Tahoe City, the steamer to Glenbrook, a bus to Carson City, then the V&T back home—a variety not frequently encountered, either in transportation or in scenery.

In 1925 the railroad was leased to the Southern Pacific. Immediately over 18,000 circulars went to travel agents all over the country announcing that the old "American Canyon Route" would now become the "Lake Tahoe Route," and that the line would be converted to standard gauge. The conversion of the track gauge became an accomplished fact on May 1, 1926, and in conjunction with the program a balloon loop was installed near the Tahoe Tavern to facilitate the turning of trains. During the summer seasons an overnight Pullman was instituted from Oakland Pier to Tahoe City, but during the winter months there was no change from normal procedures—the branch was generally closed and snows took over the line.

In spite of the changes, the railroad faced the inexorable encroachments of the automotive age. More and more traffic moved over the highway, and finally the line was abandoned on November 10, 1943.

OTHER EARLY (19TH CENTURY) LUMBER RAILROADS IN THE TRUCKEE AREA

All along the upper reaches of the Truckee River and its tributaries, from Donner Summit and/or Lake Tahoe eastward to Verdi, sawmills and lumbering blossomed and flourished following the advent of the Central Pacific Railroad. They were a heterogeneous mixture of sole proprietorships, partnerships and corporations; some large, many small; the successful and the unsuccessful. Initial impetus to their development arose with the demand for ties for the Central Pacific, then later the V&T, and finally the SP as the latter road flung its tracks across the southwest through Arizona. Then, as the railroads developed, people came, settled, discovered gold and other ores, and started mining. The Comstock, already active, went through an expanding period, and exhibited an insatiable hunger for wood, lumber and timber of every description.

In the eight miles between Truckee and Boca alone, at least a dozen sawmills were active in 1876. To bring the logs to the mills, or finished lumber from the mill to the CP railroad for shipment, various forms of transportation were utilized. Some operators boomed their logs down the river; others adopted the V-shaped flume; still others attempted land transportation—ox teams, later railroads and (less frequently) steam wagons.

TRUCKEE LUMBER CO.

Of all of these pioneer operations, one of the earliest, the most successful and the longest lived, was that of the Truckee Lumber Co. Beginning as a partnership between Brickell and Geisendorfer, the first venture was a sawmill located at Coburn's (now Truckee) in March 1867. W. H. Kruger joined the partnership shortly afterward, eventually replacing Geisendorfer as an active participant. The full story of the rapid development, expansion and coordination of the widespread activities of their enterprise has yet to be recorded, for their influence ultimately extended to a plant in Oregon, a new 150-foot lumber steamer (the *Truckee*) operating between Tillamook Bay and San Francisco in 1890, and in later years a plant near Oroville. Around 1910 a subsidiary, Butte & Plumas Railway Co., constructed a narrow gauge logging railroad to Stanwood (30 miles) and to Granite Basin (50 miles) which, together with the parent Truckee Lumber Co. was absorbed into the Swayne Lumber Company through acquisition of the stock in 1916. Of most immediate and primary interest are some of the major activities instituted along the Truckee River basin.

Conner's Fishery, six miles south of Truckee, held no interest for the Truckee Lumber Co., but the timber in the adjoining hills looked mighty appetizing. The timber was acquired, and in the late spring of 1873 a two-mile, 3½-foot gauge horse railroad was constructed to haul logs from the woods to a bluff overlooking the Truckee River. From the top of the bluff, logs were skidded down a chute to the river to be boomed to the mill at Truckee. As cutting extended deeper and deeper into the hills, the little railroad was extended, eventually to be dismantled when the land was cut over.

At Bear Creek (a tributary of the Truckee River) and again at Washington Creek, the same style of operation was repeated in 1883. Later that summer still another horse-drawn road was constructed from a point on the Truckee River three miles south of town and running eastward 1½ miles into the woods.

Dog Valley, near Verdi, was also invaded by the Truckee Lumber Co. in 1883. Purchase of the Crystal Peak Lumber Co. from Katz and Henry not only added timber holdings but a sawmill as well.

Still another large tract of timber was acquired about 11 miles southeast of Truckee, beyond the confines of Martis Valley. Distances were increasing as lands were cut over, and this time makeshift transportation would not suffice. An 11-mile narrow gauge railroad was constructed over which one small locomotive operated, a dozen flat cars being sufficient to handle the carloadings. The tracks were taken up about 1910 when operations in that sector came to an end.

At the turn of the century, the Lake Tahoe Railway and Transportation Company completed its line of railroad from Truckee to Tahoe City thus facilitating rail transportation to all points along the Truckee River between those centers. An agreement between the Truckee Lumber Co. and the railroad granted a right-of-way over the former's lands and also established contract rates for lumber company log movements via the railroad to Truckee. Before the Truckee Lumber Co. began cutting timber at Ward Creek near Tahoe City in 1903-10, it constructed a branch line of railroad to serve the area, over which logs were hauled under contract by the LTR&T Co. When the lumber company moved into Squaw Valley (now the famous ski resort) a short branch was built into that area. For all practical intents and purposes, the Truckee Lumber Co. ceased to be a railroad operator along the Truckee River Basin, relying solely upon others to meet its requirements.

GEORGE SCHAFFER

As an early lumberman in the Truckee River area, George Schaffer began business by cutting ties for the CP and the V&T, providing employment for 52 men. In 1872 he constructed a 3½-mile flume from his timber holdings in the Martis Valley to his mill near Truckee, floating the logs to the base of operations. Misfortune pursued him, however, in the prevalent manner of fires at each of two successive mills. Determined upon a change, Schaffer established a third mill on Martis Creek, six miles south of Truckee, and used a V-shaped flume to transport the finished lumber to his storage yard one mile east of town.

Since the available timber along the water supply had been logged over, Schaffer constructed a lumber railroad approximately two miles long between the logging camp and the mill. A new locomotive plus four flat cars were purchased in 1886, with which the logs were hauled from the woods to the saws. The entire operation was isolated in the back country far from civilization and communication, and little information concerning it was ever recorded. News was made one day in August 1890 when the "brakes gave way" causing the locomotive to run down hill and crash into some standing cars. H. H. Jacobs, the engineer, was injured and the locomotive was laid up for a few days pending repairs by the company blacksmith.

Just how long the short road operated, or when its activities were suspended, has not been determined. The annals were left in the woods; and the woods won't tell.

RICHARDSON BROTHERS

Warren and George W. Richardson were no novice lumbermen when they came to the Truckee River basin in 1874. They had had an operating mill at Summit Valley, near Norden on the west side of Donner Pass, before moving it to the upper waters of Martis Creek, about a mile east of the future site of Schaffer's mill. The brothers were capable and imaginative, and when a 1½-mile logging railroad was found desirable to connect their woods loading area with the mill pond, the brothers Richardson improvised one from available materials on hand.

Instead of using iron rails to form the track, 10-inch logs were laid end-to-end and partly buried in the ground to maintain the gauge. Warren

Richardson designed the "engine," using concave wheels to ride atop the log rails. Reportedly the traction of the locomotive itself was so great it could climb grades of up to 16% without a load.

Cars were deemed unnecessary (possibly foolhardy) on this short railroad-without-a-switch; in their stead a chute was fashioned of saplings and laid parallel to the log rails on the outside. By means of a cable attached to the logs, the locomotive dragged its cumbersome consist along the chute from woods to mill pond. A writer for an 1883 guide book, after watching the locomotive snake its loads through the forest, was moved to describe, ". . . its three zinc covered cylinders gleaming in the sun like eyes of some hideous dragon, its heavy flanged wheels reminding (one) of horrid tales of the Juggernaut. Slowly and ponderously it moves over its heavy log tramway . . ."

However crude or antediluvian their monster may have appeared, the Richardson brothers apparently were well satisfied with the results obtained. As a concession to the handling of milled lumber (as opposed to logs), a steam wagon was utilized to haul the finished products from the mill to the lumber yards and box factory at Martis Creek Station on the Central Pacific Railway, four miles east of Truckee. Both the locomotive and the steam wagon appear to have outlasted the lumbering operation itself, as no mention has been found of any later equipment.

PACIFIC LUMBER AND WOOD COMPANY (PL&WCO) – CLINTON

Clinton (or Camp 18, as it was called locally) was listed on the Central Pacific's timetables as a station stop during the 1880's. Located 10 miles east of Truckee and 1.8 miles east of Boca, it was the site of the mill of the Pacific Lumber and Wood Co. (not to be confused with the Pacific Wood, Lumber and Fluming Company operated on the east side of Mt. Rose in Nevada and owned by Mackay, Fair, Flood and O'Brien).

The enterprise was established in 1870 by G. N. Folsom and H. W. Bragg, although control subsequently passed to Fred Burckhalter. Timber was cut in the mountains along Juniper Creek (to the south) and the logs were hauled by horses and oxen to the top of the bluff overlooking the mill at Clinton. A steep chute, 1,600 feet long, dropped the timber down the incline to the mill pond below at the then astonishing speeds of from 35-55 miles per hour. One eyewitness account of 1874 waxed eulogistic over the novelty of the activity, proclaiming "the rapidity of descent is a sight worth seeing — greased lightning is nothing compared to it."

In common with the majority of sawmills of the times, the mill at Clinton was consumed by fire on numerous occasions. The initial conflagration occurred in 1873, scarcely three years from the commencement of operations, but failed to stir up much comment. A second holocaust in 1879 attracted far more attention when the heat from the blaze warmed the coaches of a passing CP train. Moreover, the rebuilding embodied such a number of improvements and innovations, visitors from Boca and Truckee were attracted to witness the trial run on opening day. In addition to the exhilaration of watching the logs hurtling down the chute to splash spectacularly into the water below, interest was expressed in the new telephone line which extended from the mill to the woods camp as well as to the PL&W Co's. offices in Truckee, where a general banking business was also conducted.

When Burckhalter joined the organization during the 1870's, he viewed with disfavor the slow and cumbersome procedure of hauling logs with horses and oxen. A railroad would be a faster and better solution to the problem, he reasoned, and it needn't be a large one either. So a narrow gauge railroad was constructed (locally called the Clinton Narrow Gauge Railroad), costing $40,000, and extending from the top of the chute in a southerly direction along the west side of Juniper Creek. Placed in operation on September 1, 1878, it was claimed to be the first steam logging railroad along the Truckee River, lending credence to Burckhalter's contention of having originated the method of logging by means of a narrow gauge railroad.

The business of the Pacific Lumber and Wood Company prospered and flourished. By May of 1883 timber cutters were operating seven miles deep in the woods and the little railroad had been extended to accommodate the retreating loading platforms. One visiting correspondent seemed less impressed with the activity than he was with the personalities of the people involved. In his writings that year, he reported the work to be in charge of "the immortal Phi Bates, the great bean eater of Long Valley [near Plumas Junction, California, on the N-C-O], and the man who has succeeded in hatching out and raising more grasshoppers than any other man now living. He seriously contemplated giving up the hopper business and trying his hands at crickets, but his neighbors persuaded him (with clubs) to leave the valley and he now presides over our camp. . . . His stentorian voice may be heard calling 'Time, boys'." Then, in more proper manner, the correspondent went on to acknowledge the success of Bates as a superintendent.

For a number of years some thought prevailed about building the railroad all the way to Lake Tahoe to develop the tourist business. Each natural extension of the road carried it closer in that direction. With the opening of the 1886 logging season, another extension was projected into a new timber area, and the end seemed almost in sight when suddenly, two years later, the mill at Clinton burned again. Incendiaries were blamed, for there was considerable bad feeling aroused over the hiring of two Chinese cooks. Nothing could be proved, however; the feelings subsided, and the mill was rebuilt.

Accidents of record on the railroad were practically non-existent. It is known that in November 1890 the brakes of a logging train failed to hold, and the cars jumped the track on a curve. One brakeman was fatally crushed by falling logs.

By 1892 the little road was 10 miles long and stretched to within three miles of Hot Springs (Brockway) at Lake Tahoe. Two locomotives and 10 flat cars were required to keep the mill supplied, while a total of 150 men were recruited to keep the operations going.

Mrs. M. E. Burkhalter managed the property for many years, but the railroad was never expanded above its 10-mile length, and the rails never reached the shores of Lake Tahoe. In 1901 the line was abandoned, and shortly after the machinery in the mill at Clinton was sold. Efforts were made by a son of Mrs. Burkhalter to sell the empty mill building and the timber lands to an eastern syndicate for a box factory, but before the deal could be consummated, a fire of unknown origin destroyed the mill building in June 1903. The premises were never reactivated, and the Clinton Narrow Gauge Railroad together with its bean eating superintendent have vanished into the limbo of forgotten times.

MISCELLANEA

There are other unconfirmed reports of early lumber railroads in the Truckee River area during the latter part of the nineteenth century. The Boca Mill and Ice Company operated a short line at Boca, and the Nevada and California Lumber Company is said to have built a flume together with a 5½-mile railroad in 1873 to serve its mill some eight miles to the north of Truckee. No information has been found thus far to permit either confirmation or denial of the latter's existence.

Sierra Nevada Wood and Lumber Company

As the timber in the vicinity of Incline along the north shore of Lake Tahoe started to become depleted toward the latter part of the nineteenth century (see SNW&L Co.—Incline), the Hobart interests searched elsewhere for additional holdings with which to continue their operations. They found them, to the northwest of Truckee, in the vicinity of Independence Lake around the headwaters of Prosser Creek, the Little Truckee River and Onion Creek. Following the close of the 1894 cutting season at Lake Tahoe, the moving job was started. Equipment was dismounted and removed; buildings were dismantled; the narrow gauge railway and equipment were salvaged and stockpiled.

Headquarters were centered at Overton (subsequently known as Hobart Mills), 6½ miles to the north of Truckee near the upper reaches of Prosser Creek. Here the mills were reconstructed, and during 1896 a new standard gauge railroad was built between Overton and Truckee to service the new facilities. The road followed the western contour of the valley, was well ballasted, and contained a ruling northbound grade of 2.9%, southbound of 2.4%. The maximum curve was 18° and a 1,000-foot trestle crossed the lake formed by the Bragg and Folsom dam, previously constructed on Lower Prosser Creek. (Water from a dam constructed in 1960-61 will completely inundate this area.)

By the fall of 1896 George Giffin was making regular daily runs with a 28-ton locomotive over the 40-pound steel rails of the new line. On October 10 a special train took a large crowd out from Truckee to a christening ball for the new town of Overton. The sawmill had just been erected (although no work would be done until the following summer), and the company's connecting narrow gauge logging railroad (which

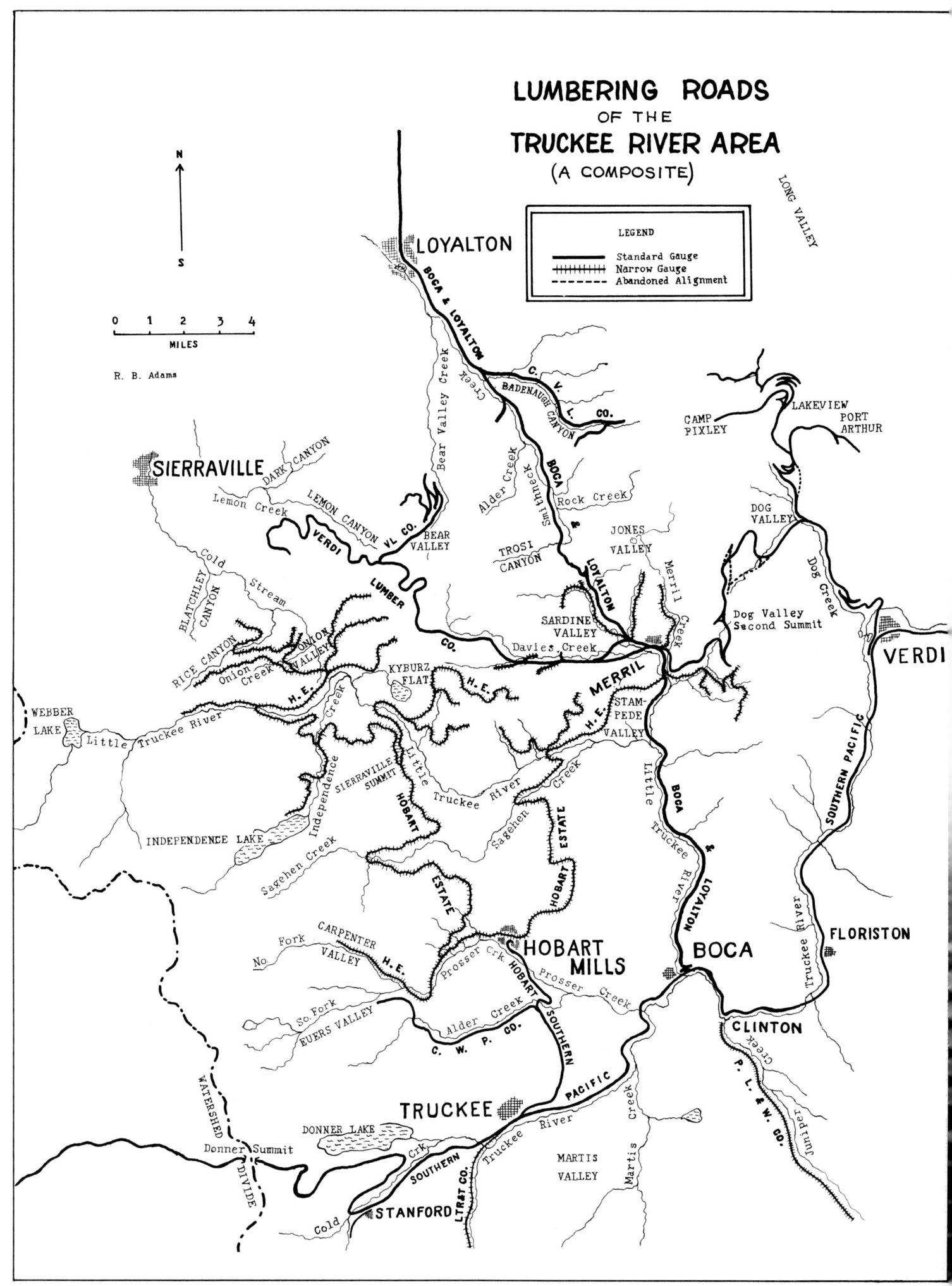

utilized the old equipment from the Lake Tahoe area) was already stretching its steel tentacles into the woods.

Changes and improvements on the standard gauge line were to follow. Not to be outdone by the Central Pacific with its 40 miles of snowsheds, Captain Overton was busy in November 1899 erecting similar structures over certain portions of his abbreviated artery. Moreover, the light 40-pound rail rapidly proved to be insufficient support for the heavy tonnage derived from the mill, and it was subsequently replaced with 60-pound rail.

George D. Oliver became superintendent of the Hobart Mills in 1900, went on to succeed Charles T. Bliss as manager in 1914, and remained with the organization in that capacity until 1936. His hobby was photography, and some of the most striking and interesting pictures of the Lake Tahoe and Hobart areas have come from his camera. Oliver's "private car" was small and self-propelled —a three-wheel gasoline speeder which could be operated on either of the two track gauges. His son, Charlie, recalls with delight various junkets to Truckee on the novel contrivance where he was met by Charles Keyser, manager of the Lake Tahoe Railway, who took him on to Tahoe City.

Hobart Mills, together with its suburbs of Flumeville and Ragtown, attained official cognizance with the establishment of a post office in 1900, a stature that survived until 1958. Hobart was the terminus of the standard gauge railroad from Truckee as well as headquarters for the SNW&L Co's narrow gauge lines which reached into the woods to the various logging camps. The first of these to be established ran east and north to the banks of Sagehen Creek, which it crossed and followed to the junction with the Little Truckee River. A second line headed west up Prosser Creek and followed the North Fork into Carpenter Valley. As operations expanded, the Carpenter Valley line became truncated into a branch by extension of the main line northward to the upper reaches of Sagehen Creek, Independence Creek, the Little Truckee River, and on into Onion Valley. Some years later a number of branches were extended into the hills and through Cold Creek Canyon, to reach within a few miles of the Verdi Lumber Company's railroad. Another cutting area to the north of the Little Truckee, but farther east, was reached by an additional branch from a point known as Sierraville Summit.

Under normal operating procedures, the main line was considered to run from Overton to Sierraville Summit (18 miles), and narrow gauge rod locomotives Nos. 5 and 6 (American and Mogul types, respectively), frequently operated as double headers over this section of the line. From Sierraville Summit into the woods, Shay locomotives normally took over, for though slower, they had additional power for the steeper grades and greater flexibility for the sharper curves.

Logging railroads, and particularly feeder lines to more remote camps, were lightly constructed and subject to change virtually without notice. Because of the temporary nature of their existence, as little heavy earthen or other work was exercised in their construction as possible; hence few scars were left on the landscape with their passing. Students of such lines frequently delve into musty archives for years to uncover traces of temporary trackage, flimsily bolstered on log trestlework, climbing seemingly impossible ravines or negotiating the faces of apparently insurmountable escarpments. Mileage figures for such lines often varied on virtually a day-to-day basis. The SNW&L CO's road was no exception to this rule, but generally speaking the total trackage expanded from approximately 8 miles of line in 1899 to 20 miles in 1908 and 26 miles in 1923.

A major change in corporate affairs occurred in 1917. The Sierra Nevada Wood and Lumber Company was dissolved and ceased to exist; all properties were transferred to the Hobart Estate Company, principal stockholder of the predecessor corporation.

Operations under the new ownership continued on an expanding basis. The east leg of the narrow gauge from Hobart to the confluence of Sagehen Creek and the Little Truckee River was rebuilt to sturdier specifications and the tracks extended during the late 1920's and early 1930's. Construction proceeded to the northeast to Merrill (at Davies Creek) and on north into Sardine Valley with branches extending in virtually every direction to new timber areas. Since the Boca & Loyalton Railroad had abandoned its line in 1916 and the Verdi Lumber Company its road in 1927, many segments of the roadbeds of these predecessor lines were rehabilitated and utilized by the narrow gauge.

Fire was the biggest threat to the little railroad. Oscar Lindsay, a Hobart veteran, recalls that there was never a summer without a fire of consequence.

One such conflagration swept through a canyon and consumed the railroad bridge along the way, effectively isolating a locomotive, a number of cars and a complete lumber camp until the bridge could be rebuilt. All available hands were required to join in the transfer of supplies around the burned sector until the bridge could be replaced. On another occasion, fire chose a Sunday afternoon while everyone was away to leap over a hill to the south of Merrill and burn locomotives Nos. 7 and 8 complete with engine shed in which they had been housed for the weekend.

In contrast to many lumber lines, the railroad became noted for the superiority of its maintenance by regular track gangs. There were some difficulties in construction, however, and some dire consequences, particularly when unauthorized short-cuts were used. One such circumstance involved Pat Thibault, construction foreman, who was instructed to build a bridge following a particular design. Pat refused, considering it unsafe; but a short time later the identical bridge was installed while Pat was on one of his three-day drunks. Several years went by uneventfully, until one day about 1915 an engine pushed a string of cars across the structure and the bridge deck gave way, dumping the locomotive 50 feet to the ground. The engine was wrecked, but was later repaired; not so the fireman, who subsequently died of his injuries.

Undoubtedly the railroad received its proportionate share of miscellaneous incidents and excitements. Occasional runaway trains stimulated action and attention. At the end of each season the annual scavenger train was assigned the job of collecting all logs along the right-of-way which had fallen off the cars during the cutting season, including the pile-up at one particular curve which was notorious for such occurrences. With the unprotected right-of-way common to most logging roads, sheep also presented a problem; one flock, herded by a Basque, crossed the tracks just as a loaded logging train rounded the curve on a downhill grade, and 30 or more sheep were ground under the siderods and wheels. Even the passive turntable pit at Hobart shared in the commotions by being the unwilling recipient of two different locomotives on separate occasions for diverse reasons—ice on the track rendered the locomotive brakes ineffective in one instance, while the other was attributed to the absent-mindedness of an experienced engineer in stepping off his engine without first "tying her down."

Operations of the standard gauge railroad under the Hobart Estate Company also received their share of attention. Probably the most major change was instituted in 1930 when it was decided to operate the line from Hobart to Truckee as a common carrier. To carry out this purpose (in order to share in the through rates), the Hobart Southern Railway was formed, on which the I.C.C. bestowed its approval in March 1932. For some time two trains were operated daily with a satisfactory volume of business. For example, 1935 was considered a reasonably good year during which 1,587 cars were moved over the 6½-mile line. Of these 1,420 constituted lumber moving to outside markets, while the balance included such diverse ladings as cattle, sheep and road building machinery.

For almost 40 years Hobart Mills was one of the principal lumber operations in the Truckee River area of California. Many men from other camps worked on the premises, including George Chubbuck and Major Gardner, former lumbermen from the Lake Tahoe area. Then, in 1936, the timber became cut over; the lumber mill was closed; plans for dismantling were made. With the cessation of operations, all activity along the narrow gauge was stilled, and the Hobart Southern Railway went back to the I.C.C. for authority to abandon its standard gauge line. Following official approval, the last train was operated on December 1, 1937.

Today there are still a few buildings standing in good condition at the former location of Hobart Mills for the tourist to see. A lake will shortly cover the valley floor, while the abandoned railroad grades of the Hobart Southern and the little narrow gauge lines are rapidly being reclaimed by the eternal forests, for the products of which they were originally spawned.

CROWN WILLAMETTE PAPER COMPANY

South of Donner Lake, near the headwaters of Cold Creek (not to be confused with Cold Stream near Sierraville or Cold Creek near Bijou), the Crown Willamette Paper Company instituted logging operations in some timber holdings. Late in 1920 they erected a tramway running from the lumber camp in the woods to a station on the Southern Pacific called Stanford, on the southeast side of the Cold Creek curve, a few miles west of Truckee. SP trains took the logs from the end of the tramway to the company's paper mill at Floriston (between Boca and Verdi).

When the area became logged out a few years later, the company shifted its operations to the north of Truckee along Alder Creek and Euers Valley on the South Fork of Prosser Creek. To service the lumber camps, a seven-mile branch line railroad was projected from the SNW&L Co's line, westward up Alder Creek and thence over the ridge into Euers Valley. Under an agreement of August 6, 1924, the paper company was granted the right to operate over the tracks of the SNW&L Co's standard gauge railroad from Truckee to the point where that line crossed Alder Creek, a distance of 3.85 miles. There a junction was made with the CWP Co's line into the woods. Operations were carried on with a 70-ton Shay locomotive until the early 1930's, when the timber gave out and the road was abandoned.

FIBREBOARD PRODUCTS, INC. HOBART MILLS

Post-mortem to the Hobart operations were those of the Fibreboard Products, Inc. (now Fibreboard Paper Products Corporation) in the years immediately following World War II. The company purchased 80,000 acres of timber in the area around Webber Lake and Hobart Mills, and arranged for logs to be cut under contract at a new small mill at Hobart, the cordwood to be shipped to the Fibreboard (paper) plant at Antioch, California. In 1946, to provide transportation from Hobart to Truckee, the company built a new standard gauge railroad on the old right-of-way of the former Hobart Southern Railway, although a problem arose over the crossing of U. S. Highway 40 just east of Truckee. As part of a plan to convert the highway into a four-lane freeway, the railroad refused to commit itself to the construction of an expensive overpass; therefore a grade crossing was arranged under provisions of a temporary permit.

Logs were cut and stored at Hobart. In 1952 and 1953 they were moved in short trains to Truckee, using a General Electric 70-ton diesel locomotive (the first and last diesel locomotive in lumbering service in the area). From Truckee, the Southern Pacific routed the cars to the Antioch plant. Then a change in technology enabled Fibreboard to utilize a newly developed debarking machine which facilitated the production of waste pulpwood and pulp at a lower cost than by logging at Hobart Mills. After 1953 the activity at Hobart dropped to a much lower scale, and in the summer of 1955 the railroad was taken up.

Ironically, today the logs are brought in by truck using an underpass at the location of the former highway crossing. Local experts advise that this underpass would have been entirely suitable for railroad use and could have been constructed for a fraction of the cost of the previously proposed overpass at the time of the grade crossing argument of several years past.

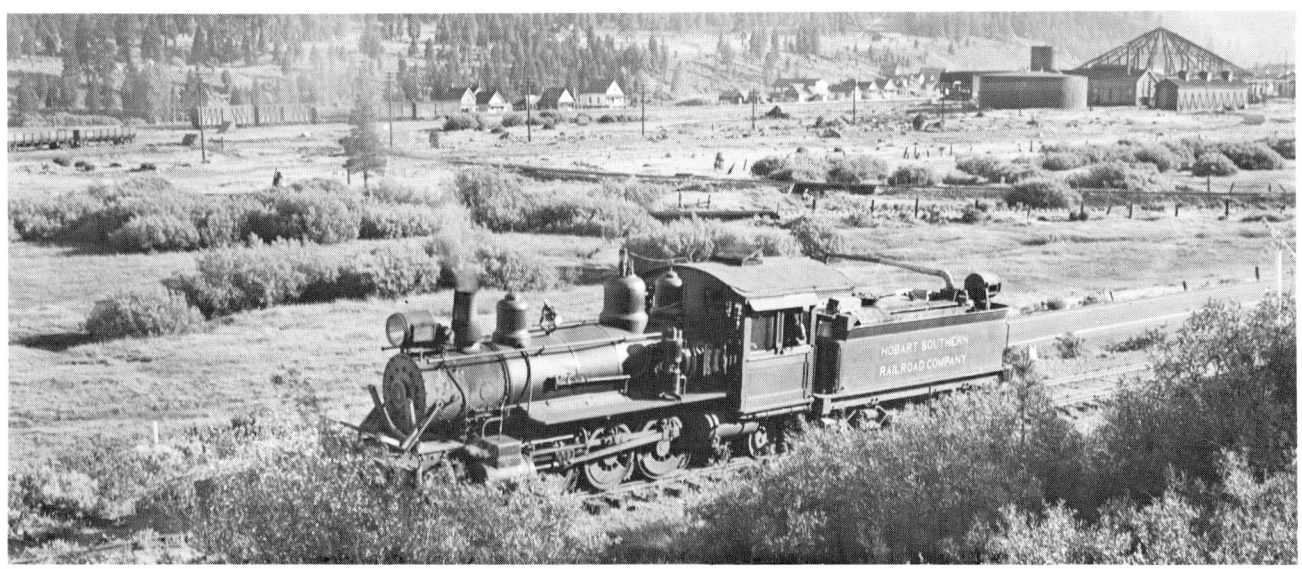

Hobart Southern No. 1 takes water near Truckee in July 1938. Remains of famed Southern Pacific roundhouse can be seen in the distance. *(Guy L. Dunscomb Photo.)*

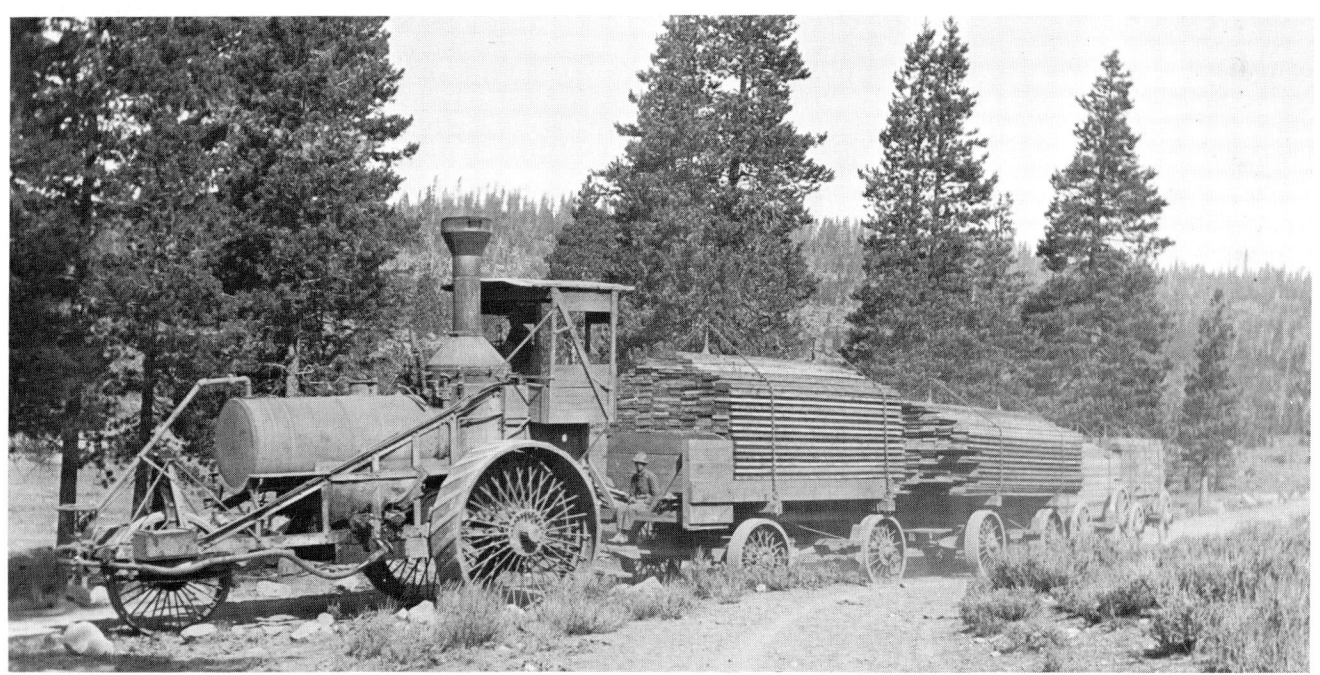

Lumbering operations in the Hobart Mills territory took many and varied forms both before and after the turn of the century. Prior to the advent of railroads, transportation was accomplished with the aid of huge steam tractors, such as the Best *(above)*. An idea of the enormity and power of these machines is amply suggested by the dwarfed figure of the man sitting on the first of the four heavily laden trailers. *(George D. Oliver Photo.)*

Teams of horses were frequently used to bring the logs out of the woods to loading docks, such as the one *(below)* on a branch of the SNW&LCo.'s narrow gauge lines. Note the log skid along the curved path of the roadway to bring logs into position for dumping on the rack. *(George D. Oliver Photo.)*

With improvements in mechanization came the Dolbeer donkey engine *(above, right)* which could snake logs through the trees faster and better than animal power and hoist them for loading on log cars as seen *(right, below)* in the wake of Sierra Nevada Wood & Lumber Co.'s narrow-gauge locomotive No. 6 pulling into Hobart Mills yard. *(George D. Oliver Photos.)*

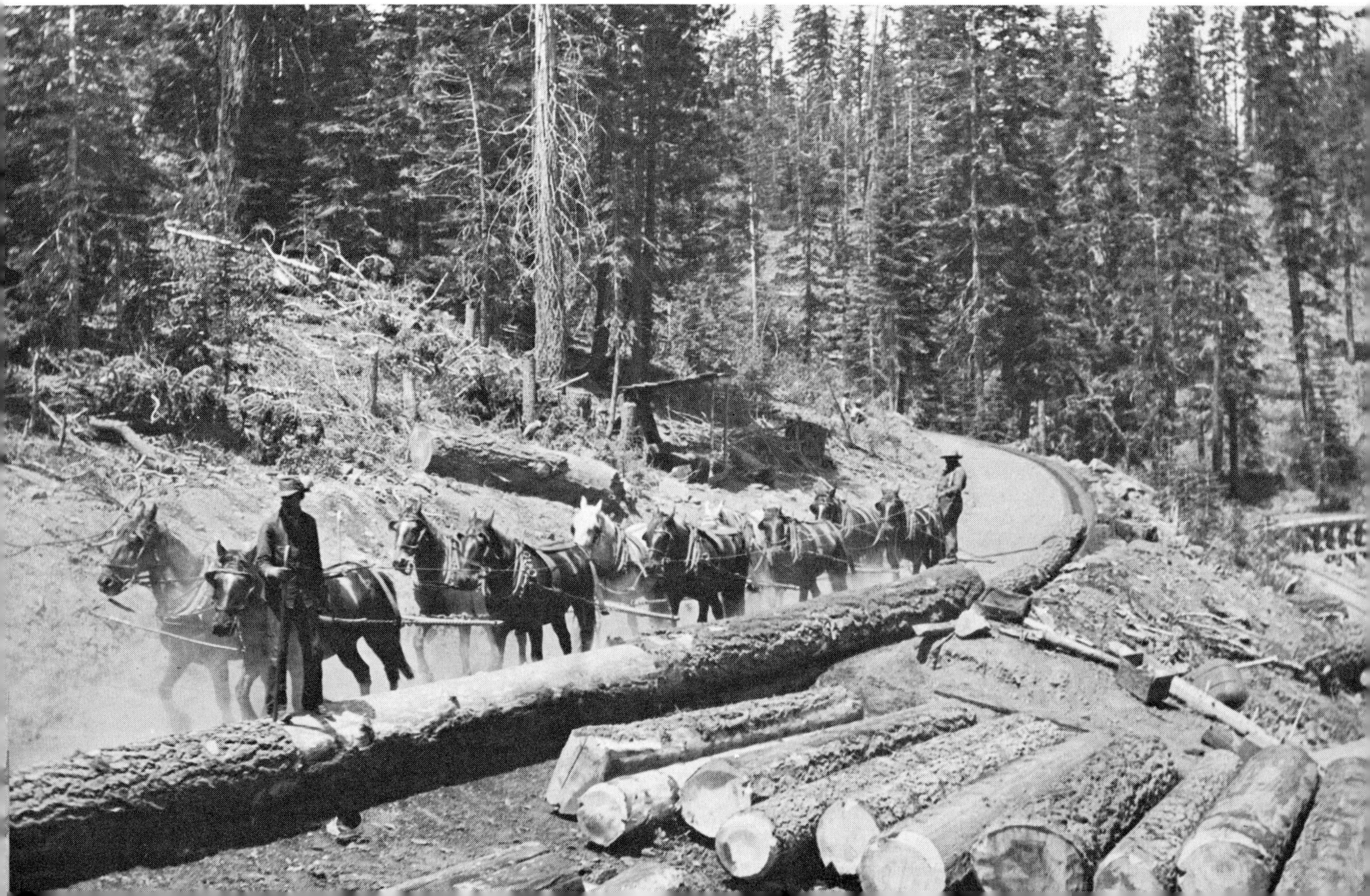

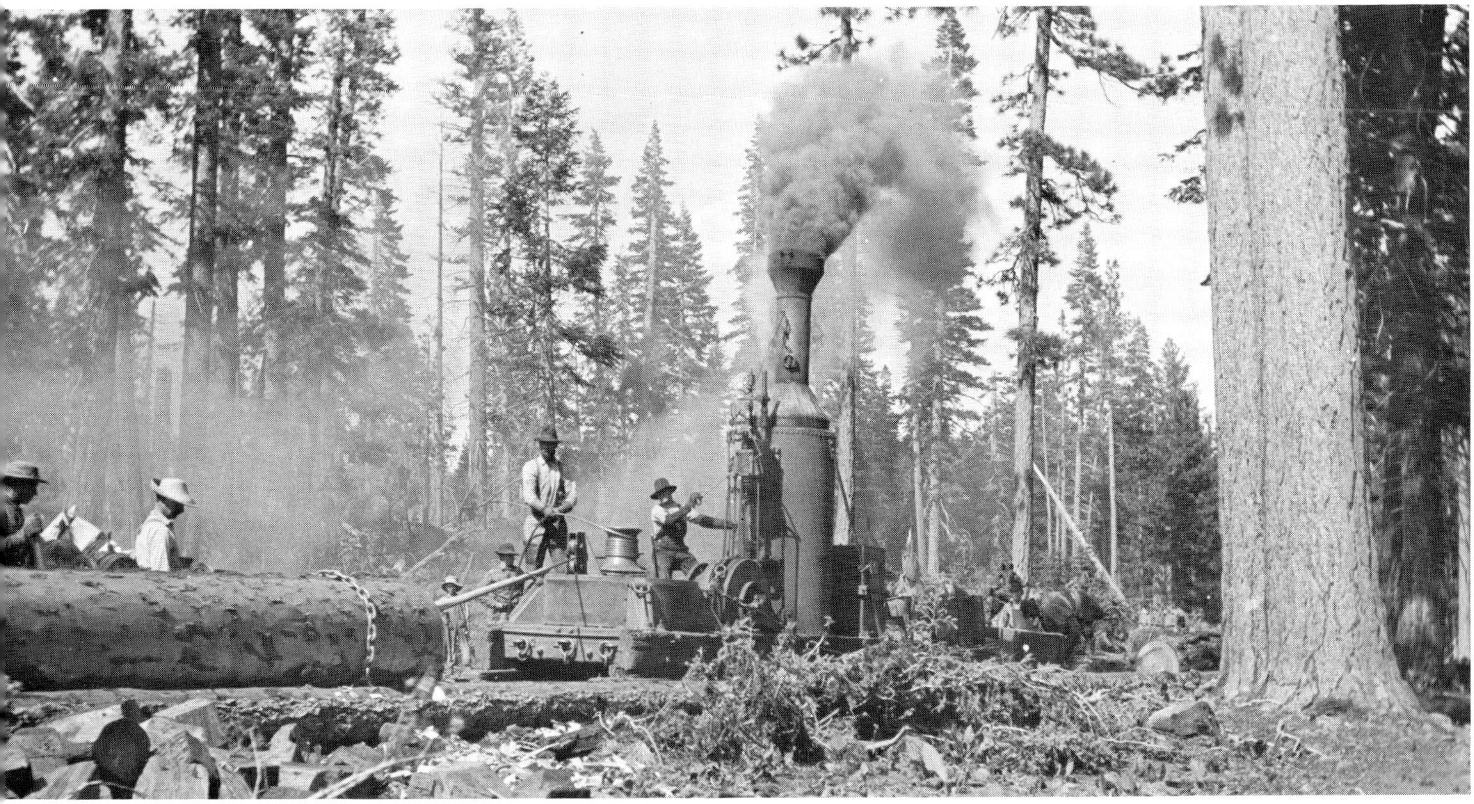

FOLLOWING PAGE:

A superb, rare, early-day panorama of the Hobart Mills buildings, railroad facilities and equipment. Of the two standard-gauge engines on the SNW&LCo.'s trackage at right, No. 3, the lead locomotive, is the former J. W. BOWKER of Virginia & Truckee fame, built by Baldwin in 1875 and sold to the SNW&LCo. in 1896. The fire pump remains affixed to her boiler top, but a back-up headlight has been added to her tender and a copious supply of links for the link-and-pin couplings of the period lie in scattered profusion on her pilot beam. To her rear is No. 4, a (2-6-2) Prairie type, garbed in early wood-burning diamond stack. The narrow-gauge locomotives on the three-rail trackage to the left all came from previous logging operations. The 4-wheel saddle tanker in front and the 0-4-0 switcher immediately behind were former Incline railroad locomotives Nos. 1 and 2, respectively. The third locomotive to the rear previously operated on the line out of Glenbrook. *(George D. Oliver Photo.)*

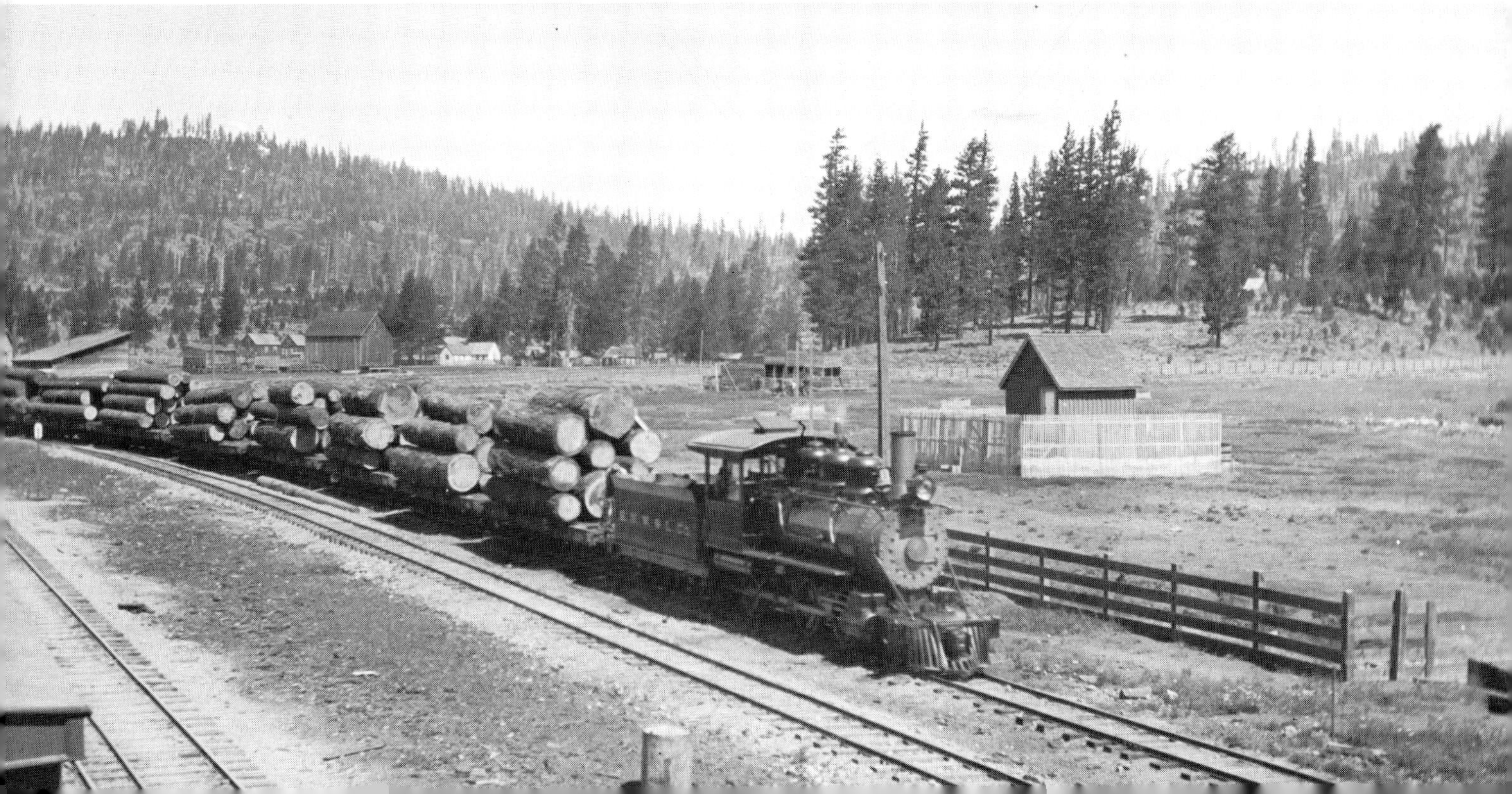

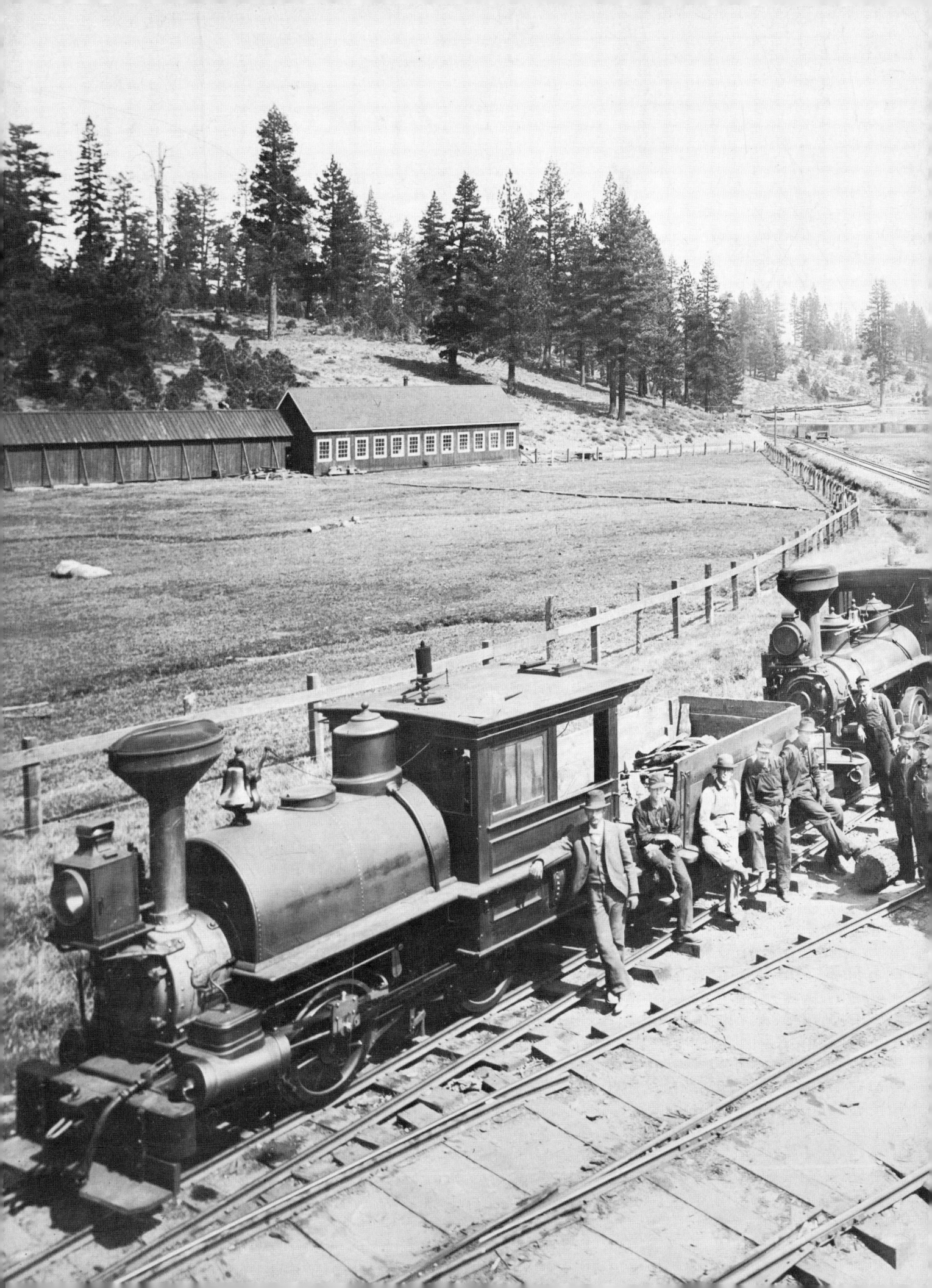

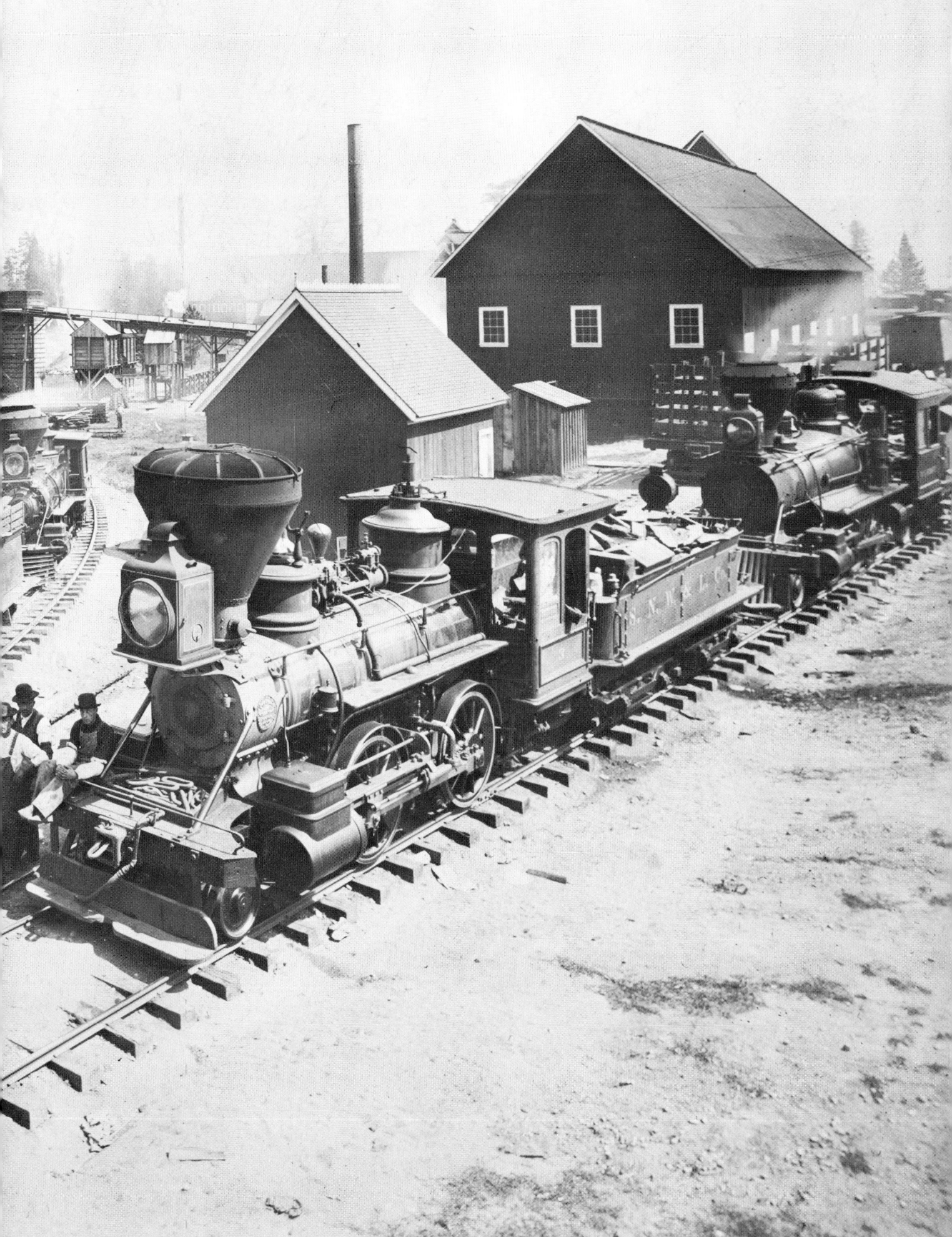

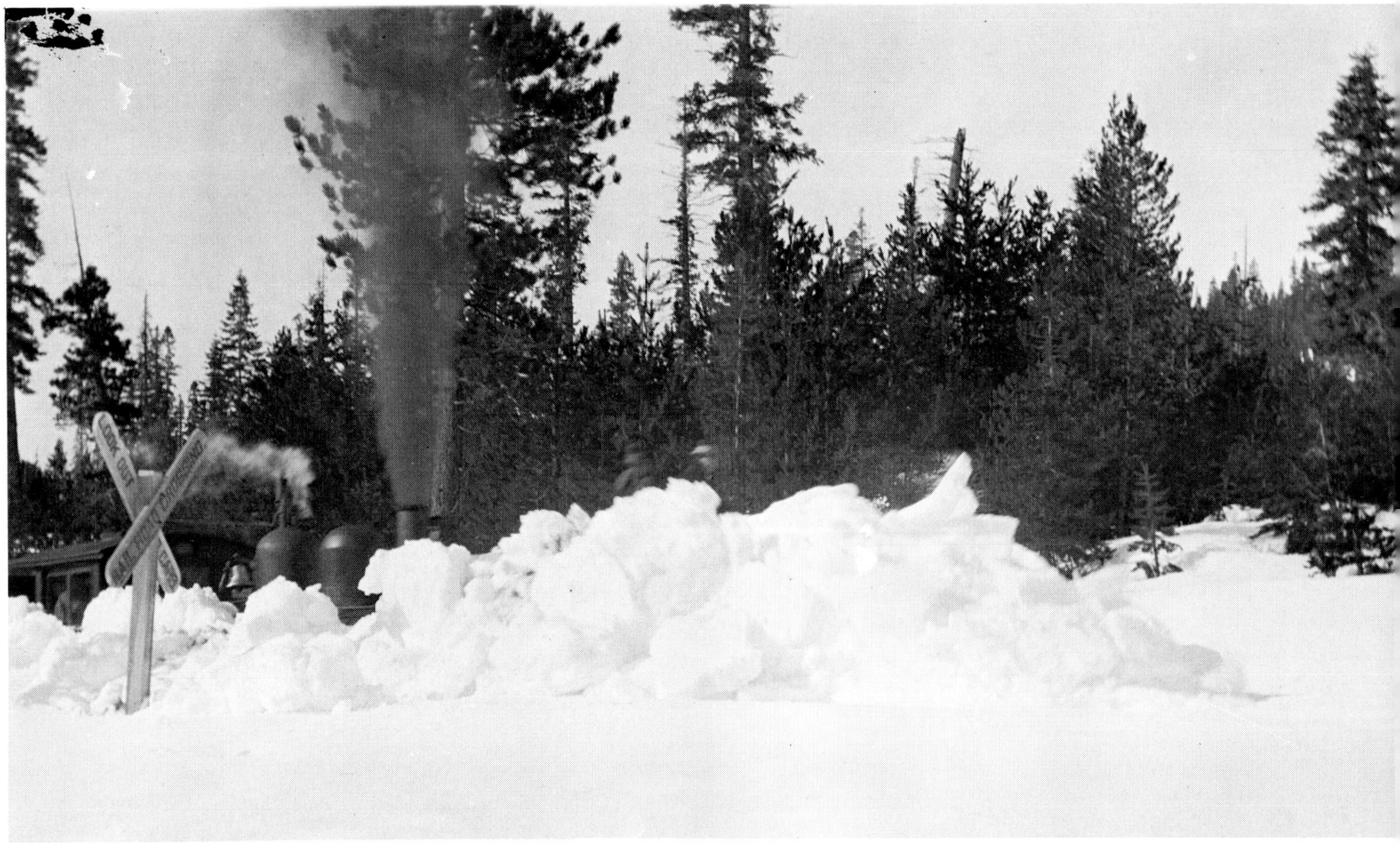

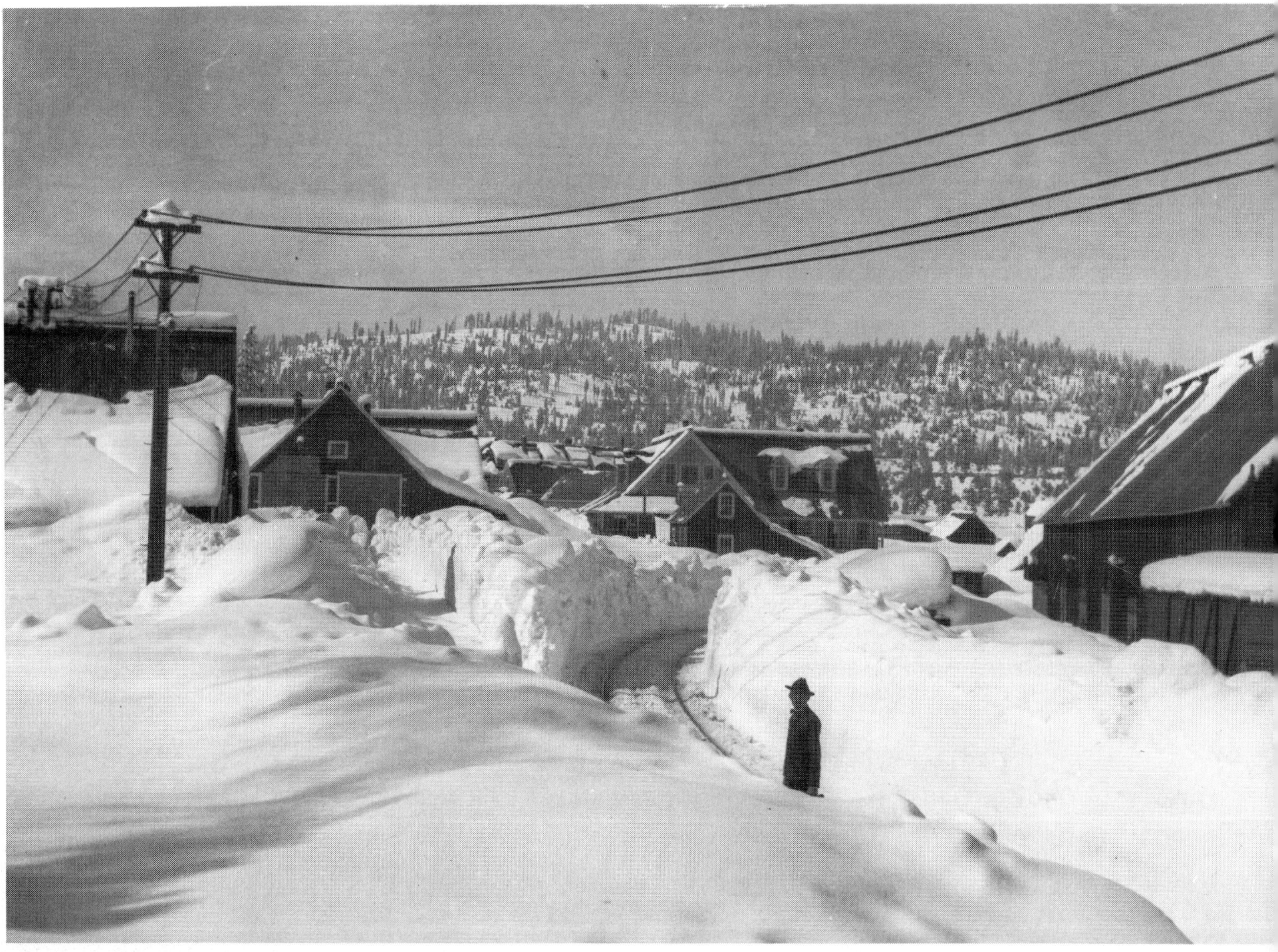

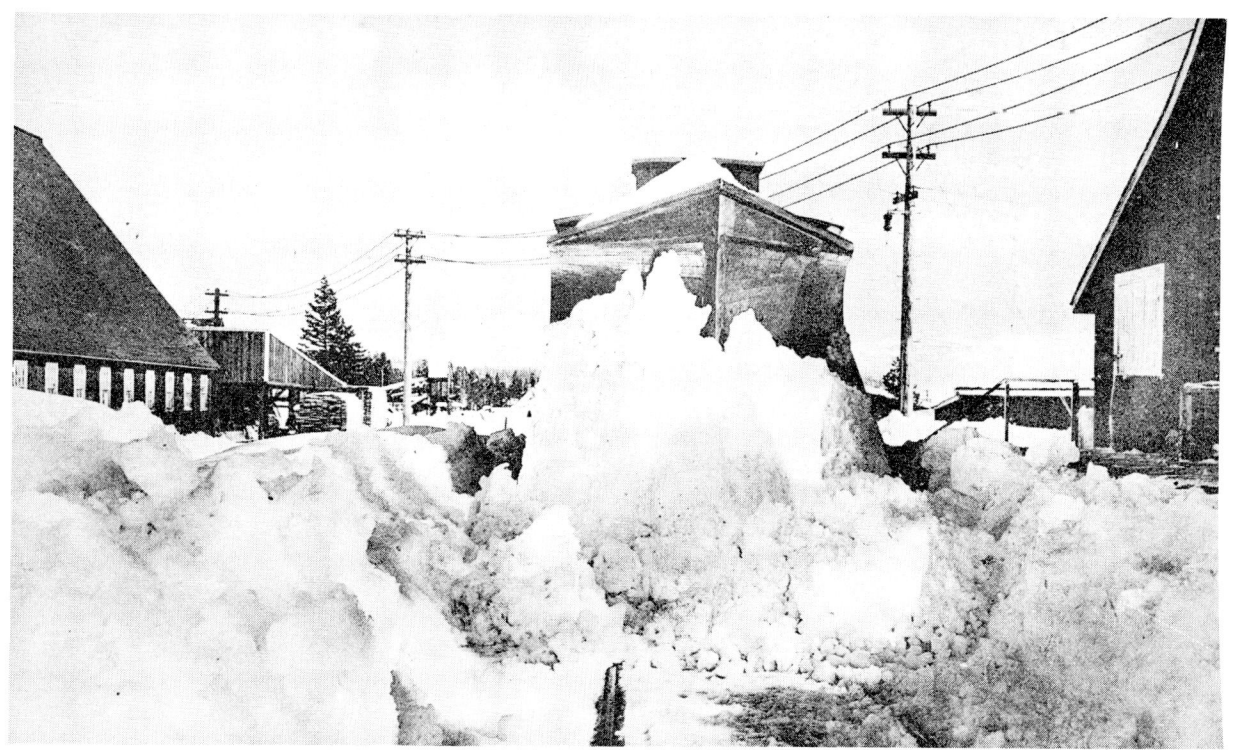

Snow became abundant and deep in the course of a Hobart Mills winter, requiring effective measures of combat. Wedge plows (above) were extra high to compensate for the extra depth of wind-blown drifts (top, left). Roof peaks on buildings (bottom, left) were steeply pitched to shed the weight of moisture-laden flakes as rapidly as possible so they would not accumulate as on the roof of the car repair shop only partially dug out in the center left of photo. When the time came to clear the track for late spring operations, home-made push plows were anchored on the ends of flat cars (below) and were forced ahead by two narrow-gauge steamers. (Left Two Photos and Bottom Right: George D. Oliver; top right, William Lawrence Collection.)

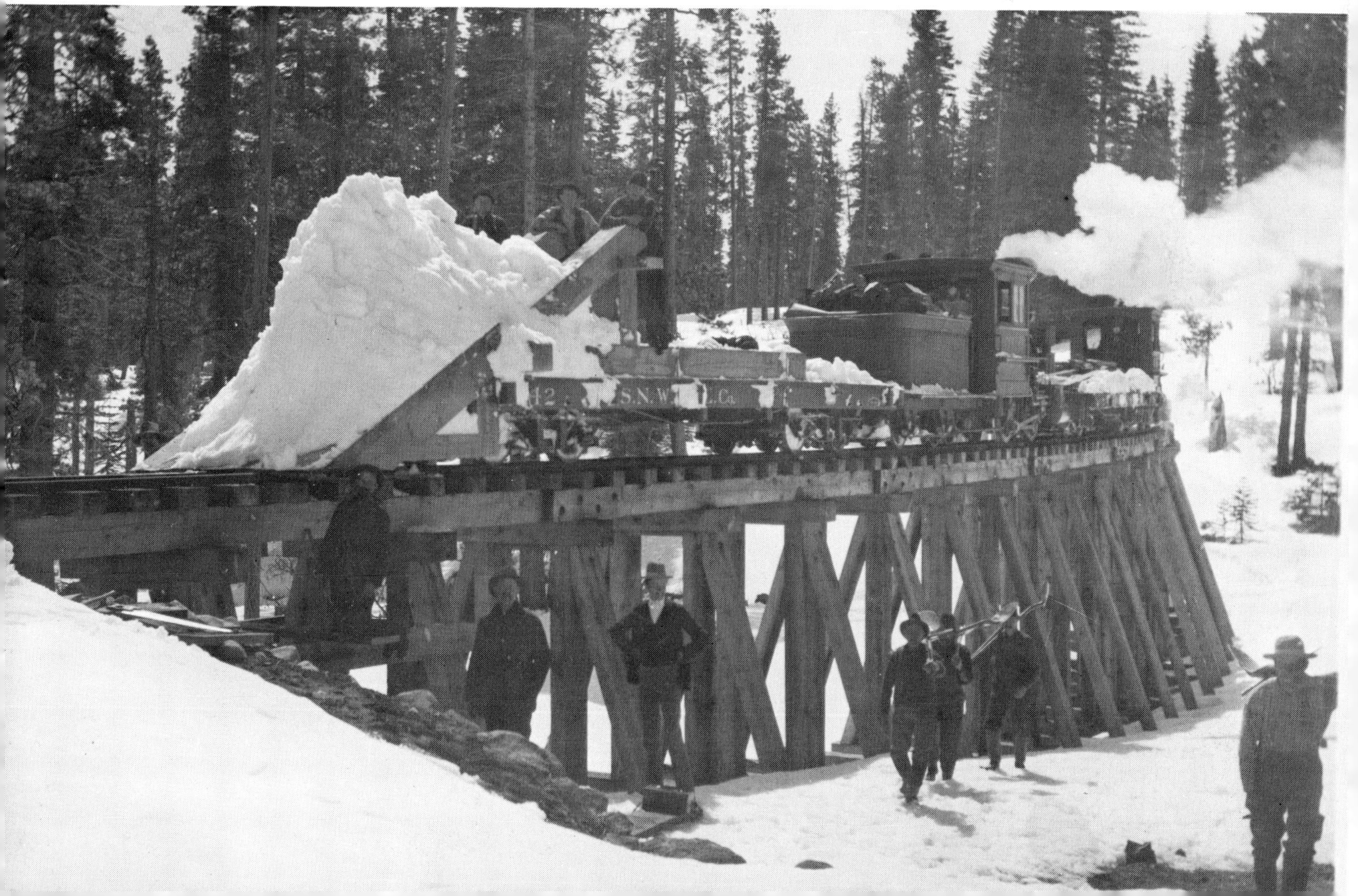

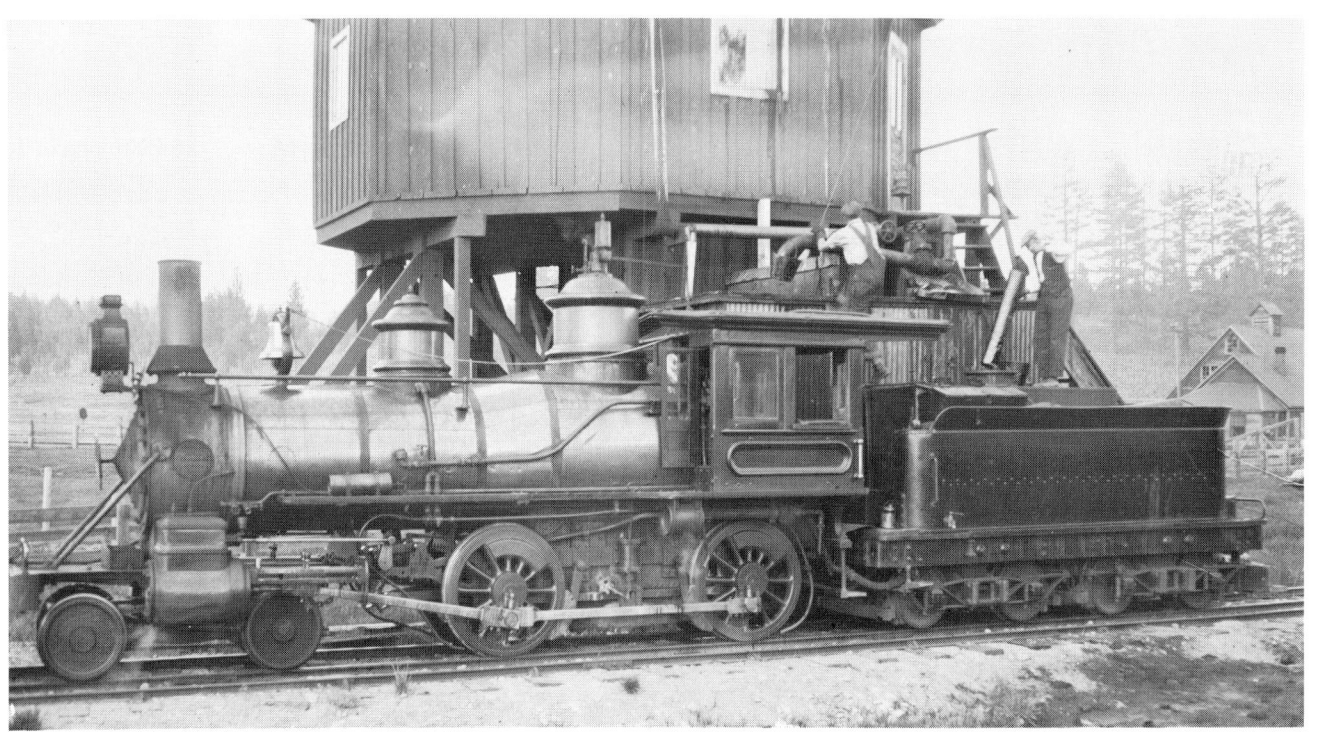

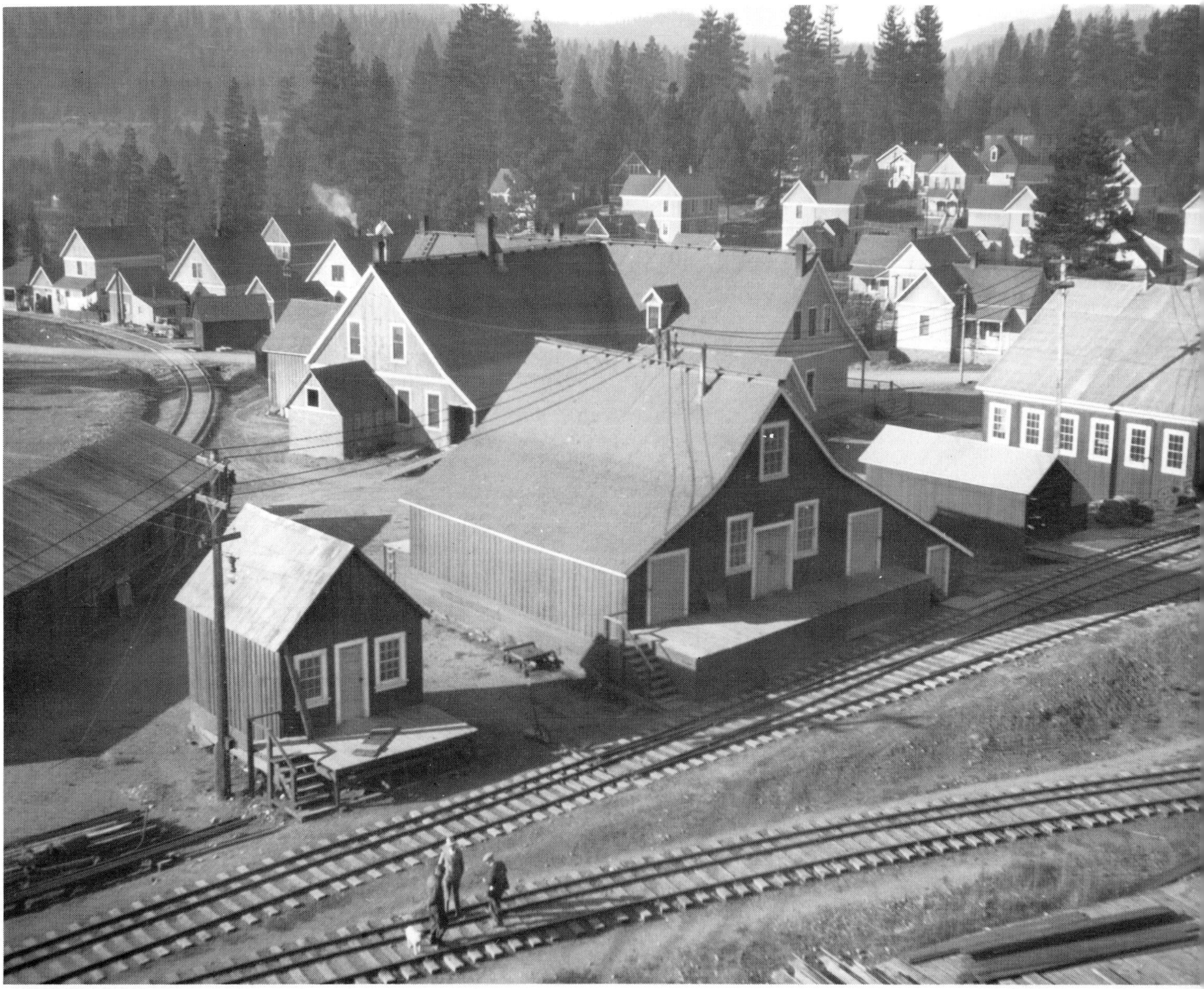

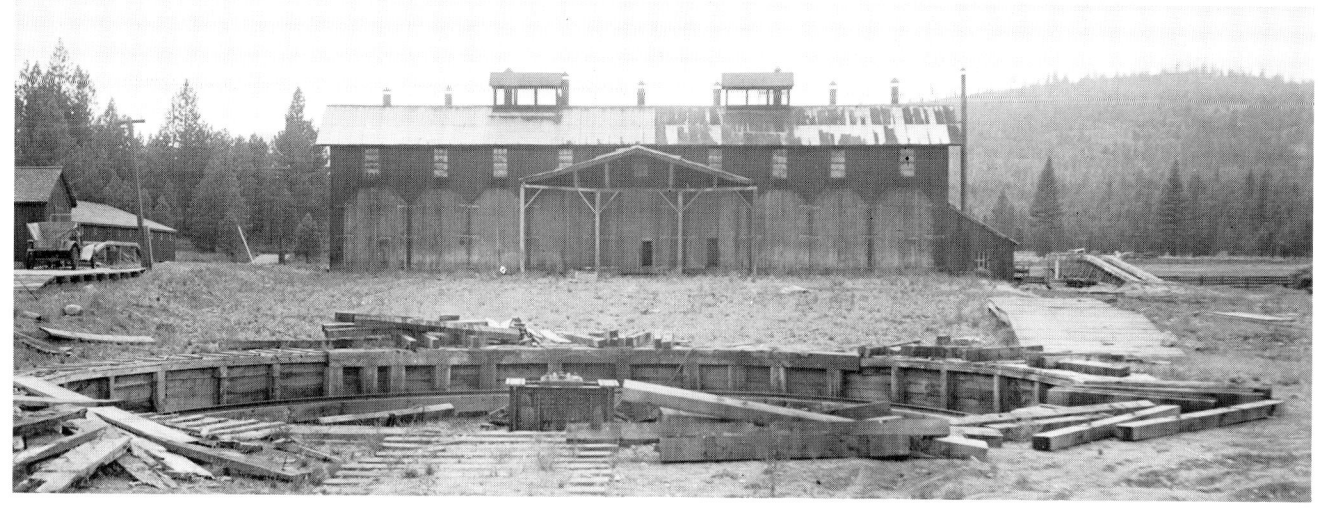

Hobart Estate's narrow-gauge (4-4-0) American No. 5 *(top, left)* appears to have been an historical mongrel of no mean proportions. Her running gear, boiler and water-spigoted tender bespeak of desert running on the Carson & Colorado; her cab, with rounded name panels might well have been borrowed from one of the former Glenbrook Moguls; but the abortive stack, the headlight, the sanders behind the rear drivers and the oil tank mounted in the former wood compartment of the tender are latter-day refinements of local ingenuity and effort some time prior to the moment of this June 1931 portrait. *(W. A. Pennington Photo.)*

The unusual, octagonal, windowed and portaled water tank behind No. 5 is located near the roundhouse (detailed *above* in 1938, the summer after abandonment), and both units may be spotted at far right in the photo *(below)* of the yards and facilities at that terminus. Were the picture *(bottom, left)* dropped just a bit more and matched to the one at *right*, the two would form a panorama of Hobart Mills trackage which, in this later era, had largely all been converted to three-rail operation with the exception of the Hobart Southern main line, seen circling southward toward Truckee at upper left in the picture. *(Top, Right: Guy L. Dunscomb; Bottom Left and Right: George D. Oliver Photos.)*

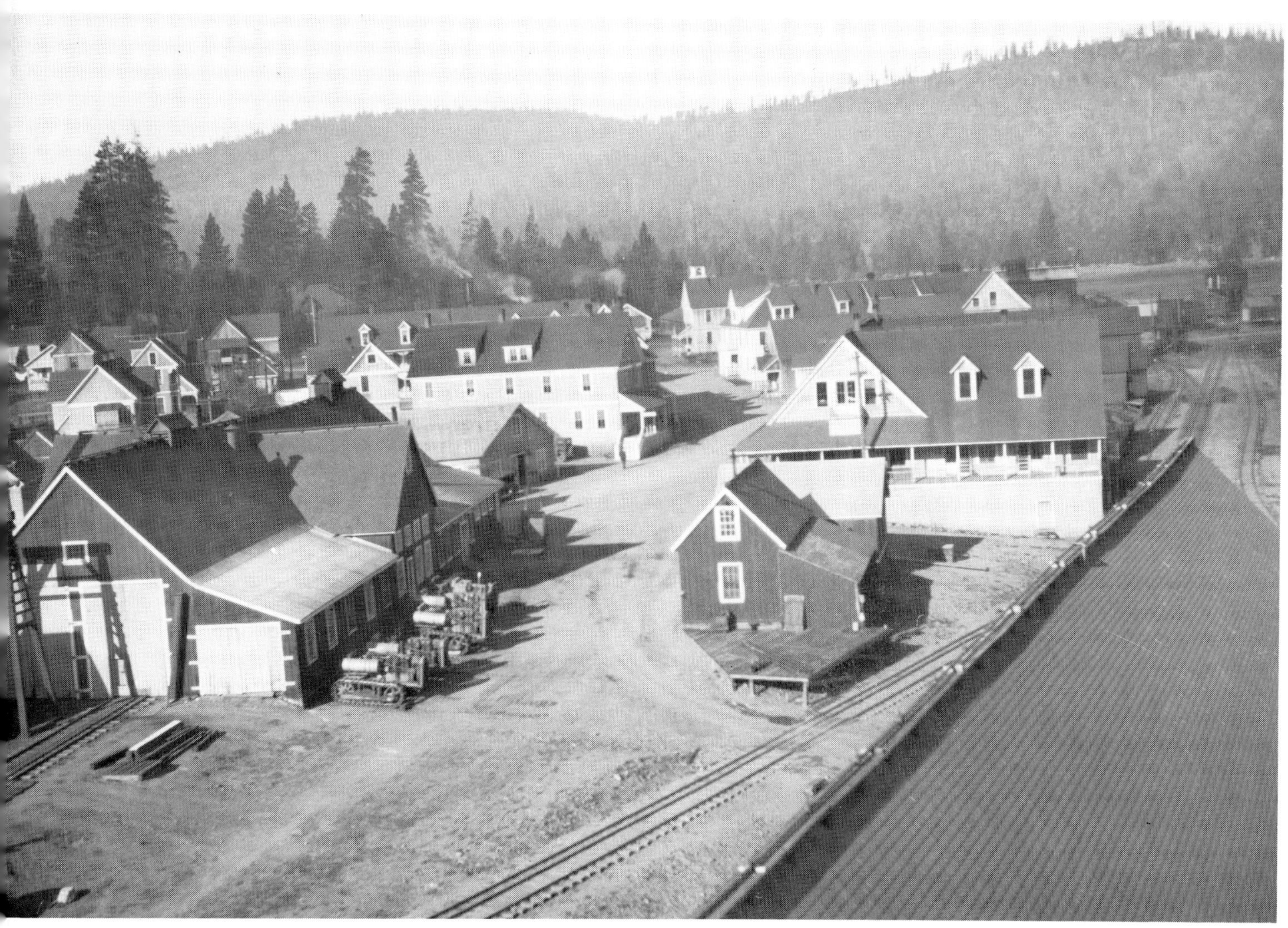

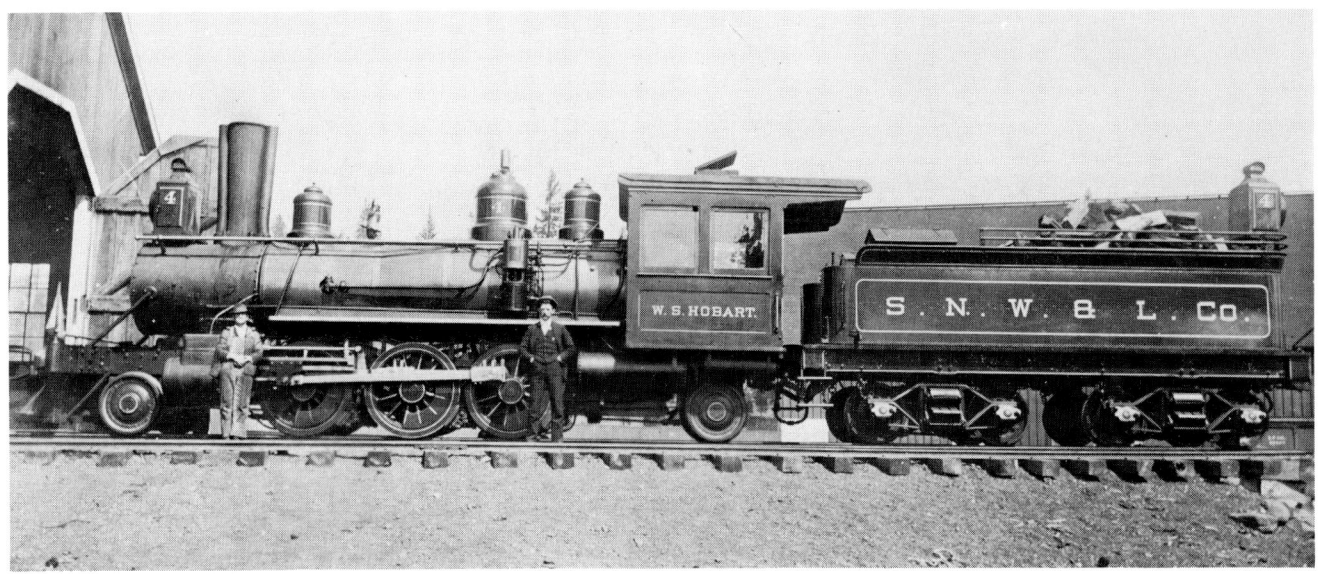

The Sierra Nevada Wood & Lumber Co. started operating its standard gauge line to Truckee in 1896, while the expansive fingers of its supplemental narrow-gauge network pushed north into the woods from Hobart Mills immediately afterward. In 1917 all properties were transferred to the Hobart Estate Company which, from 1930 to 1937, operated the standard gauge line as a common carrier under the name of Hobart Southern. Thus the apparent admixture of locomotives on these two pages in reality all belonged to the same family.

SNW&L's standard-gauge (2-6-2) Prairie type No. 4 had an elongated smokebox to accommodate the complex of spark arrester screens required by her wood burning firebox. Exhaust from the cylinders apparently was ejected fore and aft of the stack to assist in combustion. Old cronies Nos. 1 and 2 from the railroad at Incline are seen again *(below)* on the three-rail trackage at the Hobart Mills log dump. The "Hobart Southern" lettering on standard-gauge Prairie type No. 8 *(top, right)* dates its picture as post-1930. Narrow-gauge Mogul (2-6-0) No. 6 *(center, right)* has a long spread between the second and third drivers to accommodate a lengthy, narrow firebox between axles. Narrow-gauge Shay No. 9 *(bottom, right)* didn't wait to have her picture taken. A stringer gave way on the trestle over the Little Truckee River near Summit in 1915; No. 9 and her crew dove 50 feet; the fireman was killed; but the others were more fortunate. *(Top left: Louis L. Stein, Jr. Collection; Top Right: W. A. Pennington Collection; Center Right: Guy L. Dunscomb Photo; Bottom Left and Right: George D. Oliver Photos.)*

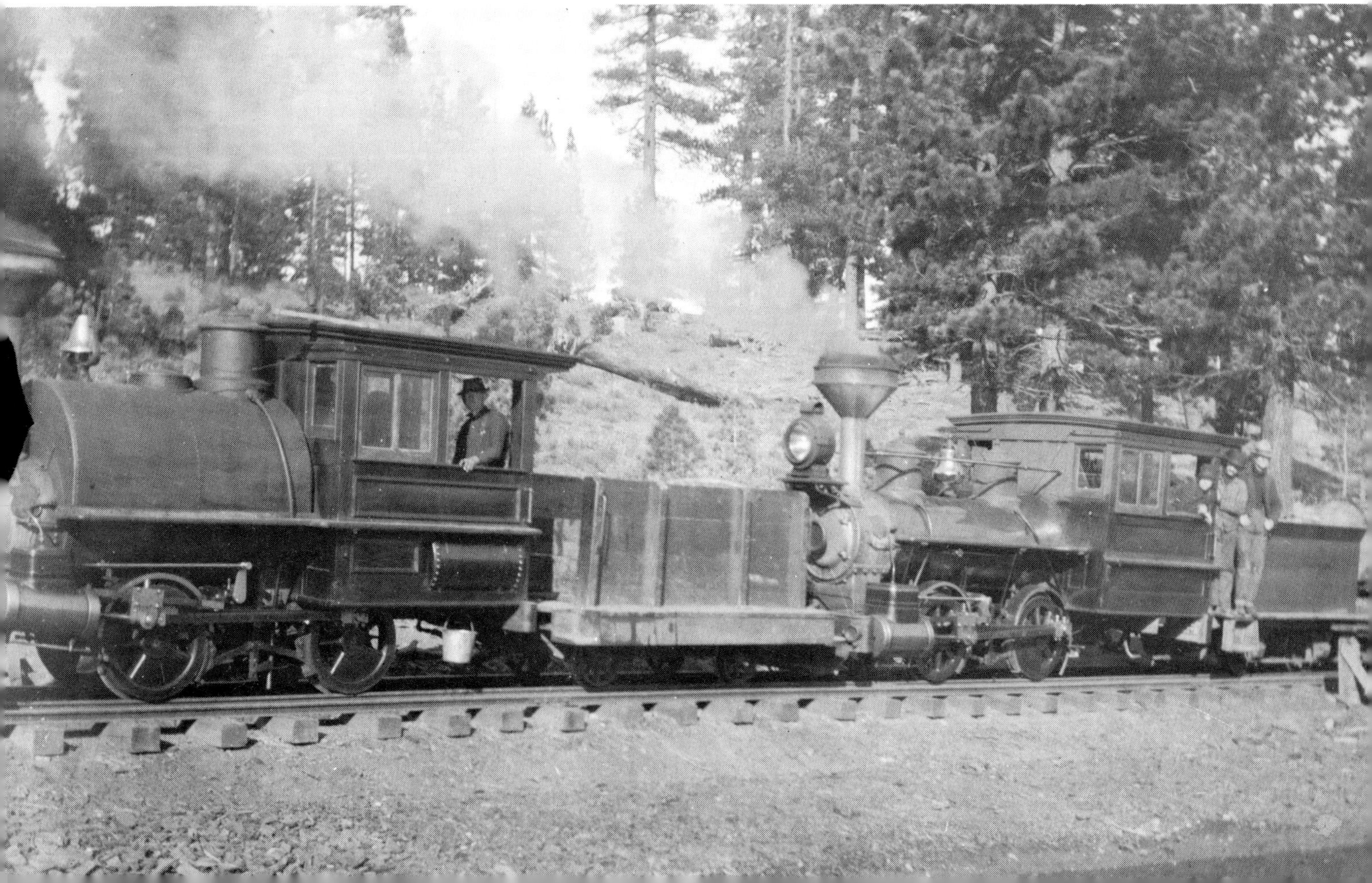

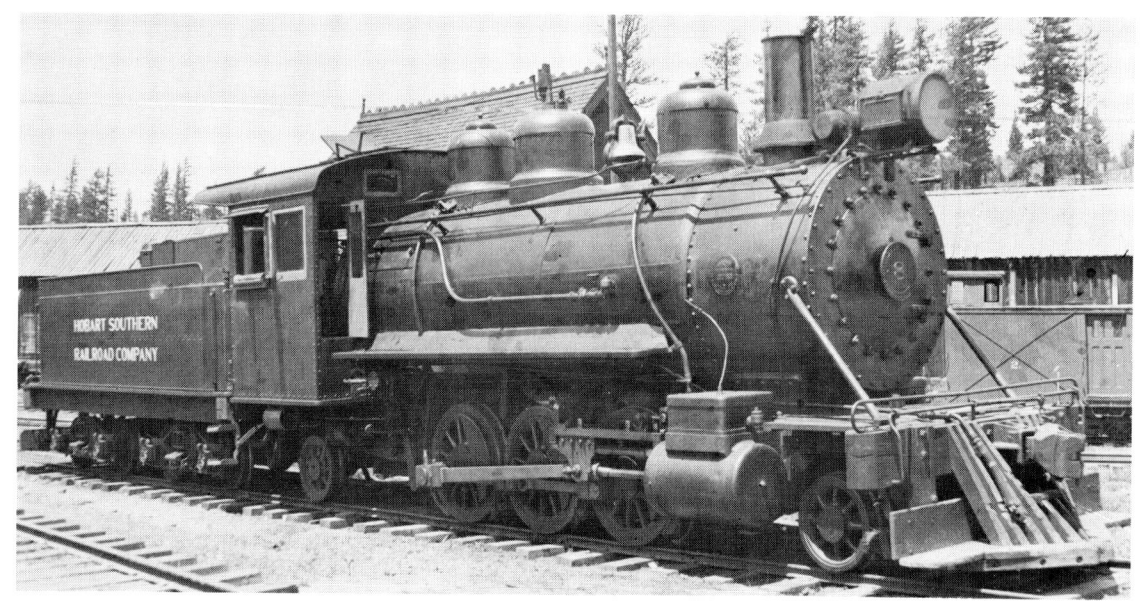

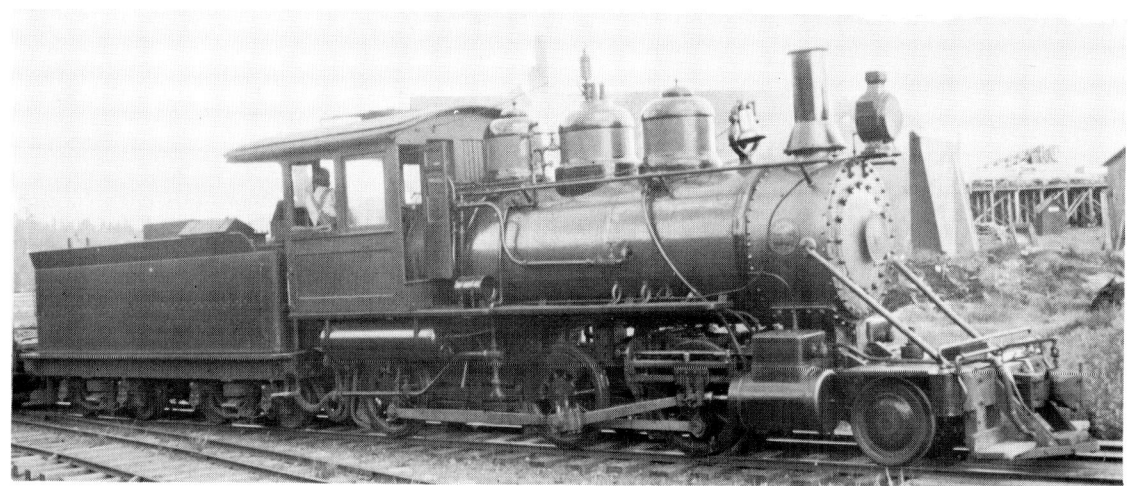

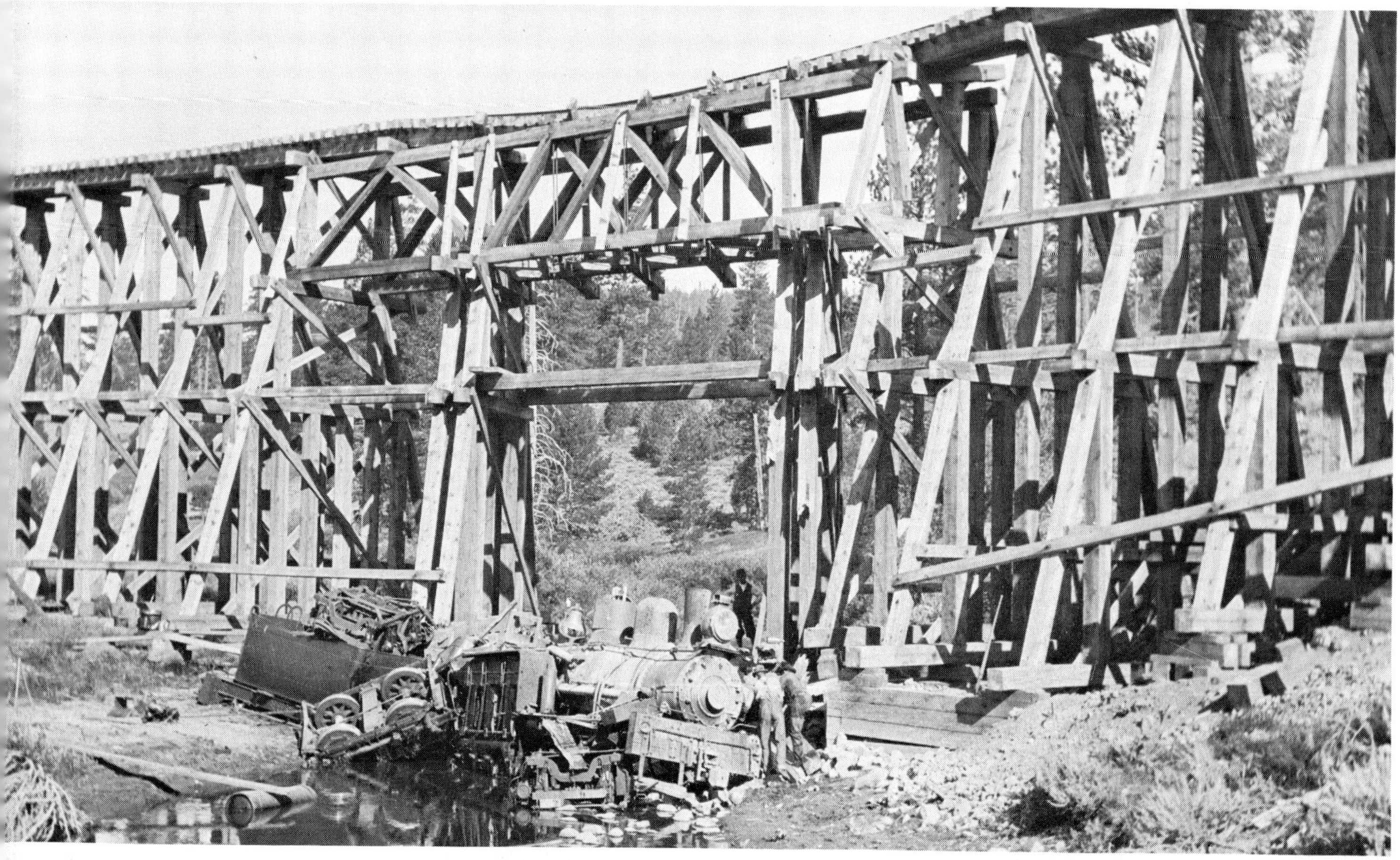